The
Macquarie
HOME GUIDE
—to—
HEALTH
&
MEDICINE

The Macquarie HOME GUIDE to HEALTH & MEDICINE

*Warwick Carter
and
Jan Bowen*

The Macquarie Library

Acknowledgments

Contributions by Peter Ryan on dentistry, Amanda Clancy on speech pathology, Gwen Jull of the University of Queensland on physiotherapy, and George Mocellin of the Lincoln School of Health Sciences on occupational therapy are gratefully acknowledged. Dr Brenda McPhee read the manuscript and provided helpful comments and advice. Staff at the North Shore Hospital in Sydney gave advice about the body scans in Section 4 — Dr Bob Cooper's assistance with nuclear scans and Dr Rein Simmul's contribution to the pulmonary function tests are acknowledged in particular.

Joanna Collard produced the black and white line drawings. The sources of the other illustrations are acknowledged in the list of illustrations.

The Australian Natural Therapists Association and the Sydney College of Chiropractic Ltd assisted with the segment on natural therapies.

Editorial Staff

The Macquarie Library Pty Ltd:
    Richard Tardif, Publisher
    Ann Atkinson, Executive Editor
    Maria Karlsson, Senior Editor

Indexing: Jill Matthews, HiTech Editing

Published by The Macquarie Library Pty Ltd
The Macquarie Dictionary, Macquarie University, NSW 2109, Australia
First published 1991
Reprinted 1991, 1992 (twice), 1993

© Copyright Warwick Carter and Jan Bowen 1991

Cover design: Karen Jeffery, Fox Badger Ferret
Typeset by Excel Imaging Pty Ltd, St Leonards, NSW
Printed in Australia by McPherson's Printing Group

National Library of Australia Cataloguing-in-Publication Data

Carter, Warwick J.
  The Macquarie home guide to health and medicine.

Includes index.
ISBN 0 949757 58 6.

1. Medicine, Popular. 2. Health. I. Bowen, Jan.
II. Collard, Joanna. III. Title. IV. Title: Home guide
to health and medicine.

All rights reserved. No part of this publication may be reproduced, stored in a retrieval system, or transmitted in any form, or by any means, electronic, photocopying, recording or otherwise without prior written permission of the publisher.

DISCLAIMER: This book is intended to give general information about health and medical matters. Every care has been taken to ensure its accuracy but medical matters are complex and exactness is not always possible in a book of this nature. The book is not intended to be used as a substitute for professional medical advice and no responsibility is accepted by the publishers, authors or consultants for any errors or omissions or for any loss, damage or injury suffered by anyone relying on the information contained in the book or from any other cause.

Contents

Preface	vi
How to use this book	vii
List of illustrations	viii

SECTION 1: The Life Cycle	1
SECTION 2: Basic Anatomy and Physiology	63
SECTION 3: Symptoms	119
SECTION 4: Investigations	191
SECTION 5: Diseases	239
SECTION 6: Treatments	563
SECTION 7: Miscellaneous	693
SECTION 8: Emergencies	765
Index	815

Preface

It is virtually impossible to go through life without encountering a medical problem. For most of us, medical questions arise all the time, either about ourselves or about our families, not necessarily because we are ill but simply because we are alive. Living is not static but ongoing, and every day we and the people close to us are in the process of change of one kind or another.

Often of course problems do arise, and when they do, questions need to be answered. Why did it happen? What should I do? What caused it? Is it normal or should I be alarmed? Will it go away? Should I call the doctor? Will there be any long-term effects? Very few of us have not been in situations involving health or medical care, routine or emergency, where we suddenly become aware of questions and do not know the answer.

The Macquarie Home Guide to Health and Medicine is a comprehensive volume aimed at meeting the needs of every Australian. Whatever your questions, you should be able to look up this book and find the answers. The people it has been written for include:
- the new mother with a baby who constantly cries,
- the sick person who wishes to know more about their newly diagnosed disease,
- the teenager concerned about contraception,
- the recently bereaved needing advice on how to cope,
- the desperate parent needing to know urgently how to treat a child with snake bite,
- the cautious person wanting to know the side effects of a recently prescribed medication,
- the sufferer needing to know the possible causes of his or her symptoms,
- the anxious person concerned about investigations the doctor has ordered,
- the student who needs information on the human body for a project,
- the school leaver wanting to know about a career in medicine,
- the traveller needing advice on vaccinations,
- the pregnant woman needing advice on childbirth,
- the overweight requiring dietary advice,
- the patient awaiting surgery who wants to know more about the operation,
- those needing advice on avoiding sexually transmitted disease,
- the teacher needing background information for a health class.

This book was written because it needed to be written. It is not merely an adaptation of a book written for other people in other countries but has been written, edited and published in Australia, for Australians. It therefore deals with conditions, circumstances and diseases particular to Australia as well, of course, as dealing with questions that arise irrespective of country or locality.

Information about health and medicine is often thought to be the province of professionals only. Our aim in writing this book has been to demystify this essential area of knowledge and to present it in everyday language so that it becomes, in effect, available to all Australians.

Warwick Carter
Jan Bowen

How to use this book

To understand the causes of health and disease, you require some knowledge of the LIFE CYCLE that takes us from cradle to grave and ensures the survival of the human species from one generation to the next.	See SECTION 1

You then need to know about the ANATOMY AND PHYSIOLOGY of the human being to understand how the body works.	See SECTION 2

When you or one of your family members are unwell, the SYMPTOMS will indicate a number of possible problems that can be assessed by your doctor.	See SECTION 3

To confirm the diagnosis, it may be necessary for your doctor to order some appropriate INVESTIGATIONS and if you understand why and how these investigations work, you will be less worried about them.	See SECTION 4

Knowledge about the specific DISEASE that is affecting you or one near to you can help you cope with the condition and possibly assist in its prevention and cure.	See SECTION 5

Understanding the various forms of TREATMENT available will encourage you to complete the prescribed regime and make an informed choice when there are alternatives.	See SECTION 6

There is a wide range of additional MISCELLANEOUS information available to help you maintain your health (e.g. diet, dentistry, preventive medicine, travel medicine, etc.), and understand how the medical profession works (e.g. medical ethics).	See SECTION 7

In an EMERGENCY you may need to know what steps to take yourself to save a life — your own or that of someone else.	See SECTION 8

List of Illustrations

Black and white figures

Line drawings are by Joanna Collard. The sources of other illustrations are acknowledged below after each figure number.

Figure 1: Temperature chart used in natural family planning
Figure 2.1: How to find the blind spot
Figure 2.2: Normal vision, short-sightedness and long-sightedness
Figure 2.3: The heart and the route of blood flow through it
Figure 2.4: The nail
Figure 2.5: An adult molar
Figure 4.1: Lumbar puncture
Figure 4.2: CT scans of different sections of abdomen
(Royal North Shore Hospital)
Figure 4.3: CT scanner
(Weldon Trannies)
Figure 4.4: Echocardiogram of heart
(Royal North Shore Hospital)
Figure 4.5: MRI scan of brain of patient with multiple sclerosis
(Royal North Shore Hospital)
Figure 4.6: Nuclear bone scan showing bony metastases in spine, ribs and pelvis from prostate carcinoma
(Royal North Shore Hospital)
Figure 4.7: How PET works
Figure 4.8: Ultrasound of uterus of pregnant woman
(Royal North Shore Hospital)
Figure 4.9: Chest X-ray
(Royal North Shore Hospital)
Figure 4.10: Electrocardiogram
(Provided by Warwick Carter)
Figure 4.11: Spirometer
(FSE Pty Ltd)
Figure 4.12: Example of an audiology report form
Figure 5.1: Demonstrating the difference between subluxation and dislocation of joint
Figure 5.2: Different types of fracture
Figure 5.3: Ganglion on tendon sheath
Figure 5.4: Wedge resection of ingrown toenail
Figure 5.5: Graph of hormone changes during menstrual cycle
Figure 6.1: Operating theatre
(Austral International)
Figure 6.2: Spinal anaesthetic
Figure 6.3: Stapling a wound
Figure 6.4: Eye operation
(Austral International)
Figure 6.5: A grommet in the ear
Figure 6.6: Artificial hip joint
Figure 6.7: Artificial heart valve
(Medtronic Australasia Pty Ltd)
Figure 6.8: Colostomy
Figure 6.9: Cross-section of body showing selective irradiation
Figure 6.10: Radiation treatment
(Medical Applications Pty Ltd)
Figure 7.1: The healthy diet pyramid
Figure 7.2: Breast self-examination
Figure 8.1: Head tilt
Figure 8.2: Mouth-to-mouth resuscitation
Figure 8.3: Resuscitation of young child
Figure 8.4: Mouth-to-nose resuscitation
Figure 8.5: Cardiopulmonary resuscitation
Figure 8.6: Putting pressure on breastbone of child
Figure 8.7: Putting pressure on breastbone of baby
Figure 8.8: Arterial pressure points
Figure 8.9: Coma position
Figure 8.10: Lateral position
Figure 8.11: Chest compression
Figure 8.12: Assisting choking child dislodge obstruction
Figure 8.13: Strapping injured joint
Figure 8.14: Tying an arm sling
Figure 8.15: Tying an elevation sling
Figure 8.16: Tying a clove hitch for a collar-and-cuff sling
Figure 8.17: Pressure immobilisation

Colour plates

Plates in Section 2 are from *Principles of Anatomy and Physiology*, Fifth Edition, by Gerard J. Tortora and Nicholas P. Anagnostakos. Copyright 1987 by Biological Sciences Textbooks Inc., A and P Textbooks Inc., and Ella-Sparta Inc. Illustrations copyright 1987 by Leonard Dank. Reprinted by permission of Harper Collins Publishers Inc. Acknowledgment of sources of plates in Section 8 appears below after each plate number.

Plate 2.1: Brain and cranial nerves
Plate 2.2: Nervous system: spinal cord and nerves
Plate 2.3: Nervous system: brachial plexus
Plate 2.4: Nervous system: lumbar plexus
Plate 2.5: Circulatory system: principal arteries (anterior view)
Plate 2.6: Circulatory system: principal veins (anterior view)
Plate 2.7: Organs of the digestive system
Plate 2.8: Location of endocrine glands
Plate 2.9: Structure of the eyeball (transverse section)
Plate 2.10: Divisions of the ear
Plate 2.11: Lymphatic system: principal components
Plate 2.12: Muscular system: principal superficial skeletal muscles (anterior view)
Plate 2.13: Muscular system: principal superficial skeletal muscles (posterior view)
Plate 2.14: Reproductive system: female organs
Plate 2.15: Reproductive system: male organs
Plate 2.16: Respiratory system
Plate 2.17: Skeletal system
Plate 2.18: Structure of the skin
Plate 2.19: Urinary system: male organs

Plate 8.1: Poisonous plants
Castor oil plant (*Ricinus communis*) (Tony Rodd)
Angel's trumpet (*Brugmansia aurea*) (Tony Rodd)
Cunjevoi plant (*Alocasia macrorrhizos*) flower (Tony Rodd)
Cunjevoi plant (*Alocasia macrorrhizos*) seeds (Tony Rodd)
Pineapple zamia palm (*Macrozamia miquelii*) (Tony Rodd)
African wintersweet (*Acokanthera oblongifolia*) (Tony Rodd)

Plate 8.2: Poisonous plants
Moreton Bay chestnut tree (*Castanospermum australe*) (Tony Rodd)
Arum lily (*Zantedeschia araceae*) (Kevin Burchett/Weldon Trannies)
Golden dewdrop (*Duranta erecta*) (Tony Rodd/Weldon Trannies)
Coral bush (*Jatropha podagrica*) (Tony Rodd)
Oleander (*Nerium oleander*) white (Tony Rodd)
Oleander (*Nerium oleander*) pink (Tony Rodd)

Plate 8.3: Venomous snakes
Death adder (L.M. Naylor/NPIAW)
Tiger snake (E. Ehmann/NPIAW)
Brown snake (J. Wombey/NPIAW)
Brown snake (G.E. Schmida/NPIAW)
Taipan (K. Griffiths/NPIAW)
Red-bellied black snake (L.F. Schick/NPIAW)

Plate 8.4: Spiders
Funnel-web spider (Weldon Trannies)
Red-back spider (Weldon Trannies)
Red-back spider: female and eggs (Weldon Trannies)

SECTION 1

THE LIFE CYCLE

SEX AND REPRODUCTION
3
CONTRACEPTION
6
PREGNANCY AND BIRTH
16
INFANT FEEDING
36
BABIES AND YOUNG CHILDREN
42
PUBERTY AND ADOLESCENCE
50
MATURITY
53
MENOPAUSE
54
AGEING
56
DEATH AND DYING
59

Sex and Reproduction

The ability to reproduce is one of the most fascinating and mysterious features of life. Generally speaking, lower forms of life simply divide by themselves without the need for a partner. In most animals, however, reproduction is sexual, meaning that a male and a female are involved, each with particular cells designed specifically to reproduce the species. These cells are called gametes. In a woman they are the ova or eggs, and in a man they are the sperm ejaculated during intercourse. If an egg is fertilised with a sperm, a new human life is begun. For this to happen an amazingly complex series of processes must occur.

Sexual intercourse

The biological purpose of sexual intercourse is to reproduce the human race. However, human beings also have sex (make love) because it feels good. In the Western world, people reproduce on average no more than three or four times in their lives, but they will probably engage in sexual intercourse thousands of times. Intercourse consists of the man inserting his penis into the woman's vagina. Before he does this, ideally, each will become sexually aroused. In the man this means that the penis will become filled with blood so that it is larger, stiff and erect. In the woman, the vagina lengthens, and glands in the vagina produce a lubricating fluid which enables the man's penis to slide in easily. Thrusting movements by both partners stimulate the penis and vagina and produce pleasurable sensations that increase in intensity until a climax or orgasm is reached. In a woman an orgasm consists of contractions of the vagina, and the man will have an ejaculation of semen, which is a mix of seminal fluid and sperm.

Positions for intercourse vary. The commonest is the so-called missionary position in which the woman lies on her back with the man on top of her. Penetration is generally deepest in this position.

In a man, orgasm and ejaculation go together. One usually does not occur without the other. Consequently a man has to have an orgasm before he can father a child. The situation is different in women. A woman does not need to have an orgasm to conceive and some women have active sex lives rarely or never achieving orgasm.

Masturbation

Masturbation is sexual stimulation of oneself. Many people masturbate, especially during adolescence and at times of their lives when they do not have a sexual partner. Some religions have

SECTION 1: THE LIFE CYCLE

frowned on the practice and insisted on their adherents regarding it as sinful. Dire threats have sometimes been made that unpleasant physical consequences such as blindness will result. This is nonsense. Masturbation is harmless, and if it provides pleasure and sexual relief there is no reason not to engage in it.

Conception

Conception occurs when, usually as a result of sexual intercourse, a female egg is fertilised by a male sperm. A woman produces an egg every month, generally 14 days before the beginning of the next menstrual period. The egg travels down the Fallopian tube towards the womb (uterus). If the woman has intercourse during this period, the male sperm deposited travel up through the uterus to the Fallopian tube where they meet the egg. If one sperm penetrates the egg, the egg is fertilised. Once an egg has been fertilised by one sperm, it immediately becomes impenetrable to other sperm, even though millions of sperm are deposited as a result of any single ejaculation.

The new cell is called a zygote. The zygote divides quickly into two and then into four, eight, 16, 32 and so on, until all the cells required for a new human being are in existence — six million by the end of pregnancy.

The ball of cells at the beginning of the division process is called a blastocyst. The blastocyst travels down the Fallopian tube to the uterus where it implants in the wall, seven days after fertilisation. At this point conception has occurred.

If, perchance, two eggs are released and fertilised, there will be two babies or twins. Twins produced from two separate eggs each have their own separate set of inherited characteristics and are not identical. Occasionally a single egg divides into two separate cells which then produce two individuals. The result is identical twins, each with the same genetic make-up, i.e. they will be the same sex, have the same colour eyes and hair, and have similar features. It is not known why this occurs.

Triplets, quads and quins usually result from both the production of more than one egg and the division of a single fertilised egg, so some of the babies will look alike and some will be different. Nowadays multiple pregnancies not infrequently result from treatment for infertility with hormones which stimulate the production of several eggs.

ARTIFICIAL CONCEPTION

In recent times, techniques have been developed to enable conception to be carried out artificially without the need for the act of intercourse. At its simplest level, this is called artificial insemination and involves male sperm being deposited into the woman usually by means of a syringe. This may be undertaken when the woman's partner is infertile and the couple decide to have a child technically fathered by another man with whom the woman does not wish to have intercourse.

In vitro fertilisation (IVF) takes place outside the human body and was first successfully carried out in England in 1978. This involves a female egg being fertilised with a male sperm in a dish ('in vitro' is Latin for in glass). The most common procedure is for several eggs to be removed surgically from the woman and placed in a dish to which sperm is added. The fertilised eggs are then incubated for two days to allow the division process to begin before being planted in the woman's uterus. If the egg implants itself in the uterus, the woman is pregnant and it can be expected that the baby will be born in the normal way. It is now possible for unused fertilised eggs to be frozen for later use if this attempt at pregnancy fails or the couple decide to have another child.

See also INFERTILITY, Section 5; COMMON OPERATIONS, Section 6.

Reproduction

The cells making up a human being all contain information that determines what characteristics the person will have, e.g. the colour of their eyes and hair, their potential height, build, intelligence and so on. This genetic information is contained in units within each cell called chromosomes. The chromosomes contain even smaller units called genes. An individual gene determines specific characteristics, e.g. hair colour. Groups of genes determine more complex characteristics, such as the potential level of intelligence.

At the moment of conception, the genetic material contained in the egg and the sperm fuses, and the individual characteristics which the new human being will have for the duration of its life are determined.

Except for the reproductive cells, each cell in the human body contains 46 chromosomes. The reproductive cells (gametes) contain 23 chromosomes, i.e. half the normal number. When the male and female reproductive cells combine, the two lots of 23 chromosomes amalgamate to make up the normal number of 46. These 46 chromosomes, half from each parent, determine what characteristics the child will have. Chromosomes are arranged in pairs, and one of these pairs carries the code for the person's sex. Looked at through a microscope, women have two X-shaped sex chromosomes, whereas men have one X and one Y-shaped chromosome. Because the reproductive cells have only half the normal number of chromosomes, the male cell may have an X or a Y chromosome. Obviously the female cell always has an X chromosome. If the X chromosome in the female cell (egg) combines with a male cell (sperm) containing a Y chromosome, the resulting child will be a boy; if the egg combines with a sperm containing an X chromosome the child will be a girl. It is thus the man who determines what sex a couple's offspring will be.

Some diseases are due to inherited recessive genes. If both parents have a similar defect contained in a recessive gene (so that it is not evident in either parent) and they each pass on that particular gene to one of their children, the child will inherit the defect. The lung disease, cystic fibrosis, is such a disease. The science of genetics is now sufficiently advanced that people known to be carriers of such disorders can obtain advice as to the likelihood of the disease occurring in their children and take decisions as to their family in the light of this.

CONTRACEPTION

Methods of contraception

Since, in human beings, sex is a pleasurable activity which is frequently engaged in for its own sake and not solely for the purposes of reproduction, a couple who want to have sex and who do not want a child will need to use some form of contraception, i.e. they will need to find some way of stopping the male sperm meeting the female egg and fertilising it.

Attempts to find some way of having sex without producing babies have a long history. Documents from Mesopotamia, 4000 years ago, record that a plug of dung was placed in the woman's vagina to stop conception. In Cleopatra's Egypt, small gold trinkets were inserted into the uterus of the courtesans as a form of early intra-uterine contraceptive device. At the same time, camel herders pushed pebbles into the wombs of the female camels so that they would not get pregnant on long caravan treks. More recently, in the eighteenth century in France, the renowned philanderer Casanova used a thin pig's bladder as an early condom or 'French letter'. Prior to this there were similar devices made from leather or gut. Finding a safe, effective and reliable contraceptive has proved a difficult task.

ORAL CONTRACEPTIVES

The pill. It is not an overstatement to say that the development of the oral contraceptive pill in 1962 revolutionised modern life. For the first time there was an effective, safe, reliable, easy to use, reversible contraceptive that did not interfere with love-making and had no aesthetic drawbacks.

The pill works by suppressing ovulation. A woman's hormone level normally rises and falls during her monthly cycle and by so doing sets in train the various reproductive processes. A woman taking the pill maintains a more constant hormone level so her eggs are not released. The most commonly prescribed pills are taken for three of the four weeks. This allows the hormone level to drop during the fourth week causing a bleeding to start and allowing as natural a cycle as possible while preventing the release of the egg. If the woman stops taking the pill, her normal cycle should resume very quickly (sometimes immediately) and she is able to become pregnant.

In its early days there were some questions raised about the wisdom of long-term reliance on the pill, but a woman on today's pill is taking a hormone dose that is some 30 times less than the original. There is no doubt that it is safer to take the pill than to have just one pregnancy — a reasonable if not entirely logical basis of comparison.

Although the pill is very safe, there are some women who should not use it. Those who have had high blood pressure, blood clots, severe liver disease, strokes or bad migraines should not take the pill. Heavy smokers, women who are excessively overweight, and those with diabetes will usually be observed closely by their doctor and probably should not use the pill after they reach 35 years of age.

The pill has several positive benefits besides prevention of pregnancy. It regulates irregular periods, reduces menstrual pain and premenstrual tension, reduces the severity of acne in some women, and may increase libido (desire for sex). It sometimes increases the size of the breasts. It also reduces the incidence of some types of cancer.

If taken correctly, the pill is very effective as a contraceptive (close to 100%). The daily dosage must be maintained, however. If more than one pill is missed it is generally wise to use some other form of contraception for seven days after the missed pill. An attack of vomiting or diarrhoea can prevent the pill from being absorbed. Some antibiotics also interfere with absorption. If any of these things occur, continue to take the pill and use another method of contraception until seven days after.

A few women have unpleasant side effects from the pill. These include headaches, breakthrough bleeding, nausea, increased appetite and mood changes. If these problems occur, see your doctor, as a pill with a different balance of hormones might be prescribed.

In the early days of the pill it was recommended that women take a break from it every few years, but this is no longer considered necessary.

The mini pill. In its most commonly used forms, the pill is a combination of the hormones oestrogen and progesterone. There is also a 'mini pill' which contains only a progestogen hormone and is suitable for some women, including breastfeeding mothers, who cannot take the combined pill. The mini pill is slightly less reliable than the combined pill and is more likely to give rise to breakthrough bleeding, but serious side effects are much less common. It is important to take it at the same time each day, and it has its greatest contraceptive effect about 4–20 hours after it is taken. Early evening is usually a good time to take it.

The morning-after pill. The morning-after pill is a short course of oral contraception which must be taken within 72 hours of sexual intercourse. The dose is repeated exactly 12 hours later, so if the first dose is taken at 10 a.m., then the second dose is due at 10 p.m. The morning-after pill prevents pregnancy in one of two ways — by preventing ovulation, or by preventing implantation of the fertilised egg in the womb. It can be used after unprotected sex at the woman's fertile period, in cases of condom or diaphragm misuse or mishap, and is also used in cases of rape.

Some women experience nausea after taking the morning-after pill, and some vomit. Anti-nausea pills are often provided together with it. Some women experience breast tenderness, headaches or light bleeding, but these symptoms usually go away without any treatment. Your period may be on time, delayed or could be early after taking the morning-after pill. In the time after you have used this pill until you have your next period, you must use some other form of contraception, as you are still at risk of pregnancy.

The morning-after pill should not be used as ongoing contraception. It should not be used more than once a month. You should discuss regular contraceptive methods with your doctor or a family planning clinic.

Depo-Provera

Depo-Provera is a means of contraception in which a synthetic form of the female sex hormone progesterone is injected into a woman's muscle and slowly released into the body, causing the ovaries to stop producing eggs. One injection lasts for 12 weeks or more. Following the first injection, it is necessary to use another method of contraception for seven days, but follow-up injections are effective immediately, provided they are administered regularly. If an injection is more than a week late, you could become pregnant and should use another method of contraception until seven days after the next injection.

During the first few months, Depo-Provera sometimes causes a change in the menstrual pattern, such as missed periods, irregular spotting, continual light bleeding, or heavy bleeding. Occasionally it gives rise to nausea, headaches, mild depression, abdominal cramps, breast tenderness and weight gain. These are not a cause for concern, but if they are prolonged or a source of discomfort you should see your doctor. Side effects cannot quickly be reversed because of the long-lasting nature of the injection.

In many women, the injections result in periods becoming lighter and less frequent, and eventually stopping. This is quite harmless and may even be welcome. It may take six months or longer after ceasing the injections for fertility to return to normal. However, there is no risk of permanent infertility.

If you are on Depo-Provera, you should tell a doctor whom you visit for any reason.

In Australia, Depo-Provera is still under study as a contraceptive, and doctors may prescribe it where they believe it is the best or only method of contraception. A woman who is on Depo-Provera should be monitored at regular intervals and should understand fully its advantages and disadvantages when making her decision.

Depo-Provera has the advantage that it is highly effective, long-acting, cannot be forgotten, is convenient, and avoids the possible side effects of the pill with its oestrogen base. However, its safety is not yet established beyond all doubt and its use as a contraceptive for some intellectually disabled women has aroused considerable controversy among people concerned with human rights.

Spermicide

There are various creams, foams, gels and tablets which act to kill sperm on contact. A tablet can be inserted high into the vagina at the opening to the womb by hand, but creams, gels and foams are usually inserted with an applicator. Generally a spermicide must be inserted no more than 20 minutes before intercourse and a new application must be used before each ejaculation. Even used strictly as directed, the failure rate of such contraceptives is very high, and they are more suitable for use in conjunction with other methods rather than on their own. Generally the use of spermicides is advised with a diaphragm. They also increase the reliability of a condom.

Condom

The condom is the simplest barrier method of artificial contraception and the only reversible contraceptive so far developed which is used by men. A condom is a thin rubber sheath which is placed on the penis before penetration. When the man ejaculates, the sperm are held in the rubber tip.

Condoms have the advantage that they are cheap and readily available. They are not completely foolproof because the rubber can tear or they can come off, but if they are used in accordance with instructions they are very effective. Used with a spermicide, the failure rate has been estimated as only 3%. Condoms have the further advantage that they not only protect the woman against becoming pregnant, they protect both partners against sexually transmitted disease, and since the advent of the AIDS virus, anyone engaging in sex with a partner who is not long-term and well known to them should use a condom. Some men complain that the rubber lessens the sensation ('like showering with a raincoat' is a common analogy), but modern ultra-thin rubbers reduce this disadvantage considerably, and the risks of engaging in unprotected sex in this day and age make such objections foolish in the extreme.

DIAPHRAGM

The diaphragm for women works on a similar principle as the condom (see above), i.e. it provides a physical barrier to the sperm meeting the egg. A diaphragm is a rubber dome with a flexible spring rim. It is inserted into the vagina before intercourse, so that it covers the cervix, or entry to the womb. It should be used with a spermicidal cream or jelly to kill any sperm that manage to wriggle around the edges. A woman must be measured by a doctor for a diaphragm of the correct size and she will also need to be instructed how to insert it properly.

Most women find a diaphragm easy enough to use, and it has a high reliability. Some women find the fact that it has to be inserted before intercourse aesthetically displeasing, but generally it presents no problems. It can be put in place some time before if necessary. It must be left in place for six hours after intercourse to ensure that all the sperm are dead before removal. Its failure rate of between 10 and 15% makes it somewhat less reliable than the condom.

A diaphragm poses no health risks unless (very rarely) either partner is allergic to the rubber.

CERVICAL CAP

Like the diaphragm, the cervical cap is a barrier method of contraception, but it is much smaller because it fits tightly over the cervix, rather than filling the vagina. There are several types of cervical caps, but the one most commonly used attaches to the cervix by suction. The cap must be fitted carefully. It should be used in the same way as the diaphragm, with spermicides and following the same precautions. It has about the same reliability as the diaphragm. The cervical cap is not widely available in Australia.

Contraceptive sponge

This recently introduced device is a sponge impregnated with spermicide which is inserted into the vagina so that it expands to cover the cervix. Like a diaphragm it is inserted before intercourse but is disposable and thrown away after use. It does not need to be fitted by a doctor and can be bought over the counter.

Intra-uterine device

The intra-uterine device (IUD) consists of a small piece of plastic, shaped like a 7, or the letter T, or a loop like an S, sometimes with fine copper wire wound round the plastic. It is inserted into the womb, and because it is a foreign body irritating the lining of the womb it stops the egg implanting (and hence the IUD can also be used as a postcoital contraceptive device if inserted within five days of unprotected intercourse). The insertion is done by a doctor and should not produce any more than minimal discomfort. A fine thread hangs down into the vagina and is used to remove the IUD when desired and also to check that it is still in place. The IUD is tiny (about 3 mm in diameter) so that it can be slid gently through the cervix into the womb; once inside it springs open into its true shape. When the time comes for it to be removed, it folds back in on itself so that it can be guided out. An IUD can be left in place for two or three years (longer if it does not have the copper) but it should be checked at least once a year by a doctor. It has the strong advantage that once it is in place it has a high degree of reliability (about 97%) and can virtually be forgotten about.

Not all women are suited to the use of IUDs. Sometimes they fall out, or they may cause heavy and painful periods. The use of an IUD results in an increased risk of pelvic infection and also an increased possibility of tubal pregnancy. IUDs seem to have fewer side effects in women who have had children, but they can be used by women who have had no children.

Natural methods

One of the so-called natural methods of contraception in which no artificial aids are used is **coitus interruptus**, in which the man withdraws his penis from the woman's vagina before orgasm so that his sperm is not ejaculated into her. This has the disadvantage of being unreliable since sperm sometimes leak out before ejaculation, and in any event the man's timing has to be accurate — not infrequently difficult to achieve. It can also take the edge off full sexual enjoyment for both partners, especially the man.

The other natural method of preventing conception is the **rhythm method**. A woman can only become pregnant for a short

Section 1: The Life Cycle

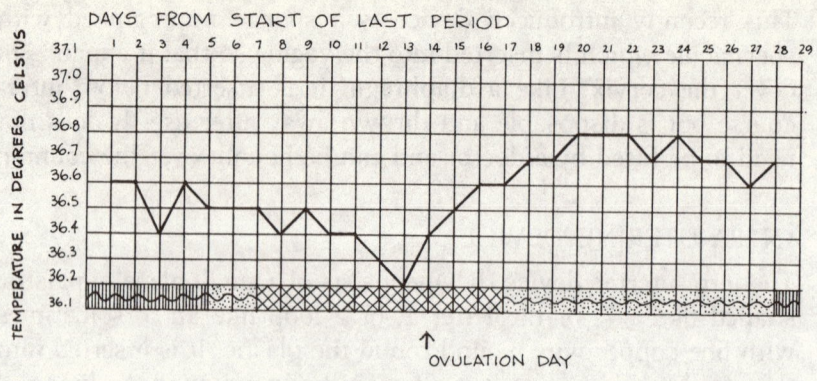

FIGURE 1: Temperature chart used in natural family planning.

period each month, a few days either side of ovulation. If she has intercourse at other times, she will not become pregnant. Theoretically, if a woman can establish when she ovulates and she and her partner refrain from having intercourse during that time and engage in sexual activity only in her 'safe period', she should not fall pregnant. Ovulation takes place in the middle of a woman's menstrual cycle, 14 days before her period, and because viable sperm may last up to seven days in her body, the time she can conceive is from seven days prior to ovulation to three days after. If a woman has a standard textbook cycle of five days bleeding out of 28, she would be 'safe' from 11 days before her period to two days after. Shorter cycles are not uncommon, and it is possible to become pregnant during periods. Many people practise this form of contraception successfully for several years, but it is notoriously unreliable. Certainly it depends on the woman having a regular cycle, but even women who are regular will sometimes vary, in which case the system breaks down. The failure rate depends a lot on the users but is generally high.

There are various more scientific means of ascertaining the safe period, involving the taking of the woman's temperature daily or analysing the appearance of the mucus produced by the cervix. These can be successful for people wishing to avoid artificial means of contraception who are prepared to be properly instructed by a doctor or family planning clinic in what to do and to follow the required procedures diligently. The Billings method (named after the Australian doctor who first recommended the technique), which combines both procedures, is said to be the most reliable.

Tubal ligation

A tubal ligation (having the tubes tied or clipped) renders a woman permanently unable to have children. As a contraceptive it is virtually 100% safe. Since it is a surgical procedure which for all practical purposes must be regarded as irreversible, it is suitable for all women who have completed their family or are sure they want no children.

A woman's Fallopian tubes are about 7 cm long and lead from each of the two ovaries to the womb. The egg released every month travels down the tube where it may be fertilised by a male sperm, in which case it will become implanted in the wall of the womb and develop into a foetus. The purpose of tying or closing the tubes is to stop the egg and the sperm meeting.

Nowadays a tubal ligation is a relatively simple operation, involving two tiny (about 1 cm) cuts in the abdomen. The surgeon then works with a telescopic device. It is generally performed under general anaesthetic with an overnight stay in hospital. The woman can expect to be off work for about a week, with minor discomfort for a few days.

Developments in microsurgery sometimes make it possible to 'untie' the tubes but the success rate is not high (about 65%) and cannot really be taken into account when deciding on the operation. Because of its permanence, a woman needs to consider all the aspects carefully and take into account all possible eventualities, for example a marriage break-up or the death of a child.

Vasectomy

A vasectomy is the procedure by which a man is rendered permanently unable to have children. It is a simpler operation than the sterilisation of a woman and is growing in popularity as men increasingly accept responsibility for family planning. Some men are concerned that a vasectomy will affect their libido or masculinity, but this is not the case. Its only effect is to stop reproduction.

A vasectomy consists of cutting and tying the vas deferens (the two tiny tubes that transport the sperm from the testicles to the penis) so that the sperm is prevented from forming part of the semen ejaculated during intercourse. Sperm is only about 5% of the seminal fluid, the other 95% being supporting and nourishing fluid which remains unchanged by the vasectomy.

The operation requires only a local anaesthetic and takes about 15 minutes. A tiny incision is made in the skin of the scrotum and each vas, which lies just under the surface, is cut. Usually a small section is removed and the two cut ends tied off. The operation is painless although there will probably be some bruising and soreness for a few days afterwards.

SECTION 1: THE LIFE CYCLE

The man does not become sterile immediately. Some sperm are stored in the sac above where the tube is tied, and this must be emptied by about a dozen ejaculations over the next few weeks. A test is normally done about six weeks after the operation to check that no sperm are getting through or remain in storage. Other forms of contraception should be used until this has been carried out and is clear.

The male hormones that establish and maintain masculinity are produced in the testicles, but these enter the bloodstream directly and are not affected in any way by the operation. The sperm themselves continue to be produced and are simply absorbed into the body without causing any problems.

As with tubal ligations, microsurgical techniques are constantly being improved so that increasingly it is possible for a vasectomy to be reversed. The success rate is higher than with a tubal ligation but by no means high enough for a couple to be able to regard it as anything but a possibility. A decision about a vasectomy needs to be taken on the basis that it is permanent and that should their marriage break down or a child die the man will be unable to have further children.

TABLE 1.1:
RELIABILITY OF CONTRACEPTIVE METHODS

Method	Percentage chance of method failure	Percentage chance of user failure
Tubal ligation	0–0.01	—
Vasectomy	0–0.01	0.15
IUD	1–1.5	1–6
Mini pill	1	2–5
Combined pill	0.3–1	2–10
Withdrawal	—	3–23
Condom	2–6	10–14
Diaphragm	2–2.5	10–20
Spermicides	2–5	15–36
No contraception	—	80–90

Fallacies

Many people believe that if a woman is breastfeeding she cannot get pregnant. It is true that breastfeeding stops ovulation in some women for some time. However, it is not a reliable or predictable method. Of women who breastfeed and have intercourse without contraception, 40% become pregnant.

Young girls often think that they can't get pregnant the 'first time'. They can and frequently do. Pregnancy depends on whether your body has released an egg, not on the number of times you have had intercourse. You can get pregnant on the first time or the tenth time or the hundredth time or any other time.

Another fallacy is 'I've had sex before and nothing happened, so I'm probably sterile.' Very few women are sterile and the chances of your being one of them are slim. You are far more likely to have been lucky and your luck is probably running out.

Pregnancy problems

Backache. A pregnant woman's pelvis has to expand at the time of birth to allow the baby through. To facilitate this expansion, the ligaments that normally hold the joints of the pelvis (and other parts of the body) together become slightly more elastic. This makes them more susceptible to strain. The joints of the spine are particularly susceptible to strains because the expanding womb shifts your centre of balance and changes your posture. Standing for any length of time is likely to impose unusual stresses on the back, and this strains the supporting ligaments and results in backache.

Slight movements of the vertebrae, one on the other, can cause nerves to be pinched and result in pain such as sciatica. This nerve pinching is further aggravated by the retention of fluid in the whole body, which causes the nerves to be slightly swollen and therefore more easily pinched.

The best way to reduce the likelihood of backache is not to gain weight excessively and to avoid all heavy lifting. If you attend antenatal classes, you will be shown the correct way of lifting, and you will also be taught exercises to help relieve the backache.

Constipation. Constipation is common in pregnancy and is thought to be due to a loosening of the muscles of the digestive tract caused by hormonal changes. In late pregnancy the enlarging womb presses on the intestines and aggravates the condition. It is not dangerous, but if it is worrying you, your doctor can recommend a faecal softener. No medication, including laxatives, should be used during pregnancy without discussing it with a doctor.

Heartburn. Indigestion or heartburn affects about half of all pregnant women. This is because during pregnancy the muscle that closes off the upper part of the stomach from the oesophagus (gullet) loosens and allows digestive juices from the stomach to flow back up the gullet and irritate it. In late pregnancy the enlarging uterus presses on the stomach and aggravates the condition.

Heartburn can be dreadfully uncomfortable but is not harmful. You may be able to lessen the symptoms by eating small, frequent meals so that there is never too much food present but always enough to absorb the stomach acid. Antacids can usually be taken safely at most stages of pregnancy, and may be used to relieve more severe symptoms. The problem disappears when the baby is born.

Morning sickness. The nausea and vomiting that affects some pregnant women between the sixth and fourteenth weeks of pregnancy is called morning sickness, but it can occur at any time of

'I'm too young to get pregnant'. If you have started menstruating, i.e. having your periods, you are not too young. You can even get pregnant before you have your first period — because the period comes after the egg has been released.

So-called astrological birth control is said to work in much the same way as the rhythm method and dictates that you will avoid pregnancy if you abstain from intercourse during your sun-moon phase — the same phase that existed on the day that you were born. According to some astrologers, women release eggs twice each month, one in mid- cycle and once during the sun-moon phase. There is no scientific basis for this belief, and for a young girl who adopts it when embarking on a sexual relationship it is likely to prove futile nonsense.

Other old wives tales say that a girl won't get pregnant if she:
- sneezes before or after having sex;
- holds her breath when the boy reaches climax;
- jumps up and down after intercourse so that the boy's sperm flows back out;
- douches after intercourse so that the sperm is washed away;
- has sex during her period.

None of these are true. Any girl and boy who are old enough to have sex are old enough not to lie to themselves with such nonsensical stories but to find out about proper contraception and how to use it.

The future

Research is continuing all the time into new methods of contraception, including the male pill. One of the methods involves the use of a hormone which regulates the release of other hormones during the ovulation cycle. This is being investigated as a nasal spray which works only on the pituitary gland and ovaries and not on other parts of the body — an obvious advance on the pill.

Research is also being carried out on a means of stopping the production of progesterone in the second half of the cycle and thus preventing the implantation of any fertilised egg in the uterus.

Other contraceptives being investigated include various devices impregnated with artificial progestogens which are inserted into the vagina or uterus and release the hormones slowly, acting directly on the reproductive organs.

Hormonal implants are already available overseas although not widespread in Australia. Their use is likely to increase. They consist of small pads, usually inserted under the skin of the upper arm, which release hormones slowly and remain active for several months or years. They mostly contain synthetic progestogens and are therefore free of the side effects of oestrogen.

SECTION 1: THE LIFE CYCLE

Research into a vaccine against pregnancy is continuing and likely to be available in the next decade. An injection every six to twelve months would give protection against pregnancy.

The so-called 'female condom' is a very old-fashioned contraceptive. Sixty years ago it consisted of a thick rubber tube, closed at one end, that was inserted into the vagina before intercourse. In recent years, a small number of women have started using these again, but now they are made of very thin rubber and are much more comfortable and aesthetic.

PREGNANCY AND BIRTH

Normal pregnancy

BEFORE PREGNANCY

Before a woman embarks on her first pregnancy, she should have a physical examination. This can reveal unknown factors in her health that may have a significant effect on her ability to fall pregnant or successfully carry a child. High blood pressure, diabetes, back disease and gynaecological problems are examples of such factors. At the pre-pregnancy checkup, the woman should be taught how to examine and care for her breasts, and one of her regular Pap smear tests should be performed. A blood test for a past history of rubella (German measles) infection will usually be arranged, and a vaccination is given if necessary. Advice on correct diet and eating patterns, weight control and bowel habits can all have a bearing on fertility. Even details on how to get pregnant can be useful (i.e. at what time of the month to try).

Smoking during pregnancy can cause small and immature babies and has been associated with birth deformities. The embryo is exposed to the hundreds of foreign chemicals that are inhaled with every puff. If you smoke and plan to get pregnant, ask your doctor now how to stop! All illegal drugs, including marijuana, will cause damage to a developing embryo. If you are addicted, discuss the problem confidentially with your doctor well before you fall pregnant so that expert help can be obtained. The consequences of a casual sniff of cocaine during pregnancy could haunt you for life every time you look at your child.

All medications and alcohol should be avoided during the vital first three months of pregnancy, unless prescribed by a doctor who knows you are pregnant. Later in pregnancy, check with your pharmacist or doctor before using even the simple grocery-type pharmaceuticals.

A pre-pregnancy checkup is of great benefit to all women.

Pregnancy diagnosis

Various tests can be used to diagnose pregnancy, most of which are based on the fact that a pregnant woman produces a hormone called human chorionic gonadotrophin (HCG), which can be detected in blood or urine as early as 12 days after conception (i.e. before a period is even missed). At this early stage, a false negative result is possible, and the tests are more reliable if carried out a couple of days after the missed period. A negative test may mean that the pregnancy is not far enough advanced to be detected, rather than that the woman is not pregnant. Some test kits are available from pharmacies, but more complex and reliable ones are used by general practitioners and obstetricians. If the test is negative, it should be repeated after a week or two to recheck the situation.

Although pregnancy actually occurs about two weeks after a woman had her last period, for convenience doctors always date a pregnancy from the first day of that last menstrual period.

There is an easy way to calculate when a pregnant woman is due to deliver. Add 7 days to the day the woman's last period started, and 9 months to the month of her last period. For example, if the last period started on 5 January 1990, she will be due to deliver on 12 October 1990.

A pregnancy lasts 40 weeks (280 days) from the beginning of the woman's last period, but only 38 weeks from conception, because she ovulates two weeks after her period starts. It is not unusual for the pregnancy to be one or two weeks shorter or longer than this.

Symptoms and body changes

The first definite sign that a woman is pregnant is that she fails to have a menstrual period when one is normally due. At about the same time as the period is missed, the woman may feel unwell, unduly tired, and her breasts may change.

When a woman becomes pregnant, her body undergoes enormous changes to cope with the new life developing within her and its eventual entry into the world. Very early, the breasts will start to prepare for the task of feeding the baby, and one of the first things the pregnant woman notices is enlarged and tender breasts and a tingling in the nipples. With a first pregnancy, the skin around the nipple (the areola) will darken, and the small lubricating glands may become more prominent to create small bumps. This darkening may also occur with the oral contraceptive pill.

Hormonal changes in early pregnancy cause the woman to want to urinate more frequently. This settles down after the twelfth week, but later in pregnancy the size of the womb puts pressure on the bladder, and frequent urination is again necessary.

Some women find that they develop dark patches on the forehead and cheeks. Called **chloasma**, these patches are caused by hormonal changes affecting the pigment cells in the skin. Such changes can also be a side effect of the contraceptive pill. The navel and a line down the centre of the woman's belly may also darken. These pigment changes fade somewhat after the pregnancy but will always remain darker than before.

As the skin of the belly stretches to accommodate the growing baby, and in other areas where fat may be found in the skin (such as breasts and buttocks), stretch marks in the form of reddish/purple streaks may develop. These will fade to a white/silver colour after the baby is born, but they will not normally disappear completely, much to the chagrin of many women. There is unfortunately nothing that can be done to prevent or treat stretch marks.

About the fourth or fifth month, the thickening waistline will turn into a bulge, and by the sixth month, the swollen belly is unmistakable. The increased bulk will change the woman's sense of balance, and this can cause muscles to become fatigued unless she can 'carry her burden with pride' and make a conscious effort to maintain an upright posture. Care of the back is vitally important in later pregnancy, as the ligaments become slightly softer and slacker with the hormonal changes, and movement between the vertebrae in the back can lead to severe and disabling pain if a nerve is pinched.

During pregnancy, the mother must supply all the food and oxygen for the developing baby and eliminate its waste materials. Because of these demands, the mother's metabolism changes, and increasing demands are made on several organs. In particular, the heart has to pump harder, and the lungs have more work to do, to supply the needs of the enlarged uterus and the placenta. Circulation to the breasts, kidneys, skin and even gums also increases. Towards the end of the pregnancy, the mother's heart is working 40% harder than normal. The lungs must keep the increased blood circulation adequately supplied with oxygen.

In the month or so before delivery, it will be difficult for the mother to get comfortable in any position, sleeplessness will be common, and the pressure of the baby's head will make passing urine a far too regular event. Aches and pains will develop in unusual areas as muscles that are not normally used are called into play to support the extra weight, normally between 7 and 12 kg (baby + fluid + placenta + enlarged uterus + enlarged breasts), that the mother is carrying around.

Development of the Foetus

Once a month, an egg that is so small that it is invisible to the human eye is released from one of a woman's ovaries and travels down the Fallopian tube towards the uterus. If during this journey the egg encounters sperm released by the woman's partner, the egg may be fertilised, and the woman has become pregnant. Once penetrated by the sperm, the egg starts multiplying, from one cell to two, then four, eight, 16, and so on, doubling in size with each division.

After ten days, the growing embryo consists of a fluid-filled ball, only a couple of millimetres across. At this point it attaches to the wall of the uterus and continues to grow, drawing all it needs from the mother through the placenta. For the first 12 weeks, the developing baby is called an embryo. The growth of the embryo is rapid to start with, but slows down as maturity approaches. The embryo soon becomes the size of a grain of rice, and then a tadpole (both in size and appearance). By the end of the first month, it is about the size of a pigeon's egg, with four small swellings at the sides, called limb buds, which will develop into arms and legs.

At eight weeks of pregnancy, the embryo is 2 cm long, and the nose, ears, fingers and toes are identifiable. Most of the internal organs form in the next four weeks, and by 12 weeks when the baby is 5.5 cm long, a pumping heart can be detected, and the baby is moving, although too weakly yet to be detected by the mother. The baby is now called a foetus.

It is during the first three months that the embryo is most prone to the development of abnormalities caused by drugs (e.g. thalidomide, isotretinoin) or infections (e.g. German measles).

At 16 weeks, the foetus is 12 cm long and its sex can be determined. The skin is bright red because it is transparent, and the blood can be seen through it. The kidneys are functioning and producing urine, which is passed into the amniotic fluid.

The 'quickening' is the time when the mother becomes aware of the baby's movements. It occurs between 16 and 18 weeks (the latter in first pregnancies). The mother usually becomes quite elated at this time, as she realises that there really is a baby inside her. The movements become gradually stronger throughout pregnancy, until it is possible to trace the movement of a limb across the belly. Babies vary dramatically in how much they move — some are very active indeed, while others are relatively quiet. During the last couple of weeks of pregnancy the baby does not move as much, as the amount of space available becomes more restricted.

By 24 weeks, the skin is the normal colour. This is the earliest that a baby has any chance of surviving outside the mother, although infants are still at high risk if born before 32 weeks. By that stage, development is complete, and the last eight weeks are merely a growth stage.

By 38 weeks, the baby has settled upside down in the uterus. During this period, the head sinks down into the mother's pelvis and is said to 'engage', ready for birth.

The miracle is completed when labour starts. The trigger for this is not accurately known, but a series of nervous and hormonal stimuli dilates the cervix that guards the opening into the womb, and starts the rhythmic contractions of the womb which will bring another human being out into the world, who in due course will start the cycle again.

THE PLACENTA

The placenta is a special outgrowth of the foetus that is firmly attached to the inside of the mother's womb. It has blood vessels that penetrate into the wall of the womb and interact with the mother's arteries and veins to enable the foetus to draw oxygen and food from the mother's system and send waste products to the mother for removal. As the foetus grows, it floats in a fluid-filled sac. It is like a water-filled balloon, and the foetus drinks the amniotic fluid and excretes into it through the kidneys. The amniotic sac and its fluid act as a very effective shock absorber so that the foetus can survive unharmed quite serious injuries to its mother (e.g. a car crash). One side of the balloon is especially modified into the placenta, while the rest is a fine but tough transparent membrane.

The foetus is connected to the placenta by the umbilical cord, which contains three intertwined blood vessels (an artery and two veins) which convey nourishment from the mother to the foetus and waste products the other way. At birth, this is between 15 and 120 cm long and runs from the navel to the placenta, where the artery and veins it contains fan out to interact with the mother's circulatory system. The mother's and baby's bloodstreams remain separate and do not mingle. Doctors will check the cord after birth, and if only one vein is present instead of two, it is probable that the baby will have some hidden birth defect.

The placenta is a flat, circular organ consisting of a spongy network of blood vessels. It acts as a combined lung, liver, kidney and digestive tract for the developing foetus. Oxygen, nutrients, waste products and other substances (e.g. alcohol and some drugs) can pass freely through the placenta from the bloodstream of the mother to the bloodstream of the foetus. Infections (particularly viruses such as German measles) may also pass to the foetus through the placenta.

Several minutes after the birth, the placenta (the afterbirth) is expelled by further contractions of the uterus, assisted by gentle traction on the cord by the doctor or midwife. Occasionally the placenta may not be expelled, which leads to appropriate intervention by a doctor (see PREGNANCY COMPLICATIONS).

HEALTH DURING PREGNANCY

After the pregnancy has been diagnosed, you should return to your general practitioner at about ten weeks of pregnancy for your first antenatal checkup or referral to an obstetrician. At this checkup you will be given a thorough examination (including an internal one), and blood and urine tests will be ordered to exclude any medical problems and to give the doctor a baseline for later comparison.

Routine antenatal checks will then be performed by your GP or obstetrician at monthly intervals until you are about 34 weeks pregnant, when the frequency will increase to fortnightly or weekly. Blood pressure and weight measurement and a quick physical check are normally performed. A small ultrasound instrument may be used to listen for the baby's heart from quite an early stage. Further blood tests will be performed once or twice during this period, and a simple test will be carried out on a urine sample at every visit. An ultrasound scan (see Section 4) may be performed to check on the size and development of the foetus, but this is not essential.

Most women are advised to take tablets containing iron and folic acid throughout pregnancy and breastfeeding, in order to prevent the mild anaemia that often accompanies pregnancy.

During the last three months of the pregnancy, antenatal classes are very beneficial. The women are taught exercises to strengthen the back and abdominal muscles, breathing exercises to cope with the various stages of labour, and strategies to cope with them. Women who attend these classes generally do far better in labour than those who do not. After the baby is born, a few more visits to a physiotherapist to get the tone back into your abdominal muscles and to strengthen the stretched muscles around the uterus and pelvis will help you regain your former figure.

Attending lectures run by the Nursing Mothers' Association (or similar organisations) to learn about breastfeeding, how to prepare for it and how to avoid problems, is also useful in the last few weeks of pregnancy and for a time after the baby is born.

Visiting the hospital or birthing centre that you have booked into for the confinement can be helpful, so that you can see the facilities and the labour ward. Then they will not appear cold and impersonal a few months later when you come to use them.

As you are the baby's sole source of nourishment during pregnancy, you should pay attention to your diet. The baby's diet depends on yours. It is not necessary to 'eat for two', but a balanced and varied diet containing plenty of fresh fruit and vegetables, as well as dairy products (calcium is required for the bones of both yourself and the baby), meat and cereal foods, is appropriate. You should not need extra vitamins if your diet is adequate. If you are a vegetarian, and particularly if you avoid all dairy and egg products too, you should discuss your special needs with a doctor.

Obviously you will gain weight when you are pregnant (about 7 to 12.5 kg by the end of the pregnancy), but excessive weight gain is bad for you. If your weight gain becomes excessive, this will be noted at one of your antenatal visits, and the doctor will give appropriate advice.

It is advisable for a pregnant woman not to smoke, because smoking adversely affects the baby's growth, and smaller babies have more problems in the early months of life. The chemicals inhaled from cigarette smoke are absorbed into the bloodstream and pass through the placenta into the baby's bloodstream, so that when the mother has a smoke, so does the baby.

Alcohol should be avoided especially during the first three months of pregnancy when the vital organs of the foetus are developing. Even in later pregnancy it is advisable to have no more than one drink every few days with a meal.

Unless a doctor has recommended otherwise (e.g. for a threatened miscarriage), there is no reason not to engage in sex during pregnancy if both partners desire it. Some women find that their sex drive decreases at certain stages of pregnancy, while other women are the opposite. A man may also be affected, being more attracted to his pregnant wife, or deterred by the new life within her. As a general rule, the foetus will not be affected by intercourse. In the last couple of months, only certain positions will be comfortable for the woman.

Labour

For weeks you have been waddling around uncomfortably. Every few hours you have Branxton-Hicks contractions that can be quite uncomfortable and sometimes wake you at night, but they always fade away. Your back aches, and you are going to the toilet every hour because your bladder has nowhere to expand. The long awaited date is due, and still nothing dramatic has occurred.

Suddenly you notice that you have lost some blood-stained fluid through the vagina, and the contractions are worse than usual. You have passed the mucus plug that seals the cervix during pregnancy, and if a lot of fluid is lost, you may have ruptured the membranes around the baby as well. Labour should start very soon after this 'show'.

Shortly afterwards you can feel the first contraction. It passes quickly, but every ten to fifteen minutes more contractions occur. Most are mild, but some make you stop in your tracks for a few seconds. When you find that two contractions have occurred only five to seven minutes apart, it is time to be taken to hospital or the birthing centre.

You are now in the first of the three stages of labour. This stage will last for about 12 hours with a first pregnancy, but will be much shorter (4 to 8 hours) with subsequent pregnancies. These times can vary significantly from one woman to another.

The hospital nurses fuss over you as you change into a nightie and answer questions. Soon afterwards, you may be given an enema. By the time the obstetrician calls in to see how you are progressing, the contractions are occurring every three or four minutes. The obstetrician examines you internally to check how far the cervix (the opening into the womb) has opened. This check will be performed several times during labour, and leads may be attached through the vagina to the baby's head to monitor its heart and general condition. The cervix steadily opens until it merges with the walls of the uterus. A fully dilated cervix is about 10 cm in diameter, and you may hear the doctors and nurses discussing the cervix dilation and measurement.

As the labour progresses, you are moved into the delivery room. In a typical hospital delivery room, white drapes hide bulky pieces of equipment, there are large lights on the ceiling, shiny sinks on one wall, and often a cheerful baby poster above them. The contractions become steadily more intense. If the pain in your abdomen doesn't attack you, the back ache does, and your partner (who has hopefully attended one or two of your antenatal classes) massages your back between pains. You begin to wonder when it will all end. The breathing exercises you were taught at the antenatal classes should prove remarkably effective in helping you with the more severe contractions. Even so, the combined backache and sharp stabs of pain may need to be relieved by an injection offered by the nurse. Breathing nitrous oxide gas on a mask when the contractions start can also make them more bearable.

Eventually you develop an irresistible desire to start pushing with all your might. Your cervix will be fully dilated by this stage, and you are now entering the second stage of labour, which will last from only a few minutes to 60 minutes or more.

Suddenly there is action around you. The obstetrician has returned and is dressed in gown, gloves and mask. You are being urged to push, and even though it hurts, it doesn't seem to matter any more, and you labour with all your might to force the head of the baby out of your body. The contractions are much more intense than before, but you should push only at the time of a contraction, as pushing at other times is wasted effort.

Another push, and another, and another, and then a sudden sweeping, elating relief, followed by a healthy cry from your new baby.

Immediately after the delivery, you are given an injection in the bottom to help contract the uterus. A minute or so after the baby is born, the umbilical cord which has been the lifeline between you and the baby for the last nine months is clamped and cut. A small sample of blood is often taken from the cord to check for any problems in the baby.

About five minutes after the baby is born, the doctor will urge you to push again and help to expel the placenta (afterbirth). This is the third stage of labour.

If you have had an episiotomy (cut) to help open your passage for the baby's head, or if there has been a tear, the doctor will now repair this with a few sutures.

You should be allowed to nurse the baby for a while (on the breast if you wish) after the birth. Then both you and the baby will be washed and cleaned, and taken back to the ward for a good rest.

THE APGAR SCORE

The Apgar score is a number that is given by doctors or midwives to a baby immediately after birth, and again five minutes later. The score gives a rough assessment of the baby's general health. The name is taken from Dr Virginia Apgar, an American anaesthetist, who devised the system in 1953. The score is derived by giving a value of 0, 1 or 2 to each of five variables — heart rate, breathing, muscle tone, reflexes and colour. The maximum score is 10.

TABLE 1.2:
APGAR SCORE

Sign	0	1	2
Heart Rate	Absent	Below 100	Above 100
Breathing	Absent	Weak	Good
Muscle Tone	Limp	Poor	Good
Reflexes	Nil	Poor	Good
Colour	Blue/pale	Blue hands and feet	Pink

When estimated at birth, a baby is considered to be seriously distressed if the Apgar score is 5, and critical if the score is 3, when urgent resuscitation is necessary. The situation becomes critical if the score remains below 5 at five minutes after birth. A score of 7 or above is considered normal.

the day. Its severity varies markedly, with about one third of pregnant women having no morning sickness, one half having it badly enough to vomit at least once, and in 5% the condition is serious enough result in prolonged bed rest or even hospitalisation.

Morning sickness is caused by the unusually high levels of oestrogen present in the mother's bloodstream during the first three months of pregnancy. Although it usually ceases after about three months, it may persist for far longer in some unlucky women. Severe cases may be associated with twins, and it is usually worse in the first pregnancy.

Because morning sickness is a self-limiting condition, treatment is usually given only when absolutely necessary. A light diet, with small, frequent meals of dry fat-free foods, is often helpful. A concentrated carbohydrate solution (Emetrol) may be taken to help relieve the nausea. Only in severe cases, and with some reluctance, will doctors prescribe more potent medications. In rare cases, fluids given by a drip into a vein are necessary for a woman hospitalised because of continued vomiting.

Morning sickness has no effect upon the development of the baby.

Pain relief in labour. Labour is usually painful, but the degree of pain and discomfort and the way it is perceived varies dramatically from one woman to another. A few decades ago, anaesthetics were routine for labour, but today the trend has swung towards natural childbirth and relaxation techniques.

Unquestionably, having a child is an experience that most women wish to experience while conscious. It is after all one of the most significant happenings in their life. However, there are many pain-relieving options, and a woman who wants to take advantage of these should never feel hesitant about doing so. A woman is not any less of a woman because she makes use of modern medical science to have a more comfortable childbirth.

One of the simplest forms of pain relief is nitrous oxide (laughing gas), usually administered through a face mask which the woman holds herself and breathes through during a contraction. The effect will last virtually only while it is being breathed and is very safe for both mother and baby. Pain-relieving injections of pethidine or similar drugs can also be given regularly, and sometimes analgesic tablets are given, but these are not particularly effective.

For women experiencing severe pain or requiring some intervention (e.g. forceps), an epidural or spinal anaesthetic (see SURGICAL TREATMENT, Section 6) is appropriate. This involves an injection into the spine, which numbs the body from the waist down. The woman feels nothing but remains quite conscious and

Pregnancy and Birth

alert, and is able to assist in the birth process. Even a caesarean section can be performed using this type of anaesthetic.

Sleep problems. Sleep disturbances during pregnancy are common. You may find it difficult to get to sleep, or to stay asleep. This may be because of the changes in hormone levels, but it may also be because you have to get up more often to urinate. In late pregnancy it can be difficult to find a comfortable position in which to lie.

Discuss the problem with your doctor, but it is unlikely the doctor will want to prescribe any sleeping medication, as it may harm the developing baby. Relaxation techniques and exercise are the most appropriate remedies. Women who are constantly tired from lack of night-time sleep should allow time for a regular afternoon nap.

Varicose veins. Many women develop varicose veins during pregnancy, especially during the later months. This is because their blood vessels have to cope with an increased supply of blood to meet the needs of the developing baby, and because of the pressure of the enlarging womb on the veins in the pelvis and abdomen. This combination of factors causes an increase in the back pressure on the superficial veins in the legs to cause them to become swollen and painful.

If you suffer from aching legs and are developing varicose veins, you should rest with your feet up as much as possible, wear loose clothing, and avoid anything tight around the top of the legs. Support stockings can both prevent the problem and relieve the symptoms. The varicose veins will become less swollen after the birth, but they will usually not disappear completely.

See also Section 5.

Pregnancy complications

ASSISTED DELIVERY

Babies are sometimes reluctant to enter into the world and must be assisted out by the doctor. Forceps have been used for 150 years to help the baby's head through the pelvis. They can be used not just to help pull out the child, but to turn the head into a more appropriate position if the head is coming out at an inappropriate angle. In a breech birth (bottom first), the forceps actually protect the following head and prevent the cervix from clamping around the neck.

Forceps consist of two spoon-shaped stainless steel blades. They slide around the side of the baby's head and fit snugly between the wall of the vagina and the head. Once placed carefully in position, the doctor, in time with the contractions, will apply traction (and sometimes rotation) to deliver the head. The baby may be born with some red marks on its face and head from the forceps, but they disappear after a week or so.

Another method of assisted delivery is vacuum extraction, in which a suction cap (ventouse) is attached to the baby's head, and traction is applied to the cap to help pull out the baby.

Bleeding from vagina during pregnancy

Extensive studies have not shown any increase in infant abnormalities after bleeding in early pregnancy. The bleeding may be due to a slight separation of the placenta from the wall of the womb as it grows, and it almost certainly does not involve the baby directly. About 30% of all pregnant women suffer from some degree of bleeding during pregnancy, and some have quite severe bleeds without losing the baby.

Bleeding in early pregnancy may also be a sign of an impending miscarriage (see below). Unfortunately nothing except rest can help the mother in this situation. Doctors cannot usually prevent miscarriages once bleeding has started.

Other causes of bleeding in pregnancy include an ectopic pregnancy (see below), vaginal ulcers or erosions, or hormonal imbalances.

Breech birth

Babies normally come into the world head first, but occasionally the wrong end fits into the mother's pelvis and cannot be dislodged. About 3% of babies are in the breech position at birth. They may be delivered by a caesarean section (see below), or normally, but with the assistance of forceps to protect the head.

Breech labours tend to take longer than head first ones, and there can be more problems for the baby, as the cord will be compressed during the delivery before the head is free to start breathing. Even so, the vast majority of breech births result in no long-term complications to the mother or child.

Caesarean section

There is a legend that Julius Caesar was delivered by surgery, giving rise to the common name for the operative delivery of a baby. This is very unlikely to have been the case as in those days surgical deliveries were only used to release an unborn child from a dying or dead mother. Julius Caesar's mother in fact bore two more children after him. In the last 2000 years the operation has been considerably refined to the point where about one in five babies are now delivered in this manner.

There are obvious situations where a caesarean section is the only choice for the obstetrician. These include a baby that is presenting side on instead of head first, a placenta (afterbirth) that is over the birth canal, a severely ill mother, a distressed infant that may not survive the rigours of the passage through the birth canal, and the woman who has been labouring for many hours with no success.

Caesarean sections may also be performed if the mother has had a previous operative birth, if she is very small, if previous children have had birth injuries or required forceps delivery, for a baby presenting bottom first, if the baby is very premature or delicate, in multiple pregnancies where the two or more babies may become entangled, and in a host of other combinations and permutations of circumstances that cannot be imagined in advance. The decision to undertake the operation is often difficult, but it will always have to be up to the judgment and clinical acumen of the obstetrician, in consultation with the mother if possible, to make the final decision.

The operation is extremely safe to both mother and child. A light anaesthetic is given to the mother, and the baby is usually delivered within five minutes. The anaesthetic is then deepened while the longer and more complex task of repairing the womb and abdominal muscles is undertaken. In many cases, the scar of a caesarean can be low and horizontal, below the bikini line, to avoid any disfigurement.

The latest innovation is epidural anaesthesia, in which a needle is placed in the middle of the mother's back, and through this an anaesthetic is introduced. The woman feels nothing below the waist, and although sedated is quite awake and able to participate in the birth of her baby, seeing it only seconds after it is delivered by the surgeon. Some doctors and hospitals allow the woman's partner to be present during these deliveries.

Recovery from a caesarean is slower than for normal child birth, but most women leave hospital within ten days. It does not affect breastfeeding or the chances of future pregnancies, and does not increase the risk of miscarriage.

DIABETES IN PREGNANCY

Pregnancy may trigger diabetes in a woman who was previously well but predisposed towards this disease. One of the reasons for regular antenatal visits to doctors and the urine tests taken at each visit is to detect diabetes at an early stage. If diabetes develops, the mother can be treated and controlled by regular injections of insulin. In some cases, the diabetes will disappear after the pregnancy, but it usually recurs in later years.

If the diabetes is not adequately controlled, serious consequences can result. In mild cases, the child may be born grossly overweight but otherwise be healthy. In more severe cases, the diabetes can cause a miscarriage, eclampsia, malformations of the foetus, urinary and kidney infections, fungal infections (thrush) of the vagina, premature labour, difficult labour, breathing problems in the baby after birth, or death of the baby within the womb.

Diabetic women tend to have difficulty in falling pregnant, unless their diabetes is very well controlled.

See also DIABETES, Section 5.

ECLAMPSIA

See pre-eclampsia and eclampsia (below).

ECTOPIC PREGNANCY

A foetus normally grows within the womb (uterus). An ectopic pregnancy is one that starts and continues to develop outside the womb. About one in every 200 pregnancies is ectopic. Conditions such as pelvic inflammatory disease and salpingitis (see separate entries) increase the risk of ectopic pregnancies, as they cause damage to the Fallopian tubes. Other infections in the pelvis (e.g. severe appendicitis) may also be responsible for tube damage.

Symptoms of an ectopic pregnancy may be minimal until a sudden crisis from rupture of blood vessels occurs, but most women have abnormal vaginal bleeding or pains low in the abdomen in the early part of the pregnancy. Many ectopic pregnancies fail to develop past an early stage, and appear to be a normal miscarriage. Serious problems can occur if the ectopic pregnancy does continue to grow.

The most common site for an ectopic pregnancy is the Fallopian tube, which leads from the ovary to the top corner of the womb. A pregnancy in the tube will slowly dilate it until it eventually bursts. This will cause severe bleeding into the abdomen and is an urgent, life-threatening situation for the mother. Other possible sites for an ectopic pregnancy include on or around the ovary, in the abdomen or pelvis, or in the narrow angle where the Fallopian tube enters the uterus.

If an ectopic pregnancy is suspected, an ultrasound scan can be performed to confirm the exact position of any pregnancy. If the pregnancy is found to be ectopic, the woman must be treated in a major hospital. Surgery to save the mother's life is essential, as a ruptured ectopic pregnancy can cause the woman very rapidly to bleed to death internally. If the ectopic site is the Fallopian tube, the tube on that side is usually removed during the operation. With early diagnosis and improved surgical techniques, the tube may not have to be removed. Even if it is lost, the woman can fall pregnant again from the tube and ovary on the other side.

It is rare for a foetus to survive any ectopic pregnancy.

Face Presentation

Normally the baby presents the crown of its head to the opening of the uterus during birth, with the neck bent and the chin on the chest. This lets the smallest diameter of the head pass through the birth canal. In a very small number of cases, the neck becomes extended (bent back) instead of flexed (bent forward), and the face presents itself to the outside. This is a significant problem, as in a face presentation the largest diameter of the head is trying to force its way through the birth canal. The result is a very long labour, and damage to both mother and baby is possible.

Obstetricians can sometimes disengage (push up) the head from the pelvis and bring it back down again with the crown of the head presenting, but in most cases a caesarean section is the treatment of choice.

Hydramnios

In the womb, the baby is surrounded by and floats in a sac filled with amniotic fluid. This fluid acts to protect the foetus from bumps and jarring, recirculates waste, and acts as a fluid for the baby to drink. If an excessive amount of fluid is present, the condition is called **polyhydramnios**.

Normally there is about a litre (1000 mL) of amniotic fluid at birth. A volume greater than 1500 mL is considered to be diagnostic of polyhydramnios, but it may not become apparent until 2500 mL or more is present.

Polyhydramnios occurs in about one in every 100 pregnancies, and it may be a sign that the foetus has a significant abnormality that prevents it from drinking or causes the excess production of urine. Other causes include a twin pregnancy, and diabetes or heart disease in the mother. In over half the cases no specific cause for the excess fluid can ever be found.

The condition is diagnosed by an ultrasound scan, and if proved, further investigations to determine the cause of the condition must follow. The treatment will depend upon the result of these tests, but often none is necessary.

The reverse condition, when insufficient amniotic fluid (less than 200 mL) is present, is called **oligohydramnios**. This may also be caused by abnormal development of the foetus, but in most cases, there is again no reason for the problem. Abnormal function of the placenta is another possible cause.

Induced Labour

A pregnancy that goes beyond about 42 weeks can put the baby at risk because the placenta starts to degenerate. It is therefore sometimes necessary to start (induce) labour artificially. Labour may also be induced for a number of other reasons, including diseases of the mother (e.g. pre-eclampsia, diabetes), and problems with the baby (e.g. foetal distress from a twisted cord or separating placenta).

Labour can be induced in a number of ways, including rupturing the membranes through the vagina, stimulating the cervix, by tablets or (most commonly) a drip into a vein in the arm. Using these methods, doctors can control the rate of labour quite accurately to ensure that there are no problems for either mother or baby.

MISCARRIAGE (SPONTANEOUS ABORTION)

A miscarriage is always most upsetting to the parents, particularly if there has been difficulty in achieving the pregnancy in the first place. A miscarriage usually starts with a slight vaginal bleed, then period-type cramps low in the abdomen. The bleeding becomes heavier, and eventually clots and tissue may pass.

The most common cause of a miscarriage is a 'blighted ovum'. This is best thought of as a growing placenta without the presence of a baby. The abnormal growth is detected, and then rejected, by the woman's body. A 'blighted ovum' is purely bad luck, and no blame can be placed on the parents for its development. A subsequent pregnancy has a normal chance of success. Other causes include abnormalities of the foetus, death of the foetus, severe infections in the mother (e.g. hepatitis), abnormalities of the womb, hormonal problems, emotional stress and a violent injury to the mother.

At least one quarter of all pregnancies end as a miscarriage, but many of these occur at a very early stage and are merely passed off as an abnormal period by the woman. Up to 15% of diagnosed pregnancies end as a miscarriage.

There is no treatment for a threatened miscarriage except bed rest. If a miscarriage occurs, it may be necessary to have a minor operation (curettage) to clean out the womb. If this operation is not performed, there may be prolonged bleeding, continued pelvic pain, and difficulty in falling pregnant again. The operation also gives the doctor an opportunity to detect any problem that may have caused the miscarriage.

Women who have repeated miscarriages will be investigated further, and may be given additional hormonal or surgical treatment by a gynaecologist.

PLACENTAL PROBLEMS

Placenta accreta is a rare condition that occurs when the placenta attaches itself too firmly to the wall of the uterus and cannot be removed after birth. Heavy bleeding often occurs after the delivery of the baby, and the usual treatment is removal of the uterus (a hysterectomy) as an emergency procedure.

Placenta praevia. Normally the placenta attaches to the front, back or side of the uterus, but if it attaches to the lower part, it may cover the opening of the uterus, through the cervix to the outside. This is placenta praevia. It is more common in women who have had several pregnancies, and it occurs in one in every 150 pregnancies.

In the later stages of pregnancy, the cervix starts to dilate to allow the head of the baby to drop, prior to labour starting. If the placenta is over the opening, it will be damaged by the dilation of the cervix and the pressure from the baby's head, and heavy bleeding may occur suddenly.

Placenta praevia may be suspected by the presence of a baby that is unusually high in the womb, and the position of the placenta can be seen accurately on an ultrasound scan (see Section 4). When diagnosed, the mother will be watched carefully, often in hospital, and about a month before the due date, a caesarean section will be performed to remove both baby and placenta safely.

A bleeding placenta praevia can be a medical emergency, as quite torrential bleeding can occur which may threaten the lives of both mother and baby. The only treatment is an urgent caesarean section (see above).

Placental abruption is the term used for a partial separation of one portion of the placenta from the wall of the uterus. It usually causes some vaginal bleeding, but usually no pain. Abruption may be caused by high blood pressure in the mother, or injury to the mother, but in the vast majority of cases, no specific cause can be found. Mild cases cause no long-term problems, but if a large portion of the placenta separates from the uterus, the blood supply to the foetus may be reduced and cause reduced growth or, in severe cases, death of the foetus.

No treatment is available or necessary in most cases, but if there is significant bleeding, the mother may need a transfusion. In the rare cases where the foetus dies, an operation to remove it is necessary.

Placental retention. After the delivery of the baby, the placenta normally separates away from the wall of the uterus and is expelled by the contractions of the uterus within a few minutes. The process may be assisted by a doctor using injections to improve the uterine contractions and manoeuvres to assist the separation of the placenta. If it fails to separate from the uterus and remains retained within the uterus, it is necessary to perform a simple procedure to remove the retained placenta. Without this procedure, the mother would continue to bleed, and this could threaten her life.

Under a general anaesthetic, the doctor slides his hand into the uterus, and uses his fingers to separate the placenta from the uterus and lift it away from the wall of the uterus, so that it can be drawn to the outside of the body through the vagina.

PRE-ECLAMPSIA AND ECLAMPSIA

Eclampsia is a very serious disease that occurs only in pregnancy. In Australia it is very uncommon, because most women undertake regular antenatal visits and checks. Pre-eclampsia is a condition that precedes eclampsia, and this is detected in about 10% of all pregnant women. The correct treatment of pre-eclampsia prevents eclampsia.

The exact cause of pre-eclampsia is unknown, but it is thought to be due to the production of abnormal quantities of hormones by the placenta. It is more common in first pregnancies, twins and diabetes. Pre-eclampsia normally develops in the last three months of pregnancy, but may not develop until labour commences, when it may progress rapidly to eclampsia if not detected.

The early detection of pre-eclampsia is essential for the good health of both mother and baby. Doctors diagnose the condition by noting high blood pressure, swollen ankles, abnormalities (excess protein) in the urine and excessive weight gain (fluid retention). Not until the condition is well established does the patient develop the symptoms of headache, nausea, vomiting, abdominal pain and disturbances of vision.

If no treatment is given, the mother may develop eclampsia. This causes convulsions, coma, strokes, heart attacks, death of the baby and possibly death of the mother.

Pre-eclampsia is treated by strict rest (which can be very effective), drugs to lower blood pressure and remove excess fluid, sedatives, and in severe cases, early delivery of the baby.

PREMATURE LABOUR

A pregnancy normally lasts 40 weeks from the last menstrual period. A birth that occurs at less than 37 weeks is considered to be premature. Before 20 weeks, any birth that occurs is considered to be a miscarriage. It is rare for an infant born before 26 weeks to survive, and only after 30 weeks are the chances of survival considered to be good (see PREMATURE INFANT below).

Premature labour occurs in about 7% of pregnancies. There is no apparent cause in over half the cases, but in others, high blood pressure, diabetes, two or more babies, more than six previous pregnancies, foetal abnormalities, polyhydramnios (see above) and abnormalities of the uterus may be responsible.

Premature labour may now be prevented or controlled in some cases by injections of drugs such as salbutamol (Ventolin — see Section 6), which is also used to treat asthma. Strict bed rest is the only other form of treatment.

Prolapsed cord

Very rarely, when the waters break, the umbilical cord slips down into the birth canal. This is a medical emergency, as the start of labour usually follows soon after the waters break, and the cord will be compressed as the baby moves down into the birth canal, cutting off its oxygen supply. This problem is more common with breech births, as the smaller bottom is more likely than the larger head to allow the cord to slip past it into the birth canal.

The only treatment for a prolapsed cord is a caesarean section as soon as possible. In the meantime, the mother may be placed in a kneeling position, with her head down on the bed and her bottom in the air. Drugs may be given to stop labour as well.

Prolonged labour

Labour may be prolonged for several reasons. The muscles of the uterus may not produce sufficiently strong contractions (a 'lazy' uterus), or may not contract regularly. Some women have incoordinate contractions, which cause different parts of the uterine muscle to contract at different times. This can result in significant discomfort but minimal progress in labour. Injections may help the contractions, but sometimes a caesarean section is necessary.

There may also be an obstruction to the passage of the baby through the birth canal. This can be caused by the baby having a large head, having the head twisted in an awkward position, or having an abnormal part of the baby presenting (e.g. shoulder instead of head); or the mother may have a narrow pelvis that does not allow sufficient room for the baby to pass. Sometimes these situations can be assisted by forceps, but often a caesarean section is necessary for the well-being of the baby.

In some women, the cervix fails to dilate and remains as a thick fibrous ring that resists any progress of the baby down the birth canal. In an emergency the cervix may be cut, but in most cases doctors would again prefer to perform a caesarean section.

Spontaneous abortion

See MISCARRIAGE (above).

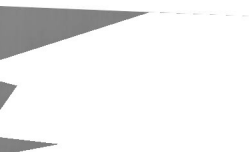

Premature infant

The survival of a baby born before 37 weeks of pregnancy depends more upon the weight of the baby than the actual number of weeks of pregnancy (see PREGNANCY COMPLICATIONS above). Babies under 500 g have only a 40% chance of survival, under 1000 g a 65% chance, and over 1500 g a nearly 100% chance of survival. These figures are for the best units in Australia, but babies born prematurely in remote areas will have far lower survival rates.

The problems that very premature babies face include liver failure and jaundice, inability to maintain body temperature, immature lungs (see RESPIRATORY DISTRESS SYNDROME, INFANT, Section 5), inability to maintain the correct balance of chemicals in the blood, patent ductus arteriosus (see Section 5), increased risk of infection due to an immature defence system, bleeding excessively, and eye problems including blindness. The smaller the baby, the greater the problems, and the more intensive the care required from specialised units in major hospitals.

The activity and processes of immature babies must be monitored carefully. Tubes and leads to and from the infant may appear to overwhelm it but are necessary to monitor the heart and breathing, supply oxygen, assist breathing in some cases, feed the baby, drain away urine, keep the temperature at the correct level, and maintain the correct chemical balance in the blood.

Even some of the treatments to help these babies can have serious complications. Many require oxygen to allow them to breathe, but too much oxygen can cause a condition called **retrolental fibroplasia** that damages the retina (light sensitive area) at the back of the eye to cause permanent blindness.

A baby born prematurely will be a little later in reaching the milestones of infancy and should have routine immunisations delayed. The delay is roughly the number of weeks of prematurity before 37 weeks (i.e. a baby born at 31 weeks is 6 weeks before 37 weeks, and can expect its milestones and vaccinations to be delayed by 6 weeks). The delay is halved by the time the child reaches six months of age, and disappears completely by one year of age.

INFANT FEEDING

Breastfeeding

When a woman has given birth, her breasts will automatically start to produce milk to feed the baby. In developed Western countries, women have a choice whether to breastfeed or bottle-feed, and the decision is one for the mother alone and depends on what she feels most comfortable doing.

'BREASTFEEDING IS BEST'.

This admonition features prominently on cans of infant formula and on advertising for breast milk substitutes in many third-world countries, and there is little doubt that it is true. Because of poverty, poor hygiene and poorly prepared formula, bottle-feeding should be actively discouraged in such areas, including among our own Aborigines.

Unfortunately, for a variety of reasons, not all mothers are capable of breastfeeding. Those who can't should not feel guilty, but should accept that this is a problem that can occur through no fault of theirs, and be grateful that there are excellent feeding formulas available for their child.

The advantages of breastfeeding include the obvious convenience of avoiding the need to sterilise bottles and prepare formulas, but more significant are the advantages it gives the child in protecting it from some childhood infections and the stimulation it gives the mothers uterus to contract to its pre-pregnant size more rapidly. Being a cost-free food, it can also help the strained budget of a young couple.

During the last three months of pregnancy, you should prepare your breasts for feeding. The skin naturally produces protective oils which help to make the nipple and areola strong. Soap should be used sparingly, as it washes away the protective oils and may lead to cracking of the nipples. The nipples also become more elastic in late pregnancy as their connective tissue softens. This process can be aided by simple exercises — hold the nipple between thumb and forefinger and gently roll it several times. To help strengthen the nipple and areola, rub in lanolin.

Babies don't consume much food for the first three or four days of life. Nevertheless, they are usually put to the breast shortly after birth. For the first few days the breasts produce colostrum, a very watery, sweet milk, which is specifically designed to nourish the newborn. It contains maternal antibodies which the baby can only get this way, and this assists the newborn to ward off infections. There is no artificial equivalent to colostrum, which is why even mothers who do not intend to breastfeed their babies are often advised to give them a few days at the breast.

Most babies know how to suck from birth, but some are a little slow to develop the technique and require some encouragement. Once they have discovered that sucking equals food equals feeling good, feeding normally proceeds smoothly. All babies are born with a sucking reflex, and will turn towards the side on which their cheek is stroked. Moving the baby's cheek gently against the nipple will cause most babies to turn towards the nipple and start sucking.

Like other beings, babies feed better if they are in a relaxed comfortable environment, with a relaxed comfortable mother. A baby who is upset will not be able to concentrate on feeding, and if the mother is tense and anxious, the baby will sense this and react, and she will not be able to produce the 'let-down reflex' which allows the milk to flow. Many babies are sleepy for the first few days of life and may go to sleep after a few sucks. This doesn't matter, and the baby should be allowed to establish its own feeding rhythm. Bouncing it awake or flicking its feet is not conducive to the baby developing a liking for being fed!

Breastfed babies regulate the amount of milk they need by themselves. Sometimes they will take a lot, sometimes a little. The milk supply is a natural supply and demand system. If the baby drinks a lot, the breasts will manufacture more milk in response to the vigorous stimulation. Mothers of twins can produce enough milk to feed both babies because of this mechanism. If the baby's demands are variable in the early stages of feeding, you may need to express some milk by hand to encourage its production until the supply becomes established.

To express milk by hand, cup your breast in one hand, placing your thumb above and forefinger blow the dark area around the nipple (the areola). Squeeze thumb and forefinger together gently, but do not slide them towards the nipple. Rotate the hand position slightly between squeezes so that all the milk ducts that radiate out from the nipple are reached. It is helpful to imagine that you are squeezing an orange — each segment must be squeezed to obtain all the juice, and each duct should be squeezed to empty milk out of each area of the breast.

While milk is being produced, a woman's reproductive hormones are suppressed and she may not have any periods. This varies greatly from woman to woman, and some have regular periods while feeding, some have irregular bleeds, and most have none. Breastfeeding is sometimes relied upon as a form of contraception. This is not safe. The chances of pregnancy are only reduced, not eliminated. The mini contraceptive pill, condoms, and the intra-uterine device can all be used during breastfeeding to prevent pregnancy.

It is important to have a very nourishing diet throughout pregnancy and lactation. The mother's daily protein intake should be increased by eating an extra egg, or about 50 g of fish or meat, and extra fresh fruit and vegetables should be eaten. Both the mother and the baby need plenty of calcium, which can be found in dairy products, green leafy vegetables and nuts. Extra iron can be obtained from egg yolk, dark green vegetables (e.g. spinach), as well as from red meat and liver. Extra fluid is also needed.

When weaning is desired, it is best done gradually over several weeks, with one breastfeed at a time being stopped in favour of solids, formula or cow's milk. The milk supply will gradually reduce, and the breasts will return to their original size. Starting an oral contraceptive pill containing oestrogen can assist in the reduction of breast milk and in weaning. When weaning is carried out too quickly, the breasts may not have time to adjust to the reduced needs, and may become engorged (see below).

Breastfeeding problems

Blocked milk duct. A small hard lump in the breast may be a blocked milk duct. If it remains after you massage it and bathe it in warm water, see your doctor, as it may also be an abscess, a breast infection, or in very rare cases a cancer (see Section 5).

Cracked nipples. A common complaint, especially in first-time mothers, is a cracked nipple. It usually starts a few days after the baby starts feeding and can be excruciatingly painful. Preparing your nipples for breastfeeding (see above) should lessen the likelihood of this problem. If a crack does appear, soothing creams are available from chemists or doctors to settle the problem, and often the baby will have to be fed from the other breast for a few days until the worst of the discomfort passes.

Excess breast milk and engorged breasts. One of the most common breast problems is engorgement, which is not only uncomfortable but may lead to difficulty in feeding and to infection. If the breasts are swollen and overfilled with milk, expressing the excess milk usually relieves the discomfort. This can be done by hand under a shower or into a container, or with the assistance of a breast pump. At other times, expressed milk may be kept and given to the baby by a carer while the mother is out or at work. Breastfeeding need not tie the mother to the home.

The infant may find it difficult to suckle on an overfilled breast, so expressing a little milk before the feed may be helpful. A well fitted, supportive bra is essential for the mother's comfort. Mild analgesics such as aspirin may be necessary, particularly before feeds, so that the feeding itself is less painful. Heat, in the form of a warm cloth or hot shower, will help with the expression of milk and with releasing milk from blocked areas of the breast.

Engorgement usually settles down after a few days or a week, but if the problem persists, fluid tablets can be used to reduce the amount of total fluid in the body and make it more difficult for the body to produce milk. In severe cases, partial suppression of the milk supply (see below) may be necessary.

Inadequate breast milk supply. Breastfeeding may be started immediately after birth in the labour ward. Babies have an instinct that enables them to turn towards the nipple when it is brushed against their cheek, and the suckling at this early stage gives comfort to both mother and child. In the next few days, relatively frequent feeds should be the rule to give stimulation to the breast and build up the milk supply. The breast milk is initially called colostrum and is relatively weak and watery. It slowly becomes thicker and heavier over the next week, naturally compensating for the infant's increasing demands.

After the first week, the frequency of feeding should be determined by the mother and child's needs, not laid down by any arbitrary authority. Each will work out what is best for them, with the number of feeds varying between five and ten a day.

If the milk supply appears to be inadequate, increasing the frequency of feeds will increase the breast stimulation, and the reflex between the breast and the pituitary gland in the brain is also stimulated. This gland then increases the supply of hormones that cause the production of milk. Sometimes, medications that stimulate the pituitary gland can be used to increase milk production, or even induce milk production in mothers who adopt a baby.

A mother who is tense and anxious about her new baby may have trouble breastfeeding. The mother should be allowed plenty of time for feeding and relaxation so that she becomes more relaxed and never feels rushed. A lack of privacy can sometimes be a hindrance to successful breastfeeding. Lots of reassurance, support from family, and advice from doctors, health centre nurses or the Nursing Mothers Association can help her through this difficult time.

The best way to determine if the baby is receiving adequate milk is regular weighing at a child welfare clinic or doctor's surgery. Provided the weight is steadily increasing, there is no need for concern. If the weight gain is very slight, or static, and increasing the frequency of feeds fails to improve the breast milk supply, then as a last resort supplementation of the breast feeds may be required. It is best to offer the breast first, and once they appear to be empty of milk, a bottle of suitable formula can be given to finish the feed.

Inverted nipples. Some women have flat or inverted nipples. Your nipple is also inverted if it retreats when you try to express milk by hand. If you intend to breastfeed, the doctor will examine your breasts, and if your nipples are flat or inverted, a nipple shield may be worn to correct the problem. The shield fits over the nipple drawing it out gently, making it protrude enough for the baby to feed. Stimulating the nipple by rolling it between finger and thumb, and exposing the breasts to fresh air (but not direct sunlight) may also help.

Mastitis. See BREAST INFECTION, Section 5.

Suppression of breast milk. If a mother desires not to feed her new baby, cannot feed because of disease or drug treatment, or the baby cannot be breastfed because of prematurity or other disease, it is necessary to suppress milk production. A firm bra should be worn and nipple stimulation should be avoided. Fluid tablets can assist reducing engorgement, and occasionally oestrogens may be prescribed. The best medication to stop the production of breast milk is bromocriptine (Parlodel) which will dry up most women's milk in three or four days, but it must be taken for at least ten days to stop it from recurring. It may cause some nausea in the first few days, but this settles with time.

Bottle-feeding

Although cow's milk is part of the normal diet of most Western nations, it is not suitable for young babies. The naturally intended food for babies is breast milk, and a baby who is not being breastfed must be fed with special formulas developed to approximate breast milk, which has more sugar and less protein than cow's milk. Most formulas are based on cow's milk but have been extensively modified by removing or adding appropriate food groups, vitamins and minerals. They are usually marketed in a dried or concentrated form, and have to be reconstituted with boiled water for use.

Provided the manufacturer's instructions are followed exactly, most babies will thrive on formula. It is quite wrong to think that a slightly stronger formula might give the baby more nourishment. If you make the mixture stronger than the manufacturer recommends, the baby will get too much fat, protein, minerals and salt, and not enough water.

A baby needs time to develop its resistance to infection. Bacteria exist in all environments, and our homes are no exception. Most of us have developed immunity to common germs, and even young babies are able to fight off germs that are inhaled or sucked off hands. Feeding is different. Milk, especially when at room temperature, is an ideal breeding ground for bacteria, and it is therefore essential that formula is prepared in a sterile environment. Bottles, utensils, measuring implements, teats and anything used in the preparation of a baby's food must be boiled and stored in one of the commercially available sterilising solutions. You should also wash your hands before embarking on preparation. Made-up formula must be stored in the refrigerator. If these precautions are not followed, the baby may develop gastroenteritis and require hospitalisation.

You should allow your baby some say in how much food s/he needs. You will generally be advised by the hospital or baby health clinic how much to offer the baby (calculated according to weight), but just as breastfed babies have different needs that can vary from feed to feed, so too do bottle-fed babies. Mothers often feel that the baby should finish the last drop in the bottle. But breastfeeding mothers have no means of measuring out the quantity the baby will receive (other than weighing the baby before and after a feed) and how much is left over, and mothers giving a bottle should adopt the same approach. Within reason, babies can generally be relied upon to assess their own needs quite satisfactorily.

Just as with breastfed babies, it is generally considered best to feed a baby as and when they are hungry. In the first few weeks this may be at irregular and frequent intervals. After all, in the womb, the baby's food was constantly replenished. It takes about three or four hours for a feed to be digested, and as the baby's digestive system matures, signs of hunger will normally settle down into a regular pattern.

A baby who is fed according to a rigid four-hourly schedule will go through the same process — except it is likely to make life miserable for everyone. After a few weeks the baby will happily accept the routine because it fits in with their natural requirements, but in the meantime you will have a fretful crying baby and have to expend a great deal of effort in trying to find other means of comfort.

The rate at which babies feed also varies. Some like to gulp down their formula, while others like to take things easy. The rate of feed can upset a baby if it is too fast or slow for its liking. Teats with different hole sizes can be purchased, and a small hole can be enlarged with a hot needle. Frequent breaks from the bottle during a feed in order to let a burp come up and the milk go down can also smooth the progress of the feed and avoid stomach discomfort afterwards.

BABIES AND YOUNG CHILDREN

Growth and development of babies

A child grows faster during babyhood than at any other stage of its life, including adolescence. By the age of 18 months a girl is usually half her adult height, and a boy is by the age of two years. There is little correlation between the rate of growth in childhood and eventual height. Many children grow quickly and then stop early so that they are short, whereas others seem to grow at a slower pace but continue until they outstrip everyone else. The most significant factor in determining height is heredity — the children of tall parents will usually also be tall. Nutrition is also significant, and a child who is poorly nourished is likely to be shorter than one who is well nourished. Advances in nutrition are the main reason for an overall increase in the height of populations of the developed world.

Body proportions of babies and children are markedly different from those in adults. A baby's head is disproportionately large compared with that of an adult, and its legs are disproportionately short. A baby's head is about a quarter of its length, but an adult's head is about one eighth of their height. Between birth and adulthood, a person's head just about doubles in size, the trunk trebles in length, the arms increase their length by four times, and the legs grow to about five times their original length.

At birth, babies have almost no ability to control their movements. At the age of about four weeks, a baby placed on its stomach can usually hold its head up. At about four months, the baby will usually be able to sit up with support, and at the age of seven months should be able to sit alone. At around eight months, most babies can stand with assistance, and will start to crawl at ten months. They can probably put one leg after the other if they are led at about 11 months, and pull themselves up on the furniture by one year. At about 14 months a baby can usually stand alone, and the major milestone of walking will probably occur around 15 months. These are average figures and many children will reach them much earlier and others much later. Physical development does not equate with mental development, and parents should not be concerned if their child takes its time about reaching the various stages — Einstein was so slow in learning to talk that his parents feared he was retarded.

TABLE 1.3:
PHYSICAL GROWTH

Age (months)	Weight (kg)	Length (cm)
GIRLS:		
Birth	2.4–3.8	45–53
3	4.2–6.8	55–63
6	5.8–8.8	61–70
9	7–10.2	66–75
12	7.8–11.2	70–79
15	8.4–12	73–83
18	9–12.8	76–86
21	9.4–13.4	79–89
24	9.8–14	81–92
BOYS:		
Birth	2.5–4.2	46–54
3	4.4–7.4	56–65
6	6.2–9.4	63–72
9	7.4–11	68–77
12	8.4–12	72–81
15	9–12.8	75–85
18	9.6–13.4	78–88
21	10–14	80–91
24	10.6–15	82–94

BEHAVIOUR

Babies are individuals from the time they are born. The age-old argument as to the relative importance in personality-terms of heredity or environment is interesting and both are unquestionably significant. However, to attribute every facet of a child's life to environmental factors must be regarded as absurd. Any mother will testify to the fact that babies are born with distinct personalities and frequently provide evidence of individual characteristics before they are born by the degree of activity they indulge in in the womb. Some babies have sunny, contented natures, others are fretful and discontented. Life can be very difficult if yours is one of the latter. However, a young baby's life revolves around physical comfort, and generally a baby will display signs of distress for a reason, e.g. it is hungry or wet, or has a pain somewhere.

Most of the so-called behaviour problems of young children are simply reactions to situations that children face as they grow up and learn to cope with the world they live in.

Thumb sucking. In a young baby, sucking is a very strong reflex, and most babies suck their thumbs or fingers at some stage. Most will stop of their own volition after a few months, or perhaps after they begin toddling around and have many more interesting activities to occupy their minds. Some parents feel they should stop a baby sucking, but this is likely to do more harm than good as the baby's sucking reflex remains unsatisfied. If a toddler of two or three is still sucking its thumb, a parent may wish to remove the thumb gently and distract the child with another activity, but to get cross or force the issue will frustrate and upset the child and usually be unsuccessful.

The use of a dummy continues to arouse different views. If a parent would prefer a child to suck a dummy to a thumb, there is no good reason why not, provided the dummy can be kept clean. To coat a dummy with honey or some other sweet substance, however, is inviting later dental problems and almost inevitably will lead to the child developing a propensity for sweet foods, which can cause lifelong problems.

Comforters. Some children develop an attachment for a particular toy or article. This may be a teddy bear or soft toy, or simply a piece of blanket which gives the child a feeling of comfort and security. Some children only require their comforter before settling down to go to sleep, others carry it around all day. Provided the object can be kept clean, clearly its presence is harmless, and the child should not be deprived of it. On the other hand, some parents seem to feel that their child 'should' have a favourite teddy or some such toy, and insist on the child taking it to bed when the child seems completely disinterested. Even young children are capable of making up their own minds about what they need in the way of comforters, and parents might sometimes ask themselves whether the behaviour they are insisting on is for the child's benefit or the parents'.

Temper tantrums. Most children will scream and cry with rage if they are frustrated. Nearly all children have the occasional tantrum, and some children have them frequently. Tantrums seem to reach their peak around the age of two when the child is beginning to assert its own independence — hence the 'terrible twos'. Toddlers who have a lot of tantrums are usually lively children, and may be very intelligent and have a strong desire to extend their horizons to things that are still beyond them. It is important to be aware that a child who has a tantrum is a child whose frustration has gone beyond the limits of their tolerance and the child can no longer help their behaviour. A tantrum is as frightening for a child as it is unpleasant for you. The best way to deal with tantrums is to prevent them by organising the child's life so that frustration is at a minimum. If a child is having a tantrum, it is pointless to try to remonstrate or argue — the child is not capable of any rational response. Try to prevent the child from getting hurt or causing damage by holding them gently but firmly on the floor. As the child calms down, they will usually find comfort in your being there. A child should neither be rewarded nor punished for a tantrum. If the tantrum was because you wouldn't let them go out to play, don't change your mind once the tantrum has taken place. On the other hand, if you were about to go for a drive in the car, continue with your plans once the tantrum has ended. As the child gets bigger, stronger and feels more confident in its ability to cope with life, the tantrums will usually come to an end.

One of the most frightening forms of tantrum (for parents) is the young baby who holds its breath, possibly until it turns blue and even loses consciousness for a brief period. Older children sometimes bang their heads on the ground or the sides of their cot. Despite their obvious unpleasantness for parents, these forms of behaviour do not seem to cause any harm, although a parent worried about some serious abnormality shouldn't hesitate to consult a doctor.

Teething

Most babies have some discomfort while they are teething. They may dribble and become fretful and irritable. Sometimes bowel movements become slightly loose, but it is a mistake to blame diarrhoea, vomiting, fever or any other sign of illness on teething. If a child is sick it needs medical help.

The reason a child cries when teething is that its gums are hurting. Chewing on a rattle or teething ring may help, as may rubbing the gums with your finger. It is generally better to avoid teething gels, as most of them contain powerful drugs.

Teeth normally start to appear around five or six months,

although babies vary widely, with some cutting a tooth as early as three months and some not until seven or eight months. A baby who cuts teeth earlier than average is not brighter or more advanced than one who cuts them later. Teeth usually appear quite rapidly in the child's second six months, and by the time they are nine or ten months, most babies have both the top and bottom four front teeth. The molars then start to appear around the age of one. These are likely to cause some discomfort even in a baby who has had none before, since the larger, broader shape makes it difficult for them to push through the gum. Most of the first or 'milk' teeth will have arrived by the age of two and a half. They will start to loosen and fall out when the child is about five, and the permanent teeth will then begin to erupt. It is a complete mistake to assume that because a child will lose their first teeth therefore dental care is of reduced importance. The second teeth are already in the gums and a child whose first teeth are allowed to decay faces a lifetime of dental problems.

Toilet-training

Babies have no control over their bladder or bowels. They simply eliminate their waste material as the organs become full. Around the age of two, the ability to exercise control develops, and gradually, in a combination of both physical development and learning, a child acquires the ability to urinate and defecate only when appropriate. Obviously there is no point in trying to toilet-train a child who is not physically ready to control its bladder or bowels. To try is the equivalent of trying to teach a six month old baby to talk and will simply lead to frustration on both sides.

Parents often feel a child should be clean by the age of two, and dry at night by the age of two and a half. In fact, only about half of all children achieve these goals and many are at least a year later. Complete control is rarely reached before three in any child.

Toilet-training usually starts around 15–18 months by placing the child on the pot after meals. This is the time they are most likely to want to void, and gradually, with much praise if the pot is used, the child will learn that this is what is required. A young child, of course, has no way of knowing what is expected and patience is needed. A child with an older brother or sister who sits on a pot will usually latch on more quickly than a child without such a model to imitate.

Most toddlers react vigorously against being forced into things, and a parent who is aggressively insistent about toilet-training is likely to find the attitude counterproductive. Toilet-training can only succeed with the voluntary cooperation of the child, and if you make the process a battle ground, you are the one likely to lose out.

It is much easier for a child to learn to be clean than dry. Most children only move their bowels once or twice a day, usually at regular intervals. You are likely to be able to recognise the signs of an approaching motion and provide a pot to collect it. Generally after a few weeks, especially if you make it clear you regard it as desirable and grown-up behaviour, your child is likely to have become proud of its new skill and will seek out the pot when it is needed.

Urinating is more haphazard. Children urinate many times in a day and, since it is a less major event, they may not even notice it if they are absorbed in play. The urge to urinate is also not enough to wake them in the early days of developing control, so they remain used to urinating in their nappy while they are asleep. If a child wakes dry, make the pot available and be liberal with praise if it is used. Gradually the child will learn that when the urge to urinate is felt they should head for the pot. It is worth remembering that children want to learn and want to acquire new skills — and also that all children do eventually stop wetting themselves, even those who seem impossibly slow. As a rule, the only children who are referred to a doctor because of failure to learn bladder control are those who have been subjected to excessive training. Bed-wetting that persists in an older child is a rather different problem, for which various types of treatment are available (see Section 5).

Feeding

A baby will normally be introduced to solids at about four months. These will consist of strained vegetables and fruits. At the beginning they are not a substitute for milk but are simply to get the baby used to them. Gradually solids become an integral part of the diet, and by six months the amount of milk can usually be reduced in proportion to solids in each meal. The best place to get advice about how to introduce solids into the diet is usually at the local clinic.

From the age of about nine months, a baby can drink ordinary cow's milk and it is safe to stop sterilising the bottles. Many babies are able to master the art of drinking out of a cup at about this time. By the time a baby is a toddler, they should be eating much the same meals as the rest of the family, assuming these are nutritious and well-balanced. It is important that food is attractively prepared and presented so that it looks appetising.

Some parents become excessively anxious because their child seems to be a 'fussy' eater, and they worry that the child will not receive adequate nutrition. Mostly this is because meals have become a battleground with a parent insisting on every last scrap being consumed. Once mealtimes become unpleasant, the child not unnaturally tries to avoid them. Children are like adults. Sometimes they are hungrier than other times, and they like some foods and dislike others. If you allow your child some individual choice in what and how much they eat, it is unlikely that problems will arise. If a child 'goes off' a particular food for a period, respect their wish — it will usually be short-lived. It is true that some children are less enthusiastic eaters than others, but it is unknown for a child voluntarily to starve itself to death.

There is growing evidence that children should not be overfed. A chubby child has long been regarded as desirably healthy and a tribute to its mother. No-one would suggest that children ought to be thin and that a little extra fat does not provide the necessary fuel for a growing and energetic youngster, but increasingly it is being realised that fat children grow into overweight adults, with all the attendant problems, such as heart disease, that this involves.

Sleep problems

Most newborn babies sleep most of the time — although as in everything else there are wide variations and some babies seem to stay awake most of the day (and some, most of the night, to the distress of their parents). As they grow, a baby's need for sleep diminishes until a toddler requires about ten or twelve hours of sleep a night, with a nap in the daytime.

Some children start to rebel against going to bed. After all, now that they are growing up, why should they not be able to participate in all the family activities, including those in the evening? Generally a child will be more amenable to an early bedtime if a regular routine is adhered to and there is no question that bedtime has arrived. A child who persistently appears for a chat after being put to bed, or constantly asks for a drink of water or to go to the toilet, should have its request met once and then be put to bed firmly with no further excuses for delay allowed. Of course, many children develop a fear of the dark at this time, and if this is the reason for a toddler's reluctance to stay in bed, a night light may solve the problem.

The childhood years

The years from two to adolescence are mostly taken up with growing, being educated, and learning to interact with the family and society at large. By the time children are five and ready to start school, most of their behaviour problems will have settled down.

A growing child needs a well-balanced diet to provide all the kilojoules, vitamins and minerals that are essential to maintain physical and mental development. The child's diet should include meat and fish with plenty of fresh vegetables and fruit, as well as

TABLE 1.4:
PHYSICAL GROWTH

Age (years)	Weight (kg)	Height (cm)
GIRLS:		
2	9.8–14	81–92
3	12–17	88–100
4	13–20	95–108
5	14.5–22.5	101–115
6	16–25.5	107–123
7	17.5–29	112–129
8	19–34	117–136
9	22–40	122–143
10	24–47	127–149
11	27–54	133–156
12	30–60	140–163
BOYS:		
2	10.6–15	82–94
3	12–18	89–102
4	14–20	96–110
5	15–23	102–117
6	17–26	107–123
7	19–30	113–130
8	20–34	118–135
9	22–39	123–142
10	24–45	128–148
11	27–51	132–155
12	30–58	137–162

adequate calcium, usually from milk, to ensure strong and healthy bones.

Children should have their teeth checked every six months to ensure that the teeth are growing as they should and that they are free from decay. Checks on hearing and vision are normally carried out through the school system. A child who is suspected of having difficulties with hearing or seeing should be tested without delay, as these handicaps can affect all areas of learning and general ability to function. It is vitally important to make sure that a child has strong, healthy feet, and this depends almost entirely on their shoes. All children should have shoes that support their feet, protect them and allow them freedom to grow.

The childhood years are years of infectious diseases, such as chicken pox. Serious diseases such as measles, mumps, rubella and whooping cough are now much less common since the introduction of immunisation programs. Scarlet fever and other bacterial infections can be cured readily by antibiotics. Coughs and colds are part and parcel of school life, and most children will get such infections at least every year or so. An otherwise healthy child will usually have a few days of feeling off-colour and then fight off the infection and return to health.

Accidents are a hazard of the childhood years. Obviously this is because a normal healthy child leads an active outdoor life, riding bicycles, swimming, climbing trees and taking part in various other activities. Falls, fractures, knee injuries, sprained ankles and dislocated shoulders are commonplace in the five to twelve age group. Fortunately, most of these heal quickly and completely if given appropriate care. Nevertheless some accidents should not happen. Parents need to give their child a basic understanding of safety, and to steer a balance between allowing the child freedom to explore and develop its independence, and sufficient supervision and protection to ensure that serious injury does not occur. The odd sprained wrist or ankle from falling off a bike is probably inevitable in an active youngster's life, but being knocked off the bike by a car with possible serious and lifelong repercussions is a quite different matter.

PUBERTY AND ADOLESCENCE

What happens and why

Adolescence is the period between the start of puberty or sexual development and full maturity. It generally begins in the early teens and ends around 18 or 20. Hence the words 'adolescent' and 'teenager' are used interchangeably. The trigger for puberty is the release of sex hormone releasing factors from the pituitary gland at the base of the brain, which cause sex hormones to be released from the gonads — oestrogen from the ovaries of females, and testosterone from the testes of males.

Adolescence is a period of rapid development, not only of sexual characteristics but of the body in general. Both sexes show a marked increase in weight and height, while boys develop more muscle and girls acquire the fatty deposits which give their rounded 'feminine' shape. There are also gender-based differences in the way the skeleton grows — boys develop wider shoulders leading to greater physical strength, and girls develop wider hips to facilitate child-bearing. As a general rule, the bones stop growing in girls by the age of about 16 and in boys by the age of about 18, although sometimes growth continues until the early twenties.

Some parts of the body are affected by the adolescent growth spurt more than others. The hands and feet mature first, then the legs, then the trunk, so children stop growing out of their jeans a year or so before they stop growing out of their jumpers.

Puberty starts in girls a year or two earlier than in boys — usually about 10 or 11 years of age in girls, and 12 or 13 in boys. These are only averages, however, and individuals vary markedly within the norm. Girls have been known to reach puberty as early as 8 and as late as 15 or 16. Boys vary similarly. Heredity is an important factor in the age of maturity. A girl whose mother started her periods late is likely also to be somewhat later than average in developing.

Puberty is also affected by general health. A child who has been undernourished or experienced a lot of illness may have the onset of maturity delayed. Children who are much smaller than the norm also may not mature as early as usual. Generally speaking there is no cause for concern unless a child shows no signs of development by the age of about 15 or 16, although a parent or child who is worried should have no hesitation in checking with their family doctor.

The physical changes of puberty are accompanied by psychological and emotional changes, also due to the production of sex hormones. In both boys and girls, there is an increased interest in sexuality as well as greater natural assertiveness, which helps to explain why teenagers are rebellious and often seen by their despairing parents as turning life into a never-ending argument. Rising levels of the male hormone testosterone are thought to be the reason adolescent boys are so often adventurous and aggressive.

Girls

The physical changes in girls include the development of the breasts, including an increase in the size of the nipples and possibly a darkening of the pigmentation. As well as the widening of the hips, the vagina and uterus develop further. Glands which will supply lubrication during sexual intercourse develop in and around the vagina. Hair grows in the armpits and the pubic region. Fine hair may develop on the forearms, parts of the legs and the upper lip.

The major change in any girl's life, however, is menstruation or the onset of her periods. Medically this is known as the menarche. It is the outward manifestation that she is physically capable of having a baby. In a mature woman, each month the ovaries release an egg. The egg is swept into the Fallopian tubes to journey down to the uterus (womb). If the woman has intercourse and the egg is fertilised by a male sperm, conception occurs, the fertilised egg implants itself in the wall of the uterus and the woman is pregnant. Every month the uterus prepares itself for a possible pregnancy by increasing the thickness of its lining so as to nourish a fertilised egg and enable it to grow into a baby. If a fertilised egg does not in fact arrive, the thickened lining is not needed and breaks down to be discarded from the body. It is this lining, together with some blood, that flows out through the vagina as the monthly period or menstrual flow. The first time a girl has a period, it shows that her body has started releasing its eggs (all of which are present from birth) and that she is capable of becoming pregnant. An entire cycle normally takes 28 days, with menstruation occurring on about four or five days.

A girl's periods are usually irregular for the first few months, since it takes a while for a pattern to be established. Some women continue to have irregular periods for their entire reproductive lives, other women are as regular as clockwork.

Unlike the male, a woman's reproductive life is limited and will cease when she reaches the menopause at the age of about 50.

Boys

The main physical signs of maturity in boys are an enlargement of the penis and testicles and the ability to produce sperm and so fertilise a female egg. Most boys will experience so-called 'wet dreams' or the involuntary emission of semen (the fluid in which sperm is contained) while they are asleep.

The boy will also grow a triangular patch of body hair in the pubic region and under the arms. (In boys, the pubic hair triangle is widest near the genitals and has its apex pointing towards the navel, whereas in girls the shape is the other way up, with the base of the triangle closest to the genitals.) Puberty is also the first time that hair appears on a boy's face, and if he does not choose to grow a beard he will need to shave. Generally the hair is soft and downy to start with and becomes thicker and more coarse as the maturing process progresses.

It is during puberty that a boy's voice 'breaks' due to the thickening of the vocal cords which cause the pitch to lower.

Once a boy reaches puberty, in essence he remains capable of fathering a child for the rest of his life.

TABLE 1.5:
PHYSICAL GROWTH

Age (years)	Weight (kg)	Height (cm)
GIRLS:		
13	34–67	145–168
14	37–73	148–171
15	41–77	150–172
16	43–81	151–173
17	44–82	152–173
18	45–82	153–174
BOYS:		
13	33–65	143–169
14	38–72	148–176
15	43–79	155–181
16	48–85	160–185
17	51–91	165–187
18	54–95	166–187

MATURITY

The period between youth and old age is the time when we are fully mature adults. Our physical growth is complete, the emotional and sexual upheavals of adolescence are over, and the more obvious deterioration of age has not yet made itself felt. For most people it is the time when they consolidate their career, marry and produce children. Youthful ardour and ideals have normally subsided and we realistically appraise our life in terms of both its potential and limitations.

Maturity is a time when most of us live our life at its optimum level. Income and job satisfaction will probably reach its highest point, the combination of energy and experience is at its peak, we are likely to have formed a stable relationship and have the pleasure of producing children, and our health is reliable.

A person in their twenties will probably not feel very different physically from the way they felt in their teens. Professional sportspeople may find that their performance has dropped to some degree, but most of us will feel as physically able and active as we ever did. From the mid-thirties on, physical changes start to become more evident. There is often a widening of the girth and hips, the face starts to show a few lines, grey hairs put in an appearance, many men show signs of baldness, and a woman's breasts may lose their firmness and start to sag.

As far as health is concerned, we probably have fewer problems from infectious diseases and accidents during maturity than in our youth, but we may find that the effects of stress affect us more so that high blood pressure can become a difficulty, as can gastric ulcers and other stress-related conditions. Degenerative disorders such as arthritis may become evident. Women, in particular, may show signs of decreased bone density or osteoporosis due to the change in their hormonal balance. Statistically people have a greater chance of developing malignancies during maturity, especially of the breast, the uterus, the prostate and bowel. This may be because the immune system no longer functions as effectively as it did.

Coronary heart disease usually first appears in middle age, as do the effects of smoking. Someone who has had a high cholesterol diet will usually find that a narrowing and hardening of the arteries becomes evident. It is important to see the early twenties as a time to review faulty living habits so that they do not become entrenched and lead to disability or early death.

In maturity it gradually becomes more difficult to learn new things, although this is offset by the enormous value of our experience, compared with when we were young.

For many people these days, middle age may involve a marriage breakdown with all its emotional trauma and possible consequent financial hardship and difficulty in rearing children. Your job may also create problems, either because of its demanding nature or because you perhaps have not progressed in the way that you had hoped. Losing a job in middle age can be catastrophic, and in such cases the stress factor and stress-related conditions that result can create very serious problems.

The positive side of maturity and middle age can be an emotional and mental stability which leads to a sense of confidence that was lacking in youth, the contentment of establishing your own home and family in a secure environment, physical well-being and a feeling of achievement in meeting your own individual challenges.

MENOPAUSE

Parents and personal development lessons at school teach girls all about periods and procreation, but nobody teaches them about what happens when it all stops. Once a woman passes her menopause, her ovaries will no longer produce eggs, her monthly periods will cease, and no more female hormones will be manufactured. The process usually occurs gradually over several years, between the early forties and the mid-fifties, but it may occur as early as 35 or as late as 58. It is therefore not unusual for a woman to spend more of her life after the menopause (or change of life, or climacteric) than she spends being fertile, but this does not mean that she loses her femininity. Many women treat the end of their periods as a blessing and lead very active lives for many years afterwards (active sexually as well as physically and mentally).

The unpleasant part of the menopause is the change from one stage to another, when the hormones go crazy, the headaches and hot flushes take over, and depression occurs. The first sign is usually an irregularity in the frequency and nature of the periods, and the gradual disappearance may be the only symptom in 25% of women. About 50% have other symptoms that cause discomfort, and the remaining 25% go through severe and very distressing symptoms.

The menopause is a natural event, and psychologically most women take it in their stride as simply another stage of life, but it is wrong to dismiss the unpleasant physical symptoms without seeking medical assistance. Doctors find the biggest problem to be the failure of their patients to tell them exactly what they are feeling and what effects the menopause is having on them. The first step in treating someone with menopausal symptoms is explanation. If they know why something is happening, it often makes the problem more bearable.

The sex hormones are controlled by the brain and released from the ovaries into the bloodstream on regular signals from the pituitary gland, which sits underneath the centre of the brain. Once in the blood, these hormones have an effect on every part of the body, but more particularly the uterus, vagina, breasts and pubic areas. It is these hormones that make the breasts grow when you are a teenage girl, give you regular periods as their levels change during the month, and cause hair to grow in your groin and armpits.

For an unknown reason, once a woman reaches an age somewhere between the early forties and early fifties, the brain breaks rhythm in sending the messages to the ovaries. The signals become irregular — sometimes too strong, at other times too weak. The ovaries respond by putting out the sex hormones in varying levels, and this causes side effects for the owner of those ovaries. The periods become irregular, vary in length and intensity, and may become painful. Other symptoms can include bloating and associated headaches and irritability as excess fluid collects in the brain, breasts and pelvis; hot flushes when hormone surges rush through the bloodstream after excess amounts are released by the ovaries; abdominal cramps caused by spasms of the uterine muscles; and depression which can be a reaction to the changes in the body, a fear of ageing or a direct effect of the hormones on the brain.

Menopause cannot be cured because it is a natural occurrence, but doctors can relieve most of the symptoms. Hormone tablets (see Section 6) are the mainstay of treatment. One hormone (oestrogen) is taken every day of the month, and a different one (progestin) is added in for 10 to 14 days of the month. Other dosage regimes are sometimes recommended. These hormones maintain a near normal balance, and some women will keep having periods while underneath the artificial hormones their natural menopause is occurring, so that when the tablets are stopped after a year or two, the menopausal symptoms will have gone. Many women are now being advised to continue the hormone tablets for ten or more years to prevent osteoporosis and to slow down ageing.

Minor symptoms can be controlled individually. Fluid tablets can help bloating and headaches, other agents can help uterine cramps and heavy bleeding. Depression can be treated with specific medications.

An obvious problem faced by a woman passing through the menopause is when to stop using contraceptives. As a rule of thumb, doctors advise that contraception should be continued for six months after the last period, or for a year if the woman is under 50. If you are taking the pill, this may actually mask many of the menopausal symptoms and cause the periods to continue. It may be necessary to use another form of contraception to determine whether you have gone through the menopause.

Doctors can also perform blood tests to determine your relative hormone levels and tell you if you are through the change of life or not. These tests are very difficult to interpret if you are taking the contraceptive pill.

Help is available, and there is no need for any woman to suffer as she changes from one stage of her life to another.

AGEING

Physical and mental changes

Everyone knows that the body ages, but no-one knows exactly how it occurs, why it occurs, and what triggers it. Ageing begins quite early in life, when we are in our twenties in the case of some organs, but it usually isn't noticed until middle age when the process accelerates.

At one time, people were 'old' when they reached their forties, and little more than a hundred years ago in Britain most people could expect to die by the time they were fifty. Advances in medical care, nutrition and general living standards have resulted in a higher life expectancy as well as a higher quality-of-life expectancy until well into the seventies and eighties.

The reasons for differences between people in life expectancy lie in a combination of factors, such as the genes we inherit from our parents, our mother's health during pregnancy, whether we undermine our health by smoking or drinking to excess, the relative poverty or otherwise of the conditions we live in. A successful businessman may be in his prime at fifty and enjoy good health, but if he is made redundant the psychological effects may cause him to 'age overnight'.

Women outlive men by an average of five to six years. No-one knows quite why. Some people believe that women are under less stress than men because women do not usually hold such demanding or responsible positions in the work force. Others say that this is nonsense, that women have to deal with far more stress than men but learn to cope with it better. The fact that until recently women have smoked far less than men could be a contributory factor to female longevity. However, younger women today are smoking more, and this could cause a major change in their life expectancy. It has been suggested that female hormones may play a part in women's longer life expectancy, but a contrary view points to the deleterious effect on women's bodies of the menopause and the cessation of oestrogen production.

As the body ages we change both physically and mentally. Needless to say, the most obvious signs are physical, and the two most common signals of approaching old age are the hair and the skin. As we age, the hair loses its pigment and turns grey and eventually white, and the skin loses its elasticity so that it wrinkles, especially around the eyes and the neck. The hair also thins and men especially may go bald. Teeth tend to decay more easily in the elderly and may have to be filled or extracted, although advances in dental techniques mean that the latter is far less common, and the days when whole sets of teeth were extracted more or less routinely in older people are mercifully a thing of the past.

Muscles tend to lose their flexibility as we age, although this is exacerbated by a sedentary life, and people who exercise adequately or do manual work show fewer signs of muscle deterioration than those who engage in little physical activity.

Bones become smaller, thinner and more brittle as they get older, and after the age of about 55 there is a measurable decrease in height. Our posture often changes so that we are no longer as erect, but round-shouldered or even stooped. Joints and ligaments deteriorate and stiffen so that movement is not as automatic as it was, but slower and more deliberate. Different body tissues and organs vary considerably as to the time at which they will begin to age. For example, hearing is never as acute as it is in the teens, whereas the heart doesn't start to deteriorate until the thirties. Most organs are slightly less efficient by the age of forty but this is generally not noticeable for another decade or so unless the body is subjected to severe stress, such as illness or extreme exertion.

Just as the external parts of the body change with age, so too do the internal organs and functions. Our lung capacity decreases (especially in smokers), our blood pressure rises, the heart increases in size and our arteries become more rigid. The levels of various minerals (such as iron) and proteins in our blood lessen. Just about every organ in our body degenerates to some extent, including the liver, kidneys, and the entire nervous system encompassing the brain, the spinal cord and the peripheral nerves.

The first mental capacity to deteriorate is the ability to formulate new concepts. Newton and Einstein were in their mid-twenties when they developed their theories. This is followed by a difficulty in learning new facts, and especially in relating them to previous knowledge — although it will usually not become obvious for a considerable period since we compensate with our increasing experience. Older people take longer to react, for example a middle-aged car driver is slower to stop in an emergency than someone in their twenties. Our ability to concentrate also lessens as we age.

The most common mental deterioration that most of us become aware of is an increasing difficulty with memory. We usually notice this for the first time around 60 and it normally relates to new things and recent happenings, not to events and skills learned in the past. Very old people can often remember perfectly what happened many years ago but have no recollection at all of the events of yesterday.

Despite the fact that our body works less efficiently as we get older, this does not mean that it is inevitable that the body will break down altogether. The ageing process of itself does not cause illness — for example arthritis has the same causes no matter what the age of the individual. But certain conditions are more likely to occur in later years simply because of a general decline in the body's strength and resistance to infection.

How to cope

All of us will either die prematurely or get old. Since we can expect to live until we are into our seventies and in the main will retire when we are 60 or 65, most of us will need to prepare for at least some years when we are classified, at least by the community at large, as old.

In general, Western societies do not cope well with old age. We don't respect our old people and, as a community, fail to provide adequate facilities for them, although as more and more people live longer, the demand and political pressure for support services is likely to be increasingly pronounced and effective.

It is important to be aware of what is likely to happen as we age and to take steps to combat any negative aspects. Since our muscles and joints will become less flexible, appropriate exercise becomes doubly important. The exercise does not have to be vigorous, but a good brisk daily walk with some gentle stretching exercises to improve muscular condition will go a long way towards maintaining mobility. It is vital to maintain an adequate diet. When there is no longer a family at home to cook for, and especially if one spouse dies, it is easy to skimp on the preparation of meals and no longer eat an adequate supply of vitamins, minerals and the necessary nutrients. Even in this day and age in Australia, it is by no means uncommon for elderly people to suffer from malnutrition. Older people often need to make a conscious effort to meet their dietary needs. Most community centres can make available easy-to-prepare recipes with a sound nutritional base.

Just as physical mobility is maintained by exercise, so too is the mind. It is important to maintain interests which have a purpose and keep the brain active and alert.

Most people will want to adapt their lifestyle as they get older so that their day-to-day living patterns are adjusted to meet their changing needs. A smaller home might be appropriate, which is near to shops or public transport if driving becomes too arduous. Proximity to family and friends becomes of increasing significance. Access to medical care is also important. Although ill health is by no means inevitable in old age, nevertheless it is more likely than before, and it is essential to have nearby a doctor and other medical facilities in which you have confidence.

DEATH AND DYING

Death

Just about everyone hopes they will die quickly. Very few of us will realise that hope. Most people die gradually over a period of weeks or months. A sudden death may be preferable for the person who has died but is usually far more difficult for relatives and friends who have had no time to prepare for the death or come to terms with it.

Until recently, death was defined as occurring when breathing ceased and the heart stopped beating. Modern advances in methods of resuscitation and artificial respiration, however, have led to the need to rethink the definition. It is now possible for the heart to be kept beating and breathing to be maintained by machines, and unless the brain has ceased to function the person may recover and start breathing independently again. Consequently death is nowadays sometimes defined as the cessation of electrical activity in the brain. Once this has occurred, there is no possibility of the person ever regaining consciousness, and life has ceased.

The process of death is essentially due to a lack of blood, and thus oxygen, first in the brain and spinal cord and then in the rest of the body. If the brain is deprived of oxygen for only about four minutes, it will irreversibly be damaged. Any longer and the damage will normally be such that the brain is no longer functioning.

The advent of transplant surgery has meant that death sometimes needs to be diagnosed promptly, since if an organ is to be transplanted it must be removed as quickly as possible while it is still healthy. A fear is sometimes expressed of being pronounced dead when there is still a faint possibility of life. In fact the tests carried out by doctors in such circumstances are quite clear-cut and definite, and there is no possibility that a person would be declared dead when they were, in fact, still alive.

Care of the dying

Most of us do not know what to expect if confronted with someone dying from a terminal illness. Generally speaking death is quite undramatic, with the person's breathing becoming irregular and slowing down until it stops altogether. The heart may continue beating for a few moments after breathing has stopped, but the beats will be weak and ineffective. Some cells take longer to die than others, and the cells of the eyes, for example, will take several hours to die.

In death, the body is still, movement and respiration are absent, no pulse can be felt or heart sounds heard over the chest. The eyes are glazed. The pupils are dilated, and when light is shone into them there is no response. Within minutes the body starts to feel cold, the skin turns pale and blood drains down to the lower part of the body (causing the flanks and buttocks to discolour). Within a period of about four hours, the body becomes stiff as the stored energy is released, causing the muscles to contract — rigor mortis. This may last for 48 hours, but it may be considerably less than this. After death many of the cell membranes break down and decomposition sets in. The undertaker will usually take steps to prevent this and preserve the body for burial or cremation.

Occasionally a dying person's last hours may be painful or distressing, for example if saliva trickles into the windpipe and cannot be coughed up or the lungs become waterlogged. In such circumstances a doctor should always be called, since relief is readily available. Most people, however, die quietly and peacefully — many die in their sleep. Obviously if you are with a dying person, it is important to give them as much quiet comfort as possible. Do not assume that because they seem to be hovering on the edge of unconsciousness they cannot hear what is said. You may feel helpless in the company of a dying person, but generally your presence is all that is required so that they are not alone.

About two thirds of deaths occur in a hospital or nursing home, and the staff will normally be experienced in dealing with dying patients and their needs. There is a growing feeling, however, that unless a person needs specialised hospital care, dying at home amid familiar surroundings is preferable to the inevitably impersonal surroundings of a hospital. In recent times there has been a growth in the number of hospices — small hospitals devoted entirely to the care of the terminally ill. These provide expert nursing care, control of pain and other symptoms, and emotional support for both the dying patient and the family.

Legal aspects of death

When someone dies, certain legal formalities must be followed. A doctor must issue a certificate stating the cause of death. If the person has died after a long illness, the attending doctor will normally complete the certificate as a matter of course, but in other cases or if there are any suspicious circumstances the coroner will be informed. The coroner may order a post-mortem examination to determine the cause of death, and if this raises further questions, an inquest (inquiry into the death by the court) may be ordered.

When a medical certificate is issued, it must be taken to the registrar of births, deaths and marriages, generally within about a week, and a death certificate will be issued. A death certificate is required before a funeral can be held and before the deceased's will can be dealt with.

Bereavement and grief

The loss of a loved one is now recognised as one of the most psychologically traumatic experiences we ever have, especially if the person is a spouse or a child. Everyone reacts to such a loss in their own way, but most people will experience a period of intense grief, which lessens as time passes so that gradually life returns to normal. The initial feeling is usually one of shock and numbness. Often the bereaved one acts as though the person is still alive. After a period varying from a few days to several weeks, realisation that the person really is dead will hit and usually be accompanied by feelings of deep sadness and loss. During this early period, thinking is usually muddled and concentration virtually non-existent. This is quite normal, and if possible it is usually wise to try to avoid making important decisions. Especially if the death has been unexpected, it is not uncommon for the bereaved person to experience feelings of anger at having been left. Financial difficulties resulting from the death may increase such feelings.

A person who has lost someone close to them may seem to lose motivation for life. They may be listless and lacking in energy, have difficulty in sleeping and lose weight. This is quite normal for a period of weeks, but if it continues for too long, medical help should be sought, as long-term depression needs treatment. It is not unusual for a bereaved person to become ill in the year following the death. There is some evidence that older people are more likely to die following the death of a partner.

Although grief is an individual matter, experience has shown that some courses of action may help. Many people find that seeing and touching the dead person helps them to come to terms with the fact that death has occurred and thus makes easier their acceptance of the loss. This seems to be particularly so with the death of a child. Someone who wants to spend time with the dead person should never be denied the opportunity of doing so.

Generally speaking the ability to experience and express grief is beneficial, and sedatives and antidepressants should be used only if necessary and only in consultation with a doctor. Grief is a perfectly natural emotion, and to deny it or try to suppress it artificially will do more harm than good. Nevertheless medications can sometimes usefully ease the pain if it becomes unbearable.

Relatives and friends need to be as supportive as they can, both immediately following the death, but also as time passes when the realisation of the loss may be actually more acute. Anniversaries, birthdays and Christmas are generally times when extra support is needed.

SECTION 2

BASIC ANATOMY AND PHYSIOLOGY

AN A–Z OF
HOW THE BODY WORKS

ADENOIDS
See PHARYNX.

ADRENAL GLANDS
The adrenal glands are part of the system that produces the body's hormones (called the endocrine system — see GLANDS). They sit on top of each kidney, a bit like a beanie. The glands are tiny — less than 5 cm long and weigh only a few grams — and yet produce more than three dozen hormones. The glands are divided into two quite distinct parts — an inner, reddish brown section called the medulla and an outer, yellow-coloured section called the cortex. Each part has its own distinct function.

Hormones are chemical messengers that help to determine the way the body functions. The hormones produced by the medulla in the adrenal gland include adrenalin which causes the well-known 'fight or flight' response to danger. The medulla is part of the autonomic (unconscious) nervous system, and when the body becomes aware of danger through one of its senses, these hormones literally spurt out making the heart beat faster, increasing the blood sugar level, altering the blood flow and generally increasing the body's capacity to deal with the emergency. Because many of the stresses of modern life do not require such a physical response, the release of adrenalin is sometimes inappropriate and the body has no way of using it up. If it happens too often it may eventually cause health problems.

The hormones produced by the cortex are steroids, of which there are three main groups. One group controls the balance of minerals in the body. Another group regulates the use the body makes of carbohydrates, and also plays a part in our ability to handle stress (cortisone is the most important hormone of this group). The third group affects the operation of our sex glands and influences our sexual development. Steroids are made from cholesterol, so a certain amount of cholesterol is necessary in our diet, provided it isn't more than we need, which can cause heart problems.

Like other glands in the endocrine system, the adrenal cortex is controlled by the pituitary gland (see separate entry).

If the adrenal glands are destroyed because of disease (e.g. tuberculosis or cancer) or are overactive, the functioning of our entire body can be impaired. The most common disorders are called Addison's disease and Cushing's syndrome (see Section 5).

ALIMENTARY TRACT
See DIGESTION.

ANUS
See DIGESTION; LARGE INTESTINE.

APPENDIX
See LARGE INTESTINE.

ARTERIES
Arteries are part of the system by which our blood circulates throughout the body (see CIRCULATORY SYSTEM). Arteries are the blood vessels going from the heart, whereas veins carry blood to the heart. Most arteries carry blood that has been enriched with oxygen by the lungs to other parts of the body. The exception is the pulmonary artery which carries blood that has been depleted of oxygen on its journey throughout the body from the heart to the lungs, so that it can be replenished with oxygen.

At any given moment about 15% of our blood supply is in our arteries. So that blood can be carried throughout the entire body as efficiently as possible, blood in the arteries is carried at much higher pressure than blood in the veins. The two major arteries are the pulmonary artery and the aorta. The aorta is shaped rather like the handle of a cane and leads out of the left side of the heart, curves across the top of the chest, then passes down the back of the chest and abdomen to a point just below the umbilicus. Other arteries, extending through the body and becoming smaller as they go, branch out from the aorta and are fed by it.

Each time the heart contracts it pumps blood into the arteries. If an artery is healthy, it has strong muscular walls which are elastic enough to expand as the blood is pumped in and then contract before the next surge. If you cut an artery, you will bleed in rhythmic spurts, each spurt relating to the surge of blood caused by the regular pumping of your heart.

In general, arteries are situated along the inner surfaces of bones, which protect them from damage. Furthermore, they are usually connected in such a way that, if one is damaged, the blood supply can still be maintained. An exception is the heart where there is no alternative method of blood supply, so that if an artery in the heart is blocked the heart muscle dies, causing a heart attack.

AUTONOMIC NERVOUS SYSTEM
See NERVOUS SYSTEM.

BACKBONE
See SPINE.

BALANCE
See EARS.

BILE
See DIGESTION; LIVER; SMALL INTESTINE.

BLADDER
The bladder is part of the urinary tract, which is one of the two waste disposal systems contained in the body. The bladder is linked to the kidneys by two long tubes called the ureters, and to the outside of the body by another tube called the urethra (see separate entries). It is situated deep in the pelvis behind the pubic bone.

The kidneys manufacture urine from the body's waste products. The manufacturing process is more or less constant, but obviously if the urine were to flow to the outside continuously, life would be very difficult. The bladder is therefore a hollow bag in which urine is stored before being excreted at some convenient time. As urine is manufactured by the kidneys, it drains into the bladder through the ureters. The bladder has a capacity of about 500 mL, and as it fills up, the elastic walls are stretched, giving rise to the urge to urinate. The bladder is the only part of the urinary system over which we have voluntary control, and on an appropriate signal from the brain, the muscles around the bladder contract at the same time as a ring of muscle at the bottom of the bladder is relaxed, allowing the collected urine to pass into the urethra and from there to the outside.

If the urge to urinate is not met, the bladder can keep expanding up to a point. Eventually however, it reaches its limit and urination then takes place involuntarily. If the nerve supply to the bladder is damaged or destroyed because of injury or disease, voluntary control of urination may be lost so that the person becomes incontinent.

Inflammation of the bladder is called cystitis, and because of their physical design, is a common disease in women. It occurs when bacteria from the surrounding organs, such as the vagina or rectum, enter the bladder. Cystitis should respond to antibiotics, but unfortunately in some women it proves to be recurrent and troublesome.

Medically the bladder is usually called the urinary bladder to distinguish it from other hollow organs containing fluid, such as the gall bladder.

See also KIDNEYS.

BLOOD

Blood is the thick fluid that flows throughout the body servicing its cells to keep them alive. On the one hand it delivers oxygen collected from the air we breathe and nutrients extracted from the food we eat, and on the other it gathers up waste products such as carbon dioxide and uric acid and transports them to appropriate organs for eventual disposal. Blood also protects us against infection and regulates our temperature and fluid levels.

The channels through which blood flows are the arteries and veins. The main pumping mechanism forcing the blood along is the heart. Veins carry the blood to the heart, and arteries carry it away from the heart.

About 55% of blood is a straw-coloured fluid called plasma. The rest of the blood is made up of cells, or corpuscles, of which there are three main types with three different functions. Red blood cells transport oxygen and carbon dioxide, white blood cells help to fight infection, and platelets assist in blood clotting.

Plasma itself is over 90% water. The remaining 10% contains just about everything the body needs to function — glucose, protein, salts, vitamins, chemical hormones and infection-fighting antibodies — as well as the waste products to be discarded. The proportions vary according to the particular needs of the body. It is because blood is so liquid that it can flow easily through the body.

Blood serum is the clear yellowish watery fluid that remains if the chemicals responsible for clotting are removed from plasma.

Red blood cells. Not surprisingly, the red colour of blood comes from its red cells. The colour is produced by an iron-containing pigment called haemoglobin. Haemoglobin acts as a carrier for oxygen. Red blood cells are shaped like a disc, hollowed out on both sides so that they have as large a surface as possible. As it passes through the lungs, one cell can attract as many as four oxygen molecules from the air that has been breathed in. Haemoglobin also attracts carbon dioxide so that, as blood travels through the body, the red blood cells operate a sort of exchange system, dropping off life-giving oxygen and picking up used and toxic carbon dioxide to be discharged in the lungs on the return journey.

The more oxygen the blood is carrying, the redder it is. Blood in the arteries flowing from the lungs, full of oxygen, is bright red, whereas blood in the veins, which has been depleted of oxygen on its journey throughout the body, is more bluish in colour. Interestingly, the red colour can only be seen if there is a lot of blood. If you were to look at a tiny smear under a microscope, it would be yellow.

Every cubic millimetre of blood contains about five million red blood cells. Women have slightly fewer than men. One red blood cell lives for about four months, during which time it will circuit the system about 300 000 times. At the end of this period it will die and eventually be discarded through the body's elimination system. New cells to replace the discarded ones are manufactured in the bone marrow (see BONE).

White blood cells. The main task of white blood cells is to fight infection. There are about 700 times fewer white blood cells than red ones. Scientifically, white cells are known as leucocytes (hence leukaemia is the name for a disease in which they multiply out of control).

Despite their name, white blood cells are in fact colourless. There are different types of white cells, but the main task of all of them is to attack harmful substances that invade the body. They may do this directly, literally by gobbling up bacteria, or by producing antibodies which work through the body's immune system. When an invader enters the body's tissues, the white cells hurry to the affected area and swing into action to destroy the interloper. At the same time, emergency supplies are produced so that an abnormally large number of white cells in the blood is frequently an indication of infection. Pus is simply the combination of white cells, together with dead germs, destroyed tissue and other waste matter.

Like red cells, white cells eventually die. Their life span depends on what they are called on to do in the body and varies from a few hours to days, months or even years. Some replacement cells are manufactured in the bone marrow, others in the lymphatic system, including the spleen (see separate entries).

Platelets. Blood clotting occurs when the blood turns from liquid to solid. A blood clot can be fatal if it forms in an artery and blocks it, but clotting is also an important part of our survival mechanism. If the blood did not clot, every time we sustained even a minor cut we would bleed to death — and indeed someone suffering from the disease haemophilia has precisely that problem. The clotting in blood is provided by the third type of blood constituent, platelets. When we are injured so that our blood comes into contact with something that is different from the lining of the blood vessels it is accustomed to, the platelets stick together and seal the wound. If the wound is serious, a further series of chemical reactions is set off which eventually cause a clot further sealing the hole.

Platelets are also manufactured in the bone marrow, and live for a relatively short period compared with red and white cells — about ten days.

The need for constant replacement of the blood cells means that the bone marrow is absolutely essential to life.

An analysis of blood by the taking of a so-called blood count, which measures the numbers of different blood cells in a particular volume of blood, is often used by doctors to detect the presence of disease.

Blood groups

Not everyone's blood is the same. Different people have blood that behaves in different ways under certain circumstances. One of the factors that dictates this behaviour is the type of antigens contained in the blood. Antigens are proteins that stimulate the production of antibodies to fight infection. If a person with antigens of one kind receives blood with antigens of a different kind, the antibodies produced will behave differently and may be fatal.

The antigens likely to cause problems have been given the names A and B. The blood group you are in depends on the presence of these antigens in your blood. The four blood types are A, B, AB, and O. People in the A-group have A antigens in their blood, people in the B- group have B antigens, and people in AB have both. O denotes people who have neither A nor B antigen. If you need a blood transfusion, you must be given blood from the same group as your own.

About 45% of Europeans have group O blood. Group O blood can also be given in an emergency because it does not have either the A or B antigen. Type B blood is the most common type in Asian races.

Another antigen contained in blood is called the Rhesus (Rh) factor, but not everyone has it. People who do have it (about 85% of the population) are said to be Rh positive. People who do not have it are Rh negative. If Rh positive blood is given to an Rh negative person, they may produce antibodies to fight off the foreign invader and so destroy the transfused blood. Once the antibodies have been produced and are in the system, a further transfusion of Rh positive blood can be fatal.

If an Rh negative woman is pregnant with an Rh positive child (who has inherited its blood group from its father), some of the baby's blood cells may pass into the mother during the final weeks of pregnancy or when the baby is being born or following a miscarriage. Since these cells are foreign to the mother, she will produce antibodies to fight them. If the woman becomes pregnant again, these antibodies may enter the bloodstream of the foetus and destroy its red blood cells, with the result that the baby may be born jaundiced or, in extreme cases, stillborn. These days, there is an injection called Anti-D which, if given to a woman within 72 hours, totally prevents any antibody formation and so protects future pregnancies and prevents these problems. This injection is given routinely to Rh negative mothers.

The blood group we are in is inherited from our parents. Sometimes blood tests are used in cases where paternity is disputed. These blood tests, however, cannot establish that a man is the father although they may establish that he is not. The inheritance patterns are complex, but basically if the child has a different blood group from its mother and the man's is different again, the man could not possibly be the father since the child must have inherited its blood group from one parent. If the man's blood is the same as the child's, it means he is possibly but not necessarily the father — the father could be some other man with the same blood group. So called genetic fingerprinting is also available nowadays. This is a blood test which checks more than the blood group, and it can tell accurately whether a man is the father or not.

See also ARTERIES; CIRCULATORY SYSTEM; HEART; VEINS.

BONE

Bone is the hard substance that makes up the body's framework — the skeleton. There are two parts to the skeleton — the central skeleton which encompasses the skull and backbone, and the peripheral skeleton which consists of the bones in the arms and legs. The central skeleton forms the shape of the body, whereas the peripheral skeleton is mainly concerned with movement.

One of the main functions of the body's bony framework is to safeguard the internal organs. The rib cage shields the heart and lungs and the skull protects the brain.

Far from being hard and inanimate, as we often think, bone is active living tissue, able to repair itself when damaged, and a major contributor to the ongoing functioning of the body.

The skeleton can be seen as early as eight weeks in a developing foetus, but at that stage it is not bone but cartilage (gristle). Among its other features, cartilage is flexible, enabling for example the baby's head to be compressed during its passage through the birth canal — hence the sometimes temporarily flattened shape of a newborn baby's skull.

Gradually the initial cartilage is transformed into bone, some while the foetus is still in the womb, some after birth. This is called ossification and consists of the laying down of calcium, phosphorus and other hard minerals in the cartilage. In most bones, the process of change is well under way by the time of birth, but it is not completed until the age of about 16 years in girls and 18 years in boys. Children's bones are therefore flexible and able to withstand the rough and tumble games they are subjected to.

In an adult body, bone makes up about 16% of its total weight. A person's height is determined by the length of their bones. Bone is also extraordinarily strong — about four times stronger under stretching than its equivalent weight in light steel or aluminium.

Adults have fewer bones than children. A baby is born with 350 bones. Many of these then fuse as the child grows, and by the time a person has reached 20 to 25 years of age, they will typically have 206 permanent bones. In the skull, for example, four separate bones, one at the front, one at the back and one on each side, fuse to form a solid skull. The soft spot on a baby's head is the point at which four of these bones meet. The fusion is complete by 12 to 18 months of age. Similarly, five small bones at the bottom of the spine fuse to form one single solid lower back bone called the sacrum.

Bone is classified into four types according to shape — long, short, flat and irregular. The long bones are those in the arms and legs, and have the classic bone shape that most of us would reproduce if asked to draw a bone — a shaft with a knob at each end. They are thin, hollow and light, enabling ease of movement. The short bones include those in the wrists and ankles and are geared to provide strength as well as limited movement. Flat bones are actually thin rather than flat and include most of those in the skull, the breast bone and the shoulder blades. Irregular bones are those that don't fit into the other categories and include some of the skull bones and the bones of the spine (the vertebrae).

All bones consist of two different types of bone — hard (compact) bone on the outside encasing spongy (cancellous) bone on the inside. The combination gives both elasticity and strength, and the proportions of hard and spongy tissue in individual bones (or even within the same bone) vary depending on which quality is the more important in the function of that particular bone. Hard bone is so hard that the only way it can be cut during surgery is with a saw.

The spongy interior of most bones is filled with marrow, a soft gelatinous substance that produces white blood cells (to fight infection), red blood cells (to carry oxygen) and platelets (which help stop bleeding). Bone marrow is crucial to the maintenance of life. Blood vessels and nerves pass into the spongy interior of a bone through small channels in the hard outer layer. Surrounding and protecting each bone is a thin tough membrane called the periosteum.

Generally speaking, bones grow from a point near each end. Bone growth is stimulated by hormones produced by the pituitary and thyroid glands. Serious illness can slow or even stop the growth of our bones. The long bones, where most growth takes place during childhood, grow from one end — the growing end. These growing ends are actually separate from the main part of the bone by cartilage, and it is by the constant formation of new cartilage which is then replaced by bone that growth takes place. It is when cartilage is no longer formed and the growing end and the parent bone become one that growth stops, usually before the age of 20.

The fact that we have stopped growing, however, does not mean that bone stops forming. All our bones are constantly renewed. Old bone is absorbed into the bloodstream to be eventually eliminated from the body and new bone is laid down. If a bone is damaged, for example because it is broken, it will eventually heal perfectly because of this ongoing regeneration. Medical science has not yet been able to develop any artificial substance with anything like the lasting qualities of natural bone. An artificial hip will usually wear out in 10 to 20 years. Most people's natural hip joints last a lifetime without causing serious trouble.

The high calcium content of bone means that it acts as a reserve store of calcium. If the calcium levels in the blood get too low, calcium is drawn from the bones. Obviously if too much calcium is taken from the bones they cannot maintain their strength and start to thin — a condition called osteoporosis (see Section 5) which is particularly common in older women.

It has long been recognised that calcium is important in children's diets to ensure healthy bone growth; consequently children have been encouraged to drink milk. Generally, however, it was believed that once bones had finished growing, calcium in the diet became less important. Because the main source of calcium is in dairy products, and most of these also contain fats that in recent years people have been advised to avoid, calcium virtually disappeared from the diet of many adults. It is now recognised that this view was wrong and that adequate calcium in the diet is essential throughout life to guard against thinning of the bones.

Bowel
See LARGE INTESTINE.

Brain
The brain is the central organ of the nervous system. It coordinates the operation of all the organs and tissues making up the body. The brain is often likened to a computer, but no computer yet developed has anything like the same complexity as the human brain.

The brain interprets signals from the senses and controls body functions, both automatic and conscious. It is also the site of memory, learning, thinking and reasoning.

The brain consists of three main divisions: the cerebrum, the cerebellum, and the brain stem.

Cerebrum. The cerebrum is the largest part of the brain, mushrooming out from the brain stem. It fills almost all of the top part of the skull and is the centre of most of the brain's activity. Nerves throughout the body travel via the spinal cord, up through the brain stem and into the cerebrum.

The cerebrum is divided into two halves or hemispheres. Because the nerve fibres cross over as they travel from the spinal cord up the brain stem, each of the two halves controls the opposite side of the body, i.e. the left side of the brain controls the right side of the body, and vice versa. For activities such as speech, one side of the brain will be dominant. Generally the left side is dominant in a right-handed person. This means that if a right-handed person has a stroke affecting the left side of the brain, they may temporarily lose the capacity to speak as well as the use of their right hand.

The outer layer of the cerebrum consists of grey-coloured matter called the cortex. This is the part of the brain that thinks, and is thought to be concerned with memory, intelligence and imagination. It also deals with information fed in from the senses, for example whether something is hot or cold or bitter, and what the response should be, for example whether your arm should be snatched away from burning heat or you should spit out the bitter substance in case it should be poisonous. The cortex selects those sensations that are important and ignores those that are irrelevant. A common analogy is to imagine yourself in a room full of people at a party. You will be conscious of the buzz of conversation but will not be aware of the specific words unless someone mentions your name, in which case, because it is important to you, you will probably pick it up. This illustrates the brain's operation perfectly. Hundreds of sensations are impinging on it at any given time, but it selects only the important ones and reacts to them.

The surface of the cortex is arranged in folds so that the area of the brain is as large as possible. It is these folds that give the brain its easily recognised ruffled appearance.

The inner part of the cerebrum is white in colour and is where emotions such as anger, pleasure, pain, fear, sexual desire and affection are thought to originate.

Cerebellum. The cerebellum is much smaller than the cerebrum and lies at the back of the brain stem. It is here that our balance is maintained, together with the coordination of our muscles and our posture.

Brain stem. The brain stem is at the bottom of the brain and extends down through an opening in the skull to merge with the spinal cord. As a continuation of the spinal cord, the brain stem is the passage for all the nerve fibres from the body to the rest of the brain. In addition, it controls most of the automatic body functions, for example the beating of the heart, breathing and digestion. By means of the hypothalamus in the upper section, the brain stem also controls our temperature, appetite and aspects of our metabolism.

Some of the substances carried by the blood to other parts of the body could damage the brain. The blood vessels servicing the brain are therefore less porous than other blood vessels. This means that oxygen, which is made up of small molecules, is allowed into the brain but harmful chemicals composed of large molecules are blocked. However, alcohol and most anaesthetics also have small molecules and can pass through, which is why we can get drunk or be anaesthetised.

The hard bony skull with its underlying cushion of fluid protects the brain from external harm.

The functioning of the brain and how information is learned and transferred to memory is still far from fully understood. It is generally acknowledged that factors such as heredity, previous experiences, the external environment, personality, character and intelligence all play a part in our brain's operation, but how and in what way is not really known.

See also NERVOUS SYSTEM.

BREASTS

The breasts are two glands in women which produce milk to feed human babies. Breasts develop in girls at puberty, and consist of fatty tissue embedded with 15 or 20 lobes containing clusters of milk-producing glands. Each cluster drains into a duct which carries the milk into a small storage space near the nipple, ready to flow out through the nipple when required. The nipple contains some 15 or 20 tiny duct openings. The nipple and the area around it, called the areola, are coloured a dark reddish pink which often darkens to brown during the first pregnancy. The nipples contain erectile tissue so that they become hard when stimulated by breastfeeding, sexual activity or cold. The breasts also consist of fibrous tissue containing nerves, blood and lymphatic vessels, but there are no muscles, so increasing the size of the breasts by exercise is impossible.

The shape and size of a woman's breasts depends largely on heredity. If your mother's breasts were small, yours probably will be too. Weight, however, plays a part — excess weight is manifested in the breasts in the same way as in other parts of the body, and a woman who loses weight will usually notice that her breasts decrease in size. Apart from weight fluctuations, the only way of significantly increasing or decreasing the size of the breasts is by cosmetic surgery. Small-breasted women sometimes choose to augment their natural size for purposes of fashion; women with large pendulous breasts may find it necessary to reduce the size for reasons of comfort (see SURGERY, Section 6).

The size of the breasts has no effect on the ability to feed a baby. The milk-producing glands exist irrespective of the amount of fatty tissue surrounding them. Breasts will get significantly larger during late pregnancy in readiness for breastfeeding. They will also swell slightly in many women just before a period when the tissues retain more water than usual.

A slight degree of breast development sometimes occurs in boys during puberty. This is because both boys and girls have male and female hormones, although in different proportions, and these sometimes take a while to settle down to normal. Unusual breast development in men beyond the stage of puberty is a sign of hormonal disturbance.

One of the major killers of women is breast cancer, and all women should examine their breasts regularly for lumps (see PREVENTIVE MEDICINE, Section 7). In fact, if a lump is found it is statistically much more likely to be benign than cancerous since there are many reasons why lumps form, but the lump should never be ignored and a doctor should be consulted immediately it becomes evident. The treatment of breast cancer is highly successful if it is detected at an early stage.

Other disorders of the breast include breast infections (see Section 5), cysts and abscesses. These normally respond readily to treatment.

See also BREASTFEEDING, Section 1.

CAECUM
See LARGE INTESTINE.

CARDIOVASCULAR SYSTEM
See CIRCULATORY SYSTEM.

CARTILAGE
See BONE; JOINTS.

CENTRAL NERVOUS SYSTEM
See NERVOUS SYSTEM.

CERVIX
The cervix is the narrow passage at the lower end of the uterus (see separate entry), which connects with the vagina. It allows blood to flow out of the uterus during the menstrual period, and sperm to enter after intercourse for possible fertilisation of an egg. The cervix is normally filled with mucus, the composition of which changes at different stages of the menstrual cycle. It is usually thick to stop bacteria and other infections from entering the uterus, but when an egg is released (ovulation) it becomes thinner so as to make it easier for sperm to enter and fertilise the egg. Some forms of birth control are based on a woman analysing the consistency of the cervical mucus she produces, since it is an obvious indicator of when an egg is about to be released.

When a baby is due to be born and the mother goes into labour, the cervix expands to many times its normal size to allow the baby out. The first stage of labour is when the muscles of the wall of the uterus start contracting while at the same time the muscle fibres of the cervix relax to allow expansion.

If the cervix opens up during pregnancy, the foetus will escape and the mother will have a miscarriage. Some women have a cervix that is prone to weakness, called an incompetent cervix. In such a case if the woman becomes pregnant, the cervix can be held firm by stitches, a procedure generally carried out under general anaesthetic. The stitches are removed when labour begins or at about the thirty-eighth week of pregnancy.

Sometimes the delicate cells forming the inner lining of the cervix spread to cover the tip and replace the stronger tissue normally occurring there. This is called cervical erosion and makes the cervix more vulnerable to infection. It may cause a heavy discharge and bleeding after intercourse. Generally the treatment for cervical erosion is to destroy the unwanted cells by heat (cauterisation) or laser. This is painless and usually requires that you attend a clinic or hospital only as an outpatient.

The main and most serious condition affecting the cervix is cervical cancer. Like most cancers, this can be effectively treated if it is detected early. The method of detection is a Pap smear (see PREVENTIVE MEDICINE, Section 7), and all women should have one annually until the menopause and every two years thereafter. Deaths from cervical cancer are second only to deaths from breast cancer, and yet it has been estimated that the death rate could be entirely eliminated if all women had regular Pap smears.

CIRCULATORY SYSTEM

The circulatory or cardiovascular system is the means by which blood circulates throughout the body. The blood travels along a complex network of narrow channels, all interlinked so that they flow into or out of the heart. These channels, or blood vessels, together with the four chambers of the heart, form a completely enclosed system. The only time any blood escapes from it is if it is damaged as a result of injury.

The vessels carrying blood from the heart out to the body organs and tissues are called arteries. They get gradually smaller the further out they extend. The smallest arteries are called arterioles. The vessels by which the used blood is returned to the heart to be pumped through the system again are called veins. The smallest veins are called venules. Linking the arterioles and venules are even tinier blood vessels called capillaries. The capillaries have tissue-thin transparent walls that allow the exchange of fluids between the blood and body cells, and blood and air in the lungs.

All cells in the body are immersed in a slightly salty liquid called tissue fluid. It is this fluid that makes possible the exchange of all the substances necessary to keep the cells alive and all the waste products that must be discarded after the life-giving substances have been utilised. For example, oxygen is carried along the arteries leading from the lungs into the smaller arterioles, and thence into the capillaries where it seeps through the walls into the tissue fluid from which it is absorbed by the cells. At the same time, the waste product carbon dioxide goes through the process in reverse, passing from the cells to be suspended in the tissue fluid until, by means of a chemical process called diffusion, it passes through the same thin walls back into the capillaries to be carried away in the bloodstream for eventual elimination.

There are two main circuits of blood vessels. Those carrying blood between the heart and the lungs for oxygenation are called the pulmonary vessels. The arteries and veins supplying the rest of the body with food and oxygen are called the systemic vessels.

See also ARTERIES; HEART; LYMPHATIC SYSTEM; VEINS.

Colon

See LARGE INTESTINE.

Digestion

The food we eat is the means by which our body is provided with nutrients and fuel to keep it functioning. Before it can be utilised, the food must be converted into a form that is able to be absorbed by the body. The process by which this occurs is called digestion, and the bodily organs involved in the process make up the digestive tract, also called the gastrointestinal tract, or the alimentary tract or canal.

The digestive tract starts at the mouth which takes in the food, breaking it up into small pieces with the teeth and tongue, and at the same time commencing the digestive process by the addition of saliva. With a swallow the food moves rapidly down the oesophagus (gullet) to splash into the stomach, which is situated just below the bottom of the breastbone.

The stomach is shaped rather like a capital J, and the food enters at the top and leaves through the lower end. The sag of the J is a lake of food and hydrochloric acid. This acid is produced by cells lining the stomach, and it breaks down the basic structure of the food. The stomach itself is protected from being attacked by the acid by a thick layer of mucus on its walls. With contractions that sweep along the muscular walls of the stomach, the food is slowly moved towards the pylorus. This is a ring of muscle that surrounds the exit tube of the stomach. As a contraction moves towards it, the muscle opens this valve to allow some but not all the food to pass into the next section of the digestive system.

The next tube is the small intestine, which starts with the duodenum, a section which is only 30–40 cm long. It is quite highly specialised, for its task is to add the final digestive juices and enzymes to the food that will break it down to its basic components. There is an opening in the side of the duodenum, and through this the bile from the liver and gall bladder is squirted onto the food, and the digestive enzymes from the pancreas are added. An enzyme is a protein that activates chemical reactions but is not itself changed or used up by the process. Each different enzyme has its own specific task and can only be used for that task. For example, one kind of enzyme deals with fats, another with carbohydrates, and yet another with proteins. Wave-like contractions from the gut steadily move the food along and churn it up so that the digestive juices are thoroughly mixed in.

The next section of the small intestine is the jejunum followed by the ileum. It is 7–10 m long, and is only loosely attached to the body so that it winds in slippery loops all over the abdominal cavity. At this stage the food is in the form of a slurry from which the fine microscopic fingers that line the intestine absorb and engulf the proteins, carbohydrates and fats that are the basic components of all foodstuffs. By the time the food reaches the end of the small intestine and enters the next section of gut, only water, fibre and waste products are left.

The large intestine comes next. This is far larger in diameter and is about 1.5 m long. The food moves very slowly through this section, as its task is to absorb as much water as necessary from the food. If the movement of food is too slow, the wastes dry out and you become constipated. If it is too fast, not enough water is removed and diarrhoea results.

The final 30 cm is the rectum. This fills the back of the pelvis and is basically a storage area for faeces. At the appropriate time, the muscle ring that forms the anus is relaxed, the muscles of the abdominal wall and rectum contract, and the unwanted wastes are eliminated after a journey that normally lasts 24 to 36 hours.

Most of the food processing is involuntary and we are unaware of it. The only voluntary control we have is chewing and swallowing at one end and eliminating at the other.

The digestive process can be affected by factors far removed from the direct intake of food, in particular, our emotions. Stress, anger, fright, fear, love and almost all extreme emotional states can cause loss of appetite, nausea, vomiting and diarrhoea.

See also MOUTH; PHARYNX; OESOPHAGUS; STOMACH; SMALL INTESTINE; LARGE INTESTINE.

DUODENUM
See DIGESTION; SMALL INTESTINE.

EARS
The ears are the organs of hearing and of balance. An ear consists of three parts — the outer, the middle and the inner ear. The outer and middle parts are concerned with hearing, and parts of the inner ear are concerned with balance as well as hearing. For hearing, the ear acts as a receiver (outer ear), an amplifier (middle ear) and a transmitter (inner ear).

The outer ear consists of the part we can see, i.e. the ear flap guarding the ear canal, which links the outer ear with the middle ear. The ear canal is also protected by tiny hairs, sweat glands and oil glands which produce wax to stop particles of dust and dirt from getting in.

At the end of the ear canal is a six-sided box which is the middle ear. Five sides of the box are made of bone but the sixth side, which is the one facing into the ear canal, is the thin, pale membrane that forms the eardrum. (The eardrum can very easily be punctured, and bobby pins, toothpicks and the like should never be used for cleaning purposes.) Inside the box are the three tiniest bones in the human body, commonly called after their respective shapes the hammer, the anvil and the stirrup, but more correctly known as the malleus, incus and stapes. Sound waves are collected by the outer ear, passed down the ear canal to vibrate the eardrum and then into the middle ear where the sounds are amplified by the tiny bones.

The middle ear has a tube connecting it to the back of the throat, called the Eustachian tube. In essence, sound consists of small fluctuations in air pressure and this tube enables the same pressure to be maintained in the middle ear as in the outside atmosphere, so that the middle ear can pick up the sound waves. If the outside pressure alters more quickly than the middle ear can adjust to, such as when we are flying or diving, the ear will hurt. The familiar 'pop' of the ears in these circumstances is the pressure adjusting by air suddenly moving through the Eustachian tube. The connection of the tube to the throat means that upper respiratory infections sometimes travel along it and become middle-ear infections.

The inner ear is filled with fluid and contains the cochlea (named because it is shaped like a cockle or snail shell) which is the part where hearing actually takes place. Sound passes from the middle ear through a fluid-filled chamber and into the cochlea where, in a tiny hair-lined section called the organ of Corti, it is converted into nerve impulses. These nerve impulses are then transmitted to the brain which registers them as sounds.

The inner ear is also the organ of balance. Above the cochlea are three semicircular canals set at different angles. These are filled with fluid which moves as the head moves. Highly sensitive hairs pick up the movement and send impulses to the brain indicating the position of the head and body.

Eustachian tubes
See EARS.

Eyes

The eyes are the organs of sight. All objects reflect light in some way and essentially what the eyes do is respond to this reflected light. The light enters the eyes and stimulates nerves which in turn transmit impulses to the brain where the information is interpreted as visual images.

Although light usually travels in straight lines, it can be bent if it passes through certain substances, such as the specially shaped glass of a camera lens or the lens made from tissue in the human eye. The degree of bending can be precisely controlled by the shape in which a lens is made. Light can, in fact, be bent inwards, or concentrated, to form tiny, but perfect images of much larger objects.

The operation of the eye is often likened to the operation of a camera but it is infinitely more varied and complex. If a camera could 'see' with anything like the complexity of the human eye, photography would take on a new dimension indeed.

Each eye is a slightly flattened sphere consisting of three layers. The outer layer is called the sclera and forms the white of the eye, except for the very front section which is transparent to allow light in and is called the cornea. The cornea is sometimes referred to as the window of the eye. The second layer is called the choroid and this contains the blood vessels that service the eye. The front of the choroid forms the iris which is the part that gives the eyes their colour — brown, blue, hazel and so on, depending on the genes we inherited from our parents. In the centre of the iris is a small gap called the pupil. Muscles in the iris enlarge or reduce the size of the pupil according to the amount of light — the more light the smaller the pupil. Just behind the iris is the lens.

The innermost layer of the eye, curving around the back of the sphere, is the retina. This is a light-sensitive structure containing nerve cells, commonly called rods and cones because of their shapes. The rods are sensitive to light and will function in dim light but do not produce a very sharp image. The cones are sensitive to colour. When you go into a darkened room such as a theatre, it is difficult to see for the first few moments. This is the time it takes the rods to adjust to the change in light. The nerves in the retina all meet together to form the optic nerve, which connects to the brain.

In the bulge between the lens and the cornea is a chamber filled with a watery fluid, called the aqueous humour. The large space behind the lens and in front of the retina is filled with a jelly-like substance called the vitreous body. It is this that gives the eyeball its firmness and maintains its spherical shape.

When we see something, light passes through all the transparent layers starting with the cornea and moving through the aqueous humour, the lens and the vitreous body to the retina. All these layers refract (bend) the light so that light from the large area outside is focused in the small area of the retina. The most important refractive body is the cornea, which is responsible for about 70% of the process. The lens focuses the light according to whether it is for near or distance vision. When the light reaches the retina, the nerve cells convert it into electrical impulses and send these along the optic nerve to the brain, which records visually the objects we are looking at. Just like the lens of a camera, the lens of the eye produces an upside down image. The brain is responsible for the right-side-up, three-dimensional view that we eventually get. If the optic nerve is damaged, it can cause blindness even

SECTION 2: BASIC ANATOMY AND PHYSIOLOGY

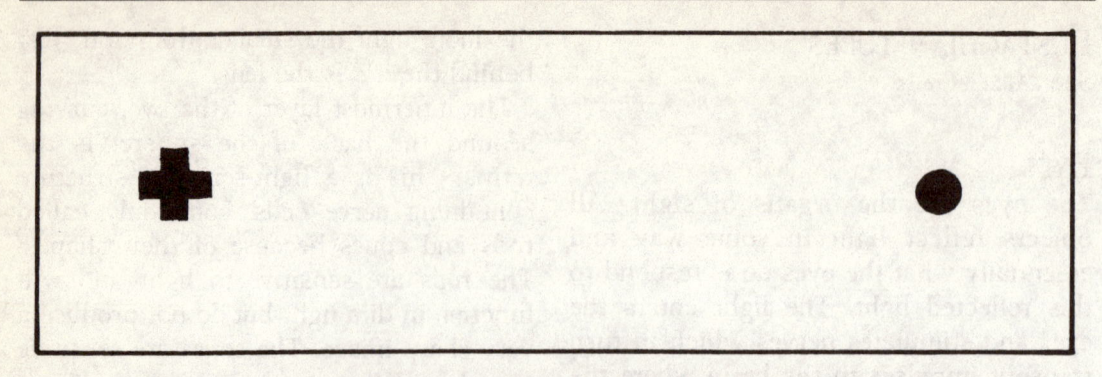

FIGURE 2.1: How to find the blind spot.
To find your blind spot, hold this book at arm's length and close your left eye. Look at the cross with the right eye, and move the book slowly towards you. When the dot disappears, its image has fallen on the blind spot of your right eye.

though the eyes themselves are still functioning.

The point where the optic nerve leaves the retina has no rods and cones and so forms a blind spot. You can find your blind spot by a simple test.

The eye is one of the most mobile organs in the body. Each eye has a set of six external muscles so that it can move in all directions to focus on objects it wishes to see. We may sometimes wish we had eyes in the back of our head, but the mobility of the eyes is such that their field of vision extends in just about every other direction.

Because the eyes are so sensitive, the body provides a great deal of protection for them. They are set in two bony sockets in the skull. Externally they are guarded by the eyebrows and the eyelids. The eyebrows help to ward off blows, shield the eyes from sunlight and deflect sweat so that it does not run into the eyes. The eyelids form a protective covering, while the fringe of eyelashes stops dust and dirt getting in. When an eyelid blinks, it wipes a film of antiseptic tears over the eye. The inner surface of both upper and lower eyelids, as well as the eyes themselves, are covered by a transparent membrane called the conjunctiva. This helps to keep the eyes moist so that they can move freely.

Tears are produced in a small gland situated at the outside corner of the eye. Small ducts lead into the eyes. Tears originate in the bloodstream and so are salty and also contain antibacterial substances to protect against infection. Tears lubricate the eyes when we blink, and may be produced in greater quantities when we are suffering from a cold or in times of intense emotion. Tears are an important part of the functioning of the eye, and an inability to produce them can lead to serious problems.

Because of their complexity, the eyes sometimes function less than perfectly. There are four main types of vision problems:

1. People who are short-sighted (myopia) have eyeballs that are too long. This means that the light cannot accurately be focused by the lens and a blurred image results.

2. The reverse problem occurs in long-sighted people (hypermetropia) where the eyeball is too short. These people can see objects at a distance but when close objects are seen, the muscles that change the shape of the lens to focus the light rays cannot cope with the shortened eyeball.

3. Older people whose sight slowly deteriorates suffer from presbyopia, or the inability of the lens to change shape sufficiently to see objects that are close to them. This is caused by a weakening of the tiny muscles that pull on the lens to change its shape.

GALL BLADDER

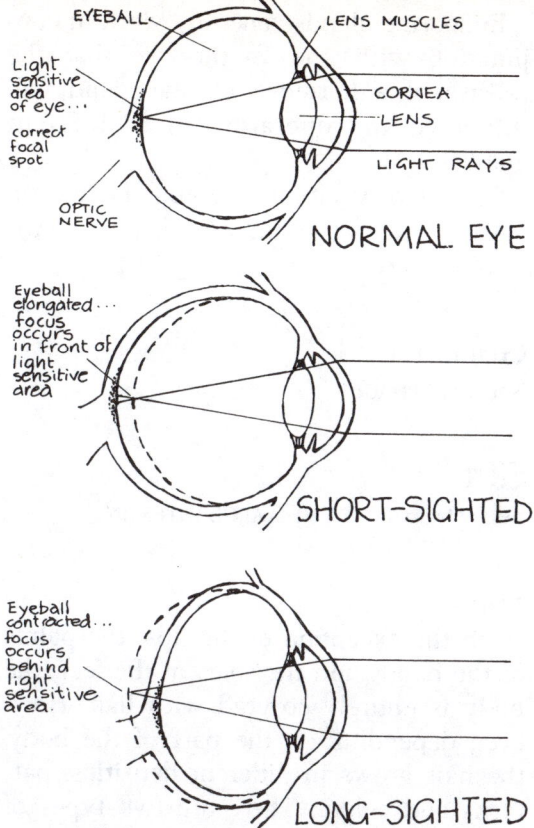

FIGURE 2.2: Normal vision, short-sightedness and long-sightedness.

4. The last group are those with astigmatism. These people have an uneven curve of the refractive surfaces at the front of the eye (i.e. the lens and cornea), so that some parts of the vision are clear while other parts are blurred at the same time.

All these problems can be corrected by placing a lens (spectacles or contact lenses) in front of the eye to help the natural lens of the eye focus the image.

See also EYE TESTS, Section 4.

Fallopian tubes

The Fallopian tubes are part of the female reproductive system. There are two Fallopian tubes and they extend from a position next to the ovaries to the uterus. They are about 10–12.5 cm long. The end near the ovaries is rather like a bent hand with its extended fingers encircling the ovary, although not actually touching it. The connection with the uterus is made by means of an opening only large enough for a bristle.

Once a month, about halfway between menstrual periods, one ovary (see separate entry) releases an egg. The egg is swept into the Fallopian tube by the waving fingers and transported down to the uterus (see separate entry). If, on its passage through the tube, the egg is fertilised by a male sperm introduced during intercourse, pregnancy will result when the fertilised egg implants itself in the wall of the uterus.

Occasionally, the fertilised egg becomes implanted in the wall of the Fallopian tube, in which case it is an ectopic pregnancy (see PREGNANCY COMPLICATIONS, Section 1). This is a dangerous and usually very painful occurrence, as the fertilised egg rapidly becomes too large for the tube and can cause it to rupture. If an ectopic pregnancy happens, the tube will usually have to be removed by surgery, but provided the woman still has one tube, she can normally still become pregnant.

If the egg passes down the tube without being fertilised, it will simply pass out of the body when the woman has her period.

A woman who is certain she does not want any more children sometimes elects to have her tubes tied (tubal ligation — see CONTRACEPTION, Section 1). This involves an operation to close the Fallopian tubes so that the egg and the sperm cannot meet. Although modern techniques of microsurgery sometimes mean this can be reversed, such an operation must be regarded as permanent and should only be carried out on that assumption.

See also REPRODUCTIVE SYSTEM.

Gall bladder
See LIVER.

Gastrointestinal tract
See DIGESTION; MOUTH; PHARYNX; OESOPHAGUS; STOMACH; SMALL INTESTINE; LARGE INTESTINE.

Genito-urinary system
See KIDNEYS; BLADDER; URETERS; URETHRA; TESTICLES; PENIS; OVARIES.

Glands
A gland is an organ or group of cells that secretes (produces) or excretes (gets rid of) various substances used in keeping the body functioning. For example, the skin contains sebaceous glands which secrete an oily material and sweat glands which help to rid the body of excess water, glands in the mouth produce saliva, and the mammary glands in the breasts produce milk.

Some glands have ducts to carry their secretions to various parts of the body, and these are called exocrine glands. Glands without ducts are called endocrine glands. These secrete hormones which are released directly into the bloodstream. (Hormones are chemical messengers that regulate and balance vital processes in the body.) Some glands are large organs such as the liver, pancreas and kidneys, but more commonly they are very tiny.

The endocrine glands are enormously important in the functioning of the body. Among other things they influence our growth, our metabolism and our sexual development. Altogether there are seven endocrine glands. The pituitary gland is situated at the base of the skull, the thyroid gland is in the lower neck and the adrenal glands lie on top of the kidneys. The pancreas, sitting just behind the stomach, not only plays a part in digestion but also functions as part of the endocrine system in regulating blood sugar levels. Other endocrine glands are the ovaries in women and the testes in men.

Endocrine glands generally work in conjunction with one another, so that the release of a hormone in one gland will influence the operation of a different gland.

See also ADRENAL GLANDS; LYMPHATIC SYSTEM; PANCREAS; PITUITARY GLAND; PROSTATE; THYROID GLAND.

Gullet
See OESOPHAGUS.

Gut
See SMALL INTESTINE; LARGE INTESTINE.

Hair
With the exception of the lips, the palms of the hands and the soles of the feet, the body is entirely covered with hair. However, depending on the part of the body, the hair grows in different densities, patterns and colour. There are two types of hair — vellus hairs which are fine and downy and which account for most of the body hair, and terminal hairs which are longer and darker and which occur in the scalp, eyebrows, eye lashes, the pubic region, the armpits and on the lower part of the male face.

The main function of hair is to act as antennae for touch sensors located at the base of each hair (see TOUCH), but it also serves other useful purposes. The hair on our head cushions blows to the head and stops the head being burnt by the sun. Hairs in the nose filter out particles of grit and dust. Eyelashes prevent foreign bodies getting into the eyes. Eyebrows serve as sweat bands absorbing and diverting perspiration so that it does not drip into our eyes.

Each thread-like hair is made up of a structure of dead cells filled with a protein called keratin. A hair develops in a tiny tube called a follicle, situated below the surface of the skin. All the follicles we will ever have are present at birth — generally about five million, of which 100 000 to 200 000 are on the head. The hair develops from cells within the follicle and pushes its way up through the top layer of the skin to the outside. By the time it reaches the outside, the cells will gradually have died and hardened to form what we normally think of as hair. The fact that visible hair is dead is evidenced by the fact that if a hair is pulled out, pain is felt at the root, whereas cutting hair, even close to the skin, is completely painless.

The hairs on the head are continuously shed and replaced by new hairs growing from the follicle. We lose about 50 to 100 hairs a day, the only obvious sign of which may be a clogged drain after washing. One hair takes about three years from the time it starts to grow to the time it drops off.

The type of hair we have depends largely on the size and shape of the hair follicle. A hair follicle that is small in diameter will produce fine hair. Conversely, coarse hair grows from a larger follicle. If the follicle is circular it will produce straight hair, and if it is oval it will produce curly hair. Whether hair is coarse or fine also depends on its structure. A single strand of hair consists of an outer scaly casing called the cuticle, and a soft fibrous inner cortex. In coarse hair the cuticle is up to four times as thick in proportion to the cortex as it is in fine hair.

Hair colour depends on the amount of pigment called melanin in the hair. We inherit the colour of our hair from our parents, although exactly how is not fully understood. It is known that dark colours are dominant over light colours, so if a child has one fair and one dark parent, the child is more likely to be dark than fair. Grey or white hair has no pigment. For some reason — no-one is quite sure why — the body stops producing melanin as we grow older, making grey or white hair one of the most familiar signs of ageing.

Although we have all our hair follicles at birth, not all are functioning. Some, such as those in the pubic area and under the arms, are inactive until puberty, when they are stimulated into production by the sex hormones. The production of hair in puberty increases far more in boys than it does in girls.

If a hair follicle is damaged, hair growth may continue, but once a follicle is destroyed, hair will not grow again in that spot.

Each hair follicle has tiny oil glands and an erector muscle that contracts under certain circumstances (e.g. fright) so that the hair 'stands on end'. Similarly if the body is cold, the muscle will contract and cause 'goose pimples'. This muscle is more apparent in animals but it can be activated in humans too.

Hair is sensitive to the body's state of health. We all know that our hair becomes dull and lifeless when we are not well, but it is also useful in the diagnosis of certain illnesses, e.g. cystic fibrosis.

Sometimes part or all of the hair falls out and we become bald (see BALDNESS, Section 3 and ALOPECIA AREATA, Section 5).

Hearing
See EARS.

Heart
Despite the emotional mystique which is often attributed to it, the heart is simply a very efficient pump. It is crucial to the maintenance of life, but no more so than many other organs such as the liver or kidney.

The heart is the centre of the circulatory system (see separate entry). It lies behind the breastbone between the lungs, and is not unlike a mango both in shape and size. One corner extends outwards towards the left nipple.

Section 2: Basic Anatomy and Physiology

Basically the heart is a muscular pump with four separate chambers into which enter the major blood vessels carrying blood to and from the rest of the body. The two upper chambers (the atria) which receive blood are much smaller than the two lower chambers (the ventricles) which pump it out.

The right side of the heart deals with blood that has been used throughout the body and so is depleted of oxygen. This blood comes into the heart via the upper right chamber, passes immediately through a valve into the lower right chamber and a split second later is pumped out into the lungs where the poisonous carbon dioxide it has collected in the body is removed and the blood is replenished with oxygen. The oxygen-enriched blood is then dealt with by the left side of the heart — it travels from the lungs into the upper left chamber and is pumped out through the lower left chamber to the rest of the body for another circuit.

The left and right sides of the heart are roughly similar in shape but the left side, which has to be strong enough to pump blood to the furthest parts of the body, even the fingers and toes, is larger and more muscular. Hence the heart has a somewhat asymmetrical appearance. The two sides of the heart are completely sealed from one another. To get from one side of the heart to another, blood has to go through the lungs or the entire circulatory system.

When it leaves the left side of the heart, the blood passes into the major artery, the aorta, and from there travels along the network of arteries into the smaller arterioles and finally into capillaries from where it is absorbed into the cells. From there it moves back through the veins to the heart again, completing the cycle. It takes about twenty seconds for one blood cell to complete the full cycle. In the major arteries blood travels at about two kilometres an hour.

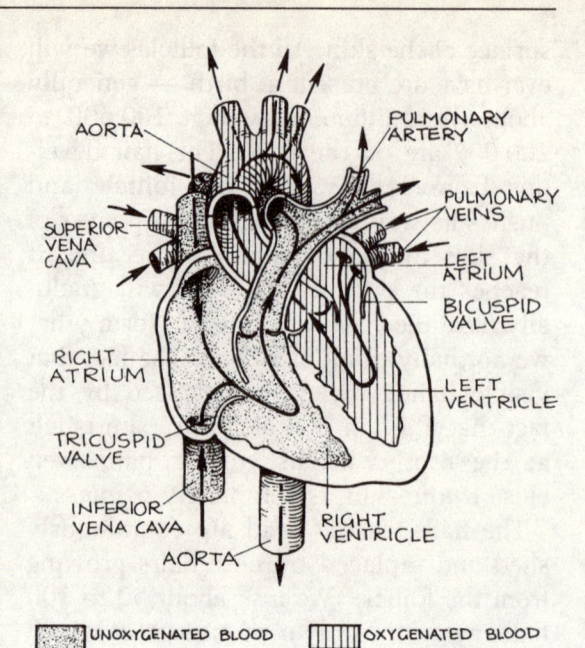

FIGURE 2.3: The heart and the route of blood flow through it.

At rest, the heart beats at about 70 times a minute. If we exercise or increase activity in some other way, the rate increases until it may reach as much as 200 times a minute. The number of beats a minute is called the heart rate or pulse. There are various parts of the body where the large arteries pass sufficiently close to the surface of the body for you to feel your pulse, the most common being the sides of the neck just under the jawbone or the under-side of the wrist. If you turn your palm upwards and gently press two fingers on the thumb side of the tendon in your wrist you should be able to feel the regular pulsation.

The heartbeat is regulated by electrical impulses generated within the heart. Without any assistance, the heart would beat at about 40 beats a minute. However, this would not be enough for all the activities the body is required to perform so there is a sort of spark plug to push the rate up higher. This consists of a group of special nerves, forming what is commonly known as a pacemaker, which produces an electrical charge and raises the heartbeat as demand requires. The pacemaker is located on the right atrium, and a large nerve (the bundle of His) connects it to the two ventricles.

The heart is made up of three main layers. The outer fibrous layer is called the pericardium and is generally surrounded by a thin protective layer of fat. The innermost layer is called the endocardium and is a thin smooth lining for the inner surfaces of the heart chambers and valves. The middle layer or myocardium is the thickest and most important. It consists mostly of muscle and it is the contraction and relaxation of this muscle that results in the heart's pumping action. In normal circumstances, this pump continues to operate without stopping for our entire life, probably 70 or 80 years. If the pumping system fails in any way, e.g. due to the heart not receiving enough oxygen, the lungs becoming damaged by disease, clots blocking an artery, extreme blood loss or any other cause, the victim will become severely ill or die.

Blood pressure

Blood pressure is just that — the pressure of the blood against the walls of the main arteries. The pumping action of the heart causes waves of pressure. As the muscle contracts, a spurt of blood is forced out into the arteries, and as the muscle relaxes so that the heart can refill, the pressure eases. The period of contraction is called the systole and the period of relaxation is known as the diastole. The pressure can be measured by a special instrument called a sphygmomanometer which measures pressure by using a column of mercury, a spring gauge, or electronically. The pressure is usually expressed as two numbers representing each extreme of pressure. The systolic pressure in a young healthy adult usually varies from about 90 to 120 mm of mercury and the diastolic pressure between 60 and 80 mm. Hence a reading might be, say, 90/60 or 120/80.

Blood pressure varies between individuals and according to age (older people tend to have slightly increased blood pressure), physical activity, and physical and emotional well-being.

In general, low blood pressure is preferable to high blood pressure. Higher than normal pressure over an extended period can be a sign of underlying disease or itself lead to major health problems. Very low blood pressure can also be a problem, e.g. severe shock can cause the blood pressure to fall so that not enough blood is transported through the body to keep it functioning properly.

Because blood pressure is such an important indicator of our state of health, doctors usually take their patients' blood pressure as a matter of routine.

ILEUM
See SMALL INTESTINE.

INTESTINE
See SMALL INTESTINE; LARGE INTESTINE.

JEJUNUM
See SMALL INTESTINE.

JOINTS
Joints occur at the intersections of bones. The main joints are in the shoulders, elbows, wrists, hips, knees, ankles and jaw. Smaller joints are in the hands and feet and the spine. Most joints are movable, but not all. Some, such as those in the skull, are completely fixed. Joints in the pubic area are fixed most of the time but move during childbirth.

The movable joints, which are what we usually think of when we use the term, can be divided into those that allow slight movement such as the ones in the breastbone and spine, and those that allow a wide range of movement such as the ones in the shoulders, hips, knees, and elbows.

The tough fibrous tissue that holds bones together at a joint are ligaments (see separate entry). Their flexibility determines the amount of movement the joint is capable of. The ends of the bones themselves are covered with a smooth layer of cartilage (gristle) providing a low-friction surface for easy movement. Joints such as the knees contain extra cartilage pads as shock absorbers. The bones in a joint never actually touch — they are always separated by a thin layer of fluid contained in a capsule surrounding the joint.

The occasional cracking noise heard when a joint is flexed or bent may be caused by the tightly stretched ligaments moving from the surface of one bone to another. Alternatively, it might be the result of air bubbles bursting in the lubricating fluid.

Both cartilage and ligaments are prone to injury. A stretched or torn ligament is commonly referred to as a sprain and can be as serious as a broken bone, needing proper rest and care until completely healed. Cartilage doesn't contain any blood vessels and so cannot heal itself if it is damaged. A torn cartilage isn't always troublesome, but if it does cause recurrent pain, e.g. in the knee, it is generally removed by surgery.

The type of movement in the various joints depends on the way they are constructed. Hinge joints such as those in the fingers, elbows and knees can move backwards and forwards. The hips and shoulders, on the other hand, are so-called ball-and-socket joints which can move in almost any direction — backwards and forwards, sideways and in circles. The wrists and ankles have gliding joints.

The movement in the joints is controlled by muscles, which are attached to the bones by tendons — strong fibrous cords similar to ligaments but not as elastic.

People who have an unusually wide range of movement and who can bend their fingers and various other parts of their body into peculiar positions are sometimes said to be double-jointed — i.e., they are alleged to have extra joints which enable their contortions. In reality there is no such thing. The likelihood is that such people have naturally slack ligaments which they have loosened still further by stretching and twisting until movement is no longer as restricted as it is in a normal person.

KIDNEYS

The kidneys are a pair of reddish-brown organs lying on each side of the spine just above the waist. If you grip your waist with your hands, your thumbs will be over your kidneys. The main function of the kidneys is to filter the blood to remove impurities and waste products. They also ensure that various elements in our blood, such as proteins, salts, vitamins and nutrients remain in perfect balance. About a litre of blood is pumped into the kidneys every minute, and the entire bloodstream is purified about every 50 minutes.

The kidneys are soft to the touch and are about 10 cm long and 6 cm wide. One side is concave and the other is convex — the classic kidney shape. The right kidney is slightly lower than the left one because of the space taken up by the liver above it.

Each kidney is cushioned by a mass of fat and is also protected by the bottom ribs. The kidneys are, nevertheless, quite vulnerable and can be injured by a blow to the small of the back.

The kidneys also monitor and regulate the balance of fluid in the body. Although the amount of water consumed in a day can vary enormously, the volume of body water at any given time remains remarkably stable. Water is lost from the body in several ways — from the skin as perspiration, from the respiratory system when we breathe out, and by passing urine. Normally the amount of water taken in is approximately equal to the amount lost. The kidneys are the main monitoring organ. If the body is short of fluid, the kidneys return more water to the bloodstream, and as a result the amount of urine is reduced and is more concentrated. Messages are also sent to the brain and we feel thirsty. Correspondingly, if the intake of water is greater than we need, the kidneys return proportionally less fluid to the blood and the amount of urine passed increases. Similarly the amount of salts contained in the body is regulated. If you eat or drink something containing substances your body doesn't want, the kidneys will filter the substances out and discard them in your urine, which will have a high concentration of waste products and may reflect what you have eaten in its colour, usually a deeper yellow. To keep the kidneys functioning as effectively as possible it is important to drink enough water and not to overload them with products the body doesn't need, such as food additives, drugs and vitamins.

The kidneys have considerable reserve capacity. If one fails, the other can generally carry the load on its own, and in fact even a third of one kidney may be enough to keep the body functioning. If the kidneys fail completely, however, the victim will die within a few days or weeks.

For many years it has been possible to transplant kidneys from one person to another. This is now a fairly common operation carried out hundreds of times a year. If a transplant is not possible for a person with failed kidneys, the work has to be carried out by an artificial kidney machine in a process known as dialysis. This involves being hooked up to a machine for eight hours at least three times a week. This must usually be in hospital unless the patient can afford to buy a (very expensive) machine for use at home. The machine is about the size of a suitcase. Modern science has not yet managed to combine the complex functions of a kidney in a package as small as the one provided by nature.

The most common diseases to affect the kidneys are infections and stones. Both of these can be effectively treated and rarely cause serious long-term damage (see Section 5).

The kidneys can also be damaged by poisons and chemicals found in the workplace or environment (e.g. lead or mercury), and as a result of complications of various diseases that individually are quite rare but collectively affect thousands of people every year.

See also BLADDER; URETERS.

LARGE INTESTINE

There are two intestines, one small and one large, forming the major part of the digestive system. The intestines are what we often refer to as the gut or the bowels. Food taken in through the mouth passes down the pharynx (throat) into the oesophagus (gullet) through the stomach and into the small intestine where the main digestive process takes place. Food that is not digested in the small intestine passes into the large intestine. Here most of the water content is extracted to be reabsorbed into the bloodstream, and the remaining semisolid waste passes into the rectum to be stored until it is eliminated from the body through the anal canal.

Like the small intestine (see separate entry), the large intestine consists of a series of loops, but it has nearly twice the diameter — about 65 mm compared with the small intestine's 35 mm. It is, however, shorter than the small intestine, measuring about 1.8 m in total length, compared with the 6.5 m of the small intestine. Dividing the small intestine from the large intestine is a muscular valve which opens to let food into the large intestine but otherwise remains closed to prevent the food passing back into the small intestine.

The large intestine begins in the lower part of the abdomen on the right side. Like the small intestine, the large intestine is divided into three parts. The first part, consisting of a small pouch into which the small intestine opens, is known as the caecum (pronounced 'sekum'). The second part is the colon, and the third part is the rectum, which passes straight down through the back part of the pelvis and opens to the exterior through the anus.

Opening off the caecum is the appendix, a small tube-like cul-de-sac, which may once have played a part in the digestive process but is no longer of any importance in it. The main relevance of the appendix in modern humans is that it is subject to inflammation and may have to be surgically removed.

The colon is the major part of the large intestine. It continues on from the caecum and at first moves upwards through the abdomen. This is called the ascending colon. When it reaches just below the liver, it takes a sharp turn right and travels across the abdomen to the left side. This section is called the transverse colon. It then takes a sharp downwards turn, when it becomes known as the descending colon. This extends down the left side to the pelvis in a line roughly parallel with the ascending colon. At the bottom of the descending colon is a sort of S-bend, called the sigmoid colon, which empties into the rectum.

Food that cannot be digested or absorbed, now called faeces or stool, is passed into the rectum for temporary storage. For the first time since the food left the mouth and was passed into the oesophagus, we have some voluntary control over it. When the rectum is full, it sends messages to the brain, and at a convenient time we can take a conscious decision to expel the waste material through the back passage or anus in a process called defecation. However, if defecation does not take place within a reasonable time and the rectum becomes overfull, the involuntary muscles will take over so that the muscle keeping the rectum closed will open and the faeces will be expelled regardless of any effort or will.

The conscious control of defecation does not occur in babies but is a response acquired in childhood. For the first couple of years of life, the anal sphincter (ring muscle) opens unconsciously in an involuntary nervous reflex. It is about the age of two that the brain is able to exercise conscious control.

See also DIGESTION.

Larynx

The larynx is the voice box where sound is produced by the vocal cords. It is also part of the mechanism that comes into play when we cough to remove excess mucus or foreign matter from the respiratory system (see separate entry). It lies below the pharynx and leads into the trachea and thence to the lungs (see separate entries).

Because the pharynx is the passageway for food as well as air, the body has to ensure that food doesn't get into the larynx by mistake. It does this by means of a leaf-shaped fold of cartilage called the epiglottis which lies at the top of the larynx and moves to cover the opening when we eat or drink, so that the food is excluded. Occasionally the epiglottis fails to move quickly enough, usually because we are trying to talk or laugh at the same time as we are eating, and food 'goes down the wrong way' and causes us to cough and splutter.

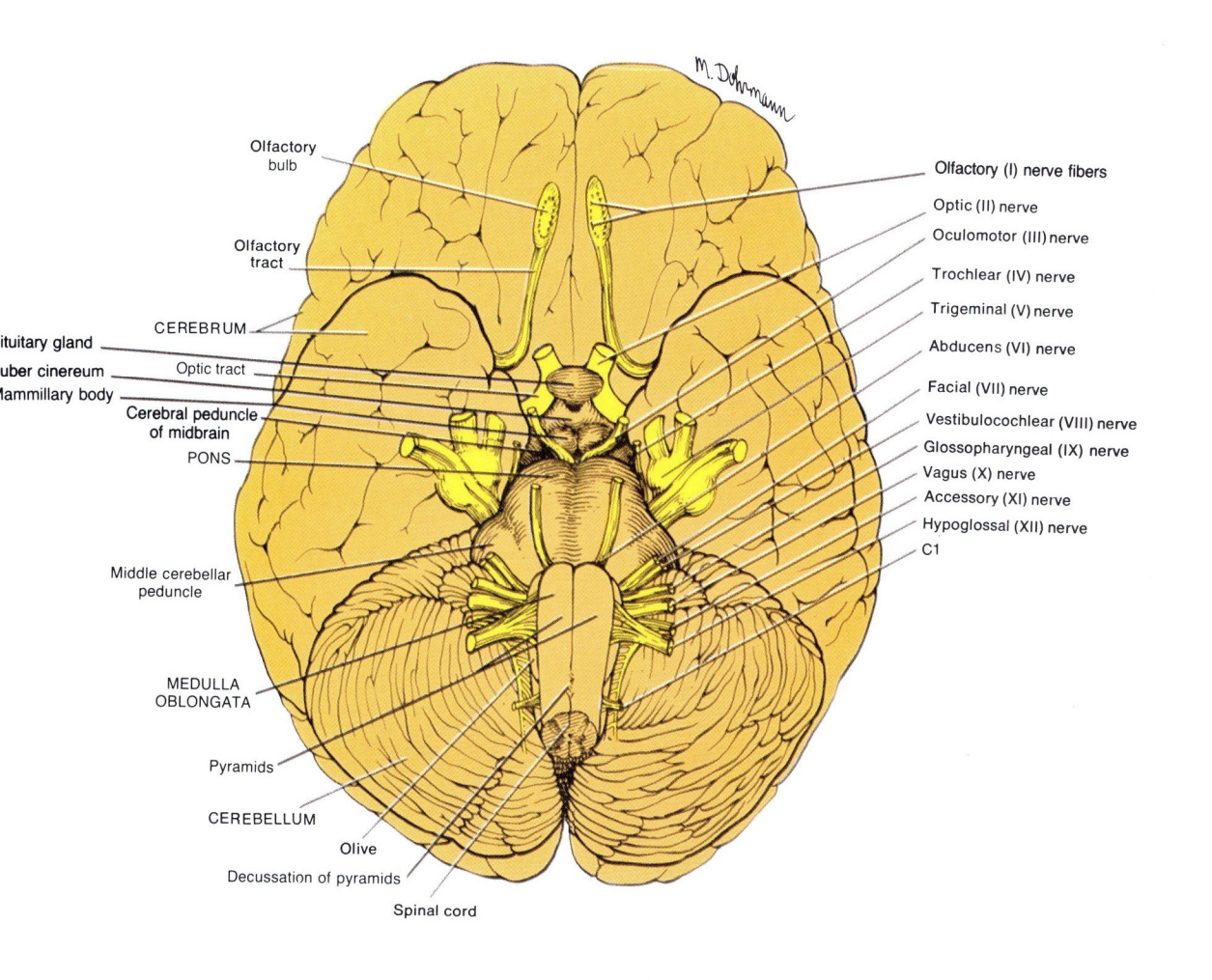

PLATE 2.1: Brain stem and cranial nerves

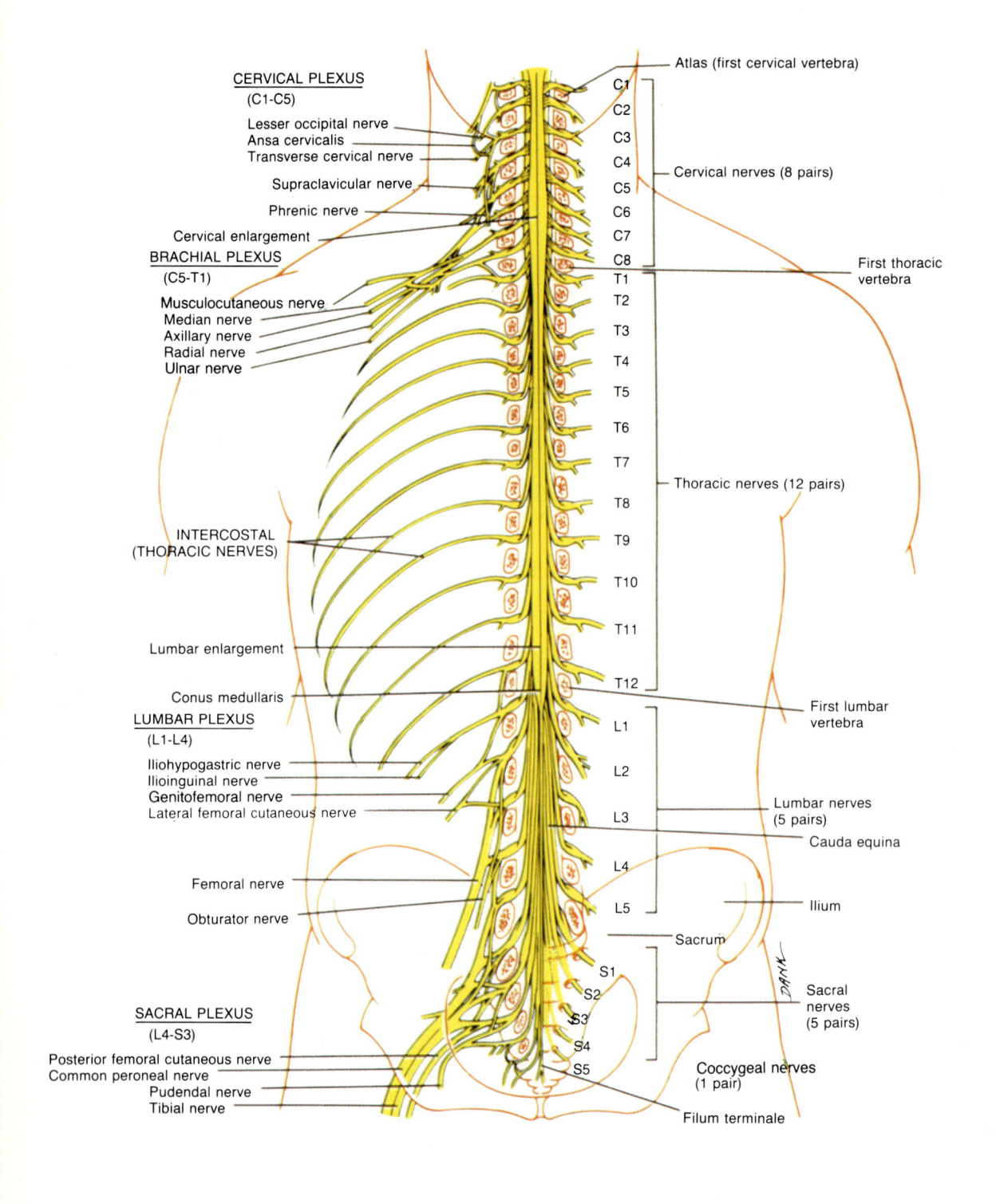

PLATE 2.2: Nervous system: spinal cord and spinal nerves

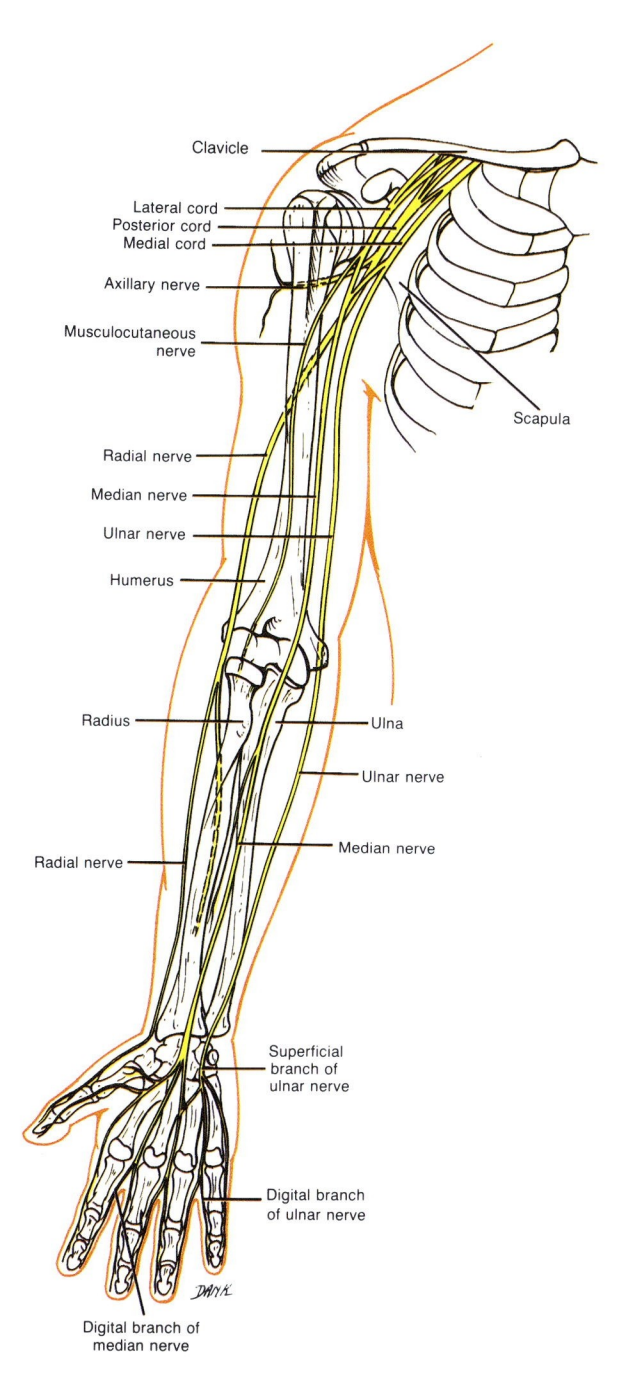

PLATE 2.3: Nervous system: brachial plexus

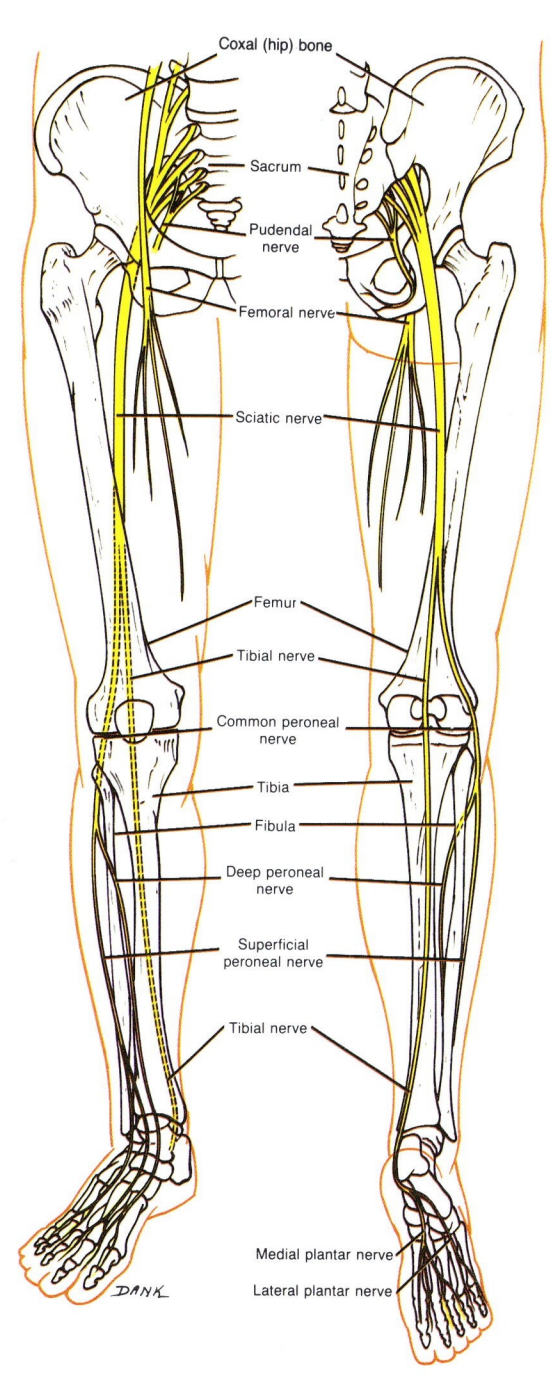

PLATE 2.4: Nervous system: lumbar plexus

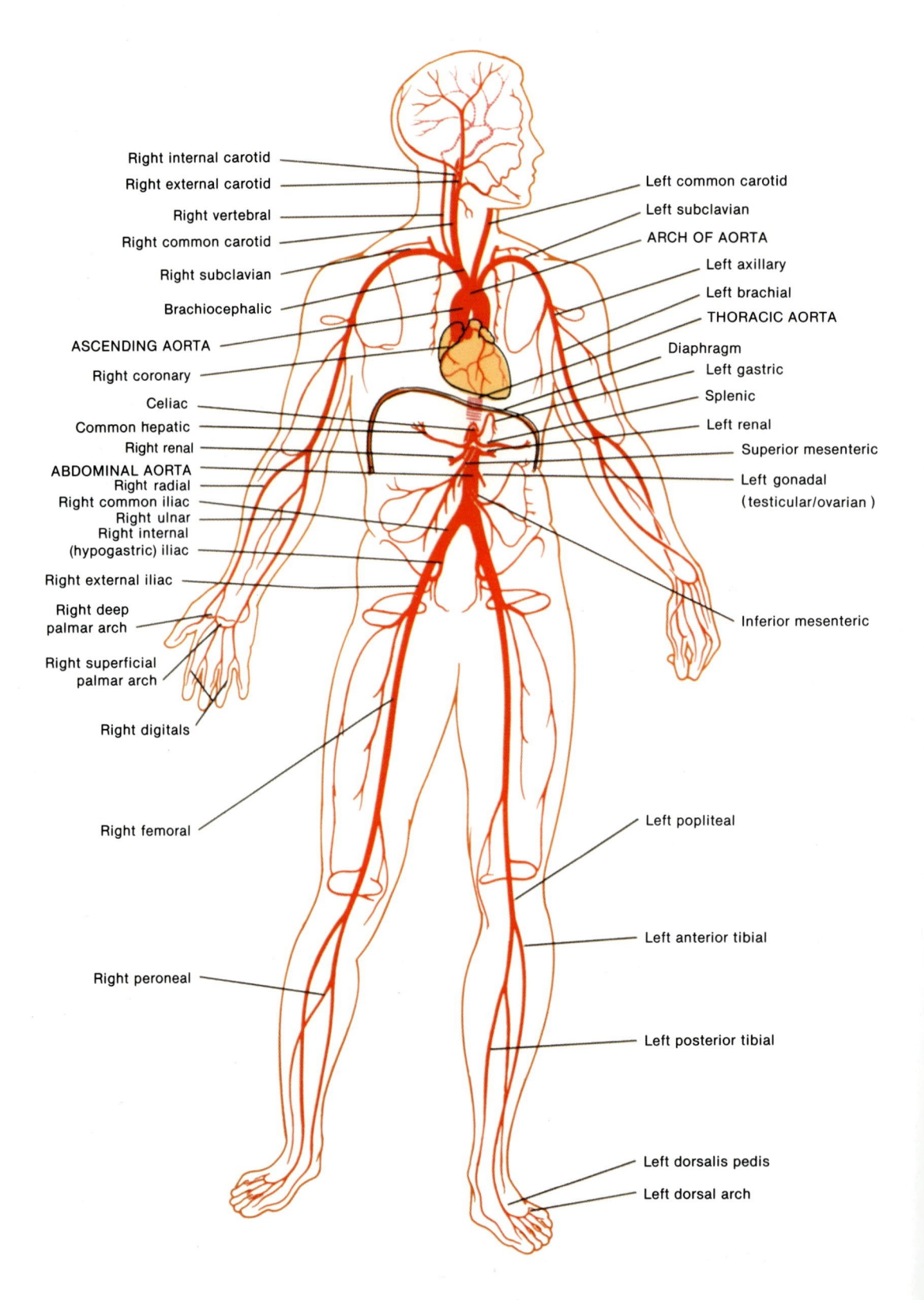

PLATE 2.5: Circulatory system: principal arteries (anterior view)

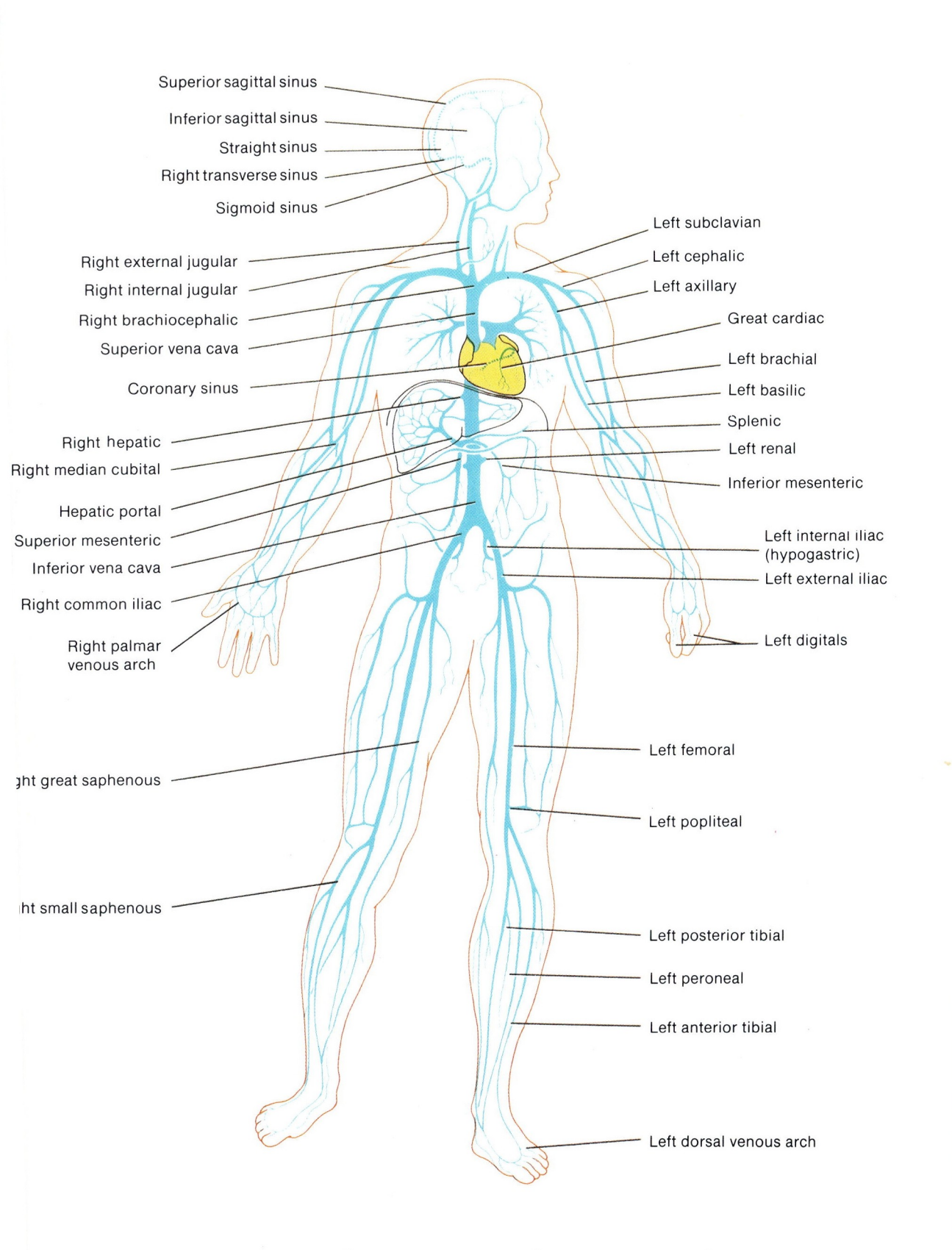

PLATE 2.6: Circulatory system: principal veins (anterior view)

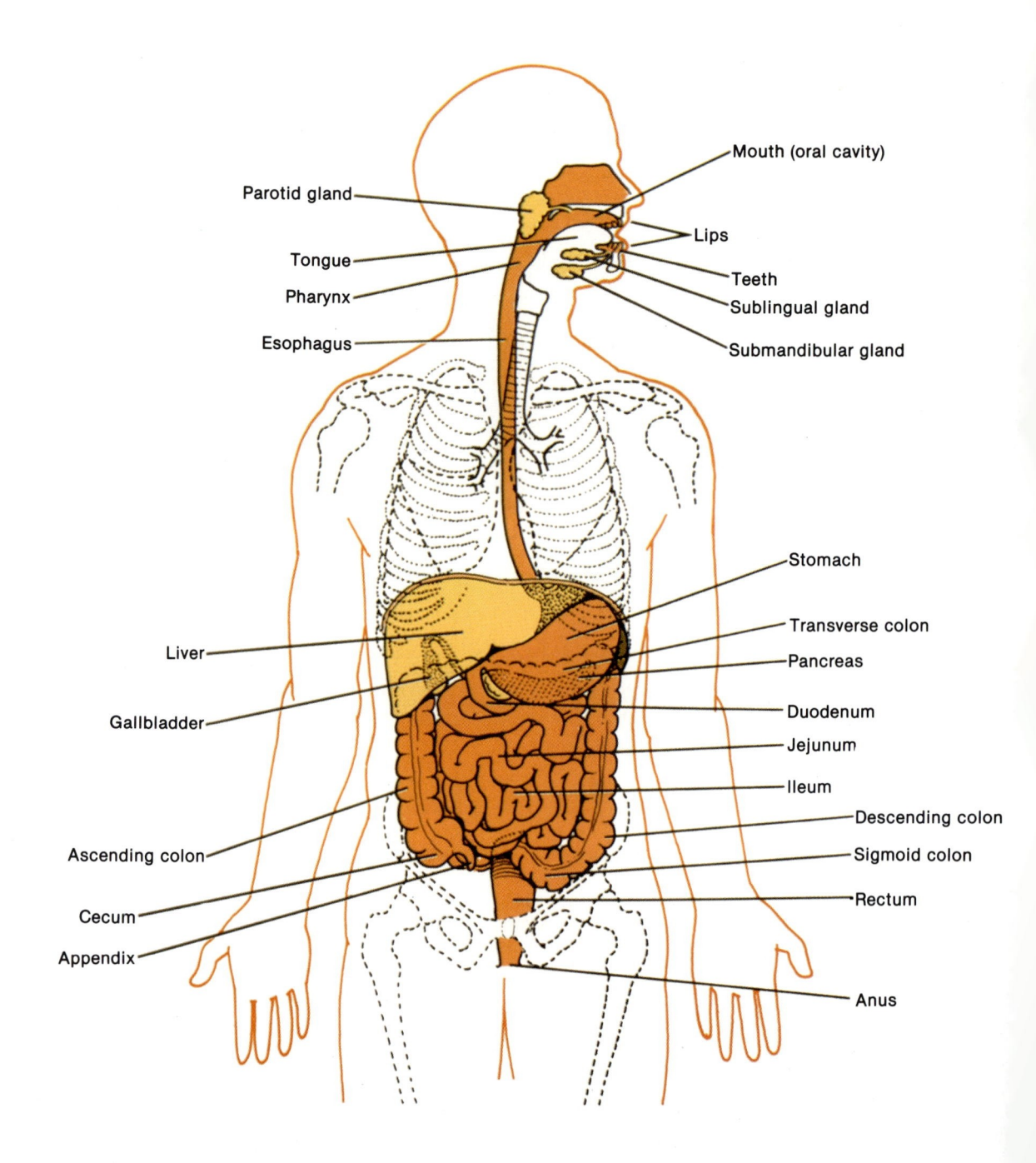

PLATE 2.7: Organs of the digestive system

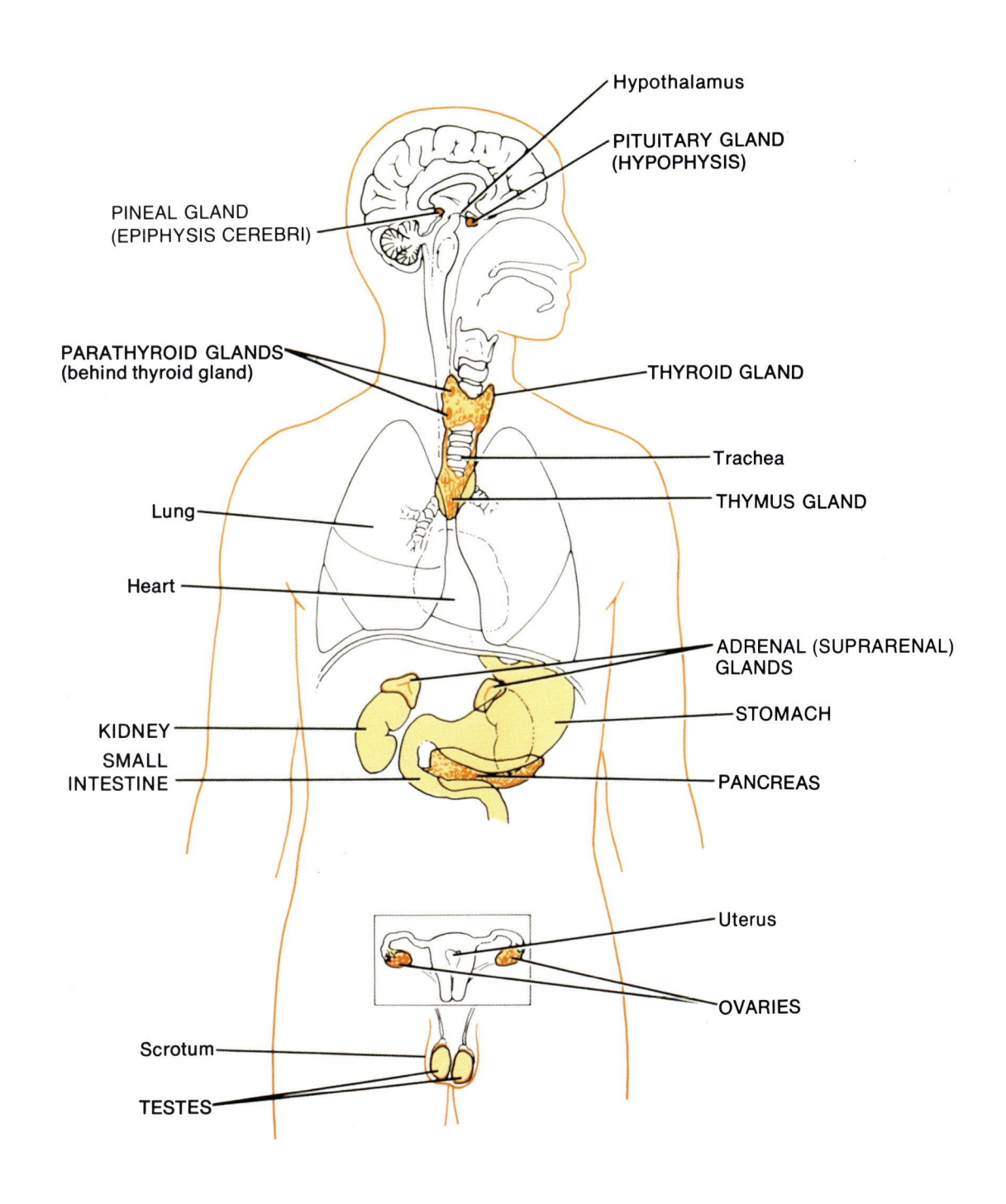

PLATE 2.8: Location of endocrine glands

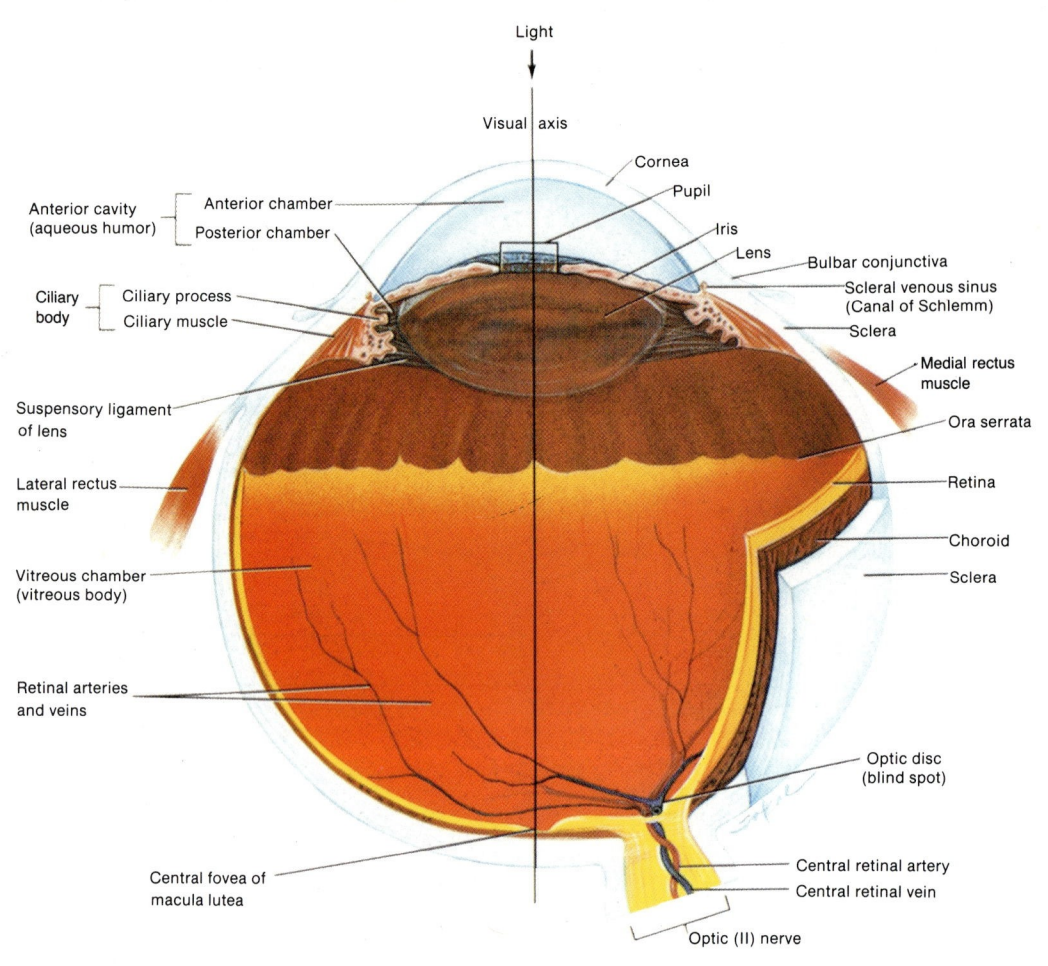

PLATE 2.9: Structure of the eyeball (transverse section)

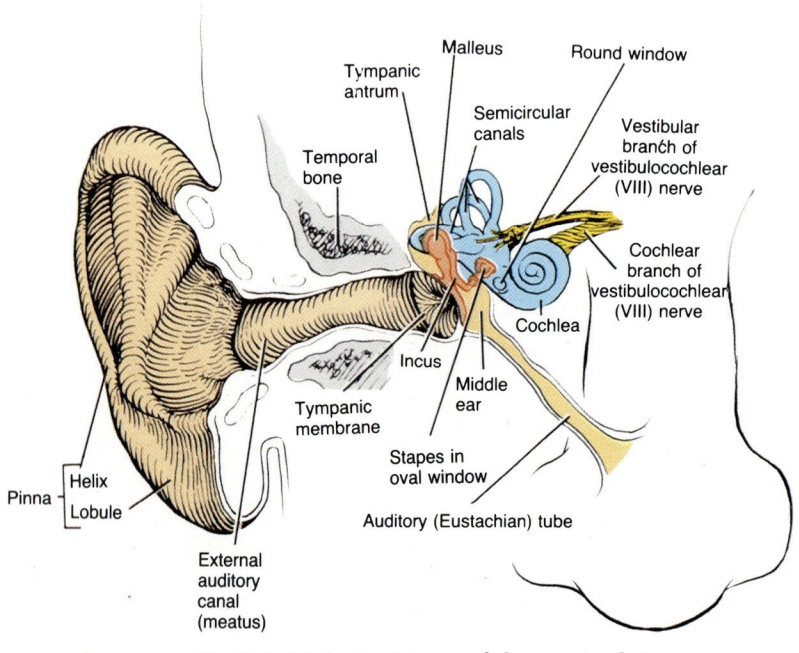

PLATE 2.10: Divisions of the ear (right)

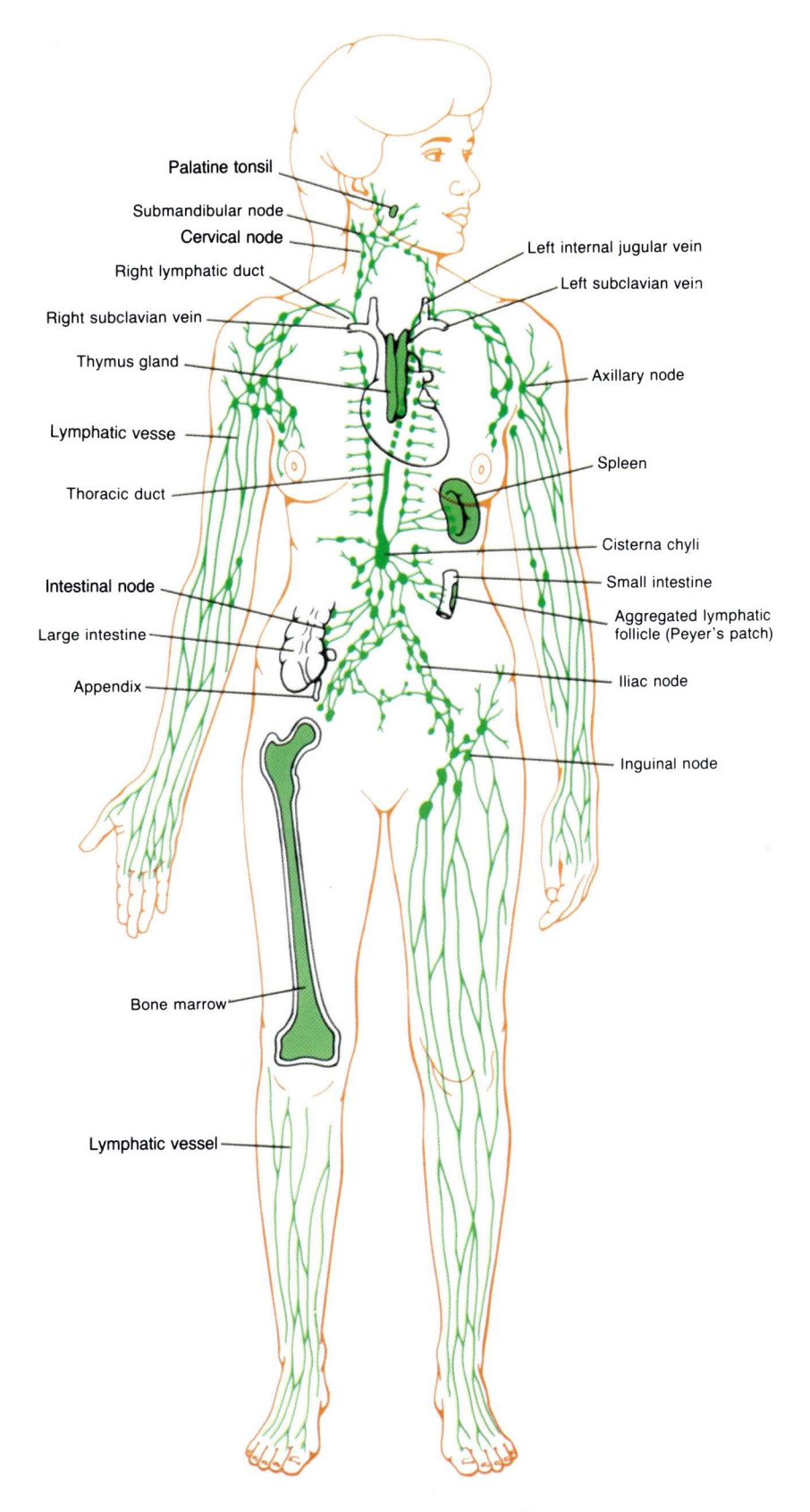

PLATE 2.11: Lymphatic system: principal components

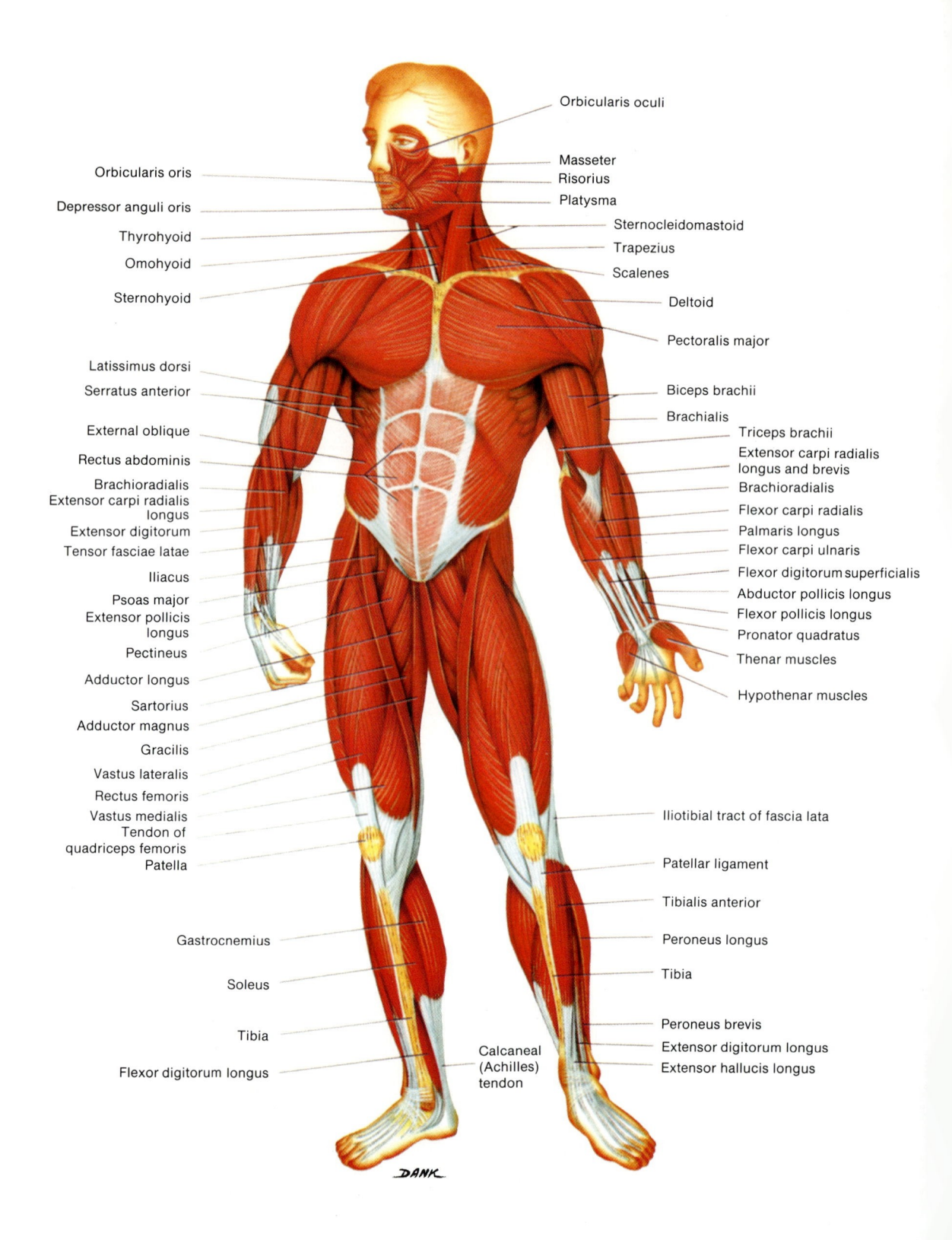

PLATE 2.12: Muscular system: principal superficial skeletal muscles (anterior view)

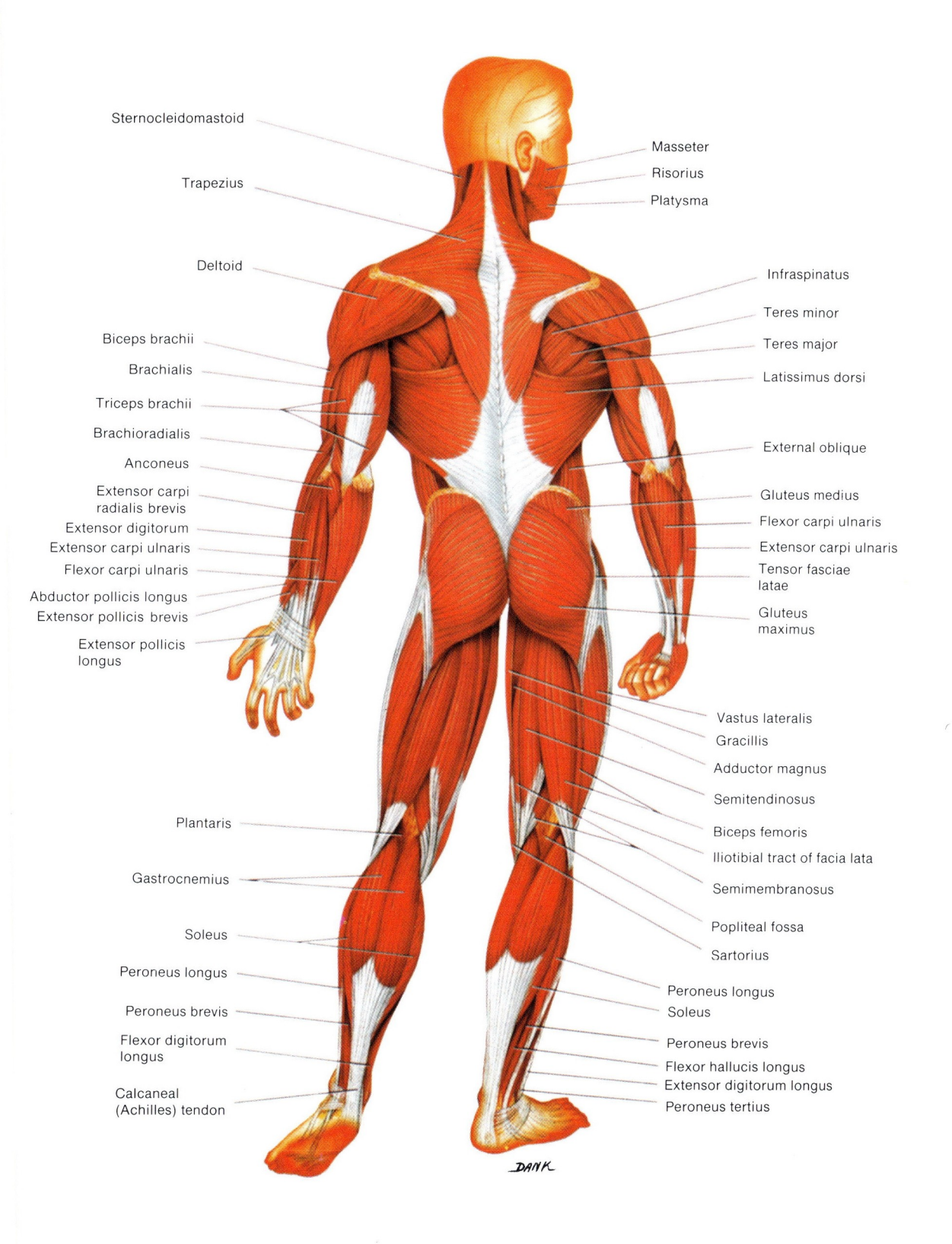

PLATE 2.13: Muscular system: principal superficial skeletal muscles (posterior view)

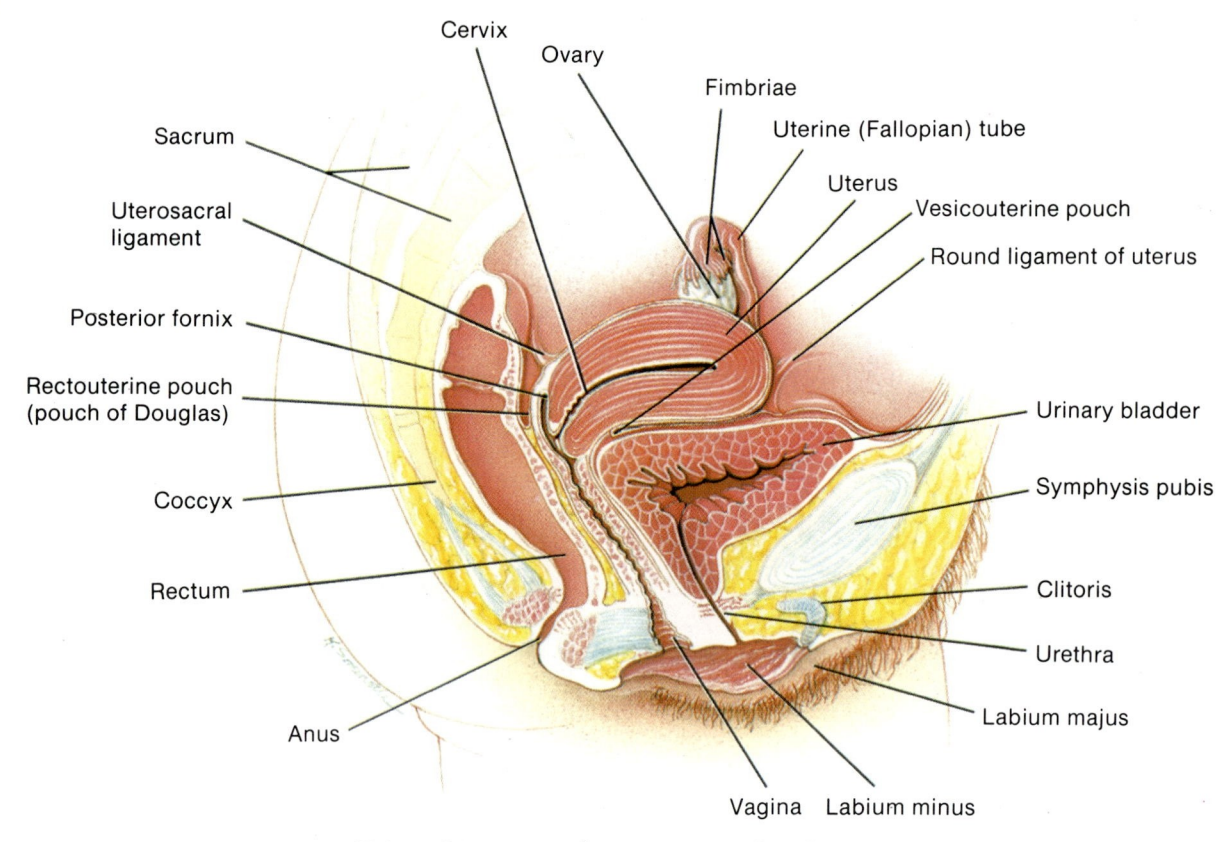

PLATE 2.14: Reproductive system: female organs

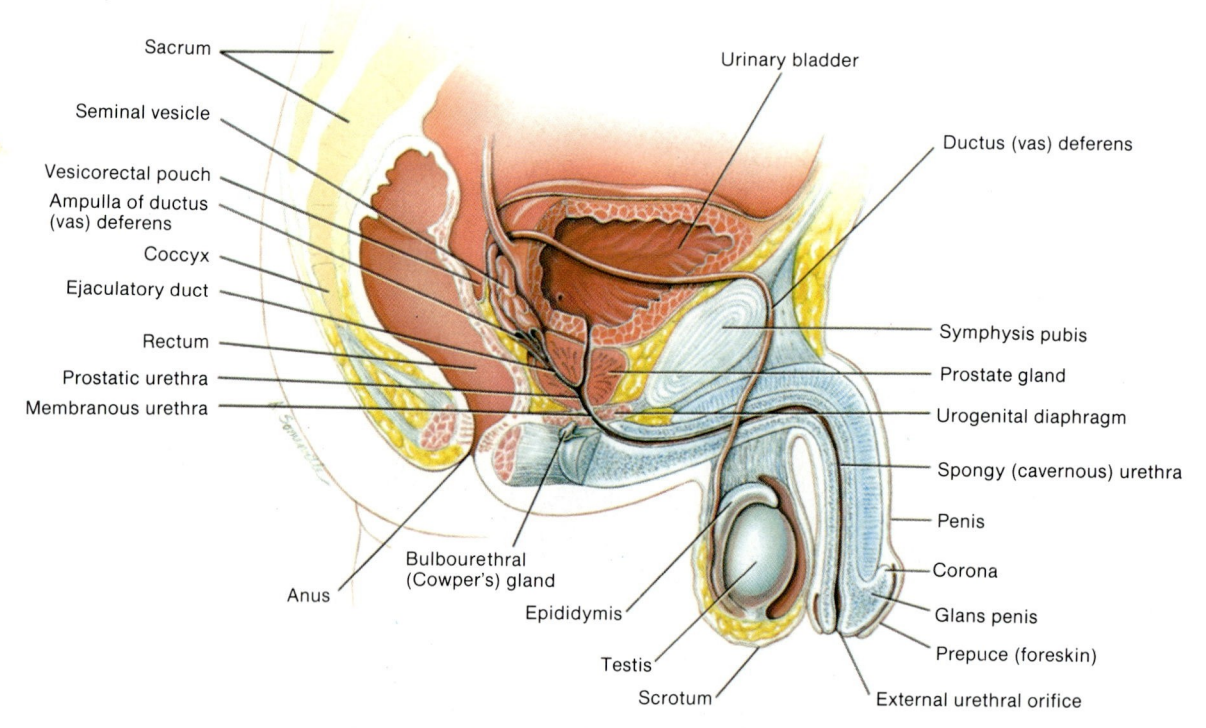

PLATE 2.15: Reproductive system: male organs

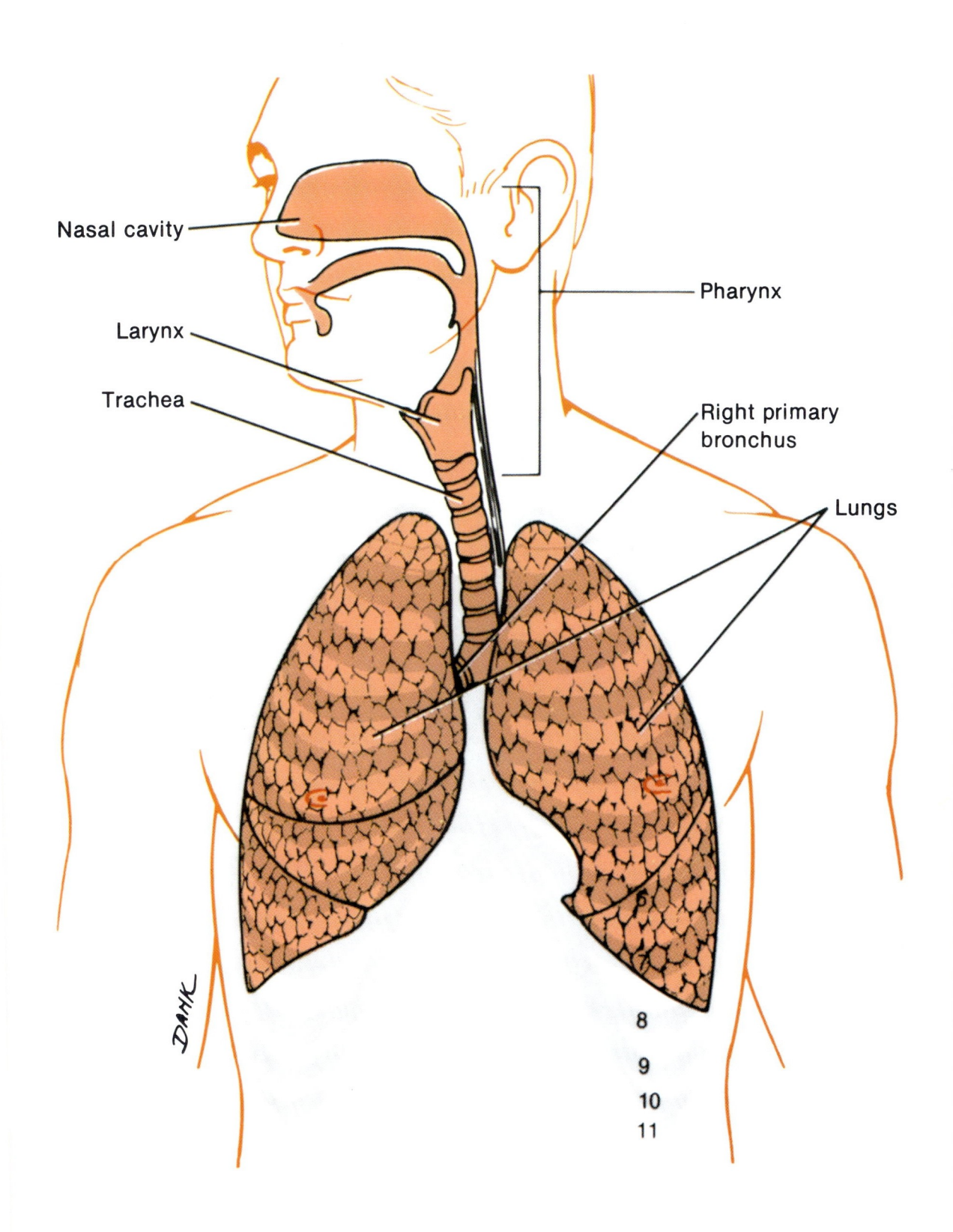

PLATE 2.16: Respiratory system

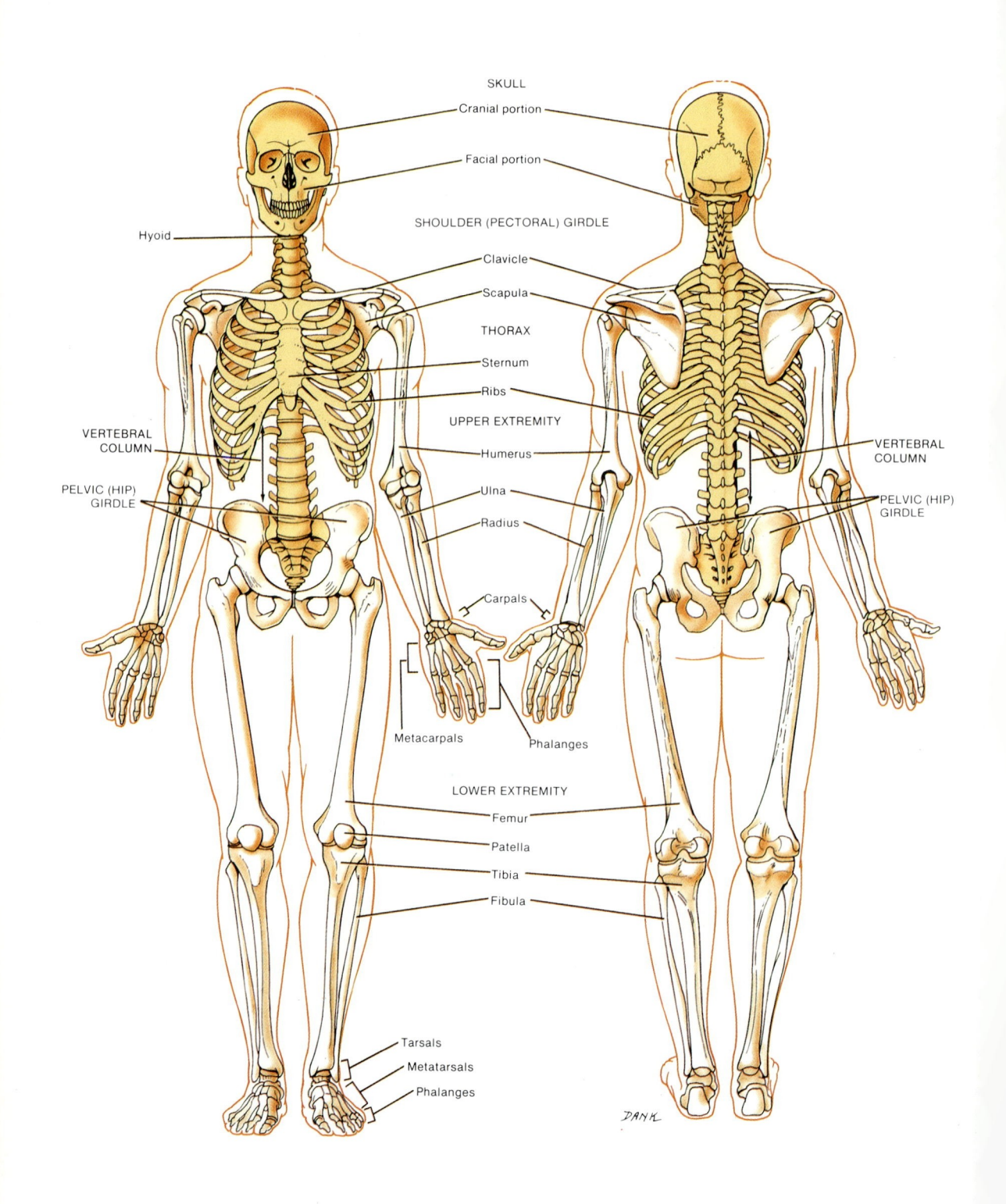

PLATE 2.17: Skeletal system

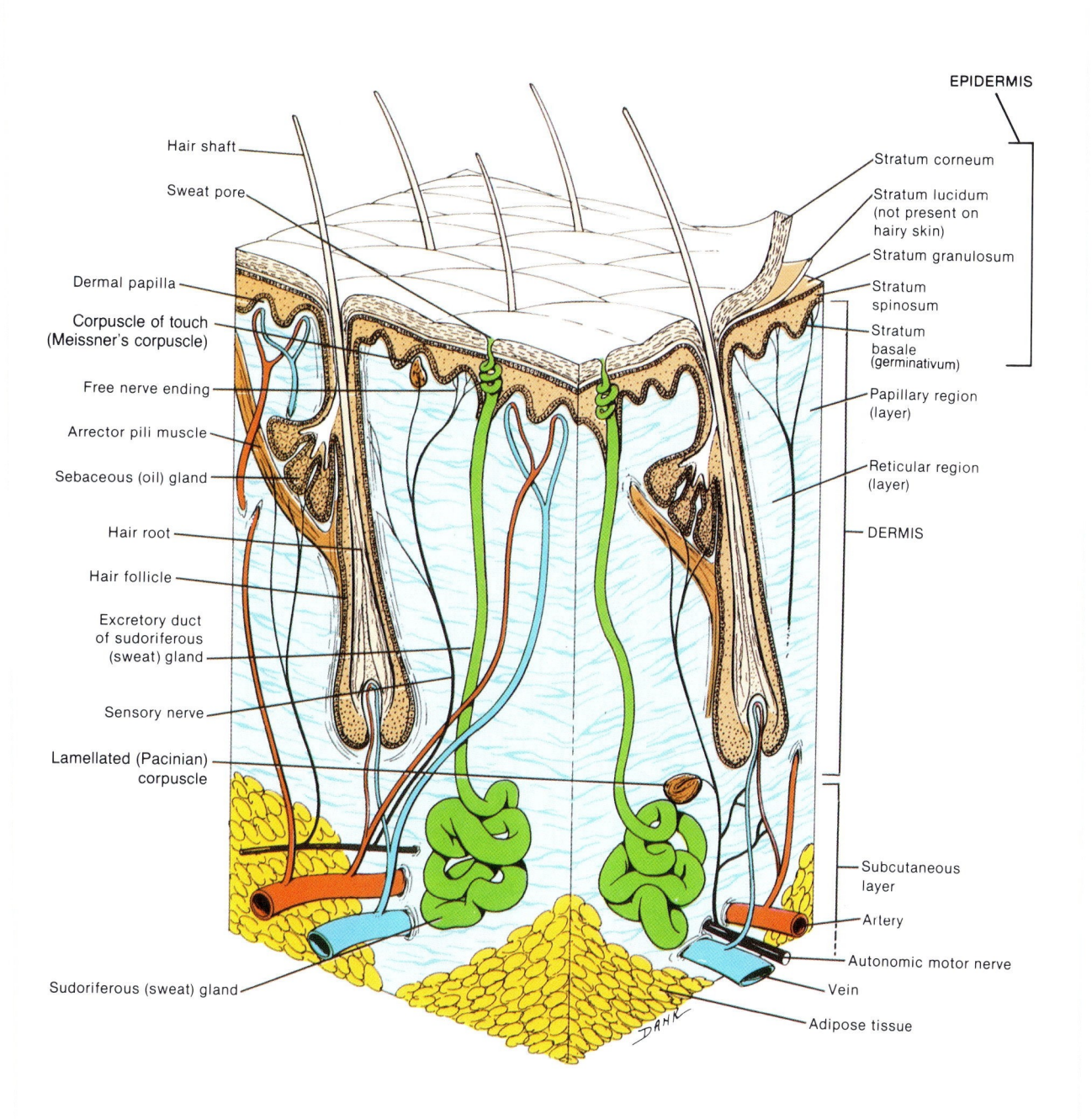

PLATE 2.18: Structure of the skin

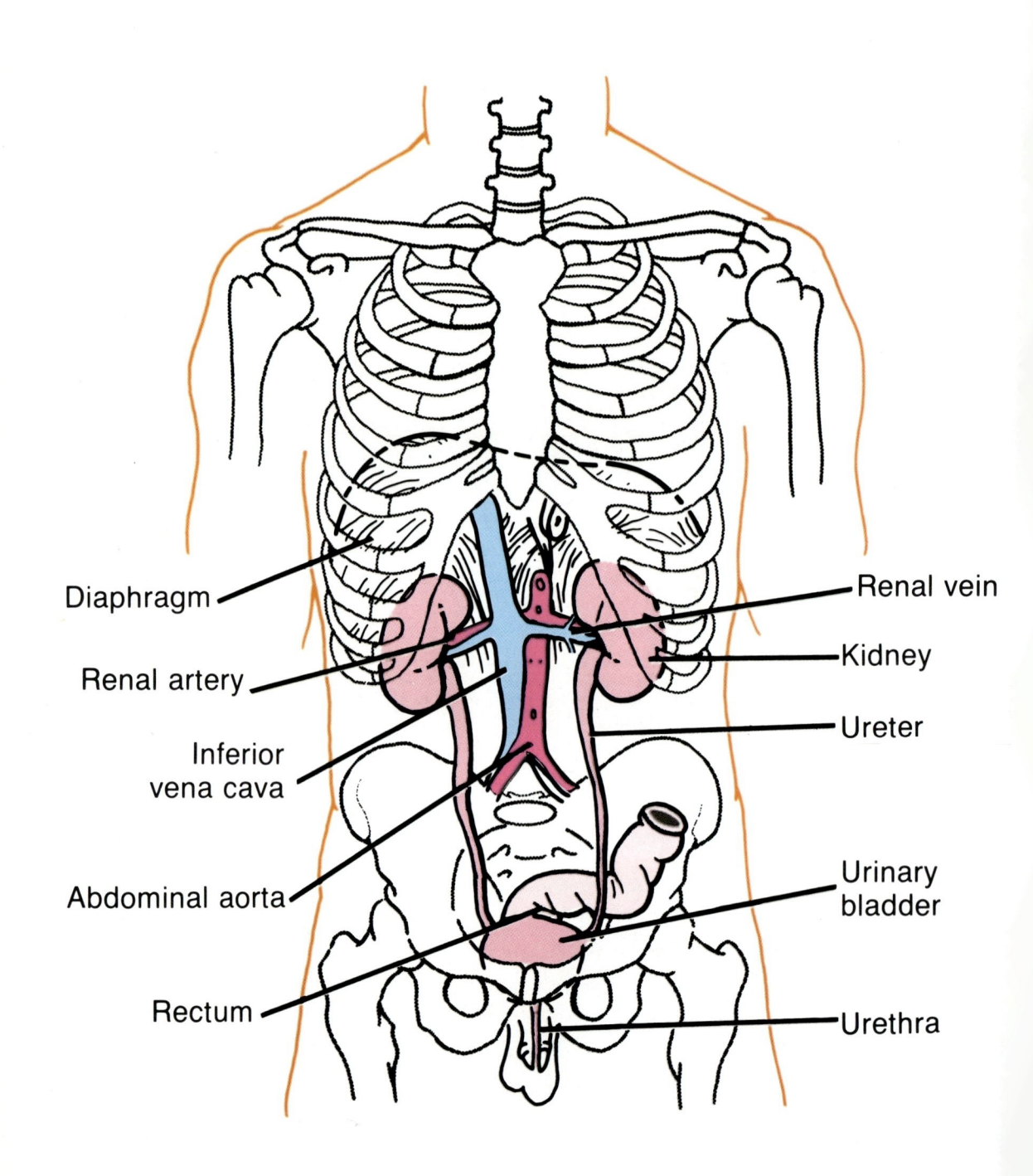

PLATE 2.19: Urinary system: male organs

The framework of the larynx protrudes slightly at the front to form the so-called Adam's apple. A man's Adam's apple is usually more obvious than a woman's because the male hormones act to enlarge the larynx and give the man a deeper voice.

The vocal cords are two folds of tissue protruding from the sides of the larynx so that the passage of air is narrowed into a small space called the glottis (situated beneath the epiglottis). As air is passed over the vocal cords, they vibrate to produce sound. By means of muscular control, this sound can be varied both in tone and pitch. The sound is then amplified by the chambers of the throat and mouth.

The type of sound depends on a number of extraordinarily complex factors, but generally speaking a large larynx with long vocal cords produces low notes. Hence men usually have a deeper voice than women and, because the larynx of a child is smaller than that of an adult, children have shriller voices than adults. The breaking of the voice in boys in puberty is due to the rapid development of the larynx at this time, together with a degree of uncertain muscular control.

Voice is also affected by sex hormones and singers often notice a slight decrease in the quality of the higher notes during menstruation and in pregnancy. Similarly the voice may change at menopause and as old age advances.

LIGAMENTS

The point where two bones meet is a joint. Joints enable the body to move (see separate entry). Consequently, bones meeting at a joint need to be held together firmly while still being sufficiently flexible to allow movement. The tough fibrous tissue that carries out this task is called a ligament. Ligaments are flexible and allow the joint to move in its intended manner while at the same time giving strength to the joint. Some ligaments are like a cord, others form flat bands. A major joint, such as the elbow, has several overlapping ligaments to support the three bones that meet there. Joints such as the knees and elbows, which need strength, are bound together by ligaments that prevent too wide a range of movement.

Despite their flexibility ligaments are not elastic, and if too much stress is placed on a ligament it will stretch or even tear, causing a sprain. Torn ligaments can be as serious as a broken bone and need proper rest and care until completely healed.

See also TENDONS.

LIVER

The liver is the largest gland and internal organ in the body. Wedge-shaped, it lies behind the lower few ribs on the right side. It weighs about 1.5 kg and has the same reddish brown colour as the animal livers we are familiar with in the butcher shop.

When food has been digested it still has to be absorbed into the body. The liver plays an integral part in this process of metabolism.

The smooth rubbery texture of the liver is deceptive. It is a mass of complex tissue containing millions of cells and blood vessels. The liver has been called the body's chemical processing plant. Among its functions, it regulates the amount of blood sugar, assists in producing the blood clotting mechanisms, helps to nourish new blood cells, destroys old blood cells, breaks down excess acids to be eliminated as urine, stores and modifies fats so they can be more efficiently utilised by cells all over the body, stores certain vitamins and minerals, and removes poisons from harmful substances such as alcohol and drugs. The liver is also an important source of the heat which is essential to maintain the body's temperature.

The liver aids the digestive process by the manufacture of bile which mixes with the digestive juices in the duodenum (see DIGESTION; SMALL INTESTINE). Bile is a thick yellowy green liquid containing salts that breaks down fat into small droplets so that it can more easily be digested. Bile is manufactured constantly, but because it may be required only a few times a day, it is carried from the liver through ducts to the gall bladder, a small pear-shaped bag lying just under the liver, where it is stored until it is needed. If the gall bladder has to be removed for some reason, the duodenum simply receives the necessary bile directly from the liver. The gall bladder is not therefore essential to life or even to good health.

Once bile salts are manufactured, the body makes the most of them. Having fulfilled their digestive purpose in the small intestine, they are not simply discarded but are recycled through the blood and back to the liver to be used again. It is estimated that this recycling process takes place about 18 times with only about 5% of salts being eliminated in the faeces each time.

One of the functions of the liver is to remove a yellow pigment called bilirubin, produced by the destruction of old red blood cells, from the blood. If the liver becomes diseased and cannot function properly, this yellow pigment stays in the bloodstream and gives a yellowish tinge to the skin and whites of the eyes — the jaundice that is such a striking symptom of the liver disease, hepatitis.

The chemical processing capabilities of the liver are amazingly complex and wide-ranging. Substances which enter as one thing frequently leave as something else, depending on the body's needs. For example, most amino acids are converted into proteins, but if the body is short of glucose, the liver will combine some of the amino acids with fat to make extra sugar. Similarly if the level of blood sugar is too high, glucose is converted into a substance that can be stored.

The liver's storage capacity is equally attuned to the body's specific needs at any given time. If more vitamins are consumed than the body immediately needs, certain of them will be stored to be released if the supply falls off. A person could survive as long as 12 months without taking in any vitamin A, and for up to four months without new supplies of vitamins B12 and D.

LUNGS

The lungs are the two main organs in our breathing apparatus, or respiratory system. They are set in the chest on either side of the heart. Each lung is shaped something like a pyramid, with the apex at the top extending into the neck and the broad base resting on the diaphragm — the dome-shaped wall of muscle dividing the chest from the abdomen. When we breathe in, muscles cause the diaphragm and chest area to increase in volume so that the lungs can expand and suck in air. When we breathe out, the lungs contract and force the air out. Breathing in involves muscular effort, but in normal circumstances breathing out does not — the muscles simply relax which allows the lungs to return to their normal size.

Each lung has an airtight cavity around it, lined with a double membrane called the pleural membrane. The outer membrane is attached to the rib cage. Between the membranes is a lubricating fluid so that they can glide smoothly over one another as the lung expands and contracts with breathing. If this area becomes inflamed, breathing becomes painful and the patient has pleurisy (see Section 5).

When we breathe in, our blood absorbs from the air the oxygen it needs to produce energy, and when we breathe out we eliminate the waste product, carbon dioxide. Air is brought into the body through the nose or mouth, and travels through the upper respiratory system to the right and left bronchial tubes branching off the trachea (windpipe) and leading to the lungs. Each bronchial tube divides further after it has entered the lung into many small branches which then subdivide again and again into smaller branches in such a way that it is called the bronchial tree. The smallest of the divisions are called the bronchioles — of which each person has about a million. At the end of the bronchial tree are clusters of air sacs, called alveoli, which look a bit like minuscule bunches of grapes. It is in these tiny sacs that the new air and the old air are exchanged. There are about 300 million alveoli providing a surface area of some 70 square metres.

The structure of the lungs means that they are like a sponge, light, fluffy and full of air. If a lung becomes infected, the affected part becomes filled with pus so that air is excluded and pneumonia results (see Section 5).

The lungs are connected with the heart by the pulmonary artery and the pulmonary vein. Used blood, low in oxygen, is pumped through the right side of the heart, via the pulmonary artery, into the lungs to be re-oxygenated. Oxygen-enriched blood is then returned to the left side of the heart through the pulmonary vein to be pumped throughout the body.

The brain and nervous system constantly check the levels of both oxygen and carbon dioxide in the blood. If the carbon dioxide level becomes too high, our breathing process is speeded up, and similarly if the level of oxygen drops too low. Yawning is not primarily due to boredom but is simply the body's way of getting more oxygen into the lungs. The faster breathing rate during exercise is also the means by which we cope with the increased demand for oxygen by the muscles. If the demand is so high that the lungs cannot keep up with it, we become 'out of breath' — gasping and panting for more air until the supply of oxygen has caught up.

We must breathe to maintain life. If we stop breathing for longer than three or four minutes, cells will start to die, beginning with the brain cells. Breathing is normally involuntary. It continues while we are asleep or even if we are completely unconscious. However, up to a point, we can switch to controlling it voluntarily if the need arises, e.g. if we want to take a deep breath before diving under water. We can also hold our breath so that the process of breathing is suspended. We cannot however stop breathing for longer than a few moments — if we try, the involuntary mechanisms will take over and breathing will resume. It is not possible to commit suicide by deliberately holding one's breath.

We don't start to breathe and therefore our lungs don't come into play until we are born. Oxygen to the foetus is supplied via the mother. The change that takes place in the lungs of a newborn baby is little short of miraculous. Before birth the lungs appear solid. They are a yellowish colour and are packed away in the back of the chest. When the baby takes its first breath immediately it is born, the lungs expand like a rapidly opening flower and the colour changes to a pinkish red. The tissue of the lungs becomes spongy and will float in water, whereas prior to birth it would sink. These changes will be evident even if the baby dies after only a few breaths. This can sometimes have medico-legal significance as it establishes whether the child was born alive or not.

See also RESPIRATORY SYSTEM.

Lymphatic system

Most of us are not very familiar with the lymphatic system, and yet it is as essential to the body's functioning as the system that circulates our blood. The lymphatic system regulates the fluid balance throughout the body. For example if you injure your knee, the surrounding tissues will generally swell up with excess fluid. This fluid will be removed and returned to circulation by the lymphatic system.

All the cells in the body are surrounded by fluid. This fluid is constantly fed with oxygen and nutrients from the bloodstream. As well as being topped up, fluid must be constantly removed, otherwise it would accumulate in the tissues. Some of it is removed through the bloodstream and some through the lymphatic system. This consists of minute lymphatic capillaries (very narrow vessels with extra thin walls) leading into progressively larger lymphatic vessels, or channels, which eventually unite to form two big ducts emptying into veins at the base of the neck — thus returning the fluid to the bloodstream. The lymphatic system thus complements the circulatory system.

The tissue fluid that is filtered into the lymphatic capillaries is called lymph. It is a colourless liquid not unlike blood plasma in its consistency and appearance, although it has a slightly different chemical composition. There are special lymph vessels in the small intestine to absorb fat after a fatty meal. These are called lacteals, because their fluid has a milky appearance.

All along the lymphatic vessels are tiny lymph nodes or glands. These are tiny, bead-like structures that filter out germs and poisons from the lymph, rather like an oil filter in a car. The lymphoid tissue which they are composed of also produces lymph cells (a type of white blood cell) and antibodies to destroy the harmful substances. There are especially high concentrations of lymph glands in the armpits, groin and neck and these may become noticeably painful and swollen if you have an infection, since the production of antibodies is stepped up.

Unlike the circulatory system which includes the heart, there is no pump to keep lymph moving along the lymphatic system. Therefore, frequent valves exist to stop the fluid flowing backwards. Circulation of lymph is maintained partly as a result of pressure, as it is forced through the capillary walls, but also as a result of breathing, muscle contraction and body movement in general. Regular exercise is therefore very important in maintaining the proper circulation of lymph.

The lymphatic network also includes three large glands — the tonsils, the spleen and the thymus. Each of these glands consists of lymphoid tissue and produces antibodies and white blood cells to fight against infection. In particular, the tonsils act as a barrier to infections entering through the mouth (see PHARYNX). The thymus is present in children's throats but shrinks after puberty. The spleen is a gland in the abdomen (see separate entry).

Mouth

The mouth, or oral cavity, is the beginning of the digestive system. Food and other nutrients are taken in through the mouth and prepared for digestion (see separate entry). The mouth is also used in the production of speech and, together with the nose, is a channel for breath.

The cavity comprising the mouth is bounded above by the hard and soft palates, and below by a layer of muscles, salivary glands and other soft tissues. The sides are formed by the inside of the cheeks. The lips form the outer opening, while at the back the cavity narrows to the pharynx, which in turn divides into the oesophagus (the tube carrying food into the stomach) and the larynx (which takes air to the lungs). Protruding into the mouth are the teeth which are used to chew food, and the tongue, used in both chewing and swallowing. In addition, there are three pairs of salivary glands, one pair situated under the tongue, another in the lower jaw, and the parotid glands in the cheeks just in front of the ear. It is the parotid glands which swell up in an attack of mumps.

When food is taken into the mouth, it is torn apart by the front teeth and ground down and pulped by the back teeth. At the same time the glands produce saliva to be mixed with the food with the help of the tongue. The production of saliva is stimulated simply by the thought of food, or even just its smell — we have all experienced 'mouth-watering' aromas. When the food is actually in the mouth and can be tasted, the production of saliva is speeded up.

The saliva not only moistens and lubricates food so that it will slide easily down the oesophagus, it actually starts the digestive process by inducing a chemical change. In particular, it starts the process of converting carbohydrates or starches into sugars which are easily absorbed. In the brief time the food is in your mouth before you swallow it, about 5% of starches will be converted. The chewed, moistened ball of food ready to start on its journey through the digestive tract is called a bolus.

Saliva also helps to keep the mouth healthy. It washes away leftover food particles and bacteria, and can even kill some of the bacteria causing tooth decay. Sometimes saliva is produced in response to indigestion, since swallowed saliva can help to dilute or neutralise acid.

While food is in the mouth, we consciously influence the digestive process — chewing and swallowing are normally carried out as a result of an effort of will. Once the food is swallowed, digestion occurs automatically.

The main problems affecting the mouth are ulcers and small sores, such as cold sores caused by the herpes virus. Usually these will appear fairly quickly without specific treatment. However, persistent sores should be checked — they may be cancerous or due to a vitamin deficiency or a sexually transmitted disease, such as syphilis. White patches on the inside of the mouth are usually due to a fungal infection called thrush. Sore and bleeding gums are a sign of teeth problems, and dental advice should be sought.

Muscles

Muscles hold various parts of the body in position and maintain posture, i.e. ensure that we don't fall over. If, when you stand, you sway too far forward or backwards, your muscles will pull you back to an upright position. Muscles are also the means by which the body moves.

Muscles act both because we instruct them to by a voluntary effort of will, and involuntarily regardless of any conscious choice on our part.

The voluntary or consciously controlled muscles are also called the skeletal muscles, because they are attached to the limbs and other bones of the skeleton. These muscles produce movement. For example, if you want to lift an arm, your brain sends a message to the appropriate muscles, and they contract to make your arm rise up. The nerves in the spinal cord keep the voluntary muscles in a state of slight tension, commonly known as muscle tone, so that they are always ready to move.

The involuntary muscles, which carry out their task without any conscious instruction, are divided into the cardiac muscle and the smooth or visceral muscles. The cardiac muscle keeps the heart

SECTION 2: BASIC ANATOMY AND PHYSIOLOGY

beating more than once every second from before birth to death, which may involve some two and a half thousand million contractions. While life exists, except in extraordinary circumstances such as open-heart surgery when a substitute is provided, the heart muscle never ever stops working. The smooth muscles are found in all the walls of cavities of the body, such as the intestines and the stomach. Among other things, they help to propel food along the digestive tract, expel waste from the bladder and control blood in the arteries and veins.

Viewed under a microscope, voluntary muscle fibres consist of alternately dark and light tissue and therefore are said to be striated or striped. Involuntary muscles are mostly unstriped or plain. There are some exceptions, however, because the heart muscle is partly striped, and certain muscles in the throat and ear, which are not controlled voluntarily, are also striped.

A typical skeletal muscle is made up of bundles of fibre which look rather like a telephone cable. On the outside the fibres contain nerves, blood vessels and connective tissue. Within this there are smaller strands called myofibrils and within these again are overlapping filaments of protein that can expand and contract like elastic.

Muscles work by contracting and relaxing. Skeletal muscles usually work in pairs, one contracting to produce the desired movement, at the same time as its pair relaxes. You can feel this by bending your arm. As it bends, you can feel the biceps in the front of the upper arm contracting and the triceps at the back relaxing. If you then straighten the arm the opposite will occur. If muscles are not adequately warmed up before vigorous exercise, they are likely to tear. This happens when a muscle is required to contract suddenly and its pair is unable to relax quickly enough.

As the body ages, in a process called fibrosis, the elastic tissue is gradually replaced by less resilient tissue, hence the reduced strength and slower muscular response of elderly people.

When a muscle contracts, its component parts slide over one another so that the muscle is shortened. This is the end result of a complex chemical process begun when the brain first gives notice via the nerves that movement is required. A muscle measuring about 15 cm can contract to approximately 10 cm, i.e. by about one third. To provide energy for the contraction a compound called glycogen, which is stored in the muscles, is converted into glucose. The conversion process involves the transfer of oxygen by the blood from the lungs to the muscle. During strenuous exercise, we may not be able to breathe in oxygen quickly enough to keep the muscles adequately supplied, in which event a waste product called lactic acid accumulates. It is the build-up of lactic acid, and not the wearing out of the muscle's power, that causes cramps and muscle fatigue (and so prevents the muscle from being destroyed from overactivity). After the exercise has stopped, we must continue to take in oxygen at an increased rate (making us puff and pant) so that the lactic acid can be taken away by the blood. A fatigued muscle will recover quite quickly after a rest, especially if accompanied by a massage to increase circulation.

When someone dies, their muscles will contract permanently, starting with the ones in the neck and lower jaw. This is the well-known rigor mortis.

There are about 650 muscles in the body. They make up approximately a third of the body weight in women and nearly half in men — hence the fact that weight for weight men are usually stronger than women.

Everyone's muscles are much the same shape. Individual differences occur when muscles are developed so that they have greater bulk, so a weight-lifter, for example, looks different from a ballet dancer. Involuntary muscles can be developed in the same way as voluntary muscles if additional demands are placed on them, although without any conscious effort. During pregnancy, for example, the muscular wall of the womb develops to more than three times its normal size to cope with the growing foetus and then decreases again in the month after the child is born.

By their movement muscles generate heat, helping to maintain the temperature of the body. It has been estimated that our muscles could keep a litre of water boiling for an hour. Shivering is simply muscles moving involuntarily as an emergency measure to combat sudden or extreme cold.

Most muscles have the ability to regenerate after injury. However, the heart muscle is an exception. If a coronary artery is blocked in a heart attack so that the muscle is deprived of oxygen, the affected muscle will die. Surrounding muscle cells may increase in size to compensate for the dead section, but the overall number of the cells will always be fewer.

Musculoskeletal system
See BONE; JOINTS; LIGAMENTS; MUSCLE; SPINE; VERTEBRAE.

Nails
Perhaps surprisingly, nails are somewhat similar to hair in their make-up and construction. Nails consist of dead cells, and the visible hard part is composed of the same protein, keratin, that makes up our hair.

Nails form a kind of armour plating for the sensitive and vulnerable ends of our fingers and toes. They lie over the top part of the fingers and toes, on what is called the nail bed — the area underneath the nail. At the bottom of the nail bed is an overlapping fold of skin topped by the cuticle. The nail bed has a very liberal blood supply, and it is this, together with the fact that the nail is thin (barely 0.5 mm thick) and transparent, which gives the nails their pinkish colour. At its base the nail becomes denser and the blood supply less generous, giving rise to the familiar white half-moon, technically called a lunula.

Hidden under the fold of skin at the base of the nail is the root from which the nail grows. The growth is continuous in finger nails and takes place at the rate of about 4 cm a year — considerably slower than hair which grows three or four times this much. Nail growth is quickest in early adulthood and slowest in infancy and old age. The right thumbnail in right-handed people usually grows faster than the other nails and similarly the left thumbnail in left-handed people — possibly because usage leads to increased blood supply. Fingernails grow more quickly than toe nails — by about four times. Nails usually grow more quickly in summer than in winter.

Nail growth also depends on nutrition and general state of health. Poor health will lead to discoloured, dry and cracked nails. An earlier patch of ill-health will sometimes be evidenced by transverse ridges in the fingernails, because the illness will have slowed the nail growth so that the density has increased. When nails grow too long, the excess is simply cut off. Since the tissue is dead, this is completely painless.

Nails are extremely porous. They can absorb 100 times as much water as an equivalent amount of skin. This causes them to swell and, although they dry out fairly efficiently and resume their normal shape, if the process is repeated too often they may split and become very painful.

See also NAIL ABNORMALITIES, Section 3.

FIGURE 2.4: The nail.

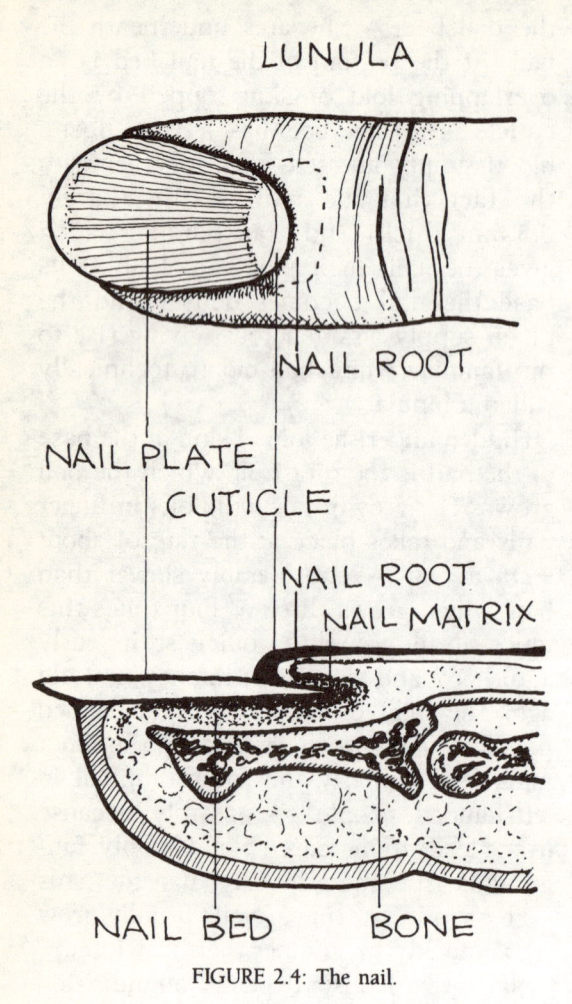

Nerves

Nerves are the means by which all the tissues of the body communicate with the central coordinating authority, the brain. Every structure in the body has its own set of nerves which, somewhat like a telephone system, come together in one central cable called the spinal cord (see separate entry). The spinal cord links with the brain, which has been likened to a central switchboard. The brain receives messages and transmits orders without ceasing throughout our lives. The entire communication system, or nervous system (see next entry), including the brain, is made up of nerve tissue.

Each nerve consists of bundles of fibres called neurones. A typical neurone is made up of a central body, or nucleus, surrounded by thread-like projections rather like a piece of coral. These are called dendrites and they carry messages to the cell body. There is also a longer cable-like projection called an axon which carries messages away from the cell body towards whatever tissue it serves, e.g. a muscle. Axons can be quite long, e.g. those from the spinal cord to the toes measure several feet.

When a nerve ending, or receptor, is activated by a stimulus, such as heat or cold or light or sound, the message is first transmitted inwards to the brain, and the response is then transmitted outwards towards the appropriate muscle or gland. All of this occurs so quickly that we are virtually unconscious of it. For example, if your hand touches a hot stove it will take only a millionth of a second for your arm muscles to receive the order to pull your hand away.

All the neurones we will ever have (many millions) are formed before birth. If neurones are damaged, at best repair is slow and uncertain. Only the extensions can regenerate, not the body. Neurones in the spinal cord and brain cannot be repaired at all, damage is permanent. However, the fact that there are so many neurones provides a safety net — even if some are destroyed the nervous system as a whole can still function.

The nerves send both chemical and electrical impulses. Like electrical wires, some nerves are insulated to prevent short-circuiting with a white coloured fatty tissue called myelin. Other nerves, including those in the outer layer of the brain, are a greyish colour — hence the popular description of the brain as 'grey matter'.

Nervous system

The nervous system is the complicated

network of cells that enable all parts of the body to communicate with the brain and with each other to bring about bodily activity. The brain is the centre of the nervous system, and together with the spinal cord forms what is called the central nervous system. The remaining nerves are called the peripheral nervous system.

There are two networks of nerves. One is under conscious control and, for example, enables us to move our legs when we want to walk. The other network is unconscious and operates irrespective of any control on our part. This network is called the autonomic nervous system and is responsible for such bodily functions as breathing and digestion.

The autonomic system, in turn, is divided into two — the sympathetic and the parasympathetic system. These work in tandem and, in general, the sympathetic system stimulates activity, whereas the parasympathetic system stops or slows activity down.

Broadly speaking, the nervous system receives messages through receptors in the skin and throughout the body which record sensations such as heat, cold, balance, heartbeat and many others (see SENSES). This is called the sensory system. Responses to these inward messages are then transmitted to the muscles and glands by the motor system.

Damage to the central nervous system can be very serious, possibly leading to paralysis of some or all of the limbs. To provide as much protection as possible, it is encased by the extremely hard, rigid bones of the skull and vertebrae of the spine.

Infections of the central nervous system include encephalitis (inflammation of the brain) and meningitis (inflammation of the membrane covering the brain and central nervous system).

See also BRAIN; NERVES; SPINAL CORD.

NEURONE
See NERVES.

NOSE
The nose is part of the upper respiratory system. Air is breathed in through the nostrils (the openings to the nose), and then passes into the pharynx (throat) and down the remainder of the respiratory system to the lungs. The nose warms the air to blood temperature and moistens it so that it will not harm the delicate tissues of the lungs.

The part of the nose we can see consists of cartilage and bone covered with skin. Behind it is the internal nose consisting of two nasal cavities divided by a ridge, which is also made up of cartilage and bone, and is called the nasal septum.

As well as providing a passage for air, one of the main functions of the upper respiratory system is to filter the air and trap infections before they reach the lungs — hence the frequency of coughs and colds and other minor upper respiratory ailments which, although tiresome, are preferable to serious lung diseases such as pneumonia.

The nose begins this filtering process very efficiently with its lining of tiny hairs, called cilia, which trap particles of foreign matter. The hairs at the front of the nose are bigger and coarser than those at the back, so that large particles such as grit and dirt are caught before they get very far. Smaller particles which manage to find their way through the front hairs will usually come to grief in the finer hairs at the back. Once particles such as dust and bacteria are trapped, we either sneeze and expel them, or they cling to the mucous membrane lining of the nose which itself has bacteria- destroying properties, and are moved by the waving of the hairs down to the throat and on to the stomach where they are processed by the digestive system. Alternatively they may be expelled in the mucus by coughing. Particularly harmful substances make us sneeze and expel the irritant at the beginning. The reason it is better to breathe through the nose than the mouth is that the nose is much more effective at dealing with foreign matter and bacteria.

A healthy adult produces about a litre of mucus in a day. If an infection takes hold, this amount will increase substantially to cope with the extra load involved in ridding the infection from the body — hence the blocked or runny nose so symptomatic of a cold.

Surrounding the nasal cavities are air spaces opening into the bones of the skull through small gaps. These are our nasal sinuses. Matching pairs of sinuses exist in the forehead, the cheeks and the front and back of the nose itself. The sinuses do not seem to fulfil any specific respiratory function but rather exist to lighten the skull and add resonance to the voice. They enlarge significantly at puberty and so are a factor in the size and shape of the face. Despite their apparent lack of usefulness, the sinuses are very vulnerable to infection.

Ducts from the eyes are connected with some of the nasal passages and draw off tears, hence the fact that crying makes us blow our nose more frequently.

The nose is also the organ of smell. Odour receptors are situated in the roof of the nasal passages and these communicate with the brain. Placed as it is, just above the mouth, the nose is in an ideal position for the smelling apparatus to function.

See also RESPIRATORY SYSTEM; SMELL.

OESOPHAGUS

The oesophagus, or gullet, is the tube connecting the mouth with the stomach. When food has been chewed in the mouth and mixed with saliva, it forms into a soft mass called a bolus, ready for swallowing. The tongue pushes the bolus into the throat, or pharynx, and from there it moves to the oesophagus.

The two outer layers of the oesophagus consist of strong muscle to propel the food along, while the lining is a mucous membrane able to keep the food lubricated. Although the food under normal circumstances moves downwards and so is assisted by gravity, gravity is not absolutely essential, and the oesophagus can do the job by itself if it has to, e.g. if you are required to lie flat in bed, or even stand on your head!

Once the process of swallowing is under way, for the first few seconds you cannot breathe or talk, and several muscular movements automatically come into play: the soft palate in the roof of the mouth is raised so that the food won't go up the nose; the pharynx rises and widens to accommodate the food; the tongue is raised to seal the back of the mouth and prevent unchewed food or other substances from sliding down as well; a flap of cartilage called the epiglottis covers the opening to the windpipe and lungs. An attempt to laugh or talk during swallowing sometimes causes one of these movements to malfunction and so food 'goes down the wrong way' or is forced up into the nasal cavity with all its attendant discomfort.

Once the food is in the oesophagus, a series of muscular contractions force it down the tube and into the stomach. A ring of muscle (the cardiac sphincter) at the top of the stomach opens to let the food through. It takes about five seconds for food to travel this far.

On its way to the stomach, the oesophagus has to pass through the diaphragm via a space called the oesophageal hiatus (hiatus means interruption or opening). If there is a weakness in the diaphragm at this point, part of the stomach may protrude through it and cause what is called a hiatus hernia (see Section 5), allowing acid to flow back up from the stomach into the oesophagus.

If a corrosive substance is swallowed, it may damage or destroy the lining of the oesophagus and make swallowing difficult or even impossible.

See also DIGESTION.

OVARIES

The two ovaries are the main female reproductive organs. Shaped like an almond, each ovary is about 3 cm long, 1.5 cm wide and 1 cm thick. They lie in the pelvis, one on either side of the uterus (see separate entry). The ovaries have two functions — the development and release of eggs, and the production of hormones. All the eggs (ova) a woman will ever have — and considerably more than she will ever need — are contained in her ovaries when she is born. At birth, there are something like two million immature eggs in each ovary. By puberty these are reduced to about 40 000, and only about 400 will be released during the child-bearing years.

Each egg (ovum) is surrounded by a small sac called a follicle. When puberty is reached, a cycle is established in which a few of the egg cells develop each month, with one reaching full maturity. When this happens the follicle bursts and releases the egg in the process called ovulation. A woman is fertile and can become pregnant a day or two either side of ovulation — and not at other times.

When an egg is released, it is swept into the adjacent Fallopian tube (see separate entry), the other end of which connects with the uterus. The egg is propelled along the tube towards the uterus by thousands of tiny hairs lining the sides. If the egg meets a sperm it may be fertilised and a completely new life may begin. The fertilised egg will implant itself in the wall of the uterus to be nourished and grow until it is ready to be born nine months later. If the egg is not fertilised, it dies within 12 to 24 hours and disintegrates to be eliminated together with the lining of the uterus during menstruation.

The ovaries also produce the hormones oestrogen and progesterone. Oestrogen is manufactured during the ripening of the egg, which takes about two weeks. It is this hormone that causes the lining of the uterus to thicken and the body to prepare for pregnancy. The second hormone, progesterone, is then produced, preparing the lining (endometrium) still further and bringing it to total readiness for a fertilised egg. If there is no conception, the oestrogen and progesterone levels fall during the next two weeks and the uterine lining is shed during menstruation. The whole process then begins again. The monthly cycle continues throughout a woman's child-bearing years from puberty to the menopause.

It is the female hormones that also give a woman her secondary sexual characteristics, for instance her broader hips than the male, her breasts and her rounder, more feminine shape.

See also REPRODUCTIVE SYSTEM.

PARATHYROID GLANDS
See THYROID GLAND.

PANCREAS

The pancreas is an organ we are usually unaware of, at least until something goes wrong. It is basically a large gland situated almost exactly in the middle of the body. It is about 15 cm long and lies across the abdomen, just above the navel. It more or less nestles in the curve of the duodenum (the upper part of the small intestine) and so is surrounded by the folds of gut making up this organ.

The pancreas has two quite distinct roles to play in the functioning of our body. Insulin, the chemical vital for the control of the body's use of sugar and the prevention of diabetes, is produced by special cells scattered throughout the tissue of the pancreas. The insulin is produced and released according to how much we eat, not only of sugar but also carbohydrate. The cells that produce the insulin have no ducts to take the chemical away, but discharge it directly into the blood vessels surrounding each cell. Once in the bloodstream, insulin controls the level of sugar inside the cells and in the blood. In diabetics, insulin is either not produced, or is made ineffective by other problems in the body.

The other function of the pancreas is to produce the main juices used in the digestion of food in our stomach. Millions of tiny glands produce powerful enzymes which are taken through a maze of ducts finally joining into one main pipe that empties into the side of the intestine, just after it leaves the stomach. As food passes through the intestine, the digestive juices produced in the pancreas are squirted onto it. The churning action produced by contractions of the intestine mix these juices into the food, where they break it down into its basic components so that it can be absorbed into the body.

The pancreas shares the opening of its duct with the bile duct coming from the gall bladder (see LIVER). Thus stones coming down from the gall bladder can block off the pancreatic juices too. This can lead to a build-up of pressure in the pancreas, forcing the powerful pancreatic enzymes to leak into the abdominal cavity. When this happens the juices digest normal tissues instead of the food they are intended for. This causes the severe pain of acute pancreatitis, and serious illness and even death can result. Pancreatitis has other causes but the condition is the same.

See also GLANDS.

PENIS

The penis is the male sexual organ inserted into the female vagina during intercourse. It is designed to allow sperm to be deposited as close to the cervix as possible.

At rest, the penis is a soft tube hanging limply down from the base of the abdomen where it is attached to the bones of the pelvis. However, it is made up of several masses of spongy tissue and these fill with blood when the man is sexually aroused so that the penis becomes erect and distended and thus able to penetrate the vagina.

Sperm are manufactured in the testicles and travel through the male reproductive system, combining with a white sticky fluid to form semen. At the height of sexual excitation, or orgasm, the semen is ejaculated. If a sperm combines with an egg a new human life begins.

The head of the penis, or glans, is a highly sensitive zone which is easily sexually stimulated. Where the glans meets the shaft of the penis, the sensitive skin covering the penis folds back on itself to form the prepuce or foreskin. It is this part of the skin that is removed by circumcision. Circumcision has been commonly performed in much of the English-speaking world for several generations, but in more recent times it has been seen as unnecessary surgery performed for no medical reason. Indeed because the foreskin is the most sexually sensitive part of the penis, it is now considered possible that a man's later sexual pleasure may be diminished by the operation. Sometimes the foreskin is so tight that the child cannot urinate properly and in this case circumcision may be essential. The condition will not usually become apparent until the age of about five.

The penis discharges both urine and semen, transported along its length by the urethra (see separate entry). This is different from women in whom the organs for sex and the organs for urinating are separate. It is not possible, however, for a man to release both urine and semen at the same time.

See also REPRODUCTIVE SYSTEM; URETHRA; TESTICLES.

Peripheral Nervous System
See NERVOUS SYSTEM.

Pharynx
The pharynx is the passageway for both food and air. It is popularly known as the throat although in fact the throat forms only part of it. Strictly speaking, the pharynx extends downwards from the back of the mouth (see separate entry) where it joins the nasal cavity, past the opening to the larynx to the top of the oesophagus (see separate entries). Its overall length is about 11 cm. Once food reaches the pharynx, swallowing becomes an involuntary reflex action and it is too late to change your mind and decide you don't want it after all. The pharynx also functions as a resonating chamber for sounds produced in the larynx.

The back of the pharynx is a solid wall of muscle, lined with mucous membrane, while the front opens into the nose, mouth and larynx. Tiny tubes called the Eustachian tubes open off the upper part of the pharynx and connect it with the ears — hence the linkage of 'ear, nose and throat'.

If you open your mouth in front of a mirror you can see the back of the middle section of the pharynx. Hanging down in front of the opening is a soft, fleshy V-shaped mass known as the uvula. It is the vibration of the uvula that causes snoring.

At the top of the pharynx is a mass of glandular tissue called the adenoids. On each side of the uvula are two similar masses called the tonsils. Both tonsils and adenoids help to combat infection but are themselves prone to chronic infection, in which case they may be surgically removed. Usually this is a relatively minor operation with no long-term adverse effects.

The pharynx is prone to inflammation because of infection or overuse, which lead to the painful symptoms of pharyngitis.

See also RESPIRATORY SYSTEM.

Pituitary Gland
The pituitary gland is situated at the base of the brain about eye level in the centre of the skull and is connected directly to the brain. The pituitary not only has its own activity but also regulates the activity of other glands. It is sometimes called the master gland of the endocrine system.

Altogether the pituitary gland produces nine different hormones. The human growth hormone is one of these hormones and possibly the most important. If too little of this hormone is produced during childhood, the child's growth will be stunted and it will be a dwarf. If too much is produced, the child will grow to an abnormal size. Other hormones stimulate the thyroid gland and the adrenal glands (see separate entries). A different hormone again acts on the kidneys and regulates the balance of water and salts in body fluids. Two further hormones stimulate the production of sex hormones in the female ovaries and the male testicles, as well as the manufacture of milk in nursing mothers. At the end of pregnancy when the time comes for the child to be born, the pituitary stimulates the muscles in the uterus to contract and so propel the child out through the birth canal. All this takes place in a gland no bigger than the size of a walnut.

The direct connection of the pituitary

gland, and through it the other endocrine glands, to the brain and thus the nervous system is the reason why our mental and emotional states can influence our hormone levels and vice versa. If the pituitary gland malfunctions, the effects can obviously be wide-ranging because of the gland's importance in so many parts of the body. Generally, however, nowadays hormones can be given artificially, so disorders can be successfully treated.

See also GLANDS.

PORTAL SYSTEM
See VEINS.

PROSTATE
The prostate is a gland whose function has only recently been understood even by doctors. It is situated in the body behind the base of the penis (see separate entry). The bladder is above and behind the gland, and the tube which carries urine from the bladder to the outside (the urethra — see separate entry) passes through the centre of the prostate. It is found only in men and there is no female equivalent.

The prostate is about the size of a golf ball and consists of glands, fibrous tissue and muscle. Its primary purpose is to produce a substance that makes up part of the semen a man ejaculates during intercourse. This substance is essential for the nutrition of the sperm as they try to fertilise an egg in the woman. Most men are totally unaware of the presence of the prostate unless it causes trouble.

In younger men, the most common cause of disease is infection, when the gland may swell up and become very tender. In older men the disease process is quite different. Up to 20% of all men over 60 may have an enlargement of the prostate which causes symptoms, and a small percentage of these may have cancer of the prostate (see Section 5).

A benign enlargement is usually associated with a drop in sexual activity. It can also affect the passing of urine. As the gland enlarges, it squeezes the urine-carrying tube which passes through it, making it steadily more difficult to pass urine. Eventually the tube can be completely blocked and the patient becomes extremely distressed as the pressure of urine in the bladder increases. This acute condition can be dealt with by inserting a rubber tube or a catheter into the bladder, but it is usually considered best to prevent it occurring by performing an operation. Milder enlargements can sometimes be relieved by medication.

The most serious disease to strike the prostate is cancer. This also usually starts with difficulty in passing urine, and any man experiencing this difficulty should have his prostate checked as soon as possible.

Doctors can often diagnose disease of the prostate by feeling the gland. This involves putting a gloved finger in the back passage so as to gauge the size and hardness of the gland. A benign enlargement of the prostate can usually be treated successfully with no subsequent effect on sexual or general health. The earlier cancer of the prostate is detected, the greater is the long-term chance of survival.

See also GLANDS.

RECTUM
See LARGE INTESTINE.

REPRODUCTIVE SYSTEM

Female
The main functions of the female reproductive organs are to produce female hormones, to release eggs for fertilisation and to nurture a fertilised egg for nine months as it grows into a baby ready to be born.

The female reproductive organs lie mostly within the pelvis. They consist of the ovaries, the Fallopian tubes, the uterus (womb), the vagina (see separate entries) and the external genitals.

Every month the ovaries release an egg (ovum) which passes down the Fallopian tube to the uterus. If the woman has intercourse so that sperm are ejaculated into her vagina while an egg is in the tube, the egg will usually be fertilised. The fertilised egg will then continue to the uterus where it will be implanted in the lining and a baby will have been conceived.

The external genitals are the area of sexual arousal. Also called the vulva, they consist of two pairs of fleshy folds or lips, and a small highly sensitive organ, called the clitoris. The outer of the two pairs of lips is called the labia majora (Latin for larger lips) and the inner pair the labia minora (Latin for smaller lips). The labia minora are sometimes hidden by the labia majora and sometimes protrude beyond them. The space surrounded by the lips is called the vestibule and contains the entrance to the vagina and the opening of the urethra — the tube through which urine is passed from the bladder.

The clitoris is located at the front junction of the labia minora and is the main centre of female sexual sensation. It contains erectile tissue and when stimulated enlarges in much the same way as the male penis.

Situated on each side of the vaginal opening are small glands which are stimulated by sexual arousal and release a mucous-like secretion to provide lubrication for intercourse.

The pad of fat covered by pubic hair at the front of the vulva is called the mons veneris (mound of Venus), or sometimes the mons pubis (pubic mound). The area extending from the back of the vulva to the anus is the perineum. The perineum is sometimes cut by the doctor during childbirth (an episiotomy) to avoid tissues being torn, and then repaired immediately afterwards.

See also Section 1.

Male

The main functions of the male reproductive system are to produce male hormones, manufacture and release sperm, and deliver it to the female for fertilisation. Some of the organs are inside the body (the prostate and various organs that collect and store sperm) and some are outside the body (the testicles and the penis). Unlike the female reproductive system, the male reproductive system shares some of its internal organs with the urinary system.

The reproductive organs become fully mature when a young boy reaches puberty between the ages of 12 and 15.

The male reproductive cells, the sperm, are manufactured in the testicles. Once mature, the sperm swim along a small tube called the vas deferens for storage in two small pouches called the seminal vesicles, situated just below the prostate gland. Both the vas deferens and the seminal vesicles produce a white sticky fluid in which the sperm are suspended. When a man has an orgasm at the climax of sexual arousal, vigorous contractions are triggered in the muscular walls of the vas, seminal vesicles and prostate, as well as rhythmic contractions of the muscles at the base of the penis. The sperm-filled fluid, called semen, is pushed into the urethra, passing through the prostate, where it collects more fluid, down the length of the penis to the tip from which it is ejaculated.

See also PENIS; PROSTATE; TESTICLES; URETHRA.

RESPIRATORY SYSTEM

The respiratory system refers to those

organs of the body used for breathing. Air enters the upper respiratory system through the nose or mouth and is conveyed by way of the pharynx (throat), larynx (voice box) and trachea (windpipe), through the two bronchial tubes to the lungs. It is in the lungs or lower part of the respiratory system that the oxygen is extracted and absorbed into the blood, which in turn is sent to the heart to be pumped throughout the body's cells. At the same time, the waste product, carbon dioxide, is extracted by the lungs from the blood and sent back up through the respiratory system to be exhaled from the body.

The upper respiratory system not only provides a passage for air but also filters it so that impurities and infections are removed before it reaches the lungs where it can have much more serious consequences. The most common problems occur in the upper respiratory system as a result of inhaling infections or allergy-causing substances from the air. Coughs, colds, hay fever and various inflammatory diseases such as sinusitis, pharyngitis and laryngitis keep the doctors busy.

Diseases of the lower respiratory tract are more serious and may include asthma, bronchitis, emphysema, pneumonia and (rarely these days) tuberculosis.

See also NOSE; PHARYNX; LARYNX; TRACHEA; LUNGS.

SALIVARY GLANDS
See GLANDS; MOUTH.

SEBACEOUS GLANDS
See SKIN.

SENSATION
See TOUCH.

SENSES
The senses are our contact point with the world. If we did not have any senses we would not be able to experience what goes on around us or what the world consists of. There are five main senses. Our eyes enable us to see, our ears to hear, our nose to smell, and taste buds in our mouth to taste. Tiny receptors all over our body, just under the skin enable us to have a sense of touch, with its associated sensations of pressure, heat, cold and pain. As well, receptors in our muscles and joints, together with those in our ears, allow us to experience position and balance.

The senses of sight, hearing, smell and taste are localised in special organs. Sight and hearing are reactions to physical stimuli, i.e. light and sound, while smell and taste are reactions to chemical stimuli. These stimuli are all external and are detected at or near the surface of the body. Other stimuli are internal, such as those by which we maintain our balance.

All senses work by means of receptors, which are specialised endings called end-organs situated in the skin, muscles and various parts of the body. These differ slightly according to what function they perform but, regardless of the type of receptor or the type of stimulus, they all communicate with the brain. A stimulus only becomes a sensation when the nerve impulse it triggers is interpreted by the brain.

See also EARS; EYES; NERVOUS SYSTEM; SMELL; TASTE; TOUCH.

SIGHT
See EYE.

SKIN
Skin is the outer covering of the body. It is much more complex than one might think from the smooth surface it presents to the

world. The skin protects the body against germs and parasites and provides a tough resilient cushion to safeguard the tissues underneath from injury. It also helps to maintain body temperature and prevent the body from becoming dehydrated. The skin is also the main organ of sensation (see TOUCH).

The skin consists of two main layers which are quite different from each other in the way they are made up and the way they function. The top layer, the one we see, is called the epidermis. This contains no blood vessels, nerves or connective tissue fibres and, in turn, is subdivided into two layers. The outer layer consists mainly of dead cells which are constantly being shed. The inner layer consists of cells with the capacity to multiply at a rapid rate, which they do continually, pushing up and replacing the discarded dead cells. The dying cells produce a protein called keratin which thickens and protects the skin. (Keratin developed in a particular way together with dead cells also forms the hair and nails.)

Under normal circumstances, from the time a skin cell is produced to the time it dies and flakes off takes about a month. However, if injury occurs, even just a minor scratch, the multiplication of cells speeds up to repair the damage. If the damage is repeated, deeper tissues may thicken to compensate and form a callus.

The inner layer of the epidermis also produces the pigment melanin, which gives the skin its colour. Freckles are simply irregular patches of melanin. We all have the same number of melanin-producing cells, irrespective of our racial origin, but dark-skinned races produce more melanin than light-skinned races. Exposure to the sun encourages the production of melanin as a protection against the sun's rays, giving a suntan. Absence of the pigment melanin leads to the abnormally white skin and general appearance of people classified as albino.

Beneath the epidermis is the dermis, which is the so-called true skin. The dermis is well supplied with blood vessels and nerves and has a framework of elastic connective tissue as well as the proteins collagen and elastin. The blood vessels provide the nourishment for the epidermis. The thickness of both the dermis and the epidermis varies so that some areas (e.g. the soles of the feet and the palms of the hands) are covered with thick layers, whereas other areas (e.g. the eyelids) are covered with thin and delicate layers.

The dermis rests on a layer of fatty tissue called the subcutaneous layer. The fat serves as both insulation and a reserve store of energy. Embedded in the dermis and extending into the subcutaneous layer are various glands integral to the proper functioning of the body.

The sweat glands are an important factor in regulating the body temperature. These glands are coiled tubes, and when it is hot they produce a mixture of water and some waste products which are evaporated through pores (tiny openings) in the surface of the skin, cooling the body's temperature in the process. Different sweat glands are located in the armpits and the groin. These react to emotional stress and sexual stimulation and secrete a fluid which, combined with bacteria, produces body odour. When the environment is too cold, the sweat glands cease to operate and surrounding tiny blood vessels contract. Cold causes the hairs on the surface to become erect, raising the skin into 'goose pimples' and trapping a layer of insulating air over the epidermis. To some extent the sweat glands also regulate the amount and composition of fluid in the body.

The sebaceous glands produce a type of oil, called sebum, which helps lubricate the skin and hair and prevent drying. The ducts of these glands open into the hair follicles (see HAIR). It is when the opening of a sebaceous gland becomes blocked with a mixture of dirt and sebum that a blackhead develops. A gland that becomes infected is called a pimple. A gland that becomes blocked by accumulated sebum so that a sebum-filled sac forms is called a sebaceous cyst and may have to be removed by surgery — generally not too difficult a procedure.

Most skin is covered by hair, with the exception of that on the soles of the feet and the palms of the hands. These areas are covered with alternately ridged and grooved patterns that increase the body's ability to grip at these points. These patterns are different in every single individual and remain the same throughout life, hence the use of fingerprints as a means of identification.

Disorders of the skin are not usually life-threatening but can be unsightly and psychologically damaging.

Small intestine

The small intestine is the organ where the main and final process of digestion takes place. By the time the ingested food reaches the small intestine, it will have passed from the mouth to the oesophagus (gullet) and down through the stomach. It is here that food is converted into tiny chemical units, small enough to pass through the wall of the intestine into blood vessels and lymphatic vessels which carry the nutrients from the food to provide fuel for the body's cells.

The small intestine is a long narrow tube consisting of a series of loosely packed loops. It is actually considerably longer than the large intestine (see separate entry) but is referred to as small because it is much narrower. Its structure is much the same as the stomach — a muscular wall that propels food along in waves, and an inner mucous lining that contains glands which produce digestive juices.

The small intestine is divided into three parts — the top part attached to the stomach is called the duodenum, the middle section is called the jejunum, and the remaining portion is called the ileum.

The duodenum is attached to the back wall of the abdomen with a fine web-like tissue containing the blood and lymphatic vessels which carry the digested food to be processed for absorption by the rest of the body.

The rate of absorption of digested food depends on the extent of the surface area over which it must pass. The larger the area, the more rapidly matter can pass over it. To increase the surface area of the small intestine, the inner lining is covered with millions of tiny finger-like projections called villi. The villi give the surface a velvety texture and facilitate the absorption of digested food into the body.

The alkaline nature of the mucus in the duodenum protects it from being damaged by the acidity of the partly digested food entering from the stomach. The mucus also contains various substances called enzymes, each designed to work on particular types of food. There is a special enzyme to break down proteins, one to break down carbohydrates and a different one again to break down fats.

Additional digestive juices from the liver and the pancreas (see separate entries) also enter the small intestine through the duodenum. The pancreas produces pancreatic juice and the liver produces bile — a thick greenish-yellow liquid containing bile salts which act to break down fat globules, not unlike detergent. These juices are conveyed to the duodenum through two ducts, respectively called the pancreatic duct and the bile duct, which normally join together just before entering the duodenum. Bile does not come directly from the liver but is stored in the gall bladder and released as needed when food enters the small intestine.

The partly digested food continues from the duodenum through the jejunum and into the ileum where digestion is completed. By the time the small intestine becomes the ileum, it has tapered from about 5 cm to about 2 cm in diameter.

The absorbable nutrients from the digested food will be passed through the villi into the blood or lymph vessels. Some (mostly fats) will go through the lymphatic system (see separate entry), and others will journey through a special series of veins to the liver for further processing so that they can be utilised by the body's cells to keep them alive and functioning.

The end products of the digestive processes consist of amino acids which come from the protein we eat, sugar in its simplest form, and fats. Those parts of the food that cannot be used are passed into the large intestine eventually to be eliminated.

See also DIGESTION.

SMELL

Our sense of smell is closely linked with our sense of taste (see separate entry). When we eat, aromas from the food pass from the mouth through the throat to the nose, where they stimulate the smell receptors. This is why there is such a strong connection between the smell of food and our appetite.

The sense of smell is extremely acute — about 10 000 times more sensitive than the sense of taste, but in modern humans it is not as important to our effective functioning as either taste or other senses, such as sight and hearing. Smell can detect a far greater variety of substances than taste (there are thousands of smells and only four tastes).

Smell operates by means of hair-like organs called the olfactory nerves which are located high in the nose. Substances that have a smell give out gases or vapours into the air. The olfactory nerves detect these gases and pass the information to the nerve centre of the brain. Substances that are converted easily to gas or vapour, such as petrol or kerosene, have a strong smell. Sometimes strong smells trigger the sense of touch in the nose, e.g. the smell of ammonia may cause the nose to sting, and the smell of camphor may cause a feeling of cold. The fact that the olfactory nerves are so far back and high up in the nose is the reason we have to sniff if we want to smell something carefully. The organ of smell is actually level with our eyebrows.

Our sense of smell adapts quickly. A smell that at first might be extremely unpleasant becomes tolerable after a relatively short period when we 'get used to it'.

Smell seems to be supported by an extremely good memory. Once we have smelt something we can usually readily recall and identify it.

Smell deteriorates with age. As we get older, we find that our sense of smell is less acute. It is important to provide attractive-looking meals for elderly people so that their appetite will be stimulated. Smell is also affected by respiratory illness. If the nose becomes congested because of a cold, air is stopped from reaching the smell receptors, and our ability to smell temporarily disappears.

Because smell is so closely linked with taste, if our sense of smell is not working, we may think we have lost our sense of taste as well. But this is not the case — what we have is actually pure taste. The close connection between smell and taste can be experienced in another way too. If we close our eyes and block our nose, onions and apples will taste almost the same!

Spinal cord

Together with the brain, the spinal cord is part of the central nervous system (see NERVOUS SYSTEM). The spinal cord is where all the nerves of the body join together in one large cable and travel up to the brain. The cord extends from the brain about two thirds of the way down the backbone (see SPINE). It is actually encased within the vertebrae so that it is well protected from harm. All nervous impulses, with the exception of those in the head, travel up and down the spinal cord.

Thirty-one pairs of nerves radiate out from the spinal cord to form (together with 12 pairs radiating from the brain) the peripheral nervous system.

Nerves that record information from the senses join at the back of the cord, and those that relay instructions for movement to various parts of the body leave from the front. The nerve root, where the nerve joins the spinal cord, runs between the spinal vertebrae, and it is this that causes such severe pain if it is squeezed because one of the discs moves out of place (popularly called a 'slipped disc').

Some nervous activity takes place in the spinal cord without involving the brain. These are the spinal reflexes. The best known is the knee-jerk. If your legs are crossed and the upper leg is tapped just below the knee, a sensory impulse will travel along the nerves to the spinal cord and make a connection with a motor nerve which will cause your leg to jerk forward. The brain is aware of what is happening but is not involved in the response. More complex reflexes involve sneezing, urinating, and digestion.

Like the brain, the spinal cord is cushioned by a layer of fluid — the cerebrospinal fluid. Some of this fluid is sometimes withdrawn by a needle inserted in the lower part of the spine in a process called a lumbar puncture or cerebrospinal fluid test (see Section 4) and used to provide information on the nervous system.

See also BRAIN.

Spine

The spine is one of the major parts of the skeleton. It consists of 26 small bones called vertebrae arranged as a column, supporting the body and surrounding and protecting the spinal cord — the nervous tissue that runs down from the brain. It extends from the base of the skull to the tail bone. The spine is also called the backbone, the spinal column, and the vertebral column.

It is the spinal cord and the surrounding vertebrae that distinguish the higher animals from the lower and that give rise to the name 'vertebrates'. Of the vertebrates, human beings are the only ones that stand absolutely erect.

Everyone's spine is much the same length once they reach adulthood — about 70 cm in men and 60 cm in women. Individual differences in height depend mainly on the length of the lower limbs.

There are seven spinal vertebrae in the neck (cervical), twelve in the region of the chest (thoracic), five in the lumbar (lower back) region, five fuse together to form the sacrum (attached to the pelvis), and four are fused in the coccyx or tail bone. The bottom two lots of vertebrae do not fuse completely until maturity, and a child's spine has 33 bones. Nearly all mammals have the same number of vertebrae in the neck, i.e. seven, regardless of their overall shape — even the giraffe.

A single vertebra is hollow, with a fairly thick piece of cylindrically shaped bone in front, called the body, and a thin circular piece curving around the back (the ring) enclosing the spinal cord which runs up through the hollow centre. Each vertebra is separated from the next one by a disc made of cartilage. The discs act as shock absorbers and give the spine its pliability. It is when an injury causes one of these discs to be squeezed by the vertebrae so that a part of it protrudes to the side and presses on a nerve branching out from the spinal cord that the acute pain of a so-called slipped disc is experienced.

Each ring has three sharp bony protrusion, two pointing sideways and one pointing backwards, to which the muscles and ligaments are attached. The protrusions can be seen or felt under the skin of the back as small spines — hence the name spinal column.

The cervical vertebrae do not have much weight to support, and they are smaller than the others. The vertebrae get progressively larger down the spine to support the greater weight they are required to bear.

The top two cervical vertebrae have special features so that the head can move. The very top vertebra has no body but a very large and strong ring, enabling nodding movements. The second vertebra fits into the first vertebra on a pivot so that the head can rotate from side to side. The seventh cervical vertebra is larger than the others and can easily be felt by placing your hand where your neck and back join.

Each of the twelve thoracic vertebrae join a pair of ribs which arch forward to the breast bone at the front of the chest, thus enclosing and protecting the heart and lungs in the ribcage. The sacrum and coccyx form part of the pelvis.

Viewed from the side, the spinal column has four curves, alternately forward and back, corresponding to the various groups of vertebrae. The two backward curves (i.e. the ones with the hollow facing towards the front), one in the thoracic region and one in the pelvis, can be seen at birth, so that the spine of a newborn baby is entirely concave from the front. As the baby begins to hold its head up at three or four months and then to sit up at about nine months, the cervical curve appears, bending the other way. When the child begins to walk, the compensating lumbar curve appears, so that the spine acquires its classic double S-shape. The curves make the spine a kind of spring, able to absorb jolting and jarring that would otherwise damage internal organs, especially the brain.

Unduly pronounced curves of the spine can cause problems. An abnormal curve in the thoracic region is the cause of a person being a so-called hunchback. Abnormal curves can be congenital, caused by disease, facture or bad posture.

Spleen

The spleen is one of the most poorly understood of the body's organs, even by doctors. It is really one of the largest and most sophisticated gland in the human body. It weighs about 100 g and is roughly the same size as a clenched fist. Shaped rather like an inverted pudding bowl, it is tucked under the bottom two ribs on the left side.

The spleen has three main functions. Firstly, it filters blood, removing damaged cells and extracting and storing re-usable elements such as iron from these cells. Secondly, it stores the antibodies developed by the body during an infection, so that when a similar infection occurs in the future the antibodies can be called into play quickly. Finally, it helps to produce new cells for use in the bloodstream — white cells to fight any infection that enters the body, and red cells to transport oxygen.

The spleen seldom causes any serious problems. The most frequent reason for medical help is that the spleen is damaged in an accident. If the chest is squashed, say, in a car accident, the spleen may be pierced by a rib or ruptured by the pressure. Because it consists of a very large number of blood vessels, it bleeds freely, and the blood loss into the abdomen may be life-threatening. It is difficult to repair surgically because it is a bit like trying to sew up sponge rubber — the stitches tear out very easily and every stitch hole bleeds. It is therefore sometimes necessary to remove it to save the victim's life. The removal of the spleen has remarkably little effect on an adult, because the bone marrow can take over most of its functions. In babies, the situation is rather different, as the spleen is essential for the early formation of blood cells, and it is removed from children only if there is no alternative.

If the spleen becomes overactive, it may destroy blood cells too rapidly so that the person becomes severely anaemic, susceptible to infection, and bleeds and bruises excessively. This can usually be controlled with medication but occasionally surgery is required.

See also LYMPHATIC SYSTEM.

STOMACH

The process of digestion (see separate entry) which begins in the mouth continues in the stomach. Chewed food is passed from the mouth down the oesophagus (gullet) to the stomach. The stomach is a bag about the size of an ordinary sausage when it is empty, and shaped something like an inflated J. It is soft and pliable when empty but becomes firm when filled with food. It is on the left side of the body, behind the lower ribs, i.e. high in the abdomen not far below the heart, and not down behind the navel as people often think.

The stomach has two main functions: it digests food itself and it also stores food, which usually has been taken in quite quickly as a meal and is released slowly to be processed by the main digestive organ, the small intestine (see separate entry).

The outside layers of the stomach consist of muscle, while the inside lining is a mucous membrane, much the same as that lining the oesophagus. The membrane in the stomach, however, forms many folds which allow it to expand as food is taken in. The stomach is capable of holding approximately 2.5 L of food and liquid. The muscles in the stomach wall grind and churn food so that it is pulverised and mixed with gastric juices. The semiliquid fairly acid product is called chyme (pronounced kime).

The gastric juices contain acid and this is neutralised by the alkaline lining of the stomach so it won't damage the stomach walls. Also, the lining is gradually shed and replaced approximately every three days. If it is damaged, it is rapidly repaired. However, if acid does manage to eat into the stomach walls, an ulcer develops.

At each end of the stomach is a muscular ring, a sphincter. These rings are normally closed, opening only to allow food in from the oesophagus and out to the small intestine. The ring at the top is called the cardiac sphincter because it is close to the heart. Sometimes this sphincter does not open properly, which leads to a feeling of being unable to swallow past this point. The sphincter at the bottom of the stomach which leads into the small intestine is called the pyloric sphincter. This sphincter occasionally malfunctions in newborn babies, leading to so-called projectile vomiting in which food is brought up in a forceful spurt. Males are more often affected than females. It can generally be successfully corrected medically or, if necessary, by surgery.

The action of the stomach consists of a series of waves propelling the contents along it towards the pyloric sphincter, which relaxes as each wave reaches it to allow some of the softened mass to pass through into the small intestine. The waves also separate out any remaining lumps and ensure that these remain in the upper part of the stomach for further digestion. Each wave takes about half a minute. Usually we are quite unaware of these wave-like movements, but if the stomach is irritated so that the digestive process is upset, it may give rise to irregular spasms causing indigestion. If the stomach is empty, it is these waves that give us a 'rumbling tummy'. Under some circumstances, e.g. if the stomach is irritated by consumption of too much alcohol, the waves will work in reverse and the cardiac sphincter will open to allow the contents of the stomach to be ejected back up the oesophagus, causing vomiting. Milder reverse action causes belching and hiccups.

The first amounts of semiliquid food will begin to leave the stomach about half an hour after a meal, with the whole process usually taking about two to six hours, depending on what has been eaten. Different types of food stay in the stomach for different periods of time. For example, fatty foods stay longer than carbohydrates — hence the ability of a meal rich in carbohydrates to provide a quick source of energy. Obviously a heavy meal will take longer to digest than a light meal. However, if the stomach is especially full, the process of digestion will be speeded up by the release of special chemicals.

Alcohol and some drugs are absorbed directly into the bloodstream from the stomach.

The passage of food through the stomach is also affected by temperature — cold, e.g. from ice cream, slows it down — and the amount of movement the body is required to make. Our natural inclination after a meal is to relax and perhaps go to sleep to enable the body to concentrate its resources on digesting food as quickly as possible, whereas strenuous exercise diverts the blood to the heart and muscles and therefore slows down the digestive process.

Sweat glands
See SKIN.

Taste
The main organ that allows us to experience different tastes is the tongue. On the upper surface of the tongue are millions of tiny projections called papillae. It is these papillae that give the tongue its rough feel. Housed within them are microscopic nerve endings known as taste buds. When food is taken into the mouth and liquefied by the chewing and the saliva, the taste buds react to the various chemicals that are released, sending messages to the taste centres of the brain. The taste buds will only be activated if there is moisture. Dry food taken into a dry mouth would have no taste at all.

There are only four primary tastes — sweet, sour, bitter and salty. The variety of flavours we experience are different combinations of these four, combined with smell. The different tastes are detected on different areas of the tongue. Bitterness is experienced at the rear, sourness at the sides, and saltiness and sweetness at the front. The tongue's centre has almost no sense of taste.

The strongest taste sensation is that of bitterness, and this has a protective aspect to it. Poisons and other toxic substances are usually bitter and, because of the extreme unpleasantness of their taste on the tongue, we are prompted to spit them out before they are swallowed and cause damage to internal organs.

It is possible for taste buds to be educated to a high degree of sensitivity, e.g. to wine. The sense of taste is closely linked with the sense of smell (see separate entry), which is some ten thousand times stronger.

Teeth

Teeth are the hard bony growths in our mouth that enable us to chew our food. During our lifetime we grow two sets of teeth. Our baby, or primary, teeth start to appear a few months after birth (although they have begun forming while we were still in the womb) and will usually have reached their full complement of 20 by about two and a half years of age. Ten are on the top and ten on the bottom jaw. The front 'cutting' teeth are called the incisors, and the back 'grinding' teeth are the molars. Dividing these are sharp pointed eyeteeth or canines.

At the age of about six, a child develops the permanent six-year-old molars. Some time after this, the roots of the baby teeth begin gradually to dissolve and the teeth fall out, in order to be replaced by the permanent teeth. This process will usually be completed during the teens, with individual children varying a great deal. The permanent teeth have started forming in the gum from the age of about two. Care and hygiene of baby teeth are no less important because the teeth will eventually be lost. Decay and infection can spread to the developing teeth and, in any event, the baby teeth are important in guiding the permanent teeth as they grow out through the jaw.

Permanent teeth are larger than baby teeth and total 32. They are accommodated by the increased size of the older child's jawbone. Sometimes the jaw isn't large enough for the third and last set of molars, often called the wisdom teeth, which may not appear until the late teens or early twenties. In this case, they may remain embedded in the jaw, and if this causes problems they may have to be removed by dental surgery. However, some people never grow their wisdom teeth and never develop any problems.

The part of the tooth we can see is

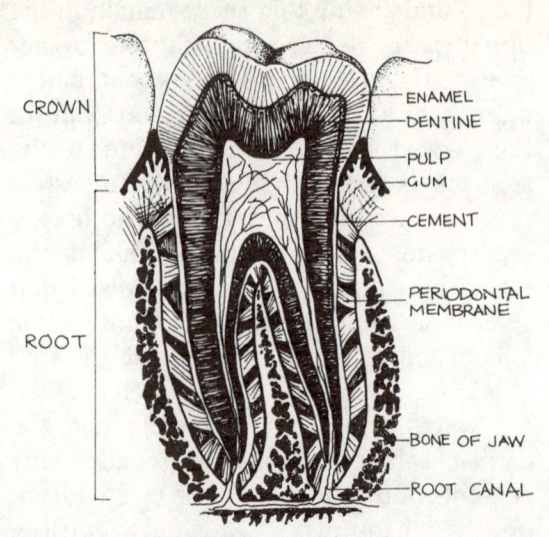

FIGURE 2.5: An adult molar.

called the crown and is covered with shiny white enamel — the hardest substance in the human body. The lower part of the tooth that fits into a socket in the jaw is called the root, and this is covered by a bony material called cementum. The area where the root and crown meet is called the neck. The root is attached to the jaw by a membrane. Under the enamel and the cementum is the bulk of the tooth consisting of a bone-like substance called dentine. In the centre of each tooth is the pulp, which contains the living matter such as nerves, blood vessels and connective tissue. This is the part that hurts if the tooth becomes infected or damaged. A fine canal (the root canal) runs from the pulp down either side of the root, and joins up with the body's main nerve and circulation systems.

The jawbone in which the teeth sit is covered by the gum, technically known as the gingiva, which is attached to the tooth enamel around the neck of the tooth. The sockets in the jaw in which the teeth sit correspond in shape to the teeth although they are slightly larger. The upper and lower teeth themselves are designed to fit perfectly one into the other when the law is closed, a feature that gives maximum chewing efficiency.

The lower jaw is joined to the base of the skull by the temporomandibular or jaw joints. These allow a greater range of movement than any other joint in the body — if you put a finger in front of each ear, open your mouth and move it up and down and from side to side, you can feel the extent of the available movement.

See also BABIES AND YOUNG CHILDREN — Teething, Section 1; and DENTISTRY, Section 7.

TENDONS

In the same way as ligaments (see separate entry) are the means by which bones are attached to other bones, tendons are the strong fibrous cords attaching muscles to bones and controlling muscular movement. Tendons are similar to ligaments but are not as elastic.

Some tendons are round and some are flat bands. Some tendons are so short that the muscle fibres are attached almost directly to the bone. Most tendons are surrounded by a sheath lined with a membrane and containing fluid so that the tendon can glide smoothly over surrounding parts. On contact with the bone, tendon fibres gradually pass into the substance of the bone and blend with it. One of the largest tendons in the body is the Achilles tendon which attaches the calf muscle to the heel bone.

The sudden imposition of an unbalanced load can result in a ruptured tendon which is extremely painful and, if the rupture is total, usually requires surgical repair and immobilisation for six weeks. The rupture of the Achilles tendon is a well-known sports injury.

Tendonitis, or inflammation of a tendon, can also result from misuse or overuse (see Section 5).

TESTICLES

The testicles, or testes, are the male sex glands and correspond to the ovaries in the female. Like chicken eggs in size and shape, they develop up near the kidneys while the child is still in the womb. Just before birth they descend through openings in the lower part of the front of the abdomen to their permanent position suspended between the thighs behind the penis in a pouch of skin called the scrotum. Like the ovaries, the testicles have two functions — to produce male sex cells, or sperm, and to manufacture male hormones.

The reason why the testicles are located outside the body is that sperm production requires a slightly lower temperature (by about 3–5 degrees) than that maintained by the rest of the body. The correct temperature is so important that if it is varied even slightly, e.g. by the wearing of tight pants, the production of sperm may temporarily cease. The scrotum provides its own temperature control, contracting to keep the testicles warm in cold weather and relaxing when the temperature rises.

Each testicle is made up of tiny coiled tubes in which sperm (spermatozoa) are continuously manufactured. About 300 million sperm are produced per day. Once manufactured, the sperm mature in a network of tubes called the epididymis, situated at the back of the testicle. After about 2–4 weeks when they acquire the ability to propel themselves or 'swim', they are transferred through ducts called the vas deferens, extending upwards into the body from the epididymis, looping beside the bladder until they reach the seminal vesicles, which are two small pouches just behind the prostate gland. Here the sperm are stored until they are either ejaculated or eventually die and are reabsorbed into the body.

The seminal vesicles produce most of the

sticky fluid in which sperm are suspended to make semen. Ejaculatory ducts carrying the semen pass from the vesicles through the prostate, where further fluid is added, into the urethra which extends down the penis, from where the semen is ejaculated. There may be as many as 500 million sperm in one ejaculation.

The testicles also produce the male hormone, testosterone, which at puberty gives rise to the development of the recognisable male characteristics, such as a deep voice, the growth of facial and bodily hair, and the development of the male genitals.

Unlike women, men's ability to reproduce does not come to a definite end in mid-life. The production of sperm and testosterone starts to decrease as early as 20 years of age, but it merely continues to decline rather than ceasing completely. Even men in their seventies can produce sperm, and a few (about 10%) can continue into their eighties.

Occasionally one or both testicles fail to descend fully as they should in a young child, in which case they will not function properly. If they remain undescended beyond the age of four or five, the condition may need to be corrected by surgery. If left undescended, testicles are more prone to cancer in adult life. One normally functioning testicle is usually adequate for a male to be fertile.

THROAT
See PHARYNX.

THYMUS
See LYMPHATIC SYSTEM.

THYROID GLAND
The thyroid gland controls the rate with which the body converts food into energy (metabolism) as well as the rate of development in adolescence. It is situated at the front of the throat just below the Adam's apple. The gland consists of two wings, rather like a butterfly, one on each side of the windpipe.

To carry out its functions, the thyroid produces two hormones. These hormones contain iodine, and a certain amount of iodine must be included in the diet to ensure the proper functioning of the thyroid. The amount of iodine required is only small and most normal diets contain enough, especially if iodised salt is used.

If the production of hormones is too much or too little, the metabolism will be either too quick or too slow. If it is too slow you will feel tired, and if it is too quick you may feel nervous and jumpy. If the variation is too far removed from normal, serious disorders may result.

If too much hormone is produced, you will become hyperactive and be unable to sleep, have palpitations and hand tremors, sweating and sometimes severe emotional disturbance. Various drug treatments are available, or more usually the gland is destroyed altogether, and substitute hormones are provided in the form of medication. This is a common condition in young and middle-aged women. The reverse occurs if too little hormone is produced. Everything will slow down and you will become tired, cold and constipated.

A goitre is an enlarged thyroid gland. It may be due to an overactive gland, or to a lack of iodine in the diet.

Some children are born without an adequate thyroid gland, in which case they will be subnormal physically and mentally in the condition known as cretinism. This is routinely tested for shortly after birth, usually before the newborn leaves the hospital. The condition is then treated, and the children grow up normally and unaffected by cretinism. It is one of the most important screening tests of the newborn, as the consequences of not detecting and treating this condition are so dire.

The most common disease of the thyroid gland is underactivity due to loss of thyroid tissue as you get older. Many elderly people suffer from this condition and take tablets to keep them functioning normally.

Cancer may also occur in the gland and is usually characterised by a painless swelling in one part of the gland. Treatment is usually very effective and may involve a combination of surgery, radiotherapy and drugs.

Embedded within the thyroid gland are the parathyroid glands, which help regulate the level of calcium in the blood. The activity of the thyroid gland itself is regulated by the pituitary gland (see separate entry) at the base of the brain.

Tongue
See MOUTH; TASTE.

Tonsils
See PHARYNX.

Touch

Touch is one of the most important of all our senses. It is the sense that enables us to experience not only contact, but also heat and cold, pressure and, most importantly of all, pain. The capacity to feel pain is one of our most fundamental protective mechanisms — without it we would lose much of our ability to recognise potential harm, e.g. burning heat, and take steps to avoid it causing damage to our body.

Unlike the other senses, such as taste, sight and hearing, which we experience in specific parts of the body, touch sensors, or receptors, are located over the entire surface of the body. They are tiny bulb-like organs (called end-organs) situated just under the skin. Touch sensors are also incorporated in the muscles where they are known as muscle spindles, and it is these that enable our bodies to remain steady and upright. Touch receptors vary in structure according to their specific purpose, i.e. to feel pain, heat, cold, or pressure.

Touch is one of the first senses we develop and is more important in the maintenance of human life than perhaps was recognised until recently. It is now generally acknowledged that newborn babies who are given all the medical care they need but are never stroked or held or touched in a normal way, will not do as well as babies who are treated in this way.

The importance we attach to touch can be seen from the use we make of it in our everyday speech — 'thick-skinned', 'thin-skinned', 'touchy', 'a soft touch', 'makes cutting remarks', 'rubs you up the wrong way', etc.

The extent to which we feel things varies greatly from one part of the body to another, depending on the number of touch receptors. The fingertips and the area around the mouth have a large number of receptors and are especially sensitive, whereas the skin on the back of the neck and the back has relatively few receptors. The greater the concentration of receptors, the easier it is to discriminate between separate points of contact. If you were to take a compass with its two points and prick your tongue, you would be able to distinguish the two pricks if the points were separated by only 1 mm. If you pricked your finger you would need to widen the points to 2 mm before you would feel two separate pricks. If you pricked an arm or leg, the points would need to be separated to 25 mm, and you would only feel separate pricks of pain on your back if the points were 50 mm apart. Different sensations are also felt more acutely in different parts of the body. For example, while the tongue and fingertips are the most sensitive to touch, they are comparatively insensitive to heat and can bear temperatures that would be intolerable to the cheek or elbow. This is why mothers are often advised to test the temperature of the water for the baby's bath with an elbow rather than a hand.

The most sensitive areas of the skin are hairless, e.g. the tongue, lips and sexual organs. These have their own special methods of recording sensation. Elsewhere the skin surface is covered with hair, varying from the long and thick hair on our head, to the less dense hair on our legs, to the fine almost invisible hairs on our trunk. These hairs act as antennae, detecting sensations and transmitting them to the touch receptors below the hair follicle. From here they are carried by the nerves to the spinal cord and finally to the brain, where they are registered so that we 'feel' whatever the original stimulus was. The hairs are amazingly sensitive. If someone touches the end of the hair on your head, even long hair, the touch receptors in your head will detect it.

There are more pain receptors than other types of receptors, and these record different qualities of sensation depending on where they are situated in the skin. The receptors in the surface layer, the epidermis, produce an itch when stimulated; the receptors a little lower down in the upper dermis produce a sharp pain; and the receptors in the lower dermis give rise to an ache. The touch receptors for pressure are located relatively deep in the body's tissues, and it has been found that pressure can sometimes be felt even under anaesthetic.

Hot and cold receptors can adapt. Anyone who has ever plunged an arm into steaming hot or icy cold water will know that, while it can seem unbearable at first, the body adjusts quite quickly and before too long the discomfort disappears. Pain receptors do not adapt nearly so readily — perhaps because nature wants to be sure that the warnings are heeded.

It is not always easy to distinguish between one sensation and another. This is because the same thing may stimulate two or more types of receptors at the same time, and the brain experiences them in the same way. For example, extremes of temperature, hot or cold, stimulate both the temperature receptors and the pain receptors and we then feel both sensations as pain.

Variations in our sense of touch are important diagnostic tools for doctors. Both excessive skin sensitivity (hyperaesthesia) and significantly decreased skin sensitivity causing a feeling of numbness (anaesthesia) can be symptoms of diseases of the spinal cord. Similarly, some diseases are manifested by abnormal sensations such as burning, pricking or tingling.

Trachea

The trachea is the medical term for the windpipe, which is the central trunk of the air passage between the larynx (voice box) and the lungs. It passes from just below the Adam's apple to the top of the chest behind the breastbone.

The trachea is not only long (about 12 cm), but thin (about 2 cm) in diameter. So that is won't collapse, it is supported by regularly spaced rings of cartilage. These rings are shaped like a horseshoe or a reversed letter C, open at the back so that the oesophagus can expand into this area when swallowing. The rings mean that whatever position the body is in, the trachea will remain open and allow air to get through.

Once it enters the chest, the trachea divides into two bronchial tubes which carry the air to the lungs.

Infection of the trachea causing inflammation is a fairly common upper respiratory ailment called tracheitis. This is generally associated with infection in the nose or throat and may cause a sore chest and painful cough.

Sometimes the trachea becomes obstructed, e.g. because of a disease such as diphtheria, or because a foreign body becomes lodged there. This is life-threatening. In an operation called a tracheotomy it is possible for a tube to be inserted to bypass the obstruction and allow air to enter directly.

See also RESPIRATORY SYSTEM.

URETERS

The two ureters are slender tubes down which urine passes from the kidneys to be stored in the bladder. Each ureter is about 30 cm long, and in parts less than 1 mm in diameter. The ureters travel from the kidneys in the small of the back through the loins and the pelvis, and enter the bladder at an angle. This enables urine to run freely into the bladder but prevents it from flowing back upwards as the bladder fills up prior to being emptied. The walls of the ureters consist of thick layers of smooth muscle which contract to force urine down into the bladder.

The main problem that occurs in the ureter is when a stone is formed in the kidney and is then passed into one of the ureters. This can be extremely painful. It may require surgery, although usually it can be treated with a process called lithotripsy, in which high intensity sound waves shatter the stone. If kidney stones form regularly, the victim will usually be put on a special diet and advised to increase fluid intake (see Section 5).

See also BLADDER; KIDNEYS; URETHRA.

URETHRA

The urethra is the final part of the urinary tract, through which the body gets rid of its waste products. The urethra is the tube leading from the bladder (see separate entry) along which urine passes to be emptied from the body.

In women, the urethra is comparatively short (about 4 cm) and has only the one purpose of conveying urine. It is set within the muscle of the front wall of the vagina and has its external opening just in front of the vaginal opening. In men, the urethra is considerably longer (about 20 cm) and runs from the bladder through the prostate down through the penis so that its external opening is at the tip of the penis. It serves as a passageway not only for urine but also for the ejaculation of semen, and so is also part of the male reproductive system. It is not possible for both semen and urine to be expelled at the same time, however, because when a man urinates, the process automatically seals the opening through which seminal fluid enters the urethra.

Inflammation of the urethra (urethritis) is caused when normally harmless bacteria existing in surrounding areas such as the rectum, or in the vagina in women, for some reason invade the urethra and give rise to infection. It may also be caused by an obstruction of the prostate in men. Urethritis tends to be more common in women because the female urethra is so short and closely related to the vagina. It can be caused by the bruising of the urethra in sexual intercourse and is sometimes called 'honeymoon cystitis' (cystitis is inflammation of the bladder).

See also KIDNEYS; URETERS.

UTERUS

The uterus or womb is the hollow muscular organ in women in which a baby grows. It is located in the pelvis and is loosely tethered to the pelvic walls by four sets of ligaments, giving it a high degree of mobility. It leans forwards when the rectum is full and backwards when the bladder is full. During pregnancy it expands upwards as far as the ribs. In a non-pregnant woman the uterus looks something like an upside-down pear. It is about 7.5 cm long and 5 cm wide. The cavity of a non-pregnant uterus is small and narrow, virtually a slit.

The upper part of the uterus is called the body, and is attached to the two egg-conducting Fallopian tubes. It narrows at the lower end to form the cervix, or neck, which protrudes into the vagina and provides a passage for sperm to enter and menstrual blood to flow out.

The wall of the uterus is made up of three separate layers. The outer layer is a tough protective covering called the perimetrium. In the middle is a thick layer of muscle called the myometrium, while the inner lining consists of a blood enriched mucous membrane called the endometrium.

Each month the endometrium thickens to prepare for the implantation of a fertilised egg. If this does not eventuate, all but the deepest part of the endometrium is discarded, leading to the monthly menstrual period. This takes place about 14 days after an egg has been released. The menstrual flow consists of the liquified dead endometrium together with some blood lost in the process. If fertilisation, or pregnancy, does occur, the embryo is implanted in the endometrium and nourished by the mother's blood supply. The mother's and the embryo's blood circulations interact through the placenta.

The muscles in the myometrium are among the strongest in the human body. They expand to accommodate the growing foetus, and when the time comes for the baby to be born they engage in a series of contractions, helping the hitherto tightly closed cervix to open and propelling the baby into the birth canal. About six weeks after pregnancy, the muscles have shrunk again and the uterus has returned to its normal size.

See also CERVIX; FALLOPIAN TUBES; REPRODUCTIVE SYSTEM — Female; VAGINA.

UVULA
See PHARYNX.

VAGINA
The vagina is the passage connecting the uterus to the external world. Usually about 8 cm long, it is joined to the uterus at the neck, or cervix, and passes through the lower part of the woman's body behind the urethra and bladder and in front of the rectum. It is the passage into which the male penis is inserted during sexual intercourse. Vaginal secretions are released during sexual arousal and facilitate intercourse. Sperm ejaculated during intercourse travel through the cervix and into the uterus and Fallopian tubes to fertilise an egg if one has been released.

The lining of the vaginal wall is made up of a mucous membrane arranged in folds which enable its muscular tissue to expand for the purpose of childbirth.

In children the external opening to the vagina is covered by a thin mucous membrane called the hymen. This will be broken at the time of first sexual intercourse, or it may break spontaneously earlier than this.

See also REPRODUCTIVE SYSTEM — Female.

VEINS
Veins are part of the circulatory system (see separate entry). They are the blood vessels that carry the blood back to the heart after it has been circulated via the arteries through the tissues of the body.

As a general rule, veins lie alongside the corresponding arteries, although there are almost twice as many veins and they have a much bigger capacity. There are also extra veins near the outside of the body which can easily be seen just below the skin.

The pressure of blood in the veins is lower than that in the arteries so the vein walls are not as thick. The pressure is also much more even, since blood in the veins flows steadily rather than being forced along in spurts by the pumping of the heart. For this reason, if a vein is cut, the flow of blood is easier to staunch than blood spouting from a cut artery.

Because the pressure in veins is so much lower than in the heart, there is a risk that blood could flow backwards (especially since much of it is flowing upwards against the force of gravity). To counteract this and to push the blood towards the heart, veins contain valves which close off as the blood moves along in them, thus preventing any backward flow. If the muscles are contracting frequently such as during exercise, the blood in the veins will be pushed more quickly towards the heart so that it can be re-oxygenated and brought back as soon as possible to keep the cells nourished and able to perform the extra work.

The tiniest veins, scattered throughout the body, where the blood begins its return journey from the cells are called venules. These flow into progressively larger veins until they reach the heart. There are two main veins flowing into the heart — one bringing the blood from the head, neck and upper limbs, and the other bringing blood from the abdomen and lower limbs. The large veins leading from the head are the jugular veins, which can usually be seen in the neck. The main veins carrying blood from the lungs to the heart are called the pulmonary veins. There are four of these, two from each lung.

Blood in all the veins except the pulmonary veins is low in oxygen and high in the waste product, carbon dioxide. Blood in the pulmonary veins, having been through the lungs, is rich in oxygen.

Totally separate to the main network of veins in the lower part of the body's trunk is the portal system. Unlike other veins which drain blood to the heart, the veins in this system drain blood from parts of the digestive tract (stomach and intestines) and various other abdominal organs into the portal vein. This empties into the liver where the nutrients are absorbed. This process having been completed, the blood links up again with the main system and proceeds to the heart.

Vertebrae
See SPINE.

Villi
See SMALL INTESTINE.

Vocal cords
See LARYNX.

Vulva
See REPRODUCTIVE SYSTEM — Female.

SECTION 3

SYMPTOMS

AN A–Z OF
WHAT YOU TELL THE DOCTOR
AND WHAT IT MEANS

ABDOMINAL FLUID, EXCESS
See ASCITES.

ABDOMINAL MASS
The abdomen is the area between the bottom of the ribs and the groin. It contains the organs involved in digesting food and eliminating the body's waste products. These organs include the stomach, intestines, liver and gall bladder, pancreas, kidneys and ureters. The abdomen also contains the spleen and the adrenal glands. The lower abdomen or pelvis contains the bladder as well as the uterus, ovaries and Fallopian tubes in women. Any one of these organs can become diseased or distended, and this can often be felt from the outside by careful examination with the hands and fingertips. Generally speaking, this is a job for a doctor rather than a layperson, since usually only doctors are sufficiently familiar with internal organs to be able to identify any abnormality and diagnose the cause.

Reasons for an abnormal mass inside the abdominal cavity range from pregnancy to cysts, tumours, abscesses, fibroids, a hernia, swelling in the wall of the aorta (the main artery from the heart), and to an enlarged spleen, liver or kidney, usually because of disease.

ABDOMINAL NOISES, EXCESSIVE (BORBORYGMI)
Abdominal noises occur when there is movement of fluid and gas in the intestines. Usually this is no more than mildly embarrassing and is the result of too much air being swallowed because you've eaten too quickly or downed a fizzy drink; or it may be due to nervousness.

If the noises are accompanied by diarrhoea, nausea and pain, it is probably a symptom of gastroenteritis — inflammation of the stomach or intestine, usually caused by an infection or eating contaminated food.

If you are also experiencing pain, constipation and vomiting, there may be an obstruction in the intestine in which case you should see a doctor.

Occasionally if the noise is excessive, it is a symptom of a condition known as irritable bowel syndrome. This occurs when there is recurrent pain and constipation and/or diarrhoea but no other symptoms of ill health. It is not known why it happens, but it is thought to be associated with stress. Sometimes it follows severe infection of the bowel.

ABDOMINAL PAIN
A 'pain in the tummy' is probably the most common symptom in existence. Causes can vary from something as minor as excess wind to major disorders of any of the organs in the abdominal cavity (see ABDOMINAL MASS), as well as various diseases of a more general nature, some minor, some serious.

Most abdominal pain is a symptom of a trivial digestive upset. However, pain can be an important indicator of something wrong with the internal organs; since these organs do not experience ordinary sensation, pain generally means a significant disturbance. The location of the pain usually indicates which organ is affected. Pain under the ribs on the left, or in the pit of the stomach, generally points to trouble in the stomach. Pain high up on the right side indicates problems in the liver or the gall bladder. Pain low down on the right may signal appendicitis. Pain low down on the left or at the exit to the bowel, may mean a disorder of the rectum. Pain that is experienced vaguely all over the front of the abdomen, especially around the navel, may indicate that the abdominal lining is inflamed (peritonitis) or that there is some irregularity in the small intestine.

If the pain is dull and aching it is generally not serious, although it should be investigated if it lasts for more than a few days. Twisting, griping pain usually indicates a digestive upset. Sudden agonising pain may be due to the passage of a gallstone. Dull pain, slightly to the right under the ribs, may indicate an ulcer.

As a general rule, recurrent or continuing abdominal pain should receive expert attention. Even chronic dyspepsia (see separate entry) can be treated and prevented from becoming permanent.

See also BURPING, EXCESSIVE.

ABDOMINAL SWELLING

A swollen abdomen may be due to excess fat, especially in elderly people and women after menopause. It may also be due to pregnancy. As a symptom of disease, a swollen abdomen can result from a minor digestive disturbance but may also be a symptom of more serious disorders. If the swelling is sudden and there is no pain, it is probably the result of wind in the bowel and will be relieved when the wind is passed. If pain is present as well, it may still be due to wind, but unless it is relieved fairly rapidly by passing wind you may have an obstruction in your intestines, in which case you will almost certainly need to go to hospital. The obstruction can often be cleared by the insertion of a tube or by an enema, but if not, you may need an operation.

Women often experience some abdominal swelling before the onset of a menstrual period. If this is distressing, and especially if it is accompanied by other symptoms such as depression or irritability, consult a doctor as there are now effective forms of treatment available.

If your ankles are puffy as well, especially if they pit when you press them, it may indicate fluid build-up and could be the result of a heart, liver or kidney disorder. You should see a doctor who will usually arrange for a series of tests. If the swelling reduces slightly when you pass urine, it may be due to retention of urine in the bladder, and in men this can be sign that the prostate is enlarged.

Gradual swelling or distension of the abdomen may also result from chronic constipation.

See also ASCITES.

AGRAPHIA
See WRITING DIFFICULTIES.

ALOPECIA
See BALDNESS.
See also Section 5.

AMENORRHOEA
See MENSTRUAL PERIOD PROBLEMS.

AMNESIA
See MEMORY LOSS.

ANAESTHESIA
See PAIN SENSATION, LACK OF.

ANAL BLEEDING

The anus is the short tube that leads from the last part of the bowel (the rectum) to the outside. Small veins lie just under the surface of the mucous membrane lining, and a common cause of bleeding from the anus is when a fissure (split) occurs as a result of straining to pass a hard motion. Anything that stretches or tears the tissue, such as the insertion of foreign objects, anal intercourse or frequent enemas, can cause a fissure. A fissure may heal itself or can sometimes be treated by over-the-counter remedies from the chemist. If it persists, it will generally need medical attention. The most common reason for anal bleeding is the development of haemorrhoids, which may be external (a lump can be felt) or internal.

Anal bleeding may also be a sign of polyps or inflammation in the colon. Or it can be a symptom of something much more serious, such as cancer of the intestine (usually the rectum or colon). In this case, as it grows, the cancer will invade an artery or a vein and blood will appear in the faeces.

Usually blood that is due to a tear in the anus, haemorrhoids or disease of the colon is bright red, whereas that coming from higher up in the intestine is a brownish or black colour. Black motions (melaena) may be caused by blood from a peptic ulcer, stomach cancer, cirrhosis of the liver or even swallowed blood from a nose bleed.

All anal bleeding should be checked by a doctor so that the reason can be found.

ANAL ITCH

An itchy anus can be a maddening condition, since scratching in the area is generally regarded as socially unacceptable. In any event, scratching usually makes the itch worse. An itchy anus may have no obvious cause, or it may be the result of irritating soap, powders, ointments or clothes to which you are sensitive. Poor anal hygiene may also lead to irritation.

A child who constantly scratches its anus is probably infested with threadworms. This is a thread-like parasite that lives in the bowel. At night the female emerges from the anus to deposit its eggs and then die, irritating and inflaming the surrounding skin, causing the itch. When the victim scratches, the fingers and nails become infected and if these are then put in the mouth or used to handle food the child is reinfected or the infection is spread to other people. The infection is common throughout the world and can almost always be treated successfully with drugs.

Some anal itching may be the result of piles (see Section 5) or a fissure (tear) in the lining of the anus. Less commonly anal itching is a symptom of disease such as diabetes or jaundice.

See also PRURITUS ANI, Section 5.

ANAL PAIN

The most common cause of anal pain is a tear in the lining of the anus (see ANAL BLEEDING) and/or haemorrhoids. However, if the pain is accompanied by diarrhoea, it may be a symptom of a problem higher up in the abdomen, such as inflammation of the colon (colitis or diverticulitis) or a growth (polyp) in the bowel.

In men, if there is a feeling of heaviness just in front of the anus, sometimes described as being like sitting on a golf ball, together with frequent and sometimes burning urination, it may indicate inflammation of the prostate. This is especially likely if the patient is feverish. Similar symptoms in a woman may mean an ovarian cyst or inflammation in the pelvis.

ANOREXIA

See APPETITE LOSS; WEIGHT LOSS, ABNORMAL.

ANOSMIA

See SMELL, LOSS OF.

ANURIA

See URINE, LACK OF.

ANXIETY

Feeling anxious or nervous is usually a temporary reaction to stress. It disappears when the problem is solved or the cause of stress is removed. Anxiety becomes an illness only when it is prolonged and interferes with our normal life. In some people this occurs because stress is constant; in other people it occurs because the individual is particularly susceptible to feeling anxious even if the stress is only slight or in some circumstances non-existent. Some people live in a constant state of anxiety for no apparent reason.

An anxiety attack usually involves a feeling of apprehension, an inability to concentrate or to think clearly, and possibly disturbed sleep. You may get sweaty palms, a pounding heart, breathlessness, trembling and diarrhoea. These symptoms may be so severe that you think you are having a heart attack. If you are in any doubt about the cause of the symptoms, get medical help.

You may experience anxiety if you have suddenly given up cigarettes, alcohol or drugs, such as sleeping pills. If constant unexplained feelings of anxiety are accompanied by a loss of weight and/or your eyes seem to be bulging, you may have an overactive thyroid gland. Alternatively unexplained tension can sometimes be a sign of heart or kidney disease. A tumour of the adrenal gland, which disturbs the production of adrenalin, can lead you to feel tense and to experience heart palpitations and high blood pressure.

If you suffer from severe and constant anxiety, you should get medical help since, even if there is no physical cause, treatment is available, and if left untreated it may lead to severe depression.

See also ANXIETY NEUROSIS, Section 5.

APHASIA
See SPEECH, LOSS OF.

APPETITE, EXCESSIVE
Appetite and hunger are two different things. Hunger is the physical need for food to keep the body's fuel supply up. Pangs of hunger are caused by the contraction of the wall of the stomach when it is empty. Even when the stomach is full, however, it is still quite possible to want to eat, i.e. to have an appetite.

Eating too much is often a symptom of unhappiness — people who are dissatisfied with their lives eat to make them feel better. Excess appetite may be an external symptom of the nervous disorder called bulimia, in which a person embarks on an eating binge and then induces vomiting to rid themselves of the food (see Section 5).

Occasionally, overeating is a sign of physical disease, especially if the person loses weight rather than gains it. The most common disorders are an overactive thyroid gland or diabetes. Sufferers of a peptic ulcer sometimes overeat, since the pain of the ulcer may be relieved when food is ingested.

Women may notice an increased appetite at the beginning of pregnancy. Generally this settles down as the pregnancy progresses, but if not, the question of diet should be discussed with the doctor, since 'eating for two' and undue weight gain has long been recognised as undesirable for both mother and baby.

See also OBESITY; WEIGHT GAIN, ABNORMAL.

APPETITE LOSS
A lack of appetite can be caused by almost any illness. Even the common cold can result in your appetite disappearing for a few days, especially since your sense of smell and taste are dulled and cannot stimulate the appetite. Emotional upsets are notorious for spoiling the appetite. Young children quite often 'go off their food' for varying periods of time, and this is usually of no special significance. Various drugs can also eliminate an interest in food, e.g. antibiotics, heart drugs, and pain-killers.

If loss of appetite lasts for a prolonged period and there is no obvious cause, it may be a general symptom of underlying disease. The possibilities are extremely wide-ranging and may be as serious as heart disease and cancer. There will usually be other symptoms as well which will indicate the need for medical advice.

An increasingly common cause of lack of appetite, especially in young women, is the nervous disorder anorexia nervosa, in which an obsession with being thin leads to a loss of desire and even a repugnance for food. The condition needs medical attention, as the sufferer will sometimes cease eating to the extent of causing malnutrition and even death (see Section 5).

See also WEIGHT LOSS, ABNORMAL.

ARM PAIN

The most common reason for pain in the arm is injury or inflammation of the shoulder, elbow or wrist joints. It can, however, be due to a number of causes, some needing urgent attention.

If pain occurs immediately after an injury, you may have a torn muscle or ligament. If the pain is severe and especially if the arm looks twisted or out of shape, you may have a broken arm. Pain in the shoulder may mean a dislocated shoulder, and pain in the wrist may signal a sprain or break in that joint. Bursitis is inflammation of a bursa, the fluid-filled sac surrounding a joint. Typical sites of bursitis are the shoulder and the elbow.

If the pain begins while you are in the middle of some strenuous physical activity, such as exercise, extends down the arm towards the wrist, and disappears after five minutes of rest, you should see a doctor immediately, especially if you are also experiencing chest pain. You may be suffering from a form of angina.

Arm pain associated with a temperature may be a sign of serious disorders, such as rheumatic fever, bone infection such as osteomyelitis, or infectious arthritis, and medical attention is imperative.

Pain down the length of your arm may be a result of pressure on a nerve in your neck because one of the vertebrae has been displaced.

Other causes of arm pain are carpal tunnel syndrome, in which the nerves of the wrist are pinched due to the swelling of the surrounding tissues, and tenosynovitis, or inflammation of the tissues in the wrist, usually resulting from constant repetitive movements such as those undertaken by computer operators.

ARTHRALGIA
See JOINTS, PAINFUL, SWOLLEN.

ASCITES (EXCESS ABDOMINAL FLUID)

Ascites is the medical term for the accumulation of fluid in the abdomen. If there is a lot of fluid, the abdomen will become swollen and distended. There are many causes, including infection, such as tuberculosis, heart failure, cirrhosis of the liver, and various cancers, especially of the ovary and liver. Ascites can be a useful warning of cancer of the ovary, which is situated so deep within the lower abdomen that swelling of the organ itself is often not noticed until the disease is well advanced. Malnutrition can cause ascites and is the reason for the typical distended stomach of children in countries suffering from severe famine or otherwise lacking enough food to feed the population.

See also OEDEMA.

ASTHENIA
See TIREDNESS, ABNORMAL.

ATAXIA
See CLUMSINESS.

ATHETOSIS
See WRITHING MOVEMENTS.

ATROPHY
See MUSCLE WASTING.

AURA (PREMONITION)
An aura is a peculiar feeling that people suffering from epilepsy sometimes experience before the onset of an attack. It may occur just prior to a seizure or as much as several hours before the seizure strikes. It is usually a feeling of a cold breeze passing over the body, but it sometimes takes the form of an odd smell or a vision of a person or animal, or even an overwhelming sense of disgust. Whatever form it takes, many epileptics learn to recognise their special aura. This can be extremely important since it gives a warning that a fit is coming and may enable the person to reach some safe place.

Migraine sufferers also sometimes experience a form of aura, e.g. as brilliant flickering lights or blurred vision.

BACK PAIN
A bad back is the most common reason for time off work in Australia. Well over five million work days are lost each year because of back pain. Back pain can be acutely painful but is normally not a symptom of serious disease. The spine is an extremely complex structure with vertebrae, discs, nerves and muscles all interacting and involved in just about every movement we make. If the joints between the vertebrae or the surrounding muscles and ligaments become strained, back pain will result. The most usual cause of back pain is damage to the muscles or ligaments due to incorrect lifting. Lifting and twisting simultaneously is particularly dangerous. Sometimes one of the spongy discs between the spinal vertebrae pushes out to one side and causes acute pain if it pinches a nerve. Normally an injury will result in the surrounding muscles going into spasm to protect the spine from moving too far, and the spasm itself can cause more distress than the pain it is meant to avoid.

Back pain sometimes occurs for no apparent reason. Some people seem to develop back pain when they are under stress, just as other people develop headaches.

In older people, arthritis may be the cause of back pain, when the smooth joints between the vertebrae become roughened and damaged by age and long years of use. In elderly women, severe back pain may be a symptom of a crush fracture of the spine due to osteoporosis.

Occasionally back pain is due to disorders affecting the abdomen or pelvis, especially the kidneys or the reproductive organs such as the prostate in men and the uterus in women. It may also be a symptom of disease, including cancer, of the vertebrae or spinal joints. Chronic back pain should always be investigated by a doctor.

See also Section 5.

BAD BREATH
The medical term for bad breath is halitosis. It does not include the bad breath caused by eating onions or garlic. By far the most common cause of halitosis is tooth decay or disease of the gums, nose, tonsils or sinuses. Improving dental hygiene is usually the most obvious treatment to begin with. However, if this is not effective and you have a persistently sore throat, or painful nasal passages or sinuses, see a doctor.

Sometimes bad breath is a sign of a disorder of the stomach or intestines or, more seriously, the lungs or the liver. Certain diseases manifest themselves by a characteristic odour of the breath, for example a sweet odour in severe diabetes and a musty odour in acute liver failure.

A bad taste in the mouth or a coated tongue is not necessarily a sign of bad breath.

BALDNESS

Going bald for no apparent reason is an affliction confined largely to men. It is usually hereditary and is almost always gradual, starting at the front of the scalp, on either the side or in a circular area on top.

Both men and women lose some hair as they grow older. If hair loss is sudden however, it may be a symptom of disease, in particular a hormonal disturbance. The most common reason is an over- or underactive thyroid gland. If this is successfully treated, the hair will grow back again. Certain other glandular diseases, especially those involving the pituitary, have similar effects. Hormonal fluctuations may occur after pregnancy and lead to hair loss, but the system will normally readjust quite quickly.

Any serious illness, especially if it is accompanied by a fever, may lead to hair loss from the whole body, not just the scalp. Drugs used in treating illness, especially cancer, can also cause the hair to fall out, as can radiation therapy. When the treatment is stopped the hair usually grows back. Too much vitamin A can lead to hair loss. You may also lose your hair if you have a sudden and excessive loss of weight — sufferers of anorexia nervosa frequently find their hair falling out and may go bald.

Children often lose small areas of hair if they have ringworm, a highly infectious fungal infection which circulates throughout the community from time to time.

See also ALOPECIA AREATA, Section 5.

BLACKOUT
See FAINTING.

BLACK SPOTS, SEEING
See VISION, BLACK SPOTS IN.

BLEEDING
See ANAL BLEEDING; BLEEDING, EXCESSIVE; BRUISING, EXCESSIVE; MENSTRUAL PERIOD PROBLEMS; NOSEBLEED; URINE, BLOODY; VAGINAL BLEEDING, EXCESSIVE; VOMITING BLOOD.

BLEEDING, EXCESSIVE

Some people bleed more than others and this is a matter of individual difference with no reason for concern. Bruising is simply bleeding into the skin, and the tendency to bruise may also vary between individuals with no special significance. Women tend to bruise more easily than men. If someone bleeds profusely and often, however, either externally or into the skin, it may be a symptom of disease and should be investigated.

If the bleeding occurs in a male child, it may be because the clotting factor is absent from the blood as a result of Christmas disease or haemophilia. If the person is excessively tired and looks pale, possibly with a skin rash, it may be due to a particularly severe form of anaemia, called aplastic anaemia. Vitamin K deficiency, either through an inadequate dietary supply or through an inability to absorb it properly, may also result in excessive bleeding. Inflamed and bleeding gums are a sign of scurvy, that scourge of early travellers to Australia caused by a lack of vitamin C.

Some drugs, including aspirin, can also cause bleeding, usually in the stomach, and aspirin should never be taken regularly or in large amounts without medical supervision.

A nosebleed or bleeding that will not stop after the extraction of a tooth isn't necessarily a sign of disease but may need medical help to stem the flow of blood.

SECTION 3: SYMPTOMS

BLINDNESS

If an eye is injured badly enough, the sight mechanism may be damaged and the capacity to see destroyed. Apart from this, there are many different causes of blindness, including some abnormality in or damage to the tissues of the brain or the optic nerve leading from the eyes to the brain. This may be due to a tumour or abscess or you may have had a stroke. A loss of vision accompanied by headaches should be investigated promptly.

Sometimes a disorder affecting the whole body, such as diabetes, will cause a loss of sight. Some forms of kidney disease, high blood pressure and disease of the carotid artery (the main artery in the neck pumping blood to the head) can cause a haemorrhage or blood clot blocking the blood vessels of the light-sensitive retina and so make the eye unable to function.

Older people are especially prone to cataracts forming an opaque film over the lens of the eye. Surgical removal of a cataract is normally highly successful, and if you become aware of your vision deteriorating, see your doctor as soon as possible. A detached retina which separates from the back of the inside wall of the eyeball will suddenly make seeing impossible and needs urgent medical attention. Other causes of blindness are inflammation of any part of the eye including the cornea (keratitis) and the iris (iritis). Glaucoma is a serious disease in which fluid pressure builds up within the eyeball and damages the retina.

Migraine headaches can cause temporary blindness which should pass in ten to twenty minutes.

As a general rule, if you notice that your sight is becoming impaired see a doctor immediately.

BLISTERS
See SKIN, BLISTERED.

BLOATING
See ABDOMINAL SWELLING; ASCITES.

BLUE SKIN
See SKIN, BLUE.

BLURRED VISION
See VISION, BLURRED.

BONE LUMPS

A lump on a bone is not always readily apparent, since it has to be felt rather than seen. If there is no pain, you may not notice it, at least for a while. Fortunately, if a painless lump is a tumour, it is probably benign and will not spread. Most bone tumours are benign. However, if it is malignant it can usually be treated successfully if diagnosed early enough, so see a doctor as soon as you become conscious of a lump.

Some bone tumours are secondary tumours, i.e. they have spread from cancer cells elsewhere in the body, commonly the breast or prostate.

If you have had a recent fracture, you may notice a lump where the bone healed. A lump on a bone may also be due to a cyst (a fluid- filled sac). This may disappear of its own accord or it can be treated if it proves troublesome.

BORBORYGMI
See ABDOMINAL NOISE, EXCESSIVE.

BOWEL MOVEMENTS, ABNORMAL COLOUR OF

A bowel movement, comprising faeces or stools, consists of the remainder of what we eat and drink after it has passed through the digestive system and had all the nutrients removed. It is normally dark brown in colour due to a pigment it absorbs from the gall bladder bile on its way through the system. However, the colour may vary according to what we have eaten, e.g. a meal of spinach will lead to dark green movements. If you are taking iron tablets your bowel movements will probably be very dark or black. If you have very dark or black bowel movements (melaena) and you are not taking iron tablets, it may be a sign of bleeding in the digestive tract, possibly from a stomach ulcer, and you should get prompt medical advice.

Bowel movements that are unusually pale can indicate that your digestive system is not absorbing the food properly, or, if your eyes look yellow as well, that you have a gall bladder or liver disease such as hepatitis. It can also signal cancer of the pancreas so expert diagnosis is essential.

If you notice blood in your bowel movements you may have a minor problem such as a tear in the anus or haemorrhoids (piles) but, especially if you feel unwell and have a temperature, it may mean something much more serious is amiss in your digestive tract, such as inflammation of the colon or rectum, or dysentery caused by an infection, which may need treatment with antibiotics.

See also ANAL BLEEDING.

BOWEL MOVEMENTS, EXCESSIVE DESIRE TO PASS (TENESMUS)

Sometimes the desire to pass a bowel movement is continuous or recurs overly frequently, without the production of significant amounts of faeces. Possibly there may be small amounts of mucus or blood. This is an uncomfortable symptom and may be due to the condition called irritable bowel syndrome which can cause either constipation or diarrhoea and for which stress seems to be the main known cause (see Section 5).

The growth of polyps (small benign growths from the mucous membrane lining of the rectum) may give rise to a desire to defecate. These will need to be surgically removed but the operation is quite simple and straightforward. Other disorders are more serious and include prolapse (downward displacement) and cancer of the rectum.

See also DIARRHOEA.

BRADYCARDIA
See PULSE, SLOW.

BREAST ENLARGEMENT

The most common reason for an increase in the size of the breasts is the onset of puberty, especially in girls, although some increase in boys' breast size may also occur (gynaecomastia). Women's breasts will increase in size from time to time throughout their lives because of hormonal fluctuations during the menstrual cycle and when they are breastfeeding. The breasts of a nursing mother may be twice their normal size. An increase in weight can also lead to the breasts becoming larger in line with the rest of the body. Treatment with hormones such as oestrogen will also usually lead to the breasts becoming larger.

If an increase in breast size in both men and women cannot be explained by any of these obvious reasons it may be a symptom of an underlying disease, including cirrhosis of the liver or cancer in the adrenal glands. It may also be an indication of overactivity or cancer of the thyroid; this will usually be accompanied by sweating, extreme tiredness and loss of weight. A form of lung cancer may also lead to increased breast size.

Men's breasts sometimes get larger as they get older. This is of no medical significance. Occasionally, enlarged breasts in a male may indicate the presence of a tumour in the testicles or a genetic condition called Klinefelter's syndrome in which there is an extra sex chromosome.

BREAST LUMP

The structure of some women's breasts is such that the tissue comprising them is uneven and lumpy. This usually gives no cause for concern. If a new lump appears, however, it should never be ignored, although it is not necessarily a sign of disaster. There are five main causes for a lump in the breast, only one of which is life- threatening.

The most common cause of a lump in the breast is a cyst (a small sac filled with fluid). An infection such as mastitis (inflammation of the breast) or a breast abscess will also cause a lump, usually together with redness, tenderness and painful swelling and possibly a temperature. Conditions such as these usually occur in women who are breastfeeding, due to bacteria entering through a cracked nipple. A third cause of a breast lump is a thickening of the milk-producing glandular tissue in a condition called fibro-adenosis. A fourth cause is a benign growth which is unlikely to spread. All these conditions can readily be treated and should not be ignored because, for example, a benign lump can sometimes turn cancerous.

The fifth cause of a lump in the breast is a malignant tumour that may spread and be fatal. This too can be successfully treated if treatment is begun early enough.

It is virtually impossible for a lay person to tell what the cause of a lump is, and you should immediately report any lump to your doctor who will usually arrange for further tests. Also if you have had a pre-existing lump which changes in some way, for example becomes painful, larger or harder, you should get medical advice without delay.

See also BREAST ENLARGEMENT.

BREAST PAIN

Some women get painful breasts every month, just before a period, due to hormonal fluctuations. Women who have painful periods are likely to find they have painful breasts as well. Breasts may swell and become extremely tender during pregnancy and while breastfeeding.

Very painful breasts that feel hot to the touch, and where there is a fever may be due to an abscess or to mastitis (inflammation of the breast). These conditions need prompt medical attention.

If the pain is connected to a lump, medical advice should be sought immediately as it may be a sign of breast cancer.

See also BREAST ENLARGEMENT.

BREATH, BAD
See BAD BREATH.

BREATHING, DIFFICULTY IN

If you are having difficulty breathing it means you are not getting enough oxygen. This may be merely because you have been engaging in undue exertion and your body's demand for oxygen has increased. It may also be due to some obstruction in the air passages, which can be as simple as the mucus that builds up in a common cold, but may be much more serious.

Breathlessness or painful breathing may be a symptom of various diseases, most of which require medical treatment. Many of these diseases involve the lungs and include asthma (a disorder of the bronchial tubes), emphysema (damage to the air sacs of the lungs), pleurisy (inflammation of the membrane surrounding the lungs) and pneumonia (acute inflammation of the lungs). Pneumonia or acute bronchitis are generally indicated by a temperature and the coughing up of greenish yellow or rusty coloured phlegm.

If breathlessness is accompanied by

severe pains in the chest, you should get help immediately as it may be angina, a heart attack, or a pulmonary embolism (blood clot in the lung). If you are having a heart attack you may find the pain radiating out to the jaw, neck or arm. If the pain is worse when you breathe in, it may mean a blood clot or a collapsed lung.

If you have developed shortness of breath (dyspnoea) over a period of time, weeks or months, are coughing up phlegm, and especially if you have worked in a dusty atmosphere, such as a mine or quarry, you may have developed a serious lung disease or one of several dust diseases such as asbestosis. Breathlessness may also be caused by chronic heart disease and certain blood disorders such as anaemia. It may also be a symptom of extreme tension and anxiety. People who are overweight may find themselves out of breath after only slight exertion, as may heavy smokers.

Whether accompanied by other symptoms or not, if difficulty in breathing is severe and/or the victim has a bluish colour around the lips, this is an emergency and immediate medical attention is essential (see FIRST AID, Section 8).

See also WHEEZE.

BREATHING, RAPID (HYPERVENTILATION)

Overly rapid breathing, or hyperventilation to use its medical term, is usually a reaction to stress or anxiety. It generally refers to an adult breathing rate of more than 35 breaths a minute. Because the normal breathing rhythm is disturbed, the balance of oxygen and carbon dioxide is upset and this leads to tingling, light-headedness and even fainting. It may also result in chest pains and palpitations. Hyperventilation can be alleviated with treatment.

Hyperventilation is a common accompaniment to general infections and may sometimes signal a more serious disorder such as a cerebral haemorrhage or a collapsed lung or anything that causes the tissues of the body to receive inadequate amounts of oxygen, including being at a high altitude. It is also caused by some drugs, such as adrenaline and its derivatives which may be found in some asthma and cold remedies.

BRUISING, EXCESSIVE

Bruising occurs when small blood vessels under the skin are damaged and bleed below the surface of the skin so that the blood can be seen as a dark mark. Most bruises are the result of minor injuries and will heal comparatively quickly as a result of the body's natural processes. Women tend to bruise more easily than men. Abnormal bruising which occurs frequently as a result of even minor knocks and which does not heal readily can be a different matter and may indicate serious disease, including haemophilia (where the blood's clotting mechanism is defective) and leukaemia (cancer of the white blood cells). Another condition is thrombocytopenia in which the sufferer has insufficient platelets in their blood.

Excessive bruising may be a sign of kidney or liver failure. It is also caused by various drugs such as steroids, arsenic, quinine and aspirin. These should never be taken except as prescribed by a doctor or recommended by a chemist.

There are various other causes of excessive bruising, all of them serious, and as a symptom it should never be ignored.

See also BLEEDING, EXCESSIVE.

BULIMIA

See APPETITE, EXCESSIVE.

See also Section 5.

Burping, excessive

Burping, or belching, occurs when air is swallowed and is then released through the mouth, sometimes accompanied by noise. It is generally a sign that too much gassy food or liquid has been eaten too quickly, or that air has been swallowed at the same time as food, possibly as a result of nervous tension.

If pain in the chest or abdomen is associated with the burping, it may be a sign of an inflamed oesophagus (gullet) or of a hiatus hernia in which the stomach protrudes through the diaphragm into the chest. Pain and tenderness in the abdomen associated with burping may signal an ulcer in the stomach or duodenum.

Cachexia
See WEIGHT LOSS, ABNORMAL.

Chest pain

Pains in the chest can be due to gastric problems, heart problems, lung disorders, numerous general diseases and the fact that you have injured yourself. The most likely cause of chest pain is indigestion (see DYSPEPSIA). The pain can be acute and is easy to mistake for something more serious; if in doubt, see a doctor. A hiatus hernia occurs where the stomach protrudes through an opening in the diaphragm into the chest and can cause extreme pain.

If indigestion is not the cause, chest pain is usually associated either with breathing difficulties or heart problems. If the pain is crushing and radiates from the chest to the neck, jaw or arm, it is likely to be a heart attack and you should get medical help immediately. Similarly if you have previously had a heart attack and the pain seems the same, get help.

If the pain is accompanied by shortness of breath and you have recently been confined to bed, you may have a blood clot in the lung. If you have a cough or a high temperature, it may be pneumonia or acute bronchitis.

Chest pain which causes a burning feeling in the skin and is unaffected by breathing may be a symptom of a viral infection attacking the nerves, e.g. shingles. Arthritis in the spine and an underactive thyroid are other conditions that can give rise to pains in the chest and any unexplained and continuing or recurrent pain should always be investigated.

See also Section 8.

Chloasma
See SKIN PIGMENTATION.

Chorea
See JERKING MOVEMENTS.

Clubbing of fingers
See FINGER TIPS, SWOLLEN.

Clumsiness

Clumsiness in very young children usually means merely that they have not yet learnt to coordinate their body movements properly. Most children under three are relatively uncoordinated.

Some people are described as clumsy all their lives. This simply seems to be a matter of individual difference — some of us do not have the same degree of control over our body movements as others. However, an unusual lack of coordination not previously apparent may be a symptom of disease affecting the brain or spinal cord, or certain muscular disorders, and should be investigated. In elderly people clumsiness may be an indication of Alzheimer's disease.

Difficulty in coordinating body movements may also be caused by alcohol and certain drugs, including those prescribed for epilepsy.

COLIC
See ABDOMINAL PAIN.
   See also Section 5.

COMA
A coma is a state of deep unconsciousness from which the patient cannot be aroused. The brain stops functioning normally and cannot be stimulated. A coma is much deeper and longer lasting than a fainting attack (see separate entry). Some comas last for years; cases have been reported where a patient has been in a coma for more than thirty years.

A coma can result from disease, alcoholism, drugs, poison or injury. In the case of diabetes, too much or too little insulin or glucose can result in the sufferer lapsing into a coma.

A coma is always serious and needs immediate medical treatment.

CONFUSION
Temporary and mild confusion can result from any of a number of commonplace causes ranging from jet lag to too much to drink to simple tiredness or the use of sedatives. Similarly a blow to the head or concussion may lead to mild confusion, although if it lasts for more than an hour or so it should be reported to a doctor.

Extreme and prolonged confusion may be serious and symptomatic of kidney or brain disorders, or of injury to or disease of the central nervous system. It may also be indicative of epilepsy. A high level of confusion may also be present in certain psychiatric conditions such as schizophrenia.

CONJUNCTIVITIS
See EYE PAIN; EYE RED.
   See also Section 5.

CONSTIPATION
People often think they are constipated when they fail to pass a motion every day. In fact 'normal' bowel habits can vary from two or three times a day to two or three times a week, or even once a week in some individuals.

Difficulty in passing motions because the stools have become hard and dry is usually a result of eating too much junk food with too little fibre, or lack of exercise. It may also be due to repeatedly ignoring signals that the bowel needs emptying. The bowel becomes distended, the urge to eliminate is reduced and the problem becomes self-perpetuating.

Other causes of constipation include pregnancy and the side effect of many commonly used medications, for example codeine in cough mixtures and pain relievers.

To be medically significant, constipation must cause discomfort in the abdomen, pain around the anus, tears in the anus that bleed, piles or some other problem. Continuing constipation is sometimes an indication of an underlying disorder, for example an underactive thyroid gland, a tumour in the intestines, or diabetes. It can also indicate certain psychiatric conditions. It should not be ignored but assessed by a doctor.

CONVULSIONS
A convulsion is a fit or seizure caused by abnormal activity of nerve cells in the brain. A convulsion may be caused by many factors — interruption of the blood flow to the brain, a brain tumour, injury to the brain, epilepsy, or inflammation of the brain as a result of diseases such as meningitis and encephalitis. In older people, convulsions may sometimes be associated with arteriosclerosis (hardening of the

arteries) of the brain. An overdose of insulin in diabetes can also lead to convulsions, as can an excessive intake of alcohol or drugs.

Convulsions occur more often in children than in adults because a child's brain is still developing and is more sensitive to disturbances. Any infection or disease involving a high fever may cause a child to have a convulsion (see also FEBRILE CONVULSIONS, Section 5). Some children have a convulsion for no apparent reason. This is generally regarded as a form of epilepsy and can be extremely alarming, but it may occur once and never again or at very rare intervals.

Many convulsions end by themselves but a doctor should always be consulted.

See also JERKING MOVEMENTS.

See also EPILEPSY, Section 5; and FITS/CONVULSIONS, Section 8.

COUGH

Coughing is the way the body rids itself of irritants or mucus. Most commonly it is a symptom of respiratory tract (breathing apparatus) infections or influenza.

The coughing up of yellowish or brownish phlegm may indicate lung disorders such as bronchitis, pneumonia and pleurisy to name a few of the most common. There are many others, including emphysema, tuberculosis and legionnaire's disease. Coughing together with a wheeze may be a sign of asthma.

A persistent cough can indicate various dust diseases such as asbestosis and silicosis in people who have been living or working near a mine or quarry. Some heart problems are accompanied by coughing, as are diseases such as goitre (an enlarged thyroid) and measles. A persistent cough should always be investigated, and if there are other symptoms as well, a doctor should be consulted for an accurate diagnosis.

CRAMPS, MUSCULAR

Muscular cramps, particularly of the calf muscles, tend to occur at night as the body relaxes (then also called **nocturnal cramps**) and after exercise. Although they usually only last a few minutes, they can be excruciatingly painful. The pain is caused by a sudden spasm of the affected muscles that is far more intense than any normal contraction of the muscle. The exact reason for the development of a cramp is unknown, but both dehydration (e.g. after a bout of diarrhoea) and a build-up of waste products within a muscle after exercise have been implicated. Warming up the muscles adequately before exercise may prevent cramps. Conditions such as pregnancy, poor circulation, kidney diseases and old age are known to increase the incidence of night time cramps. The use of diuretics (fluid-removing drugs) and a lack of salt are other possible causes. More serious causes of muscular cramps include an underactive thyroid gland, diseases of the nervous system and muscles, and (most seriously, but rarely) tetanus.

Immediate relief can be gained by stretching the cramping muscle. Massage and heat (e.g. a hot shower) may also ease the spasm.

Muscular cramps may be prevented by ensuring an adequate fluid intake and by using medications such as quinine sulphate tablets (also found in small amounts in tonic water), biperiden, procainamide or diazepam before going to bed. Unfortunatley some sufferers appear to be resistant to all treatment measures.

See also MUSCLE SPASM.

CYANOSIS
See SKIN, BLUE.

DEAFNESS
Deafness is a partial or total inability to

hear. It can be present at birth or it may develop at any stage afterwards. For many reasons, some still not fully understood, hearing tends to deteriorate with age. Other kinds of deafness are usually the result of something blocking the sound waves from getting through to the inner ear, such as ear wax (see separate entry) or a foreign body that has become lodged in the ear canal. A damaged eardrum, an accumulation of mucus in the middle ear (glue ears) and infections in the middle ear, such as an abscess, can also lead to impaired hearing, as can infections of the adenoids at the back of the nose which block the tubes leading from the throat to the ear.

Deafness that develops without an obvious cause is usually due to any one of a number of disorders specific to the ear. Otosclerosis is a condition in which the bones in the middle ear become stiffened by a new deposit of bone, impeding the transmission of sound waves.

Measles or mumps, or an underactive thyroid, can also lead to impaired hearing, as can an injury to the head. A not uncommon condition in older people is Ménière's disease, which affects the inner ear and in which deafness is associated with buzzing in the ears (tinnitus) and possibly dizziness.

Exposure to loud noise over a long period can lead to impaired hearing, and people in jobs with excessive noise levels should always wear ear protectors.

Deja vu

Deja vu is the medical term for the feeling that whatever is happening at present has happened before. Most of us have this feeling from time to time but it is a common feature of a type of epilepsy. It may also signal certain psychiatric disorders or brain damage, possibly from a stroke.

Dementia

Dementia is a serious loss of mental capacity, usually together with emotional and behavioural disturbances. What used to be called dementia in elderly people is now usually referred to as Alzheimer's disease, an extremely distressing condition in which the sufferer becomes increasingly confused and unable to cope with everyday life (see Section 5).

In people of all ages, dementia can be symptom of a number of diseases including meningitis and encephalitis (inflammation of the brain or surrounding tissues), arteriosclerosis (hardening of the arteries of the brain), the sexually transmitted disease syphilis, and a brain tumour. It may also indicate disorders of the pituitary or adrenal glands and liver failure.

Certain drugs such as barbiturates and bromides may lead to a severe loss of mental capacity, as may alcoholism. Glue sniffing can also be a cause.

Depigmentation of skin
See SKIN, DEPIGMENTATION OF.

Depression

Depression is a disorder of its own (see Section 5). Sometimes however, depression is a symptom of something else. Generally there will be other symptoms as well, but disorders where depression may be a feature include over- or underactivity of the thyroid and parathyroid glands, a brain tumour or other brain diseases, anaemia, and multiple sclerosis, which attacks the nervous system. One of the commonest causes of depression is a bout of the flu (or other viral infection) which can leave you feeling under the weather and depressed for weeks. Women may find attacks of irritability and depression an uncomfortable side effect of the menopause.

Many drugs can induce a feeling of

depression, in particular the contraceptive pill, drugs used to treat heart conditions such as angina, and cortisone.

While occasionally feeling down in the dumps is part of everyone's life and nothing to worry about, a person with persistent depression needs help. Treatment is available and no-one should feel they have to put up with what is a very uncomfortable condition.

Dermographia
See SKIN WEALS.

Diarrhoea

Diarrhoea is the frequent and excessive discharge of watery fluid from the bowel. Very few of us would not have suffered from an attack at one time or another in our lives. There are many different causes. If you have eaten or drunk unwisely, a brief attack of diarrhoea is one of the ways your body may handle the substances it cannot absorb. Or you may be allergic to certain foods or medications which will give rise to a similar bodily reaction. Antibiotics may cause diarrhoea by altering the balance of normal germs found in the gut. Emotional stress or excitement can have the same effect. Inflammation of the stomach (gastritis) or a viral infection of the intestines (gastroenteritis) can interfere with the normal processes of digestion (see Section 5).

More serious causes of diarrhoea include food poisoning as a result of eating contaminated food. You will generally have nausea and vomiting as well. Arsenic or lead poisoning can also cause looseness of the bowels. Various infections such as dysentery will cause diarrhoea. These are commonly acquired in foreign countries, where you are exposed to bugs in the food and water to which you have no immunity. It is generally wise to avoid uncooked food and drinking the water in such places unless it has been boiled. Many general conditions may cause diarrhoea (e.g. thyroid disorders, diabetes and tumours in the intestines), but there will generally be other symptoms as well.

Mild attacks of diarrhoea can usually be dealt with by diet (see Section 7) and over-the-counter remedies from the chemist. However, if it persists for more than a day or so, you should see a doctor. The chief danger with diarrhoea is dehydration, so it is important to keep up your fluid intake.

Diarrhoea can be somewhat more serious in babies than adults, since babies cannot stand the loss of very much fluid. Most babies have attacks occasionally, but unless the diarrhoea is very mild indeed, medical attention is always a wise precaution.

Diplopia
See VISION, DOUBLE.

Discharge
See EAR DISCHARGE; NIPPLE DISCHARGE; NOSE DISCHARGE; URETHRAL DISCHARGE; VAGINAL DISCHARGE.

Dizziness (Vertigo)

Dizziness or vertigo is the feeling you get when the world seems to be spinning around. The ground may actually seem to tilt. Vertigo is often associated with nausea and vomiting, and sometimes with ringing in the ears.

Our sense of balance is maintained by fluid in the inner ear moving around three small semicircular canals. If there is some external disturbance of this fluid, for example by the movement of a boat, we are likely to feel sick and dizzy. Some people feel giddy when looking down from heights or at fast moving objects.

Physical causes of vertigo include viral infections, some drugs (quinine), alcohol, migraine, epilepsy, brain disease such as tumour or stroke, and some eye nerve problems. Ménière's disease occurs mainly middle age and causes repeated episodes of severe giddiness, often accompanied by ringing or buzzing in the ears, and in severe cases nausea and vomiting.

Sometimes dizziness is really lightheadedness or faintness. Causes include disorders of circulation (where the brain does not get enough blood), heart disease (where the heart beat is too slow, too fast, or irregular), stress and anxiety. A common cause, especially in the elderly, may be due to nothing more than getting up too quickly when you have been lying down. The blood supply to the head has not had quite enough time to adjust. This will pass within a minute or so.

See also FAINTING.

Double vision (diplopia)
See VISION, DOUBLE.

Dry eye
See EYE, DRY.

Dry mouth
See MOUTH, DRY.

Dry skin
See SKIN, SCALY.

Dwarfism
See GROWTH, REDUCED.

Dysarthria
See SPEECH, DIFFICULTY WITH.

Dysmenorrhoea
See MENSTRUAL PERIOD PROBLEMS.

Dyspepsia
Dyspepsia is another name for indigestion. It is characterised by a burning sensation in the chest, burping, and sometimes distension of the abdomen. In severe cases it may be accompanied by nausea and vomiting. Dyspepsia is usually the result of eating or drinking too much too quickly, especially rich or spicy food. It can become particularly troublesome in people who are anxious and stressed. However, almost any inflammation of the digestive organs, such as gastritis or duodenitis, may manifest itself as dyspepsia.

Less often, dyspepsia is a symptom of more serious diseases, such as gastric ulcer (in the stomach) or a duodenal ulcer (in the upper part of the small intestine) or a hiatus hernia where the wall of the stomach pushes up the oesophagus (gullet). Occasionally it is a sign of disease of the gall bladder, the pancreas, or the kidneys.

See also HEARTBURN.

Dysphagia
See SWALLOWING, DIFFICULTY IN.

Dyspnoea
See BREATHING, DIFFICULTY IN.

Dysuria
See URINE, PAINFUL PASSING OF.

Earache
Children seem to have a penchant for stuffing things into the openings in their body, and the ears are no exception. Generally the first thing to do if a child has an earache is to look into the ear with a torch to see if there is a pea or part of a toy or something similar lodged in it. If you can remove it easily it may solve the problem but never poke or probe in the ear as it is very vulnerable to damage. Take the child to the doctor. Apart from foreign bodies, the most common cause of earache is

Section 3: Symptoms

infection of either the outer ear or the middle ear. Middle ear infections are particularly common in children.

Because the middle ear is so closely connected with the nose and the throat (see EARS, Section 2) infections in these parts, such as colds, flu or tonsillitis, often spread to the ear. Inflammation of the sinuses can also be responsible for earaches.

Sometimes earache may be indicative of a disorder of the facial nerves (e.g. neuralgia). In rare cases it may indicate cancer of the ear, tonsils, mouth or pharynx.

Ear troubles should always be diagnosed by a doctor with the proper equipment, and treated early. Infections of the middle ear may spread to the mastoid bone, the part of the skull behind the ear, causing mastoiditis. Although this can now be very effectively treated with drugs, it is a serious condition and if left untreated can spread to the brain.

Sometimes the ear aches because of what is called referred pain, i.e. the cause of the pain is elsewhere but you feel it in the ear. For example, if you have an infected tooth, or your teeth or jaw are not aligned properly, you may first become conscious of it as pain in your ear.

EAR DISCHARGE

A discharge from the ear of yellowish pus will usually have been preceded by an earache and at least the more common causes are much the same — the presence of a foreign body or an infection in the outer or middle ear (see EARACHE). In a middle ear infection, the pain is caused by the pus stretching the eardrum; if the pus perforates the drum, the pain stops and the pus appears at the opening to the ear as a discharge.

Bleeding from the ear may simply result from eczema or some other skin irritation in the ear canal. If the eardrum becomes infected there may be a small amount of bleeding from the ear canal. Injury, such as a blow to the head, or a sudden change of pressure for example in an aeroplane, can damage your ears and cause them to bleed.

If you have had a blow to the head and your nose is bleeding as well as your ear, or there are signs that you are bleeding elsewhere, you may have a fractured skull.

EAR NOISES (TINNITUS)

Sometimes we get a ringing in the ear or hear noises in the ear without any external sound being present. This is called tinnitus and is quite common, affecting about one in six adults at some time in their life. The many causes include wax in the ear, damage to the eardrum, diseases of the inner ear, including Ménière's disease, abnormalities of the main nerve leading from the ear to the brain, low blood pressure, high blood pressure and clogging of the arteries. Drugs such as aspirin and quinine can also cause the condition.

If the underlying cause can be identified, tinnitus may be successfully treated. However, in most cases no cause can be found, and then it is only possible to try to relieve the tinnitus itself. Various drugs are available but tinnitus can prove a maddening condition which is hard to eliminate completely.

EAR PAIN
See EARACHE.

EAR WAX

One of the most common reasons for a gradual loss of hearing in adults is an excessive build-up of ear wax.

The ear consists of three parts. The outer ear is a canal, 2–3 cm long, that leads from the ear lobe into the eardrum.

Beyond the eardrum is the middle ear which contains three tiny bones that conduct sound to the inner ear. This contains special nerve cells capable of sensing vibration, and thus sound. It is only in the outer ear that wax is formed.

Wax is meant to be found in the ear. It is secreted by special glands in the outer ear canal, and slowly moves out to clear away dust and debris that enter the ear. It is not only the normal cleaning mechanism of the ear, but also acts to keep the skin lining the canal lubricated and to protect it from water and other irritants.

Only if excess amounts of wax are produced, the wax is too thick, the canal is narrow, or the person works in a dusty and dirty environment, is the wax likely to cause problems. When wax builds up on the eardrum, it is unable to receive the vibrations in the air produced by sound, and it cannot transmit the vibrations on to the inner ear. Because the ear is designed to be self-cleaning, attempts to clean the ear may aggravate the problem. Cotton buds should be banned from ears. They irritate the skin lining the outer canal and tend to pack the wax down hard on the eardrum rather than clean it out. Bobby pins, pen tops and other such objects that people use in attempts to clean their ears have similar effects. 'Nothing except your own elbow should enter your ear' is a very old but very true aphorism.

Water entering the ear during bathing or swimming may cause the wax to swell. Pain and deafness can then develop quite quickly.

Once excess wax is present, an infection may start in the skin under it causing itching and pain. This, and the deafness that occurs, takes the patient to a doctor.

Ear wax is removed by syringing, suction or fine forceps. In syringing, warm water is gently squirted into the ear to dislodge the wax, with large lumps being removed by forceps. The use of wax- softening drops may be necessary to facilitate the removal of particularly large or hard accumulations of wax. Once the wax is removed, any infection present usually settles without further treatment, and normal hearing returns immediately. Those unlucky enough to have recurrent problems with ear wax may find it beneficial to use the wax-softening drops on a regular basis.

No-one should attempt to clean their own or someone else's ears. It is very easy to scratch and damage the sensitive skin lining the ear canal, spread an infection or even pierce an inflamed eardrum to cause permanent hearing loss.

Ejaculation, lack of

The male ejaculation or discharge of semen at the time of sexual intercourse sometimes goes awry, and instead of travelling from the testes into the penis and out through the urethra, the ejaculate goes backwards into the urinary bladder. Medically this is called retrograde ejaculation and it can have many causes, including prostate surgery or disease, injury to the pelvis or the spinal cord, diabetes, or a tumour of the spinal cord. It may also be due to psychological stress, or to an abnormality the individual was born with (when it will usually become evident soon after puberty). Sometimes no cause can be found.

Energy, lack of
See TIREDNESS, ABNORMAL.

Enophthalmos
See EYE, SUNKEN.

Epistaxis
See NOSEBLEED.

ERYTHEMA
See SKIN, RED.

EXOPHTHALMOS
See EYE, PROTRUDING.

EYE DISCHARGE
We only have one pair of eyes and any problem with them should be treated seriously. If we lose our sight or it is impaired, it may be difficult or impossible to get it back.

The most common cause of a discharge from the eyes is inflammation of the eye or conjunctivitis. This may be caused by a viral or bacterial infection, or by an allergy. Another common reason for a painful and discharging eye is that some foreign body has got into the eye. Generally a doctor will need to get it out.

If you have been sitting under a sun lamp for too long without protecting your eyes, the fact that your eye is discharging may mean you have developed a condition called arc eye, in which the surface of the cornea is damaged by overexposure to ultra violet rays. Welders who do not protect their eyes adequately can also develop this condition.

If severe pain is present with the discharge, you may be suffering from more serious conditions, such as inflammation of the iris or the sclera (the white of the eye), an ulcer, or glaucoma.

EYE, DRY
Dry eyes occur when the normal lubricating fluid (tears) covering the cornea is lacking. The cornea may also be inflamed and ulcerated.

Dryness of the eyes is generally a symptom of a lack of vitamin A in the diet, and anyone suffering from it will normally be advised to increase their intake of yellow foods such as butter, egg yolks and carrots. The old wives' tale that eating plenty of carrots will improve your ability to see at night perhaps should not be dismissed too lightly. Dry eyes may also occur in people suffering from rheumatoid arthritis. Sometimes it is due to an allergy to an eye ointment or drops. Sometimes no reason can be found.

Dryness of the eyes associated with a dry mouth can sometimes indicate disease of the bile duct or wasting of the salivary glands in a rare condition called Sjögren's syndrome (see Section 5).

EYE PAIN
The first thing to ask yourself if you have a painful eye is whether you might have injured it. Have you recently poked something into it or knocked it, or otherwise done something that might have damaged it? If the answer is yes and you can see that the eye has been damaged, go to the doctor. Damage to the eye always needs urgent medical attention.

Alternatively, if the eye is painful and watering, you may have a foreign body in it. You may be able to remove this quite simply yourself (see Section 8), but if not you will need to visit the doctor.

If you have a red swelling on one of your eye lids, you are probably developing a sty.

If your vision is blurred and light hurts your eyes, you may have acute glaucoma (pressure build-up behind the eyeball), and again you should get rapid medical advice.

There are many other disorders that may be indicated by painful eyes, including inflammation of the sinuses, meningitis (inflammation of the tissue surrounding the brain), and inflammation of the arteries in your forehead. Sore eyes can also be a symptom of measles, an overactive thyroid, syphilis and yellow fever.

Always seek immediate medical advice if you have pain in the eyes accompanied by a severe headache, dislike of bright light, pain when you bend your head forward, drowsiness or confusion.

Eye, protruding (exophthalmos)

A condition in which a person's eyeball protrudes abnormally is usually a sign of an overactive thyroid gland. The thyroid gland is situated in the neck, and an overactive thyroid will generally be observed as swelling in the neck. The combination of a swollen neck and bulging eyes is what we commonly call goitre.

Protruding eyeballs may also be a symptom of infection or, occasionally, of a tumour at the back of the eyeball.

Eye, red

Red eyes are a common complaint and their causes are many. Everything from minor infections to tiredness to too much to drink may cause redness of the white part of the eye.

Conjunctivitis, an infection of the outer surface of the eye by a virus or by bacteria, is the most common medical cause of red eyes. Generally there is also a sticky discharge.

Pain or blurring of the vision in association with a red eye is a serious situation and medical treatment should be sought urgently. It may indicate glaucoma (a build-up of pressure in the eyeball) which can lead to loss of sight if treatment is delayed.

Iritis, an inflammation of the coloured part of the eye, may also cause pain and reduced vision with a red eye. It is not as serious as glaucoma but still needs medical attention to relieve the discomfort and prevent further damage.

Any foreign body in the eye will cause it to become red, watery and sore. A foreign body may be an inturned eyelash, a barely noticed speck of dust, or a larger fragment of dirt, grit or metal.

Allergic conjunctivitis or hay fever may also cause red, itchy and watery eyes, especially in spring when pollen levels are highest.

Trachoma is a severe eye infection that has caused havoc in the Aboriginal population of Australia.

Eye, sunken (enophthalmos)

An eye that is abnormally sunken into the socket may follow a fracture of the cavity in the skull in which the eye sits, allowing the eye to sink downwards and backwards. It can also indicate paralysis of nerves in the neck.

Eye, watery

Tears are produced to keep the eyeballs lubricated and clean. Sometimes, however, too many tears are produced so that the eyes become watery. Most commonly this is due to extreme emotion when we cry or laugh a lot. If emotion is not the reason and the eyes are red and inflamed as well, it may be due to an infection or the presence of a foreign body, such as dirt or dust. It may also result from an eyelash growing towards the eye from a lid that turns inwards. Iritis is an inflammation of the coloured part of the eye. Sometimes the tear ducts become blocked, either because a foreign body gets into them or because they have an in-built defect present from birth. Either will need medical attention.

Less common serious diseases giving rise to watery eyes are glaucoma and cataracts (see Section 5).

See also EYE, RED.

Eyelid disease

The eyelids exist to protect our eyes, but sometimes they themselves become diseased. The most commonly occurring eyelid problem is a sty. A more generalised inflammation of the eyelid with white scales accumulating along the lashes is often associated with dandruff on the scalp and is a condition known as blepharitis. Allergic blepharitis may occur in response to drugs or cosmetics.

If an eyelid turns in, it may mean that the lashes rub against the eye and irritate it. The eyelid turning away from the eyeball is usually a consequence of ageing and the decreasing elasticity of the tissue around the eye.

Small scaly patches on the eyelid that do not heal may be a small rodent ulcer, which is something between a chronic ulcer and a cancer. It should be treated.

See also EYELID, DROOPING, EYELID, SWOLLEN.

EYELID, DROOPING (PTOSIS)

The drooping of the upper eyelids is a sign that the nerve that leads from the brain and controls the muscle keeping the upper eyelid elevated or open is paralysed. It is sometimes present from birth, when it usually affects only one eyelid and often runs in families. If it happens later in life it can be a symptom of the disease known as Bell's palsy, in which nerves in the face become paralysed and cause weakness down one side of the face and an inability to close the eye.

A drooping eyelid may also indicate myasthenia gravis, in which certain muscles become so fatigued that they are effectively paralysed. The Guillain-Barr syndrome is a disease of the peripheral nerves leading to numbness and weakness of the limbs. It usually follows a couple of weeks after a respiratory infection. Horner's syndrome is a group of symptoms including a drooping upper eyelid, due to a disorder of nerves in the neck. A brain tumour can cause an eyelid to droop, in which case it will often be accompanied by double vision.

A drooping eyelid is cosmetically unattractive and can be treated by surgery, medication or a support built into spectacles, so if you suffer from the condition, see your doctor.

EYELID, SWOLLEN

The simplest reason you may develop a swollen eyelid is because you have been bitten by an insect or injured it in some way.

If the eyelid is itchy as well as swollen, you may have an allergy, perhaps to something you have eaten, to dust or pollen that has blown into the eye, or to a medication you have been taking.

If you are unduly fatigued, losing weight and sweating more than usual, swollen eyelids may be a sign that your thyroid is malfunctioning and you have too many thyroid hormones in your blood. Swollen eyelids can also be a symptom of an underactive thyroid, in which case they will be accompanied by dry skin, aching muscles and loss of hearing.

FACIAL PAIN

A face ache is a miserable condition and can be caused by almost anything that goes wrong in the mouth, the jaw or the surrounding areas, such as the head and the sinuses. It can also be a reflection of something wrong somewhere else in the body, so persistent facial pain should be investigated by a doctor, especially if it is accompanied by swelling and/or fever. Serious causes of facial pain can range from a stroke to muscular disorders such as Parkinson's disease. However, the causes are usually far more obvious, and include various infections of the mouth. If you have an infected or abscessed tooth, you will probably have a very sore face. If your sinuses have become infected, perhaps because of a cold, the ache radiating out from under the eyes can be almost unbearable. Brief paroxysms of searing pain can indicate a nerve disorder called trigeminal neuralgia.

Failure to thrive (in babies)

The regular gaining of weight is one of the most important signs of a healthy baby. There are generally accepted standards for weight gain in babies (see Section 1), and normally your GP or the local clinic will weigh the baby on its regular visits. Although individual babies can vary considerably, up or down, from the standards, a baby who is consistently significantly below the normal weight for age and who seems generally listless is said to be failing to thrive.

The most obvious reason for a failure to thrive is that the baby is not getting adequate nourishment. This may be simply because the baby needs more to eat, the mother's milk supply isn't enough, or it may be due to neglect. However, it may be a symptom of an underlying disease, ranging from congenital heart disease to a disorder of the central nervous system to kidney malfunctions and various other conditions. A not infrequent cause is an inability to absorb food, e.g. because the child is allergic to wheat products (see COELIAC DISEASE, Section 5). As a general rule, a baby who fails to gain weight over a period of two weeks should be checked, at least by the clinic, who will then be able to assess whether medical assessment is needed.

Fainting (syncope)

A sudden feeling of weakness and unsteadiness that may result in a brief loss of consciousness can have literally dozens of causes. Essentially it is caused by a lack of blood reaching the brain, and this may occur simply because you stand up too quickly after sitting or lying down, so that your blood pressure has not had enough time to adjust (see also DIZZINESS). Similarly if you were exercising more vigorously than normal, it may cause you to feel faint while your supply of oxygen catches up. Standing for long periods, especially in a hot stuffy room or without adequate refreshment, can bring on an attack of fainting.

There are many other reasons for fainting, ranging from emotional upsets to heat exhaustion to a vigorous attack of coughing. As a general rule, a loss of consciousness for a minute or two is not a cause for concern and can be treated by lying down with the feet raised (see also UNCONSCIOUSNESS, Section 8). If the feeling of faintness is accompanied by numbness or tingling in any part of the body, blurred vision, confusion, difficulty in speaking or loss of movement in the limbs, you may have had a mild stroke and should call the doctor immediately.

Other serious conditions of which fainting is a symptom may involve the heart and lungs, and if the person having the attack has any pain, especially in the chest, or if their pulse seems unduly slow or irregular, get medical help quickly.

If you are over 50 and turning your head slowly makes you feel faint, you may be suffering from cervical osteoarthritis, a disorder that affects the nerves and bones in the neck. If the faintness is accompanied by inexplicable tiredness and you are often short of breath, it may be due to a form of anaemia.

See also COMA.

Familiarity

See DEJA VU.

Farting

See FLATULENCE.

Section 3: Symptoms

Fasciculation
See TREMOR.

Fat
See OBESITY; WEIGHT GAIN, ABNORMAL.

Fatigue, abnormal
See TIREDNESS, ABNORMAL.

Fear (phobia)
There would not be a human being alive who is not fearful of something. Events occur in all our lives which make us feel nervous and frightened. To some extent fear is a protection against embarking on hazardous and potentially dangerous undertakings. It is when our feelings of fear are out of all proportion to the danger that exists, or indeed there is no danger at all, that it becomes medically significant. If irrational fear is directed at something in particular, it is called a phobia, e.g. claustrophobia (fear of closed spaces), agoraphobia (fear of open spaces), acrophobia (fear of heights). Some people have compulsive fears, e.g. they may constantly wash their hands or the kitchen floor because of fear of germs, and may be suffering from an obsessional neurosis.

Abnormal fears associated with delusions and hallucinations may be a sign of severe mental illness, such as schizophrenia. If abnormal fears are accompanied by an inability to sleep, it is usually a symptom of depression.

See also PHOBIA, Section 5.

Fever (high temperature, pyrexia)
Our normal temperature is about 37 degrees Celsius. This is by no means absolute and may vary according to the individual, the climate, or even the time of day. A woman's temperature rises by up to half a degree after she ovulates in the middle of her menstrual cycle. A temperature that is more than half a degree or so above the norm, however, is a fever and is an important sign of disease. It may indicate anything from a common cold to a generalised form of cancer.

Different diseases cause different types of fever. A virus often causes a rise in temperature in the morning and evening when the trillions of virus particles reproduce all at once. A constant high fever over 40 degrees is typical of a severe bacterial infection. A fever that returns every three or four days is typical of malaria.

You can take your own temperature by using a thermometer — readily available from the chemist. The most comfortable way is to put it under the tongue for at least two minutes. If you are taking a child's temperature and are afraid the child may bite the glass of the thermometer, you can slide it into the anus. The thermometer can also be placed under the arm, but this will give a reading about half a degree lower than the correct one.

For a fever above 40 degrees, or if the fever persists for more than 24 hours, you should call a doctor.

See also Section 8.

Fingernails
See NAIL ABNORMALITIES.

Finger pain
See JOINTS, PAINFUL, SWOLLEN.

Fingertips, swollen (clubbing of fingers)
Some people's fingers become deformed in a strange way. The cuticles seem to disappear and the fingernails curve around the ends of the fingers. The tips of the fingers may also flatten out so that they resemble a spatula. This is called clubbing and is a

symptom of chronic heart or lung disease, or sometimes of disorders of the digestive system. In particularly bad cases the toes are deformed in the same way.

FITS
See CONVULSIONS.

FLATULENCE (FARTING)
Various foods cause gas to form in the digestive tract. If the gas forms in the stomach, it is generally expelled through the mouth. If it forms in the bowel, it will usually pass out through the anus. When gas is present in large amounts in the bowel, it is usually due to fermentation by bacteria. If you have recently embarked on a high-fibre diet, you will almost certainly notice an increase in flatulence, as high-fibre foods such as oats and bran are well-known generators of gas. Other foods that produce gas are onions, cucumber, cabbage and eggs. Provided your family can stand it, there is no cause for concern.

If the cause of your flatulence cannot be explained this way, and you have bouts of abdominal pain that are relieved when you pass wind or have a bowel movement, you may have a disorder of the colon. If your bowel movements are pale and particularly foul-smelling, the flatulence may be because you are not absorbing your food. If you have diarrhoea or alternatively constipation and pain, it might be due to inflammation or ulceration of the digestive tract, or to diverticulitis, a disorder of the colon.

FLUID, EXCESS
See ASCITES; OEDEMA.

FLUSH
A flush is when the face or neck becomes diffused with a red glow. Most of us will have been flushed with anger at some stage in our life. Other extreme emotions may also cause us to flush. The most serious causes of flushing can be cancer of the liver, a condition where there are too many thyroid hormones in the bloodstream, or some forms of heart disease. It can also indicate a disease of the pituitary gland. The flushed look of someone with high blood pressure is familiar to most of us. Many women going through the menopause suffer from hot flushes when the reddening is accompanied by a feeling of heat. Hormone treatment can sometimes have the same effect.

FOOT PAIN
We kick, tread and jump on them. We constrict, squash and rub them. We generally ignore them, but when they give even the slightest trouble, we are very quick to complain. Our feet are vital to our health, work, sport and play. Virtually no thought is given to preventive foot care, but when one of the many diseases and disorders of the feet occurs, our lives and livelihood are thrown into chaos. Correct shoes for work, sport or home, and care of nails are the most important ways to maintain good foot health.

A pain in the instep can mean that the blood supply to your foot is inadequate because of clogged arteries. The pain will first appear while walking and usually disappear with rest. As the condition worsens, the pain may not ease with rest. Those who have hardening of the arteries, diabetes and smoke are more likely to develop this problem, which is called claudication by doctors.

If a foot suddenly becomes painful, cold and numb, a blood clot (embolism) may have blocked off an artery. This requires urgent medical attention.

Pain under the heel is one of the common problems. It can be caused by a **spur** on the bottom of the heel bone, by inflammation of the large fibrous band that maintains the arch of the foot, or from damage to the heel tissues from running on hard surfaces. Joggers are particularly susceptible to heel pain and should ensure that they wear good running shoes and run on grass rather than roads. Rest is the most important part of treatment for heel pain. Swimming and cycling can be substituted for exercise while the damaged tissue recovers. Anti-inflammatory medications prescribed by a doctor may ease the discomfort, but some patients require injections of steroids into the heel. These are very successful in curing what can become a chronic problem, although they may be rather painful to receive. Many doctors inject local anaesthetic with the steroid to minimise the discomfort.

A **march fracture** of the forefoot bones is caused by prolonged running, jumping or walking, usually on hard surfaces. Severe pain may develop in the ball of the foot. Soldiers on route marches may develop the condition. There are minimal changes on X-ray, but excruciating pain on attempting to walk. Six weeks rest heals these fractures.

In the elderly, foot pain may be the first sign of poor circulation, diabetes, rheumatoid arthritis or neuralgia. Because these conditions can be serious, the cause of the pain must be investigated by a doctor and the correct treatment started.

Doctors work together with podiatrists (chiropodists) to keep our feet healthy.

Many other foot problems are dealt with separately in this book. See BUNION; CLUB FOOT; FLAT FOOT; FUNGAL INFECTIONS — Tinea; GANGLION; METATARSALGIA; WARTS, Section 5.

Frequent Micturition
See URINE, EXCESSIVE OR FREQUENT.

Frigidity
See SEXUAL PROBLEMS, Section 5.

Gait, Abnormal
See WALK, ABNORMAL.

Galactorrhoea
See NIPPLE DISCHARGE.

Gassy Urine
See URINE, GASSY.

Giant
See GROWTH, EXCESSIVE.

Giddiness
See DIZZINESS.

Gigantism
See GROWTH, EXCESSIVE.

Gingivitis
See GUM PAIN.

Glands, Swollen
The fluid surrounding the cells in our body is regulated by the lymphatic system, and invading germs are filtered out by tiny lymph glands (see LYMPHATIC SYSTEM, Section 2). Lymph glands are most apparent in our armpits, groin and neck, and when an infection is present they go into overdrive to fight it off. The extra antibodies the glands need to carry out their work causes them to swell up. Consequently enlarged or swollen glands in these areas can be a symptom of a simple infection such as a cut or graze that has failed to clear up, or a wide range of viral infections, such as measles, German measles (rubella), chicken pox, glandular fever and, increasingly, AIDS.

A swollen gland under the arm may be due to an infection in the arm, possibly as a result of a cut or graze, but occasionally it may be the first sign of breast cancer and if there is no obvious explanation a doctor should be consulted immediately. Swelling in the centre of the neck, near the Adam's apple indicates a problem with the thyroid gland (see GOITRE). Swelling of the glands in the neck, just below the ears is the most obvious symptom of mumps, a common childhood disease but one that often afflicts adults as well, with possible serious consequences. A swelling in the groin that disappears when you press it or increases in size when you cough may be a hernia (rupture).

Swollen glands can also be a symptom of various malignancies such as Hodgkin's disease (a disease of the lymphatic tissues) and leukaemia. Serious diseases will usually have other symptoms as well such as a high temperature or, for example in the case of leukaemia, excessive tiredness and lethargy.

See also ADENITIS, Section 5.

GOITRE

Goitre is the name commonly given to an enlarged thyroid gland. The thyroid gland lies over the windpipe just below the Adam's apple. It cannot normally be felt, unless you are very thin, except when you swallow. If you become conscious of a lump or swelling in the front of the neck and you can feel it move under your fingers when you swallow some water, the swelling is in the thyroid.

The thyroid hormone, thyroxine, is necessary in the body's metabolism (chemical processes). An enlarged thyroid can indicate that it is malfunctioning either by producing too much thyroxine (hyperthyroidism) or too little (hypothyroidism). Among other things, this can be due to the development of cysts in the gland or to tumours, either benign or cancerous, or to growths in the larynx (throat). The most common disease associated with an overactive thyroid is Grave's disease in which the victim also has protruding, 'staring' eyes. At one time goitre was common due to a lack of iodine in the diet (a small amount of iodine is necessary in the production of thyroxine). This could afflict whole populations of people since it was generally due to a deficiency of iodine in the drinking water, and was known as endemic goitre. In Australia and most developed countries it has largely been overcome since the introduction of table salt, bread and milk with the addition of iodine compounds.

GROIN PAIN

The groin is the area at the front of the body at the top of the leg. It includes the lower part of the abdomen and the upper part of the thigh. A pain in the groin is generally caused by a strained muscle or ligament. If there is also a lump or swelling, it may be a sign of a hernia (rupture), or of an inflamed lymph gland (see GLANDS, SWOLLEN). In men, a pain in the groin can indicate a problem in the testicles, and in women it is sometimes a signal of a tumour in the ovaries, or if the pain occurs at regular intervals, endometriosis (see Section 5). It can also be a symptom of osteoarthritis of the hip, or if the area is tender to the touch and you feel feverish, an abscess in the abdomen. Pain can also arise if the nerves in the area become disturbed for any reason.

GROWTH, EXCESSIVE (GIGANTISM)

The average height is 175 cm for men and 160 cm for women. Of course individual heights vary a great deal from the average but 200 cm in men and 180 cm in women would be regarded as significantly above average. Excess height can be caused by overproduction of the growth hormone by the pituitary gland and is called gigantism. The condition is often caused by a non-cancerous tumour of the pituitary gland, in which case the sufferer will usually also experience headaches, weakness and general lethargy, and difficulties with sight. These other symptoms are due to overgrowth of the bones of the face and skull, resulting in a typical appearance of prominent heavy jaw bone and eyebrow ridge. Sometimes the pituitary tumour presses on the optic nerve (the nerve of vision) and causes visual disturbances. People with gigantism will generally not develop normally at puberty. Gigantism can usually be treated by radiation or hormone therapy or by surgery.

Occasionally excessive height is due to a genetic abnormality in the chromosomes.

Growth, reduced (dwarfism)

Dwarfism is abnormally stunted growth. It has many causes including inadequate nutrition, which can itself be due to a disorder such as coeliac disease in which there is an inability to absorb nourishment. Dwarfism may also be due to a deficiency of vitamin D (the lack of which hinders bone growth leading to rickets in children; it is obtained from sunlight and so is uncommon in Australia), or an inadequate production of growth hormone by the pituitary gland. If this last is the cause, the dwarf will be well proportioned though small. A more common type of dwarfism is achondroplastic dwarfism, in which the head and body are normal in size but the long bones in the limbs are abnormally short. This is due to an inherited or genetic chromosomal abnormality. If the cause of the dwarfism is underactivity of the thyroid, the dwarf will be mentally retarded, but in other types of dwarfism, mental development is usually normal.

Almost any chronic disorder affecting major organs, including heart disease, kidney failure and severe asthma are among other conditions that may impede normal growth. A child with cystic fibrosis will generally not grow to normal size. Extreme cases of the psychiatric disorder, anorexia nervosa, may stunt growth.

Gum pain (gingivitis)

Gingivitis is the medical name for painful, bleeding gums. Its most common cause is decayed and improperly maintained teeth. In most cases regular dental checks and good dental hygiene will prevent it. It is necessary also to ensure properly fitted dentures. In addition, bleeding gums can be a sign of generally poor health and nutrition.

Occasionally bleeding gums are a symptom of a serious disease such as leukaemia or a form of anaemia caused by a deficiency of vitamin B12. In this case other symptoms will normally be present, but persistently bleeding gums should be checked by a dentist or doctor.

Gynaecomastia
See BREAST ENLARGEMENT.

Haematemesis
See VOMITING BLOOD.

Haematuria
See URINE, BLOODY.

Haemorrhage
See BLEEDING.

Hair, excess (hirsutism, hypertrichosis)

On the whole, men don't consider having too much hair as a problem but women do. The amount of hair you have is generally an individual characteristic whether you are a man or a woman. It may be influenced by your ethnic background, e.g. Asian races tend to have less hair than other races. Too much hair on any part of the body is called hypertrichosis, and there is usually no specific cause for it over and above ordinary racial or genetic tendencies.

Hirsutism describes the condition of a woman who has hair where it would not normally be because of a hormonal abnormality. Some of the more common reasons why a woman develops excessive hair growth include: puberty — the male/female balance takes a while to settle down; the menopause — the amount of oestrogen being manufactured decreases; an overactive adrenal gland, and therefore too many adrenal hormones, due to a benign or malignant tumour; ovarian cysts or tumours which cause the male hormone testosterone to be produced and so lead to an increase in the amount of hair; a tumour in the pituitary gland also causing hormonal disturbances; hormone therapy consisting of testosterone, sometimes prescribed for the relief of menopausal symptoms. Some women also grow extra hair during pregnancy or if they are taking an oral contraceptive. Drugs such as cortisone and some antibiotics can lead to hair growth.

Excess hair combined with a moon-shaped face and a fatty hump on the upper back are symptoms of a condition called Cushing's syndrome in which the body produces too many steroid hormones.

HAIR, LOSS AND LACK OF
See BALDNESS.

HALITOSIS
See BAD BREATH.

HALLUCINATIONS
We are generally said to be hallucinating when we see or hear something that we think is real but it is not. In fact hallucinations can apply to any of the senses including taste, smell and touch.

Hallucinations may be a result of sleeplessness, overwork or fever, but they may also be a symptom of serious psychiatric illness, in particular schizophrenia, and anyone who experiences hallucinations needs medical help. Epileptics sometimes hallucinate.

Sometimes hallucinations are brought on by alcoholism or may be drug induced, e.g. by LSD, marihuana, heroin or amphetamines.

HAND PAIN
Painful hands are one of the most disabling conditions we can experience since we use our hands in almost every task we undertake. The most obvious cause of pain in the hand, wrist or fingers is a specific injury such as a sprain or broken bone. Painful joints are often a symptom of arthritis, especially as we get older. Pain in the wrists leading into the fingers can be due to the inflammatory conditions known as tenosynovitis and carpal tunnel syndrome, both caused by constantly repetitive tasks such as operating a word processor without adequate breaks and proper seating arrangements. Carpal tunnel syndrome is sometimes caused by an underactive thyroid, is more common in women, and can occur during pregnancy. Because the skin of the palm of the hand is thick and fixed to the tendons and bones, it will not swell in the usual way if it is injured or becomes infected. Consequently if you have a painful hand and do not get it treated properly, you risk the tendons becoming fixed in one position so that the hand becomes useless.

Sharp radiating pain is usually caused

by a damaged nerve (neuralgia). If the damage is severe, the muscles may contract so that the hand takes on the shape of a claw.

Raynaud's disease is a condition in which the arteries in the fingers react unduly to cold and go into spasm causing numbness and discomfort.

Headache

A headache is probably the most common medical symptom that exists. There are more than a hundred different causes. Headaches of various kinds are conditions in themselves (see Section 5). Often, however, a headache is a symptom of some other disorder, most commonly bacterial or viral infections, inflamed sinuses, dental problems, ear blockages and disease, psychiatric disorders and hormonal disturbances. Serious diseases of which headaches may be a symptom include strokes, brain tumours, nerve compressions, diabetes, high blood pressure and kidney disease.

Because headaches can be a symptom of so many disorders, it is important to consult a doctor if you have a headache that persists or is not relieved by one of the milder pain relievers available from the chemist.

Hearing loss
See DEAFNESS.

Heart
See BREATHING, DIFFICULTY IN; CHEST PAIN; HEARTBEAT, FAST; PALPITATIONS; PULSE, SLOW; SKIN, BLUE.

See also Section 2 and Section 5.

Heartbeat, fast (tachycardia)

Normally our heart beats away, day in and day out, without us being conscious of it. If we become aware of it, it is usually because it is beating faster than normal. This can be for any one of a number of reasons, such as exertion, fear or emotion, which in themselves normally give no cause for concern. If you are conscious of an increased heart rate, or palpitations, while you are sitting quietly at rest, you should ask yourself why. It might be because you eat or drink or smoke too much, or you drink too much coffee. It could also be because of drugs you are taking, such as thyroid pills or appetite suppressants.

The heart will often beat faster due to anaemia, because if your blood is deficient in red blood cells, the tissues need more blood to service their needs, and the heart therefore has to beat faster to supply the extra blood.

If you have a fast heart beat, feel tired all the time, and feel the cold more than normal, it might be due to an overactive thyroid.

The heart will also speed up if it is diseased, since it has to compensate for the lack of strength to pump out enough blood for the body's needs. Cancer or any chronic kidney or liver disease can also trigger an abnormally rapid heartbeat.

Heartburn

Heartburn or dyspepsia (see separate entry) is one of the most common medical complaints in existence and has nothing to do with the heart. Mostly it is due to overeating or overindulging in alcohol. A sensation of burning pain is felt behind the breastbone. The pain may spread all the way from the top of the stomach to the back of the mouth.

Heartburn appears to be related to the regurgitation of hydrochloric acid from the stomach into the lower part of the oesophagus (gullet). The mucous lining of the stomach has an acid-protecting quality but the lining of the oesophagus does not, and can be damaged if it is exposed to the potent stomach acid. Some foods are more likely to cause heartburn than others. These include highly spiced foods, fatty or fried foods, salad dressings, citrus fruits, pineapple, peppermints and coffee. Medications such as aspirin and some arthritis-treating drugs may also cause heartburn. If you have a hiatus hernia, where part of the stomach slips through into the chest cavity, acid can more easily escape up into the oesophagus to cause heartburn. If tenderness and nausea is present, heartburn may be a sign of a peptic ulcer. Heartburn is very common during pregnancy because of the pressure of the enlarging womb and the hormonal effect on muscle tissue in the oesophagus and stomach.

Heartburn is usually a temporary annoyance that can be relieved by antacids from the chemist, but sometimes it can be sufficiently debilitating to require medical attention.

See also CHEST PAIN.

HEMIPLEGIA
See PARALYSIS.

HICCUPS (HICCOUGHS)
The diaphragm is a sheet of muscle that stretches across the body to separate the chest from the abdomen. It has holes in it to allow the major blood vessels and the gullet (oesophagus) to pass through. Hiccups are due to spasms of the diaphragm. When it contracts, a small amount of air is suddenly forced out of the lungs, causing the characteristic sound. The diaphragm goes into spasm because it, or the nerve that controls it, becomes irritated. If you swallow large chunks of food, swallow quickly, or overfill the stomach, it causes pressure on the diaphragm, and therefore irritation. Sudden laughing may also trigger an attack of hiccups. The nervous swallowing of air can cause the stomach to become bloated and put pressure on the diaphragm to cause hiccups. A large number of rarer conditions may also be responsible, particularly if the hiccups are long-lasting and constant. These include pneumonia, pancreatitis, abscesses in the abdomen, brain disorders (e.g. strokes, tumours), chemical imbalances in the bloodstream and heart disease.

Attacks of hiccups usually last no more than a few minutes or an hour or two, but in uncommon cases they may persist for days, and even for weeks, months or years. One recent case reported in Australia concerned a whole family consisting of a sister, two brothers, grandfather, father, uncle and aunt with uncontrollable hiccups. One of the victims was 70 years old and had been hiccuping almost constantly for 30 years.

The cure for the condition is to cause a counterirritation or relieve the pressure. Drinking water may remove a piece of food lodged in the oesophagus. Holding a deep breath causes counterpressure on the diaphragm. A fright can cause a sudden generalised muscular spasm. Burping can relieve pressure too. Most of the well-known remedies work this way.

In the rare cases where the hiccups are prolonged, the possible causes need to be investigated and treated. If no specific cause can be demonstrated, medications can be given to relax the diaphragm muscle.

HIP PAIN
The hip is a complicated structure. The whole joint is bound together by fibrous bands called ligaments. Inside the ligaments is a joint capsule lined by a thin membrane that continuously produces tiny amounts of fluid to lubricate the joint. Where the bone ends are in contact, their surfaces are covered with a smooth, firm

substance called articular cartilage. Constantly used as they are, it is hardly surprising that, as we grow older, hips are very vulnerable to degenerative joint disease such as osteoarthritis. Generally there will be pain, swelling and stiffness occurring at intervals of months or years. The pain may not cause more than minor discomfort, but if it becomes severe enough to disturb sleep and everyday life, it is possible to replace the joint with an artificial hip.

Hip fractures are common in elderly people, especially women.

See also JOINTS, PAINFUL, SWOLLEN.

HIRSUTISM
See HAIR, EXCESS.

HIVES
See SKIN WEALS.

HOARSENESS
The voice is produced by the vibration of the vocal cords within the larynx (voice box). If we overuse our voice, the vocal cords become tired and inflamed, reducing their elasticity so that our voice loses its usual clarity and sounds hoarse and strained. Generally this will disappear within a few days if the voice is given a rest. (If we don't heed the warning signals, we may find that the voice insists on a rest by refusing to function altogether so that we 'lose our voice'.) Inflammation of the larynx (laryngitis) can also result from smoking, too much alcohol, depression and anxiety, and from minor infections such as a cold or sore throat.

Persistent hoarseness, lasting more than about a week, may signal something more serious and should be investigated by a doctor. The most likely reason is that a small benign nodule, which can readily be removed, has formed on the vocal cord. There is, however, the possibility of a cancerous growth.

The voice can also become hoarse if the muscles and nerves servicing the vocal cords are interfered with by infection or disease, especially the long nerve leading from the brain down through the throat to the chest and branching out to the vocal cords. A widening of the artery leading from the heart to the rest of the body (called an aortic aneurysm) can also interfere with the nerve that opens and shuts the vocal cords and so cause hoarseness.

If your voice is hoarse and you are feeling the cold more than you used to, your skin and hair are unusually dry, you have put on weight for no reason or you are inexplicably tired, you may have an underactive thyroid.

HUNGER, EXCESSIVE
See APPETITE, EXCESSIVE.

HYPERTRICHOSIS
See HAIR, EXCESS.

HYPERVENTILATION
See BREATHING, RAPID.

ICHTHYOSIS
See SKIN, SCALY.

ICTERUS
See SKIN, YELLOW.

IMPOTENCE
See SEXUAL PROBLEMS, Section 5.

INCOORDINATION
See CLUMSINESS.

INCONTINENCE OF URINE
See URINE INCONTINENCE.

INDIGESTION
See ABDOMINAL PAIN; BURPING, EXCESSIVE; CHEST PAIN; DYSPEPSIA; HEARTBURN.

INGUINAL PAIN
See GROIN PAIN.

INSOMNIA (INABILITY TO SLEEP)
In the main, sleeping difficulties are indicative of psychological problems such as stress and anxiety or depression. On occasion a severe psychiatric disorder such as schizophrenia may be the cause. In women sleep disturbance is a common symptom of menopause.

In rare cases, inability to sleep may be indicative of physical disease, usually only if there are other symptoms as well such as involuntary jerking movements, memory loss and weakness. People suffering from Cushing's syndrome, a condition resulting from too many steroid hormones in the body, may also be unable to sleep in addition to having other symptoms, such as a moon face and overweight.

See also Section 5.

INTERCOURSE, PAINFUL
See SEXUAL PROBLEMS, Section 5.

ITCH (PRURITUS)
Itching occurs when the myriads of tiny nerve endings in the skin are irritated. It can be caused by dozens of different things, from skin irritations themselves, either minor, local ones such as those caused by an insect bite, to more widespread and troublesome conditions such as eczema and dermatitis. Other skin disorders include fungal infections such as tinea or ringworm (which tends to attack the scalp and feet), bacterial infections such as that scourge of most primary schools, impetigo, and psoriasis, a chronic condition often with no known cause in which unsightly itchy scaly red patches form on various parts of the body such as the elbows and knees, forearms and legs causing great distress to the sufferer. There are many more.

Another common cause of itching is parasitic infestations such as lice and various tropical bugs. An allergy to a substance or food or some medications will frequently also cause the skin to break out in an itchy rash.

Most skin conditions are not life-threatening, although they can be extremely distressing and uncomfortable.

Sometimes itching is a symptom of underlying disease. Again these are numerous and include liver disease, diabetes, kidney problems, forms of anaemia and even some malignancies.

Because itching can be a symptom of so many different conditions, any itch that is more than a minor irritation which does not clear up within week or so should be checked by a doctor.

See also ANAL ITCH; VULVAL ITCH.

JAUNDICE
See SKIN, YELLOW.

JERKING MOVEMENTS (CHOREA)
Irregular involuntary jerking movements, particularly involving the shoulders, hips and face are a symptom of various diseases affecting the nervous system. The medical name for the general condition is chorea. One type of disease is Sydenham's chorea, also called St Vitus dance, which is associated with rheumatic fever in children. An earlier sign of the diminishing muscular control is unusual clumsiness. It usually responds to rest and sedatives. In Huntington's chorea (see Section 5) the nerves in the brain degenerate and eventually mental functioning becomes impaired. Senile chorea occurs in elderly people

although in this case there is no mental deterioration.

See also CONVULSIONS; MUSCLE SPASM; TIC; TREMOR.

JOINTS, PAINFUL, SWOLLEN

The joints in our body are where our bones meet. Most joints have to hold two bones securely together as well as allowing a substantial degree of movement without causing friction and therefore wear between the bones. To carry out their tasks, joints are made up of a complex combination of elastic tissue called cartilage to allow movement, strong fibrous tissue called ligaments to keep the bones together, and lubricating fluid. Injury to any of these parts because of a sprain, dislocation or fracture can result in pain and swelling.

If there has been no injury but your joints hurt (i.e. you have arthralgia), you probably have some disease. It is not generally realised that all the joints in the body are interrelated, irrespective of where they are. If you ache all over and you feel feverish you probably have a general viral infection such as the flu. Hepatitis B can also cause pain and swelling of several joints. Bacterial infections sometimes get into the bloodstream and penetrate a joint, which becomes swollen, painful and full of pus. Generally only one joint will be affected. If you have constantly aching, swollen deformed joints, feel feverish and generally tired and unwell, you may have rheumatoid arthritis. If you feel all right but you have pain in particular joints, such as your fingers or knees or hips, you probably have osteoarthritis. This generally strikes as we get older and our joints begin to 'wear out'.

Someone under 20 who has had a sore throat followed by aching joints where the pain seems to move from one joint to the other may have rheumatic fever. Pain in the joints can even be caused by certain cancers, bleeding problems (where the blood seeps into the joint), venereal disease such as gonorrhoea, and diseases of the intestines.

Medications can sometimes cause painful joints, for example, oral contraceptives, some tranquillisers, drugs taken to lower blood pressure and penicillin, so if there does not seem to be any other reason for your joints suddenly to have started hurting and you have recently been put on a course of drugs, ask the doctor if they could be the culprit.

If the pain in your joints is acute, or if it lasts for more than about a week and there is no obvious cause such as injury, see a doctor to establish the cause.

See also HIP PAIN; KNEE PAIN; SHOULDER PAIN; TOE, PAINFUL.

KIDNEY PAIN

See LOIN PAIN; URINE, BLOODY; URINE, PAINFUL PASSING OF.

KNEE PAIN

Pain in the knee can be caused by any of the conditions to which joints in general are susceptible (see JOINTS, PAINFUL, SWOLLEN).

Bursitis in the knee occurs when the pouch (the bursa) that supplies the lubricating fluid to the joint becomes inflamed due to an accumulation of fluid. It generally results from the strain and pressure of a great deal of time spent kneeling on hard floors and is often referred to as housemaid's knee. This can generally be relieved by applying alternating hot and cold wet compresses and by taking aspirin. If the pain or swelling is severe, see a doctor who may decide it should be drained.

Paget's disease is a chronic disease of the bones that tends to strike elderly people. An affected bone becomes thickened and its structure disorganised so that the leg bows outwards to put abnormal stress on the knee to cause pain in the joint.

Common causes of knee pain in older children and teenagers who are growing rapidly and active in sport include osteochondritis, Osgood-Schlatter disease and chondromalacia (see Section 5).

LACTATION, ABNORMAL
See NIPPLE DISCHARGE.

LEG PAIN
After a bad back, aching legs are probably the next most common complaint. There can be numerous causes, mostly related to the circulation of blood. Trouble can arise in the arteries (the vessels carrying blood to the leg muscles) which may become narrowed because of arteriosclerosis, or in the veins (the vessels carrying blood back to the heart) which may become enlarged as varicose veins, or develop clots. Alternatively the pain may be a symptom of diseased or irritated nerves to the legs. This can be caused by neurological disorders, diabetes, smoking and alcohol abuse.

Cramps in the legs due to muscle fatigue, strain or injury, are so common that most people regard them as nothing but a temporary annoyance. Persistent unexplained cramps, however, may be due to a deficiency in certain minerals or, if they occur in the calf after you have been walking, to arteriosclerosis.

Sometimes leg pain has nothing to do with blood supply but is caused because of a disc problem in the back, causing the pinching of one of the nerves running down into the leg from the spine.

See also JOINTS, PAINFUL, SWOLLEN; KNEE PAIN.

LETHARGY
See TIREDNESS, ABNORMAL.

LEUCORRHOEA
See VAGINAL DISCHARGE.

LIBIDO, REDUCED
See SEXUAL PROBLEMS, Section 5.

LIGHT-HEADEDNESS
See DIZZINESS; FAINTING.

LIMB PAIN
See ARM PAIN; LEG PAIN.

LOIN PAIN
The loin is the region of the back and side of the body between the lowest rib and the pelvis. Pain is generally due to disease of the internal organs situated in the area. Most commonly the kidney is responsible, but other organs such as the pancreas, the liver or bile duct, or the spleen may also be involved. It may also be caused by diverticulitis or an ulcer in the colon (the large intestine).

See also ABDOMINAL PAIN; GROIN PAIN.

LOSS OF SKIN COLOUR
See SKIN, DEPIGMENTATION OF.

LUMPS
See BONE LUMPS; BREAST LUMP; NECK LUMP; SKIN PAPULES.

MALABSORPTION
Malabsorption means that although you are eating enough, your system is not absorbing sufficient nutrients. Consequently despite an adequate diet, you lose weight and are generally unwell. There are many diseases which can cause the condition, perhaps the commonest of which is coeliac disease. People who have this disease have an in-built intolerance to wheat flour which causes the lining of the small

intestine to be damaged and this in turn means that fat cannot be absorbed, leading to a wasting away.

There are many rare diseases that cause malabsorption, but some other common causes include an overactive thyroid gland, cystic fibrosis, Crohn's disease and diabetes. It may also be a side effect of some drugs and radiation therapy for cancer.

See also DIARRHOEA.

MALNUTRITION
See APPETITE LOSS; FAILURE TO THRIVE (IN BABIES); WEIGHT LOSS, ABNORMAL.

MELAENA
See ANAL BLEEDING; BOWEL MOVEMENTS, ABNORMAL COLOUR OF.

MEMORY LOSS (AMNESIA)
Most of us suffer from a loss of memory from time to time, usually when we especially want to bring something to mind. Difficulty in remembering individual events and facts is normally simple absent-mindedness and can be cured by a greater effort at concentration. Difficulty in remembering whole periods of time, however, is amnesia and may be a symptom of something more serious. If you have had a blow to the head and cannot remember the period immediately before or after the accident, you should get medical help immediately as it may be a sign of brain injury.

Emotional stress can affect the ability to concentrate and therefore may lead to memory difficulties of even quite long periods. Depressive illnesses can be particularly to blame.

If you find you have forgotten the events surrounding a severe feverish illness, the period before or after an operation, or a diabetic coma or epileptic seizure, this is quite common and is usually no cause for concern.

A deteriorating memory is common as we grow older and usually means no more than that we have to write things down. If the loss of memory is associated with other signs of deterioration, however, such as personality change, difficulty in coping with everyday matters, a decline in personal hygiene and the like, it may be a symptom of Alzheimer's disease.

Certain medications, especially those used for sleeping problems can cause lapses of memory. If these are troublesome, discuss them with your doctor.

MENORRHAGIA
See MENSTRUAL PERIOD PROBLEMS.

MENSTRUAL PERIOD PROBLEMS
Once a month, just after a woman releases the egg (at ovulation) from her ovary, the lining of the womb (uterus) is at its peak to allow the embedding of a fertilised egg. If pregnancy does not occur, the lining of the womb starts to deteriorate as the hormones that sustain it in peak condition alter. After a few days, the lining (endometrium) breaks down completely, sloughs off the wall of the uterus, and is washed away by the blood released from the arteries that supplied it, and a menstrual period occurs. Contractions of the uterus also help remove the debris. After 3 to 5 days, the bleeding stops, and a new lining starts to develop, ready for the next month's ovulation. This very complex process can easily be disrupted so that the woman experiences excessive pain, heavy bleeding or very frequent periods. Some women are unlucky to suffer two or all three of these problems simultaneously.

Amenorrhoea is a lack of periods, dysmenorrhoea is painful periods, polymenorrhoea is frequent periods, and heavy periods are called menorrhagia. Polymenorrhagia is the technical term for frequent and excessively heavy periods. Metrorrhagia covers all possibilities and describes heavy, frequent, irregular and often painful periods.

Amenorrhoea, primary (failure of periods to start, delayed puberty)

Most girls commence their menstrual periods between 12 and 14 years of age, but they may start as early as ten or as late as 16. Over the last century, the average age of puberty in girls has dropped by 18 months in western countries due to better general health, hygiene and nutrition. In third-world countries today, the age of puberty is significantly higher than in the average Australian girl.

Any girl who has not started her periods by 15 should be checked by a doctor. In most cases all is well, and reassurance and more time are the only treatments necessary. In a small number of cases, a significant reason for the failure of the periods to start may be found. These reasons vary from chromosomal abnormalities that have been present since birth (e.g. Turner's syndrome, genital malformations) and ovarian disease to tumours of the pituitary gland in the brain or of the brain itself. The treatment in these circumstances will depend on the cause, but birth defects usually cannot be corrected.

Amenorrhoea, secondary (stopping of periods)

Once a woman has started her periods, the only natural reasons for them to stop are that she is pregnant, breastfeeding, or has reached the menopause. Other reasons for the periods stopping include prolonged and strenuous exercise (athletes undertaking rigorous training sometimes find that their periods stop), inadequate nutrition and psychiatric conditions such as anorexia nervosa. Drugs such as steroids, hormone therapy and the contraceptive pill can also lead to the cessation of periods.

Periods may also stop because of lifestyle changes such as moving house, travelling, or working a different shift. This is because the body regards a major change from normal as not conducive to reproduction, so the controlling mechanism in the brain switches off the reproductive ability. Periods normally return once the woman has adjusted to the new regime.

Less common causes for secondary amenorrhoea include hormonal disorders, tumours or cysts of the ovaries, and turmours in other parts of the body.

Any woman whose periods stop for more than two months should see a doctor to eliminate any serious cause.

Dysmenorrhoea (painful periods)

Painful periods are caused by excessive contractions of the uterus or by passing clots of blood. The cramping pain resulting from such contractions can be so severe that the woman is completely disabled, very distressed, and requires potent pain-killers. The pain often starts 12 to 24 hours before the bleeding and usually settles within a day of the bleeding starting. It may be accompanied by nausea, vomiting and a bloated feeling in the pelvis. It is much more common in teenagers than older women, and it is uncommon after a pregnancy.

Painful periods that develop when they were previously painless may be a symptom of pelvic inflammatory disease, tumours of the uterus, fibroids of the uterus or endometriosis (see Section 5). Some women find that the intra-uterine device (IUD) aggravates both painful periods and heavy periods.

There are many different treatment regimes available for period pain, depending upon the attitudes and needs of the individual woman. The oral contraceptive pill can be used for all forms of period problems, as it modifies the body's natural hormone balance into an artificial but beneficial balance. Some experimentation may be necessary to find the pill that gives the correct hormonal balance, but once this is done, the periods should be regular, light, and free of pain. The pain can also be eased by mefenamic acid, indomethacin, hormone-blocking agents, nifedipine or pain-killers (see Section 6), but none of these should be used without discussing the problem with a doctor. In very resistant cases, a uterine curettage (dilation and curettage — see SURGERY, Section 6) to clean out the contents of the uterus may be beneficial.

Period pain can usually be treated, and no woman should try to struggle on without help.

Menorrhagia (excessively heavy periods)

The amount of bleeding during a period varies considerably from woman to woman, but the fact that the bleeding is heavy does not necessarily signal that there is anything wrong. Excessively heavy bleeding, especially if it is a change from the normal pattern, may indicate the presence of some problem.

Women with menorrhagia have a normal cycle length but excessively heavy and prolonged periods. Some women suffer massive blood loss for up to ten days, passing clots, and losing so much blood that it is impossible for them to leave home or undertake normal activities. This blood loss can cause significant anaemia, tiredness and weakness if left untreated.

Menorrhagia is usually caused by ovarian conditions such as a cyst or tumour that causes an imbalance between the two female hormones (oestrogen and progesterone), but it may also be due to an abnormality of the uterus itself, such as the formation of fibroids within the uterine muscle wall (see UTERINE FIBROIDS, Section 5), infections in the pelvis, nervous tension, excess alcohol intake, or the presence of an IUD. In older women, heavy periods may indicate the start of the menopause.

Once again, the oral contraceptive pill can be used to control the problem by altering the woman's hormonal balance. As an alternative, other hormones (e.g. norethisterone, a progestogen) can also be used for the last half of the monthly cycle to reduce the amount of material and blood lost during the period. In severe cases in older women, particularly where there is an abnormality of the uterus, a hysterectomy may be the best available option.

Polymenorrhoea (frequent periods)

Women with polymenorrhoea have normal pain-free periods, but they occur very frequently. It is not considered to be a problem unless the periods occur more often than every 24 days, and treatment is often reserved for those women in which it occurs more often than once every three weeks.

It is important to distinguish from polymenorrhoea, the small break-through bleed that may occur at the time of ovulation in the middle of some women's monthly cycle. These mid-cycle bleeds are usually only 12 to 36 hours in length, and are characterised by minimal blood loss. A similar break-through bleed can occur while taking an oral contraceptive pill that is too low in hormone dose for that woman.

Frequent periods can be caused by a disturbance to the pituitary gland under the brain, which is releasing the ovary-stimulating hormones at the incorrect time. In other women, damaged ovaries (e.g. due to cysts) may be the cause of polymenorrhoea.

The only practical treatment for polymenorrhoea is the oral contraceptive pill, as this can hold the hormone levels at an artificially high level until the period is desired (usually every 28 days). If the woman objects to the use of the pill, other hormones may be used, but they are not generally as effective.

The problem of treating women with menstrual period problems who are trying to become pregnant is quite difficult, but if a pregnancy is achieved, the problem often does not recur when the periods return at the cessation of breastfeeding.

See also ENDOMETRIOSIS; PREMENSTRUAL TENSION SYNDROME, Section 5.

MOUTH, DRY

There are numerous salivary glands in the mouth which produce the liquid that starts the digestive process and helps us swallow. Under some circumstances the secretion of saliva is reduced, in which case your mouth will feel dry. This may be caused by drugs or poisons, following radiation therapy for cancer, or it may be a symptom of disease. A high fever is a common cause of a dry mouth.

A condition sometimes indicated by a dry mouth is Sjögren's syndrome in which the salivary glands waste away. This may be associated with rheumatoid arthritis, in which the eyes will normally lose their normal lubricating fluid as well and become dry. Botulism, a severe and often fatal form of food poisoning, is also characterised by a dry mouth.

The most common cause of a dry mouth, however, is prescription drugs, especially antihistamines (used in cold remedies) and those used to treat depression.

MOUTH PIGMENTATION

A healthy mouth is a reddish pink colour. If it takes on a dark hue, it can sometimes signal a hormone imbalance resulting from malfunctioning adrenal glands or a hereditary disorder in which too much iron is absorbed by the body. A malignant melanoma may appear as a black patch in the mouth.

MOUTH, SORE

A sore mouth can have many causes, including gum inflammation and ulcers, the herpes virus infection leading to a cold sore in the surrounding area, and an allergy to cosmetics. General ill health can lead to the mucous membrane lining the mouth becoming inflamed and sore. A sore mouth with white patches on the tongue or inside the cheeks is an infection called thrush. It sometimes results from antibiotics and can be treated with antifungals.

Tobacco, spices and some drugs can lead to mouth inflammation, while jagged teeth or poorly fitting dentures can result in abrasion or injury. Another cause of a sore mouth can be the formation of a stone in the salivary glands or a cyst associated with the salivary glands under the tongue.

Together with other more significant symptoms, a sore mouth can accompany several diseases, including leukaemia, anaemia due to vitamin deficiency, and tuberculosis. A swollen tongue and bleeding gums is a symptom of scurvy.

See also GUM PAIN; MOUTH ULCERS.

MOUTH, SWOLLEN

A swollen mouth is generally due to an allergy of the type that produces hives. Usually it is a reaction to certain foods such as shellfish or strawberries. Its medical name is angioneurotic oedema, and in it the tissues under the skin swell up at the affected area, particularly on the face. In severe cases the skin around the eyes, the lips and tongue swell enormously. This is serious because the swelling may spread to the throat in which case breathing can become obstructed. Urgent medical attention is essential.

See also SALIVARY GLANDS, PAINFUL OR SWOLLEN.

Mouth ulcers

Mouth ulcers may form as a result of a scratch or injury to the inside of the mouth, or for no apparent reason. Small ulcers can be extremely painful but are usually harmless and heal without medical treatment. There are various remedies available from the chemist that may relieve the pain and assist the healing process.

A cold sore is an ulcer on the lip caused by the herpes virus. Generally this is difficult to treat and time is the only remedy.

Occasionally mouth ulcers are associated with diseases such as leukaemia, glandular fever, pernicious anaemia, diphtheria and cancer.

Movements, abnormal

See CONVULSIONS; JERKING MOVEMENTS; TIC; TREMOR; WRITHING MOVEMENTS.

Muscle pain (myalgia)

There are about 650 muscles in the body and some of them will almost inevitably cause pain at some stage of your life. If you undertake any unusual activity with muscles you have not used for a while, such as a new sport or exercise or gardening, you will generally feel sore and stiff for a few days.

If a muscle cramps, it will generally cause acute pain. This will subside as the cramp disappears, but sometimes it can take what seems like an agonisingly long time. Pain will also be caused if you strain or pull a muscle, or if a muscle becomes inflamed, or because of muscular rheumatism.

A great many infections cause muscles to ache, such as flu, hepatitis, encephalitis, malaria, measles and several others. Muscle aches and pains can also result from kidney disorders and underactivity of the parathyroid gland (situated near the thyroid). Some drugs to combat high blood pressure can give rise to aching muscles.

Much muscle pain can be treated with a warm bath and pain-killers. However, unless the pain subsides quickly, you should see a doctor to investigate the cause.

Muscle spasm

The most common muscle spasm is a cramp, which is a sharp stitch-like pain. Muscle cramp often occurs as a result of cold, or it may strike while in bed, especially in older people (see CRAMPS, MUSCULAR).

In a severe spasm, the muscles are more firmly contracted than in cramp. Spasms may occur if the chemistry of the body is upset by an infection such as tetanus or acute pancreatitis (inflammation of the pancreas), or a poison such as strychnine. Spasms also typically occur in people who engage in repetitive movements such as operating a word processor, or who write (writer's cramp). Muscle spasm is also often associated with epileptic seizures.

See also CONVULSIONS; JERKING MOVEMENTS; TIC; TREMOR.

Muscle wasting

Muscles will waste away if they are not used. Anyone who has had an injured limb in plaster for a period of time will usually be shocked at the reduction in size of the muscles when the plaster is removed. Usually the muscles will regain their former size quite quickly once they are back in use, perhaps with some extra exercise.

Muscle wasting (atrophy) is associated with various diseases such as poliomyelitis as well as several conditions grouped together under the heading of muscular dystrophy (see Section 5).

Muscle weakness
See PARALYSIS.

Myalgia
See MUSCLE PAIN.

Nail abnormalities

Nails are the hard protective tissue that grows on the end of the furthermost extremities of our body, our fingers and toes. They often seem inconsequential compared with other organs and yet doctors can frequently tell a great deal about a patient simply by looking at the nails. Everything from compulsive nail-biting, to anaemia, lung disease, heart trouble and infection can be diagnosed from the nails.

The existence of transverse white bands going across the nails indicates a deficiency of a protein called albumin. It is usually caused by a serious infection, illness, or by various drugs used in the treatment of cancer, but if this does not apply, someone may be trying to poison you with arsenic!

Brittle nails are usually something we are born with, but they may be exacerbated by constantly putting our hands in water, especially if there are also detergents and harsh chemicals. Brittle nails are sometimes a sign of an over- or underactive thyroid gland.

The normal colour for healthy nails is pink, reflecting the liberal blood supply to the skin beneath. A discoloured nail is usually a sign that something is amiss. Discoloured nails can be black, brown, blue, yellow, white or red. The causes may be as simple as slamming your finger in the door so that bleeding under the skin causes the nail to turn black, or the familiar brown stain on the fingernails of a heavy smoker, to the presence of some underlying disorder such as hepatitis (yellow nails), disease of the kidneys (brown nails), anaemia (pale or whitish nails), or heart failure (red half-moons). Bluish nails mean that there is not enough oxygen in the blood. In babies this can be due to a congenital heart condition (so-called blue babies) which needs surgery. In an adult it may mean they have been exposed to poisonous chemicals, or if you

TABLE 3.1:
NAIL ABNORMALITIES

Abnormality	Possible causes
Bands across nails	Severe infections, steroid therapy, cancer drugs, arsenic.
Black nail	Bleeding under nail, melanoma, recurrent infection of nail.
Blue nails	Cyanosis from inadequate blood or oxygen supply, heart disease, copper, mepacrine or chloroquine poisoning.
Brown nails	Nicotine or other chemical stains, kidney failure, psoriasis, Addison's disease, silver or mercury poisoning.
Curved nail (finger clubbing)	Severe heart or lung disease, Crohn's disease, hereditary.
Green nail	Fungal or bacterial infection under nail.
Lifting nail (not attached at the end)	Injury, fungal infections, psoriasis, eczema, Raynaud's phenomenon, diabetes, poor circulation of blood, thyroid disease.
Pitted nails	Psoriasis, recurrent nail infections, eczema of fingers.
Red nail	Bleeding under nail, cold exposure.
Red nail half moons	Heart failure.
Ridges across nail	Eczema, recurrent nail bed infections, nails irritated by soaps and detergents, severe period problems.
Ridges along nail	Cysts of nail bed, poor blood supply to nail, common in elderly.
Single ridge across nail	Episode of severe physical or emotional illness.
Spoon-shaped nails	Iron deficiency.
Thickened nail	Recurrent injury, tight shoes, fungal infection, psoriasis, old age.
White nails	Liver disease, severe anaemia, cancer drugs, arsenic.
Yellow nails	Jaundice from hepatitis or liver failure, fungal infection, tetracycline antibiotics.

are short of breath and coughing, you might have a heart or lung problem and should see a doctor as soon as possible. A black spot under a nail may also be caused by a malignant melanoma.

Pitted or dimpled nails may indicate psoriasis of the nails — a disorder that also appears as white scaly patches on the skin.

A thick ridge going across the nails is usually a sign that you've had a period of ill-health in the not too distant past. While you were ill, the nail stopped growing so that it thickened, and this thick band then moves up as the nail starts growing again. Ridges going up and down may simply be a sign of getting older but they can also indicate various diseases such as diabetes or a poor blood supply to the finger.

If the skin around or underneath the nail is swollen, inflamed and painful, and especially if your hands are in water a lot, you may have an infection called paronychia. This can generally be treated with creams and wearing rubber gloves.

A nail, especially a toenail that is discoloured, thickened and flaky, is usually an indication that a fungal infection is present. Thick, distorted nails can also result from a number of diseases, ranging from a vitamin deficiency to thickening of the walls of the arteries.

Small white flecks in the nails are usually caused by air pockets and of no medical significance.

The causes of a wide range of nail abnormalities have been summarised in table form.

Nausea and vomiting

There would be few people who have not experienced nausea and vomiting at some stage of their lives. The two frequently accompany one another because nausea, a sick or queasy feeling in the stomach, is usually relieved by vomiting, eliminating the contents of the stomach. Basically it is the body's way of getting rid of something it would rather not have.

Vomiting occurs when the stomach, and sometimes the upper part of the small intestine, goes into spasm and discharges its contents via the oesophagus and mouth for a wide variety of reasons. Some causes are common and innocuous but others may indicate serious disease.

By far the most common reason to feel sick and vomit is a toxin irritating the gut. This is food poisoning, and a contaminated prawn, sausage or other foodstuff is usually responsible. The vomiting occurs two to eight hours after eating the food and is usually sudden, violent and short-lived. It is unusual for the problem to persist more than a few hours, and is only occasionally accompanied by diarrhoea.

Gastroenteritis is another very common cause of nausea and vomiting. In this a virus enters the stomach causing it to become inflamed. In this state it secretes excessive amounts of digestive juices and can go into spasm very easily, particularly if any further food is eaten. Initially the upper part of the gut is affected, and as the virus moves down through the digestive system, the large bowel is involved. When the gut goes into spasm, its contents are expelled through the nearest appropriate opening causing vomiting and/or diarrhoea, and may be associated with painful abdominal cramps.

Nausea and vomiting often accompany migraine-type headaches. Sometimes the migraine actually eases after vomiting.

Overindulgence in food and alcohol is another cause of nausea and vomiting. Sometimes it is due to an allergy to certain foodstuffs, for example shellfish, eggs or pork.

Anything that disturbs our sense of balance, for example motion sickness (see TRAVEL MEDICINE, Section 7) or Ménière's disease (a disorder of the middle ear), can make us feel nauseated.

It is possible to feel sick simply at the sight, the smell or even the thought of something, for example putrefied food or extreme violence, or perhaps images on the nightly television news of especially horrible injuries.

Many other conditions from meningitis and stomach cancer to liver disease and pregnancy may be associated with vomiting. If you are suffering and it does not settle rapidly, have the cause investigated and treated by your family doctor.

Neck lump

Lumps in the neck are usually due to enlarged lymph glands. This might be because of a sore throat or because you have had a visit to the dentist, or you have an infection such as mumps, rubella (German measles) or glandular fever. A lump in the front of the neck is usually due to an enlarged thyroid gland (see GOITRE).

Various cysts and tumours may also be felt as a lump in the neck. There may not be any pain associated with these; you will most likely become aware of them when shaving or applying make-up. Any unexplained lump should be investigated promptly.

Neck pain

Apart from someone or something we don't like very much, a pain in the neck has several causes. If swallowing hurts on the outside rather than in the throat, you may have an inflamed thyroid. If the pain is not in the front but on either side of the neck, the large arteries carrying blood to the brain (the carotid arteries) may be inflamed. If your glands are swollen the pain will usually be due to infection (see GLANDS, SWOLLEN). Tension or sitting or sleeping for long periods in an uncomfortable position can lead to a stiff neck which may last for several days. If you are developing arthritis in the upper part of your spine, your neck will feel stiff and be difficult to move freely.

See also NECK LUMP.

Nipple discharge

If you have a whitish or greenish discharge from your nipples, you have probably just had a baby or are just about to have one and the discharge is breast milk. If you are breast feeding, leaking breast milk is likely to be a frequent occurrence.

In rare cases, such discharge occurs at other times in women and sometimes even in men. It may not look like milk, but is simply a watery discharge of white, clear or greenish fluid. It is called galactorrhoea (literally 'too much milk'). In women it may be a result of taking the pill. Galactorrhoea may also be caused by other hormone imbalances or because of certain tranquillisers. It can sometimes be a symptom of a disorder of the pituitary gland, such as a tumour, so have it checked out by a doctor.

Any dark coloured discharge (usually dark red or black), especially if it comes only from one nipple should be reported immediately to a doctor. It is probably due to a blood discharge caused by a small benign growth called a duct papilloma, but it might be a sign of breast cancer.

Nipple lump
See BREAST LUMP.

Nipple pain
See BREAST PAIN.

Nodules
See SKIN PAPULES.

Section 3: Symptoms

Noise, abdominal
See ABDOMINAL NOISES, EXCESSIVE.

Noise in ears
See EAR NOISES.

Nosebleed (epistaxis)
Some people seem prone to a bleeding nose; other people rarely, if ever, experience one. The nose bleeds easily because, in order to warm the air breathed in, the blood vessels lining the nasal cavity are very close to the surface; consequently they can be damaged easily.

Nosebleeds seem to occur from time to time in many children, often for no apparent reason. Some children have a habit of pushing things up their nose, which may damage the blood vessels and cause it to bleed.

The most common cause of a nosebleed is an injury to the nose or blowing your nose too vigorously. You will usually only need medical treatment if it won't stop. Hot, dry weather may cause the nose to dry out, crack and bleed.

Nosebleed can accompany various diseases ranging from local infections in which the mucous lining of the nose is inflamed, to rheumatic fever, measles, and polyps or tumours in the nose. High blood pressure can cause the tiny blood vessels to rupture and start to bleed.

If you are a mountain climber or thinking of a holiday trekking in Nepal you may find a bleeding nose one of the hazards of going into a high altitude.

See also Section 8.

Nose discharge
The most likely reason your nose is discharging is because you have a cold, sinusitis or the flu. When the infection enters through the nose, the mucus secreted in the nasal passages increases to try to fight it off, and your nose becomes stuffed up and runny. You will usually also feel headachy and generally below par, perhaps a bit feverish. The infection may spread to your sinuses or adenoids.

If you have been sneezing and have a runny nose with none of the other symptoms of a cold, and the discharge is clear rather than thick and cloudy, your runny nose may be due to an allergy. You will probably have itchy red eyes as well.

Polyps, foreign bodies in the nose and nasal tumours can all cause a discharge. Sometimes more general diseases involve a running nose, especially in the early stages, but there will usually be other symptoms as well to suggest that you see a doctor.

Nose, obstructed
A constantly obstructed nose with which you find it hard to breathe normally is generally the result of an overgrowth of the glandular tissue at the back of the nose forming the adenoids. This mostly occurs in children who typically go around with their mouth open and talk in a 'nasal' way. Usually the condition rights itself during the teens. In extreme cases, however, if the child finds it hard to hear and is subject to constant attacks of bronchitis because of always breathing through the mouth, the adenoids will probably be removed surgically — a relatively simple matter. The tonsils will probably also prove to be enlarged and may be removed at the same time.

Soft jelly-like growths called polyps sometimes obstruct breathing through the nose. These can be removed comparatively easily, although they tend to recur and the process may have to be repeated several times before they finally disappear.

Malignant tumours are very rare in the nose but occur occasionally. They are hard to the touch, unlike a soft polyp.

Numbness
See PAIN SENSATION, LACK OF; PINS AND NEEDLES SENSATION.

Obesity
If you are more than 20% above the recommended weight for your particular height, you are considered obese (see table under WEIGHT-REDUCING DIETS, Section 7). Obesity results mostly from eating more than your body needs for its energy requirements. Occasionally it is a sign that there is something wrong with one of the organs concerned with how the body functions, e.g. an underactive thyroid or a disorder of the hypothalamus (the part of the brain controlling many body functions, including thirst, hunger and eating, and water balance). For treatment of obesity, see Section 5.

Excessive weight gain can also be a symptom of a disease called Cushing's syndrome in which there is an overproduction of steroid hormones in the body. People with this disease typically have a puffy moon face.

See also WEIGHT GAIN, ABNORMAL.

Oedema
Oedema is abnormal accumulation of fluid beneath the skin or in the body cavities. It is also known as dropsy. It may be a symptom of a disease, or the result of an injury, a deficiency in the diet, or of taking some kinds of drugs.

Probably the most common occurrence is oedema of the ankles. If you are on your feet a great deal you may find your ankles are puffy. This is not serious and the swelling will usually subside with adequate rest. Some women find that their ankles swell before their period. Severe ankle swelling should be reported to a doctor, as it maybe a symptom of disease of the heart, kidneys, lungs or other major organs. Oedema in pregnancy is also common but should be reported to a doctor if the swelling does not go down with rest.

In diseases of the kidneys, such as nephritis or Bright's disease, the ankles may be puffy or there may be swelling around the eyes, and accumulation of fluid may also occur in other parts of the body.

Tissues may also swell because of starvation, an allergic reaction, or drugs, especially the cortisone-based drugs.

See also ASCITES; MOUTH, SWOLLEN.

Oliguria
See URINE, LACK OF.

Ovary Pain
See PELVIC PAIN.

Overeating
See APPETITE, EXCESSIVE; WEIGHT GAIN, ABNORMAL.

Overweight
See OBESITY; WEIGHT GAIN, ABNORMAL.

Pain
See ABDOMINAL PAIN; ANAL PAIN; ARM PAIN; BACK PAIN; BREAST PAIN; BREATHING, DIFFICULTY IN; CHEST PAIN; CRAMPS, MUSCULAR; EARACHE; EYE PAIN; FACIAL PAIN; FOOT PAIN; GROIN PAIN; GUM PAIN; HAND PAIN; HEADACHE; HIP PAIN; KNEE PAIN; LEG PAIN; LOIN PAIN; MENSTRUAL PERIOD PROBLEMS; MOUTH, SORE; MUSCLE PAIN; NECK PAIN; PELVIC PAIN; PENIS PAIN; PREGNANCY, PAIN DURING; SALIVARY GLANDS, PAINFUL OR SWOLLEN; SHOULDER PAIN; SKIN PAIN; TESTICLES, PAINFUL OR SWOLLEN; THROAT, SORE; TOE, PAINFUL; TONGUE, SORE; TOOTHACHE; URINE, PAINFUL PASSING OF; VISION, PAIN WITH BRIGHT LIGHT.

Pain Sensation, Lack of (Anaesthesia)

When we talk about anaesthesia, we usually mean the deliberate suspension of feeling by the use of drugs for an operation. Medically, however, anaesthesia means loss of sensation for any reason.

The involuntary loss of the sensations of touch, pain, temperature or vibration, not deliberately induced, will usually be regarded seriously by a doctor since it means that there is some interference with the nervous system. This may be a symptom of injury to or disease of the brain or spinal cord. Sometimes it can be caused by disease or blockage of an artery, or by a disc in the spine having slipped out of place so that it pinches a nerve. Diabetes can cause a loss of sensation in the peripheral nerves (those other than the ones in the brain and spinal cord), as can alcohol and leprosy. Sometimes sensation is inhibited because of drug use.

Pallor (Pale Skin)

A healthy skin reflects a good supply of red blood cells and is a pinkish colour. However, a pale skin is not necessarily a sign that there is anything wrong. Some people are pale because they don't go outside very often or because they were born that way, e.g. Swedes and Danes are normally pale compared with Italians or Spaniards. Extreme pallor, however, perhaps accompanied by pale lips, palms of the hands and various other parts of the body that are coloured even in people of pale complexion, is due to a reduced flow of blood or a lack of red blood cells. This may be nothing more significant than that you have just had a nasty shock or are unduly tired or have a hangover. But if you have a persistent pallor and you feel generally unwell in other respects, you are probably anaemic. This may be for any one of many reasons, ranging from malnutrition or loss of too much blood during your period to cancer. If you are constantly pale and unwell, or if you have noticed that you are short of breath or have heart palpitations, have a checkup by a doctor.

Palpitations

A feeling that your heart is beating irregularly can be extremely uncomfortable. It is often of no great medical significance and may be due to anxiety or stress, or to the substances in tea, coffee, cola drinks or tobacco. Sometimes, however, the atrial chambers of the heart beat rapidly and chaotically, making it impossible for the heart to maintain its normal regular beat. This is called atrial fibrillation and needs medical attention. The main causes are atherosclerosis (narrowing of the arteries because of fatty deposits on the walls), chronic rheumatic heart disease, and heart disease resulting from high blood pressure. It can also be a complication of other conditions, including chest infections and an overactive thyroid. A generalised infection or fever can also cause palpitations, as can the menopause.

See also HEART, IRREGULAR RHYTHM, Section 5.

Papules

See SKIN PAPULES.

Paraesthesia

See PINS AND NEEDLES.

Paralysis

The inability to move, or paralysis, can have numerous causes, such as a blow on the head, a brain tumour, a stroke, a disorder of the nervous system such as multiple sclerosis or poliomyelitis, muscular disease, bone disease, thyroid disease, severe food poisoning, and the sexually transmitted disease syphilis.

If one side of the face is paralysed, it may be due to a stroke or a brain tumour, or to a condition called Bell's palsy which is caused by an inflammation of the facial nerve as it leaves the skull. The facial distortion caused by Bell's palsy is often unpleasant to have to live with, but the condition is usually not permanent and gets better after a few weeks. The distinguishing feature between a stroke and Bell's palsy is normally that you can close your eye on the affected side of the face if you have had a stroke, but not if you are suffering from Bell's palsy.

If you become paralysed in any part of your body, you should get immediate medical attention.

See also PARAPLEGIA AND QUADRIPLEGIA.

PARAPLEGIA AND QUADRIPLEGIA

In paraplegia the legs and the lower part of the body are paralysed; in quadriplegia all four limbs are paralysed. The most common cause of both conditions is injury to the spine and the spinal cord. If the spinal cord is severed, the entire nervous system below that point is made inoperative, and there is no way the affected part of the body can function. The nerves can never be repaired. The cause of paraplegia or quadriplegia may also sometimes be disease or infection of the spinal cord, including cancer and multiple sclerosis.

See also PARALYSIS.
See also Section 5.

PARESIS
See PARALYSIS.

PELVIC PAIN

The pelvis is the bony structure that connects the legs with the spine. It consists of the hip bones on each side and the sacrum and coccyx, or tail bone, behind. In the front is the pubic bone. The bladder and rectum lie inside the pelvis, together with, in men, the seminal vesicle sex glands and the prostate. In women, the pelvis contains the ovaries and the womb. Pelvic pain can relate to any of these parts.

A common cause of pelvic pain in women, especially young women, is pelvic inflammatory disease (PID). This occurs when an infection invades the uterus and spreads to the Fallopian tubes, ovaries and surrounding tissues. If you have severe pain and tenderness in the lower abdomen, and possibly feel feverish, you should see a doctor since PID is the likely cause. If the pain is mild but recurrent, you may have a chronic form of the disease.

Other causes of pelvic pain are periods, a miscarriage, ectopic pregnancy, endometriosis, appendicitis, constipation and cancer.

In both men and women, pelvic pain should be investigated by a doctor, since there are so many possible reasons for its occurrence.

See also ABDOMINAL PAIN; PREGNANCY, PAIN DURING.

PENIS PAIN

The average male is extremely sensitive about anything to do with his penis, particularly if it hurts. The most common reason for a sore penis is an injury of one kind or another, not infrequently relating to overenthusiastic sexual practices. Another common source of pain is genital herpes. There will usually be five or six days of burning, itching or pain at the site of infection, followed by the outbreak of the actual blisters. When these close over and heal, the pain disappears. Once the herpes virus has taken hold, it remains in the system and the attacks may recur, although some people have no further symptoms for months or years, or occasionally forever.

Other causes of penile pain are inflammation of the prostate gland, various sexually transmitted diseases such as non-specific urethritis and gonorrhoea, and, less frequently, cancer of the penis and an auto-immune disease (a disease in which the body's own antibodies attack the tissues) known as Reiter's syndrome which causes aching joints and red eyes as well. If a man is uncircumcised, an infection under the foreskin can produce a swollen painful penis.

Occasionally for various reasons, a man's penis remains persistently erect. This is called priapism and is an extremely painful condition.

See also URETHRAL DISCHARGE; URINE, PAINFUL PASSING OF.

PENIS PROBLEMS
See EJACULATION, LACK OF; IMPOTENCE; PENIS PAIN; URETHRAL DISCHARGE; URINE, PAINFUL PASSING OF.

PERIOD PROBLEMS
See MENSTRUAL PERIOD PROBLEMS.

PETECHIA
See SKIN, BLEEDING INTO.

PHOBIA
See FEAR.

PHOTOPHOBIA
See VISION, PAIN WITH BRIGHT LIGHT.

PHOTOSENSITIVE
See SKIN, SUN-SENSITIVE.

PIGMENTATION
See MOUTH PIGMENTATION; SKIN, DEPIGMENTATION OF; SKIN PIGMENTATION.

PINS AND NEEDLES SENSATION (PARAESTHESIA)
A sensation of numbness and prickling is something we all experience from time to time. It indicates that the blood supply to a nerve has been interrupted, usually because a limb has been in an awkward position, e.g. if you sleep with an arm underneath part of your body. Once the pressure is removed, feeling should return to normal in a few moments.

If pins and needles become frequent, it may be a sign of a nervous disorder, either physical or psychiatric, and you should check with your doctor. If your hands are affected and you have a stiff neck, you may have cervical osteoarthritis, a disorder of the nerves and bones in the neck. Sharp pains in the hands suggest the possibility of carpal tunnel syndrome, a disorder of the nerves passing through the wrist.

Types of anaemia, diabetes, kidney failure and some drugs can also be responsible for pins and needles. More exotic causes can be beri-beri (a deficiency of vitamin B1, widespread in rice-eating communities), rabies, leprosy, and ciguatera (poisoning by tropical fish).

POLYDIPSIA
See THIRST, EXCESSIVE.

POLYURIA
See URINE, EXCESSIVE OR FREQUENT.

PREGNANCY, BLEEDING DURING
See PREGNANCY COMPLICATIONS, Section 1.

PREGNANCY, PAIN DURING
Many pregnant women suffer varying degrees of pain which may be exceedingly

uncomfortable but not medically significant. Two of the most common types of pain are backache and heartburn (see NORMAL PREGNANCY, Section 1).

Abdominal pain early in pregnancy may also signal significant complications, such as a miscarriage or an ectopic pregnancy.

Premonition
See AURA; DEJA VU.

Priapism
See PENIS PAIN.

Pruritus
See ITCH.

Ptosis
See EYELID, DROOPING.

Puberty, delayed
The age at which puberty is reached depends on many factors, individual and inherited. Girls tend to follow the pattern of their mothers, i.e., a girl whose mother started her periods late is likely to be later than average herself.

Girls generally reach puberty between the ages of ten to twelve, boys a year or two later than this. However, the range is broad and generally there is no cause for concern unless maturity is delayed beyond the mid to late teens.

Reasons for a delay in the onset of puberty, other than normal inherited characteristics, can be generally poor health and nutrition, certain forms of drug treatment and, rarely, hormonal or chromosomal abnormalities.

See also Section 1.

Puberty, early
On occasions, puberty starts much earlier than normal. Just as with delayed puberty, there may be no special reason, other than individual variations. Girls as young as eight have been known to start their periods with no adverse inferences. Excessively early development may, however, be triggered by tumours affecting sexual functioning, hormone treatment, abnormal activity of the thyroid, pituitary or adrenal glands and various other causes.

See also Section 1.

Pulse, fast
See HEARTBEAT, FAST; PALPITATIONS.

Pulse, slow (bradycardia)
A very slow pulse or heartbeat (less than 60 per minute), can often be found in very fit athletes, in whom it is normal. In other people, an abnormally slow pulse can be a result of various medications to control high blood pressure, angina, a heart rhythm disorder, migraine and excessive anxiety. If you are not an athlete or on any likely medication, among other possible causes you may have an underactive thyroid, especially if you feel constantly tired and abnormally cold.

A very slow pulse may sometimes signal disease of the heart's natural electric pacemaker which regulates the rate at which the heart beats. This may lead to heart block, when the system fails, either partially or completely. Heart block can occur for no obvious reason, but is often associated with a heart attack caused by a thrombosis (clot) or blockage of one of the coronary arteries.

Purpura
See SKIN, BLEEDING INTO.

Pustules
See SKIN, PUSTULAR.

Section 3: Symptoms

Pyrexia
See FEVER.

Quadriplegia
See PARAPLEGIA AND QUADRIPLEGIA.

Rash
See SKIN RASH.

Renal pain
See LOIN PAIN.

Retention of urine
See URINE, INABILITY TO PASS.

Rigidity, muscular
See CONVULSIONS; MUSCLE SPASM.

Salivary glands, painful or swollen
Salivary glands are situated in our mouth to help us swallow and digest food. There are three pairs, one pair under the tongue, one pair in the lower jaw and one in the cheeks just in front of the ears. If the pair in the cheeks (the parotid glands) are sore and swollen, the most likely explanation is that you have caught the mumps. Mumps is often thought of as a childhood disease, as indeed it is, but not exclusively so. Adults are often stricken with it, and in them it can be a serious illness with unpleasant after effects. A parotid tumour or cancer also causes swelling, similar to mumps, but only on the affected side.

Your salivary glands can also become infected by bacteria, especially if you are run down or if one of your glands has been damaged by salivary duct stones. An infected salivary gland becomes swollen and painful, and the lymph glands in your neck underneath the jaw may also feel enlarged and tender. You may have a bitter taste caused by pus from the infected gland trickling into your mouth. A persistent infection can cause so much scarring in the gland that it can no longer function, so swelling in your mouth or around your chin or jaw should be attended to.

A salivary duct stone occurs when a minute particle of solid material becomes trapped in one of the glands and encrusted with chemicals and salts. When you eat, the saliva produced by the gland to moisten the food cannot get past the stone and so the gland swells up. The glands in the floor of the mouth are the most likely to be affected by this disorder, which usually occurs in middle-aged and elderly people.

See also MOUTH, SWOLLEN.

Scrotal pain
See TESTICLES, PAINFUL OR SWOLLEN.

Sensation, loss of
See PAIN SENSATION, LACK OF.

Sexual intercourse pain
See SEXUAL PROBLEMS, Section 5.

Sexual problems
See Section 5.

Shivering
The reason most of us shiver is because we are cold. Shivering generates heat in the muscles and so helps us to warm up. Shivering when the weather isn't cold however may be sign of disease.

Any infection involving a fever may cause you to feel alternately hot and cold with uncontrollable shivering during the bouts of cold. Some of the infections you may be going down with include the flu, pneumonia, tonsillitis, glandular fever, malaria or polio. Uncontrollable shivering may also be caused by withdrawal from addictive drugs such as heroin.

SHORTNESS OF BREATH
See BREATHING, DIFFICULTY IN.

SHORT STATURE
See GROWTH, REDUCED.

SHOULDER PAIN
Anyone with a painful shoulder should ask themselves whether they have injured it in the last 24 hours. If so, the pain may be due to a torn muscle, tendon or ligament, or a sprain.

If you cannot move the shoulder and it looks out of place, you have probably dislocated it. If the tissues around the joint are inflamed you may have bursitis, in which case pain will occur when you move your arm. If the shoulder has become increasingly stiff and painful over a period of weeks, you may have a frozen shoulder caused by inflammation of the tendons and tendon sheaths. This can take a long time to clear up. Sometimes following an injury, deposits of calcium form on a tendon causing severe discomfort. If you feel ill and your shoulder pain is accompanied by a temperature, you may have rheumatic fever. If you also have pain and swelling in other joints you may be suffering from rheumatoid arthritis.

Referred pain (that is pain that is caused by one part of the body but felt in another) may be felt in the shoulder. For example in some heart problems, pain starts in the left shoulder and spreads down to the fingertips. Referred pain in the shoulder can also be due to conditions such as ruptured ectopic pregnancy and perforated peptic ulcer, but with conditions such as those there are usually other symptoms as well.

SKIN, BLEEDING INTO (PURPURA)
There are a number of disorders in which blood leaks through the walls of the small blood vessels and into the skin. This causes a rash consisting of flat, dark red or purplish spots or blotches (petechiae). In one of the diseases called thrombocytopenia, the blood contains only about a third (or even less) of the platelets responsible for causing the blood to clot. This may occur for no known reason, because of drug or radiation therapy for cancer, or it may be a symptom of other blood disorders such as leukaemia (cancer of the white blood cells). In senile purpura, reddish-brown or purplish areas, sometimes as large as 5 cm across, appear on an elderly person. They may occur on any part of the body but are usually most noticeable on the legs, the forearms and the back of the hands. Other causes of bleeding into the skin may be allergies and certain vitamin deficiencies, for example lack of vitamin C, causing scurvy.

SKIN, BLISTERED
A blister is a small pouch occurring beneath the surface of the skin, filled with clear fluid consisting of serum, which is the watery component of blood. A blister is usually the result of some form of irritation, such as continuous friction (e.g. a shoe rubbing on a heel), or an insect bite, or excessive heat (including that from the sun) so that the skin is burned. Where blisters are not the result of external injury, they may be caused by an infection, such as the herpes virus (cold sores or shingles), chickenpox, and impetigo. Eczema may also cause a rash accompanied by small blisters that weep and become encrusted. Pemphigus is a condition that produces large blisters in babies or middle-aged and elderly people.

If a blister bursts it is liable to become

infected, so care should be taken to keep it clean and dry.

Skin, blue (cyanosis)

A normal healthy skin has a pinkish hue reflecting the bright red cells in normal blood. If the skin takes on a blue or purplish tinge, it indicates a lack of oxygen in the blood, possibly due to a disorder of the heart or lungs. If someone takes on a blue colour medical help should be sought immediately.

A so-called 'blue baby' is a baby whose lips and skin have a bluish tinge because of a heart defect present at birth, in which the blood is not pumped into the lungs as it should be, but bypasses them and does not receive the oxygen that it needs. These days this condition can usually be rectified by surgery.

Skin, depigmentation of (loss of skin colour)

The darkness or lightness of our skin depends on the amount of the pigment melanin it contains. In the main this is determined by our forbears and their racial origins. If your family migrated from Ireland you probably have a pink, freckled complexion, whereas if your parents hail from a Mediterranean country, your skin will be much darker.

Occasionally areas of skin lose their pigmentation in a condition called vitiligo. This may be a symptom of diabetes, a form of anaemia or a malfunctioning thyroid gland, but usually it has no connection with general health and its cause is unknown.

A few people are born with an absence of pigmentation in their skin, hair and eyes, so that they have an abnormally light skin and hair, with pinkish eyes. This is called albinism, and a person inheriting the condition is called an albino.

Pityriasis refers to a group of fungal skin diseases in which pink or very pale spots develop, usually on the trunk, mostly in young adults or adolescents. These spots of fungal infection prevent suntanning of the skin, so even after the infection is cured, white spots will remain.

Skin, itchy
See ITCH.

Skin pain

Since our skin is the first point of contact for whatever touches our body, anything that is likely to be harmful will usually cause the skin to react by registering pain as a protective mechanism. Extreme heat or extreme cold will be painful, as will acid that may burn. Sitting out in the sun for too long is one of the surest ways to suffer from painful skin. Sunburn varies from a reddening of the skin to the development of large painful blisters. If you are fair-skinned you are more vulnerable to being burned by the sun than if you are dark-skinned. A small isolated area of soreness on the skin usually means you have suffered an injury, such as a cut or a bruise.

Many skin disorders generate pain, although they more commonly lead to itchiness. If you are suffering from shingles, however, which affects the nerves as well as the surface of the skin, you can probably expect a considerable degree of pain.

Skin, pale
See PALLOR.

Skin papules

A papule is a small superficial raised abnormality or spot on the skin. There can be a number of causes ranging from insignificant to sinister. Acne is the most common cause of a papular rash. A xanthoma is a yellowish swelling in the skin resulting from a deposit of fat. It may indicate a raised blood cholesterol level. A basal cell carcinoma, or rodent ulcer, is a slow growing malignant tumour, often at the edge of the eyelids, lips or nostrils, or on the ears. These take a long time to spread but ultimately can be very descructive of nearby tissues and should be removed. The appearance of a dark coloured papule may be a malignant melanoma and should be investigated promptly. Molluscum contagiosum is a common viral infection of the skin that causes multiple small papules to appear.

Skin pigmentation

Normal skin has a skin colouring pigment called melanin. Sometimes the cells producing melanin are more numerous or more active than usual. This may lead to patches of skin with darker pigment than others.

A person who is born with an area of discoloured skin is said to have a birthmark. These can be tiny and almost unnoticeable, or they may be large and disfiguring, in which case plastic surgery when the child is older (over about three) may come to the rescue.

Moles are small dark areas of skin consisting of dense collections of melanin-producing cells. Occasionally a mole may be malignant; if you have a mole that changes its shape or size, see a doctor.

Seborrhoeic warts are patches of dark skin varying from 1-3 cm across. They have a crusty greasy surface and are common after middle age. Seborrhoeic warts are not contagious but are named for their wart-like appearance.

Certain diseases, e.g. Addison's disease (in which the adrenal glands do not produce enough steroid hormones), and some drugs can cause a person to develop a 'suntan' even though they haven't been out in the sun. If you develop a tan for no apparent reason you should see your doctor.

Hormone changes during pregnancy or while taking oral contraceptives cause some women to develop darker patches of skin on the face (chloasma). Cirrhosis of the liver can have a similar effect, and liver disease can also cause yellow skin (jaundice) due to bile salts being deposited in the skin.

Dark, almost black pigmentation in the gums is a sign of a disorder in which the intestines become studded with polyps from the stomach to the end of the colon. These are precancerous and usually have to be removed.

Skin, pustular

A rash on the skin consisting of raised spots filled with pus is a very common condition indeed. The simplest and most usual explanation is a blocked sebaceous (oil-producing) gland that has become infected and formed into a pimple. Pimples occurring in large numbers on the face, chest and back are usually described as acne, that scourge of adolescents. Itchy pus-filled spots may signify chicken pox. Other common skin disorders manifesting themselves in this way include shingles, cold sores (both caused by the herpes virus) and impetigo.

Skin rash

The eruption of a red area on the skin, typically with many small spots, can be caused by anything from nappy rash in babies to prickly heat, hives, an allergy rash, or an infectious disease (e.g. measles, rubella, scarlet fever or shingles). Sometimes a rash can simply be caused by emotional stress.

Various creams and lotions are available to soothe rashes. If a rash persists or is accompanied by a temperature, headache or a general feeling of being unwell, you should see a doctor.

Skin, red (erythema)

Abnormal skin redness is caused by the accumulation of blood in the blood vessels just below the surface of the skin. It can be due to various forms of dermatitis as well as almost all common skin disorders, including sunburn, hives and psoriasis. Bacterial infections of the skin (cellulitis) is a serious cause of skin redness that requires urgent medical attention.

Diseases of the tissue under the skin may cause redness, including gout, arthritis and an abscess. A high fever is a common cause of generalised skin redness, and exertion usually also causes the skin to redden to some extent.

See also SKIN RASH.

Skin, scaly

Scaly skin can vary from a few small patches to a generalised rash that covers most of the body. A fine scale may occur in association with red underlying skin in a wide range of conditions, including pityriasis versicolor (a fungal infection), eczema and psoriasis.

Ichthyosis is a condition in which the skin is dry and scaly. It is often inherited, so that a child has extremely dry, scaly skin all over the body, but the palms of the hands and the soles of the feet are the most severely affected areas. The skin breaks up into tiny diamond-shaped plates, rather like fish scales, and it may be darker than normal.

Excessively dry skin due to overexposure to sun, or due to lack of oil in the skin, may also produce scaling.

Skin, sun-sensitive

Most Australians regard lying in the sun as their divine right, notwithstanding the current knowledge of the damage it can do, especially with regard to skin cancer.

Under certain circumstances, skin may become even more sensitive to the sun than is normally the case. By far the most common reason for this is that you are taking at least one of a very wide range of medications, including some tranquillisers, sulpha drugs and the tetracycline group of antibiotics. It is worth being aware of this possible side effect and taking extra precautions to avoid sunburn if you are prescribed such medication. Various other conditions, in particular dermatitis, can make sunbaking even more of a hazard than usual.

Skin, thickened

When eczema or other skin disorder is healing, the skin may roughen or thicken. Sometimes this follows excessive itching or scratching. If the skin is constantly subjected to friction or abnormal pressure, it may thicken as a protective mechanism and form a callus. Calluses often develop on the sole of the foot, usually when there is an existing problem such as ill-fitting shoes or if you are walking with the foot turned inwards.

Scleroderma is a serious disease which is characterised by skin thickening and arthritis.

Skin, thinned

As we get older, the skin fibres and elements that give it its elasticity gradually change so that it becomes less flexible, wrinkled and thinner. This is an irreversible part of the ageing process.

Occasionally thin skin occurs in a young person, in which case it may be because of disease, in particular, a condition known as Cushing's syndrome where the body produces too many steroid hormones. The most obvious symptom of Cushing's syndrome is a rounded moon-shaped face.

SKIN WEALS (DERMOGRAPHIA, HIVES)

If you are a person who suffers from allergies, you will likely be familiar with hives — raised red weals on the skin. Hives range in size from small to several inches across, and they usually itch incessantly. They may last for a few hours or several days. Foodstuffs which not infrequently cause hives are shellfish and strawberries. The medical name for hives is urticaria, and sometimes this can affect areas other than the skin, causing swelling on the tongue and lips. This is a serious condition that needs urgent medical attention.

Some people's skin is so highly sensitive that they can 'write' on it with a finger or blunt instrument and the pressure produces weals.

See also ALLERGY, Section 5.

SKIN, YELLOW (JAUNDICE, ICTERUS)

A person is said to be jaundiced if their skin takes on a yellow colour. This can have a number of causes, including eating an overly large quantity of carrots or other yellow vegetables and fruit. As a symptom of disease, however, a yellow skin is caused by an excess of one of the components of bile, called bilirubin. This is a waste product of the normal breakdown of red blood cells and is normally removed from the bloodstream by the liver. If the liver becomes diseased and cannot function properly, too much bilirubin builds up and shows up as a yellowish tinge in the skin and in the whites of the eyes. The most common liver disorders are hepatitis and cirrhosis, the latter often as a result of alcoholism.

A second reason for a yellow skin is a blocked bile duct. This may happen because a stone forms in the gall bladder and travels into the bile duct where it lodges. Inflammation and pain are common and it may lead to jaundice as well.

It is not unusual for newborn babies to show slight signs of jaundice. This is because their liver is not yet functioning properly and breaks down too many red blood cells. It usually clears up within a few days. A similar disorder in an adult, in which the spleen breaks down an excess of red blood cells is called haemolytic anaemia.

Other diseases that can lead to a yellowish-looking skin include various different kinds of anaemia, malaria and yellow fever, syphilis and Hodgkin's disease (a malignant disease of the lymphatic system).

Some drugs, such as the sulpha drugs, can also cause the skin to take on a yellow hue.

SLEEP, INABILITY TO
See INSOMNIA.

SMELL, LOSS OF (ANOSMIA)

Almost everyone loses their sense of smell to some extent as they get older. A loss of smell in a younger person usually indicates a recent heavy cold or other viral infection. The clogging of the nasal passages interferes with the ability of the smell receptors to detect smells, and this may continue for weeks or even months after the infection has cleared up. The sense will generally return in time, although some people seem to find their sense of smell has been permanently impaired. Hay fever will also interfere with the ability to smell, as will the growth of nasal polyps which are common in allergy sufferers. Occasionally loss of smell is a symptom of an abscess or even a tumour on the brain, but this is very rare.

The ability to smell may also disappear because of a head injury. This is because such an injury sometimes damages the nerves that carry smell sensations to the brain.

Snoring

The noises, sounds, eruptions, gargles and other auditory traumas associated with snoring are impossible to express adequately in print. The effects upon a spouse or entire family may be sufficient to lead to arguments, fights or even divorce and mental illness. The greatest problem with snoring is that the snorer is often unaffected, but those around him (and most snorers are male) are the victims.

Snoring is the production of a harsh, rough sound caused by the passage of air through the mouth, throat and nose during sleep. It can occur intermittently during colds, flu or throat infections because of the excess production of phlegm and the swelling of tissues at these times, or it may occur almost every night.

In chronic cases, snoring is due to the vibration of the uvula or soft palate with the movement of air in and out of the mouth. The uvula is the piece of tissue that can be seen hanging down the back of the throat when the mouth is wide open, and the soft palate is the back part of the roof of the mouth, to which the uvula is attached. In some cases, long-lasting snoring is associated with periods when the breathing stops completely for up to a minute. This problem is sleep apnoea (see Section 5), and is due to collapse of the soft tissues of the throat during sleep. It may cause significant health problems to the sufferer.

The first step in the management of snoring is changing the position of the snorer. Sleeping on the back is worse than sleeping on the side. If the snorer is overweight, loss of weight is often very beneficial. Sedatives, alcohol and smoking will all aggravate snoring. Nose clips sometimes prove successful.

After these steps have been tried, it is probably wise to seek the help of a doctor, as there are a few rare diseases that may cause snoring, and these must be excluded. If no underlying cause can be found, certain drugs have been successful in some cases. These vary from antidepressants that vary the depth of sleep, to respiratory stimulants, anti-inflammatory drugs, and rarely steroids. Your doctor can discuss the pros and cons of these with you.

Sore throat
See THROAT, SORE.

Spasm, muscular
See CONVULSION; MUSCLE SPASM; TIC; TREMOR.

Speech, difficulty with (dysarthria)

A person who is not affected by alcohol or sedatives, who suddenly finds it difficult to speak properly may need urgent medical help. If they are dizzy and complain of numbness or tingling in any part of the body, weakness in the legs or arms, and/or blurred vision, it may signal a stroke, either actual or impending.

Some emotional and psychiatric disorders, e.g. schizophrenia, are characterised by a difficulty with speech. In this case, it is likely to be not so much how the person pronounces words, but the content of what they say, which will be increasingly nonsensical. If there is also an inability to cope with ordinary everyday matters and a lack of concern with cleanliness and overall personal appearance, it may signal the onset of Alzheimer's disease in older people, or, more rarely, a brain tumour.

Any disease affecting the facial nerves,

such as Bell's palsy, multiple sclerosis, or Parkinson's disease, can affect our ability to speak.

See also SPEECH, LOSS OF.

Speech, loss of (Aphasia)
A complete loss of the ability to speak is called aphasia and almost always results from damage to the language centres of the brain. It is characterised by a complete or partial loss of the ability to use words but, depending on the extent of the brain damage, some language functions may be impaired and not others. For example, the person may be able to write and not speak or vice versa, or they might have problems with particular categories of words, such as names. Aphasia may follow a stroke affecting the dominant half of the brain (usually the left side in a right-handed person).

See also SPEECH, DIFFICULTY WITH.

Spots in vision
See VISION, BLACK SPOTS IN.

Squint
See Section 5.

Stridor
Stridor is a shrill wheezing or grunting noise, caused by breathing through a narrowed larynx (voice box) or trachea (windpipe). It usually occurs in children and may be due to a respiratory infection such as a cold, bronchitis or laryngitis. It is commonly associated with croup. A child who suddenly develops stridor, and does not have a respiratory infection may have swallowed a foreign object; you will need to see a doctor urgently for advice about removing it.

Any disease that causes a narrowing of the breathing passages can lead to stridor, and on occasion it may be a symptom of glandular fever, diphtheria and even the existence of a tumour. The onset of stridor should always be regarded seriously.

See also WHEEZE.

Swallowing, difficulty in (Dysphagia)
We almost always take our ability to swallow for granted and yet it is an exceedingly complex process which can malfunction for any one of a number of reasons.

We often find it difficult to swallow if we are anxious or emotional, simply because our state of nervous tension causes the muscles to seize up and fail to work as efficiently as they should. We have all experienced a lump in the throat as a result of extreme feelings. Alternatively, the nerves associated with swallowing might be damaged as a result of disease or a stroke, or the muscles may be weakened by a chronic muscle disorder such as myasthenia gravis.

If the difficulty is when you begin to swallow, the problem is in the pharynx (throat). The cause can be anything from a minor infection to tonsillitis, to nerve damage from a stroke or poliomyelitis. If the problem is further down, you have something wrong with the oesophagus (gullet). This could be due to an enlarged gland or a tumour or a dilated aorta (the main artery from the heart) or, low down in the oesophagus, a hiatus hernia. If you cannot swallow either liquids or solids, you probably have a serious infection or a tumour. If you can get liquids down but not solids this usually indicates a mechanical blockage. If the reverse is the case, that is you can cope with solids but not liquids, the nerves and muscles of the throat are the problem rather than a blockage.

A difficulty in swallowing can be potentially very serious, and there are so many possible causes that you should always see a doctor quickly.

Sweating, excessive

We all sweat when we get hot. If we get very hot we may sweat or perspire a great deal. This is the body's way of getting rid of excess heat and is quite normal. Similarly, most of us break out into a sweat if we are highly emotional about something, for example if we are angry, nervous or afraid. If there is no cause such as this, however, and the sweating is all over our body, rather than where the sweat glands are most numerous under the arms, the palms of the hands, soles of the feet and groin, we can look to disease as the cause.

Any disease that causes a fever will lead to sweating. This may be the flu or rheumatic fever or cancer or any one of dozens of others. An overactive thyroid will cause sweating since the body's metabolism is working at a faster rate than normal. Some diseases have individual patterns, for example tuberculosis is commonly characterised by sweating at night.

A hormonal imbalance is a common cause of sweating, either because of disease, or hormone treatment or menopause in women. You might also sweat because you drink too much coffee, or because you are going to have a heart attack.

Sweating usually matters little in a medical sense. However if you sweat excessively for no apparent reason, or you have other symptoms such as faintness or a feeling of being unwell, you should see a doctor to find out why.

See also Section 5.

Swelling

See ABDOMINAL SWELLING; ASCITES; EYELID, SWOLLEN; FINGERTIPS, SWOLLEN; GLANDS, SWOLLEN; MOUTH, SWOLLEN; OEDEMA; SALIVARY GLANDS, PAINFUL OR SWOLLEN; TESTICLES, PAINFUL OR SWOLLEN.

Syncope
See FAINTING.

Tachycardia
See HEARTBEAT, FAST.

Taste, abnormal

We have all experienced losing our sense of taste from time to time. Usually it means that our taste receptors have lost their sensitivity, and it is caused by something fairly minor such as a mouth infection, a sinus infection or a cold. Sometimes it can signal something more serious, such as a stroke.

Tasting something different from what we are eating means that the taste signals to the brain have become jumbled, and this may be a sign of a migraine, a stroke, epilepsy or a brain tumour.

Teeth, painful
See TOOTHACHE.

Tenesmus
See BOWEL MOVEMENTS, EXCESSIVE DESIRE TO PASS.

Testicles, painful or swollen

Any lump or swelling in the testicles may be a symptom of disease irrespective of whether there is pain as well, so medical advice should be sought.

If one or both testicles suddenly becomes painful, the first thing to consider is whether you have injured your genitals within the past 48 hours. Injury to the testicles can cause severe pain, but if it subsides within a hour or so and your scrotum is not bruised or swollen, there is probably no reason for alarm. If you have had a recent attack of mumps you may have developed orchitis, or inflammation of the testicles. A sausage shaped swelling at the back of a testicle, which is hot, tender and very painful, indicates an infection originating in the sperm duct, called epididymitis.

Torsion of the testicle is a disorder in which a testicle becomes twisted within the scrotum. This can happen at any time, even while you are asleep, and is indicated by a sudden pain in the testicle. It may be accompanied by nausea and vomiting. The testicle is suspended in the scrotum by the blood vessels that supply it. When it twists, the blood supply is cut off and the testicle will become gangrenous unless urgent surgery to untwist it restores the blood supply. Urgent attention within six hours is therefore essential to prevent the testicle from being permanently damaged.

A hydrocele is an accumulation of fluid around the testicles and is quite common, especially in older men although it can occur at any age. It normally causes a generalised painless swelling of the scrotum.

Cancer of the testicles is one of the most easily cured types of cancer, but it needs to be treated at an early stage or it may spread throughout the lymphatic system. Just as women are advised to examine their breasts at regular intervals, so men should carry out the same process on their testicles. A lump in the scrotum may not always be distinguishable from a lump in the testicle. A lump in the testicle is almost always a cause for concern — a scrotal lump may be a hernia, or may be due to a cyst which is probably harmless.

Tetany
See MUSCLE SPASM.

Thirst, excessive (polydipsia)
The first thing the doctor will look for if you complain of feeling abnormally thirsty is the most common type of diabetes, diabetes mellitus, in which the body is unable to utilise sugar. The system tries to get rid of the excess sugar in the urine and to do this the kidneys need extra water. Consequently a sufferer feels constantly thirsty.

There is another type of diabetes called diabetes insipidus in which, because of a disorder of the pituitary gland, the body produces too much urine. A constant feeling of thirst is the body's way of signalling it needs a replenishment of fluid. Diabetes insipidus is relatively rare.

Other reasons for feeling very thirsty are dehydration (when the fluid level in the body is too low because you don't drink enough water, or you have lost fluid due to excessive vomiting or diarrhoea), kidney disease, and (rarely) brain disease.

Whatever the cause, fluid is essential for the body to function and if your thirst is not quenched by drinking water, you should see a doctor to find out why.

Thoracic pain
See CHEST PAIN.

Throat, sore
You may develop a sore throat because you have been talking too much. Or you may smoke too much. Apart from these reasons, however, a sore throat is one of the body's early warning signals. Generally it means you have picked up an infection, commonly a cold or tonsillitis or any one of many germs that invade the respiratory system. If you have a temperature you may have the flu. If the area of your jaw just below the ear is swollen and sore, you are possibly in for an attack of the mumps. If you had fish for dinner, you may have swallowed a bone which has lodged in your throat. The causes of a sore throat are almost never-ending and can include such serious disorders as measles and glandular fever, sexually transmitted diseases like syphilis and gonorrhoea, and leukaemia.

You can soothe a sore throat by taking pain-killers or gargling with aspirin. However if it persists for longer than a few days, consult a doctor.

TIC (REPETITIVE MUSCULAR MOVEMENT)

A repeated and involuntary movement, usually in the face, is generally described as a tic. It can vary from a small twitching muscle to quite large movements. A common reason for developing a tic is emotional stress.

There are also various physiological causes. The inflammation of a major nerve in the face giving rise to a tic and shooting pains in the face is called trigeminal neuralgia or tic douloureux. This is most common in elderly people and may be triggered by something quite commonplace, such as brushing your teeth. A tic may also be a facet of epilepsy, or occasionally it may signal that there are growths in the brain tissue.

TINGLING

See PINS AND NEEDLES SENSATION.

TINNITUS

See EAR NOISE.

TIREDNESS, ABNORMAL

A feeling of unusual tiredness is something we all experience from time to time. It is a common symptom of many disorders, both trivial and serious, and it is generally the presence of other symptoms that indicates what it is due to.

The most obvious reasons for tiredness are overwork, the need for a holiday, or lack of enough sleep. Tiredness is a very common symptom early in pregnancy and is often noticed even before the woman is aware she is pregnant. Tiredness is also common in women going through the menopause. Recovering from an illness, in particular viral illnesses, often leads to several weeks of tiredness. If it lasts for more than four weeks and does not respond to commonsense measures such as adequate rest and sleep and proper nourishment, see your doctor.

Other more serious causes of abnormal tiredness are goitre (swelling in the throat due to an overactive or underactive thyroid). If you suffer from an underactive thyroid, you will usually feel the cold more than you used to, and have a dry skin, thinning or brittle hair and unexplained weight gain. If you are unusually pale, faint and suffer from breathlessness and palpitations, you may be anaemic.

Tiredness associated with an inability to concentrate or make decisions, a lack of interest in sex, recurrent headaches and generally low spirits is likely to mean depression and should be treated — it can have serious consequences.

The sudden onset of extreme tiredness, together with discomfort in the chest may sometimes be a sign of impending heart trouble.

Other important causes of abnormal tiredness include an inadequate diet, cancer, poisons, many lung diseases, diabetes, a stroke, kidney or liver failure and alcoholism.

TOE, PAINFUL

The joints of the toes may give rise to any of the symptoms common to other joints (see JOINTS, PAINFUL, SWOLLEN). Gout, however, is a disease that especially attacks the big toe, which will become swollen, red and extremely tender. If you have these symptoms and have been taking a diuretic (medication to rid the body of excess fluids) you almost certainly have gout. Gout is generally regarded as the result of an excessive indulgence in rich food and drink, but this is not always the case. Gout is not exclusively manifested in the big toe joint, but about 75% of cases are.

Another reason for a painful big toe can be a bunion, generally caused by ill-fitting shoes that put pressure on the lower joint connecting the toe with the foot. The constant pressure and irritation causes a spur of bone to form, and this is then covered by a sac of fluid-filled tissue (a bursa). The skin covering the pressure point often thickens into a corn or a callus, adding to the pain.

TONGUE, DISCOLOURED

A normal-looking tongue is pink, usually with deep red showing through the fissures running along it. From time to time, something happens to change the colour, but generally this is no cause for concern. Everyone has bacteria in their mouth and occasionally these accumulate so that the tongue appears to be dark brown or black. If you wish you can clean it gently with a toothbrush dipped in antiseptic.

A white or yellowish furry tongue is sometimes thought to be a sign of disease, but this is not necessarily the case. It is produced by cast-off cells on the surface of the tongue which act as a trap for food particles and other substances. It may be a result of smoking or show that you are not cleaning your teeth with sufficient thoroughness. Sometimes a coated tongue accompanies illness of a general kind, especially if you have a fever, but it will usually return to normal when the illness clears up.

A patchy white tongue may, however, be a symptom that something is wrong. It can signal a fungal infection such as thrush, or a disease called leukoplakia in which there is overgrowth of the tissue. This may be caused by excessive smoking or alcohol, or by certain infections. Occasionally it may be malignant. Lichen planus is an inflammatory condition which often causes white patches in the mouth.

A black tongue can be caused by smoking, or it may be a result of drugs such as penicillin or those used to combat arthritis. It may also be caused by a malignant melanoma.

A smooth red tongue is a common symptom in people who are anaemic or suffering from either vitamin B12 or iron deficiency. A red tongue also occurs as a result of scarlet fever or some streptococcal infections. Sometimes it indicates a disease known as pellagra, in which there is a deficiency of vitamin B and which is common in maize- eating communities.

A blue tongue can be a sign of heart or lung disease. And jaundice can give rise to a tongue with a yellowish tinge.

TONGUE, SORE

The most common reason for a sore tongue is an ulcer — one of those nasty little sores that appear for no apparent reason and can give rise to pain out of all proportion to its size and significance. Ulcers are often caused by a virus and so are difficult to treat, but the chemist may be able to give you something to relieve the acute soreness.

If you bite your tongue it will generally hurt, as it will if it is constantly being rubbed by badly fitting dentures.

A persistently sore tongue may be a sign of anaemia due to a lack of iron or vitamin B12. It is also possible for tiny cancers to develop on the underside of the tongue, so you should have the cause checked out.

Sometimes the nerves supplying the mouth become irritated and are felt as a sore tongue, although the pain may in fact be coming from the teeth and gums. This is generally referred to as neuralgia.

It is not unknown for heart trouble to be felt as pain in the tongue. This is called referred pain.

TOOTHACHE
Toothache generally occurs because a tooth or teeth have decayed. Food particles that have remained in the mouth after a meal eat into the tooth enamel and expose the more sensitive nerve tissue, dentine, that lies beneath. Untreated tooth decay (caries) can lead to diseased gums, and a sore tooth should always signal the need for a visit to the dentist.

Toothache or pain can occur even though there is no decay. Decay of the gum and supporting tooth bone (gingivitis and periodontitis) can mimic tooth pain, particularly when the pain is vague and cannot be isolated to a particular area. The dentine can also be exposed if the gums recede, so that if you eat or drink anything hot or cold you will experience what feels like severe toothache.

Your teeth may be painful after a visit to the dentist, as with any surgical procedure. An incorrectly shaped filling that has to be trimmed further may also cause pain.

Children whose new teeth are coming through may experience pain in the same way as babies. This may continue to the late teens when the wisdom teeth finally appear.

Most pain in the face comes from the teeth, and most causes are easily diagnosed and treated — generally the sooner the treatment the faster the relief.

See also DENTISTRY, Section 7.

TREMOR
Your hands may display a tremor or shake because you are nervous, angry or distressed, or because you drink too much coffee or alcohol. If you develop a tremor and it has no obvious cause, you may be unfortunate enough to have Parkinson's disease, which affects the nervous system. The first and most prominent symptom is usually a tremor, often affecting one hand, spreading first to the leg on the same side and then to the other limbs. The trembling will be worse when you are at rest.

Tremor can accompany a variety of diseases, including advanced liver trouble, kidney malfunction and an overactive thyroid. It can also signal brain disorders other than Parkinson's, such as multiple sclerosis, a stroke or a head injury.

If you are a diabetic and take too much insulin, you may get the shakes, and similarly if you indulge in cocaine and other 'recreational' drug taking.

A fine tremor in elderly people, usually in the hands and possibly the lower jaw, is quite common and not an indication of disease.

See also JERKING MOVEMENTS; TIC.

TUMOUR
See BONE LUMPS; BREAST LUMP; NECK LUMP; SKIN PAPULES; TESTICLES, PAINFUL OR SWOLLEN; VIOLENCE, ABNORMAL.

TWITCH
See TIC; TREMOR.

ULCER
See ABDOMINAL PAIN; MOUTH ULCERS.

See also EYE ULCER; ULCER, PEPTIC; ULCER, SKIN, Section 5.

UNCONSCIOUSNESS
See FAINTING; COMA.

See also Section 8.

URETHRAL DISCHARGE
Urethritis is inflammation of the urethra, the tube leading from the bladder to the outside. Typical symptoms of urethritis

include local pain, frequent urination and a discharge from the opening to the outside. In women, urethritis is generally the result of bruising during sexual intercourse. In men it is generally caused by sexually transmitted disease — notably non-specific urethritis and gonorrhoea.

A urinary tract infection that spreads to the prostate may cause prostatitis (inflammation of the prostate). If pus accumulates it will find its way to the outside via the urethra.

See also URINE, BLOODY; URINE INCONTINENCE; URINE, PAINFUL PASSING OF.

URETHRAL PAIN
See PENIS PAIN; URETHRAL DISCHARGE; URINE, PAINFUL PASSING OF.

URINE, ABNORMAL COLOUR
Urine is usually a straw colour, but if you have been eating a lot of rhubarb your urine might look dark yellow or orange. Laxatives can have the same effect. Your urine may also be concentrated and therefore darker than usual because you are hot and losing fluid through sweating. This may be due to a summer's day or because your own temperature has risen because of a fever. Similarly if you have had a gastric attack with vomiting and diarrhoea, you will have lost fluid this way.

Clear dark brown urine may signal jaundice if the whites of your eyes are yellow and you have pale bowel movements as well.

Almost anything you have eaten may pass into your urine and, for example, artificial colouring in food, blackberries, beetroot and various drugs can cause a change in colour. This is no cause for concern. However, if you pass pink, red or smoky-brown urine for no apparent reason, it may be due to blood in the urine (see below) and you should see a doctor.

URINE, BLOODY
Blood in the urine should never be ignored. It means that there is a problem somewhere in the urinary tract, from the kidneys where urine is made to the urethra which passes it to the outside. In the kidneys, the problem might be an injury, for example a blow, a kidney stone or infection, or a tumour. Further down in the bladder, bleeding might be caused by an infection (cystitis), inflammation, polyps or a tumour. Similarly, the urethra may be inflamed or infected. Prostate problems can also lead to blood in the urine.

Generally speaking, blood passed from higher up, for example in the kidneys, will be brownish, while blood originating from lower down will be bright red. The fact that urine is red is not always due to blood — it might be caused by something you've eaten.

See also URINE, ABNORMAL COLOUR.

URINE, EXCESSIVE OR FREQUENT (POLYURIA)
Passing an abnormal amount of urine may mean no more than that you've consumed a large amount of fluid, particularly alcohol. Cold or excitement can also cause you to pass water more frequently than usual. Some drugs, called diuretics, are prescribed specifically to rid the body of excess fluids, and these work by stimulating the kidneys to produce more urine. They include drugs to combat heart disease and high blood pressure. If none of these reasons apply, the production of an abnormal amount of urine can be a symptom of innumerable other conditions, starting with pregnancy and including almost all disorders of the urinary tract as well as diabetes. In women a commonly occurring complaint leading to frequent urination, usually with a burning sensation, is cystitis or inflammation of the bladder. This needs medical attention.

Other possible causes of excess urination are inflammation of the prostate in men, an over- or underactive thyroid and kidney disease.

Urine, gassy

The presence of bubbles of air or other gas in your urine can be due to the formation of gas by bacteria infecting the urinary tract. It can also occur if there is an opening between the urinary tract and the bowel or vagina so that gas formed in the bowel can leak through. Such an opening is called a fistula and may be due to injury, tumour, or an infection, or the person may have been born with it.

Urine, inability to pass

If it is difficult to pass urine which is manufactured by the body, the cause is usually some physical blockage in the bladder such as a tumour or blood clot. Or it may be due to an enlarged prostate. Foreign bodies sometimes find their way into the bladder or urethra and cause a blockage, or the urethra may become narrowed because of infection or disease.

Urine incontinence

Passing urine is a complex process involving an interaction between numerous muscles that are controlled by the brain through a network of nerves. Messages must be sent from the bladder when it is full to the brain to be interpreted and evaluated, and then messages sent back to the various muscles controlling the opening of the bladder instructing them to open. If any part of this process is faulty, urine may be passed involuntarily instead of being held in the bladder until it is convenient. This can be caused by coughing or sneezing or laughing too much, when the muscle control is poor, and it may also be caused by injury or disease. Any injury or infection or tumour affecting the spinal cord may interrupt the pathway of the nerves to and from the brain and so the messages won't get through. Similarly if the brain itself is affected by some disorder such as a stroke or tumour or Alzheimer's disease, its ability to interpret incoming signals may be impaired. Anxiety and stress can also affect the control we have over our bladder. In men, incontinence can sometimes result from an inflamed or infected prostate. In women, it is a frequent result of the weakening of the pelvic floor muscles in childbirth.

See also INCONTINENCE OF URINE, Section 5.

Urine, lack of (oliguria, anuria)

A condition in which the body manufactures an abnormally small amount of urine is called oliguria. If there is no urine at all it is called anuria. You may have a reduced volume of urine if you have perspired a lot in hot weather and you haven't drunk enough fluid to replace the water you have lost. It is of no consequence if you are otherwise healthy. If this is not the explanation, oliguria is usually caused by diseases that impair the functioning of the kidneys, or because of certain heart or liver diseases which lead to excessive retention of water in the tissues. Shock may also cause a reduced urine output, as may certain infectious diseases such as cholera and yellow fever.

Urine, painful passing of (dysuria)

Urination is sometimes accompanied by pain in the abdomen or urinary passage. If the pain is in one side of the small of the back, just above the waist, it may signal a kidney infection. In men, if the pain is lower down nearer the opening and they have a discharge, it may indicate a sexually transmitted disease. In women, pain on passing urine is usually due to cystitis. Vaginal thrush causes pain when urinating only if the external genitals of the woman have become inflamed.

In general. difficulty and pain in urinating is a symptom of various disorders of the bladder, urethra or prostate gland, i.e. cystitis, urethritis and prostatitis.

URINE, RED
See URINE, ABNORMAL COLOUR; URINE, BLOODY.

UTERINE BLEEDING
See MENSTRUAL PERIOD PROBLEMS; VAGINAL BLEEDING, EXCESSIVE.

VAGINAL BLEEDING, EXCESSIVE
Bleeding that occurs between normal menstrual periods or after menopause should be investigated. The bleeding may be a result of non- malignant growths such as polyps or fibroids, but it may also signal cancer. A woman of child-bearing age who has bleeding accompanied by severe abdominal pain should get immediate medical help, as she may have a pregnancy developing outside the womb (an ectopic pregnancy).

Endometritis is inflammation of the lining of the womb and may lead to excessive menstrual bleeding and pain in the lower regions of the back and abdomen.

Other causes of excessive vaginal bleeding include an intra-uterine contraceptive device (IUD), an early miscarriage, various disorders of the reproductive organs, breakthrough bleeding from the pill, a prolapse of the uterus or vagina, an underactive thyroid, and unusual stress and tension.

Irregular and increased bleeding in women in their forties usually heralds the onset of the menopause. If there are other unpleasant symptoms, consult a doctor, as these can usually be treated (see Section 1). Bleeding after the menopause is over, say six months after the last period, may indicate cancer and should be investigated promptly.

See also PREGNANCY COMPLICATIONS, Section 1.

VAGINAL DISCHARGE
A discharge from the vagina that is different in colour, consistency or quantity from that normally experienced between periods may simply be a reaction to the pill if you have recently begun taking it, or it may be due to an irritation of the vagina, in which case it will usually be accompanied by an itch or soreness. Sometimes you may notice a slightly increased discharge between periods when ovulation takes place — this is normal and not a cause for concern.

If you have a white curdy discharge, you may have a fungal infection. Yellow or grey discharge which may be frothy and have an offensive smell may be due to various bacterial infections. If the discharge is greenish-yellow with an unpleasant smell, check if you have forgotten to remove a tampon or diaphragm. If so, and you feel ill or feverish, see a doctor. You should also see a doctor as soon as possible if the discharge is accompanied by pain in the lower abdomen, as it may be caused by acute infection of the Fallopian tubes or the uterus.

Other reasons for vaginal discharge include sexually transmitted diseases such as gonorrhoea and chlamydia, pelvic inflammatory disease, and growths such as polyps and fibroids. If the discharge does not clear up within a few days, see a doctor.

VERTEBRAL PAIN
See BACK PAIN.

Section 3: Symptoms

Vertigo
See DIZZINESS.

Violence, abnormal
Abnormally violent behaviour is usually considered to be (and is) a personality disorder rather than a medical problem, but sometimes it is due to a malfunction of the behaviour centre of the brain and is a symptom with medical implications.

Excessive aggression and violent behaviour may indicate alcohol or drug abuse, a deficiency of glucose in the blood, or it may be a result of an injury to the head. It may also be a sign that there is something acutely wrong with the brain (e.g. a tumour) or that the perpetrator is suffering from schizophrenia or other psychotic disorders.

Vision, black spots in
Many of us see spots before our eyes from time to time. Generally they are due to floaters — small protein or cellular deposits in the fluid within the eyeball — and are harmless. However, if the spots persist and are troublesome, ask your doctor about them. They can occasionally signal something serious, such as a brain tumour. Black or floating or cobweb-like shapes in one eye may be a sign that the retina is becoming detached from the surrounding tissue. This is more likely if you are older or may follow an injury, and it needs immediate medical attention. If there is a cloudy area in the centre of your vision, you may be getting a cataract. In epileptics the seeing of spots may be a warning of an impending seizure (see AURA). Migraine sufferers are often prone to see spots or patterns just prior to or during an attack.

Vision, blurred
If, when you try to see something, it looks blurry, the most likely explanation is that your sight is abnormal, e.g. you are either short-sighted or long-sighted. This can be corrected with spectacles or contact lenses. Certain drugs, too much alcohol, a heavy concentration of nicotine, and even extreme tiredness can make things seem blurry. Inflammation of the eye causing conjunctivitis can also cause blurry vision, as can a deficiency of the vitamin riboflavin (contained in liver).

You may experience blurred vision if you suffer from high blood pressure, diabetes, liver or kidney complaints, or clogged arteries. It is also a characteristic of migraine.

Occasionally blurred vision is a symptom of serious eye disease such as a cataract (clouding of the lens), damage to the retina (for example a detached retina), damage to the optic nerve, glaucoma, iritis (inflammation of the iris) or scarring of the cornea, possibly due to the eye disease, trachoma.

If your vision becomes blurry suddenly or is accompanied by pain, see your doctor as soon as possible. Blurred vision after a head injury or blow to the head of any kind is a serious symptom, and medical advice should be sought.

Vision, double (diplopia)
Seeing double is usually due to weakness or paralysis of the eye muscles. This may be caused by a stroke, migraine, a disease of the nervous system such as multiple sclerosis, or a tumour on the brain. Sometimes it is due to botulism, an extreme form of food poisoning, or to thyroid disease. It can also be caused by a blow to the head leading to concussion.

Vision, pain with bright light (photophobia)
If looking at bright light causes pain in your eyes, it can be a sign of anything

causing inflammation of the eyes or eyelids. You may have some foreign matter in your eye or an infection causing conjunctivitis. More seriously, you may have an inflamed iris (iritis) or acute glaucoma. Migraine can also make it painful to look at bright light. It can be a symptom of viral infections such as measles, and rare diseases caused by tiny parasitic organisms, usually passed on through animals or insects. Sometimes a disorder of the parathyroid gland (surrounding the thyroid in the neck) is involved.

Vitiligo
See SKIN, DEPIGMENTATION OF.

Vomiting
See NAUSEA AND VOMITING; VOMITING BLOOD.
See also TRAVEL MEDICINE, Section 7.

Vomiting blood (haematemesis)
If you vomit because of an upset stomach or you have eaten contaminated food or have a 'wog', you will bring up the contents of your last meal. Continued vomiting will usually consist of green bile. If the vomiting is prolonged and vigorous, it may cause a tear in the small blood vessels of the throat or the oesophagus (gullet), so there are small streaks of blood in what you bring up. However, vomiting blood is usually a sign that you have a peptic ulcer (in the stomach or duodenum), severe irritation leading to a breakdown in the lining of your upper digestive organs, or advanced liver disease. Less often it indicates cancer of the stomach.

Vomiting blood should always be treated seriously and medical attention sought.

Vulval itch
The skin surrounding the external female genitals, the vulva, is very sensitive because it is designed to respond to sexual stimulation. It is also situated in a part of the body that generates moisture and is without much airflow. If you cut off the air even more than usual, by wearing tight clothes so that the skin gets even less ventilation, it is likely to protest by developing an extreme itch. On the other hand, if you dry out the area by overly frequent washing, especially with perfumer soaps, the skin will itch in rebellion against the interference to its normal environment.

If an infection, such as thrush, or an allergy takes hold in the genital area, the sensitive skin will almost always develop an itch in addition to a rash or any other symptoms. Occasionally, the vulva develops cancer, in which case it will not only be red and itchy but hard to the touch.

Vulval itching is common in young girls before they begin their periods and in older women after menopause. It is thought to be related to the production of sex hormones, especially to the lower level of oestrogen present after menopause. Women with diabetes also sometimes experience irritation in the genital area, because they are more likely to develop thrush and other infections.

Generally your doctor will prescribe a soothing cream and advise you to wash with a mild unscented soap once a day, or with no soap at all but using sorbolene or some similar substitute. Cotton underwear allows the skin to breathe. The area will probably be dry and sore as well as itching, and a lubricant during intercourse may be helpful.

See also ITCH.

Walk, abnormal (abnormal gait)
The way we walk is one of our personal characteristics. We can often recognise someone by their walk well before it is possible to distinguish their features. Our walk in this sense is simply a mannerism,

with no special significance. However, doctors can often tell quite a lot about a patient by the way they walk. A person with Parkinson's disease, for example, takes short rapid steps, leaning forward to the extent that it appears they may overbalance. Inflamed nerves (neuritis) in the legs may lead to walking with abnormally high steps. A stroke victim will frequently be unable to lift the affected leg very high at all, and will walk by swinging the leg outwards and dragging the foot along the ground. Someone who reels from side to side with a staggering 'drunken' walk may have brain damage affecting their balance.

WATERBRASH

Most of us will have experienced a bitter taste in our mouth from time to time. This is called waterbrash and is generally due to indigestion when acids used in the stomach to digest food are regurgitated into the mouth. If, as well as a bad taste, you have a tender abdomen after you have eaten, it is possible that you have a hiatus hernia, in which part of the stomach bulges through a weak point in the muscular wall of the diaphragm. Alternatively you might have a peptic ulcer, where the digestive acids have eaten into the wall of part of the intestine.

WEAKNESS, MUSCULAR
See PARALYSIS; TIREDNESS, ABNORMAL.

WEALS
See SKIN WEALS.

WEIGHT GAIN, ABNORMAL

Most people put on weight because they eat too much. However, if you suddenly start to gain weight, and on an honest assessment of your lifestyle it cannot be attributed to the intake of too much food, there are other possibilities.

If you are feeling the cold more than everyone else and are generally feeling tired and run-down, possibly with menstrual irregularities or hair loss, you might have an underactive thyroid gland. Swollen feet and shortness of breath in addition to extra weight means you are retaining fluid and may have kidney trouble, a heart problem, or sometimes liver disease. If you are at times uncontrollably hungry and have palpitations, tremors and sweating, your pancreas could be producing too much insulin and cause low blood sugar, which makes you hungry so that you eat more and put on weight. Severe headaches or a change in your vision could indicate a tumour in the part of the brain which regulates appetite. Cushing's syndrome is a condition where there is too much cortisone in the body, so the torso becomes fat and the face becomes moon-shaped while the arms and legs remain thin.

Certain drugs, notably the contraceptive pill and several tranquillisers can lead to an increase in weight.

See also APPETITE, EXCESSIVE; OBESITY.

WEIGHT LOSS, ABNORMAL

Quite obviously, if you go on a diet or increase your amount of exercise you should expect to lose weight. However, if you have not changed your eating or exercise habits and you lose more than about 4.5 kg in two or three months, you should begin asking why.

The most straightforward reason for losing weight, apart from not eating, is a problem in the digestive system that stops food being absorbed. This can be anything from inflammation of one of the organs (e.g. the pancreas) to an infestation of worms, an ulcer in the stomach or duodenum, or a narrowing of the throat, possibly because of disease. The failure of an adequate amount of bile to reach the intestine can also lead to weight loss. This might be because of a blockage, such as a stone in the bile duct, or it might be due to liver disease, but whatever the cause you will usually have the characteristic yellow colour of jaundice as well.

Other reasons for weight loss are legion and include chronic infections such as hepatitis, an overactive thyroid, heart problems (you will generally be short of breath as well), asthma, diabetes, tumours (both benign and malignant), depression, drug abuse and alcoholism. Abnormal weight loss in young girls may be due to anorexia nervosa, in which the victim loses the desire to eat or even finds eating repugnant.

See also APPETITE LOSS.

WHEEZE

Noisy, difficult breathing is usually due to obstruction in the breathing passages or respiratory tract. The most widespread cause is asthma, a condition in which the tubes through which the air passes into the lungs become narrowed. Wheezing is also a result of emphysema (in which the air sacs in the lungs are damaged, often as a result of smoking), bronchitis (inflammation of the bronchial tubes), cancer of the bronchial tubes, an especially nasty disease called hydatids, in which a parasitic worm penetrates the lungs and forms cysts, cystic fibrosis (a hereditary disease in which the lungs become persistently blocked with mucus) and pneumonitis (inflammation of the air sacs within the lungs). If an otherwise seemingly healthy child starts wheezing, it may be because they have swallowed something that has become lodged in the windpipe or the bronchial tubes. If coughing does not dislodge it you will need to see a doctor to get it out — quickly if the child is finding it difficult to breathe (see CHOKING, Section 8).

See also STRIDOR.

WRITHING MOVEMENTS (ATHETOSIS)

Athetosis is the name given to slow, involuntary writhing movements of the arms and legs caused by a brain disorder. This may be due to certain drugs or disease, or it may be a result of cerebral palsy, usually occurring at birth, in which the brain cannot coordinate the limbs. Athetosis can also be caused by a stroke and some brain diseases afflicting children.

WRITING DIFFICULTIES

Any disease causing severely weakened muscles or a tremor may make it difficult or impossible to hold a pen to write. A stroke affecting the dominant side of the body will usually mean the victim has not the required degree of coordination to carry out the process of writing or they may have lost the power to express ideas by writing.

YELLOW SKIN
See SKIN, YELLOW.

SECTION 4

INVESTIGATIONS

HOW DOCTORS DIAGNOSE
WHAT IS WRONG

DIAGNOSIS

193

PATHOLOGY

195

BODY SCANS AND X-RAYS

210

ENDOSCOPY

224

ELECTRICAL TESTS

230

PHYSICAL TESTS

232

SIGHT TESTS

235

HEARING TESTS

238

Diagnosis

When you go to a doctor with a complaint, the first thing the doctor must do is find out what symptoms you have and what they mean, i.e. make a diagnosis. To do this the doctor will ask you a number of questions and may use some implements to test various parts of your body. Diagnosis requires considerable skill and is a systematic procedure — questions that may seem to you to have little to do with your suffering, such as whether your mother is still alive, are all designed to help the doctor reach a conclusion about what is wrong with you.

Most common illnesses can be diagnosed by the doctor in the surgery, but if specialist knowledge is needed you may have to go to a hospital for further tests. If the doctor requires a sample of your blood or urine to be tested, the sample is sometimes collected by the doctor, but in most cases nowadays you will go to a central clinic staffed by trained nurses, associated with a laboratory.

To make the diagnosis, doctors use a number of diagnostic aids. These include their senses (Do you look pale? Did you walk in with a limp? Was it difficult to lower yourself into the chair?), their knowledge gained during training, their experience, and a wide range of instruments. All these provide information about what is happening inside your body. Some of the tests may be designed to eliminate various possibilities. The doctor will not only try to find out what is wrong but also to assess how far a particular diseases has progressed, what course it may take and therefore what treatment and advice you need, both in the short term and the long term.

The doctor will usually begin by asking questions about your symptoms, what they are, when they started, and whether you have experienced them before. You may be asked whether a member of your family has suffered from the same or a similar ailment. You will probably be asked about your diet, how much you drink and if you smoke. You may be asked what kind of job you do, in particular whether it is sedentary or manual, whether you are under any stress at work or at home, if you play sport and what exercise you get. Your answers to these questions will help the doctor build up a picture of you as a patient and indicate the likelihood of a particular illness.

Following the initial questions, the doctor will usually carry out a physical examination taking a closer look at your body, examining your skin, eyes, tongue and general condition which often reflect a patient's state of health. Your tongue may be pressed down with a spatula so that your throat and tonsils can be seen. Depending on your symptoms, the doctor may take your temperature, and if you are obese or underweight, you may be weighed and measured.

These general observations may be followed with more detailed

Section 4: Investigations

tests on the different body systems, starting with the one under suspicion. To investigate the circulatory system, the doctor will take your pulse and blood pressure. The blood vessels of your eye may then be examined by pulling down your lower lid. Examination of the vessels on the retina at the back of the eye is done with an instrument called an ophthalmoscope which shines a bright light through the pupil of the eye, and contains a tiny magnifying glass through which the doctor can peer. Diseases of the blood or circulation often become apparent during such eye examinations. Finally the doctor will listen to your heart with a stethoscope and note any abnormal sounds.

The doctor will assess your respiratory system by tapping on your chest and listening to the sound produced. You will be asked to breathe in and out deeply while the doctor listens to your lungs through the stethoscope, first at the front of the body and then at the back.

Apart from looking at the mouth and teeth and examining the anal area, the doctor can examine the digestive system and the internal organs by feeling them through the anal canal or, in women, via the vagina, and by pressing carefully and systematically on the abdominal wall.

Problems in the muscular system usually make themselves evident by means of pain or discomfort when you move. The doctor will check to find out exactly which movements cause pain, e.g. by bending your knee into different positions.

To test your central nervous system, the doctor will ask you to cross your knee, and will then tap below the knee with a small rubber hammer to elicit a jerking reflex response. A similar process is repeated for other reflexes in the knee, elbow and sole of the foot. The doctor will also check your muscle power and tone, look for any muscle wasting or abnormal muscle action, check eye movements, vision and pupil reactions, and may test your memory.

To examine your sense organs, the doctor will look at your eyes with an ophthalmoscope, and into your ears with an auriscope to detect any signs of damage or infection in the middle ear or eardrum. A wide range of tests will also be done to make sure that the senses of touch, pain, temperature and movement or position are functioning as they should.

If a complete diagnosis is impossible, or the doctor wants to confirm a suspected diagnosis, you may need to go for additional tests at a hospital where equipment and specialist knowledge are available.

The role of the hospital in diagnosis ranges from taking X-rays and conducting chemical and microscopic examinations of blood and urine, to scanning with sophisticated and expensive machinery, to performing operations conducted under general anaesthetic in which the interior of the body is examined with a lighted tube called an endoscope. The tests will often be carried out by technicians, and the results will be interpreted by specialists.

When the diagnosis has been made, treatment can be decided upon.

Pathology

Pathology is the study and analysis of diseased body organs and cells. Pathologists (doctors who specialise in pathology) normally work in laboratories, and if a pathology test is ordered, you are unlikely to meet the pathologist in the normal course of events.

For a pathology test to be carried out, a sample of body tissue or fluid will be taken and sent to the laboratory for analysis. The sample might be of blood, urine, faeces, sputum, pus, a discharge of some kind such as from the vagina or penis, cerebrospinal fluid (from the brain or spinal cord), fluid drawn out from a joint or a cyst, or tissue obtained by scraping or biopsy. The sample may be taken by the doctor, but more commonly you will visit a central pathology clinic where it will be taken by a trained nursing sister. If, for example, a biopsy or a sample of cerebrospinal fluid is needed, you may have to go to hospital.

Samples taken by the doctor or at the clinic will be sent by courier to a laboratory. Modern laboratories are usually large organisations with 20 to 200 staff or more. The sample will be tested by a medical technologist under the pathologist's supervision. If the required tests are complex, a scientist may be called in to help, and the pathologist may examine the specimen, especially if a finding is unusual.

The first examination will usually be under a microscope. This may be in the specimen's natural state, or it may be stained with a dye so that its various elements can be isolated (e.g. acids respond to one particular stain whereas alkaline elements react to a different one). Some of the sample may then be cultured. This means that it is added to a culture medium, which is usually a liquid or jelly-like substance containing nutrients in which bacteria or other micro-organisms will grow. The culture is incubated for a period, and if the bacteria or other organisms do in fact grow, they can be identified under a microscope or by various tests. If necessary, the organisms can be tested to see if they are sensitive to antibiotics, and if so, to which ones.

Once the results are obtained they will be fed into a computer for collation. If a serious disease is detected, the doctor who ordered the test will be telephoned with the result. Printed results are sent back by courier to the doctor's office.

Depending on what tests are necessary, the results will be available in a day or so, or in a couple of hours if it is an emergency. Culturing may take a couple of days, in the case of bacteria, or possibly several weeks if a virus is involved.

Almost any part of the human body or its secretions can be tested for disease. Urine samples can be tested to see if the patient is taking medication, or has infections or gout. Faeces can tell a pathologist if the patient is absorbing food properly, or keeping to a diet. The fluid around the brain and spinal cord will provide details of a head injury or infection. Cancer can be detected in many different tissues that a surgeon has removed. If cancer is suspected during an operation, a pathologist may be called to the operating theatre to examine the tissue under a microscope so that the surgeon can decide how to finish the operation. Cancer of the cervix can also be detected at a very early stage by the pathologist's examination of the Pap smear that all women should have every year or two (see Section 7). Unusual tests can be performed on sweat to check for cystic fibrosis (an inherited lung disease in children), on the fluid around the baby in the womb to detect congenital diseases and to find out its sex, on semen to determine a man's fertility, on the fluid in joints for arthritis, and on bone marrow to detect leukaemia.

Amniocentesis

While a foetus is in the womb, it is surrounded by the amniotic sac which contains fluid that protects it from harm. Amniotic fluid is swallowed by the foetus and passed out through the anus and bladder, so it contains cells of the baby's skin and other organs. Amniocentesis is a procedure in which a small amount of the amniotic fluid is drawn off, and the cells it contains are cultured and analysed under a microscope to give information about the health of the baby. It will also disclose the baby's sex. The cells contain the baby's chromosomes which it has inherited from its parents. These chromosomes can be analysed to give information about 75 different genetic disorders, such as Down's syndrome. Not all the tests will be carried out routinely, so it is important for the doctor to be aware of your particular family and medical history.

There is a slightly increased possibility of miscarriage as a result of amniocentesis, and it will not usually be carried out unless there is some risk of abnormality.

Risk factors include:
- A woman who is over 37 years of age, especially if it is her first child. Older mothers are significantly more at risk of giving birth to a Down's syndrome child and will usually be offered this test as a matter of routine at between 16 and 18 weeks of pregnancy.
- One or other parent with a known chromosomal abnormality. For example, a woman may be a carrier of a genetic disorder

such as haemophilia which does not affect her but which her sons have a 50% chance of inheriting. Amniocentesis reveals the baby's sex and so gives the parents the opportunity of terminating the pregnancy.
- Certain diseases that run in either parent's family (e.g. muscular dystrophy).
- The fact that the mother has had three or more miscarriages.
- An earlier abnormal child, or a close family member with an abnormal child.

Amniocentesis is also performed late in the pregnancy to establish the baby's lung maturity if it is to be induced prematurely or delivered early by caesarean section. One of the main dangers faced by premature babies is that their lungs are not sufficiently mature to function properly, and amniocentesis can give early warning of the need to overcome this. Late amniocentesis is also carried out in cases of Rh incompatibility (see BLOOD, Section 2) and will show if the baby needs a blood transfusion while it is still in the womb, or whether it needs careful monitoring after the birth.

How amniocentesis is done
An ultrasound scan (see separate entry) will be performed first so that the position of the foetus and placenta can be pinpointed. The woman will then be given a local anaesthetic in the abdomen, following which a hollow needle will be inserted through the abdominal wall into the uterus. About 14 mL (roughly two dessertspoons) of fluid will be removed by a syringe attached to the needle. The fluid will be placed in a centrifuge and spun, so that the cells are separated out. The cells are then cultured for two and a half to five weeks.

Amniocentesis is performed not less than 14 weeks (and usually 16–18 weeks) after the last period, because until then there is not enough amniotic fluid or cells to analyse.

The pros and cons of amniocentesis
Amniocentesis is 99% reliable. The risk of injury to the baby is practically nil. The risk of a miscarriage occurring is very slight — about one in 200. Complications such as infection and bleeding are also rare, although some of the baby's blood cells may leak into the mother's system and this can cause complications if the mother is Rh negative.

It is not, however, a procedure that should be undertaken lightly. There is a risk, albeit a slight one. You will need to think about what your reaction will be if the results should prove to be abnormal. If you would not consider having the pregnancy terminated under any circumstances, the test is probably pointless. There is a long wait for the results and this can be stressful.

Terminating a pregnancy at the stage the results become known is distressing and may need to be the same as an induced labour.

See also CHORIONIC VILLUS SAMPLING.

BIOPSY

A biopsy is the removal of a small piece of tissue from an organ or part of the body so that it can be examined under a microscope to detect the presence of abnormal or diseased cells. It is one of the surest ways to determine if disease is present.

Biopsies are particularly important in the diagnosis of cancer and will often be performed when there is a lump, a tumour, a cyst or a swelling for which there is no apparent cause and when the doctor feels that the only way to reach an accurate diagnosis is by taking a piece of that lump and looking at the cells directly.

If the tissue to be sampled is skin, the procedure is quite simple — a piece of skin is merely cut away, using a local anaesthetic. If the required tissue is from an internal organ, e.g. the liver, kidney or lung, a special hollow needle is inserted which will suck the tissue out. A local anaesthetic may be applied to the skin, and the procedure is quite quick and usually painless. In a biopsy such as a cervical smear test, the tissue is removed by scraping a thin film of surface cells. In an endoscopic biopsy, a fine tube with both a lens and a light is passed into the body so that the inside can be seen. A tiny knife in the head of the tube then removes a small specimen of tissue. This is done for ovarian cysts, if it is suspected that a peptic ulcer might be malignant, or to investigate a growth in the colon or rectum (see ENDOSCOPY).

Once the tissue has been extracted, it is usually placed in preservative and sent to the laboratory, where it is set in wax and finely sliced. The slices are then mounted on a glass slide and stained with various dyes which highlight different characteristics. Abnormal cells can be identified and treatment can be decided upon according to the results.

A biopsy is sometimes performed as part of an operation, e.g. when the surgeon needs to know whether a lump is benign or malignant. In this case, the tissue can be snap-frozen, sliced and examined under a microscope immediately. The operation will then proceed on the basis of the result, and if cancer is found, the surgeon will try to ensure that all the diseased tissue is removed then and there rather than subjecting the patient to another general anaesthetic and operation.

Bone marrow biopsy

A bone marrow biopsy is most commonly carried out in cases of suspected leukaemia and certain anaemias. The bone marrow is responsible for the production of new blood cells, and an analysis of bone marrow can give vital information if this production seems to have been disrupted and caused disease.

Marrow is obtained through a needle inserted into the cavity of either the breastbone or the hip bone. A local anaesthetic is given, but there will usually be some pain as the needle reaches the interior. A smear of the bone marrow extracted is examined to assess such things as the number of cells, the internal chemistry and the maturity of the cells, and the presence of abnormal cells.

Leukaemia is a type of cancer of the blood in which developing white blood cells fail to mature properly and as a result multiply abnormally fast, eventually overpowering the normal cells in the bloodstream. A bone marrow biopsy will show whether this is happening.

Pernicious anaemia is a disease in which red cells fail to develop in the normal way, resulting in vast numbers of abnormal cells in the bone marrow. This too can be diagnosed by an analysis of a sample of bone marrow.

Lymph node biopsy

Lymph nodes are tiny glands in the lymphatic system that filter out infections and poisons that occur in the body. A lymph node biopsy is a procedure in which a lymph node is removed and analysed for abnormalities. It may give information about certain infections or about one of the cancers attacking the lymphatic system, including the spleen, such as Hodgkin's disease.

To remove a lymph node, the area of skin over the node is anaesthetised and then cut so that access can be gained to the node, which then is removed. The cut is then stitched with one or two stitches. The procedure takes about 15-30 minutes and is not painful, although as with any cut the area will be sore for a day or so. A child may be given a general anaesthetic.

Breast biopsy

If preliminary examinations of a lump in the breast indicate that it might be malignant, the doctor may order a breast biopsy. This may be performed in either of the two basic ways, i.e. a hollow needle may be inserted into the breast to extract fluid that contains cells, or some of the tissue may be removed with a knife. The first method is called a needle biopsy, and the second is called a surgical biopsy. A needle biopsy may or may not require a local anaesthetic and takes only a few minutes; it is usually done in the outpatient's department of the hospital, or sometimes in the surgery by the doctor. A surgical biopsy may also be done in the outpatient's department with a local anaesthetic, but more frequently it involves admission to hospital and a general anaesthetic, especially if the lump is large and deep-seated or has showed up on an X-ray but cannot be felt.

At one time, if a surgical biopsy proved positive, the operation continued and the woman's breast was removed immediately. This practice is now rare. It will usually only be followed if a needle biopsy has already indicated that cancer is present and the woman and her doctor have discussed the options fully and reached a considered decision. Even in these circumstances, the woman may choose to defer the removal of the breast until after the confirmatory results are known and she has had time to prepare emotionally and to explore all the alternatives to their fullest extent. See BREAST CANCER, Section 5.

BLOOD TESTS

Blood tests are among the most useful and commonly ordered of all diagnostic tests. A blood test can give information not only about your blood (e.g. whether it contains infection-causing bacteria, drugs or alcohol), but since the blood is linked to all parts of the body, it also reflects many changes involving quite separate organs. For example, if your liver is malfunctioning, the problem will almost certainly show up in your blood. Consequently, blood tests are used not only for information on the blood itself but to diagnose disorders of many of the organs and systems of the body.

Among the things that can be detected by analysing your blood are bone disease, whether you have a bone fracture that is healing, liver diseases caused by hepatitis, cancer or alcohol abuse, heart disease, gallstones, thyroid and parathyroid disorders, kidney disease, a too high level of cholesterol leading to increased likelihood of heart disease, diabetes, anaemia, malnutrition, gout and if you have too much or too little vitamin D. It can also tell what medications or drugs you are taking.

How the blood is taken

The doctor may take the blood in the surgery or you may be asked to go to a nearby pathology clinic. Either way, the sample will be sent to a laboratory for analysis, unless a relatively simple test is required, in which case the doctor may have the necessary equipment in the surgery to perform the analysis (e.g. for anaemia).

Blood is extracted by inserting a hollow needle into a vein and allowing an amount of blood to flow into an attached tube. The blood will usually be taken from a vein at the bend in your elbow, but if that is not sufficiently prominent, the nurse may try your forearm or the back of your hand. It takes only a minute or so.

For very minor blood tests where not much blood is needed, such as for a simple cholesterol test, enough blood may be obtained from a prick in your finger. Once the nurse has sufficient blood for the tests that have been ordered, the needle will be withdrawn and a pad of dressing or cotton wool pressed on to the point of entry to stop the flow. You will need to leave it in place for half an hour or so until the blood clots naturally.

If the blood test is to measure the proportions of oxygen and carbon dioxide in your blood (a blood gas analysis), it will be taken from an artery, because arterial blood contains oxygen absorbed from the air in your lungs. In this case, blood will be taken with a needle and syringe from the arm, wrist or groin. This is more uncomfortable than taking blood from a vein and you may be given a local anaesthetic.

Usually the blood can be taken at any time of the day, unless the test is to measure your metabolism (roughly, how your body converts food into energy), in which case the test might be ordered in the early morning after a 12 hour fast, or at particular times after you have eaten a certain measured amount of food. Blood tests to measure the amount of certain drugs in the system are also taken at specific times after the tablets are swallowed.

Types of blood analysis
There are several types of blood analysis, depending on what the test is aimed at discovering. Different groups of tests may be carried out by different laboratories.

Haematology tests deal with blood cells, blood groups and clotting functions and can disclose diseases of the blood, such as anaemia. Biochemistry measures the concentration of the chemicals contained in the blood. Microbiology tests are to investigate the presence of bacteria and viruses. Other specialised laboratories measure hormones and antibodies in blood. Mostly blood will be subjected to a battery of tests.

Full blood count
A full blood count (FBC) is the most frequently performed of all blood tests and is a series of several tests which give an enormous amount of information about your blood and the state of your overall health. Blood cells consist of three different types — red cells, white cells and platelets. Red cells transport oxygen, white cells fight infection, and platelets are one of the main factors in enabling the blood to clot. A blood count determines the number of all these cells, their size, the amount of haemoglobin (oxygen-carrying red pigment in the red cells) and the proportions in which they exist. If you consult a doctor because you are unduly tired and lacking in energy, it may mean that you are anaemic, or that you have an infection, or simply that you are

SECTION 4: INVESTIGATIONS

working too hard. By ordering a blood count, the doctor can find out which it is. If you are anaemic, you will have too few red blood cells; if you have an infection it is likely that your white blood cells will have increased to fight it. If both your red cells and white cells are normal, the doctor will probably suggest that you have a holiday.

Clotting test

A clotting or coagulation test measures how long it takes the blood to clot and the levels of the many factors involved in the clotting process. This test may be ordered for someone who bruises or bleeds excessively to find out if they are a sufferer from the hereditary disease haemophilia (in which the blood does not clot and so even a minor accident can cause them to bleed excessively), or one of the many other diseases that can reduce clotting.

Patients with a high risk of clots forming in an artery and causing a heart attack may be placed on anticoagulant drugs. Clotting tests may be carried out to monitor the effect of these drugs and to ensure that a balance is maintained between preventing a clot forming and stopping the blood clotting at all.

Blood gas analysis

Oxygen from the air we breathe is extracted by our lungs and transferred to our blood to be pumped throughout the body. The oxygen is exchanged with the waste product, carbon dioxide, which is contained in blood that has been used. If the lungs are diseased, this exchange process will not take place efficiently, and our blood will retain the poisonous carbon dioxide and not adequately be rejuvenated with fresh oxygen. A blood gas analysis measures the concentration of oxygen and carbon dioxide in the blood and can tell the doctor if lung diseases such as asthma, pneumonia, emphysema or pneumoconiosis may be present.

Blood sugar test

Blood sugar tests are used to diagnose hyperglycaemia and hypoglycaemia (too much or too little sugar in the bloodstream) which may be associated with diabetes.

Glucose (a type of sugar) is essential for the efficient working of every cell in the body. Sugar we eat is processed for use in the body by a chemical called insulin, produced by the pancreas. If insulin is not being produced as it should, the sugar cannot be metabolised and accumulates in the bloodstream. This is diabetes, and a blood sugar test will be ordered for a patient suspected of suffering from diabetes.

As a first step the test will normally be taken at any convenient time of the day, and if the blood sugar level is abnormally high you will be required to have another test after a 12 hour fast. If the fasting blood sugar is raised, a glucose tolerance test will normally be given. In this test a fasting blood sample is collected as a base. You will then be given a drink containing a measured amount of glucose. For the next three hours (roughly the time the digestive process takes), samples of blood are collected at half-hourly intervals. The glucose level of each sample is measured and plotted on a graph. The finished graph will show if, and at what rate, the glucose is being absorbed. If the absorption rate is abnormally low, it establishes that you are not producing enough insulin and so have diabetes. Thereafter, treatment by diet, insulin injections or other medication in tablet form will be necessary.

Blood urea test

Urea is a chemical produced by the liver in the process of the body's use of proteins. It is normally excreted by the kidneys, and if the kidneys are not functioning properly it will accumulate in the blood. Hence a high level of urea in the blood indicates possible kidney disease.

Immune tests

If you get an infection, your blood produces antibodies to fight it off. These antibodies remain even after the infection has cleared up, and in many instances mean that the particular infection cannot take hold again, in other words that you are immune to it. Rubella (German measles) is an infection which, once suffered, will not usually recur. A doctor will often order a blood test to find out if a patient is at risk from various diseases. For example, the doctor will want to know if a pregnant woman has had rubella (which can harm the foetus) or whether she should be immunised against it — although immunisation during pregnancy is not advisable.

For some reason not yet fully understood, a person's body can start producing antibodies to their own tissues. This means, in effect, that the body fights against itself and is the cause of its own destruction. This is called auto-immune disease, an example of which is rheumatoid arthritis. The presence of these antibodies can also be determined by a blood test.

Sometimes tests are carried out to detect the presence of antigens themselves (antigens are substances that the body regards as foreign and to which it will develop antibodies). The presence of particular antigens in the blood indicates that the organism is still active and that, even though the symptoms have subsided, the person may be a carrier of the disease, e.g. hepatitis B.

The progress of certain diseases can be assessed by testing the blood for substances called immunoglobulins (disease-fighting organisms much like antibodies) which are different according to whether the disease is current or past.

A T cell count tests the number and proportion in the blood of substances called T lymphocytes, which are an indication of the progress of immune deficiency diseases such as AIDS.

How the blood test is carried out

Blood is made up of cells suspended in straw coloured fluid called plasma. Blood serum is the fluid that separates from clotted blood or blood plasma when it is allowed to stand. Most tests are carried out on serum. When your blood is collected, it is placed in a plain glass or plastic tube in which it clots. If the blood cells or plasma are to be examined, some of the sample is put into a different tube containing a chemical that stops it clotting, so that it forms what is called a whole blood sample. The cells and clot are then separated from the plasma or serum by spinning the tube in a centrifuge.

Nowadays, most of the common blood tests are carried out by machines called auto-analysers and are available within 24 hours of the sample reaching the laboratory. Unusual or specialised tests may take a few days, since they will normally be performed in batches once or twice a week.

CEREBROSPINAL FLUID TEST (SPINAL TAP, LUMBAR PUNCTURE)

Cerebrospinal fluid (CSF) is the clear watery fluid that surrounds the brain and spinal cord. The chemical composition of CSF changes in the presence of certain diseases of the nervous system, and in cases of suspected multiple sclerosis, stroke, poliomyelitis, meningitis, tumour and similar disorders, a sample of the spinal fluid may be analysed as a help in diagnosing the disease. Other diagnostic techniques used in such investigations are radiography and electroencephalography (see separate entries).

The extraction of CSF is commonly called a spinal tap or lumbar puncture. The procedure is carried out in hospital where local anaesthetic is injected just under the skin. The patient lies on the side, legs drawn up to the abdomen and chin bent down to the chest so that the spine is stretched and the spaces between the vertebrae are opened up. A hollow needle is then passed between the vertebrae in the lower part of the spine. A probe from the centre of the needle is removed and fluid flows up the hollow channel. A pressure-measuring manometer is connected so that the spinal fluid pressure can be measured and then, using a three-way tap, a sample of fluid is run off into a bottle. The procedure takes about 15 minutes, and some people find it

FIGURE 4.1: Lumbar puncture.

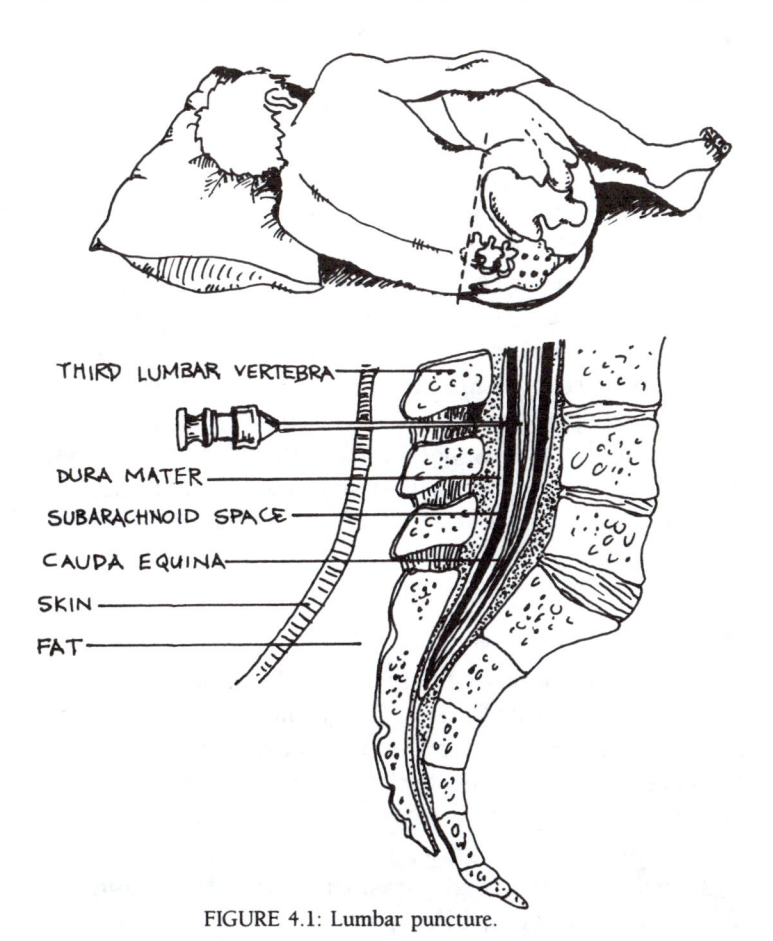

uncomfortable although not usually painful. You will normally be required to remain lying down for several hours to reduce the likelihood of headache, although you may have a moderate to severe headache for up to 24 hours afterwards.

Chorionic villus sampling (CVS)

Chorionic villus sampling is a relatively new technique that can be used in the same situations and for the same reasons as amniocentesis (see separate entry). Primarily it checks for chromosomal abnormalities in a developing foetus. CVS has the advantage over amniocentesis in that it can be performed as early as eight weeks after conception. The results are therefore known earlier, and if a termination of pregnancy is desired because of a serious abnormality in the foetus, this can be undertaken at a far earlier stage of pregnancy when it is physically safer and less stressful to the mother.

The chorionic villi are the microscopic fingers of the placenta that penetrate into the wall of the mother's uterus to enable the blood supplies of the foetus and mother to interact and exchange nutrition, wastes and oxygen. The placenta has the same chromosomal make-up as the foetus, so analysing a sample of cells from the chorionic villi of the placenta gives the same result as analysing cells from the foetus itself.

CVS involves collecting a small amount of placental tissue by passing a very fine tube into the vagina and through the cervix into the uterus, and sucking up a small amount of the placenta into a syringe. Only a tiny number of cells is required, as after removal they are cultured to increase their number before being examined for abnormal chromosomes.

There is a risk of miscarriage with this procedure, as with amniocentesis, but it is only two or three in every 100 tests. For this reason the test is only undertaken if there is some initial suspicion that an abnormal result may be obtained (e.g. if a previous child or a close family member has some chromosomal abnormality).

FAECES TESTS

Faeces are the solid waste eliminated from our body. Like urine, because faeces have passed through much of the body, an analysis of their composition can be an indication of abnormalities and disorders existing in the body. A faeces sample is collected by defecating directly into a clean dry container.

One of the most straightforward reasons for testing the faeces is the suspected presence of parasites or worms in the intestines. In such a case, the eggs, body parts or entire bodies can often be seen quite easily in the faeces. As well, the colour of the faeces can indicate something abnormal. For example, black or red faeces may indicate bleeding in the stomach or intestines, while tan or white faeces may be a sign of liver or gall bladder problems.

Even if nothing untoward can be seen in the faeces, chemical tests may show, for example, that blood is in fact present. An analysis of the fat and salt content of the faeces provides a means of assessing if food is being properly digested and absorbed, or if there is some digestive disorder present. A culture test performed on the faeces may be carried out to determine a possible infectious cause of diarrhoea.

LUMBAR PUNCTURE

See CEREBROSPINAL FLUID TEST.

SEMEN TEST

The purpose of a semen test is to determine the health of a man's sperm if he and his partner are having difficulty in conceiving a child. The man will ejaculate a sperm sample into a sterile container, which will be sent to a laboratory and examined to establish the number of sperm, whether they are normal, and if they are able to swim sufficiently strongly to make their way to the woman's ovaries to fertilise an egg. The semen sample must reach the laboratory as soon as possible after ejaculation.

Semen tests are also performed about six weeks after a vasectomy to ensure that the operation has been a success and the man is infertile.

Skin tests

Allergy tests

The most common reason skin tests are carried out is to test for allergies. If a person has all the symptoms of an allergy (e.g. a rash, hives or swelling, or sometimes respiratory difficulties such as in hay fever) and does not know what is causing it, they may need to be tested to find out. The tests consist of the injection of various substances under the skin. These substances, called allergens, are found in cat fur, house dust, pollen from various plants, etc. Allergies to certain foods and drugs can also be tested. If you react to a particular injection, then the source of the allergy has been identified. The process is one of elimination, and consequently may be very slow.

Allergy testing can be especially important for people who react violently to things such as bee stings, since they may need desensitising treatment or to carry a supply of adrenaline in case of emergency.

Mantoux test

A Mantoux test establishes if someone has ever had tuberculosis. It is similar to an allergy test in that a solution containing dead tuberculosis bacteria is injected into the skin. If the person has had the disease or has been immunised against it, their system will contain antibodies and these will rush to the site of the injection (normally the arm) leading to a raised red swelling. The reaction takes 48 to 72 hours. The larger the patch, the more likely it is that the person has, or has had, tuberculosis, or has developed immunity to it following vaccination.

Schick test

A Schick test establishes a person's immunity to diphtheria. In this test a weak solution of the toxins produced by the bacteria which causes diphtheria is injected into the skin on the forearm. In this case, there will be no reaction if the antibodies are present, since the toxin will be neutralised. Instead the reaction occurs within three or four days if the person has not had the disease and so needs immunising against it.

Spinal Tap

See CEREBROSPINAL FLUID TEST.

Sputum Tests

Sputum is a kind of messenger from the respiratory system. It consists of mucus and fluids produced by the lungs and other air passages, and if there is an infection in any of these areas, the organisms will usually be found in the sputum. Generally a sputum sample will be obtained quite easily by your coughing it up. If you have trouble producing it in the doctor's office, you may be given a container to take home overnight or be sent to a physiotherapist to be given chest draining treatment.

The sample will be sent to a laboratory and usually examined first under a microscope. If you have a bacterial infection, it will generally be pinpointed at this stage and treatment can begin. If the result is uncertain, the specimen may be cultured in a special liquid or jelly to see what disease-causing organisms grow.

A problem which sometimes arises with sputum tests is that the sample may be contaminated with organisms from the mouth. In this case, the test becomes largely useless.

Urine Tests

Next to blood tests, urine tests are the most frequently ordered of the diagnostic tests. During the course of the day, all our blood is filtered through our kidneys, which means that not only are diseases of the urinary system and kidneys detectable in urine, but also a number of diseases which occur elsewhere in the body, the most common of which is diabetes. However, for something to show up in the urine, it must be a substance that is isolated by the kidneys or picked up as the urine flows from the kidneys to the bladder and out of the body. This does not include disease-fighting antibodies, some hormones, proteins and fats, and many other substances which are symptoms of disease — blood tests are necessary for these. Substances that are found in the urine include sugar, blood, pus, crystals, bile and some proteins.

Urine can be analysed by its appearance, by mixing it with various chemicals and noting the reaction, and by placing a specimen under a microscope to see if organisms are present.

To provide a urine sample or specimen, you will usually urinate into a clean glass container. The doctor may give you one provided by the laboratory, or you can use any bottle or jar of a suitable size and shape provided it has been carefully washed and dried. You will sometimes be asked to provide the sample first thing in the morning. However, sometimes the doctor will want urine samples collected throughout the day. This is because the kidneys function differently at different times of the day, due to eating, drinking, physical activity and various hormonal activities. They may retain more or less water, or different kinds of salts. As a result, the amount and concentration of the various substances contained in the urine varies throughout the day. Substances that are high at one time of the day may be quite low at another time. The only way to obtain a full picture of what the urine contains and whether it is abnormal or simply part of the daily variation is to collect and analyse all the urine discharged over a whole 24 hour period, and this will normally be done, for example, when disorders of the endocrine system (the system that produces the body's hormones) are suspected.

On occasions a urine sample is collected straight from the bladder by means of a catheter. Modern day catheters are usually made from plastic or rubber, with a solid tip so that it is easier to insert. Great care must be taken in the sterilisation of catheters to avoid passing any infection into the bladder. Not only will the instrument be thoroughly sterilised itself, but the hands of anyone who is involved in its use will be prepared as if for an operation. The catheter must be introduced very gently, especially in men with their much longer urethra.

What the urine tests reveal

A routine urinalysis begins with an evaluation of the colour, clarity and odour of the sample. Normal urine is clear, pale yellow to dark amber, and has an easily recognisable odour. If the urine is cloudy or has a foul odour, it may indicate the presence of infection. If it has a pinkish tinge, blood may be present, and if it is brownish, there is too much bilirubin — a pigment produced by the liver which is present in excess if the person is suffering from liver disease such as hepatitis. Certain foods, food colourings and drugs turn urine orange.

Urine that smells of ammonia may be a sign of cystitis, whereas the urine of someone suffering from diabetes smells like new-mown hay. What we eat is reflected in the smell our urine gives off — the pungent smell of garlic is evident in the urine as well as in the breath, spinach produces an acrid smell, mushrooms produce a fetid odour, and truffles a stagnant smell. Even certain deodorants and talcum powders can be detected in the urine.

Nowadays the most common form of chemical analysis is a dipstick — a paper or plastic strip impregnated with bands of chemicals that change colour when exposed to certain substances. Diabetes, kidney disease, stones, liver disease, dehydration can all be diagnosed in this way.

Urine can also be examined under the microscope for the presence of various bacteria and cells. Although blood may be visible to the naked eye, the presence of blood cells will normally be confirmed by a microscope analysis. Blood indicates kidney disease or a stone, an ulcer or tumour in the urinary system. If pus is present it generally shows that there is inflammation or ulceration somewhere in the urinary passages.

Pregnancy testing
A urine test will normally be carried out to confirm pregnancy. When a woman is pregnant, her body releases a hormone called HCG (human chorionic gonadotrophin) which is not present at other times. This hormone is produced by the placenta and appears in the urine from about the tenth day after the baby has been conceived.

The pregnancy test simply consists of mixing a few drops of the woman's urine with certain chemicals. If HCG is present, a particular chemical reaction will take place. In a test carried out in a test tube, the mix of urine and chemicals will form a characteristic deposit; if the test is carried out using a dipstick, the chemicals will change colour. To ensure a reliable result, the test is generally carried out 2–7 days after the first missed period (i.e. 16–21 days after conception).

A pregnancy test can be carried out at home with a kit purchased from the chemist, but more reliable tests are performed by doctors.

Schilling test
A patient suspected of being anaemic may be given a Schilling test to find out how well the body is absorbing vitamin B12. You will be given two doses of vitamin B12, one as an injection and one in tablet form, and then have your urine collected over a 24 hour period and analysed to establish how much of the vitamin has been absorbed. If a deficiency is established, another test may be taken and, if necessary, you will be prescribed injections of vitamin B12.

Certain neurological disorders can be caused by vitamin B12 deficiency.

Body scans and X-rays

Bone scan
See DUAL PHOTON ABSORPTIOMETRY OR DENSITOMETRY.
See also NUCLEAR SCAN.

CT scan
CT stands for computerised tomography. The term CAT scan (computerised axial tomography scan) is less used by the medical

profession nowadays. CT scans are a combination of X-rays (see separate entry) and computers.

When X-ray machines were first developed, they were a marvellous way of enabling doctors to see breaks and abnormalities in bones. They were not so successful at showing up soft tissues. Furthermore they took pictures from only one direction at one point in the body, thus limiting how much of the body could be seen at any one time and at what angle. Modern day CT scanners take pictures of soft tissue such as tumours, and send X-rays from all sides — around the entire circumference of 360 degrees — with no greater amount of radiation than regular X-rays. The computer then builds these cross-sectional images up into a two dimensional slice. This means that the doctor can see a total picture. CT scanners can also take pictures at every point through the body, fractions of millimetres apart. This means not only that the picture is extraordinarily accurate, but also that very precise measurements are possible, e.g. in the case of a tumour.

CT scanners have meant that doctors can make very reliable diagnoses and thus a better assessment of what treatment is most suitable. They can also guide the technician during a biopsy and may help in surgery. By far the greatest application of the scanners is in the area of malignancies to assess whether there is a tumour, how big it is and how far it has spread. A CT scan can be used after a stroke if it is not possible to tell what part of the brain has been affected. Scanning is invaluable for suspected cancers deep within the abdomen, such as in the liver. A scanner enables a doctor to see inside the body, not only without subjecting the patient to an operation, but even without having to insert a tube in an endoscopy (see separate entry).

The drawback of CT scanners is that they are enormously expensive both to buy and to run. Generally only the main hospitals can afford not only to acquire them but also to employ the skilled technicians needed to operate them. This means that one machine must usually service a large area with many people, so the demand and waiting time for use is always high. A scanner will therefore not be used for routine examinations which can just as easily be done by cheaper means, not in such heavy demand.

Having a CT scan is quick, painless and safe. Sometimes you will have some dye introduced into your body before the scan is started, either by injection or swallowing, so that the particular organ under investigation will show up more clearly. For the scan itself, you may lie on an ordinary bed while the scanner moves over your body, or the bed might be a movable one which is placed inside a circular machine, according to what part of the body is to be scanned. The machine rotates around you as it

SECTION 4: INVESTIGATIONS

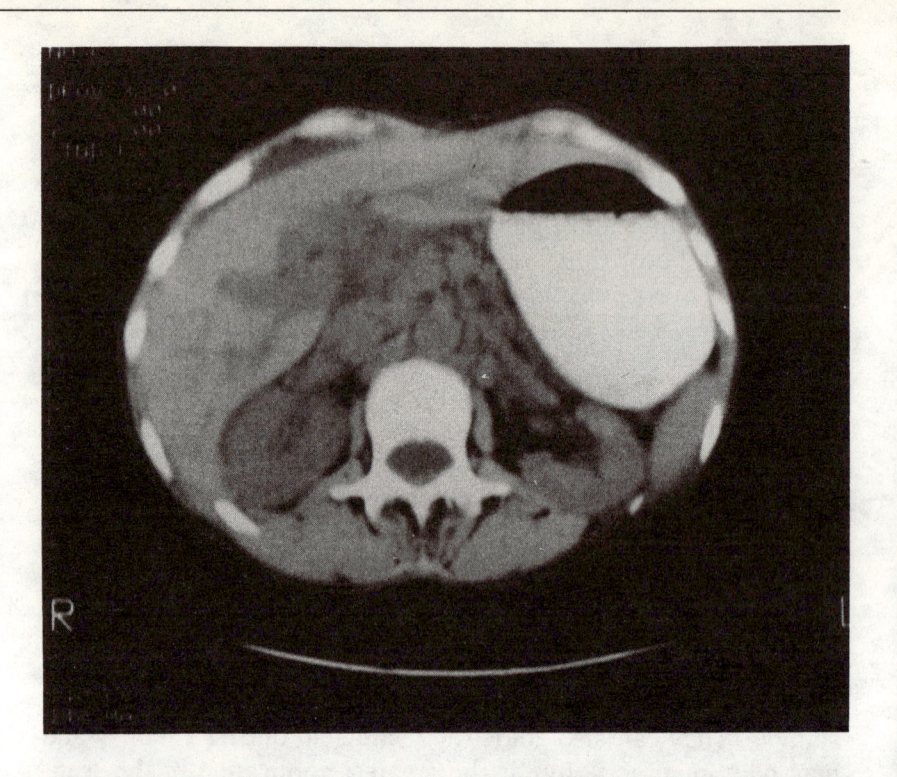

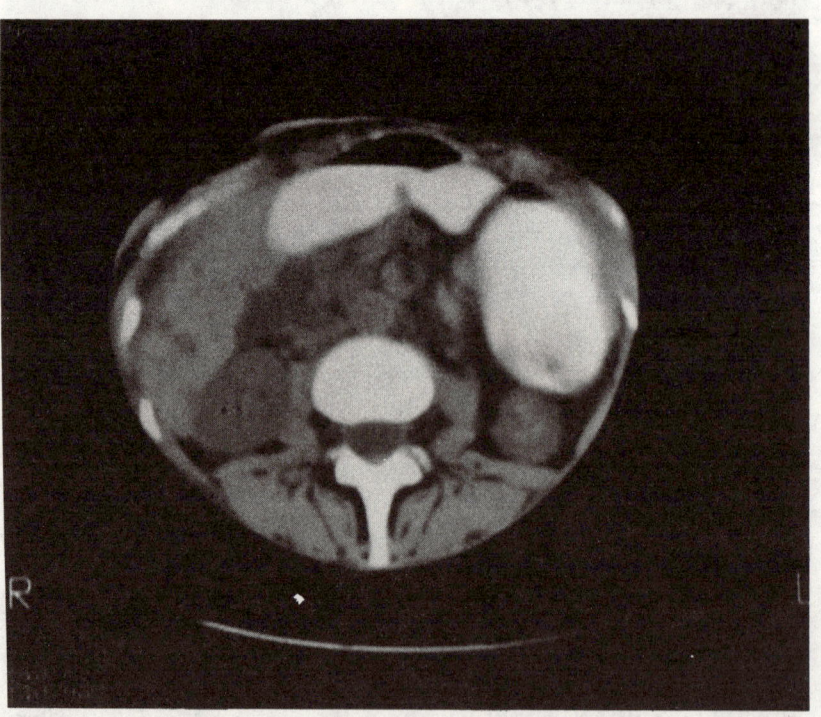

FIGURE 4.2: CT scans of different sections of abdomen.

FIGURE 4.3: CT scanner.

takes the pictures. You may be firmly strapped to the bed to avoid any movement which would blur the pictures.

Dual photon absorptiometry/densitometry (bone scan)

The density of bone can be ascertained from the amount of mineral contained in it. This type of scan is able to measure the mineral content of bone and is a way of diagnosing the onset of osteoporosis, or thinning of the bones. The machine is called an osteodensitometer. The patient lies on a bed with a flat plate underneath as a (very mild) source of radiation, and a long-armed scanner then moves slowly down the body emitting photon beams which can determine the density of the tissue they are passing through. The procedure takes about half an hour and is completely painless.

A bone scan cannot necessarily predict osteoporosis in normal people but is very useful for high-risk subjects or people who already have signs of osteoporosis, so that remedial treatment such as hormone replacement therapy and calcium supplements can be administered.

Echocardiography

Echocardiography is a highly sophisticated form of ultrasound (see separate entry) used to investigate the inner workings of the heart and in particular the heart valves.

While lying down, the patient's chest is smeared with gel, and

SECTION 4: INVESTIGATIONS

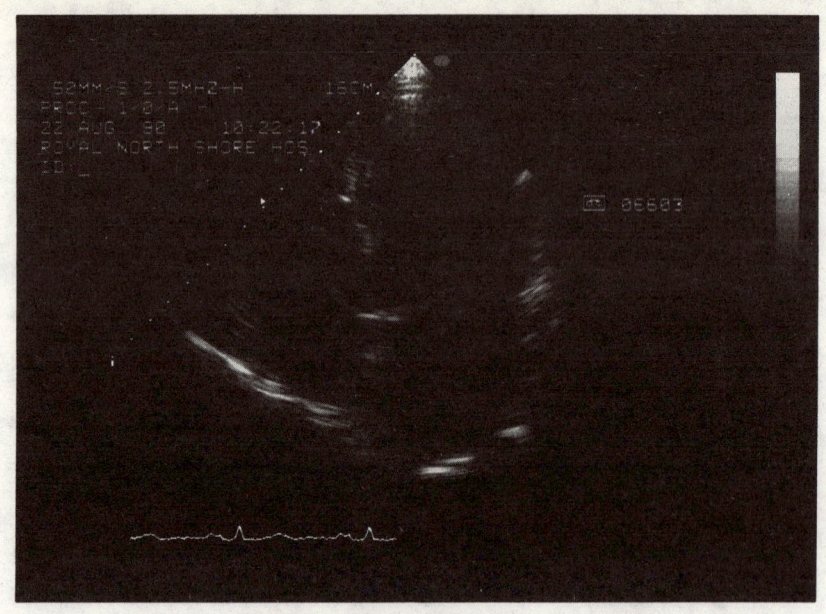

FIGURE 4.4: Echocardiogram of heart.

an instrument is placed on the chest and moved slowly from one point to another over the heart. The instrument sends out high frequency sound waves and receives back an echo of these waves as they are reflected by the heart. The reflected waves are recorded on a moving sheet of paper to give a complex tracing. Specialist doctors (usually cardiologists) interpret this tracing to see if the heart valves are working properly (e.g. if they are leaking or narrowed) and to check the contraction of each chamber of the heart.

Because performing echocardiography involves no risk, no pain and no discomfort for the patient, the procedure is often carried out before progressing to more sophisticated and invasive tests on the heart. If no abnormalities show on the echocardiogram, the other tests may be unnecessary.

MAGNETIC RESONANCE IMAGING (MRI)

Magnetic resonance imaging (MRI), or nuclear magnetic resonance (NMR) as it is sometimes called, is a new technique of scanning the body, especially the tissues that are hidden deep inside, and is a further advance on X-rays and CT scans (see separate entries). It is based on the fact that living tissues give off their own special electromagnetic signals, depending largely on their water content, and if the tissues are exposed to a magnetic field the signals can be picked up and read. Hence, a very strong magnetic field is created by special magnets, and different areas of the body absorb different amounts of magnetism according to their water content. A magnetic absorption photograph is then

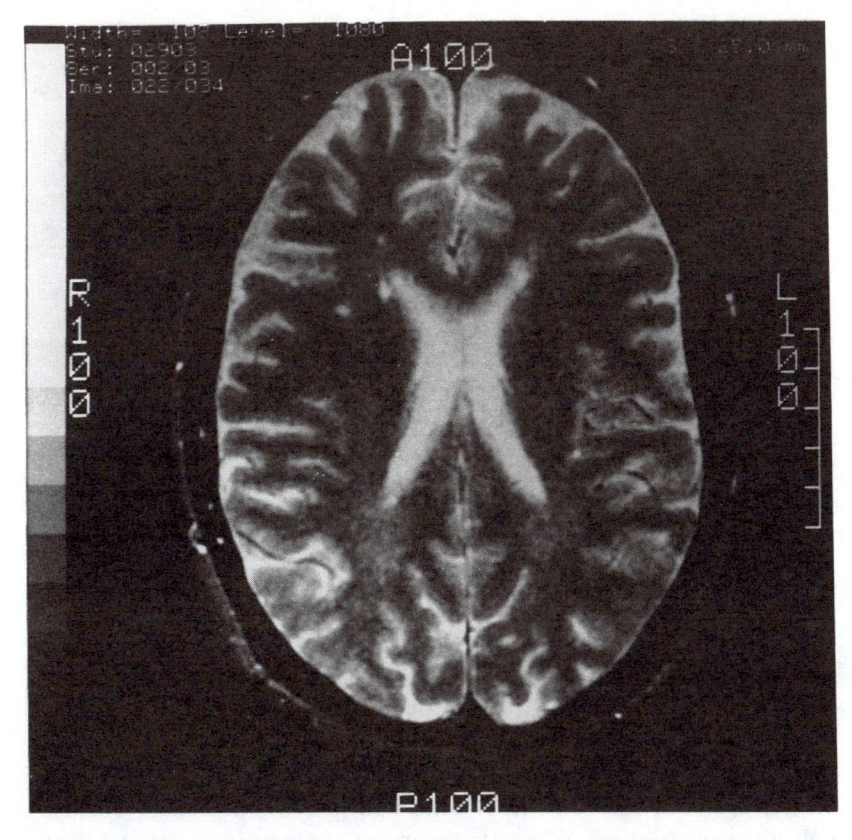

FIGURE 4.5: MRI scan of brain of patient with multiple sclerosis.

built up, and can be seen and analysed, slice by slice, on a computer screen in much the same way as a CT scan. MRI is particularly useful as it ignores bones (which contain little water) and shows up soft tissue, which is the opposite of X- rays.

MRI is especially helpful in diagnosing diseases in the brain and spinal cord, e.g. multiple sclerosis which involves abnormalities of the nerve fibres. The picture obtained by MRI of the brain clearly shows the difference between the white matter (nerve fibres) and the grey matter (nerve cells). Tumours that are not apparent on a CT scan are sometimes revealed by MRI, not only in the brain but in organs deep within the abdomen such as the liver.

MRI is completely safe. Its main disadvantage is that the equipment is enormously expensive (approximately twice as expensive as a CT scanner) and must be housed in a special magnetically sealed room.

Nuclear scan (radionuclide scan)

Nuclear scanning or imaging (also called isotope scanning) is used to measure the function of various organs, rather than

SECTION 4: INVESTIGATIONS

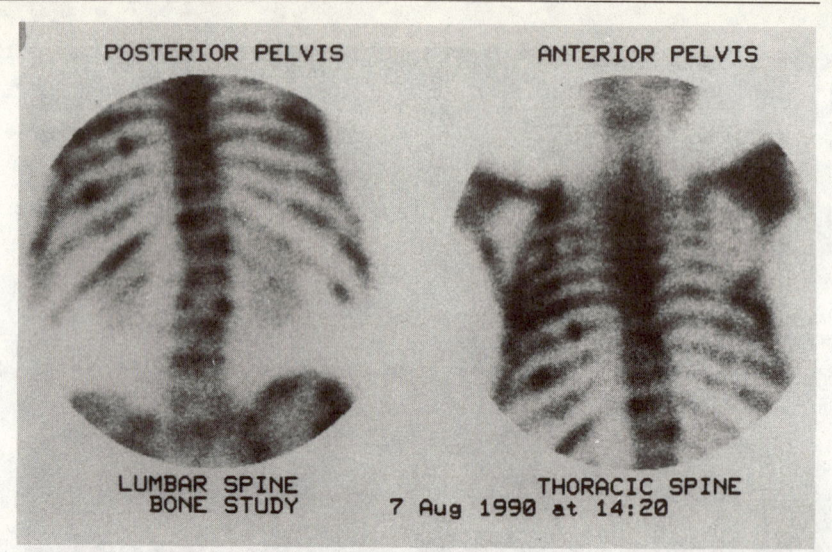

FIGURE 4.6: Nuclear bone scan showing bony metastases in spine, ribs and pelvis from prostate carcinoma.

examine their structure. It involves introducing into the body a radioactive chemical that is specifically tailored to go to the part of the body being investigated, and the nuclear energy it gives off will then be picked up by a gamma camera (working like a normal camera but picking up radiation instead of light) which is moved over the relevant area. This will provide a picture of how well the organ under investigation is functioning. An area of under- or overactivity may indicate a cyst, abscess, tumour or other abnormality, depending on the organ and on the radioactive chemical being used.

Nuclear scanning can be used to look at many different organs in the body, including the heart, bones, lungs, thyroid gland, liver, spleen and kidneys. It is particularly useful in detecting abnormal heart function and cancer in bone, where normal X-rays are not able to give enough information.

A nuclear heart scan may be performed for angina, cardiomyopathy or a heart attack to locate and measure damage to heart muscle caused by a clot or embolism. A radioactive substance that is specifically attracted to heart muscle is injected into a vein in the patient's arm. It travels through the circulation to the heart, where it is concentrated in the heart muscle, and will clearly show the site of any damage when photographed with a camera that can detect the rays released from the radioactive substance. The whole process takes less than an hour, and will be performed in a major hospital.

Bone cancer may just show as an abnormality of bone on a normal X-ray, and to differentiate normal bone from a bone cancer, a similar technique to the heart scan is undertaken, but with a different radioactive substance that concentrates in the abnormal bone.

Nuclear scanning is very safe because the amount of radiation given off by the radioactive chemical is very small — less than that from a detailed kidney X-ray (IVP). The residual chemical is eliminated from the body through the kidneys and bowels in a matter of days or hours, depending on where it has been concentrated. Nevertheless, the test is avoided in pregnant and breastfeeding women, unless absolutely essential, to protect the unborn or newborn baby from any irradiation.

PET SCAN

'PET' stands for positron emission tomography, and a PET scan is a way of measuring the chemical activity of the brain, which varies under different conditions. Unlike CT and MRI scanning, which show what the brain looks like, PET provides information

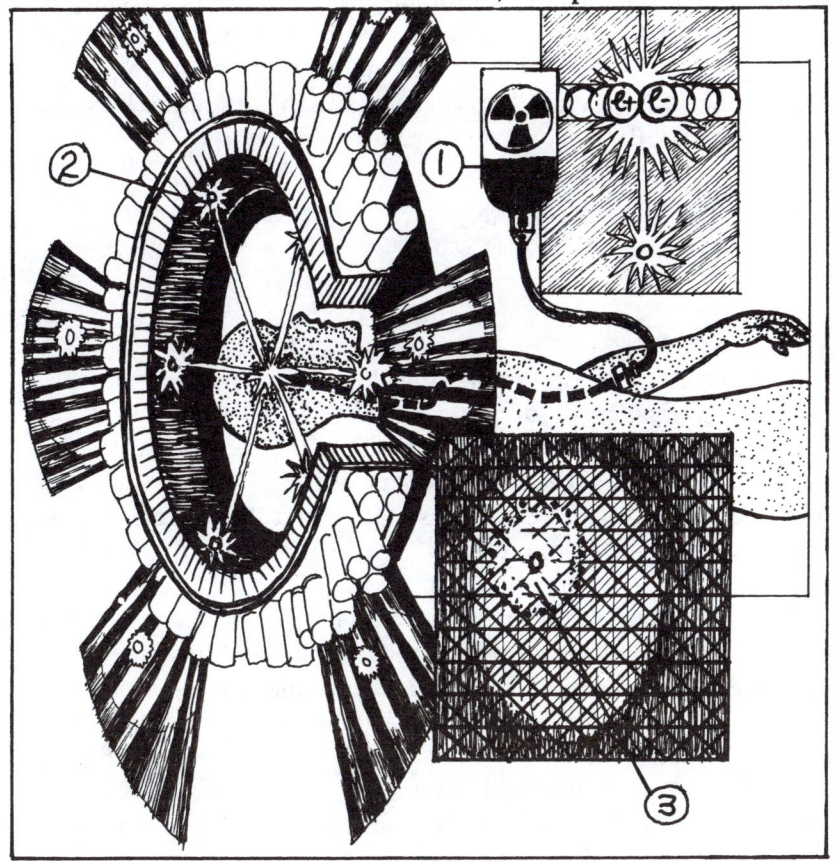

FIGURE 4.7: How PET works.
1. Tagged substance is injected, moves normally through patient and accumulates in targeted organ.
2. Patient enters PET camera, which translates data on the movement of the tagged substance into computer images.
3. Malfunctions are immediately apparent by the abnormal distribution of the tagged substance.

about how the brain is working. It produces a three-dimensional 'map' that differentiates those areas where a lot of chemical activity is taking place from those where there is little chemical activity. For example, some tumours produce more and some less chemical activity than the surrounding tissue, and a PET scan will identify them.

To carry out the scan, a radioactive chemical is injected, and as it flows throughout the brain's blood vessels it is absorbed in the greatest amounts by the most chemically active areas. As the radioactive substance breaks down, minute particles called positrons are given off. These are picked up by the scan, analysed by computer as to what part of the brain they came from, and a picture is built up of how the radioactive chemical is distributed. The number of positrons emitted from a particular area reflects how much radioactive substance has been taken up, and therefore how chemically active that section of the brain is.

PET can help to diagnose tumours (where there is virtually no chemical activity) and epilepsy (where there is excessive activity), and also give information about the functioning of the brain in various mental illnesses such as schizophrenia. It is also used to assess Parkinson's disease.

Radionucleotide scan
See NUCLEAR SCAN.

Ultrasound
Ultrasound is based on the fact that high-frequency sound waves bounce off tissues of different density at different rates. For example, bone reflects back nearly all sound waves that hit it, whereas fluids allow the waves to pass through. Sound waves are bounced off the organ being investigated, and the reflected waves are translated into a picture so the doctor can see what they mean.

Most ultrasound scans are performed by the same doctors who take X-rays (radiologists), but some GPs, obstetricians and others have their own machines for patient convenience.

There are two main types of ultrasound machines. 'Real-time' machines produce a moving image from which selected still photographs are taken. Part of the patient's body is coated with oil, and a small box that contains the sound recorder and microphone is placed on the skin. Once the area has been scanned, the instrument is moved a few centimetres and another scan is taken, and so on, until the entire area under investigation has been covered.

The other type of instrument that has been used in the past for ultrasound scanning but is now becoming obsolete involved immersing the organ to be investigated in water, which transmitted the sound waves. This type of ultrasound was used for examining the breasts and testicles, which could then be scanned in all directions without the need for the patient to move.

Almost any part of the body can be examined by ultrasound, with the exception of the head because the sound waves cannot penetrate bone. Because of the ribs, it is also difficult to see into the chest.

The most useful aspect of ultrasound is its ability to examine the foetus of a pregnant woman without the risks associated with X-rays. The size, position and sometimes sex of the baby can all be seen, and some of the internal organs of the baby, particularly the heart, can be checked. Abnormalities such as spina bifida, hydrocephalus and certain other congenital disorders can be identified. A routine scan may be performed between the sixteenth and eighteenth week of pregnancy when the foetus can easily be seen and transformed into an image. Another scan is sometimes performed later in the pregnancy, after about 32 weeks.

The breasts can be carefully checked for cysts, fibrous lumps or cancer by ultrasound, as the cancer cells reflect sound in a different way from normal cells. The gall bladder and liver can be checked for damage and stones, the kidneys and pancreas for cysts and stones, the thyroid gland and spleen for enlargement, tumours and cysts, among many other uses.

Ultrasound can also be used to study the flow of the blood. Among other interesting pieces of information to emerge is that the blood flow in the carotid artery (the main artery carrying blood to the brain) is strongly influenced by external stimuli, such as the phone ringing or someone coming into the room.

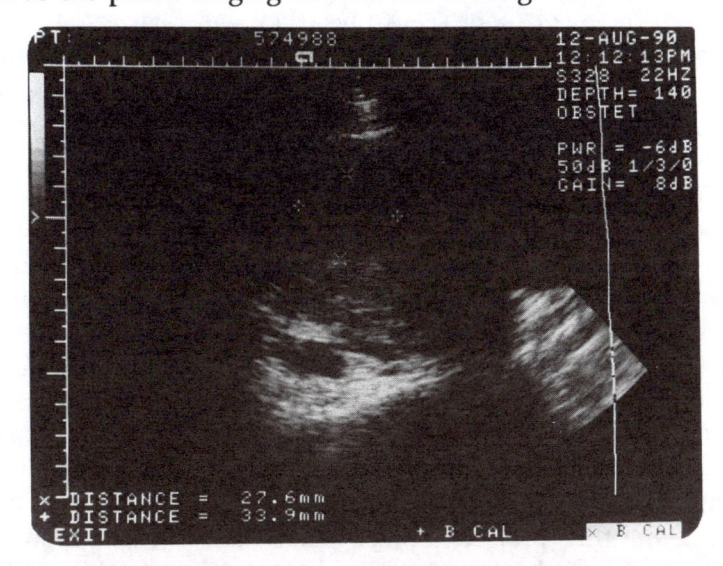

FIGURE 4.8: Ultrasound of uterus of pregnant woman.

Ultrasound is frequently used to facilitate other tests, e.g. to guide the needle towards its destination in a biopsy.

Unlike X-rays, sound waves have no effect on the tissues exposed to them, so, as far as is known, ultrasound is completely safe. It can be repeated as often as required without concern.

Ultrasound is quick, safe, painless, inexpensive and yields immediate results. Although its application is not universal, ultrasound can often complement the investigation of patients by X-ray and radioactive isotope scanning.

X-RAYS

X-rays were discovered in 1896 in Germany and virtually revolutionised medicine. It meant that for the first time it was possible to see inside the human body without cutting it open. They were called X-rays because in the beginning no-one knew exactly what they were. The study of X-rays and other types of radiation for use in diagnosis, treatment and medical research generally is called radiology. X-ray pictures of internal organs can be used to diagnose many conditions, including broken or diseased bones, pneumonia, tuberculosis, gastric ulcers, and obstructions in the intestines.

X-rays are a form of energy similar to light rays and radio waves but with the power to penetrate soft tissue. If you turn on a bright torch in a darkened room and then place a leaf over the torch lens, a shadow of the leaf showing its internal structure will be projected onto the wall. X-rays work in the same way as the torch, but because they have to penetrate the human body, the intensity of the light required is far greater. The frequency of these waves is so great that they are invisible to the eye. Although the eye cannot see X-rays, they will register on photographic film and, in essence, the taking of X-rays is a form of photography. However, no lens is used for an X-ray photograph which is different from an ordinary photograph in that it reproduces shadows rather than a pictorial image.

To take an X-ray, a photographic plate is placed in a yellow envelope, which in turn is placed in a black envelope to shield it from the light in the same way as photographic film is shielded by the camera body. The plate is then placed in close proximity to the limb or whatever part of the body is to be X-rayed. The X-ray tube is placed opposite the plate and on the other side of the limb. The tube must be some distance away from the limb to avoid distortion. When the X-ray tube is activated, the X-rays pass in parallel lines through the body opposite to the plate behind. Dense tissue such as bone prevents some of the rays from passing and thus projects a paler image than soft tissue, so that the image as a whole appears as dark and light shadows. The

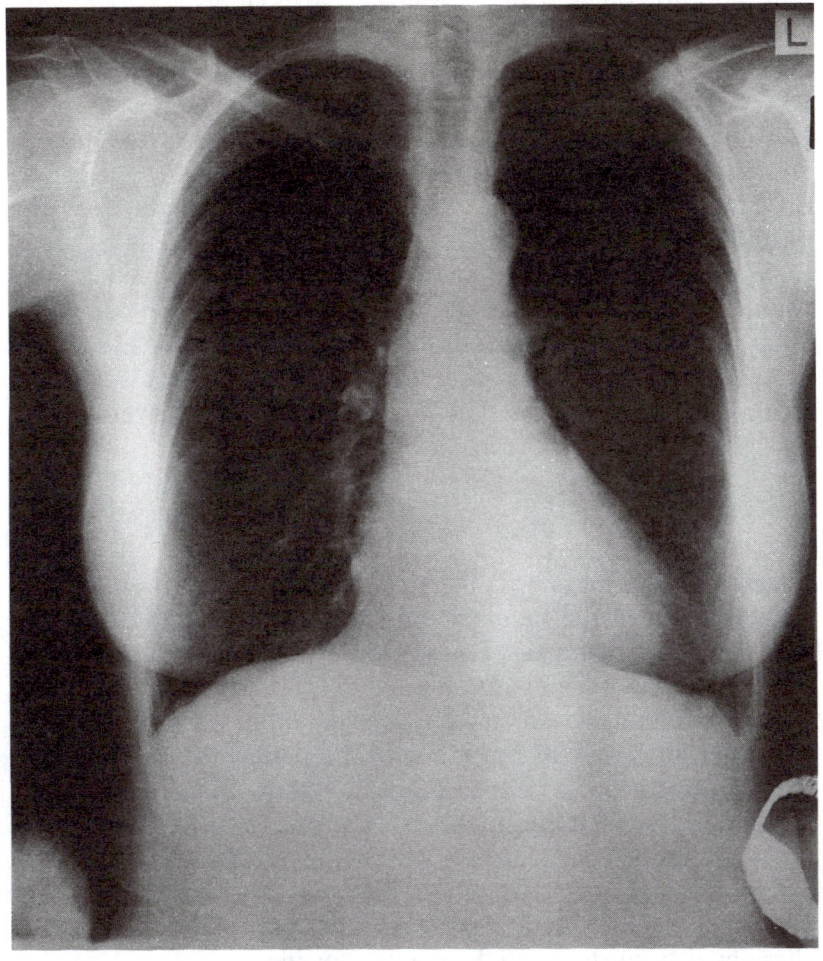

FIGURE 4.9: Chest X-ray.

recorded image is developed in the same way as in ordinary photography. The taking of X-ray photographs is called radiography.

Because an X-ray picture is a shadow, it does not matter if the X- ray beam goes from front to back, or from back to front — the same picture will be produced. X-rays cannot show depth for the same reason, and side and oblique views are usually taken so the exact position of a bone or other structure in the body can be determined.

It is now possible, using the X-ray technique, to photograph hollow interior organs to study their position and shape, and whether there is any obstruction either in the organ itself or in the ducts leading from it. To do this, harmless substances which do not transmit X-rays are either given to the patient to swallow or are injected into the organs being investigated. These throw a dense shadow on the photographic plate, corresponding to the interior of the organ being examined. For example, a patient with a suspected gastric ulcer or other digestive tract disorder will usually be asked to swallow a glass of barium sulphate which will pass down into the stomach and duodenum, showing up the existence of any abnormality in the smooth wall of the organs. Similarly, organs that are not part of the digestive tract, such as the lungs, gall bladder and kidneys, can be highlighted by the injection of radio-opaque dyes which make it possible to see if there are stones or other obstructions. X-rays obtained in this way are called contrast X-rays.

Large doses of X-rays can destroy tissues. This means that they are sometimes used in a therapeutic way to destroy abnormal tissue, but it also means that X-rays should not be given unnecessarily, and these days their use as a diagnostic tool is kept to a minimum.

Special X-rays

Intravenous pyelogram (IVP). An intravenous pyelogram (IVP) is a photograph of the kidneys and the urinary system, using the contrast X-ray technique. The soft tissues of the kidneys and the ureters (the tubes leading from the kidneys to the bladder) do not show up well on an ordinary X-ray, so an iodine compound which is opaque to X-rays is injected into the patient. The dye is normally injected into a vein in the arm ('intravenous' — within a vein) and travels through the bloodstream until it reaches the kidneys a few seconds later, at which time the X-ray is taken. The dye is then removed from the blood by the normal filtering process of the kidneys so that it becomes part of the urine and is eliminated from the body. It is quite harmless.

The pyelogram shows the sizes of the kidneys and ureters, whether their shapes are normal, and the position of any stone which exists there. If there is a stone blocking one of the ureters, only the kidney and that part of the ureter above the blockage shows.

A tight belt around the belly compresses the ureters for the first few minutes of the procedure and concentrates the dye in the kidneys. When the belt is released, the X-rays show the dye flowing down the ureters to the bladder.

In a retrograde pyelogram, dye is introduced through a tube passed into the bladder and up a ureter into the kidney's drainage system.

Myelogram. A myelogram is a special X-ray used to detect abnormalities in the spinal canal, such as tumours, fractures or damage to the vertebrae or discs, and other conditions that compress the spinal cord or the nerve roots. You will have to go to hospital and will be sedated, sometimes even given a general anaesthetic. A radio-opaque dye is injected into the space surrounding the spinal cord by means of a spinal tap (see separate entry). You will have been placed on a special table which can be tipped so that the dye can be distributed along the length of the spinal cord. The X-ray pictures are then taken.

Barium meal and **barium enema**. Barium sulphate is a heavy white radio-opaque powder used for contrast X-rays of the intestinal tract. If your upper intestines (e.g. the duodenum or stomach) are being investigated, the powder will generally be flavoured and mixed with liquid which you swallow from a glass, as a so-called barium meal. You will have been asked to fast for six hours before your appointment. The mixture passes quickly into your digestive system, enabling a picture to be taken and the presence of abnormalities to be investigated. The doctor will probably prod your abdomen and ask you to move around to enable clear photographs to be obtained of the areas needing particular examination.

If part of the lower intestine (the colon) is under investigation, you will usually be given a barium enema, in which the barium is introduced through the rectum.

You will possibly find that you are constipated following a barium meal, and that you suffer from cramps and a strong desire to defecate after a barium enema.

Angiogram. An angiogram is a contrast X-ray of a blood vessel. A radioactive dye is injected into the vessel being investigated and a picture taken of the area where the problem is suspected. You will usually be sedated but conscious during the procedure. An angiogram of an artery is called an arteriogram, and a venogram is an angiogram of a vein. Angiograms are usually used to detect blockages, such as a clot, or the narrowing of the wall of a blood vessel, such as occurs in arteriosclerosis.

If you have had a heart attack, if heart disease is suspected, or if you are to undergo a heart bypass operation, you may have a cardiac angiogram to see how much blood is getting through to the heart. This involves a catheter (thin tube) being inserted into an artery in your groin or arm and guided towards the heart where the dye is injected, and X-rays are then taken of the heart and coronary arteries. You may be given a general anaesthetic.

Mammogram. A mammogram is an X-ray of the breast using a special technique to reveal the structure of the breast. It is one of the most significant diagnostic tools available for the detection of breast cancer.

A mammogram may be ordered to investigate a lump that has emerged during a physical examination of the breasts, either by the patient herself, or by her doctor. However, more and more women are being urged to have routine mammograms since it is the only reliable method of detecting cancer at the earliest possible stage, even before a lump can be felt. Unfortunately they are not 100% reliable, and a mammogram should always be preceded or followed by a breast examination by a doctor.

Cancer cells are denser than ordinary cells and are impenetrable to certain X-rays. A tumour will therefore appear as a white patch on the mammogram picture. Mammography can sometimes detect the difference between benign and malignant tumours.

The rate of breast cancer rises markedly in women above 45, and regular mammograms are recommended for all women over this age, generally once every two years. Women younger than this should have regular mammograms if there is a high risk of developing breast cancer. Studies carried out in various parts of the world estimate that the death rate from breast cancer is reduced by up to 70% in screened women.

To have a mammogram, the woman will strip to the waist and sit in front of a small table, leaning in such a way that her breast is resting on the table, where it will be placed in various positions and photographed by the X-ray machine above. The breasts will be compressed to reduce the distance the X-rays must pass through them, and to reduce distortion caused by the curvature of the breast surface. The technique is especially valuable in the examination of large breasts, because the contrast is greater. However, a trained radiologist will detect any abnormalities in even the smallest breasts.

Having a mammogram is painless, although some women find the compression of their breasts uncomfortable. For routine mammograms, it is better to make the appointment in the first two weeks of the menstrual cycle when the breasts are not swollen and painful because of normal hormonal changes.

Modern mammography equipment delivers very little radiation and so is considered safe. Nevertheless, even small amounts of radiation increase the likelihood of getting cancer to a degree, and this needs to be taken into account when deciding on the frequency of routine tests. The older a woman gets, the less she is at risk from radiation, so those for whom a mammogram is of most value are at least risk from exposure to radiation.

Endoscopy

At one time the only way to examine the insides of a patient was to cut them open. These days sophisticated X-ray machines allow photographs to be taken deep inside the human body from every angle, scanners enable electrical impulses to be recorded and analysed so as to diagnose abnormalities, and the technique of endoscopy enables the insertion of instruments with magnifying lenses and lights, so that a doctor standing outside the patient can see exactly what is going on inside.

An endoscope is a long, usually flexible tube, with a lens at one end and a light source and a telescope at the other. The end with the lens is inserted into the patient, light passes down the tube so that the relevant area is illuminated, and the telescopic eyepiece enables the area to be magnified so that the doctor can see what is there.

Early endoscopes, which are still used and are very effective for some diagnoses, consisted of a hollow tube made of metal, often with a light bulb. More sophisticated endoscopes have since been developed, such as the fibre-optic endoscope which consists of hundreds of small bundles of glass fibres down which a light is directed and which reflects back the image by means of what are effectively tubular mirrors. The glass rods are so thin that they bend easily, making the endoscope flexible enough to bend around any organ. This kind of endoscope can literally see around corners.

An endoscope is usually inserted into the body through one of its normal openings, e.g. the mouth, the urethra or the anus. Sometimes, however, there is a need for a small incision in the skin.

Individual endoscopes have been developed for many parts of the body, including the abdominal cavity, oesophagus, rectum, bladder, lungs, stomach, intestines, uterus and several joints. Each has its own name, depending on what part of the body it is intended to investigate, so a gastroscope looks the stomach, a bronchoscope looks at the bronchial passages and the lungs, and an arthroscope examines the inside of joints.

Some endoscopes have special equipment so that a sample of tissue can be removed for further analysis (a biopsy). It is even possible for surgery to be performed using an endoscope, and a tubal ligation (tying a woman's Fallopian tubes), for example, is nowadays usually performed by endoscopy, using an instrument called a laparoscope (see LAPAROSCOPY below). Endoscopes are also used to locate and remove foreign objects that have found their way into organs such as the stomach and lungs.

Some endoscopies can be carried out in the doctor's surgery, others need a trip to hospital, and a few need a general anaesthetic. Generally you will be sedated and possibly given pain-killing medication, but the procedure may still be uncomfortable. Nevertheless an endoscopy is a good deal easier and safer than a major operation and may save your life. For example, a tiny polyp in the intestines would probably once have remained undetected until it developed into full-blown cancer. Even were it discovered, the risks of an operation had to be balanced against the possibility that the polyp was harmless. With an endoscope, such a polyp can easily be observed and simply snipped off.

Arthroscopy

Arthroscopy is a relatively new technique for the diagnosis and treatment of joint problems. It has virtually revolutionised the treatment of knee injuries, but other joints, as small as the jaw joint, can also be entered by an arthroscope.

A knee arthroscopy is performed by an orthopaedic surgeon who makes a small incision in the knee and inserts the thin lighted tube that is the arthroscope. This enables an examination of the knee to establish what particular part is damaged, e.g. the cartilage, tendon or ligament, and then, if necessary, remedial surgery can be carried out there and then, such as the removal of bits of damaged cartilage. If required, separate incisions can be made to enable the surgeon access to the damaged tissue, but these are tiny and the whole operation is viewed by the surgeon through the arthroscope. The advantages of having tiny cuts over a large incision are obvious, not least from the point of view of recuperation. The patient may be given a general anaesthetic.

Bronchoscopy

Bronchoscopy is the examination of the bronchial tubes and the inside of the lungs through a type of endoscope. It may be used if a tumour is suspected or you have a serious disease such as chronic pneumonia.

Bronchoscopy involves a trip to hospital and you will be asked to fast for six hours before the test is performed. Although your throat and airways will be anaesthetised, the procedure is quite uncomfortable. It takes about half an hour.

Colonoscopy

Just as a gastroscopy is an examination of the upper digestive tract, a colonoscopy is an examination of the lower digestive tract, or colon. A colonoscope is flexible and like other endoscopes combines the features of magnification and illumination. It is fairly long and enables the doctor to view the entire colon.

For the lower third of the colon, an instrument called a sigmoidoscope is used, which is rigid but shorter than the colonoscope which enables an examination of the bowel for polyps, tumours and other diseases. The instrument used for seeing inside the rectum and anus is called a proctoscope.

If you are to have a colonoscopy, you will normally be given a laxative or an enema and then be instructed to drink only clear fluids until the test is performed. You may experience some discomfort and will possibly be mildly sedated. The examination takes about an hour.

Colposcopy

A colposcope is a microscope that illuminates and magnifies the cells covering the cervix and vaginal walls. It is especially useful in the early diagnosis of cancer of the cervix, and if you have an abnormal result from a Pap smear (see Section 7) you will almost always have a colposcopy.

For this test, a metal instrument called a speculum is used to open up the vagina in the same way as for a smear test. The colposcope is then moved into position just outside the vagina (it never actually enters the vagina and therefore is not, strictly speaking, an endoscope) and focused on the cervix which is magnified about 10–15 times. The cervix may be painted with solutions of water and vinegar and water and iodine, which shows up abnormal cells. A tissue sample will be taken of anything suspicious.

Colposcopy is painless and takes only about 15 minutes. However, you may be asked to go to a hospital or clinic to enable a curette to be performed at the same time. This is a scraping of the lining of the uterus and may be given a general anaesthetic. In the case of a curette, there will be bleeding for some days but otherwise there should be no side effects.

If the colposcopy fails to pinpoint the diseased cells (most likely in women over 35 since cervical tissue retracts with age and cannot be seen as easily) or the full extent of the suspicious cells cannot be determined, a cone biopsy may be taken. Because of the larger amount of tissue removed in a cone biopsy, it also serves as a form of treatment. More recently, laser techniques have been developed as a form of treatment to burn off abnormal cells after a normal biopsy has been taken — a much less invasive procedure than a cone biopsy and with considerably reduced risk of bleeding and other complications.

Culdoscopy

Culdoscopy is a type of endoscopy for observing a woman's internal reproductive organs. The culdoscope is inserted through a tiny incision in the top of the vagina. It is used in the diagnosis of disorders of the uterus and the endometrium (the lining of the uterus). The woman will normally be given a general anaesthetic. Culdoscopy is now less commonly used than laparoscopy.

See also HYSTEROSCOPY.

Cystoscopy

A cystoscopy is an examination of the inside of the bladder and urinary tract. The end of a tube called a cystoscope is inserted through the urethra (the tube linking the bladder with the outside) into the bladder, where the combination of light and magnification enables the doctor to observe any abnormalities, such as stones, tumours or disorders of the bladder lining.

In men, a cystoscope may be used in the investigation of cancer of the prostate. The man will be given an anaesthetic, general or local, depending on the circumstances, and the tiny tube will be gently guided up through the penis until it reaches the prostate which is situated at the base of the bladder.

Small tumours or stones can often be removed by means of a special instrument inserted through the cystoscope, and if so there will be no need for surgery.

Fine tubes called catheters can be passed along a cystoscope and guided into each ureter (the tubes leading from the bladder up to the kidneys). This enables a specimen of urine to be obtained from each kidney so that the doctor can find out which one is diseased.

Gastroscopy

Gastroscopy is a technique by which a doctor can look inside your upper digestive tract (oesophagus, stomach and small intestine), e.g. to determine whether you have a peptic ulcer, or sometimes to investigate other disorders such as a tumour.

A gastroscope is an instrument about 1 m long, consisting of a highly flexible thin tube. There is a light to illuminate your insides at the end that is inserted, and a box at the end remaining outside with various controls so that the doctor can manipulate the tube on its way down and see everything that is present. Long flexible forceps pass down the tube and take a sample of tissue from inside the small intestine.

To have a gastroscopy, you will have to fast overnight and then go to hospital for a few hours. In hospital you will be sedated and possibly have a local anaesthetic applied to your throat and mouth. When you are sufficiently relaxed and drowsy, a gastroscope will be passed through your mouth and throat and into your stomach (the sedation will stop you retching). The procedure is not painful, but some people find having a tube passed down their throat uncomfortable. The doctor will turn on the light in the endoscope and darken the room to maximise the degree of illumination. You may be asked to lie in different positions to bring areas into view. Patients have been known to feel so comfortable at this point that they go to sleep. When the investigation is complete, the doctor will slowly withdraw the instrument. The whole procedure takes about ten minutes.

You will be allowed to go home when the sedation wears off, but you should arrange for someone to escort you.

See also COLONOSCOPY.

HYSTEROSCOPY

A hysteroscopy is an endoscopic examination of the inside of the uterus using a hysteroscope, which is passed through the vagina and cervix into the womb. A hysteroscopy is used to help diagnose disorders of the womb and the endometrium (lining of the womb). The patient will be sedated or given a general anaesthetic.

See also CULDOSCOPY; LAPAROSCOPY.

LAPAROSCOPY

A laparoscopy is an endoscopic examination of a woman's internal reproductive organs. It allows a very clear view of the tubes of the womb and the ovaries. This has made it very useful in diagnosing various gynaecological diseases, such as pelvic infection and ovarian cysts and tumours. It has also proved to be valuable as a means of checking that some gynaecological complaints such as endometriosis (tissue resembling the lining of the womb, growing outside the womb) and cancer of the ovaries are responding to treatment.

As a test for infertility which may be caused by blocked Fallopian tubes, it is possible to send dye into the uterus and see by laparoscopy if it spills out of the Fallopian tube into the abdomen. If it does, it means that the passages that allow the egg and the sperm to meet are open. At the same time, a piece of tissue from the lining of the womb can be removed for examination in the laboratory to see if the woman is ovulating.

An increasing use for laparoscopy is the removal of a woman's eggs by suction for fertilisation in a dish as part of IVF (in vitro fertilisation) procedures.

A laparoscopy involves a stay in hospital, usually with a general anaesthetic, although sometimes an epidural anaesthetic is performed in which the anaesthetic is injected into the spinal cord and the woman remains conscious. Under some circumstances only a local anaesthetic is required. A small incision is made in the abdomen just below the navel so that no scar is visible afterwards. A needle is inserted into the abdomen, and carbon dioxide gas is pumped into the abdominal cavity to inflate it so that the area can be seen more easily. The needle is withdrawn and the laparoscope is inserted. The doctor (usually a specialist gynaecologist) will then be able to see any abnormalities, and if necessary will take a small sample of tissue for further analysis. The procedure usually takes about half an hour and will be concluded with one or two stitches in the cut. You may be allowed home within a few hours, provided you have someone to assist you, or you may stay in hospital overnight. The cut and some remaining gas may produce a degree of discomfort for a day or so.

It is even possible for some surgery to be performed by means of a laparoscopy, and tubal ligation (tying of the woman's tubes for the purposes of sterilisation) is now invariably done this way. For this operation there may be two incisions, the second of which is generally made just inside the line of the pubic hair (its tiny size and the fact that the hair grows back mean that the scar is invisible in even the briefest bikini).

Electrical tests

Electrocardiogram (ECG)

The heart is a muscular bag that pumps blood by contracting and relaxing. Messages for the muscle to contract are carried electrically from one part of the heart to another. An electrocardiograph (ECG) is a machine that measures the electrical activity of the heart and can tell if it is irregular, which may signal heart disease.

Early ECG recordings were made by putting both the patient's arms and a leg in a bucket of salty water (which conducts electricity), and putting a wire from an instrument for measuring changes in electrical current (a galvanometer) into each bucket. Modern electrocardiographs are more sophisticated but work on the same principle, using electrodes (metal plates) and leads instead of wires and buckets of water. A present day ECG is relatively small — about one-quarter the size of a television set — but infinitely more expensive. An electrocardiogram is the single most important test for coronary heart disease due to narrowing of the arteries.

To have an ECG you will be asked to strip to the waist so that ten electrodes can be attached to your chest, arms and legs. They are held in place by elastic straps, suction caps or sticky pads. There is no discomfort or pain of any kind. While you lie quietly, the doctor will twist dials and move levers on the machine to measure the electrical activity being picked up from your body by the ten different leads. If you move to any significant degree, the electrical activity generated in your muscles may interfere with the reading.

The machine will produce a graph consisting of a continuous wriggly line that looks like a landscape of steep mountains and deep valleys and represents the activity of your heart. The graph may appear on either a screen or on a long strip of paper. A normal healthy heart has a characteristic pattern. Any irregularity in the heart rhythm or damage to the heart muscle will show up as being different from the normal pattern.

The ECG may show enlargement of the heart, irregular beats,

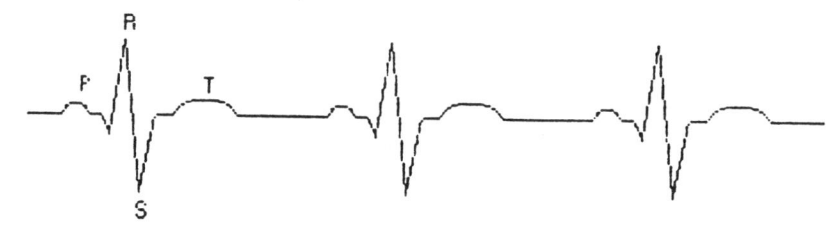

FIGURE 4.10: Electrocardiogram.
The different bumps in the print-out are identified by letters of the alphabet. The small bump marked P shows the activity of the atrium (the upper chamber of the heart). The RS zigzag is the contraction of the ventricles (lower heart chamber), and the T wave is the recharging of the heart ready for the next beat.

damage to the heart (e.g. by a heart attack), poor blood supply to the heart, abnormal position of the heart, high blood pressure, abnormal nerve pathways, and even an imbalance in the blood chemicals that control heart activity.

Unfortunately the cardiograph only shows what is happening to the heart at the moment the reading is taken. It cannot always predict what will happen to the heart in the future. It is not unknown for a patient to have a heart attack only minutes after a normal ECG. For this reason, if there is significant suspicion (not just for routine investigations), an exercise ECG, or stress test, will be performed.

Electrocardiograms are sometimes performed as a routine part of a medical examination, but more commonly if a doctor is suspicious about a patient's health.

See also STRESS TEST.

ELECTROENCEPHALOGRAM (EEG)

An electroencephalogram (EEG) is a recording of the electrical activity of the brain in the same way as an ECG measures the electrical activity of the heart.

For an EEG, electrodes will be attached to your scalp. There will normally be about eight electrodes attached to the electroencephalograph (the machine that does the recording). The procedure is completely painless. The minute electrical waves produced by the nerve cells of the brain as it sends messages throughout the body are transmitted to the machine and reproduced as a wavy line on a strip of paper. You will usually lie quietly while the recording is taking place. You may be asked to open and close your eyes and to breathe heavily. Lights may be flashed before your eyes. If there is no abnormality, the pattern will be fairly regular. If you were excited, the pattern would be different. The recording will take roughly half an hour to an hour.

Normal 'brain waves' occur at a rate of about 50 per second. A departure from this can indicate abnormalities such as epilepsy, a tumour, degeneration of the tissues of the brain, or other serious disorders of the central nervous system. In someone with epilepsy, brain activity can suddenly jump to as many as 500 messages a second.

The most common reason for an EEG is suspected epilepsy. But, of course, the machine only measures the activity at the time the test is being carried out. There are EEG test patterns typical of epileptic seizures, but it is possible to have epilepsy and to have a normal EEG, simply because there is no unusual brain activity at the time of the test. If a person is having seizures and produces a normal EEG, there will be a need for further testing.

An EEG can be used to establish death. Nowadays, it is possible for the heart to be kept beating artificially, virtually indefinitely. Consequently it may be necessary to establish that the person's brain has ceased to function and therefore that there is no possibility of a return to consciousness. A completely flat EEG, with no peaks and valleys, which persists for an extended period of time, can provide irrefutable evidence that life no longer exists.

Electromyogram (EMG)

An electromyogram shows the electrical activity of the muscles. Every time they move, muscles create an electric current, and if a person is paralysed, an EMG can determine whether the paralysis is due to a muscle disorder or to a disorder of the nerves.

For an EMG, an electrode is passed through the skin and attached to a muscle. The electricity is then picked up and transferred to the electromyograph (the machine that does the recording). A graph of the activity is then projected onto a screen or printed out onto a continuous strip of paper. There may be some brief discomfort as the electrode needle is inserted, and a tingling sensation from the current may persist for about a day. The test generally lasts for about half and hour to an hour. Periodic EMGs are often used to measure the progress of someone who is recovering from some form of paralysis.

A similar test can be carried out on the nerves. In this case, an electrode is taped to the skin over the nerve.

Physical tests

Cardiac stress test

A cardiac stress test explores the activity of your heart, not the amount of mental tension to which you are being subjected. It is generally carried out if heart disease is suspected.

Just like an ordinary pump, the heart is more likely to break down when it is called on to work hard. Consequently, if you are suffering from chest pain and an electrocardiogram (ECG — see separate entry) recorded in the doctor's surgery is normal, you may be asked to undergo an exercise ECG or so-called stress test. It involves having an ECG done while you are exercising in a carefully controlled manner, and also having your blood pressure measured. First, a calculation is made of your maximum safe heart rate, based on variables such as your age and weight. You are then connected to the ECG machine and start off walking slowly on a treadmill machine, or possibly riding an exercise bicycle. The pace is gradually increased by speeding up the machine until your heart is beating steadily at the calculated rate. An ECG is taken before, during and after the exercise, so that adverse results of the increased activity on the heart quickly become apparent.

People whose arteries have narrowed so that the heart is not getting enough blood often have a characteristic ECG pattern. A stress test is also used for someone who is recovering from a heart attack to determine how much blood is getting through to the heart.

The test is painless, but it is possible that you may feel dizzy or weak, or become conscious of your heartbeat becoming irregular, or even experience some chest pain. However, it is obviously vital for the person taking the test to ensure that the exercise does not bring on a heart attack, and your ECG readings will constantly be monitored so that the test can be stopped if there is any hint of cardiac distress.

If a stress test is found to be abnormal, you may have a coronary angiogram (see X-RAYS), in which X-ray photographs are taken of the arteries supplying the heart muscle after dye has been injected into them so that they can be seen clearly. If the angiogram shows that your arteries are narrowed or blocked, you may have to undergo surgery — which these days is extremely safe and effective.

In the same way as an ordinary ECG, an exercise ECG can only show what is happening at the time it is taken. It is not unknown for a person to have a stress test which seems normal and then have a heart attack shortly afterwards.

Pulmonary (respiratory) function tests

Pulmonary (respiratory) function tests are used to measure how effectively the lungs are working. These tests are useful in determining the severity of diseases such as asthma, chronic bronchitis, emphysema and cystic fibrosis. A wide range of tests are available, ranging from simple ones performed by a general practitioner to very complex ones undertaken in special units or hospitals.

Peak expiratory flow rate (PEFR) is the maximum rate at which you can exhale (breath out). The patient is asked to blow

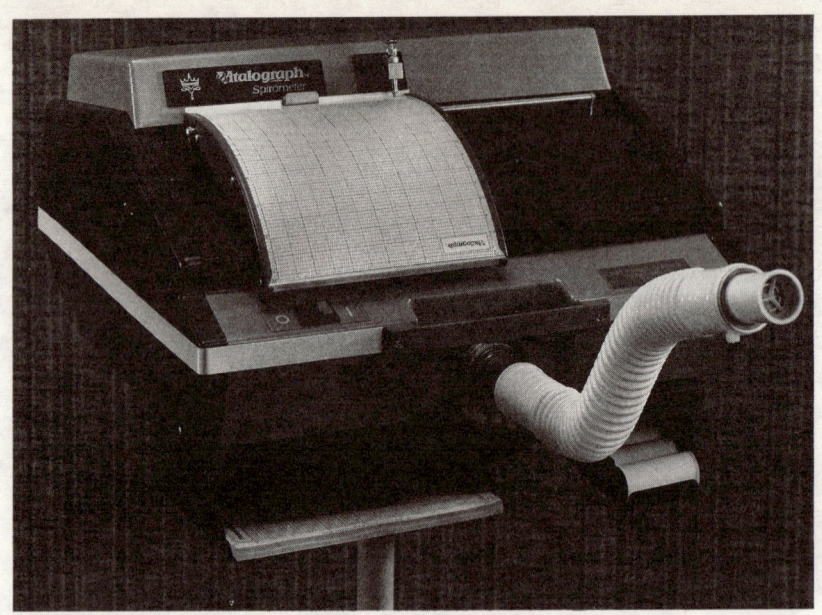

FIGURE 4.11: Spirometer.

as hard as possible into a small hand-held tube with a gauge and a mouthpiece attached (a peak flow meter). The rate at which you blow is measured in litres per minute, and the normal value will vary significantly depending on your sex, age and height. Doctors have tables which can compare the patient's performance to that of the average person. A poor result is characteristic of asthma, and some asthmatics have these simple measuring devices at home to determine the severity of their asthma attacks.

The **vital capacity** (VC) of the lungs is the difference in lung volume between the deepest breath you can take in and the maximum lung emptying possible by breathing out. This is measured by a machine called a spirometer, into which you will be asked to blow as long and hard as you can after first having taken a deep breath in. These machines may produce a line on a piece of graph paper, or may have an electronic print-out. The recordings of PEFR and VC and other measurements that can be made from the results enable doctors to obtain a very accurate picture of lung function in disease.

Total lung capacity (TLC) is sometimes measured in special laboratories. This involves breathing a mixture of helium and oxygen into a complex machine that can use the information obtained to measure quite accurately the total amount of gas in the lungs. TLC can also be measured with the patient seated inside a body plethysmograph ('body box') while performing various breathing manoeuvres.

Gas transfer tests also use complex automated machines, and a helium/carbon monoxide gas mixture to measure how effectively the lungs are transferring gas into and out of the bloodstream.

Arterial blood gas measurements can also be used to measure how effectively the lungs are able to transfer oxygen and carbon dioxide to and from the bloodstream. An artery in the arm is pierced by a needle, and a small amount of blood is withdrawn. The blood is then injected into a sealed chamber of an automated machine that can measure the amount of oxygen and carbon dioxide in the blood. If the oxygen level is low and the carbon dioxide is high, the lungs are not working effectively, and the patient would need appropriate treatment.

Exercise stress tests are performed in patients who experience a shortness of breath when they perform activities requiring some form of exertion (e.g. walking up stairs). The patient is asked to pedal a stationary bicycle or walk on a treadmill while connected to a mouthpiece which is in turn connected to various pieces of equipment that enable the amount of air breathed to be measured. The amount of oxygen consumed and the amount of carbon dioxide produced is also measured with gas analysers. An electrocardiograph (see separate entry) is also performed, and oxygen levels (saturation) are measured in the blood. The load on the bicycle or treadmill is progressively increased while the above parameters are monitored. If the lungs are not working properly, the patients will not be able to reach their 'maximal oxygen uptake' level, which is a reflection of their exercise capacity.

Sleep studies are performed mainly on patients with respiration-related problems during sleep, but also sometimes on patients with neurological problems, insomnia, etc. Obstructive sleep apnoea (see Section 5) is diagnosed by having various instruments attached and a series of measurements made throughout the night while the patient is sleeping — electrodes on the head to establish sleep states, special bands around the chest and abdomen to detect movement, a sensor to detect air flow at the nose and mouth, and an oximeter on the finger or ear to detect oxygen levels in the blood.

Sight tests

OPHTHALMOSCOPY

Ophthalmoscopy is examination of the eye using an ophthalmoscope — a small device, held by hand, which shines a beam of light into the eye. The instrument has a series of lenses, and by focusing these the light beam can be directed through the pupil so that all the structures of the eye from the cornea in the front to the retina at the back are magnified and can easily be seen and investigated.

Ophthalmoscopy can help the ophthalmologist (eye specialist) diagnose cataracts (a clouding of the lens in the eye resulting in blurred vision, particularly common in elderly people), corneal ulcers, foreign bodies in the eye, and many other problems. Even the light-sensitive retina at the back of the eye can be inspected, together with the retinal blood vessels and the beginning of the optic nerve which links the eye with the brain, and detachment of the retina can be diagnosed. The blood vessels in the retina can also signal vascular abnormalities in other parts of the body and may give early warning of narrowing arteries to the heart, high blood pressure, anaemia, and diseases such as diabetes. The eye is the only place in the body where blood vessels can be seen directly.

An ophthalmoscope is also used to test how well the cornea and lens of the eye refract light, i.e. whether the patient's sight is as good as it should be or if they need glasses or contact lenses.

You may be given eye drops before an ophthalmoscopy so that your pupils dilate and allow the inside of the eye to be more easily examined. The drops will probably make your vision blurry for an hour or so afterwards and you may need someone to accompany you home. If a more detailed examination of the retina is required, this may be carried out with a retinoscope which is similar to an ophthalmoscope but provides higher magnification and is more sensitive.

TONOMETER

Glaucoma is a serious eye disease that can lead to blindness (see Section 5). There are various types, but the most common one, chronic glaucoma, typically develops in older people and is basically a build-up of pressure in the eyeball which arises if a blockage prevents normal drainage of fluid from the eye. If the pressure gets too high for too long, the sight may be permanently damaged. Because chronic glaucoma develops very gradually and in its initial stages causes no pain, it is possible to have it and not know until it is too late. Everyone over 40 should have their eyes regularly checked, especially if they have a family history of the disease. Glaucoma can be controlled successfully if it is discovered early enough.

Whether you go to an ophthalmologist (an eye specialist) or an optometrist (a person trained to test for glasses), you will usually be tested for glaucoma as a matter of routine with an instrument called a tonometer. This is a relatively simple instrument consisting of a gauge with a pointer. A few drops of anaesthetic will be put into your eye and the lid held open while the doctor places the tonometer on your eyeball. The handle of the tonometer will be lowered until it hovers at a point on the dial, indicating the tension of your eyeball. If the reading is greater than a certain amount, disease may be indicated.

Visual acuity tests

Visual acuity tests are a tests administered to determine if there are any defects in vision, what they are, and how severe they are.

The tests are quite simple. You will be shown a chart on a wall 6 m away with letters on it and asked to read it line by line. The letters vary in size from row to row. The top row has one large letter, the next row smaller letters, the next, smaller letters still, and so on. A person with normal vision should be able to read letters 6 mm high at a distance of 6 m.

The doctor will generally guess at which line you will be able to see, and ask you to start there and read the letters out. If you cannot see them, you will move up a line until you reach a line you can read without difficulty. The result is given as two figures, e.g. 6/12. The first figure refers to the distance at which you read the letters (6 m). The second figure describes the distance at which a person with normal vision can read the smallest letters that you were able to read correctly. For example, the smallest letters that you were able to see from a distance of 6 m would be seen from 12 m by a person with normal sight. The results may be different for each eye.

Poor reading of the chart usually means that your eyes have an impaired ability to refract light — the basis of sight. You will be either near-sighted (myopic) or far-sighted (hypermetropic). Occasionally it indicates a serious eye disease, such as glaucoma.

If your vision is faulty, the doctor or optometrist will ask you to look through a selection of lenses of different magnifications and to read the chart again, covering up one eye at a time. The combination of lenses which enable you to see best are then prescribed as glasses or contact lenses.

Even people with previously good sight usually find that they are having difficulty reading and seeing things up close as they get older, and most of us will need a visual acuity test by the time we are in our mid-forties, if not before that.

See also EYES, Section 2.

Colour blindness test

Colour blindness is tested by means of specially designed plates with patterns made up of different coloured dots. For example, to test whether you can distinguish between red and green, you will be shown a plate covered with dots in various shades of green with a numeral in the middle composed of red dots. People who are able to distinguish between red and green will be able to pick out the figure, whereas the plate will appear to be all the one colour to those who can't tell the difference between red and green.

SECTION 4: INVESTIGATIONS

Other plates with different patterns and colour combinations test other types of colour blindness.

Hearing tests

The most basic test for hearing simply involves the doctor talking to you and making sounds to see if you can hear them. Generally the doctor will sit about 6 m away from you, whisper numbers and then repeat them in a normal voice. You will listen first with one ear and then with the other. An experienced doctor can assess hearing loss quite accurately using this method.

A similar test uses a ticking watch. You cover first one ear and then the other, and the doctor determines at what distance you can hear the sound of the watch. A tuning fork may be used to test your ability to hear tones conducted by air and by the bones of your head.

A more scientific way of evaluating hearing is using an audiometer. This is a device that produces pure tones of a certain pitch and loudness. The first part of the test measures your ability to hear air-conducted sounds and involves you listening through earphones to tones of different pitch and volume, or to spoken words. You are asked to signal when you can hear something, or to repeat the words. The second part of the test measures your ability to hear bone-conducted sounds. For this, an oscillating device is placed on the bone behind each ear, and you will be asked to signal when you hear a tone.

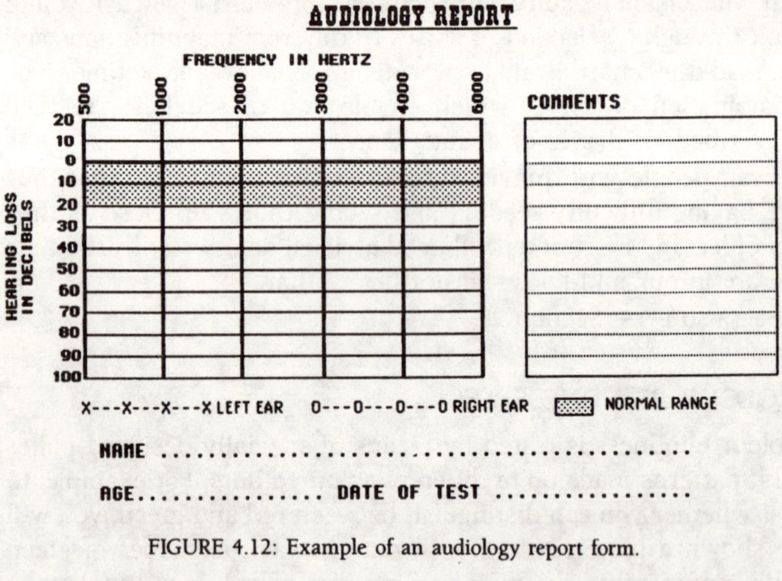

FIGURE 4.12: Example of an audiology report form.

SECTION 5

AN A–Z OF
DISEASES

Abortion, Spontaneous
See PREGNANCY COMPLICATIONS, Section 1.

Abscess
An abscess is a collection of pus in a tissue-lined cavity. Abscesses occur due to the destruction of normal tissue by bacterial infection. In rare cases, a fungal infection may also cause an abscess. When bacteria infect an area, they destroy the normal cells. The wastes produced can usually be removed through the blood circulation in the area, but if the destruction is too great, the waste products accumulate as pus, and an abscess forms. There are two main types of abscesses — those that occur in or under the skin, and those that occur in internal body organs.

Skin abscess
An abscess in or under the skin appears as a red, painful swelling. It is initially hard to touch, but as the pus formation increases, it becomes soft and obviously fluid-filled. In due course, it will 'point' and form a head that will eventually burst and allow the pus to escape. Treatment in the early stages will involve antibiotics by mouth or injection, and hot compresses on the area. Once there is obvious fluid present, the abscess should (under local or general anaesthetic) be drained, scraped out, and the drain hole kept open by a small piece of cloth (a wick) to allow any further pus to escape quickly. The wick is changed regularly, and the abscess cavity will slowly reduce in size until it heals. Particularly nasty abscesses may develop around the anus and require quite major surgery to allow for the adequate drainage of pus.

Internal abscess
Abscesses can occur in almost any organ of the body, and are often not found until they have progressed to quite a large size. They may be the cause of a previously undiagnosed illness that is usually accompanied by a fever and a general feeling of being unwell. The organs most commonly affected include the brain, liver, breast, lung, tonsils (see QUINSY) and teeth. All these abscesses must have their pus removed by an open operation under a general or local anaesthetic.

Sometimes, a collection of pus will occur outside an organ but inside the abdominal cavity. These most commonly develop in the pelvis and around the liver, and may follow after an operation or another type of abdominal infection such as appendicitis. Antibiotics may be used to stop the spread of the infection but will not cure the abscess. If left untreated, a patient may become severely ill, with new abscesses forming in surrounding tissues.

Acne (Pimples)
Acne can vary from the occasional spot to a severe disease that may cause both skin and psychological scarring. It is generally a curse of the teenage years but may strike later in life — particularly in women.

Pimples are due to a blockage in the outflow of oil from the thousands of tiny oil glands in the skin. This blockage can be due to dirt, flakes of dead skin, or a thickening and excess production of the oil itself. Once the opening of the oil duct becomes blocked, the gland becomes dilated with the thick oil, then inflamed and eventually infected. The result is a white head, with the surrounding red area of infection. The face, upper chest, upper back and neck are the areas commonly affected. Fringes and long hair can aggravate the condition. The severity of your acne will also depend greatly on your choice of parents. If one or both of them had severe acne, you have a good chance of developing the same problem.

There are many different subtypes of

acne that enable doctors (especially skin specialists) to determine more accurately the type of treatment necessary, and the likely outcome. **Acne vulgaris** is one of the most severe forms and almost invariably results in scarring of the face, back and chest.

The hormonal changes associated with the transition from childhood to adult life are the major aggravating factor in acne, as the hormones cause changes to the skin and to the thickness of the oil, and may worsen (or occasionally improve) acne. Pregnancy, menopause and the oral contraceptive pill may all influence pimples in this way. There is no evidence that vitamins, diet or herbs have any effect on pimples.

Acne cannot be cured, but in the majority of cases it can be reasonably controlled. You should ensure that your skin is kept clean with a mild soap and face cloth. Then some of the many creams and lotions available from pharmacists can be tried. These should be used carefully and regularly, and the instructions for their use should be scrupulously followed. Some can cause quite severe reactions if not used strictly as directed. The vast majority of sufferers can have their acne controlled in this way.

If these simple measures are not successful, doctors can prescribe further treatment. This will involve combinations of antibiotics by mouth that may be taken in the short term for acute flare ups, or in the long term to prevent the occurrence of acne. Antibiotics in the tetracycline class (see Section 6) are most commonly used for this purpose. Skin lotions or creams containing antibiotics and/or steroids can also be prescribed. Sometimes, changing a woman's hormonal balance by putting her on the oral contraceptive pill or using other hormones can control acne.

In rare cases, referral to a skin specialist for more exotic forms of treatment is required. These would include a potent drug called isotretinoin (which can cause birth deformities if used during pregnancy), injections of a steroid called triamcinolone into the skin around particularly bad eruptions of acne, and abrading away the skin around the scars that are left behind after acne attacks.

Unfortunately, the treatment of adults with maturity onset acne is far harder than the juvenile acne.

ACOUSTIC NEUROMA (ACOUSTIC NEURINOMA)

All nerves are covered with an insulating sheath, rather like the insulation around an electrical wire. An acoustic neuroma is a benign (non-cancerous) tumour (abnormal growth) of the tissue which covers the auditory nerve, i.e. the nerve that transmits sound from the ear to the brain. The tumour often develops at the point where the nerve passes through a small hole into the inside of the skull, and a relatively small growth in this cramped space can apply considerable pressure to the auditory nerve and stop it from functioning. The result is initially a ringing noise, followed by deafness in the affected ear.

As the tumour increases in size, it can apply pressure to the lower part of the brain, causing further symptoms. Other symptoms may include pain, dizziness and, because of pressure on other nearby nerves that supply the eye, a lack of tears in the eye and double vision. Headache does not occur until the tumour is very large.

When acoustic neuroma is suspected, the patient will proceed through a series of blood tests, X-rays and hearing tests, until a CT scan (see Section 4) is performed. This can usually show the tumour quite accurately. The only treatment is surgical removal of the tumour in a very intricate operation performed by both neurosurgeons and ear, nose and throat surgeons. The smaller the tumour at the time of surgery, the better the final result. Tumours less than 2 cm in diameter can normally be removed without any problem. Removing larger tumours may result in unavoidable permanent deafness and possibly other nerve damage.

ACQUIRED IMMUNE DEFICIENCY SYNDROME
See AIDS.

ACROMEGALY
Acromegaly is characterised by the excessive growth of the hands, feet, jaw, face, tongue and internal organs. Patients also suffer from headaches, sweating, weakness, and loss of vision. A woman's periods will stop. It is caused by excess production of growth hormone in the pituitary gland (see Section 2) which sits underneath the brain. This hormone is required during the normal growth of a child, but if it is produced inappropriately later in life, acromegaly results. The most common reason for this excess production is the development of a tumour in the pituitary gland, but occasionally tumours elsewhere can secrete abnormal amounts of the hormone. Laboratory tests can be used to prove the diagnosis, and X-rays and CT scans (see Section 4) of the skull can detect the tumour.

Treatment will involve specialised microsurgery through the nose, and up into the base of the brain, to remove the tumour. Occasionally irradiation of the tumour may be performed. Treatment is very successful, particularly in younger adults. Sometimes hormone supplements must be taken in the long term to replace the normal hormones produced by the destroyed pituitary gland. Diabetes insipidus is a common complication of the disease and its treatment.

ACTINOMYCOSIS
Actinomycosis is a bacterial infection of the skin, particularly on the face, which causes the formation of hard, inflamed lumps that develop into abscesses (see separate entry) and discharge pus. Other areas that may be infected include tooth sockets after an extraction, and the gut.

Patients usually have a fever, and if the infection is internal, constant severe pain will be felt in that area. The bacteria that cause this uncommon infection live normally in the mouth and assist with food digestion. Only when they enter into damaged tissue in a different part of the body do they cause problems. The abscesses formed may persist for many months. The bacteria causing the abscesses are difficult to identify, and are resistant to simple treatments.

Treatment involves a 6-week or longer course of penicillin and other antibiotics, initially by injection, and surgically draining and/or cutting out the affected tissue.

ACUTE HAEMOLYTIC ANAEMIA
See ANAEMIA.

ADDICTION
See ALCOHOLISM; DRUG ADDICTION.
See also ALCOHOL; SMOKING, Section 7.

ADDISON'S DISEASE (CHRONIC HYPOADRENOCORTICISM)
The adrenal glands (see Section 2) sit on top of each kidney, and produce hormones (chemical messengers) that control the levels of vital elements in the body and regulate the breakdown of food. Addison's disease occurs when the adrenal glands do not produce sufficient quantities of these vital hormones. In most cases, the cause for the failure of the adrenal glands is unknown, but tuberculosis was a common cause in years past. It is a rare disease,

and the common symptoms are weakness, lack of appetite, diarrhoea and vomiting, skin pigmentation, mental instability, low blood pressure, loss of body hair and absence of sweating. It is diagnosed by special laboratory tests that measure the body's response to stimulation of the adrenal gland.

Treatment involves taking a combination of medications (different types of steroids) to replace the hormones missing from the body. The dosages vary greatly from one patient to another. Frequent small meals high in carbohydrate and protein should be taken, and any infections must be treated rapidly.

Patients with Addison's disease must wear a bracelet warning doctors of their condition and carry an emergency supply of hydrocortisone (see Section 6) with them at all times.

Treatment can give most patients a long and useful life, but they cannot react to stress (both physical and mental) adequately, and additional treatment (e.g. hydrocortisone) must be given to cover these situations. The ultimate outcome of the disease depends greatly on the patient's ability to follow strictly all treatment regimes. Complications include diabetes, thyroid disease, anaemia, and eventual death.

ADENITIS (SWOLLEN AND INFLAMED GLANDS)

Adenitis is an infection of one or more of the lymph glands (see LYMPHATIC SYSTEM, Section 2) in the body. These glands are designed to remove and destroy invading bacteria and viruses (see Section 7) from the bloodstream. In some cases, the infection overwhelms the gland, and it becomes red, sore and swollen and the patient develops a fever and feels ill.

The most commonly affected areas are the neck, armpit, and groin. Glands around the intestine can be infected to cause a condition called mesenteric adenitis (see separate entry), which may mimic appendicitis. Cancer spreading from another part of the body can also cause a gland to become painful and enlarged. All glands that cause discomfort must therefore be examined by a doctor.

If the infection is bacterial, the treatment will involve the use of antibiotics. Viral infections of the glands, such as mumps and glandular fever, will need to run their course, with rest and pain-killers being the only treatment. Cancerous glands will need to be removed, and further treatment will depend on the type of cancer present.

See also GLANDULAR FEVER; MUMPS.

ADHESIONS

Adhesions are a relatively uncommon but potentially serious and disabling complication of any surgery within the abdomen. When you are cut, inflammation occurs to stick the edges of the wound together and eventually heal the wound. During an operation, minor damage to all tissue in the area is inevitable, and this becomes slightly inflamed. If two areas of damaged internal tissue come into contact after an operation, they will heal together and form an adhesion. The adhesions form tough fibrous bands across the abdominal cavity between two points that have been inflamed or damaged during surgery. They are more common if there is an infection in the abdomen (e.g. a burst appendix), but they sometimes occur after a relatively minor operation. They appear to develop more readily in short, fat females, but the reason for this is unknown.

Most adhesions produce no symptoms but can occasionally trap a loop of bowel and cause an obstruction. More commonly, they cause a persistent colic in the gut as the intestine winds tightly around these fibrous bands, or the adhesion may tear and bleed, leading to more pain.

The only treatment available is more surgery to cut away the adhesions. During this further surgery, extreme care is taken to prevent any bleeding into the abdomen and any unnecessary injury to the bowel. Unfortunately, after a few months or years, the adhesions may re-form, and the symptoms start again. It is therefore a very difficult problem to deal with, and there is no permanent solution.

AGAMMAGLOBULINAEMIA
See IMMUNODEFICIENCY.

AIDS (ACQUIRED IMMUNE DEFICIENCY SYNDROME)

Until 1983, doctors were barely aware that AIDS existed, but since then it has swept the world. In 1984, no general practitioner ever expected to see a case of AIDS in their own surgery, but now many GPs have had the shock of discovering a victim amongst their own patients.

The story begins in central Africa, where it is now believed a mild form of the human immunodeficiency virus (HIV) has existed for centuries. This mild form (known technically as HIV 1) has been isolated from old stored blood samples dated in the 1950s. From Africa, it spread to Haiti in the Caribbean. Haiti was ruled by a vicious dictator, and many Haitians fled to Africa to avoid persecution. Once the dictator was removed from power, these exiles returned, bringing AIDS with them. In the process, it mutated (to HIV 3) and became more virulent, causing a faster and more severe onset of symptoms. There may also have been some movement of the disease directly through Africa to Algeria and France. American homosexuals frequented Haiti because it was very poor and sexual favours could be bought cheaply. They returned home from their holiday with the AIDS virus, and it has spread around the world from there.

Those who are infected with the human immunodeficiency virus are said to be HIV positive. Doctors have classified the disease into several categories, but these classifications are still changing as more information about the disease becomes available. A patient's disease category can progress to more severe levels but cannot revert to less severe levels.

HIV category 1 is a glandular fever-like disease that lasts a few days to weeks. The patient has inflamed lymph nodes, fever, rash and tiredness, and a blood test is positive.

HIV category 2. A blood test is positive but the patient has no symptoms.

HIV category 3. The patient has persistent generalised enlarged lymph glands.

HIV category 4 (AIDS). Patients have varied symptoms and signs depending on the areas of the body affected. Problems include fever, weight loss, diarrhoea, nerve and brain disorders, severe infections, lymph gland cancer, sarcomas, and other cancers.

The disease may remain at the HIV 2 level for many years, possibly even decades, and some doctors believe that a small number of patients may never develop the full-blown HIV 4 AIDS. Statistically, approximately 50% of those who are HIV positive have not developed category 4 disease after ten years. On the other hand, no-one with category 4 HIV (AIDS) has lived more than a few months. The immune system that protects the body is destroyed by the virus, and sufferers develop severe lung infections and multiple rare cancers that eventually kill them.

Fortunately for most of us, AIDS is a relatively hard disease to catch. It can *NOT* be caught from any casual contact, or from spa baths, kissing, mosquitoes, tears, towels or clothing. Only by homosexual or heterosexual intercourse with a carrier of the disease, by using contaminated needles, or blood from a carrier, can the disease be caught. There is no cure or vaccine, and it is unlikely that one will be available for many years.

Once the AIDS virus enters your body, it may lie dormant for months or years. During this time you may have no or minimal symptoms, but it may be possible for you to pass the infection on to another sex partner, and babies can become infected in the uterus of an infected mother. Blood tests can detect the disease at this early stage, but there may be a lag period of up to three months or more from when the disease is caught until it can be detected.

Once someone is diagnosed as HIV positive, they should not give up all hope, because they may remain in the second stage for a long time. Prolonging this second stage can be achieved by stopping smoking, exercising regularly, eating a well-balanced diet, resting adequately, avoiding illegal drugs, and preventing the spread of the disease to sex partners.

Prevention is the only practical way to deal with AIDS. Condoms give very good, but not total, protection from the virus. Drug addicts need to be educated not to share needles. Tests are now available to allow blood banks and pathologists to screen for AIDS.

For the majority of the community who are not promiscuous or intravenous drug users, AIDS is far more a mouse than a lion. The tragedy occurs when a man or woman has a casual affair with an AIDS carrier (who may not know they have the disease) and brings the deadly virus back to their spouse.

ALCOHOLISM

Alcoholism is a disease in the same way that malaria and lung cancer are diseases. You catch malaria if you are bitten by an infected mosquito. You can develop lung cancer if you smoke too much. You can become an alcoholic if you consume too much alcohol. Alcohol is a powerful drug. Alcoholic drinks contain the drug ethanol (ethyl alcohol), which can poison the human body if taken in large quantities, or in combination with other drugs such as sleeping pills, tranquillisers, marijuana, prescribed medicines and cold remedies.

It does no good to tell an alcoholic to 'pull yourself together' or 'stop drinking before it kills you'. They need professional counselling and treatment. The biggest problem faced by families and doctors is the denial by so many alcoholics that they have a problem. Unfortunately, it is not possible to force these people into treatment centres until they are well down the path of chronic alcoholism and become a danger to themselves and others. At this point, doctors and families (the law varies between states) can certify the person to be an alcoholic and they are then forcibly placed in a treatment centre. Forced-entry patients never progress as well in treatment programs as voluntary patients, so, in times of sobriety, every effort must be made to convince these men and women to accept the advice of their family doctor to enter a voluntary treatment program.

Alcoholism has two stages of development — problem drinking, and alcohol addiction. Problem drinking is the use of alcohol intermittently to ease tension and anxiety. It may be associated with the use of prescription drugs to control emotional problems. Alcohol addiction is more serious.

Signs of alcohol addiction

An alcoholic is someone who has three or more of the following symptoms or signs:
- drinks alone;
- tries to hide drinking habits from others;
- continues to drink despite convincing evidence that it is damaging their health;

- disrupts work or social life because of alcohol;
- craves alcohol when none is available;
- appears to tolerate the effects of alcohol well;
- blacks out for no apparent reason;
- binges on alcohol;
- averages six standard alcoholic drinks a day;
- has abnormal liver function blood tests.

Alcoholism may be suspected in someone who has a flushed face, alcohol on their breath, unexplained work absences, frequent accidents and cigarette burns to their body.

Complications of alcoholism

The social complications of alcohol are obvious and include the disruption to family life with verbal and physical abuse of children and wife/husband, poor performance at work and repeated loss of jobs or failure to gain promotion, loss of friends and chastisement from relatives, the physical risks of drink-driving and being injured in falls or industrial accidents, and the increased risk of eventual suicide.

The medical effects of alcoholism can be serious to the point where they can significantly alter the quality of life and shorten the life of the alcoholic.

Cirrhosis is hardening of the liver (see separate entry). The soft normal liver tissue is replaced by firm scar tissue that is unable to process the waste products of the body adequately, allowing them to build up in the blood stream. The other vital actions of the liver in converting and storing food products and producing chemicals essential to the body are also inhibited. This can lead to an inability to clot blood properly and an increased tendency to bleed and bruise. As a result, fatal bleeding into or around the brain can occur more easily after a fall in alcoholics. The spider-like fine red blood vessels that occur on the skin of many alcoholics is another effect.

Brain damage can cause depression, irrational behaviour and a form of insanity known as the Wernicke-Korsakoff psychosis (see separate entry). These conditions are related to vitamin deficiencies caused by an inadequate diet while on alcoholic binges.

Damage to the nerves supplying the rest of the body can also occur, and result in a condition known as peripheral neuropathy, which causes muscle cramps, pins and needles sensations and muscle pains.

Degeneration of the cerebellum (the part of the brain that is at the back of the head) caused by alcoholism can cause permanent incoordination, difficulties in walking and performing simple tasks.

The foetal alcohol syndrome occurs when a pregnant woman is an alcoholic and her child is born damaged by the alcohol she has consumed. The forms of damage include an underweight baby, mental retardation, heart defects and behavioral problems. Breech births are more common in alcoholic mothers, as the baby moves around less, and may not turn into the correct position.

Withdrawal from alcohol

Many problems can occur when an alcoholic is deprived of alcohol, and this should therefore be done under medical supervision. Mild cases may merely experience anxiety and tremor, while worse cases may become highly agitated and develop delirium tremens.

Delirium tremens develops up to seven days after alcohol is ceased but is more common in the first two or three days. The patient hallucinates, has tremors, becomes confused and irrational, may have convulsions, refuse food and water and become acutely dehydrated. It can be so severe as to cause an irregular heart beat, biochemical abnormalities in the blood, and death. Death is uncommon in hospital but may occur in up to a third of all victims who go through this condition without adequate medical care. For these reasons, hospitalisation is essential in all patients withdrawing from chronic alcoholism.

Treatment of alcoholism
Support for the patient from family, friends, therapists and doctors is essential. Total abstinence from alcohol is the goal to be achieved, and not 'controlled drinking'. It is too easy to relapse from a so-called controlled state, and alcoholics must stop drinking completely to be cured. Alcoholics Anonymous, church groups and similar support organisations, doctors who specialise in treating alcoholics, and specialised clinics where alcoholics can be admitted, all play a role. The level of intervention required is best assessed by the family doctor, as the requirements of a problem drinker differ from those of an alcohol addict.

At the time of diagnosis, a complete physical examination and blood tests should be ordered by the doctor to assess the severity of the condition. Sedatives and other drugs should not be used as a replacement for alcohol, but may be briefly necessary in controlled dosages to overcome a crisis or to ease the symptoms of withdrawal.

Aversion therapy by psychiatrists or psychologists will teach alcoholics to avoid alcohol as they learn to associate unpleasant stimuli, triggered by the therapist, with the taking of alcohol. Antabuse (disulfiram) is a drug that will cause severe vomiting if alcohol is taken. It must be used with the consent of the patient and not secretively, as serious consequences could result. The drug is taken regularly for weeks or months as a disincentive to drinking. The patient is given small amounts of alcohol by the doctor after starting the medication to demonstrate what may occur, and then the patient merely reports every few weeks for physical and blood tests to ensure s/he is following the regime correctly and without side effects.

A good diet is essential in alcoholics, as they are often malnourished. Vitamin supplements, particularly vitamins B and C, are necessary in the early stages of recovery. It has been reasonably suggested that thiamine (a B-group vitamin) should be added to beer to prevent some of the brain damage caused by alcohol.

Unfortunately, many of the complications of alcoholism (e.g. cirrhosis and brain damage) are permanent and do not respond to any treatment, and may result in the need for long-term medical care. The support of family, Alcoholics Anonymous and doctors will be required for many years to obtain a successful outcome.

See also CIRRHOSIS; WERNICKE-KORSAKOFF PSYCHOSIS.

See also PREVENTIVE MEDICINE, Section 7.

ALDOSTERONISM
See CONN'S SYNDROME.

ALLERGIC RHINITIS
See HAY FEVER.

ALLERGY
An allergy is an excessive reaction to a substance which in most people causes no reaction. An allergy can occur to almost any substance in our environment. It may be triggered by foods, pollens, dusts, plants, animals, feathers, furs, mould, drugs, natural or artificial chemicals, insect bites and gases. No-one is totally immune to all possible allergic substances, but some individuals are far more suscep-

tible to a wide range of substances than other people. This tendency towards allergies tends to run through a family, but the form the allergy takes (e.g. hay fever or asthma) and the substances that the person reacts to (e.g. strawberries and bee stings) can vary from one generation to the next. Allergy reactions may be very localised (e.g. at the site of an insect bite, or in just one eye), may occur suddenly or gradually, may last for a few minutes or a few months. They may involve internal organs (e.g. lungs), or be limited to the body surface (e.g. skin or nose lining). Allergies that cause significant discomfort or distress to the patient occur in 10% of the population.

An allergy differs subtly from a hypersensitivity reaction, where a normal reaction, experienced by most people, is exaggerated in some individuals. Often the difference is of little consequence to the sufferer and may only be determined by measuring specific substances (called immunoglobulins) in the blood. Side effects of drugs, psychological reactions, personal dislikes and the results of overexposure to substances, all must be differentiated from a true allergy.

When a person is exposed to a substance to which he or she is allergic, the body reacts by releasing excessive amounts of a substance called histamine from 'mast cells' that are found in the lining of every body cavity, and in the skin. Histamine is required at times to fight invading substances, but when released in excess, it causes inflammation, redness, and swelling, and in body cavities, the excess secretion of fluid from the involved surface. Intense itching often also occurs.

Allergies to specific substances can be detected by skin tests or blood tests. In the skin test, a minute amount of the suspected substance is scratched into a very small area of skin. The reaction of that skin area is then checked regularly over several days. In blood tests, specific antigens (chemicals produced in the body in response to invading allergic substances) are sought and identified.

The treatment of an acute allergic reaction will depend on where it occurs, its severity, and its duration. Antihistamine drugs (see Section 6) are the mainstay of treatment and may be given by tablet, mixture, injection or cream. They are best used early in the course of an allergic reaction or if an exposure to an allergy-provoking situation is expected. Unfortunately, many antihistamines cause drowsiness, which may be an unacceptable side effect, but in recent years a number of non-sedating antihistamines have been developed and marketed.

Once the reaction is established, a severe attack may require steroid tablets or injections (see Section 6), adrenaline injections, or, in very severe cases, emergency resuscitation (see anaphylaxis below). Other drugs may be used in specific allergy situations (e.g. lung opening drugs in acute asthma). Severe allergic reactions may kill a patient by causing the throat to swell shut, acting on the heart to cause irregular beats, or inducing a critical lung spasm.

There are a number of substances that can be used on a regular basis to prevent certain allergic reactions. One of these is Intal (sodium cromoglycate) which may prevent hay fever, asthma and allergic conjunctivitis (called Opticrom as eye drops) if used several times a day throughout the allergy season (often spring). A small number of patients are so allergic to certain substances (e.g. bee stings or ant bites) that they must carry an emergency supply of an injectable drug (usually adrenaline) with them at all times, and must inject themselves if they suspect that they have been exposed to the allergic substance.

Once the substances that cause an

allergy in an individual have been identified, further episodes of allergic reaction may be prevented by desensitisation. This involves giving extremely small doses of the allergy-causing substance to the patient, and then slowly increasing the dose over many weeks or months until the patient can tolerate the substance at the maximum likely exposure level. The desensitisation may be given by weekly injections, or more frequent drops of the substance placed under the tongue.

Allergies can cause a wide range of symptoms, from itchy eyes and diarrhoea, to a runny nose and skin lumps. Some of these types of allergy will now be discussed individually.

Hives (urticaria, angioedema)

Hives is an allergic reaction that occurs in the skin. Red, raised, itchy weals may be limited to a small area, or spread widely over the skin. The rash develops rapidly over a few minutes or a couple of hours, and may persist for up to two weeks, although two or three days is the average. Some rarer forms may become chronic and last for months or years. Hives may also occur in a non-allergic form, and may be a response to stress, but often the cause cannot be determined. The treatment for both allergic and non-allergic hives is the same.

Angioedema is a term used more commonly when the lips or eyelid is involved and becomes severely swollen, with only slight itchiness and redness.

Common causes of hives include brushing against plants that may have stinging nettles on their surface, insect bites and chemicals (in creams, cosmetics, soaps, etc.) that are applied to the skin.

Some patients with long-term and recurrent forms of urticaria may be reacting to salicylates and tartrazine, chemicals that occur naturally in a wide range of foods. A diet, which must be especially formulated, free of these substances, is sometimes of benefit.

Treatment involves the use of antihistamines or steroids (see Section 6) by mouth or injection. Strangely, tricyclic antidepressants (see Section 6) also seem to benefit some patients. Soothing creams, lotions (e.g. calamine) and baths can give relief to patients during the worst stages of an attack.

Familial angioedema is a rare, severe form of reaction that runs in families and may cause fatal swelling of the tongue or throat. This is treated with a wide variety of rather unusual drugs including danazol (also used for infertility) and the sex hormone, methyltestosterone.

Anaphylaxis

Anaphylactic reactions are immediate, severe, life-threatening reactions to an allergy-causing substance. Death may occur within minutes if medical help is not immediately available. The patient becomes rapidly sweaty, develops widespread pins and needles, may develop a generalised flush or red rash, or swelling in one or more parts of the body (possibly including the tongue, throat and eyelids), starts wheezing, becomes blue around the lips, may become incontinent of urine, loses consciousness, convulses and stops breathing. Swelling of the tongue and throat alone may be enough to cause death if air is unable to pass into the lungs. The terrified victim suffocates.

First aid can give only limited assistance. The patient must be placed on their back with the neck extended to give the best possible airway, and mouth-to-mouth resuscitation and external cardiac massage may be necessary.

Medical treatment must be sought urgently, as an injection of a drug such as adrenaline, hydrocortisone, aminophylline or an antihistamine (this is the preferred order) can reverse the allergic reaction rapidly and save the patient's life. Patients who are aware that they may have an anaphylactic reaction usually carry an injectable form of adrenaline with them at all times to be used in an emergency.

Insect stings (e.g. bees, hornets, wasps and ants) and injected drugs are the most likely substances to produce acute anaphylaxis. It is rare for inhaled, touched or eaten substances to cause this reaction.

See also ALLERGIC REACTIONS, SEVERE, Section 8.

Allergic conjunctivitis

If a pollen, dust or other substance to which a person is allergic is blown or rubbed into an eye, an allergic reaction can occur in that eye. It will normally take the form of redness, itching, blurred vision and watering, but in severe cases the white of the eye may swell dramatically and balloon out between the eyelids. This appearance causes great concern but is not dangerous, provided appropriate medical attention is given promptly. There may be a clear, stringy discharge from the eyes, as well as excessive tears, and if the lower eyelid is turned down, it appears to be covered with a large number of tiny red bumps. This is also the itchy area of the eye. Allergic conjunctivitis is often associated with hay fever, and may occur regularly at certain times of the year.

The condition can be prevented by the regular use of Opticrom (sodium cromoglycate) drops throughout the allergy time of year, and attacks of the condition can be treated by antihistamine tablets and eye drops (see Section 6). Simple eye preparations available over the counter from chemists and containing artery-constricting medications can be used in milder cases. These usually settle the symptoms rapidly.

See also ASTHMA; HAY FEVER.

ALOPECIA AREATA

A sudden loss of hair in a well-defined patch on the scalp or other areas of body hair (e.g. pubic area, beard, chest, eyebrows) is commonly caused by alopecia (meaning hair loss) areata (meaning a specific area). It is different to baldness in that it can occur at any age, in either sex, and in any race. It starts suddenly, and a bare patch 2 cm or more across may be present before it is noticed. It is more common under 25 years of age, and is quite common, with about 2% of patients seeing skin specialists having the condition. The hairless area may slowly extend for several weeks before stabilising. Several spots may occur simultaneously, and may merge together as they enlarge. If the entire body is affected, the disease is called alopecia totalis, but this is not a different disease, just a severe case of alopecia areata.

There is a family history of the disease in up to 20% of patients, but in the majority, no specific cause for the disease can be found. Stress and anxiety are not considered to be a common cause. Although these may cause diffuse hair loss, they do not cause total loss of hair in an area. Fungal infections and drugs used to treat cancer may also cause patchy hair loss, and these causes must be excluded by a doctor.

Treatment of alopecia areata will involve using strong steroid creams, injections of steroids into the affected area, and irritant lotions. There are many other treatments undergoing trial, with varying results. In 90% of patients, regrowth of hair eventually recurs, although the new hair may be totally white. Sometimes the regrowth may take many months. The further the bare patch is from the top of the scalp, the slower and less likely regrowth of the hair becomes. It is rare for recovery from total hair loss to occur.

Altitude sickness (mountain sickness)

This condition occurs when ascending rapidly to heights over 3000 m. As Mount Kosciusko is only 2230 m high, it is a condition unknown in Australia, but the common Australian overseas experience of trekking in the Himalayas may bring on an attack. It is impossible to predict who will be affected, how rapidly or at what altitude. A slow ascent is less likely to cause problems than a rapid one.

The symptoms start with headache, shortness of breath, and excessive tiredness. These may be rapidly followed by inability to sleep, nausea, vomiting, diarrhoea, abdominal pains and a fever. The symptoms may become so debilitating as to become life-threatening. Fluid can fill the lungs, victims start coughing up blood, the heart races, and the patient may eventually drown as their own blood fills their lungs.

A rapid descent to a lower altitude is the only effective treatment for severe cases, although mild cases may recover with rest at the high altitude. Fluid removing drugs (see DIURETICS, Section 6) may be used in an emergency to remove some fluid from the lungs.

A drug called acetazolamide given during the climb may prevent altitude sickness in some climbers. Oxygen used by very high altitude climbers protects against the disease, but the heavy cylinders must be carried up by the climbers, slowing their progress.

Alzheimer's disease

Alzheimer's disease, which is receiving more and more media attention, is named after a German physician who lived in the latter part of the nineteenth century and was the first to describe the disease. It is one of the most common forms of dementia (see separate entry) in the elderly, but unfortunately it may strike as early as the mid-fifties and cause extreme distress to spouses, family and friends. It is characterised by loss of recent memory, loss of initiative, reduced physical activity, confusion, loss of orientation (patients become confused about where they are and dates), and then it gradually progresses to loss of speech, difficulty in swallowing (drooling results), stiff muscles, incontinence of both faeces and urine, and a bedridden state in which the patients are totally unaware of themselves or anything that is happening around them. The brain ceases to function at any conscious level. From diagnosis to this tragic final condition takes on average seven years, and eventually death results.

Alzheimer's disease is caused by a faster than normal loss of nerve cells in the brain. Every person has a set number of brain cells, which reach their maximum number in the mid teen years. From then on, the number of brain cells slowly decreases, the rate of cell loss increasing with age. If this rate of cell loss becomes excessive, and affects particularly the front and sides of the brain that are responsible for our thoughts, personality and ingenuity, this disease occurs. The dead cells are replaced by plaques of inactive scar tissue in the brain. The exact cause for the increased rate of brain cell loss is not known, but research is continuing, and several interesting changes in the chemistry of the brain have been discovered. Whether these discoveries will lead to the cause will have to await further investigations. Recent studies suggest specific genes may predispose a person to Alzheimer's disease, and certainly there is a familial tendency, i.e. the most accurate predicting factor in whether you will develop the disease is if your parents did.

There is no easy way to diagnose the condition until the disease is far advanced and a reduced brain volume may show on a CT scan (see Section 4). The diagnosis is primarily one that is made by the doctor after excluding all other forms of dementia in an elderly patient. Blood tests, X-rays, electroencephalograms (see Section 4) and possibly taking a sample of the spinal fluid may all be used to ensure that there is not a treatable cause for the dementia.

The progress of the disease can be assessed by neurologists and psychologists who conduct specific tests of skill, general knowledge, simple maths, etc., to determine the rate of deterioration. Some patients may not deteriorate for some time, then drop to a lower level of activity quite suddenly.

There is no cure, and treatments are aimed at keeping the patient content and ensuring that the family is able to cope with him/her at home for as long as possible. Medication is only useful for restlessness and insomnia. Physiotherapists, occupational therapists, home nursing care and health visitors are the mainstay of management. The family general practitioner can prove to be an invaluable source of regular encouragement and support. When necessary, the doctor can arrange for admission to a respite care centre to give the family a holiday from the patient, and in due course can arrange for admission to a nursing home or hospital.

Many claims have been made for various herbal extracts, vitamins and secret elixirs, but unfortunately, when subjected to careful trials, none have proved to be beneficial. Many of these remedies are expensive and only add to the financial distress of the affected family.

Amenorrhoea
See MENSTRUAL PERIOD PROBLEMS, Section 3.

Amoebiasis
Single-celled animals called amoebae may infect the body to cause amoebiasis. The most common areas affected are the gut and liver, and very rarely the brain and lung. It is a rare condition in Australia but relatively common in many third-world countries.

The amoebae in the gut are passed out with the faeces, and if human wastes then contaminate food or water, the infection can be picked up by other persons. Some people may have very mild infections and act as carriers, steadily infecting more and more people with the disease.

The symptoms include abdominal pain, diarrhoea, mucus and blood in the faeces, fever, and in severe cases the bowel may rupture, leading to peritonitis and death. If the amoebae enter the liver from the gut, an abscess (see separate entry) can form in the liver and cause severe pain.

The disease is diagnosed by finding the amoebae in the faeces when it is examined under a microscope. There are also special blood tests (see Section 4) that can detect antibody changes in the bloodstream caused by the infecting amoebae.

The disease is best controlled by strict attention to personal hygiene, cooking food and boiling water. Treatment will involve one or more of a number of drugs to kill the amoebae. Many of these drugs have significant side effects and may need to be used for several weeks. Any abscess will need to be drained surgically.

If left untreated, those with severe cases will die, but modern treatment methods lead to the total recovery of the majority.

Amyloidosis
Amyloidosis is a rare disease in which millions of microscopic fibres made of a dense protein infiltrate and replace the normal tissue of different parts of the body. The kidneys, lungs, heart and intestine are commonly involved. When these tissues are examined, they appear to be made of a dense jelly formed by the protein fibres,

rather than normal tissue. The symptoms of the disease are very variable, depending on which organs are involved. The disease may be triggered by another disease, such as tuberculosis, rheumatoid arthritis, cancer or drug abuse, but in many cases, no apparent cause can be found.

The diagnosis is proved by taking a small sample of the affected organ during surgery under an anaesthetic. The abnormal protein fibres can be easily seen under a microscope.

Complications of the disease such as pneumonia and kidney infections may be treated effectively, but amyloidosis is incurable, and most patients die within three years of the diagnosis.

Anaemia

Anaemia is defined as a low level of haemoglobin in the blood. This complex compound is found in red blood cells and gives them their red colour. The role of haemoglobin in the blood is to transport the oxygen from the lungs to the organs. If the level of haemoglobin is low, you feel tired and weak, as insufficient oxygen (which is required by all cells to burn fuel for energy) is being transported to the cells. Other symptoms can include pins and needles in the arms and legs, palpitations, abnormal finger nails, dizziness and shortness of breath. There are many different types of anaemia, and they vary in their cause and severity.

Acute haemolytic anaemia

Haemolytic anaemia occurs when the red blood cells are destroyed at a rate faster than they can be made. This cell destruction may be an uncommon complication of many diseases including kidney failure, liver failure, cancer and both viral and bacterial infections. Transfusion with blood that is not completely compatible is another cause, as is exposure to some drugs and poisons.

The symptoms are the same as for any anaemia, with tiredness and weakness, but fever and jaundice (yellow skin) may also be present. In severe cases, the patient may become semiconscious, have severe abdominal pain, and bruise easily.

The disease is easily diagnosed by blood tests and examining the red blood cells under a microscope, but the exact reason for the disease may be very difficult or impossible to determine.

Emergency treatment involves repeatedly transfusing the patient with concentrated red blood cells to give them sufficient for normal bodily functions, but this will not cure the condition. Prednisone (a steroid — see Section 6) is the main drug used in treatment, but some patients do not respond, and more exotic and toxic drugs are then required. The spleen (see Section 2) is the organ responsible for destroying red blood cells normally, and if this becomes overactive, surgically removing the spleen may control the disease.

The outcome of the disease depends greatly on its cause. Most cases respond well to treatment and recover in a few months. Some patients require years of treatment, and in a small number the condition is resistant to treatment and fatal.

Aplastic anaemia

Aplastic anaemia is the most serious form of anaemia, and up to half the patients with this form will eventually die. Fortunately it is rare, and fewer than one hundred patients a year are diagnosed in Australia. It is caused by a failure of the body to produce blood cells. All cells have a fixed life, and as the old red blood cells die, they are not replaced, leading to a rapidly progressive and severe anaemia.

There are many reasons for the failure of the blood cell production, including poisons, toxins (including insecticides), nuclear irradiation, severe viral infections and some drugs. In more than half the cases, no cause can be found.

In addition to the normal symptoms of anaemia, these patients have a fever, bleeding into the skin, a rapid heart rate, and they are susceptible to infection. Repeated blood transfusion can keep the patient alive in the short term, but other complications can prevent this from continuing for too long.

Any cause must be eliminated if it can be found. Steroids (see Section 6) may control the condition and eventually lead to a cure, but the only effective long term cure is given by a bone marrow transplant.

Marrow transplantation is a simple procedure, but the selection and preparation of the donor is very complex, as the donor must usually be closely related to the patient, but cannot be one of the parents. Brothers and sisters are usually the best potential donors, but their marrow must still be very closely compatible with the patient. It involves taking a small amount of bone marrow from the pelvic bone or breast bone of the donor, and injecting it into the bone marrow of the patient. Rejection is a far greater problem with this type of transplant than with any other form of organ transplant.

Iron deficiency anaemia

Iron deficiency anaemia is the most common form. Iron is an essential element for the functioning of the human body. Between 5 and 8 mg of iron is required in a man's diet every day for good health, and because of the iron loss in their monthly period, women require twice as much as men. Pregnant and breastfeeding women require even more iron than this, sometimes up to 35 mg per day, and as this amount may be difficult to obtain in the diet, most pregnant and breastfeeding women are advised to take a daily iron tablet.

The primary use of iron in the body is to be the core element in the manufacture of haemoglobin. If iron levels are low, haemoglobin levels drop and the body becomes starved of oxygen.

In Western societies, iron deficiency anaemia is usually found in women who have very heavy periods or are pregnant, and in those with a poor diet. Serious causes for this condition include a slow bleed into the gut from a peptic ulcer, or cancer. Anyone with this type of anaemia must therefore be thoroughly assessed by a doctor.

Iron is found naturally in many foods, including meat, poultry, fish, eggs, cereals and vegetables. Red meat, oysters, liver, beans, nuts and wheat contain particularly high levels of iron. Vitamin C and folic acid, present in fruit and vegetables, assist in the absorption of iron from the gut into the bloodstream. Because of this, commercially prepared iron tablets often contain folic acid, and sometimes vitamin C as well.

Some patients with severe degrees of anaemia due to lack of iron, or to intestinal diseases that reduce the absorption of iron, may require injections of this element. Usually they can return to tablets, and then a good diet, after only a few shots.

Pernicious anaemia

Vitamin B12 (cyanocobalamin) is essential for the formation of haemoglobin, the oxygen-carrying chemical in red blood cells. Vitamins (see Section 6) cannot be produced in the body, and must be found in the diet. There is normally more than sufficient vitamin B12 in an Australian's diet, but for it to be absorbed from the stomach and into the bloodstream, another chemical (called intrinsic factor) is required. This attaches to the vitamin B12, and transports it from the stomach and into the blood. Patients with pernicious anaemia lack intrinsic factor and therefore develop a lack of vitamin B12. This in turn leads to an inability to produce haemoglobin, and anaemia results.

In addition to tiredness and pallor, patients with this type of anaemia have a smooth and sore tongue, indigestion, lack of appetite, and occasionally jaundice (yellow skin). Once anaemia is found on a routine blood test, further tests, and the presence of certain types of blood cells, give the definite diagnosis of pernicious anaemia. It is given its name because of its very gradual and 'pernicious' onset over many years.

Because people with pernicious anaemia cannot absorb vitamin B12 from the stomach, treatment involves regular injections of this vitamin for the rest of the patient's life. The injections may be weekly at first, then reduced to one every two or three months. Pernicious anaemia cannot be cured, but it can be effectively controlled. The symptoms will reverse with treatment, and patients can lead a healthy life of normal length. Untreated, the disease is fatal.

ANAL ITCH
See PRURITUS ANI.

ANAPHYLAXIS
See ALLERGY.

See also ALLERGIC REACTIONS, SEVERE, Section 8.

ANEURYSM
An aneurysm is the ballooning out of one part of an artery (or the heart), at a point where the artery becomes weakened. The blood moves in the arteries under pressure (the blood pressure). If there is a weakness at one point on the side of an artery, the pressure will cause that point to balloon out. An aneurysm may be a slight bump on the side of an artery, a quite large bubble, or a long sausage-shaped extension along an artery.

Weakness in arteries may be caused by plaques of atheroma (hardening of the artery), high blood pressure, or injury to the artery. A congenital weakness (present since birth) in the wall of an artery may also lead to the development of an aneurysm. The heart may be weakened by a heart attack, when some of the muscle in the heart wall dies. This weakened area can also bulge out as an aneurysm.

Any artery in the entire body may be affected by an aneurysm, but the most serious ones to be involved are the aorta (the main artery down the back of the chest and abdomen) and those in the brain.

There are several different types of aneurysms that are categorised by their shape. The most common are saccular or berry aneurysms which are direct balloonings on the side of an artery. The most sinister are the dissecting aneurysms, where only part of the artery wall is damaged (often by atheroma) and the blood penetrates in between the layers of the artery wall, slowly splitting them apart, and extending along the artery.

The aneurysm itself usually causes no symptoms, unless it is very large or presses on a nerve. The major problem with aneurysms is that they may burst, leading to a massive loss of blood or damage to surrounding organs (e.g. brain), or they may extend to the point where they put pressure on other arteries, and cut off the blood supply to other vital areas (e.g. the kidney).

An aneurysm can only be diagnosed if seen on an X-ray after special dye has been injected into the artery. Very large aneurysms may be felt on examination, seen on a plain X-ray, and may be picked up incidentally when an X-ray of the chest or abdomen is performed for another reason. CT scans and magnetic resonance imaging (see Section 4) may also be used to detect an aneurysm.

The rupture of an aneurysm of a major artery can lead to death within a few minutes, or a slow leak may allow surgeons enough time to undertake a major operation to repair or replace the leaking artery. Obviously, seconds count in this situation, and the patient must be urgently transported to a major hospital where such an operation is feasible. If an aneurysm is found incidentally, it will be a difficult decision as to whether it should be operated upon to prevent it bursting, or left alone in the hope that it will not burst or leak. The site, size and type of aneurysm, and the age, general health and occupation of the patient will all enter into consideration in making this difficult decision.

In the brain, a small aneurysm may be clipped with a tiny piece of silver to prevent it from leaking in future. Some unlucky people are born with many 'berry aneurysms' (named because they look like a red berry on the side of an artery), and it is not practical to surgically clip every one of them.

In all patients with aneurysms, it is obviously vital to control blood pressure and avoid other aggravating factors such as smoking and strenuous exercise.

The prognosis of an aneurysm is extremely variable, depending on the site and severity of any rupture. There is a significant overall mortality rate.

ANGINA

Angina is a pressure-like, squeezing pain or tightness in the chest, usually central, that starts suddenly, often during exercise, and settles with rest. It may extend into the left arm, neck, upper abdomen and back. It is due to a narrowing of one or more of the three small arteries that supply blood to the heart muscle. This narrowing can be due to hardening of the arteries (see ATHEROSCLEROSIS), or a spasm of the artery caused by another disease or stress. If the heart is deprived of blood because of these narrowed arteries, it does not receive sufficient oxygen, it cannot work effectively, and waste products build up in the heart muscle. This inflames the nerves in the muscle to cause the characteristic pain of angina.

Diagnosis may be difficult, as the pain has usually subsided when the patient sees a doctor, and all blood tests and electrocardiographs (see Section 4) may be completely normal at this time. Quite often the history from the patient is sufficient to make the diagnosis, but sometimes a stress ECG must be performed (under strict medical supervision) to recreate the pain and observe the abnormal pattern on the cardiograph. Coronary angiography is a special type of X-ray (see Section 4) that can detect the narrowed arteries around the heart.

Treatment involves two different approaches — prevention of further attacks, and treatment of any acute attacks that may occur. Prevention is always better than treatment, and tablets (e.g. Isordil, beta-blockers or calcium channel blockers — see Section 6) may be taken regularly to keep the arteries as widely dilated as possible. Skin patches or ointments containing similar drugs, which can be absorbed through the skin and into the blood stream, can be used instead of, or as well as, tablets.

Treatment of the acute attack involves immediately resting, and placing a tablet containing nitroglycerine, nifedipine or a similar drug (see Section 6) under the tongue, from where it will be rapidly absorbed into the bloodstream and dilate the heart arteries to relieve the attack.

About 5% of all patients with angina will have a heart attack each year, and half of these will die from that heart attack. Heart failure can gradually affect those remaining, reducing their mobility and eventually leading to premature death. High blood pressure, diabetes and an irregular heart beat are unfavourable findings and will also lead to an early death. For this reason, if a narrowed artery can be demonstrated by coronary angiography, it is sensible to have this narrowing bypassed in an operation called a coronary artery bypass graft (CABG). It involves using a small piece of vein from elsewhere in the body to provide a channel around the narrowed section of artery. These are now a routine procedure in many major city hospitals and help to improve the quality and length of life of many angina sufferers.

Another technique involves passing a tiny deflated balloon through the arteries in the leg or arm, into the heart, and then into the small narrowed arteries around the heart. The balloon is then inflated, enlarges the artery, and improves the blood flow. Balloon angiography is not appropriate for all patients but is proving effective in a specially selected category of angina sufferers.

ANGINA, VINCENT'S
See VINCENT'S ANGINA.

ANGIOEDEMA
See ALLERGY — Hives.

ANKYLOSING SPONDYLITIS
Ankylosing spondylitis is a long-term inflammation of the small joints between the vertebrae in the back, which leads to pain, stiffness and eventually a fixed forward curvature of the back. It is more common in men, usually starts in the late twenties or early thirties, but takes many years to become a serious problem for the patient. It may be associated with a number of apparently unrelated conditions, including arthritis of other joints, heart valve disease, weakening of the aorta and inflammation of the eyes. These problems must be treated separately.

The disease starts gradually with a constant backache that may radiate down the legs. Stiffness of the back becomes steadily worse, and eventually an old patient may be bent almost double by a solidly fused backbone. Diagnosis in the early stages involves X-rays of the back, which may show characteristic changes, and blood tests that are now quite accurate in making the diagnosis.

Treatment involves the use of anti-inflammatory drugs (NSAIDs — see Section 6) such as indomethacin, aspirin and (in resistant cases only) phenylbutazone. Physiotherapy plays an important part, and regular therapy can keep the back supple for far longer than would be expected. Other forms of physiotherapy can relieve the pain and stiffness even in advanced cases.

The disease may settle spontaneously for a few months or years, before progressing further. There is no cure available, but treatment can give most patients a full life of normal length.

ANOREXIA NERVOSA
Anorexia nervosa is an eating disorder that is almost exclusively a disease of young women, and as many as one in every 200 women in Australia between 13 and 30 may be affected. It is a disease of white Western society, and is almost unknown in American Negroes and British Indians. It is totally unknown in third-world countries.

The patient has an extreme dislike of food, due to an inappropriate body image which makes them feel grossly overweight, or have an abnormal fear of becoming overweight when in fact they may be very underweight. The dislike of food is usually accompanied by excessive exercising, especially since aerobics and jobbing became so popular. The fixation that they are obese, or may become so, cannot be easily broken, and mirrors, scales and other props seem to be disbelieved by the patient. The patient can become seriously undernourished and emaciated, to the point of death, if adequate treatment is not available. Other symptoms include a cessation of menstrual periods, diffuse hair loss, an intolerance of cold, a slow pulse, irregular heart beat and other complex hormonal disorders. Patients practice deceit to fool their family and doctors by appearing to eat normal meals but later vomit the food, use purgatives to clean out their bowel, or hide food during the meal.

The treatment is extraordinarily difficult and prolonged and requires the attention of psychiatrists and physicians who are expert in the field. Initial hospital admission is almost mandatory, and any relapses should also be treated by hospitalisation. Punishment for not eating must be avoided, but friendly encouragement and persuasion by family and friends is beneficial in both improving the patient's self-esteem and food intake. Medication is not successful without the accompanying psychiatric help. Tricyclic antidepressants (see Section 6) are the most commonly used drugs.

Relapses are common, and suicide is frequently attempted. Psychotherapy to control and monitor the patient is required for many years, but even in the best centres deaths do occur.

See also BULIMIA.

ANTERIOR CHEST WALL SYNDROME
See TIETZE'S SYNDROME.

ANTHRAX
Anthrax is caused by a bacterium in cattle, horses, sheep, goats and pigs, but only rarely in people. It is most common in farmers, meat workers, veterinarians and others who come into close contact with these animals. It is caught by the bacteria entering the body through scratches and grazes, or rarely by inhalation into the lungs.

Initially, a sore appears at the site of entry. Then the nearby glands become inflamed, a fever develops, followed by nausea, vomiting, headaches and collapse. If the infection enters the lung, a severe form of pneumonia results. The diagnosis is confirmed by microscopic examination of smears from the skin sores, or from sputum samples. Specific blood tests may also detect the disease.

Treatment involves antibiotics (penicillin injections or tetracycline) which will clear the skin form of the disease effectively in most cases. Anthrax pneumonia, or a spread of the disease into the bloodstream, is very serious, and a significant proportion of these patients will die.

ANXIETY NEUROSIS
It is normal to be anxious about many situations that arise in everyday life. Problems with your children at school, extra responsibility at work, financial problems, disagreements with others, illness in the family and many other circumstances will cause anxiety. There are two main ways to deal with this type of anxiety — you can take action to remove the cause of the stress, or you can rationalise the problem. The anxiety about financial problems will be removed if you work overtime and earn more money. The anxiety over problems with your children may be resolved by a discussion with their teacher. Some causes of anxiety cannot be removed as easily. In these cases, discussing the problem with relatives, friends, your family doctor or another sympathetic person may help you

to put the problem into perspective. You may find after these discussions that there is some action that can be taken to relieve the pressure you are suffering. If there is nothing you can do, your friends and counsellors can offer moral support.

Doctors become more concerned when you become anxious about routine matters that the majority of people take for granted. Anxiety about catching a bus, meeting new people, going shopping or using household appliances is not normal, and if allowed to continue, it may cause you to become steadily more anxious about more and more things. This is an anxiety neurosis, and it can become so severe that the patient is unable to lead a normal life. Unfortunately, some of these people are also anxious about seeing doctors and may not seek help until the situation has reached a crisis. It is important for close friends and relatives to intervene in this situation, in order to ensure that medical assistance is obtained at an early stage.

Treatment may only involve regular counselling sessions with your general practitioner or, for more severe cases, in-depth assessment and psychoanalysis by a psychiatrist. Sometimes medication is required to give the patient an initial boost back to the normal world. Medications used include benzodiazepines, such as Serepax, Valium, Tranxene, Frisium, Ativan and Xanax (see Section 6). These should only be used for short periods of time, and preferably intermittently, as dependence may occur. Other drugs used in this situation are safer in the long term and include the tricyclic antidepressants (see Section 6), such as Sinequan, Tryptanol and Prothiaden. Other medications that may be used include Equanil, Melleril and Parnate. The earlier treatment is started, the shorter the course required, and the more successful the eventual outcome.

See also STRESS.

AORTIC STENOSIS (COARCTATION OF THE AORTA)

The aorta is the main artery running from the heart through the chest and down the back of the abdomen. It ends just bellow the navel, where it splits into the major arteries that lead down the legs. A stenosis is a narrowing, and so aortic stenosis is a narrowing of the aorta. The term coarctation of the aorta is also used. Aortic valve stenosis is a narrowing of the valve in the heart that leads to the aorta and is dealt with separately under heart valve disease.

Coarctation of the aorta is a congenital condition (present since birth) that is more common in boys than girls. It is often associated with abnormalities of the aortic heart valve. Only a short segment of the aorta is normally narrowed. The severity of the symptoms depends upon the degree of narrowing of the aorta. A very narrow segment can restrict blood flow to the lower half of the body and cause heart failure as the heart strives to pump the blood past the obstruction.

It is a condition that should be diagnosed at birth or shortly afterwards, although milder cases may not be detected until the child undergoes rapid growth in the early teenage years. Symptoms in these children include headaches, leg pain with exercise and frequent nose bleeds. They are also found to have high blood pressure in the arms, and low blood pressure in the legs.

Aortic stenosis is usually discovered during a routine examination on the birth of the baby, when a doctor hears a characteristic murmur when listening to the heart. This murmur is caused by the blood rushing through the narrowed section of the aorta.

The treatment involves surgical correction of the narrowing as soon as practical after the diagnosis is made, with attachment of a synthetic patch to open up the aorta to its correct diameter. The results of surgery are very good, but without surgery, 75% of these babies die in the first year of life.

Aortic valve disease
See HEART VALVE DISEASE.

Aphthous ulcer
See ULCER, MOUTH.

Appendicitis
Appendicitis is almost totally unknown in the poorer countries of the world, but in Australia, a significant number of us will have our appendix removed at some stage of our lives. The reason for this seems to be dietary, and the lack of fibre in the Western diet is often blamed. The incidence of appendicitis has actually fallen in recent years, due to the better dietary education of the population.

When we eat, food passes down the gullet into the stomach. From there it passes through about eight metres of small intestine, before entering into the side of the large intestine and slowly moving the last one and a half metres to the anus (see LARGE INTESTINE, Section 2). At the point where the small intestine enters the large intestine, there is a dead ending of large intestine (the caecum) going in one direction, and the main part of the large intestine leading to the outside going in the other. Running off the caecum is a narrow tube about 12 cm long that is also a dead end. This tube is the appendix.

In other mammals, particularly those that eat grass, the appendix is an important structure which aids in the digestion of cellulose. In man it serves no useful purpose, and a few people are even born without an appendix.

If the narrow tube of the appendix becomes blocked by faeces, food, mucus or some foreign body, bacteria can start breeding in the closed-off area behind the blockage. This bacterial infection causes appendicitis. The victim usually starts to complain of pain around the navel, but soon after the pain moves to the right side of the abdomen just above the pelvic bone. The infection is often associated with loss of appetite, slight diarrhoea and a mild fever. The pain steadily worsens until medical aid is sought. The diagnosis is confirmed by the doctor carefully examining the patient, and usually blood and urine tests are done to exclude other causes of the pain.

If the disease is left without treatment, the appendix becomes steadily more infected, and so full of pus that it eventually bursts. The pus and infection can then spread around the entire abdomen, causing the patient to become extremely ill.

The only effective treatment is surgery, and because of the serious consequences of a ruptured appendix, if there is a significant suspicion of appendicitis, surgeons will remove the offending organ. Occasionally a normal appendix will be found, but it is far better to be safe than very sorry.

The operation is simple and takes about 20 minutes. Unless there are complications, you should only have a small scar low down on the right side of your belly, often below the bikini line in women (see COMMON OPERATIONS, Section 6). You will be in hospital between two and four days, and you can return to work in seven to ten days.

The removed appendix will be sent to a pathologist for further checking under a microscope so that the diagnosis can be confirmed and any other disease excluded (see PATHOLOGY, Section 4).

Arrhythmia
See HEART, IRREGULAR RHYTHM.

Arterial gas embolism
See BENDS.

Arterial hardening
See ATHEROSCLEROSIS.

Arteriosclerosis
See ATHEROSCLEROSIS.

Arteritis
Arteritis is an auto-immune inflammation of arteries. Auto-immune means that the body's immune system is inappropriately attacking its own cells, in this case the arteries. The arteries most commonly involved are those in the temples at the side of the head and those supplying the eye, and the condition is then called **temporal arteritis** or **giant cell arteritis**.

The symptoms include headache, tiredness, weight loss, and loss of appetite. The arteries on the side of the head become exquisitely tender. The most serious consequence is the possible loss of vision. Treatment involves the use of steroids (see Section 6).

Arthritis
Arthritis is a pain in a joint — any joint, from the big toe to the jaw. To say that a patient has arthritis therefore means very little. The cause of the arthritis and the type of arthritis must be determined before the correct treatment can be commenced.

There are many different types of arthritis, some common, others very rare, and it may take a number of blood, X-ray and other tests before the final diagnosis can be made. Sometimes a disease may be in its early stages or occur only fleetingly, in which case treatment of a non-specific nature may be started while awaiting further developments that will allow a more definite diagnosis and appropriate treatment.

Many injuries, from sport, work, motor vehicle or domestic accidents, can cause joint pain, and these traumatic forms of arthritis can be treated simply and effectively with combinations of hot/cold packs, rest, physiotherapy, anti-inflammatory drugs (NSAID — see Section 6), pain-killers, liniments and immobilisation. Some of these injuries (usually only a very small percentage) may progress to a more chronic form of arthritis, and a patient who is experiencing prolonged problems after an injury should bring these to the attention of their general practitioner sooner rather than later.

Juvenile rheumatoid arthritis
See Still's disease (below).

Osteoarthritis
Osteoarthritis is a degeneration of one or more joints. It is a disease limited to these affected joints, and differs from rheumatoid arthritis in that there are no effects from the disease elsewhere in the body. It is the most common form of arthritis and affects up to 15% of the total population, most of them being elderly. It is caused by a degeneration in the cartilage within joints, and inflammation of the bone exposed by the damaged cartilage. There is a hereditary tendency to the disease, which is aggravated by injury and overuse of joints.

The symptoms are usually mild at first, but slowly worsen with time and joint use. Any joint in the body may be affected, but particularly vulnerable are the knee, back, hip, feet, and hands. Stiffness and pain that are relieved by rest are the initial symptoms. As the disease progresses, limitation of movement, deformity and partial dislocation (subluxation) of a joint may occur. The joint may become swollen during acute episodes, and a crackling noise may come from the joint when it is moved. Nodules (Bouchard's or Heberden's nodes) may develop on the fingers in severe cases.

There are no blood tests available to confirm the diagnosis, but X-rays show characteristic changes from a relatively early stage. Repeated X-rays over the years are used to follow the course of the disease.

The mainstay of treatment is to avoid any movement or action that causes pain in the affected joints. If the leg or back are involved, climbing stairs and carrying loads should be avoided or minimised. An overweight patient is constantly carrying a load, and weight reduction may give considerable relief to a weight-bearing joint. Heat to the affected joints gives considerable relief, and may be best applied by hot wax baths administered by a physiotherapist.

Non-steroidal anti-inflammatory drugs (NSAID — see Section 6) such as aspirin, Indocid, Naprosyn, Voltaren, Feldene, etc., may be used to reduce the pain in a damaged joint. They often must be used in the long term, and may cause indigestion or stomach ulceration in some patients. Pain-relieving medications of varying strength that can be used as required are the only other form of drug treatment available.

Surgery to replace major joints affected by osteoarthritis is very successful. The most common joints to be totally replaced by steel and plastic prostheses are the hip and knee. Previously crippled patients are often able to walk normally again within a couple of months of the operation. Surgery to the joints in the back is sometimes necessary, but these joints have to be fused together to prevent movement between them, as they cannot be replaced. Spinal fusion and laminectomy can give enormous relief to patients who have chronic lower back pain from osteoarthritis.

Injections of steroids into an acutely inflamed joint may give rapid relief, but this treatment cannot be repeated frequently because of the risk of further damage to the joint caused by the side effects of the steroid.

The prognosis of osteoarthritis is variable, depending on the joints involved and the severity of the disease. Quite remarkable cures can be performed by joint replacement surgery, but other patients can achieve reasonable control with medications. In any one joint, the general prognosis is a slow and steady deterioration, but some severely affected joints can become relatively pain-free with time.

Rheumatoid arthritis

Rheumatoid arthritis is a disease that affects the entire body in different ways and is not limited to the joints. The cause is unknown, although there are many theories that include hereditary factors, unidentified viruses, environmental factors and combinations of these. It causes inflammation (swelling and redness) of the smooth moist membrane that lines joint surfaces.

Rheumatoid arthritis occurs in one in every 100 people, and females are three times more likely to develop it than males. It usually starts in the prime of life, between 20 and 40 years of age, while the other common arthritis, osteoarthritis, is worse in the elderly.

The early symptoms include early morning stiffness in the small joints of the hands and feet, loss of weight, a feeling of tiredness and being unwell, pins and needles sensations, and sometimes a slight intermittent fever. The onset is slow and insidious, and it may be months or years before the symptoms are bad enough to take the victim to a doctor. Occasionally the disease has a sudden, acute onset, with severe symptoms flaring in a few days, often after emotional stress, or a serious illness that may lower the body's natural defences.

As the disease worsens, it causes increasing pain and stiffness in the small joints, progressing steadily up the arms and legs to larger and larger joints, the back being only rarely affected. The pain becomes more severe and constant, and the joints become swollen, tender and deformed. Other manifestations of the disease can include wasting of muscle, lumps under the skin, inflamed blood vessels, heart and lung inflammation, an enlarged spleen and lymph nodes, dry eyes and mouth, and changes to the number and type of cells in the bloodstream.

The diagnosis is made on the results of blood tests, X-rays and the clinical findings. A 'rheumatoid factor' (RF) can be found in the blood of 75% of patients with rheumatoid arthritis, but this can also occur in some other rare diseases, so is not an absolute diagnosis. The level of RF and other indicators in the blood stream can give doctors a gauge to measure the severity of the disease and the response to treatment.

X-rays show characteristic changes around the affected joints, but sometimes not until the disease has been causing discomfort to the patient for some time. Examination of the fluid drawn out from an affected joint may also be used to confirm the diagnosis.

There is no cure for rheumatoid arthritis, but effective controls are available for most patients, and the disease tends to burn out and become less debilitating in old age. Treatment will be prolonged and require the careful control by doctors, physiotherapists and occupational therapists. The severity of cases varies greatly, so not all these treatments will be tried in all patients, and the majority will only require minimal medical care.

Rest of both body and mind are important, as it has been shown that emotional problems and anxiety, as well as physical exhaustion, can cause a deterioration in the disease. Rest of the affected joints in splints is also important, provided physiotherapists control regular passive movement of the joints to prevent permanent stiffness developing, and apply heat or cold as appropriate to reduce the inflammation. After the acute stage has passed, carefully graded exercise, again under the care of a physiotherapist, is vital for the long-term control of the disease in a particular joint.

Medication will be prescribed by doctors to relieve the painful swollen joints. Aspirin and more sophisticated non-steroidal anti-inflammatory drugs (NSAID — see Section 6) are the mainstays of treatment. A wide variety of these are available, and there may be some trial and error necessary to find the one that is most beneficial to an individual patient. Unfortunately, all these drugs have some tendency to cause irritation and bleeding in the gut, and occasionally ulcers, so they must be used with some caution.

A number of unusual drugs are also used for this form of arthritis, and in most cases their mode of action is unknown, and their successful use in rheumatoid disease has been found by chance rather than research. Gold, as a salt, can be given by injection or tablet on a long-term basis to stop the progression of the disease, but regular blood tests and physical examination is necessary to avoid toxic effects. Antimalarial drugs such as chloroquine have also been found useful in high doses, but they occasionally cause eye pigmentation, so regular examination by an eye specialist is necessary while using them. Penicillamine (not an antibiotic) is also used, but it has significant side effects in some patients. The dosage is started at a very low level and slowly built up over several months to avoid toxicity. A number of cell-destroying drugs (see CYTOTOXICS, Section 6) may also be tried in very severe cases but must be used with great care, under strictly supervised conditions.

Steroid drugs such as prednisone give dramatic, rapid relief from all the symptoms of rheumatoid arthritis in most patients. There are few short-term side effects, and patients are keen to keep taking them, but they do have severe long-term side effects (e.g. bone and skin thinning, fluid retention, weight gain, peptic ulcers, lowered resistance to infection, etc.), and doctors must carefully balance the benefits against the risks. Usually, the lowest possible dose is used for constant treatment, or better still, they are given for a short period of time in high doses to control flare-ups of the disease. In some cases, steroids may be injected into a particularly troublesome joint.

Surgery to isolated, painful joints can be useful in a limited number of patients. The small finger joints can be replaced by artificial ones, as can most of the major joints of the body. Removing the lining of the joint surgically is sometimes performed, but the results have been only fair. Joint destruction and fusion can also be performed.

The prognosis of rheumatoid arthritis is extremely variable. Some patients have irregular acute attacks throughout their lives, others may have only one or two acute episodes at times of physical or emotional stress, while others steadily progress until they become totally crippled by the disease. Even in severe cases, there are cases of sudden, total remission and recovery, but this is uncommon.

The vast majority of patients can be controlled by the above measures to the point where they can lead comfortable, useful, and long lives.

Septic arthritis

Septic arthritis is a bacterial infection of a joint. It is a serious condition that requires urgent and effective medical treatment to prevent long-term damage to the joint. The disease starts with the sudden onset of severe pain in a joint that is tender to touch, swollen, hot, red, and painful to move. The patient usually has a fever, and the knees, hips and wrists are the most commonly involved joints. Other joints may become painful intermittently before, and during, the acute stage of the disease.

A number of different bacteria may be responsible for the disease, and they usually enter the joint through the bloodstream. Occasionally, obvious injury to the joint or adjacent bone can allow a route of entry for the bacteria. It may follow the injection of drugs into a joint, or the draining of fluid from a swollen joint.

It is a relatively uncommon disease, and the average general practitioner would see less than one case a year. Premature babies are at a particularly high risk of developing the disease.

Blood tests can show that an infection is present in the body, but they are not able to identify the location or type of bacteria. Fluid drawn from the joint through a needle can be cultured, and the offending bacteria can be identified to give a definite diagnosis. X-rays do not reveal the early stages of the disease, but only show changes after the bacteria has eaten away part of the bone that forms the joint.

Investigations should be started before treatment is commenced, so that the infecting bacteria can be correctly identified. While awaiting results, the doctor will usually start the patient on a potent antibiotic. This may be changed at a later time when the results become available. The appropriate antibiotic to treat the disease can then be chosen. Antibiotics may need to be given by injection initially.

Removal of the infected fluid from the

joint by needle aspiration on a regular basis is also necessary. Hot compresses, elevation and immobilisation of the joint, and pain relieving medication complete the necessary treatments.

As the joint recovers, movement of the joint, without causing pain, should commence under the supervision of a physiotherapist to prevent later limitation of movement.

Recovery within a week to ten days is normal with adequate care, but joint destruction, severe chronic arthritis, or complete fusion and stiffness of a joint can occur if the disease is not treated correctly.

Still's disease (juvenile rheumatoid arthritis)

Still's disease is a rare condition that is also known as juvenile rheumatoid arthritis. In simple terms, it is a rheumatoid arthritis- type disease that occurs in children and teenagers. The cause is unknown. There are several forms of the disease that vary in their symptoms, severity and outcome.

Still's disease is characterised by a widespread measles-type rash, a fever that rises and falls rapidly, enlarged lymph glands, spleen and liver, and one or more hot, red, painful, swollen joints. Nodules may develop under the skin near joints, and the heart, lungs and muscles may also become inflamed. The knees, hips, elbows and ankles are the joints most commonly affected. The onset is rare under one year of age and over fourteen, and girls are twice as likely as boys to develop the disease. Blood tests show signs of generalised inflammation, but the tests that diagnose adult rheumatoid arthritis are usually normal.

Treatment involves prolonged rest, with passive movement of affected joints by physiotherapists on a regular basis. Heat often relieves the pain and swelling. Drug treatment includes aspirin, other anti-inflammatory drugs (NSAIDs — see Section 6), and in severe cases, steroids. The course may be prolonged, but most children eventually recover. Unfortunately, some have chronic joint damage and deformity that can cause long term problems.

A large number of other diseases can cause arthritis, including ankylosing spondylitis, gout, lupus erythematosus, polymyalgia rheumatica, pseudogout, psoriasis, Reiter's syndrome, rheumatic fever, Ross river fever, scleroderma, Sjögren's syndrome.

ASBESTOSIS

Asbestosis is a lung disease caused by the inhalation of fine asbestos particles over a prolonged period of time. It is similar to the disease caused by coal dust in miners (pneumoconiosis), silica dust from rock mining and stone cutting (silicosis) and talcum powder in milling and the rubber industry (talcosis)

The asbestos particles are long, thin filaments, that easily become trapped in the small air tubes (bronchioles) of the lung. The lower part of the lungs is most commonly affected, and a characteristic appearance develops on X-rays of the chest. The disease occurs almost exclusively in asbestos factory workers, processors and miners who inhale free-floating particles of asbestos in the workplace.

The asbestos particles are harmless when combined with cement and other materials in pipes and sheeting, and can only cause harm if inhaled during sawing or cutting of these pipes or sheets. Swallowing small amounts of asbestos or touching asbestos in any form is harmless. Asbestos dust has been used as an insulating material in the past, and may be harmful if the roof or wall cavity in which it is situated is opened, and the dust therein inhaled. This form of asbestos is being steadily removed from most buildings in Western countries.

Sufferers from asbestosis develop shortness of breath, cough, and, in advanced cases, blue lips and clubbed finger tips. The lungs become progressively more damaged with time and further exposure, to the point where the patient may have no exercise tolerance and suffer symptoms similar to severe asthma or emphysema. The disease may progress for long after asbestos exposure has ceased. Smoking will obviously aggravate the condition.

The most serious complication of asbestosis is the development of a virulent form of lung cancer known as **mesothelioma** (see separate entry) and caused by exposure to asbestos. Up to 7% of patients with asbestosis will develop mesothelioma. This type of cancer occurs half the time in non-asbestosis sufferers, but it is more common in smokers who have been exposed to asbestos. The average age of onset of this cancer is 60, and the latent period between exposure to asbestos and development of mesothelioma can be up to 40 years.

Mesothelioma has a very insidious onset, with symptoms little different to asbestosis itself, and X-ray changes may not be apparent until the disease is quite advanced. CT scans (see Section 4) are more useful in making the diagnosis in suspicious cases. A biopsy of the cancerous area is the only way to make a definite diagnosis. The cancer is extremely virulent and spreads rapidly. Three quarters of victims die within a year of the diagnosis, and 98% within two years. Treatment with surgery, drugs and radiation has been tried, but with virtually no success.

See also LUNG CANCER; PNEUMOCONIOSIS.

ASCARIASIS

See ROUNDWORMS.

ASTHMA

Asthma is a temporary narrowing of the tubes through which air flows into and out of the lungs. This narrowing is caused by a spasm in the tiny muscles which surround the air tubes. The problem is further aggravated by the excess production of phlegm in the lungs and swelling of the lung tissue through inflammation.

The narrowing of the airways causes shortness of breath and wheezing. Asthmatics usually find they cannot breathe out easily because, as they try to exhale the lung collapses further, and the small amount of space left in the airways is obliterated. Asthmatic symptoms also include coughing, particularly in children, or a mild tightness and discomfort in the chest.

If asthma is suspected, the first step is to perform tests on the lungs to assess their function. This involves blowing into a number of different machines which either draw a graph a doctor can interpret, or give a reading on a gauge (see PULMONARY FUNCTION TESTS, Section 4). The tests are performed on several occasions at different times of the day before a definite diagnosis of asthma is made. The patient's response to medication is also checked on these machines.

Many people who have asthma never see a doctor, even though they may be aware of the diagnosis. Although they may feel well, they often do not have their asthma under adequate control. Their quality of life and exercise tolerance could be improved dramatically if a doctor saw them regularly to keep their asthma under review. Attacks may build up slowly over many weeks, and the individual may be unaware of the deterioration in his lung function until it is measured.

The absolute cause of asthma is unknown, but certain triggers can start an attack in susceptible individuals. The triggers include colds and other viral infections, temperature changes, allergies, exercise, smoke, dust and other irritants. Once the diagnosis has been established, it is important to identify any trigger substances which might start an attack. This can often be done by the patient on a trial and error basis, but an allergist is usually called upon in severe cases to help in the identification of potential risk factors.

A tendency to develop asthma runs in families, along with hay fever and some forms of eczema. If you have a parent with asthma, you have a 15 times greater chance of developing it than the average person.

The treatment of asthma is divided into two broad categories — prevention of attacks, and treatment of the acute attacks when they occur. It is true that asthma cannot be cured, but doctors can control the disease very effectively in the vast majority of patients. Asthma treatment is a team effort involving the doctor, physiotherapists and other health professionals, and the cooperation of the patient and his/her parents and family is vital.

Prevention is always better than cure, and all but the mildest of asthmatics should be using one or more of several different types of sprays or tablets to prevent attacks. These include steroid sprays such as Aldecin, and anti-allergy sprays such as Intal. If one form of prevention does not work, other types should be tried, or combinations used. Severe asthmatics may need to use prednisone tablets (a type of steroid — see Section 6) to both prevent and treat their attacks. These may have significant side effects if used over long periods of time, and their dosage must be kept to a minimum under the strict guidance of a doctor. Some asthmatics who react to specific substances may benefit from allergen desensitisation.

The best way to treat an asthma attack is by aerosol sprays which take the drug directly into the lungs where it is needed. These can be in the form of pressure pack sprays, motor or gas driven nebulisers, or capsules which can be broken and their powder inhaled. They act to dilate the airways and liquefy the thick mucus. These are a class of drugs called sympathomimetics (see Section 6) and include Ventolin, Respolin, Bricanyl and Berotec. A spray called Atrovent is often used as an adjunct to these. Many of these sprays can have their effectiveness and ease of use improved, particularly in children, if a spacing device such as a Misthaler or Nebuhaler is used with the spray.

Mixtures and tablets are also available for the treatment of asthma attacks, but they work more slowly and have greater side effects. Most of these are in a class called xanthinates (see Section 6) and include Nuelin, Theo-Dur, Somophyllin, Brondecon and others. Very severe attacks may require oxygen by mask and injections of theophylline or steroids.

People can die rapidly from a sudden, severe asthma attack. If an attack of asthma does not respond rapidly to the normally used treatments, seek further medical assistance immediately.

Research into asthma and its control is continuing apace, with the assistance of the Asthma Foundation and other research organisations, and new treatments and control methods are being marketed every year. Asthma is no longer the torture of years past, and the future is looking brighter all the time.

Astrocytoma
See BRAIN CANCER.

Atherosclerosis
Arteries (see Section 2) are normally elastic, and can expand and contract slightly

to allow for variations in the pressure of the blood caused by each beat of the heart. Degeneration of the arteries in the body, making them hard and inelastic, is **arteriosclerosis**. This is usually associated with, and caused by, atherosclerosis, which is the excessive deposition of hard fatty plaques and nodules within the artery, and in the tissue forming the artery wall. It is usually found in the elderly, and those who have an above average level of cholesterol in their blood. High blood pressure may also cause, and aggravate, arteriosclerosis.

If an artery becomes hardened, it is less able to cope with pressure changes within the blood stream and more likely to rupture, causing a leak of blood, sometimes into vital structures such as the brain, which may lead to a stroke. Patients find they cannot cope with sudden changes in position (e.g. getting out of bed) without becoming dizzy or light-headed, as the blood supply is suddenly reduced by the changing effects of gravity and the inelastic arteries are unable to respond.

Fatty deposits from an excessive cholesterol level form at points of turbulence within an artery (e.g. the junction of two arteries, or a bend in the artery). The deposits are hard, not soft, and steadily splint the artery wall so that it cannot move freely. These deposits are more common in the major arteries such as the aorta, the arteries of the legs, and those in the neck. With time, the deposits can narrow the artery and gradually restrict the flow of blood to the tissues beyond. If the leg arteries are involved, the leg muscles may not be able to obtain sufficient blood (and therefore oxygen) during exercise. The patient then develops severe leg pain, particularly when climbing slopes or stairs. With a few minutes rest, the pain eases, and the victim can walk a few metres more before the pain strikes again. This condition is called arterial claudication.

If the tiny arteries that supply blood to the heart muscle are involved, angina occurs (see separate entry) and the patient develops chest pain with exertion. If arteries to the brain are involved, the patient may develop a multitude of bizarre symptoms, become light headed, dizzy, confused, or black out as the brain does not receive sufficient blood to operate correctly.

Blocked arteries can be treated with medication to relax the tiny muscles in the artery walls, allowing them to open as far as possible (e.g. Adalat, Duvadilan — see Section 6), or with medication that eases the passage of blood cells through the narrowing (e.g. Trental), and by surgery. Surgery can be extremely successful in relieving and curing this condition. There are two types — bypass grafts, and cleaning out the deposits inside the artery.

Bypass grafts use tubes of synthetic material to form a new artery to bypass the blocked area. These can be quite large, and amazingly long if necessary. An alternative is to use pieces of vein from elsewhere in the body to form a bypass passage for the blood. This is the method commonly used in heart artery bypass surgery for angina.

The other surgical technique, which can be used most successfully on the legs, involves opening the blocked artery and actually cleaning out the fatty deposits that are blocking it. This procedure is called endarterectomy.

Recently a technique called balloon angioplasty has also been used to open blocked arteries. In this, a fine tube, with a deflated balloon at the end, is passed along an artery and into the narrowed segment. The balloon is then inflated, forcing open the blockage. After deflation, the balloon and tube are withdrawn, leaving a more open artery than before.

Another serious problem associated with atherosclerosis is embolism. An embolism occurs when a piece of the hard fat within the artery, breaks away, and travels with the blood along the artery. Eventually it reaches an artery which is too narrow for it to pass, and this small artery can become totally blocked by the piece of fat. This causes little problem in most parts of the body, but if the blocked artery happens to be in the heart or brain, a heart attack or stroke will occur, as the tissue beyond the blockage dies from lack of blood.

Atherosclerosis is better prevented than treated, and everyone should have their cholesterol checked in their thirties, and every five years thereafter, to ensure the level is not high enough to predispose to the development of this condition. If the levels are high, diets and medication can be used to lower it.

ATHLETE'S FOOT
See FUNGAL INFECTIONS — Tinea.

ATRIAL FIBRILLATION
See HEART, IRREGULAR RHYTHM.

AUTISM
Autism is a developmental disorder in which a child fails to develop normal social skills, language skills and communication skills. Such children are often excessively preoccupied with a particular type of behaviour and are very resistant to change or education. Repetitive habits are common.

Autism is thought to be an abnormality in the development of the brain, and may be due to brain damage during growth in the womb, at birth, or in the first years of life. The absolute cause is not yet known.

There are no blood tests to diagnose the condition, but CT scans (see Section 4) sometimes show non-specific abnormalities. Electroencephalograms (see Section 4) are usually normal, except in those who develop epilepsy, which may occur in up to 30% of cases.

Occasionally autistic children have exceptional talents in a particular area (e.g. maths or music — the 'idiot savant syndrome'), but unfortunately the majority remain mentally retarded and require care from responsible parents or institutions throughout their life. There is no effective treatment, and their life expectancy is close to normal.

AUTO-IMMUNE DISEASE
See ARTERITIS; DERMATOMYOSITIS; PEMPHIGOID; PEMPHIGUS; POLYARTERITIS NODOSA; PSORIASIS; RHEUMATOID ARTHRITIS; SCLERODERMA; SJÖGREN'S SYNDROME; VITILIGO.

BACK DISEASE
See ANKYLOSING SPONDYLITIS; ARTHRITIS; BACK PAIN; KYPHOSIS; PARAPLEGIA; SCHEUERMANN'S DISEASE; SCOLIOSIS; SPINA BIFIDA; WHIPLASH.

BACK PAIN
Back pain can reduce a person to crawling on hands and knees. It can strike down national sportsmen in their prime and is responsible for more workers compensation claims than any other illness.

The back is made from 24 bones, called vertebrae, that sit one on top of the other. The bottom vertebra sits on top of the sacrum, which is really another five vertebrae that have fused together. The sacrum forms the back part of the pelvis. The top vertebra is specially modified to allow the skull to sit on it and swivel in all directions (see SPINE, Section 2).

When looked at from behind, the vertebrae form a straight line. From the side though, the bones of the back are aligned in several smooth curves. The back curves in at the waist, out over the back of the chest, and in again at the neck. This careful alignment of bones is maintained by ligaments (stout bands of fibrous tissue) and muscles that run along the length of the back.

Between each vertebra is a cushion of cartilaginous material known as a disc. This has a semiliquid centre (like a jelly-filled balloon), and the discs absorb the shocks the body receives in walking, running and jumping. The spinal cord runs through holes in the centre of each vertebra. The cord is an extension of the brain and passes through every vertebra from the skull to waist level. Between each vertebra, the spinal cord sends out nerves that supply that section of the body. Nerves run out from the neck to supply the arms, and from the lower vertebrae to supply the legs.

The sacrum, that big bone at the bottom of the spine, is attached to the pelvis by a complex network of ligaments positioned just under the dimples that many people have on either side of their back, just above their buttocks.

Back pain occurs when this intricate arrangement of bones, ligaments, discs, muscles and nerves becomes strained, torn, broken, stretched or otherwise disrupted. The most common cause of back pain is ligamentous and muscular damage from incorrect lifting. Lifting and twisting simultaneously is particularly dangerous. In older people, arthritis may be the cause of back pain, when the smooth joints between the vertebrae become roughened and damaged by age and long years of use.

Direct injuries may fracture or dislocate the bones in the back and cause the spinal cord to be pinched and paralysis of the body below that point. A slight shift in the position of one vertebra on another, or inflammation of the surrounding tissues, may put pressure on a nerve and cause sciatica or localised back pain.

Treatment of back problems is often complex and slow but can be quite successful. The use of medications to reduce inflammation, pain-killers and physiotherapy are the usual methods. The physiotherapist is invaluable in the treatment of all back conditions, and a good physio can often return a worker to his/her job faster than the use of tablets alone. Exercises, traction, manipulation, corsets and braces are some of the treatments physiotherapists use. The treatments of last resort are injections into the damaged area, and surgery to realign the vertebrae and unpinch nerves.

The best treatment is prevention. Lifting correctly protects your back from injury. If a sore back develops, the sooner medical assistance is sought, the sooner the pain will go, and the sooner you will be able to resume your normal activities.

See also ANKYLOSING SPONDYLITIS; ARTHRITIS; KYPHOSIS; LUMBAGO; PARAPLEGIA; SCOLIOSIS; WHIPLASH.

See also Section 3; and SURGERY and PHYSIOTHERAPY, Section 6.

BALANITIS

Balanitis is an inflammation or infection of the head of the penis (the area normally covered by the foreskin in uncircumcised men). It may also occur at the tip of the clitoris in women. The infection may be caused by bacteria (common), fungi (i.e. thrush — also common), and micro-organisms such as amoebae and Trichomonas (uncommon). Irritants such as chemicals, urine (in incontinent men) and dermatitis may also cause balanitis. The head of the penis becomes tender, sore and there may be weeping sores present.

Treatment involves antibiotic creams and/or tablets to destroy any infecting organism. Irritants must be removed, or the penis protected by a barrier cream or condom. Dermatitis may be difficult to treat and require a variety of creams and ointments. In recurrent cases, circumcision may be required.

Bartholin's cyst
Bartholin's glands are mucus-secreting glands that open through small ducts onto the inside lips of a woman's vulva. They produce mucus to keep the female genitals moist, and secrete extra fluid to act as a lubricant during sexual intercourse. If the gland becomes infected with bacteria, the duct becomes blocked with pus, and the gland swells up to form a tender, painful lump in the vulva. An abscess may form, and cause severe discomfort and embarrassment to the female victim. Sex is obviously very painful, and even sitting may be uncomfortable. Occasionally, the duct may block intermittently, causing a less painful but still distressing cyst to swell and subside in the area.

Treatment of an acute infection requires antibiotics by mouth, but in most cases, adding surgery to drain away the pus, or removing a chronically recurring cyst, is the best long-term solution.

Basal cell carcinoma
See SKIN CANCER.

BCC (basal cell carcinoma)
See SKIN CANCER.

Bed sores (pressure sores)
The skin, as with every other part of the body, needs an adequate blood supply to function correctly. If the blood supply is cut off or significantly reduced, the area affected dies. If you press on your skin firmly, the area under pressure becomes white because of the lack of blood. If the pressure is applied for many hours without relief, the area of skin being pressed will die. This is what happens with bed/pressure sores.

Elderly, infirm, paralysed or unconscious patients who spend long periods in bed, or sitting, may not have the ability to move themselves or the sensation necessary to prompt movement, so that a particular area of skin may be carrying a great deal of the body's weight for a prolonged period of time. The involved skin eventually breaks down, and a deep ulcer can develop that may be very difficult to heal. The most commonly affected areas are the heels, buttocks, back of the head and over the lower part of the backbone.

To prevent this problem, nurses attend to these patients frequently, moving them from side to side every hour, so that no area bears pressure for a prolonged period of time. Sheep skins, ripple mattresses, water beds and other devices are placed under affected patients to spread their weight as much as possible. Once present, the sores become infected very easily, further complicating their recovery.

Treatment involves the avoidance of any further pressure to the area, antibiotic dressings, special absorbent bandages or dressings, and, in resistant cases, surgical treatment to cover the area with a skin graft.

Once affected, the same area is very susceptible to future damage, and extra precautions must be taken to avoid their recurrence.

Bed-wetting (enuresis)
Bed-wetting is a medical problem that makes businessmen dread overnight trips to a conference, causes marriages to break up, stops teenagers from spending the night at a friend's, and drives the mothers of some children to desperation. The technical medical name for bed-wetting is enuresis. People with this problem are often too embarrassed to see their family

doctor about it, but it may cause severe disruption to home life and a career.

Normally, urine is retained in the bladder by the contraction of a ring-shaped bundle of muscle that surrounds the bladder opening (see Section 2). When you wish to pass urine, this ring muscle (sphincter) relaxes, and the muscles in the wall of the bladder and around the abdominal cavity, contract to squirt the urine out in a steady stream. Those who are bed-wetters tend to sleep very deeply, and during the deepest phases of this sleep, when all the main muscles of the body are totally relaxed, the ring muscle that retains the urine in the bladder also relaxes. Because there is no associated contraction of the muscles in the bladder wall or elsewhere, the urine just dribbles out slowly in the night, not in a hard stream.

Some children are slower at controlling their bladder at night than others. Some may be three or four years old before control is obtained. The important thing to remember is that, in most cases, the problem can be controlled by cooperation between doctor, patient and family.

The first step is to investigate the patient to exclude any physical cause for bed-wetting. Chronic infections, structural abnormalities, and other rarer conditions may cause a weakness or excessive irritability of the bladder. Once these problems have been excluded by urine tests and X-rays, the treatment of a true bed-wetter can begin.

In children, the simple steps of restricting fluids for three hours before bedtime, taking the child to the toilet during the night, and establishing a reward system, can be tried. Unfortunately, these methods are often unsuccessful, and more specific remedies are required.

The best form of treatment is the bed-wetting alarm. This consists of a moisture-sensitive pad that is placed under the patient, a battery and an alarm. When it becomes wet from the first small dribble of urine, it closes an electrical circuit, and sounds the alarm. The patient is then woken, and can empty the bladder in the toilet before returning to sleep. After a few weeks use, most people learn to waken before the alarm, and the problem is solved, but some patients require an extraordinarily loud alarm to wake them.

Another effective form of treatment is the use of a medication called amitriptyline (Tryptanol) every night to alter the type of sleep. The muscles do not relax as much, thus retaining the urine in the bladder, and the patient can sleep quite normally. Over a few weeks, the dosage is slowly lowered, until the medication is stopped completely. Hopefully, the bad sleep habits and bed-wetting do not return.

The final form of treatment is psychotherapy by a psychiatrist, but this is used in only the most resistant cases.

Up to 10% of five-year-olds still wet the bed, so parents should not become too anxious until the child is past this age. Premature treatment can cause permanent sleep disturbances in a child, but delaying treatment beyond five can lead to the problem becoming a major influence in the child's life.

Adults should overcome any false embarrassment, and discuss the matter with their general practitioner to obtain sympathetic and confidential treatment.

See also INCONTINENCE OF URINE.

BELL'S PALSY

The muscles of the face are controlled by the facial nerve, which comes out of a hole in the skull just below and in front of the ear. From there, it spreads like a fan across the face, with branches going to each of the many tiny muscles that control our facial expressions. Damage to this nerve causes all these facial muscles to stop working, because the nerve tells the muscles when to contract and when to relax. The patient can no longer smile or close the eye properly. There are some rare serious causes for this type of paralysis, but by far the most common is Bell's palsy.

Bell's palsy is caused by an inflammation of the facial nerve as it leaves the skull. The exact reason for this inflammation and the subsequent paralysis is unknown. When the condition starts, the patient develops a sudden paralysis of the face muscles on one side only. There may be some mild to moderate pain at the point where the nerve leaves the skull beside the ear, but this settles after a few days. There may also be a disturbance to taste sensation. Two thirds of patients recover completely within a few weeks with no treatment. Most of the others obtain partial recovery, but 10% are significantly affected long term by facial paralysis.

No treatment is necessary for most patients, but if the victim is elderly, the paralysis is total, or if there is severe pain, treatment may be tried. High doses of prednisone (a steroid — see Section 6) to reduce the inflammation in the facial nerve is the usual medication. It is important that the treatment start within five days of the onset of the condition. Unfortunately, there is varying evidence about the value of any treatment, but at least it rarely causes any harm.

BENDS (ARTERIAL GAS EMBOLISM, CAISSON DISEASE)

When we breathe, the oxygen and nitrogen in the air are taken into the lungs, and fill up millions of tiny bubbles (called alveoli) that are covered by a fine network of capillaries (very small blood vessels). The gases pass across a fine membrane and are dissolved into the blood stream. If the air pressure is high, more gases (oxygen and nitrogen) will be dissolved into the blood than if the air pressure is low.

Divers must breathe air at a pressure equivalent to the depth of water in which they are diving. As a result, more oxygen and nitrogen than normal is dissolved into their bloodstream. If the air pressure were kept low, their lungs would collapse with the water pressure around them. At 30 m, the pressure on the lungs is four times that at the surface. When divers surface, they must do so slowly (following rates of ascent that have been worked out from tables that allow for depth and time), or the lower pressure around their bodies and in their lungs will allow the previously dissolved gases to come out of solution and form actual tiny bubbles within the blood. Exactly the same phenomenon can be seen when the top is removed from a bottle of carbonated soft drink or beer, and it starts to fizz. Divers who develop the bends have blood that fizzes.

The gas primarily responsible for the bends is nitrogen, which makes up 78% of the air we breathe. To overcome this problem, the nitrogen is replaced with the far lighter gas helium in some gas mixtures designed for prolonged dives at great depths. Helium comes out of solution in blood far faster than nitrogen, so the excess can escape through the lungs as the diver ascends.

The symptoms of the bends may occur immediately after a too rapid ascent, or it may develop up to 6 hours later. The symptoms depend greatly on the fitness, age, and weight of the diver, as well as on the amount of physical exertion he or she has undertaken. Joint pain, weakness, shortness of breath, dizziness, visual disturbances, pins and needles sensation, rashes, loss of the power of speech, headaches and confusion are the most common symptoms. The pain may be excruciatingly severe, and permanent joint damage can result. If the bends remains untreated, it may progress to coma and death.

The name of the disease, 'the bends', derives from the posture the victims adopt in an attempt to relieve the pain. It is also known as caisson disease. Caissons are pressurised chambers that are lowered to the floor of rivers, etc., to enable workers to excavate for the foundations of bridges. The high air pressure inside the caisson kept water from entering. Caissons are rarely used today, as modern surface drilling has replaced this dangerous form of underwater excavation.

The only safe medication for the pain of the bends is aspirin, as stronger drugs may confuse the doctor's assessment of the victim. Oxygen should be administered by mask to anyone who develops the bends, or who has surfaced too quickly.

The only effective treatment is to recompress the patient as rapidly as possible. Anyone who has surfaced too quickly should, if possible, dive again to the appropriate depth, and resurface slowly, while being supervised by another competent diver. Once the bends is present, or if it develops while diving, it is generally too dangerous to manage the patient underwater, and transportation to the nearest decompression chamber as quickly as possible should be undertaken.

The benefits of transportation by air from remote centres to a decompression chamber must be balanced against the dangers of an even lower air pressure in an aircraft flying at any significant altitude. Special clearance for low level flights to transport emergencies of this type has been granted in the past.

Decompression chambers are maintained by the navy, Commonwealth and state governments, and private institutions at a number of points around the Australian coastline. They are a reinforced cylinder that can have air pumped into it at the required pressure. The patient, and often a medical attendant, are placed in the chamber, the air pressure inside is increased to the necessary level, and then over several hours or days slowly reduced back to normal again. This has the effect of re-dissolving the nitrogen bubbles into the bloodstream, and then allowing the gas to escape slowly and naturally through the lungs.

The outcome of the bends is extremely variable, as it depends on the depth of the dive, the length of the dive, the individual diver's characteristics, and the delay before recompression commences.

Prevention is better than treatment, and all divers should be aware of the correct procedures for the dive they undertake, and should avoid diving to greater depths or for longer periods than planned.

BERI-BERI

Beri-beri is caused by an acute lack of thiamine (vitamin B1). This vitamin is relatively common in the diet, and significant amounts can be found in liver, lean pork, yeast and all cereal grains. The disease occurs in those who are malnourished, have food idiosyncrasies, who overcook their food, in alcoholics and in those who require larger than normal amounts of thiamine (e.g. due to an overactive thyroid gland, or prolonged fever). The most common cause in Australia is alcoholism, as alcoholics obtain most of their calorie intake in the form of alcohol and neglect their normal food intake.

In the early stages, the patient has a multitude of vague complaints, including tiredness, loss of appetite, twitching and muscle cramps and pains. Swollen joints, shooting pains, paralysis of feet and hands, and heart abnormalities are late symptoms of a very advanced form of the disease.

Beri-beri is easily treated by giving the patient thiamine and a well-balanced diet. It may be necessary to administer the thiamine by injection in the acute stages of the disease. Patients respond very rapidly to treatment, and recover significantly within 48 hours.

Some authorities have argued that thiamine should be added to alcoholic drinks to prevent beri-beri, in the same way that iodine is added to salt to prevent goitre.

Bilharzia (schistosomiasis)

Bilharzia cannot be caught in Australia, as it is transmitted by a species of snail that is not found in this country. Doctors do see cases of bilharzia though, as patients migrating from overseas may bring the disease with them, and in rare cases tourists may be infected when visiting endemic areas. It can be caught by bathing in fresh-water streams, rivers and lakes in Egypt, tropical Africa as far south as Zimbabwe, the Caribbean and eastern South America.

Bilharzia is caused by a microscopic animal called a fluke (trematode) that enters into the body by burrowing through the skin, often of the foot. Once in the bloodstream, the fluke travels to the veins around the large intestine. Here, eggs are laid, and pass out with the faeces or urine to infect water supplies. Once in the water, the eggs hatch, and the larvae seek out and burrow into the flesh of certain species of fresh-water snail. Here they mature, and emerge from the snail ready to enter and infect another human host.

Infected humans do not pass out all the eggs that are laid by the fluke, and eggs may infect the liver, lungs or spinal cord to cause symptoms involving these organs.

The first symptom is an itchy patch at the site of skin penetration. Varying symptoms then follow, depending on the areas affected by the fluke as it moves through the body, and the individual's reaction to those changes. Long-term symptoms include diarrhoea, abdominal pain and bloody urine. The disease may cause a low-grade chronic illness, or may progress to death in a matter of months. Diagnosis involves blood tests, urine tests, skin tests and liver and gut biopsies.

Treatment is difficult, particularly late in the disease. A number of drugs can be used to kill the fluke inside the body. Damage caused to organs by the fluke may be permanent.

The outcome of treatment is good if commenced early in the course of the disease. Advanced disease may be incurable.

Bites
See Section 8.

Black death
See PLAGUE, BUBONIC.

Blackwater fever
See MALARIA.

Bladder infection
See CYSTITIS.

Bleeding
See BLOOD DISEASE.
 See also Section 3.

Blepharitis

Blepharitis is a common inflammation of the eyelid edges. It may be caused by bacteria or can be a reaction to some environmental factor. The eyelids become red, covered with scales, sore and itchy. Almost invariably, both eyes are involved. As the disease advances, the eyelashes may fall out, and ulcers may form on the lid margins.

Treatment involves cleaning away the scales several times a day with moist cotton wool, and applying antibiotic ointment to the affected areas of the eyelids. A cure is usual within a few days.

Blood Disease
See ANAEMIA; CHRISTMAS DISEASE; EMBOLISM, LUNG; HAEMOPHILIA; LEUKAEMIA; MULTIPLE MYELOMA; POLYCYTHAEMIA RUBRA VERA; THALASSAEMIA; THROMBOSIS; TRANSFUSION REACTION, BLOOD; VON WILLEBRAND'S DISEASE.

Blood Poisoning
See SEPTICAEMIA.

Blood Pressure Disease
See HYPERTENSION; HYPOTENSION; PHAEOCHROMOCYTOMA.

Blood Transfusion Reaction
See TRANSFUSION REACTION, BLOOD.

Boil (Furuncle)
A boil or furuncle starts as an infected hair follicle and develops into a small superficial abscess (see separate entry) that is acutely painful, red and tender. Because these bacterial infections start in hair follicles, people who are very hairy, particularly on areas which are irritated frequently such as the bottom, will develop more boils than others. Other commonly affected areas are the armpits and groin.

A boil gradually enlarges, causing more and more pain (particularly in areas where the skin is tight) until it eventually ruptures, discharging its contained pus. The infection then gradually settles. Once a boil is present, the infection can easily spread across the skin or via the fingers to cause the eruption of boils in other areas. In severe cases, the infection may enter the blood stream to cause septicaemia, fever, and a general feeling of illness. Boils should never be squeezed, as the pus they contain may rupture internally, and spread through the blood stream to the brain and other vital organs.

A **carbuncle** is several boils in a limited area that join together to form an interconnecting infected mass.

Fungal infections can also cause boil-like eruptions, as can a number of less common diseases, including anthrax and orf (see separate entries).

Treatment involves antibiotic tablets or capsules by mouth, applying antiseptic or antibiotic ointment to the boil, and when pus is obviously present, lancing the boil with a scalpel or needle to release the pus. Immobilisation of an infected joint may help ease the pain.

Repeated attacks may require long-term antibiotic treatment, antiseptic soaps and antiseptic lotions applied regularly, to prevent recurrences. Patients with diabetes or kidney failure are particularly susceptible to boils, and recurrent attacks should lead the doctor to exclude these diseases as a possible cause.

See also ABSCESS; FURUNCULOSIS, EAR.

Bone Cancer
See BONE TUMOUR.

Bone Disease
See BONE TUMOUR; MULTIPLE MYELOMA; OSTEOMALACIA; OSTEOMYELITIS; OSTEOPOROSIS; PAGET'S DISEASE OF BONE; PERTHE'S DISEASE; RICKETS.

Bone Tumour
There are many different types of bone cancer, but generally they are some of the nastiest types of cancers that can attack humans. As with all cancers, early diagnosis and treatment gives a far better outcome.

The most common type of bone cancer is that which has spread from another site in the body. Many different cancers tend to spread to bone, including breast and prostate cancer. These have a far poorer outcome than most cancers that actually start in the bone.

The most common symptoms are bone pain and swelling, although many types of bone cancer may show no symptoms until the disease is quite advanced. Fractures that occur very easily, painful or swollen joints, and limitation of joint movement are other possible symptoms of bone cancer.

Diagnosis will involve X-rays, biopsy (taking a sample of a suspicious area) and blood tests to confirm the type of cancer that is present. An exact diagnosis is essential before treatment, as different tumours react in different ways.

Treatment will involve a combination of amputation, surgical removal, irradiation and drugs, depending on that exact diagnosis, and the experience gained over many years from patients with similar problems. The outcome of treatment is extremely variable, depending on the type of cancer, the stage at which it is diagnosed, the position in the body, the age of the patient and the response to treatment.

The different types of bone tumour include osteomas, fibrosarcoma, enchondroma (start in cartilage), chondrosarcoma, osteoclastoma (giant cell tumours), osteosarcoma and Ewing's tumours. The last two will be discussed in more detail.

Osteosarcoma (osteogenic sarcoma)
This cancer occurs in teenagers and young adults, and is more common in males than females. The patient first notices gradually increasing pain in the arm or leg, and less frequently in other parts of the body. The knee and elbow are the most commonly affected areas. The cancer gradually swells, causing the covering skin to become warm, and the swelling is tender to touch. Blood tests can give clues to the existence of the cancer, but X-ray and biopsy are the more important investigations.

Amputation of the affected arm or leg is the usual treatment, with surgical removal of as much bone as possible if the cancer occurs in other areas of the body. Drugs and irradiation may also be used, particularly if the cancer has spread (most commonly to the lungs) or if it cannot be removed at operation.

The outcome is better the further out along the limb the cancer develops. The overall cure rate is only 50%, for cancer in the forearm or lower leg it is 70%, but for cancers in the pelvis or breast bone, there are virtually no survivors.

Ewing's tumour
This form of bone cancer usually occurs in young adults but can develop in children too. Almost any bone in the body may be affected, including the vertebrae of the back. There is pain, swelling and tenderness at the site of the tumour, and the patient develops a fever and becomes anaemic. The diagnosis is made by X-ray and biopsy, blood tests being of little use.

Treatment involves surgical removal if possible, plus irradiation and potent anticancer (cytotoxic) drugs. With intensive treatment in good hospitals, a 50% cure rate can be achieved.

BORNHOLM DISEASE
See PLEURODYNIA.

BOWEL DISEASE
See GUT DISEASE.

BRAIN CANCER
Cancer of the brain is rare, and most general practitioners would see a case only once every three or four years. There are many different types of cell in the brain,

including nerve cells, membrane cells, glandular cells, and cells that secrete the fluid that surrounds the brain. Each of these different types of cells can develop one or more different cancers. Cancers can also form in the brain after migrating through the blood stream from other parts of the body including the lung, kidney and breast.

More than half of all brain cancers are gliomas. These develop from the support cells that surround and separate the nerve cells in the brain and spinal cord.

The symptoms of brain cancers and tumours (abnormal growths that are not necessarily cancer) are very varied, depending on the type, size, and position in the brain. Symptoms that may occur by themselves or in combinations include convulsions, twitching, personality changes, nausea and vomiting, intellectual decline, strange sensations, loss of speech or sight, confusion and headaches. Contrary to popular belief, in only 20% of all cases is headache the first symptom noted by patients. Later in the development of the condition, the patient may become paralysed, unconscious and have difficulty in breathing.

When a brain tumour is suspected, investigation will include blood tests, X-rays (sometimes involving the injection of dye into the arteries supplying the brain), measuring the brain waves electrically (electroencephalogram), CT scans (see Section 4), taking samples of the fluid around the brain (spinal tap), injecting safe radioactive material into the blood stream and using scanners to see how it is concentrated in the brain, and magnetic resonance imaging (see Section 4). A biopsy is often necessary to confirm the diagnosis.

Treatment also varies depending on the type and position of the cancer. Surgery to remove the cancer is obviously the prime choice, but sometimes it is not possible because of the position of the cancer or the part of the brain involved. Irradiation and cancer-killing drugs are often used alone or in combination with surgery. Steroids are often given to reduce the swelling of the brain that occurs around the tumour. The result of treatment varies dramatically between patients.

Brain cancers include gliomas, astrocytomas, medulloblastomas, ependymomas, pinealomas, neurinomas and meningiomas. Some of these are discussed in more detail below.

Astrocytoma

An astrocytoma arises in the connective cells of the brain and is the most common type of glioma (cancer of connective cells). Its symptoms are often very mild and confusing in the early stages, and as a result it may be quite large before it is detected. Because of its size when diagnosed, it often cannot be totally removed surgically. The outcome is often better in children. Irradiation does not help in most cases, and the parts that cannot be removed are treated by drugs.

Medulloblastoma

A medulloblastoma starts in brain nerve cells, and is more common in children. It increases the pressure in the brain to cause nausea and headaches. It is treated with a combination of surgery, irradiation and drugs. They are very sensitive to irradiation, but because they spread rapidly through the brain, only 30% can be cured.

Meningioma

The meninges are the thin membranes that surround the brain, and meningiomas develop from these. They are more common in older people, and the tumour compresses the brain, causing symptoms that relate to the part of the brain compressed. For example, if the area of the brain controlling the arm is compressed, the arm may become weak or paralysed. These are not very malignant tumours, and can be easily seen on a CT scan, and sometimes on a normal X-ray. They are treated by surgical removal, which is usually curative.

BRAIN DISEASE
See BRAIN CANCER; ENCEPHALITIS; EPILEPSY; FEBRILE CONVULSIONS; HUNTINGTON'S CHOREA; HYPOPITUITARISM; MENINGITIS; MIGRAINE; MOTOR NEURONE DISEASE; NARCOLEPSY; PARKINSON'S DISEASE; STROKE; TRANSIENT ISCHAEMIC ATTACK.

BREAKBONE FEVER
See DENGUE FEVER.

BREAST CANCER
Breast lumps probably arouse more concern among women than any other condition. This is because of the fear of cancer in an organ that is so significantly associated with femininity and sexuality. It is important to understand that there are many other causes of lumps in the breast, so if a lump develops — particularly in a young woman — the chances are that it is NOT a cancer. Fewer than one breast lump in ten seen by a doctor proves to be malignant. However, if doctors knew that all breast lumps were benign (non-cancerous) they wouldn't bother about them at all, but it's because there is a chance that any lump may be malignant that doctors treat all breast lumps with suspicion until the precise diagnosis is made.

The most important method of detecting breast cancer and lumps is self examination by the woman. All women should be taught how to check their breasts for lumps by a doctor and should perform this easy procedure every month. Women who are still menstruating should do this after their period has just finished. The technique is demonstrated in Section 7.

If a lump is found in the breast, you should see your general practitioner today or tomorrow, not next week or next month! After further examining the breast, the GP may arrange for an X-ray mammogram, needle biopsy or an ultrasound scan of the breast (see Section 4). These tests show the inside structure of the breast and can sometimes differentiate between cysts, cancers and fibrous lumps. If all the features of the examination and investigations in a young woman indicate that the lump is benign, it is safe to watch the lump, with regular checks by your doctor, because many disappear after a few months.

In an older woman, or if the lump persists, it should be removed by a small operation. If possible, this will be through a cosmetic incision that follows the line of the coloured area around the nipple, or the skin fold under the breast. In the majority of cases this is the only treatment necessary, and the scar should be almost invisible. If the lump is found to be cancerous, a more extensive operation may be necessary.

The treatment of breast cancer has continued to advance over the past few decades, but by far the most important feature in determining the outcome is the time of presentation. If breast cancer is operated on when detected early, the outcome is dramatically better than a late diagnosis. 25% of all cancers in women occur in the breast. Up to two thirds of all patients with breast cancer can be cured. In early cases this rises to over 90%.

Radical mastectomy (removal of the breast and underlying muscles), and its accompanying disfigurement is an operation of the past. It has been replaced by simple mastectomy in which only the breast is removed, leaving a cosmetically acceptable scar and scope for reconstruction of the breast by plastic surgery at a later date. Often the lymph glands under the arm will be removed at the same time, because this is the area that cancer spreads to first. Alternatively, or combined with this, a course of radiotherapy or chemotherapy (drugs) may be recommended.

In some women, equally good results in controlling the cancer can be obtained by removal of the lump alone, coupled with radiotherapy to the breast and excision of the underarm glands. This is such a major departure from the traditional treatment of breast cancer by mastectomy that some surgeons are reluctant to recommend this approach, but experience and carefully planned studies show that the results of lump removal are often just as good as removal of the breast, and a gradually increasing proportion of women are being treated this way. Lumpectomy is only suitable for early cancers; more advanced cancers still require mastectomy. Thus delay in presentation can have a dramatic cosmetic effect as well as a prognostic one, and a return to a normal lifestyle may be only a couple of weeks away with the simpler procedure.

Evidence that *early* breast cancer can be treated effectively without removing the breast should encourage early diagnosis and help to remove some of the fears about the disease.

See also PAGET'S DISEASE OF NIPPLE.

BREASTFEEDING PROBLEMS
See Section 1.

BREAST INFECTION (MASTITIS)
Mastitis is an infection of the breast that requires rapid treatment to prevent the formation of an abscess. In a breastfeeding mother, if one of the many lobes in the breast does not empty its milk, the milk may become infected, and the breast becomes very tender, red and sore. It may start with a sore, cracked nipple, but often the woman wakes in the morning with breast pain as the first symptom. She may become feverish, and feel quite unwell. Women nursing for the first time are more frequently affected.

Fortunately, antibiotics can usually settle the problem, and it does not mean that the woman must stop feeding. If an abscess forms, an operation to drain away the accumulated pus is necessary.

BRONCHIAL CARCINOMA
See LUNG CANCER.

BRONCHIECTASIS
Bronchiectasis occurs if the tubes within the lung that carry air (the bronchi) are damaged, scarred and permanently overdilated. The bronchi can be damaged from birth by diseases such as cystic fibrosis, or in childhood by immune deficiencies. The condition may develop in adult life due to recurrent attacks of pneumonia or to the inhalation of toxic gases. Patients with this condition have a constant cough that brings up large amounts of foul phlegm. They may cough up blood, become anaemic, lose weight, and develop frequent attacks of pneumonia and other lung infections that are triggered by minor stress, a cold or flu. An X-ray of the chest reveals characteristic changes that allow the diagnosis to be made.

Regular physiotherapy to clear the chest of sputum is the main treatment, and antibiotics are used when necessary to control infection. Other medications to open up the clogged airways (bronchodilators), liquefy sputum (mucolytics) and assist the coughing (expectorants) are also prescribed. It is essential for smokers to stop, as smoking further damages the lung and may have been responsible for the bronchiectasis in the first place.

In severe cases where a limited part of the lung is badly affected by bronchiectasis, that section of the lung may be surgically removed.

Bronchiolitis

Bronchiolitis is a lung infection of children under two years and especially under six months of age that is most commonly caused by a virus called the respiratory syncytial virus. It tends to occur in epidemics. The child has a cough and wheeze, may be short of breath and a have a runny nose. In severe cases, the child may be very weak, blue around the mouth, and dehydrated. Doctors can hear sounds in the chest through a stethoscope that enable the diagnosis to be made. In the early stages, chest X-rays can be normal, but later a characteristic pattern may show in the lungs that enables the diagnosis to be confirmed.

Antibiotics cannot cure this viral condition but are sometimes given to prevent the development of any further bronchitis or pneumonia. Bronchodilator medications may be used but often are of little help, and placing the child in a warm room with a humidifier, or in a steam tent may give relief. Some children who do not settle quickly, or who are more severe cases, will require hospitalisation, where oxygen may be administered into the steam tent to assist with breathing.

The vast majority of cases settle without complications in a few days to a week, but in rare cases permanent lung damage and even death may result.

Bronchitis

When you breathe in, air passes through your mouth or nose into your pharynx. This divides into the gullet which takes food to the stomach, and the larynx which contains the vocal cords. The oxygen-rich air continues on down the trachea (windpipe), which is a cartilaginous tube of 1–2 cm diameter, situated in the front of the neck (see Section 2). Behind the top of your breast bone, the trachea divides into a left and right main bronchus, one for each lung. In the lung, the bronchi divide into smaller and smaller tubes called bronchioles before ending up in an intricate network of billions of microscopic bubbles called alveoli. The alveoli are covered in a fine network of blood-containing capillaries, and it is here that oxygen is taken from the air into the blood. When you exhale, the air makes the long reverse journey from the alveoli to the outside carrying the waste carbon dioxide.

The dust, pollens and other fine particles of matter that enter the lungs are removed by a watery mucus that lines the air passages. This mucus is moved rapidly along and out of the lungs by the waving motion of fine microscopic hairs that cover the inner surface of all the bronchi and bronchioles.

Bronchitis is an infection of the major tubes (the bronchi) that carry air within the lungs. Pneumonia is an infection of the smaller bronchioles and alveoli. Bronchitis is a very common condition, and occurs in two very different forms, acute and chronic.

Acute bronchitis is most commonly caused by a viral infection, frequently by infection with bacteria, and rarely by a fungus. Once the invading organism settles on the inside of the bronchi, it starts multiplying into vast numbers. This causes swelling and inflammation of the tissue, and the mucus in the tubes becomes thick and purulent with the infection. The cleaning mechanism of the lungs no longer works efficiently, phlegm plugs up the bronchi, and coughing is stimulated by the body in an attempt to clear the blockage.

The diagnosis is made by the doctor listening through a stethoscope to the pops, squeaks and whistles made by the air as it rushes in and out of the partly blocked bronchi. In the early stages, X-rays may be quite normal. Viral bronchitis cannot be cured, but it settles with time, rest, inhalations, bronchodilators (drugs to open up the bronchi) and physiotherapy. If a bacterial cause is suspected, antibiotics will also be prescribed.

Chronic bronchitis is due to repeated attacks of acute bronchitis, long-standing allergies, or constant irritation of the bronchi by noxious gases, particularly those found in tobacco smoke. Patients have a chronic cough, are short of breath, are unable to take much exertion, and may be blue around the lips. Their finger tips may become rounded and swollen in a process known as 'clubbing'. X-rays can easily make the diagnosis as the thickened, scarred bronchi and poor air entry to the lungs show up quite markedly.

Chronic bronchitis is a semi-permanent condition for which there is no effective cure, but physiotherapy and medications to improve air flow, and antibiotics to treat any infection can be used to keep the condition under control for many years. The vast majority of victims are smokers. The disease may progress on to emphysema, and is sometimes associated with lung cancer.

Bronchopneumonia
See PNEUMONIA.

Brucellosis (undulant fever)
Brucellosis is an infection of cattle, goats and pigs, which can spread to man. The most commonly infected people are meat workers, veterinarians and farmers. It is caught by humans when the bacteria infecting the animal enter the human system through a cut or graze in the skin, or is swallowed. The bacterium is called *Brucella*, and there are several different types, depending on the host animal. It can be found in raw meat and unprocessed milk. Once the bacteria enter the system, the patient develops a fever, tiredness and intermittent sweats. The onset can be very slow over several weeks, and may be thought by the patient to be a passing chill or viral infection. As a result, it is often not until the disease has been present for several weeks and further symptoms of headache, joint pains and swellings, loss of appetite and abdominal pains (from a large spleen and/or liver) develop that the patient sees a doctor. Because the fever may come and go for many months in a low-grade chronic form of the disease, brucellosis is also known as undulant fever. Occasionally a brucellosis infection may involve the lung, brain, and heart, causing specific problems in those areas. Long-term complications include arthritis, and bone weakness. Specific blood tests can diagnose the disease quite easily, and can be used to follow the progress of the condition.

Treatment involves antibiotics (usually a tetracycline — see Section 6) and rest until all symptoms have settled and blood tests have returned to normal. It may recur over the years and require further courses of treatment.

Prevention involves seeking out infected herds of cattle, pigs or goats and destroying them. The disease causes pregnant cattle to miscarry, and can spread rapidly through a herd. Animals may also be vaccinated to prevent them from catching the disease, and in this way, large areas of Australia have been kept free of brucellosis.

Bruise
A bruise occurs when part of the body is struck by a blunt object to cause rupture of blood vessels under the skin, when internal structures rupture blood vessels by their movement (e.g. a fracture of a bone), or blood vessels are ruptured by

overstretching when a joint is overextended (e.g. a severe sprain). If an artery ruptures, a bruise will form very rapidly, with swelling and a blue/black tinge to the overlying skin. A bruise develops more slowly and with less swelling if a vein ruptures. It is far harder to rupture a muscular, thick-walled artery than a thin-walled vein.

Blood under pressure can track its way between layers of tissue so that bruising may occur not only at the site of the injury, but some distance away (e.g. a kick to the calf may cause a spot bruise on the calf, but a day or two later bruising may appear around the ankle).

Patients on medication (e.g. warfarin) which is prescribed to reduce the speed at which blood clots (e.g. patients who have had strokes, thromboses or heart attacks) will bruise far more easily than normal people. Aspirin, anti-inflammatory medications and other less commonly used drugs may also increase bleeding, and therefore bruising. Women bruise more than men, particularly around the menopause, because hormonal changes may make blood vessel walls weaker and allow them to rupture easily. Many women complain of multiple small bruises on their arms and legs in places where they cannot recall any significant injury. A number of diseases, most of them quite rare (e.g. haemophilia, scurvy, aplastic anaemia) reduce the speed at which clots form, and sufferers from these conditions also bruise easily.

When a bruise is likely, or first develops after an injury, the affected area should be cooled with ice, elevated and rested. The ice should not be applied directly to the skin, but wrapped inside a cloth. Elevation of the area reduces the pressure in the veins, and slows blood loss from the ruptured blood vessel. Any exercise or movement involving an area with a ruptured blood vessel will force more blood out into the tissues.

Paracetamol or codeine should be used as a pain reliever, as aspirin may increase the amount of bruising. A firm supportive bandage can be wrapped around the damaged area once it is stabilised, to give support, reduce movement, and prevent further bleeding.

With time, the swelling will reduce, the bruise will go from blue/black to purple, brown and finally yellow before disappearing. There may be some residual swelling and firmness at the bruise site due to the formation of fibrous scar tissue for some time after the bruise disappears. The skin over the area may dry out and flake off. Provided there is no graze or open injury, moisturising cream may be applied to protect the skin.

Anyone who feels that they bruise excessively should have a blood test performed to check that their clotting mechanism is working normally. The vast majority will be normal, but occasionally, a significant disease may be discovered, which can then be effectively treated.

BUBONIC PLAGUE
See PLAGUE, BUBONIC.

BUERGER'S DISEASE (THROMBOANGIITIS OBLITERANS, SMOKER'S FOOT)

The technical name for Buerger's disease is thromboangiitis obliterans, which means 'clotting, inflammation and obliteration of arteries'. Dr Buerger, who first described the disease, was an American urologist (urinary tract specialist) who worked in New York and Los Angeles in the first half of this century.

Thromboangiitis obliterans is a dreadful disease which causes the loss of fingers, toes, then arms and legs, and it occurs only in smokers (thus the common name — smoker's foot), nearly always in men, and often young men. Due to the influences of toxins within tobacco smoke, segments of the small arteries in the hands and feet become inflamed. This inflammation causes a clot to form in the artery, which becomes completely blocked. The tissue beyond this blockage is then starved of blood, becomes painful, white and eventually gangrenous.

The process starts in the fingers and toes, and slowly moves along the arteries, further and further up the arms and legs. A limb may eventually be totally amputated, but often over several operations as each successive area becomes deprived of blood.

The first symptoms are a pain in the foot when walking, which settles with rest, red tender cords caused by involved blood vessels may be felt under the skin, and a finger or toe may be white and have reduced sensation. The next stage is characterised by pain at rest, loss of pulses in the hands and feet, ulcers may form around the nails, and cold weather may aggravate the symptoms. If the disease progresses further, gangrene results.

Treatment involves trying to stop these patients from smoking, but because they are even more addicted to their habit than the average smoker, this is extremely difficult. If smoking is stopped, the disease usually does not spread any further. If the disease progresses, surgery to the nerves supplying the arteries to make them totally relax and open up as much as possible may be tried, but progressive amputation of the limbs is often necessary. If the patient cannot stop smoking, clots may form in vital organs and cause death.

Bulimia

Bulimia is defined as the voracious and continuous consumption of huge quantities of food. The patient (almost invariably middle to upper class young females) may gorge themselves for minutes, hours, days or weeks — and then attempt to lose weight by purging, vomiting and the use of fluid tablets. The condition may be associated with anorexia nervosa (see separate entry). The main difference between these diseases being the way in which the patients see themselves — the bulimic has a fear of being fat, the anorexic has a desire to be thin. Bulimics often maintain a near-normal weight, despite their habits, and are often secretive, appearing to eat normally in public, but are binge eating and vomiting in private.

Complications can include menstrual irregularities, sore throat, bowel problems, dehydration, lethargy, and dental problems due to the repeated exposure of the teeth to stomach acid. Blood tests may show changes in the balance of some chemicals within the blood, due to their loss with repeated vomiting and purging.

Treatment requires close family support, psychotherapy and careful medical monitoring over a period of several years. Most patients recover, and go on to lead normal lives, although suicide can be a risk in severe cases.

See also APPETITE, EXCESS, Section 3.

Bunion

If the big toe is constantly pushed across towards the smaller toes by high heeled shoes, tight shoes, or a poor way of walking, the big toe may become semi-permanently deformed in this direction. The end of the long bone behind the two big toe bones in the front half of the foot (called a metatarsal) is exposed by the deflection of the toe bones, and starts pushing against the skin. A protective, fluid-filled sac (called a bursa) forms between to bone end and the skin to protect the bone. This sac slowly enlarges to

SECTION 5: DISEASES

cause a lump that may become tender and painful. This is a bunion.

Bunions are becoming less common with more sensible and better made footwear, and with a wealthier society in which correctly fitted shoes can be purchased regularly for a child's growing feet. Bunions usually start in childhood but may not cause significant discomfort until adult life.

A number of surgical procedures are available to cure a bunion, but in elderly people it may be preferable for a protective pad to be worn inside soft or especially made shoes.

BURNS

Any burn, no matter how mild or serious, should be initially treated by immersion in cool water, or covering the area with a wet cloth, for at least twenty minutes. For first-aid treatment of burns, see Section 8.

A burn may be caused by hot fluids (a scald), flame (e.g. clothing catching alight, often with careless cigarette smoking), or by dry heat (e.g. touching a stove hot plate). Most of the victims who die in house or other enclosed fires usually die of suffocation before they receive any burns. The severity of a burn depends on the area covered by the burn and the depth of the burn. The patient's age and general health also play a part in survival in severe burns.

First-degree (superficial) burns are red or grey in colour, and are not blistered initially. They do not cause major problems and heal readily without scarring, with the aid of soothing antiseptic creams. They can be very painful, and moderate to strong pain-killers may be required for the first two or three days.

Second-degree (partial thickness) burns are blistered, or the blister may have burst and the area is moist and red or white by the time it is seen. The tissue under the burn becomes progressively more swollen for several days. These burns are often not as painful as first-degree burns, as the nerve endings have been partially destroyed and cannot react. Medical treatment is essential but scarring only results if the burn becomes infected or otherwise further damaged. They take between two and four weeks to heal.

Third-degree (full thickness) burns are sometimes difficult to differentiate from second-degree burns unless there is obvious tissue charring or exposed fat, muscle or bone. They may appear tough and leathery, and be almost any colour. There is usually no pain, as the sensory nerve endings have been totally destroyed. Skin grafts are required for all but small areas, and scarring does develop.

Extensive second- and third-degree burns threaten a patient's life because of the loss of vital body fluids through the burn area and the absorption of large amounts of toxic waste products into the bloodstream. These toxins can cause both kidney and liver failure. Inhalation of hot gases may also burn the inside of the mouth, throat and lungs, and make breathing difficult.

A good airway may need to be established by an ambulance officer or doctor, as burns patients can die from suffocation. Mouth-to-mouth resuscitation can keep a victim alive until trained help arrives. Shock can cause the heart to beat irregularly or stop, and external cardiac massage by regular chest compression may be life-saving.

Severe burns cases will need urgent hospitalisation in a special burns unit where they can be kept alive on a ventilator and fluids can be replaced through drips into a vein. Special feeding solutions will also need to be given through the drip if the patient is unable to eat or drink. Pneumonia and heart failure are common complications of severe burns. Once the patient has been stabilised, the burn can be treated effectively. Severe burns are treated in many different ways, depending on their site, severity and the age of the patient. In some cases, the burn is left open to dry out and only antiseptic paints are applied. Other cases are covered with creams, or amniotic sac membrane (recovered from the afterbirth of mothers who have just delivered a baby) to protect the area while it heals. New artificial skins developed from pig skin or human tissue cultures are now being developed to protect wounds after the dead, burnt tissue has been cleaned or cut away (surgical debridement). Often a lot of blood is lost during this process and transfusions may be needed. Pressure may be applied to some areas in various ways to reduce scarring. Antibiotics are often given to prevent the burn area from becoming infected. Skin grafts to areas that have been totally destroyed are a late stage of treatment, starting ten or more days after the injury.

Many exciting and innovative treatments for severe burns are being developed around the world. Tissue cultures of the patients own skin cells, or those of a donor, look to be one of the most effective of these developments. In this, a few skin cells are taken and grown in dishes to form flat tissue thin sheets, that can then be grafted onto the burn area.

The outcome and survival of acute burns varies dramatically, depending on the extent, position and severity of the burn, and the availability of specially trained burns unit doctors and nurses. Patients under two years and over sixty have a higher death rate from burns. Burns to the face, hands, feet and groin are also far more difficult to treat, and have a poorer outcome than burns elsewhere. Any victim with more than 20% of the body surface burnt is considered to be critically injured, and it is rare for patients to survive a burn of more than 70% of the body surface.

Rehabilitation may take many months or years, and may involve plastic surgery to correct contractures (tight scars) or improve the appearance of scars. Physiotherapists, occupational therapists, and even speech pathologists (for inhaled hot gas burns) will all play a part in bringing the patient back into the mainstream of society.

BURSITIS

Every joint in the body contains a lubricating fluid called synovial fluid. This fluid is produced in small sacs that surround the joint. These sacs are called bursae. The fluid they produce passes through tiny tubes into the joint space, and is slowly absorbed from there into the bone ends and bloodstream. There is thus a constant renewal of the synovial fluid within a joint. If a bursa becomes inflamed, a patient has bursitis.

Bursitis may be caused by an injury to the area, an infection entering the joint or bursa, or by arthritis. The most common sites for bursitis are the point of the elbow, over the kneecap (housemaid's knee), and the buttocks.

In cases of simple inflammation, local heat, rest, splinting and pain-killers may be the only treatment required. If arthritis is present, this should be treated first. Recurrent or persistent cases may need to have the fluid in the bursa removed by a needle, and steroids injected back into the sac to prevent further accumulation of fluid.

If the bursa is infected, antibiotic therapy and drainage of pus from the bursa are the normal treatments.

CAISSON DISEASE
See BENDS.

Section 5: Diseases

Calculi
See GALL STONES; KIDNEY STONES; SALIVARY STONES.

Cancer (neoplasm)
The word that patients fear most to hear from a doctor is 'cancer'. Cancer, the crab of astrology, is so named because the ancients could see the abnormal cancer cells clawing their way into the normal tissue, destroying everything in their path. Doctors now understand a great deal about cancer, but we do not fully understand what starts the process. Although the specific cause of cancer is unknown, sun exposure, a low-fibre diet and smoking are well-known precipitating factors.

Cancer occurs when otherwise normal cells start multiplying at an excessive rate, and the cells made by the rapid process of reproduction are abnormal in shape, size and function. Although they may have some slight resemblance to the cells around them, cancer cells cannot perform the correct work of that type of cell, and they prevent the normal cells around them from working properly, thus enabling the cancerous cells to spread. The situation is rather like a disruptive child in a large class, disturbing the children around him, who in turn disturb the children around them, and so on.

Cancer is not just one disease process — dozens of different types of cancer occur in different parts of the body, and each type causes different problems and responds differently to treatment. Several different types of cancer can be found in the lungs for example. There are however two main groups of cancers according to the type of tissue affected — **sarcomas** are tumours originating in connective tissue (bone, cartilage, muscle and fibre), and **carcinomas** are tumours originating in the epithelial cells (tissue comprising the external and internal linings of the body).

Nothing can be done to help a patient with cancer until they present to a doctor, and this is one of the most frustrating aspects of medicine for general practitioners, because so many people wait for far too long before seeing a doctor with their symptoms. At times, an otherwise intelligent human being will suspect cancer, but do nothing about it until the symptoms become so bad they are beyond help.

Over half of all cancers can be cured, and that excludes the skin cancers that rarely cause death. The cure rate is far higher in those who present early to a doctor, because the less the cancer has spread, the easier it is to treat.

Treatment may involve surgery to remove the growth, drugs that are attracted to and destroy abnormal cells, irradiation of the tumour with high-powered X-rays, or combinations of these three methods.

The **early signs of cancer** are:
- a lump or thickening anywhere in the body,
- sores that will not heal,
- unusual bleeding or discharge,
- change in bowel or bladder habits,
- persistent cough or hoarseness,
- change in a wart or mole,
- indigestion or difficulty in swallowing,
- loss of weight for no apparent reason.

If you note one of these changes in yourself, or a friend, seek immediate expert medical advice. It is far better to be reassured that there is nothing wrong now, than to worry for months unnecessarily. If the condition is serious, early treatment may save your life.

Many of the different types of cancer are described in greater detail individually. See BONE TUMOUR; BRAIN CANCER; BREAST CANCER; CARCINOID SYNDROME; CERVICAL CANCER; COLO-RECTAL CANCER; HEPATOMA; HODGKIN'S DISEASE; LEUKAEMIA; LUNG CANCER; OVARIAN CANCER; PAGET'S DISEASE OF NIPPLE; PROSTATE GLAND DISEASE; SKIN CANCER;

STOMACH CANCER; TESTICULAR CANCER; THYROID CANCER; UTERINE MOLE; WILM'S TUMOUR.

CANDIDIASIS
See THRUSH.

CARBUNCLE
See BOIL.

CARCINOID SYNDROME
Carcinoid tumours are a type of cancer that starts in specialised cells inside the small intestine, stomach or lung. The cells involved are called argentaffin cells, and they are responsible for producing a number of essential chemicals for the functioning of the gut and body in general. When these cells become cancerous, they produce excessive amounts of these chemicals, which causes the unusual symptoms that are characteristic of the carcinoid syndrome. These symptoms include hot flushes of the face, swelling of the head and neck, diarrhoea and stomach cramps, asthma and bleeding into the skin.

Once the disease is suspected, blood or urine tests can be carried out to identify the high levels of chemicals in the bloodstream or urine that are causing the symptoms. The symptoms can develop very rapidly, and victims can deteriorate from apparent perfect health to being severely ill in a few days. Prednisone (a steroid — see Section 6) is used in the emergency treatment of the disease, and other medications are given to control the other symptoms.

The site of the cancer is often very difficult to find, as it is usually very small and slow growing. It also tends to spread at an early stage to other areas, so even if the original is removed, the syndrome may continue due to the production of chemicals in high levels by newly formed and very small cancers in multiple sites. Drugs such as Interferon can sometimes be used to destroy the cancer cells, but with variable success.

Because of its slow growth rate, it may take 10 or 15 years for the disease to progress from the stage of being a nuisance that requires constant medication, to being a life-threatening condition.

CARCINOMA
See CANCER; LUNG CANCER.

CARDIAC DISEASES
See HEART DISEASES.

CARDIAC FAILURE
See HEART FAILURE.

CARDIOMYOPATHY
Cardiomyopathy means heart muscle disease ('cardio' refers to the heart, 'myo' to muscle, and 'pathy' to disease). Diseases and weakness of the heart muscle are very common in older people due to the ageing process. Almost any disease from an infection to a heart attack can cause cardiomyopathy, and so the term is often used when the exact nature of the heart disease present is unknown. Drugs, tumours and high blood pressure can also cause a cardiomyopathy. A cardiomyopathy may be a trivial illness that is barely noticed by the patient, or it can be a progressive disease that leads inevitably to death or the need for a heart transplant.

Medications such as digoxin, and a number of others, may be prescribed to strengthen the heart muscle and make it contract more efficiently.

See also MYOCARDITIS.

CAROTENAEMIA
(HYPERVITAMINOSIS A)
Vitamin A is primarily derived from leafy

green vegetables, dairy products, liver and yellow coloured foods such as carrots, pumpkin, mangoes, pawpaws, oranges and apricots that contain large quantities of a yellow substance known as carotene. Excess levels of carotene and vitamin A (hypervitaminosis A) therefore occur simultaneously in most cases.

Carotenaemia and hypervitaminosis A are caused by the excessive eating of vitamin A tablets or yellow fruit and vegetables. Huge quantities must be consumed, but patients who develop a craving for one particular type of fruit or vegetable can consume sufficient in a few weeks for the symptoms to appear. The symptoms include loss of appetite and weight, yellow colouring of the skin (particularly the palms and soles, but unlike hepatitis, not the whites of the eyes), brittle nails, dry and cracked skin, sore gums, headaches and other more bizarre conditions.

Treatment involves stopping the eating of the offending foods and vitamin supplements. The condition almost invariably resolves slowly over a few weeks without long-term damage. There is some evidence that the disease can cause deformities to the foetus of a pregnant woman, and therefore large doses of vitamin A should be avoided during pregnancy.

Carpal tunnel syndrome

The carpal tunnel syndrome is caused by the excessive compression of the arteries, veins and nerves that supply the hand as they pass through a narrow area in the wrist. The carpal tunnel consists of an arch of small bones which is held in place by a band of fibrous tissue, forming a shape rather like a D lying on its side. Vital supplies for the hand run through this tunnel. If the ligaments become slack, the arch will flatten, and the nerves, arteries, etc., will become squashed. This then causes numbness, tingling, pain and weakness in the hand.

The condition is far more common in women and in those undertaking repetitive tasks such as typing, using a sewing machine, or playing the piano. Pregnancy can induce very sudden and severe attacks that require immediate surgery.

The treatments available include splinting, fluid tablets (to reduce swelling), anti-inflammatory drugs, and occasionally injections of steroids into the wrist, but most patients will eventually require minor surgery to release the pressure, although the other treatments may delay this for many years. The surgery involves only a one-day stay in hospital, and sometimes it is done under local anaesthetic in a doctor's rooms. A small cut is made across the palm side of the wrist in a 'lazy S-shape', and through this the band of ligament causing the pressure is cut. The operation normally gives a lifelong cure.

Cataracts

High technology helps people in many ways. Cataract surgery is an area which has seen many dramatic improvements in recent years to help patients with severely reduced sight achieve normal or near-normal vision after an operation.

The lens sits behind the pupil in the centre of the eye. All light entering the eye must pass through the lens to be focused onto the light-sensitive cells on the back of the eye. A cataract is a cloudy lens in the eye, which causes reduced vision. Cataracts may be present at birth, or may be caused by injury or infection in the eye, but the cause of most cataracts, which normally develop in older people, is unknown.

A patient who has a cataract is initially treated with powerful spectacles, but the cloudiness in the lens gradually worsens in most cases, and the victim finds that their vision is similar to looking through a frosted glass window. Eye surgery to remove the damaged lens is the only solution.

Only if the rest of the eye is healthy and you are likely to have long-term benefit from the surgery will the operation be contemplated. If both eyes are affected by cataracts, as is often the case, only one eye (usually the worst one) will be operated upon. Once this has recovered successfully, the second eye may be repaired. The procedure can be done under a general or local anaesthetic, depending on the circumstances. If you have a local anaesthetic, you will be given a sedative to help you relax, and prevent eye movement. Before the operation, antibiotic eye drops are used for several days to reduce the number of germs that will be present during the operation.

The operation involves cutting open the top of the eye at the edge of the iris (the coloured part of the eye). An extremely fine, diamond-tipped scalpel is used to do this. The damaged lens is then totally removed by gentle suction, but the membrane that held the lens in place is left behind. After the lens is removed from the eye, an artificial lens is often inserted to enable the light to be correctly focused. Without this lens, the patient would have very blurred vision or require extremely thick spectacles that would distort objects, particularly those at the edge of the vision. A plastic lens is slid through the incision, into the eye, and held in place within the fine membrane that held the original lens. The small cut in the eye is then closed with very small sutures. Because of the delicate nature of the operation, the whole procedure is carried out by the eye surgeon while looking through a microscope.

After the operation, it is important not to bump or rub the eye, and to prevent this, a small plastic shield is usually put over the eye. Drops must be put into the eye several times a day to prevent swelling and infection, but after a few weeks, the dressings are removed, and the patient should have far clearer vision than before.

Spectacles are still required for most patients, but modern thin lenses can be used, and not the thick, distorting, goggle-eye ones of years gone by.

Cat scratch disease

Cat scratch disease is a curious condition caused by bacteria that appear to be present on cat paws. When a person is scratched by a cat, the bacteria enter the tissue. A few days later, some patients (about one third) develop a scab-covered sore at the site of the scratch. Between one and three weeks later, a fever and headache occur, and are accompanied by enlarged glands in the groin and the side of the neck or armpit nearest the scratch. Occasionally the infected glands cause an abscess that bursts or needs to be lanced by a doctor. There are no specific tests available to confirm the diagnosis, and blood tests merely show that an infection is present, but not what has caused the infection.

There is no treatment available or necessary. Antibiotics are not effective, and the only required medical intervention may involve draining an abscess. The disease usually settles spontaneously within a week or two. Complications are very rare, but a form of encephalitis and skin rashes have been described.

Catarrh (postnasal drip)

The inside of the nose and sinuses is lined with a moist membrane. This remains moist because it contains microscopic glands that constantly secrete mucus. If this lining (called a mucus membrane) becomes inflamed, the glands it contains swell up (therefore causing all the tissue lining the nose and sinuses to swell) and secrete extra amounts of mucus. This excess mucus overflows the sinus cavities, and runs down the back of the throat. This is a postnasal (at the back of the nose) drip, or catarrh.

The glands in the mucus membranes may become inflamed for one or more of many reasons. Infections with bacteria (e.g. sinusitis) or a virus (e.g. the common cold or flu) are common causes. Bacterial infections can be cured by a course of antibiotics, but a virus cannot be killed. Medications to shrink down the swollen mucus membranes and reduce the production of mucus can be taken. Other causes of catarrh include allergies (e.g. hay fever, cigarette smoke), temperature changes (a condition known as the vasomotor response), hormone changes (more mucus may be produced at certain times in a woman's monthly cycle), anxiety and stress (catarrh may develop at the worst possible time before an exam or interview) and changes in position (e.g. getting out of bed may start a sneezing fit).

It is often a combination of two or more of the above that causes any individual's catarrh. None of these can be cured, but most can be controlled by using antihistamines (see Section 6) to reduce the amount of mucus, mucolytics to liquefy the phlegm and let it run away more freely, decongestants in tablets and nasal sprays to clear the airways, and steroid or Rynacrom nasal sprays to prevent the nose from reacting excessively. Unfortunately, most of these treatments give only partial relief, and patients continue to suffer the irritated throat, recurrent cough, blocked nose and nausea (from swallowed mucus) that characterise catarrh.

Most patients with catarrh are troubled by it for only a few days or weeks. There are an unfortunate minority who continue to have it for months on end. These patients may be helped by surgery which reduces the amount of mucus membrane in the nose. There are several different operations available including destroying part of the nose lining by diathermy with an electrically heated needle, and removing some curled up bones inside the nose (called turbinates) that are covered with mucus secreting membranes.

See also HAY FEVER; SINUSITIS.

CELLULITIS

Cellulitis is an infection of the tissue immediately under the skin. It may start from a bite or wound, but sometimes for no apparent reason. The infected area slowly spreads, and once the lymphatic system becomes involved, red streaks may run from the infected area towards the nearest lymph glands.

The area affected by cellulitis is hot, red, tender, swollen and painful. If the infection spreads to the lymph glands, they will become infected and the patient will develop a fever and become quite ill.

Cellulitis responds rapidly to antibiotic tablets or injections (e.g. penicillin) in most cases.

See also ERYSIPELAS.

CEREBRAL PALSY (SPASTICITY)

Cerebral palsy (CP) is the correct medical term for most forms of spasticity. It is caused by the abnormal development of the brain while the baby is growing in its mother's womb, or to brain damage which may occur around the time of birth, usually because the brain is deprived of oxygen for several minutes.

Children who suffer from CP are trapped inside a crippled body for the rest of their lives. They may be subjected to cruel jests, rude stares, and an acute lack of understanding. Try to imagine yourself, a normal, intelligent human being, having a body which refuses to respond to your commands and needs — a body that twists itself uncontrollably because of the inexorable spasms of your muscles. The frustration of such a situation is hard to comprehend. Many sufferers from cerebral palsy have normal intelligence, and some are university graduates.

Cerebral palsy can vary dramatically from one person to another. Some have slight difficulty in controlling one limb, others may be unable to talk clearly, yet others may be totally unable to care for themselves in any way. Understandably there may be emotional and social problems associated with this incurable disease.

Doctors do their best to control the muscle spasms, give emotional and psychiatric support and treat the skin, chest and orthopaedic problems that beset the sufferers, but the most effective help comes from teams of nurses, physiotherapists, occupational therapists, social workers and volunteers who devote their lives to the management of these patients in a lifestyle which is as near to normal as possible. Early recognition that an infant has cerebral palsy can be very beneficial, because the sooner treatment is started, the less severe the long-term problems are likely to be. Operations to correct deformities and release spasm in limbs can complement medications which also reduce the uncontrollable twitching that may occur. Paramedical staff can instruct the child in the control of an unwilling body.

On average, three children a day are born with cerebral palsy in Australia. As a result, there is a growing need for further facilities for these people. There is no likelihood in the future of any cure being found for spasticity, because once part of the brain is damaged, it is unable to repair itself.

Cerebrovascular accident (CVA)
See STROKE.

Cervical cancer
Cancer of the cervix of the uterus is the second most common of the female cancers, after breast cancer. It can be detected in the early stage by the Pap smear test. As this kind of cancer has a very high cure rate if detected early enough, all sexually active women and women over 40 should have an annual Pap smear. Treatment may include surgery or radiotherapy or both. Early cancer zones may be treated with local excision (conisation) or the abnormal cells may be burnt away by diathermy or laser. Many factors have been associated with the development of cervical cancer, including genital herpes infections (see HERPES SIMPLEX INFECTIONS) and genital warts (see WARTS).

See also PREVENTIVE MEDICINE, Section 7.

Cestodes
See TAPEWORMS.

Chancroid
Chancroid is a sexually transmitted disease caused by bacteria. It is rare in Australia, more a disease of the tropics, but is sometimes seen in people born in or returning from a visit to Asian countries. About three to five days after sexual contact with a person who has the disease, a sore develops on the penis or vulva. This rapidly breaks down to form a painful ulcer. Several sores and ulcers may be present at the same time. The infection may then move to the glands in the groin, which swell up into a hard, painful lump, that may develop into an abscess and discharge pus. During this process, the patient is feverish and feels quite ill.

Some patients may develop a mild form of the disease, with minimal signs of infection. They can then transmit the disease to others, while not knowing that they are infected themselves. This is particularly common in women, where the sores may be hidden internally in the vagina.

A number of other diseases can cause sores and ulcers on the genitals (e.g. syphilis) and these must be excluded before treatment is started. The disease can be proved by taking swabs from the sores and identifying the bacteria present in the pus. Skin tests (that often remain positive for life) can also be performed to determine the past or present existence of the disease. Once the diagnosis has been made, treatment with the appropriate antibiotic can be given in tablet form to kill the responsible bacteria.

CHARCOT-MARIE-TOOTH DISEASE

Charcot-Marie-Tooth disease is an inherited nerve disease in which patients initially have an abnormal gait and foot deformities in late childhood or early adult life. A gradual worsening over several years causes weakness and loss of sensation in the legs, and later the arms. Paralysis of both arms and legs is the eventual result. It is caused by a gradually progressive degeneration of the nerves that supply these areas.

The disease is named after Jean Marie Charcot (Parisian neurologist born in 1825), Pierre Marie (Parisian neurologist born in 1853) and Howard Henry Tooth (London neurologist born in 1856), who were the first doctors to describe the condition.

CHICKENPOX (VARICELLA)

Chickenpox is one of the most annoying childhood diseases, but it has absolutely nothing to do with poultry. The name comes from the observation in medieval times that the skin of a patient with severe chickenpox looked vaguely like that of a plucked chicken! A virus called *Herpes zoster* causes chickenpox. It can be found in the fluid-containing blisters that cover the body of the victim, and in their breath and saliva. Infection occurs when some of these virus particles pass from the patient to another person.

Patients are infectious for a day or two before the spots appear, and remain infectious until all the sores are covered by scabs and no new blisters are appearing — usually about eight days. It takes 10 to 21 days from exposure to the virus for the first spots of the disease to appear. The early signs of infection are symptoms similar to those of a cold, with a vague feeling of being unwell, headache, fever and sore throat. The rash usually starts on the head or chest as red pimples. They then spread onto the legs and arms, and develop into blisters before drying up and scabbing over. New spots may develop for three to five days, and it may be two weeks or more before the last spot disappears.

Chickenpox is generally a mild disease, but it is highly contagious and usually occurs in epidemics every couple of years. Once you have contracted chickenpox, it is unlikely (but not impossible) that you will ever have it again.

Complications may occur in some patients, particularly adults. These are usually chest infections such as bronchitis, but a type of meningitis (brain infection) can occur in rare cases. It is not really a disease to be avoided though, as it is almost inevitable and far better to catch as a child than an adult.

Parents often worry that the pock sites will scar. This is quite unusual, unless a secondary bacterial infection occurs. This is more likely if the spot is constantly picked and scratched, but by no means inevitable.

Treatment involves bed and home rest until the patient feels well, and medications to relieve the itch, fever and headache. The disease has no specific cure, and there is no vaccine available. Children should be kept home from school until the spots are obviously healing, i.e. for at least seven days after the appearance of the rash. Calamine or other soothing lotions may be applied frequently to relieve the intense itch. Baths containing anti-itch additives such as sodium bicarbonate or other preparations available from chemists, are also beneficial. Children's nails should be cut short, to prevent picking and scratching. Doctors can, as a last resort, prescribe drugs to relieve an extremely distressing itch and give relief to a sleepless victim. A doctor's advice should also be sought if the patient does not settle quickly, or develops a productive cough. He or she can then act to prevent any complications.

Once you have had chickenpox, the virus never leaves your body but migrates to the nerves along your spinal cord where it remains for the rest of your life. It may be reactivated at times of stress or other illness to give the patient the painful rash of shingles many decades after the original infection.

See also SHINGLES.

CHILBLAINS

Chilblains are itchy, red skin spots that can develop as a result of exposure to extreme cold, normally on the fingers and toes, but other exposed areas such as the nose may also become involved. The spot may form a blister, and the itching is aggravated by warmth. Recurrent chilblains can lead to a permanent scar forming at the site.

Treatment involves gradual warming in a warm room. The fingers or toes should NOT be immersed in hot water or placed near a heater or fire, nor should the area be rubbed or massaged as this may cause further damage. If not exposed to further cold, the skin spots will heal in a day or two. The only complication associated with the condition is the invasion of the damaged skin to give an infection that will require antibiotics.

CHILD ABUSE
See Section 7.

CHLAMYDIAL INFECTIONS

Chlamydiae are a group of organisms that are not bacteria, but closely resemble bacteria. They act as parasites inside human cells, cause the destruction of the cell where they multiply, and then move on to infect more cells. There are many different types of *chlamydiae*, but fortunately only two are of significance to humans. Others can cause severe diseases in birds (particularly parrots), and another type is believed to be causing a rapid decline in koala populations in Australia.

One of the forms of chlamydia that infects birds can be transmitted to humans to cause a disease known as psittacosis (see separate entry). The other form of chlamydia that can infect humans is responsible for an eye infection called trachoma (see separate entry) and a rare type of pneumonia. This second type is also responsible for the better known chlamydial infections that are spread sexually and cause infections of the penis or vagina that may spread internally in women to cause (along with bacteria and other organisms) pelvic inflammatory disease (see separate entry). Sexually transmitted chlamydial infection can be present both in males and females without symptoms. Because of this, all sexual contacts should be treated when the infection is discovered.

Male genital chlamydial infection
There is a condition called non-specific urethritis (NSU) or non-gonococcal urethritis (NGU) in which the male has a white discharge from the penis, painful

passing of urine, but rarely other symptoms, and from which it was not possible to isolate the infecting organism. It is now known that many (but not all) cases of NSU are caused by a chlamydial infection.

The chlamydia can spread from the penis up into the testes or prostate gland to cause infection in these areas as well. It is spread by passing from the man to female sexual partners. In homosexuals, the infection may occur around the anus.

The chlamydia organism can now be identified by special tests, but it is not always reliable, and a negative test does not mean that the infection is not present.

Once suspected, antibiotics such as tetracyclines and erythromycins (see Section 6) can be used to kill the organism and cure the infection.

Female genital chlamydial infection
Chlamydia can live in the vagina without causing any symptoms. The infection can be readily passed on to any male sexual contact of an infected woman. Only if the infection becomes severe enough to cause a slight discharge, or migrates internally to cause a painful infection of the Fallopian tubes or other pelvic organs (see REPRODUCTIVE SYSTEM, Section 2), is the woman aware that she has the disease. These infections can cause damage to the Fallopian tubes that is severe enough to result in infertility. For this reason, any sexual partners of men with the infection must be treated to protect the woman's future ability to have children and to prevent them reinfecting their partner or others.

If a pregnant woman has a chlamydial infection, it can infect the baby during birth and cause a type of conjunctivitis that may become chronic and cause permanent damage to the surface of the eye. In rare cases, the baby may also catch a type of chlamydial pneumonia that may be difficult to diagnose and treat.

Lymphogranuloma venereum
This sexually transmitted disease is also caused by the chlamydia organism. It is rare in Australia but is sometimes seen in people coming from Africa or Asia. Patients develop a sore on the penis or vulva, which is followed by infection of the glands in the groin. These glands soften and suppurate (drain pus) onto the skin. The infection may spread into the body to cause joint, skin, brain and eye infections. If anal intercourse has occurred, sores and pus discharging glands may form in and around the anus.

The incubation period after sexual contact with a carrier of the disease is one to three weeks. The initial sore is not painful, and may be easily missed. Even the pus discharging glands are remarkably pain free, and only if the disease spreads into the body does a fever develop. The disease is diagnosed by a special skin and blood tests.

Antibiotic treatment using tetracyclines results in a cure in the majority of cases. Surgical procedures to drain all the pus from the groin and anus may be necessary. If left untreated for weeks, it is harder to eradicate the chlamydial infection, and permanent disfiguring scarring will occur in the groin at the site of the pus discharging infected glands, and the genitals may become permanently swollen.

CHOLECYSTITIS
See GALLSTONES.

CHOLELITHIASIS
See GALLSTONES.

CHOLERA
We are very fortunate in Australia that cholera and many other serious tropical diseases are virtually unknown here. Very occasionally, wild cases of a mild form of

cholera do occur in this country (e.g. Logan river of south-east Queensland in the early 1980s), but most cases are caught by travellers to countries where the disease is endemic.

Cholera is a disease that causes severe diarrhoea and rapid dehydration that may lead to death. Vast amounts of fluid are lost in a short time, and blood may be present in the faeces. The patient shivers, has a below normal temperature, shallow breathing, muscle cramps and may become comatose. From the time of onset to death from dehydration can be a matter of only a day or two. In children, it may be hours.

Cholera is caused by a bacterium called *Vibrio cholerae* that is taken into the body in contaminated water or food. The bacteria multiply rapidly in the body to irritate the gut and cause the diarrhoea. The bacteria then pass out of the body in the faeces, to contaminate water supplies, and infect other victims. Doctors may need to prove the diagnosis of cholera by taking a sample of the faeces and culturing it in the laboratory.

Treatment involves replacing the massive fluid loss by a drip into a vein or an electrolyte mixture by mouth. The intravenous method is better, but not always available in poor third-world countries. Untreated, the death rate is 35–80%, but with proper treatment, 98% should survive.

An emergency mixture to rehydrate a victim can be made by mixing a level teaspoon of salt and eight level teaspoons of sugar or glucose into a litre of boiled water. This should be given freely to more than replace the fluid lost in the diarrhoea. The only further treatment required is a brief course of a tetracycline antibiotic to kill any of the infecting bacteria in the gut.

A vaccination against cholera is available but only gives limited protection (probably less than 60%) and is not useful in controlling epidemics. It is only recommended for travellers who are planning to spend time in rural areas of affected countries in central Asia, tropical Africa and central America (see Section 7). Two injections, 7 to 28 days apart are required, and side effects of the vaccination such as fever, and pain and swelling at the injection site may occur.

CHOLESTEROL EXCESS (HYPERCHOLESTEROLAEMIA)

A yellow/white fatty substance called cholesterol is responsible for a large proportion of the heart attacks, strokes circulatory problems and kidney disease in the Western world. Yet cholesterol is essential for the normal functioning of the human body. It is responsible for cementing cells together, is a major constituent of bile and the basic building block for sex hormones. Only in excess is it harmful.

If too much cholesterol is carried around in our blood stream, it may be deposited in gradually increasing amounts inside the arteries. Slowly, the affected artery narrows until the flow of blood is sufficiently obstructed to cause the area supplied by that artery, to suffer. If that area is the heart, a heart attack will result — if it is the brain, a stroke will occur. This deposition of fat is known as arteriosclerosis, or hardening of the arteries.

The people most affected by high levels of cholesterol are overweight middle-aged men. Women, and people of normal weight, may be affected too, but not as frequently.

It has been proved that if you have cholesterol levels that are within normal limits, your risk of heart attack or stroke is greatly reduced. It is therefore important for anyone who feels they may be at risk to have a blood test to determine their cholesterol level. For this test to be accurate, it is necessary to starve for 12 hours (usually over night) and avoid alcohol for 72 hours before the blood sample is taken.

The actual cholesterol levels that are considered safe is a matter of some controversy in the medical profession. A level below 6.5 mmol/L is probably reasonable for patients over 40. Younger patients should aim for a level below 5.5 mmol/L, while the elderly are probably safe with levels as high as 7.0 mmol/L. A higher value is accepted in females than in younger males. There is no evidence that a very low cholesterol level is of any added benefit to health.

Cholesterol is divided into high-density and low-density fats. If the amount of high-density fats is high, there is less to be concerned about, as it is the low-density fats that are a factor in heart disease and hardening of the arteries. These ratios can be measured if the total cholesterol is found to be high.

If you are found to be in the high-risk group, there are several measures you can take to bring you back to normal. The first step is to stop smoking, limit your alcohol intake, take more exercise and lose weight if you are obese. If these measures are insufficient, doctors will recommend a diet that is low in cholesterol. On this, the majority of people return to within the normal levels after a month or two.

A low-cholesterol diet involves avoiding all dairy products, fatty meats, sausages, offal, fried foods, nuts and egg yolk. There is no evidence that this diet will benefit people whose blood cholesterol level is within normal limits while already consuming the forbidden foods. The foods that are allowed include skim milk, polyunsaturated margarine, lean meats, fish, all vegetables and fruits, cereals and soft drinks.

Despite a strict diet, there are still some people who cannot keep their cholesterol levels under control. They will require further lifelong medical management by the regular use of tablets or drinks that are designed to lower the level of fat in the blood (see HYPOLIPIDAEMICS, Section 6). These are prescribed by a doctor only when necessary.

Once the fatty deposits of cholesterol are deposited inside the arteries, they remain there permanently. There are new surgical techniques available to clean out clogged arteries, but diet has little effect at this late stage. As in all diseases, prevention is much better than cure.

See also TRIGLYCERIDE EXCESS.

CHONDROMALACIA

Chondromalacia is a disease usually of the knee cap (patella) that occurs only in teenagers and young adults.

The knee cap is designed to glide smoothly over the end of the femur (the thigh bone) as the knee is bent and straightened. The under-surface of the knee cap is covered with a very smooth layer of cartilage. In patients with chondromalacia, this cartilage becomes softened, pitted, uneven and damaged, and the knee cap is grating across the femur instead of gliding. The cause of chondromalacia is often difficult to determine, but it can certainly be caused by recurrent dislocation of the knee cap, or by falling repeatedly on the knee.

Patients complain of a pain deep in the knee, and pain on bending the knee or kneeling. When the knee is bent, a fine grating may be felt by the patient, and by a doctor when s/he places his/her hand over the knee cap.

Treatment involves firm bandaging and rest for the knee. With this the majority of cases settle. Sometimes splinting or a plaster cast may be required to totally rest the knee cap for a few weeks. After many months, if pain persists, surgery to modify or remove the knee cap may be necessary.

CHOREA
See HUNTINGTON'S CHOREA.

CHORIOCARCINOMA
See UTERINE MOLE.

CHRISTMAS DISEASE (FACTOR IX DEFICIT)

This inherited disease of males has absolutely nothing to do with the festive season. It is named after a boy whose surname was Christmas and who was the first patient to be diagnosed with the disease. It is closely related to haemophilia, but haemophilia is seven times more common than Christmas disease.

The blood flows freely around the body in the arteries and veins, but once exposed to the air in a cut or other wound, it rapidly clots and solidifies. Thirteen different chemicals (called factors) and some specialised blood cells are required to cause blood to clot. If even one of these factors is missing, blood will not clot easily, and these patients are known as bleeders. In Christmas disease, Factor 9 (IX) is missing. In haemophilia, Factor 8 (VIII) is the one that is absent. These are not diseases that you catch, but they are caused by a defect that occurs at the moment of conception when the egg and sperm fuse.

Every individual has two sets of genes, one from the mother and one from the father. These are carried on 46 chromosomes, 23 from each parent. The chromosomes that determine the individuals sex are called the X and Y chromosomes. The only difference between the cells of a male and female is that females have two X chromosomes while men have only one. In place of a second X chromosome, men have a very small Y chromosome. In genetic terms, females can be described as XX and males as XY. After intercourse, if a sperm and egg meet and join, a pregnancy will result. If the sperm joining with the egg (which all contain only X chromosomes) also contains an X chromosome, a female (XX) will be produced. If the sperm contains a Y chromosome, a male (XY) child will result. The sex of any child is therefore determined by the father.

Christmas disease and haemophilia are transmitted through the genes that are carried on the X chromosome. Because females have two X chromosomes, the good X chromosome can suppress the action of the diseased one. In men there is no such balance, so they show evidence of the disease, while the woman may act as a carrier from one generation to another.

Patients with Christmas disease not only bleed freely when cut, but may bleed internally, particularly into a joint that may be injured by excessive use. This leads to a painful swollen joint and premature arthritis. Another problem that may be encountered is passing blood in the urine. Sufferers from this and other bleeding diseases must be constantly alert for injury. A simple pat on the back can cause a massive bruise that takes weeks to settle.

Fortunately, the missing Factor IX can be replaced. It is obtained from blood donations, purified, and given to these patients by injection. Unfortunately it only lasts about 12 hours after injection and is in short supply, so it cannot be used routinely to control the disease. The injection is used to control a serious bleed once it is started, or to prevent bleeding during any necessary surgical procedure.

The disease can be diagnosed by special blood tests that are performed soon after birth when excessive bruising causes suspicion that the disease may be present.

Most families who have the disease in their background are aware of the dangers involved for their children. Men with Christmas disease rarely father children. Statistically, half of the male children of women who are carriers will have Christmas disease, and half of the girl children will be carriers. Genetic histories can be worked out to determine whether or not a woman is likely to be a carrier, but there is no test at present available to determine absolutely the carrier status of a woman.

Chronic fatigue syndrome
See MYALGIC ENCEPHALOMYELITIS.

Chronic hypoadrenocorticism
See ADDISON'S DISEASE.

Chronic obstructive airways disease
See BRONCHITIS; EMPHYSEMA.

Chronic pulmonary heart disease
See COR PULMONALE.

Ciguatera poisoning
Ciguatera poisoning results from eating reef fish that contain the ciguatera toxin. Over 400 different species of tropical reef fish have been implicated at different times, but generally the larger the fish, the more likely it is to be toxic. The fish itself is not affected by the poison, and there are no tests for differentiating non-toxic from toxic fish.

The poison is produced at certain seasons by a microscopic animal (Dinoflagellida) that proliferates on tropical reefs. This is eaten by very small fish, who are then eaten by bigger fish, who are then eaten by still bigger fish. There may be a dozen steps along this chain, with the poison being steadily concentrated in the fish tissue at every step, until the fish is caught and eaten by the unsuspecting victim.

The ciguatera poison is present in a low concentration in most reef fish, but only when it exceeds a certain concentration does it cause problems in humans. It cannot be destroyed by cooking. There are far higher concentrations of the poison in the gut, liver, head and roe of reef fish, which should never be eaten or used to make fish soup.

The symptoms of the poisoning vary dramatically from one victim to another, depending on the amount of toxin eaten, the size of the victim, and the individual reaction to the poison. Symptoms can include unusual skin sensations and tingling, diarrhoea, nausea, abnormal sensation, headaches and irregular heartbeats. Sufferers of mild forms of the disease will recover in a few days, but severe attacks may cause symptoms for a couple of months. Unusual tingling sensations may persist for years, and subsequent serious attacks may be triggered by eating the tiny amounts of ciguatera poison that may be present in fish that others can eat without adverse effects. Death is rare, but possible, and is caused by the effects of the toxin on the heart and blood vessels. Death normally occurs within 36 hours of the onset of the attack.

There is no treatment or antidote, but medication may be used to control the worst symptoms of the disease until the toxin is naturally eliminated from the body.

Cirrhosis
The liver is a soft fleshy organ tucked under the ribs on the right side of the body. It is responsible for the control of the blood contents, manufacturing essential chemicals and breaking down foodstuffs (see Section 2). If it is damaged, it may become hard and enlarged as the liver tissue is replaced by fibrous scar tissue. This is cirrhosis. The disease develops slowly over many years, and may be detected by a doctor during a routine examination, or not until the patient becomes quite ill with itchy skin without a

rash, jaundice (yellow skin), diarrhoea or abdominal discomfort. The liver damage may be caused by recurrent attacks of hepatitis A, one attack of hepatitis B, other liver infections, excess alcohol intake, gall stones, a number of rare diseases that affect the liver (e.g. haemochromatosis, Wilson's disease, Gaucher's disease, etc.), toxins, poisons (e.g. arsenic) and drugs (e.g. methotrexate, isoniazid). The diagnosis of cirrhosis is confirmed by blood tests, and ultrasound and/or CT scans (see Section 4) of the liver.

Other than the major surgery involved in a liver transplant, there is no cure for cirrhosis, and the liver tends to become steadily more damaged until it ceases to function completely. Liver transplants are only considered in very select cases. Doctors concentrate on minimising further liver damage and relieving the symptoms of the disease. Patients must stop all alcohol intake, and avoid substances that may be toxic to the liver. Vitamin supplements are usually prescribed, and medication can be used to control itching and diarrhoea. The final outcome depends on many factors, including the original cause of the cirrhosis, the age and general health of the patient, and the compliance with the doctor's recommendations regarding diet and alcohol.

See also ALCOHOLISM; HEPATITIS.

CLOSTRIDIAL MYOSITIS
See GAS GANGRENE.

CLOTS
See EMBOLISM, LUNG; THROMBOSIS.

CLUB FOOT
A club foot is caused by a defect in the development of the foot in the foetus before birth. Technically, a club foot is called *talipes equinovarus*. A baby with a club foot has the foot turned in so that the sole of the foot faces the other foot, and if the baby was to walk, it would walk on the outside edge of the foot. It is often associated with underdevelopment of the muscles that move the ankle joint.

Club feet are more common in boys than girls, and one or both feet may be affected. The defect is usually obvious at birth, and treatment should begin soon afterwards. If treatment is delayed, there may be permanent deformity of the foot, due to a distorted growth of the bones around the ankle.

Treatment involves splinting the foot into the correct position for many months in mild cases, and surgery to correct the deformity in more severe cases and those that do not respond to splinting.

CLUSTER HEADACHES
Severe, one-sided pain around the eye that occurs daily for weeks and then subsides, only to flare again months later, is a characteristic of cluster headaches. Because of their severity, these headaches can be quite disabling, and they are resistant to most common pain relievers. They are more common in middle-aged men, and may be accompanied by a congested nostril on the same side as the headache, a watery red eye and weakness on the affected side of the face. The headache is not normally constant, but comes on suddenly and lasts for a few hours before subsiding. Attacks may be triggered by alcohol, stress, exercise, certain foods and glare. Once present, these headaches are very difficult to control. A number of different medications can be prescribed by a doctor, and it is normally a matter of trial and error to determine the most effective regime in any individual.

Prevention is far better than cure, and medications such as propranolol, ergotamine, lithium and amitriptyline can be used on a regular basis to prevent further attacks once a cluster of headaches has started. In severe cases, prednisone can be prescribed in an attempt to relieve an otherwise intractable series of headaches.

See also HEADACHE, Section 3.

CMV
See CYTOMEGALOVIRUS INFECTION.

COARCTATION OF THE AORTA
See AORTIC STENOSIS.

COCAINE ADDICTION
See DRUG ADDICTION.

COELIAC DISEASE (COELIAC SPRUE, NON-TROPICAL SPRUE)

Coeliac disease (spelt celiac in the USA) is a disease of the small intestine that causes patients to pass large, foul-smelling, frothy, fatty motions. This causes weight loss, anaemia and generalised weakness due to lack of nutrition and a failure to absorb vitamins A, D, E and K (the fat soluble vitamins). The disease usually starts in childhood, and persists into early adult life, often settling in middle age. It is a congenital condition caused by an error in one of the genes that act on the small intestine. Other symptoms include rashes and weak bones, as well as a failure to grow and foul frequent motions.

The small intestine of coeliacs is unable to absorb fats and, to a lesser extent, carbohydrates and protein, because the intestine has been sensitised to a substance called gluten. Gluten is found in wheat, oats, barley and rye cereals, and may be used as a bulking agent in prepared foods such as sausages. Patients with coeliac disease are unable to tolerate any form of gluten in their intestine.

Coeliac sprue, i.e. chronic malabsorption due to coeliac disease, is diagnosed by taking a biopsy (sample) of the lining of the small intestine. This is performed by the patient swallowing a capsule that has a hole in one side, and is attached to a long fine tube. After the capsule is swallowed, the tube follows after it, but the other end remains outside the body. Once the capsule is in the small intestine, suction is applied to the end of the tube to suck a small amount of the lining of the intestine through the hole in the side of the capsule. The capsule is then pulled up the gut and out through the mouth, and the sample of intestine lining it contains is examined under a microscope to prove the diagnosis.

Coeliac sprue responds to a diet free of gluten, high in calories and protein, and low in fat. With this regime, the disease in most patients is completely controlled. Gluten-free breads, flour, biscuits and other foods are now widely available from health food stores and bakeries. Once they reach adult life, many patients with coeliac sprue find that they can slowly introduce gluten containing products to their diet without ill effect.

COLD, COMMON (CORYZA)

The common cold is only common while it belongs to someone else. Once you are the victim, it is a week of wet-nosed, sore-throated misery.

The common cold (or coryza as it is technically known) may be caused by one or more of several hundred different viruses. It is a distinct entity from influenza, which is caused by a specific virus, even though that virus may mutate to many different forms.

When you catch a viral infection, the body develops antibodies to that virus. These protect the body from further attack by that virus (see VIRUSES, Section 7). For example, you only catch measles or mumps once, and the antibodies produced give lifelong protection. Immunity can also be given by a vaccination, which also acts to raise the antibody level against a specific virus. Unfortunately, because so many different viruses, and versions of these viruses, may cause the common cold, the immunity you develop against one gives no immunity against another. Thus a vaccine is not possible.

Bacteria are microscopic animals that can be destroyed by antibiotics. A virus is a particle of protein one thousandth the size of a bacterium. The virus particles can remain in an inactive form for a short time (depending on the type) outside a cell, but before they can cause any infection, they must invade a cell. A virus may in fact infect not only human cells, but any animal, including a bacterium.

The cold virus spreads from one person to another in the tiny droplets of moisture in your breath, in a cough or in a sneeze. Once inhaled, they settle in the nose or throat of their new host, and start multiplying rapidly.

Scientists have found it almost impossible to destroy viruses because they are barely alive. It is usually necessary to kill the cell containing the virus in order to kill the virus itself. With a cold, billions of the cells in your nose, throat and chest are infected.

If you catch a cold, there is nothing a doctor can do to cure it. He or she can certainly prescribe medications to ease the symptoms and make you feel more comfortable, but please do not pester him or her for antibiotics, because they do not help the problem at all. The more you rest, the faster the problem will go away. Those who insist on working while feverish and miserable prevent the body from building up its defences rapidly, and pass the infection on to their work mates. Aspirin or paracetamol, rest at home and medications for the cough, sore throat, runny nose and blocked sinuses are the best remedy. The usual cold will last for a week, but some people are luckier and have a brief course, while others are particularly unlucky, and the first cold may so lower their defences that they can catch another one, and then another, causing cold symptoms to last for many weeks.

Unfortunately, there is no cure or prevention likely before next century. Many vitamin and herbal remedies are touted as cures or preventatives for colds, but when subjected to detailed trials, none of them can be proved to be successful.

COLD EXPOSURE
See HYPOTHERMIA.

COLD SORES
See HERPES SIMPLEX INFECTIONS.

COLIC, INTESTINAL
Colic is an intermittent spasm of a muscular tube in the body (e.g. gut, bile duct, ureter) that causes recurrent attacks of pain. Colic is more a symptom of disease than a disease itself.

Infantile colic

As new parents begin to establish a routine in the management of their infant, the pattern may be rudely shattered by the onset of 'six week colic'. The baby starts screaming for no apparent reason, draws the legs up and looks pale. After a few minutes, the attack subsides, and although a little reticent, the infant appears quite normal again. After another short interval, the screaming starts again. This pattern can repeat itself for quite some time (for the parents it seems to be an eternity!), several times a day.

There are many arguments about infantile colic, whether it really exists, what

Section 5: Diseases

causes it, what (if anything) should be used to treat it, and if it is a disease restricted to western society rather than infants of all economic and ethnic backgrounds. There are no tests that can be performed to confirm the diagnosis, and there are no clinical examinations that can be considered objectively. Nevertheless, parents of babies who have suffered are in no doubt that it is a real entity.

It is probably caused by a spontaneous spasm of the small intestine, but no reason for this spasm has ever been proved. Changes in diet and formula, different foods for the mother of breastfed infants, alterations to feeding times and positions, vitamin and naturopathic supplements, increases or decreases in the degree of attention paid to the child have all been tried to ease the problem. Some experts blame anxiety in the parents, particularly with a first child in a family without extended family support, for causing anxiety in the infant, and subsequent gut spasms. Eventually, usually at 12 to 16 weeks of age, the colic eases, the parents relax, and the treatment being tried at that time is credited with a miraculous cure.

Parents who are faced with this problem can certainly try all the above remedies, plus the available anti-spasmodic drugs and pain relievers such as paracetamol. More importantly, these babies should be checked by a doctor to ensure that there is no more serious cause for their apparent stomach pain, such as those listed under the adult form of colic below.

Infantile colic always goes away in due course, and assistance from family and friends in caring for the baby can often give a new mother a little free time for herself, to gather her composure, and prepare for the next interrupted night of intermittent screaming.

Adult colic
Intermittent colicky pain in the abdomen of an adult can be caused by any one of a number of conditions. The most serious disease causing intestinal colic is an obstruction to the gut, where a blockage prevents food from passing naturally through the intestine. The gut goes into recurrent painful spasm in an attempt to force the food past the obstruction, which may be caused by cancer, tumours, twisting of the gut, adhesions, infections, swallowed foreign bodies or a number of rarer diseases. This type of colic requires urgent medical attention.

Infections of the intestine such as gastroenteritis, food poisoning, overindulgence in food, parasites in the gut, dehydration and even extreme stress and anxiety can all cause the intestine to go into spasm that results in colic. If there is no obvious cause for the recurrent abdominal pain, medical attention should be sought, so that appropriate treatment can be given before any serious consequences develop.

COLITIS, ULCERATIVE
See ULCERATIVE COLITIS.

COLO-RECTAL CANCER
Anyone who experiences an alteration in their normal bowel habits, passes blood with their faeces, is losing weight, has colicky pains in the abdomen and feels constantly tired needs to see a doctor urgently, because these are the cardinal symptoms of a cancer in the colon or rectum.

The colon and rectum form the large intestine (see Section 2), the last one to one and a half metres of the gut, starting just inside the anus. Cancer of this area is responsible for more cancer deaths than any other form of cancer. Colo-rectal cancer is more common in men, and more than half develop in the last 10 cm of the gut, so it can be felt by a doctor doing a finger examination through the anus. A large cancer can also be felt as a hard lump in the abdomen, particularly in thin patients. Other patients with suspicious symptoms will need a colonoscopy and/or barium enema (see Section 4) to confirm the diagnosis.

Patients who have a bad family history of bowel cancer, or symptoms that are less definitely suspicious, can have a sample of their faeces tested for blood. Three samples are usually necessary over several days, and certain foods such as red meat, cauliflower, broccoli, turnips, bananas and radishes must be avoided before the test. A negative test does not positively exclude the presence of cancer, but lessens its likelihood. A positive test is an indication to investigate further. Some doctors now advocate a routine, regular faeces blood testing for all men over 40.

The most common complication of this cancer is obstruction, when the cancer grows to a size where the faeces cannot pass, and the intestine ceases to function. Another complication that can occur is a hole developing in the gut through or beside the cancer. This allows faeces to leak into the abdomen, which leads to peritonitis and a critical illness.

There are no specific blood tests that will detect this type of cancer, but blood tests may show anaemia caused by the constant slow leaking of blood from the cancer into the bowel.

The only curative treatment is major surgery to remove the cancer, the bowel for some distance above and below the cancer, and the surrounding lymph nodes. This is one of the most major operations routinely undertaken, and up to 5% of patients may die during or immediately after the operation. Without the operation, death from the cancer is inevitable.

If the cancer has not spread away from the large intestine, two out of three patients will survive for five years. If the cancer has spread, the survival rate drops steadily, depending on the degree of spread.

After the operation, regular examinations of the colon are required to detect at the earliest possible stage any recurrence of the cancer, or the development of a new bowel cancer (a phenomenon that is quite common in these patients).

COMMON COLD
See COLD, COMMON.

CONCUSSION
See HEAD INJURY.

CONDYLOMATA ACUMINATA
See WARTS — Genital warts.

CONJUNCTIVITIS, ALLERGIC
See ALLERGY.

CONJUNCTIVITIS, INFECTED
Conjunctivitis is a term that covers several different diseases. Literally, the word means an inflammation of the outer surface of the eye, and this is usually accompanied by pain or an itch, redness of the eye and often a discharge.

Any eye problem that does not settle rapidly should be seen by a doctor. Even simple conditions, if allowed to persist, may cause scarring of the eye surface and a deterioration in the most vital of our senses — sight.

There are two main types of infection causing conjunctivitis — viral and bacterial.

Viral conjunctivitis
Viral conjunctivitis is the most difficult form to treat. Doctors are unable to cure most viral infections, but there are some

types that infect the eye surface that antiviral drops can control. Unfortunately, most viruses cause low-grade irritation, a clear sticky exudate and red eyes for several weeks until the body's own defences overcome the infection. Soothing drops and ointment may be used, but time is the main treatment.

Bacterial conjunctivitis

The most common form of conjunctivitis is that caused by a bacterial infection of the thin film of tears that always covers the eye. These bacteria are very easily passed from one person to another as the patient rubs the eyes with a hand, then shakes hands, and the second person then rubs their eyes. It is obviously easy for all the children in a family or a school class to develop the infection one after another.

Bacterial conjunctivitis is characterised by yellow pus that forms in the eyes and may stick the eyelids together when waking. The eyes are bloodshot and they may be a little sore. It almost invariably involves both eyes. Once correctly diagnosed by a doctor, treatment is simple by using antibiotic drops or ointment on a regular basis until the infection clears. The drops only last a very short time in the eye and so must be used every two or three hours during the day. The ointment will last for longer, but may blur the vision, so is often used only at night.

Babies who develop recurrent attacks of bacterial conjunctivitis are often suffering from a **blocked tear duct** as well. Your tears are produced in a small gland beyond the outer edge of your eye. They move across the surface of the eye, and then through a tiny tube at the inner edge of the eye that ends in the nose. This is why you get the salty taste of tears in your mouth when crying. If the duct is too small in an infant, or is blocked by pus, the circulation of tears is prevented and infection easily results.

A blocked tear duct may be probed and cleared by a doctor if the conjunctivitis persists in a baby for several months, but most grow out of the problem.

CONN'S SYNDROME (HYPERALDOSTERONISM)

The adrenal glands sit on top of each kidney at the back of the abdomen (see Section 2). Conn's syndrome is a rare disease caused by a tumour in one of the adrenal glands that produces excessive amounts of a substance called aldosterone — thus another name for this disease is hyperaldosteronism (the Latin 'hyper' means excess). There are other rare diseases that can also cause excess aldosterone production.

Aldosterone is a hormone (substance secreted by a gland) that controls the amount of salt in the body. If the level of salt in the blood drops, more aldosterone is secreted by the adrenal gland, and it acts on the kidney to reduce the amount being lost in the urine. Salt levels in the body are critical for good health, as the amount of salt in the body also determines the total amount of water in the body.

The aldosterone-secreting tumour of Conn's syndrome is not a cancer, but it causes excess amounts of salt to be retained in the body. This in turn causes high blood pressure, an excessive production of urine, muscle weakness, pins and needles sensations, headache and thirst. The diagnosis can be confirmed by blood tests that show markedly abnormal levels of salt (NaCl) and other chemicals in the blood stream. The tumour can usually be seen by a CT scan or by magnetic resonance imaging (see Section 4). Radioactive substances that concentrate in the abnormal adrenal gland may also be given to a patient in whom the disease is suspected, and the degree of concentration of the substance in each adrenal gland can then be measured.

Conn's syndrome may be the cause of high blood pressure that does not respond to normal treatments. When high blood pressure is discovered, blood tests are normally performed to exclude this, and other diseases, as a cause of the high blood pressure.

Once diagnosed, the tumour of the adrenal gland can be removed surgically to cure most cases of the condition. Medications may be required to control the symptoms and high blood pressure before the operation. Other types of hyperaldosteronism not caused by Conn's syndrome will require long-term treatment with drugs such as spironolactone.

CONSTIPATION
See Section 3.

CONTRACTURE, DUPUYTREN'S
See DUPUYTREN'S CONTRACTURE.

CONVULSION
See EPILEPSY; FEBRILE CONVULSION.
See also Section 3; Section 8.

CORNEAL ULCERS
See EYE ULCERS.

COR PULMONALE (PULMONARY HYPERTENSION, CHRONIC PULMONARY HEART DISEASE)

Patients with cor pulmonale have the symptoms of a long-lasting bronchitis, but there is no infection of the lungs present. The symptoms include a cough that produces clear or blood-stained phlegm, a wheeze, shortness of breath with any exertion and general weakness. In advanced forms of the disease the ankles may be swollen, nausea and indigestion may occur, and the liver enlarges.

Cor pulmonale is an enlargement of the right side of the heart. This is the part of the heart that pumps blood into the lungs. If the lungs are damaged by emphysema (see separate entry), smoking, inhaled coal dust or asbestos, recurrent lung infections or a number of rarer lung diseases, the lung tissue may be so abnormal that the blood has difficulty in passing through it. The right side of the heart, over many years, must work harder and harder to force the blood through the damaged lung. This causes a significant rise in the blood pressure in the right side of the heart and the lung, while the blood pressure in the rest of the body may remain normal. The increased blood pressure in the lungs causes further damage to the blood vessels, and worsens the disease. Because of the extra work it must do, the heart muscle thickens and enlarges, and the characteristic symptoms of cor pulmonale develop. Because of the lung damage, inadequate oxygen enters the blood, which further compounds the problem, as the rest of the body then lacks oxygen to function correctly.

The disease can be diagnosed by an X-ray which shows the enlarged heart, and by an electrocardiogram (see Section 4) which shows characteristic changes. Other investigations that may be necessary include passing a tube through a vein into the heart to measure the blood pressure (cardiac catheterisation), echocardiography and angiography (see Section 4).

Patients with cor pulmonale are susceptible to lung infections such as bronchitis and pneumonia, and become steadily weaker as the disease progresses. Medication for infections can be prescribed to ease the disease, strengthen the heart and open the lungs, but no cure is possible. Physiotherapy can help drain phlegm from the lungs, and oxygen may be used to relieve the shortness of breath. The patients steadily deteriorate over several years, and eventually die from heart attacks, pneumonia or other complications of the disease.

Coryza
See COLD, COMMON.

Costochondral syndrome
See TIETZE'S SYNDROME.

Cot death (sudden infant death syndrome, SIDS)

Cot death is the sudden unexpected death of an apparently normal healthy child in whom a subsequent detailed post-mortem examination reveals no cause for the death. Cot deaths are at present unpredictable and cannot be prevented. Every year, about 500 Australian babies die from cot death or sudden infant death syndrome. Or to put it another way, two or three out of every 1000 children between the ages of one month and one year will die from this distressing condition. Cot deaths have been documented since biblical times, so they are not something new, but they have come into prominence in the last few decades because most of the other causes of death in infants have been prevented by vaccination, or can be cured by antibiotics, other medications or surgery.

The typical history is of a baby that is put to bed in its cot and some hours later, or the next morning, is found dead. There is no evidence of disturbed sleep and no cry is heard, even by parents who are awake nearby. The baby just stops breathing during sleep. For the parents, the discovery of a dead baby that they have just begun to know and love is an overwhelming tragedy. They cannot understand how such a normal, healthy, happy infant could die so suddenly and without warning. Once the diagnosis has been confirmed by autopsy, it is imperative that the parents receive adequate and immediate counselling by trained professionals. Other parents who have suffered a similar loss may be involved in the counselling. The bereaved parents develop an acute sense of guilt, thinking that they are in some way responsible, and they fear that someone will blame them for the death of their child due to neglect or mistreatment. But of course, this is not so. These feelings are normal and natural. Other children in the family will also be affected, despite the fact that they may deny it or appear unconcerned. This is because they are often unable to understand or accept the tragedy. These children should also be involved in the counselling and be given constant reassurance that any minor aggression or hateful thoughts they may have shown to the baby are in no way responsible for the tragedy.

As with any death for which the cause is unknown, theories abound, but none have yet been proved. Cot deaths are not infectious or contagious, nor are they due to suffocation, choking or allergies. They occur in both bottle- and breastfed babies and there is no relationship between immunisation and cot deaths. There is no evidence that vitamins, dietary supplements or any other medications can prevent the syndrome. A recent theory implicates high body temperatures due to over-wrapping or dressing a baby, so that it cannot sweat effectively. If one baby in a family dies from cot death, there is some evidence that subsequent babies are at a higher risk, but the reason for this is unknown.

Some parents have found their children on the verge of cot death, lying in the cot blue and not breathing, and rousing them has started breathing again. After such an event, these babies can be monitored by a sensing device that sounds an alarm if breathing stops for more than a few seconds. Only a very select group of infants require this type of care.

A vast amount of research is being carried out into cot death, and a large amount of information is being built up and gradually collated in the hope that a reason, and then a form of prevention, will eventually be found.

CP
See CEREBRAL PALSY.

CRABS (PEDICULOSIS)
Pubic pediculosis, commonly known as crabs, is the infestation of the pubic hair with a parasitic insect. The lice that cause the infestation (scientifically called *Phthirus pubis*), live by sucking blood in tiny amounts from their human host. The infestation is often asymptomatic, and many people have it and are totally unaware of it. In others the lice cause an itchy rash in the pubic area, which may be raw and bleeding from constant scratching. Secondary skin infections may develop in these sores, and this infection can cause further symptoms including a fever and enlarged glands in the groin. The condition is caught by being in close bodily contact with someone who already has an infestation (e.g. during sex), but as the lice can survive away from humans for a time, it can also be caught from borrowed clothing, bedding or toilet seats.

A number of lotions are available to kill the crabs. The affected individual, and all sex partners, must be treated simultaneously to prevent reinfestations occurring. All clothing and bedding that may be affected must be thoroughly washed in hot water. A repeat treatment after 24 hours and again after seven days is advisable in order to kill any lice that have hatched in the interim. Antibiotics may be required to treat secondary infections. Correct treatment should result in a complete cure.

See also LICE.

CRAMPS, INTESTINAL
See ABDOMINAL PAIN, Section 3.

CRAMPS, MUSCULAR
See Section 3.

CRETINISM
The thyroid gland in the front of the neck is responsible for producing a substance called thyroxine which acts on every cell in the body to control the rate at which it works (see Section 2). Thyroxine is the accelerator of cell action. In cretinism, the thyroid gland fails to function correctly from birth, which results in impaired brain development and severe mental retardation. Blood tests performed on all babies immediately after birth are designed to detect cretinism (which occurs at the rate of one in every 4000 births) and other serious diseases.

Once detected, treatment to replace the missing thyroxine is undertaken. This will reduce the amount of brain damage, but unfortunately there is usually some degree of impairment due to lack of thyroxine in the foetus before birth.

Most cretins can function normally in society with their intelligence and functional capacity only slightly below average.

See also HYPOTHYROIDISM.

CROHN'S DISEASE (REGIONAL ENTERITIS)
Crohn's disease is named after the New York physician, Burrill Crohn (born 1884), who first described the disease. It is a chronic inflammation and thickening of the wall of the intestine, for which there is

no known cause or permanent cure. It usually occurs in the lower part of the small intestine (the ileum), but may occur anywhere between the stomach and the anus. It is a disease of young adults that in some cases, and despite treatment, continues for the rest of the patient's life. If the intestine of these patients is examined at operation, segments of bowel from a few centimetres to a metre or more in length are found to have a wall that is several times thicker and much firmer than normal.

Patients describe moderate to severe intermittent lower abdominal pain (colic), alternating diarrhoea and constipation (with the diarrhoea being more common), intermittent fever, loss of appetite, passing excess wind and weight loss. The disease can range through the full spectrum of being a minor irritation to being a very severe disease that may cause bowel perforation and, in rare cases, death. Patients may have episodes of comparatively good health for years, then become acutely ill for a few months. In severe cases, the bowel may rupture into the bladder, vagina or through the skin around the anus. Obstruction to the passage of food may occur, as the affected segment of gut cannot contract properly. The diagnosis is confirmed by a barium meal X-ray, where a substance that shows on X-ray is swallowed, and followed on an X-ray screen as it passes through the intestine. If the lower part (the colon) is involved, a barium enema is necessary.

Treatment involves surgically removing the worst affected segments of the intestine, and controlling the symptoms such as diarrhoea and pain with medication. Surgery must be limited in severe cases, as removing too much of the affected intestine will lead to the inability to absorb adequate food. Patients are given a high-calorie, high- vitamin, low-residue diet with calcium supplements. Vitamin injections are sometimes necessary if food absorption is very poor. Anaemia, dehydration and diarrhoea are signs of a poorly maintained diet. Antibiotics are given to treat bowel infections, and steroids to control flare-ups of the disease.

Even after surgery that appears to have removed all of the affected intestine, 60% of cases develop new affected segments of intestine. Patients with Crohn's disease find it places some restrictions on their lifestyle, but although the mortality rate of these patients is slightly increased, most live relatively normal and long lives.

CROUP

The characteristics of croup include a seal-like barking cough, difficulty on breathing in, and excessive chest movement with breathing in a child. There is usually only a slight fever, and minimal pain in the throat.

Croup is caused by a viral infection of the throat, usually at a low level, so no abnormality is seen on examination of the throat through the mouth. The throat when examined by a mirror can be seen to be very swollen and partly blocking the airway. This is the cause of the typical cough.

The most effective treatment is placing the child in a warm, moist environment. The steam produced in a bathroom with a hot shower running is most effective, but commercial vaporisers can be used to produce steam in a bedroom. Other effective substitutes include a wet towel hung over an oil-filled space heater or a simmering crock-pot in the room. The other treatments required are paracetamol for any fever or discomfort, and adequate amounts of fluid to prevent dehydration. Antibiotics are not required unless a secondary infection develops. The vast majority of children recover spontaneously within a day or two. In more serious cases, a steam tent may be used in hospital to assist the breathing. Very rarely, the child may develop a severe degree of swelling in the throat that totally obstructs breathing. This is a critical emergency requiring life-saving procedures by a doctor.

CURVATURE OF SPINE
See KYPHOSIS; SCOLIOSIS.

CUSHING'S SYNDROME
Cushing's syndrome is named after Harvey William Cushing, a prominent brain surgeon from Boston (USA), who pioneered many brain surgery techniques in the latter part of the nineteenth century. The syndrome is caused by excessive amounts of steroids in the bloodstream. These may be produced by an overactive adrenal gland (see Section 2), or by taking excessive amounts of steroids (e.g. prednisone) for medical reasons.

Part of the brain called the hypothalamus decides how much natural steroid is required by the body. It then sends a nerve message to the pituitary gland (see Section 2), which sits under the centre of the brain. This in turn sends a chemical message to the adrenal glands, which are responsible for producing the steroids required by the body. Faults in any of the hypothalamus, pituitary gland or adrenal gland can result in the overproduction of steroids, and Cushing's syndrome. Tumours in one of these three areas are the most common cause for overactivity. Cushing's syndrome due to overactivity of a gland, rather than a tumour, may be triggered by pregnancy or other stress.

Cushing's syndrome causes a fat face, fatty deposits on the upper back (called a buffalo hump), obesity of the abdomen and chest with thin arms and legs, high blood pressure, impotence, cessation of menstrual periods, skin infections and pimples, headaches, backache, excess hair growth on the face and body, mood changes, excessive bruising, thinning of the bones (osteoporosis — which can cause bones to fracture easily), stretch marks on the breasts and abdomen, kidney stones, and generalised weakness.

Specialised and sometimes complex blood tests can confirm the presence of the syndrome, but diagnosis of the actual cause (i.e. where the tumour or activity is present) can be very difficult. CT scans and magnetic resonance imaging (see Section 4) are used in an attempt to find these very small tumours. The complications of Cushing's syndrome include strokes, heart attacks, broken bones, diabetes, increased susceptibility to infections (particularly of the skin and urine), and psychiatric diseases.

If a tumour can be found in the adrenal or pituitary gland, it is surgically removed and the patient is cured. The adrenal gland tumour can be removed through an incision in the loin, but to remove a pituitary tumour in the centre of the brain, extraordinarily delicate surgery is performed with long instruments that are passed up through the nose into the base of the brain. Other treatment methods include irradiation of the pituitary gland, or removal of both adrenal glands.

Medical treatment using drugs is generally unsuccessful, but if a patient has both adrenal glands removed it will be necessary to supply the body with its required level of steroids by taking tablets regularly. Other hormones may be necessary to correct impotence and restart menstrual periods. Insulin will be required if diabetes develops.

The outcome of this syndrome depends on its cause. Some tumours of the adrenal gland or pituitary gland are very aggressive and spread to other areas to continue the syndrome. These patients have a poor life expectancy. In others, a lifelong cure may be obtained by removing the offending localised tumour. Patients whose Cushing's syndrome is caused by excessive intake of steroid tablets can have the syndrome controlled by stopping their medication. Unfortunately, they may require this medication for control of asthma, rheumatoid arthritis or other diseases, and the patient and his/her doctors must tread a very narrow path between the side effects of the medication and the underlying disease.

CVA (CEREBROVASCULAR ACCIDENT)
See STROKE.

CYST
A cyst is a collection of fluid, fat, oil, blood, pus, air, parasites or other liquid or semiliquid substance within the body that is surrounded by, and contained in, a wall of cells or fibrous tissue. Cysts can occur in almost any part of the body from the brain to the bone, but are most common in the skin, ovaries, breast, lung and kidney.

See also BARTHOLIN'S CYST; MEIBOMIAN CYST INFECTIONS; OVARIAN CYST; POLYCYSTIC KIDNEY; SEBACEOUS CYST.

CYSTIC FIBROSIS (FIBROCYSTIC DISEASE)
Cystic fibrosis is a congenital disorder (one present from birth) that causes the glands of the body to secrete abnormally thick mucus. It mainly affects the gut, lungs and skin. Normally, glands lining the gut and lungs, secrete a thin watery mucus that keeps these organs lubricated and functioning properly. In cystic fibrosis, the mucus is so thick that it plugs up the airways in the lungs and blocks the absorption of food from the gut. On the skin, the sweat glands secrete excessive amounts of salt, so that when kissed, an infant will taste salty. This may be the first sign of the disease, and if a mother comments that her baby tastes salty, a doctor is alerted to the possibility of cystic fibrosis being present.

The disease is not normally diagnosed until a child is several years old, when the recurrence of frequent attacks of bronchitis or pneumonia, shortness of breath, inability to exercise and a chronic cough cause suspicion. Other symptoms include diarrhoea with fatty faeces, an enlarged chest and thickened finger tips ('clubbing' — see Section 3). Due to the presence of thick secretions in the testes and Fallopian tubes, these patients are also sterile. The diagnosis may be confirmed by a test to determine the amount of salt in the sweat. Chest X-rays and pulmonary function tests using a spirometer (see Section 4) may also be abnormal.

There is no cure for cystic fibrosis, and the outcome of the disease depends on the patient's dedication to following a comprehensive treatment program. Physiotherapy several times every day to clear the lungs is critical. Antibiotics are used to treat any lung infection, and medications to open up the airways (bronchodilators — see Section 6) and loosen the thick mucus (mucolytics) are prescribed.

Until the 1960s, survival beyond 20 years of age was rare. Death was due to uncontrolled pneumonia or cor pulmonale (see separate entry). Today, survival into the twenties is common, and many victims are now alive and well over 30 with continued intensive therapy. Some of the heart-lung transplants carried out today are for cystic fibrosis. The patient receives a new heart and lungs, as lungs cannot be transplanted on their own, and donates his/her own heart to someone with heart disease.

CYSTINOSIS
Cystinosis is a very rare inherited disorder

that results in the deposition of crystals of a substance called cystine in the eye, bone marrow, lymph nodes, white blood cells, kidneys and other organs. There are two forms of the disease — that which commences shortly after birth, and an adult form.

Babies with cystinosis are very small, feverish, vomit constantly, pass excess urine and become dehydrated. Death from kidney failure before the age of ten is usual. In the adult form, only the eyes are affected, and painful eyes, intolerance to bright lights and headaches are the main symptoms. Kidney failure may be a late complication.

The diagnosis of the condition is difficult and is usually picked up by noting the presence of crystals in the white blood cells when examined under a microscope.

There are a number of experimental treatments, but nothing that has proved effective in the long term is available yet.

CYSTITIS (BLADDER INFECTION)

Uncomfortable, embarrassing and common — cystitis (a bladder infection) is all three to many women. Cystitis is one of the most common conditions seen by general practitioners, but some women can barely get away from the toilet for long enough to visit the surgery!

The symptoms of burning pain on passing urine, pain in the pelvis, and the desire to pass urine every 10 minutes that are associated with cystitis are not limited entirely to women, but less than 10% of cases occur in men because the longer length of their urethra (the tube leading from the bladder to the outside) gives them considerable protection from infection. When it does affect males, it is often more serious and requires more aggressive investigation and treatment. Most women will have at least one bladder infection in their lives, and some have repeated attacks that require constant medication to prevent them.

Cystitis is due to bacteria that can reproduce rapidly in the warm urine. The bacteria can enter the bladder in one of two ways — by coming up the urethra from outside the body, or coming through the bloodstream to the kidneys and then the bladder. Entry of the bacteria from the outside is far more common, and is often due to sex. Because the urethra is very short in women (as little as 1 cm), bacteria on the skin can easily pass into the bladder with the massaging that area receives during intercourse. Passing urine immediately after sex can help to remove any bacteria that may have entered.

Slackness of the muscle ring that controls the release of urine from the bladder can also allow bacteria to enter the bladder. This damage may be caused by childbirth or prolapse of the womb, and may eventually cause incontinence with a cough or laugh. There are physiotherapy and surgical procedures available to correct this problem.

When a patient arrives at a surgery with symptoms of cystitis, a urine sample will be checked for infection. A plastic strip covered with spots that are sensitive to different constituents of the urine is used for this purpose. This can give a quite accurate picture of what is happening to cause the patient's symptoms. The sample is then sent to a laboratory for further testing to find out which bacteria are causing the infection, and which antibiotics will kill them. These tests may take a few days to complete, so the patient is usually started on an appropriate antibiotic immediately, which can be changed at a later date if the tests results indicate that this is necessary. Other medications (in the form of a powder that makes a fizzy drink) to alkalise the urine and remove the unpleasant burning sensation are also prescribed. Drinking extra fluid will help wash the infection out of the kidneys and bladder. If several infections occur, further investigations such as X-rays of the bladder and kidneys are performed, to exclude some of the rarer more serious causes of recurrent cystitis.

In most patients, cystitis is a considerable nuisance, not a serious disease, which can be easily and effectively treated provided the patient presents to a doctor at the first sign of trouble.

Cytomegalovirus infections

Infections with cytomegalovirus (CMV) are extremely common, and at any one time, between 10% and 25% of the entire population are infected with this virus. In all but a tiny percentage of these infected people, there are absolutely no symptoms, and they appear and feel totally well. Infection rates may be in excess of 80% in homosexual men, where the virus is sexually transmitted. Normally, CMV passes from one person to another in saliva or as droplets in the breath. In some cases, infection has spread through blood transfusions.

A CMV infection may be a serious illness in patients who have reduced immunity due to treatment with cytotoxic drugs (see Section 6) for cancer, have suffered other serious illnesses, are anaemic, suffering from AIDS or other immune affecting diseases, or who are extremely run-down from stress or overwork. If a pregnant woman with reduced immunity acquires a significant CMV infection, her baby may be affected in the womb. The baby can be born with liver damage (jaundice), enlarged liver and spleen, poor ability to clot blood, and bruises. More seriously, up to a third of affected babies may be born with mental retardation, and one in six are deaf. Adults with reduced immunity who develop a significant infection with CMV, will suffer from a fever, headaches, overwhelming tiredness, muscle and joint pains, enlarged glands and an inflamed liver.

The disease can be detected by specific blood tests, and the virus may be found in sputum, saliva, urine and other body fluids. There is no specific treatment for CMV infections, although some anti-viral drugs are being used experimentally. Aspirin and/or paracetamol is used to control fever and pain, and prolonged rest is required for recovery. In patients with severely reduced immunity, pneumonia and hepatitis may develop, and these can prove fatal.

See also VIRAL INFECTION.

Dandruff

Over a period of a few weeks, our skin totally replaces itself. New cells are produced deep in the skin, slowly move out as new cells are produced beneath them, thin out to form a hard scaly layer, and eventually slough off as we wash and our skin rubs on clothing or bedding. Dandruff is an acceleration of this natural process in which the rate at which cells are produced on the scalp is increased, so that the excess cells produced form a scale on the skin. The underlying skin may become inflamed and itchy. It is now thought that a fungal infection of the scalp causes this increased rate of cell loss. Emotional stress, overworking, hot climates and a poor diet all aggravate dandruff.

Dandruff must be differentiated from other skin diseases such as psoriasis of the scalp (see separate entry), which is a far more serious form of dermatitis, and other fungal infections.

Treatment of dandruff should involve good scalp hygiene, and one of the many anti-dandruff lotions or shampoos available. These include selenium sulphide (e.g. Selsun), coal tar (e.g. Ionil T), and zinc pyrithione (e.g. Dan-Gard). Resistant cases may be helped by steroid scalp lotions (e.g. Diprosone, Betnovate — prescription required) and antifungal lotions (e.g. miconazole, econazole, clotrimazole).

Most patients with dandruff have recurrences throughout life, with bad and good periods, often for no apparent reason. Control is normally possible by using one of the above methods.

DEAFNESS
See Section 3.

DEHYDRATION
Dehydration occurs when there is less than the normal amount of water in the body. Our body weight is 80% water, but even a decrease of 5% in this level can cause significant disease, and a 10% loss may be fatal in children. The early signs of dehydration are thirst, dry mouth, slack skin, sunken eyes, weight loss, rapid heart rate, weakness and lethargy. Blood tests are available that will accurately determine the degree of dehydration.

Dehydration may be caused by severe diarrhoea and/or vomiting, water deprivation, burns, diabetes mellitus, diabetes insipidus, peritonitis and kidney disease. Because of their lower body weight, children will dehydrate far more rapidly than adults.

Treatment involves giving water to the patient in a form that will be retained in the body. It is better to give a correctly formulated electrolyte solution (available from chemists) by mouth if possible, but in an emergency, a mixture containing a level teaspoon of salt and eight level teaspoons of sugar or glucose into a litre of boiled water may be given. Plain water may pass straight through the body, and should only be used if the other solutions mentioned are not available. In severe cases, fluid will need to be given by a drip into a vein. Care must be taken not to give too much too quickly.

DELIRIUM TREMENS
See ALCOHOLISM.

DEMENTIA
Dementia is a problem common in elderly people, and as our population ages, it will become a major social and economic problem in Australia. Patients with dementia require constant care and attention, and as the condition is normally incurable, it will become a significant financial problem to the patients, their family and government.

Dementia is a generalised deterioration in intellect, leading to confusion, irrational behaviour, inappropriate reactions, poor or jumbled speech patterns, hallucinations (both visual and auditory), and loss of short term memory. The symptoms are often worse at night. Some patients may become uninhibited in both their language and habits, and may act in a manner that is quite socially unacceptable. It is a progressive condition, with a slow and gradual onset, and a continued steady deterioration over many years. It is rarely reversible, even in younger patients, unless a specific underlying disease (e.g. an underactive thyroid gland) can be found and treated. Depressed patients may appear demented, but recover remarkably when their depression is treated. Dementia in the elderly usually has no specific cause, but may be worsened by arteriosclerosis (hardening of the arteries), and alcohol or drug abuse. Alzheimer's disease (see separate entry) is a form of dementia.

There are no specific blood tests that can diagnose the condition, but in advanced stages, a CT scan (see Section 4) of the brain will show a shrinking of the brain cortex and opening up of the natural fissures in the brain.

Treatment is basically custodial. The

patient should be kept in a pleasant, safe, non-threatening environment with adequate medical, nursing, physiotherapy, occupational therapy and general support services. Medications may be given to control irrational behaviour, hallucinations and violent tempers, but do not improve the overall condition of the patient. Patients gradually deteriorate to a vegetative state, and die from diseases such as pneumonia, caused by being constantly in bed.

Dengue fever (breakbone fever)

Mosquitoes throughout the tropics are responsible for the transmission from one person to another of the virus that causes dengue fever. In the vicinity of Australia, cases of this disease have been reported from south-east Asia, Indonesia, New Guinea, Vanuatu and Fiji.

After being bitten by an *Aedes* mosquito carrying the virus, the incubation period before the first symptoms of the disease appears is three to seven days, but may stretch out to two weeks. Patients experience the sudden onset of a high fever, chills, and a severe aching of the back, head and legs (hence the alternative name, breakbone fever). Other symptoms that develop over the next few days are a sore throat, blotchy skin and depression. After three or four days, these symptoms totally cease for a day or two, to be followed by the second phase of the disease. This is similar to the first phase, but generally milder, and is usually accompanied by a rash that starts on the hands and feet and spreads to cover the entire body with the exception of the face. In severe cases, skin bleeding, and bleeding into the gut with accompanying diarrhoea can occur. Blood tests show that a viral infection is present, but not until a specific test for dengue fever is performed can the diagnosis be confirmed. Patients with dengue fever may be thought to have influenza or another severe viral illness unless they tell their doctor about their recent trip to a tropical area. Even then, the disease may be easily confused with malaria or yellow fever.

The only protection from the disease is prevention of mosquito bites by the use of insect repellents, clothing to cover arms and legs, and netting. A vaccine is not yet available, but one is likely in the future.

Patients may become dehydrated because of diarrhoea, and require fluid replacement, but there are not normally any other serious complications. The only treatment available is aspirin for the fevers and pains, and prolonged rest. It may take several months for complete recovery from the infection.

Dental disease
See DENTISTRY, Section 7.

Depression

All of us have our good and bad times. Days when we are happy, days when we are sad. Sometimes these changes can occur from one hour to the next, or may last for many days. They may be associated with hormonal changes that occur during a woman's menstrual cycle or with menopause. Fortunately, most of us bounce back fairly quickly, and our periods of unhappiness are not too prolonged. Others are not so lucky, and may be depressed for weeks or months on end. Prolonged depression can be broadly defined as falling into one of two categories — reactive or endogenous depression. Those who suffer from **endogenous depression** (also known as affective depression) can find no reason at all for their constant state of unhappiness. They slowly become sadder and sadder, more irritable, unable to sleep, lose appetite and weight, and may feel there is no purpose in living. They may feel unnecessarily guilty, have a very poor opinion of themselves, feel life is hopeless and find it difficult to think or concentrate. After several months they usually improve, but sometimes it can take years. When they do start to improve, some patients with depression go too far the other way and become over-happy or manic. These patients are said to be manic depressives or have bipolar (generally severe swings of mood) or cyclothymic (milder mood changes) disorder.

People with endogenous depression are not able to pull themselves together and overcome the depression without medical aid. Certainly, a determination to improve the situation helps the outcome, but like other diseases such as diabetes or high blood pressure, these patients require regular medication to control their disease. Depression in these cases is due to an imbalance of chemicals that normally occur in the brain to control mood. If too much of one chemical is produced, the patient becomes depressed — if too much of another, the patient becomes manic. So, as with other chronic diseases, it is necessary for doctors to alter this balance by giving medications that can control the production or activity of the depressing chemicals. With appropriate medication, a patient can progress from the depths of depression to normal life in a few weeks. Most of the antidepressant drugs (see Section 6) do not work quickly, so patients and relatives should not expect an overnight recovery. Hospitalisation in order to use high doses of drugs or other treatments, and to protect the patient from the possibility of suicide, is sometimes necessary when the disease is first diagnosed.

Reactive depression is the sadness that occurs after a death in the family, loss of a job, a marriage break-up or other disaster. You are depressed for a definite reason, and with time, you will be able to cope with the situation yourself. Some patients do require medical help, but only until the worst reaction to the situation has passed.

The worst problem with untreated depression is suicide, and this can be seen as a desperate plea for help in many people. The disease may not be detected or treated until a radical attempt to end life has occurred. Depression is not a fashionable disease, and as a result, many people delay in asking for help until it is too late. But it is a disease, not just a state of mind, and there are very effective methods of treatment available for it.

There are no blood tests or brain scans that can be performed to diagnose depression, and the diagnosis must depend on the clinical acumen of the doctor and information supplied by the patient, relatives and friends.

Medication and counselling by a general practitioner or psychiatrist will control the vast majority of cases. The other form of treatment used is shock therapy (see ELECTROCONVULSIVE THERAPY, Section 6). This has been surrounded by some controversy in the past but is a safe and often very effective method of giving relief to patients with severe chronic depression.

If you have this readily treated disease, but have avoided seeking treatment or have stopped treatment, you are wasting your life. Discuss it with your doctor. The doctor is not going to laugh at or about you, but will arrange to bring you back to leading a full and happy life.

See also MANIA.
See also DEPRESSION, Section 3.

DERMATITIS

Dermatitis means inflammation of the skin, so for a doctor to say that a patient has dermatitis is a rather meaningless statement, because almost any rash is dermatitis. What is important is the type of dermatitis that is present, so after stating that a rash is dermatitis, the doctor must determine the cause of that dermatitis before any reasonable treatment program can be instituted. This is often very difficult, for although the skin is the most visible of our organs, its diseases are very diverse and often difficult to diagnose accurately. For this reason, the specialty of dermatology has developed and grown rapidly over the past decade, to the point that there is now a significant shortage of dermatologists in Australia.

In some mild, early stages of a disease, a general practitioner may try simple anti-inflammatory creams to settle down an undiagnosed dermatitis, but if the problem persists or recurs, further investigation is essential.

Contact dermatitis

Contact dermatitis is one of the most common forms of dermatitis. The skin is red, itchy, swollen, burning and may be blistered in an area that has come into contact with a substance to which the patient has reacted. After a few days, the area may become crusted, weeping and infected with bacteria. Contact dermatitis is most common on exposed parts of the body, but may occur on other areas if, for example, underclothes are washed in a detergent to which the patient reacts. Soaps, detergents, chemicals, solvents, cosmetics, perfume, jewellery, metals, rubber and plants are the most common substances causing contact dermatitis. Sometimes the creams used by doctors to treat other rashes can cause this type of dermatitis. Substances that a person has used or touched regularly for many years without any adverse effect may suddenly sensitise them, and cause a reaction. This is particularly common in the workplace (e.g. solvents, dyes, rubber, inks) and with cosmetics.

Investigations to test a person's reaction to suspect agents may be undertaken, but these tests, in which a patch of skin is exposed to a substance to test its response, are often inconclusive. The best treatment is prevention, and if the substance causing the dermatitis can be identified and avoided, the problem is solved. Gloves can be used to avoid detergents, soap substitutes used for washing, and changes in occupation to avoid solvents. Unfortunately, all to often the offending substance is widespread and cannot be reasonably avoided. In these situations, it may be possible to desensitise an individual to a particular allergen (see ALLERGY), but in most cases the dermatitis must be treated when it occurs.

The mainstays of treatment are steroid creams, lotions and ointments (see Section 6). These are available in many different forms and strengths. Placing an occlusive dressing over the dermatitis and cream increases the effectiveness of the treatment but must only be done for short periods of time. In severe cases, steroids may need to be given in tablet form, or even by injection. If the dermatitis has been secondarily infected by bacteria, antibiotics may also be required. Provided the causative agent is not touched again, the dermatitis should settle with treatment, and not recur.

Exfoliative dermatitis

With exfoliative dermatitis, there is widespread scaling, peeling and redness of the skin. It is often associated with drugs or foods, and removal of the offending substance causes the rash to subside. Commonly used medications that may cause this rash are gold injections (used for rheumatoid arthritis), sulphonamide antibiotics, some diabetes tablets and some anti-inflammatory arthritis tablets (see Section 6). Exposure to heavy metals (such as lead in battery factories) may also be responsible.

Dermatitis artefacta

Dermatitis artefacta is the term used to

describe a rash that is deliberately self-inflicted to attract attention or obtain special treatment. The rash can be extraordinarily varied in its form, and quite bizarre in its presentation. It usually does not respond to treatment, and occurs on unusual parts of the body. Patients who produce these rashes may be disturbed psychiatrically, prisoners, deprived of affection or attention, senile or confused. They may use heat, sharp instruments, sandpaper, chemicals or their fingernails to create the rash. Women are five times more likely to have the condition than men. Once created, the rash may become infected or gangrenous, and thus disguise its origins.

Treatment involves psychiatric counselling and medication, and dressings that cannot be easily removed by the patient. Plaster casts may occasionally be necessary to stop a patient constantly picking at an ulcer that will not otherwise heal.

Dermatitis herpetiformis
Dermatitis herpetiformis occurs on the elbows, knees and backside. It consists of small, intensely itchy, fluid-filled blisters on red, inflamed skin. It often appears scratched and bleeding because of the almost irresistible itching.

There are several different causes for this relatively uncommon type of dermatitis. In some cases it is caused by a substance called gluten in the diet. This is found in many cereals, and the dermatitis can be cured by avoiding them. The other types are more resistant to treatment, and may require very potent tablets for their control.

See also ECZEMA; ERYTHEMA NODOSUM; INTERTRIGO; LICHEN SIMPLEX; PSORIASIS.

DERMATOMYOSITIS (POLYMYOSITIS)
Dermatomyositis is a rare and dreadful disease that combines a persistent rash with muscle weakness. The cause is unknown, and it most commonly attacks those in late middle-age. When it occurs without the rash (which is present in only 40% of cases) it is called polymyositis. Patients present with a dusky red rash on the cheeks and nose, shoulders and upper chest and back. The eyelids are often swollen and appear bruised. Other unusual symptoms include redness and bleeding under the nails, cold hands, and a scaly rash over the knuckles. The main characteristic of the disease is a gradually progressive weakness and pain of the muscles in the neck, upper arms, shoulder, buttocks and thighs. This eventually can cripple the patient unless effective treatment is instigated. Rare complications can also develop to involve the heart and lungs. One in ten of these patients develops cancer — a far higher rate than expected.

Once suspected by a doctor, the disease can be diagnosed by blood tests and by taking a reading of the muscle's electrical activity (see ELECTROMYOGRAM, Section 4). Although there is no cure, most patients can have the disease controlled to the extent that they can lead a relatively normal life. Drugs such as steroids, methotrexate and azathioprine are commonly used.

DIABETES INSIPIDUS
Diabetes insipidus has almost nothing to do with the common sugar diabetes (diabetes mellitus). The word 'diabetes' suggests a condition characterised by frequent and excessive passing of urine, and it is this symptom, along with excessive thirst, that the victims of both diabetes mellitus and diabetes insipidus share. Diabetes insipidus is an uncommon disease that may be triggered suddenly by a head injury, or develop slowly over many months because of a brain infection,

tumour or stroke. It is caused by a failure of the pituitary gland (see Section 2), situated in the centre of the head, to produce the hormone (called vasopressin or antidiuretic hormone) that controls the rate at which the kidney produces urine. Without this hormone, the kidney constantly produces large amounts of dilute urine. A rare variation of diabetes insipidus occurs when the kidney fails to respond to this hormone, even when it is being produced normally by the pituitary gland.

Because of their huge urine output, the patients are constantly thirsty, and they may take ten litres or more of fluid a day. They lose weight, develop headaches and muscle pains, become easily dehydrated, and may have an irregular heart beat. The disease can be diagnosed by a series of ingenious blood and urine tests after exposing the patient to varying degrees of water intake.

Diabetes insipidus cannot be cured, but it is controlled by regular injections of vasopressin which last from one to three days. Milder cases can be treated with a nasal spray of a synthetic form of vasopressin, but this only lasts for a few hours. The hormone cannot be given as a tablet because it is destroyed by the stomach acid. A number of other drugs are under trial for use in mild cases of the disease.

The outcome of the disease depends upon its cause. Some cases do settle spontaneously, but most continue throughout life, and require long-term treatment.

Diabetes mellitus (sugar diabetes)

Glucose, a type of sugar, is essential for the efficient working of every cell in the body. It is burned chemically (metabolised) to produce the energy for the cell to operate, and is found in most fruit and vegetables. When glucose is eaten, it is absorbed into the bloodstream from the small intestine. It then travels to all the body's microscopic cells through the arteries and capillaries. Once it reaches a cell, it must enter across the fine membrane that forms its outer skin. This skin is normally impermeable to all substances, but insulin has the ability to combine with glucose and transport it from the bloodstream through the cell membrane and into the interior of the cell, where it can be used as an energy source for that cell.

Insulin is a chemical of very great complexity. It is made in the pancreas, which sits in the abdomen below the stomach (see Section 2). The insulin it produces enters the bloodstream, and is attracted to those cells that are running short of energy and require more glucose. If there is no glucose available to the cells because you have not been eating, because a lack of insulin prevents glucose from entering the cell, or because the cell membrane fails to allow the insulin to work, the cell weakens and eventually stops working altogether. If insulin is the problem, the patient has diabetes mellitus. The physiology of diabetes, and the use of insulin, was discovered by the American doctors Banting and Best in the 1920s.

The early symptoms of diabetes are excessive tiredness, thirst, excess passing of urine, weight loss despite a large food intake, itchy rashes, recurrent vaginal thrush infections, pins and needles and blurred vision.

The earlier diabetes is controlled, the better the outcome for the patient, as side effects and body damage are less likely.

If you suspect that you may have diabetes, your doctor can perform a simple test on your blood or urine to determine the diagnosis within minutes. It is far better to have the disease diagnosed now than to wait for months while the high blood glucose levels cause damage to your body. A glucose tolerance test is the main test performed to determine the severity of diabetes. This test may also be able to tell if you are likely to develop diabetes in the near future. After fasting for 12 hours, a blood sample is taken. A sweet drink is then swallowed, and further blood samples are taken at regular intervals for two or three hours. The pattern of absorption and elimination of blood glucose will give the diagnosis.

There are two totally different types of diabetes — juvenile diabetes (type 1) and maturity onset diabetes (type 2). Diabetes effects approximately 2% of the population, with 90% of diabetics suffering from the maturity onset form. Although they both are caused by the inability to utilise glucose, the cause of the disease in the two types is quite different.

Juvenile diabetes (type 1 diabetes, insulin-dependent diabetes)
People who lack the insulin necessary to take the glucose into the cells have juvenile diabetes, and if the insulin is not supplied, they become steadily weaker because their muscles and other organs cannot work properly. There may be very high levels of glucose in their bloodstream, but because it cannot enter the cells, it cannot help them. These diabetics therefore require regular supplements of insulin to keep them well.

The biggest problem with insulin is that it cannot be taken by mouth as it is destroyed by acid in the stomach. It must be given by injection once, twice or more times a day. This way insulin enters the bloodstream directly and can start transporting the necessary glucose into the cells immediately. Most people who develop diabetes which requires insulin injections do so as a child or in early adult life. They must use the injections for the rest of their lives, as there is no cure for diabetes, only an effective form of control.

Insulin can be injected into any part of the body covered by loose skin. The same site should not be used repeatedly. Commonly used sites are the abdomen, thighs, buttocks and upper arm.

When first diagnosed, patients with juvenile diabetes are often quite ill, and most are hospitalised for a few days to stabilise their condition with frequent injections of insulin.

Insulin from pigs and cattle has been available for many decades, but in the last few years, human insulin has been produced by genetic engineering techniques to enable diabetics to lead relatively normal lives. Human insulin will replace the animal form completely in the near future, as allergy reactions to the animal products do occur in some diabetics.

The newer pen-style delivery systems enable diabetics to easily dial the required dose and inject themselves as necessary with minimal inconvenience. Insulin pumps are another method of introducing insulin. These are small machines that hook onto the belt, and through a fine tube that is inserted into a vein pump small amounts of insulin almost constantly into the blood. These are used mainly in diabetics who are very difficult to control with regular injections.

There are many different types of insulin that vary in their speed of onset and duration of action. Some have a rapid onset and last a short time, others start slowly and last a long time. All possible permutations of speed of onset and duration of action are available, and the doctor will choose whichever will best suit the individual patient.

Diet is essential for all diabetics, because the amount of glucose you eat is not normally constant, and diabetics lack the means of adjusting the amount of glucose in their blood with insulin. As the insulin injections remain at a constant strength, the glucose intake must also remain constant.

A diabetic diet must restrict the number of kilojoules (calories) being eaten. Sugar in all its forms should be eaten only with caution. Fat should not account for more than a third of the total calories, and cholesterol intake should be restricted. Protein should be obtained more from poultry and fish than red meats. Carbohydrates other than sugar can be consumed freely. Grains and cereals with a high fibre content should be the main part of any diabetic diet. Artificial sweeteners such as aspartame (NutraSweet) can be used to flavour food and drinks. See also DIET, Section 7.

Fat cells can react abnormally to insulin very easily, and so overweight diabetics must lose weight and remain within certain strict limits.

Exercise should be encouraged in diabetics, but on a regular daily basis. Extra exercise will require a greater food intake, while less exercise may require more insulin. Variations between weekdays and weekends must be allowed for.

Once on treatment, diabetics must undertake regular self-testing to ensure that the control of their diabetes is adequate. Both blood and urine tests for glucose are available, but the blood tests are far superior. Most diabetics will test their own blood glucose using a tiny drop of blood that is placed on a sensitised stick. This is then placed in a small instrument called a glucometer which, by reading the colour change caused to the sensitised stick by the glucose in the blood, can give a relatively accurate reading of the blood glucose. These glucometers must be calibrated regularly by the patient, using standard solutions of glucose, to ensure that the readings remain accurate.

Blood tests can be performed by doctors to determine not only the level of glucose at that time, but by measuring the amount of glucose in certain blood cells, they can determine what the blood glucose level has been over a couple of months.

There are many complications of diabetes, including an increased risk of both bacterial and fungal skin and vaginal infections, the premature development of cataracts in the eye, microscopic haemorrhages and exudates that destroy the retina at the back of the eye, damage to the kidneys that prevents them from filtering blood effectively, poor circulation to the extremities (hands and feet) that may cause chronic ulcers and even gangrene to the feet, the development of brown skin spots on the shins, and sensory nerve damage that alters the patient's perception of vibration, pain and temperature.

There are also complications associated with treatment. The best known is a 'hypo' in which a diabetic has too much insulin, exercises more than usual or does not eat enough food, and his/her blood glucose level drops (hypoglycaemia) to an unacceptably low level. The patient becomes light-headed, sweats, develops a rapid heart beat and tremor, becomes hungry, then nauseated before finally collapsing unconscious. Glucose drinks or sweets given before collapse can reverse the process, but after collapse, an injection of glucose given by a doctor is essential. In an emergency, a sugary syrup or honey introduced through the anus into the rectum may allow a diabetic to recover sufficiently to take further sugar by mouth. Do not try to give an unconscious diabetic sugar by mouth, as they could choke or inhale the sugar.

Even if they are well controlled, diabetics should carry glucose sweets with them at all times to use in an emergency situation. All diabetics should wear a bracelet or charm that alerts doctors and other health workers to their condition and may allow life-giving treatment to be given in the event of a coma.

Other complications of insulin treatment include adverse reactions to pork or beef insulin, and damage to the fat under the skin if the same injection site is used too frequently.

Maturity onset diabetes (type 2 diabetes, non-insulin dependent diabetes)

Older people who develop diabetes can often have the disease controlled by diet alone or a combination of tablets and diet. This is because there is not a lack of insulin in these patients, but a lack of response by the cells to the insulin. The tablets make the cell membrane respond to insulin again. Commonly used tablets include tolbutamide, chlorpropamide, glibenclamide and glipizide (see HYPOGLYCAEMICS, Section 6).

The symptoms of the two types of diabetes are similar, but those with maturity onset diabetes have less thirst and urinary frequency, but more visual problems, skin infections and sensory nerve problems than those with the juvenile form. Many patients are totally without symptoms when the diagnosis is discovered on a routine blood or urine test.

Maturity onset diabetes is far more common in obese patients, and weight loss is a vital part of their treatment. If normal weight levels can be maintained, the disease may disappear. High blood pressure is more common in mature diabetics than the average person of their age.

Education of patients with this type of diabetes is very important, so that they understand what they can and cannot eat and drink. Regular testing of blood glucose levels is also necessary for the patients, but normally on a weekly rather than daily basis. Urine tests are often inaccurate in the elderly, as their kidney function may be reduced to the point where glucose cannot enter the urine. The elderly are very susceptible to the complications of diabetes listed above, particularly foot damage and eye damage.

With the correct treatment and careful control, patients with both types of diabetes should live a near-normal life, with a near-normal life span. A diabetic patient's motivation, intelligence and compliance with treatment will determine whether or not he or she develops any of the long-term complications associated with the disease or its treatment.

On diabetes in pregnancy, see PREGNANCY COMPLICATIONS, Section 1.

Diabetic ketoacidosis

This is the most severe way in which a patient with diabetes can present to a doctor. It is caused by a build-up of waste products and glucose in the bloodstream because of untreated or under-treated diabetes. Patients who are careless about their treatment, diet and self-testing may develop diabetic ketoacidosis. Almost invariably, it is the juvenile-type diabetics that develop this complication.

The patient is in a mental stupor, nauseated, vomiting, short of breath and may become comatose. If left untreated, death will occur due to kidney, heart or brain damage. Doctors can give injections of insulin when the condition is discovered, but emergency hospital treatment is necessary to control the situation adequately.

DIARRHOEA
See DYSENTERY; FOOD POISONING; GASTROENTERITIS, VIRAL.

See also Section 3.

DIGEORGE'S SYNDROME
See IMMUNODEFICIENCY.

DIPHTHERIA
Most young doctors have never seen a case

of diphtheria. Those who have seen one will agree that it isn't a pleasant sight. The incidence of this disease is now low, but older citizens may recall losing childhood friends to it. Diphtheria is still around though, and many children still catch the disease each year and suffer the difficulty in breathing and possible heart complications that can accompany it.

The infection is caused by a bacterium called *Corynebacterium diphtheriae* which attacks the throat and trachea (the tube leading to the lungs). It spreads from one person to another in the tiny droplets of water that are exhaled with every breath. The infection becomes apparent between two and seven days after inhaling the bacteria-containing droplets. The symptoms are a sore throat, fever, nasal discharge, hoarse voice and obvious illness, with overwhelming tiredness and muscle aches. A thick, grey, sticky discharge from the infected tissue forms a membrane across the throat that the patient is constantly fighting to clear. The throat is also very swollen and narrowed. The combination of these two factors makes it difficult for the patient to breathe, and in severe cases a tracheotomy must be performed to allow air into the lungs. This involves surgically inserting a tube through the front of the neck into the trachea. The patient becomes very ill very quickly, and most deaths occur within the first day of the disease. The infection may spread to the heart, nose, skin and nerves, to cause further complications.

Diagnosis of the disease can be confirmed by throat swabs, but treatment in the early stages is critical and must be commenced before the results are available. The heart involvement can be diagnosed by using an electrocardiograph (ECG). Treatment involves injecting the diphtheria antitoxin, which assists the body's natural defences in fighting the disease. Antibiotics are also prescribed, but as the worst complications of the disease are caused by a toxin that is produced by the bacteria, killing the bacteria will not cure the disease, as the toxin is still present in the body. Potent medications can be prescribed to control or prevent complications such as inflammation of the heart. The patient will appear to improve in a few days, but must be kept at rest for at least three weeks until all the toxin has been removed from the body.

Diphtheria can be totally prevented by a series of vaccinations as an infant. The triple antigen vaccine given to children at two, four, six and 18 months of age contains the diphtheria, tetanus and whooping cough vaccines. Boosters are given at five years of age, and every ten years thereafter, in combination with the tetanus vaccine.

The death rate in diphtheria varies between 10% and 30%, and for a disease that can be totally prevented by vaccination, it is obviously inexcusable for any parent to neglect the protection of their child and expose them to the high risk of this life threatening disease. Those that do survive may be affected for life by resultant damage to the heart or lungs.

DISLOCATION

A dislocation occurs when the surfaces of a joint that normally slide across each other are totally displaced, one from the other. If there is partial separation of the joint surfaces, the condition is called subluxation.

A dislocation can be a birth defect (e.g. congenital dislocation of the hips), due to a severe injury (almost any joint in the body), spontaneous for no apparent reason but caused by disease in a joint (e.g. the dislocation of a toe joint severely affected by arthritis), or recurrent, when after previous dislocation the joint dislocates very easily in the future (e.g. shoulder). A dislocation caused by injury may also be associated with a fracture, and anyone treating a dislocation must be aware of this possibility.

Inevitably, cartilages and ligaments, and possibly muscles and tendons around a dislocated joint will also be stretched, strained or torn by the dislocation. A dislocated joint will be painful, swollen and difficult or impossible to move. The skin over the dislocated joint will have different contours to the same joint on the other side of the body. An X-ray is the only definitive way to make the diagnosis.

A dislocation can be associated with complications, such as pinching a nerve or blood vessel, which may cause severe pain beyond the dislocation, and a poor blood supply that can result in tissue death and gangrene. Other complications involve the joint itself, and repeated dislocations can damage the smooth surfaces of the joint and lead to persistent pain after the dislocation has been reduced and to the premature development of arthritis.

A dislocation is treated by replacing the bones of the joint back into their correct position. Immediately after the injury, this can sometimes be done quite easily, even with major joints, as the damaged muscles around the joint will not yet have gone into a spasm. This spasm can later make the reduction of dislocations very difficult without an anaesthetic to relax the muscles.

Those giving first aid may attempt the reduction of a dislocation, but if not readily successful should not persist, as there may be a fracture or other complication present. In severe cases, a joint may need to be replaced in its correct position by an open operation. The hip is a common example of this. Severely damaged ligaments and cartilages around a joint may also need to be surgically repaired.

After the joint has been correctly replaced, little or no rest is required. A major joint may require one or two days of limited use, but prolonged rest of the joint can lead to the formation of scar tissue and a permanent limitation of movement. Movement of the joint through its maximum possible range, without putting it under any stress (e.g. avoid weights), is the best way of bringing a joint back to full recovery as quickly as possible. The exception to this rule is the situation when a fracture is also present. The fracture will require immobilisation to allow healing. Physiotherapy will then be required at a later date to fully mobilise the joint once the fracture has healed.

Joints that dislocate repeatedly (e.g. the shoulder) may require an operation to tighten the ligaments and muscles around the joint to prevent further dislocations.

The more common dislocations of the hip and shoulder are dealt with separately in this section.

See also SPRAINS, STRAINS AND DISLOCATIONS, Section 8.

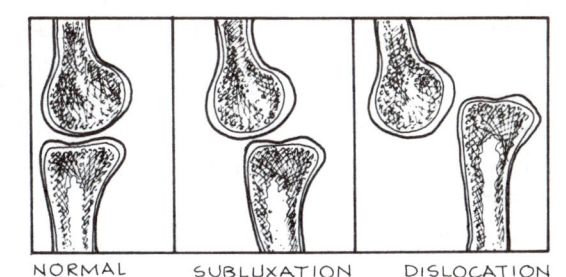

FIGURE 5.1: Demonstrating the difference between subluxation and dislocation of joint.

DIVERTICULITIS

Many of the more horrendous diseases of history are now almost unknown in our modern technological society, but some diseases have developed because of our high standard of living. One of these diseases is diverticulitis.

In more primitive times and countries, a large part of the human diet comprised unprocessed cereals, vegetables and fruit.

Today we eat far more meat, dairy products, sugars and processed cereals. The main difference is the amount of fibre in the diet. If fibre is lacking from your food, almost everything that you eat is absorbed, and there is little to pass on in your faeces. If there is no bulk in your motions, you tend towards constipation, and pressure can build up in the large bowel as the hard, dry food remnants are moved along towards the anus. This pressure increase in the last metre or so of the bowel, and can cause ballooning out of the bowel wall between the muscle bands that run along the length of the gut. With time, these outpocketings become permanent and form small diverticulae. It is easy for faecal particles to lodge semi-permanently in these small pockets, and then infection and inflammation occur to cause the disease known as diverticulitis. The '-itis' at the end of the word merely indicates inflammation or infection, as in 'appendicitis' or 'tonsillitis'.

Once the diverticulae are present, they usually become permanent, and periodic infections lead to the uncomfortable symptoms of this condition. Intermittent cramping pains in the lower abdomen, alternating constipation and diarrhoea, excess flatus, and excessively noisy bowels are the most common complaints. If the diet is changed once the disease is present, it will not lead to a cure, but it will prevent the formation of more diverticulae and therefore limit the severity of the disease.

The only certain ways to diagnose diverticular disease are by an X-ray of the large bowel (a barium enema), or by looking up the large bowel with an instrument known as a colonoscope. With these investigations, the small pockets can be seen poking out from inside the gut.

Acute attacks of diverticulitis are treated with antibiotics and medications that reduce gut spasm. These normally settle the situation fairly quickly, but sometimes the treatment must be continued for a long time to prevent recurrences. It is sometimes necessary to add specific fibre supplements to the diet, as well as faecal softeners to prevent constipation. Sometimes, in severe cases, surgery may be necessary to remove the affected sections of bowel, particularly if the bowel starts to bleed from chronic irritation or if an abscess forms.

It is always wise to check the symptoms of irregular bowel habits and abdominal pain with a doctor, so that any serious cause can be detected and treated at an early stage.

DOWN SYNDROME (TRISOMY 21)

Down syndrome, previously known as Down's syndrome (after the London physician who first described it), is a congenital condition that occurs at the moment of conception due to the presence of three copies of chromosome 21 instead of two (one from each parent). Thus the alternate name for this syndrome is trisomy 21.

Over 120 features have been described and there is considerable variation between individuals. The most common characteristics include poor muscle tone, joints that move further than normal, slanted eyes, a flattened facial appearance (accounting for the former name of "mongolism"), small stature, some measure of intellectual disability, small nose and a short broad hand. Other characteristics that may be present include a fissured protruding tongue, short neck, widely spaced first and second toes, dry skin, sparse hair, small genitals, small ears, poorly formed teeth, and a squint. Sometimes there are more severe health problems such as abnormal heart formation, abnormal formation of the intestines (especially the duodenum), a clouded lens in the eye and infertility. There is also evidence of a higher than normal incidence of leukemia.

Close examination of the hands of people with Down syndrome reveals finger prints that have a whorl with the loop on the thumb side of the finger tip and other characteristic features. The condition can usually be easily recognised and diagnosed at birth.

Down syndrome occurs at a rate of one in every 600 births overall, but rises to a rate of one in every 100 for mothers over 40 years of age.

Diagnosis of the condition before the birth of the child is possible from the fifteenth week of pregnancy by a process known as amniocentesis or chorionic biopsy (see Section 4).

Provided there are no serious heart abnormalities, the life expectancy of people with Down syndrome is relatively normal and most people have quite good health. Additional health check-ups for babies and young children are recommended to ensure satisfactory development. Also more than average medical attention for ear, nose and throat infections is often necessary. It is a good idea for children with Down syndrome to have regular hearing and sight checks with a specialist to ensure there are no problems to hinder language development. An early establishment of a balanced diet and exercise routine will help to overcome any tendency to become overweight.

Although there is no cure, in recent years a variety of educational techniques, physiotherapy and other methods have been shown to be effective in helping Down syndrome people achieve a higher potential than once thought possible. Many complete near normal schooling, find employment and are able to live independently, while others will require lifelong care. Of particular importance is early intervention.

Drug addiction (illicit drugs)

In some sections of the community, addiction to illicit drugs is a major problem, and it is responsible for a significant proportion of the crimes committed in Australia. Robbery, fraud and prostitution to finance the cost of prohibited and addictive drugs is a serious social problem. Police forces estimate that they spend more than one third of their time on drug- or drug-related offences. Possibly one in every 100 people is dependent upon illicit drugs, and a far higher percentage has experimented with them at one time or another.

There are hundreds of substances that can be used to obtain artificial sensations of happiness, forgetfulness, relaxation, or exaggerated experiences. These have varied results, side effects, levels of addiction, medical problems and social consequences. Some, such as LSD, are synthesised in the laboratory, glue can be purchased from any grocery and sniffed, and some mushrooms can be picked straight from the field and eaten to create the desired effect.

The treatment of drug addiction is swinging away from prosecution and persecution of drug abusers to studying and hopefully removing the factors that cause drug-taking to start. Unemployment, divorce and broken families, poverty, overcrowding and loss of community spirit all may have roles to play in the increase in drug addiction that occurred in the 1960s. Treatment of drug addiction varies dramatically from place to place, doctor to doctor, and drug to drug. The treatment options available are:

- Gradual withdrawal from a drug by a tiny decrease in the daily intake of the drug over a prolonged period while receiving regular counselling and medical support as a hospital patient or at home.
- Immediate drug withdrawal ('cold turkey') while hospitalised in a specialised unit, sometimes combined with other

drugs that are used temporarily to reduce the symptoms associated with the drug withdrawal.
- Substitution of the prohibited drug (e.g. heroin) with a prescribed medication (e.g. methadone) on a medium- to long-term basis.
- Half-way houses and rehabilitation units that remove the patient from the environment in which drug taking is encouraged.
- Individual or group psychotherapy as an adjunct to any of the above regimes.
- Education of intravenous drug users of the dangers associated with their habit (e.g. the development of AIDS or hepatitis B).

A representative sample of addictive illicit drugs will be discussed further.

Cocaine

Cocaine is a stimulant that is used in medicine as a local anaesthetic and constrictor of blood vessels. It is manufactured from the leaves of the coca plant (not to be confused with the cacao plant from which chocolate is obtained) which is native to South America. The drug is available illegally as a white, crystalline powder, which is usually diluted with sugars such as lactose and glucose to less than 50% purity. 'Crack' is a concentrated form of cocaine. Cocaine use is growing rapidly, particularly in the United States, where it is described as a 'recreational' drug. Users tend to be depressed and have a poor self-image and ego.

Cocaine can be administered by sniffing it into the nostrils (most common), injection into a vein, or smoking. Its effect is only brief, and it causes mood enhancement, increased energy and generalised stimulation of all senses. With continued use, the duration of the pleasant effects becomes shorter and shorter, requiring further doses every 15 to 30 minutes to maintain the desired effect.

Adverse effects of the drug include a high fever (which may cause brain damage and death), high blood pressure (which may cause strokes), reduction of the desire to breath (which may stop breathing completely and cause death), irregular heart beats (which may cause a heart attack), delusions, paranoia, hallucinations, insomnia and convulsions (which may lead to loss of consciousness and unintentional self-injury).

Heroin

Heroin is refined from the milky juice of the opium poppy, which is grown legally for medical purposes in Australia in northern Tasmania. Most illegal supplies reaching this country originate in south-east Asia, particularly northern Thailand and Burma. Heroin is one of the most addictive substances known. Codeine, pethidine, morphine and oxycodone are all derived from heroin and can be abused if taken regularly or excessively. These substances are collectively called **narcotics**. Codeine and oxycodone are found in low doses in many readily available pain-killers and cough mixtures. Codeine in higher doses, along with pethidine and morphine, are used by doctors as tablets or injections to relieve severe pain after operations, in cancer patients, and in other similar situations.

Heroin causes exaggerated happiness, relief of pain, a feeling of unreality, and a sensation of bodily detachment. It is normally administered by addicts to themselves as an injection directly into the veins. As sterile techniques are often not followed, the veins and skin at the injection site become infected and scarred. Heroin and other narcotics may also be inhaled or eaten, but they have a much slower effect than if injected.

Most abusers of heroin have personality disorders, antisocial behaviour, or are placed in situations of extreme stress. One quarter of heroin addicts will die within ten years of commencing the habit as a direct result of the heroin use. A rising proportion will die from complications of the intravenous injections such as AIDS, septicaemia and hepatitis B. Heroin abuse is often combined with abuse of alcohol, smoking and synthetic drugs. Physiological problems associated with narcotic addiction include vomiting, constipation, brain damage (personality changes, paranoia), nerve damage (persistent pins and needles or numbness), infertility, impotence, stunting of growth in children, difficulty in breathing (to the point of stopping breathing if given in high doses) and low blood pressure.

Withdrawal causes vomiting, diarrhoea, coughing, twitching, fever, crying, excessive sweating, generalised muscle pain, rapid breathing and an intense desire for the drug. These symptoms can commence within 8 to 12 hours of the last dose, and peaks at 48 to 72 hours after withdrawal. Mild symptoms may persist for up to six months.

Marijuana (marihuana, cannabis, 'pot', 'hash')

'It's no worse than alcohol.'

This is the main defence heard from marijuana users. Considering the social and medical problems associated with the two most readily available addictive drugs (alcohol and nicotine), this is not a good argument.

Marijuana is made from the hemp plant, *Cannabis sativa*. Pot, cannabis, hash, dagga, ganja, bhang or marijuana — no matter what it is called, it still comes down to the same active ingredient, a chemical called tetrahydrocannabinol (abbreviated to THC for obvious reasons). THC occurs in all parts of the cannabis plant and is a depressant drug, not a stimulant as many people think.

Marijuana can be taken into the body in two main ways — by smoking or eating. The plant leaves can be dried and smoked like a cigarette, or can be cooked into biscuits or soup. More dangerous is the habit of using the concentrated resin from the plant — hashish. It is stronger than marijuana and produces a more noticeable effect, causing excessive happiness, followed by a long period of depression and drowsiness.

Like other sensual drugs, cannabis used daily for a few weeks eventually ceases to have its original effect, and the user must increase the dose to reach the same level of intoxication. This is how addiction develops, and is proved by the withdrawal symptoms experienced when a regular user ceases the drug. Most drugs dissolve in water, but THC dissolves in the body's fat, and so stores of the drug can be established in the system. This leads to a prolonged withdrawal stage, and the frightening flash-backs that regular users experience when a sudden release of the drug from the body's fat stores occurs. These flash-backs can occur without warning for weeks after the last use of marijuana, and may cause hallucinations while working or driving and can therefore place others at risk.

Cannabis cannot be considered a harmless drug. The willingness to use it by many young people comes from the false belief that it will not cause damage. However, there is evidence that long-term use or dependence on cannabis can cause problems such as increased risk of bronchitis, lung cancer and other respiratory diseases associated with smoking; decreased concentration, memory and learning abilities; interference with sex hormone production; and cannabis psychosis, which is a condition with symptoms similar to schizophrenia.

Cannabis is often also used in combination with other drugs, and this can intensify its effects, often in unpredictable ways. Using cannabis and alcohol together

— a common combination — can be much more dangerous than using either drug by itself.

See also ALCOHOLISM.

LSD

LSD (lysergic acid diethylamide) is a synthetic psychedelic drug that was first developed in 1947. Its use peaked in the late 1960s, and it is no longer in favour amongst the underground cult of drug abusers.

LSD is taken by mouth in pill form. It causes a rapid heart rate, high blood pressure, dilation of pupils, tremor, terror, panic and high fever within a few minutes of being swallowed. Addicts seek the hallucinations, illusions and happy mood that also occur. The actions last for 12 to 18 hours after swallowing the tablet. Long-term effects include psychoses, personality changes, schizophrenia, deterioration in intelligence, poor memory and inability to think in abstract terms. Tolerance to LSD develops rapidly, and higher and higher doses must be taken to obtain the same effect. Death as a direct effect of LSD is rare, and there are no significant effects after withdrawal of the drug.

DUCTUS ARTERIOSUS
See PATENT DUCTUS ARTERIOSUS.

DUODENAL ULCER
See ULCER, PEPTIC.

DUPUYTREN'S CONTRACTURE OF HAND

Across the palm of the hand, under the skin, stretches a fibrous sheet (the palmar aponeurosis) that acts to give the palm its smooth appearance, strength and firmness, and to protect and control the movement of the muscle tendons that cross the palm under it. If you look at the back of your hand with the fingers straight, you can easily see the tendons standing out under the skin. On the palm side of the hand, this does not occur because of the presence of the fibrous sheet of the palmar aponeurosis.

In some people, the palmar aponeurosis becomes damaged and scarred, and contracts and thickens into hard lumps that can be felt under the skin. As the condition progresses, the contraction of the fibrous sheet can pull on the tendons that run underneath it to prevent their free movement. The fingers cannot be fully extended, and gradually contract into a claw-like appearance. This condition is called Dupuytren's contracture, and is named after Baron Guillaume Dupuytren, a Parisian surgeon, who first described the condition nearly 200 years ago.

The cause of Dupuytren's contractures is unknown, but it may be caused by a poor blood supply to the hand, by the use of vibrating tools (e.g. jack hammers), injury to the hand from repeated blows (e.g. catching cricket balls), and there is a tendency for the condition to occur in successive generations. The ring and little fingers are usually more severely affected than the others, and men are affected more than twice as often as women — possibly because women don't normally use jack hammers.

The first sign of the disease is a hard, fixed nodule under the skin of the palm. Treatment is not usually undertaken until the patient experiences discomfort or loss of finger mobility. The only effective treatment is an operation to carefully cut away the thickened part of the palmar aponeurosis and free the tendons. A slow recurrence after operation, which may require further surgery, is quite common.

In rare cases, a similar condition can occur in the sole of the foot.

DVT (DEEP VENOUS THROMBOSIS)
See THROMBOSIS.

DYSENTERY, BACTERIAL (SHIGELLOSIS)
A number of different bacteria from a group known as *Shigella* can infect the gut and cause severe intermittent abdominal pain, copious diarrhoea with blood and mucus mixed in with the faeces, and a high fever. This is bacillary (bacterial) dysentery or shigellosis. It is a relatively common disease in third-world countries and the poorer areas of some relatively developed countries. It is now uncommon in Australia. It is caused by poor sanitary conditions, and spreads from one person to another when the bacteria in the faeces is able to enter the food and mouth of a second person. In children under three years of age and the elderly, the disease can be dangerous to the point of causing life-threatening diarrhoea. In older children and adults, the disease can be readily treated, or it may persist for several weeks without adequate treatment.

The disease is diagnosed by examining a sample of faeces for the presence of the infecting bacteria. Once this has been identified, the appropriate antibiotic can be prescribed to destroy it. Other treatments required include adequate fluid intake, by an intravenous drip in severe cases, and a strict diet to avoid foods that may irritate the gut (e.g. milk products, eggs and fatty foods). Medications to relieve the severe abdominal cramps may also be prescribed.

It is important to be very careful in the disposal of the faeces and soiled linen to prevent others in the home or hospital from becoming infected.

See also CHOLERA; GASTROENTERITIS, VIRAL; TYPHOID FEVER.

DYSIDROSIS
See POMPHOLYX.

DYSMENORRHOEA
See MENSTRUAL PERIOD PROBLEMS, Section 3.

EAR DISEASE
See FURUNCULOSIS, EAR; MASTOIDITIS; MÉNIÈRE'S DISEASE; OTITIS EXTERNA; OTITIS MEDIA.

EAR WAX
See Section 3.

ECHINOCOCCOSIS
See HYDATID CYST.

ECLAMPSIA
See PREGNANCY COMPLICATIONS, Section 1.

ECTOPIC PREGNANCY
See PREGNANCY COMPLICATIONS, Section 1.

ECZEMA
The term eczema describes a large range of skin diseases that cause itching and burning of the skin. It typically appears as red, swollen skin that is initially covered with small fluid-filled blisters that later break down to a scale or crust. The many different forms of eczema also have innumerable causes, both from within the body (e.g. stress) and outside (e.g. allergies, chemicals). The appearance of an eczema depends more on its position on the body, duration, severity and degree of scratching than the actual cause. The specific diagnosis of the type of eczema is therefore quite difficult.

A representative sample of the more common forms of eczema will be described further.

Allergic eczema
Many substances have the ability to cause an allergic reaction in an individual. They are called allergens. Some people are far more sensitive to allergens than others. There are some strong chemicals to which nearly everyone will react, whereas other substances are relatively inert, and very few people react to them.

In most cases, the first exposure of a patient to a substance causes no reaction, but this initial contact commences the sensitisation of the patient to that substance. Subsequent exposure, be it hours, days or years later, can then cause an allergic reaction, sometimes to a substance that has been handled without any problem in the past. Drugs are sometimes responsible for these reactions, particularly if present in creams. Chemicals, metals, elements, plants, preservatives, rubber, cement, etc., may all cause allergic eczema. A comprehensive list of all substances that can cause allergy reactions would double the size of this book.

The reaction to a substance is increased if the patient is hot and sweaty, as the substance is held on the skin in the sweat. Other situations that aggravate allergic eczema occur if the substance is caught in clothing, or is present at a point of skin flexion (e.g. in the groin, under breasts, armpit). The older the patient, the more severe the reaction. Allergic eczema is therefore relatively uncommon in the young, and very common in the elderly.

The sites of the eczema rash on the body correspond to the points where the allergen has been present on the skin. This may give a clue to the nature of the substance, but it is often very difficult to identify.

Once certain substances are suspected, the reaction to them can be confirmed by 'patch testing', where a patch of the substance is applied to the skin, and the reaction of the underlying skin is noted. If it is possible, the condition can be controlled by avoiding the substance, but pollens and dusts may be impossible to avoid.

Treatment involves the use of steroid creams to weeping areas, steroid ointments (see Section 6) to dry and scaling areas. If the reaction is very severe, steroids may need to be given by tablet or injection. Most patients respond well to treatment for a particular attack, but the rash may recur on subsequent exposure to the allergen. Unavoidable exposure to an allergen can cause a persistent rash that is difficult to treat.

Atopic eczema
Atopic eczema occurs almost exclusively in children and young adults, and the vast majority are under five years of age. Up to a third of the population are potentially atopic, but only 5% of children will develop this skin disease.

Atopy is the tendency to develop a sudden, excessive sensitivity to a wide range of substances. It is a reaction similar to allergy, but not the same, as no previous exposure to the substance is required, and there must be a genetic predisposition to atopy present.

Atopic eczema may be triggered by changes in climate or diet, stress or fibres in clothing. In the majority of cases, the substance causing the atopic reaction cannot be identified. The rash occurs in areas where the skin folds in upon itself (e.g. groin, arm pits, inside elbows, neck and eyelids). It is more common in winter and urban areas (possibly due to pollutants such as vehicle exhausts), has a peak incidence between 6 and 12 months of age, and may cause lymph nodes in the neck, groin and armpit to become enlarged and tender.

The rash is extremely itchy, and invariably any blisters that form are rapidly destroyed by scratching. The scratching changes the normal appearance of the eczema, so that it appears as red, scaly, grazed skin that may be weeping because of a secondary bacterial infection that has entered the damaged skin. With time, and repeated irritation by scratching, the skin may become hard, thickened, and have the appearance of a large number of tiny pebbles under the skin.

Skin tests and blood tests can be performed to determine whether or not an individual has an atopic tendency, but as only 15% of these people will develop atopic eczema, they cannot prove that the rash is caused by this disease.

The high incidence in childhood, and the spontaneous settling of the rash with time, has led to a number of theories regarding atopy. It is possible that there is an hereditary lack of a specific type of immunoglobulin (immune system protein) or white blood cell in childhood that corrects itself as the child matures. This does not affect their health in any other way.

Treatment involves the use of moisturising creams to soothe the inflamed and scratched skin, steroid creams to reduce the inflammation and itch, and soap substitutes to prevent drying of skin when bathing. Antibiotic creams may be required if there is an infection present. In severe cases, steroid tablets may be required to control the rash, and antihistamines (see Section 6) to control the itch.

Steroid creams may be needed repeatedly over many months or years to keep the condition under control, but the vast majority grow out of the condition in later childhood or the early teen years. There is no specific cure, but effective control can be obtained in the majority of cases.

Discoid eczema (nummular eczema)
Discoid eczema effects mainly young adults, and both sexes. It appears as discs or 'coins' of scaling, red, thickened skin on the back of the forearms and elbows, back of the hands, front of the legs and the tops of the feet. The affected areas can vary in size from a few millimetres to three centimetres or more. The cause is unknown. Diagnosis can be confirmed by a biopsy (cutting out a piece) of the edge of one affected skin patch. It is frequently confused with fungal infections.

Discoid eczema is treated with steroid creams, which cause rapid healing of the rash. Antihistamines (see Section 6) are occasionally necessary for the itch. Unfortunately, there is a tendency for recurrences, and repeated treatments may be required for each attack. After a period of many months, or a couple of years, the attacks cease.

Hypostatic eczema
See *varicose eczema* (below).

Irritant eczema (housewives dermatitis)
Irritant eczema is due to the skin being exposed to irritating substances such as caustics, acids, detergents, bleaches, oils, soaps, solvents, washing powders and a host of other chemicals. The hands are obviously the part of the body most likely to be exposed, and the majority of cases of irritant eczema occur on the hands. Because of the likelihood of detergents and soaps causing the problem, this condition has also been named housewives dermatitis. However, in babies, drooling saliva, and faeces and urine in nappies may cause the eczema. It can occur at any age, in both sexes, and at any site on the body. The affected skin becomes dry, cracked, red, swollen and in severe cases, painful and ulcerated.

Treatment involves removal of the irritant substance if possible. Cotton-lined gloves should be used for household chores. Soap should be avoided, substituted with moisturising creams. In the workplace, a change in work practices, or even a new job may be necessary to stop the eczema from recurring. Barrier creams and protective clothing can also be useful.

Removal of the irritant results in a cure. Unfortunately, this is not always practical, and steroid creams can be prescribed in various strengths and forms to control acute attacks and prevent recurrences.

Photosensitive eczema

This uncommon type of eczema affects the areas of skin that are exposed to light, usually in middle-aged and elderly men. The rash is red and covered with scales and is intensely itchy. The face, forearms and hands are the most common areas affected. It is caused by a reaction in the skin to ultraviolet wavelengths in sunlight. In rare cases, it can become so severe that the patient cannot go outside during the day. Fluorescent lights also give off ultraviolet radiation and can cause this reaction.

Treatment involves use of long-sleeved shirts, hats and UV sun screen creams to reduce exposure to sunlight, and very strong steroid creams to settle the rash. Occasionally steroid tablets (see Section 6) are also required.

Once established, the condition persists for life. It may force some patients to reverse their lifestyle — sleeping during the day and being active at night — in order to avoid the sun.

Seborrhoeic eczema

Seborrhoeic eczema is a widespread, common eczema that can occur at any age. It results from inflammation of the sebaceous glands in the skin, which are responsible for producing the oil that lubricates and moistens the skin, but the basic cause of this inflammation is unknown.

In infants, seborrhoeic eczema frequently affects the scalp to cause 'cradle cap' or the buttocks to cause 'nappy eczema'. Other frequently affected areas are the cheeks, neck, armpits, groin and folds behind the knees and elbows and under the breasts. In adults, it is responsible for some forms of dandruff. On the scalp, it appears as a red, scaly, greasy rash. In skin folds, the skin is red, moist and breaking down into tiny ulcers. On exposed areas such as the face, the rash is red, scaling and may contain tiny blisters. There is often a secondary fungal infection present in seborrhoeic eczema, and this must be treated as well as the rash.

The scalp is treated with a lotion or cream to remove the oil and scale from the skin, and regular shampooing. Tar solutions can be applied in resistant cases. In other areas, mild steroid lotions or creams are used. Soap substitutes should be used.

Seborrhoeic eczema tends to be chronic and recurrent. Children often grow out of it in the early teens, but in adults it may persist for years with good and bad periods that occur for no apparent reason.

Varicose eczema (hypostatic eczema)

More women than men have varicose eczema, and it is far more common in the elderly. It affects the inside of the shin, just above the ankle, in patients with and without varicose veins, though it is more common if varicose veins are present. The skin is itchy, red, shiny, swollen, dry and covered with scales. It is easily injured by even slight bumps, and very slow to heal. Varicose eczema is caused by a poor return of blood through the veins from the feet to the heart. Blood pools in the feet, and causes pressure on the skin, which reacts to give this type of eczema. Ulcers are a common complication, as are bacterial skin infections, and allergy reactions. These must be treated separately from the varicose eczema.

Treatment involves elevating the leg as much as possible, using support stockings or pressure bandages, and raising the foot of the bed slightly. If varicose veins are present, it may be appropriate to remove them surgically. Mild steroid creams and coal tar solutions are used on the eczema. The condition is usually chronic, and the results of treatment poor. Controlling the rash and preventing ulcers and other complications are the aims of treatment.

See also DERMATITIS; LICHEN SIMPLEX; POMPHOLYX.

EJACULATION PROBLEMS
See SEXUAL PROBLEMS.

ELEPHANTIASIS (FILARIASIS)

Filariasis is a disease of the tropical parts of Asia, Africa and America. It cannot be caught in Australia, but in rare cases travellers or migrants from those areas develop the disease. It is caused by a microscopic animal (filarial nematodes of several different species) that is injected into the bloodstream of the victim by an infected mosquito. It results in inflammation of the lymph glands and fever. After repeated attacks, the lymph channels of the lymphatic system (see Section 2) that carry waste products away from the arms and legs become blocked because of the damage caused to them by the infecting animal. When wastes and fluid cannot escape from the legs, arms and scrotum, they blow up to a huge size over a period of months to give the characteristic appearance of elephantiasis.

The disease is diagnosed by seeing the infecting animal in a drop of blood under a microscope.

Treatment involves elevation of the affected limb, medication to kill the filarial organism, and surgery to remove the swollen tissue.

Residents of areas that are affected by this disease should be careful to avoid mosquito bites by using insect repellents and nets over their beds. Medication can be taken constantly to prevent the disease but may have side effects in some people. It is not normal for travellers passing through these areas to take any extraordinary precautions.

EMBOLISM, LUNG (PULMONARY EMBOLISM, LUNG CLOT)

Blood is extraordinary in that it remains a liquid while in the body, and flows smoothly through the arteries and veins, but if exposed to air, it rapidly clots into a hard lump. An embolism occurs when a blood clot or other substance capable of blocking a blood vessel is transported by the blood to a smaller vessel which it then obstructs. Blood clots often occur in the veins of the calf at the back of the leg (see THROMBOSIS), but may also arise in many other parts of the body. From there, they move along through larger and larger veins to the right side of the heart, which pumps the blood and clot into the lung. In the lung, the clot blocks an artery, cutting off the blood supply to the segment of lung beyond that point. The section of lung involved will collapse and die, and form an area of fibrosed scar tissue. This part of the lung can no longer function. Some clots are so tiny and have so little effect upon the lung that the patient never knows that they have occurred. If the area of lung involved is large, this damage can lead rapidly to death. This occurs in about 10% of all diagnosed lung clots. More commonly, only a small area of lung is involved, but the clot acts on the blood flowing by it to slowly increase in size. This extending clot can cut off more and more arteries, and gradually destroy a larger and larger area of lung. The aim of medical treatment is to prevent this enlargement of the clot.

Lung clots are common after operations, in patients who are bedridden for long periods, and in the elderly. The patient develops chest pain, shortness of breath,

Section 5: Diseases

coughing of blood and may faint. The heart rate increases, and a fever develops within an hour or so. The condition is diagnosed by an X-ray that may show the collapsed segment of lung, by blood tests that show signs of clotting within the body, and by an electrocardiogram (see Section 4) that shows strain on the heart. Specialised tests of lung function are sometimes necessary to determine the position and extent of damage. An X-ray in which dye is injected into the veins and can be seen moving through the arteries in the lung is the best available test in cases of doubt. This test is not routine.

Treatment must be as rapid as possible to prevent further extension of the clot. Anticoagulants are drugs that prevent blood clotting (see Section 6). These are given initially as an injection, and later as tablets, to ensure that no further clots form. As a side effect, they also prevent clots from forming when you cut or bruise yourself. The dosage must be very finely tuned to prevent abnormal clots from forming, while at the same time preventing excessive bleeding in other areas. Regular blood tests are performed throughout treatment with anticoagulants to fine-tune the dosage required. The anticoagulant therapy is continued for three to six months after the attack. In patients who are at high risk, it may be continued for life.

The other treatment available is the destruction of the blood clot that is blocking the artery in the vein. This can be done by injecting drugs known as thrombolytics. These are normally only used in patients with very large clots and significant lung damage. In rare circumstances, surgery to remove the clot from the lungs or leg is undertaken, or a filter is inserted surgically into the main vein of the body leading from the legs to the heart, to filter out any blood clots that may form in the future.

The prevention of blood clots in the legs is important to prevent pulmonary emboli. This can be done by using pressure stockings during long operations and in high-risk patients. Early mobilisation after surgery, physiotherapy to keep leg muscles active, and elevation of the legs to drain out blood in bed-bound patients all help prevent clots.

The vast majority of patients who survive the first hour after a lung clot will go on to lead normal lives, provided appropriate treatment is given quickly. After a large amount of lung damage, the increased back pressure of blood on the heart may lead to the development of a condition called cor pulmonale (see separate entry).

Emphysema

All of us have been short of breath at some time — most commonly after strenuous exercise or during a bout of coughing. You gasp for air, and wonder where the next breath is coming from, but then the problem slowly passes. But try and imagine the way you would feel if the shortness of breath did not go away. Imagine constantly gasping for breath — even while resting in front of the television — even while trying to sleep! This is the way patients with emphysema feel. Emphysema is an incurable disease that is frequently caused by smoking or exposure to other noxious gases. Recurrent attacks of bronchitis or pneumonia may also be responsible for it.

The lung is made from millions of tiny bubbles (called alveoli), rather like the foam that detergent makes while you are washing the dishes. These tiny bubbles are all interconnected by fine tubes that join together into successively larger tubes (called bronchi) to eventually form the windpipe (trachea). Air enters and leaves the lungs through the tubes, and essential oxygen is absorbed into the bloodstream through the walls of the tiny bubbles. With constant exposure to noxious gases, or repeated lung infections, these bubbles start to break down into larger cavities. If you watch detergent foam in the sink, this too will gradually merge into fewer larger bubbles in much the same way as a lung affected by emphysema. These larger cavities have less surface area to absorb oxygen, and there is a great deal of scar tissue also affecting their function. Oxygen is essential for the function of the body, and when it is lacking, signals are sent to make you breathe faster and deeper. With emphysema, these signals go unanswered because the lungs are already working to their full capacity.

Emphysema is most common in the elderly, and in addition to their constant shortness of breath, sufferers have a constant cough, a barrel shaped chest and excessive sputum. Because of their constant exertion to breathe, they are wasted and emaciated. This worsens as the disease progresses.

The disease is diagnosed by X-rays, and by breathing into machines (e.g. spirometers, peak flow meters) that can analyse the lung function. There may be changes found in blood tests and electrocardiograms (ECG) indicating chronic oxygen starvation. Once diagnosed, it is essential to avoid any further deterioration as the damage is permanent.

Treatment is aimed at trying to control the situation. It involves physiotherapy to make the damaged lung work as effectively as possible, drugs by tablet or spray to open up the lungs to their maximum capacity, and antibiotics to treat infection at the earliest possible stage. In severe cases, steroids by inhalation or tablet, are given to reduce any inflammation in the lungs, and as a last resort oxygen may be given to make more effective what breathing can be managed. Oxygen can be provided by cylinders of compressed gas or, more efficiently in chronic cases, by a machine that concentrates oxygen from the atmosphere.

Complications of emphysema include recurrent attacks of bronchitis and pneumonia, heart failure and pneumothorax. It is these complications that eventually cause death in emphysemic patients. Vaccination against influenza with annual flu shots, and the use of Broncostat to prevent bronchitis may prevent a fatal illness.

The best form of treatment is prevention. Emphysema is a terrible and distressing disease, and if you smoke you have a reasonable chance of developing it.

ENCEPHALITIS

Encephalitis is an infection of the brain. It is often confused with meningitis (see separate entry), which is an inflammation of the membranes that surround the brain. There are several different types of encephalitis, but all have much the same symptoms. These include headache, intolerance of bright lights, fever, stiff neck, lethargy, nausea, vomiting, sore throat, tremors, convulsions, stiffness and paralysis. This can progress to coma, and sometimes to death. The disease can occur at any age, but is more common in children and the elderly.

The diagnosis is confirmed by taking a small sample of the fluid around the brain and spinal cord (the cerebrospinal fluid) through a needle that is placed into the spine, just above the pelvis. This fluid is analysed under a microscope and cultured to determine the presence of any germs. Blood tests can also be useful in giving an indication to the cause of the encephalitis.

Complications include pneumonia, and if the infection is prolonged, mental deterioration and epilepsy.

Treatment in most cases is not available. The patient is supported in hospital, and medications are given to control the symptoms and complications. The disease may last for a few days or several weeks, and the final outcome may not be apparent for months after apparent recovery. Most cases of death occur in very young children or the frail elderly.

Toxic (bacterial) encephalitis
Toxic encephalitis is uncommon and occurs when a bacterium, or the toxin produced by a bacterium (e.g. *Shigella*), attacks the brain. Antibiotics may be useful in this situation.

Viral encephalitis
Viral encephalitis is the most common form of encephalitis. There are many different types of viruses that can cause infections in the brain, one of the most serious being caused by *Herpes simplex*. This infection may be caught by a baby during birth when the mother has a genital herpes infection. A new antiviral drug called acyclovir may be useful with herpes encephalitis.

Other viruses that can cause encephalitis include those responsible for mumps, measles, polio and rabies.

Murray Valley encephalitis
Murray Valley encephalitis is the Australian version of encephalitis caused by a group of viruses that are spread by mosquito bites from one victim to another. It tends to occur in epidemics every few years, and often follows flooding, when mosquito populations increase dramatically. The reservoir of the virus occurs in water fowl, and it is transmitted from them to humans by the mosquito. It has a higher mortality rate than other forms of encephalitis.

In the Americas, similar viruses cause California encephalitis, eastern and western equine encephalitis (which also effects horses, and rats act as a source of the virus), St Louis encephalitis (for which domestic hens are the source) and Venezuelan encephalitis. Russian summer encephalitis, western Nile encephalitis and Japanese B encephalitis (found in monkeys and throughout eastern Asia) are mosquito-borne forms of encephalitis in other parts of the world. A vaccine is now available against Japanese B encephalitis, but not the other types.

See also REYE'S SYNDROME.

ENDOCARDITIS
Endocarditis is an infection that occurs inside the heart. It can develop slowly over many weeks or months in an already damaged heart (the more common form), or cause sudden illness in a previously healthy individual.

The heart valves control the flow of blood into and out of the heart. These may be malformed from birth, damaged by disease (e.g. rheumatic fever), distorted by cholesterol deposits, or scarred by heart attacks. An artificial heart valve may be inserted operatively into the heart to replace a damaged valve. Some babies are born with holes in the heart of varying severity that may or may not require surgical repair. In all these circumstances, it is possible for a bacterial infection to develop on and around the damaged part of the heart to cause endocarditis.

The symptoms of endocarditis can be many and varied, and some patients, particularly the elderly, may have almost no sign of the disease at all. Most patients have a fever, and other complaints include night sweats, fatigue, tiredness, palpitations, rapid heart rate, loss of appetite, chills, joint pains, muscle pains, weight loss, swollen joints, paralysis, headache, chest pain, nose bleeds and a host of other minor problems.

The disease is not entirely limited to the heart. The infection causes clumps of bacteria to grow like moss inside the heart. Doctors refer to these growths as 'vegetation', and pieces of this very delicate growth can break off and travel through the arteries to cause severe problems elsewhere in the body. If these clumps of bacteria enter the brain, they can block an artery and cause a stroke. In other organs they may cause blindness, kidney failure, joint damage and bowel problems. Almost any part of the body may be affected. The endocarditis may not be detected until another organ becomes seriously affected by the spread of the disease and the patient becomes acutely ill with lung, kidney or heart failure.

The disease is diagnosed by taking blood and culturing it in the laboratory in order to detect any bacteria. Other blood tests may also indicate the presence of disease.

As with all diseases, prevention is far better than cure, and patients who have had rheumatic fever or any other heart disease should tell doctors and dentists about it so that measures can be taken to prevent endocarditis.

During any operation, including dental ones, some bacteria are released into the blood stream. Patients with damaged hearts are vulnerable to these bacteria, which may settle on the damaged area, and cause endocarditis. A course of penicillin, given before and during the operation or dental procedure, will destroy the bacteria and prevent endocarditis.

Once the disease is diagnosed, urgent hospital treatment is essential. Large doses of antibiotics, often penicillin or one of its derivatives, are given by injection. These may need to be continued for several weeks. Other treatment may include correction of any anaemia, and controlling the damage done to other organs by using the appropriate medications.

Only 60% of patients with endocarditis recover completely, and this may take months of intensive treatment. Another 30% survive, but with significant restrictions on their lifestyle caused by damage to the heart or other organs. In approximately 10% of cases, death occurs. If the disease is left untreated, death is inevitable.

Complications such as heart attack and stroke can occur years after the disease appears to have been cured.

In the rare cases where a fungus rather than a bacterium causes the endocarditis, the outcome is far worse. This type of infection occurs most commonly in intravenous drug abusers, and the majority die within a few weeks. Major heart surgery is often required in survivors.

See also MYOCARDITIS.

ENDOMETRIOSIS

The uterus (womb) is lined with special endometrial cells that during the second half of a woman's monthly cycle are prepared to accept any fertilised egg and allow it to grow into a baby. If no pregnancy occurs, these cells degenerate, break away from the inside of the uterus, and with the resultant bleeding are carried out of the body in the woman's period.

From the top of the uterus, a Fallopian tube leads out to each of the two ovaries. In a small number of unlucky women, the cells that normally go out during a period, may go into and through these Fallopian tubes. The cells are then in an abnormal position around the ovary on the outside of the uterus, or in the pelvic cavity, and they can attach to these tissues and start growing and spreading further. These are normal endometrial cells, and in no way are they cancerous or malignant, but because of their position in the body, they will cause considerable trouble to the patient. They will still respond to the woman's hormonal cycle every month, as these hormones pass through the blood stream to every cell in the body. As a result, these cells in abnormal positions, will bleed with every period, releasing blood in places where it can cause pain and other symptoms. The cells may also block the Fallopian tubes to cause infertility, irritate the bladder, or settle on the outside of the intestine to cause cramps and diarrhoea.

A doctor will often suspect the diagnosis of endometriosis after hearing of a woman's symptoms and examining her internally. The condition can only be definitely diagnosed by examining a woman's pelvis by means of an operation or a laparoscopy. X-rays and blood tests are not particularly useful.

Laparoscopy requires a general anaesthetic in most cases, and involves a small tube being put through the navel into the abdomen. Through this a doctor can see the spots of endometriosis in its abnormal positions. If the spots are easily accessible, a second tube may be put through the front of the abdomen, low down on one side. This can be used to pass a probe which will burn away the worst of the abnormal endometrial tissue. Other patients may require an open operation to remove large amounts of abnormal tissue. As a last resort, a hysterectomy may be performed.

Medical treatment is also available, but surgery is usually required as well in severe cases. For many years, hormones have been used to completely stop a woman's periods for 6 to 12 months. Many of the abnormally placed endometrial cells will die off during this time, curing the disease. In the last few years, an extremely expensive drug called Danocrine has been used to treat endometriosis with great success. Again this must be used for many months, and some patients develop uncomfortable side effects whilst using it.

Women with endometriosis can suffer terribly every month, and sometimes have pain through the month as well. If they are also infertile because of the disease, they will tolerate almost any treatment in order to be rid of this unusual but very distressing condition.

ENTERITIS
See CROHN'S DISEASE; GASTROENTERITIS, VIRAL.

ENTEROBIASIS
See PINWORM.

ENTEROCOLITIS, NECROTISING
See NECROTISING ENTEROCOLITIS.

ENURESIS
See BED-WETTING.

EPICONDYLITIS
See TENNIS ELBOW.

EPIDEMIC POLYARTHRITIS
See ROSS RIVER FEVER.

EPIDERMOLYSIS BULLOSA
Epidermolysis bullosa is a rare, inherited skin disease in which the slightest injury to the skin causes the development of large, firm blisters. In infants, the blisters develop on knees and hands as the child starts to crawl, but later they may develop anywhere.

There are several subtypes of epidermolysis bullosa that vary in severity from an inconvenience to life-threatening. In severe forms, the blisters may occur from birth and re-occur throughout life. On healing, they leave a scar that causes significant disfigurement. In the worst forms, the fingers may become bound together by scar tissue, the mouth and throat may be involved, and cancer may develop in the affected tissue. The nails and teeth may also be damaged.

There is no cure. Steroids (see Section 6) are the only treatment available, but they are not particularly effective. Avoiding any injury to the skin is imperative.

Epididymo-orchitis

The testis hangs in the male scrotum, and the sperm it produces pass out of the testis into a dense network of fine tubes that forms a lump on one side of the testis called the epididymis. These fine tubes eventually join up to form the sperm tube (vas deferens) that takes the sperm to the penis.

In Greek, the word 'orchis' refers to the testes. The suffix '-itis' means inflammation or infection, as in 'appendicitis' and 'tonsillitis'. The rather tongue-twisting and complex term epididymo-orchitis therefore refers to an infection of the epididymis and testis. Orchitis is an infection of the testis alone, but because of the close connection of the epididymis to the testis, the infection almost invariably is present in both places.

Men with a bacterial epididymo-orchitis have a painful, swollen testicle, and an associated fever. They are acutely uncomfortable, and usually seek treatment early.

A painful testicle can also be caused by torsion of the testis (see separate entry). This is an acute emergency that requires immediate surgical treatment. Any boy or man, particularly in the teenage years or early twenties, who develops a painful testicle, must see a doctor at once — day or night.

If the cause of the testicular pain is confirmed to be due to an infection, it is treated with the appropriate antibiotics. Aspirin or paracetamol is used for pain relief, and a supportive bandage or jockstrap should be worn. Ice applied to the scrotum may give some additional relief from the pain. Occasionally an abscess will form, and needs to be surgically drained. With the correct treatment, the bacterial epididymo-orchitis resolves in a couple of days, and usually does not cause any problems with fertility or masculinity. If the infection is caused by a virus, as in mumps orchitis, there is no effective treatment other than time and rest. In some cases, this can cause problems with fertility in later life.

Epiglottitis

This uncommon disease is an acute medical emergency that requires urgent hospitalisation. It can occur at any age, but is most common in children under five years of age.

The epiglottis is a piece of cartilage that sticks up at the back of the tongue. It can be seen in people who can open their mouths very wide, if a stick is used to push their tongue down against the floor of the mouth. Its job is to stop food from entering the wind pipe (trachea) when we swallow. If this structure becomes infected by bacteria, it can swell up rapidly and cause a very sore throat, fever and obvious illness. If the epiglottis swells excessively, or is disturbed by trying to eat solids or by the tongue depressing stick of a doctor examining the mouth, it can cover the wind pipe completely and rapidly cause death through suffocation. This complication is far more likely in young children than older ones. For this reason, if a doctor suspects epiglottitis, he or she will give the throat only a cursory examination before arranging the immediate transfer of the child to hospital. If the airway is obstructed in hospital, an emergency tracheotomy (an operation to make a hole into the wind pipe through the front of the neck) can be performed to allow the child to breathe. Some hospitals routinely anaesthetise such children, and put a tube through the mouth or nose and down the throat to prevent the airway from blocking, rather than operating after any blockage has occurred.

The diagnosis can be confirmed by a side-on X-ray of the neck that will show the swollen epiglottis. Throat swabs are carefully taken to identify the infecting bacteria. Sometimes blood tests are also performed to detect the bacteria in the bloodstream and to measure the cells in the blood to enable the severity of the infection to be estimated.

Further treatment involves antibiotics to cure the infection and paracetamol to reduce fever and pain. The infection usually settles in a few days, and any tubes that have been inserted can then be removed. Provided there has been no airway obstruction, the outcome is excellent.

Epilepsy

Epilepsy is defined as any condition causing recurrent seizures (fits). People with epilepsy are not subnormal, not retarded, not violent, not abnormal in any way — except for the fact that they have a disease which can affect their bodies in a most unpleasant and unpredictable way. It is unusual for epileptics to have a fit in public these days, as most sufferers can be very well controlled by some of the many forms of medication available.

Some people are born with epilepsy, while others acquire the disease later in life after a brain infection, tumour or injury. Brain degeneration in the elderly can also cause epilepsy to develop. An excess or lack of certain chemicals in the body may also cause epilepsy. If the kidney fails, waste products can build up in the blood to the point where fits occur. Removing alcohol from an alcoholic or heroin from an addict may also result in epilepsy.

Epilepsy can affect people in many different ways, and can vary from very mild absences in which people just seem to loose concentration for a few seconds, to uncontrolled bizarre movements of an arm or leg, to the grand mal convulsion in which an epileptic can thrash around quite violently.

It is a disease which can affect anyone, and once stricken, most people are ashamed of the affliction — it is not as socially acceptable as high blood pressure or diabetes. But in epilepsy the treatment is much the same in that tablets are taken regularly throughout life, and these normally prevent most of the attacks.

Epilepsy can be explained most easily by an analogy to a computer that develops a short circuit. Parts of the brain are able to short- circuit after very minor and localised damage. This can stimulate another part of the brain, and then another, causing the responses that we see.

After the first convulsion the patient is naturally extremely anxious to find out why it is happening and to prevent a recurrence. Several tests are performed, including an electroencephalogram (see Section 4) to measure the brain waves and find out exactly where the short circuit exists, and hopefully what is causing it. Other investigations will include blood tests and a CT scan (see Section 4) of the brain. Unless there is some underlying disease to explain the epilepsy, blood test results are normal.

Once diagnosed, treatment can be prescribed and regular blood tests ensure that it is adequate to control the disease. Medication to prevent further fits is the mainstay of the treatment. There are many different anti-epileptic drugs (see ANTICONVULSANTS, Section 6) and the drug or combination of drugs used to control the condition will depend on the type of epilepsy present, the individual patient's reaction to that medication, and the side effects of the medication. These drugs are given as tablets or mixtures several times a day.

Medication must be continued for a long time, but after several years without fits, a trial without medication may be undertaken. Those who are mentally subnormal in association with epilepsy are less likely to be removed successfully from medication. Injections can be given by doctors to control an acute attack once it occurs, but there are no long-acting injections to prevent the fits.

Epileptic attacks can be triggered by outside factors in some patients. Flickering lights (e.g. poorly adjusted televisions) can start some fits, while others may be precipitated by certain foods, emotional upsets, infections or stress. If an epileptic knows that exercise, alcohol, lack of sleep or other factors can trigger an attack, these must obviously be avoided.

Many, but not all, patients with epilepsy develop warnings that an attack will occur in the next few minutes or even hours. These warnings can be a particular type of headache, change in mood, tingling, lightheadedness or twitching. An aura is an extension of these feelings that is far more intense and precedes the attack by only a few seconds.

Epileptics must not put themselves in a position where they can injure themselves or others. They must never swim unsupervised, drive a car, or operate machinery until they have been free of fits for at least two years.

Convulsions in children due to a high fever are not true epilepsy and do not lead to epilepsy in later life. They are caused by a temporary short circuit in the brain when it is overheated.

Epilepsy is arbitrarily classified by the types of seizures that occur, but as there is a steady progression between one type and another and several different types of seizure may occur in the one person at different times, the groupings that follow cannot be exact or exclusive.

Grand mal epilepsy
Grand mal is the massive fit which most people associate with epilepsy. The patient becomes rigid, falls to the ground and stops breathing. The muscles in different parts of the body become alternately rigid and slack, causing gross abnormal movements and twitching of the arms, legs and trunk. The patient may urinate, pass faeces and become blue.

The fits usually only last two or three minutes, but because of the violence of the attack, the victims must be protected from injuring themselves. It is possible for them to bite or 'swallow' their tongue, but attendants must *NOT* place their own hand in the mouth to protect the victim's tongue — they will only end up with badly bitten fingers. A piece of rubber or wood may be placed between the teeth, but do not attempt to prise the teeth apart to insert it. Merely placing the patient in the coma position (see UNCONSCIOUSNESS, Section 8) and keeping the chin forward and neck extended will prevent the tongue from being bitten or from blocking the airway.

Epileptics who have grand mal fits have no knowledge of what happens during the attack. They may have a brief warning aura, but then they lose consciousness and wake up some time after the fit has finished, not knowing if they have been unconscious for a few seconds or an hour. After recovering from the fit, the patient is confused, drowsy, disoriented and may have a severe headache, nausea and muscle aches.

Status epilepticus
Status epilepticus is the condition where one grand mal attack follows another without the patient regaining consciousness between attacks. Urgent medical attention is required for these patients.

Section 5: Diseases

Petit mal (absences, drop attacks)

Petit mal attacks are periods of unconsciousness that may last from one or two seconds to a minute or more. There may be some unusual movements associated with them but nothing as violent as in a grand mal attack. The patient may appear totally normal during the attack, may stumble momentarily, or drop to the ground and rapidly recover. The attacks come without warning, and may appear merely as an unusual break of several seconds in a sentence while speaking. Patients are often unaware that they have had an attack.

Petit mal epilepsy is far more common in children and teenagers than adults.

Partial seizures (temporal lobe epilepsy)

Epilepsy may be restricted to only one part of the brain, usually the temporal lobe of the brain on one side. The seizures can vary greatly in their severity, and in some cases the patient remains conscious while one arm and/or leg contracts and relaxes, thrashing about outside the conscious control of the patient. The fit can vary from minor twitches of the fingers or eyelid, to apparent grand mal fits, but involving only one side of the body. In other cases they may present as difficulty in talking or swallowing, as an unexplained loss of memory, or an abnormal shift of mood and emotion (e.g. a sudden unexplained fear or terror, or ecstasy). At other times, partial seizures may be unnoticed by others but felt as abnormal sensations (e.g. tingling, burning) by the patient. Other manifestations include flashes of light, strange smells, buzzing noises, sweats, flushes and hallucinations.

Deja vu

Deja vu is a feeling of intense familiarity when confronted with someone, something, or a place that is actually totally unfamiliar to the individual. This happens occasionally in normal people but is more commonly associated with some types of epilepsy or psychiatric disorders. *Deja vu* means 'already seen' in French.

Further assistance and information can be obtained from the epilepsy associations that operate in all major cities.

See also NARCOLEPSY.

ERB'S MUSCULAR DYSTROPHY (LIMB GIRDLE DYSTROPHY)

Erb's muscular dystrophy is a rare type of gradually progressive muscle-wasting that affects the muscles around the shoulder and pelvis. It progresses at a variable rate from its onset to cause severe disability in mid-life. It may start at any age from late childhood to the late twenties, but most commence in the mid-teen years.

The severity of the disease varies significantly between patients, some being only moderately inconvenienced while others may be severely disabled and unable to care for themselves. There is a tendency for the disease to occur in the one family in successive generations. No treatment is available other than physiotherapy and occupational therapy.

ERB'S PALSY

Wilhelm Erb was a nineteenth century neurologist from Heidelberg in Germany. He was the first to describe a type of paralysis that involved the muscles around the shoulder and elbow. Patient's with Erb's palsy are unable to move the upper arm away from the body, fully bend the elbow, or turn the hand so that the palm faces backwards when the arm is beside the body. The muscles involved in this paralysis are the biceps, deltoid, brachialis and brachioradialis, and they run from the shoulder through the upper arm and finish just beyond the elbow. The biceps is the muscle at the front of the upper arm that is traditionally flexed by muscle men to demonstrate their strength.

Erb's palsy is rare today, as it is caused by pulling too hard upon the head during the difficult delivery of a baby. During this procedure, the nerves running from the neck across the top of the shoulder to the muscles mentioned are stretched and torn, so that no messages can pass from the brain to the muscles. Although the muscles are not damaged, without a nerve supply, they cannot function. The arm hangs limply by the side, and if treatment is unsuccessful, it appears withered and wasted as the child grows older.

Treatment involves splinting the shoulder in a position that allows the nerves to grow back and recover. This may take as long as six months, but most show some improvement within a month. More than nine out of ten cases recover with adequate treatment.

ERYSIPELAS

Erysipelas is a bacterial infection of the layer of fat that occurs just under the skin. The area most commonly involved is the cheek, but any area of the body may be affected. The skin becomes swollen, red, painful and hot. The patient is also feverish, may have shivering, and feels very ill. The infection starts as a red spot that slowly enlarges over several days. It may start at the site of a scratch, crack or bite, but often there is no apparent cause. Fluid-filled blisters may develop on the infected area of skin.

Erysipelas may be confused with cellulitis (see separate entry) which is an infection of the skin itself, rather than the tissue immediately under the skin. The treatment for both is the same, and involves giving antibiotic tablets or liquids by mouth, or by injection in severe cases, to control the infection.

Erysipelas used to be a very serious disease and often killed children 50 years ago before effective antibiotics were available. Today, recovery is rapid once the antibiotics are started, and the infected skin heals without scarring.

ERYTHEMA MULTIFORME

Erythema multiforme is an acute inflammation (redness) of the skin, which may be triggered by drugs, bacterial or viral infections, cold sores and other herpes infections, or it may appear for no apparent reason. 75% of cases occur after a herpes or cold sore infection, and half of the remainder are caused by drugs — particularly sulpha antibiotics. The attacks that are caused by cold sores and other infections tend to be mild, but those that occur as a result of drug sensitivity can be very severe.

Patients with erythema multiforme suddenly develop several types of rash simultaneously. This gives the disease its name, which can be loosely translated as 'red spots of many shapes'. The easiest rash to identify appears as red, sore rings on the skin with a pale centre. They may be any size from a few millimetres to 2 or 3 cm in diameter. They may be even circles or quite distorted in outline. There may be only a few of these spots, or several dozen. Other forms of the rash include red patches, swollen lumps, fluid-filled blisters, itchy red stripes, and painful hard dome-shaped bumps. Almost any imaginable skin problem can occur. The insides of the mouth and the vagina, and also the eyes, may be involved. General soreness of the moist membranes and eye surface occur, with ulcers developing in some cases. In the worst cases, ulceration, pain and swelling can extend down the throat and into the lungs to give a form of bronchitis.

The rash may occur anywhere on the body, but is most common on the front of the leg, over the shoulders, and above and below the elbow on the outside of the arm. The soles and palms are other areas that are commonly attacked. In most cases, the rash is evenly distributed on both sides of the body. Most patients have only a mild fever, but severely affected victims may be acutely ill with a very high fever and generalised weakness.

The diagnosis must be made by the doctor on the appearance of the patient, as there are no blood tests or other investigations that can confirm the presence of erythema multiforme. If a drug is suspected as the cause, it must be immediately ceased. If an infection is thought responsible, this is treated appropriately.

There is no cure for this condition, but the vast majority of cases are mild and settle in two to four weeks. Severe cases may persist for up to six weeks, and in rare cases, with lung involvement in the elderly or chronically ill, death may occur. These more serious cases are described as the Stevens-Johnson syndrome (see separate entry). Recurrent attacks are quite common.

Treatment is aimed at minimising the symptoms and discomfort with painkillers such as paracetamol and aspirin, and with creams, lotions and dressings to ease the irritation of the rash. Steroids (see Section 6) may be prescribed in severe cases.

Erythema nodosum

Erythema nodosum can be translated as 'red lumps', and the disease is characterised by the development of very tender, painful red lumps that develop on the front of the leg, usually below the knees. Other areas that are affected less commonly include the arms, face and chest. The lumps persist for about six weeks before slowly disappearing. Patients also have a fever, joint pains and general tiredness.

The full cause of this disease is unknown, but it often appears to be a reaction to certain types of bacterial infection, drugs (e.g. penicillin) or more serious underlying diseases (e.g. leukaemia, tuberculosis, syphilis, hepatitis B or ulcerative colitis). As a result, all patients with this condition need to be thoroughly investigated to find any otherwise hidden disease.

The diagnosis can be confirmed by cutting out one of the sore lumps and examining it under a microscope. Other tests are done to determine the cause of the erythema nodosum. If a cause can be found, this is treated (e.g. infections) or removed (e.g. drugs). There is no specific treatment available, but steroids (see Section 6) may ease the symptoms, and painkillers may be prescribed. There are no serious after-effects of the disease, but recurrences are quite common.

Ewing's tumour
See BONE TUMOUR.

Exposure
See HYPOTHERMIA.

Eye disease
See BLEPHARITIS; CATARACTS; CONJUNCTIVITIS; EYE, FOREIGN BODIES IN; EYE ULCERS; FLASH BURNS TO EYE; FLOATERS IN EYE; GLAUCOMA; IRITIS; MEIBOMIAN CYST INFECTIONS; RETINAL DETACHMENT; STY; TRACHOMA.

Eye, foreign bodies in
Grass, dust, hair, metal, pins, glass, staples, chalk, dirt — every imaginable substance and object has at some time been found in a human eye. Patients are immediately aware of the presence of an eye injury, and in most cases the discomfort persists until the object is removed. Everyone who feels they have a foreign body in

their eye should see a doctor, and have the vision in the affected eye tested.

Foreign bodies in the eye fall into three different categories — those that are floating freely on the surface of the eye, those that are imbedded into the cornea (eye surface), and those that have penetrated through the cornea into the interior of the eye. The treatment of these three types is very different.

Objects that penetrate into the eye may be obvious (e.g. a pin sticking out of the eye) or hidden (e.g. a metal fragment that flies into the eye when hammering may be hidden deep in the eyeball, or air gun pellets). Under no circumstances should a person giving first aid attempt to remove a foreign body that is penetrating an eye. Both eyes should be carefully bandaged (movement in the good eye causes movement in the damaged eye) and the patient should be taken quickly to a doctor. Do not transport these patients by air unless the flight can occur at a constantly low altitude, as even a small drop in air pressure may cause the contents of the eyeball to extrude through the wound.

Any doctor may be able to carefully remove an object that is sticking out through an eyeball, but if an ophthalmologist (eye specialist) is available, his/her assistance should be sought. Objects deep inside the eye can only be removed by intricate surgery in special units attached to major hospitals. Very powerful magnets are sometimes used to draw out pieces of metal. X-rays can be used to show metal and some glass particles inside the eye, but wood splinters and many other substances may not show on X-ray.

Some small particles of inert metals or glass that penetrate the eye are better left alone, as their removal may cause more damage than leaving the object inside the eye.

Penetrating wounds can cause infection inside the eye, and many patients are left with some sight defect after even the most careful repair. Major damage may result in the removal of the eye.

Objects that are embedded in the surface of the eye can be seen as spots on the eye. Sometimes the spot can be very difficult to see if it is over the pupil or matches the colour of the iris around the pupil. Doctors use special lenses to examine the eye to find even the smallest particles. Once the object is found, anaesthetic eye drops are put into the eye, and the object can be delicately removed by the tip of a needle or similar instrument. The eye will need to be covered until the anaesthetic wears off, and antibiotic ointment or drops may be prescribed to prevent any infection.

A scratch to the eye may feel like a foreign body, and scratches can be seen by a doctor after a special dye is placed in the eye. These scratches usually heal, often with the help of antibiotic ointment or drops, in a day or two.

Objects that are free on the surface of the eye may not be easily seen, as they can be caught under the upper or lower lids. Washing the eye out with copious amounts of water under a trickling tap or in an eye bath, may remove sand, grass, dirt, grit and hairs that are caught in the eye, but sometimes it is necessary to turn up the upper lid to find the offending particle.

If an object cannot be easily removed by washing or the gentle application of a cotton bud to the undersurface of an eyelid, seek medical assistance. Persisting may cause eye damage.

See also CONJUNCTIVITIS.

EYE ULCERS (CORNEAL ULCERS)

The cornea is the transparent outside covering on the front of the eye. If this becomes scarred and opaque, blindness results. Ulcers on the cornea, particularly if they are long-lasting or recurrent, can cause such a scar to form. All corneal ulcers cause pain in the eye, and watering. Generalised redness of the whites of the eye, and the discharge of sticky pus may also occur.

There are many different causes for ulcers on the surface of the eye. They are simply divided into injuries and infections. Ulcers caused by an injury (e.g. scratch) usually heal within a few days without treatment, although antiseptic drops are a wise precaution to prevent any infection developing. Dozens of different viruses, fungi and bacteria can cause infections on the surface of the eye and, subsequently, eye ulcers.

Bacterial infections can be readily treated with the appropriate antibiotic ointment or drops to cure the infection. Occasionally, antibiotic tablets are also required. Provided the infection is treated early and does not recur, no ulcers or scars should develop. Unfortunately, in many third-world countries and amongst our Aborigines, treatment is not sought, not available or not followed, and the infection persists to cause ulceration and permanent damage.

Fungal infections causing ulcers are seen most commonly in farm workers, but may develop in others when steroid eye drops are being used to treat other eye conditions. Appropriate eye drops can be prescribed to cure the infection.

Virus eye infections are common, but occasionally viral eye infections can cause serious eye ulceration. Herpes simplex, the virus that causes cold sores and genital herpes, is the most common cause of all eye ulcers. Most cases settle without treatment after a few weeks of discomfort, but in some patients, particularly those who are otherwise in poor health or on potent drugs for other serious diseases, the infection can steadily worsen to cause severe eye ulceration. These ulcers are irregularly shaped and branching in appearance, and are called 'dendritic ulcers'. Herpes zoster, which causes chickenpox and shingles, can also infect the eye and cause serious ulcers that are likely to leave a scar.

Serious viral eye infections can be treated with special anti-viral eye drops and ointment, and through a microscope, minor surgery to remove the active viral areas at the edge of the ulcer may be undertaken.

Two rare causes of eye ulceration are a deficiency in vitamin A (e.g. in people on fad diets, or with inability to absorb vitamin A because of diseases of the bile duct) which results in a very dry eye, and prolonged exposure of the eye in unconscious patients who do not blink.

The outcome of any eye ulcer will depend upon the severity of the infection and the response to treatment. If necessary, a scarred cornea can be surgically replaced by a corneal transplant.

See also CONJUNCTIVITIS.

FACTOR VIII DEFICIT
See HAEMOPHILIA.

FACTOR IX DEFICIT
See CHRISTMAS DISEASE.

FALLOT'S TETRALOGY
See HEART VALVE DISEASE.

FEAR, ABNORMAL
See PHOBIA.

FEBRILE CONVULSIONS
A child under the age of three years, and usually over six months, who has a high fever, may suddenly have a fit (convulsion). These fits are more likely if the rise in the child's temperature has been rapid. Up to 5% of all children have a febrile

convulsion at some time. These are usually only brief single episodes, but some children may convulse many times with every minor fever over a year or two. Febrile convulsions are more common in males and tend to run in families, so if the parents suffered from febrile convulsions in their childhood, their children are more likely to do the same.

The fever can be caused by a bacterial or viral infection, and it does not have to be a severe disease. A common cold may be sufficient to cause an attack. The convulsions almost invariably occur within the first 24 hours of the onset of fever, and usually in the first six hours.

A parent faced with a fitting, feverish child should immediately immerse the child in a bath of tepid water, ensuring that the head is kept well out of the water. The head can be sponged with cool water. An alternative is to wrap the child in a wet towel. The child should be protected from injuring itself while the fit continues. Once the fit ceases (most only last a few seconds, or a minute or two), seek medical attention to treat the cause of the fever. A prolonged fit, or recurrent fits, will require an injection by a doctor to stop them. It may be necessary, particularly if there have been several fits, to investigate the child further to exclude epilepsy. Febrile convulsions do NOT increase the risk of epilepsy in later life. On the other hand, febrile convulsions are more common in children with epilepsy and in those who have had brain damage at birth or who are already mentally retarded.

Paracetamol is the only useful medication in children to keep their fever under control. Regular sponging with cool water and having a fan on in the child's room are also very useful.

More than one third of children who have one febrile convulsion will have further convulsions with subsequent fevers. They should be given paracetamol and kept physically cool at the first sign of any fever. If these measures are inadequate, doctors will prescribe anticonvulsant drugs (see Section 6) to be taken regularly for a couple of years to prevent any further fits.

See also EPILEPSY.

See also CONVULSIONS, Section 3; FITS/CONVULSIONS, Section 8.

FELTY'S SYNDROME

The spleen, along with the bone marrow, is responsible for making many of the cells that circulate in the bloodstream. It also acts to destroy and remove old blood cells. It sits under the ribs on the left side, just below the heart (see Section 2). Patients with Felty's syndrome have a grossly enlarged spleen and a low level of both red and white blood cells in the bloodstream because the spleen is destroying them prematurely. It is usually associated with advanced rheumatoid arthritis. The people affected may have significant discomfort in their abdomen because of the enlarged spleen.

When the spleen becomes very big, it puts pressure on veins that pass through it. This pressure can extend back through the venous system and cause dilation of the veins that surround the upper part of the stomach at the point where the gullet (oesophagus) enters the stomach. These dilated veins can be attacked by the acid in the stomach, put under stress by vomiting, and damaged by food entering the stomach, so that they can become ulcerated and bleed. The patients then may become quite ill, very anaemic and vomit blood. If this bleeding is allowed to continue, it may become extremely serious, and occasionally patients die from losing blood out of their arteries and veins because it has leaked into their stomach. Other symptoms that may occur in Felty's syndrome are arthritis, a fever, leg ulcers, darkly pigmented skin patches, and tiny blood blisters under the skin. The diagnosis can be confirmed by blood tests that estimate the type and age of cells in the blood stream.

Treatment involves removal of the spleen by surgery, and medication to control the rheumatoid arthritis. The cells necessary for the blood continue to be produced by the bone marrow in the absence of the spleen. After removal of the spleen, patients react more slowly to invading germs, and they must ensure that they are treated early in the course of any bacterial or viral infection. Regular influenza and pneumococcal vaccinations are recommended.

FIBROCYSTIC DISEASE
See CYSTIC FIBROSIS.

FIBROIDS OF UTERUS
See UTERINE FIBROIDS.

FIBROSITIS
Aching, tender and stiff muscles in varying parts of the body are the characteristic symptoms of fibrositis. Other complaints include tiredness, insomnia, and even bladder irritability and passing urine frequently. Touching certain areas of muscle causes sudden, severe pain, while nearby areas are quite unaffected. Muscle strength and use is usually unaffected. The cause is unknown, but it is more common in women, particularly in middle age. It may be aggravated by disturbed or poor sleep. There are no specific tests that can be performed to confirm the diagnosis.

The disease may be temporary, recur regularly, or in rare cases last for many years. Heat, massage and exercise seem to help the affected muscles. Anti-inflammatory drugs (NSAIDs — see Section 6) will reduce the pain and tenderness, and medication to relax the patient and assist in sleeping may also be prescribed. Some patients are helped further by physiotherapy.

FILARIASIS
See ELEPHANTIASIS.

FITS
See EPILEPSY; FEBRILE CONVULSIONS.

See also CONVULSIONS, Section 3; FITS/CONVULSIONS, Section 8.

FLASH BURNS TO EYE
All welders are well aware of the risks involved in looking at a welding arc without protective eye wear, but even so, they sometimes take short cuts, or forget the rules of their trade and develop so-called flash burns to the eye. Other workers in an area where welding is being done, and even passers-by, who have no eye protection, may be affected. The eye is very painful, red and sometimes swollen. There is the equivalent of a superficial burn to the surface of the cornea (the clear outer part of the eye). The same damage can be caused by dropping a hot liquid into the eye. Severe or recurrent eye burns can cause scarring and blindness that can only be corrected by a corneal transplant.

The pain of a flash burn may not develop until 6 to 12 hours after exposure. Medical treatment is essential to relieve the pain, prevent infection, and ensure that the eye heals without scarring. Appropriate eye drops and pain-killing tablets will be prescribed by a doctor, and the eye will be covered by a patch until it has recovered. The only effective first-aid measure is a cold, wet compress applied to the eye.

Ultraviolet light may also cause a similar eye condition, and ultraviolet burns to the eye can occur if excessive use is made of ultraviolet lighting at discos, dances and other entertainment venues. Constant ultraviolet light should be used for no more than one third of the time in such venues, and for no more than five minutes at a time. It is better medically (but less aesthetically pleasing) to mix normal and ultraviolet light together with no more than one third of the total lighting wattage being ultraviolet.

Radiant energy (e.g. extremely intense light, or watching the sun) may also burn the eye. This type of burn does not damage the surface of the eye but the light sensitive cells at the back of the eye. Once these cells are destroyed by the concentrated light, they usually never recover, and a permanent black spot appears in the vision.

FLAT FOOT

Flat feet have traditionally been an excuse to avoid military service and the cause of a great deal of anxiety in parents. *Pes planus* (medical jargon for flat feet) is no longer considered to be a serious condition, and no treatment other than well fitting shoes is required.

A foot is considered to be flat when the arch on the inside of the foot is in continuous contact with the ground when the person is standing barefoot on a smooth hard surface. The foot may be slightly twisted outwards at the same time. A flat foot is an inherited or congenital disorder (present since birth). There is no specific or serious cause for the condition.

All newborn children are flat-footed, as the arch of the foot only starts to develop at about the age of two. If the flat foot is still present at 12 or 13 years of age, it will persist throughout life. The vast majority of patients with flat feet have absolutely no symptoms or discomfort. In later life, these people are more likely to develop arthritis in the foot and strain their feet more easily than the person with a normal foot arch. An adult who develops a flat foot after having a normal arch in earlier life is more likely to suffer symptoms. The cause is often obesity, when the foot must take far more weight than nature's design will allow. Other causes include severe foot arthritis, and occupations that requires prolonged standing on hard floors.

Children with flat feet require no treatment at all. Wedging of the shoes to tilt the foot outwards is occasionally used if the parents demand treatment. The commonest complications are an awkward gait and distorted shoes, but rarely any pain or discomfort. In some children it may cause knock-knees, but only gross deformities require surgery.

Adult flat foot can be helped by weight reduction, arch supports, foot exercises and physiotherapy. Appropriate additional treatment is given for any arthritis.

FLOATERS IN EYE

'I've got a spot in my eye that won't go away, and it's always there, no matter where I look.' This is the most common presenting complaint of a patient with a floater in the eye. The patient often further classifies the spot as a speck of soot, a tiny worm, a spider or cobweb. The spot continues to move across the vision after the moving eye comes to rest — thus the name floater for what is actually a collection of cells or protein in the half-set jelly-like substance that fills the eyeball. These abnormal clumps of cells in the centre of the eyeball cast a shadow on the light-sensitive retina at the back of the eye, and the brain perceives this shadow as an object in front of the eye. The floater can occur at any point in the field of vision, but the closer it is to the centre (i.e. when looking straight ahead), the more annoying it becomes. The cells can form in the centre of the eye because of bleeding into the eye, a detached retina, infection, or no apparent cause may be found. Diseases such as diabetes, leukaemia, high blood pressure, and a number of rarer conditions may cause bleeding into the eye. A detached retina can be repaired by laser therapy in the early stages, but, if left, may result in permanent blindness.

Because there may be a serious disease causing the problem, all patients with floaters must be appropriately investigated to exclude these problems. The condition is only treated if it is causing significant trouble, as most floaters dissipate with time. If treatment is necessary, a laser can be used by an eye specialist to destroy the floater (if it can be found) while using a powerful microscope to look inside the eye.

FLU
See INFLUENZA.

FOLLICULITIS
Hair grows out of a hair follicle, which slowly produces new hair substance and pushes it steadily out until it appears above the skin. The hair length will depend upon the strength and thickness of the hair (scalp hair is far stronger and thicker than pubic hair), and the rate of growth. Folliculitis is a bacterial infection of a hair follicle and tends to occur in areas where hairs can be easily irritated or damaged, such as the neck, upper lip and groin. It is a disease that (for obvious reasons) is far more common in men than women. It is a condition that is also more common in diabetics, in those with poor personal hygiene, and in those with oily skin.

In folliculitis, a pus-filled blister, sometimes still containing a hair, appears on the skin. It is surrounded by an area of red skin, and is sore, tender, and sometimes itchy.

Treatment involves antibiotic ointments or creams applied to the sores, and in severe cases, antibiotic tablets or capsules by mouth. Personal hygiene should be scrupulous. Untreated, an abscess or boil may form, which will need to be incised and drained. Once established, some patients find that the infection is extremely difficult to cure, and attacks may recur for several months or years. Long-term use of antibiotics and antiseptic soaps may be required.

FOOD POISONING
The term food poisoning is applied to any combination of vomiting, diarrhoea, nausea, fever and stomach cramps that the patient attributes to eating a certain food. Almost certainly, many attacks are not due to any toxin, infection or other substance in the food, but are caused by viral gut infections, stress and anxiety, exercise, excitement, drugs, allergies (e.g. to preservatives or colouring in food) or food intolerance. To be accurately called food poisoning, bacteria or a toxin produced by bacteria present in food must cause a reaction in an individual's gut. Many different types of bacteria are capable of causing food poisoning directly, or producing a toxic chemical that has the same effect. The diagnosis is most strongly suspected when a whole family or group of people is affected simultaneously.

The symptoms and the severity of the attack will depend upon the bacteria causing the poisoning, the amount eaten, and the age and general health of the victim. Most attacks of food poisoning occur abruptly, within eight hours (and often one or two hours) of eating the contaminated food, but some types may take up to 24 hours to give symptoms. The patient suddenly starts vomiting, and has explosive diarrhoea associated with intermittent stomach pain. Blood may be vomited or passed in the motions, but provided it is not excessive, no further treatment is required. Foods that are particularly likely to be infected are dairy products, fish, chicken or other meat that has been inadequately refrigerated, fried foods and meat dishes that have been reheated, and stale bread.

In most cases, no treatment is necessary other than a clear fluid diet. Most attacks settle within six to twelve hours, and go almost as quickly as they arrived. In the very young and elderly, dehydration may be a problem, and intravenous drips in hospital may be required in severe cases. Antibiotics to clear the gut of the infection are rarely necessary.

Botulism is an extremely severe form of food poisoning. Twelve to 36 hours after eating inadequately preserved food, the victim develops double vision, difficulty in swallowing and talking, a dry mouth, nausea and vomiting. The muscles become weak, and breathing becomes steadily more difficult. This can progress to death in up to 70% of patients unless adequate medical treatment in a major hospital is readily available.

Home-preserved fruits and vegetables, and very rarely commercially canned foods, are responsible for harbouring a bacterium called *Clostridium botulinum* which is capable of producing an extremely potent poison that attacks the nervous system. If this condition is suspected, the patient must be hospitalised immediately and put upon an artificial breathing machine (ventilator) to maintain lung function once the paralysis occurs. An antitoxin is also available for injection.

In the best circumstances, up to 25% of patients will still die from botulism poisoning. If they do survive, there are no after-effects at all. Fortunately, the incidence of botulism in Australia is now very low, as comparatively few people now preserve their own fruit and vegetables.

See also GASTROENTERITIS, VIRAL.

FOOT PROBLEMS
See BUNION; CLUB FOOT; FLAT FOOT; FUNGAL INFECTIONS — Tinea; GANGLION; METATARSALGIA; WARTS.
See also FOOT PAIN, Section 3.

FRACTURES
A break (or fracture — the terms are identical) of a bone can vary from mildly annoying to the very serious. The bones support the body and all its structures and any break disables that part of the body until healing is complete. Fractures can be caused by direct violence to a bone (e.g. a fall or a blow), or indirect violence such as twisting an ankle or wrist excessively.

Fractures can be diagnosed by an X-ray in most cases, but sometimes the fracture is obvious because of the deformity of the body part affected. X-rays must always be taken, even in the most obvious fractures, to determine exactly where the bone pieces are located. In rare cases, X-rays may not show a fracture, and a bone scan is performed.

After a fracture has been manipulated or operated upon, further X-rays are taken to confirm that the bones are in a satisfactory position. X-rays are sometimes taken at stages through the healing process, and after the plaster or screws are removed, to ensure that healing is complete. The more complex the fracture, the more X-rays will be required.

Types of fracture
Doctors divide fractures into several different types and categories:

Hair line fractures are the most minor of all. The bone is only just cracked, and the bone ends have not moved apart. These fractures are often quite difficult to detect on X-ray. The bones in the wrist are commonly involved, but because of the poor blood supply to these bones (particularly the scaphoid bone), healing may be slow or not occur at all, and part of the bone may actually die.

Another form of minor break is the **greenstick fracture** that a child may sustain. Because a child's bones are still slightly flexible, they do not snap in the same way as an adult's. A fall can bend the bone, but it breaks on only one side, before returning to its correct shape and position, just like trying to break a greenstick from a tree.

The next type in order of seriousness is an **avulsion fracture**. In this, a small piece of bone is torn from a major bone where a ligament or tendon is imbedded in it. This often occurs around the ankle when it is twisted. Sometimes it is necessary to sew the piece of bone back on in an operation, but most heal in plaster.

Normal or **simple fractures** of the long bones in the arm and leg can occur straight across the bone, in a spiral or obliquely. All these factors influence the healing time. The bone ends may be displaced sideways from each other, or may meet at an abnormal angle, or may even overlap. Manipulation of the bone ends under an anaesthetic is necessary in all these cases, as the bone ends must be in almost perfect alignment to allow for healing and satisfactory long term appearance and function. After manipulation, a plaster, or screws or wires inserted surgically, will be used to keep the bones in the correct position.

Impacted fractures occur when a bone is forcibly shortened, and one fragment of bone is pushed into the other. Minor degrees of impaction can be left alone and the fracture placed in plaster. Severe impaction may cause shortening of a limb, and an operation to fix the bones in their correct position is then necessary.

If a bone is broken in two places (a **comminuted fracture**), an operation to screw or wire the three pieces together will usually be needed. Operations of this type are necessary whenever it is difficult to keep the bone ends together.

The most serious fractures are those where one end of the broken bone protrudes through the skin (called a **compound fracture**). These are likely to become infected and great care must be taken in the care of the skin wound and the bone.

Flat bones such as the skull can have a **depressed fracture**, where part of the skull is pushed down into the brain. The depressed bone fragment must be surgically elevated into its correct position, and sometimes kept in position with wires. If the bone is badly damaged, a small metal plate may be inserted to replace part of the skull.

A **joint fracture**, where the line of the break enters a joint, can cause arthritis and stiffness after even the best treatment. Patients may be left with an irregular joint surface and inability to move the joint through its full range of movement. The elbow is particularly susceptible to limited movement after such a fracture. Long-term physiotherapy is required for the best possible result.

A **fracture and dislocation** may occur simultaneously, particularly around the shoulder, and these injuries are very difficult to treat. Long-term stiffness and poor joint function are common complications.

A **pathological fracture** occurs when a bone that is already weakened by disease, such as a cancer deposit in a bone, breaks with only a small amount of force. These fractures are very difficult to heal. Elderly women with osteoporosis may also fracture their bones (particularly the hip) very easily.

Common fractures
Some common types of fractures have

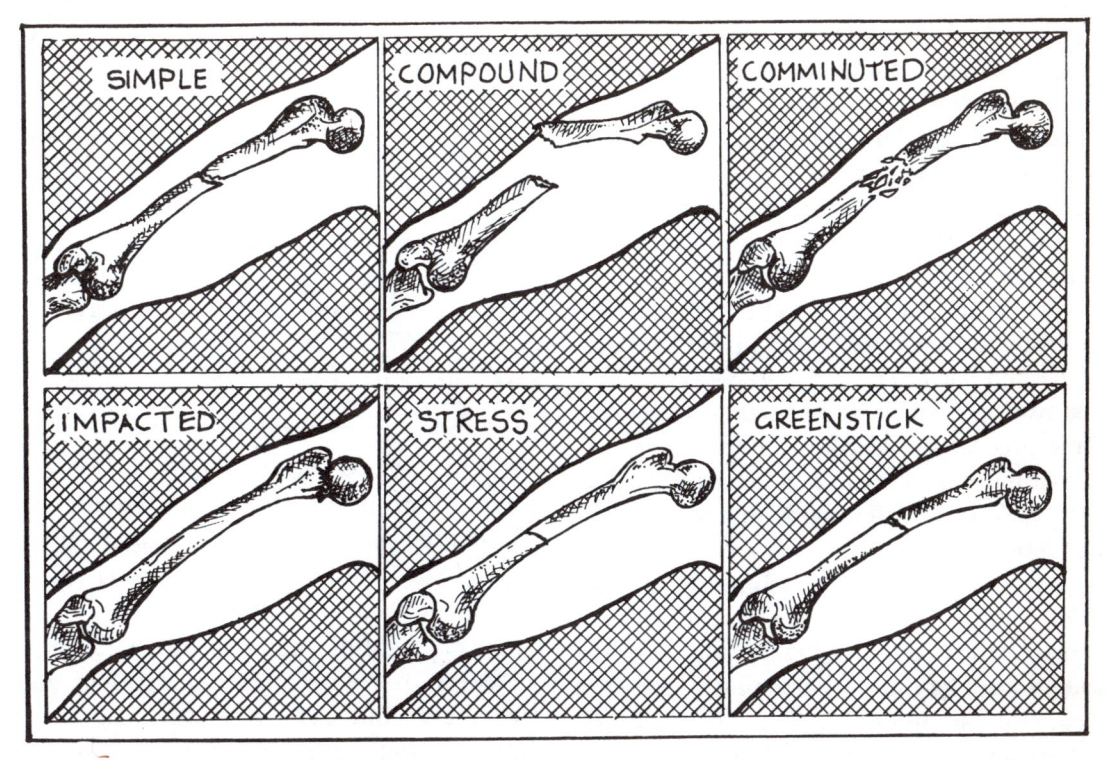

FIGURE 5.2: Different types of fracture.

been given individual names by the medical profession, while others are merely named after the involved bone or nearest joint. As any bone in the body may be fractured, only a few of the most common types can be discussed in detail.

One of the most common named fractures is a **Colles' fracture**, which is named after Abraham Colles, a Dublin surgeon who practised in the early part of the nineteenth century. This occurs when a person lands on the outstretched hand while attempting to save themselves from a fall. The forearm bones (the ulna and radius) are bent back and fractured just above the wrist. The bones must be put back into place under an anaesthetic and held in position by a plaster for six weeks in an adult.

A **Smith's fracture** is the reverse of a Colles' fracture. In a Smith's fracture, the wrist is bent forward excessively to cause a fracture of the forearm bones just above the wrist. Treatment is the same as a Colles' fracture.

A **Pott's fracture** (named after Percival Pott, an eighteenth century London surgeon) occurs at the ankle, when the ends of the two bones in the lower leg (the tibia and fibula) are broken off. These fractures require up to three months in a plaster to heal adequately.

Hip fractures (see also HIP DISLOCATED) in elderly people are also serious because they are difficult to heal. Technically, they are actually a fracture of the top of the thigh bone (the femur) and in most cases do not directly involve the hip joint itself. Orthopaedic surgeons often totally replace the hip joint and the top of the femur, and patients are mobile again in only a few weeks. In other cases, surgery to fix the fracture in position with steel pins or screws, or many weeks in traction in bed are required to allow healing. The greatest complication associated with this fracture is that the blood supply to the top of the femur, where it forms the hip joint, will be inadequate, and this area of bone will die. These fractures are uncommon in younger adults and children.

Fractures of the scaphoid bone in the wrist can be serious, because in a small number of cases, part of this small bone may die after a fracture and cause a constantly painful wrist joint. These fractures are often hard to detect, and X-rays a week or two apart may be necessary to see the fracture. Most heal after four to six weeks of immobilisation in plaster. An artificial scaphoid bone can now be inserted if complications occur.

A **fracture of the collar bone** (the clavicle) commonly occurs after a fall onto the outstretched arm, or by a fall onto the shoulder. They are a particularly common fracture in children. Most cases can be treated by placing the arm in a sling for three (in children) to six (in adults) weeks. In cases where there is significant displacement of the bone fragments, the bone may need to be repaired surgically.

Treatment of fractures

The treatment of any fracture involves keeping the bone ends perfectly still. If there is any movement of the pieces, healing will be slow or will not occur at all. This is where the age-old treatment with plaster casts comes to the fore. A plaster (or one of the newer, lighter and more expensive fibreglass and synthetic substitutes) is designed to immobilise the joint above and below the fracture. Once this is done, the slow process of repairing the bone can begin.

As a rough estimate of the time it takes for a simple fracture of various bones to heal is outlined in this table. These times can be halved for children, and increased by up to 50% in the elderly.

If a plaster cannot keep the bone ends in position, screws, rods or wires are surgically placed inside or through the bones to force them into the correct alignment. These may be left in place either for only a part of the healing time or, in some cases, permanently (e.g. hip fractures).

During healing, cells at the bone ends send out fibres to meet each other, and then new bone cells migrate along these fibres, laying down the new bone. This is soft to start with and takes several weeks to harden. Thus care must be taken in protecting the fracture site for some weeks after it has apparently healed. After a fracture has healed, physiotherapy is essential to mobilise joints that have been in a splint for a long time. Physiotherapists can also assist in teaching the elderly to walk again, getting younger people back to work quickly, strengthening muscles that may have wasted from lack of use, and teaching patients to deal with any residual disability.

Orthopaedics has come a long way in treating the more severe fractures with artificial bones and joints and the surgical screwing or wiring together of difficult fractures, but the basic fracture has been treated the same way for centuries, with plaster immobilising the break.

See also Section 8.

TABLE 5.1:
HEALING OF FRACTURES

Fractured bone	Time to heal (weeks)
Finger, toe	1 to 2
Thumb	3 to 4
Hand or forefoot (carpal and metacarpal bones), big toe	4 to 6
Wrist (carpal bones), forearm (radius, ulna), collar bone (clavicle), jaw	5 to 7
Upper arm (humerus), breast bone (sacrum)	6 to 8
Ankle, lower leg (tibia, fibula)	10 to 12
Thigh bone (femur)	12 to 16

FRIGIDITY

See SEXUAL PROBLEMS.

Frostbite

Although not nearly as common in Australia as in Europe and North America, frostbite does occur amongst residents of, and visitors to, the snow country in the Southern Alps and Tasmania. Frostbite is caused by freezing living tissue, and occurs most commonly in the toes, but the fingers and nose may also be affected. The severity of the frostbite depends on the depth to which the freezing has penetrated in the tissue. Freezing of the skin itself is not particularly serious, but if the freezing penetrates to the bone, the tissue will die, and the finger or toe requires amputation.

The early symptoms are numbness, itching and a pricking sensation. As the freezing penetrates deeper into the tissue, stiffness and shooting pains will occur. The skin is white or yellow, and the toe or finger becomes immobile. Late stages of frostbite are characterised by blistering, swelling, black colouration and gangrene. Wet socks or gloves will dramatically increase the risk of frostbite. Any other dry clothing wrapped around the foot or hand as a substitute is preferable to persisting with the wet socks or gloves.

If frostbite is suspected, immediate rewarming is the obvious treatment. Rapid re-warming or overheating further damages the tissue. Thawing in front of a fire or with other direct heat is not appropriate. It is far better to use the fire to heat snow or water for use in thawing. Placing the affected foot or hand in a bowl of water warmed to 40 degrees Celsius (just slightly warmer than normal body temperature) is the ideal. Thirty minutes is usually sufficient time for thawing of the frozen tissue.

Unfortunately, frostbite often occurs in skiers or hikers who are lost, injured or inadequately prepared, and the ideal methods of rewarming are not available. If re-freezing is possible, it is better not to thaw in the first place. Continuing to walk on frozen toes in order to reach suitable shelter is better than thawing them out and then allowing them to freeze a second time.

If two people are present, thawing each others toes by placing them in the other person's armpit is an ideal method. After thawing, the toes should be kept protected and warm by adequately thick, dry socks. If only one person is present, thawing fingers by this method is still practical, but the toes are rather more awkward! Once the hands have been thawed, they can be used to apply steady pressure to the frozen toes, and gradually thaw them. Never warm an area affected by frostbite by rubbing or massaging, as this will further damage the already fragile tissue.

After thawing, the affected fingers or toes should be protected from all injury, and the patient should rest in bed if possible. No dressings should be applied, but the affected areas should be left exposed in a warm room. Antiseptics may be applied to blisters and antibiotics given for infection. Only after several days or weeks is amputation of affected fingers or toes considered, as recovery may occur from an apparently hopeless situation. Moist gangrene on the other hand is an indication for immediate amputation.

Any area that has been frostbitten will be more susceptible to frostbite in future, and victims must be made aware of this so that they can take appropriate precautions.

See also HYPOTHERMIA.

Frozen Shoulder

A shoulder that for no apparent reason becomes stiff and limited in its range of movement is often referred to as a frozen shoulder. Technically, the condition may be referred to as adhesive capsulitis.

The cause of frozen shoulder is

unknown. Injury is not always present, but overuse of the joint may be an aggravating factor. The condition usually starts slowly and worsens gradually over a period of days or weeks. As well as being unable to move the shoulder more than a small distance in any direction, the patient may also complain of a constant ache in the joint.

X-rays are usually taken to exclude other possible causes of shoulder pain and stiffness such as arthritis, but in a frozen shoulder, the X-rays are normal. There are no blood tests that can give any useful information.

Treatment involves rest of the shoulder in a sling, with periods of gentle movement several times a day under the supervision of physiotherapist. Anti-inflammatory drugs (NSAIDs — see Section 6) and mild to moderate strength pain-killers can be prescribed. In severe cases, steroid tablets or injections into the joint may also be given.

Most cases last 6 to 12 months, then slowly recover regardless of any treatment. If recovery of movement is delayed long after the pain has eased, the shoulder may be moved around while the patient is anaesthetised to break down any adhesions that may have formed within the joint.

Fungal infections

Fungi are members of the plant family, and a limited number of them can cause infections in humans. The vast majority of fungal infections occur on the skin, but other commonly affected areas include the vagina (see THRUSH), mouth and gut. In rare cases, fungal infections can spread to the lungs (see HISTOPLASMOSIS), brain and other internal organs.

See also FUNGI, Section 7.

Tinea (ringworm)

Tinea is a term that includes almost every fungal infection of the skin. Fungal infections prefer areas of the body where there is heat (under clothing, in shoes), friction (from tight clothes or skin folds rubbing together) and moisture (from sweat). Tinea is more common in the tropics than in temperate climates.

Ringworm is *NOT* caused by a worm, but is a fungal infection of the skin. The fungus settles in one spot on the skin, and after the infection starts, a red dot may be seen but is often missed because it is quite small. This dot slowly enlarges as the fungus spreads away from its central base. After a few days, the centre of the red patch becomes pale again and similar to normal skin, because the infection is no longer active at this point. Meanwhile the infection continues to spread and forms an ever enlarging red ring on the skin. The same phenomenon can be seen in nature with mushroom rings that form on the ground after damp weather, because mushrooms are a giant, distant relation to the microscopic fungi that are responsible for ringworm.

The term tinea is often followed by a further Latin word which indicates the area of the body affected.

Tinea pedis is the term for fungal infections of the foot (including athlete's foot). It is far more common in men than women, and uncommon in children. The most common site for the infection is in the skin folds under the toes, where it may cause cracking and pain. The clefts between the toes are another common site, but almost any part of the foot, including the sole, may become involved. On the sole of the foot, the fungal infection may appear as deep-seated blisters rather than a red rash. The infection is caught from infected skin fragments that may be found on damp floors (e.g. communal showers, swimming pool change rooms).

Tinea cruris (also colloquially called 'crotch rot') is the term for fungal infections of the groin. These are also more common in men than women, and have a peak incidence in the 20s and 30s. A red, scaly rash can spread out from the skin folds in the groin to cover the inside of the thighs, the lower abdomen and the buttocks. The rash is often itchy and feels constantly uncomfortable. It tends to recur in summer and with exercise.

Tinea corporis is the traditional ring-shaped ringworm seen on the chest, abdomen and back. It appears as a red ring on the skin, with a pale centre. It affects both sexes and all ages equally. The infection may be caught by close contact with another infected human or animal (often cats, cattle and dogs). Without treatment, the ringworm may persist for many months, but it does not usually cause much itching or discomfort.

Tinea manum is a fungal infection of the hand. It is uncommon in children, and usually affects the palms and palm side of the fingers. It appears as a fine scale with a faint red edge. It is best treated by tablets rather than cream, because the thick skin of the palm makes it difficult for creams to penetrate.

Tinea capitis is a fungal infection of the scalp that occurs almost exclusively in children. The infection appears as an irregular, relatively bald patch on the scalp, which is covered by broken hair stubble rather than the flexible long hair elsewhere on the head. The fungi invades the hairs and causes them to become fragile and break. The affected area of the scalp is also covered in a fine scale. A severely affected patch may develop a thick build-up of scale, and the disease is then called **kerion**. The infection is treated by a long course of tablets, and the result of this treatment is good.

Tinea unguium is the notoriously difficult-to-treat fungal infection that occurs under the nails. It is more common in the middle-aged and elderly. The nails appear white or yellow and gradually thicken. A very long course of tablets is the best treatment. Despite treatment, some of these infections persist for many years, particularly in toe nails, which are usually more severely affected than the fingers.

Doctors may occasionally refer to fungal infections by the name of the actual fungus that is causing the infection, rather than by the area that is affected. The common fungi affecting humans come from the *Trichophyton, Microsporum* and *Epidermophyton* families.

If a fungal infection is suspected, its presence can be proved by taking skin scrapings (obtained by scraping the edge of a knife or scalpel across the skin) and examining them under a microscope to find the spores of the fungi. Similar spores can also be identified on hair and nail clippings if these areas are affected. Ultraviolet light can also be used to diagnose some fungal infections, particularly of hairy areas. In an otherwise dark room, an ultraviolet light (referred to as a Wood's light medically) will cause a bright green fluorescence of hair and skin affected by a fungus.

Fungal skin infections can be treated with a wide range of antifungal creams, ointments, lotions, tinctures and shampoos (see Section 6). The choice of form will depend on the position and severity of the infection. There are now a number of antifungal tablets available, the most common being griseofulvin (see Section 6), but they are very slow to work, and must be taken for one to six months, again depending on the site of the infection.

Pityriasis versicolor (tinea versicolor)
Pityriasis versicolor is a fungal skin disease of the tropics that is relatively common in Queensland and the Northern Territory. It affects young adults more than the elderly and children. Initially, the

fungus causes the development of pink/brown patches on the body, which may have a very faint scale upon them. After the disease has been present for a few weeks, the skin underlying the infection has the pigment reduced, so that the rash appears as white patches. These patches are due to sunlight being unable to tan the skin underlying the patches of fungus, because the fungus produces a chemical (carboxylic acid) that prevents the formation of the brown pigment (melanin) that causes tanning. On the one patient, areas not exposed to sunlight (e.g. armpits, breasts) may retain the pink/brown patch appearance, while in sun-exposed areas (e.g. back, arms) the same infection can cause white patches to appear on the sun-tanned skin. This effect does not occur on Aborigines, Chinese and other dark-skinned races.

The chest, upper arms, neck, upper back and armpits are the most commonly affected areas. There are usually no other symptoms other than a occasional very mild itch, and patients see a doctor because of the adverse cosmetic effect caused by the rash. The diagnosis can be proved by examining skin scrapings under a microscope, but in most cases, the diagnosis is obvious to the doctor, and no investigations are needed.

Treatment involves the regular use of antifungal lotions, rinses or creams. The white patches will remain for some time after the fungus has been destroyed, until the sun is given the chance to tan the area again. In years past, selenium sulphide (the active ingredient of the anti-dandruff shampoo Selsun) has been used to treat this condition, but more potent and effective antifungals are now readily available. An antifungal tablet (Nizoral — see Section 6) is now used to kill chronic and widespread attacks of pityriasis versicolor.

Episodes of infection are quite easy to clear, but the infection recurs in the majority of victims, usually in the next summer. Some people appear to be susceptible to the infection, while others are resistant. The reason for this is unknown.

FURUNCLE
See BOIL.

FURUNCULOSIS, EAR
A furuncle is a boil that involves a hair follicle. It is a significant infection when occurring on the skin, but far more serious and painful when it occurs in the outer canal of the ear. Bacteria invade the roots of the fine hairs in the ear canal (often after an injury to the ear canal from a cotton bud, hair pin or other foreign object), and produce an excruciatingly painful swelling that may completely close the ear canal. If the infection is deeper in the tissue, there may be less swelling and only a patch of redness on one side of the ear canal. The pain can be aggravated by chewing (the jaw joint is just in front of the ear) and may spread to the glands on that side of the neck. In due course, the furuncle may burst and discharge copious amounts of pus.

A swab may be taken from the ear to culture the particular bacteria that is causing the infection, and to select the correct antibiotic to treat them. A bacterium called *Staphylococcus aureus* (the golden staph) is one of the most common to cause this infection. X-rays are occasionally necessary to ensure that surrounding bone has not been damaged by the infection.

Heat in the form of a hot-water bottle, or short-wave therapy by a physiotherapist, can help relieve the pain. Because the pain is caused by an increase in pressure in the area, normal pain-killing tablets are relatively ineffective. A wick (thin ribbon of cloth) soaked in an antibiotic and soothing ointment may be gently placed in the ear canal and changed daily.

The mainstay of treatment is a course of antibiotics by mouth (or occasionally injection) to kill the invading bacteria. A form of penicillin is the normal first choice antibiotic. Scratching the ear canal with any object (including a finger) is forbidden, whether the ear is infected or not. Most furuncles burst spontaneously, but some deep-seated infections may need to be lanced to drain the pus.

Furuncles are more common in diabetics and others who are generally unwell. In cases of recurrent ear furunculosis, tests should be done to exclude any other disease.

Gallstones (cholelithiasis, cholecystitis)

Fair, fat, female, forty and flatulent. These are the people who, according to traditional medical textbooks, are more likely than others to suffer from gallstones. Of course the problem can occur in many people outside this group, but it is quite surprising just how many do belong to this group of 5 Fs.

The liver, which sits behind the lower ribs on the right side of the body, produces bile at a more or less constant rate. This bile moves through a series of collecting ducts, which join up to form the common bile duct. This duct leads to the small intestine. There are two side ducts to the common bile duct. The first one is called the cystic duct and leads to the gall bladder. The lower side duct leads to the pancreas. Bile is required to help in the digestion of food, but as we do not eat constantly, it is not needed in the gut all the time. There is a valve at the lower end of the common bile duct where it opens into the intestine. This valve opens when food passes to allow bile to be added to the food in the gut. When the valve is closed, the bile must be stored, and this is where the gall bladder fits into the picture. It is a storage area for bile not immediately required, and the bile from the liver is directed into it when the valve is closed. When extra bile is required in the gut to digest food, the gall bladder contracts to squeeze the bile out through the open valve onto the food. The pancreas also produces enzymes which are used in digestion.

Problems occur when the bile in the gall bladder becomes too concentrated and precipitates out as a crystal or stone. Up to 10% of men over 60 years of age, and 20% of women over 60 have some gallstones. The incidence is increased in diabetics. Small stones can pass out along the ducts, but larger stones block up the bile ducts, and when the gall bladder contracts, the movement of the stone in the duct causes severe intermittent pain in the upper right side of the abdomen. This pain also tends to run through to the back and can be felt at the lower end of the shoulder blade. It often occurs when eating, as the gall bladder tries to contract and discharge its contents onto the food. If the stone becomes stuck in the common bile duct, constant severe pain results, and an emergency operation is required to clear it. Because bile is not reaching food when it is required, indigestion and burping, or passing wind rectally (farting), are common problems in patients with gallstones. The other common complication is infection, because it is easy for the gall bladder to become infected when its exit is blocked by a stone. The patient is then feverish, nauseated and in constant pain.

The presence of gallstones can be confirmed by an ultrasound scan (see Section 4) of the gall bladder, where the sound waves reflected back from the harder gallstones differentiate them from the softer surrounding tissue. A series of special X-rays (cholecystograms) can be taken, after a dye which concentrates in the bile has been swallowed or injected, from the liver to the gall bladder to show the presence of stones. Sometimes the dye is pushed up the bile duct from the gut by using an endoscope. Blood tests are normal unless the gallstone is blocking the bile duct. In this situation, waste products cannot escape from the liver, and build up in the bloodstream where they can be measured.

The most effective treatment is surgery to remove the gall bladder and the stones it contains. If there are no acute problems, it can be carried out routinely at the patient's convenience, but often after the patient has lost any excess weight. An incision is made diagonally under the ribs on the right side, or vertically from below the breast bone to the navel. The operation last between 45 and 90 minutes and patients must remain in hospital for five to seven days afterwards. It usually takes a month or more before they can return to work.

Some patients can have stones that are very low in the common bile duct removed by an instrument that is passed through the mouth and stomach into the intestine (an endoscope). A side piece on this endoscope can pass up the bile duct to remove an obstructing stone.

Patients who are too old or ill for an operation may use an expensive drug that slowly dissolves some gallstones over many months.

The most recently developed form of treatment is lithotripsy (see Section 6), in which the stones are shattered by a high-frequency sound wave, but it is not suitable for all cases of gallstones.

Ganglion

A hard lump that develops on a tendon on the back of the hand, or (less commonly) on the top of the foot, is most likely to be a ganglion. The term ganglion is a confusing one in medicine, because it also refers to the microscopic connections between nerve fibres. The ganglions referred to here usually have nothing to do with nerves; they are thin-walled cysts that are filled with a thick, clear fluid.

Tendons slide backwards and forwards as muscles contract and relax. Around the wrist and ankle, they are confined within fibrous tubes called tendon sheaths. The sheaths prevent the tendon from slipping out of position around the joint, and from raising the skin excessively when the wrist or toes are bent back. The solid tendon is surrounded by a thin film of lubricating fluid within the tendon sheath. The ganglion is attached to this sheath that surrounds the tendon. One theory to explain their cause is that there is a small puncture in the tendon sheath which allows some of the lubricating fluid around the tendon to escape and form a firm lump under the skin. Ganglions may also form as attachments to joints within the wrist.

Ganglions are not dangerous, and they usually cause no problems other than being unsightly and uncomfortable. Occasionally, the ganglion may press on a nerve and cause pain and/or weakness in the hand or finger beyond that point. Very occasionally they may become infected, and as this infection can spread into the tendon, it must be treated rapidly and effectively.

The traditional treatment of a ganglion was to place the hand flat on a hard surface and hit it firmly with the family Bible. This usually caused the cyst to burst and disappear. This form of treatment can no longer be recommended, as the ganglions tend to come back, a local inflammatory reaction can occur at the site of the burst ganglion, and the hand may become quite bruised.

The more orthodox treatment involves a minor operation in which the ganglion is cut away from the tendon or joint to give a permanent cure. Another treatment method involves inserting a needle into

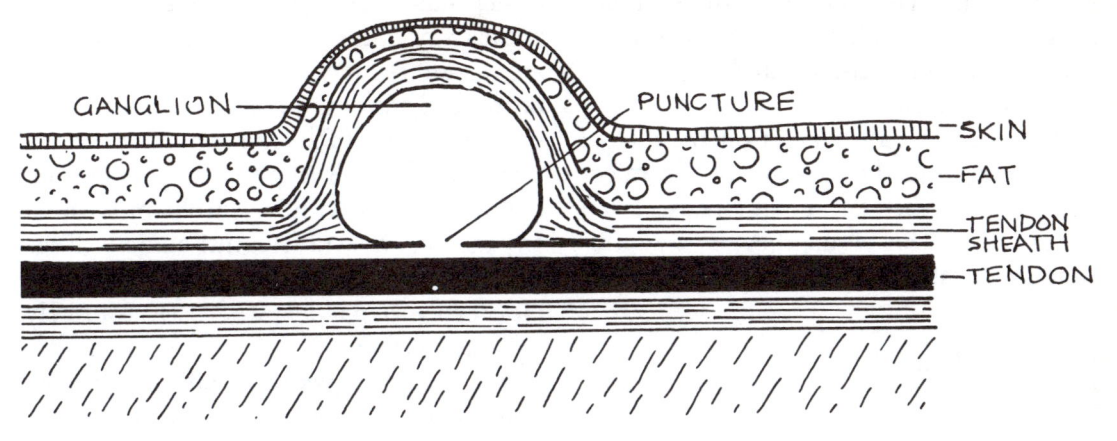

FIGURE 5.3: Ganglion on tendon sheath.

the ganglion, withdrawing the thick fluid in it, and injecting back a small amount of a steroid solution that often prevents the ganglion reforming.

GANGRENE
See GAS GANGRENE.

GAS GANGRENE (CLOSTRIDIAL MYOSITIS)

For millennia, soldiers about to enter battle have had a morbid fear. They did not fear a quick death at the end of a lance (at which time they presumably rose to their Valhalla or its equivalent) but a foul lingering death caused by gas gangrene. Gas gangrene (also known as clostridial myositis — *Clostridium* is the name of the responsible bacterium and 'myositis' means muscle inflammation) can occur in any deep wound into which air (or more correctly, oxygen) cannot penetrate.

The bacteria that can grow in these deep wounds are relatively widespread in the environment, but they cannot survive if exposed to oxygen. They are referred to medically as 'anaerobic' (without air) bacteria. Once in a deep wound, they multiply and produce a chemical (toxin) that destroys damaged muscle and produces a foul-smelling gas. The wound becomes painful and swollen, and the skin around it is discoloured. Pressure over this discoloured skin produces a crackling sound as the tiny gas bubbles in the damaged muscle burst. These gas bubbles can also be seen on an X-ray of the area.

As the disease progresses, a smelly discharge issues from the wound as the muscle within rots away. The patient becomes feverish, delirious, and comatose. The toxins enter the blood stream, circulate throughout the body, destroy red blood cells, and damage the liver and kidney. Death is almost inevitable within a few days without adequate treatment. The diagnosis is usually obvious, but a swab taken from the wound will show the infecting bacteria when examined under a microscope.

Treatment involves massive doses of penicillin by injection. A gas gangrene antitoxin is available and should also be given routinely, but it is only beneficial if given very early in the course of the disease. Surgery to cut away all the affected tissue is also essential. This may involve the amputation of a limb, or massive disfiguring surgery to the trunk.

The high-pressure oxygen chambers used to treat divers with the bends (see separate entry) may also be used to treat gas gangrene. The oxygen in these chambers may be at a high enough pressure to penetrate into the tissues and destroy the invading bacteria.

The outcome will depend on the site of the wound, and the severity of the infection when treatment commences. Even today in good hospitals, there is a significant death rate.

Gastric ulcer
See ULCER, PEPTIC.

Gastritis
Strictly speaking, the term gastritis means inflammation of the stomach. In medical usage, it often refers to any minor illness of the stomach. Gastritis may cause intermittent symptoms for a few hours or days, or it may be the early stages of a peptic ulcer (see ULCER, PEPTIC) that will cause constant discomfort for weeks or months. The symptoms of gastritis include nausea (feeling of wanting to vomit), vomiting, loss of appetite, a feeling of fullness, upper abdominal discomfort or pain, and possibly indigestion.

Gastritis may be caused by many factors including stress, gut infections, drugs (particularly aspirin and anti-arthritis drugs), alcohol excess, overindulgence in food, stomach cancer and allergies. A formal diagnosis may be made after a gastroscopic examination (see Section 4) of the stomach, when the inflamed red stomach lining is seen through a flexible tube that is passed through the mouth and into the stomach. Because of the risk of cancer or other serious disease, anyone with persistent gastritis, or who vomits blood, must have a gastroscopic examination.

The treatment of gastritis will depend upon the cause. If stress is responsible, removing the source of the stress is the obvious treatment, but this is usually far easier said than done. As a result, milk, antacids or anti-ulcer drugs (see Section 6) are given regularly, or when symptoms occur, to control the condition. Sometimes reassurance that the stomach pains are not serious is enough to give the patient confidence to deal with the problem without any medical assistance. Anti-anxiety drugs may be used on a short-term basis, but may cause dependency if used routinely for long periods.

Drug-induced gastritis will require the removal of the drugs, substituting other drugs, or if the medication is essential, adding anti-ulcer or antacid medications to control the continuing symptoms.

Peptic ulcers and stomach cancer have to be dealt with appropriately if they are responsible for the gastritis.

The outcome of the disease is also dependent upon the cause, and will vary dramatically from one individual to another.

Gastroenteritis, viral
You wake with that uncomfortable feeling in your stomach. Something is brewing down there, and it doesn't feel good. The gurgling grows steadily louder, the cramping pains become worse, and then there's the mad rush to the bathroom as the vomiting starts. A few hours later when you are beginning to feel that the dry retching will never stop, the vomiting starts to ease, and then the diarrhoea starts. For a while you are not sure which end should be over the toilet bowl! For between 24 and 72 hours you are tormented by your intestinal tract as it heaves and squeezes to rid the body of every trace of food and fluid. Eventually it ceases and you can rest, feeling drained and exhausted.

Very few of us have escaped the trial of gastroenteritis, which is usually a viral infection of the gut. The rotavirus is one of the most common viruses responsible for this type of infection, particularly in children. There may be other causes of diarrhoea and vomiting, including food poisoning (see separate entry), toxins and bacterial infections. During the one to three days or more of the disease, the violent contractions of the bowel have not only expunged the entire contents of your gut, they have also washed out most of the infecting viruses, and antibodies have developed in the bloodstream to fight off the infection from the inside.

Gastroenteritis often appears in epidemics, and usually in spring or early summer. It passes from one person to another through contamination of the hands, and then food. Children are more commonly affected than adults, and infants can be quite dangerously ill from the disease. The great danger in the little ones is dehydration.

The treatment in both adults and children is primarily diet to replace the fluid and vital salts that are rinsed out of the body by the vomiting and diarrhoea, and then to carefully reintroduce foods and gradually increase the food intake to restore it to normal. A gastroenteritis diet plan is suggested in Section 7 (see SPECIAL DIETS FOR HEALTH DISORDERS).

In adults, medications can be used to slow down the rush to the toilet and ease the gut cramps, but these do not work well in children or have unacceptable side effects. Paracetamol can be used for the abdominal pain. Children must be checked by a doctor if they have diarrhoea or vomiting that lasts more than 12 hours. A few may become rapidly dehydrated and require urgent hospitalisation so that the lost fluid can be replaced through a drip into a vein. Some children develop an intolerance to milk sugar (lactose) after a viral gut infection, and this may prevent them from returning to a normal diet for several weeks or months.

See also DYSENTERY, BACTERIAL.

GENITAL HERPES
See HERPES SIMPLEX INFECTIONS.

GENITAL WARTS
See WARTS.

GENU VALGUM
See KNOCK-KNEES.

GERMAN MEASLES
See RUBELLA.

GIARDIA INFECTION (GIARDIASIS)
Giardia lamblia is a microscopic animal that is classified zoologically as a protozoa. This parasite can easily enter the body and cause an infection in the small intestine. It passes from one person to another by poor personal hygiene. The eggs are found in the faeces, and can be picked up on the hands that then touch food and enter another person's gut. Faecal contamination of water supplies is another common way of spreading the infection. Giardiasis is widespread in third-world countries, but even in Australia up to 20% of all children will be infected every year. The condition is far more common in children than adults.

Most people with giardiasis have no symptoms and are unaware that they are infected. Those that do have infections most commonly develop a mild diarrhoea with foul-smelling stools, smelly flatus (farts), general tiredness, an uncomfortable feeling in the abdomen, nausea, vomiting, burping and cramping pains in the abdomen. A long-term result may be malnutrition, particularly amongst Aborigines and children in third-world countries, as the constant diarrhoea prevents them from absorbing the small amount of food that they are able to obtain and eat.

The disease is diagnosed by examining a

sample of the faeces under a microscope and identifying the eggs or live giardia. From the time the eggs of the giardia are swallowed, it may be one to three weeks before symptoms develop or the parasite can be found in the faeces.

Most cases clear spontaneously without treatment, but this may take many weeks or months. When treating giardiasis, it is essential to treat all members of the patient's family, and any other close contacts (e.g. a child's playmates). People with the parasite but without symptoms can easily pass the infection back to children who have been treated successfully.

A number of different medications can be given to cure the condition. Most are a single-dose treatment, and they are available as tablets or mixtures. The commonly used drugs in Australia include tinidazole, metronidazole, mepacrine and furazolidone (see Section 6). These are marketed under a number of different brand names. The vast majority of cases settle rapidly with this treatment. The only form of prevention is scrupulous personal hygiene.

GINGIVOSTOMATITIS

See PERIODONTITIS; STOMATITIS; VINCENT'S ANGINA.

GLANDULAR FEVER (INFECTIOUS MONONUCLEOSIS; IM)

Although romantically named the 'kissing disease', glandular fever is a most unpleasant disease to catch, and doctors are completely powerless to prevent it or treat it. Also known as infectious mononucleosis (IM), glandular fever is caused by a virus. These are particles of protein so small that they cannot be seen under a normal microscope, and only the very sophisticated scanning electron microscope can detect them (see VIRUSES, Section 7). Billions (not just millions) of them could fit onto the sharp end of a pin!

The virus is passed from one person to another through all the bodily fluids, but most commonly in the tiny droplets of water that you exhale when breathing. These droplets can be seen as 'steam' when breathing in cold, dry air. If you are unlucky enough to inhale some of these virus-carrying droplets from a person with glandular fever, you may catch the disease yourself. Fortunately, most of us have a good defence system built into our bodies, and the white cells in our bloodstream can destroy the virus and prevent infection. If the defence system is overwhelmed by a large number of virus particles, or if our defences are reduced because we are tired or recovering from another illness, then we become victims of the disease and can pass it on to even more people.

Patients with glandular fever usually have a sore throat, raised temperature, large glands in the neck and other parts of the body, extreme lethargy, and generally feel absolutely lousy. Doctors can perform a blood test to prove the diagnosis, but these may not prove positive until ten days after the onset of the disease. Doctors can also give advice on how to cope with the disease, but unfortunately, this advice will not cure the disease. The patient must rest as much as possible, take aspirin or paracetamol for the fever and aches, use gargles for the sore throat, and then wait until the illness passes. Antibiotics are designed to destroy the much larger infecting animals called bacteria, and have no effect on viruses. Some antibiotics (penicillin most commonly) can actually cause patients with glandular fever to develop a widespread rash.

The disease lasts about four weeks, but some patients are unlucky enough to have it persist for several months. The patient is considered infectious while s/he has the large tender glands, and during this time should avoid close contact with others. Kissing is obviously a very easy way to catch the disease from a sufferer, and so the nickname of this disease developed. Personal hygiene at the toilet, in bathing and in the use of cutlery and china is also important to prevent further spread.

After the symptoms have settled, the patient is often left very tired and weak, and it may be another week or two before he or she is fit to resume school or work. Complications of the disease are rare. Some people develop secondary bacterial infections while their resistance is lowered by the glandular fever. Others may have their spleen infected by the virus, or in even rarer cases the liver, heart and brain may be involved. Doctors can usually deal adequately with these complications.

The sooner a person with the disease is diagnosed, the sooner he or she can be isolated from others, and so the spread of this disabling but generally not serious disease can be limited. It is therefore important to see a doctor early in the course of the illness to ensure that it is correctly diagnosed.

Glaucoma

'For all the discomforts that will accompany my being blind, may the good God prepare me'.

These were the last words ever written by the seventeenth century English diarist, Samuel Pepys. The fear of blindness continues to this day, but one common cause until well into this century can now been controlled in most cases. The disease is glaucoma. To understand this relatively common condition (one in every 75 people over 40 years of age have it), it is necessary to understand the eye.

The eye is filled with a clear fluid (called aqueous humour) that has the consistency of half-set jelly. This fluid is slowly secreted by special cells within the eye, while in another part of the eye, the fluid is slowly removed, causing a steady renewal of the eye's contents. This exchange occurs quite slowly, but when it is disrupted, glaucoma occurs.

The fluid is produced by a structure called the ciliary body which sits just behind the iris (the coloured part of the eye). The fluid moves through the pupil (the black hole in the centre of the iris), and is drained back into the body through tiny canals that are situated around the outer edge and in front of the iris. The usual disruption to this circulation of the eye contents involves a blockage to the drainage of the fluid from the eye. The new fluid continues to be secreted, and as a result the pressure inside the eye increases. With this increase in pressure, damage occurs to the light-sensitive areas at the back of the eye, eventually causing them to be permanently scarred, and blindness results.

Glaucoma is diagnosed in most cases by measuring the actual pressure of the fluid within the eye. This involves briefly anaesthetising the eye surface with eye drops, and then resting an instrument called a tonometer on the surface of the eye while the patient is lying down. The procedure takes only a few seconds and involves no discomfort. Other more complex tests, including examining the eye through a microscope, are undertaken by eye specialists to ascertain the nature and seriousness of the glaucoma.

Measurement of the damage to the field of vision may also be undertaken by asking a patient to stare at a black dot in the centre of a large white sheet. Another black dot is then moved in from the side of the white area until it can be seen by the patient. The sideways limit of vision can then be marked on the sheet, and the procedure is repeated from different angles so that the field of vision can be mapped out in all directions.

Glaucoma occurs in three main types. **Chronic glaucoma** (also known as open-angle glaucoma) is by far the most common type. It has a slow onset over months or years and is usually detected because of a deterioration in vision. This type of glaucoma tends to occur in both eyes simultaneously and also runs through families from one generation to the next. Anyone over 40 with glaucoma in the family should have the pressure in their eyes tested every couple of years to detect the onset of glaucoma before it causes any damage. Patients with diabetes and arteriosclerosis (hardening of the arteries) are also more liable to develop this form of glaucoma.

Acute glaucoma (also called angle-closure glaucoma) is the worst type, as it can develop in a few hours or days. It usually occurs in only one eye, and blindness can result if medical attention is not sought urgently. The symptoms include a rapid deterioration in vision, severe pain, rainbow-coloured halos around lights, nausea and vomiting. A blow to the eye may precipitate acute glaucoma, or it may develop for no discernible reason. Immediate treatment is essential if the sight of the eye is to be saved.

The alternative names for these two types of glaucoma refer to the angle between the iris and cornea, at which point the fluid in the eye is normally resorbed back into the body.

The third type of glaucoma is **congenital glaucoma**. Babies born with this disease require surgical treatment to give them some chance of retaining their sight. The earliest sign of this condition is the continual overflow of tears from the eye. It may also be noted that the baby turns away from lights, rather than towards them as a normal baby does.

A number of other conditions may also cause glaucoma. These include eye tumours, eye infections and eye injury. In rare cases, some drugs (e.g. steroids) may also be responsible.

Both the acute and chronic types of glaucoma can be treated medically in the majority of cases. This involves the regular use of eye drops (miotics and/or timolol — see Section 6) that are designed to reduce the pressure in the eye. These drops do not cure the disease but keep it under control while they are used. If the eye drops are not successful, or the situation is very serious, microsurgery on the tiny drainage canals in the front of the eye may be necessary. Lasers are being used in some centres for this procedure. The surgery may cure the disease, but usually it merely brings the pressure in the eye to a level where the drops are able to work.

Without treatment, glaucoma progresses inexorably to total blindness. If the disease is detected early, glaucoma in most patients can be successfully controlled.

Blindness is a terrifying affliction, but blindness that could have been avoided if adequate treatment had been sought is even worse. If you notice a deterioration in your sight, particularly if it is accompanied by eye pain or headaches, see your doctor immediately, so that the appropriate diagnosis can be made at an early stage of the disease.

See also EYES, Section 2.

GLIOMA
See BRAIN CANCER.

GLOMERULONEPHRITIS
Glomerulonephritis is a kidney disease that occurs in two forms — acute and chronic. They are similar in that they both involve the degeneration of that part of the kidney where the waste products are filtered out of the blood to form urine.

In the kidney, there are millions of microscopically small cups into which blood pours. The cups are made of cells that can allow certain waste products and fluid to pass through, while the major part of the blood flows out of the other side of this invisibly small cup. These cups are called glomeruli, and the nephron is the microscopic tube that carries the urine away from the glomerular cup, thus giving the term glomerulonephritis (inflammation of the glomeruli and nephrons).

Acute glomerulonephritis (acute nephritis)
Acute glomerulonephritis is often triggered by a bacterial infection (e.g. throat infection, tonsillitis) but may start as a result of other diseases in the body (e.g. systemic lupus erythematosus) or for no identifiable reason. Many patients develop a very mild form of glomerulonephritis after an infection but do not realise they have it until it is detected in a urine test. Most of these cases settle spontaneously after a week or two without any treatment. The disease usually affects both kidneys, and it is far more common in children than adults. It is a relatively common condition in third-world countries and amongst Aborigines, but quite rare in affluent white middle-class society.

The patient feels tired, has no appetite, develops headaches and has a low-grade fever. Other symptoms can include a low urine output, loin (kidney) pain, swelling of the ankles and around the eyes, and cloudy urine. Doctors may detect an increase in blood pressure. The diagnosis is confirmed by examining the urine under a microscope, when blood cells and cell fragments are seen. Blood tests can determine how effectively the kidneys are functioning.

Treatment in most cases merely involves antibiotics for any infection that is present, and keeping the patient at rest until the kidneys recover. In severe cases, a special low-protein, high-carbohydrate diet is required, and medication may be required to lower the blood pressure. In the rare cases that deteriorate further, an artificial kidney machine may be needed for a short time.

Most patients with acute glomerulonephritis recover completely after a month or two, but in severe cases it may take up to a year or more. About 5% of patients who have a severe case of acute nephritis are left with some permanent kidney damage. Death may occur during an attack but is extremely rare in Australia.

Chronic glomerulonephritis
Some patients do not recover from acute glomerulonephritis, and if it continues for more than a year, with persistent and worsening kidney function as measured by blood tests, the patient is considered to have chronic glomerulonephritis. There are usually no symptoms until the kidneys start to fail and excessive levels of waste products build up in the bloodstream.

There is no specific treatment other than continuation of the low-protein, high-carbohydrate diet. A large intake of fluids is also desirable.

Infection, injury or strenuous exercise may cause a sudden deterioration in kidney function, but most patients live relatively normal lives for 20 or 30 years before kidney failure (see separate entry) occurs.

See also NEPHROTIC SYNDROME.

GOITRE
See Section 3.

GOLFER'S ELBOW
See TENNIS ELBOW.

GONORRHOEA ('CLAP')
Gonorrhoea is a common sexually transmitted disease, which has faded somewhat in the public's awareness since the AIDS

epidemic and the fear of genital herpes have hit the newspaper headlines. Even so, gonorrhoea is still extremely common, with nearly 200 000 cases estimated to occur in Australia every year. It is caused by a bacterium called *Neisseria gonorrhoeae* and can only be caught by having sex with a person who already has the disease. It has an incubation period of three to seven days after contact.

The symptoms vary significantly between men and women. In **women**, there may be minimal symptoms with a mild attack, and this allows prostitutes and others to transmit the disease from one man to another without being aware that they are themselves a carrier. When symptoms do occur, they include a foul discharge from the vagina, pain on passing urine, pain in the lower abdomen, passing urine frequently, tender glands in the groin, and fever.

Whether symptoms are present or not, the infection can move further into the body, and involve the womb (uterus) and Fallopian tubes. In these situations gonorrhoea may cause salpingitis and pelvic inflammatory disease (see separate entry) which can have infertility and persistent pelvic pain as complications.

In **men**, the symptoms are usually obvious, with a yellow milky discharge from the penis, pain on passing urine and, in advanced cases, inflamed glands in the groin. If left untreated, the prostate can become infected, which can cause scarring of the urine tube (urethra), permanent difficulty in passing urine and reduced fertility.

Through anal intercourse, a rectal infection with gonorrhoea can develop. An anal discharge, mild diarrhoea, rectal discomfort and pain on passing faeces are the common symptoms. Oral sex can lead to the development of a gonococcal throat infection.

The disease can be confirmed by examining a swab from the urethra, vagina or anus under a microscope and culturing the bacteria on a nutrient substance. There are no blood tests available to detect gonorrhoea. Other sexually transmitted diseases should also be tested for when gonorrhoea is diagnosed, as they may be contracted at the same time. For this reason, blood tests are often ordered by doctors when treating anyone with any form of venereal disease.

A couple of decades ago, gonorrhoea was readily treated with a course of penicillin. Unfortunately, many strains of gonorrhoea are now resistant to penicillin, and more potent antibiotics are required to effect a cure. The antibiotics can be given by mouth or injection, and in some cases a single dose is all that is required. All contacts of the infected person need to be notified, as they may be carriers of the disease and unaware of the presence of the infection. After treatment, a follow-up swab is important in women and homosexuals to ensure that the infection has been adequately treated.

Some degree of protection from catching gonorrhoea can be obtained by using a condom, but this is not a total protection and has a failure rate of 5% to 10%.

There are a number of other less common complications of gonorrhoea. Babies born to mothers with the infection can develop a gonococcal conjunctivitis (eye infection), which can be treated by eye drops and/or antibiotic injections. The gonorrhoea may also enter the bloodstream and cause a form of septicaemia (see separate entry), which causes fevers and skin sores. The most unusual complication is gonococcal arthritis, which causes pain in the knees, ankles and wrists. This must be treated with both antibiotics and the normal anti-arthritis medications, but if joint damage has occurred, the arthritis may be long-lasting. Other rarer complications of gonorrhoea include infections of the heart, brain and tendons.

More than 95% of cases of gonorrhoea can be cured by the appropriate antibiotics, but some of the complications can cause long-lasting effects. The most common persistent problem is infertility due to adhesions and scarring in the Fallopian tubes and the uterus of a woman.

Gout

Gout has the very obvious symptoms of a very red, swollen and excruciatingly painful joint. The most common joint to be involved is the ball of the foot, but almost any joint in the body may be involved. In severe attacks, a fever may develop, along with a rapid heart rate, loss of appetite and flaking of skin over the affected joint. Victims describe the exquisite pain of gout as having a joint full of barbed wire, with the wire being constantly twisted and turned so that it stabs repeatedly. The attacks start very suddenly, often at night, and may occur every week or so, or only once in a lifetime. The tendency to develop the disease runs in families, so that if your father had gout, your chances of developing the disease are above average. Nearly all gout victims are men (one out of every 150 males in Australia) and it usually starts between 30 and 50 years of age.

Gout is caused by excess blood levels of uric acid, which is produced as a normal breakdown product of certain foods. Normally it is removed by the kidneys, but if excess is produced or the kidneys fail to work efficiently, excess levels build up in the body. The excess acid can precipitate as crystals in the cavity of a joint. Under a microscope the crystals look like fine needles, and this is why they cause severe pain in the patient who has millions of these tiny crystals jabbing into the lining of his joint. The acid crystals can also form lumps (called tophi) under the skin around joints and in the ear lobes, but this disfiguring complication is rare with modern treatment. More seriously, the crystals may damage the kidneys and form kidney stones. Patients may have high levels of uric acid (hyperuricaemia) in their bloodstream, which may be causing kidney damage but not painful joints. The only way to detect this situation is with a blood test. Once detected, treatment is just as important as in gouty arthritis in order to stop the formation of kidney stones and to protect the kidneys from irreparable damage.

Gout is traditionally said to be caused by high living and drinking alcohol. This is not strictly true, but a drinking binge or eating a lot of meat can start an attack in someone who is susceptible to the disease. Sufferers should avoid foods that contain high levels of purine, which metabolises to uric acid. These include prawns, shellfish, liver, sardines, meat concentrates and game birds.

The treatment of gout takes two forms — treatment of the acute attack, and prevention of any further attacks.

Doctors will prescribe a combination of anti-inflammatory drugs and a medication called colchicine (see Section 6) that will relieve the acute attack rapidly. Rest of the affected joint to control the pain and prevent further joint damage is also important. After blood tests to confirm the disease and exclude any complications, the patient must start taking one or more tablets a day for the rest of his life to prevent the pain and kidney damage of further attacks.

Patients can help themselves by avoiding the foods listed above, not consuming excess alcohol, keeping their weight under control, drinking plenty of liquids to prevent dehydration, avoiding overexposure to cold, not exercising to extremes and remembering to take the gout- preventing tablets. If the tablets are missed, an attack of gout can follow very quickly.

Gout was dreaded a century ago because of the pain and crippling it caused, but doctors can control and prevent it quite easily these days, provided the patient understands the problem and cooperates with the treatment program.

See also ARTHRITIS; PSEUDOGOUT.

GRAND MAL
See EPILEPSY.

GRAVE'S DISEASE
See HYPERTHYROIDISM.

GROWING PAINS (LIMB PAIN SYNDROME)
Most medical textbooks and many doctors deny the existence of growing pains, but many general practitioners have seen children who appear to have significant pain in their legs and (less commonly) their arms that is worse at times of rapid growth. The term 'limb pain syndrome' is now sometimes used to give the condition of growing pains some medical respectability. The symptoms include a deep ache in the limbs that occurs between joints, and not at the joint. It is often worse at night, and equal on both sides. The pains are intermittent, and occur with the same frequency in both sexes between the ages of six and fourteen years. It is important for the doctor to exclude any other causes of arm or leg pain (see Section 3) before making the diagnosis.

Treatment involves reassurance, paracetamol and heat (e.g. hot water bottle). The condition always settles spontaneously but may affect up to one third of all children. There is also a tendency for the condition to recur within the one family in successive generations.

GUILLAIN-BARR SYNDROME
The Guillain-Barr syndrome is a rare inflammation of the nerves that usually follows a viral infection, injury, surgery, vaccination or a period of stress. The nerves in any part of the body may be affected, but the nerves in the legs are most commonly involved. The muscles that these nerves supply become paralysed, and sensation to the affected areas may also be lost. Most patients slowly recover, but up to 20% may be left with a permanent disability. In rare cases the muscles that allow breathing may be paralysed, which can result in death.

Steroids (see Section 6) are used in treatment, but their use is controversial.

GUT DISEASE
See CHOLERA; COLIC, INTESTINAL; COLO-RECTAL CANCER; CROHN'S DISEASE; DIVERTICULITIS; DYSENTERY, BACTERIAL; FOOD POISONING; GASTRITIS; GASTROENTERITIS, VIRAL; GIARDIA INFECTION; HAEMORRHOIDS; HIATUS HERNIA; INCONTINENCE OF FAECES; IRRITABLE BOWEL SYNDROME; PERITONITIS; PROLAPSE; REFLUX OESOPHAGITIS; STOMACH CANCER; ULCER, PEPTIC; ULCERATIVE COLITIS; ZOLLINGER-ELLISON SYNDROME.

GUT CANCER
See COLO-RECTAL CANCER.

HAEMOCHROMATOSIS
Haemochromatosis is a congenital disease (present since birth), in which the body stores excessive amounts of iron in the liver, pancreas, kidneys, heart, testes and other tissues. It is far more common in males than females, and because it is a very slowly progressive condition, it usually causes no problems until the patient is in his 50s or 60s. The common symptoms are liver enlargement and reduced liver function, joint pains, heart enlargement, impaired heart function, dia-

betes, dark skin discolouration and impotence. The disease can be diagnosed by specific blood tests and liver biopsy.

The treatment of haemochromatosis appears to be extremely old-fashioned. Blood-letting on a regular basis to remove iron from the body is the main method of dealing with the disease. This may need to be continued weekly for some years to adequately drain iron out of the system. Drugs are also available to increase the rate at which iron is excreted through the kidneys and urine. Damage already caused to the body's vital organs by the excess levels of iron (e.g. diabetes, liver and heart failure) cannot be reversed by these treatments, and specific additional medications are required.

Haemophilia (factor VIII deficit)

One of the many miracles of human life is blood. It is a liquid that transports the necessary elements of existence to every cell in the body, but if allowed to leak out of a vein, artery or capillary, it will rapidly solidify to prevent further loss of this vital fluid. Clotting is accepted as normal, and we have all experienced the stickiness of blood that occurs during the clotting process, but this is not a simple occurrence. More than a dozen different chemicals, cells and enzymes are involved in an extremely complex interaction to convert this liquid into a solid. There are some people who are born with defects in these chemical pathways and are bleeders. Instead of stopping within a few minutes of an injury, bleeding may persist for hours, and the slightest injury may cause massive bruises or bleeding into joints, which leads to arthritis.

Haemophilia and Christmas disease (see separate entry) are inherited diseases of excessive bleeding. These diseases only occur in males, but females act as the carriers from one generation to the next. Approximately one in every 10 000 males has haemophilia. This can occur because the female has two X chromosomes, while the male has only one. Some of the chemicals (known as factors) essential for clotting are produced by genes attached to the X chromosome. If one X chromosome is faulty, there is in the female another one to take over, but there is no equivalent back-up system in the male. The two diseases vary in the nature of the missing factor.

The severity of haemophilia can vary from one patient to another. Some only bleed excessively during surgery or if wounded, while others may bruise terribly with only a minor blow. The bleeding may occur anywhere within the body, but because of the stress placed upon them by normal activity, the most common sites for bleeding are the joints and muscles. The disease can be confirmed by performing specific blood tests.

There is no cure for haemophilia. However, it is possible to replace the factors missing from the blood and control the bleeding. Factor VIII (missing in haemophilia) and factor IX (missing in Christmas disease) may be extracted from plasma obtained from blood donated to the Red Cross blood bank. Unfortunately it does not last long after injection into the patient and must be given frequently to control any excess bleeding. Other measures to control the condition include avoiding situations and occupations where even minor injury is possible, and not using aspirin or anti-arthritis drugs, as these may cause bleeding within the gut. Because of repeated bleeds into joints, haemophiliacs often develop severe arthritis and joint deformities that require complex treatment from specially trained orthopaedic surgeons.

When you donate blood, most people think that it will be used in major surgical procedures or to help the victims of road accidents, but the essential cells and factors that are extracted from some donations can help a far wider range of Australians lead normal, healthy lives.

Haemorrhoids (piles)

Haemorrhoids, or piles as they are also sometimes called, can occur very suddenly or build up over many years.

Around the anus is a circular vein, close to the skin surface. The anal canal is about 2 cm long, and at the inner end of the canal, another vein circles around it, close to the surface. When a motion is passed, the anal canal dilates to let it pass. If this dilation is excessive due to constipation, these fine veins can be stretched, then rupture and form piles. Haemorrhoids may appear as an intermittent, painless swelling beside the anus, or they can be excruciatingly tender and painful, and bleed profusely. If the outer vein ring is damaged, an external haemorrhoid results; if the inner vein ring is damaged, an internal haemorrhoid is formed. Once a haemorrhoid has developed, a weak area will always be present, and even though one attack may settle, the same haemorrhoid may flare up time after time.

The best treatment for this distressing problem is prevention. There are two chief causes of haemorrhoids — hard large motions, and straining with heavy lifting. Haemorrhoids are a common complaint amongst Olympic weight-lifters.

Keeping the bowels regular and soft is the most important preventive measure. This involves diet and habit. The diet should be high in fibre (bulk), and low in refined foods such as sweets, cakes, white bread and sugar. High-fibre foods include unrefined cereals, wholemeal breads, green vegetables, fruit and unpolished rice. The habit of opening the bowels at a regular time each day, and not suppressing the urge to pass a motion, will also ensure that no extra stress is put on those fine veins around the anus. Once piles are present, it is even more vital to prevent further stresses to the sensitive area.

Treatment of haemorrhoids follows several steps. Initially, the soothing creams available over the counter from chemists can be used, but if relief is not rapidly obtained, assistance should be sought from your general practitioner.

After examining the area to determine exactly what damage has occurred, the doctor will prescribe appropriate treatment. This usually takes the form of anti-inflammatory (e.g. steroid) and antiseptic creams that can be used directly on the haemorrhoids, and soothing suppositories. These are bomb shaped tablets that are inserted through the anus into the rectum, where they dissolve to help internal piles. If there is a clot of blood in the dilated haemorrhoid, it may be cut open to allow the congealed blood to escape. Although momentarily painful, this is usually followed by significant relief.

If the haemorrhoids fail to settle after simple treatments, further intervention is necessary. This can vary from simply clipping a rubber band around the base of the pile, to a full scale operation to cut away part of the anal canal. Haemorrhoids may also be injected or electrically coagulated. The operation can be rather uncomfortable and painful for some days afterwards, so more conservative measures are used whenever possible. If an operation is necessary, it is normally successful in permanently removing the problem.

Although rarely serious, piles can be a distressing condition and should be treated sooner rather than later. If the appropriate creams and suppositories are used soon enough, it may be possible to avoid surgery for many years.

Hair, excess (hirsutism)

There are many causes for hirsutism, and

the treatment will depend on the cause. All cases of hirsutism should be adequately investigated to exclude any specific cause before treatment commences. In many cases, particularly in women, there is no specific identifiable cause for the excessive hair growth and it is considered to be an inherited or congenital trait (present since birth).

Treatment can range from bleaching dark hairs and shaving, to removal of hairs by commercially available depilatory creams, and permanent destruction of hair follicles by electrolysis.

Spironolactone is a drug that has been used for many years to treat heart and kidney diseases. It has recently been noticed that it also causes excessive facial and body hair in women to disappear if taken in large doses for a long period of time (6 months or more). Many women are now benefiting from this new use for an old medication.

See also Section 3.

Hair loss
See ALOPECIA.

Hand contracture
See DUPUYTREN'S CONTRACTURE.

Hansen's disease
See LEPROSY.

Hardening of arteries
See ATHEROSCLEROSIS.

Hay fever (allergic rhinitis)
The symptoms of hay fever are well known to the 10% of the population who suffer from this annoying and distressing condition. It starts with a sneeze, followed by another sneeze, then another, and dozens, scores or hundreds more. The nose drips constantly but remains so clogged you cannot breathe, you have bad breath, a constant drip of phlegm in your throat, red eyes, and a feeling that you just can't take any more of this devious torment. Most victims have the condition for only a few weeks or months of the year, when the pollens or dusts to which they react are present in the atmosphere. Although called hay fever, **allergic rhinitis** (to give it its technical tag) can be due to any one or more of several hundred different minute particles floating in the air. These can be the pollen which many plants release to fertilise others of their species, or they may be microscopic animals such as the house dust mite, or skin, scale or hair particles from animals.

Whatever the cause, the response is the same. When the sensitive, moist membranes that lines your nose and sinuses first comes into contact with the sensitising particle (called an allergen), there is no reaction, but the body's immune system is primed to react to the next invasion by these allergens. On the second exposure, the large immunoglobulin proteins that act to defend the body against invasion by any foreign matter react violently. They cluster around special cells (called mast cells) that rupture and release a substance called histamine into the nasal tissues. Histamine causes the tissue to become inflamed. The lining of the nose swells, blocking the airway, and it secretes large amounts of clear mucus in an attempt to wash away the offending particles of pollen or dust. After a few hours or days, the body destroys the histamine released, and the tissues return to normal, until a further inhalation of allergens triggers the reaction again.

The diagnosis of hay fever is relatively obvious, but not all people with runny noses are its victims. Changes in temperature and position, emotional upsets, hormonal changes (some women find their runny noses to be worse at certain times of the month), and virus infections can all cause blocked and runny noses, and the treatment for these conditions can be quite different. Blood tests may show an increase in certain types of blood cells and other chemicals in patients with hay fever, but other diseases may produce similar changes.

Hay fever can be treated by using antihistamines (see Section 6) to counteract the histamine released into the tissue. These are effective, but many of them cause drowsiness in patients. Some recently released and more expensive antihistamines overcome this problem. Antihistamine nasal sprays are also available. Another method of relief is to use pseudoephedrine nasal sprays and tablets. A doctor may also prescribe special steroid sprays (e.g. Beconase, Aldecin), and/or anti-allergy sprays (e.g. Rynacrom) in chronic cases. These are designed to be used regularly to prevent the nose from reacting to the allergens in the air.

Maintaining an allergy-free environment around the victim can often be beneficial. Covering mattresses and pillows with plastic, removing carpets and curtains from bedrooms, using synthetic stuffing and materials in pillows and furniture rather than animal hair, feathers or wool, and avoiding dust-collecting wickerwork and similar furniture are some of the steps that can be taken.

Victims who suffer regularly can have blood or skin tests performed to determine exactly which dusts and pollens cause the hay fever. Once this is known, a course of ten or more weekly injections may be used to desensitise the patient. An allergy specialist or general practitioner may give them, and they are effective in permanently preventing hay fever in some cases.

The last resort is surgery. In this, part of the lining of the nasal cavity may be removed by burning (diathermy), and some of the curly bones within the nose (called turbinates) may be cut out so that there is less area of membrane to secrete the excessive amounts of watery phlegm.

The exact form of treatment will depend on the severity of the disease and can only be reasonably determined after consultation with your general practitioner.

See also ALLERGY.

HEADACHE

One of the most common conditions seen by a general practitioner is a headache. As there are several hundred causes for several dozen different types of headache, the condition can be quite difficult — and therefore interesting — for the GP to deal with. Some causes of headache are discussed in Section 3. Cluster headaches, muscle spasm headaches, meningitis, migraine and sinus headaches are dealt with separately.

There are many rare causes for headaches, too numerous to mention here, but common reasons include bacterial or viral infections anywhere in the body, fevers, dental problems, ear blockages and disease, psychiatric disorders, jaw joint dysfunction, strokes, brain tumours, nerve compression, diabetes, thyroid disease, high blood pressure, kidney disease, and hormonal disturbances. Because this list of possible causes is so long, it is important to consult a doctor if you have a headache that persists and does not settle after use of the milder analgesics available from chemists.

See also SINUSITIS.

HEADACHE, MUSCLE SPASM (TENSION HEADACHE)

In patients with a muscle spasm headache,

the muscles at the top of the neck, in the forehead and over both temples go into prolonged contraction. This tightens the scalp, causing pressure on the skull, and increases the strain on the muscles. Victims usually complain of a constant unrelieved pressure across the head, but also sharp pains and tenderness around the hairline and neck. Poor concentration, tiredness and worsening of the headache by stress, noise and glare are symptoms that accompany tension headaches.

Muscle spasm headaches can usually be treated by aspirin or paracetamol preparations, but in some severe cases, doctors prescribe muscle relaxants. Commercially available combinations of pain-killers and mild muscle relaxants (e.g. Mersyndol, Fiorinal — see Section 6) are useful in the short term, but often cause drowsiness. Mild heat and massaging the tense muscles is a pleasant way to obtain relief. More importantly, the cause of the pain should be determined. Stress is the most common trigger, but allergies, infections and injury can also cause muscle spasm. Relief of chronic anxiety by talking through the problems with a doctor or counsellor, accepting help to deal with a stressful situation, and for a brief period in acute situations using an anti-anxiety medication may also give relief. Anyone with persistent tension headaches should have the cause of their headaches, and the correct treatment, checked by a doctor.

See also HEADACHE, Section 3.

HEAD INJURY

Your mind, your self, your very being — all these and much more are found amongst the intricate network of nerves in that delicate organ known as the brain. It is the best protected part of our bodies. It is housed in a solid case of bone, and in front and below, several layers of bone separated by air spaces (known as sinuses) protect the brain from injury. Inside its bony case, the brain floats in cerebrospinal fluid, a liquid that is very similar to sea water in its make-up. The spinal cord is the part of the brain that runs from the skull down the back, through the centre of the 24 vertebrae, and carries the brain's messages to the body. The soft brain, inside the rigid skull, cannot tolerate any increase in pressure. If this occurs due to bleeding or swelling, then pressure is exerted on the base of the brain which contains the vital centres controlling such functions as breathing and heart action.

Despite its defences, the brain may still be injured, and sometimes that injury can be very severe. Additional protection for the head in certain circumstances is therefore prudent and necessary. Motorbike riders are now compelled by law to wear protective helmets, but in other situations where head injuries are common, this type of protection is often ignored. Pony clubs usually enforce helmets during their competitions, but far too many riders fail to use them when riding socially. A fall when moving rapidly is bad enough, but when the height of a rider on a horse is added, the trauma becomes significantly greater. The major area of neglect is for bicycle riders. When slow-moving cyclists and rapidly moving motor vehicles (that are many times larger and harder than the cyclist) are mixed, the result is often lethal. Cyclists be warned — your heads are just as delicate as those of motorbike riders!

When the head is injured, it may be damaged in many different ways. The mildest form of head injury is **concussion**. In this, the sudden movement or stopping of the head causes the brain to hit against the inside of the skull as it floats in its watery cerebrospinal fluid. This pummelling causes headaches, nausea, drowsiness and confusion, but should pass in a few hours or a day or two.

More serious is the situation where this sudden movement of the brain causes bruising to occur, and a blood vessel starts to leak slowly into the tissue that supports the brain. This is known as a **sub-dural haematoma**, and the collection of blood can slowly enlarge over days or weeks until the pressure affects the brain. Surgery is then necessary to remove the clot and relieve the pressure.

If an artery in the brain itself bursts as a result of severe injury, blood rapidly spreads through the tissues, and high pressures build up to rapidly cause severe damage to the function and structure of the brain. This is an emergency, in which rapid surgery may decide the difference between a normal life, permanent mental impairment, and death.

If the skull is fractured, the vital fluid around the brain may leak out, again causing severe effects upon the functioning of the brain.

After a head injury, a patient should always be checked by a doctor, and this is even more important if the victim was knocked out. Immediately after an obvious head injury, those administering first aid should clear the airway and ensure that the patient is able to breathe freely. The neck should be immobilised by wrapping a folded towel or something similar around it. The patient may then be rolled into the coma position if unconscious. A conscious patient who is not delirious can be allowed to determine the most comfortable position for himself. The patient should be kept warm and be transported to hospital as quickly as is reasonably allowable. Skull X-rays are often performed routinely on any patient who has been knocked out, but they are probably unnecessary unless there are some further signs of brain damage. See also Section 8.

Patients with a head injury should consume food and drink in moderation for the first 24 hours. Alcohol should be totally avoided for at least a day, and no medication other than paracetamol should be taken unless instructed by a doctor. The patient should rest, use a flat pillow, avoid exercise, and not drive a car or operate machinery for 24 hours after being knocked out.

After the initial assessment for a head injury and being discharged from a doctor's care, someone in the patient's home should keep them under close observation for at least 24 hours. Problems may occur gradually, and certain warning signs will develop that indicate that pressure will have to be relieved by surgery. The patient must be returned to medical care immediately if any unusual signs develop.

Signs that indicate a serious head injury are:
- loss of consciousness
- confusion
- irrational behaviour
- severe headache that worsens
- bleeding from the ear
- repeated vomiting
- convulsions
- pupils of unequal size
- blurred or double vision.

HEAD LICE
See LICE.

HEART ATTACK (MYOCARDIAL INFARCT)
A heart attack is due to part of the heart not receiving sufficient blood. The heart is made almost entirely of muscle, but it cannot obtain the necessary oxygen and other vital elements from the blood within it, because the chambers of the heart are lined with an impervious membrane and there are no fine blood vessels leading into the heart muscle from the chambers. All the blood to keep the heart alive and well passes through three small arteries that

circle around the heart and send small vessels into the muscle. If one of these arteries is blocked, one part of the heart muscle cannot obtain sufficient blood, and dies. This is a heart attack or myocardial infarct. If you put a tight rubber band around your finger, you cut off the finger's blood supply. It rapidly becomes painful and would eventually wither and die. The same thing happens in the heart, but more rapidly, because the heart must keep working hard with every beat, while your finger is at rest.

The arteries of the heart can be blocked by fatty deposits that build up in the arteries because the patient is overweight or has high cholesterol levels, by clots or fat globules breaking off from damaged blood vessels elsewhere in the body and blocking an artery, or by damage to the artery from many years of high blood pressure.

Many patients feel unusual chest discomfort, a change in their angina pattern, or complain of 'indigestion' for hours, days or even weeks before a heart attack. When the heart attack occurs, the patient feels a severe crushing pain in the chest and shortness of breath. The pain builds up rapidly in waves, and then persists for some time before gradually fading. The pain may be accompanied by sweating, weakness, anxiety, dizziness, cough, nausea and vomiting. Most patients seek medical aid rapidly because of the severity of the symptoms, and this is vital, because doctors can give medications by injection that stabilise the heart and prevent it from stopping completely. Unfortunately, some heart attacks create minimal discomfort, and may be dismissed by the patient as a passing attack of severe indigestion.

If you feel that you, or someone with you, is having a heart attack, call an ambulance (use the 000 number) and your general practitioner. Once you are under the care of a doctor, your chances of survival are good, because of the many medications and treatments available to stop abnormal heartbeats, which are the normal cause of death in a heart attack. Doctors can also give injections to relieve the crushing, severe pain, and relieve the intense anxiety of the patient. Less than 20% of patients die immediately from a heart attack.

Once in hospital, the victim will be kept in a coronary care ward under the constant eye of specially trained nurses and doctors who can instantly deal with any further deterioration.

Treatment will include drugs to break up the blood clot blocking the coronary artery that supplies the heart with blood, and a complex cocktail of other medications to regulate the functioning of the heart. Most of these will be given into an intravenous drip in the arm. After a few days, you will be allowed to rest in a normal ward while the heart heals. Then after 10 to 14 days, you can go home for a further six or more weeks rest.

The heart attack is diagnosed by an electrocardiogram (see Section 4) and by blood tests that can detect abnormal chemicals produced by the heart muscle damage. Chest X-rays will be performed, but more to check the state of the lungs and size of the heart than to diagnose the presence of a heart attack.

The secret of recovery lies in gradually increasing levels of exercise over many weeks in order to slowly strengthen the heart. Manual workers can often return to their jobs after a couple of months, and provided they look after their general health, most heart attack victims will lead a normal and full life.

After the initial recovery period, further investigations will be undertaken to determine the cause of the heart attack and to see if further surgical or medical treatment can be undertaken to prevent another heart attack. These investigations may include echocardiography, coronary angiography and nuclear scans (see Section 4).

Virtually every heart attack victim will be put on medication (e.g. beta-blockers and aspirin — see Section 6) to prevent another attack. These may need to be continued for life. It is also necessary to have regular checkups by your GP to ensure that you and your heart remain in peak condition.

If a particular artery can be found to be blocked, coronary artery bypass graft (CABG) surgery (see Section 6) may be performed to bypass this blockage.

The long-term complications of a heart attack include angina (see separate entry), an irregular heartbeat (which can normally be adequately controlled by medication), heart failure (see separate entry) and an aneurysm (see separate entry).

Statistically, after a heart attack, 20% of patients will die within the first hour, a further 10% will die in hospital, 5% will die within three months of leaving hospital and another 3% in every year thereafter. The death rate has been significantly lowered in recent years by the use of medication in the long term after a heart attack.

The main things that you can do to prevent a heart attack are to keep your weight within reasonable limits, have your blood pressure checked and treated if necessary, avoid excess cholesterol in your diet, exercise regularly, and stop smoking. Smokers are at a far higher risk than others in the community because nicotine can cause spasm of the arteries in the heart.

HEART DISEASES
See ANEURYSM; CARDIOMYOPATHY; COR PULMONALE; ENDOCARDITIS; HEART ATTACK; HEART FAILURE; HEART, IRREGULAR RHYTHM; HEART VALVE DISEASE; HYPERTENSION; HYPOTENSION; MARFAN'S SYNDROME; MYOCARDITIS; PAROXYSMAL ATRIAL TACHYCARDIA; PATENT DUCTUS ARTERIOSUS; PERICARDITIS; RHEUMATIC FEVER.

HEART FAILURE (CARDIAC FAILURE)
Heart failure occurs when the heart is no longer capable of pumping blood around the body effectively. Many conditions can cause heart failure. These include heart attacks (which damage the heart muscle), heart infection (see ENDOCARDITIS; MYOCARDITIS; PERICARDITIS), narrowing or leaking of heart valves, high blood pressure, narrowing of the aorta (see AORTIC STENOSIS), irregular heart rhythm (see following entry), alcoholic heart damage, severe anaemia (inadequate oxygen being transported by the blood) and an overactive thyroid gland (increased rate of body activity results in greater demands for blood).

Patients with cardiac failure ('cardiac' means 'of the heart'), complain of being short of breath when exercising or climbing stairs, but as the condition worsens they are constantly out of breath, particularly when lying down at night. Other symptoms include a hard dry cough, having to get out of bed to pass urine at night, general tiredness and weakness, a rapid heart rate, chest and abdominal discomfort and swelling of the feet, ankles and hands. These patients may be noticed by others to be losing weight, unable to speak a full sentence without taking a breath, and in advanced cases a blue tinge develops on and around the lips.

The diagnosis can often be made by a doctor without resorting to any sophisticated tests, but it is important to discover the cause of the heart failure, particularly in younger patients, and this may involve extensive investigations over a considerable period. Blood tests, chest X-rays and electrocardiograms (see Section 4) are the main tests performed. Further tests may be indicated after the results of these are obtained. Echocardiograms (see Section 4) and cardiac catheterisation (passing a tube through a vein into the heart) are sometimes undertaken if surgical treatment of a heart defect is being contemplated.

Treatment involves correction of any specific cause for the heart failure if possible. If the thyroid is overactive or the patient is anaemic, these can be treated and the heart failure may disappear. Correction of high blood pressure, controlling an irregular heart rhythm and treating heart infections are other methods of dealing with a specific cause of heart failure. Sometimes surgical correction of a heart valve deformity is also possible.

A diet low in salt, and avoiding strenuous exercise can often be beneficial. Medications to remove excess fluid from the body (diuretics — see Section 6) and to strengthen the action of the heart (e.g. digoxin) are in common use. A number of more sophisticated drugs are available for use in resistant or difficult cases. Oxygen may be supplied to seriously ill patients.

In many elderly patients, there can be a multitude of causes, or no specific cause at all for the heart failure. In these cases, the condition is treated as a disease in itself.

Unless an underlying correctable cause can be found, heart failure cannot be cured, only controlled. As the years pass, the condition usually slowly worsens and becomes steadily harder to control. Some patients succumb to heart attacks, while others become more and more incapacitated so that they cannot leave a bed, and develop pneumonia. The actual outcome in any individual is very difficult to predict, but it may take many years before serious incapacitation or death occurs.

See also COR PULMONALE.

HEART, IRREGULAR RHYTHM (ARRHYTHMIA)

Cardiac arrhythmias (irregular heartbeats) can vary from the totally harmless to the rapidly fatal. The rate at which the heart beats is controlled by a collection of nerve fibres near the top of the heart called the pacemaker. This fires off at regular intervals to produce an electrical charge that causes the upper chambers of the heart (the atria — see HEART, Section 2) to contract, and a fraction of a second later, the lower chambers (the ventricles) of the heart are stimulated to contract. Normally the pacemaker sends out its signals 70 times a minute, but at times of exercise or stress this can increase to three or more times this normal rate. In many individuals, particularly in fit athletes, the normal rate is lower, while in others, such as small women, the natural rate may be higher. If the pacemaker does not act at all, the heart muscles will contract anyway, as they have an in-built ability to contract rhythmically. This rate is very slow though — about 40 beats per minute. Many diseases can alter the heart rhythm. Anaemia and an overactive thyroid can cause an increase in rate, while an underactive thyroid may cause a decrease.

Occasional **dropped beats** are very common in older people and are no cause for concern. If the dropped beats are more frequent (say one in every five), then it is necessary for tests such as an electrocardiogram (ECG) to be done to determine the cause. Even in this situation, there may be no serious problem. The occasional extra heartbeat fits into this category also. Stress, alcohol, smoking and exercise are common causes of dropped or extra beats. More serious diseases may also be responsible, such as high blood pressure, rheumatic heart disease and as an after effect of a heart attack.

A totally irregular heartbeat may occur if the upper heart chambers (the atria) are fibrillating (vibrating rapidly) rather than contracting correctly. **Atrial fibrillation** will cause the patient to be tired and breathless, but often minimal symptoms are present. The condition can be corrected in most cases by using drugs such as digoxin or verapamil (see Section 6). It should not be allowed to persist for long periods unless control is difficult or impossible.

There are many combinations and permutations of heartbeat irregularities, the fine details of which need to be assessed on an individual basis by a doctor.

See also PAROXYSMAL ATRIAL TACHYCARDIA.

See also PALPITATIONS, Section 3.

HEART VALVE DISEASE

The heart has four valves that control the inflow and outflow of blood. There is a valve between the upper chambers (the atria) and lower chambers (the ventricles) of the heart on both the right side, where the tricuspid valve is situated, and on the left side, where the mitral valve can be found. There are also valves at the point where the large arteries leave the right ventricle to go to the lungs (the pulmonary valve) and where the aorta leaves the left side of the heart to take blood to the body (the aortic valve — see HEART, Section 2). These four valves can be either incompetent (leak, and allow blood to flow the wrong way) or stenosed (narrowed, and impeding the flow of blood). Incompetent valves are sometimes described as causing valve regurgitation or valve insufficiency.

Diseases of heart valves are investigated and diagnosed by a combination of electrocardiograms (ECG), echocardiograms, special X-rays of the heart, cardiac catheterisation (passing a tube through a vein into the heart), CT scans and other more sophisticated tests (see Section 4).

Treatment of damaged heart valves almost invariably involves surgery. Faulty valves can be replaced with artificial valves or animal (e.g. calf, pig) heart valves in operations that are now quite routine. Narrowed (stenosed) valves can sometimes be opened up by passing a deflated balloon on the end of a tube through an artery or vein until it reaches the valve. The balloon is then blown up to force open the narrowed valve.

Aortic valve

The aortic valve sits between the left ventricle and the aorta, and stops blood that has been pumped out to the body from running back into the heart.

Aortic valve stenosis (narrowing) prevents the blood from easily leaving the heart and moving to the body. It is a disease that may be congenital (present at birth) or develop because of rheumatic fever (see separate entry) or hardening of the valve from high blood pressure and/or high cholesterol levels.

The stenosis is diagnosed by a doctor hearing the typical murmur produced by the blood rushing through the narrowed valve. Symptoms are often absent in mild cases, but when the stenosis is more advanced they include chest pain (that may progress to angina), fainting with exercise, and an irregular heartbeat. Once symptoms occur, surgery to correct the narrowing should be performed, as half those with symptomatic aortic valve stenosis will die within three years without surgery.

Aortic valve incompetence (regurgitation or leakage) allows blood that has just been pumped out of the heart and into the aorta to run back into the heart as it relaxes in preparation for the next beat. It may be caused by rheumatic fever, endocarditis, high blood pressure, and syphilis, or it may be a birth defect. If only a slight leak is present, there will be no symptoms, but if the leak worsens, the patient will become short of breath, develop chest pain, and be very tired. The condition can be quite advanced before the patient notices any problem, and then s/he may deteriorate rapidly.

Some drugs to reduce the blood pressure may give relief, but if possible, surgical correction should be undertaken once symptoms are present.

Mitral valve

The mitral valve is the large valve between the upper and lower chambers on the left side of the heart. The valve receives its name because its two halves resemble a bishop's mitre.

Mitral valve stenosis (narrowing) is caused by rheumatic fever in most patients, and as the incidence of this infection decreases, so does the incidence of mitral stenosis. The symptoms include shortness of breath, tiredness, an irregular heartbeat (caused by atrial fibrillation — see HEART, IRREGULAR RHYTHM), coughing of blood, and cor pulmonale (see separate entry). A common complication can be an embolism (a blood clot that travels to the brain) that may cause a stroke or death. Anticoagulant drugs (see Section 6) are given to prevent emboli, but if the condition is uncontrolled, surgery to correct the narrowing should be undertaken.

Mitral valve incompetence (regurgitation or leaking) can be caused by rheumatic fever, endocarditis and heart tumours. It may also accompany Marfan's syndrome (see separate entry). In this situation, when the large left ventricle (lower heart chamber) contracts, blood is forced not only into the aorta (where it should go) but back through the damaged valve and up into the smaller left atrium (upper heart chamber) from where it has just come. This puts pressure back into the lungs to cause shortness of breath and fatigue. Complications of this incompetence are an irregular heartbeat and infections of the damaged valve.

Patients with only minimal symptoms require no treatment, but if complications or progressive symptoms develop, surgical repair or replacement of the valve is necessary.

Pulmonary valve

The pulmonary valve is one between the right ventricle (right lower chamber) of the heart and the pulmonary artery, which takes the blood from the heart to the lungs. The word 'pulmonary' refers to the lungs.

Pulmonary valve stenosis (narrowing) is usually a birth defect. Severe narrowing causes chest pain, fainting on exertion, and shortness of breath. If the stenosis is causing symptoms it must be corrected surgically, because if it is left untreated, sudden death or heart failure may occur.

Tricuspid valve

The tricuspid valve has three parts (cusps) to give it its name. It controls the flow of blood between the upper chamber (the atrium) and lower chamber (the ventricle) on the right side of the heart.

Tricuspid valve stenosis (narrowing) is an uncommon condition in Australia and usually occurs as a result of rheumatic fever. It causes dilation of the veins in the neck and a redness in the neck and face, as blood finds it difficult to progress from the body and into the heart. The treatment is surgical.

Tricuspid valve incompetence (leaking, regurgitation) may occur in cor pulmonale (see separate entry), because of a heart attack, with heart tumours, or with endocarditis in intravenous drug abusers. There are a number of rarer causes. Control of this condition is often by medication rather than surgery, which is performed only in severe cases.

Fallot's tetralogy

Fallot was a French physician who practised in Marseilles during the latter part of the nineteenth century. He described a relatively common but complex birth defect of the heart that has four components (thus the name tetralogy — four parts).

Babies born with Fallot's tetralogy have a hole between the left and right ventricles, and the aorta starts from the wrong position within the heart, there is a narrowing of the pulmonary artery or valve that leads from the right ventricle to the lung, and an enlargement of the right ventricle. Babies usually have no symptoms at birth, but doctors can hear abnormal murmurs within the heart. Shortly after birth, the time depending on the severity of the pulmonary valve narrowing, the baby becomes blue and short of breath. These babies also grow very slowly.

Treatment involves extensive open heart surgery, usually within the first year or two of life. Without surgery, death is inevitable as the child slowly grows and puts added demands upon the damaged heart.

Hepatic disease
See LIVER DISEASE.

Hepatitis

Unfortunately there are still some diseases where medical science has been unable to significantly improve the method of treatment for many decades. One such disease is hepatitis. Most people know of hepatitis as a liver infection that makes a patient turn yellow. Fewer know that there are two main forms of hepatitis — type A and type B — which differ greatly in the way they are caught and in their long-term outcome. To confuse matters slightly, there is also another less common type of hepatitis called 'non-A, non-B', or hepatitis C. All these types of hepatitis are caused by those smallest of all living particles, viruses, and doctors are unable to cure the vast majority of these infections anywhere in the body.

There is no cure for hepatitis, but it is rare for hepatitis A to cause long-term problems in the same way as hepatitis B.

Hepatitis A (infective hepatitis)

Hepatitis A is caught by eating food that has been handled by someone else who has the disease. The virus lives in the liver, but large numbers pass down the bile duct and into the gut, and contaminate the faeces. If a sufferer is not careful with his/her personal hygiene, the virus may be passed onto someone else. Contrary to earlier beliefs, it is now thought that there are no long-term carriers of hepatitis A in the community.

If virus particles are swallowed, they are absorbed with the food into the bloodstream and migrate to the liver, where after an incubation period lasting two to six weeks they start causing damage to the liver cells.

The liver is used by the body to process food and eliminate waste products through the bile. If it is damaged, it cannot work efficiently, and the main constituent of the bile (bilirubin) builds up in the blood stream. Because of the yellow colour of bilirubin, the victim's skin slowly turns a dark yellow. The whites of the eyes are affected first, and this may be the only sign of the disease in a dark-skinned person. The other symptoms are nausea, vomiting, marked tiredness, loss of appetite, generalised aches and pains, fever and a large tender liver.

Sophisticated tests are now available to diagnose hepatitis and monitor its progress. Blood tests are performed frequently during the disease, so that doctors can detect any deterioration. The main treatment available is the same one that has been in use for almost a century — rest, and a good diet that is low in protein and high in carbohydrate. Alcohol is forbidden.

The usual course of the disease is an initial worsening of symptoms after diagnosis to a peak when jaundice (yellowing of the skin) is most marked, followed by a slow recovery period that may take from one to four months. If the disease continues to worsen, drugs may be used in an attempt to reduce the liver damage, but nothing can be done to kill the infecting virus. In rare cases (2 in 1000), the disease may progress despite all efforts of doctors and result in death. This is more common in the elderly.

Hepatitis A can be prevented in the short term by an injection of gammaglobulin, and close contacts and family members of a patient are usually given this to prevent them from developing the disease. Unfortunately its effects last only a few months. The vital preventative factor is the standard of hygiene in the community. As a result, hepatitis A is far more common in third-world countries than in Australia. Gammaglobulin injections can also be given to travellers who plan a visit to third-world countries (e.g. Indonesia, India), particularly if they are camping or backpacking.

Hepatitis B (serum hepatitis)
Until 25 years ago, doctors did not realise that there were two different types of hepatitis, and it is only in the last decade that we have been able to easily differentiate between them using sophisticated blood tests. These tests are now routine for anyone who catches hepatitis.

Hepatitis B was first identified as a separate disease in Australian Aborigines, and the specific antigen that could be detected in the bloodstream to diagnose the disease was called the 'Australia antigen' for many years. There is no way for a doctor to tell which form of hepatitis a patient has without these tests. Both types cause the patient to be very ill with a liver infection, fever, jaundice (yellow skin), nausea and loss of appetite. Most recover from this episode after a few weeks, but about 1% of patients will develop rapidly progressive liver damage that will lead to death. Unfortunately some people who have hepatitis B develop a very mild form of the disease which may be passed off by the patient as being slightly unwell for a few days, but that illness may be enough to totally alter his/her future life.

Hepatitis B can only be caught by intimate contact with the body fluids of a person who has the disease or is a carrier of the disease. These body fluids are generally blood and semen, so you can catch Hepatitis B by receiving blood from such a person, using a contaminated needle, rubbing your graze or cut on an infected person's graze or cut, being bitten by an infected person, or having sex with them. Babies born to mothers who are hepatitis B carriers have a more than 50% chance of catching the disease. Blood banks screen all donations for hepatitis B, so it is virtually impossible to catch the disease by this route. Drug addicts who share needles are at great risk. Splashes of blood into an eye or onto a cut or graze can be enough to spread the disease. For this reason, doctors, dentists, nurses and other health workers are at greater risk than the rest of the community. Nine out of ten people who catch hepatitis B will recover from it completely, but the other one in ten will become chronic carriers of the disease and may be able to pass it on to others for the rest of their lives.

Hepatitis B has a long incubation period of six weeks to six months from initially coming into contact with the virus. The infection cannot be detected during this period.

The long-term problem with hepatitis B is that a significant percentage of all people who catch the disease will develop cirrhosis and failure of the liver, which may ultimately prove fatal. Liver cancer (hepatoma) is also more common in these patients. It is for this reason that the medical profession is becoming so concerned by the spread of the disease through the community by promiscuous sex and drug abuse. Some patients are found to have a 'Delta agent' present in their blood as well, and they are more likely to develop the long- term, severe complications of hepatitis B.

On the other hand, it is possible to vaccinate against hepatitis B, but not against hepatitis A. Three vaccinations are necessary within six months and then another after five years to give lifelong immunity to the disease. It is currently recommended that everyone in the medical or dental profession who is exposed to blood should be vaccinated against hepatitis B. Others who feel their lifestyle puts them at risk (e.g. other health workers, policemen, prison guards and others who may be in direct contact with people who have the disease) should also have this series of injections. At present the vaccine is quite expensive, but its manufacture is extremely complex, involving genetic engineering to make an exact but safe copy of the hepatitis B virus, in order to stimulate a person's immune system appropriately.

If you have had hepatitis B, you must ensure that you are no longer infectious before having sex with anyone and have regular blood tests throughout your life to detect any liver damage at an early stage.

Non-A non-B hepatitis (hepatitis C)
This is a form of hepatitis, presumably caused by a virus, in which the specific blood tests for the A and B types remain negative. Because it cannot be detected by blood tests, it is possible although unlikely to catch this form of hepatitis by a blood transfusion.

The incubation period is variable between two and 20 weeks, but otherwise the symptoms and treatment are the same as hepatitis A.

HEPATOLENTICULAR DEGENERATION
See WILSON'S DISEASE.

HEPATOMA (LIVER CANCER)
A hepatoma is a cancer that starts in the liver. Most liver cancers are secondary cancers and have started in other parts of the body before spreading to the liver. Hepatomas are far more common in developing countries where the occurrence is associated with hepatitis B, liver parasites and malnutrition. In Australia, hepatomas occur most commonly in patients who have long-standing alcoholic cirrhosis (see separate entry). There is often no sign that a patient has a hepatoma until it is well advanced, at which point the liver begins to fail and the patient becomes jaundiced (yellow), nauseated, very weak, loses weight and is unable to eat. In a late stage, the abdomen may become swollen with fluid. The diagnosis can be confirmed by blood tests, a liver biopsy (taking a sample of the liver through a needle), ultrasound scans and CT scans (see Section 4).

In the vast majority of cases, there is no surgical or medical treatment available, as almost invariably the cancer has spread too far by the time it is diagnosed. Death within a short time of the condition being diagnosed is the usual result.

HERNIA
To say that someone has a hernia really means very little, as a hernia is merely the rupture of tissue out of its normal position into a place where it is not normally situated. There are therefore many different types of hernia in the body. Some are quite rare, but amongst the more common types are the hiatus hernia (see separate entry),

the umbilical hernia (where fat or gut bursts out through the wall of the abdomen to lie under the skin around the navel), the femoral hernia (which can occur in a woman's groin), and the most common of all, the inguinal hernia in the groin.

Inguinal hernia
Inguinal hernias occur almost invariably in men, and the reason for this goes back to the time when the man was still a foetus in his mother's womb. The testicles develop inside the abdomen, and before birth they migrate down into the scrotum. Behind them as they move down, they leave a tube (called the inguinal canal) that in the adult is 10 to 12 cm long. Through this tube run the arteries, veins and nerves that supply the testicles. The small vas deferens, a duct that carries the sperm from the testicle to the base of the penis, also passes through the tube left by the descending testicle. Shortly before birth, the inguinal canal closes down so that it is almost shut, leaving just enough room for the vital supplies to pass to and from the testes. In some little boys, the tube does not close properly, and this allows a small amount of fat or intestine to move down the tube from the inside of the abdomen, to form a hernia just under the skin beside the penis. It should now be fairly obvious why this type of hernia is rare in women!

In most men, the tube shuts effectively, but it remains a source of weakness in the strong muscle wall of the abdomen. If excess pressure is put on the lower part of the belly by heavy lifting, prolonged coughing or some other form of strain, the closed inguinal canal may tear open again, allowing some of the gut to protrude as a hernia. Men who are overweight and have their muscles weakened by fat deposits are more likely to develop this type of hernia, and the slackening of muscle tone with advancing age can also lead to a rupture. There is also an hereditary tendency, so that if your father had a hernia, your chances of developing one are increased.

Once a hernia is present, it may be only mildly annoying after exercise, or it may become very painful, and occasionally the gut inside the hernia may become strangled in the inguinal canal, causing that section of gut to become gangrenous. This is a surgical emergency.

To prevent this emergency from occurring, and to relieve the discomfort of the hernia, doctors usually recommend that it be surgically repaired. This is a relatively common and simple operation in which the inguinal canal is opened, the protruding gut is replaced in the abdomen, and the tube is sutured closed in several layers to prevent a further rupture. Sometimes material similar to mosquito netting is stitched into the muscle layers to further strengthen the area. There is some post-operative soreness, but most people can return to office work after two or three weeks, and heavy labour after six to eight weeks. Even in the best surgical hands, however, about 10% of inguinal hernias will recur.

In some older men, particularly if the hernia is very large, surgical repair is not practical, and a suitable truss is used to hold the bulging hernia in place. These larger hernias are less likely to strangle.

Femoral hernia
There is another point of weakness in the groin, just underneath the skin where the femoral artery passes through a small hole as it leaves the abdomen and starts its journey down the front of the thigh. Under pressure from heavy work or childbirth, a small piece of intestine may be forced into this narrow hole and appear as a small lump under the skin of the groin. Because it is often quite small, it is very easy for the trapped intestine to become pinched,

twisted, and gangrenous. Femoral hernias are more common in women than men, but may occur in both sexes.

Femoral hernias may either cause no symptoms or be responsible for vague, intermittent abdominal pains. The lump under the skin may not be noticed until the hernia becomes painful, particularly in fat women. Once the intestine becomes trapped, it will become very painful and obvious to the patient.

Whenever discovered, a femoral hernia should be surgically repaired because of the high risk of gangrene. Once pain has developed in the hernia, surgery becomes a matter of urgency. The recurrence rate after surgery is about 5%.

Umbilical hernia

Umbilical hernias (protrusions of the navel) come in two forms — those that occur in children, and those that develop in elderly adults.

In **children**, there is a hole between the muscle layers of the abdomen where the arteries and veins that passed down the umbilical cord from the mother entered the baby. This hole normally closes quickly after birth, but in some children the hole is very large, or is slow to close. In these cases, bulging of the intestine into the area just below the skin of the umbilicus can occur. Umbilical hernias are more common in premature babies, as their systems are not as mature, and the processes involved in closing the hole behind the umbilicus are slower.

Umbilical hernias bulge out while the infant is crying or active, but usually disappear when the child is lying quietly. The hernia almost never gives pain or discomfort to the child. It is very rare for the intestine to become trapped and gangrenous.

The vast majority of umbilical hernias in children close spontaneously without any surgical intervention. This usually occurs within twelve months but may take until three years of age. There is no benefit from strapping or taping the hernia, and no matter how much it bulges, the skin covering the hernia never bursts. If the hernia persists beyond three years of age, surgery may be contemplated, but in Africa, where umbilical hernias appear to be more common, spontaneous repair may occur as late as six years of age.

In **adults**, the hernia is not strictly speaking an umbilical hernia, but a **paraumbilical hernia**, as the rupture occurs not immediately underneath the umbilicus but in the slightly weakened fibrous tissue just above (more common) or below the navel. This type of hernia is common in women who have had multiple pregnancies, in the very obese and those who have other causes of excess pressure in the abdomen.

In contrast to the situation in children, umbilical hernias in adults do not reduce in size but steadily increase with time, until they can form the major part of the front of the abdomen. These large hernias can contain a significant amount of intestine and may cause significant discomfort and constipation.

Small umbilical hernias are best repaired surgically when discovered, as delay will only lead to a larger hernia and more difficult repair later. In older patients with particularly large hernias, surgical repair may not be practical as a routine procedure, but if pain occurs as a result of strangulation of the intestine and impending gangrene, emergency surgery is essential. The recurrence rate after surgery depends upon the original size of the hernia, but is generally low.

Heroin addiction

See DRUG ADDICTION.

HERPANGINA
See STOMATITIS.

HERPES SIMPLEX INFECTIONS
Herpes simplex is a virus that causes infections of moist membranes and skin. The most common areas affected are around the nose, lips, vulva, vagina and penis, but the surface anywhere on the body may be involved. The herpes virus is widely distributed in the community, and infections are very common.

The herpes simplex virus comes in two main types, labelled simply 1 and 2. Herpes simplex 1 tends to cause infections around the nose and mouth (cold sores) and herpes simplex 2 tends to cause genital infections, but they are interchangeable and not mutually exclusive. A distantly related virus, *Herpes zoster*, is responsible for shingles and chickenpox (see separate entries).

Cold sores (herpes simplex 1)
Approximately 60% of the population are infected with herpes simplex 1 and remain carriers of the virus for the rest of their lives. The virus is passed from one person to another by direct contact (e.g. kissing).

Cold sores are rare before six months of age, but as the immunity passed on by the mother at birth and through breastfeeding has worn off, the infection can develop on the lips, inside the mouth or around the nostrils. Serious infection before five years of age is uncommon, and the incidence also seems to decrease in old age.

Cold sores are characterised by redness and soreness of the affected area, followed a day or two later by an eruption of small blisters, which rapidly burst to leave a shallow, weeping, painful ulcer. In severe cases, there may be a mild fever, and the glands in the neck may become tender and enlarged. After about a week, the sore heals and the pain eases.

Infections with herpes simplex 1 can also develop on the fingers, particularly at the edge of the nail, when it is given the name **whitlow**. Herpes simplex 1 infections occasionally occur on the genitals, where the herpes simplex 2 infection is more common, and vice versa. In rare cases, the infection can spread into the throat and lungs, and these patients become extremely ill.

Recurrences of cold sores tend to develop at the same spot time after time. They occur when the patient is under stress, run-down or has an infection (e.g. a cold — hence the name, cold sores), or when the skin is damaged by drying, sun burn or wind burn. At these times, the virus is able to overcome the body's defence mechanisms, start multiplying and cause the typical sore. After an attack, the virus lies dormant in the nerve cells under the skin until the opportunity to cause a further infection arises.

The diagnosis can be confirmed by taking special swabs from the sore and identifying the virus in a laboratory. Normally no investigations are required, and the diagnosis can be made on the appearance of the sore.

If treatment of a particular cold sore infection is undertaken immediately the redness and discomfort is felt and before the blisters form, it may be possible to stop it progressing further. Creams or lotions containing idoxuridine (see Section 6) are used for this purpose. Once the cold sore is established, a cure is not possible, but drying, antiseptic and anaesthetic creams or lotions may be used to control the symptoms and prevent any secondary infection from developing.

A bacterial infection, in addition to the original herpes viral infection, is the only common complication. Antibiotic creams or ointments are then necessary.

Some patients have only one attack of cold sores in their lives, while others are unlucky enough to become a victim every month (it may follow a woman's menstrual cycle). There appears to be no obvious reason why some people are affected more than others. Patients who are severely affected on a regular basis may use Zovirax tablets (see Section 6) continuously to prevent most of the infections, but these are very expensive and beyond the financial means of most people.

Genital herpes (herpes simplex 2)
Herpes simplex 2 is the technical name for a disease that is second only to AIDS in its effect upon the sexual mores of the world. Genital herpes is not a new disease, but it has become more widely spread in the past two decades.

It is sometimes possible to develop a genital form of herpes sore from a herpes simplex 1 virus. The blisters from both types of herpes infection are identical. The majority of cases of genital herpes are caught by sexual contact with someone, male or female, who already has the disease. It is possible, but unlikely, for the virus to be caught in hot spa baths and from a shared wet towel, but these and similar incidents are not common.

Once a person is infected with the virus, it settles in the nerve endings around the vulva or penis. It remains there for the rest of that person's life. At times of stress, illness or reduced resistance, the virus starts reproducing and causes the painful blisters and ulcers that characterise the disease. The first attack may occur only a week, or up to some years, after the initial infection. Blisters and ulcers may develop anywhere on the penis or scrotum (sac) in the male; and on the vulva (vaginal lips), and in the vagina and cervix (opening into the womb) of the female. When they occur internally on the cervix or high in the vagina, the symptoms are reduced, and the woman may pass on the infection without being aware of its presence.

The attack will last for two to four weeks and then subside. After weeks, months or years, a further attack may occur, but the usual pattern is for the attacks to become less severe and to occur further apart. Some victims have only one attack in their lives — others who are less fortunate may have repeated attacks for long periods of time that seriously affect their lifestyle. Herpes infection can also in rare cases cause an encephalitis. Genital herpes appears to affect women more severely and frequently than men.

The infection can be definitely diagnosed by taking a swab from the ulcer and having this examined in a laboratory. This is sometimes necessary to exclude other causes of ulcers on the genitals, and for legal reasons.

Until recently, herpes was incurable. Medications were available to shorten an attack and reduce its severity, but they were not always effective. Soothing anaesthetic creams and lotions are still the mainstay of treatment and control until an attack passes. Recently, the first anti-viral drug ever produced (acyclovir or Zovirax — see Section 6) was released on the market in Australia. These tablets are extraordinarily expensive (approximately $250 for a 2-week course), but they will cure an attack of genital herpes and, if taken for several months, will prevent further attacks and possibly cure the disease. It is also available as an ointment.

If sores are present, there is a very good chance of passing the disease on to your sexual partner. A victim is also infectious for several days before a new crop of sores develop, as the virus is rapidly reproducing at this stage. An absence of sores does not guarantee that the infection will not be transmitted, but condoms will give some protection (but not 100%) against spreading the disease.

The most serious side of this normally distressing but not life-threatening disease is the effect it may have on the babies of women who develop an attack at the end of their pregnancy. If a baby catches the infection during delivery, it can cause severe brain damage in the child. For this reason, if a woman has a history of repeated herpes infections, she may be delivered by caesarean section so that the baby does not come into contact with the virus particles that may be present in the birth canal.

There is also evidence that the incidence of gynaecological cancer is increased in women with genital herpes. All women should have regular smear tests, but particularly so if they have this annoying, but rarely serious disease.

HERPES ZOSTER INFECTIONS
See CHICKENPOX; SHINGLES.

HIATUS HERNIA

A hernia occurs when a part of the body slides through an opening into a position that is not its normal position. The stomach (see Section 2) sits in the abdomen immediately below the diaphragm, which is a sheet of muscle that separates the chest from the abdomen. The oesophagus (gullet) runs from the back of the throat, down the back of the chest, through the diaphragm to join the stomach. The duodenum drains food and digestive juices from the other end of the stomach and into the intestine. There is a hole in the diaphragm through which the oesophagus passes just before it enters the stomach. If part of the stomach moves up through this hole into the chest cavity, the patient has a hiatus hernia.

Pressure in the abdominal cavity from heavy lifting, obesity, and tension (muscle spasm occurs), or slack ligaments in the diaphragm in the elderly, may all lead to the formation of a hiatus hernia. There are two types of hiatus hernia — the paraoesophageal hiatus hernia, and the sliding hiatus hernia.

Paraoesophageal hiatus hernias occur when a pocket of stomach pops up beside the oesophagus and through the hole in the diaphragm. These may cause no symptoms, but patients usually describe difficulty in swallowing and sometimes pain from ulceration inside the hernia or pinching of the hernia. Further symptoms can include burping, a feeling of fullness, bleeding from the damaged part of the stomach, and palpitations if a large hernia pushes onto the heart. Most of these hernias are small, but sometimes a large proportion of the stomach may push up into the chest. Once this type of hernia is discovered, it should be surgically repaired, unless the patient is elderly or in poor health. The results of surgery are generally good.

Sliding hiatus hernias are far more common, and 90% of all hiatus hernias fit into this category. In this type of hiatus hernia, the stomach slides up into the chest, displacing the lower end of the oesophagus. The stomach does not share the hole in the diaphragm with the oesophagus, but pushes the oesophagus further up into the chest.

Patients complain of heartburn (which may be very severe), burping excessively, a bitter taste on the back of the tongue (waterbrash), and difficulty in swallowing. The heartburn is usually worse at night when lying down, or after a meal. It is usually eased by drinking milk or an antacid, but this relief may only be temporary. Some patients believe that they are having a heart attack, as the pain of the heartburn is so severe. The pain causes a rapid pulse rate and cold sweats, which may also make it difficult for a doctor to correctly differentiate between heartburn and heart pain.

The cells lining the stomach secrete a

mucus that protects them from the concentrated hydrochloric acid that is secreted by the stomach to digest food. The cells lining the oesophagus are not protected against acid, as the oesophagus is never meant to be exposed to it. When a sliding hiatus hernia develops, the valve at the lower end of the oesophagus that normally prevents the acid from flowing into it is damaged and no longer works effectively, so that when the patient lies down or bends over, the acid can flow freely back up into the oesophagus and start to attack its lining. This naturally causes pain, and causes a condition known as reflux oesophagitis (see separate entry). Long-standing reflux of acid into the oesophagus can cause peptic ulcers (see separate entry) which may bleed and cause serious complications. The acid taste on the back of the tongue (waterbrash) occurs when the stomach acid is able to flow all the way up to the throat. The same acidic taste is also experienced after vomiting.

In some patients the hernia remains fixed in the one position, but in others, the hernia may slide up and down, depending on the patients position or activity. A large meal may be sufficient to push the overloaded stomach up into the chest.

The diagnosis can be confirmed by a barium meal X-ray (see Section 4), or by gastroscopy (see Section 4) in which a flexible tube is passed through the mouth and into the stomach.

Many sliding hiatus hernias are discovered incidentally on routine X-rays for other conditions, and cause no symptoms. Only when the patient is discomforted by the hernia is treatment necessary.

Most cases of sliding hiatus hernia can be treated with medication, posture and diet. Antacids (see Section 6) that neutralise the acid, liquids and gels that coat the lower oesophagus, anaesthetic mixtures, foaming granules that float top of the stomach acid, and tablets that reduce the amount of acid secreted by the stomach (e.g. Tagamet, Zantac etc. — see Section 6) can all be used alone or in combination. Tablets that increase the emptying rate of the stomach and strengthen the valve at the lower end of the oesophagus (e.g. Maxolon) are also useful. Frequent small meals, rather than three large meals a day, and a diet low in fat and high in protein is beneficial. Obese patients must lose weight.

Gravity is the most important factor in keeping the stomach in the abdomen rather than the chest and the acid in the stomach rather than the oesophagus. Bending over to garden or to lift and any heavy lifting are banned. The head of the bed should be elevated, and three or more pillows should be used to raise the chest higher than the abdomen. Lying on the right side rather than the left can also be tried to enhance the drainage of the stomach.

In only a small percentage of patients who do not respond adequately to the above regime should surgery be contemplated. A number of different operations can be performed. Some are done through the abdomen, others through the chest, and yet another through the back. All have their good and bad points, and it will depend very much on the experiences of the surgeon and the individual problems of the patient as to which procedure will be performed. These are major operations that require a significant time in hospital, but more than 80% of patients obtain a satisfactory result.

See also HERNIA.

HICCUPS (HICCOUGHS)
See Section 3.

HIGH BLOOD PRESSURE
See HYPERTENSION.

Hip, dislocated

The hip may be dislocated at birth (congenital dislocation), dislocated in a major injury (traumatic dislocation), or dislocated because of severe disease (pathological dislocation — e.g. infection, arthritis). These three forms of hip dislocation are very different in their presentation and treatment and will be discussed separately.

Congenital dislocation

Some babies are unlucky enough to be born with one or (in one third of cases) both hips dislocated, or in a position where dislocation can readily occur. Girls are five times more likely than boys to have this condition. Congenitally dislocated hips are usually detected shortly after birth at a routine examination of the infant. The doctor can detect the abnormal position or movement of the hips, and this can be confirmed by an X-ray. Later signs of the condition include a delay in walking, uneven skin folds on the buttocks and back of the legs, and limping.

If detected and treated early, most patients can be effectively cured without surgery. This involves putting the baby's legs in a 'frog position' (widely spread) in a special splint or double nappies for three months or more. This position forces the hip joint back into its socket. If these measures are not successful, or if the condition is not diagnosed until after the child is six months old, an operation to correct the dislocation is required. In severe cases, an artificial hip may need to be inserted once adulthood and full growth is achieved.

Traumatic dislocation

Traumatic dislocation of the hip is a very serious injury that can occur in motorbike accidents, industrial accidents and other major causes of injury. The hip joint is forcibly torn from its socket, and the surrounding ligaments and muscles are invariably severely damaged. The dislocation may be accompanied by a fracture. An operation is usually necessary to repair the damage, and many months convalescence are required. Permanent arthritis is often a consequence.

Pathological dislocation

Patients with very severe arthritis of the hip joint may develop a pathological dislocation of the hip because the joint is worn away by the degeneration of bone and cartilage caused by the arthritis. These patients are invariably elderly and have very poor muscle strength and slack ligaments. The treatment will depend on the disability arising from the dislocation and the patient's general health. An operation to replace the hip joint may be undertaken if appropriate.

In younger patients, a severe infection of the hip joint may partially destroy the joint and allow it to dislocate.

See also FRACTURES.

Hirschsprung's disease

Hirschsprung's disease is a congenital disease (present since birth) of the large intestine which is far more common in boys than girls. There is a tendency for it to run from one generation of a family to the next. It is caused by a failure of the nerves supplying the large intestine (colon) to develop correctly. Without these nerves, the intestine cannot contract, and faeces collect in the area to dilate it to an enormous size. Gut contractions are necessary to move the faeces along and down through the intestine.

The condition is usually diagnosed soon after birth. The baby is severely constipated, has a distended belly, refuses to feed, is lethargic, small in size, and is very irritable. Foul smelling diarrhoea may develop as a late complication. The diagnosis can be confirmed by an X-ray of the gut, and taking a biopsy (small sample) of the colon for examination under a microscope.

Treatment in Hirschsprung's disease is essential, because without treatment most of the affected babies will die. Initially the excess faeces can be removed through a tube placed up through the anus, but in due course an operation to remove the affected section of gut is necessary. After the operation, most of these children progress very well and have only minor long-term problems.

HIRSUTISM
See HAIR, EXCESS.

HISTOPLASMOSIS

Histoplasmosis is a fungal (mould) infection that can be caught in south-east Asia, North and South America and Africa. It is very rare in Australia. The spores that cause the infection are present in the soil and can be inhaled to cause a form of pneumonia. Most cases of histoplasmosis are very mild and may pass unnoticed or cause mild flu- like symptoms. Sometimes a moderately severe case of pneumonia may develop, and in rare cases a severe and fatal form of pneumonia may occur.

The symptoms depend on the severity of the infection but in severe cases resemble those of a normal pneumonia with a cough, wheeze, shortness of breath, marked tiredness and a fever. The disease is diagnosed after examining a sample of sputum under a microscope and culturing it to determine the type of infecting germ. There is also a specific blood test that can diagnose whether histoplasmosis is present, or has ever been present in the past. X-rays of the chest also show a characteristic pattern.

Minor cases require no treatment, but the more severe ones are treated with specific antifungal medications that can be given as tablets or injections. With correct treatment, only the elderly or otherwise ill are likely to die or develop long-term complications of the disease.

HIVES
See ALLERGY.

HODGKIN'S DISEASE (LYMPHOMA)

Hodgkin's disease is a form of cancer of the lymph glands and takes its name from Thomas Hodgkin, who was a physician in London in the mid 1800s and who first described the disease in the medical literature. Cancers of the lymph glands are called lymphomas. The group of lymphomas that do not fulfil all the criteria to be called Hodgkin's disease are called 'non-Hodgkin's lymphomas'.

The lymph glands contain large numbers of cells that are designed to fight infection. They are concentrated in the neck, groin, armpit and inside the abdomen. Patients with Hodgkin's disease develop painless swellings of the lymph glands, often in the neck. Other symptoms include tiredness, fever, weight loss, night sweats and a generalised itch. The disease slowly spreads to other lymph nodes in the immediate area, and only later to lymph nodes and organs in other parts of the body. The diagnosis can be confirmed by removing an involved lymph node and examining it under a microscope. The abnormal cancer cells can then be seen.

Most patients with Hodgkin's disease can be classified into different stages depending upon the degree of spread of the disease. The treatment that is appropriate varies depending on the stage of the disease and involves various combinations of radiation, cytotoxic (anti-cancer) drugs (see Section 6), and sometimes surgery.

The survival rate of patients with Hodgkin's disease has improved dramatically in recent years. This also depends upon the staging. It should always be remembered that survival rates vary from one place to another and apply to a large group of patients, which makes it difficult, if not impossible, to extrapolate these rates to the individual patient.

TABLE 5.2:
HODGKIN'S DISEASE

Stage	Symptoms	Average 10 year survival rate with treatment
Stage One:	Only one area of lymph nodes (e.g. one side of neck) affected by cancer cells.	80–90%
Stage Two:	Two lymph node areas affected, but within one half (top or bottom) of the body.	75–85%
Stage Three:	Two or more lymph node areas affected in widely separated areas of the body.	30–60%
Stage Four:	Several lymph node areas, liver and/or bone marrow affected.	20–40%

The staging may also be broken down further into A and B (e.g. Stage 2B, Stage 3A). Those with A stage disease have no fever, weight loss or night sweats — those with B stage disease do have these symptoms. The outcome is worse for B stage disease than A stage.

The treatment of non-Hodgkin's lymphomas is primarily cytotoxic drugs, and those cases generally have a worse outcome than patients with the true Hodgkin's disease.

HOOKWORM

Hookworm infestations do not occur naturally in Australia but may be found in migrants and travellers. The hookworm is widespread in all the tropical countries of the world, including south-east Asia, India, China, the Middle East, North Africa and tropical America.

The adult hookworm is 1 cm long and lives in the gut. Eggs pass out in the faeces, and if the faeces fall onto moist ground, the larvae will hatch from the eggs. The larvae remain active in the moist soil for up to a week, and during that time, a larva may penetrate the skin of the foot of any person who treads on it. The larva then migrates through the bloodstream to the lung, where it breaks into the air-carrying passageways of the lung. From there it is carried with sputum up into the throat, where it is swallowed, enters the gut, develops into an adult worm and starts the process all over again.

The symptoms include an itch at the site of skin penetration, a cough, wheeze and fever while the larvae are in the lung, and mild abdominal discomfort and diarrhoea when there are a large number of worms in the gut.

Drugs are available to destroy the worms. Only in patients who are otherwise ill or malnourished does a hookworm infestation cause significant problems.

HORDEOLUM
See STY.

HORNER'S SYNDROME
Johann Friedrich Horner was an eye doctor in Zurich, Switzerland, in the late 1800s. He described a condition that was characterised by a drooping eyelid, contracted pupil and a sunken eye, associated with reduced sweating. This bizarre combination of symptoms is caused by compression of a special network of nerves. The compression often occurs in the chest due to lung cancer or pneumothorax (see separate entries) but may also be caused by nerve compression in the brain itself. In many patients, Horner's syndrome is the first sign of a quite advanced lung cancer.

The only treatment is to deal with the underlying cause of the nerve compression.

HOUSEWIVES DERMATITIS
See ECZEMA — Irritant eczema.

HUNTINGTON'S CHOREA
Huntington's chorea is a distressing, incurable disease that is passed from one generation to the next. Statistically, half the children of a sufferer will develop the condition, but because the symptoms of Huntington's chorea do not become apparent until a person is between 30 and 50 years of age, it has often already been passed to the next generation who has been born to the victim at an earlier age. There is some doubt as to whether any new families are developing the disease. It is highly likely that all cases in existence can trace their disease back to previous generations.

Huntington's chorea was first described by George Huntington, a New York doctor, in a paper he wrote in 1872. Chorea is a medical term which refers to irregular, random movements of the arms, legs and face. The symptoms of Huntington's chorea are (in the most common order of appearance) irritability, mood changes, antisocial behaviour, restlessness, fidgeting, abnormal movements of the body, mental deterioration, premature senility, and rigid muscles. These symptoms may develop very slowly over several years.

There is no effective treatment available, and the inevitable progression of Huntington's chorea cannot be halted. Death within 10 to 20 years of symptoms developing is usual. Some drugs used in psychiatry can control mood changes, and muscle relaxants may ease the abnormal movements.

It is important for children in affected families to seek genetic counselling, but there is no test yet that can differentiate those who will develop the condition from those who will not. Research to find a method of identifying the carriers of Huntington's chorea is continuing, and with the continued advances in DNA technology it is likely to be successful in the future.

HYALINE MEMBRANE DISEASE
See RESPIRATORY DISTRESS SYNDROME, INFANT.

HYDATID CYST (ECHINOCOCCOSIS)
Echinococcus is the name of a microscopic larva that enters a human who eats food that has been contaminated by the faeces of an infected animal (usually dogs or other meat-eating animals). Once in the human, the larva migrates to the liver, lung, spleen or brain, where it forms a cyst.

The normal life cycle of *Echinococcus* requires the affected part of the body to be eaten by a dog or other carnivore, in which it enters the gut and grows into a tape worm. The tape worm then passes eggs out in the faeces to contaminate grass and other food. The normal hosts other than humans are cattle, sheep and other grazing animals, which eat the contaminated grass or food and are eventually killed by the *Echinococcus* infestation in their body. This allows the carcass to be eaten by meat-eating animals, and the life cycle of the parasite continues. The disease is uncommon in Australia, but widespread in South America, around the Mediterranean, in east Africa and central Asia.

After the cyst forms in the body, it usually remain dormant for many years, often causing no symptoms. Over a decade or more, the cyst slowly enlarges, until the pressure it exerts on its surroundings causes problems. With liver cysts, there may be pain in the upper part of the abdomen, nausea, vomiting and jaundice. In the lung, the cysts may cause part of the lung to collapse, pain and shortness of breath. In the brain symptoms occur earlier, and even a small cyst may cause convulsions or severe headaches. If a cyst ruptures, the reaction in the body to the sudden release of a large number of larvae may cause sudden death or severe illness and the formation of multiple cysts in other parts of the body.

The diagnosis can be made by seeing the cyst on a CT or ultrasound scan (see Section 4). Special X-rays are also sometimes used. Specific blood tests can be performed to determine whether or not a person has a cyst somewhere in their body. Discovering the actual site of the cyst may then prove very difficult or impossible.

If possible, a cyst (or cysts — 20% of patients have more than one) should be removed surgically. It is vital for the surgeon not to rupture the cyst during its removal, because the spilled larvae can then spread through the body. In other cases, or as an additional form of treatment, potent medications may be prescribed to kill the larvae, but the cyst will remain.

Provided the disease is not widespread, the results of treatment are good. If multiple cysts are present, the long-term outlook is grave. Dogs in affected areas can be treated regularly to prevent them carrying the disease to humans.

Hydatid of Morgagni

Giovanni Battista Morgagni was a seventeenth century Paduan (Italian) anatomist who has had a large number of relatively minor anatomical structures named after him. The hydatid of Morgagni is a small, unnecessary tissue sac that hangs loosely from the top of the testis in the male and the Fallopian tube in the female. It is present from birth, and normally causes no problems.

In the male, it is possible for the sac to become twisted about its neck, and become gangrenous and acutely painful. The patient complains of the sudden onset of pain, and has a very tender testis. Torsion of the testis (see TESTICULAR DISEASE) is an emergency that requires surgical treatment within a few hours and also has the symptoms of a very painful, tender testis. For this reason, the diagnosis of a twisted hydatid of Morgagni is only made at operation, after ensuring that the testis itself has not become twisted and potentially gangrenous.

The operation is simple and minor. The offending piece of tissue is removed, with no subsequent adverse effects upon the potency or masculinity of the patient, and the wound is sutured. Recovery is usually complete within three or four days.

Hydatidiform Mole
See UTERINE MOLE.

Hydramnios
See PREGNANCY COMPLICATIONS, Section 1.

Hydrocele
See TESTICULAR DISEASES.

Hydrocephalus

The brain and spinal cord are surrounded by cerebrospinal fluid (CSF). The brain also contains a number of cavities that are filled with this fluid. In one of the cavities is a network of veins (the choroid plexus) that secretes the cerebrospinal fluid. This fluid has a circulatory pattern. After being produced in the cavities within the brain, it passes through small tunnels in the brain tissue to the outside of the brain. From there it flows down and around the spinal cord in the back, from where the cerebrospinal fluid is absorbed into the bloodstream. Hydrocephalus (which means water head) occurs when an excessive amount of CSF accumulates in or around the brain.

There are two main types of hydrocephalus. When the CSF cannot escape from the cavities within the brain due to a blockage in the draining tunnels, the obstructive (or non-communicating) form of hydrocephalus occurs, and the brain is blown up by the fluid it contains. The expanding brain distends the skull in an infant.

The other type of hydrocephalus occurs when there is a blockage of the circulation down the spinal cord and the fluid cannot be absorbed back into the bloodstream. In this communicating form of hydrocephalus, the brain remains the normal size, but the baby's soft skull is grossly dilated by the excess fluid inside it. In an older child or adult, a severe headache, partial paralysis and loss of consciousness may be the presenting symptoms, as the harder skull is unable to expand.

Hydrocephalus is usually caused by a developmental abnormality during the growth of a foetus within the mother's womb. It may develop in later life because of brain infections, tumours in the brain or skull, cysts in the brain, thromboses and several rarer conditions.

In children with hydrocephalus, the head is larger than normal at birth, but not always remarkably so. The fontanelle (soft spot) on top of the baby's head is larger than normal and bulges. Other symptoms will depend upon the effect of the increased fluid pressure on the brain.

Hydrocephalus is treated by inserting a tube (called a shunt) into the brain or skull, to drain away the excess amounts of CSF. The tube has a one way valve along it, allowing the CSF to escape, but preventing other fluids or infection from entering the brain. The far end of the tube is inserted into a vein in the neck or chest, or is run all the way through the chest, and allowed to drain into the abdominal cavity. These drains are very successful in controlling the condition, and although they may become blocked and require replacement or clearing occasionally, they generally allow the patient to lead a normal life with minimal impairment of body function or intelligence.

HYPERACTIVITY (IN CHILDREN)

Many children are overactive, particularly boys between the ages of two and five, but very few are truly hyperactive. Hyperactive children are totally uncontrollable and destructive and do not appear to respond to normal discipline. They are also more often at the extremes of intelligence. Very intelligent children may be bored by the activities available to them, and misbehave to obtain further stimulation. Children with low intelligence may be confused and not understand what is expected of them.

In all cases, a detailed assessment of the child's capabilities by a psychologist is necessary, together with a thorough examination by a doctor to exclude any physical or mental diseases that may be responsible for the child's hyperactivity. Parents and teachers will need to be counselled with regard to the results of these tests.

Consistent, appropriate, non-violent discipline is essential. The child must learn that certain consequences will always result from behaviour that is not appropriate. The 'time-out' concept of isolating the child for a short time is often effective. Conversely, appropriate rewards must be instituted for correct behaviour. These rewards may only need to be a word of encouragement or a cuddle, and not necessarily a gift. Bribes are never appropriate, nor are threats. 'If you do this I'll buy you that' and 'Wait till your father gets home' are phrases that should never be used. A reward after spontaneous correct behaviour is far more effective, as is punishment at the time rather than later. The child can learn to dread the father's return home, which only worsens his/her insecurity.

Behaviour modification under the guidance of an experienced and well-trained psychologist is the next step in a treatment program, and if still no success is achieved, a psychiatrist may undertake psychotherapy, with or without the assistance of medication. These treatments take many months, and overnight success should not be expected.

A number of medications have been found to be successful in controlling hyperactive children, but their long-term use is not recommended, and they should be used only in combination with psychotherapy, or as an additional form of control in a subnormal and mentally disturbed child.

There is no evidence that special diets or vitamins themselves are responsible for any improvement in an individual child's behaviour. It is likely though that the additional attention directed towards a child when on a special diet is sufficient for him/her to respond more appropriately to the wishes of the parents and improve his/her behaviour.

The long-term results are usually good, particularly in intelligent children. There are remarkably few hyperactive adults in society.

HYPERALDOSTERONISM
See CONN'S SYNDROME.

HYPERCHOLESTEROLAEMIA
See CHOLESTEROL EXCESS.

HYPERLIPIDAEMIA
Hyperlipidaemia is an excess of all blood fats. Cholesterol and triglyceride are the two main types of fat found in the blood. See CHOLESTEROL EXCESS; TRIGLYCERIDE EXCESS.

HYPERPARATHYROIDISM
The four small parathyroid glands sit behind the thyroid gland in the neck (see Section 2). They secrete a hormone called calcitonin that is responsible for controlling the amount of calcium in the bones and bloodstream. If the parathyroid glands become overactive (hyperparathyroidism), excess amounts of calcitonin are secreted by the gland. This results in calcium being taken out of the bones and into the bloodstream. The bones become brittle and painful and break more easily. The high levels of calcium in the bloodstream causes kidney stones and damage (which can result in thirst and the passing of large quantities of urine), high blood pressure, constipation and peptic ulcers in the stomach.

Hyperparathyroidism is a rare disease that may be caused by a tumour or cancer in one of the four parathyroid glands, but often no cause for the over activity can be found. The diagnosis can be readily confirmed by finding high levels of calcium in the blood and urine when it is tested in a laboratory. More specific blood tests and CT scans (see Section 4) are then used to determine the site of the affected gland and the possible cause of its overactivity.

The most serious consequence of the disease is the damage caused to the kidneys, which may eventually fail to work effectively if the disease remains untreated.

The main form of treatment is surgical removal of the overactive gland. This is not major surgery, but very intricate and time-consuming because the parathyroid gland must be separated from behind the thyroid gland, which is surrounded by many other vital structures in the neck. A large fluid intake is necessary to flush out the kidneys. There are no drugs that can be effectively used to cure the disease.

Surgery is successful in most cases, but without this treatment, hyperparathyroidism will steadily progress until serious complications result.

See also HYPOPARATHYROIDISM.

HYPERTENSION (HIGH BLOOD PRESSURE)

Any plumber will tell you that if a pipe carries water at a pressure higher than the pressure it was designed for, it will eventually rupture. If the pressure in the pipe is not only too high but varies rapidly in its level, the rupture will occur even sooner because of the excessive stresses on the pipe. Exactly the same situation occurs in the human body when the pressure of blood in the arteries becomes too high. The arteries of a person with high blood pressure will become hardened, brittle and eventually rupture, causing a stroke, heart attack or other serious injury to vital organs.

The heart contracts regularly to pump blood through the arteries to the arms, legs, head and other organs. The blood returns to the heart along veins. When the heart contracts, the blood is moved along under high (systolic) pressure. When the heart relaxes between beats, the blood continues to flow due to the lower (diastolic) pressure exerted by the elasticity of the artery walls. When one, or both, of these pressures exceeds a safe level, the person is said to suffer from high blood pressure or hypertension.

A blood pressure reading is written by a doctor as systolic pressure/diastolic pressure (e.g. 125/70). The actual values for blood pressure vary with many things, such as exercise, anxiety, age, fitness, smoking and drinking habits, weight and medications. All these must be assessed by a doctor over several visits before the diagnosis of hypertension is made.

When a doctor is asked what a normal blood pressure should be, the answer is often evasive, because so many factors must be considered. In an elderly person, a blood pressure of 160/95 may be acceptable, but this would be considered very high in a young woman, where 110/60 would be more appropriate. Life insurance companies generally require the blood pressure to be under 136/86 for the person to be acceptable at the normal rates. The numbers are a standard measure of pressure in units of millimetres of mercury (mmHg).

There is no simple method for any individual to measure their own blood pressure, so it is a good idea to have your doctor check the pressure with a sphygmomanometer at regular intervals, particularly if you are over 40.

A **sphygmomanometer** works by compressing the artery in your upper arm. The cuff is inflated to a high pressure so that the artery is completely compressed and no blood can pass. The pressure is then slowly lowered until the blood can squirt past the constriction when the variable pressure is at its maximum. This squirting can be heard by a doctor through a stethoscope which is placed over the artery, just below the cuff on the inside of the elbow. As the pressure drops further, the lower pressure is eventually sufficient to keep the artery open at all times, so that the squirting through the narrowed segment that occurs at a higher pressure can no longer be heard. The doctor notes on the gauge of the sphygmomanometer the pressures at which the noise can first be heard, and when it disappears.

You can help prevent and treat hypertension by keeping your weight within reasonable limits, not eating excessive amounts of salt, not smoking, and by exercising regularly.

The majority of people with high blood pressure have no symptoms of the problem for many years, and when they do it may be too late. Up to 20% of adults over 40 years of age may have hypertension, but it can occur at any age and may be a particular problem in pregnant women. Those who do have symptoms complain of headaches and tiredness, but only when the blood pressure is very high do the further symptoms of nausea, confusion, and disturbances in vision occur.

Once diagnosed, blood tests are performed to see if there is any specific cause for the increased blood pressure, but the majority of people have 'essential' hypertension, for which there is no single identifiable cause. X-rays of the kidneys and an electrocardiograph (ECG) may also be included in the initial work-up by a doctor. The identifiable causes of hypertension include kidney disease, oestrogen- containing medications (e.g. the contraceptive pill), hyperparathyroidism, phaeochromocytoma (see separate entries) and a number of other rare diseases. High blood pressure may also be a complication of pregnancy, when it can lead to quite serious consequences (see PREGNANCY COMPLICATIONS — Pre-eclampsia, Section 1).

A rapidly progressive condition known as malignant hypertension can sometimes develop and cause remarkably high levels of blood pressure. This requires urgent hospital treatment.

The major complications of untreated high blood pressure are strokes and heart attacks at an earlier age than would be expected with normal blood pressure. Other complications include kidney damage and bleeding into an eye.

Treatment is necessary in all cases of hypertension to prevent the serious long-term problems that may occur. There is no cure for high blood pressure, but it can be very successfully controlled in the majority of patients by taking one or two tablets a day. Some patients require higher doses of medication, but all must be continued for life, or until circumstances change (e.g. the patient is no longer obese) and enable a doctor to gradually withdraw them.

A wide range of medications are available, and some types will suit some patients better than others. It may take days or weeks for the tablets to work, and regular checks are essential until the correct dosage is determined. After that, blood pressure checks every 3 to 6 months are all that is necessary. Once controlled, there is no reason why the patient should not lead a full and active working, sporting and sexual life. Before effective treatments for blood pressure were available, most patients with moderate hypertension died within 20 years of the diagnosis. The causes of death, in order of importance, were heart disease, strokes and kidney failure.

The biggest problem facing doctors in treating patients with hypertension is that patients do not take their advice, stop the pills or fail to attend for follow-up checks. The patient who does this usually has no symptoms but is risking his or her life, because the continued excess pressure on the walls of the arteries may have fatal results.

See also HYPOTENSION.

HYPERTHYROIDISM (THYROTOXICOSIS, GRAVE'S DISEASE)

The thyroid gland sits in the front of the neck (see Section 2). It is shaped like a number 8 lying on its side, with the large lobes on either side of the windpipe (trachea). It is responsible for secreting a number of hormones that are collectively called thyroxine. These hormones act as the accelerators for every cell in the body. If the level of thyroxine is high, the cells function at an increased rate — if the level of thyroxine is low, the cells function at a less than normal rate. Overactivity of the thyroid gland is called thyrotoxicosis, Grave's disease or hyperthyroidism ('hyper' means excess).

The functioning and interactions of the thyroid gland with the body are extraordinarily complex. Depending on the cause of the overactivity, the thyroid gland may be grossly enlarged (a goitre) or normal size. There are many different causes for thyroid overactivity, but the most common is an auto-immune disease, in which antibodies (which are normally used to attack invading infections or foreign material) attack the thyroid gland and over stimulate it.

Patients with hyperthyroidism sweat excessively, lose weight, are nervous, tired, cannot tolerate hot weather and have a mild diarrhoea. Other effects of the excess levels of thyroxine in the blood include a rapid heart rate, slightly protruding eyes, warm skin, and a slight tremor. Patients tend to fidget, dart quickly in their activity, and speak rapidly.

The activity of the thyroid gland can be determined by measuring the amount of hormone and other substances acting on the gland that are present in the blood. Because of the rapid heart rate, abnormalities may also be seen on an electrocardiogram (see Section 4). Once diagnosed, the overactivity can be controlled by medication, but medication is only useful in the short-term situation in most patients and does not permanently cure the condition.

A cure can be obtained by surgically removing most of the thyroid gland (in an operation called sub-total thyroidectomy) or destroying most of the cells in the gland by giving the patient radioactive iodine (Iodine 131). Iodine concentrates in the thyroid gland as it is an essential component of thyroxine. Radioactive thyroxine decays rapidly and in the process destroys the overactive cells. It is a very effective and safe method of achieving a surgical result without actually resorting to surgery.

It is not possible for doctors to estimate exactly how much of the thyroid gland must be removed to result in normal hormone production. If any excess gland substance is present, the thyroid gland will continue to secrete excess thyroxine, and the patient will need further treatment. It is therefore better to remove too much gland rather than too little. Because there is usually insufficient thyroid gland left behind to produce adequate amounts of thyroxine for the normal functioning of the body, it is necessary for most patients to take thyroxine tablets on a daily basis for the rest of their lives after a subtotal thyroidectomy or radioactive iodine destruction of the thyroid gland.

The complications of untreated thyrotoxicosis are serious. The weight loss and muscle wasting may become permanent, liver damage and heart failure may be fatal, psychiatric disturbances may lead to hospitalisation, eye scarring may lead to blindness, and infertility may occur. If treated early, thyrotoxicosis has an excellent prognosis. If treatment is delayed until complications, particularly heart and liver failure, become apparent, the outcome is far less favourable.

See also HYPOTHYROIDISM.

HYPERTRIGLYCERIDAEMIA
See TRIGLYCERIDE EXCESS.

HYPERVITAMINOSIS A
See CAROTENAEMIA.

HYPOADRENOCORTICISM
See ADDISON'S DISEASE.

Hypoglycaemia

In medical terms, 'hypo' means low, 'glyc-' refers to glucose and 'aemia' to blood (as in anaemia), so hypoglycaemia is the technical term for low blood glucose. It should be remembered that glucose is just one of a number of different types of sugar (e.g. sucrose, fructose) that are present in the normal diet. Other types of sugar can be converted by the body into glucose. The amount of glucose in the body can be easily measured by a blood test. A less accurate method is to test the amount of sugar present in the urine.

Hypoglycaemia obviously occurs during starvation or malnutrition, when inadequate amounts of sugar are eaten. This can be corrected by adding sugar to the diet. Other causes of hypoglycaemia are very rare, and very serious. They include tumours of the pancreas (see Section 2) that secrete excessive amounts of insulin (a hormone that removes sugar from the blood), a reaction to extensive bowel and stomach surgery, and alcoholism. All of these will need to be extensively investigated and appropriately treated.

There is no evidence that low blood sugar levels are a cause of illness in people who are on a normal diet and have no signs of serious disease.

Hypoparathyroidism

The function of the parathyroid glands (which are situated behind the thyroid gland in the neck) is to regulate the amount of calcium in the blood and bones. In hypoparathyroidism, the parathyroid glands secrete inadequate amounts of a hormone called calcitonin. This allows excessive amounts of calcium to be drained from the blood and into the bones.

Patients with underactive parathyroid glands develop spasms of the small muscles in the hands and feet, tingling lips, tiredness, wheezing, muscle cramps, fungal infections, abdominal pains, anxiety attacks, and behavioural alterations. If present for some time, the nails will become thin and brittle, the teeth will be deformed, cataracts may develop in the eyes, and the skin becomes dry and scaly. Hypoparathyroidism is a rare condition that may occur after thyroid gland surgery, or may be spontaneous for no apparent reason.

The diagnosis can be confirmed by measuring the amount of calcium present in the blood. A number of other abnormalities can be found in the blood of these patients, including high levels of phosphorus. X-rays show very dense bones and calcium deposits in areas where it should not occur (e.g. brain).

Untreated, the condition may lead to heartbeat irregularities, reduced growth in children, anaemia and mental retardation. Treatment may be an emergency in serious cases, and involves calcium injections and tablets, and vitamin D tablets. Once stabilised on treatment, the long-term outlook is good, but damage already done to eyes, teeth and other tissues may be irreversible. Very regular blood tests, follow-up visits, and lifelong medication are essential.

See also HYPERPARATHYROIDISM.

Hypotension

Hypotension is excessively low blood pressure. The intricacies of blood pressure and its measurement are discussed fully under the section on hypertension. Low blood pressure only causes concern when it causes symptoms or is detected in the course of investigation of other diseases (e.g. someone with a suspected heart attack). A person (particularly a young woman) may have a blood pressure of 90/50 and be perfectly well, but the same pressure in an elderly person may have serious consequences and require treatment. Hypotension (low blood pressure) is thus a relative term — the blood pressure is low compared to what is should be — and not an absolute one.

Low blood pressure may occur with a serious injury resulting in blood loss (shock), heart attack, heart failure, dehydration, alcoholism, serious infections, heat stroke, pregnancy, a large number of less common diseases, and with some drugs. In each case, the cause of the low blood pressure needs to be treated, rather than the blood pressure itself.

Anyone who has low blood pressure that is causing symptoms, such as dizziness and headaches, must be thoroughly investigated to find and treat any possible cause. In a very small number of people no specific cause can be found, and in these cases a medication may be given to raise the blood pressure slightly.

Postural hypotension

Many people experience light-headedness and dizziness, and sometimes even blackouts or faints, when rising quickly from lying or sitting to a standing position. This is postural hypotension, and it is caused by a brief drop in blood pressure caused by the altered relative positions of the brain and the heart. The heart must pump harder, and the arteries must contract more to maintain blood flow by means of the blood pressure to a brain that is 30 cm above the heart, rather than one that is at the same level as the heart. It takes a few seconds for this adjustment to be made, particularly in those who have some degree of hardening of the arteries.

The best treatment for patients with hypotension, who are usually elderly, is to advise them to be slow in their position changes. This is far better treatment than adding further medications. On the other hand, those medications that are being taken by the patient may be aggravating the hypotension, and should be reviewed. Doctors can readily detect the problem by measuring the blood pressure when the patient is lying, and again immediately after they stand up.

Therapeutic hypotension

In some forms of surgery it is necessary to reduce the blood pressure in order to reduce the amount of bleeding or swelling of certain tissues. Therapeutic hypotension is a procedure carried out under strictly controlled conditions in an operating theatre by an anaesthetist. Brain and heart surgery are some examples where therapeutic hypotension is required.

See also HYPERTENSION; SHOCK.

HYPOTHERMIA (EXPOSURE)

Hypothermia is an abnormally low body temperature. A temperature below 35 degrees Celsius is generally considered to be serious and require treatment. The most common cause of hypothermia is exposure to cold conditions without adequate protection. Cold air alone can cause hypothermia, but if combined with wind, the chill factor rises dramatically, and hypothermia occurs more rapidly. Snow may be used as an insulator against cold in low sub-zero temperatures, and may also be used to help protect against wind. Cold water is the most serious cause of hypothermia, and a drop in temperature sufficient to cause death may occur in as little as three or four minutes in icy water.

The victims of accidents are often hypothermic as an additional complication, and it is important for people giving first aid to be aware that the reason the victim is suffering from hypothermia may be due to some injury (e.g. cross-country skier with a broken leg).

It is not necessary for the weather to be very cold for someone to suffer from hypothermia. An inadequately clad person may suffer hypothermia after hours or days exposed in a climate where the air temperature does not drop below 20 degrees Celsius. Even in tropical waters, shipwrecked swimmers may die from hypothermia before drowning or being taken by sharks. Alcoholics may neglect themselves and even in relatively mild conditions suffer from hypothermia due to inadequate clothing, shelter and nutrition.

In people with hypothermia, the blood vessels to the skin have contracted so that the victims feel far colder to the touch than expected. Other symptoms are weakness, drowsiness, irritability, irrational behaviour and poor coordination. These factors can make it even harder for the victim to escape from his/her predicament. As the temperature drops further, delirium, coma and death from an irregular heartbeat occur.

Doctors diagnose the condition by measuring the temperature using a rectal (through the anus) thermometer. The skin temperature and even the mouth temperature are often inaccurate.

Treatment depends on the severity of the hypothermia. Mild cases will respond well to good warm clothing, warm bed and rest. Moderate to severe cases will require hospitalisation. Rapid warming, and warming the surface of the body only (which may cause premature dilation of the arteries in the skin), can cause heart irregularities and death. Warmed air or oxygen, warm drinks, and warm fluids through a needle into a vein will heat the core of the body effectively. This may be followed by immersion in a lukewarm bath that may have its temperature increased slowly over several hours. Heated blankets may also be used.

Patients who appear to have died because of hypothermia must be treated with mouth-to-mouth resuscitation and external heart massage for several hours while continuing to warm the body. Recovery may not occur until the body temperature rises to 32 degrees Celsius or more. Patients (particularly children) have been known to recover fully after prolonged periods of immersion or apparent death, with appropriate resuscitation, as the low temperatures protect the brain and body against damage.

See also FROSTBITE.

HYPOTHYROIDISM (MYXOEDEMA)

The thyroid gland sits in the front of the neck (see Section 2). It is shaped like a number 8 lying on its side, with the large lobes on either side of the windpipe (trachea). It is responsible for secreting a number of hormones that are called collectively thyroxine. These hormones act as the accelerators for every cell in the body. If the level of thyroxine is high, the cells function at an increased rate — if the level of thyroxine is low, the cells function at a less than normal rate. Underactivity of the thyroid gland is called myxoedema or hypothyroidism ('hypo' means reduced or less). It is common in elderly women, as the thyroid gland tends to fail with advancing age. Hypothyroidism may be associated with an enlarged thyroid gland (goitre), or the thyroid may be normal in size.

Patients with hypothyroidism complain of tiredness, weakness, muscle cramps, constipation, dry skin, headaches, nervousness, an intolerance to cold weather and a hoarse voice. Other signs in more severe cases include thinning of the hair (particularly of the eyebrows), brittle nails, weight gain, shortness of breath, a thick tongue and a slow heart rate. Because the drop in thyroxine levels is usually gradual over many years, the symptoms may be overlooked until the disease is quite advanced. The condition can be diagnosed by a specific blood test that measures the amount of thyroxine, and other thyroid-related substances.

Treatment is relatively simple — thyroxine tablets are taken in the long term in the appropriate dosage to replace the thyroxine not being produced by the thyroid glands. Doctors normally start with a low dosage and slowly increase it, depending upon the results of subsequent blood tests. Patients usually notice a remarkable improvement in their quality of life as the thyroxine acts upon the body and removes the symptoms, which individually are often minor collectively can have a significant impact upon an individual.

If left untreated, the patient has an increased risk of developing severe infections, and these, or heart failure, may cause death. With adequate treatment, the patient should lead a normal, active and healthy life, without any expectation of a reduced life span.

See also CRETINISM; HYPERTHYROIDISM.

IBS
See IRRITABLE BOWEL SYNDROME.

IM (INFECTIOUS MONONUCLEOSIS)
See GLANDULAR FEVER.

IMMUNODEFICIENCY
Our immune system is centred on the thymus gland (which sits behind the top of the breast bone), the bone marrow and lymph glands (in the armpit, groin, etc.). These produce special white blood cells, antibodies (chemicals that attack specific viruses or bacteria), and other substances which can circulate in the bloodstream to detect and destroy invading germs. Immunodeficiency (a lack of immunity to infection) is a rare condition that is caused by a lack of white blood cells, abnormal white blood cells, a lack of other special chemicals or cells, or a lack of immunoglobulin, which is a substance that is capable of reacting to infections. Almost invariably, immunodeficiency occurs in children, and is usually detected within a year of birth. Protection against infection in the first few months of life may be given by the antibodies from the mother and breastfeeding.

A number of very rare diseases are responsible for immunodeficiency. These include DiGeorge's syndrome (a failure of the thymus to develop), Wiskott-Aldrich syndrome (an inherited failure to produce white cells), and agammaglobulinaemia (a lack of gamma immunoglobulin).

Children with immunodeficiency cannot be cured. They develop many severe infections, and sometimes bleed and bruise easily. They often die early in life.

Acquired immune deficiency syndrome (AIDS — see separate entry) is a form of immunodeficiency. The white cells are destroyed by the virus causing AIDS, and allow these patients to develop severe infections and cancers.

IMPETIGO
See SCHOOL SORES.

IMPOTENCE
See SEXUAL PROBLEMS.

INCONTINENCE OF FAECES
Incontinence is the inability to control the discharge of body waste products. Incontinence of faeces takes two forms. There are those patients who are aware of passing a small amount of faeces through the anus but are physically incapable of stopping it, and there are those who are not aware of passing the faeces but could have stopped it if they had been aware.

The first group includes patients with severe diarrhoea (e.g. gastroenteritis, cholera, etc.), women after childbirth when the anal canal may be torn, and patients who have had operations on the anus (e.g. dilation for an anal tear). In these cases, the condition causing the incontinence is usually of short duration and may be treatable. It is a considerable inconvenience when the incontinence occurs, but it is rarely a long-term problem.

The sadder and more difficult situation occurs with those who are not sufficiently aware of their own body to know that they are soiling themselves. This includes patients who are in a coma or unconscious (because of injury or disease), cases of paralysis of the lower half of the body (paraplegics and quadriplegics), mentally deranged people, the confused elderly (e.g. advanced Alzheimer's disease), and those with subnormal mentality. Most of these cases cannot be cured, and the problem is a long-term one. The wearing of nappies and use of protective sheeting in beds must become routine. Careful attention by attendants to hygiene and cleanliness is essential to avoid rashes and sores developing on the buttocks and around the anus.

INCONTINENCE OF URINE

Embarrassing, unpleasant, uncomfortable, distasteful, offensive, distressing, intolerable and very annoying. Urinary incontinence is all these things, and more, but it is a topic that is never discussed with friends or family, and mentioned to doctors often only after many visits for other more socially acceptable diseases. Incontinence is usually associated with the old man lying semiconscious in a nursing home bed. But it is far more common in women, and many relatively young women in their thirties or earlier can be victims.

Incontinence is the loss of urine from the bladder at times when such loss is not desirable. It can vary from constant bed-wetting, to the occasional dribble when the woman jumps, coughs or laughs.

The most common cause of incontinence is the damage done to the genitals during childbirth, and this is the reason for women being the victims far more frequently than men. Other causes include urinary infections, strokes, confusion in the elderly, bladder injury, epilepsy and damage to the spinal cord in paraplegics and quadriplegics.

The urethra is the tube that carries urine from the bladder to the outside of the body. In women it is only 1 cm long. It leaves the bladder at an acute angle, and this angle causes the pressure of the urine inside the bladder to keep the urethra closed. It requires a voluntary muscular effort to open the urethra and allow the urine to escape. The stretching that occurs during childbirth can cause this critical angle to be lost and the urethra to become a straight tube leading from the bladder to the outside. Any pressure put on the bladder, or any significant volume of urine, can then cause incontinence. Unfortunately this straightened tube can also allow bacteria and infection to enter the bladder more easily and cause the pain and discomfort of cystitis (see separate entry).

Because the bladder is controlled by nerves, damage to the nervous system by a stroke or the cutting of the spinal cord in paraplegics may also lead to incontinence.

As with most diseases, the earlier incontinence is treated, the better the results. Prevention is even better than cure. Exercises to strengthen the muscles of the pelvic floor should be undertaken by all women immediately after childbirth. These can also be done in the early stages of incontinence to help control the bladder function as normally as possible. A patient can start by practising stopping and starting the urinary stream several times whenever they go to the toilet. Physiotherapists can teach the finer details of these exercises.

If the problem has progressed beyond control by exercises alone, the options are rather limited. In younger women, an operation to correct the abnormal bladder/

urethra angle is usually successful. In older women, a specially shaped rubber ring may be worn inside the vagina to put pressure on the urethra and prevent urine from escaping. These rings must be fitted and regularly checked by a doctor. A woman's concern about incontinence can become a significant mental problem and a social barrier, and should therefore be treated sooner rather than later.

Men can also have an operation, but it is not as successful as in women. In elderly and paralysed men, it is often more practical to use a collecting bag, as this can be easily attached to the penis.

See also BED-WETTING.
See also URINE INCONTINENCE, Section 3.

INFARCT
See HEART ATTACK.

INFECTION
An infection is the invasion of the body by viruses (most common), bacteria (common) or fungi (uncommon). When microscopic animals invade the inside or outside of the body (e.g. lice, amoebiasis) the condition is called an infestation. There are about one hundred bacteria that cause significant infections in mankind, but several thousand viruses may attack the body. Fewer than 20 fungi cause serious problems.

Infections may enter the body when you inhale, eat or drink droplets containing germs, when germs come into contact with a wound, or when germs enter through other natural body openings (e.g. ears, anus, vagina), or by the skin being directly attacked (e.g. school sores).

As a general rule, bacterial and fungal infections can be treated and cured by the appropriate antibiotics and antifungal medications (see Section 6). Viral infections, with a few rare exceptions (e.g. shingles), cannot be cured, but it is possible to vaccinate against some of them (e.g. measles, influenza).

Viruses are generally classified by code numbers (e.g. HIV three that causes AIDS), or disease names (e.g. Hong Kong flu), and occasionally by a specific name (e.g. Rota viruses that cause gastroenteritis in children). Viruses are constantly changing their form, so detailed classification is difficult. Because of their incredibly tiny size, even identification prior to classification can be a major problem.

Bacteria and fungi can be more readily identified and classified. They have a family name which is followed by a species name. The infamous golden staph bacterium is correctly called *Staphylococcus aureus* because it comes from the Staphylococcus family, and appears golden in colour ('aureus' means golden) under a microscope. It may cause infections in the throat, lungs, skin or almost any other part of the body. Other common examples of bacteria are *Mycoplasma pneumoniae* (causing a nasty form of pneumonia), *Neisseria meningitidis* (causing a type of meningitis), *Salmonella typhi* (causing typhoid), *Neisseria gonorrhoeae* (causing gonorrhoea), and *Escherichia coli* (causing some types of gastroenteritis).

Many diseases (e.g. bronchitis, meningitis, tonsillitis, urinary infections) can be caused by many different types of bacteria. Some bacteria are more susceptible to one antibiotic than another, and antibiotics do not always cure an infection by killing the bacteria, because in most cases there is no easy way for a doctor to tell which of the many possible bacteria is causing the infection. This can be determined by sending a sample of the infected material (e.g. urine or pus) to a laboratory for identification of the bacteria in it and establishing which antibiotics will kill them.

Fungi normally cause infections of the

skin, mouth and vagina but may invade the inside of the body, particularly the gut and lung. *Candida albicans* is the fungus responsible for thrush in the mouth and vagina, while *Trichophyton rubrum* is responsible for some cases of tinea.

An infection is normally classified by the area infected rather than the bacteria or fungus causing the infection. Doctors (and patients) therefore talk about 'tonsillitis' rather than a 'staphylococcal infection of the tonsil'. Some infections have specific names (e.g. pneumonia) which are and indication of both place (the lung in this instance) and the seriousness of the infection. Specific common infections are dealt with under their name or the place infected. In addition to those mentioned above, see ABSCESS; APPENDICITIS; BALANITIS; BLEPHARITIS; BOIL; BREAST INFECTION; CELLULITIS; CHLAMYDIAL INFECTIONS; CHOLERA; COLD, COMMON; CONJUNCTIVITIS; CYSTITIS; DENGUE FEVER; DIPHTHERIA; DIVERTICULITIS; DYSENTERY; ELEPHANTIASIS; ENCEPHALITIS; ENDOCARDITIS; EPIDIDYMO-ORCHITIS; ERYSIPELAS; FOLLICULITIS; GAS GANGRENE; GIARDIA INFECTION; GLANDULAR FEVER; HEPATITIS; HERPES; LARYNGITIS; LEGIONNAIRE'S DISEASE; MASTOIDITIS; MUMPS; MYOCARDITIS; NAIL INFECTION; OSTEOMYELITIS; OTITIS EXTERNA; OTITIS MEDIA; PANCREATITIS; PELVIC INFLAMMATORY DISEASE; PERICARDITIS; PERITONITIS; PHARYNGITIS; POLIO; PSITTACOSIS; PYELONEPHRITIS; Q FEVER; QUINSY; ROSEOLA INFANTUM; ROSS RIVER FEVER; RUBELLA; SCARLET FEVER; SEPTICAEMIA; SEXUALLY TRANSMITTED DISEASE; SINUSITIS; STOMATITIS; SYNOVITIS; SYPHILIS; TETANUS; TOXOPLASMOSIS; TRICHOMONIASIS; TUBERCULOSIS; TYPHUS; URETHRITIS; URTI; VAGINITIS; WHOOPING COUGH.

See also FUNGAL INFECTION; VIRAL INFECTION.

See also GERMS, Section 7.

INFECTIOUS MONONUCLEOSIS
See GLANDULAR FEVER.

INFERTILITY

Infertility — the very word causes a chill in the hearts of many couples! As teenagers though, no thought is given to the possibility that you may not be able to have a child. At the time of marriage, the idea may fleetingly cross your mind. But after the decision to start a family has been made, there is that nagging doubt in the back of your mind — could I be infertile?

After 12 months of 'normal marital endeavour' (as the textbooks so politely put it), 85% of couples should have conceived. The remaining 15% can be considered to have below-normal fertility. With the aid of medical techniques, all but 3% of couples can eventually have children.

It must be remembered that fertility is a joint property, not just a feature of the male or female. One third of infertility is due to the male partner. It takes two to tango!

In the male, the causes of infertility include premature ejaculation, undescended testes (which fail to work because of overheating), injury to the testicles, mumps infection of the testes, testicular and sperm tube venereal infections (e.g. syphilis, gonorrhoea), chromosome abnormalities, and hormonal disorders.

Infertility in the female may be caused by failure of the ovaries to develop (e.g. Turner's syndrome), endometriosis, abnormal development of the uterus, pelvic inflammatory disease, venereal infections of the Fallopian tubes (e.g. syphilis, gonorrhoea), hormonal imbalances, and in rare cases a reaction to the husband's sperm can develop.

When a couple present to their general practitioner because of a difficulty in falling pregnant, the doctor will be reluctant to undertake any specific investigations until they have been trying for at least a year. It is not unusual for several months to pass before falling pregnant after the oral contraceptive pill is ceased.

Doctors start their investigations by checking the couple's sexual habits. A woman is only fertile for four to six days a month, and if sex is infrequent, it is quite easy to miss these days.

The first step in specific testing is a sperm analysis in the man. The sperm from an ejaculation is collected in a sterile container and must be examined in a laboratory within two hours. The number of sperm, their shape and their activity are all checked to ensure that they are adequate to fertilise the woman's egg. If these tests are normal, it is not usually necessary to perform any further tests on the man.

In a woman, the first step is a temperature chart. This involves marking on a graph the woman's temperature immediately upon waking every morning, the days of the period or other bleeding, and the days when intercourse has occurred. From this and a blood test, a doctor can often see problems with ovulation. There is normally a rise in temperature for the second half of the cycle after the egg has been released from the ovary.

After these simple tests, investigations become more complex. It is necessary to exclude any blockage in the tubes leading from the ovary to the womb, and to assess the woman's hormonal and biochemical function by a series of blood tests. A careful gynaecological examination is performed, and this may be followed by special X-rays that outline the uterus (womb) and tubes. The final stage of investigation is an operation called a laparoscopy, in which a small tube is poked through a cut in the lower part of the abdomen. To prevent scarring, the navel is often used for this purpose. Through this tube the doctor can directly examine the female reproductive organs to detect any problems.

Once a problem is found, treatment can start. In the male, hormone supplements, storage and concentration of sperm (artificial insemination by husband — AIH), or fertilisation by donor sperm (artificial insemination by donor — AID) can be tried. In the woman, fertility drugs can be used to promote ovulation (e.g. Clomiphene — see Section 6), other drugs may be used to treat endometriosis (see separate entry), or antibiotics may be needed to treat infections. If there is an anatomical abnormality, it may be correctable by surgery.

As a last resort, a very small number of couples may be considered suitable for IVF (in-vitro fertilisation or 'test-tube babies' — see Section 6), or GIFT (gamete intra-Fallopian transfer). GIFT involves transferring an unfertilised egg and sperm into the Fallopian tube of an infertile woman through a laparoscope. The husband's sperm is used, but the egg may come from the wife or may be donated by another woman. Centres in every Australian capital now perform both IVF and GIFT. Australia is one of the leading countries in the world with this technology.

The treatment of infertility has progressed by leaps and bounds over the past few years, and the techniques used are at the leading edge of medical technology. Even so, the greatest miracle of all is what happens when a sperm meets an egg and fertilisation occurs.

INFLUENZA (FLU)

Singapore, Mississippi, the Philippines, Dunedin (New Zealand), Victoria, Hong Kong, Leningrad (the Soviet Union), and Taiwan all have one thing in common. They are places where strains of influenza experienced in recent Australian winters were first isolated. Unfortunately, every winter, doctors' surgeries are filled with patients who neglected to take a simple precaution in autumn, because like all other viral illnesses, such as measles, mumps, hepatitis, glandular fever and the common cold, influenza cannot be cured.

Influenza was once thought to be due to 'influences in the atmosphere', thus giving the disease its name, but it is now known to be one of many diseases that are caused by a virus. Medical science has drugs that can kill bacteria, funguses and microscopic animals that may enter the body, but it is unable to kill viruses. Viruses are barely alive and are therefore very difficult to kill. They are self- replicating crystals that are so small they cannot be seen by the most powerful light microscope. Bacteria on the other hand are microscopic animals, and they can be killed by antibiotics. The only effective treatment for the flu is prevention by an annual influenza vaccination. Some viral diseases, such as measles, can be prevented by a once in a lifetime shot, but the influenza virus has the most unfortunate ability to change its form slightly every year, so the resistance developed by the body to one form does not prevent infection by a marginally different form. Thus the flu shot has to be an annual event, with the contents of the vaccine varying from year to year depending on the types of influenza about. The vaccine gives more than 80% protection from contracting influenza. Unfortunately it does not prevent the common cold, and many people who complain that their flu shot has not worked are suffering from a cold caused by yet another group of viruses.

Influenza was, and still can be, a very serious disease. Millions of people died from it in severe epidemics earlier this century, but deaths are now rare except in the elderly and debilitated. Asthmatics, those with other chronic chest and heart conditions, the elderly, and patients with debilitating illnesses are at particular risk and should always be vaccinated. Health care workers, essential industry workers, and those in regular contact with the public are other groups who should seriously consider having an annual vaccination.

Flu is spread by microscopic droplets in a cough or sneeze from one person to another. The droplets may be inhaled by a passer-by, and the millions of virus particles it contains can settle in the nose and throat and start reproducing rapidly. Eventually there will be uncountable trillions of the virus particles, and they will cause the tissue to become inflamed, swell up and secrete excess amounts of phlegm. The runny nose, stuffed sinuses, painful throat, headache, tiredness, nausea, fever and a dozen other symptoms then attack you. Over several days the body builds up immunity to the virus particles and develops specific cells to fight and destroy the infection, killing all the viruses and curing the patient. In the meantime, the victim suffers.

Rest and time are the most effective cures, and aspirin in high doses is very useful. Other medicines to stop the cough, ease the stuffy nose and relieve pain may be useful. If symptoms persist, a doctor should be consulted. There are also some tablets called amantadine available on prescription that will prevent some forms of flu while they are being taken. They are useful to prevent a wife contracting flu while her husband is suffering at home in bed, or similar circumstances.

The one good thing about influenza is that once you have had it this year, you are unlikely to contract it again until next year. Better still, be prepared, and have a flu shot in autumn rather than suffer later.

See also REYE'S SYNDROME.

INGROWN NAIL
See NAIL INFECTION.

Insecticide poisoning
See ORGANOPHOSPHATE POISONING.

Insomnia (inability to sleep)
Sleep is as essential for the normal functioning of the human body as food and drink. Doctors do not completely understand why we need sleep, but we do understand what happens when we are asleep.

There are two types of sleep — deep sleep and REM sleep. REM stands for rapid eye movements. Several times a night, the level of sleep lightens, and while the eyelids remain closed, the eyes themselves move around rapidly. It is during this stage of sleep that dreams occur, and it is the more valuable form of sleep. If a volunteer is woken every time he or she starts REM sleep, he or she will remain tired and irritable and obtain little benefit from the sleep. REM sleep does not start until an hour or so after first falling asleep, and long periods of deep sleep occur between each episode. Unfortunately, many sleeping tablets induce deep sleep but tend to prevent REM sleep, so that people using them do not benefit from their sleep as much as those who sleep naturally. This is one of the reasons that doctors are reluctant to use them until all other avenues have been explored.

The amount of sleep needed varies dramatically from one person to another. Some require only three or four hours a day; most require seven or eight hours; others may need ten hours. As we age, our sleep needs change too. An infant requires 16 or more hours of sleep a day; in middle age, eight hours is normal; but the elderly need only five or six hours sleep. The problem here is that older people may have less to occupy their days with and look forward to the escape of eight hours sleep every night, but then find they cannot obtain it because their bodies do not require that much. This is further exacerbated by the low activity levels of many elderly people and any midday naps they take. As a result, some elderly people seek help in obtaining extra sleep from their doctors by means of sleeping pills. This is not true insomnia, merely a desire for extra sleep above what is biologically necessary.

There are, of course, those who genuinely cannot get to sleep for a variety of reasons, and 15% of the population fall into this category. There are many things other than medication that can be done to ease the problem. Simple steps that anyone can use to aid sleep include:
- Avoid exercise immediately before bed. Take time to wind down before going to bed.
- Avoid drinks containing caffeine such as tea, coffee or cola. Caffeine is a stimulant.
- Lose weight if you are obese. A slight weight loss can significantly improve sleep.
- Avoid eating a full meal immediately before bed time. Give your food a couple of hours to settle.
- If you cannot sleep once in bed, get up and read a book or watch television for half an hour before returning to bed. Never lie there tossing and turning.
- Learn to relax by attending specific relaxation classes which your doctor may recommend. Follow up by listening to relaxation tapes.
- Instead of counting sheep or worrying about your problems, focus your mind on a pleasant incident in your past (such as a holiday, journey or party) and remember the whole event slowly in great detail from beginning to end.

If all else fails, and you still find you are unable to sleep, consult your general practitioner. He or she can prescribe medications (sedatives, hypnotics — see Section 6) that can be taken, ideally for a short time only, to relieve the problem.

See also Section 3.

INTERCOURSE PROBLEMS
See SEXUAL PROBLEMS.

INTERTRIGO
Heat, sweat and friction are the causes of intertrigo. These factors result in an area of red, damaged, moist, itchy and burning skin in places where the skin folds back upon itself. The most commonly involved areas are under the breasts, in the groin and armpit, and in skin folds of the abdomen and neck in obese people. In advanced cases, the skin may crack, bleed and become painful. Fungal and/or bacterial infections may also develop on the damaged skin. Those who are overweight, have poor personal hygiene, live in the tropics, or suffer from diabetes have a higher risk of developing this rash.

Treatment involves scrupulous hygiene, treating any diabetes, using antibiotics and antifungals to remove infection, losing weight, and applying drying powders to the affected areas. A piece of soft cloth placed under bulky breasts, and a well fitted bra may help the intertrigo in this area. Plastic surgery to reduce large breasts or remove excessive skin on the belly may be appropriate in a small number of patients.

Unfortunately, most patients remain overweight, are not consistent in their hygiene, and the problem persists or recurs every summer.

INVASIVE MOLE
See UTERINE MOLE.

IRITIS (UVEITIS)
The iris is the coloured part of the eye, and the pupil is in the centre of the iris. Iritis is an inflammation of the iris. When the surrounding tissues are involved, it is called uveitis. The inflammation can be due to an infection such as toxoplasmosis, tuberculosis or syphilis (exogenous iritis), or it may be associated with inflammatory diseases in other parts of the body, including psoriasis, ankylosing spondylitis, and some bowel conditions (endogenous iritis). The latter form is more common.

Almost invariably, only one eye is involved. It will suddenly become red and painful, and the vision is blurred. Bright lights will aggravate the eye pain and the pupil is small. In the exogenous form, there is less pain and the onset is slower.

In all cases, the underlying infection or disease must be treated if possible. The eye itself can be made more comfortable with warm compresses. Steroid and other eye drops are used regularly to reduce the inflammation and prevent any complications from developing. The endogenous form of iritis usually recovers satisfactorily, but recurrences are common. The exogenous form often results in some long-term deterioration in vision.

IRON POISONING AND IRON DEFICIENCY
Iron is not only a metal that is usually seen in ingots or machinery, it is also an essential element for the functioning of the human body. Between 5 and 8 mg of iron is required in a man's diet every day for good health, and women require twice as much as men because of the iron loss in their monthly period. Infants and rapidly growing teenagers also require more iron in their diet. Pregnant and lactating women require even more iron than other women, up to 35 mg per day, and as this amount may be difficult to obtain in the diet, most pregnant and breastfeeding women are advised to take a daily iron tablet. These tablets contain iron in a form that is readily absorbed into the body.

Section 5: Diseases

Only one tablet a day is necessary for prevention of iron deficiency, but two may be prescribed for a severe deficiency. Iron tablets commonly contain between 250 and 300 mg of iron. Pure iron (e.g. iron filings) is not well absorbed, and would pass out with the faeces.

People who take excessive amounts of iron into their systems, either deliberately or accidentally, are said to be suffering from **iron poisoning**. As well as being found in tablets used to treat iron deficiency states and anaemia, iron may be present in many tonics and anti-vomiting drugs. 2000 mg of iron taken at once is sufficient to cause iron poisoning in an adult. Lesser amounts can be very serious in a child. Overdoses in children are not uncommon, as brightly coloured and sugar-coated iron tablets can look very attractive. Adults may overdose because they regard the tablets simply as vitamins.

Iron poisoning causes vomiting, diarrhoea, black coloured faeces, a rapid and irregular heart rate, low blood pressure, convulsions, and eventually coma and death. These symptoms may commence in as little as an hour after taking excessive amounts of iron. Treatment requires urgent hospitalisation. Medications to bind the iron and remove it from the body will be given, and drips into a vein to correct the dehydration caused by vomiting and diarrhoea. The outcome of iron poisoning will depend upon the amount of iron taken. It is not always possible to save all patients with modern medical care, and even after apparent recovery, liver, pancreas and kidney failure may occur at a later date.

The primary use of iron in the body is to be the core element in the manufacture of haemoglobin. This compound is found in red blood cells and transports the oxygen from the lungs to the organs. An **iron deficiency** will cause haemoglobin levels to drop and the body to become starved of oxygen. You then feel tired and weak, as oxygen is required by all cells to burn fuel for energy. Other symptoms can include pins and needles in the arms and legs, palpitations, abnormal finger nails and dizziness.

Iron deficiency anaemia (see separate entry) is the disease resulting from lack of iron. In Western societies, it is usually found in women who have very heavy periods, in pregnancy, and in those with a poor diet. Sinister causes for this condition include a bleed into the gut from a peptic ulcer or cancer. Anyone with this type of anaemia must therefore be thoroughly assessed by a doctor.

Iron is found naturally in many foods including meat, poultry, fish, eggs, cereals and vegetables. Red meat, oysters, liver, beans, nuts and wheat contain particularly high levels of iron. Vitamin C is essential for iron to be absorbed from the gut into the bloodstream, and folic acid is useful in the treatment of some types of anaemia. Both these vitamins are present in fruit and vegetables. Because of this requirement, commercially prepared iron tablets often contain folic acid, and sometimes vitamin C as well. Some food (e.g. bran) and drinks (e.g. strong tea) can prevent the absorption of iron, and should be taken in moderation.

Some patients with severe degrees of anaemia due to lack of iron, or with intestinal diseases that reduce the absorption of iron, may require injections of this element. Usually they can return to tablets, and then a good diet, after only a few shots.

Our modern lifestyle which causes people to eat inadequate snacks on the run can lead to a combination of stress, overwork and iron deficiency anaemia which causes a 'burnt-out' feeling. Doctors can perform a simple blood test to measure the level of iron in your body, and if low can recommend one of the courses of treatments mentioned above.

See also HAEMOCHROMATOSIS.

IRRITABLE BOWEL SYNDROME (IBS)

Your gut is a very long tube lined with a wet membrane, and with bands of muscle running along and around the tube. Food goes into one end of the tube, and faeces comes out the other end. The movement of the food from one end to the other is the result of rhythmic contractions of the muscles in the gut wall. This sends waves and ripples along the gut, always pushing the food further down. Nutrients are removed from the gut as the food moves along, and only the non-absorbable fibre and roughage remains to be passed out through the anus.

Our modern diet tends to consist of large quantities of refined foods that have remarkably little fibre content. As a result, the bulk of our faeces is far less than that of our forefathers and those who live in primitive societies. When the muscles in the gut contract, they may have very little in the way of faeces to push along, and this may lead to spasm of the gut. People with tense personalities or continuing stress will find that their 'stomach is in knots'. This is merely the sensation that the intestine is acting more rapidly than is necessary due to the overstimulation of the nervous system. Over a number of years, the combination of a low-fibre diet, anxiety, stress and hereditary factors may lead to the development of the irritable bowel syndrome. This syndrome is characterised by abdominal pain caused by intense spasms of the bowel muscle, alternating constipation and diarrhoea, passage of wind by mouth and anus, nausea, loss of appetite and mucus on the stools. Once established, the pattern may be very difficult to break, as the symptoms cause further anxiety in the victim, which in turn exacerbates the original symptoms. The disease has been given many different names over the years, and may also be known as nervous dyspepsia, mucus colitis and functional indigestion.

There are no definite tests to prove the presence of the syndrome, and so all other causes of the symptoms must be excluded by exhaustive tests. An X-ray of the large intestine (a barium enema) may show the excessive spasms of the gut in some patients.

Once diagnosed, the treatment consists of a diet high in fibre and low in dairy products and processed foods. High-fibre dietary supplements are often recommended. Regular meal and toilet habits should be established, and tobacco and alcohol intake should be restricted. Reassurance is very important, and anti-anxiety drugs, antidepressants (see Section 6) and psychotherapy may all prove useful. In the acute situation, doctors can prescribe one or more of a number of drugs that are used to reduce the activity of gut muscles. Occasionally pain-killers are also necessary.

The usual course is for the syndrome to occur intermittently over many years. The continued attention by a sympathetic doctor is necessary for all sufferers because the greater the confidence the patient has in the treatment and the doctor, the more likely the regime is to succeed.

ISCHAEMIC HEART DISEASE

Ischaemic heart disease occurs when the heart is deprived of adequate supplies of blood, and therefore oxygen. Mild degrees of ischaemic heart disease cause angina, and more severe degrees result in a heart attack (see separate entries).

JAUNDICE

See SKIN, YELLOW, Section 3.

Jet lag
See TRAVEL MEDICINE, Section 7.

Joint diseases
See ARTHRITIS; BUNIONS; BURSITIS; CHONDROMALACIA; FROZEN SHOULDER; GOUT; KNOCK-KNEES; METATARSALGIA; OSGOOD-SCHLATTER'S DISEASE; PERTHE'S DISEASE; PSEUDOGOUT; ROTATOR CUFF SYNDROME; SHOULDER DISLOCATION.

See also SPRAINS, STRAINS AND DISLOCATIONS, Section 8.

Keratoacanthoma
Keratoacanthomas (KA) are often confused with skin cancers, but except for the temporary disfigurement they cause, they are quite harmless. KAs are more common in the elderly and occur on the face, hands and other sun-exposed areas of the body. They are rare in dark-skinned races. They appear initially as small, scale-covered lumps. Over a period of a couple of months, the lumps enlarge rapidly to red, shiny, firm blisters that may be 2 cm or more in diameter and topped with a plug of hard scaly material. Over the next few months, the lumps will slowly disappear, and eventually little or no trace of their presence remains. They take roughly twice as long to resolve as they take to develop.

If a doctor is certain about the diagnosis, no treatment is required unless the KA is very disfiguring. If there is any doubt at all about the diagnosis and it may involve a skin cancer, a biopsy (sample) must be taken to confirm the diagnosis. Unsightly keratoacanthomas may be removed surgically.

See also SKIN CANCER.

Kerion
See FUNGAL INFECTIONS — Tinea.

Kidney disease
See GLOMERULONEPHRITIS; KIDNEY FAILURE; KIDNEY STONES; NEPHROTIC SYNDROME; POLYCYSTIC KIDNEY; PYELONEPHRITIS; WILM'S TUMOUR.

See also CYSTITIS.

Kidney failure (renal failure)
The kidney acts to remove waste products from the body and to retain the correct amount of water in the body (see Section 2). If the kidney fails to work correctly, the patient may become very ill. There are two quite separate forms of kidney (or renal) failure — the acute form which occurs rapidly, and the chronic form which develops over many months or years.

Acute kidney failure

The patient notes a sudden dramatic reduction in the output of urine, associated with a loss of appetite, nausea, tiredness and vomiting. A doctor will note a raised blood pressure. After a few days or weeks, the kidney usually starts to work again, and the patient starts to pass copious quantities of clear urine. Over a few more weeks, the urine and kidney function gradually return to normal.

Acute renal failure may be triggered by a severe injury (particularly crush injuries), major surgery, poisons (e.g. mercury, dry cleaning fluid, mushrooms), heart attacks, severe burns, severe infections, and a number of rarer causes. It may also occur as a complication of pregnancy. The diagnosis can be confirmed by blood and urine tests, which will show excess waste products in the blood and very dilute urine.

In treating the condition, any specific cause of the renal failure should also be treated (e.g. resuscitate a patient with severe burns). In severe cases, an artificial kidney machine may be needed to clean the blood in a process known as dialysis. The amount of fluids that the patient drinks must be very carefully regulated, and a strict diet that limits the number of waste products in the body is given. Infections are a common complication, and these must be treated appropriately.

The outcome will depend upon the cause, and although some patients will die within a couple of days of the disease starting, most can be managed in a good hospital to a successful outcome. There is usually no long-lasting kidney damage, and the patient can lead a normal life.

Chronic kidney failure (uraemia)
The slow, gradual failure of the kidneys is called chronic renal failure or uraemia. Because of its slow onset, patients may not present to a doctor until the condition is well advanced. The symptoms include weakness, tiredness, lack of appetite, weight loss, nausea, headaches, passing urine frequently and at night, and in advanced cases itchy skin and vomiting.

Chronic kidney failure can be caused by many diseases, including a damaged blood supply to the kidney from hardened arteries, poisons, infections, the body trying to reject the kidney in auto-immune conditions such as systemic lupus erythematosus, and a large number of rarer diseases. Old age is a common cause of very gradual renal failure.

Doctors will note that the patient usually has high blood pressure and abnormal results for both blood and urine tests. Anaemia is a common finding. Further investigations are always carried out in an attempt to discover the cause of the kidney failure. Treatment involves treating any detectable cause of the condition, a strict diet (low in protein), and control of all fluids that are drunk.

Patients with renal failure must be very careful about any medications that they take, as they are likely to be far more effective and last longer in the body than normal. This means that side effects and toxicity problems are more likely to occur.

Unless the cause of the kidney failure can be corrected, the only treatment available is long-term treatment with an artificial kidney machine (dialysis), or a kidney transplant operation. Patients can be maintained for many years on dialysis, in which they hook themselves up to a kidney machine at a hospital or their own home for 6 to 12 hours several times a week. Blood is taken from a vein in the patient's arm, passed through the kidney machine, and back to the patient.

Kidney transplants have more than an 80% success rate and effectively cure the condition, but they are only practical in otherwise healthy young and middle-aged victims.

See also NEPHROTIC SYNDROME.

KIDNEY STONES (NEPHROLITHIASIS)

A long sharp knife is plunged into your loin. Then the knife is slowly twisted around before being slashed across your groin. Then there is a respite for a few minutes before the knife is thrust back again! This is how victims of kidney stones describe the excruciating pain caused by a kidney stone that is moving down the ureter from the kidney to the bladder.

The kidney acts to filter the blood, and removes excess water and wastes. If these wastes become too concentrated or altered in some way, they can precipitate out and form a crystal that slowly grows into a stone. Once the stone has formed, one of three things can happen to it. Most stones are flushed down the tube that leads to the bladder from the kidney (the ureter) and are passed out of the body with the urine while still microscopic in size. These cause no trouble at all, and you do not know that they have been present. A small number of stones may slowly and steadily grow in size until they are the size of a grape, or even a ping-pong ball. These big stones may completely fill the urine collection chamber of the kidney. They sometimes cause no trouble, but they are often the source of repeated kidney infections and pain.

The third group of stones is the most troublesome. Being from one to five millimetres in length, they can enter the ureter. This fine tube is very sensitive, and as the stone is pushed along the tube by the pressure of urine behind, it scrapes the tube wall to cause the intense pain that sufferers experience. The pain of renal colic ('renal' refers to the kidney, while 'colic' means a recurrent rather than constant pain) stops and starts because the stone stops and starts on its journey down the ureter. When the pressure of urine builds up behind it sufficiently, the stone moves and causes pain. When the pressure drops, the stone stops. The pain can thus come and go for several days as the stone slowly moves along. Patients often note blood in their urine because the stone is damaging the ureter to the point where it bleeds. Doctors can perform X-rays of the kidney to see the stone, its size and position. The progress of the stone can be carefully watched by repeat X-rays, and the treatment decided upon accordingly.

Most patients are merely given pain relief and lots of fluids to wash the stone down and out. After a few hours, or a day or two, the stone enters the bladder and can pass to the outside without causing any further trouble. Blood tests are then done to check for the cause of the stone formation, and if possible measures are taken to prevent a recurrence.

Unfortunately some stones get stuck halfway down the ureter, and this causes severe problems because little or no urine can escape from that kidney, and the back pressure of urine on the kidney tissue can cause significant damage. In this situation, an operation or other procedure is needed to remove the stone. This can be done by passing a tiny umbrella into the bladder and up the ureter to a point above the stone. The umbrella is then opened, and slowly removed, dragging the stone along with it.

At other times an open operation through the abdominal wall may be necessary, but in the last few years two radical new treatments have become available. Under the control of a highly skilled radiologist (X-ray specialist), a tube can be placed through the skin into the kidney, and through this the stone may be removed. Lithotripsy is the more amazing breakthrough (see Section 6). In this procedure, the patient is immersed in a bath of water, and pulses of extremely high-frequency sound waves are directed in a narrow beam through the body and onto the stone. The stone is harder than the surrounding tissue, and starts vibrating with the sound waves to the point where it breaks up into a fine powder that is then passed with the urine.

KLINEFELTER'S SYNDROME

This syndrome is named after Harry Fitch Klinefelter, who practised as a physician in Baltimore, USA, until very recently. He described a condition in which males have very small testes, small breasts, a small penis, scanty body hair and impotence. They are always sterile. It is caused by an abnormality in the chromosomes that govern the activity of every cell. At the moment of conception when the sperm fuses with the egg, the chromosomes from the mother and father of these men combine incorrectly. Because every cell in the body is affected by the abnormal chromosomes, no cure is possible. Testosterone (male hormone) tablets or injections can be given to improve the general body shape and impotence of the man, but the infertility cannot be corrected. Plastic surgery to remove the breasts is sometimes necessary.

KNOCK-KNEES (GENU VALGUM)
Knock-knees is a common condition in children, and in the vast majority of cases it corrects itself without any treatment. In rare cases it can be due to rickets, poorly healed fractures of the leg bones, and a number of other very uncommon diseases.

Knock-knees (technically called *genu valgum*) can be diagnosed when a child who is standing straight tries to bring the bony bumps on the inside of the ankles together. If they are unable to do this because the knees come together first, the diagnosis is confirmed. In severe cases, a wedge may be inserted into the inside edge of the shoes to turn the foot slightly outwards.

If the problem continues into the early teenage years and is causing difficulty in walking or abnormal appearance and posture, an operation may be necessary to correct the deformity. A number of different procedures are available, but they are only undertaken after careful discussion with the child and parents.

The reverse condition, when the knees are widely spread, is called bowlegs or *genu varum*. This is very normal in toddlers, and it is extremely rare for any treatment to be necessary.

KORSAKOFF'S PSYCHOSIS
See WERNICKE-KORSAKOFF PSYCHOSIS.

KUGELBERG-WELANDER SYNDROME
See MOTOR NEURONE DISEASE.

KWASHIORKOR
See MALNUTRITION.

KYPHOSIS
The backbone when looked at from the side, curves gently from front to back in a double S-shape. It curves in at the neck, out over the back of the chest, in at the small of the back, and out again between the buttocks. Kyphosis is an excessive outward curve of the spine at the back of the chest. It may be a slightly increased prominence, or a severe hunchback deformity.

There are many causes for kyphosis, including ankylosing spondylitis (see separate entry) in the elderly, osteoporosis (see separate entry) in older women, compressed and collapsed vertebrae, tuberculosis, tumours, constant muscle spasm in spastics, and a number of less common diseases. The diagnosis can be confirmed by X-rays of the spine, which often show the cause of the kyphosis at the same time.

Treatment involves treating the cause, if possible. Many patients have remarkably pain free backs despite quite horrendous deformities.

See also LORDOSIS.

LARGE INTESTINE CANCER
See COLO-RECTAL CANCER.

LARYNGITIS
The larynx is the voice box or Adam's apple at the front of the throat. It is made of cartilage and contains the vocal cords which are responsible for much of our speech. An infection of the larynx is called laryngitis. The suffix '-itis' means infection, as in 'appendicitis' and 'tonsillitis'.

Laryngitis causes hoarseness or total loss of voice, pain, difficulty in swallowing, a dry cough and a fever. Almost invariably, laryngitis is a viral infection and cannot be cured by antibiotics, which act only against bacteria.

Laryngitis will settle after five to ten days, but recovery will be delayed in smokers and those who persist in using their voice excessively. Recurrent attacks of laryngitis or hoarseness caused by excessive shouting or singing may cause small nodules to form on the vocal cords, and huskiness in later life.

The only treatments available are time, voice rest and aspirin. Aspirin is useful not only as a pain-killer, but also to reduce the inflammation and swelling of the vocal cords, and to ease an associated fever.

Lassa fever

Lassa fever is named after a town in northeast Nigeria where the disease was first isolated in 1969. It is an extremely contagious and frequently fatal viral infection of the blood stream and throat. It is more common in women. No cases have ever been reported in Australia, although there have been a couple of scares when visitors from West Africa have become ill.

There is no prevention available, and it is believed to be spread by rats and in conditions of poor hygiene. Patients must be nursed in strict isolation to prevent the infection spreading. No cure is available, but a number of drugs are being used experimentally to modify the course of the disease.

Lead poisoning

Lead poisoning is far less common in Australia now than it was a couple of decades ago when lead was routinely used in paint products. In old houses with flaking paint chips, high levels of lead could be swallowed, particularly by children. Renovators of old homes must still be careful when sanding and stripping many layers of paint that they do not inhale the lead-containing paint dust or allow it to contaminate food or drinks. Lead poisoning is most commonly found amongst battery workers today. Modern car batteries contain a large amount of lead. Poisonous levels of lead are rarely found after one episode of swallowing or inhaling lead — it is usually a gradual build-up due to exposure to lead in the workplace.

The symptoms of lead poisoning include loss of appetite, irritability, nausea, stomach cramps, diarrhoea, vomiting, headache, and leg cramps. Severe cases may have black faeces, reduced urine output, forgetfulness and eventually convulsions, coma and death. The condition can be readily diagnosed by measuring the amount of lead in the blood.

Treatment will depend upon the extent of the poisoning. In mild cases, complete removal from exposure to lead may enable the body to clean itself of the substance naturally. Moderate cases will be treated with a drug (called BAL) that actively removes lead from the body. Severe cases will need additional treatment in hospital.

All workers in lead smelters and battery factories should be screened by blood tests for lead poisoning on a regular basis.

Left-handedness

In the past, there has been something of a stigma attached to being left-handed. Left-handed people make up nearly 10% of the population, and there are more left-handed males than females. Unflattering words used to describe these people include 'southpaw' and the Australianism 'mollydooker' which literally means 'woman-handed'. The word 'sinister' is the Latin word for left, while dexterity, implying a high level of manual skills and ability, comes from the Latin word for right. Since biblical times the left hand has been reserved for the damned. It has been suggested that the bias against the left-hander may have its origin in early civilisations when the left hand was used for toilet purposes and the right for more hygienic activities. The lefties in our society should not feel apologetic for their 'preferred laterality', to use the correct medical term for left-handedness. There is an impressive list of left-handed leaders, artists and sportspeople including Queen Victoria, Harry Truman, Gerald Ford, Michelangelo, Paul McCartney, Judy Garland, Picasso, Jimmy Connors and John McEnroe.

There is good evidence that left-handedness is more common in persons with reading disabilities, stuttering and poor coordination. Ex-president Ford was noted for his clumsiness both on and off the golf course. Stuttering may be precipitated if a naturally left-handed child is forced to use the right hand, but of course many people in the past have made this transition without problems developing.

Hand preference does not appear to be a characteristic of animals, but is exclusive to humans. There are many theories to explain this. Some experts claim it is due to emotional contrariness in childhood, others that it is inherited, still others that it is an acquired learning process. It may well be a combination of these factors. Because most sporting equipment, tools and appliances are designed for right-handed people, this has created preference in the community for the right hand. Parents tend to give children toys and the like in their right hand, thereby adding to the learning process of the child. Hand preference usually begins around 9 months of age, and is established around 18 months to two years.

There is increasing research interest in the proficiency with which left-handers are able to use their right hand. Some left-handers are quite hopeless using their right hand, while others are much better. There is a suggestion that this might be related to some problem with the dominant side of the brain. Reading ability might also be tied up with this, as some left-handers have poor reading ability while others are quite normal. One side of the brain is responsible for both reading ability and speech. This may vary in left-handers leading to some confusion in the brain and clumsiness and stuttering as well as reading difficulties. A lot of research remains to be done in this area.

Parents often ask should they try to change their child's handedness. The short answer is NO!

LEGIONNAIRE'S DISEASE

Legionnaire's disease is a form of pneumonia caused by a bacterium called *Legionella pneumophila*. It derives its name from the 1976 American Legion Convention in Philadelphia, USA, where 220 cases of pneumonia developed within a few days due to contamination of the air-conditioning system at the convention centre with the responsible bacteria, and 34 of the victims died. Since then, air-conditioning systems in large buildings with water cooling towers (but not domestic air-conditioners) have been responsible for outbreaks of legionnaire's disease all over the world. Many outbreaks have occurred in Australia, including epidemics in Burnie, Tasmania, and in Newcastle, New South Wales, in 1989.

Once an epidemic occurs, it is essential for the responsible building and air-conditioning system to be identified so that it can be thoroughly cleaned and disinfected. Shopping malls, office buildings, hospitals and even the old parliament house in Canberra have been implicated in outbreaks. Correct regular maintenance of air-conditioning systems should prevent any contamination.

Victims inhale the *Legionella* bacteria in microscopic droplets of water. They enter the lungs and cause a severe pneumonia. Patients may develop only a mild infection and recover without treatment, but some (particularly smokers) will rapidly deteriorate and die. It is not possible, except by tests on the sputum, to differentiate legionnaire's disease from other types of pneumonia. The pneumonia itself can be readily diagnosed by a doctor listening to the chest with a stethoscope, and by chest X-rays.

Fortunately, it has been discovered that a commonly used antibiotic, erythromycin, will kill the *Legionella* bacteria and slowly cure most cases of pneumonia. Other ancillary treatment, such as physiotherapy and expectorant medications (see Section 6), are also necessary. Even with good hospital care, up to 15% of patients who develop legionnaire's disease will die, particularly if they are elderly or have other lung disease (e.g. chronic bronchitis in smokers).

LEPROSY (HANSEN'S DISEASE)

In the mind, leprosy conjures up an image of grossly disfigured individuals, whose fingers, toes and nose have dropped off partially or completely. For millennia it has been a feared disease, and sufferers have been banished to isolated areas so that they do not transmit the disease to others. Unfortunately these traditional and false ideas die hard. Until the early 1980s, a leper colony existed on Fantome Island, off the Queensland coast near Townsville. The reality is that the majority of victims suffer only minor symptoms, the disease is not easily transmitted, and with modern medical management, patients can live normally in the community. The disease is caused by a bacterium called *Mycobacterium leprae*, which is spread from one person to another by prolonged close contact, most commonly in childhood. The armadillo is the only animal that can catch leprosy.

Leprosy starts and progresses very slowly. The cooler parts of the body, furthest from the heart, are affected first. Pale, thick patches of skin on the hands and feet are the first sign. These are followed by nodules that slowly enlarge to 5 cm in diameter. The nerves supplying the affected areas of skin become involved and sensation is lost. As the disease progresses, a pins and needles sensation may be felt, ulcers form, and bones in the fingers and toes begin to disintegrate. There is rarely any pain. A lot of the damage and deformity in leprosy is due to unintentional burns and injuries to totally numb fingers, toes, etc. Eventually, in very severe cases, fingers and toes do fall off, but this late stage is now very rare, as most patients receive adequate treatment to cure the disease before deformity occurs.

A small number of new cases are still diagnosed each year in Australia, mainly in migrants from south-east Asia and in Aborigines. The diagnosis can be confirmed by examining samples of affected skin under the microscope.

A number of antileprotic drugs (see Section 6) are now available that will slowly cure leprosy over several years. Any existing deformities must be treated with plastic surgery. Untreated, the disease progresses to death over 10 to 20 years.

LEPTOSPIROSIS

Leptospirosis is a bacterial infection of the liver and other organs that is caught from infected cattle and pigs by abattoir workers, veterinarians and farmers. In third-world countries, dogs and rats may also carry the disease. The bacteria enter the body through minor abrasions on the hands or by being swallowed. The incubation period varies from three days to three weeks.

Patients who develop the disease suffer from a sudden high fever, headache, stomach pain, muscle aches and inflamed eyes. After a couple of days, these symptoms disappear, and the second stage of the infection commences. This lasts for one to four weeks, and the patient complains of swollen glands, a generalised rash, eye pain, and in severe cases yellowing of the skin (jaundice). The second stage may be very mild or so severe as to be life-threatening.

The diagnosis of leptospirosis can be confirmed by a specific blood test. Once diagnosed, antibiotics such as penicillin are usually prescribed, but sometimes it has remarkably little effect. Careful nursing of seriously ill patients is important. If jaundice develops, the death rate may be as high as 10%.

The disease can be prevented in most cases by taking a doxycycline (see Section 6) antibiotic tablet once a week.

LEUKAEMIA

Leukaemia! It is a diagnosis that will turn a parent's heart to ice. Fear is the only thing that floods into the brain. But there are many different types of leukaemia, and it is not an inevitable death sentence any more.

Leukaemia can best be described as a cancer of the white blood cells. Blood contains two main types of cells — red cells that carry oxygen, and white cells that fight infection and carry out many other functions to control the body. There are many different types of white blood cells, and so there are many types of leukaemia.

White blood cells are formed as identical cells in the bone marrow, and then gradually change into many specialised different types of white blood cell. The primitive forms of white blood cell in the marrow are frequently involved in leukaemia. At the simplest level, white blood cells are divided into two groups called lymphocytes and myelocytes. Cancer in these can cause lymphatic (or lymphocytic) leukaemia and myeloid leukaemia.

There are two other large divisions in leukaemia — the rapidly developing forms (acute leukaemias), and the slowly developing forms (chronic leukaemias). Combining the two types of white cells that can be involved, and the two rates of onset, we come up with four possible combinations — acute lymphatic, acute myeloid, chronic lymphatic and chronic myeloid leukaemia. Because of significant differences between them, they will be discussed separately. There are many further subtypes and rarer types of leukaemia known (e.g. hairy cell leukaemia).

Acute lymphatic (lymphocytic) leukaemia

Acute lymphatic leukaemia is the main leukaemia of childhood, and its usual age of onset is between three and seven years, but about 20% of cases occur in adults.

The symptoms include tiredness, recurrent infections, bruising, nose bleeds and bleeding from the gums. Every child in the country will have at least one of these symptoms at one time or another, so parents should not start worrying until several of them occur at one time. Only 33 in every one million children will develop leukaemia. These children develop progressively more severe infections, including skin infections, abscesses and pneumonia. Bleeding into joints may cause arthritic pains. The liver, spleen and lymph glands in the neck, armpit and groin may be enlarged. The diagnosis can be confirmed by blood tests and taking a sample of the bone marrow. Many patients are diagnosed after a routine blood test for vague symptoms. In other cases, the child may become rapidly very ill with multiple serious infections.

The aim of treatment in this type of leukaemia is to cure the patient permanently. The treatment will continue intermittently or continuously for some years, and a wide range of drugs are used, including cytotoxics and immunosuppressants (see Section 6). There are significant side effects from most of these drugs, and constant monitoring and testing of the patient is required. Other treatments that may be used include blood transfusions, radiotherapy, spinal injections and bone marrow transplants. The choice of treatment will depend upon the individual patient's reactions to treatments, the results of the investigations, and the preference of the treating doctor.

Acute lymphoblastic leukaemia can now be cured in 60% of children, and 95% achieve some remission of the disease. Adults with this form of leukaemia have slightly poorer results.

Acute myeloid leukaemia

Acute myeloid leukaemia has the same symptoms as the acute lymphoblastic form. It is normally a disease of the elderly but may also occur in children and young adults.

The only way to differentiate the different types of leukaemia is by the results obtained from blood tests and bone marrow examination. The marrow sample is usually taken from the breast bone or the pelvic bone. Under a local anaesthetic, a needle with a large diameter is bored through the bone and into the marrow. A small amount of marrow is then sucked out. The local anaesthetic can give relief from most of the pain, but the marrow itself is quite sensitive.

The treatment of acute myeloid leukaemia is also similar to that of acute lymphatic leukaemia, although different drugs may be used. Blood transfusions and more intensive radiotherapy are commonly required. Of adults with this form of leukaemia, 70% can be given remission from the disease, but fewer than 30% can be cured. If bone marrow transplantation is possible in younger patients, the cure rate rises to 50%.

Chronic lymphatic (lymphocytic) leukaemia

Chronic lymphatic leukaemia is a slowly progressive form of leukaemia that is found almost entirely in the elderly. Most patients have only vague symptoms of tiredness or enlarged glands, and the diagnosis is frequently made after a routine blood test for another reason. The liver and spleen may be enlarged, and in severe cases bleeding from nose and gums and into the skin may occur. Most cases progress very slowly over many years, but about 10% progress at a faster rate. Because of its relatively slow progress in elderly patients, many sufferers are given no treatment at all for chronic lymphatic leukaemia. If the disease becomes more active, steroid and cytotoxic drugs (see Section 6) are given. Severe anaemia or excessive bleeding may require an operation to remove the spleen.

The disease is slowly but relentlessly progressive, with an average survival time of eight years. No cure is possible, but the progression of the disease in its advanced stages may be slowed by medication. Because the patients are elderly, they frequently succumb to other diseases before the leukaemia.

Chronic myeloid leukaemia

Chronic myeloid leukaemia is a disorder of middle-aged to elderly people. Patients complain of an intermittent fever, tiredness, excessive sweating, and fullness in the abdomen. The disease is often discovered incidentally on a blood test. The diagnosis is confirmed when a blood test shows a very large number of abnormal white cells present in the blood. The spleen (see Section 2) may also be enlarged. Further tests may be performed on the bone marrow to estimate the severity of the leukaemia.

There is no great urgency in treatment of this disease until the blood test results reach certain levels. At that point, cytotoxic or immunosuppressive drugs (see Section 6) are given to reduce the number of abnormal white blood cells. Many different combinations of drugs are used by different doctors in different hospitals. The medication does not cure the disease, but slows its progress and makes the patient feel better. Unfortunately some of the drugs can have rather unpleasant side effects in some patients. On drug therapy alone, the average survival time is four years.

The other available form of treatment is bone marrow transplantation. Finding a compatible donor is difficult, but if a donor can be found and marrow can be transplanted, 60% of patients with chronic myeloid leukaemia can be cured.

LICE (PEDICULOSIS)

The human head louse is an insect, 2–3 mm long, which lives on human hairs and survives by sucking tiny amounts of blood from the skin. There are three distinct types of louse which live in different areas of the body — the head louse, pubic louse and body louse (which lives on the chest of hairy men). Technically they are called respectively *Pediculus capitis*, *Phthirus pubis*, and *Pediculus corporis*. Except for their location on the body, their symptoms, mode of transmission and treatment are similar.

To the great embarrassment of parents, the school teacher is often the first person to notice that a child has head lice. Head lice are very common, even in the most meticulous households, because the louse can spread from one person to another very quickly. Children are most commonly affected, but adults may catch these tiny insects too. They spread by close contact, such as when children are huddled head to head in discussion, by sharing a brush or comb, or by wearing another person's hat. The pubic louse usually spreads through sexual contact.

The female louse lays eggs and glues them to the hairs. The eggs hatch after six days, and grow into adults capable of further reproduction in about ten days. They live for four to six weeks. The nits that can be seen attached to hairs are actually egg cases. They can be differentiated from dandruff and other scalp diseases because they are stuck firmly to the hair, and will not brush out easily. The most common areas for the head lice to congregate are the forehead and behind the ears.

There are often no symptoms of an infestation with lice, but in severe cases there may be a mild itching from the bites on the skin or scalp. The only way to diagnose the problem is to actually see the insects or nits. Once the problem is discovered, treatment is necessary to prevent any further spread. Exclusion of children with head lice from school is only necessary until proper treatment has been given.

It is usually advisable to treat all the members of a family, even if only one is obviously affected. Preparations available from chemists that contain malathion or gamma benzene hexachloride kill the insects. They are available in both lotion and shampoo form. The treatment should be given weekly for two or three weeks to kill any insects as they hatch from the eggs. The hair does not need to be cut short unless there are repeated infestations that prove difficult to control. Eggs that remain after treatment may be removed by combing with a very fine metal comb.

Some 'old wives tales' that are associated with head lice must be put to rest. Head lice are *NOT* associated with a lack of cleanliness. Lice cannot survive for long away from humans, so clothing and pillows need only normal washing and no special treatment. Ordinary hair and body washing cannot prevent or cure lice.

Most cases of louse infestation can be

easily treated at home, but if there is any doubt about the diagnosis, or the problem becomes recurrent, the advice of a doctor should be sought.

See also CRABS.

LICHEN SIMPLEX

Lichen simplex is a type of persistent dermatitis that is characterised by intensely itchy, dry, scaling, thick plaques on the skin. They can appear anywhere on the body, but usually occur in places which are easy to scratch, such as the wrist, neck, thigh and groin. The condition is thought to be a form of nerve rash, and patients who are anxious, tense, nervous or aggressive are more likely to develop the condition. In some cases, mild stimulants such as tea or coffee may aggravate the condition, and cessation of these drinks may dramatically improve the itching.

The most important part of the treatment is to avoid any further damage to the skin from scratching. Bandages may be wrapped around the affected area, but patients often rub through the bandage or push sticks under the dressing to scratch the area. In extreme cases, a plaster may be applied. Steroid creams on the dermatitis, and steroid injections into the affected areas of skin may also be given by a doctor. Avoiding stressful situations is helpful, but often not practical. If the patient can be prevented from irritating the lichen simplex, the disease will cure itself.

See also ECZEMA.

LIMB GIRDLE DYSTROPHY
See ERB'S MUSCULAR DYSTROPHY.

LIMB PAIN SYNDROME
See GROWING PAINS.

LIVER CANCER
See HEPATOMA.

LIVER DISEASE
See CIRRHOSIS; GALL STONES; HEPATITIS; HEPATOMA; HYDATID CYST; WILSON'S DISEASE; YELLOW FEVER.

LOCKJAW
See TETANUS.

LORDOSIS

The backbone, when looked at from the side, curves gently from front to back in a double S-shape. It curves in at the neck, out over the back of the chest, in at the small of the back, and out again between the buttocks. Lordosis occurs when there is excessive inward curvature of the lumbar vertebrae in the small of the back. It is the opposite of kyphosis (see separate entry).

Lordosis is often associated with poor posture, slack muscles and obesity. It may be present to compensate for kyphosis (outward curvature) of the vertebrae at the back of the chest, or an abnormal hip.

No treatment is required unless pain and discomfort are present. If treatment is necessary, weight loss, exercise and physiotherapy are appropriate.

LOUSE
See LICE.

LUMBAGO

Lumbago is a term that is now old-fashioned, as it describes a collection of symptoms rather than a specific disease. Patients experience a sudden, severe pain in the lower back, often while lifting, coughing or straining. Any movement of the lower back causes further stabs of excruciating pain, and the patient may be totally unable to stand and is forced to crawl around on hands and knees. In some cases the pain will run across the buttock and down a leg, and can be described as sciatica.

The cause of the pain is the pinching of a nerve as it leaves the spinal cord in the lower back. The pinching may be due to a ligamentous strain, disc injury, to arthritis or a misplaced vertebra. Investigations should include an X-ray of the spine, and in recurrent cases a CT scan (see Section 4) may be appropriate.

Treatment will involve bed rest, a corset, physiotherapy, pain-killers and anti-inflammatory drugs (NSAID — see Section 6).

See also BACK PAIN.

LUNG CANCER

'Smoking is a health hazard'.

Every packet of cigarettes sold carries this or a similar warning. Lung cancer is the greatest health hazard caused by smoking. Smoking causes 90% of all lung cancers, and 90% of those who get lung cancer will die from the disease within five years. Smoking is thus a form of slow suicide, but many people are reluctant to cease because they enjoy smoking, or because they cannot stand the withdrawal symptoms that occur when smoking ceases. Other causes of lung cancer include asbestos dust, irradiation and chrome dust.

The incidence of lung cancer is steadily increasing in Australia, particularly in women, and it is now the most common form of internal cancer in the community. This is because the effects of smoking are often delayed, and the high proportion of the population that smoked in the 1950s are now entering the age at which this type of cancer develops. Most cases present between 55 and 75 years of age, and fewer than 5% of cases occur in patients under 40.

The early warning signs of lung cancer are weight loss, a persistent cough, a change in the normal type of cough, coughing blood and worsening breathlessness. Later symptoms include loss of appetite, chest pain, hoarseness and enlarged tender glands in the armpit. Your only chance of survival if you do develop lung cancer is to note these changes early, and obtain immediate treatment.

As many as one quarter of patients with lung cancer have no symptoms when the diagnosis is made, often by a routine chest X-ray. Lung cancer is therefore a very insidious and sinister form of cancer, and smokers should consider having a routine chest X-ray every few years.

There are many different types of lung cancer, depending on what type of cell in the lungs becomes cancerous. The common types are oat cell (or small cell) carcinoma, squamous cell carcinoma, adenocarcinoma and large cell carcinoma. Many rarer types are known.

Squamous cell carcinomas are a relatively common form, and symptoms usually occur early. The cancer doubles in size every three months on average, and spreads early to lymph glands.

Oat cell (small cell) carcinomas double every month on average, are far more serious, spread rapidly to other parts of the body, and are almost impossible to cure.

Adenocarcinomas and **large cell carcinomas** develop at the edge of the lung, have few symptoms, and are not easily detected. They double in size every three to six months, but spread early to distant parts of the body.

Secondary cancers that have spread from other parts of the body are also common in the lung. These are not connected to smoking, and their treatment involves the treatment of the original cancer as well as the tumour in the lung.

Lung cancer is diagnosed by chest X-rays, CT scans (see Section 4), and sputum examination. Occasionally a biopsy of the tumour is necessary to determine which type of cancer is present, but normally the cancer cells can be found in a sputum sample.

The treatment of lung cancer involves a mixture of major surgery, irradiation, and potent drugs, depending on the type of cancer present. Only a quarter of patients are diagnosed early enough for surgery to be considered, and the surgery required is usually major, with the entire affected lung often being removed. Chemotherapy with potent cytotoxic drugs (see Section 6) is the next option. These have significant side effects and seldom effect a cure, but they can often extend life considerably. Radiation may be used to shrink the original tumour, but is primarily used to treat the secondary cancers that have developed in other parts of the body. Common sites for the cancer to spread to are the bone and brain.

Overall, only 10% of patients with lung cancer survive more than five years from diagnosis. Those with small cell (oat cell) carcinoma usually die within a year, those with squamous cell carcinoma tend to live a little longer than average.

Prevention is always better than cure, and the only effective way to prevent lung cancer is to stop smoking. Even if you have been a heavy smoker, after five years of non-smoking, your risk of developing lung cancer will return to that of a lifelong non-smoker.

Lung cancer is a dreaded diagnosis to give to anyone, and far too many people receive it.

See also ASBESTOSIS; MESOTHELIOMA.

See also SMOKING, Section 7.

LUNG DISEASE

See ASBESTOSIS; ASTHMA; BRONCHIECTASIS; BRONCHIOLITIS; BRONCHITIS; COR PULMONALE; EMBOLISM, LUNG; EMPHYSEMA; LUNG CANCER; MESOTHELIOMA; MYCOPLASMA INFECTIONS; PLEURISY; PNEUMONIA; PNEUMOTHORAX; PSITTACOSIS; PNEUMOCONIOSIS; RESPIRATORY DISTRESS SYNDROME, INFANT; SILICOSIS; TUBERCULOSIS.

LUPUS ERYTHEMATOSUS, SYSTEMIC

Systemic lupus erythematosus (SLE) is an auto-immune disorder. There are many diseases in this category, one of the most common being rheumatoid arthritis.

Auto-immune diseases can be explained as the body rejecting part of its normal tissue which for an unexplained reason it suddenly considers to be foreign tissue. When the body receives a transplant (e.g. kidney, heart, etc.), the body detects the implant as foreign tissue and starts an intense inflammatory reaction in an attempt to reject it. In auto-immune diseases, this same reaction occurs but inappropriately, and directed against selected parts of the body. In SLE, the auto-immune reaction attacks joints, skin, liver, and kidney most commonly, but almost any tissue in the body can be affected.

Of all SLE cases, 85% occur in women, usually young women. SLE can have a very variable course, from a mild arthritic complaint that causes only slight intermittent discomfort to a rapidly progressive disease that leads to death within a few months. Most patients are towards the milder end of the scale.

The common characteristics of SLE are a red rash across both cheeks and the bridge of the nose ('butterfly rash'), rashes on other areas that are exposed to sunlight, mouth ulcers, arthritis of several joints, poorly functioning kidneys and anaemia. In addition, patients may complain of a fever, loss of appetite, tiredness, weight loss, damaged nails, loss of hair and painfully cold fingers. Less common complaints include conjunctivitis, blurred vision, chest pain, pneumonia, heart failure, abdominal pain, constipation, depression and convulsions. The symptoms vary dramatically from one patient to another, and none will have all these problems, and most have only half a dozen of the symptoms. Arthritis is the most common link.

Because of the varied symptoms and progress of the disease, it is often difficult for doctors to diagnose SLE. Once suspected, specific blood tests can diagnose the condition. Anaemia and reduced kidney and liver function may also be detected on blood tests.

Treatment will depend upon the severity of the disease. Many patients with relatively mild symptoms will require no treatment, or only occasional treatment for arthritis. Sun exposure should be avoided, and because some drugs are known to precipitate the condition, all non-essential medications should be ceased. In more severe cases, a wide range of drugs, including steroids, cytotoxics, immunosuppressives and antimalarials (used for their anti-arthritis properties — see Section 6), may all be used in various combinations and dosages. Patients are followed closely after the diagnosis, and while on medication, very frequent blood tests and doctor visits may be required.

There is no cure available for SLE, but nearly 90% of patients are still alive more than ten years after the diagnosis is made. Many patients are free of symptoms for months on end before a further relapse requires another course of treatment. After each attack, there is slightly more residual liver, kidney or heart damage, and eventually these problems accumulate to the point where the disease becomes life-threatening. In rare cases the SLE proceeds relentlessly to death within a relatively short time.

With careful management, compliance with treatment, and regular checkups, the outlook for most patients with SLE is quite favourable.

LYMPHOGRANULOMA VENEREUM
See CHLAMYDIAL INFECTIONS.

LYMPHOMA
See HODGKIN'S DISEASE.

MALARIA

One of the most frustrating problems a doctor faces is the patient who presents with a disease that could have been prevented if readily available advice had been heeded. Many diseases fit this category, but one of the most serious is not often considered in Australia. Malaria is a disease that many who fought in the Second World War will remember, and it caused as many deaths in New Guinea as enemy action. It is a disease which was eradicated from this country a century ago, but which could flare up again if the correct circumstances were allowed to develop. Malaria still attacks several hundred people annually in this country, and virtually all of them have caught it overseas, often while on a brief trip to south-east Asia.

A bite from the *Anopheles* mosquito spreads malaria from one person to another. During a bite, the mosquito draws the malaria sufferer's blood into its belly to be digested. That mosquito is now a carrier of malaria to every subsequent person it bites. When the next person is bitten, a small amount of the insect's saliva is injected before the blood is drawn up. This saliva contains the malaria parasite, which immediately starts multiplying in the bloodstream and liver of the victim. The malaria parasite is called *Plasmodium*, and there are four different types of *Plasmodium* that cause slightly different types of malaria. Some are more common in one area than another.

SECTION 5: DISEASES

The sufferer usually develops symptoms of the disease 8 to 30 days after being bitten, but in some cases symptoms may not occur until six months or more after catching the disease. Attacks of severe fevers, sweats and chills every three to four days are the first signs. The patient becomes obviously very ill as the blood cells are destroyed to cause jaundice (yellow skin), headaches, and muscle pain. Late symptoms include delirium, convulsions, coma and sometimes death. It is not a pleasant disease. The pattern of attacks of fever and temporary recovery varies from one type of malaria to another. Some forms are also more likely to progress more rapidly or cause complications.

If suspected, the diagnosis can be confirmed and the type of malaria determined by examining a sample of the patient's blood under a microscope. Because the malarial parasite goes through cycles of infecting the liver and then the blood, it is sometimes necessary to take several tests before the parasite can be detected.

Appropriate treatment can usually kill the parasite responsible, but this can take some time, and relapses caused by new showers of parasites into the blood stream from the liver can occur for months or years afterwards. A number of different drug combinations are used to treat malaria, and prevention is often given by using the same drugs but in a much lower dosage (see ANTIMALARIALS, Section 6).

The complications of malaria include brain infections, extremely high fevers that may cause brain and other organ damage, and gut infections. **Blackwater fever** is a complication of malaria in which large amounts of blood are passed in the urine ('black water'). It is caused by the massive breakdown of red blood cells in patients who have been inadequately treated with quinine. The patient is very anaemic, a deep yellow colour, feverish and desperately ill. The death rate exceeds 25%.

The geographic situation of Australia places us close to the world's worst types of malaria. Throughout Indonesia, New Guinea, Thailand, and other south-east Asian and west-Pacific nations, a form of malaria has developed which is resistant to chloroquine, the most commonly used form of treatment. This new strain can still be treated, but more importantly, it can be prevented. Every traveller in the tropics should ensure they take the appropriate medication to prevent the onset of malaria. The tropical areas of America, Africa and central Asia also have malaria-carrying mosquitoes. Prevention is remarkably simple. No injection is needed, just one or two tablets that are taken once or twice a week, from two weeks before entering a malarial area until four weeks after leaving the area. As an added precaution, use of an appropriate insect repellent, with long sleeved shirts and slacks or trousers, reduces the chance of being bitten.

No vaccine against malaria is yet available, but Australian scientists are at the forefront of research to make this breakthrough. Malaria kills millions of people who live in the tropics every year, and an effective vaccine would make an enormous difference to the lifestyle in many tropical third-world countries.

The worst situation that could occur is the reintroduction of malaria to tropical Australia. We have the right mosquitoes here, and it would only take one traveller returning from overseas with malaria to be bitten by an Australian mosquito, and the cycle could establish itself again. If you are travelling to a malarial area, don't take chances. It only takes one mosquito bite to catch a disease that could leave your health permanently affected.

MALNUTRITION, KWASHIORKOR AND MARASMUS

Fortunately, Australians are rarely faced with the prospect of starvation or an inadequate diet, but we frequently see scenes on our television screens of mass malnutrition in third-world countries.

Starvation or an inadequate diet causes two different problems. **Marasmus** is caused by a lack of both protein and carbohydrates, and is a result of a lack of all food (starvation). **Kwashiorkor** is caused by a lack of protein, although adequate amounts of carbohydrates may be eaten (malnutrition).

In Australia, patients with anorexia nervosa, cancer, depression, diarrhoea, malabsorption, kidney failure and a number of other diseases may suffer from malnutrition as a result of their disease. Some elderly and intellectually handicapped people become malnourished because they are unable to care for themselves adequately. Malnutrition obviously causes weight loss, but if this weight loss exceeds one third of the normal body weight, heart, liver, kidney and other organ damage becomes significant and sudden death may occur. Resistance to infection is also reduced, and severe lung and skin infections may also cause death.

Patients with marasmus have wasted muscles, retarded growth, no fat under the skin, dry skin, and look older than their years. In contrast, those with kwashiorkor have swollen bellies, tiredness, thin limbs with swollen ankles, wasted muscles, a dry dermatitis, sparse hair, conjunctivitis and inflamed gums. The lack of protein in the diet allows protein levels in the blood to drop to a very low level. At these low levels, water escapes from the blood and into the tissues to give the characteristic bloated belly appearance.

Treatment of both conditions requires a slow and steady replacement diet. Trying to feed even normal quantities of food to these people can result in an imbalance of chemicals in the blood. Small amounts of nutritious food frequently over a couple of weeks before returning to a normal diet is essential.

MANIA

A manic episode is the opposite of depression, but it is often associated with depression, as patients with depression usually swing from one extreme of mood to the other. Patients with mania change their ideas rapidly, speak quickly on different topics that are not apparently connected, become over-involved in activities, move very quickly to the point where minor accidents are common, require little sleep, are very irritable and lose their temper easily. In severe cases, marked aggression may occur, the patient may have exceedingly grand ideas about his/her importance and ability, and may make rash decisions such as resigning from a job or making inappropriate major purchases. Exhibitionism, excessive sexual desires, pointless travel and attempting to obtain media coverage are other symptoms. The patient may believe that others are persecuting him/her (paranoia), have hallucinations, hear imaginary voices, and feel rejected by society.

Episodes usually commence suddenly, and may last from hours to months. They may be preceded or followed by a period of intense depression during which suicide is a risk. The attacks may be triggered by stress and anxiety, drug abuse or epilepsy. Some patients with mania are actually suffering from schizophrenia (see separate entry).

There is a risk that patients who are manic will injure themselves or others by their actions, so urgent treatment is necessary. If the patient is perceived by a doctor to be at risk of suicide or injuring

SECTION 5: DISEASES

others and refuses to accept treatment, the doctor may, with the cooperation of relatives or another doctor, certify the patient so that the police are empowered to take the patient to a psychiatric hospital for compulsory treatment. The regulations covering certification under the mental health acts vary from state to state.

Treatment will involve the use of one or more antipsychotic medications (see Section 6). Lithium is one of the most common drugs used in this situation. If the patient can be convinced to remain on medication, good control can be obtained. Unfortunately, many patients cannot see why they should take drugs for many months or years, and stop them prematurely which leads to a relapse into the mania or depression.

See also DEPRESSION.

MARASMUS
See MALNUTRITION.

MARFAN'S SYNDROME
Marfan's syndrome is an uncommon inherited condition that affects the skeleton, heart and eye, and occurs in all races but only in one out of every 20 000 people.

The skeletal characteristics of the syndrome include very long thin bones in the arms, legs, fingers and toes, a tall skull, excessive joint movement and a humped back. More than half the patients are born with an eye lens that is in the wrong position, and they may develop a detached retina (the light-sensitive area) at the back of the eyes, which results in partial or total blindness. An abnormality in the elastic tissue of the heart valves and major arteries causes the heart valves to fail and the pumping of the heart to be inefficient. The main artery of the body, the aorta, also becomes overly dilated and distorted and may eventually rupture. Because of the heart damage, heart infections (endocarditis) are common. Most patients will not have all these symptoms and problems, as there is great variation between one patient and another. Some people may be totally unaware that they are affected and just appear to be very tall and thin.

The condition can be diagnosed by the characteristic appearance of the bones on an X-ray, and by assessing the heart abnormalities with special techniques.

There is no cure, but treatment to control and correct the problems in the heart and aorta by both medication and surgery are necessary. Death from these complications in middle age is common unless the surgery to correct the problems is successful.

MARIJUANA ABUSE
See DRUG ADDICTION.

MASTITIS
See BREAST INFECTION.

MASTOIDITIS
Immediately behind the ear, there is a small bump of bone at the bottom of the skull. This bone is called the mastoid, and it contains a honeycomb of air filled spaces. If it becomes infected, the patient is said to suffer from mastoiditis. Almost invariably, mastoid infections occur as a result of infection spreading from the middle ear. Patients who have recurrent or severe attacks of middle ear infection may develop an infection of the mastoid bone. The symptoms include severe pain and tenderness behind the ear, fever, and redness over the mastoid bone. The patient is obviously quite ill. An X-ray of the mastoid shows the air spaces within it to be destroyed and replaced by pus (an abscess). The ear may also be discharging pus if the eardrum or mastoid abscess has ruptured.

Immediate effective treatment is essential if permanent ear damage is to be avoided. Potent antibiotics (often penicillin) will be prescribed and are sometimes given by injection. If these fail to control the infection within a couple of days, an operation to drain the pus out of the mastoid bone will be necessary.

The operation (called a mastoidectomy) involves making a hole behind the ear into the mastoid bone, and removing the pus it contains. In some cases the infection in the mastoid will eat away the bone at the back of the ear canal and allow the pus to escape into the ear. This hole between the ear canal and the mastoid air cells, and the cavity in the mastoid bone that results from the infection, are permanent and will need to be carefully checked by doctors for many years. If left untreated, the infection causing the mastoiditis may spread through the bone at the bottom of the skull and into the brain.

ME
See MYALGIC ENCEPHALOMYELITIS.

Measles (Rubeola, Morbilli)
Only one disease in mankind's history has been totally eradicated by medical science, and that was smallpox, the last case being in Somalia in 1978. Medical science continues to advance, and the next disease on the international hit list is measles. This may seem a strange choice, as many people consider this to be a relatively minor disease, and in Australia it usually is. However, serious complications may be associated with measles, and in more primitive countries where there is no natural immunity, a measles epidemic can be devastating.

Measles usually starts with the cold-like symptoms of a snuffly nose, cough and conjunctivitis. Not until the rash develops a few days later can the diagnosis be made. The rash starts in the mouth, where tiny white spots may appear on the lining of the cheeks. The skin rash usually starts on the face about four days after the cold symptoms, and gradually spreads as dark red blotches across the body. The rash remains for a week or more before gradually fading. Other symptoms include a high fever and avoidance of bright lights. Light does not actually harm the patient's eyes, but because of the inflammation of the eye, bright lights cause significant eye discomfort, and for this reason patients prefer to rest in a dimly lit room.

The patient often starts to feel better once the rash has reached its maximum spread, but is contagious from five days before the rash appears until it disappears. The incubation period (time from exposure to the virus until the disease appears) is 10 to 14 days. The diagnosis can be confirmed by blood tests if necessary, but it is usually quite obvious. Previous exposure to the measles virus can also be confirmed by blood tests.

Measles is due to a viral infection, and like all other viral infections there is no specific treatment. All doctors can do is ease the symptoms of the disease, and in the case of measles they can also prevent the disease by vaccination. If everyone is vaccinated, then the disease ceases to exist. Some small countries in Europe and Africa have carried out comprehensive vaccination campaigns and have already eradicated the disease. In Australia, many general practitioners have not seen cases for several years. But because vaccination against measles is voluntary, and not compulsory, some parents neglect to have their children vaccinated, and outbreaks are still occurring. Not until over 90% of the population has been vaccinated, or developed natural immunity by catching measles, will the disease die out.

The ideal time to vaccinate a child is between 12 and 15 months of age, but older children and adults can be vaccinated at any age. The vaccination is normally combined with the mumps and rubella (German measles) vaccine, and is given as one injection that gives lifelong protection. The obvious reason for vaccinating your child is to prevent them from catching the disease and its nastier complications. These include encephalitis (a serious brain infection) that may result in permanent brain damage, pneumonia, ear infections and damage, and the increased risk of developing multiple sclerosis later in life. Death, although rare (approximately one in every 5000 cases), can occur, even in our lucky country, but in third-world countries, one in ten children or adults who catch measles will die.

Immediately after an attack of measles, patients are susceptible to other infections, and a significant number will develop bacterial infections such as tonsillitis, ear and gland infections that can be treated with antibiotics.

If your child catches measles, have the diagnosis confirmed by a doctor, who will probably prescribe rest, pain-killers and medicine to relieve the cold symptoms. If the child worsens, immediately seek further medical help.

If you or your child have not been vaccinated, see your doctor as soon as possible and arrange a vaccination to prevent this slowly disappearing but still serious disease.

MEASLES, GERMAN
See RUBELLA.

MEDULLOBLASTOMA
See BRAIN CANCER.

MEIBOMIAN CYST INFECTIONS
The upper and lower eyelids contain about 20 meibomian glands each. These glands secrete an oily substance that helps to lubricate the surface of the eye. If the tiny tube leading out of one of these glands becomes blocked, the gland will swell up into a cyst, which is felt and seen as a lump in the eyelid. This cyst usually becomes infected, red and painful, at which point patients usually seek treatment.

This infection is more common in those over 40 years of age, and often no apparent cause can be found, but it may follow a period of eye irritation. It may be associated with conjunctivitis and a yellow pus discharge in the eye.

The treatment involves the use of antibiotic eye ointment for a few days to cure the infection. In resistant or recurrent cases, it may be necessary to give antibiotic tablets by mouth and to put a small cut into the cyst to drain out the pus it contains.

MELANOMA
See SKIN CANCER.

MÉNIÈRE'S DISEASE
Ménière was a physician in Paris in the early part of the nineteenth century who described a syndrome that consisted of dizziness, deafness and a constant noise in the ears. Other symptoms that may be associated with the disease are sweating, nausea and vomiting. There are no specific tests to diagnose the disease. Doctors make the diagnosis on what they find when they question and examine the patient.

The ear is a complex organ composed of three main parts. The outer ear is where the wax forms and this ends at the eardrum. Beyond this is the middle ear, which connects via a small tube with the back of the nose. Three small bones transmit the vibrations of the eardrum across the middle ear to the inner ear. It is in the inner ear that the problems leading to Ménière's disease occur.

The inner ear contains a hearing mechanism, which is shaped like a spiral, rather like a snail's shell, but only a few millimetres across. The other part of the inner ear is responsible for balance and consists of three semicircular canals full of fluid. Again, this is a very small structure.

The disease may occur after a head injury or ear infection, but in most patients it has no apparent cause. It is more common in men, and becomes more common with age. The exact cause is not known, but there is usually a build-up in the pressure of the fluid inside the hearing and balance mechanisms of the inner ear. The increase in pressure causes the distressing symptoms of the disease. Attacks of dizziness and nausea can come and go for no apparent reason, but the deafness is usually slowly progressive and permanent.

The most distressing symptom is the constant noise (tinnitus is the technical term) in the ear. It is usually a high-pitched ringing, but may be a dull roar in some people. This noise is what drives patients to desperation in finding a cure. It keeps them awake at night, and blots out the sounds they do want to hear.

Unfortunately, treatment is not very satisfactory, and new drugs and devices are constantly being tried to give relief. Among the drugs, one called Serc (available on prescription only) which increases the blood supply to the inner ear has been successful in some people. Other drugs tried with varying success are various antihistamines, diuretics, prochlorperazine, amitriptyline and chlorpromazine (most are on prescription — see Section 6). None of these have more than a 50–50 chance of success but may be tried to see if they give relief.

If medication is successful in controlling the nausea and dizziness, but not the noises, a tinnitus masker may be beneficial. This is a hearing-aid type of device that is worn in the ear and emits a constant tone that counteracts the noise already heard in the ear. It may take some experimentation to find the right one for each patient, but with persistence many can be helped.

There are also microsurgical techniques to help the sufferers of Ménière's disease. These usually involve draining the high-pressure fluid from the affected parts of the inner ear, or as a last resort destroying the auditory nerve, leaving the patient deaf in that ear but without the distressing buzz saw noise.

Those who do suffer should not despair but keep trying the various methods of treatment that are available in the hope that one will suit them.

MENINGIOMA
See BRAIN CANCER.

MENINGITIS
Between the brain and the skull are membranes called the meninges which wrap all the way around the brain and act to contain the fluid in which the brain is supported (the cerebrospinal fluid — CSF) and to protect the brain. If the meninges become infected, the patient is said to suffer from meningitis. If the brain itself is infected, the patient has encephalitis (see separate entry). The meninges can be infected by either viruses or bacteria. These two types of infection will be discussed separately.

The diagnosis of both types of meningitis is confirmed by taking a sample of cerebrospinal fluid and examining it under a microscope for the presence of certain cells. The sample is taken by putting a needle into the lower part of the back in a procedure called a spinal tap. The spinal cord is an extension of the brain that runs down from the head through the vertebrae. The spinal cord is also surrounded by meninges and cerebrospinal fluid.

Aseptic (viral) meningitis
Viral (or aseptic) meningitis is a relatively benign condition that may be caught like any other viral infection, or it may be a complication of diseases such as mumps, glandular fever and herpes. The patient experiences fever, headache, nausea and vomiting, tiredness and sometimes muscle weakness or paralysis. Doctors may note that the patient has a stiff neck.

There is no specific treatment available for viral meningitis. With bed rest, good nursing, paracetamol, and sometimes medication for vomiting, patients will recover in one or two weeks, and it is rare for there to be any after-effects.

Bacterial meningitis
Bacterial meningitis is a much more serious condition, with the severity and symptoms varying depending upon which type of bacteria is infecting the meninges. These infections are caught from people who are carriers of the bacteria, but the victims are usually weak, ill, under stress or have their ability to resist infection reduced in some way.

Patients experience severe headaches, vomiting, confusion, high fevers, become delirious, unconscious and may convulse. Some types of bacterial meningitis are accompanied by a rash on the skin and inside the mouth. Neck stiffness is quite obvious, and patients may lie with their neck constantly extended as though they are looking up.

As well as examining the cerebrospinal fluid for cells, it can be cultured to find the exact bacteria that is causing the infection. Blood tests also show abnormalities.

Treatment involves giving the appropriate antibiotic in high doses, usually by injection or a continuous drip into a vein. Other serious effects of the infection must also be treated, and these patients always require hospitalisation.

Despite the best treatment, a number of complications are possible from bacterial meningitis. They can include permanent deafness in one or both ears, damage to different parts of the brain, heart or kidney damage, arthritis and the excess production of cerebrospinal fluid which can put pressure on the brain. The worst complication is called intravascular coagulation, which involves the blood clotting within the arteries and blocking them. It is frequently fatal.

Patients deteriorate very rapidly with bacterial meningitis, and most deaths occur within the first 24 hours. The overall mortality rate is about 20%, although it is higher in children.

MENOPAUSE
See Section 1.

MENORRHAGIA
See MENSTRUAL PERIOD PROBLEMS, Section 3.

MENSTRUAL PERIOD PROBLEMS
See Section 3.

See also PREMENSTRUAL TENSION SYNDROME.

MENTAL DISEASE
See ALCOHOLISM; ANOREXIA NERVOSA; ANXIETY NEUROSIS; AUTISM; BULIMIA; DEMENTIA; DEPRESSION; MANIA; MULTIPLE PERSONALITY DISORDER; NEUROSIS; OBSESSIVE COMPULSIVE NEUROSIS; PARANOID DISORDERS; PHOBIA; PSYCHOSIS; SCHIZOPHRENIA; WERNICKE-KORSAKOFF PSYCHOSIS.

MERCURY POISONING
Swallowing mercury or mercury-containing compounds or inhaling mercury vapour may cause mercury

poisoning. The problem of contamination of the food chain with mercuric compounds gained some media exposure in the 1970s, when a number of children from Minamata in Japan were born with severe birth defects (subsequently called Minamata disease) because their mothers suffered from chronic mercury poisoning after eating fish contaminated by a nearby chemical factory.

Acute poisoning, when a relatively large amount of mercury is swallowed at one time, produces a metallic taste, thirst, burning in the throat, excessive saliva formation, abdominal pain, vomiting, bloody diarrhoea and collapse. Patients may die from kidney failure. Inhaling mercury vapour can cause an intractable form of pneumonia.

Chronic mercury poisoning, in which small amounts of mercury are swallowed over a long period of time, can cause 'pink disease' in which the hands and feet are red and swollen, the patient is irritable, feverish, loses hair and the nails are damaged. Later problems include a tremor, convulsions and brain damage.

Acute mercury poisoning can be treated by making the patient vomit up any recently swallowed mercury, and then by giving egg whites and milk. Doctors can give medications to help remove recently swallowed mercury from the body.

There is no treatment for mercury pneumonia or long-term mercury poisoning.

See also POISONING, Section 8.

Mesenteric adenitis

The mesentery is a thin membrane which connects the small intestine within the abdomen with the back wall of the abdomen. It carries the arteries, veins and nerves to the intestine. Scattered through the mesentery are numerous lymph glands, similar to those found in the neck, armpit and groin. If these glands become infected or inflamed, the patient is suffering from mesenteric adenitis.

The symptoms of this disease are identical to those of appendicitis, and many patients who at operation for acute appendicitis are found to have a normal appendix are actually suffering from mesenteric adenitis instead. It is very difficult for doctors to distinguish the two diseases. Both cause severe abdominal pain, nausea, diarrhoea and fever. Mesenteric adenitis is far more common in children than adults, and is often preceded by another infection such as a bad cold or bronchitis. Blood tests are also unable to differentiate between the two diseases, as the infected appendix causes the same changes in the blood cells as infected glands. In many cases, it is better to perform an appendectomy and find mesenteric adenitis, rather than risk the dangers of a ruptured appendix.

Mesenteric adenitis is almost invariably a viral infection, and no specific treatment is available. The pain usually settles after five to ten days.

See also ADENITIS.

Mesothelioma

Lining the inside of the chest cavity and abdomen are smooth, shiny membranes. In the chest this membrane is called the pleura, and in the abdomen it is called the peritoneum. A mesothelioma is a tumour of either the pleura (80% of cases) or the peritoneum.

Mesotheliomas can be malignant cancers (75% of cases), or localised benign (non-cancerous) growths. The vast majority of cases occur in men, and there is a high incidence of the malignant form among workers exposed to asbestos dust. It is a disease of men who may not have worked with asbestos for 20 years or more. The symptoms include shortness of breath, weight loss and chest pain.

The diagnosis can be confirmed by chest X-rays and CT scans (see Section 4). If a suspicious area is seen, a biopsy is performed to obtain a small amount of the tumour for examination under a microscope.

The malignant form of mesothelioma spreads very rapidly around the lung and abdomen, and patients become progressively more breathless and suffer considerably from pain, as every movement of the chest with breathing irritates the cancer. A number of treatments with potent drugs and irradiation have been tried, but with minimal success, and the majority of victims die within eight months of diagnosis. Survival beyond two years is rare.

The benign form of the disease is readily treated by surgically removing the affected area of pleura or peritoneum.

See also LUNG CANCER.

METATARSALGIA

The long bones in the front half of the foot are called metatarsals. Inflammation of one or more of these bones is referred to as metatarsalgia, and usually causes pain at the far end of the bone near the toes.

Metatarsalgia may be caused by a stress fracture to one of the metatarsal bones, by inflammation of one of the nerves that run beside the metatarsal bone (**Morton's metatarsalgia** or neuroma), or by flattening and thinning of the forefoot fat pad and transverse arch that protects the ends of the metatarsals when walking or running.

Joggers, particularly those who run on hard surfaces such as roads and in poor footwear, are particularly susceptible to metatarsalgia. An unusually long walk, or climbing, may also trigger an attack. Patients experience varying degrees of pain in the ball of the foot, or in the front half of the foot beside the ball of the foot. Every step may be painful, and running excruciating, as the far ends of the metatarsal bones supports the full weight of the body with every step. Victims often adopt an unusual way of walking by taking the weight on their heels or one side of the foot.

Treatment will depend upon the cause. Stress fractures will heal without plaster in most cases, provided the patient rests and walks carefully, and does not run for about a month.

Morton's metatarsalgia is more common in middle-aged women, and is treated by inserting a shock absorbing insole into the shoes, taking anti-inflammatory medications (NSAIDs — see Section 6), or in severe cases having an operation to remove the damaged section of nerve.

Damage to the forefoot arch and fat pad can be helped by physiotherapy to strengthen the small muscles within the foot. In older patients, sponge rubber insoles and anti-inflammatory medications (NSAIDs — see Section 6) may be necessary to give relief from persistent pain.

METRORRHAGIA
See MENSTRUAL PERIOD PROBLEMS, Section 3.

MIDDLE EAR INFECTION
See OTITIS MEDIA.

MIKULICZ'S DISEASE
See SJÖGREN'S SYNDROME.

MIGRAINE

A migraine may occur once in a person's life, or three times a week. They may cause a relatively mild head pain, or may totally disable the victim for days on end. Headaches can be caused by spasm of muscles in the scalp, pressure in the sinuses, inflammation of the brain tissue with infection, eye strain and a build-up of pressure within the skull. Migraines are quite distinct from all these other headaches, because they are a condition associated with the arteries of the brain. Migraines are caused by the initial contraction of an artery in the brain, which may give the patient an unusual sensation and warning of an attack, followed within a few seconds or minutes by an over-dilation of the artery.

The size of an artery is controlled by muscles in its wall, and if these muscles totally relax, excess blood passes to the part of the brain that the artery supplies. This section of the brain is then unable to function properly, and the patient feels the intense pressure, pain and other symptoms that occur with a migraine. Usually, only one artery at a time is affected.

The actual effects of a migraine can vary dramatically from one person to another, depending on what part of the brain is involved. As well as the intense head pain, most patients suffer from nausea and vomiting and find that loud noises or bright lights aggravate the pain. Other symptoms that may occur with attacks in different parts of the brain include partial blindness, personality changes, loss of hearing, noises in the ears, paralysis, numbness, and violence.

If you close your eyes, patterns can be seen on the back of the eyelids. These patterns are actually the random activity of the nerves in the light sensitive retina at the back of the eye and in the visual centre of the brain. In normal people, a swirling smooth pattern will be seen. If a patient with a migraine closes their eyes, flashes of light and jagged patterns will be seen instead. This test can be used to differentiate migraines from other types of headache, as the eye is an extension of the brain.

Migraines may occur for no apparent reason, or may be triggered by certain foods, anxiety and stress, hormonal changes, allergies, loud noises or flashing lights. The frequency and severity of migraines tend to decrease with age, and an initial attack over the age of 40 is unusual. Many victims find that, as they age, the migraines will suddenly cease for no apparent reason.

Doctors manage migraines by using medications on a regular basis to prevent them, and by giving drugs to control the acute attacks. It is far better to prevent than cure, and unless your migraines are infrequent or mild, you should be taking medication all the time to prevent attacks. There are many different prescription drugs that can be used to prevent migraine, and it is often a matter of trial and error over several months to find the one that suits you best. Common drugs used for prevention include propranolol (Inderal), methysergide (Deseril), clonidine (Dixarit) and pizotifen (Sandomigran — see Section 6). If you persevere, it should be possible to find the correct combination to prevent the vast majority of these disabling attacks.

Once a migraine is present it can be very difficult to cure. Pain-killers become less effective the longer the migraine has been present. The very strong narcotic pain-killers should normally be avoided in treating the condition, as it is possible for patients with recurrent attacks to become dependent upon them. Medications taken as soon as the attack occurs to control the over-dilation of the artery causing the migraine (e.g. ergotamine) have a better result, and a supply of these drugs should be carried by all migraine sufferers. Using these tablets, and at the same time resting in a cool, dark room, is probably the best way to deal with the early stage of a migraine. Paracetamol, aspirin, mild sedatives and medication to ease the nausea and vomiting are also useful. If these simple measures are unsuccessful, see your doctor sooner rather than later.

MINAMATA DISEASE
See MERCURY POISONING.

MISCARRIAGE
See PREGNANCY COMPLICATIONS, Section 1.

MITRAL VALVE DISEASE
See HEART VALVE DISEASE.

MOLE
See UTERINE MOLE.
 See also SKIN PIGMENTATION, Section 3.

MOLLUSCUM CONTAGIOSUM
As can be determined by its name, molluscum contagiosum is a contagious disease, but the term 'molluscum' does not refer not to a disease caught from shellfish but to a rash that vaguely resembles tiny molluscs (shells) on the skin. Patients with this viral infection discover multiple small (3–5 m), dome-shaped, white blisters on scattered parts of their body. The blister often has a central dimple. Any part of the body can be affected, but the abdomen, chest and face are the most common areas affected. The infection is spread from one person to another by close contact, and if the blisters occur on the genitals, it has probably been caught by sexual contact. The diagnosis is usually quite obvious to a doctor, and rarely are any specific tests required.

 In most cases, no treatment is required, because the rash disappears spontaneously after six to ten weeks. Particularly unsightly or persistent blisters can be removed by a doctor scraping out their contents or heating them with an electrical cautery needle.

MONGOLISM
See DOWN'S SYNDROME.

MONILIASIS
See THRUSH.

MONONUCLEOSIS
See GLANDULAR FEVER.

MORBILLI
See MEASLES.

MORGAGNI, HYDATID OF
See HYDATID OF MORGAGNI.

MORNING SICKNESS
See NORMAL PREGNANCY, Section 1.

MORTON'S METATARSALGIA
See METATARSALGIA.

MOTION SICKNESS
See TRAVEL MEDICINE, Section 7.

MOTOR NEURONE DISEASE
This insidious disease is one of the most unpleasant a doctor ever has to deal with. There are several different forms of motor neurone disease, but they all affect the nerves that supply the muscles of the body.

 Your nerves are divided into two main groups — sensory nerves that feel heat, cold, touch and pain, and motor nerves that take the signals from the brain to the muscles and instruct the muscles to contract or relax. Motor neurone ('neurone' means nerve) disease is a steadily progressive degeneration of the motor nerves in the body, or the areas in the brain that control motor nerves. It is normally a disease of adults between 35 and 70 years of age. Children may be affected by similar diseases that are called **Werdnig-Hoffman syndrome** and **Kugelberg-Welander syndrome**.

Patients find that muscles in various parts of the body become steadily weaker until complete paralysis results. The muscles affected, and therefore the symptoms, vary between one patient and another. Common symptoms include difficulty in swallowing and talking, drooling of saliva, inability to cough effectively, reduced tongue movement, and weakness of the arms and legs. As the disease progresses, weakness of the muscles required for breathing cause severe shortness of breath, and allow lung infections such as pneumonia to develop. It is usually secondary infections such as pneumonia that cause the death of these patients. Some muscles go into involuntary spasm to cause jerking movements and speech.

Investigations are concentrated on electrical tests of the motor nerves to determine how well they are functioning, and taking a small piece of affected nerve tissue (a biopsy) for examination under a microscope. There are no blood tests available to make the diagnosis.

There is no cure available, and treatment is aimed at relieving muscle spasm, assisting feeding, preventing infections, aiding breathing and making the patient as comfortable as possible. Physiotherapy on a very regular basis is essential. The disease is steadily progressive to death within three to five years.

MOUNTAIN SICKNESS
See ALTITUDE SICKNESS.

MOUTH ULCER
See ULCER, MOUTH.

MS
See MULTIPLE SCLEROSIS.

MULTIPLE MYELOMA (MYELOMATOSIS)
Multiple myeloma is a cancer of the cells in the bone marrow of the elderly. This causes destruction of the bone marrow and damage to the surrounding bone. Patients experience bone pain (back, ribs and thighs are the most common sites), tiredness from anaemia, and recurrent infections because of reduced immunity. Further complications include fractures of the weakened bones, and kidney and heart failure caused by the toxic by-products of the marrow and bone destruction. Another complication may cause the blood to become excessively thick and viscous, and this leads to a wide range of other symptoms including dizziness, vomiting, bleeding gums, mental changes and partial blindness.

Because the bone is being destroyed by the marrow cancer, calcium is released from the bone into the blood stream, and excessively high levels of calcium are found on blood tests. This gives a clue to the diagnosis, which can then be confirmed by more specific tests on the blood and taking a sample of the bone marrow for examination. X-rays show a 'moth-eaten' appearance of the bone in areas where it has been eaten away, particularly in the skull, ribs and long bones of the arms and legs.

There is no cure for multiple myeloma, and treatment is aimed to reduce the symptoms and prolong life. Potent cytotoxic drugs (see Section 6) and radiotherapy are the most common forms of treatment used. Patients survive for one to four years after diagnosis, depending upon their age, the aggressiveness of the cancer, and their general health.

MULTIPLE PERSONALITY DISORDER
The movie, *The Three Faces of Eve*, has made this rare disorder better known, but

the average medical practitioner will never see a case in his or her career. Patients with this condition have two or more (sometimes more than 20) different personalities within the same body and brain. These personalities may switch from being dominant and obvious to being totally suppressed in a matter of seconds. One personality is usually present for most of the time, and the others are present for far shorter periods, but in some patients it is difficult to determine which personality is the most common one. Each personality is totally independent of the others, with its own likes and dislikes, friends and hobbies; but the different personalities may be aware of each others presence in the one body, and there may be friends and enemies between the personalities. At other times, one personality may not be aware of the activities of the other. The change from one personality to another is often triggered by stress, but sometimes a particular action, activity, place or word may trigger the change. The personalities are often opposites — shy or extrovert, teetotaller or alcoholic, sportsman or studious. A normally faithful husband may suddenly become involved with prostitutes, a rabid anti- smoker may change into a chain-smoker. The possibilities are endless. Schizophrenia (see separate entry) is a totally separate disease, and is not a disorder of multiple personalities.

The disorder may be started by stress in childhood or adolescence (e.g. a sexual assault, emotional cruelty, repressed aggression), but in most cases, no specific cause can be found.

The aim of psychiatrists in treating this difficult disorder is to determine which personality is dominant and to promote that personality over the others in a long course (sometimes life-long) of psychotherapy. The outcome of the condition will vary significantly from one patient to another, but the incidence of suicide while in one of the alternate personalities is high.

MULTIPLE SCLEROSIS (MS)

Multiple sclerosis (or MS for short) is not a particularly common disease, but it is one that can strike anyone, and it often attacks people in the prime of life rather than old age. It is a disease of the brain and spinal cord, and interferes with the brain's ability to control the body. Sufferers can experience difficulty in controlling an arm or leg, or cannot talk, or may have periods of blindness.

The cause of multiple sclerosis is not known precisely, but there are several theories. It is possibly due to an unidentified virus, or may be the result of the body's reaction to a virus. Viruses are so small that they cannot be seen under a normal microscope, and billions of them could fit on this full stop. There is increasing evidence that the measles virus may be responsible for MS in some patients. The other theory is that the body becomes allergic to itself, and starts attacking its own cells in an immune response. Rheumatoid arthritis is thought to be due to an immunological reaction like this, and the rejection of transplanted hearts and kidneys is caused by a similar reaction.

Many scattered parts of the brain and spinal cord are damaged with multiple sclerosis. The damaged areas occur at random, and when damaged, the area affected can no longer function properly. As a result, the symptoms of MS vary greatly from one patient to another. They usually have vision problems, unusual forms of paralysis, tremor, loss of balance, poor coordination, general tiredness and numbness.

To make the situation even more complex, the symptoms keep changing in any one patient because the damaged tissue can repair itself and start functioning again, while another area becomes damaged in the nervous system, causing yet another set of problems. When an area of nerve tissue is damaged, the electrical messages from the brain to the muscles cannot flow smoothly. Sometimes the message cannot get through at all, and paralysis results. At other times the message may go to the wrong place, causing abnormal movement or a tremor. Because of the varying nature of the condition, the diagnosis can be quite difficult to confirm. There is no simple laboratory test for MS, but combining a wide range of test results, measuring the activity of nerves, and scanning the brain with a magnetic resonance imaging scanner (see Section 4) may build up a picture that fits the diagnosis.

Once the diagnosis is made, the patient is NOT condemned to life as an invalid. The disease goes through a series of attacks and remissions, and periods of good health can last for many months or years. Most patients can lead independent, active and satisfying lives and take care of their own needs for many years after the diagnosis is made.

The life span of victims is not significantly altered, but young adults are the most commonly afflicted age group. All that these people ask from the public is understanding. MS is not a mental disease, it is not contagious and it is not preventable. Unfortunately, no effective treatments are available to cure the disease either, but doctors combine with physiotherapists, speech pathologists and occupational therapists to help these young patients cope with a most unpredictable and distressing condition. A number of medications, particularly steroids (see Section 6), can be used to control and shorten acute attacks.

Mumps

Mumps is usually thought to be a mildly annoying disease of childhood, but it can occur in adults too, and may cause severe illness in both adults and children. Along with most of the other childhood diseases, such as measles and chickenpox, mumps is a viral illness. Thus antibiotics, which act only against bacteria, have no effect on the mumps virus. There is no cure for the disease, and once contracted, it has to take its course.

Since 1980, there has been a vaccine available in Australia that will give lifelong protection. The vaccine is usually combined with those against measles and German measles, and is given between 12 and 15 months of age. Children born before 1979 may not be protected, and should have the vaccine now to protect them in the future. It is important to vaccinate against mumps, not just because it may cause your children to become ill at an inconvenient time, but because mumps may be a significant disease, particularly in adults. Inflammation of the brain, testicles and ovaries may occur. The kidneys, heart and thyroid gland may also be damaged. Very rarely, death may occur. Although many of these complications are uncommon, prevention of mumps is far better than cure, particularly as there is no cure.

Mumps is spread from one person to another in microscopic droplets of fluid that come from your nose and mouth whenever you breathe out. It takes two to three weeks from the time of contact for the disease to develop. The patient is infectious from one or two days before the symptoms appear, until all the swelling of the glands has disappeared. The degree of infectivity declines steadily as the disease progresses, so that the chance of catching mumps from a victim who has had symptoms for several days is far less than when the symptoms first start.

Most people know the main symptoms of the disease from personal experience.

Fever, swollen tender glands just under the jaw, headache, and a general feeling of ill-being. Sometimes one side of the neck is involved, and not the other. In this situation, the other side may swell up several days after the first side has subsided, prolonging the disease beyond its normal eight to twelve day course.

The glands in the neck that are normally involved are called the parotid glands. Their task is to make most of the saliva that is in our mouth, and a small tube leads from the gland to deliver the saliva to the back of the mouth, just behind the last bottom tooth on each side. For this reason, patients with mumps often experience pain in the gland if spicy or highly flavoured food is eaten, or even smelled.

Once you have had mumps, it is extremely unlikely that you will develop the illness again.

Treatment is simple and straightforward. Rest is the most important element, with aspirin, paracetamol and/or codeine for the pain and fever. Recovery is usually uneventful, but if complications do occur, medical advice should be sought. Even if inflammation of the testicles occurs, sterility is unusual. Obviously, exclusion from school is mandatory for the course of the disease.

If you or your children have not had mumps or the vaccination, see your general practitioner to obtain lifelong protection.

Munchausen's syndrome

Baron von Munchhausen was a noted sixteenth century traveller — and liar! Munchausen's syndrome was first named in the early 1950s, and describes patients who travel from one hospital and doctor to another, and tell extraordinary lies in order to obtain the most elaborate and extensive medical investigations and treatment possible.

Patients with this syndrome have usually studied medical textbooks, and are able to describe and mimic a wide range of medical symptoms and diseases. They may convulse, roll in agony, vomit, pretend to be unconscious and even mutilate themselves so that they bleed in front of examining doctors. By these means, they convince doctors to subject them to numerous operations for imaginary ills, and then they discharge themselves prematurely from hospital so that they can present to another doctor or hospital for further treatment of the 'complications' of the last operation or to complain about the 'incompetence' of the previous doctor. These patients are actually suffering from a serious psychiatric condition which, once suspected, needs to be thoroughly assessed by a psychiatrist for prolonged counselling and psychotherapy. Unfortunately, the relapse rate is high, and patients may actually succeed in committing suicide by proxy, by the actions of unsuspecting, but caring doctors.

A disturbing form of Munchausen's syndrome occurs when parents induce false illnesses in their children, and demand inappropriate investigations and surgery for them.

Murray Valley encephalitis
See ENCEPHALITIS.

Muscle disease
See MUSCULAR DYSTROPHY; TENOSYNOVITIS AND TENDONITIS.
See also CRAMPS, MUSCULAR, Section 3.

Muscle spasm headache
See HEADACHE, MUSCLE SPASM.

Muscular dystrophy
There are many different types of muscular dystrophy, some of which are inher-

ited, some are present at birth, and others develop later in childhood or adult life. They all share one common characteristic — the progressive and permanent weakening and wasting of muscles in one part of the body. These diseases are diagnosed by specific blood tests in some cases, electrical studies of muscle action, and taking samples of muscle tissue for examination. No effective treatment or cure is available for any of them, but physiotherapy is beneficial.

Becker's muscular dystrophy is an inherited condition that has its onset in late childhood or the early teens. It affects the muscles around the shoulder and hip, and progresses very slowly. Patients often have a normal life span.

Distal muscular dystrophy is an inherited condition that has its onset in middle age and the elderly. It progresses very slowly, and affects the hands and feet initially, before slowly moving up the arms and legs.

Duchenne's muscular dystrophy is an inherited condition that starts in infancy or early childhood, and progresses rapidly. The pelvic, shoulder, arm and leg muscles are progressively affected, and eventually involvement of the muscles essential for breathing leads to death in the teens or early twenties.

Erb's (limb-girdle) muscular dystrophy may be a spontaneous or inherited condition. It has its onset between 10 and 30 years of age and involves the shoulder and hip muscles. The rate of progression is variable, and it may lead to severe disability in later life.

Fascioscapulohumeral muscular dystrophy is an inherited condition that may commence at any age. It is very slowly progressive and initially involves the face muscles and the shoulder. Later the hip and leg muscles are involved. A normal life span is usual.

Oculopharyngeal muscular dystrophy is an inherited disorder that affects the muscles that move the eye and allow swallowing. It may commence at any age.

MYALGIC ENCEPHALOMYELITIS (ME, CHRONIC FATIGUE SYNDROME)

Myalgic encephalomyelitis is difficult enough to pronounce, but far more difficult to live with. It is also known as chronic fatigue syndrome and Tapanui (New Zealand) flu. It is far more common in women than in men. The condition may affect anyone, as it is thought to be caused by a virus. ME (the reason for the abbreviation is obvious) may start as a flu-like illness that recurs several times until it becomes constant. The patient is extremely tired all the time, every muscle in the body aches constantly, a severe headache occurs, skin rashes can develop, and there may be weakness of the arms and legs. It is like having the worst possible case of influenza, but without the runny nose and cough, and without improving for many years.

There are no tests to prove the presence of the condition. In fact, every blood test performed is usually completely normal. This makes the diagnosis very difficult, and some doctors doubt that the condition exists and explain it as a psychiatric problem rather than a medical one.

With time, most cases slowly improve, but some patients are left with tiredness so severe that they are unable to work or to undertake normal daily activities.

Unfortunately there are no miracle cures available, but antidepressants, anti-inflammatory medication, steroids (see Section 6) and other drugs may be helpful. There are also a few new medications being used on an experimental basis by some specialist physicians.

Myasthenia gravis

Myasthenia gravis is a condition characterised by a varying weakness of the muscles that control the eyelids, the movement of the eyes and swallowing. These weaknesses cause the patient to have drooping eyelids (called ptosis), double vision and difficulty in swallowing. In severe cases, the muscles used in breathing and walking are also affected. The weakness varies in severity during the day and may disappear entirely for days or weeks before recurring. Over a period of months or years, the attacks become more severe, and unless adequate treatment is obtained, death eventually results from breathing difficulties.

Myasthenia gravis may occur at any age, but is most common in young women and may be associated with rheumatoid arthritis, lupus erythematosus (see separate entry), thymus and thyroid disease. The symptoms are caused by a blocking of the nerves that supply the affected muscles, and it is believed that there is an immunological cause for the condition. This means that the antibodies that normally fight off infection are actually attacking the nerve tissue. The reason for this abnormal antibody reaction is unknown. The diagnosis is confirmed by the patients reaction to a drug from the anticholinergic group (see Section 6) which immediately reverses all the muscle weakness.

Treatment involves removing the thymus gland which is the source of most of the antibodies in the blood, and using anticholinergic drugs on a regular basis to control the muscle weakness. Steroids (see Section 6) can be used in patients who respond poorly to other treatments. Patients require treatment for the rest of their lives, but some patients have lengthy periods when the disease is inactive, during which they can cease their medication.

Mycoplasma pneumonia

Mycoplasma pneumoniae is a bacterium that may cause a particularly insidious form of pneumonia (see separate entry). It tends to attack teenagers and young adults, and often in summer rather than winter. The symptoms are frequently mild at the beginning and slowly worsen over many weeks. A wheeze, persistent cough, tiredness, intermittent fever and loss of appetite are the most common symptoms.

The patient may be initially diagnosed as suffering from a viral infection or asthma, until their failure to respond to treatment leads the doctor to order a chest X-ray. This shows a typical pneumonia pattern in the lungs, and a sputum sample can then be cultured to determine the type of bacteria present. Blood tests show the presence of infection, but not the type of infection.

Once diagnosed, antibiotics such as erythromycin and tetracycline can be used to cure the infection.

Myelomatosis
See MULTIPLE MYELOMA.

Myocardial infarct
See HEART ATTACK.

Myocarditis

'Myo' means muscle, 'cardium' means heart and the suffix '-itis' indicates infection or inflammation. Myocarditis is therefore a heart muscle infection, and quite a serious disease.

Infections of the heart muscle are unusual but may be caused by viruses (most common), bacteria, fungi or parasites. Inflammation of the heart muscle may be caused by some poisons (e.g. arsenic), toxins, irradiation and potent drugs (e.g. cytotoxics used in cancer treatment).

Patients usually remember another infection a week or two prior to the onset of infective myocarditis. Chest pain is the most common symptom, and may be accompanied by a rapid pulse, tiredness, shortness of breath, swollen ankles and a cough. These symptoms are the result of the damaged heart muscle being unable to contract as forcefully as normally, and the patient develops heart failure (see separate entry). The diagnosis can be confirmed by an electrocardiogram (see Section 4), blood tests, and other heart tests.

The treatment will depend upon the cause. If bacteria are present, antibiotics are prescribed, but if a virus is responsible, no specific treatment to cure the infection can be prescribed, and the resultant heart failure must be treated. Viral myocarditis tends to persist for many months and then slowly resolve, but after any form of myocarditis, permanent heart damage is a common result.

See also ENDOCARDITIS.

MYXOEDEMA
See HYPOTHYROIDISM.

NAIL INFECTION
The nail may become infected in two areas — at the point at the side of the nail where it emerges from the skin (a paronychia), and where one outside corner of the nail digs into the flesh of the toe or finger (an ingrown nail).

Paronychia causes a red, tender, painful swelling at the side and base of the nail. If not treated, the swollen area of infection can break down to an abscess full of pus, which may damage the nail bed and cause the nail to drop off. The infection can be caused by damage to the side and base of the nail from habitually picking at the area, working in water, working with chemicals (including detergents and soaps), dermatitis, and gardening when

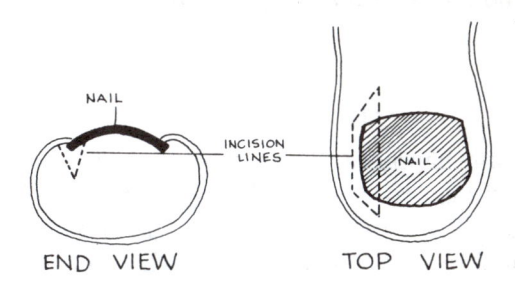

FIGURE 5.4: Wedge resection of ingrown toenail.

particles of dirt may be pushed between nail and skin.

Treatment involves applying antibiotic ointments to the infected area of skin around the nail, taking antibiotic tablets, and if an abscess is present, having it lanced to drain away the pus within. Most paronychias settle quickly on this treatment, and only gross neglect leads to loss of the nail.

Ingrown nails occur almost invariably on the toes, and most commonly on the big toe. The nail has usually been torn, or cut too short, or the shoes are too tight. This allows the skin at the end of the toe to override the end of the nail, so that when the nail grows, the corner of the nail cuts into the flesh and causes damage, pain and infection. The infection is dealt with in the same way as a paronychia, but an abscess is less likely to develop. The ingrown corner of the nail must be allowed to break free of the skin, and this may be achieved by avoiding shoes, and pulling the flesh away from the ingrowing nail corner with tape or regular massage. If these simple measures are unsuccessful, a number of minor operations may be necessary.

The most common operations involve cutting away the excess flesh that is growing over the nail, or cutting away a wedge of the nail, nail bed and tissue beside the nail (a wedge resection) to permanently narrow the nail. This latter procedure should permanently cure an ingrown toe nail.

Nappy rash

Many nappy rashes are normal. This is not a statement of infant heresy, but a simple fact. Many babies develop angry red areas of skin under their nappies, which usually cause more concern to the mother than the child. There are other rashes that should not be present and require medical treatment. It is far better to prevent these rashes than to later find it necessary to take aggressive treatment measures.

Prevention involves changing wet nappies as soon as possible, and avoiding, when practical, the use of pilchers or plastic overpants. Many mothers and baby-cuddling friends will know how impractical the latter can be at times. Nappy liners can protect the skin and should be used routinely with cloth nappies. When nappies are washed, rinse them thoroughly afterwards to remove chemicals and detergents. When bathing the infant, use a small amount of the mildest soap possible (as soap can remove the protective oils that coat an infant's skin), and apply zinc cream, lanolin or petroleum jelly to the bottom afterwards. Despite all these precautions, many mothers still present to a doctor's surgery with a happy baby who has a nappy rash. This does NOT mean that these women are poor mothers — in most cases it is merely the excess sensitivity of their child's skin.

Nappy rashes are generally due to wetness. Sweat can play a part as well as urine, so it is important not to overdress the child, particularly in summer. It is not unusual to see a baby with a nappy liner, nappy, pilchers, pants and jumpsuit covering its overheated lower half. Rough textured nappies are also a problem, and nappy liners or disposable nappies can overcome this, as can the correct selection of material when making nappies.

Nappy rashes that require medical treatment are usually due to infection or oversensitive skin. The most common infection is fungal, and may be called tinea, thrush or monilia. This may appear first in the mouth, before migration through the gut to cause problems around the anus. This type of rash often avoids the deep creases of the bottom, has a bright red edge with a paler centre, and there may be small spots beyond the edge of the main rash. It is treated by antifungal creams for the bottom, and antifungal drops or paint for the mouth.

Babies who may develop eczema later in life, have more sensitive skin than normal, and this may cause angry red rashes in the fold lines. These may require a mild steroid cream to clear them. Other nasty types of nappy rash, such as bacterial infections, are uncommon. Most can be treated, controlled and prevented by the mother with some advice from her general practitioner.

All nappy rashes are aggravated by urine, and it is often worth while to allow the baby to lie without a nappy on, but with a nappy or two underneath it in the cot to catch any accidents. Overbathing may also aggravate nappy rashes, and it may help to bathe only every second day, wiping dirty areas with a damp cloth (without soap) at other times.

Creams and ointments from chemists can be used on mild rashes, but ensure that the preparation is designed for this purpose, as some treatments not specifically designed for babies' bottoms may aggravate the rash.

A nappy rash is not a reflection on the mother or a sign of neglect. If the rash does not settle after simple remedies, it is sensible to be reassured by your doctor that it is not one of the more serious forms that requires specific treatment.

NARCOLEPSY

Narcolepsy is an unusual form of epilepsy (see separate entry) that is characterised by sudden periods of sleeping for 5 to 30 minutes several times a day, sudden muscle weakness, hallucinations before and during sleep periods, and paralysis immediately before and during sleep. Not all of these symptoms occur in all patients, and there is a wide range of severity from those who merely appear to sleep excessively, to those who are barely able to function or care for themselves. Patients may suddenly fall asleep, sometimes in the middle of a sentence, or when halfway across a pedestrian crossing. Narcolepsy therefore has obvious dangers and requires urgent treatment.

The diagnosis can only be confirmed by an electroencephalogram (see Section 4) and by observing the patient in a sleep laboratory. Patients with narcolepsy go from wakefulness almost immediately into the deepest type of sleep known as REM (rapid eye movement) sleep, without passing through the normal intermediate stages.

Treatment of narcolepsy involves using stimulants, such as amphetamine, on a regular basis. Patients must not be allowed to drive, swim or operate machinery until they have been well controlled for a long time. In many patients, good control of symptoms is quite difficult to achieve.

As narcolepsy is a rare condition, it is far more likely that patients who sleep excessively are merely over-tired from work, play and activities. Many medical conditions from anaemia and chronic infections to an underactive thyroid gland and the side effects of medications can also cause tiredness and falling asleep rapidly.

NARCOTIC ADDICTION
See DRUG ADDICTION.

NECK INJURY
See PARAPLEGIA AND QUADRIPLEGIA; WHIPLASH INJURY.

NECROTISING ENTEROCOLITIS

Necrotising enterocolitis is a rare and fatal disease of infants in which large segments of the small and large intestines become gangrenous. The cause is unknown, but may be associated with gut infections. The disease is more common in premature babies. The baby passes bloody diarrhoea, vomits, and rapidly becomes extremely ill as the intestine ruptures and allows its contents to escape into the abdominal cavity. The diagnosis is readily confirmed by an X-ray of the abdomen. Urgent surgery, massive doses of antibiotics and intensive care are sometimes successful, but the majority of these babies die within a couple of days.

NECROTISING ULCERATIVE GINGIVOSTOMATITIS
See VINCENT'S ANGINA.

NEMATODES
See ROUNDWORMS.

NEOPLASM
See CANCER.

NEPHRITIS
See GLOMERULONEPHRITIS.

NEPHROBLASTOMA
See WILM'S TUMOUR.

NEPHROLITHIASIS
See KIDNEY STONES.

NEPHROTIC SYNDROME
The nephrotic syndrome is a form of

kidney failure (see separate entry), and the symptoms are a result of the kidney's inability to remove fluid and waste products from the body. The major symptom is a dramatic swelling (caused by fluid) of the body — the feet, abdomen and hands being the most commonly affected areas. If the chest is affected, the patient becomes very short of breath. Other changes include a high blood pressure, stretch marks (striae) on the skin of the swollen belly, loss of appetite and a pale complexion.

The nephrotic syndrome is usually caused by glomerulonephritis (see separate entry), but may be a complication of diabetes, multiple myeloma, poisons or other diseases. It is far more common in third-world countries where there are poorer standards of nutrition and hygiene.

The patient is obviously very ill and may deteriorate rapidly, although some cases develop very slowly. Doctors will test the urine and blood, and make the diagnosis on the results of these tests. A biopsy (see Section 4) of the kidney is often performed to determine the degree of kidney damage.

There is no specific treatment available for the nephrotic syndrome, but prolonged bed rest, usually in a hospital, is essential. Steroids (see Section 6) are often prescribed to limit further damage to the kidneys. If a specific cause for the disease is present (e.g. diabetes), this can be treated.

The outcome in children is far better than in adults, and the majority of children recover after a few weeks of complete rest. In adults, long-term kidney problems are more likely, and total kidney failure may require kidney transplantation or dialysis.

Nerve disease

See MULTIPLE SCLEROSIS; NEURALGIA; TRIGEMINAL NEURALGIA.

Neuralgia

Neuralgia is pain in a nerve. Any nerve in the body may be affected, so the pain may occur anywhere, but the chest, face and arms are the most frequently affected areas. The nerve pain (neuralgia) may be caused by pinching of the nerve between other tissues, by a reduced blood supply, by an infection of the nerve, by an injury to the nerve, or by arthritis.

When you hit your 'funny bone' in your elbow, you are actually knocking a nerve, and the resulting pain in the elbow and down the arm is a neuralgia. Prolonged coughing, straining or sport may cause an injury to the small muscles between the ribs. These can pinch the nerve that runs around the chest between the ribs, and cause a sudden, stabbing and shooting pain that is another form of neuralgia. Arthritis in the back, or in any other joints, can cause a nerve to be pinched when the joint is moved in a certain direction, yet again causing neuralgia. Sciatica is a form of neuralgia that occurs when the sciatic nerve in the buttock becomes pinched by arthritis in the back.

Migraines can cause the blood supply to certain nerves to be reduced due to spasm of the tiny arteries supplying the nerve. This may be responsible for intense neuralgia in the head or other parts of the body.

Infections of the nerves, such as shingles (see separate entry), can cause intense neuralgia in the affected nerve. This pain may persist for months or years after the attack of shingles, due to damage and inflammation to the nerve. This condition is known as post-herpetic (the herpes zoster virus causes shingles) neuralgia.

The treatment of neuralgia will depend upon the cause. Anti-inflammatory drugs (NSAID — see Section 6) can reduce inflammation associated with muscle strain and arthritis, and steroids (see Section 6) given as injections into the damaged area or as a tablet may also give relief.

See also TRIGEMINAL NEURALGIA.

NEUROFIBROMATOSIS
See VON RECKLINGHAUSEN'S DISEASE.

NEUROSIS

A neurosis is defined as an illness of the personality in which the patient is aware that a problem is present. In many psychiatric conditions, such as schizophrenia and psychosis (see separate entries), the patient is not aware that there is a problem present. People who are neurotic (have a neurosis) are excessively anxious, may be unduly scared of something or some place (a phobia), and may become obviously distressed by their anxiety and/or fear. The distress may take the form of shortness of breath, palpitations, nausea, abdominal pain, headaches or a faint.

Both severe neuroses and depression may be politely referred to as 'nervous breakdowns'. There is a tendency for neuroses to run in families from one generation to the next, and most are present before the age of 25 years.

It is often not possible to define the cause of the anxiety in patients with neuroses. They may try to explain the anxiety as a result of some stress in their lives, but in most situations, when questioned closely, the anxiety is found to be 'free floating' and have no real basis.

Most phobias (fears) also have no rational explanation. The phobia is most commonly associated with crowds and associating with people (agoraphobia — 'agora' means market place in Latin), with closed areas such as lifts or small rooms (claustrophobia), with heights, or with any number of less common circumstances. Sometimes psychiatrists can determine that a phobia has been triggered by an unpleasant experience in childhood, but in the majority of cases, no specific trigger to the fear can be found.

Both anxiety and fear can lead to panic attacks. During such an attack the patient becomes breathless, tight in the chest, dizzy, nauseated, bloated, may vomit and collapse in a faint. These usually occur without warning, but once experienced, the patient will be extremely reluctant to place herself in similar circumstances again. This can lead to the reinforcement of a phobia about a particular place or circumstance. Panic attacks and neurotic episodes tend to be more common in the week immediately before a menstrual period. Caffeine (in coffee and cola drinks) has also been associated with the onset of attacks.

Treatment of neuroses will involve a mixture of behavioral therapy, psychotherapy, social counselling and medication. Behavioral therapy involves talking, and then taking the patient through stressful and fear-producing circumstances. The patient is relaxed, and then asked to imagine more and more anxiety-producing circumstances. Once the patient can tolerate thinking about the situation, the therapist will take the patient into the same situation that had been previously only imagined. Gradually harder and harder tasks are set for the patient, until a complete return to normality is achieved. In some cases, 'flooding' is employed, where the patient is constantly exposed to the phobia, until the anxiety response wears off. Psychotherapy involves analysing the patient's reaction to their past and present situation, their friends, relatives and family. Group therapy may be employed to give additional encouragement so that the patients realise that they are not alone in their fears. Social counselling requires a doctor, psychologist or social worker to advise the family and friends on how they should assist the patient. Activities that accentuate any phobias or anxieties will be discouraged, and the family will be taught how to encourage a more normal interaction with society by the patient.

Many medications are available to assist the patient through a crisis situation. Anxiolytics and sedatives (see Section 6) are better used in the short term only, but a number of antidepressants may be used for long periods without adverse effects or dependence developing.

The longer the neurosis has been present, the harder it will be to treat. Long-term treatment and encouragement by a sympathetic doctor is essential in all cases, and with the assistance of the family and friends, a more normal and pleasant lifestyle can normally be established for the patient.

See also OBSESSIVE COMPULSIVE NEUROSIS.

NGU (NON-GONOCOCCAL URETHRITIS)
See NON-SPECIFIC URETHRITIS.

NON-SPECIFIC URETHRITIS (NON-GONOCOCCAL URETHRITIS, NSU, NGU)

For many years, it was noticed that some men presenting with a discharge from their urethra did not fit the normal criteria for gonorrhoea. The discharge could not be demonstrated to contain the gonorrhoea bacteria, and they often did not get better if treated for gonorrhoea. This condition was therefore called non-specific or non-gonococcal urethritis (NSU or NGU). In the 1970s, it was found that many of these men actually had an infection with bacteria called *Chlamydia trachomatis* or *Ureaplasma urealyticum*. Even today though, there are still men in whom no specific infecting organism can be identified, possibly because it is very difficult to detect both these bacteria, or because another as yet unidentified bacterium is responsible. As the symptoms and treatment are the same for all these types of infection, the condition is still referred to as NSU or NGU.

Men with NSU have a cloudy discharge from the penis that stains the underpants, and there is often discomfort on passing urine. In severe cases, the lymph glands in the groin may become inflamed and tender.

Women may also develop the infection, and have a slight vaginal discharge and irritation, but in the majority of cases, no symptoms are present. Unfortunately, if the disease is not treated in these women, it may spread to the Fallopian tubes and cause infertility. If a woman gives birth to a baby while infected with NSU, she may give the baby a form of conjunctivitis that can result in permanent eye damage or a low-grade persistent pneumonia.

The disease is diagnosed by taking samples from the urethra in men and the cervix in women, but a negative result does not mean that the infection is not present, as it can be very difficult to detect in the laboratory. There are no blood tests for NSU or chlamydial infections.

Treatment involves a course of antibiotics — usually a tetracycline or erythromycin (see Section 6) — for both sexual partners. It is important to trace all contacts of a person with NSU, as the disease is spread from one person to another by sex, and symptoms may not occur in the woman until the disease is far advanced.

See also CHLAMYDIAL INFECTIONS.

NON-TROPICAL SPRUE
See COELIAC DISEASE.

NOSEBLEED
See Section 3; Section 8.

NSU
See NON-SPECIFIC URETHRITIS.

Obesity
In Roman times, a beautiful woman was considered to be well proportioned and rounded in the style of Venus de Milo (plus arms of course!). During the Renaissance, voluptuous females of Junoesque proportions were appreciated. Today the tall, skinny fashion model is considered to be in vogue. It is possible that those overweight by today's standards were merely born in the wrong era!

Obesity is often blamed on 'glands' or medical problems, but the factors that will determine your weight are (in order of importance) your food intake, the amount of exercise you undertake, and your parents. The vast majority of cases of obesity are due to excessive food and physical inactivity (but see also Section 3). If the amount of energy used (calories/kilojoules) in exercise and normal body function exceeds the amount of energy taken in as food and drink, the person will always lose weight. If the reverse is true, weight will increase. It should be remembered that calories and kilojoules are a measure of the energy content of food, and not the fat content.

Obese men and women tend to spend an incredible amount of money in their attempts to become thin by buying special foods and medicines. The cheapest and most effective way to loose weight is to spend less, by buying less food, particularly less of the expensive processed foods. If you find your willpower is lacking, or the craving for rich foods becomes unbearable, doctors can prescribe tablets that are designed to reduce your appetite (ANORECTICS — see Section 6). These drugs are expensive, and should not be used for long periods, but they are effective.

Those whose weight is within 20% of their recommended weight have little to fear health-wise. Those who exceed this limit are more likely to develop strokes, heart disease, diabetes, arthritis and liver disease. See also PREVENTIVE MEDICINE, Section 7.

If you are serious about losing weight, the following diet plan is effective, and it is not expensive. The simple rules you must follow are:

1. EAT ONLY THREE TIMES A DAY. Never eat between, before or after your normal meals. Drink only water, black tea/coffee or diet drinks if thirsty.
2. EAT THE RIGHT FOODS. Eat a balanced selection of the correct foods. This means that those foods with low kilojoule values, selected from all food groups (fruit, vegetables, meats, cereals) are the only ones to eat. Do not stick to one food group for long periods of time, as this can seriously upset the body's metabolism. Tables of relative food values are readily obtainable from doctors. For example, avocado is very rich in kilojoules, cucumber is low. See also DIET, Section 7.
3. EXERCISE DAILY to the point where you are hot, sweaty and breathless. If you are over 40, you should check with your doctor to determine what level of exercise is appropriate. 400 kilojoules (100 calories) will be used by walking briskly for 20 minutes, swimming for 10 minutes, or running flat out for 7 minutes.
4. IF NECESSARY, EAT LESS. If you are not losing weight at the rate of 1 kg per week, you need to eat less!
5. KEEP GOING until you reach your target weight, and continue dieting to maintain that weight.

Obsessive Compulsive Neurosis
This is a form of neurosis (see separate entry) in which the patient has a totally irrational desire to undertake a repetitive task. The desire to perform this task is

constantly intruding into the patient's thoughts, and even after completing the task, the patient feels that he or she must do it again and again.

One of the most common desires is hand washing. The patient cannot be convinced that his/her hands are clean, and must scrub them repeatedly, often to the point where a serious dermatitis of the hands develops. Other repetitive desires include constantly checking that a tap is turned off, a door is closed, the fly is zipped up, a window is locked, or innumerable other similar routine tasks have been carried out. Compulsive exercise or running to the point of total exhaustion is another form of obsessive compulsive neurosis. The patient may feel that by performing the rituals, he or she will regain control of a personality and emotions that are felt to be out of control. The patient is well aware that the habit is abnormal, but is powerless to stop it.

Other more frightening compulsions may occur. These may be the constant desire to hit or hurt someone else, to steal, to vandalise or to injure themselves in some way. In extreme cases, these desires may lead to criminal acts or suicide. Obsessive compulsive neurosis is more common in women than in men and is occasionally related to previous brain injury or infection (e.g. encephalitis).

Treatment involves psychotherapy, behavioral therapy and medication. No medications are particularly successful in treating this disorder, but a number of different ones may be tried.

See also PHOBIA.

OESOPHAGITIS, REFLUX
See REFLUX OESOPHAGITIS.

ORCHITIS
See EPIDIDYMO-ORCHITIS.

ORF
Orf is an unusual viral infection of sheep and goats that can infect the skin, particularly of the fingers and hands, of people (e.g. shearers, abattoir workers, veterinarians) who come into close contact with the infected animals. If the virus enters a minor injury to the skin, a sore will develop at that site four to ten days later. This enlarges to become a large, fluid-filled, ulcerating and scabbing lump that may be several centimetres across. The lump becomes soft, breaks down, and heals completely after four to eight weeks, leaving no scar. The glands in the armpit or other areas may flare up and become tender in some patients.

There is no treatment available or necessary, and good hygiene of the sore to prevent a secondary bacterial infection is all that is required.

ORGANOPHOSPHATE (INSECTICIDE) POISONING
Many of the potent insecticides available today contain a group of chemicals called organophosphates. These can cause poisoning by being swallowed, inhaled or absorbed through the skin. Parathion, fenthion and malathion are examples of chemicals in this class, but parathion is 100 times more toxic than malathion. Patients who have been poisoned have wheezing, contracted pupils, excessive sweating, nausea and vomiting, watery eyes, and diarrhoea. In severe cases, this can progress to muscle weakness, convulsions, coma and death.

If the poison has been swallowed, the patient should be made to vomit, and then given milk. The patient must be thoroughly washed to remove any poison from the skin, and contaminated clothing must be removed. Mouth-to-mouth resuscitation and external cardiac massage (see Section 8) may be necessary. Persons giving first aid must be careful not to contaminate themselves. The patient must then be taken to hospital as quickly as possible, where emergency treatment and medication to neutralise the poison can be given. The outcome will depend upon the type of poison, its dosage, and the age and fitness of the patient.

See also POISONING, Section 8.

ORNITHOSIS
See PSITTACOSIS.

OSGOOD-SCHLATTER'S DISEASE
Osgood-Schlatter's disease may appear to be a rather long and clumsy name for a relatively common but minor disease of children, but when compared to its alternative — apophysitis of the tibial tuberosity — you can understand why doctors tend to stay with the eponymous title. Dr Robert Bailey Osgood (born 1873) was an orthopaedic surgeon in Boston, and Carl Schlatter was a surgeon in Zurich, Switzerland, in the early part of this century.

At the top and front of the tibia (shin bone) in the leg, there is a lump just below the knee. This is the tibial tuberosity. Attached to this is the large patellar tendon, which runs up to the knee cap (patella) and through this is connected to the large muscles on the front of the thigh (quadriceps). When you straighten your knee, the thigh muscles contract, which pulls the knee cap (patella) up, which pulls on the patellar tendon, which is attached to the tibial tuberosity, which pulls the tibia (shin bone) into position. Children who are growing rapidly tend to have slightly softened bones. The growth area of the tibia is just behind the tibial tuberosity, and in a child who exercises a great deal it is possible for the tibial tuberosity to be pulled slightly away from the softened growing area of the tibia behind it. This separation of the tibial tuberosity from the upper part of the tibia causes considerable pain and is called Osgood-Schlatter's disease.

The patient is more often a boy, a keen sportsman, and commonly between 9 and 15 years of age. There is pain and tenderness and sometimes an obvious swelling just below the knee. The pain is worse, or may only occur, whenever the knee is straightened, particularly when walking or running. The knee joint itself is normal and pain-free. The diagnosis can be confirmed by X-rays that show the separation of the tibial tuberosity from the tibia.

The only treatment is time and rest. If the condition is mild, stopping sport may be the only treatment required, but in severe cases, strapping or plaster and crutches may be necessary to rest the area adequately. Up to two months rest may be required, and sport should not be resumed until the area is totally free of pain.

OSTEITIS DEFORMANS
See PAGET'S DISEASE OF BONE.

OSTEOGENESIS IMPERFECTA
Osteogenesis imperfecta is a very rare disease in which a child is born with fragile, brittle bones that break easily and heal poorly. Other characteristics of the condition include deafness, a blue colour to the whites of the eyes, spinal deformities and teeth defects. The disease tends to run in families, although in an irregular pattern. Varying degrees of severity are possible, and some patients are far more severely affected than others. The condition can be diagnosed by X-rays which show a typical appearance in the long bones of the legs and arms.

No treatment is available, and children with the disease suffer from multiple painful fractures that may take months to heal and leave a permanent deformity. Many die before puberty, but if they survive to adult life, the disease tends to become less severe, and a relatively normal life expectancy is possible.

Osteomalacia

Osteomalacia is now rare in Australia but still common in many third-world countries. It is the adult form of rickets in children. Both diseases are caused by a lack of calcium and the resultant softening of the bones. In adults, the most common cause is a disease of the parathyroid gland in the neck, which controls the calcium balance of the body. If this gland is overactive, calcium is drawn out of the bones and osteomalacia results. Other causes of osteomalacia include a deficiency in vitamin D or phosphate (both are essential to control calcium activity within the body), kidney failure, alcoholism, poisons and a number of rarer diseases.

The symptoms may be very mild, and the disease is detected by a routine blood test or X-ray; or the patient may have muscle weakness, tiredness, and bone pain. Fractures are only slightly more common than would normally be expected. Blood tests, X-rays and bone biopsy are used to confirm the diagnosis.

The treatment involves correcting the cause. This may involve improving the diet, prescribing vitamin D, and giving calcium supplements.

See also RICKETS.

Osteomyelitis

Osteomyelitis is a serious but uncommon infection of a bone. These infections are more common in children, and the femur (thigh bone), tibia (shin bone) and humerus (upper arm bone) are the most commonly affected, but any bone in the body may be involved. Any cut that penetrates through the flesh to the bone leaves the bone open to infection, but osteomyelitis often commences without any obvious cause and the infecting bacteria must therefore reach the bone through the blood stream. The infected bone becomes painful, tender and warm, and the tissue over the infected bone is swollen. The patient is feverish and feels ill. X-rays can show the bone damage caused by osteomyelitis, but often not until several days after the infection has started.

Treatment before this stage is desirable, and so testing the blood for the presence of bacteria, plus the appearance of the patient, are usually sufficient to allow the commencement of a potent antibiotic, which is often given as an injection. Once the infecting bacteria have been correctly identified, the antibiotic may be changed. Several weeks of antibiotic treatment, and strict bed rest during this time, are necessary. If pus is present in the bone, an operation to drain it is essential.

Complications of osteomyelitis include septicaemia (see separate entry), permanent damage to the bone and nearby joints, bone death and collapse, persistent infection and damage to the growing area of a bone in a child. With modern antibiotics, the majority of osteomyelitis cases are controlled and cured soon after the diagnosis. Complications are more likely in remote areas with poor access to medical services, in disabled patients who cannot adequately communicate their problems, and in underdeveloped countries.

Osteoporosis

A multistorey building is held up by the steel girders inside it. The human body is held erect by bones. If the steel in a skyscraper rusts and weakens, the building will collapse. Bones do not rust, but their basic constituent, calcium, may drop to a dangerously low level. When this occurs, the bones soften and they may bend or collapse. This condition is known to doctors as osteoporosis. In Latin, 'osteo' means bone, and 'porosis' means porous, or full of holes.

Despite the fact that women live on average four years longer than men, they seem to suffer a higher proportion of the diseases known to affect humans. Osteoporosis is another in this category, and up to one quarter of women over the age of 50 will suffer from this disease.

Calcium is found in your diet in all dairy food (particularly cheese), sardines, shellfish, beans, nuts and tripe. Adults require up to 800 mg of calcium, and children and pregnant women up to 1400 mg a day, but as 200 mg of calcium is found in a 25 g piece of cheese, it is fairly easy to obtain adequate amounts in your diet. Nevertheless, many older people do not consume adequate amounts of calcium, and as the structure of our bones is being constantly renewed, this lack of calcium over many years leads to a gradual deterioration in bone strength.

Once women reach the menopause, the drop in hormone levels exacerbates the problem, and the loss of calcium from the bones accelerates. This is why women are more susceptible to the disease than men, who go through a more gradual drop in hormone levels as they age. All of us have seen the sweet little old lady shuffling along the street with a hump back. Almost certainly she is suffering from osteoporosis, and she may have been 20 cm taller or more in her youth. Her present posture and height are due to the gradual collapse of her weakened bones.

Most sufferers do not know they have the disease until they fracture a bone (particularly the hip) with minimal injury, or if on a routine X-ray their bones are seen to be more transparent than normal. A procedure similar to an X-ray, called dual photon densitometry (see Section 4), is now available to diagnose osteoporosis at an early stage. There are no blood tests available to diagnose the condition.

The main problem with this disease is the ease with which fractures may occur. Other complications include deformity of the back, severe arthritis, and neuralgia caused by the collapsing bones pinching nerves.

Treatment involves adding calcium to the diet by permanently altering your eating habits, and by taking calcium supplements in a tablet form. Some of these tablets dissolve in water to make them easier to swallow. Regular exercise is also important, as the minor stresses on the bones from exercise keep them stronger. Hormone replacement therapy is also necessary for women sufferers and will actually prevent the disease if commenced at the time of menopause. This involves taking the necessary female hormones as one or two tablets a day for several years. With a calcium-rich diet, the bones will stop deteriorating and may slowly regain their strength. Other factors that can aid the treatment are reducing your intake of coffee and alcohol, and stopping smoking.

Osteoporosis may be hereditary and more common in petite, small-boned women. If your mother was a victim, it may be wise to watch your diet and exercise level from an early age.

Osteosarcoma
See BONE TUMOUR.

Otitis externa (outer ear infection, swimmer's ear)
Summer is the time of year when Australian children live in swimming pools and often seem to spend more time under water than on the surface. The most significant medical problem associated with this phenomenon is otitis externa, or swimmer's ear. With this disease, the

outer ear canal and the outer surface of the eardrum become infected and very painful. It can come on very rapidly, and a child may go from being perfectly well to rolling around in agony in an hour or two. Pain may be the only symptom, but as the infection progresses, a discharge from the ear usually develops.

Otitis externa may occur under many circumstances, but by far the most common is retained water in the ear canal. Other causes include irritating the ear canal with a cotton bud, hair pin or similar object ('nothing except your own elbow should ever be put into your ear'), badly fitting hearing aids, sweating in dirty and dusty conditions, and dermatitis in the ear canal. Bacteria normally live in the outer ear, but if the canal remains constantly wet, the type of bacteria can change from the good ones that are meant to be there to a type that can cause tissue damage and infection. If a fungus causes the outer ear infection, alone or in combination with bacteria, the condition is referred to as **tropical ear**.

Water of any type can start this infection, but sea water is less likely to be a problem. Hot spa baths (particularly public ones) and swimming pools are the worst causes. Private facilities are less likely to cause problems than public ones, not because the public pools and saunas are poorly cared for, but because far more people use them and introduce more bacteria. Warm water is also a greater problem than cold.

Adults too can catch this infection, but it is less common because an adult's ear is larger and less likely to catch and retain water than the narrow canal of a child.

Another common cause of outer ear infections is wax. Excess wax will aid the retention of water in the ear, and itself can cause infections under hot and sweaty conditions.

Prevention is always better than cure, so if you or your children suffer from ear infections, you should take steps to prevent their recurrence. The cleanliness of the water that you swim in is of primary importance, and if you have a pool or spa of your own, you should maintain it in peak condition by regular water tests. For the majority who must use public pools, drying drops used in the ear after each period of swimming can prevent most infections. These are readily available from chemists. Ear plugs are the only other method of prevention. The ready-made ones often leak or fall out. Custom made ones are available and are very good, but also rather expensive. Vaseline and cotton wool plugs make a cheap alternative.

Once you have an outer ear infection, it is important to obtain medical attention as soon as possible. This is because untreated infections can spread through the eardrum and cause a more serious middle ear infection (otitis media — see below). In most cases, no investigations are necessary, but if the infection is persistent or recurrent, swabs may be taken from the ear and sent to a laboratory so that the responsible bacteria and fungi can be identified.

Treatment of swimmer's ear involves cleaning the ear of any wax or debris that may be present in the canal, so that the ear can dry out. Antibiotic drops or ointment are then prescribed. In difficult cases, a wick (piece of light material) soaked in an ointment may be put in the ear, and antibiotic tablets may be given.

Tropical ear is more difficult to cure and control, and a prolonged course of antifungal drops or ointment and antifungal tablets is necessary.

It is important that a child with recurrent infections is treated adequately, because each infection can injure the ear and in due course cause permanent damage.

Otitis media (middle ear infections)

The ear is divided into three main parts, outer, middle and inner (see Section 2). The outer ear is the canal from the outside to the eardrum. Wax can accumulate here, and the infections collectively known as otitis externa, swimmer's ear or tropical ear (see above) are the most common ones to occur.

The middle ear contains three tiny bones that transmit the vibrations of the eardrum to the hearing mechanism which constitutes the inner ear. There is a small tube (the Eustachian tube) connecting the middle ear to the back of the nose, and infection can enter the middle ear from there. If the tube becomes blocked with phlegm, pressure may build up in the middle ear, causing intense pain that often develops during the night. Until the blockage is relieved, and the pressure drops, the pain will continue.

If phlegm and mucus fill the middle ear, the condition is known as 'glue ear'. If this 'glue' or other fluid within the middle ear becomes infected, the patient has otitis media ('otic' refers to the ear, '-itis' means infection, and 'media' means middle). Infection can also spread from the outer ear to the middle ear.

The patient experiences the sudden onset of severe pain, often at night, and will usually have a fever. Pressure on the outside of the ear aggravates the pain. Children are far more commonly affected than adults.

Treatment involves antibiotics by mouth and medications to dry up phlegm. It is sometimes necessary for an ear nose and throat specialist to perform a small operation on the eardrum to relieve the pressure.

If the otitis media is left untreated or progresses rapidly, the bulging eardrum may burst, and blood and pus will ooze out of the ear canal. The pain may be relieved by a **rupture of the eardrum**, but effective continuing treatment with antibiotics is essential to ensure that the eardrum repairs itself completely. This normally occurs in one or two weeks. If the hole in the eardrum fails to heal after several months, it may be necessary to have a small operation in which the eardrum is repaired using a tiny skin graft. Rarer complications of otitis media include a spread of the infection into the surrounding bone (see MASTOIDITIS), or into the bloodstream or brain.

Prevention is always better than cure, and using cold treatments to clear away the excess secretions at an early stage may prevent the blockage of the tube and infection in the middle ear. Any child who complains of ear pain must be seen by a doctor at the earliest opportunity.

Children who have recurrent ear infections or glue ear may require a tube to be inserted through the eardrum to allow the constant equalisation of pressure. These tubes are known as grommets, and their insertion is one of the simplest and most common operations required in children (see Section 6).

Outer ear infection
See OTITIS EXTERNA.

Ovarian cancer

There are several different types of cancer of the ovary, and as the ovary is the source of eggs for fertilisation and growth into new humans, the cells in the ovary, when cancerous, may develop into many different types of tissue. One of the most unusual and serious types of ovarian cancer is a **teratoma**, in which all types of strange tissue may develop, including gland tissue, muscle tissue and even teeth. Cancer of the ovary is a relatively uncommon cancer, but it is a particularly nasty one as there are few symptoms and it cannot be detected until it is well advanced.

About 900 women in Australia will develop cancer of the ovary every year, and the majority of them will be over 60 years of age. Interestingly, the incidence in Tasmania is almost twice that of mainland states, but the reason for this is unknown. The overall Australian incidence is considerably lower than that of most developed countries.

Most women present with a large, painless lump in the lower abdomen, or with a pelvic discomfort. A CT scan (see Section 4) of the pelvis is the easiest way to diagnose the presence of a tumour, and an operation will then be performed to remove the tumour and determine its type.

Drug treatment (chemotherapy) with cytotoxics (see Section 6) is important in the treatment of ovarian cancer. A number of different drugs may be used, and they often slow or control the spread of the cancer to other parts of the body.

The overall five-year survival rate for all ovarian cancer patients is only 35%.

OVARIAN CYST

A cyst is a fluid-filled sac. Every time a woman produces an egg from the ovary, it is surrounded by a tiny sac of fluid. This is a normal cyst, and rarely causes problems, but some women experience a slight stab of pain ('*Mittelschmerz*') in the region of the ovary as the fluid around the egg is released when ovulating in the middle of each month. If these normal tiny cysts reform and enlarge after releasing the egg, a true cyst of the ovary results. This is a 'follicle cyst', and these are quite common in teenage girls and young women. They are usually less than 5 cm across, and may cause some irregularity of the periods. The woman is often not aware that the cyst is present unless it is discovered at surgery, or bursts. Occasionally they may form giant cysts the size of a football, and although a swelling similar to that of pregnancy may be noted in the abdomen, there still may be minimal pain or discomfort. If these cysts burst, the woman experiences sudden, severe pain on one side, low down in her abdomen. The pain eases slowly over several hours or days, as the irritating fluid contained in the cyst disperses, and no further treatment is necessary unless the cyst has been very large.

Women who are found to have follicle cysts, or who develop them frequently, can be given the oral contraceptive pill, which will prevent ovulation, and therefore the formation of further cysts. The pill will also shrink existing cysts, but large cysts will need to be removed surgically.

Many other types of ovarian cysts are known. These may be luteal cysts, which cause delayed or irregular periods; cysts caused by infections of the ovary and tubes; cysts associated with endometriosis (see separate entry); and in rare cases, cysts associated with some types of ovarian cancers.

The **polycystic ovarian syndrome** occurs when multiple small cysts form in one or both ovaries. The production of hormones by the ovaries is interfered with, and as a result the woman develops facial hairs, gains weight, stops her periods and is infertile. It is often discovered during investigations for infertility. Treatment of this syndrome involves cutting away part of the affected ovary tissue, and using hormones to stimulate the ovary to restart its correct function.

See also STEIN-LEVENTHAL SYNDROME.

OVERACTIVE CHILD
See HYPERACTIVITY (IN CHILDREN).

OVERDOSE OF DRUGS
See OVERDOSES, Section 8.

See also SUICIDE ATTEMPT.

PAGET'S DISEASE OF BONE (OSTEITIS DEFORMANS)

Sir James Paget was a noted London surgeon in the middle of the nineteenth century, and has five diseases (three very rare), a type of cell, and a clinical test named after him. Paget's disease of bone is a disorder for which there is no known cause. The bone in scattered parts of the body becomes grossly thickened and soft, causing compression of nerves and collapse of those bones that support weight. Fractures may occur with only slight injury, and the back becomes bent and deformed. Bone pain is the earliest symptom.

In the early stages, the patient may have no symptoms, and the diagnosis is made on the characteristic X-ray appearance. Blood tests show specific chemical imbalances, including excess calcium, which may cause kidney damage. The skull, thighbone (femur) and shinbone (tibia) are particularly involved, giving a characteristic head appearance and bowing of the legs as they bend under the body's weight. The skull enlargement can cause pressure on nerves and a variety of unpleasant consequences, including pressure on the brain and constant headaches. The extra blood flow to the bones can also cause circulatory and heart problems.

The disease has a very insidious onset and may be quite advanced before diagnosis. It can vary from very mild to rapidly progressive, and although there are drugs available to slow its progress, there is no known cure. Tablets and/or injections will be required regularly for the rest of the patient's life to prevent the complications of the disease.

It is unusual for this disease to occur under 60 years of age, and the earlier it occurs in life, the more likely it is to be severe. A small number of patients will develop a form of bone cancer.

PAGET'S DISEASE OF NIPPLE

Paget's disease of the nipple is a type of cancer that starts in the milk ducts of the nipple, and may spread rapidly along these ducts, deep into the breast. Only one in every 100 breast cancers is due to this disease. There are often very few symptoms until the disease is well advanced, and no lump is felt. Symptoms include itching and irritation of the nipple, and a thickening of the nipple that may be thought to be a dermatitis by the patient. As the disease advances, the nipple will develop an ulcer.

The only treatment is surgery, and the more advanced the condition, the poorer the survival rate.

See also BREAST CANCER.

PAN

See POLYARTERITIS NODOSA.

PANCREATITIS

The pancreas sits in the centre of your abdomen directly behind your navel, and one of its main tasks is to produce the digestive enzymes that attack your food. A tiny duct leads from the pancreas to the bile duct and then to the small intestine to transport these enzymes to the food. The pancreas may become infected, damaged by excess alcohol intake, injured in an accident, or the duct leading from it may be blocked by a gallstone. In these circumstances the digestive enzymes may leak out of the pancreas and start dissolving the pancreas itself, your intestine and other abdominal organs — this is pancreatitis. It is an excruciatingly painful disease with pain in the centre of the abdomen that may also be felt in the back and sides. This usually leads to very rapid consultation with a medical practitioner. The patient is also nauseated, vomiting, weak, feverish and sweaty. The diagnosis can be confirmed by a test that shows enormous levels of enzymes present in the blood.

The treatment is difficult and often involves long hospital stays. It involves resuscitating a patient who is usually very ill and shocked, pain relief, then treating the cause of the pancreatitis. This may involve antibiotics and prolonged bed rest, and occasionally surgery.

Pancreatitis is not a common disease, but it is a well recognised complication of alcoholism. Anyone who drinks excessive amounts of alcohol, either constantly or intermittently, is placing their health at risk in many ways. Recurrences of pancreatitis, particularly in alcoholics, are common. There is a significant death rate with all attacks of pancreatitis, and it rises with subsequent attacks.

Paralysis
See BELL'S PALSY; CEREBRAL PALSY; ERB'S PALSY; PARAPLEGIA AND QUADRIPLEGIA.

See also Section 3.

Paraplegia and Quadriplegia
Unfortunately, more and more Australians, and even more tragically, young Australians, are ending up in wheelchairs because of broken backs or necks. Most cases are due to motor vehicle or motorbike accidents, but injuries from diving into shallow water account for many broken necks, and broken backs can occur in many different types of falls.

Those with broken necks are referred to as **quadriplegics**, those with broken backs as **paraplegics**. These technical terms merely mean quadruple paralysis (both arms and legs paralysed) and half paralysis (paralysed below the waist).

If you cut yourself or break a bone, the body immediately sets out to heal the injury, and after a time, the skin or bone is as good as before. All parts of the human body are capable of this self-repair function, with one dramatic exception — the central nervous system. The central nervous system comprises the brain and spinal cord. The spinal cord runs from the base of the brain, down through the vertebrae that form the backbone, and ends just below the waist. Throughout its length, the spinal cord has nerves running out from it to the muscles, skin and other tissues. One bundle of nerves emerges from the spinal cord as it passes through each of the 24 vertebrae. In the brain is an area known as the motor cortex. This sends signals on command to make the body work. If you want to move your leg, a message goes from the conscious part of the brain to the motor cortex. From there the message is sent down the spinal cord to the appropriate level, and then along the nerve that comes from the spinal cord to the muscle that must act to move the leg. In reverse, all the senses of touch and feeling are sent along nerves to the spinal cord, and then up to the sensory cortex of the brain. If the spinal cord is cut, it is impossible for these nerve signals to pass backwards and forwards from the brain to the body. And once damaged, the body is unable to repair the nerve tissue in the spinal cord.

Those who have severed or severely damaged their spinal cord cannot feel heat or cold, hard or soft, sharp or dull, or any sensation below the level of the injury. There is no control of muscles either, so they cannot walk, or use their arms if they are quadriplegic. To add insult to injury, they have no control of their bladder either, and have problems with the collection of urine.

Muscles are of two types — voluntary muscles that you can control by deliberate thought, such as the muscles that move your arms and legs, and involuntary muscles that you have no conscious control over, which control the internal organs such as the gut and heart movements. These involuntary muscles are supplied by a different set of nerves, and are not affected by spinal injury.

The only help that can be offered to paraplegics and quadriplegics is rehabilitation so they can cope with their disability. The future may hold some hope, because, as computers and computer components can be made smaller and smaller, it may become possible to implant a computer that can transmit the appropriate signals across the cut section of cord, enabling some degree of function to the previously paralysed part. Unfortunately, this advance is still more than a decade away from fulfilment.

See also Section 3.

PARANOID DISORDERS

Patients with paranoid disorders are deluded in that they believe that they are being persecuted by individuals or organisations. They can usually live relatively normally in society, but may express these unreasoned fears of persecution at inappropriate times. The preoccupation with the imagined persecution can have a marked effect upon the patient's home life, and may cause disruption to a marriage or family. Examples of paranoid delusions include the belief that the CIA has bugged the home and is listening to all the conversations of the family, or that the next-door neighbour is deliberately undertaking activities that are constantly irritating.

Paranoid disorders may occur alone, or as a part of schizophrenia (see separate entry).

Treatment involves the use of antipsychotic medications (see Section 6) and psychotherapy.

PARATHYROID DISEASE
See HYPERPARATHYROIDISM; HYPO-PARATHYROIDISM.

PARKINSON'S DISEASE

Many people recall grandparents who had an uncontrollable tremor, and used to sit twitching and shaking in their favourite chair. When they walked, it was with a short-stepped shuffle, and they were prone to falls. There are many causes for a tremor in elderly people, but one of the more common is Parkinson's disease.

In 1817, Dr James Parkinson, an Englishman, wrote an essay about 'a disease of long and steady progression' that had all these symptoms. He called it a 'shaking palsy' and noted its inexorable progression over many years or decades, until the patient became a total invalid. There is still no cure for Parkinson's disease, but we now have some very effective forms of control that enable many sufferers to lead normal lives.

There is no known cause for the disease, but what happens in the brain to cause the symptoms is understood. When a muscle contracts, the opposite muscle must relax. For example, when you bend your finger, the muscles on the palm side of the finger contract, while those on the back of the finger must relax. This coordination occurs in the brain. In parkinsonism, the brain cells that control this coordination have degenerated so that smooth control of movement is lost. This also leads to the general stiffness that occurs in these patients, and to their typical way of walking. The intelligence and mental powers of victims are not affected in the early stages of the disease, and this causes great frustration, particularly when speech may be impaired. They can quite understandably become depressed, anxious and emotionally disturbed. The disease progresses steadily over the years, rarely causing death, but causing otherwise normal people to become invalids, totally dependent on others for everyday tasks.

Patients and relatives should not give up hope though. Until 25 years ago there was no effective treatment, but today a number of drugs (see ANTIPARKINSONIANS, Section 6) are available to control the symptoms and slow the progress of the disease. More new drugs are being marketed all the time, and some combinations of older drugs have been found to be very effective. It is very much a matter of trial and error to determine which medications will help any particular patient, as everyone reacts in different ways to each drug or combination of drugs. The medications are available only on prescription and go by many different names. One of these drugs (Parlodel), as well as dramatically helping Parkinsonism, is also used to dry up breast milk and treat the overgrowth of bones. That's what can be called a very versatile drug!

Physiotherapy is a very important adjunctive treatment that should be continued throughout the course of Parkinson's disease. In rare cases, brain surgery, in which part of the brain is destroyed in an attempt to block nerve pathways that cause the constant tremor, is undertaken to help the victims. It is only considered when all medical treatment fails, and it is not always successful.

It is important for doctors to recognise Parkinson's disease as early as possible in its course, so that adequate treatment can be undertaken to prevent irreversible damage. The early signs are failure to swing the arm when walking, a deterioration in handwriting, and poor balance. Unfortunately, there is no specific blood or other test that can be used to make the diagnosis, which has to depend on the clinical acumen of the doctor.

PARONYCHIA
See NAIL INFECTION.

PAROXYSMAL ATRIAL TACHYCARDIA (PAT)

Paroxysmal means occurring suddenly and irregularly for no apparent reason. 'Atrial' refers to the atrium, which is the small upper chamber of the heart and which regulates the rate at which the heart beats. 'Tachycardia' means rapid heart in Latin and indicates that the heart is beating far faster than it should. Paroxysmal atrial tachycardia is therefore a sudden rapid beating of the heart, which starts in the atrium. The diagnosis can be confirmed by performing an electrocardiogram (see Section 4) while an attack is present, but this is often difficult to arrange.

PAT is relatively common in women, may be triggered by hormonal, emotional or other factors, and is not harmful. Most attacks last only a few minutes and cause minimal discomfort to the victim. The main problem is often the anxiety caused, as many patients believe that they are having, or are about to have, a heart attack.

If the attacks last for longer periods or occur very frequently, medication can be given to prevent them. There are also a few tricks that can be used to stop the attacks once they have developed. These can be taught by a doctor and include firm massage of the eyeballs and dunking your face in icy water.

The need for long-term treatment depends on the severity and frequency of attacks. Antiarrhythmics and beta-blockers (see Section 6) are the main drugs used.

See also HEART, IRREGULAR RHYTHM.

PAT
See PAROXYSMAL ATRIAL TACHYCARDIA.

PATENT DUCTUS ARTERIOSUS (PDA)

While a baby is still a foetus inside the mother's womb (uterus), it is not breathing but obtains its oxygen from the mother's blood. The lungs therefore do not need a large blood supply. The blood is diverted away from the lungs immediately after it leaves the right side of the heart, through an artery called the ductus arteriosus. The ductus arteriosus connects the pulmonary artery to the aorta. Immediately after birth, this special artery contracts and closes, diverting the full supply of blood into the lungs, which assists in their expansion, and enables the newborn baby to obtain its oxygen requirements by breathing. If the ductus arteriosus remains open after birth, it is said to be 'patent'. A patent ductus arteriosus (PDA) will divert unoxygenated blood away from the lungs and into the general circulation. This prevents sufficient oxygen from reaching the body, and eventually the baby may become blue. In most babies with PDA, there are no symptoms initially, but as the heart has to work harder, it will gradually enlarge, and over a period of several months or years, the heart will gradually fail because of the extra work it is required to undertake.

Doctors normally diagnose PDA shortly after birth when they examine the baby and listen to its heart. A heart murmur, characteristic of PDA, can be heard. The diagnosis can be confirmed by sophisticated X- rays of the heart, electrocardiographs (see Section 4) and other specialised tests. In some patients, the ductus arteriosus may be partially closed, and the problem is not significant enough to warrant treatment. In others, the dilated patent ductus arteriosus may be life-threatening.

Until recently, the only treatment available was surgery, and in some cases that is still necessary. A few years ago, it was found that a drug called indomethacin (see Section 6), commonly used for treating arthritis, also caused a patent ductus arteriosus to close. Because there may be other malformations of the heart present, the heart is always carefully investigated before indomethacin is given to a baby.

PDA
See PATENT DUCTUS ARTERIOSUS.

PEDICULOSIS
See CRABS; LICE.

PELVIC INFLAMMATORY DISEASE

Pelvic inflammatory disease (PID) is usually associated with the sexual transmission of bacteria from one person to another, although less commonly it may occur as a result of non-sexually transmitted infections. PID is most common in young, sexually promiscuous women. The use of intra-uterine devices (see Section 1) doubles the risk of developing PID, while the use of condoms provides significant protection from catching the disease.

A wide range of different bacteria may be responsible for PID, and frequently two, three or more different types of bacteria may be present.

PID is an infection of the uterus (womb), Fallopian tubes, ovaries and the tissues immediately around these organs. If the Fallopian tubes alone are infected, the condition is called **salpingitis**.

The symptoms include pain low in the abdomen, fevers, a vaginal discharge, abnormal menstrual periods, pain with intercourse, and infertility. The pain may become so severe, and the patient appear so ill, that sometimes the diagnosis is thought to be appendicitis, until blood tests and vaginal examination give a clue to the infection being in the pelvis and not the appendix. There may be no symptoms in the male partner of the patient, although a discharge from the penis is sometimes present.

Treatment involves the use of the appropriate antibiotics to clear the infection. Swabs are usually taken from the vagina and cervix (opening into the womb) in order to determine which bacteria are present and which antibiotic is the best one to kill them. Injected antibiotics may be necessary in severe cases. Sex should be avoided until complete recovery has occurred, which may take several weeks, or even months. If an abscess develops in the pelvis, an operation will be necessary to drain it.

Infections in the pelvis can cause the womb and Fallopian tubes to be damaged so that the sperm and egg have difficulty in meeting, or the fertilised egg has difficulty in growing. This results in a form of infertility that may only be treated by in-vitro fertilisation (see Section 6) or intricate surgery to repair the damaged Fallopian tubes.

One quarter of all women who develop PID will have long-term problems due to the infection. These include repeat infections, infertility (10% after one attack of PID, 55% after three attacks of PID), persistent pain in the pelvis or with sex, and ectopic pregnancy (pregnancy that develops in the wrong position).

See also CHLAMYDIAL INFECTIONS.

PEMPHIGOID

Pemphigoid is a skin disease of elderly women, although men may sometimes be affected. Patients develop red, scaling, itchy patches, which after a few days break down into large, fluid-filled blisters on widespread areas of the body. These huge, soft bubbles develop on the arms and legs initially, but soon spread to the trunk. The face and head are rarely affected.

Pemphigoid is an auto-immune disease. This means that there is an incorrect immune reaction within the body that causes part of the body (in this case the skin) to be rejected in the same way as a transplanted kidney or heart is rejected by the body. The actual cause of the auto-immune reaction is unknown. The diagnosis can be confirmed by taking a sample of the affected skin, and examining it under a microscope, where characteristic changes can be seen by a specialist pathologist.

The disease is treated with high doses of prednisone tablets. Prednisone is a steroid (see Section 6) that reduces the immune response and allows the skin to repair itself naturally. Once the disease is under control, the dosage is slowly reduced over a period of many months. Most patients will need to remain on a low dose of prednisone for years. Cytotoxic drugs (see Section 6) may also be used in treatment.

Without treatment, pemphigoid is fatal in one third of patients. With treatment, deaths are very rare, and one third of patients will require no treatment after two years.

PEMPHIGUS

Pemphigus, like pemphigoid above, is an auto-immune skin disease, but a totally separate disease entity. It occurs in all age groups and both sexes, but is rare in children. The rash varies dramatically in its form. Some patients may have shallow ulcers, others multiple blisters, and yet others red scaling patches. Any part of the body, including the face and the inside of the mouth, may be affected. A biopsy (sample) of the affected skin is examined under a microscope by a pathologist to make the diagnosis.

Treatment involves the use of large doses of prednisone or other steroids (see Section 6), which may have significant side effects. Long-term treatment is usually necessary. Immunosuppressive and cytotoxic drugs (see Section 6) are also used.

Without treatment, pemphigus is invariably fatal. With adequate treatment, the mortality rate is below 25%.

PENIS INFECTION
See BALANITIS; HERPES SIMPLEX INFECTIONS; NON-SPECIFIC URETHRITIS; REITER'S SYNDROME; SEXUALLY TRANSMITTED DISEASE.

PEPTIC ULCER
See ULCER, PEPTIC.

PERICARDITIS
The heart is contained within a fibrous sack called the pericardium ('peri-' means around, and 'cardium' is the heart in Latin). The heart normally slides and moves freely within this sack as it contracts and relaxes. If the pericardium becomes infected or inflamed, the patient has pericarditis. There are many different forms of pericarditis, depending upon the cause and effects of the disease. All are relatively uncommon. The common symptoms to all forms include chest pain, shortness of breath and a fever.

Pericarditis may be caused by a viral (common) or bacterial (rare) infection. The viral form may be secondary to mumps, hepatitis, influenza and other common viral infections. There is no specific cure for this viral infection, and the treatment involves aspirin, anti-inflammatory drugs (NSAID — see Section 6) and prednisone. Bacterial pericarditis can be treated with antibiotics.

Pericarditis may also occur if the pericardium is affected by the spread of cancer cells from the lung, lymph glands or elsewhere. Other causes include heart attacks, tuberculosis, kidney failure (due to the build up of waste products within the blood stream), and irradiation.

The complications of the disease, in all forms, include the secretion of fluid by the damaged pericardium into the tiny space between the pericardium and heart (pericardial effusion) which puts pressure on the heart, and scarring of the pericardium from infection which contracts and constricts the heart. In both these cases, the heart may not be able to expand fully between each beat, and becomes steadily more constricted (constrictive pericarditis), causing the heart to fail as a pump (see HEART FAILURE).

The disease is diagnosed by a combination of X-ray, CT scan, electrocardiogram, blood tests and biopsy examinations (see Section 4).

The outcome of the disease will depend upon the cause and severity. Death occurs in a significant number of cases, particularly if the patient is elderly or debilitated.

PERIOD PROBLEMS, MENSTRUAL
See MENSTRUAL PERIOD PROBLEMS, Section 3.

PERIODONTITIS
By their mid-teens, four out of five people have the beginning of gum (periodontal) disease, which can slowly and often painlessly destroy the supporting structure of the teeth, in a similar way to termites chewing up the foundations of a house. The eventual result can be a set of dentures, instead of the teeth that should have lasted through even the longest life. Periodontal means 'around the tooth', and refers to any disease of the gums and other structures that support the tooth.

Inflammation of the gums (periodontitis) is primarily the result of the destructive action of products from bacteria that invade the mouth. The bacteria colonies are part of the sticky film called plaque which forms constantly on teeth, especially in the protected areas in the crevice at the point where the tooth joins the gum. If the plaque is not removed daily, it can harden into calculus ('tartar'), and this can only be removed by a dentist. The plaque bacteria produce toxins (poisons) which cause an inflammation of the gums called gingivitis. This causes the gums to swell, pull away from the teeth, and sometimes bleed. The space between the gum and tooth enlarges, allowing more plaque and calculus to move down towards the roots of the tooth, and the bone which supports them. Eventually the bone is destroyed, and the tooth loosens and falls out.

Other conditions, such as diabetes and pregnancy, can make existing periodontitis worse, but more important in the aggravation of the disease is the consumption of excessive amounts of sticky, sugary food. Other factors that can worsen the disease include crowded and poorly aligned teeth, poorly fitted dentures, and a severe vitamin C deficiency (see SCURVY).

Most people with periodontal disease are not aware of its presence, because there are few symptoms. Early warning signs include bleeding gums after brushing teeth, a bad taste in the mouth, bad breath and swollen puffy gums. Very often, the condition is first diagnosed by a dentist.

It is important to realise that prevention of periodontitis is relatively simple, effective, inexpensive, and entirely up to the individual. It involves the daily removal of soft plaque before it can damage the gums and harden into calculus. Effective tooth brushing, twice a day, using a small, soft-bristled brush moved in small circles is the first step. A toothbrush, however, cannot penetrate between teeth to remove plaque where most periodontal disease (and decay) occurs. It is therefore necessary to supplement tooth brushing with the use of dental floss or tape. The floss or tape should be dragged against each adjacent tooth surface, and eased down carefully onto the gum. Once a day use is sufficient, but it is a technique that is best taught by a dentist. Mouthwashes provide only temporary freshening of the breath, and cannot remove plaque or stop the progression of periodontal disease.

If periodontitis has not been prevented, it can be treated by a dentist or specialist periodontist. This involves mechanical removal of plaque and calculus from the crowns and roots of your teeth, and instruction in daily plaque control.

See also DENTISTRY, Section 7.

Peritonitis

Your belly (abdomen) is a large, hollow sack that contains the gut and other organs. The inside of the sack is covered with a shiny, slippery membrane called the peritoneum. If this becomes inflamed or infected, the patient has peritonitis.

A wide range of diseases of any organ within the abdomen may cause peritonitis. Examples include gut infections such as appendicitis or diverticulitis, a hole in the gut from an ulcer that allows the gut contents to escape into the abdominal cavity, liver infections such as hepatitis and cirrhosis, pancreatitis, pelvic inflammatory disease, bleeding within the abdomen from injury, a ruptured ovarian cyst, advanced cancer of any organ in the abdomen, mesenteric adenitis (see separate entries), or as a rare side effect of some drugs or poisons.

A diagnosis of peritonitis is not adequate to give complete treatment to a patient. It is essential that the cause of the peritonitis be determined by further investigations. These may include blood tests, X-rays, placing a needle into the abdomen to sample any fluid that may be present, vaginal and rectal examinations, or an operation to explore the abdomen. Once the cause of the peritonitis is known, the appropriate treatment may be given.

Regardless of cause, patients with peritonitis suffer from severe abdominal pain, nausea, fever and sometimes diarrhoea. They may become very shocked and collapse. Complications may include the temporary paralysis of the gut, abscess formation in the abdomen, liver damage and adhesions.

With good treatment, recovery is normal, but without adequate medical care, death can occur.

PERITONSILLAR ABSCESS
See QUINSY.

PERTHES' DISEASE
George Clement Perthes was a surgeon in Leipzig, Germany, who nearly 100 years ago described a disease of the hip that is now named after him. Perthes' disease is caused by a softening of the growing area of the thigh bone (femur) in children, immediately below the hip joint. The disease occurs in children between 5 and 11 years of age, and is believed to be due to an abnormal blood supply to the bone. All bones in children have growing areas near one end that are slightly soft, but in Perthes' disease, this becomes excessive, and the softened bone becomes distorted and damaged as the child continues to walk on it.

The first sign is usually a limp, as the affected leg does not grow as well as the other one, and becomes slightly shorter. Pain is the next symptom, and any walking may become impossible. The diagnosis is confirmed by an X-ray of the hip. The child's general health is unaffected by the disease, and the only consequence is permanent deformity of the hip, and the development of early arthritis.

A number of treatments have been tried with varying success. Resting the affected leg by keeping the child in bed, on crutches or in a calliper, is the mainstay of most treatment regimes. If there is significant deformity, or the bone in the hip dies, an operation may be necessary. In most cases, the condition settles after two years.

PERTUSSIS
See WHOOPING COUGH.

PETIT MAL
See EPILEPSY.

PHAEOCHROMOCYTOMA
Phaeochromocytoma can be loosely translated from the Latin as black-celled tumour, and this abnormal growth in the adrenal glands does contain an excessive number of black phaeochrome cells when examined under a microscope. One adrenal gland (see Section 2) sits on top of each kidney. This rare tumour releases a substance into the blood stream that causes very high blood pressure, severe headaches, palpitations of the heart, abnormal sweating, nausea and vomiting, abdominal pains, blurred vision, and brain damage that may result in loss of speech, blindness or unconsciousness. Other associated symptoms may include increased appetite, nervousness and irritability, shortness of breath, weight loss, light-headedness and chest pain (angina).

In some cases, there is an hereditary tendency to develop this tumour, but most arise for no apparent reason. There are several forms of phaeochromocytoma, some of which are associated with cancer, but a phaeochromocytoma is not a cancer itself.

The diagnosis is made by special blood tests that can measure the excessive levels of catecholamines (the chemical released by the tumour). A CT scan or a magnetic resonance imaging scan (see Section 4) is then performed to locate the exact position of the tumour.

Treatment involves controlling the high blood pressure with medication, and then surgically removing the tumour. Long-term management with medication, but without surgery, is not practical.

The outcome of the disease depends on how much damage has been caused by the high blood pressure before the diagnosis is made. If the tumour is removed early in the course of the disease, a complete recovery can be expected. Some patients have multiple tumours in other parts of the body, and their prognosis is poorer.

Without treatment, the disease is invariably fatal, and even in the best medical centres, a small percentage of patients will die from complications of the disease or the surgery. It is believed that some unexplained sudden deaths, may be due to a heart attack caused by an undiagnosed phaeochromocytoma.

PHARYNGITIS (THROAT INFECTION)

The pharynx is the throat, and pharyngitis is a throat infection (the suffix '-itis' means inflammation or infection). A throat infection is one of the most common ailments of mankind, but the vast majority of these infections are caused by viruses (see Section 7) and not bacteria, so they cannot be cured. The germ (virus or bacterium) is passed from one person to another in tiny water droplets in their breath. If you breathe in one of these contaminated droplets, the germ can settle on the back of your throat, start multiplying, and cause another case of pharyngitis. Most cases occur in winter, but in the more equable climate of northern Australia they occur year round.

Pharyngitis can vary from one day of mild discomfort to a severe bacterial infection that may cause dramatic swelling of the throat and threaten life. The vast majority tend towards the milder end of the spectrum. The symptoms include a fever, throat pain and soreness, pain on swallowing, a dry cough from the irritation, and sometimes enlarged glands in the neck. Most cases require no investigation, but if there is some doubt about the causative organism, a throat swab may be taken and sent to a laboratory to identify the bacteria so that the appropriate antibiotic can be prescribed. Blood tests may be performed if diseases such as glandular fever (see separate entry) which also cause throat pain are suspected.

If the pharyngitis is viral, the only treatments are minor pain-killers (e.g. aspirin, paracetamol), anaesthetic gargles, and soothing lozenges. The infection may last for a week or ten days.

If a bacterial pharyngitis is present, antibiotics (e.g. penicillin) can be prescribed that will cure the condition in a day or two. The most serious bacterial pharyngitis is caused by *Staphylococcus aureus* (golden staph), but by far the most common is caused by a class of bacteria called *Streptococci*.

PHENYLKETONURIA (PKU)

Every baby in Australia is routinely tested for this rare but serious disease a couple of days after birth. A single drop of blood, taken from a heel prick, is all that is required. Phenylketonuria (PKU) is a congenital (present from birth) disease that runs in families from one generation to the next. Genetic counselling is required for all families in which a case of PKU is diagnosed. PKU is more common in people of Scottish or Irish descent (1 in 5000 children), but extremely rare in Negroes (1 in 300 000).

A baby with PKU cannot tolerate foodstuffs which contain the amino acid, phenylalanine, and a build-up of the phenylalanine in the blood causes brain damage, mental retardation, epilepsy, behaviour problems and eczema. Removing phenylalanine completely from the diet of these babies until they are at least eight years old will prevent the disease from damaging the brain, and they will grow up to be normal adults with normal intelligence. The phenylalanine-free diet must be started before two months of age. Phenylalanine is found in most proteins, and these children must be given a diet free of all proteins, but other amino acids (the building blocks of protein) are provided in a special formula.

Blood tests are performed regularly to ensure that the amount of phenylalanine in the child's blood does not rise above normal levels.

Phobia

A phobia is a fear, and in medical terms, an unreasonable fear. In many cases, an anxious patient rationalises the anxiety and the symptoms it causes (e.g. palpitations, sweating, nausea, headaches, etc.) by considering it to be a fear of something. There are people who fear enclosed spaces (claustrophobia), spiders (arachnophobia), open spaces (agoraphobia), heights (acrophobia), sharp implements, specific animals, eating in public or almost any thing or activity imaginable.

A phobia may be a form of obsession (see OBSESSIVE COMPULSIVE NEUROSIS) that dominates the patients life, particularly if the fear is of contamination, dirt or disease, which leads to repetitive actions such as constant, excessive hand-washing. In other situations, patients may go to extreme lengths to avoid the object of their fear (e.g. stay in rooms on the ground floor of hotels), or undertake rituals that make a fearful activity safe (e.g. always wear a certain piece of clothing when flying). Phobias most commonly develop in the late teens and early adult years, and are more common in women than men. The patient with one serious phobia usually develops more and more phobias of less and less fearful objects and situations, as the neurotic disease or anxiety worsens.

Some patients have a fear of a particular circumstance because of an unpleasant experience in the past (e.g. claustrophobia after being trapped in a lift). This is not a true phobia in the psychiatric sense, but a quite rational fear triggered by a previous unpleasant experience.

Patients with phobias that are causing disruption to their normal activities of daily living should see a psychiatrist. The psychiatrist can help the patient deal with the underlying anxieties, give behavioral treatment that gradually exposes the patient to the fear, and prescribe medication that may control the problem.

Minor degrees of phobia, and rational fears may be dealt with by a general practitioner, sometimes with the assistance of a psychologist.

See also NEUROSIS.

PID
See PELVIC INFLAMMATORY DISEASE.

Pigmented Villonodular Synovitis

The synovium is the tissue that lines the inside of the joint, and it is normally very smooth and slippery so that the bones can move freely one on the other. If the synovium becomes diseased (i.e. synovitis — see separate entry), it becomes painful and there is excess fluid secreted into the joint so that it becomes swollen and red. Pigmented villonodular synovitis is caused by the smooth joint lining becoming covered with dark-coloured (i.e. pigmented) microscopic protuberances and lumps. It may be due to injury to the knee, or can be associated with rheumatoid arthritis.

The pain can be controlled by anti-inflammatory drugs (NSAID — see Section 6), and the swelling can be eased by removing the excess fluid from the joint through a needle. Unfortunately these measures are only temporary, and the patient will probably need surgery to the joint in the long term. The options are to have the whole knee joint replaced, or to have the knee fused stiff. If the problem has persisted for many months without relief, a knee replacement operation may be the best treatment.

PILES
See HAEMORRHOIDS.

PIMPLES
See ACNE.

PINWORM (ENTEROBIASIS)
Enterobius vermicularis is the technical name for the pinworm that may infect the gut of humans. Children are the most commonly affected group, and they spread the infestation to others by poor personal hygiene. It is very easy for all the members of one family to be affected.

The worm, 1 cm long, lives in the large intestine, but migrates to around the anus to lay eggs, from where they may be transferred to the fingers during wiping or scratching, and then re-enter the original patient's mouth or pass to another person, where the cycle starts again. The worm dies after depositing the eggs and passes out with the faeces, where they may sometimes be seen. If the patient does not reinfected themselves, the worms will die out in six to seven weeks. The eggs can survive for up to three weeks outside the body.

Most patients have no symptoms of the infestation, but some will experience anal itching (particularly at night), mild diarrhoea and minor abdominal pains. In rare cases, the worms may migrate to the vagina and urethra in women and girls.

The diagnosis can be confirmed by examining the faeces for the presence of worms or eggs. A better test is to place clear sticky tape on the skin immediately beside the anus first thing in the morning, then lifting the tape off, and sticking it to a glass slide before taking it to a doctor for examination under a microscope to see if eggs are present.

Treatment should involve all members of the patient's immediate family. A number of medications (see ANTHELMINTICS, Section 6) can be used to kill the worms.

Although annoying, there are no serious consequences of a pinworm infestation, and virtually all patients will recover with time and good personal hygiene (e.g. careful hand-washing after going to the toilet, and not scratching the anus).

PITYRIASIS ROSEA
Pityriasis rosea is a skin disease of older children and adults up to middle age. It causes dark red, scaling, slightly raised, oval-shaped patches to form on the chest, upper arms, thighs, neck, abdomen and back. The lower arms, lower legs and face are not usually affected. The cause is unknown. Usually a larger patch called the 'herald patch' occurs first, preceding the other smaller patches by a week or two. There is only very slight itching or irritation, and the rash causes the patient only minimal discomfort.

No investigations are required, as the diagnosis is relatively obvious, and the rash settles without treatment in six to eight weeks. Sometimes a blood test may be suggested to exclude more serious but unlikely diagnoses. If the skin irritation is of concern to the patient, antihistamine tablets (see Section 6) may be taken at night, and steroid creams (see Section 6) may be applied.

Pityriasis versicolor
See FUNGAL INFECTIONS.

PKU
See PHENYLKETONURIA.

Placental disease
See PREGNANCY COMPLICATIONS, Section 1.

Plague, bubonic (black death)
An epidemic of bubonic plague swept through Europe in the middle of the fourteenth century and killed every person in some villages and up to one third of the population of some countries. It took almost a century for Europe to recover economically and socially from the aptly named black death. The epidemic began in the far east of Asia, and plague is still present in many third-world Asian and African countries. Cases in Australia now occur only in migrants or travellers from these countries.

A bacterium called *Yersinia pestis* is responsible for bubonic plague. It normally infects rats, and passes from one rat to another in fleas. If a flea carrying the bacteria bites a human, that person will develop the disease. The infected patient will develop large, pus-filled glands (buboes) in the neck, groin and armpit. This is accompanied by a high fever, severe muscle pain, headache, rapid heart rate, profound tiredness and a coma. The infection may spread to the blood and cause black spots (bruises — thus the 'black death') under the skin. A plague pneumonia or meningitis may develop, and almost invariably these complications are fatal without excellent medical care. The diagnosis can be confirmed by special blood tests and cultures from the discharging glands.

Treatment involves isolation in hospital, antibiotics and intravenous drip feeding. In good hospitals, virtually all patients will recover, but untreated the mortality rate can exceed 50%, and death may occur within a few hours of onset in those who are already malnourished or in poor health.

A plague vaccine is available to give partial protection to travellers and residents in areas where the disease is endemic. Tetracycline (see Section 6) tablets can be taken on a daily basis to give good protection against the infection.

Pleurisy (pleuritis)
The inside of the chest cavity is lined with a smooth, slippery, shiny membrane called the pleura. As the lung contracts and expands with breathing, it slides across the pleura, which is covered with a very thin layer of fluid that acts as a lubricant. If the pleura becomes inflamed or infected, the patient has pleurisy or pleuritis.

Pleurisy causes severe pain that can often be localised to one point on the chest or back and that is worse with breathing, sneezing, coughing, laughing or any movement of the chest. Pleurisy is quite common in association with viral infections of the chest, and will settle with rest and minor pain-killers or anti-inflammatory medication (e.g. NSAID such as indomethacin — see Section 6). Other common causes of pleurisy include a fractured rib that damages the pleura, and bacterial infections associated with pneumonia which will require the use of antibiotics and stronger pain-killers.

A **pleural effusion** occurs when a large amount of fluid is found between the pleura and lung. The fluid can restrict the movement of the lung, and may cause significant shortness of breath and a dry cough. There are many causes for pleural effusions, including heart failure, cirrhosis, nephrotic syndrome, lung embolus, cancer, tuberculosis (see separate entries) and other infections. The excess fluid can be readily seen on a chest X-ray, and in some cases the fluid can be removed by putting a needle through the chest wall and into the fluid collection, then drawing it off into a syringe. The fluid may be examined to determine the type of the disease present. Further treatment will depend upon the cause of the effusion.

Pleurodynia (Bornholm disease)

Pleurodynia is a viral infection that attacks the pleura at the point where the diaphragm attaches to the back of the ribs at the bottom of the chest (see also PLEURISY). The diaphragm is a horizontal sheet of muscle that separates the chest and abdominal cavities. The upper (chest) surface of the diaphragm is covered with the slippery, shiny membrane called pleura. Patients experience sudden, severe, lower chest pain that is aggravated by chest movements such as a deep breath or cough. Other symptoms include a fever, headache, nausea, and sore throat. There is marked tenderness of the lower ribs. In rare cases it is possible for the virus to spread to the testes and brain.

No treatment is possible for a viral infection, and the patient is given rest and minor pain-killers until the disease settles spontaneously after two or three weeks.

PMR

See POLYMYALGIA RHEUMATICA.

PMT

See PREMENSTRUAL TENSION SYNDROME.

Pneumoconiosis

Pneumoconiosis is a replacement of normal lung tissue by fibrous scar tissue due to the long-term inhalation of fine dust particles. If the particles are asbestos, asbestosis will result (see separate entry), if silica (rock) dust, silicosis occurs (see separate entry). The most common pneumoconiosis is caused by the inhalation of coal dust in underground coal miners. A chest X-ray of a victim of coal miner's pneumoconiosis shows numerous small pellets of coal dust concentrated in the lungs. The upper part of the lung is more affected than the lower.

Patients have no symptoms until the condition is quite advanced, when they may become short of breath. There is no cure, but the disease does not necessarily lead to lung cancer in the same way as asbestosis. The problem may be aggravated by cigarette smoking.

Another less common form of pneumoconiosis is **talcosis**, from talcum powder in the milling and rubber industry.

Pneumonia

The lung is like a sponge — light, fluffy and full of air. Imagine dipping that sponge in a jar of honey. When it comes out it will be heavy, solid and sticky. When someone develops pneumonia, the section of lung affected becomes like that honey soaked sponge, except that thick sticky pus replaces the honey.

Pneumonia is an infection of the tiny air bubbles that form the major part of the lung and enable the oxygen to cross into the bloodstream. The infection is caused by bacteria, miniature microscopic animals that are inhaled with every breath. Normally these bacteria are destroyed by the body's defence mechanisms, but if the person is tired, run-down, overworked, bedridden or suffering from other illnesses, the bacteria may be able to get a hold and start multiplying. Usually only one part of the lungs, often at the bottom of your chest, is affected at first, but the infection may spread to other parts of the lung.

The symptoms of pneumonia may be obvious, with fever, cough and chest pains, but some bacteria are far more insidious and cause minimal symptoms for some months. The patient may just feel tired, short of breath and have intermittent sweats.

A chest X-ray is always necessary when a doctor suspects pneumonia, as the damaged section of lung can be seen, and the extent of the infection assessed. A sample of sputum is taken before treatment is started, and this is sent to a laboratory where the infecting bacteria can be identified. Once one type of bacteria are in residence, your resistance to further infection is lowered, and it is much easier for a second type of bacteria to infect the lungs as well. When this happens, both types of bacteria can be identified by the laboratory, and you are said to have **double pneumonia**. It is possible to have triple, and rarely even quadruple pneumonia if you are particularly unlucky! The laboratory will also be able to tell which antibiotics will kill the various types of bacteria infecting your lungs. The appropriate combination of antibiotics can then be given by the doctor to cure the condition.

Treatment may be started before the laboratory results are received, but sometimes the antibiotic has to be changed to a more appropriate one at a later date. Medications to open up the airways and loosen the phlegm (see EXPECTORANTS, Section 6) may also be prescribed, along with cough mixtures and pain-killers. Regular physiotherapy is very important to drain the foul collection of pus out of the chest. While this remains, the patient cannot recover.

The other important factors in treatment are rest and the cessation of smoking. If the patient tries to keep working, the body cannot gain enough energy to help the antibiotics fight off the infection. Anyone who continues to smoke while they have pneumonia is effectively frustrating every effort of the doctors and therapists to cure them.

X-rays will be taken at regular intervals throughout the treatment to ensure that the pneumonia is resolving. Most patients settle in a couple of weeks, but some may take months. Occasionally oxygen is required for seriously ill patients with a large area of lung affected by pneumonia. In rare cases, surgery to drain out collections of pus or remove areas of chronically infected lung is required.

Inadequately treated pneumonia can cause chronic ill health, and lead to permanent lung damage. Once the lung is damaged, the chances of developing a subsequent attack of pneumonia is increased, and smoking will again accelerate this process. Pneumonia, particularly recurrent attacks, puts a great strain on the heart, and this vital organ may fail in older or more debilitated patients.

Pneumonia is one of man's oldest enemies, but with the correct treatment and the cooperation of the patient, the majority of patients can soon return to a normal active life.

See also MYCOPLASMA PNEUMONIA.

PNEUMOTHORAX

The lung is made up of millions of air bubbles that all connect together by means of fine air-filled tubes. The entire lung lies in a sack that has a smooth inner surface (the pleura), allowing the lung tissue to slide over it as you breathe in and out. If the lung develops a puncture (i.e. one or more of the tiny air bubbles or tubes bursts), air will leak into the sack around the lung and will be unable to escape. More and more air steadily accumulates in the sack, causing pressure on the lung, shortness of breath and severe pain. This is a pneumothorax ('pneumo' means air, and 'thorax' means chest in Latin — therefore 'air in chest').

A pneumothorax often occurs for no apparent reason (**spontaneous pneumothorax**), or may be due to lung diseases such as asthma, which put an excessive stress on the lungs. Other causes include injury, tuberculosis, cancer or cystic fibrosis.

The diagnosis can be made by a doctor listening to the chest with a stethoscope, when reduced breath sounds will be heard at the site of the pneumothorax. A chest X-ray will show the partly collapsed lung. Once diagnosed, medical attention is required. A small pneumothorax may merely be observed and its progress checked by X-rays every 12 hours or so, as the escaped air may slowly be absorbed back into the body. If the pneumothorax is large or growing larger, urgent treatment is necessary. A tube is placed through the chest wall to remove the escaped air, and this allows the lung to expand and refill the sack. The outside end of the tube is placed under water to stop air re-entering the lungs again.

Pneumothorax resembles asthma in that the patient is short of breath, but asthmatics are not normally in pain.

Most forms of pneumothorax do not become life-threatening unless many hours or days have elapsed, but one type of pneumothorax, known as a **tension pneumothorax**, may be fatal in a few minutes, as every breath pumps air out of the lungs and into the cavity of the chest. The pressure of this air builds up rapidly and causes the lungs to collapse. The harder the victim tries to breathe, the more air is pumped out of the lungs and the more the lungs collapse. Doctors, nurses, ambulance officers and others who can make the sometimes difficult diagnosis of tension pneumothorax have saved a patient's life by plunging a knife or other sharp implement into the chest and releasing the trapped air. In hospital, a sterile tube is pushed through the chest wall into the cavity to achieve the same result.

Patients who have repeated attacks of spontaneous pneumothorax, may require surgery to repair the damaged area of lung. All patients who have had any form of pneumothorax must stop smoking.

POISONING

See CIGUATERA POISONING; FOOD POISONING; IRON POISONING; LEAD POISONING; MERCURY POISONING; ORGANOPHOSPHATE (INSECTICIDE) POISONING.

See also Section 8.

POLIO (POLIOMYELITIS)

Polio is a frightening disease that can be totally prevented but cannot be cured. Once you catch this virus, doctors can do very little to prevent permanent paralysis, maimed and withered limbs, and possible death. The public still consider poliomyelitis to be a disease of the past, but this is not so. Polio is endemic in many third-world countries, and a drop in community vaccination rates could result in several hundred Australian children developing the frightening symptoms of polio.

You cannot even claim fear of injections as a reason for avoiding the vaccination. Thanks to a New York bacteriologist, Albert Sabin, we have a vaccine named after him that can be taken as two drops by mouth. Polio is therefore a potentially fatal disease that can be prevented by a simple oral vaccination that is given on four occasions before 18 months of age. The vaccine is extremely effective, safe, and has no side effects. Yet, polio still exists. Why? The only possible answer is laziness and ignorance, and after reading this, you can no longer plead ignorance, only laziness.

Talk to people who were parents of young children in 1956. That was the last year before the original Salk injectable vaccine became available, and it was the year of the last polio epidemic in Australia. Those parents were scared, so scared for their children, that when the vaccine became available, there were queues down the street from the clinic front doors that rivalled the scene before a modern pop concert. They wanted their children protected, and as soon as possible. Today, the vaccine is available from most general practitioners — no fuss, no pain and no queues.

Children are not the only people at risk, adults too may catch polio. Many older members of the community have never had any form of polio vaccine, and those who had the Salk vaccine in childhood may no longer be protected. Although excellent in its time, the Salk vaccine may not give lifelong protection. As a result, all adults who have not had four oral Sabin vaccines, should have a full course of these as well.

Polio is due to a virus, one of those incredibly small particles of matter that cause disease as diverse as measles and hepatitis, the common cold and shingles. Antibiotics have no effect upon them, and there is no cure. The polio virus causes muscle spasm and paralysis, and if the muscles of breathing or the heart are affected, the patient may die or remain on a respirator for life. The virus passes from one person to another through droplets in the breath or by touch.

Please ensure that you and your children are adequately protected against this still dangerous disease.

POLYARTERITIS NODOSA (PAN)

Polyarteritis nodosa (PAN) is an inflammation of small to medium-sized arteries. The damaged artery may become weakened and balloon out to several times its normal diameter, it may scar and shrink down, or the blood passing through the inflamed section of artery may clot and completely block the artery (a thrombosis). The arteries affected may be anywhere in the body, but the gut, liver, heart, testes, kidney, and muscles are most commonly involved.

The cause of PAN is unknown, but it is known to occur more commonly in drug abusers and those who have suffered from hepatitis B. In rare cases, it may be a side effect of some drugs. Men are three times more likely to develop the disease than women, and it is most common in young adults, but may occur at any age.

The symptoms are very varied, depending upon which arteries and organs are involved. The patient is usually feverish, and has pain in the area involved. Specific complaints may include muscle pain, palpitations, arthritis, skin ulcers, spots in the vision, abdominal pain, nausea, vomiting, diarrhoea, etc. Most patients are found to have high blood pressure when examined by a doctor. There are no specific blood tests that can diagnose PAN, but the presence of inflammation somewhere in the body can be detected by some blood tests. A biopsy (sample) taken from an involved artery is the only definite way to confirm the diagnosis.

The treatment involves taking steroids (e.g. prednisone — see Section 6) in high doses for a long period of time. Immunosuppressive drugs (see Section 6) may also be used.

The outcome varies markedly from one patient to another, depending upon the areas and arteries involved. Some patients do recover, but the majority slowly deteriorate to die within a few months or years.

POLYCYSTIC KIDNEY

Polycystic kidney is an inherited disease that results in the formation of multiple fluid-filled cysts in the kidneys. The liver and pancreas is also involved in a small number of patients. The cysts are formed from tiny urine-collecting tubes within the kidney that are blocked or do not connect up to the main urine-collecting system of the kidney.

Patients often have no symptoms, and the disease is found as part of the investigations of a family that is known to have the disease, during an operation or other routine investigation. In other cases, polycystic kidneys may be a cause of high blood pressure, responsible for blood in the urine, or result in a constant pain in one loin.

Most patients require no treatment, because, although damaged, the kidney tissue remaining between the cysts is able to clean the blood of waste products adequately. In the serious cases where the kidneys do fail, dialysis using an artificial kidney machine, or a kidney transplant, are the only treatments available.

POLYCYSTIC OVARY SYNDROME
See OVARIAN CYST; STEIN-LEVENTHAL SYNDROME.

POLYCYTHAEMIA RUBRA VERA (POLYCYTHAEMIA VERA)
Polycythaemia rubra vera is a disease characterised by the excess production of red blood cells. It is most common in middle-aged to elderly, overweight men, but may occur in both sexes. It is rare under 40 years of age.

The red blood cells are made in the bone marrow, primarily of the breastbone, pelvis and thighbone (femur). If the marrow becomes overactive, excessive numbers of cells may be produced.

The common symptoms of polycythaemia rubra vera include headache, dizziness, tiredness, blurred vision, generalised itching and noises in the ears. Doctors may find high blood pressure and an enlarged spleen. The diagnosis can easily be confirmed by a blood test that measures the number of cells present in a sample of blood. Further tests may be performed upon the bone marrow to determine the severity of the disease.

A century ago, leeches were used to drain blood from the body, and two centuries ago, blood-letting from various veins was a common treatment for almost all ailments. Modern doctors have abandoned these practices in the treatment of all diseases — except for one. The treatment for polycythaemia rubra vera is blood-letting. By draining large quantities of blood initially, and smaller amounts on a regular basis in the long term, the disease can be adequately controlled although not cured. The excess cells are drained away by the blood-letting, and extra fluid can be produced faster by the body than the excessive cells to return the blood volume to normal.

Medications to reduce the activity of the bone marrow are now being tried in some patients.

The main complication of the disease is blood clots in vital organs, and some patients develop a form of chronic leukaemia (see separate entry). The average survival time after diagnosis is about twelve years.

POLYHYDRAMNIOS
See PREGNANCY COMPLICATIONS, Section 1.

POLYMENORRHAGIA
See MENSTRUAL PERIOD PROBLEMS, Section 3.

POLYMENORRHOEA
See MENSTRUAL PERIOD PROBLEMS, Section 3.

POLYMYALGIA RHEUMATICA (PMR)
Polymyalgia rheumatica (PMR for short) is a most distressing condition, but not

serious or fatal. It involves inflammation of the muscles and can attack any muscle group at random. Women are affected five times more often than men. PMR is one of a number of diseases categorised as post-viral syndromes. No-one can fully explain these conditions, because they have only recently been recognised, and remarkably little is known about them. It appears that in some people a viral infection such as influenza or the common cold is followed by a chronic inflammation of many organs of the body. It is rather like a prolonged dose of the flu, but without the runny nose and fever — just aches and pains and tiredness.

The symptoms of PMR vary dramatically from one patient to another, and there are no specific blood or other tests to make the diagnosis. This makes the task for doctors very difficult and explains why some of the sufferers have at times been described as malingerers.

The patient suffers severe aches and pains in a group of muscles for a few days before the pain subsides, then another muscle group is attacked. The muscles are also very weak during an attack. He or she is usually irritable, tired, unable to concentrate, and depressed. Other symptoms can include nausea, headache, arthritis and loss of appetite. Good days and weeks will alternate with bad periods. The condition can last for weeks or months, then recur after a long absence. Its exact cause is unknown, but blood tests indicate a generalised inflammation of the body tissues.

The treatment involves heat, pain-killers and anti-inflammatory medications (NSAID — see Section 6). If these are not successful, steroids (see Section 6) can be used. Steroids are potent drugs that reduce the swelling, pain and tenderness associated with many diseases. They may have serious side effects, but if taken strictly as directed they are unlikely to do any harm.

It is probably better to have your attack of PMR settled by steroids rather than suffer for many weeks to come.

Eventually recovery occurs, but the sufferer may have had many weeks off work and considerable discomfort in the meantime.

Polymyositis
See DERMATOMYOSITIS.

Pompholyx (Dysidrosis)
Pompholyx is a skin condition that affects the sides of the palms of the hands and soles of the feet, and may be associated with excess sweating, emotional stress, fungal infections of the skin, and touching irritating substances or plants. The patient develops small blisters that are deep in the skin and moderately itchy. With irritation, the blisters burst, the skin peels and leaves small brown and scale-covered ulcers. Treatment involves avoiding all soaps, irritants, detergents and chemicals. No further treatment is necessary for mild cases. Prescribed steroid or coal tar creams can be used to treat moderate attacks, and severe attacks may require steroid tablets. The condition is more common in young adults, and it frequently recurs after settling.

Porphyria
Patients with porphyria have the unique ability to pass clear urine that turns a dark purple colour, and then brown if left standing for a few minutes in sunlight. Porphyria's other claim to fame is that it affects one branch of the British royal family (but not the immediate family of the present Queen). There are several types of porphyria, all of which are liver diseases. The two most common forms of these quite uncommon diseases will be discussed.

Section 5: Diseases

Acute hepatic porphyria

Acute hepatic porphyria is an inherited disease that passes from one generation to the next but causes symptoms in only 10% of those affected. Those who do show symptoms develop them at the time of puberty.

The patient usually complains of vague abdominal pains, nausea, vomiting and abnormal sensations. As the disease progresses, the abdominal pains may become severe, causing doctors to operate upon the patient, but often finding nothing abnormal in the abdomen. In advanced cases, nerve pain, paralysis, personality changes and fits may occur. Some patients may have the otherwise quiescent disease triggered by severe infections, starvation, some drugs or steroids. The disease can be confirmed by specialised blood tests.

Death may occur due to the paralysis of the muscles that act during breathing.

Porphyria cutanea tarda (latent hepatic porphyria)

Porphyria cutanea tarda is the most common form of porphyria, and again is usually an inherited disease but may be triggered by some poisons. It can occur in varying degrees of severity from so mild that it is undetected to a severe rapidly fatal form. It occurs in all races but is far more common amongst the Bantu tribes of Africa.

The main symptom of the disease is skin that is very sensitive to sunlight, with skin thickening and pigmentation occurring in sun exposed areas such as the face and forearms. It is diagnosed by special blood tests.

The main complication of this disease is liver damage, which may progress to liver failure or liver cancer (hepatoma).

Treatment of both types of porphyria involves careful genetic counselling of families with the disease and avoiding the possible precipitating factors (e.g. crash diets, emotional stress, alcohol, certain drugs). Once present, the disease may be controlled, but not cured, by the use of a complex drug regime.

Postnasal Drip
See CATARRH.

Prader-Willi Syndrome

Prader-Willi syndrome is a rare congenital condition (present since birth) that affects only boys. It is characterised by babies who are small at birth but develop into obese children due to compulsive overeating as a result of an abnormality in the part of the brain that controls hunger. They are usually short, have underdeveloped genitals, and are mentally retarded. The muscles are weak and have very poor tone, which combined with the excess fat results in a very flabbly belly. Children with this syndrome have a significant tendency to develop diabetes later in life. The cause of the syndrome is unknown, and there is no effective treatment.

Pre-eclampsia
See PREGNANCY COMPLICATIONS, Section 1.

Pregnancy Complications
See Section 1.

Premature Ejaculation
See SEXUAL PROBLEMS.

Premature Infant
See Section 1.

Premature Labour
See PREGNANCY COMPLICATIONS, Section 1.

Premenstrual Tension Syndrome

Only in the past decade or two have doctors accepted as a disease entity a condi-

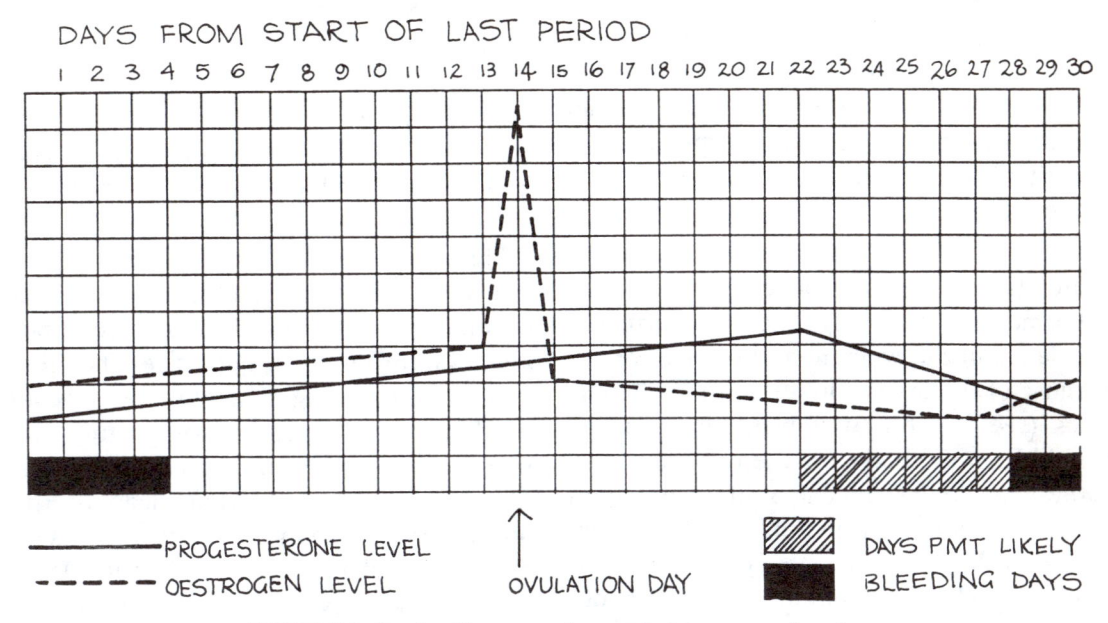

```
DAYS FROM START OF LAST PERIOD
1 2 3 4 5 6 7 8 9 10 11 12 13 14 15 16 17 18 19 20 21 22 23 24 25 26 27 28 29 30
```

——— PROGESTERONE LEVEL ↑ OVULATION DAY   ▨ DAYS PMT LIKELY
- - - - OESTROGEN LEVEL   ■ BLEEDING DAYS

FIGURE 5.5: Graph of hormone changes during menstrual cycle.

tion that affects, will affect, or has affected, half the population of the world to a greater or lesser extent. Premenstrual tension (PMT) syndrome may vary from a slight discomfort for a couple of hours before the onset of a woman's period to a severely distressing condition that has been used in court as a defence for murder.

During the four weeks of a woman's hormonal cycle, two hormones, oestrogen and progesterone, play an important part. During the first half of the cycle, there is a relatively high concentration of oestrogen released from the ovary. After two weeks, the relationship changes, and the hormones in the progesterone group predominate. This changeover precipitates the release of an egg from the ovary that may be fertilised during the next two or three days. When these hormones revert to their previous relationship, the lining of the uterus (womb) breaks down, and a period occurs. See Figure 5.5 above.

During the two weeks leading up to a period, the body starts to retain fluid. If the balance between the two hormones is not quite right for that woman, excessive amounts of fluid are retained, and this is believed to be the main cause of the premenstrual tension syndrome.

The usual complaint is of gradually increasing discomfort in the pelvis and breasts, with swelling of the hands and feet to the point where it is uncomfortable to wear rings or tight shoes. Pounding headaches and depression, very rarely severe enough to lead to suicide, are also very common, possibly due to the retention of excess amounts of fluid in the brain. As the period approaches, those women who are the worst sufferers will experience abdominal pain, anxiety, irritability and clumsiness, and may be unable to concentrate, work or exercise effectively. Then relief comes. The period starts, and within a few hours, or a day or two, the woman returns to normal and is able to function as she wishes, not as her body dictates.

There is no reason why any woman should tolerate a condition that affects her so dramatically. If she feels that her lifestyle is being adversely affected by PMT, she should complain to her doctor, and if not satisfied with the result, she should complain, complain and complain again until all available forms of treatment have been tried.

The most effective forms of treatment are the oral contraceptive pill or similar hormones. These regulate the hormonal balance in the woman, and so remove the cause of the excess fluid retention. Diuretics (see Section 6), tablets that remove fluid from the body, are the next step, and these may be used alone or in combination with the contraceptive pill. Some doctors believe that moderate doses of vitamin B6 are helpful, but others feel that the benefits are minimal. Medications that block the action of hormones may also be used. There are many drugs in this group, but the most commonly used ones include Ponstan, Naprosyn and Indocid (see Section 6). There are other drugs available for those women who demonstrate a specific cause for their PMT or who are resistant to the commonly used medications.

Other approaches to PMT include a sensible balanced diet (avoiding coffee, chocolate and rich foods in the two weeks before the period), regular exercise, and herbal remedies such as evening primrose oil.

Help is available, and there is no reason why the majority of women, provided they are prepared to try different treatments over several months, should not be helped adequately.

PRESSURE SORES
See BED SORES.

PROGRESSIVE SYSTEMIC SCLEROSIS
See SCLERODERMA.

PROLAPSE

A prolapse is a protrusion of an organ into an abnormal place, caused primarily by gravity. The most common prolapses are those of the rectum (last part of the bowel), the bladder, and the uterus into the vagina.

The vagina leads from the outside up to the uterus. During childbirth, the vagina becomes very stretched, and it does not always return to its original size. The muscles around the vagina may become weakened and the ligaments supporting the uterus may also become stretched and sag. After some years, this may lead to the uterus slowly moving down the vagina to a point where it completely fills it. Occasionally the cervix, which is the lowest part of the uterus, may even protrude through the vulva to the outside. This is a uterine prolapse. In other women, part of the bladder which is in front of the vagina, may push back into the vagina causing a bladder prolapse (cystocele) and difficulty with passing urine and various forms of urinary incontinence. The large intestine which is behind the vagina may push forward into the vagina as a rectal prolapse (rectocele), this time causing bowel problems. Occasionally there is a combination of the three types of prolapse into the vagina.

Another form of rectal prolapse occurs in babies of both sexes who have constipation and straining at stool, or severe diarrhoea, when part of the lower gut slips out through the anus. This may occur in the elderly also.

Treatment of all types of prolapse is usually successful by means of an operation that uses strong natural material in the pelvis and artificial slings to support the prolapsing organ. In some older women, a ring inserted into the vagina may be used to hold everything in the correct place. Younger women can help prevent the problem by undertaking special pelvic floor exercises under the guidance of a physiotherapist both before and after the delivery of their babies.

Prostate gland disease

The prostate gland is a mystery to most people, and doctors have not understood its function until quite recently (see Section 2). It is situated in the body behind the base of the penis. The bladder is above and behind the gland, and the tube which carries the urine from the bladder to the outside (the urethra) passes through the centre of the prostate. It is found only in men, and there is no female equivalent.

It is the size of a golf ball, is made of glands, fibrous tissue and muscle, and its prime purpose is the production of a secretion which makes up part of the semen a man ejaculates during intercourse. The contents of this secretion are essential for the nutrition of the sperm as they try to fertilise an egg (ovum) in the woman. Most men are totally unaware of the presence of the prostate unless it causes trouble.

Prostatic cancer

The most serious disease to strike the prostate is cancer. Because this is a very slow-growing cancer, it may give no symptoms until many years after it has developed. The symptoms usually start with difficulty in passing urine, but the condition may not be diagnosed until pain occurs due to the spread of cancer to the bones of the pelvis and back.

Cancer of the prostate is rare before 50 years of age, and its incidence rises steadily with age. A very large proportion of men over 90 years of age have some degree of prostatic cancer. There are specific blood tests available that can detect most cases of prostatic cancer. It is treated with a combination of surgery, drugs and irradiation. Unless it is highly malignant, early stages of cancer of the prostate may not be treated in the very elderly, because it is unlikely to cause trouble in their life time.

Doctors can often diagnose disease of the prostate by feeling the gland. This is done by putting a gloved finger in the back passage, and the size and hardness of the gland can then be gauged.

The earlier any cancer of the gland is detected, the higher the chance of long-term survival. If the cancer is localised to the gland itself, the five-year survival rate is over 90%. With local spread, the survival rate drops to about 70%, but with spread to the bone, only 30% of patients survive five years.

Because of the discomfort, and the more serious possibility of cancer, any man who has difficulty in passing urine is risking fate if he delays having his prostate gland checked by a doctor.

Prostate enlargement

Up to 20% of all men over 60 may have an enlargement of the prostate which causes difficulty in passing urine. This benign enlargement is usually associated with a drop in sexual activity. As the gland enlarges, it squeezes the urine-carrying tube which passes through it, making it steadily harder to urinate. Eventually the tube can be completely blocked, and the patient becomes extremely distressed as the pressure of urine in the bladder increases.

In the acute situation, doctors can normally pass a rubber tube through the penis into the bladder to relieve the sufferer, but sometimes a needle must be pushed through the lower wall of the abdomen, into the bladder, to release the urine. To prevent this acute situation, an operation is usually performed, although there are some medications that can relieve milder enlargements of the gland.

The operation can take several forms, from simply dilating the urine tube, to scraping away the part of the prostate constricting the tube by passing a specially shaped knife up the urine tube (trans-urethral resection of prostate, or TURP), or completely removing the gland.

In some cases, a drug called prazosin (see Section 6) can be used to shrink the enlarged prostate slightly, and allow urine to escape more easily from the bladder.

The treatment for a benign enlargement of the prostate gland is almost invariably successful, with no subsequent effect on the sexual or general health of the patient.

Prostatitis (prostate infection)
In younger men, the most common cause of disease in the prostate is infection, when the gland may swell up and become very tender. Prostatitis can occur due to bacteria moving up the urethra from the outside, or uncommonly, from an infection spreading from other parts of the body. The symptoms include pain behind the base of the penis, a discharge from the penis, pain on passing urine, fever and passing urine frequently. The diagnosis can be confirmed by taking a swab from the urethra, and identifying the bacteria present.

Treatment involves a long course of antibiotics. The acute case usually settles with this treatment, but recurrences are common and a low-grade chronic infection may develop. These recurrent infections may become difficult to treat.

It is possible for the infection to spread to the man's sexual partner, in whom it may cause pelvic inflammatory disease (see separate entry).

Pruritus Ani

Pruritus ani is an excruciatingly itchy anus. Possible causes include fungal infections, diabetes, worm infestations, antibiotics, cancer and a number of skin diseases, but usually there is no obvious cause for the itching, and except for the scratch marks left by the victim's finger nails, there is often no rash. The itch is far more annoying at night, and some patients find it is made worse by red wine and spicy food. Any underlying causes must be excluded by examination of the faeces, skin scrapings for fungi, and blood tests for diabetes.

In the treatment, it is vital that scratching be stopped, as scratching will prolong and exacerbate the problem. The anal area must be kept cool and dry by avoiding nylon underwear, tight clothing and sweating. The area should be rinsed with warm water for washing, but no soap should be used, and the area should be patted dry, and not rubbed.

If these measures are insufficient to give relief, a mild steroid cream (see Section 6) may be prescribed by a doctor to control the itch. Sitz baths in potassium permanganate or silver nitrate may also be beneficial.

The condition is not serious, but often recurrent, long-lasting and very annoying.

Pseudogout

Gout (see separate entry) is caused by the deposition of excess uric acid crystals in a joint. Pseudogout has exactly the same symptoms as gout, but is caused by the deposition of a different crystal (calcium pyrophosphate dehydrate) in the knees and other large joints. Patients are usually elderly, and complain of recurrent, severe pain in the affected joints. The disease is diagnosed by identifying the responsible crystals in the fluid that may be drawn out of the affected joint through a needle. X-rays show arthritis and calcification around the joint.

Treatment involves use of anti-inflammatory drugs (NSAID — see Section 6), and injections of steroids (see Section 6) into the joint. Unlike gout, there are no medications that can be used in the long term to prevent further attacks.

Pseudomonas infections

A pseudomonas infection is serious and usually causes a form of bronchitis that produces yellow to green phlegm. *Pseudomonas aeruginosa* is the full name of the bacterium which causes this type of bronchitis and pneumonia (see separate entries). If left untreated, it can cause permanent lung damage and chronic poor health.

Sputum samples should be taken and sent to a laboratory to determine which antibiotic is appropriate to kill the infection. Gentamicin (see Section 6) is commonly used to treat this type of infection, but there are others available.

Psittacosis (ornithosis)

Psittacosis is a bacterial infection of parrots, pigeons, chickens and ducks that may very occasionally be transmitted to humans, in whom it causes a form of pneumonia (see separate entry). It rarely passes from one person to another. Patients experience a gradual onset of fever, headache, muscle pains, tiredness, dry cough and nose bleeds. It takes one to two weeks for the disease to develop after exposure to an infected bird. Some patients develop skin spots, shortness of breath, and abdominal pains.

The diagnosis is suspected in bird fanciers, chicken farmers and veterinarians who have these symptoms. It may be confirmed by a laboratory pathologist finding the responsible bacteria in a sample of sputum. There is also a specific blood test available to confirm that the patient has been exposed to the disease. A chest X-ray can show the presence of pneumonia, but not that the pneumonia is caused by psittacosis.

Psittacosis is treated by using the appropriate antibiotics, sometimes by injection. The complications include a spread of the infection to the heart or brain, and sometimes a second bacterium may cause double pneumonia.

Although sometimes prolonged, the vast majority of patients can be completely cured.

See also CHLAMYDIAL INFECTIONS.

Psoriasis

The most complex organ in the body after the brain is probably the skin (see Section 2). It must be waterproof, and yet let out water in the form of sweat. It must be strong to resist damage, yet flexible and sensitive to touch. Skin must repair itself rapidly when damaged, or vital body fluids may escape in a quantity sufficient to threaten life. It is easy to see, but difficult to treat, because few medications can penetrate through it. Because of the complexity of skin, many diseases can arise in our outer covering, and dermatologists are the doctors who specialise in diagnosing and treating its ailments.

One of the most annoying and distressing skin diseases, because it tends to be chronic and difficult to treat, is psoriasis. Psoriasis (the P is silent, and it is pronounced almost as 'sore-eye-asis') affects up to 2% of the population. It is unusual in children but becomes more common as age increases. One of the most frustrating aspects of this disfiguring dermatitis is the way in which it can come and go without any treatment. It almost invariably returns, and often in a worse form than previously. Because of this tendency to improve spontaneously, many forms of alternative medical treatment have claimed success in its management. The truth is that there is no cure for psoriasis, but doctors do have a number of quite successful forms of control that help most patients. It is important to realise that many diseases cannot be cured, but can be controlled. Control usually means that the sufferer must continue to take regular treatment to prevent the disease from progressing.

Psoriasis first appears as a small patch of red skin covered with fine scales. The elbows, knees and scalp are the most common sites affected, but the rash may cover any part of the body. The small spot gradually enlarges, roughens and the skin thickens. Then other spots start in other areas of the body over a period of months, until a large part of the body is affected. In the scalp, it may appear to be a bad case of dandruff until the doctor makes the diagnosis. The nails may also be affected, and they become rough and pitted.

Psoriasis has many subtypes, and it is not always easy to make the diagnosis. It may be necessary to cut out a small piece of skin for a pathologist to examine under a microscope before the diagnosis is finally confirmed. One of the more unusual features of psoriasis is that in severe cases the joints may be attacked to cause a type of arthritis.

Treatment can begin once the psoriasis has been diagnosed. This usually involves one or more of a number of creams or ointments that are used regularly on the skin. Coal tar in various forms is the mainstay of treatment, but steroid creams are also widely used. Other skin preparations include drugs called dithranol, salicylic acid and psoralen. Ultraviolet light may be used in conjunction with psoralen to promote healing. In very severe cases, steroid tablets or injections may be given, and in recent years a new drug called etretinate (see Section 6) has become available to treat the most severe cases. Although it is a chronic and sometimes severe disease, psoriasis can usually be successfully controlled.

PSYCHIATRIC DISEASE
See ALCOHOLISM; ANOREXIA NERVOSA; ANXIETY NEUROSIS; BULIMIA; DEMENTIA; DEPRESSION; MANIA; MULTIPLE PERSONALITY DISORDER; NEUROSIS; PARANOID DISORDERS; PHOBIA; PSYCHOSIS; SCHIZOPHRENIA; SUICIDE ATTEMPT; WERNICKE-KORSAKOFF PSYCHOSIS.

PSYCHOSIS
A psychosis is broadly defined as any mental disorder in which the patient has no understanding that he or she are mentally ill and so has lost touch with reality. It is a classification that covers a large group of mental diseases. Psychoses tend to be the more serious mental diseases, and are further classified into groups such as schizophrenia, paranoid disorders and manic depressive states. These are all discussed separately.

See also NEUROSIS.

PULMONARY EMBOLISM
See EMBOLISM, LUNG.

PULMONARY HYPERTENSION
See COR PULMONALE.

PULMONARY VALVE DISEASE
See HEART VALVE DISEASE.

PYELONEPHRITIS
Pyelonephritis is an infection of the kidney. It comes in two forms, acute and chronic.

Acute pyelonephritis
Acute pyelonephritis is a kidney infection that starts suddenly and, with correct treatment, has a brief course. The infection may come to the kidney through the blood

stream, or up from the bladder. Patients complain of pain in the loin, fever, nausea, headaches and sometimes nausea and vomiting. There may be associated cystitis (see separate entry), with pain on passing urine, and urinary frequency. Pyelonephritis is more common in women, after operations to the urinary tract, during pregnancy, and in those who are very sexually active.

The diagnosis can be confirmed by examining a sample of urine in a laboratory, where the bacteria responsible for the infection and the correct antibiotic to treat the infection can be determined. Blood tests are not particularly helpful, except to exclude other causes of the symptoms.

The treatment involves a course of the appropriate antibiotic (see Section 6), usually as a tablet or capsule by mouth for five to ten days, but occasionally by injection. Patients should take as much fluid as possible to flush out the infection from the kidneys.

If there are recurrent attacks of acute pyelonephritis, it is essential for further investigations to be undertaken to determine the reason for the recurrences. These investigations will include X-rays of the kidney and possibly cystoscopy (see Section 4), in which a fine flexible tube made of glass fibres and through which a doctor can see is passed up into the bladder.

Some patients will require long courses of antibiotics to prevent further attacks. Passing urine after sex is another method of reducing the incidence of recurrences.

Chronic pyelonephritis

Chronic pyelonephritis is a constant or recurrent infection of the kidney that often has no symptoms but is detected on a routine urine test. Although it may occur in both sexes and at any age, those most commonly affected are elderly, incontinent (unable to control their bladder), and may have a catheter into the bladder.

In most patients, there is no long-term harm caused by the low-grade persistent infection, but if there is some abnormality in the kidney or obstruction to the passage of urine from the kidney to the outside, significant damage may be caused to the kidney. In the worst cases, the chronic infection may cause scarring of the kidney, high blood pressure, anaemia and functional failure of the kidney.

Doctors will undertake a detailed investigation of the kidneys whenever chronic pyelonephritis is discovered. These will include X-rays, blood tests, urine tests, and cystoscopy (see Section 4). If an abnormality is found, this may be surgically corrected in some cases.

The usual treatment is to give a very long course of the appropriate antibiotic, as determined by special urine tests. Urinary antiseptics and acidifying agents (e.g. Ural, Citravescent — see Section 6) are also useful. Patients are encouraged to drink large quantities of fluids.

One third of patients will be cured by a six-week course of antibiotics, another third will be cured after six months of antibiotics and antiseptics, 10% will progress to severe kidney damage and failure, and the remainder will continue to have a chronic infection without symptoms or kidney damage.

PYLORIC ULCER
See ULCER, PEPTIC.

Q FEVER (RICKETTSIAL INFECTION)
Q fever is caused by primitive bacteria of the genus *Rickettsia*. The specific type of bacteria was not identified for many years, and as a result, the cause of the fever in patients was unknown and a continual nagging question in the minds of the doctors who had to deal with it. The disease derives its name from the fact that these doctors were constantly questioning (Q)

the cause of the fever. Another argument has been put forward that the Q stands for Queensland, where the disease was very common and first researched.

Coxiella burnetti is the rickettsia that causes Q fever. It is named after Sir Macfarlane Burnet, a distinguished Australian microbiologist, who first discovered the cause of this mysterious world-wide disease. The bacterium is a parasite of sheep, cattle and goats, but causes only a mild infection in these animals. It passes from these animals in the milk and faeces. Droplets and dust containing the bacteria may then be inhaled by humans, allowing them to catch the disease. Farmers, shearers and abattoir workers are obviously at a high risk of catching the disease. It does not spread from one human to another.

The incubation period is one to three weeks. Many cases of infection cause very mild, barely noticeable symptoms, but in more severe cases, the patient will develop a fever, weakness, headache, muscle pains and a dry cough. In advanced cases, jaundice (yellow skin), stomach pains, and heart and brain involvement are possible. A specific blood test can now diagnose the disease accurately. A chest X-ray may show some abnormalities in the lung in severe cases.

The infection can be prevented by a vaccination that is given to those who are at high risk of developing the disease.

Treatment is not completely satisfactory. Tetracyclines (a type of antibiotic — see Section 6) can be used to suppress the infection, but it does not always eliminate the disease completely, and relapses are common. Death is rare unless the heart becomes involved.

QUADRIPLEGIA
See PARAPLEGIA AND QUADRIPLEGIA.

See also Section 3.

QUINSY (PERITONSILLAR ABSCESS)
An abscess (see separate entry) is a collection of pus caused by an infection. If the tonsil at the side and back of your throat becomes infected, you suffer from tonsillitis. If the infection is severe enough to cause destruction of the tonsil tissue, pus will form and collect between the tonsil and the wall of the throat. This abscess around the tonsil (peritonsillar) is called quinsy. The tonsillitis may initially appear to settle, but then the patient develops a high fever, severe pain on one side of the throat, a swollen throat, and difficulty in swallowing and opening the mouth. Attacks of quinsy are more common in adults and males, but may develop at any age.

The treatment includes large doses of antibiotics (often penicillin — see Section 6) by injection or tablet, and an operation to either drain the abscess or remove the tonsil and abscess together. If the pus alone is drained, the tonsils are often removed a few weeks later to prevent a recurrence of the quinsy.

See also TONSILLITIS.

RABIES
Rabies is unknown in Australia, but travellers to most other parts of the world may be exposed to the disease if they are bitten by an affected dog, cat, bat, monkey, or in rare cases by rats or other animals. Rabies exists in Indonesia and throughout Asia, eastern Europe, Africa and the Americas. This is one of the reasons for Australia's strict animal quarantine laws.

Travellers overseas should avoid animals that may be infected, and must always have any animal bite attended to by a doctor. Thorough washing of any wound with soap and water is the best first aid.

In animals, it affects the salivary glands, so that any bite causes the injection of the responsible virus into the victim's wound.

The usual incubation period after a bite is three to seven weeks, but it may be a much shorter or longer period. If possible, the animal causing the bite should be isolated and observed. If it dies from rabies, it is essential for the patient to receive a special vaccine to counteract the effects of the rabies. In countries where rabies is endemic, a vaccine is available to protect both animals and man from the disease, but it is not widely used in man because of side effects.

The classic symptom of rabies is a fear of water (hydrophobia), but this fear is due to the severe pain that swallowing any food or liquid causes as a result of muscle spasm in the throat caused by the rabies. The fear is not a true phobia in the psychiatric sense. Further symptoms include skin pain and tingling, generalised muscle spasms, fits and the production of copious amounts of thick saliva. These symptoms progress to paralysis, and death is almost certain within two or three days. There is no treatment available once the symptoms of the disease appear.

RADIATION SICKNESS

Exposure to ionising radiation can occur as a result of a nuclear reactor accident, the mishandling of radioactive material used in medicine (see RADIOTHERAPY, Section 6) or industry, or as the result of an atomic bomb. First aid involves removal of the patient from the contaminated area, thorough washing of the patient, providing fresh uncontaminated clothing, and purging the gut. If evacuation from a contaminated area is not immediately practical, placing as many walls of a house between the outside and any people is advisable. A cellar is ideal.

A high dose of irradiation will cause damage to all the tissues in the body. The bone marrow, which is responsible for producing cells that maintain our immune system, is particularly susceptible to damage and will cease to function and allow the body to be overwhelmed by what would otherwise be minor infections. Other particularly vulnerable organs include the liver, lung, thyroid and breast.

Patients will exhibit symptoms that depend upon the dose of radiation and the areas irradiated. A piece of heavy furniture, a building or other object may partly shield a person from the worst effects of any radiation and cause people in the same area to exhibit different symptoms. Symptoms may include nausea, vomiting, weakness, delirium, blindness (the cornea of the eye being damaged to cause a cataract), mouth ulcers, bleeding gums, bleeding into the skin (bruises), and convulsions. These symptoms may develop slowly over weeks, or within a few hours, and the risk of death will depend upon the dosage of radiation received. The testes and ovaries may be affected as well, to cause deformities or infertility. Unborn babies are at particular risk of irradiation, and miscarriages are common.

With time, natural repair of radiation damage is possible, but nature can be assisted in the acute situation by blood transfusions, marrow transplants and drugs that will remove any inhaled or swallowed radioactive dust from the body. Some body damage may be permanent (e.g. skin scarring, thyroid destruction), and there are long-term risks of increased cancer rates.

RASH
See SKIN RASH, Section 3.

RAYNAUD'S PHENOMENON
A nineteenth century Parisian physician called Raynaud has given his name to a phenomenon that is extremely distressing to the thousands of women who suffer

from it but is little known in the community. Raynaud's phenomenon is taught to medical students as the 'loyal disease' because the hands of these people go 'red, white and blue and swell up with pride'. Unfortunately it does not end there, because the colour changes and swelling of the hands are also accompanied by considerable pain. The symptoms are caused by spasm of the small arteries which restricts the blood flow. This causes the hands to go white, then blue, and finally to flush red when the blood rushes back into the then dilated vessels. The attacks are usually triggered by cold, and so the condition is far commoner in the cooler states, but many find the condition so distressing that they migrate to the northern parts of Australia to escape the pain. But even in Cairns or Darwin, entering an air-conditioned building may be sufficient to trigger an attack that causes agony for many hours. Other trigger factors may be hormonal changes, stress and anxiety, exercise and some foods. The disease usually starts in the teenage years or early twenties and may remain lifelong. Fortunately, many women find that it eases after the menopause.

One in every five women will suffer from Raynaud's phenomenon at some time in their lives. What must be detected and, if possible, treated in all these victims is any underlying cause for the problem. Unfortunately, in the majority of patients, no specific cause can be found. **Raynaud's disease** is the most common cause. This is different from the Raynaud's phenomenon in that it has many symptoms other than the cold, painful hands. These include constriction of the blood vessels to the feet, face, chest, abdomen and sometimes internal organs. The patient will have intense feelings of cold in these areas. The poor blood supply to the fingers and toes may lead to ulceration and eventually gangrene.

Rheumatoid arthritis is often associated with Raynaud's phenomenon, and scleroderma is a rare disease that may be a cause. This is characterised by gross thickening of the skin and damage to the heart, lungs and kidneys.

Treatment of Raynaud's phenomenon is difficult, and there is no cure, only control. Keeping the hands warm is the first step, but this is far easier said than done and not always effective. Alcohol in low doses may be useful. A wide range of drugs can be used to dilate the tiny arteries in the fingers which go into spasm to cause the blanching and pain. They include prazosin, nifedipine and methyldopa (see Section 6). All these medications require prescriptions, and the pros and cons of their use should be discussed with your doctor. An ointment called Nitro-Bid (see Section 6), which is normally used to prevent angina in the heart, may also be useful in very small doses when rubbed into the affected fingers. As a last resort, operations to cut the nerves that cause the artery spasm can be performed.

Those who suffer from this distressing condition should be under the regular care of a doctor so that all avenues of treatment can be tried to give the best possible relief.

RECTUM CANCER
See COLO-RECTAL CANCER.

REFLUX OESOPHAGITIS
Babies and overweight elderly men — these are the two groups that are most likely to suffer from reflux oesophagitis. The oesophagus (see Section 2) runs from the throat to the stomach through the back of the chest. At its lower end, it passes through the diaphragm, which is a sheet of muscle that separates the chest from the abdomen. At the point where it passes through the diaphragm, there is a muscle ring which opens when you swal-

low food but remains closed at other times to prevent the concentrated hydrochloric acid in the stomach from coming back up (refluxing) into the oesophagus when lying down or bending over. The cells lining the inside of the stomach are acid-resistant, but those lining the oesophagus are not. If acid (along with food and other digestive juices) is able to flow back up into the oesophagus, the acid will attack the unprotected cells and can cause inflammation, ulceration, pain and scarring. This is reflux oesophagitis.

Some **babies** are unlucky enough to have a defect or temporary weakness in the muscle ring at the bottom of the oesophagus. The reflux of acid into the oesophagus causes considerable pain to the infant. Most children will grow out of the problem, but medication must be given in the meantime to prevent the burning and pain. This is usually in the form of a mixture (e.g. Gaviscon — see Section 6) which is given after every feed. More sophisticated treatments are available for the intractable cases. It is important that the baby is fed in an upright position and is not allowed to lie down flat after the feed.

In **adults**, factors such as obesity, smoking, overeating, a hiatus hernia, rapid eating, alcohol, stress and anxiety, and poor posture may cause the excessive production of acid in the stomach and/or slackness in the muscle ring. The patient experiences a burning sensation behind the breast bone (see HEARTBURN, Section 3), a bitter taste on the back of the tongue and burping as gas escapes easily from the stomach. It is often worse at night after a large meal when the patient is lying down, as it is then easier for the acid to flow up out of the stomach.

If the attacks of acid reflux are intermittent and mild, the lower end of the oesophagus can recover between each episode, but if the attacks are regular or constant, the pain will become more severe, and significant damage may occur to the area. If ulcers form, they may erode down to a vein or artery, and severe bleeding may occur that in extreme cases may be life-threatening. The other main complication is scarring and narrowing of the lower end of the oesophagus to the point where it may be difficult, or even impossible, to swallow food. Long before these advance stages, most patients have sought medical assistance for the problem.

When reflux oesophagitis is suspected, it will be proved by either gastroscopy, in which a flexible tube is passed down into the stomach, and through which a doctor can see exactly what is happening; or by a barium meal, in which a special fluid is swallowed, and its passage into the stomach (and sometimes its reflux back up into the oesophagus) can be followed by a series of X-rays (see Section 4).

Treatment will involve the appropriate advice with regard to losing weight, propping up the head of the bed, having the main meal in the middle of the day, avoiding bending and heavy lifting, stopping smoking and reducing alcohol (nicotine and alcohol relax the muscle ring). Medication can be given to reduce the acid concentration in the stomach (see ANTACIDS, Section 6) and to act as a foam that floats on the stomach acid to protect the lower end of the oesophagus. Further treatment will involve the use of medication to help empty the stomach, and reduce acid production (see ANTIULCERANTS, Section 6).

Only in severe, resistant cases is it necessary to resort to quite major surgery to treat the problem. The majority of patients can be controlled if they follow a doctor's advice and use the appropriate medication.

See also HIATUS HERNIA.

REGIONAL ENTERITIS
See CROHN'S DISEASE.

Reiter's syndrome

A syndrome is the concurrence of several apparently unconnected symptoms in a disease. Reiter's syndrome has the unusual and apparently totally unconnected symptoms of conjunctivitis (eye inflammation), urethritis (inflammation of the urine tube — the urethra) and arthritis (joint inflammation). Other symptoms that may be associated with the syndrome include mouth ulcers, skin sores, inflammation of the foreskin of the penis and a fever. In rare cases, the heart may become inflamed. The cause of the syndrome is unknown, but it tends to occur more commonly in young men, and often follows a bacterial infection. The diagnosis is suspected when these symptoms occur, and a blood test can be performed that will make the diagnosis more likely. X-rays can show arthritis in the joints of the back after several attacks.

The disease will heal itself without treatment after a few days or weeks, but the arthritis tends to last far longer and recurrences are common. The course of the disease can be shortened by the use of anti-inflammatory drugs such as indomethacin (see Section 6).

Renal colic
See KIDNEY STONES.

Renal failure
See KIDNEY FAILURE.

Repetitive strain injury (RSI)

Repetitive strain injury is a controversial disease, and may in fact be diseases such as tenosynovitis and tendonitis, carpal tunnel syndrome, arthritis, synovitis (see separate entries), or a combination of these.

The symptoms of RSI are usually pain, swelling and stiffness of the wrist, elbow or the small joints in the hand. It tends to occur in those undertaking repetitive tasks such as typing, playing the piano, or working on a production line. The pain may actually be worse on the weekend while the patient is at rest and immediately upon returning to work after a break. A prolonged rest such as a holiday often settles the disorder. RSI may result in long-term stiffness, pain, and limited joint movement.

The diagnosis is made only after all other possible conditions have been excluded by X-ray and other investigations.

Treatment involves resting the affected joint in a splint for a short time, altering the type of work undertaken, physiotherapy, alternating heat and cold to the area, and anti-inflammatory medications (NSAID — See Section 6).

The diagnosis is controversial and there have been no long-term follow-up studies to determine the outcome of the condition. It appears that some cases become chronic and some resolve completely after treatment.

Respiratory distress syndrome, infant (hyaline membrane disease)

The respiratory distress syndrome (hyaline membrane disease) is a lung disease that occurs in babies who are born prematurely. The more premature the infant, the greater the risk of developing the condition. Of babies born 8 weeks premature, 75% will be affected. It is the most important problem doctors face in dealing with these tiny babies.

A substance called 'surfactant' is essential within the lungs to enable them to open up and fill with air after birth. Surfactant is not produced in adequate quantity in some premature babies, so their lungs do not open adequately and they cannot obtain sufficient air and oxygen. A membrane that lines the inside of the tiny airways within the lungs, the hyaline membrane, is responsible for producing surfactant, thus giving the condition its alternative name. Hyaline membranes are not anatomical structures but restrictive membranes, formed by proteins exuded from the tiny blood vessels in the immature lungs of premature babies, which decrease the elasticity of the lungs and make breathing harded.

The condition does not develop until some hours after birth, when the baby starts to breath rapidly, grunt with each breath, and has very marked movements of the chest and abdomen as it tries to breath. As the condition advances, the baby will become blue in colour (cyanosed), lapse into a coma and die.

The diagnosis can be confirmed by an X-ray of the chest and lungs. A special test performed on a sample of the amniotic fluid in which the baby floats in the womb and obtained through a needle that is put through the mothers belly can assess the risk of developing the disease in any individual baby.

The respiratory distress syndrome can be prevented in most cases, if the mother is given an injection of a steroid (see Section 6) at least 48 hours before the birth. This is now routinely given to all mothers who come into premature labour, and it is also given to some mothers who have a history of giving birth prematurely. Every effort will be made to delay a birth until the 48 hours has elapsed.

Once the disease is present, there is very little treatment available except for giving oxygen in a humidicrib. If the baby survives for 48 hours, it is almost certain to recover fully, although a small number of children do have permanent lung damage.

RESTLESS LEGS SYNDROME
When some people go to bed, they can't get to sleep because they feel that they have to keep moving their legs. They constantly feel as though they want to go on a marathon run. This rather strange medical entity, and very distressing problem, is the restless legs syndrome. Its cause is not understood, and it does not seem to be related to exercise. Getting out of bed and going for a run doesn't help either. It is more common in women, it is made worse by pregnancy and heat, and sometimes antihistamine medications (see Section 6) can aggravate it.

Treatment involves keeping the legs cooler than the body, and the use of a very small dose of a mild muscle relaxant such as Valium (see Section 6), or one of a number of similar drugs that may be prescribed by a doctor.

RETINAL DETACHMENT
The retina is the light-sensitive area at the back of the eye (see Section 2). Normally it is loosely attached to the eyeball, but if it becomes detached from the back of the eye, full or partial blindness results. The retina may become detached if a blood vessel ruptures and bleeds into the area between the retina and back of the eyeball, or if the fluid in the eye leaks into this area. It may follow an injury to the eye, or be caused by high blood pressure or a tumour in the eye. Frequently, there is no obvious cause for the retinal detachment.

A patient affected by a retinal detachment describes a black curtain slowly moving across the field of vision, as the retina progressively lifts away from the back of the eyeball and causes at first partial, and later complete blindness. The retina may detach very slowly over a period of years, or the process may be complete in a few minutes. A doctor can readily see most detachments by examining the eye with an ophthalmoscope (small magnifying glass attached to a light). Early treatment is essential to save the sight, and treatment is very effective — up to 95% of retinal detachments can now be cured or controlled. Surgical procedures, or a laser that is shone in short, sharp, accurately aimed bursts into the eye, can be used to seal the retina back onto the eyeball.

Retinitis pigmentosa

Retinitis pigmentosa is an inherited disease of the light-sensitive cells that form the retina at the back of the eye, which passes from one generation to the next. It starts with night blindness in childhood and slowly progresses to cause near total blindness in old age. The light-sensitive cells at the back of the eye steadily deteriorate, and pigment cells proliferate and give a characteristic pigmented appearance to the retina when viewed by a doctor using an ophthalmoscope.

The degeneration of cells starts at the edge of the retina and progressively moves towards the centre over many years, so that the field of vision slowly decreases until the patient can only see straight ahead as though through a tunnel and has no peripheral vision.

No treatment is available.

Reye's syndrome

This very rare and often rapidly fatal disease is named after a contemporary Sydney pathologist, Ralph Douglas Kenneth Reye. It is more common in children under six years of age, and may be associated with the use of aspirin. Its cause is unknown. It is because of this disease that paracetamol and NOT aspirin is recommended for any fevers in young children and babies. The condition invariably follows two to three weeks after a viral infection such as influenza, chickenpox or a cold, and causes liver failure and brain inflammation. The inflamed brain swells to cause vomiting, mental confusion and convulsions.

No specific treatment is available, but attempts are made to control the brain swelling and assist breathing. The death rate is in excess of 30%.

See also ENCEPHALITIS.

Rheumatic fever

Many diseases that were common a few decades ago are now rarely seen by doctors. One such disease is rheumatic fever, which is an inflammation (tissue damage) of the heart valves that follows some types of bacterial infections. In Australia, bacterial infections are now cured rapidly at an early stage by the use of appropriate antibiotics. Only in third-world countries, where medical attention is not readily available, is rheumatic fever still a significant problem. Because antibiotics were not readily available until the mid-1950s, some middle-aged and elderly people are still affected by the sequelae of rheumatic fever suffered in earlier years. There is no direct connection between rheumatoid arthritis and rheumatic fever, although both are caused by a disruption to the immune system, and both may cause arthritis.

Patients with rheumatic fever have two or more of a number of widely different symptoms. Every case is therefore completely different. Patients commonly develop inflammation of the heart and the valves it contains (see Section 2), which may cause a rapid pulse and irregular heart beat; irregular shaped red patches and rings on the skin; uncontrolled twitching of the arms, legs and face (technically called chorea); a high temperature; and arthritis that moves from one large joint to another. The diagnosis is confirmed by performing blood tests to detect the presence of a previous bacterial infection and other abnormalities, and an electrocardiogram (see Section 4) to detect heart damage.

The disease is treated with antibiotics (commonly penicillin) to remove any remaining bacterial infection, aspirin to reduce fever and joint pains, and strict bed rest for several weeks or months.

The greatest problem with rheumatic fever is that it often causes permanent damage to heart valves. These valves may leak and fail in later life, and are very susceptible to infection (see ENDOCARDITIS). Because of this high infection risk and the possible further heart damage that an attack of endocarditis could cause, all patients who have had rheumatic fever must take antibiotics whenever they have any dental treatment or operation.

Rheumatic fever usually lasts a few weeks to months, with children taking far longer to recover than adults. A significant number of patients have recurrences of the disease for years afterwards. 98% of patients recover from the first attack, but multiple repeat attacks in a small number of patients may also lead to death. Two thirds of all patients suffer some permanent heart valve damage.

RHINITIS
See HAY FEVER.

RHINOPHYMA
Rhinophyma is enlargement of the nose due to a dramatic enlargement of the oil glands in the nose and an excessive deposition of fat and other tissue under the skin. The name is derived from the Greek 'rhino' for nose (as in rhinoceros) and 'phyma' for tumour. In advanced cases, the condition is very disfiguring and gives the appearance of a large growth on the nose. It is almost always restricted to men, and is really a severe form of rosacea (see separate entry). The only effective treatment is plastic surgery to remove the excess tissue.

RICKETS
Rickets is now a rare disease in Australia but still common in areas of the world where children receive an inadequate diet. Rickets and osteomalacia are the same disease, the difference being that rickets occurs in children whose bones are still growing, while osteomalacia (see separate entry) occurs in adults.

Children develop rickets if they have an inadequate intake of vitamin D (see VITAMINS, Section 6), or in rare cases, if their body has an inherited inability to deal with vitamin D. Vitamin D is essential for the body to absorb calcium, which is the main constituent of bone.

The major supplies of vitamin D are obtained from dairy products (milk, cheese, yogurt, etc.), eggs and fish. Oatmeal, which is often used in porridge, may actually prevent the body from absorbing vitamin D. Vitamin D can also be formed in the body by the action of sunlight on certain substances in the skin. In earlier times, rickets was very common in Scotland, where sunshine was lacking, the diet of poor crofters was often inadequate, and oatmeal formed a large part of the diet.

Children with rickets have soft bones and grow slowly. The legs tend to bow outwards because of the deformity caused by weight-bearing and walking on the soft long bones of the legs. There are also abnormalities in the growth of the ribs which develop knobbly ends beside the breast bone, and excessive enlargement of the forehead. These children may also be 'double-jointed', with slack ligaments around the joints, and may have weak muscles.

The treatment involves supplying adequate amounts of vitamin D in the diet.

If the condition is diagnosed late, any bone deformity present may become permanent.

RICKETTSIAL INFECTION
See Q FEVER; TYPHUS.

RINGWORM
See FUNGAL INFECTIONS — Tinea.

RODENT ULCER
See SKIN CANCER.

ROSACEA
Rosacea is a skin disease of the face, found most commonly in middle-aged women, but it may occur in adults of either sex and any age. The cause is unknown. In the early stages, the victim has excessive intermittent flushing of the face, but this soon becomes a permanent redness of the facial skin. After a few days or weeks, sores develop on the face, rather similar to a severe case of pimples. It usually affects both sides of the face equally, and in advanced cases, the surface of the eyes may be involved in a form of conjunctivitis.

Tetracyclines, a type of antibiotic (see Section 6), are effective in controlling most cases, but the course of capsules or tablets must be continued for two or three months. Relapses are common for years afterwards, but if tetracyclines are used immediately, they suppress each attack effectively.

See also RHINOPHYMA.

ROSEOLA INFANTUM
Virtually every child will contract the viral disease roseola infantum in the first two or three years of life, but most will have such a mild attack that it will be passed off as a mild 24-hour 'wog'. Children who have a severe attack will develop a fever and a measles-like rash on the trunk and neck, which usually appears after the high temperature has gone. One attack gives lifelong immunity, and the incubation period from contact with the disease to the development of symptoms varies from 7 to 17 days.

No treatment other than paracetamol for the fever is required, as the child recovers completely within two or three days.

ROSS RIVER FEVER (EPIDEMIC POLYARTHRITIS)
Ross River fever is an infection carried from one person to another by mosquitoes. When the mosquito bites an infected person, the germ enters the mosquito with the blood and is injected back into the next person the mosquito bites, infecting them also. It is caused by an organism that is halfway between a virus and a bacterium.

Ross River fever is named after the river flowing through Townsville in north Queensland, but it is a worldwide disease and takes the name epidemic polymyalgia in other tropical countries. It is found throughout northern Australia, and is also known in the Riverina irrigation area.

The patient suffers from fevers, muscle aches, arthritis, headaches, swollen glands, poor appetite, nausea, flu-like symptoms, and is very tired. It may last for a couple of weeks or a couple of months. There is no cure. The only treatment is symptomatic — aspirin and other anti-inflammatory medications to ease the aches and pains and remove the fever. Tetracycline antibiotics (see Section 6) are sometimes used in the early stages of the disease to ease the severity of the infection, but their usefulness is not established.

The only form of prevention is control of mosquitoes and the liberal use of insect repellents, screening houses and long sleeves.

The disease has no serious consequences but may be debilitating for a long time and may recur after recovery seems complete.

Rotator cuff syndrome

The shoulder is able to move through a greater range than any other joint in the body. This is because the socket of this ball and socket joint is very shallow. The upper part of the humerus (upper arm bone) forms the ball, while the socket is formed by the outer end of the shoulder blade (scapula). Because the socket is very shallow, the shoulder joint is very unstable and dislocates relatively easily. To stabilise the joint, a number of muscles and tendons crowd around the joint as a 'cuff' of firm tissue, inside which the shoulder can still freely rotate. Damage to this rotator cuff causes the rotator cuff syndrome.

Any tear, stretching or rupture of the muscles, ligaments or tendons forming the rotator cuff around the shoulder joint, caused by an obvious injury, overuse or aging, will result in the pain and tenderness around the shoulder joint that is characteristic of the rotator cuff syndrome. Depending upon the muscles injured, some movements of the joint may be very painful, while others cause no discomfort.

The treatment is a combination of rest, physiotherapy, anti-inflammatory medications (NSAIDs — see Section 6), and in severe cases injections of steroids and anaesthetics (see Section 6) into the affected muscles. If a muscle or tendon has torn badly or completely ruptured, surgery to repair the damage will be necessary.

Roundworm infestation (ascariasis, nematode infestation)

Roundworms (ascaris or nematodes) are worms that infect the human gut. Infections with roundworms are uncommon in Australia but very widespread in Indonesia, south-east Asia and other less developed countries. They live in the small intestine as adult worms, between 20 and 40 cm long, and after fertilisation, the females release a large number of microscopic eggs that pass out in the faeces.

The eggs can survive for many years in the soil. In areas where human faeces is used as a fertiliser, it is easy for them to be swallowed again on food; or if sewerage contaminates the water supply, they may be swallowed in a drink. Once the eggs are swallowed, an extraordinarily complex life cycle follows. The eggs hatch into larvae that burrow through the gut wall into the bloodstream. In the blood they move to the heart, and then into the lungs. In the lungs, they move out of the blood and into the small air tubes (bronchioles) of the lung. The tiny larvae then wiggle their way up through larger and larger airways to the windpipe (trachea), and eventually to the back of the throat. From there they are swallowed again, to enter the small intestine and grow into mature adults that may live for up to a year. At all these stages, the larvae and worms can cause symptoms in the human. These include a cough, shortness of breath, fever, wheezing, chest pain, abdominal pains and discomfort, nausea and gut obstruction. The diagnosis is confirmed by finding eggs in the faeces.

A number of drugs are available to treat the disease, but they often have side effects. If patients are given the correct treatment at a relatively early stage of the disease, full recovery is normal. If severe infestations are left uncontrolled, the worms may move into the gall bladder and pancreas, rupture the bowel, and cause other severe complications that may result in death.

RSI
See REPETITIVE STRAIN INJURY.

RUBELLA (GERMAN MEASLES)
Before 1969 there was no vaccination available for rubella, a disease that causes blindness, deafness and other serious damage to the babies of pregnant mothers who catch the disease. Since then, rubella (or German measles) has been attacked in a world-wide campaign to totally eradicate it.

Although relatively mild if caught by a child or adult, the virus causing rubella can cross from the mother to her child in the womb. It is only between the sixth and twelfth weeks of pregnancy that the virus can cause damage, but the damage it does cause is quite catastrophic. By preventing the correct development of the eye, ear, heart and sometimes other organs, the baby is born with severe defects in these areas that cannot be adequately corrected by later treatment.

Rubella resembles measles in that it occurs commonly in children, produces a fine rash over the body, and can be caught only once in your life, but it may cause so little in the way of sickness and be so mild that it is completely overlooked. The rash lasts only two or three days, is not itchy, and is not accompanied by the sore eyes and cold symptoms associated with common measles. There are often some enlarged glands at the back of the neck, and the patient in bad cases may have a fever, runny nose and joint pains. The incubation period from exposure to the disease developing is two to three weeks.

German measles, common measles and baby measles (roseola infantum) are totally different diseases, and there is no protection against one if you catch the other.

Vaccination against rubella is simple and effective. There are no side effects, and every woman should ensure that she has had the vaccination before she plans her first pregnancy. As a routine, all children are now given mumps, measles and rubella as a combined vaccine at 12 to 15 months of age. All twelve-year-old girls should be given a further rubella vaccination to ensure that they have long-lasting protection.

If all girls received this vaccine, rubella as a cause of deformity in children would be eliminated. But many older women have not had the vaccine, and some girls do not attend clinics or their general practitioner for the vaccine. As a result, babies are still being born deaf and blind. Some women do not have the vaccine because they are positive that they had rubella as a child. This is a most unreliable guide, as many other mild viral infections of childhood can cause a rash and mimic rubella. If a woman is unsure about her vaccination history, a blood test is available from doctors which will determine her immune status.

RUBEOLA
See MEASLES.

SALIVARY STONES
Under your tongue and in the side of your jaw you have salivary glands — three on each side of your mouth. They are called the parotid glands (at the angle of the jaw), submandibular glands (under the side of the jaw) and submental glands (under the chin). These produce the saliva to keep your mouth moist and to start the digestion of food. A small tube leads from each gland to open into the mouth under the tongue or at the back corner of the mouth. If a salivary gland becomes infected or injured, or the saliva becomes too concentrated, a stone may form in the gland. This stone then moves along the duct towards the mouth, causing excruci-

ating pain with every movement.

When you see, smell or taste food you automatically salivate. In patients with a salivary stone, this salivation causes pain because the pressure of saliva behind the stone moves it in the delicate duct. These patients require urgent treatment to temporarily dry up their saliva and ease the pain. Surgery is often necessary to remove the stone and relieve the condition. Fortunately, salivary stones are fairly uncommon.

SALMONELLA INFECTION
See TYPHOID FEVER.

SALPINGITIS
See PELVIC INFLAMMATORY DISEASE.

SARCOIDOSIS
Sarcoidosis is an uncommon disease of unknown origin which causes damage and inflammation to a wide range of organs within the body, most commonly to the lungs. The tissue affected becomes abnormal and fails to function correctly. Patients frequently have a fever, tiredness and shortness of breath, but because almost any part of the body may be involved, the symptoms can be very varied and sometimes bizarre, and may include rashes, enlarged glands, liver or spleen enlargement, pain, arthritis, pins and needles sensation and heart failure. Women are more commonly affected than men, and the usual age of onset is between 40 and 60.

Blood tests show abnormalities, but cannot specifically diagnose sarcoidosis. X-rays also show abnormalities in the lungs that may indicate the presence of sarcoidosis but that may also be caused by other diseases. The only definite way to diagnose the condition is to take a biopsy (sample) of the damaged tissue and examine it under a microscope.

Treatment involves the use of steroids (see Section 6) to reduce the inflammation. The disease is slowly progressive and cannot be cured, but the control of the inflammation is usually sufficient to give the victim a relatively long life.

SARCOMA
See BONE TUMOUR; CANCER.

SCABIES
Over the past decade since the late 1970s, the incidence of scabies has increased so that it is now quite common for general practitioners to see a case in their surgeries. In many third-world countries, the disease is in epidemic proportions, and it is unusual in some areas to find a person without the infection.

A description of exactly what causes scabies makes patients even more agitated, because, to be pedantically accurate, scabies is an infestation, rather than an infection. An infestation occurs when a tiny animal is found living in large numbers in or on a person. In scabies, a tiny insect called *Sarcoptes scabiei* burrows under the skin. It is rather like a microscopic mole, digging burrows that can be 1 cm or more in length in the outer layers of your skin. These burrows and the tissue around them then become red, itchy and inflamed. The scratching that follows often damages the skin further, making it difficult for a doctor to diagnose the condition, and it sometimes allows a secondary infection caused by bacteria to enter the area. This will further aggravate the discomfort.

The only way to catch scabies is by close contact with someone who already has the disease. The problem is that, in its early stages, a person may not realise that a couple of itchy spots that they have on their hands are scabies, and so shaking hands with another person could spread the disease.

Once on your skin, the mite starts burrowing, but it may be several days before you are aware of its unwelcome presence. The most common areas for it to settle are the fingers, palms, heels, groin and wrists; but it can spread across the entire body. It is unusual for the head and neck to be involved.

The scabies mite is just visible to the naked eye but appears like a spot of dust on a piece of black paper. It cannot be seen on the skin. If there is any doubt about the diagnosis, your doctor will gently scrape some of the affected area with the edge of a scalpel, and send the scrapings collected to a pathologist for examination under a microscope. The mites and their eggs can then be seen.

The incessant itching usually sends most victims to a doctor fairly quickly. Treatment can then be given to kill all the mites. This usually involves painting the entire body with a lotion or cream (e.g. Ascabiol — see Section 6). All other members of the family, and anyone else closely connected with the sufferer, should also be treated at the same time. It is advisable to change all the bed linen that night too, and to repeat the treatment on the patient after a week, so that any mites that hatch from the remaining eggs after the initial treatment will be killed. Occasionally there can be a reaction to the creams and lotions that are used, but this is only temporary. Often the itch continues for 10–20 days after completion of the treatment. This is due to an allergy to the scabies bodies or their products (eggs, droppings, etc.) and not necessarily a failure of the treatment.

Scabies is not a disease of unhygienic families and can occur in the children of the most scrupulously clean mother. No one can be blamed for the spread of the disease, but obviously the sooner it is treated, the less it will spread.

SCARLET FEVER

This scourge of children in earlier centuries is now very uncommon in Australia, to the point where many younger general practitioners have never seen a case. Scarlet fever is a bacterial infection caused by bacteria from the streptococcal family. It attacks the throat, tonsils and skin to give the characteristic 'scarlet red' appearance to the cheeks and to skin on other parts of the body. The patient is unwell with a fever and sore throat for a few hours to two days before the typical rash develops. The rash consists of bright red, pin-head size dots that may appear on the face, neck, in the armpit, groin and other areas. The skin immediately around the mouth often remains a normal white colour. The tonsils are usually enlarged, red and painful, and the tongue may be red and swollen. The skin of the palms and soles may flake away in severe cases. The diagnosis can be confirmed by taking a swab from the throat, and by specific blood tests.

The disease can be both treated and prevented by antibiotics such as penicillin and erythromycin (see Section 6), and the wide use of antibiotics for minor infections has almost completely eradicated this infection.

SCC (SQUAMOUS CELL CARCINOMA)
See SKIN CANCER.

SCHEUERMANN'S DISEASE

Scheuermann's disease is a relatively uncommon bone condition that affects the shape of the vertebrae in rapidly growing teenagers but may not become apparent until later in life when pain develops in the back.

The back consists of 24 vertebrae which sit one on top of the other in precise positions to give the back its correct curvature.

The vertebrae are joined together by ligaments, and their exact position and movement is controlled by muscles.

In Scheuermann's disease, the vertebrae in the middle part of the back, behind the chest, do not grow properly, and instead of being roughly square in shape, they become slightly wedge-shaped. This causes the back to curve excessively giving a slightly humped appearance. The movement of the back is reduced, pain may be present due to compression of nerves, and osteoarthritis develops prematurely. The diagnosis can be made by seeing the abnormal vertebrae on an X-ray.

The main treatment is physiotherapy to correct the posture, anti-inflammatory medications (NSAID — see Section 6), and exercise. In rare cases surgery is recommended.

SCHISTOSOMIASIS
See BILHARZIA.

SCHIZOPHRENIA
Dr Jekyll and Mr Hyde — two personalities in the one body. That is what most people think when the term schizophrenia is used, but this is *NOT* the case with this severe and sometimes disabling disease. Patients with schizophrenia often change the topic of conversation for no apparent reason. They may not look after themselves, become dishevelled in appearance, withdrawn, and fail to communicate properly with others. When treatment starts, the majority of patients return to the person you knew them to be. This gives the impression of two different personalities, but there is only the treated and untreated patient.

No-one knows exactly what causes schizophrenia, but there are many theories. There is certainly a family tendency for developing the disease. If your parents, or brothers or sisters have the disease, it is more likely, but by no means inevitable, that you could develop symptoms. Another factor is the environment in which the patient is raised. Family, school or work stresses, particularly in early childhood, may lead a person to escape these stresses by developing schizophrenia.

Schizophrenia, like all mental illnesses, is a disease, and is no different to asthma, high blood pressure or a stomach ulcer, except it is the brain that is involved.

There are many different types of schizophrenia, but most patients who are diagnosed with this condition have the symptoms mentioned above, as well as other mood and behaviour changes that seem bizarre to others. Schizophrenics often believe that people are trying to persecute them. They may hear unfriendly voices, or have frightening hallucinations.

The diagnosis is not an easy one for doctors to be certain about, because patients must be observed for several months, and their reaction to treatment must be assessed. A general practitioner may be concerned about a patient and refer them to a psychiatrist, who can usually make a definite diagnosis. Once the diagnosis is made, appropriate treatment can start. Doctors have a wide range of effective medications (antipsychotics — see Section 6) to control the disease. This is not the end of treatment though. Just as important as the medication is the environment in which the patients live and are cared for. Their psychological needs must be catered for, they must be made to feel part of the community again, and their families will probably require counselling so that they can overcome the stress of coping with someone who may not want to be part of modern society.

Permanent cure is not always possible, and many schizophrenics must remain on medication for the rest of their lives. Provided they attend regular follow-up by a psychiatrist or general practitioner, there should be no reason why their lives shouldn't be as long, normal and productive as any other citizen's. The number of people with this disease is greater than you may realise. This is because most sufferers are ashamed, for no good reason, of the diagnosis.

Mental illnesses are rapidly losing the accursed name they had in years past. Anyone can suffer from a mental illness, and anyone can be appropriately treated. The understanding of the general public can only help these people.

See also MULTIPLE PERSONALITY DISORDER.

School sores (impetigo)

School sores, or impetigo as it is technically known, is a very common skin infection and does not reflect upon the cleanliness of the child or family. Virtually every child will at some stage catch this bacterial infection, but some children appear to be more susceptible than others. The infection may spread to adults too. One of several different bacteria are responsible for this condition, but the one that is most common is *Staphylococcus aureus*, commonly known as the 'golden staph'. This is a serious disease inside the body, but relatively mild on the skin.

The infection spreads from one person to another, and is called school sores because the close contact between school children allows the bacteria to flourish. Sometimes an infected dog, cat or other animal may act as a source of the disease. Once one sore develops on the body, self inoculation can occur, so that if the sore is touched, the fingers can spread the infection to another part of the body. The sores can thus rapidly develop in varied parts of the anatomy.

The most common symptom is an itchy, red, raised, weeping or crusting sore. If there are a large number, the victim may begin to feel generally unwell, but normally there are no signs of infection inside the body. If impetigo occurs in new born babies, it may spread very rapidly and become quite serious. For this reason, older children with school sores should be kept away from their newborn siblings.

Once the disease is suspected, medical treatment should be started as soon as possible. This will involve antibiotic mixtures or tablets, and an antibiotic cream or lotion may also be prescribed. Antiseptic soaps can be used to prevent the spread of infection. To prevent spreading the infection to other members of the family, the patient should use their own towel and face washer, and not share a bed. The child should be excluded from school for a few days until the sores start to heal, but if there are only one or two sores present which can be easily covered by an adhesive bandage, contagion is unlikely, and the child can continue their studies.

School sores are more common in warm climates and in summer. It is possible for the sores to be confused with other diseases such as chickenpox, eczema, and cold sores, so if there is any doubt, a doctor's opinion should be sought. If necessary, swabs can be taken from the sores and sent to a laboratory for further investigation to confirm the diagnosis, determine the infecting bacteria, and select the correct antibiotic to effectively treat it. If correct treatment is obtained, the sores will heal without scarring in a few days.

Sciatica

Sciatica is caused by the pinching of a nerve as it emerges from the spinal cord and passes between two vertebrae low in your back. The pain is not always felt at the point of pinching, but where the nerve runs. The nerve pinching may be caused by arthritis, ligament strains or disc damage in the back. In some cases, more sinister diseases may be the cause of sciatica. The sciatic nerve is made up of many spinal nerves that join together in the middle of your buttock, at a point where the pain of sciatica is often first felt. The nerve then runs down the back of your thigh and calf, giving off branch nerves to supply the muscles and other structures of the leg. Some unlucky victims feel the shooting pains associated with sciatica all the way from the back to the foot.

Investigation of sciatica will involve careful examination of your back by a doctor, and having X-rays taken to determine why the nerve is being pinched. Most patients can be helped by adequate treatment in the form of anti-inflammatory medications (NSAID — see Section 6), physiotherapy, and occasionally surgery.

Scleroderma (progressive systemic sclerosis)

Scleroderma is an auto-immune disease of no known cause. This means that some parts of the body set off an immune reaction that is not appropriate, and the body tries to reject part of itself. In kidney transplants, the body attempts to reject the transplanted kidney. In scleroderma the skin and gut are most commonly affected, followed by the oesophagus (gullet), lungs, heart and other internal organs. It usually starts between 30 and 50 years of age, and women are affected far more often than men. The symptoms vary from one patient to another but include thickening of the skin, arthritis that moves between joints, patchy changes in skin colouration, poor circulation to the hands, difficulty in swallowing, lung infections, fevers and diarrhoea.

Blood tests can show vague abnormalities but cannot specifically diagnose the condition. A biopsy (sample) of skin or other affected tissue can be examined to confirm the suspected diagnosis.

The disease is slowly progressive over many years. The treatment is merely supportive, as there is no cure. Men and older patients deteriorate more rapidly than others.

Scoliosis

If a school nurse or doctor tells you that your child has scoliosis, you immediately think of Quasimodo — the hunchback of Notre Dame. Even without medical intervention, very few children with curvature of the spine would ever deteriorate to that extent, and with proper medical care it is almost unknown. Scoliosis is abnormal lateral (side-to-side) curvature of the spine. Minor degrees of this condition are seen in many teenagers as they go through rapid growth spurts. These children often have poor posture, which accentuates the deformity. Only significant curvature warrants medical attention.

Spine curves are usually double. If there is a curve in one direction, there must also be a curve in the opposite direction further up or down the spine. If this were not so, the shoulders would tilt to one side.

The easiest way to detect curvature is to have the child touch their toes. When looking along their back, one side will be seen to rise higher than the other, even though the spine may appear relatively straight when erect. If scoliosis is detected, the cause must be determined. If one leg is shorter than the other due to injury or other causes, the pelvis will be tilted, and the spine will curve to compensate. Abnormal vertebrae in the back that may have been present since birth or damaged by a severe injury may also lead to scoliosis. Diseases of the muscles that support the vertebral bones are another cause. This occurs in patients with polio or quadriplegia. Spasm of the same muscles in spastics can pull the backbone out of shape.

The commonest form of scoliosis in teenagers and children has no apparent cause. This is the type that must be watched most carefully to prevent permanent deformity. The younger the onset of the problem, the greater the need for concern, but babies nearly always recover spontaneously.

Initially, careful measurements and X-rays will be taken, along with other tests to exclude complicating diseases. The patient is then checked at regular intervals to assess the progress of the scoliosis. If there is continued deterioration and the curvature exceeds 15–20 degrees, treatment is essential. This may be by means of physiotherapy and structured exercises, or by using braces. Only in severe cases is surgery contemplated.

Surgery to correct scoliosis can involve insertion of steel rods into the back to keep it straight, or fusing several vertebrae together in a straight line to prevent them from moving. These procedures are only undertaken after careful consideration by several doctors, but have a very good success rate.

Any parent who is concerned about their child's growth should see their general practitioner for a check. It is far better to do this now than to leave it until more radical treatments may be necessary.

SCROFULA

Scrofula is extremely rare in Australia but still occurs in third-world countries. It is tuberculosis (see separate entry) occurring in the glands of the neck to cause large, hard masses that may drain pus out onto the skin.

The disease rates a mention for historical reasons, as in past centuries it was called 'King's evil', and it was believed that if a victim was touched by the King, the sores would heal. The modern treatment involves cutting out the affected glands and giving antituberculotic medications (see Section 6).

SCURVY

Scurvy is intimately connected with Australia's past but is very uncommon today. It was the scourge of sailors on long voyages, particularly voyages of exploration to places where fresh food supplies could not be relied upon. Captain James Cook made a name for himself early in his career by insisting that all his crew had rations of lime juice (which contains high levels of vitamin C) every day to counteract scurvy. His success was notable in that none of the crew on his long voyages exploring the Pacific ever contracted the disease. The early convicts were not as lucky, as Cook's knowledge and experience in these matters was not accepted by all captains. As a result, many convicts, and some members of the crew, particularly in the notorious second fleet, arrived in this country suffering terribly from scurvy.

Scurvy is caused by a lack of ascorbic acid (vitamin C — see Section 6) in the diet. It may still be found in people who are on unusual fad diets or in alcoholics who are malnourished.

In the early stages, the symptoms are vague and include tiredness and weakness. As the deficiency of vitamin C becomes more severe, symptoms include bleeding into the skin, rashes, bleeding gums, joint pain and bleeding into joints, slow wound healing and tender bones. The patient is severely anaemic, and bleeds readily. In advanced cases, the kidneys fail, the tissues of the body swell, bleeding into the brain occurs, and death follows.

The diagnosis can be confirmed by specifically measuring the amount of ascorbic acid in the blood, and by noting the marked anaemia. Between 100 and 300 mg of vitamin C a day is all that is required to treat scurvy. To prevent the disease, 50 mg a day is sufficient. There is no benefit in taking larger doses of vitamin C, which may in fact cause toxic problems in higher doses, particularly in children.

SEA SICKNESS
See TRAVEL MEDICINE, Section 7.

SEBACEOUS CYST
Sebum is the oil-like substance that keeps our skin moist and supple. It is produced in glands beneath the skin, and is discharged through small ducts. These glands are present all over the body, but in areas that may become sweaty, dirty or injured it is possible to block the duct leading from the gland. The sebum continues to be produced, and a cyst (known as a sebaceous cyst) slowly fills up under the skin. The cysts appear frequently on the back, chest and neck, are slightly soft and often have a tiny dimple at the point where the original duct opened onto the skin. Sometimes the pressure in the cyst is sufficient for its contents to be discharged through the previously blocked duct. Unfortunately, the cyst usually regrows again. The worst thing that can happen is for these cysts to become infected, and if antibiotics are not given soon enough, an abscess may form. Any cyst that is unsightly or becomes infected should be cut out. This is a simple procedure that can be performed under local anaesthetic by most general practitioners.

SEPTICAEMIA (BLOOD POISONING)
Septicaemia can be simply defined as a bacterial infection of the blood. Many different bacteria may be responsible for the infection, and it is important to identify them by blood tests before antibiotic treatment commences.

The infection usually starts in another part of the body, such as the lungs, tonsils or after childbirth (now very rare), but in some cases the origin of the infection may never be found. The original site of infection must also be treated. Many different bacterial infections have septicaemia as a complication. Patients are usually very ill, with a high fever, prostration and generalised aches and pains.

Provided an appropriate antibiotic can be found, most patients can be cured, but often injected antibiotics in a hospital are required. A small number of patients will have an overwhelming infection with resistant bacteria, which leads to death.

SERUM SICKNESS
Serum sickness is an uncommon allergy reaction that occurs in the blood as a reaction to the use of a drug, or more commonly after a blood transfusion or use of a blood product (e.g. globulin or proteins). The reaction may be immediate, or delayed for up to two weeks. The patient feels unwell, tired, nauseated and feverish. The glands in the neck, armpit and groin are enlarged, an itchy rash develops, cramps occur in the abdomen, and the joints may become painful. Serum sickness may be a mild reaction that passes almost unnoticed, or a very severe condition that can lead to death in a few hours. The result depends upon the severity of the allergic reaction (see ALLERGY).

Treatment involves using drugs to counteract the allergy reaction (e.g. antihistamines — see Section 6), and to treat the results of the reaction (e.g. steroids, adrenaline — see Section 6).

SEXUAL PROBLEMS
Normal sexuality is discussed in Section 1, and the reproductive systems are

described in Section 2. Only problems with sexual intercourse are discussed in this section. All patients should be aware that the correct treatment of nearly all sexual dysfunction will require the assistance of a general practitioner, psychiatrist, psychologist or qualified sex therapist. Unqualified sex therapists should be approached with considerable caution.

Ejaculation problems

Ejaculation of semen by the male normally occurs a couple of minutes to 20 minutes or more after penetration during sex. Problems with ejaculation include failure to ejaculate, premature ejaculation, and retrograde ejaculation (see below).

Ejaculatory failure (or retarded ejaculation) is the male equivalent of a failed orgasm in the female. The condition is far less common in men than its equivalent is in women.

Some men find that they can ejaculate when masturbating, or with oral sex, but not at all, or only with difficulty, in vaginal sex. The cause (when not a side effect of some drug) is usually psychological, and secondary to inhibitions or fears that may be subconscious or conscious. The problem may have started after an unwanted pregnancy occurred in a sex partner, or due to fear of losing self-control.

Treatment involves progressive desensitisation with the assistance of a cooperative sex partner, who initially masturbates him to ejaculation, and over a series of weeks, learns to bring him to almost the point of ejaculation by hand stimulation before allowing vaginal sex. Another technique involves additional stimulation of the penis during intercourse by the woman massaging the penis with her fingers while the man thrusts into and out of the vagina. Distracting the man from consciously holding back the ejaculation may also help. This can be achieved by passionate kissing or other stimulation of the face or back during intercourse.

Premature ejaculation (ejaculating before you wish to) is a far more common problem. Ejaculation cannot be brought about by conscious effort, but it can be prevented by specific techniques.

Treatment again requires the cooperation of the sex partner. There are two techniques that have proved successful — the 'stop-start' and the 'squeeze'. Experimenting with masturbation to detect and memorise the feelings that occur just before ejaculation may be necessary before trying these techniques.

The 'stop-start' technique involves stopping all sexual activity at a point just short of orgasm. The man indicates by a signal or word that ejaculation is imminent, at which point the partners lie still until the urge to ejaculate has subsided. This may occur several times until the couple are ready to orgasm. The 'stop' may occur before any penetration is attempted in those men who ejaculate very early, and with practice, the pre-intercourse petting and intercourse itself can be prolonged to the satisfaction of both partners.

In the 'squeeze' technique, the man again indicates when ejaculation is imminent, but instead of stopping all activity, the woman grasps the man's penis firmly just behind the head (glans) of the penis, and squeezes firmly until the man loses part of his erection, and the penis becomes slightly soft, at which point she lets go and continues uninhibited sexual activity. This process can also be repeated several times before allowing ejaculation to occur. With practice, the man can learn to control his ejaculation more and more until these techniques are no longer required.

Retrograde ejaculation occurs when the semen is ejaculated from the sac at the base of the penis, but instead of passing along the urethra to the outside, it travels in the other direction and enters the bladder. This condition is a complication of surgery in the area (e.g. to the prostate), due to advanced diabetes or a side effect of some uncommon drugs.

Frigidity

A woman who is unable to experience any pleasure or arousal from sexual stimulation is described as frigid. There is no lubrication of the vagina, enlargement of the nipples or clitoral tenseness, but it is a psychological problem and not a physical one. The frigidity may be a result of a woman's strict upbringing, a loathing for sex that has been conditioned by an oppressive mother or violent father, an unfortunate early sexual experience, an unwanted pregnancy, or it may develop after a rape or other assault. Other causes of frigidity include pain with intercourse (see below), stress from a new baby or postnatal depression after birth, moving house or changing jobs, and the hormone drop associated with menopause. Certain prescribed drugs and hormones may also be responsible.

Treatment of frigidity requires a very understanding partner and a very slow teaching process, usually with the help of a psychiatrist or psychologist. Stimulation of non-erotic parts of the body to relax the woman over a period of weeks, followed by stimulation of more erotically sensitive areas, slowly breaks down the barriers. The back may be the starting point, followed by the face, ears, lips, and after many sessions and several weeks or months, the breasts and finally the genital area may be stimulated.

Impotence

An erection cannot be willed consciously but occurs as a nervous reflex which is outside the voluntary control of the man. The factors that are necessary for an erection to occur are adequate levels of testosterone (male hormone), healthy arteries to the penis (they may be blocked in men with diabetes or hardening of the arteries), and normal anatomy of the penis. Impotence, the failure of a male to obtain or sustain an erection, occurs for many diverse reasons.

Any form of anxiety can interfere with the complex reflex of an erection and prevent it from occurring.

Far from being a sexual stimulant, as is often thought, alcohol actually suppresses the ability to perform sexually. An alcoholic with liver damage may ultimately become totally impotent, since it is the liver that controls the balance between male and female hormones in the body.

Athletes and body builders who use anabolic steroids to enhance their performance and physique also become impotent, sometimes permanently, because of the effect these drugs have on the testes. Some types of treatment for high blood pressure can also affect a man's ability to have an erection, and he should discuss the side effects of any medication with his doctor. A prostate operation has no direct effect on sexuality, unless it is a total prostatectomy.

The main reason for a failed erection is psychological pressure to perform. If a man is anxious about sex because of a new partner, conditions that are not ideal, or other stress and worries, there is a good chance that these nervous signals will override the stimulating signals and the penis will not become erect. If he has failed previously, then there is even more anxiety, and every successive failure makes him more anxious to perform and therefore less likely to succeed. The way to overcome this is not to plan sex, but to relax and wait until it occurs spontaneously. A couple should find a private and relaxed place and time, engage in mutual heavy petting and erotic stimulation, but without the expectation that sex will occur. The man should not worry about whether or not an erection occurs, or how hard it is if one does arise, but should relax and enjoy the stimulation his partner is giving his body. In this less tense situation, an erection may arise, but should not be used for intercourse on the first occasion. Once spontaneous erections develop, sex may start again.

Libido, reduced
Libido simply means sexual desire, and refers to both men and women. A woman whose libido is virtually non-existent is described as frigid (see above). Reduced libido may be caused by several disorders, including diabetes, Parkinson's disease, thyroid disease, pituitary gland disorders, hormone imbalances and many other diseases. Stress, anxiety and depression are very common causes of reduced libido, as is alcohol in excess and drug abuse. Prescribed medications, especially those used to treat high blood pressure, drug addiction and emotional or psychiatric disorders, may reduce the person's libido. Libido also drops with age.

Reduced libido requires appropriate investigation, and any cause (including anxiety or depression) should be appropriately treated. Some women find that their libido increases on the contraceptive pill, because of its effects on the woman's hormonal balance, and sometimes because of the psychological effect of being free of the risk of pregnancy.

Orgasm problems
A woman may be sexually responsive, enjoy sex and have the physical signs of erotic arousal, but she may still fail to have an orgasm. The orgasm is a reflex, in the same way as a tap on the knee causes a reflex. Some people have a vigorous response to a knee tap, others have little. Thus it is difficult to determine what is a normal and abnormal reflex or orgasm.

Different women require different degrees and types of stimulation to have an orgasm. Some can only orgasm by stimulation of the clitoris, others require prolonged intercourse, while others may orgasm frequently and easily with merely breast stimulation or thinking about sex. A woman may find that one particular sex position causes orgasm more easily than other positions.

The treatment of a woman who complains of no or an inadequate orgasm is difficult. She should be taught relaxation techniques which are accompanied by masturbation by hand or mechanical devices in order to bring herself to orgasm. Once she has experienced orgasm in this manner, she can move to the next stage of treatment with a male partner. This may involve the man using his hand to stimulate her to orgasm before or after he has climaxed, or by using different sex positions (e.g. man behind woman) during which the woman can stimulate her own clitoris.

The supervision of a sex therapist (psychiatrist or psychologist) in this process is invaluable.

Painful intercourse
Pain with sexual intercourse can affect both men and women.

In **women**, the causes of painful sexual activity can be physical or psychological. Vaginismus (see below) is one of the most common causes of pain in women. Other causes include infections in the vagina, bladder or pelvis; sores such as herpes on the vulva; tumours or cysts of the uterus (e.g. fibroids) and ovaries; and endometriosis. Scarring of the vagina after childbirth may also cause discomfort with sex for many months after the birth.

Sexual difficulties can also arise from diseases of other areas of the body. Arthritis of the lower back or hips can obviously cause problems, but more distant diseases, such as an underactive thyroid gland reducing the vaginal secretions, may also be responsible. At the time of menopause, the vaginal secretions may also be reduced.

Pain during intercourse in **men** is far less common than in women, but it may be due to infection or irritation of the skin of the penis, herpes infections, allergies, or infections of the prostate, urethra or testes. Vaginismus or dryness in the man's partner may increase friction and cause pain. The nylon string from a woman's intra-uterine device can sometimes graze the head of the penis. On rare occasions painful intercourse can be due to cancer of the penis or testes.

In some instances, a man may be allergic to contraceptive creams or douching solutions used by his partner. If a man is allergic to rubber, a condom may cause problems, although this is rare.

Sex problems in the elderly

There is no reason why elderly people should not maintain an active sex life until well into their seventies, but there are a number of factors which will make the task more difficult.

The main factor that can affect the elderly is the menopause in both men and women. Both sexes are affected, but the male menopause is often forgotten, although there is no doubt that it does occur. From the mid-fifties onwards, the amount of male hormone in the system slowly decreases. Unlike the female menopause, where there is a relatively sudden drop in hormone levels, the drop in men is so gradual that it may not be noticed until the early seventies when sexual responsiveness and libido (desire for sex) starts to decrease. This will obviously vary from one man to another. The drop in libido in a woman may be more sudden, but a woman can still appreciate and enjoy the closeness and intimacy that sexual intercourse gives until an advanced age.

Other factors affecting the elderly can include medical problems as diverse as heart failure and arthritis which may make sex physically more difficult, and medications (particularly those for blood pressure) that may affect a man's erection. Diseases such as diabetes and atherosclerosis cause the partial blockage of small arteries, and may also affect the ability to have an erection.

As other activities are undertaken at a slower pace in old age, so should sexual activity. Most problems can be overcome by patience, mutual understanding and sometimes the assistance of a doctor in modifying medication.

Small penis

A small penis has no effect upon a man's ability to father children or satisfy his sexual partner, and continued reassurance on this point will help a patient gain confidence in his 'manhood'. The size of the penis varies from one person to another, in the same way that some people have big noses while others are small. There are no prizes for having the largest nose on the block, nor are there for the size of any other parts of your anatomy. The only people who will ever need to be aware of the size of a man's penis are the man himself and his wife or other sex partners.

The size of the penis does not determine whether a man is a good lover or not. Women appreciate the foreplay and fondling as much as the sex act itself, and if a man can become skilled in the former, he can keep any woman sexually satisfied. Even during intercourse, the most sensitive part of a woman's sexual organs are the clitoris, which is at the outside entrance to the vagina, and the so-called 'G spot' which is just inside, and on the front wall of the vagina, at a point where even the shortest penis can give stimulation.

SECTION 5: DISEASES

No man with a relatively small penis should underestimate his sexual prowess, as he will be able to satisfy the sexual appetite of any woman if he approaches her in the right way.

Vaginismus

Vaginismus is a spasm of the muscles around the vagina that is so strong that sexual intercourse becomes impossible as the man is unable to penetrate the woman. It is an unconscious reaction, normally triggered by anxiety related to the sex act. The initial trigger for vaginismus may be fear (of pregnancy, pain, etc.), guilt, lack of privacy, anxiety about expectations, lack of self confidence, previous rape or sexual assault, and a wide range of other psychological factors. It is not a disease or physical abnormality.

Treatment of vaginismus involves using vaginal dilators (artificial penises) of gradually increasing width. A pencil-sized object may be used initially, and then objects of gradually increasing diameter are introduced into the vagina. This may be done by the woman privately, by a doctor or by her sex partner. Once an object the size of a penis can be introduced, the woman is cured, but the process must not be rushed, and confidence must be gained in using one size of dildo before the next size is attempted.

See also SEXUALLY TRANSMITTED DISEASE; and Section 1.

SEXUALLY TRANSMITTED DISEASE (STD)

Sexually transmitted disease (STD) has taken over from venereal disease (VD) as the accepted term for a large group of socially unacceptable diseases. The STDs include all diseases caused and transmitted by sexual contact, from syphilis to hepatitis B and NSU; from the relatively common genital warts and genital herpes to the uncommon chancres, and the worst of them all — AIDS. They are described separately under the name of each disease. The risk of catching these diseases can be reduced, but not completely eliminated, by using condoms.

Sometimes patients may exhibit no symptoms of a disease but be able to pass it on to any subsequent sex partners. To prevent the spread of serious STDs, some of them have to be reported to authorities so that all the contacts of a patient can be found, tested, and treated if necessary. These so-called communicable diseases include gonorrhoea, syphilis and AIDS. The tracing of the contacts is often left to the patient, assisted by a counsellor. The police don't come knocking at your lover's door — that would scare anybody away from having a checkup. Those who are at risk of contracting any form of sexually transmitted disease should not hesitate to have regular checks by their doctor. The undetected development of any such disease could have lifelong consequences.

See also AIDS; CHANCROID; CHLAMYDIAL INFECTIONS; GONORRHOEA; HEPATITIS B; NON-SPECIFIC URETHRITIS; SYPHILIS; TRICHOMONIASIS; WARTS, GENITAL.

SHIGELLA INFECTION
See DYSENTERY, BACTERIAL.

SHINGLES (VARICELLA, HERPES ZOSTER)

One of the most unpleasant diseases of the skin is shingles, particularly as it occasionally leaves permanent scarring and pain in its wake. Shingles is caused by a virus called *Herpes zoster*, which is the same virus that causes chickenpox (see separate entry).

When you were a child, you probably had chickenpox at some stage. Since then, the virus has not left your body, but has migrated to the roots of the nerves along your spinal cord, where it can remain in an inactive stage for the rest of your life. At times of stress, either emotional or physical, or when you have another illness that lowers your resistance, the virus may become active again and start to multiply and move along the nerve. This causes the skin and other tissues around the area the nerve supplies to become very painful, and this is the first symptom of shingles. Usually only one or two nerves are affected, and almost invariably on only one side of the body. Any nerve may be affected, and it can occur on the abdomen or chest (most common sites), or on the face or legs. The worst variety occurs around the eye and ear, where dizziness, ear noises and rarely blindness may occur.

When the rapidly multiplying virus particles reach the end of the nerve, an acutely tender blistering rash occurs. This often forms a belt-like line around one half of the body, and it is from this appearance that the disease gets its name, for *cingulum*, from which the term shingles is derived, means belt in Latin. Even the slightest touch on an affected area can cause severe shooting pain. The rash dries out slowly and disappears over several weeks, usually healing completely, but occasionally leaving some scarring on sensitive areas such as the neck and face. The pain is slower to disappear, and may last a month longer than the rash. A small number of people, particularly elderly women, can be even more unlucky and may develop chronic inflammation in the nerve. In these cases, the pain may persist for years.

Anyone can develop shingles, but it is far more common in older people, as their natural immunity to the chickenpox virus has waned over the years. It is quite uncommon in children. You cannot catch shingles from another person, but a child who has not had chickenpox may catch this from a person who has active shingles.

Shingles can now be cured, but only if treatment is started within 72 hours of the rash first appearing, so seeing a doctor as soon as the diagnosis is suspected is important. A tablet called Zovirax (see Section 6) is used for this purpose, but it must be taken in quite high doses. Side effects from the medication are uncommon. If treatment is neglected until three or more days after the onset of the rash, Zovirax is ineffective and treatment returns to the traditional ones of painkillers, drying antiseptic lotions and mild sedatives. Steroids may be used in severe cases.

Shingles is rarely a dangerous disease and the vast majority of people make an excellent recovery, but it is still a most unpleasant few weeks for the patient.

SHOCK (SHOCK SYNDROME)

Medically, the term shock has nothing to do with a fright or upset, but is a condition in which there is an inadequate circulation of blood around the body. Medical shock may be caused by a very wide range of problems, including loss of blood from a major injury, severe burns, several fractures, extensive bleeding into the gut from an ulcer or other disease, massive diarrhoea, various forms of heart damage and failure, lung disease (e.g. thrombosis or embolism), heart valve disease, septicaemia (see separate entry), and many other serious conditions.

The patient will collapse, be obviously very ill, pale, sweaty and have a weak, thready pulse. The blood pressure will be very low, and consciousness may be disturbed. Further symptoms will depend upon the cause of the shock, and may vary from pain to shortness of breath and fever.

Shock is a medical emergency that is best dealt with in hospital casualty departments, but a patient who is remote from ready access to a hospital may be adequately stabilised by any doctor who has access to basic equipment and facilities. The patient should be lying down flat with their legs raised, if conscious, to improve the blood flow to the brain, or lying down flat and on the side if unconscious. Treatment will certainly involve the use of intravenous fluids (or blood) through a drip. Other treatments will include controlling any obvious bleeding, oxygen, maintaining body temperature by the use of warm blankets, splinting fractures, protecting burnt areas and pain-killing injections when appropriate. If the patient deteriorates, mouth-to-mouth resuscitation and external cardiac massage (see Section 8) may be necessary. Further treatment will depend upon the cause of the shock and may include a wide range of drugs and possibly surgery. Almost certainly, the patient will be managed in an intensive care unit of the hospital until the shock is adequately controlled.

The prognosis depends upon a multitude of factors including the cause of the shock, the patient's age and general health, and the speed with which medical assistance can be obtained.

See also HYPOTENSION.

SHOULDER DISEASE
See FROZEN SHOULDER; ROTATOR CUFF SYNDROME; SHOULDER DISLOCATION.

SHOULDER DISLOCATION
The shoulder joint can move through a greater range than any other joint in the body. This freedom of movement comes at the price of relative instability, and the shoulder joint is the most commonly dislocated major joint (the minor fingers and toe joints are more commonly dislocated) in the body. The shoulder is a ball and socket joint, but the socket is very shallow to allow maximum movement. A cuff of muscles and ligaments (the rotator cuff — see separate entry) surrounds the shoulder joint to keep it in the correct position. If excessive force is applied to the shoulder joint, it may dislocate forwards, or backwards (less common). Any shoulder dislocation is associated with tearing and damage to the surrounding muscles and ligaments of the rotator cuff and joint capsule.

It is often difficult for a doctor to differentiate a dislocation from a fracture of the humerus (upper arm bone), and X-rays are often necessary before any reduction of a dislocated shoulder can be attempted. Patients with a dislocated shoulder experience severe pain, do not like the shoulder joint to be moved, and often hold the elbow of the affected arm at right angles and against their side with the other hand.

Once correctly diagnosed, the dislocated shoulder can be reduced (put back into place) by one of a number of different techniques. If applied soon after the injury, little or no anaesthetic may be necessary and the shoulder may slip back quite easily. After an hour or so, spasm of muscles around the joint may make the reduction more difficult, and pain-killing injections or even a brief general anaesthetic may be necessary. Once the shoulder dislocation has been reduced, the arm is kept in a sling for about a month to allow the damaged tissue around the shoulder to heal.

If the shoulder dislocates several times, a totally different problem must be dealt with. **Recurrent shoulder dislocation** can be a significant handicap, as the shoulder may dislocate by merely picking up a heavy object or raising the arm above the head. There is far less pain in these situations, and the dislocation can be easily reduced, but there is no gain from immobilising the arm in a sling for weeks after the incident, and normal activity can normally be undertaken again within a couple of days. Each dislocation further damages the supporting muscles and ligaments of the joint, so that a subsequent dislocation becomes easier. This vicious circle can only be broken by an operation (called the Putti-Platt procedure) to repair and tighten the damaged tissues. This is quite major surgery, and it will take six to eight weeks to recover normal use of the joint.

SIDS (SUDDEN INFANT DEATH SYNDROME)
See COT DEATH.

SILICOSIS
There are a number of lung diseases caused by the long-term inhalation of harmful particles. Silicosis is caused by the inhalation of tiny particles of silica, asbestosis from inhaling asbestos particles (see separate entry), and pneumoconiosis from inhaling coal dust (see separate entry). Silicosis occurs in workers involved in rock quarrying, stone cutting, tunnelling, pottery and those who use diatomaceous earth. It causes the formation of multiple small hard round nodules in the lung. These can be readily seen on an X-ray. Most victims are unaware that they have the disease, and it is usually diagnosed after a routine chest X-ray. In advanced cases there may be shortness of breath, and a poor tolerance to exercise. No treatment is available.

SINUSITIS
Below, above, between and even behind your eyes, your skull bone is riddled with spaces called sinuses. All these sinuses are connected together by small holes and tubes, making a complex interconnecting system rather like a cave-explorer's nightmare in miniature. The exact purpose of the sinuses is obscure, but they certainly lighten the skull and may act as resonance chambers for speech. Lining this network of sinuses is a moist membrane, the same as that inside your nostrils. The whole system is thus kept constantly moist, and the moisture slowly flows out of the drain holes in the sinuses into the back of your nose and throat. The system is designed to keep the sinuses clean, as any dust or other small particles that may enter them, is washed out. Unfortunately it does not always work perfectly. Some people secrete excess amounts of fluid in the sinuses, while others may have drainage holes and tubes that are too small to cope with the secretions produced.

With hay fever, particles to which the person reacts adversely enter the sinuses and set up an irritation that stimulates the excess production of watery phlegm. A constantly runny nose and a postnasal drip then result. If bacteria or viruses enter the sinuses, an infection may result. The phlegm produced is no longer watery, but thick and pus-like. It is very easy in this situation for the drain holes to become blocked, and the infection then concentrates in a small number of sinuses. Pus is constantly being formed by the rapidly multiplying bacteria, and soon the sinus becomes very painful and tender. Waste products from the infection enter the blood stream, and cause a fever, headaches and the other unpleasant sensations of any major infection. This is sinusitis. It is quite easy for the infection to spread to the middle ear too, as the Eustachian tube connects the back of the nose to the middle ear.

The easiest way to prove the presence of sinusitis is to take an X-ray of the sinuses which shows if they are clear or full of fluid. Swabs may be taken from the back of the nose and sent to a pathologist so that the type of bacteria causing the infection can be determined and the correct treatment selected.

Once infection is present, it can persist for a long time unless the appropriate treatment is given. Untreated the infection can spread to the teeth, eyes and even the brain, and severe abscesses may form. Treatment usually takes the form of the appropriate antibiotic (see Section 6), and other medications (e.g. mucolytics — see Section 6) to help dry up the production of phlegm and clear the sinuses. Many people find inhalations of steam and nasal decongestant drops beneficial. In severe cases, it may be necessary to insert needles through the nose into the sinuses to wash out the pus.

Prevention is always better than cure, and in people who suffer from repeated attacks of sinusitis, procedures to reduce the likelihood of attacks can be performed by ear, nose and throat surgeons. These can vary from burning away the moist membrane lining the nose, to drilling larger drain holes into the sinuses.

There are also special nasal sprays available on prescription from doctors that can be used regularly to prevent the lining of the nose from reacting to any allergies. These must be used long term to give maximum benefit.

Sinusitis is a very common and often very distressing condition, but provided treatment is sought promptly, it should not cause any serious complications.

Sjögren's syndrome (Mikulicz's disease

Sjögren's syndrome is an auto-immune disease (the immune system attacks part of the body inappropriately) consisting of arthritis, dry eyes, dry mouth, dry skin and dry throat. Other symptoms include difficulty in swallowing, teeth affected by holes, loss of taste and smell, and a hoarse voice. Complications can involve the pancreas, thyroid and other organs. It was first described by a Swedish ophthalmologist earlier this century.

Nearly all the patients with Sjögren's syndrome are women, and it most commonly commences in those who are in their fifties. The disease can be diagnosed by specific blood tests.

Sjögren's syndrome is closely related to rheumatoid arthritis and is treated in much the same way, with the addition of artificial tears and skin moisturisers for the dryness problems, and good dental hygiene. There is no permanent cure, but reasonable long-term control is normally possible.

Skin cancer

Australia is blessed with far more sunshine than most nations with a predominantly white-skinned population. As a result, it is also blessed with a far greater percentage of sun-induced skin cancers.

There are many sun-induced skin sores which are not the nasty cancerous type, but there are also some which can spread rapidly enough to eventually kill the unfortunate owner of the spot. It is often difficult for doctors to be absolutely certain about a spot when examined on the patient, and so if there is any doubt at all, the spot is cut out. This can be done very easily in a general practitioner's surgery. The lesion is then sent to a pathologist, who will examine it further under a microscope to make the exact diagnosis.

Nasty skin spots fall into several different categories. Cancers of the outermost layer of skin are commonly called skin cancers, or squamous cell carcinomas (SCC). Another type of tumour develops if the next layer down in the skin is involved. These growths are called basal cell carcinomas (BCC) and are generally not as serious as the more superficial cancers. Malignant melanomas are the most serious and deadly of them all. Even with the best medical care, a significant proportion of these patients will die, often because they have been seen too late by a doctor. However, Australia leads the world in malignant melanoma management, and complete cures are now possible if the patient presents early in the disease. In the last 10–20 years, the outcome for malignant melanoma sufferers has changed greatly and for the better.

Signs to watch for in a spot or sore are:
- any irregularity in colour, shape or outline,
- soreness or itchiness,
- bleeding or weeping.

If any of these signs occur, see your doctor immediately! It is far better to find out the truth now, be it good or bad, than to worry for months unnecessarily, or have a far worse outcome because of the delay.

Squamous cell carcinoma (SCC)

Cancers of the outermost layer of skin are called squamous cell carcinomas (SCC). They occur most commonly on the exposed parts of the body, such as the rims of the ears, the face, scalp, arms and hands. Men with receding hairlines are at greatest risk, because they lack nature's own sunshade.

The stage before an SCC is called a **hyperkeratosis** or solar keratosis. These are patches of raised and scaling skin, but they are not red or itchy. These may be treated by acid ointments or surgical procedures to remove them and prevent them from becoming SCCs. In some elderly patients with very large areas affected by keratoses, it may not be practical to remove all the spots, but they should be checked regularly by a doctor so that any which change can be treated immediately.

Another type of skin condition that can progress to an SCC is called **Bowen's disease**. These are less common than keratoses but are more likely to develop into a skin cancer. They appear as a sharply edged red patch covered with a fine scale. They may be found anywhere on the body and are caused by exposure to sunlight or arsenic compounds. They should be removed or chemically destroyed.

A squamous cell carcinoma looks like a red spot covered in fine white scales. They may be itchy or sore but often attract attention because they are unsightly. They occur on sun-exposed parts of the body, usually in patients who are over 50 years of age. They are caused by prolonged exposure to sunlight or irritant chemicals. Most of them can be very easily removed, and the doctor, if sure of the diagnosis, may burn the cancer off with a diathermy machine or freeze it off with liquid nitrogen. Both methods are very effective in early stages of the disease.

If the skin cancer is larger, or if the diagnosis is not certain, it is necessary to cut out the spot and the surrounding tissue to prevent it from spreading further. SCCs can spread by blood or lymphatics to distant parts of the body. This is why they are more serious than basal cell carcinomas (see below).

Basal cell carcinoma (BCC, rodent ulcer)

Cancers of the deeper layers of the skin are called basal cell carcinomas (BCC) and are generally not as serious as the more superficial cancers. They occur at an earlier age than SCCs but rarely before 25 years of age. They are caused by prolonged exposure to sunlight, and so occur most commonly on the face and back, but they are uncommon on the arms and legs.

BCCs may appear as shiny, rounded lumps that often change in size and colour, or they may present as an ulcer that fails to heal. The ulcer often has a pearly, rounded edge.

Whenever a BCC is suspected, it should be removed surgically. The specimen is then sent to a pathologist for examination to ensure that the diagnosis is correct, and that all the tumour has been removed. Other forms of treatment include irradiation and diathermy.

If correctly treated, these growths can be completely healed, but if left until large, significant plastic surgery may be necessary to correct the defect left behind after the BCC is removed. Untreated, the cancer will slowly invade deeper tissues, become very obvious and repulsive in appearance, and after many years may cause death. BCCs do not spread to other parts of the body.

Melanoma
Melanomas are the most serious form of skin cancer, and one third of all patients who develop a melanoma will eventually die from this disease. Melanomas may be black, brown, pink or blue, and when found individually or mixed in a skin spot, these colours could be deadly.

The melanocytes are the cells in the skin that create pigment. In Europeans (Caucasians), these cells are relatively inactive, giving a pale colour to the skin. In Asians (Mongols) they are moderately active, and in Africans (Negroes) they are very active, giving a steadily darker skin colour. Cancer can develop in any type of cell in the body. When the melanocytes start multiplying abnormally, they form melanomas, which appear as irregularly edged, dark (or rarely pink), enlarging spots on the skin. The surface of the melanoma is often uneven and bumpy, and the pigment can be seen advancing into the surrounding skin. They may enlarge very rapidly, and advanced cases will bleed, scab and ulcerate.

Melanomas can occur in unusual situations such as under the nail (where they may be mistaken for a bruise), in the mouth, under the eyelids, on the retina inside the eye, and in the anus, but the sun-exposed parts of the skin are by far the most commonly affected areas.

This type of cancer is rare in children, and slightly more common in women than men. Their greatest incidence is between 30 and 50 years of age, and the most common sites are the legs and back. One in every 150 people in Australia will develop a melanoma at some time in their lives. Fair-skinned people are far more likely to develop this cancer than those with dark complexions.

The actual cause is unknown, but exposure to sunlight, particularly in childhood and the teen years, dramatically increases the risk of developing a melanoma. Melanomas are therefore more common in the warmer climates of northern Australia than in Tasmania. Ultraviolet radiation, most of which is filtered out of sunlight by the ozone layer in the upper atmosphere, is the part of the spectrum that causes the damage. Any depletion in the ozone layers around the globe will inevitably lead to a dramatic increase in the incidence of melanomas.

When discovered, the melanoma, and a large area of skin around and under it, must be cut out. This usually leaves a hole that must be covered by a skin graft. The lymph nodes around the melanoma may also need to be removed in some patients.

Melanomas have a tendency to grow deep into the body and migrate to other organs. If the melanoma is a particularly virulent one, or there is evidence that it has spread through the bloodstream to other areas, the patient will also be treated with irradiation and injected medications to control its further growth. The liver, lungs and glands in the armpit and groin are the most common areas for secondary melanomas to develop.

It is very difficult to predict the course of the disease in any particular patient. Some cases are completely cured by local excision, others will advance rapidly despite all treatment, and another group may appear to be cured but the disease can flare up decades later.

In the very early stages, melanomas have a 97% cure rate. As the cancer enlarges, the cure rate drops dramatically. The lesson from this is to protect yourself from the sun, and have any spot on your skin that is enlarging, changing, darkening, itchy, weeping, bleeding or sore checked by a doctor.

See also KERATOACANTHOMA.

Skin disease
See ACNE; ALLERGY; ALOPECIA AREATA; BED SORES; BOIL; BURNS; CHICKENPOX; CONDYLOMATA ACUMINATA; CRABS; DANDRUFF; DERMATITIS; DERMATOMYOSITIS; ECZEMA; EPIDERMOLYSIS BULLOSA; ERYSIPELAS; ERYTHEMA MULTIFORME; ERYTHEMA NODOSUM; FOLLICULITIS; FROSTBITE; FUNGAL INFECTIONS; HAIR, EXCESS; HERPES SIMPLEX INFECTIONS; INTERTRIGO; KERATOACANTHOMA; LICHEN SIMPLEX; LUPUS ERYTHEMATOSUS, SYSTEMIC; MOLLUSCUM CONTAGIOSUM; NAPPY RASH; ORF; PEMPHIGOID; PEMPHIGUS; PITYRIASIS ROSEA; POMPHOLYX; PRURITUS ANI; PSORIASIS; ROSACEA; SCABIES; SCHOOL SORES; SCLERODERMA; SCROFULA; SEBACEOUS CYST; SHINGLES; SKIN CANCER; ULCER, SKIN; VITILIGO; VON RECKLINGHAUSEN'S DISEASE; WARTS; YAWS.

SLE (systemic lupus erythematosus)
See LUPUS ERYTHEMATOSUS, SYSTEMIC.

Sleep apnoea
Adequate sleep is essential for the good health of everyone, but when sleep apnoea occurs, a significant deterioration in the quality of life may develop. 'Apnoea' means 'no breathing', and patients with sleep apnoea stop breathing for periods from 10 to 60 seconds on many occasions whilst asleep during the night.

There are two reasons for sleep apnoea developing. The most common cause is due to the small muscles at the back of the throat and in the roof of the mouth relaxing completely and allowing this tissue to become very soft and flabby. The airway tends to collapse as the patient breathes in, closing it off and preventing breathing. Snoring is also caused in the same way. Most patients with this form of sleep apnoea are overweight middle-aged men. The other cause is an effect in the brain, whereby the urge to breathe is suppressed during very deep sleep. Elderly men with high blood pressure most commonly fit into this category.

Patients complain of tiredness during the day, morning headaches, personality changes, poor concentration, bed-wetting and impotence. The sleeping partner complains about the other person's loud snoring and thrashing restless sleep. The diagnosis can best be made in a sleep laboratory, where the patients sleep and breathing pattern can be monitored through an entire night (see PULMONARY FUNCTION TESTS, Section 4).

Treatment involves weight loss, and avoiding alcohol, sedatives and smoking, and these steps alone may be sufficient to cure the problem. In persistent cases, treatment can involve a small mask being fitted to the patient's nose, and air being blown up the nose at a slight pressure (with a small electrically driven blower called a continuous positive airway pressure blower). This 'splints' the airway open, causing air to enter the lungs and breathing to continue normally. In severe cases, a clear airway may also be established by surgery to the back of the throat and nose to remove the uvula and part of the soft palate.

Sleep problems
See INSOMNIA; SLEEP APNOEA.

Sleeping sickness (African trypanosomiasis)

Sleeping sickness is unknown in Australia. It is caused by a tiny parasite called *Trypanosoma brucei* (of which there are three further subtypes), which is transmitted to humans living in tropical Africa by the bite of the tsetse fly. The parasite lives in game animals, cattle and sheep, and a tsetse fly that bites an infected animal carries the infection to other animals it bites, including man.

The patient develops a sore at the site of the tsetse fly bite, followed a few days later by further symptoms that include infected glands, fever, headache, rashes and joint pain. The patient often has periods of two or more weeks when s/he is in perfect health, followed by a recurrence of the symptoms. As the disease progresses, the patient loses weight, becomes very tired and, as the brain becomes involved, wants to sleep constantly. Eventually, the patient becomes comatose and dies. The disease may take many months to run its course.

Travellers to areas of Africa where the disease occurs should avoid tsetse bites by wearing trousers and long-sleeved shirts, and using insect nets at night and an insect repellent by day. There are drugs available to treat the disease, but early treatment is essential to avoid long-term complications. Without treatment, the disease is almost invariably fatal.

Smallpox

Only one disease in mankind's history has been totally eradicated by medical science, and that was smallpox, the last case being in Somalia in 1978. From being one of mankind's most feared diseases, it now rates only a couple of paragraphs as an historical curiosity in medical textbooks due to an intensive world-wide vaccination campaign.

Smallpox was a highly contagious virus infection that caused sores on the skin and was associated with a severe headache and high fever. There was no treatment available, and more than half the patients died. Edward Jenner was the English physician who developed the first smallpox vaccination in the late 1700s. He used cowpox scabs as the vaccinating material, and this gave a cross protection against smallpox.

People in third-world countries who have recovered from smallpox still show the scars of the disease, but once it has run its course, survivors are no longer infectious.

Vaccination against smallpox is no longer necessary for travellers anywhere in the world.

Smoker's foot
See BUERGER'S DISEASE.

Smoking-related diseases
See BRONCHIECTASIS; BUERGER'S DISEASE; EMPHYSEMA; HYPERTENSION; LUNG CANCER; THROMBOSIS.

See also SMOKING, Section 7.

Snake bite
See Section 8.

Snoring
See Section 3.

Sores
See BED SORES; BOIL; SCHOOL SORES.

Spasticity
See CEREBRAL PALSY.

Spider bite
See Section 8.

Spina bifida

The spinal cord runs from the base of the brain, down through the vertebrae that form the back (see Section 2), and ends at about waist level. The spinal cord is responsible for carrying the nervous messages from the brain to the rest of the body, and the bones in the back protect this vital structure. As a foetus in the mother's womb, the growing baby develops its spinal cord and vertebrae from a flat strip of nerve tissue that folds in upon itself lengthwise, and fuses into a rod of nerve tissue. It is then surrounded by the bony arch of the vertebrae. This process occurs in the first three months of pregnancy. Spina bifida is the failure of this process. Usually, it fails to fuse only at the lower part of the spinal cord, and this vital nerve tissue may be left covered by merely a very thin layer of skin. The spinal cord may not work below the level of failed fusion, and victims are often paraplegics (paralysed below the waist — see separate entry). The vertebral arch also fails to fuse and form, and has a double pointed (bifid) appearance on examination.

The cause of spina bifida is unknown, but its incidence is higher in subsequent pregnancies after one child has been born with the condition. It is also more common in those of Irish and Welsh ancestry. In mothers who are at high risk of having a baby with this deformity, a test performed on the amniotic fluid that surrounds the baby in the womb can indicate the condition between the 14th and 16th week of pregnancy.

There are many different degrees of spina bifida, depending upon the severity of the failed fusion. The mildest form, which affects many people, is **spina bifida occulta**, in which only the vertebral arch is affected, and the spinal cord works normally.

A **meningocele** is the next most serious form, and in this there is a protuberant sac at the level of the failed fusion, which contains cerebrospinal fluid only. The spinal cord has some damage and often only transmits some of the necessary nerve messages to the legs and bladder.

Those who have a **meningomyelocele** are paralysed below the level of damage and have no control of their bladder or legs. These babies have a raw, uncovered sac of nerve tissue and cerebrospinal fluid that protrudes onto the surface of the back. There is a significant risk of infection in the spine and brain of these babies, and an operation to close the defect in the back is usually undertaken early in life. Unfortunately, this does not cure the paraplegia — it only stops later complications from developing.

There are a number of other rarer combinations and permutations of failed nerve and bone development in the lower back. Spina bifida may be associated with other birth deformities such as hydrocephalus (see separate entry) and anencephaly (failure of the brain to develop).

There is no cure for spina bifida, but control of the condition enables the sufferers to have a normal life span.

Spinal disease
See BACK DISEASE.

Spleen, ruptured

The spleen is one of the most poorly understood of the body's organs, even by doctors. It weighs about 100 g, and is roughly the same size as your fist. It is shaped rather like an inverted pudding bowl, and is tucked under the last couple of ribs on your left side (see Section 2). It has three main functions. It filters blood to remove damaged cells and store the vital elements, such as iron, that it salvages from these cells. Secondly, it stores the antibodies that the body develops after an infection, so that when a similar infection occurs in the future, the antibodies to attack the infecting germ can be produced and released rapidly. Finally, it helps to produce new white cells that act to fight any infection that enters the body, and red cells to transport oxygen around in the blood stream.

In a car or other accident, the chest may be squashed, and the spleen may be pierced by a rib or ruptured by the pressure. Because it is made of a very large number of blood vessels, it bleeds freely, and this blood loss into the abdomen can be life-threatening. Repairing the spleen surgically is difficult, as it is rather like trying to sew up fine sponge rubber — the stitches tear out of the tissue very easily, and every stitch hole bleeds. As a result, it is sometimes necessary to remove the spleen in order to save the accident victim's life.

The removal of the spleen has remarkably little effect on an adult, as the bone marrow can take over most of its functions. In babies, the situation is rather different, as the spleen is essential for the early formation of blood cells, and it is removed from children only in extreme circumstances, or with some rare diseases.

SPRAIN, JOINT
See SPRAINS, STRAINS AND DISLOCATIONS, Section 8.

SPRUE, NON-TROPICAL
See COELIAC DISEASE.

SPRUE, TROPICAL
Sprue is the failure to absorb fat from the gut, resulting in bulky, frothy, pale, foul-smelling motions. People with sprue are underweight, and as a result of the failed fat absorption, they also fail to absorb vitamins A, D, E and K, which are all soluble in fat.

There are two types of sprue — **tropical sprue** which develops in Westerners who live for prolonged periods in tropical countries, and **coeliac sprue** (see COELIAC DISEASE) which is a defect present from birth, but which may not show up until the child is several years old.

Tropical sprue is characterised by explosive diarrhoea with watery stools, rapid weight loss, indigestion, burping, abdominal cramps and muscle cramps. The diagnosis is made by examination of the faeces, which is found to contain high levels of fat, and by X-rays of the small intestine. Blood tests show a particular type of anaemia.

Tropical sprue is treated by giving tetracycline (an antibiotic — see Section 6) for a week, and folic acid for several months. Further treatment may be required if severe anaemia has developed. Recovery within a few weeks is usual.

SQUAMOUS CELL CARCINOMA
See SKIN CANCER.

SQUINT (STRABISMUS)
The evil eye! That is the way a squint was thought of a century ago. Today, the early diagnosis and correction of this common eye problem prevents lifelong visual problems that cursed sufferers in the past.

A squint (or strabismus, to give it its correct medical name) occurs when the two eyes do not align equally when looking at a distant object. One eye appears to be looking in one direction, while the other is looking in a different direction. This is quite normal when looking at something very close, as both eyes turn in to look at it.

The diagnosis of squint is not as easy as one might expect. A number of normal conditions may mimic a squint, or the eye problem may not be constant and occur only when the child is very tired. One of the commonest reasons for confusion is a child who has a very broad nasal bridge (e.g. in the Chinese), as this may give the false impression that the eyes are not parallel. If a child does have a significant squint, the brain will gradually suppress the sight in one eye to avoid double vision. If the squint remains uncorrected, the affected eye may never learn to see again, resulting in the child becoming blind in that eye. The correction of a squint at an early age is therefore vital.

Once a doctor suspects the diagnosis, he or she will carefully check the eyes to see if there is any specific reason for the squint and may then prescribe special spectacles to correct the problem. Spectacles do not, as is sometimes thought, weaken the vision but are designed to reduce the angle of the squint, thereby curing the condition, provided the spectacles are worn for a sufficient length of time. If the squint is more severe, spectacles alone may not correct it, and eye exercises may be added.

In marked degrees of squint, it is necessary to operate on the child to correct the deformity. This involves changing the tightness of the tiny muscles that control eye movement to shorten those that are not pulling the eye around far enough and/or lengthen those that are pulling the eye around excessively. Although technically a difficult operation, because of the microscopic size of the structures being altered, it is relatively minor surgery for the patient and the success rate is very high.

Unfortunately for parents and their children, the successful management of a squint is a slow process that takes several years rather than months, and there can be a temptation for the patient to become slack in undertaking the correct treatment and to drop follow-up appointments, but for the long-term future vision of the child, good and careful care is essential. Provided the medical advice is followed, the long-term cosmetic and vision results are excellent.

STAMMERING
See STUTTERING.

STAPHYLOCOCCAL INFECTIONS
The bacterium *Staphylococcus aureus* (golden staph) is responsible for infections in the lungs (pneumonia), eye, skin, brain (meningitis), gut and other parts of the body. Most staphylococcal infections are susceptible to antibiotics (see Section 6) such as penicillin and cephalosporins, but in some cases this particular bacterium has mutated to become highly resistant to even the stronger antibiotics. Methicillin is one of the most potent forms of penicillin, and methicillin-resistant staphylococcus aureus (MRSA) is becoming a serious problem, because it is difficult to treat and tends to occur in hospitals where large quantities of antibiotics are used.

A patient who develops MRSA will need to be isolated and nursed in such a way that the hospital staff cannot transmit the infection to other patients (barrier nursing). Most patients with MRSA can be successfully treated, but it may take far longer and require far more potent antibiotics than normal, often given as injections rather than tablets, to achieve this result.

STD
See SEXUALLY TRANSMITTED DISEASE.

STEIN-LEVENTHAL SYNDROME
Women with the Stein-Leventhal syndrome have multiple cysts in their ovaries (polycystic disease of the ovaries) that causes the menstrual periods to stop. Disruption to the normal hormone production by the ovaries also causes sterility, excessive hair growth on the face and body, weight gain, and a loss of breast firmness.

The syndrome is named after the American gynaecologists Irving Stein (born 1887) and Michael Leventhal (born 1901) who first described the condition.

The cause of the syndrome is unknown, but the abnormal levels of hormones can be measured in the bloodstream. The diagnosis is confirmed by an ultrasound scan (see Section 4) of the pelvis which shows the large cyst-filled ovaries.

Treatment will depend upon whether the patient desires to fall pregnant or not. A combination of surgery to remove some of the cysts, hormones to replace those that are not being produced, and ovarian stimulating drugs are used in treatment. Excessive hair growth can be treated separately by using spironolactone or progestagens (see Section 6). Some women who find the discomfort of the condition and the side effects of the medication unacceptable decide to have a total hysterectomy.

There are no serious long-term effects caused by the disease, and control by one means or another is normally achieved.

STEVENS-JOHNSON SYNDROME

Erythema multiforme (see separate entry) is a reaction of the body to drugs, virus infections or other stresses. The Stevens-Johnson syndrome is a severe form of erythema multiforme which is triggered by drugs such as sulpha antibiotics. It is named after the New York paediatrician Albert Mason Stevens (born 1884), and F.C. Johnson (born 1894), an American physician.

Patients with this uncommon syndrome have a widespread red rash that varies in its form, conjunctivitis and ulcers on the eye, a fever, and an ulcerated and painful mouth, nose, anus, urethra and vagina.

Treatment involves removing any offending drug, and large doses of steroids (see Section 6). Unfortunately, despite the best treatment, some patients develop kidney damage which may be fatal.

STILL'S DISEASE
See ARTHRITIS.

STOMACH CANCER

Cancer of the stomach is one of the less common cancers in Australians (4% of all cancers), but it is very common amongst the Japanese. It is more than twice as common in men than women, and usually occurs over the age of 60 years.

It is believed that the consumption of green and yellow vegetables decreases the risk of stomach cancer, but the risk rises in the lower socioeconomic groups and in those who have pernicious anaemia.

Stomach cancer often has mild symptoms, such as indigestion and heartburn, so patients frequently treat themselves with antacids and other medications and do not present to a doctor until the condition is quite advanced. This makes the cancer harder to treat successfully and accounts for the relatively poor long-term cure rate. Other symptoms of stomach cancer include burping, feeling very full in the upper belly, nausea, weight loss and a loss in appetite. Vomiting blood and excreting black faeces are late complications.

The diagnosis is confirmed by gastroscopy (see Section 4), which involves swallowing a tube, through which the doctor can see inside the stomach and take a biopsy (sample) of any suspicious areas. A stomach cancer often looks like, and may be confused with, an ulcer.

The only treatment is surgical removal of the stomach, and the surrounding glands to which the cancer may have spread. The liver is another common site for the spread of the cancer, but once this is involved, a cure is most unlikely. Irradiation may be used as an adjunctive treatment. The five-year survival rate is about 20%.

STOMACH ULCER
See ULCER, PEPTIC.

STOMATITIS
A stoma is any opening into the human body, but in this instance stomatitis refers to an infection of the mouth. Stomatitis may be the result of one or more mouth ulcers (see ULCER, MOUTH), a fungal infection (see THRUSH), viral infection (e.g. herpes) or a bacterial infection.

Fungal infections of the mouth are common in babies and in those who are on antibiotics or taking anti-cancer drugs (cytotoxics). The inside of the mouth and tongue have patches of off-white slough sticking to them, and if this is scratched away, a red sore area is exposed. The infection is often painful and aggravated by sweet or spicy foods. Treatment with anti-fungal drops, ointments or lozenges is rapidly effective.

Viral infections in the mouth include chickenpox (see separate entry), hand foot and mouth disease, and, most seriously, herpes simplex.

Herpes viruses cause painful ulcers that prevent the victim from eating or drinking. In children this may lead to dehydration and malnutrition. The ulcers heal after seven to ten days, and the only treatment is anaesthetic gels.

Herpangina is a special type of stomatitis caused by an organism known as coxsackievirus. It occurs in children under 6 years of age and causes sudden pain in the mouth, fever, difficulty in swallowing, mouth ulcers and grey coloured blisters.

Bacterial infections of the mouth may arise from poor dental hygiene. They cause generalised soreness of the mouth and bad breath. Treatment involves hydrogen peroxide mouth washes and antibiotics.

STONES
See GALL STONES; KIDNEY STONES; SALIVARY STONES.
See also LITHOTRIPSY, Section 6.

STRABISMUS
See SQUINT.

STREPTOCOCCAL INFECTIONS
Beta-haemolytic streptococci are very commonly the cause of infections in humans. They are divided into two major groups — A and B. Group A is responsible for infections in the throat and on the skin. They may have the complication of subsequently causing rheumatic fever and glomerulonephritis (see separate entries). Group B causes some types of genital infections, meningitis and pneumonia.

A specific blood test is available to detect the presence of the A group streptococci anywhere in the body. The B group can be detected by a culture of the blood, sputum or other infected tissue. These infections can be readily treated by antibiotics such as penicillin, erythromycin and cephalosporins (see Section 6).
See also SCARLET FEVER.

STRESS
Mortgage repayments. Marriage strife. Young children. Job security. Your relatives. Family finances. Separation and divorce. Leaving home. Unemployment. Poor health. Work responsibility. Death in the family. All of these, and hundreds of other situations, are causes of stress. Stress is not something new to modern humanity. Stress has always been with us, but the form has changed over the years. Many of the above problems were experienced thousands of years ago, but we at

least do not have to worry about starvation and a life-expectancy half that of today.

Stress can cause a very wide range of physical illnesses. Chronic headaches and peptic ulcers are probably the best known diseases due to stress, but depression, heart disease, migraines, diarrhoea, shortness of breath, sweating, passing excess urine, rashes, vomiting, and a host of other symptoms may be an outward manifestation of inward emotional turmoil.

There are three basic ways to treat stress:

1. The obvious, most successful, but hardest to achieve, is removing the cause of the stress. If your mortgage repayments are in arrears, winning the pools will solve your problems and remove the stress, but this is a solution for the minority, not the majority. Marriage stress is probably one of the most difficult forms of stress to remove, as bitterness and wrangling over children and property may last for many years after the divorce.

2. The next way to deal with stress is to rationalise it. This can involve a combination of several different techniques. Talking is an excellent way of relieving anxiety. Discuss the problem with your spouse, relatives, friends, doctor, priest, work mates or anyone else who will listen. Problems often do not appear as insurmountable once bought into the open.

Writing down the details of the problem is another excellent way of relieving anxiety. An insurmountable problem in your mind often appears more manageable on paper, particularly when all your possible options are diagrammatically attached to it to enable a rational view of the situation to be obtained.

Professional assistance in discussing your problems is also very helpful. This may be given by your own general practitioner (who can often be a friend as well as counsellor), a psychiatrist (not because you may be insane, but because they have specialist skills in this area), a psychologist, marriage guidance counsellor, child guidance officer or social worker. Many people are reluctant to seek this type of assistance, but it is far preferable to the third type of treatment for stress — drugs.

3. Drugs that alter your mood, sedate or relieve anxiety are very successful in dealing with stress, but should only be used in a crisis, intermittently or for short periods of time. Some antidepressant drugs and treatments for psychiatric conditions are designed for long-term use, but most of the anxiety-relieving drugs can cause dependency if used regularly. When prescribed and taken correctly, they act as a very useful crutch to help patients through a few weeks of extreme stress, and allow them to cope until such time as the cause of the stress is removed or counselling can be started.

See also ANXIETY NEUROSIS.

STROKE (CEREBROVASCULAR ACCIDENT, CVA)

Strokes are the third major cause of death in Australia after heart disease and cancer. The risk of developing a stroke is higher in those who smoke, have high blood pressure, high cholesterol levels in their blood, are diabetic, and drink alcohol to excess.

Doctors technically refer to a stroke as a cerebrovascular accident (CVA). This translates as an accident involving the blood vessels in the brain. If a clot, or piece of material from elsewhere in the body blocks an artery in the brain, or if an artery burst in the brain, a stroke may occur.

Because any blood vessel in the brain can be involved, almost any part of the brain may be damaged, and the area damaged determines the adverse effects in the normal operation of that person's body.

The symptoms of a stroke can therefore be many and varied.

If a motor area of the brain which controls movement is affected, the patient becomes paralysed down the opposite side of the body. This occurs because the nerves supplying the body cross over to the opposite side at the base of the brain. Thus the right side of the brain controls the left arm and leg. Other victims may lose their memory or power of speech, or may become uncoordinated, unbalanced, start fitting or any of several dozen other possibilities.

Both the ambulance and the family general practitioner should be called when someone suffers a stroke. The GP will be able to stabilise the patient for the trip to hospital where investigations will begin. The GP can also answer the many questions which the family will certainly ask and can help them cope with a very stressful situation.

Doctors can often work out which part of the brain is involved by analysing the patient's complaints. More information about the stroke can be obtained with special X-rays, CT scans and magnetic resonance imaging (see Section 4), blood tests, tests on the fluid around the brain, and measuring the brain waves electrically. Using these techniques, a specialist physician can determine the precise cause of the stroke and commence the appropriate treatment.

Surgery to the bleeding or blocked artery in the brain may be necessary in some cases, particularly if the stroke and resultant brain damage worsen.

When it comes to treatment, a wait-and-watch attitude is adopted in most cases, with medication given to protect the patient from any further damage to other vital organs.

The brain unfortunately does not repair itself, but it can often find different ways of doing a task and bypassing the damaged areas. This is where paramedical therapists are vital to the person's eventual recovery. Physiotherapists, speech pathologists and occupational therapists will start treating the victim as soon as possible after arrival in hospital.

The biggest changes are usually noted in the first week. The patient may recover completely and have no residual disability. Some impairment is all too often left behind, and occasionally a steady deterioration may lead to death or a permanent semi-comatose state. Those patients who become unconscious during a stroke generally have a poorer outcome than those who do not.

Recovery may take months, and attendance at therapy clinics and constant encouragement from family and friends during this stage is essential to maintain the patient's optimism and self esteem. Nothing is worse for a person than to be fully intelligent and aware of what is happening, but to look a fool because he is drooling, unable to speak, and uncoordinated. Stroke victims with these problems become extremely depressed because they are treated as idiots and everyone speaks to them in baby talk.

If a relative has a stroke, it will be several days or even weeks before doctors will be able to give you an accurate idea as to the final outcome. Keep in contact with your GP and the specialists involved during this time so that appropriate advice about the patient's rehabilitation can be given.

See also TRANSIENT ISCHAEMIC ATTACK.

Stuttering (stammering)

Stuttering is the involutary repetition of a sound during speech. The speaker is unable to proceed past a certain point in speech for some seconds but eventually overcomes the barrier, and the remaining part of the sentence or phrase comes out in a rush.

The cause of stuttering is unknown, but it tends to start with the commencement of speech between two and four years of age. It is more common in boys than girls, and more likely if one parent is or was a stutterer. Some experts believe that enotional insecurity, anxiety and disturbances in childhood can be a trigger for stuttering, but this theory is not accepted by all. It may be that the insecurity and anxiety is caused by the stammer, rather than the converse. An association between left-right confusion and stuttering has also been noted.

If the person is tense, hurried or confused, the stammer will be worse. Helping a stammerer to finish a sentence only agitates him/her more and worsens the problem with the next sentence. The consonants are the usual blocks for stammerers, and the letters 'p' and 'b' are the most commonly involved.

Interestingly, stammerers can usually sing without stammering, even if it is a sentence they had been totally unable to complete previously. Some stammerers use a sing-song cadence to their speech pattern to overcome their problem, and speech pathologists may use singing as a starting point in their treatment of stuttering. A metronome may also be used during treatment to correctly pace the speech patterns.

Treatment involves assessment by a paediatrician to exclude any of the rare underlying brain conditions that may contribute to stuttering, followed by long-term treatment by a speech pathologist. Psychologists and/or psychiatrists may also be involved in counselling at intervals through this treatment.

Other than brief use of minor anti-anxiety drugs, no medication can help stuttering, but given persistence over many months or years, most patients can learn to cope with their disorder with the dedicated assistance of a speech pathologist.

STY (EXTERNAL HORDEOLUM)

A sty is a bacterial infection of one of the tiny sweat or oil glands on the margin of the eyelid. The oil glands (called glands of Zeiss) keep the eyelashes moist and lubricated. There is often no apparent reason for a sty developing, but rubbing the eye, or an injury to the eye, makes it easier for a sty to develop. The infected gland becomes painful, red and swollen, and fills with pus. A sty is really a miniature abscess.

Treatment of sties involves the use of frequent warm compresses to the eye, and antibiotic ointment under the upper eyelid. A persistent sty can be incised by a doctor to drain away the pus it contains.

SUBDURAL HAEMATOMA
See HEAD INJURY.

SUDDEN INFANT DEATH SYNDROME
See COT DEATH.

SUGAR DIABETES
See DIABETES MELLITUS; HYPOGLYCAEMIA.

SUICIDE ATTEMPT

Suicide is eighth in importance as a cause of all deaths in Australia, but in young adults it is placed far higher in the rankings. Suicide attempts are at least ten times more common than successful suicides, and twice as many women as men attempt suicide, but men are three times more successful in committing suicide than women. Men are more likely to use violent means of suicide (e.g. gun, jumping) than women.

Suicide may be triggered by an emotional crisis such as divorce, death of a close family member, loss of a job, financial crisis or as a result of some other form of rejection. Alcoholism makes suicide attempts more likely, and the sudden excessive use of alcohol in an already stressed or depressed person is cause for considerable concern. Those who live alone and who have poor general health are also at a higher risk than the average person.

Those who contemplate suicide often provide clues of their intentions to those around them, but unfortunately these clues are sometimes not obvious enough, or they are ignored. The saying 'many a truth is told in jest' may hold true in this case, and a person who jokes about 'ending it all', or that the family is 'better off without me', may well be trying to judge the reaction of others to this idea. Other similar conversational clues to a possible suicide attempt may be introduced in the third person by expressing ideas such as 'my friend often talks of suicide' or 'did you read about that suicide in the paper today'. Further clues that a suicide attempt is possible will include changes in behaviour such as giving away prized possessions, enquiring about cremations, or sudden changes in religious attitudes and investigating alternative religions to the one which the person has traditionally followed. A decision to attempt suicide may be a long slow process over many weeks or months, in which cases clues may be identified and a doctor alerted, so that appropriate treatment may be given. In other circumstances, a sudden bout of deep depression may result in the decision to suicide being made in a matter of minutes, and in this situation medical intervention is almost impossible.

Once there is reasonable suspicion that an individual may attempt suicide, action must be taken to prevent that attempt. In most cases that means involving a medical practitioner (usually the person's general practitioner) by making him or her aware of the clues that have been noticed. The doctor will then take all possible measures to ensure that the person is treated and counselled appropriately. No-one can be forced to undergo medical treatment, but if the doctor's efforts to persuade the person to accept treatment are unsuccessful, and if the doctor is convinced that a suicide attempt is imminent, documents may be signed to allow the person to be taken into a hospital for further assessment and treatment. The rules governing this procedure vary from state to state, and it is a measure that is undertaken only as a last resort.

If the patient accepts treatment, it will involve doctors in counselling the patient about the problems he or she faces and how to overcome them, and medication to correct the biochemical imbalance in the brain that may be causing depression (see separate entry). Suicides can be prevented, and the patients can be successfully treated so that they can lead a happy and productive life for many years to come, but the early involvement of general practitioners and psychiatrists is essential.

See also Section 8.

SUNBURN
See BURNS.
See also Section 8.

SVT (SUPERFICIAL VENOUS THROMBOSIS)
See THROMBOSIS.

SWEATING, EXCESSIVE
Damp armpits, stained shorts, and a moist forehead — excess sweating can be a curse to those afflicted. The many possible causes of excessive sweating are covered in Section 3. Any course of treatment must deal with these factors first. However, if

the victim has no apparent cause, but merely excessive numbers of sweat glands or overactive sweat glands, other treatments are available.

The 'roll-on' type preparations available from supermarkets and chemists should be tried first. If these are unsuccessful, doctors can prescribe a number of more potent lotions or tablets. In those who are severely afflicted, surgical techniques to cut the nerves supplying the sweat glands in the armpits, totally removing the armpit sweat glands, or using a process known as iontophoresis to neutralise the sweat glands may be tried. Although they sound rather radical, they are often very successful techniques and can give remarkable relief.

See also Section 3.

SWIMMER'S EAR
See OTITIS EXTERNA.

SYNOVITIS
A synovial membrane lines all joint cavities, covering all surfaces within the joint except those where the weight-bearing cartilage is present. This membrane secretes a lubricating fluid (the synovial fluid) which acts as the 'oil' within a joint, and allows it to move smoothly and freely. If the synovial membrane becomes inflamed, the patient has synovitis.

Synovitis is usually associated with the excessive secretion of synovial fluid into the joint to cause swelling, restricted movement, pain and sometimes redness and heat in the joint. Any joint in the body may be involved, but the hip, knee and ankle are the most commonly affected ones.

Synovitis may be caused by a bacterial infection, injury to the joint, rheumatoid arthritis, tuberculosis (now rare), gonorrhoea (see separate entry) or other infecting organisms.

Treatment of synovitis involves dealing with the cause (e.g. giving antibiotics for a bacterial infection) and resting the joint until the pain and swelling subside. Patients may have the joint strapped and supported, i.e., may have an arm in a sling, or use crutches if a leg joint is involved. If left untreated, permanent damage to the joint may occur, or arthritis may develop prematurely.

See also PIGMENTED VILLONODULAR SYNOVITIS.

SYPHILIS
Syphilis is a potentially fatal sexually transmitted disease caused by a bacterium (spirochete) called *Treponema pallidum*. The same organism causes another disease called yaws (see separate entry) which is transmitted by close body contact (but not necessarily sexual contact). There is some argument about whether Columbus brought syphilis back with him from America, or whether yaws developed into a sexually transmitted disease at this time because of improving hygiene and housing in Europe.

Syphilis is transmitted from one person to another by heterosexual or homosexual contact, or it may pass in the blood from an infected person with the use of shared needles or blood transfusions. All blood donations in Australia are tested to prevent this last form of transmission. The disease can also be transmitted from the mother to her child during pregnancy to cause congenital syphilis.

Congenital syphilis is one of the greatest medical tragedies and occurs when a woman with active syphilis becomes pregnant. A newborn infant of such a mother may suffer from any one of a number of problems, including teeth abnormalities, deafness, misshapen bones, deformed nose, pneumonia, and mental retardation. The child is infectious when born and may develop more serious problems if the condition is not treated aggressively with antibiotics. Unfortunately, many of the defects suffered by these children cannot be cured, but plastic surgeons may correct the more obvious ones. To prevent this problem, all pregnant women are routinely tested for syphilis in the early months of pregnancy.

An infection with **acquired syphilis** passes through three main stages in a victim over many months or years. In its first stage, syphilis causes a sore (chancre) on the penis, the female genitals, or around the anus of homosexuals. This sore is painless, and heals itself after three to six weeks. There may be painless enlarged glands present in the armpit and groin that also disappear with time.

This is followed a few weeks or months later by a second stage that is characterised by a widespread rash, mouth and vaginal ulcers, and a slight fever. The patient is highly infectious at this stage and can easily pass on the disease to a sexual contact. The patient will usually recover from this stage and enter a latent period that may last many years. Complications that may develop during the rash stage include spread of the infection to involve the joints, brain, liver and kidney. These organs may be severely damaged and cause further symptoms in the patient.

After the latent stage, a relapsing stage with further attacks of the second stage may occur, but more commonly a third stage develops. In the third stage, which may occur many years after the other stages, tumours (gumma) develop in the liver, major arteries, bones, brain, skin and other organs. Depending upon the areas affected, the patient may develop many varying symptoms.

In the liver, cirrhosis and blockage of the bile ducts may lead to liver failure and jaundice. If arteries are involved, they can weaken to form aneurysms (see separate entry), dilate to cause pressure on other vital structures, and rupture to cause strokes, heart attacks and massive lethal internal bleeding. In the bones and joints, third-stage syphilis causes arthritis, bone weakness and severe bone pain. The skin and membranes in the mouth, nose and vagina may develop ulcers, scars and nodules that damage the tissue underneath them. These can spread down the larynx and into the lungs.

The brain is the most severely affected organ in long-standing syphilis, and here there are many different complications, including degeneration of the spinal cord to cause paralysis, blindness, headaches, muscle spasms, vomiting, confusion, insanity and death.

Syphilis is obviously not a pleasant disease to develop, and it is vital to diagnose its presence and treat it at an early stage. It can be diagnosed at all stages by one or more of a number of blood tests, or by finding the responsible bacteria on a swab taken from a genital sore in the first stage of the disease. The blood tests can show whether a person has ever had syphilis in their life, and whether they are still infectious. In advanced cases of third-stage syphilis, tests may also be carried out on the fluid around the brain (the cerebrospinal fluid).

Treatment of syphilis is highly effective, but only in the first two stages. Once the third stage of the disease has developed, any organ damage caused is irreversible. Treatment at this stage can merely prevent further damage. Penicillin (often as an injection) is the mainstay of treatment, but other antibiotics (see Section 6) such as tetracycline and erythromycin may also be used. A course of antibiotics for a few weeks almost invariably cures the disease.

Because of the availability of effective antibiotics, the incidence of syphilis dropped markedly in the 1950s and 1960s, but in recent years its incidence is starting to rise again, particularly amongst homosexuals and prostitutes.

Systemic lupus erythematosus
See LUPUS ERYTHEMATOSUS, SYSTEMIC.

Tachycardia
See PAROXYSMAL ATRIAL TACHYCARDIA.
See also HEARTBEAT, FAST, Section 3.

Talcosis
See PNEUMOCONIOSIS.

Tapeworms (cestodes)
The tapeworm is so called because it is divided into segments in much the same way as a tape measure. At one end there is a head (scolex) that has a large sucker on it, and this is used to attach the worm to the inside of the gut. Six different types of tapeworm can infect man, and they vary in length from half a centimetre (dwarf tapeworm) to more than 25 m (beef tapeworm). Tapeworms are unknown in Australia, but different types may be caught in almost every other part of the world.

The mature tapeworm lives in the gut of humans or other animals. Segments that are full of eggs are constantly dropping off from the end of the worm and are passed out with the faeces. These eggs remain in the soil until eaten by another animal. When the egg is swallowed, it hatches an embryo that burrows into the muscle of the animal and remains there for the rest of that animal's life. If the animal's flesh is eaten, the embryo enters the gut of the new host, attaches to the inside wall of the gut, and grows into a mature tapeworm.

Tapeworm embryos may be found in the flesh of cattle, pigs, and fish. The tiny embryos are destroyed by cooking, and can only survive to infect a human if raw or partly cooked meat is eaten. Less common tapeworms can be transmitted by fleas and other insects from rats and dogs to man, and another uncommon form passes directly from the gut of one human to another through faeces and contaminated food.

There may be no symptoms of a tapeworm infestation until the numbers of worms present is quite high. At this stage nausea, diarrhoea, abdominal discomfort, hunger, weight loss and tiredness may occur. The presence of tapeworms can be confirmed by examining the faeces under a microscope for the presence of eggs. Sometimes patients find segments of the worm in their underclothes or bedding.

Medications are available to rid the gut of tapeworm. Except for the rare cases where the embryo stage spreads to the brain, there are no long-term complications after treatment.

TB
See TUBERCULOSIS.

Tendonitis
See TENOSYNOVITIS AND TENDONITIS.

Tennis elbow (lateral epicondylitis)
Sport is part of the Australian way of life, and those sports requiring skill with club or racquet are increasing in popularity at a rapid rate. As a consequence, injuries in tennis, golf, squash and similar sports are also increasing, mainly in the form of overstraining parts of the body which are exposed to excessive stress. The most common of these injuries, and one of the most difficult to treat, is tennis elbow, or lateral epicondylitis.

To be more precise, tennis elbow occurs when the forearm muscle tendon that runs around the outside of the elbow is inflamed. If the tendon on the inside of the elbow is involved, the disease is called **golfer's elbow**. These injuries, which are due to excessive bending and twisting movements of the arm, can occur in tradesmen who undertake repetitive tasks, housewives, musicians and many others who may put excessive strain on their elbows.

In tennis, the injury is more likely if the backhand action is faulty, with excessive wrist action and insufficient follow-through. Being unfit, having a tautly strung racquet, a heavy racquet and wet balls all add to the strain on the elbow.

It is not normally one hit that strains the elbow tendon, but repeated episodes of overstretching that tear the minute fibres in the tendon. This leads to scarring in the tissues, which is then broken down again by further strains. Eventually, painful inflammation occurs, which can be constant or may only occur when the elbow is moved or strained. The whole forearm can ache in some patients, especially when trying to grip or twist with the hand.

Tennis elbow is not easy to treat, and it can easily become chronic. Rest is the most important component, and quite prolonged rest may be necessary. Exercises to strengthen the elbow are also important, and anti-inflammatory drugs may be used in the acute stage. Cortisone injections may be useful in resistant cases.

The strengthening exercises are best done under the supervision of a doctor or physiotherapist, because it is easy to do too much too soon. Generally, they involve using your wrist to raise and lower a weight, the palm facing down in tennis elbow, but facing up in golfer's elbow.

Some players find pressure pads over the tendon, or elbow guards (elastic tubes around the elbow) help relieve the symptoms and prevent recurrences by adding extra support to this rather vulnerable joint.

TENOSYNOVITIS AND TENDONITIS

Tendons are the ropes of the body. They connect a muscle to a bone so that when a muscle contracts, the bone is pulled by the tendon. The tendons run inside a fibrous sheath in many parts of the body, particularly the hands and feet. Between the sheath and the tendon is a very thin film of lubricating oil called synovial fluid. Tenosynovitis is an inflammation of the sheath around a tendon, and tendonitis is inflammation of a tendon itself. These conditions usually occur due to overuse or injury. Whenever you see the suffix '- itis' after a word, it means inflammation. Thus appendicitis is an inflamed appendix, tonsillitis is an inflamed tonsil, and tendonitis is an inflamed tendon.

If you start at a new job, sport or hobby, it is possible to use tendons (and muscles) that cannot adequately withstand the new type of repetitive strain. This will result in inflammation and pain in the tendon. It may also be caused by one sudden overstretching injury of the tendon. The primary treatment of both conditions is rest. The affected part may be strapped, bandaged or even plastered to ensure adequate rest of the tendon. Anti-inflammatory medicines (NSAIDs — see Section 6) may also be used along with physiotherapy. Physiotherapy is particularly valuable on return to work to prevent a recurrence of the problem. In severe or chronic cases, injections of steroids may be given, but these cannot be repeated too frequently. With tenosynovitis, a last resort is an operation to remove the tendon sheath.

See also REPETITIVE STRAIN INJURY.

TENSION HEADACHE
See HEADACHE, MUSCLE SPASM.

TERATOMA
See OVARIAN CANCER.

Section 5: Diseases

Testicular disease

A man's testes and a woman's ovaries both start life together inside the abdomen of a foetus. Just before the birth of a boy, the testes start migrating through the wall of the lower abdomen to settle in the scrotum, while in a girl the ovaries remain behind in the abdomen to lie beside the womb. As they migrate through the muscles, fat and fibrous tissue of the abdominal wall, the testes trail behind them the arteries, veins, nerves and sperm tube that connect them to the body and keep them nourished and healthy. These pass through a tube called the inguinal canal back into the abdomen. This canal remains a point of weakness in the muscles of a man, and an inguinal hernia (see separate entry) may develop there later in life. Once in the scrotum, the left testicle hangs lower than the right, except in some dominant left-handed men where the reverse is true. This uneven appearance of the testes worries many teenage boys, but is completely normal.

In babies, the testes may move back towards the abdomen quite easily, but as they mature, this occurs less and less. The testes require a slightly lower temperature than the rest of the body to operate effectively, and this is why they are placed in the scrotum where they are not as readily exposed to body heat. In very hot weather, the supporting muscle of the testes relaxes, letting them drop further away from the body. In cold weather the reverse is true, and the muscle draws them higher up in the scrotum to keep them warm. Testes that are kept too hot (e.g. cyclists wearing tight clothing) do not function effectively, and the man may be sterile until the testes cool down for a few weeks.

All men should be aware of the functioning and problems possible with this private organ, and parents should be very aware of a teenage son who may be too embarrassed to discuss a problem he may be having, a problem that could vitally affect his future.

Several diseases may occur in the testes, and these will be discussed below.

Hydrocele

A common testicular problem from infancy to adult life is a hydrocele. This is a collection of fluid around the testicle. It is painless and there is no discomfort, but the testicle may slowly enlarge to two or three times its normal size.

The testes are surrounded by a fine layer of tissue called the tunica vaginalis. Fluid may accumulate between the testes and the tunica to cause an apparent swelling of the testicle. Hydroceles may enlarge to the size of a tennis ball or more, but cause no permanent damage to the testicle or its function. The problem may occur at almost any age, and may follow an injury or infection in the scrotum, or may occur for no apparent reason. In infants the problem sometimes settles without treatment, but in adults a needle can be used to drain off the fluid. Unfortunately the fluid often re-accumulates, and a minor surgical procedure may be necessary to drain off the excess fluid and give a permanent cure.

There are other cysts and growths that can occur in the scrotum, including cancer, which may not be painful. For this reason, any swelling of the testes, whether painful or not, must be checked by a doctor.

Testicular cancer

Any firm lump, hardening of the testicle or gradual enlargement of the organ may be due to testicular cancer. There is often no pain, and as a result, patients may not see a doctor until the condition is quite advanced. One unusual symptom that is sometimes associated with testicular cancer is the patient's development of small breasts. About 350 men every year in Australia develop this condition, so it is not a particularly common form of cancer. It most commonly occurs in the early adult and middle-aged men.

There are several different types of cancer that can develop in the testes. These include embryomas, seminomas (most common and least serious), choriocarcinoma, teratomas (in which unusual types of tissue may be found), and a number of others. Most are relatively responsive to treatment, so the overall cure rate is close to 90%. Testicular cancer may spread to the lymph glands in the groin, and if left untreated eventually reach the lungs and liver.

Some types of cancer can be detected by blood tests, but any hard lump in the scrotum must be surgically examined to determine the exact cause. Treatment involves removing the affected testicle and the nearby lymph glands. This may be followed by irradiation or cytotoxic drugs (see Section 6) depending upon the type of cancer present.

Testicular infection
See EPIDIDYMO-ORCHITIS.

Testicular torsion
If a testicle, hanging from its network of veins, arteries and nerves, twists horizontally, these vital connections to the body may have undue pressure placed upon them, and the blood supply to the testicle can be cut off. This is torsion of the testis, and the testis will die unless the tubes are surgically untwisted.

Torsion of the testes is a medical emergency, and treatment delayed for more than 12 hours can have serious consequences. The victim experiences pain, and the testes become red, swollen and tender. This problem usually occurs in teenage boys, and is almost unknown over 30 years of age. Any such symptoms should result in immediately seeing a doctor.

Infection of the testes can also occur (see epididymo-orchitis), and may be confused with torsion, but the pain is usually less severe, the patient is febrile and both testes may be involved.

See also MORGAGNI, HYDATID OF.

Undescended testes
The migration of the testes from inside the abdomen to outside in the scrotum has occurred in 97% of boys by the time they are born, but it may be delayed in premature babies. If this migration fails to occur and the testes remain inside the abdomen, the child is suffering from undescended testes.

One or both testes may not descend, and in some little boys the testes may appear undescended but can be found in the groin and manipulated into the scrotum by gentle finger movements. In this latter case, no treatment is usually required, but the testes must be checked regularly to ensure that they do eventually descend by themselves.

A testicle that remains undescended will eventually fail to function due to overheating, and if both testes are involved, sterility will result. Long-term problems of undescended testes include the increased likelihood of inguinal hernias, torsion of the testicle and the development of cancer of the testicle.

If the testes do not descend by themselves in the first few years of life, an operation to place them in the correct position in the scrotum is necessary.

TETANUS (LOCKJAW)
Tetanus is a disease, the seeds of which are in the soil around us. Tetanus is not restricted to the third-world nations of Asia and Africa but is also present in Australia. It causes the death of nearly half the people who catch it, and causes excruciating pain from muscle spasms triggered by

the slightest noise. We are fortunate in Australia to have access to vaccinations which prevent this terrible disease, and the number of people who catch it is not therefore high. In less fortunate countries, the population is not as well educated and medical services are not as readily available. Thousands of people die a terrifying and tortured death because of the unavailability of a simple vaccine.

A bacterium called *Clostridium tetani* can live quite harmlessly in the gut of many animals, particularly horses. When it passes out of their bodies in faeces it forms a hard microscopic cyst which then contaminates the soil and waits for a chance to return to active life. The bacterium can remain inactive for many years until it enters a cut or wound in the dirt or dust that may be around when the tissues are exposed. Once it has infected a cut, it starts multiplying and produces a chemical which is absorbed into the bloodstream and spreads throughout the body. This chemical (a toxin) attacks the small muscles used for chewing our food, making it difficult to open the mouth. Thus the common name for tetanus is lockjaw. The toxin gradually attacks larger and larger muscles, irritating them and causing them to go into severe spasm. These spasms are similar to the cramps you may experience in your leg at night, except they are more severe and can attack every muscle in your body. The patient remains conscious throughout the disease, but eventually the muscles which control breathing and the heart are affected, and the patient dies.

There are very few effective treatments for tetanus, because although the bacteria may be killed, the toxin remains in the body.

All children should have a series of vaccinations known as triple antigen at two, four, six and 18 months of age. This contains vaccines against whooping cough and diphtheria as well as tetanus. A further booster is given prior to school entry at five years of age. Adults are still at risk. The tetanus vaccine does not give lifelong protection, and revaccination is necessary every ten years.

If you have a wound likely to be contaminated by tetanus, the vaccination should be given again after only five years. Deep wounds, such as treading on a nail, are particularly likely to cause tetanus.

The tetanus vaccine is one of the smallest and least painful injections of all, and it has no side effects. There are no excuses for you and your children not being adequately protected.

THALASSAEMIA

Thalassaemia is a blood disease that may cause severe anaemia. It is found in people who live in an area that stretches across Europe and Asia from southern Italy to Malaya, and in some Negro tribes. It is a genetically transmitted disease (passes from one generation to the next), and occurs in two main forms, minor and major. There are a number of further subdivisions.

Thalassaemia minor

Thalassaemia minor is only an inconvenience and is the most common form of the disease. There is only slight anaemia present, and usually no symptoms. Blood tests can be used to determine whether a person has the condition.

If someone with thalassaemia minor marries a normal person, half their children have the chance of having thalassaemia minor. If two people with thalassaemia minor marry, one quarter of their children will have the far more serious and disabling disease of thalassaemia major. One half will have thalassaemia minor, and the other quarter will be normal.

Those with a family history of the disease should arrange through their GP to have the tests to see if they have the minor form of the disease. If a person does have thalassaemia minor, any likely marriage partner should also have the same test. They can then decide on their future.

Thalassaemia major
Patients with thalassaemia major are very anaemic, weak, and susceptible to other diseases. They lead a very restricted life as a result. These children grow slowly, require blood transfusions for the severe anaemia, develop large livers and spleens, and may become jaundiced (yellow).

The heart is put under great strain trying to cope with supplying adequate amounts of oxygen to a body with severe anaemia, and usually becomes very enlarged. Death from heart failure, infection or other complications is common in early adult life.

The exact outcome in any patient will depend upon which subtype of the disease they have.

THROAT INFECTION
See PHARYNGITIS.

THROMBOANGIITIS OBLITERANS
See BUERGER'S DISEASE.

THROMBOSIS
A thrombus occurs when blood clots inside a vein or artery, partially or completely blocking it. If a thrombus occurs in an artery supplying the heart muscle, a heart attack (see separate entry) occurs. If an artery in the brain is affected, the patient suffers a stroke (see separate entry). The heart, brain and lung (see EMBOLISM, LUNG) are the organs most seriously affected by an arterial thrombosis, but any part of the body may be involved.

Thrombosis in an artery may be caused by an injury, prolonged immobility, hardening of the arteries from cholesterol deposits (atherosclerosis), cancer, operations and a number of rarer conditions.

A **deep venous thrombosis** (DVT) in one of the veins inside the calf or thigh muscles is another serious form of thrombosis. The blood returns from the feet to the heart through two sets of veins — a superficial set that is just under the skin and may dilate to form varicose veins (see separate entry), and a deep set that lie under and in the muscles of the leg. These two systems connect with each other at numerous points.

Patients may develop a DVT after surgery, with heart failure and poor circulation, due to cancer or varicose veins, or as an uncommon side effect of oral contraceptives. The symptoms include pain and tightness in the calf which is worse when walking.

If the clot in the veins becomes fragile, small pieces can break off and travel through the larger veins in the trunk to the heart and then into the lungs. In the lungs, the arteries supplying the blood become steadily smaller, until the piece of clot blocks off one of them. The part of the lung beyond this blockage in the artery then dies. This is a lung embolism, which is a serious complication of a DVT. In some cases, there are no signs of the condition in the legs, and the diagnosis is made only when the pulmonary embolism occurs.

If a DVT is found, the patient will be put on anticoagulant drugs (see Section 6), the legs will be elevated, firm elastic stockings will be applied and strict bed rest enforced. In complex or persistent cases surgery will be undertaken to remove the clot or prevent its spread to the lungs.

Prevention is always better than cure, and patients having major operations may be given special stockings to wear during and after the operation, the foot of the bed

Section 5: Diseases

can be elevated, and leg exercises encouraged. Women who have had blood clots anywhere in the body should not use the contraceptive pill.

With appropriate treatment, most patients with deep venous thrombosis recover in four to six weeks without complications.

A **superficial venous thrombosis (SVT)** is not nearly as severe. The affected vein becomes red, hard and tender, and may follow an injury to the area, an intravenous drip insertion, or other disease.

Treatment of an SVT involves heat, rest of the limb, and the use of aspirin or other anti-inflammatory medication (NSAID — see Section 6). Recovery without complications in a week or two is normal.

Thrush (Candidiasis, Moniliasis)

Thrush, also known as candidiasis or moniliasis, is a fungal infection caused by *Candida albicans*. It is a distant cousin to the fungus that can grow on rotting food. *Candida* can cause infections in many different areas, but the most common are the mouth and the vagina. The mouth infections usually occur in babies, but it is the vaginal form that causes the greatest problem.

Oral thrush

A mouth (oral) infection caused by *Candida albicans* is quite common in infancy, particularly in those babies who are bottle-fed. The mouth develops grey/white patches on the tongue, gums and inside of the cheeks. Unlike milk curd, these patches cannot be rubbed away with a finger tip or cotton bud. The infection may spread down into the gullet, and emerge from the anus to infect the skin around the bottom, where it causes a bright red rash that is slightly paler towards the centre of the rash.

Oral thrush may be triggered by a course of antibiotics that destroys the 'good' bacteria in the mouth that normally control the growth of excess fungi.

Treatment involves the use of antifungal drops or ointments (see Section 6) in the mouth, and antifungal creams around the bottom. Complications are rare, and most babies respond rapidly to the correct treatment.

Vaginal thrush

Tight jeans, pantihose, the contraceptive pill, nylon bathers, antibiotics and sex. All these have one thing in common — they are the common aggravating factors involved in catching the modern woman's curse of vaginal thrush.

The fungus *Candida albicans* lives in the gut where it causes little or no trouble. Usually when it comes out on to the skin around the anus, it dies off; but if that skin is warm, moist and irritated, it can grow and spread forward to the lips of the vagina (the vulva). A warm climate and these aggravating factors give the area between a woman's legs the right degree of warmth, moisture and irritation to make the spread of the fungus relatively easy. Antibiotics aggravate the problem because, as well as killing infecting bacteria, they can kill off the bacteria that normally keep the number of fungi under control. Entry of the fungus into the vagina from the skin outside is aided by the mechanical action of sex and by the alteration in the acidity of the vagina caused by the contraceptive pill.

Once established, this fungus causes an unpleasant white vaginal discharge, intense itching of the vulva and surrounding skin, and often inflammation of the urine opening so that passing urine causes discomfort. The almost irresistible, but socially unacceptable itch is what drives most patients to the doctor.

The treatment of vaginal thrush revolves around antifungal vaginal pessaries (tablets), vaginal creams and antifungal oral tablets. These can give rapid relief, and are given in a course that can vary from one to ten days depending on the severity of the infection and the method of treatment used. Unfortunately, many women have repeated attacks, and this is due to inadequate treatment, contamination from the gut, or reinfection from their sex partner. The husband/boyfriend must also be treated with a cream, because although he may show no signs of the infection, it may be present under his foreskin, and he can give the thrush back to the woman after she has been successfully treated.

Thrush rarely causes serious medical problems, but because of its troublesome nature, it should always be treated promptly and effectively.

Women can prevent vaginal thrush infections by wearing loose cotton panties, drying the genital area carefully after swimming or showering, avoiding tight clothing, wiping from front to back after going to the toilet and not using tampons when an infection is likely. Even using all these measures, it is a fortunate woman who avoids catching thrush at some time in her life.

See also FUNGAL INFECTIONS.

THYROID CANCER

The thyroid gland sits in the front of the neck between the Adam's apple and the top of the breast bone (see Section 2). It produces a hormone that controls the metabolic rate of the body. Cancer of the thyroid gland is usually detected as a painless lump in the gland, and may not concern a patient until it is quite large. The cancer does not normally interfere with the workings of the gland until it is very advanced, and so there are no other symptoms in the early stages, and the cancer cannot be detected by a blood test.

For these reasons, any hard lump in the thyroid gland is considered to be a cancer until proved otherwise. The proof usually involves scanning the thyroid gland with radioactive iodine (^{131}I), taking a biopsy (sample) of the lump through a needle, or removing the lump surgically.

Several different types of cancer are possible in the thyroid, and the treatment and outcome will depend upon the type present. Anaplastic carcinoma of the thyroid has the worst prognosis and usually proceeds rapidly to death, while papillary tumours rarely are fatal. Depending upon the type, the cancer may spread to surrounding lymph glands, bone, liver and other tissues.

The main form of treatment for all types of thyroid cancer is surgery, but irradiation and cytotoxic drugs (see Section 6) may be added in some cases.

THYROID DISEASE
See CRETINISM; HYPERTHYROIDISM; HYPOTHYROIDISM; THYROID CANCER.

THYROTOXICOSIS
See HYPERTHYROIDISM.

TIA
See TRANSIENT ISCHAEMIC ATTACK.

TIC DOULOUREUX
See TRIGEMINAL NEURALGIA.

TICK BITE
See Section 8.

TIETZE'S SYNDROME (COSTOCHONDRAL SYNDROME, ANTERIOR CHEST WALL SYNDROME)
Tietze's syndrome is a relatively common condition which tends to mimic the pain

of a heart attack but can be easily differentiated from this far more serious condition by a doctor.

The ribs sweep around the chest from the backbone towards the breast bone (sternum) but stop a few centimetres short. The ribs are joined to the breast bone by a strip of cartilage. The point where the cartilage joins onto the rib is called the costochondral joint (or junction) and it is inflammation at this point that causes Tietze's syndrome.

Alexander Tietze (born 1864) was a German surgeon who first described this inflammation of the costochondral joint that results in painful, tender swellings of the cartilage. The second rib is most commonly involved, but any rib, and any number of ribs may be involved. The cause of the disease is unknown.

Patients with Tietze's syndrome are usually in middle life, and there is normally only one attack of this painful but harmless condition. It will settle spontaneously in two weeks to six months, but its symptoms can be eased by the use of anti-inflammatory drugs (NSAID — see Section 6), steroid injections (see Section 6) and pain-killers.

TINEA
See FUNGAL INFECTIONS.

TOENAIL, INGROWN
See NAIL INFECTION.

TONSILLITIS
The tonsils are modified lymph glands that sit at either side of the throat at the back of the mouth. They normally act to intercept and destroy bacteria and viruses that are entering the body. If a tonsil is overwhelmed by the germs it is trying to destroy, tonsillitis occurs and the gland becomes enlarged, red, painful and covered in pus. The infection can easily spread to the other tonsil and to glands below the jaw and around the ear. The patient develops a sudden high fever, headache, throat pain, has offensive breath and finds it difficult to swallow or speak. Tonsillitis may occur at any age, but is far more common amongst children than adults.

A number of different bacteria (e.g. *Streptococci, Staphylococci, Haemophilus*) may cause tonsillitis, and these can only be differentiated by a throat swab. A cotton or synthetic swab is rubbed across the tonsil and then sent to a laboratory for culture. The infecting organism and the correct antibiotic to kill it can then be identified. In some mild to moderate cases, swabs are not necessary, and a broad spectrum antibiotic (e.g. penicillin, erythromycin, tetracycline) can be used by a doctor with reasonable confidence that it will be successful. Even when a swab is taken, antibiotics are usually started while awaiting the result. If tonsillitis is left untreated, the infection may spread to cause an abscess (see QUINSY) or septicaemia (see separate entry).

Before antibiotics became readily available in the late 1940s, the vast majority of patients with tonsillitis did recover, but often after a very uncomfortable and distressing few weeks. As a result, tonsils were removed to prevent further attacks of the disease. In the last two decades, because attacks of tonsillitis can be easily controlled by safe and effective antibiotics, the rate of tonsillectomy (see Section 6) has steadily decreased so that it is now only performed if the patient has recurrent attacks of tonsillitis, excessively large tonsils, or other significant reasons for the procedure to be performed.

Treatment of acute tonsillitis involves bed rest, fluid diet, aspirin or paracetamol, antiseptic mouth washes and antibiotics. It is important to finish the course of antibiotics. Although symptoms may rapidly disappear, the tonsillitis may recur if the antibiotic course is not completed, and the responsible bacteria may no longer respond adequately to the previous antibiotic as it may have developed resistance to it.

Viral infections of the tonsils may also be severe but will not respond to antibiotics. One of the more common causes of viral tonsillitis is glandular fever. This can be diagnosed by a specific blood test. Unfortunately no treatment is available, and pain-killing tablets and gargles must be used to give relief, while prolonged rest allows a cure. Another cause of tonsillitis, which is rare today due to vaccinations, is diphtheria (see separate entry).

Tonsillitis is infectious, and the causative bacteria or viruses may be passed to another person who has close contact with the patient.

Toxic shock syndrome

The toxic shock syndrome was responsible for considerable media activity in the mid 1980s, when a number of American women died from it due to infections that developed in tampons. The syndrome is not a new one though, and may be associated with the after-effects of confinement, the use of contraceptive diaphragms, after surgery, with an abscess, or even as a complication of influenza. More than 90% of cases of this syndrome have occurred in women, and almost invariably within five days of the onset of the menstrual period.

The syndrome is caused by a toxin (poison) released by the bacterium *Staphylococcus aureus* (golden staph). The blood-soaked material in a tampon may become invaded by the bacteria, which release the toxin, which enters the bloodstream of the woman through the vaginal wall. The woman herself is not infected by the bacteria. Once the toxin starts to circulate in the blood, the patient becomes feverish, develops a widespread red rash, headache, muscle aches, vomiting and diarrhoea, and the blood pressure drops to dangerously low levels. This low blood pressure may threaten the blood supply to the brain, liver, kidney and other vital organs, and eventually causes them to fail, at which point the patient dies. The overall mortality rate is 15%.

Treatment involves steroids (see Section 6), artificial kidney machines, transfusions, antibiotics and intensive care in hospital.

Toxoplasmosis

Toxoplasma gondii is a single-celled animal that is found world-wide as a parasite of cats, other animals and birds, from whom it may spread to humans. The eggs pass out in the faeces of the animal and may then enter a human mouth, e.g. after careless handling of cat litters or soil contamination of fingers or food. Once in the gut, the microscopic egg hatches and multiplies into millions of single-celled animals.

In many patients, the symptoms are so mild that they are ignored, but in severe cases the patient complains of a low-grade fever, tiredness, muscle aches, joint pains, headache, sore throat, a mild rash and enlarged glands. In the rare severe cases, the liver, spleen, lungs, eye, heart and brain may be involved.

Patients usually recover without treatment in four to eight weeks. If symptoms are significant or complications develop, medications are available (e.g. pyrimethamine — see Section 6) to destroy the infection.

The worst complication of toxoplasmosis occurs in women who are pregnant. The infection may cause miscarriages, still birth, and deformities in the baby (e.g. small head, hydrocephalus, mental retardation, fits, blindness). The disease can be detected by a blood test, and this test is often routinely performed during antenatal blood examinations. If toxoplasmosis is detected in pregnancy, treatment will be given to cure the disease. Unfortunately, because the disease has already occurred, there may still be some damage to the foetus.

There is no vaccination or other form of prevention available. Pregnant women should not associate closely with cats.

TRACHOMA

Trachoma is a type of conjunctivitis (superficial eye infection) caused by an organism known as *Chlamydia* (see CHLAMYDIAL INFECTIONS). It is very common in all areas of the world, but particularly in areas of low hygiene where flies can transmit the infection from one person to another. It is particularly common among Australian Aborigines.

A trachoma infection may not be very noticeable, and particularly in children may cause no symptoms at all. In more severe cases, eye pain, intolerance to bright lights, and a weeping swollen eye may develop. Small bubbles on the underside of the eyelids are the earliest sign of the disease. Chronic trachoma causes scarring of the cornea (the outer surface of the eye) and subsequent blindness. Blood vessels grow into the scar tissue, and the coloured part of the eye and the pupil may be covered with a thick scar and obvious small arteries and veins. The gland that produces tears (the lacrimal gland) can also be damaged by the infection so that tears are no longer formed, the eye dries out, and again becomes damaged and scarred. Trachoma (along with diabetes) is responsible for most of the blindness in Aborigines and is a common cause of blindness in third-world countries.

The disease can be diagnosed by a doctor sending a swab from the eye to a laboratory for culture and examination. The infection is treated and usually cured in its early stages by a one to three month course of antibiotics and antibiotic eye ointment. Once blindness has occurred from corneal scarring, the only treatment is surgical replacement of the damaged cornea by one donated by a deceased person. If treated within the first year, the outcome is excellent, but if left longer, some scarring of the eye surface may occur.

The disease is under control in most Australian Aboriginal communities, but millions of older people in countries with poorer medical services are blinded by it.

TRANSFUSION REACTION, BLOOD

Most people know that it is necessary to cross-match blood before it is given to a patient, so that the blood of the patient and the donor are compatible. There are four main blood groups — A, B, O and AB. These are further divided into those that are Rhesus negative and Rhesus positive. A person can therefore be one of eight different combinations, i.e., A+ or A-, O+ or O-, B+ or B-, and AB+ or AB-.

This is complex enough, and for most purposes, this is all that is required. Unfortunately there are several dozen subgroups beyond this classification. In most cases these further subgroups make no significant difference to the patient receiving the blood, but in some cases a transfusion reaction can occur if there is a very slight mismatch of the blood with regard to one of these minor subgroups.

The most common transfusion reaction is a raised temperature. Other problems that can occur are muscle pains, headaches, and shortness of breath. Very rarely does any transfusion reaction become worse than this, and most patients have no reaction at all.

Transient ischaemic attack (TIA)

Many types of funny turns in elderly people are due to miniature strokes, or transient ischaemic attacks, in the brain. These are not serious but can make the person feel strange and act peculiarly at times. Transient ischaemic attacks (TIAs) may be an early warning of narrowed arteries in the brain, and can forewarn of strokes and other serious disorders.

A patient experiencing a TIA will describe weakness in one arm or leg, abnormal sensations (e.g. pins and needles, numbness), disturbances in vision, abnormally slurred speech, dizziness, confusion, tremor and blackouts. These episodes may last for a few seconds or several hours. Any patient experiencing a TIA needs to be examined by a doctor as it may lead to a stroke.

TIAs are transient events, and the patient returns to normal within 24 hours. Most TIAs are caused by the hardening and narrowing of arteries in the neck and brain by excessive deposition of cholesterol. These plaques of hard fat can cause small blood clots to form. These clots, or part of the cholesterol plaque itself, may break free from the artery wall and travel through the artery into the brain, where it may temporarily obstruct an artery, causing some damage to the brain tissue beyond the blockage. Spasms of arteries may also cause TIAs. These spasms may be caused by stress, toxins, allergies or many other triggers.

Aspirin in low doses has recently been found to prevent TIAs, and often prevents large strokes too. Aspirin acts by preventing blood clots. Only half to one tablet a day is required, but it should be continued in the long term.

See also STROKE.

Trench mouth
See VINCENT'S ANGINA.

Trichomoniasis, venereal

A single-celled animal, *Trichomonas vaginalis*, may cause infections in a woman's vagina, and the urethra (urine tube) of both men and women. The infection is transmitted from one victim to another by heterosexual or homosexual intercourse.

In men, there are often minimal symptoms, and the condition may persist undiagnosed for many months. Discomfort on passing urine, often first thing in the morning, is the most common symptom.

In women, the vaginal infection causes a foul-smelling, yellow/green, frothy discharge. There may be mild itching or soreness around the outside of the vagina. The diagnosis can be confirmed by examining a swab taken from the vagina. Treatment involves a course of the appropriate antibiotic tablets and/or vaginal cream. All sexual contacts need to be treated at the same time. Often treatment is a single dose of tablets.

Tricuspid valve disease
See HEART VALVE DISEASE.

Trigeminal neuralgia (tic douloureux)

The trigeminal nerve leaves the brain and passes through a hole in the skull just beside the ear. From there it fans out across the face, to receive sensations from the skin of the face, and to give instructions to the muscles in the face. Neuralgia is nerve pain, and patients with trigeminal neuralgia experience sudden severe pain in the trigeminal nerve. The pain often arises beside the mouth and spreads almost instantly up to the eye, down to the jaw, and across to the ear. The pain may last a few seconds or several minutes. Only one side of the face is affected. Attacks of pain may be started by cold winds, eating, yawning, or touching the face. The pains tend to come in episodes, with attacks coming every few minutes for a few days or weeks, and then disappearing for a time. Unfortunately, each successive attack tends to last longer than the preceding one, and the pain-free periods become shorter. Spontaneous, permanent cures do occur.

Occasionally, trigeminal neuralgia may be caused by a brain or nerve disease such as multiple sclerosis, but usually there is no specific cause, and there are no tests available to prove the diagnosis.

A number of drugs can be used to control the condition. Pain-killers are not particularly effective, but anti-epileptic drugs such as carbamazepine and phenytoin (see Section 6) are quite successful. If these medications prove unsuccessful, surgical exploration of the nerve may find an area of compression or abnormality as a cause of the pain. Very rarely, as a last resort, the nerve may be destroyed to give relief from intractable pain, but this leaves the face numb and paralysed.

Triglyceride excess (hypertriglyceridaemia)

Triglycerides are formed when one of a group of fatty acids (oleic acid, stearic acid and palmitic acid) combines with glycerol. Triglycerides are found in most animal and vegetable fats and form an essential part of the human diet. Only when eaten in excess, or excessively concentrated in the bloodstream, do they become a problem. High levels of triglycerides in the blood (hypertriglyceridaemia) predisposes towards an increased risk of strokes and heart attacks, as the excess triglyceride is deposited along with cholesterol on the inside wall of arteries to cause hardening of the arteries (see ATHEROSCLEROSIS). The cholesterol levels are more important than those of triglyceride in this process (see CHOLESTEROL EXCESS).

The amount of triglyceride present in the blood can be readily measured in a pathology laboratory. For an accurate result, it is necessary for the patient to fast for twelve hours before the test.

Some patients have an inherited type of excess triglyceride level in their blood, and this cannot be adequately corrected by diet alone but requires medication to reduce it to an acceptable level. Oral contraceptives may also be responsible for raising the blood triglyceride level. Patients with no signs of any hereditary disease can usually be controlled by a diet that excludes most animal and vegetable fat. A low triglyceride diet would exclude all fried food, most dairy products and fatty meats (e.g. sausages, lamb chops).

Patients with obesity, diabetes, alcoholism, an underactive thyroid gland, and a number of rarer diseases have an increased risk of developing high blood levels of triglycerides.

Trisomy 21
See DOWN'S SYNDROME.

Tropical ear
See OTITIS EXTERNA.

Trypanosomiasis
See SLEEPING SICKNESS.

Tuberculosis (TB)
Tuberculosis is an infection caused by a bacterium called *Mycobacterium tuberculosis*. It may cause infection in bone, skin, joints, lymph glands, kidney, gut, heart and brain, but by far the most important and common site for tuberculosis infections is the lung. Evidence of tuberculosis

has been found in the remains of a Neolithic man who lived 7000 years ago, and the disease continued to ravage mankind without check until the first of the sulpha drugs was isolated 50 years ago.

A German rural doctor, Robert Koch (1843–1910), made the first breakthrough in the fight against TB by discovering *Mycobacterium tuberculosis* and proving that it was responsible for the disease. Under a microscope, he found the now infamous rod-shaped bacteria, and from them he derived a substance called tuberculin, which he hoped would be a cure for the disease. This hope proved to be unfounded, but tuberculin became the basis of a useful skin test that is still used to diagnose the presence of the tuberculosis.

In the centuries before 1940, millions of people in every corner of the globe died from TB. Huge hospitals were erected in every major city of Australia to cope with the large number of previously fit young men and women who became afflicted with the characteristic productive cough, night sweats, loss of appetite, fever, weight loss and generalised tiredness that are the main symptoms of the disease. Rest and fresh air were the only treatments available, and sanatoriums were established in areas where the air was supposed to be the freshest and cleanest possible. Switzerland was the destination of those with sufficient financial means, while the middle class retreated to the mountains behind Australia's capital cities. The poorer classes suffered at home and spread the disease further.

Effective antibiotics changed the picture almost over night, and within a couple of decades, mass X-ray screening with mobile vans visiting every community and suburb on a regular basis had identified every case of tuberculosis in the country, and these patients had been treated and cured. The chest hospitals changed their emphasis, and instead of having wards full of those with TB, they accepted patients with a full range of illnesses. The hilltop and rural sanatoriums closed down, and the pattern of society was significantly changed.

Today, tuberculosis is uncommon in Australia, and is found mainly amongst migrants from Asia and South America and in some isolated Aboriginal communities. Cattle and other animals may carry TB and make its total eradication difficult.

The bacteria responsible for tuberculosis pass from one person to another in the moist droplets that are carried out through the mouth and nose in every breath. When inhaled by a second person, the bacteria can infect the lung and the surrounding lymph glands. The bacteria may lie dormant for years, and then start multiplying to cause an initial or subsequent attack of the disease at a time when the patient's resistance is down. For this reason, even today, the treatment of TB requires the long-term use of antibiotics. From the lungs, it is possible for the bacteria to gradually spread to almost every other organ of the body in untreated patients. The symptoms depend upon which areas are affected.

Once TB is suspected, the disease may be confirmed by collecting sputum samples and identifying the bacteria through a microscope. X-rays show a characteristic appearance once the infection is well established, and skin tests can determine whether the person has ever been exposed to tuberculosis.

Treatment involves using a combination of different antibiotics and antituberculotics (see Section 6) for a year or more. Patients must be hospitalised and isolated until they are no longer infectious. All the other members of the patient's family must be investigated for early signs of the disease, and may be given treatment as a routine preventative measure.

An effective vaccine that gives lifelong protection against TB has been available for many years. The BCG vaccine is given routinely at birth to babies in many overseas countries, but in Australia it is only offered to those at risk of catching the infection. Today, with effective treatment regimes, a complete cure can be expected, and most recurrences of infection are due to patients failing to complete the full course of treatment.

Over the last 50 years, medical science has in developed countries reduced one of the greatest threats to the general health of the entire population to a rarity, but in third-world nations with inadequate health resources, tuberculosis still rages virtually unchecked.

See also SCROFULA.

TUBEROUS SCLEROSIS

Tuberous sclerosis is an uncommon congenital condition (present since birth) that may occur in successive generations in the one family or develop randomly. Its cause is unknown. Young children with the condition have repreated convulsions and are mentally retarded. Later in childhood, a rash consisting of red nodules appears on the face and neck. Other unusual rashes may develop elsewhere on the body, and lumps may form under the nails. Numerous other complications develop in some victims, including eye damage, cysts in the heart, bone and lungs, and benign growths in the bowel. The mental retardation steadily worsens with age. Other than medication to control the convulsions, and surgery for some of the more serious cysts, no treatment is available.

TURNER'S SYNDROME (XO SYNDROME)

At the moment of conception when the male sperm and female egg fuse, the two sets of chromosomes from the parents pair up (see Section 1). The sex chromosomes are named X and Y — a person with two X chromosomes (XX) is female, and with one of each (XY) is male. In the rare Turner's syndrome, the person is born with only one X chromosome, and no matching X or Y (XO). The syndrome is named after the Oklahoma (USA) physician, Henry Hubert Turner (born 1892), who first described it.

To all intents and purposes, people with Turner's syndrome look female, but they are really asexual, as they do not develop testes or ovaries and are infertile. At puberty, the breasts and pubic hair fail to develop, the genitals remain child-like in appearance, and there are no menstrual periods. Other signs that may be noticed in these people are their short stature and a web of skin that runs from the base of the skull down the neck and onto the top of the shoulder. Less common problems include eye disorders, heart valve defects, narrowing of the aorta (main body artery), a stocky chest, the early development of diabetes and thin frail bones (osteoporosis).

The diagnosis can be confirmed by blood and cell tests that show the chromosome structure.

Treatment involves helping these people become as female as possible by giving them female hormones (oestrogens) in a cyclical manner from the time of expected puberty. Growth hormone can be used to improve their growth, and surgery can correct the heart defects and neck webbing. With correct management, these patients can function as females in every way except fertility, and they can lead a normal life.

TYPHOID FEVER (SALMONELLOSIS)

Fortunately, typhoid fever is now unknown in Australia, but it remains widespread in many of the less developed countries to our north. Typhoid fever is a bacterial infection of the gut and surrounding lymph nodes, including the spleen. It is caught by eating food that has been contaminated with *Salmonella typhi* bacteria, which pass out in the faeces and urine of those who have the infection or are symptom-free carriers of the bacteria. In severe cases, it is possible for the infection to spread to the lungs, brain, kidneys and gall bladder.

It takes 5–14 days from the time the bacteria are first swallowed to the development of symptoms, so international travellers who have visited third-world countries where typhoid fever is endemic may return to Australia before the symptoms develop. It is therefore important for travellers to tell doctors that they have been overseas when presenting with any illness within several weeks of their return.

Patients with typhoid fever gradually develop a fever with headache, tiredness, cough, sore throat, abdominal pain and constipation. After a day or two, the constipation suddenly gives way to a massive diarrhoea. With no treatment, the patient who survives the severe dehydration that accompanies the diarrhoea will slowly improve after about ten days, but relapses may occur for the next two or three weeks. Complications include massive bleeding into the gut and perforation of the gut, which usually cause the death of the patient. Death may occur in up to 30% of untreated cases, but only in 2% of those who are treated in good facilities.

The presence of the infection can be confirmed by blood, urine and faeces tests.

Treatment involves the use of antibiotics to destroy the invading bacteria, steroids (see Section 6) to reduce inflammation, a low-residue diet and intravenous fluids. The infection may be almost impossible to eradicate from those people who become symptom-free carriers of the disease.

Prevention is available in the form of a course of three tablets that give twelve months protection, or two injections that give three years protection. These precautions should be taken by travellers to any country where typhoid is known to occur (see Section 7).

Typhus (Rickettsiosis)

Typhus is a disease caused by an organism called *Rickettsia*, which is transmitted from animals to man by insects. *Rickettsiae* are unusual organisms that fit halfway between bacteria and viruses. They live inside the cells of the patient's body like a virus, rather than leading the independent existence of bacteria. Except for the uncommon and usually mild **Queensland tick typhus**, which uses ticks to move from marsupials to man, the disease is unknown in Australia.

There are three main types of typhus — **epidemic typhus** which is carried from one human to another by body lice, **murine typhus** which is carried from rats to humans by fleas, and **scrub typhus** which uses mites to move from rats to humans. Epidemic typhus occurs in Africa, South and Central America and Asia. Murine typhus occurs world-wide in areas of poor hygiene, and scrub typhus is limited to south-east Asia and Japan.

The symptoms of typhus vary slightly between one type and another, but generally after an incubation period of 10 to 14 days, patients develop a fever, generalised rash, overwhelming tiredness, chills, headache and muscle pains. The blood pressure drops to very low levels, and this may cause heart failure.

Treatment involves using an antibiotic (e.g. tetracycline — see Section 6) to kill the *Rickettsiae*, and pain relief. The mortality rate again varies from one form of the disease to another, but is generally around 10%.

A number of vaccinations are being used experimentally, but none are currently in widespread use. Control of the disease must therefore depend on control of the insects that transmit it.

ULCER, MOUTH (APHTHOUS ULCER)

Mouth ulcers can vary from one or two millimetres in diameter to over a centimetre, and can cause considerable distress and discomfort. There are many reasons for the development of a mouth ulcer, but the most common is an imbalance between the normal bacteria, viruses and fungi that are meant to be present in the mouth. An infection, allergy, being overtired or run-down, or a course of antibiotics may be sufficient to alter this delicate balance and allow one type of germ to overgrow, attack the lining of the mouth, and form an ulcer.

Other causes include injuries to the mouth from false teeth, biting on hard food, dental disorders, burns from hot liquids, food allergies, infections of the mouth and numerous less common but sometimes quite serious diseases. Some women develop them before their periods every month.

If the mouth ulcers are recurrent, it is essential to have a checkup by your doctor to see if there is some significant disease causing the problem. Cancers in the mouth may first appear as a mouth ulcer, particularly in smokers.

The best treatment involves using one of the innumerable mouth ulcer preparations available from chemists. All of these work to some extent, but it will be a matter of trial and error to find the preparation that suits you best. A combination of a mouthwash and paints or pastes to put on the ulcer is probably the best form of management. Some doctors believe that vitamin B and folic acid supplements can be beneficial.

ULCER, PEPTIC

Hydrochloric acid is known to most high-school students as a potent acid that can eat through many substances and cause nasty burns on your skin. This acid is also naturally produced in the body, and in its correct place in the stomach does no harm to the body but aids food digestion. Specialised cells lining the stomach make the acid and release it in response to the sight or smell of food. We also start to produce more saliva when food is nearby, and if the food is not forthcoming, we are left drooling and with an ache in the gut, because no food has been eaten to soak up the saliva and acid. We normally end up eating the food we expect, and the acid works in the stomach to break it down to its basic components. Further digestive enzymes are added to the food when it passes out of the stomach into the small intestine.

The cells lining the stomach protect themselves from attack by the acid with a thin layer of mucus. If there is excess acid, or insufficient mucus present, the acid may be able to attack the stomach wall. Many factors can produce either or both of these stomach problems. The most common triggers are smoking, stress, alcohol, and aspirin-type medications. Anxiety can cause excess acid to be produced, which can then eat into the stomach. Smoking can reduce the mucus secretions that protect the stomach, while aspirin and some anti-arthritis drugs can directly damage the mucus layer.

As the acid attacks the stomach wall, it causes a **gastric** or **stomach ulcer**, the same as an acid burn on the skin. The first part of the small intestine (the duodenum) may also develop an ulcer (**duodenal ulcer**), as excess acid overflows from the stomach. **Pyloric ulcers** develop at the point where a muscle ring acts as a valve between the stomach and duodenum. The term peptic ulcer refers to all three types of ulcer.

Unlike the skin, the stomach has few nerve cells, and the acid may eat through to a blood vessel and cause bleeding, anaemia and weakness before any pain is felt. Most ulcers cause pain, which may be severe because the acid is attacking a nerve. The pain is often at its worst just before a meal when the acid levels are highest, and food (particularly milk) may relieve the pain. Once a person has the severe pain high up in the abdomen that is characteristic of an ulcer, it is important to have the diagnosis proved and treatment started quickly in order to avoid complications. Other symptoms can include a feeling of fullness, burping excessively, and indigestion. Doctors will prove the presence of an ulcer by a barium meal X-ray or gastroscopy (see Section 4). Surgery for ulcers is rarely required these days, as the majority of patients can be cured or controlled by medication (antiulcerants and antacids — see Section 6). The patient's diet needs to be sensible and well balanced, but most foods can be taken in moderation. The victim can also help by not smoking and by learning to relax.

A very small percentage of ulcers can be cancerous, so it is vital that the disease is correctly diagnosed and treated.

See also STOMACH CANCER; ZOLLINGER-ELLISON SYNDROME.

ULCER, SKIN

An ulcer occurs on the skin when the outer layers of the skin are destroyed and the underlying tissue is exposed. A skin ulcer can be caused by constant pressure (see BED SORES), injury or poor blood supply (venous ulcer). A cut or sore that is constantly irritated by scratching or rubbing from clothing may develop into an ulcer. Sometimes mentally disturbed patients, prisoners and people trying to draw attention to themselves deliberately irritate an ulcer to prevent it from healing. Covering the ulcer with a dressing that prevents irritation almost invariably results in its cure.

Venous ulcers occur on the shin and ankle in the middle-aged and elderly due to a poor return of blood from the ankles and feet to the heart. The ankles may be swollen, and the skin may be thin and discoloured by eczema, but not necessarily so. The condition is aggravated by varicose veins and diabetes. Women are affected far more often than men. A slight injury may cause the ulcer to start, and because of the high pressure from the swollen veins in the area, the poor quality of the skin, and the poor blood supply, healing may be very slow.

Treatment of venous ulcers requires prolonged elevation of the leg to reduce the pressure in the veins, wearing compression bandages or stockings when walking, avoiding standing still for prolonged periods, and careful dressing of the ulcer with antiseptics and specialised pads or powders. In persistent cases, surgery to the swollen veins to relieve the pressure may be necessary before healing can occur.

ULCERATIVE COLITIS

Bloody diarrhoea with severe abdominal cramps and pain are the principal symptoms of ulcerative colitis. Large amounts of mucus may also be present in the diarrhoea, and in severe cases the diarrhoea may occur 20 times a day and consist entirely of blood and mucus, with no faeces being present. Occasionally, periods of apparent constipation can occur between attacks of diarrhoea which are severe enough to cause the patient to collapse. Further symptoms include fever, loss of appetite, weight loss and overwhelming tiredness.

Ulcerative colitis is an inflammation and subsequent ulceration of the section of large intestine known as the colon (see Section 2). Repeated attacks cause thickening and scarring of the colon to the point where it cannot adequately undertake its task of absorbing excess fluid from the faeces. The cause is unknown. The symptoms may be quite mild at first, but subsequent attacks steadily worsen to give the picture above. Occasionally, an initial attack may be very severe.

Once suspected, doctors can confirm the diagnosis by performing an X-ray of the colon known as a barium enema (see Section 4) or sigmoidoscopy, in which a tube is passed through the anus into the colon to allow it to be examined. Blood and faeces tests will be performed to exclude other possible causes of the diarrhoea.

The inflammation of the large intestine can cause a number of complications including abscesses around the anus, a rupture of the gut, cancer, or false connections from the gut to the bladder or vagina caused by ulcers breaking through to these adjacent organs. The inflammation in the gut may be associated with inflammation in other parts of the body, including the skin, joints, eye, mouth and liver. There are numerous other rarer complications of the condition.

Ulcerative colitis is a severe and potentially life-threatening disease that needs effective, continuing treatment to keep it under control, as there is no permanent cure. The disease passes through phases of active disease and remission, and treatment is aimed at treating the active disease when it occurs and preventing an attack from developing when the patient is in good health. Severe attacks require admission to hospital for intensive therapy that will include drips into a vein, antibiotics, and steroids (see Section 6). If the gut ruptures, urgent surgery may be necessary. Milder attacks may be treated by steroid tablets or suppositories (given through the anus).

Prevention and the treatment of mild attacks require a specific diet that is high in protein but excludes dairy products and other foods that are known to aggravate the condition, and the regular use of a drug called sulphasalazine (see Section 6) that reduces the gut inflammation.

Uncontrolled disease may require the surgical removal of the entire colon. The patient's small intestine is opened out onto the skin of the abdomen (an ileostomy — see STOMAS, Section 6), and the wastes are collected in a bag.

Patients with ulcerative colitis have a much higher incidence of bowel cancer than the normal population, and must have regular bowel examinations to exclude this possibility, as well as checking on the severity of the colitis. Most cases can be adequately controlled by medication, but the cooperation of the patient is vital. Because of the long-term complications and related conditions in other organs, the average life expectancy of these patients is slightly less than normal.

UNDESCENDED TESTES
See TESTICULAR DISEASE.

UNDULANT FEVER
See BRUCELLOSIS.

UPPER RESPIRATORY TRACT INFECTION
See URTI.

URAEMIA
See KIDNEY FAILURE.

URETHRITIS
Urethritis is an inflammation or infection

of the urethra, which is the tube that leads from the bladder to the outside of the body in both men and women. The usual cause is a bacterial infection, which may be related to cystitis (usually women), non-specific urethritis (both sexes), or prostatitis (men only). Patients complain of burning and/or pain on passing urine, the desire to pass urine frequently, and sometimes a clear discharge from the urethra.

Treatment involves taking a course of the appropriate antibiotic.

See also CYSTITIS; NON-SPECIFIC URETHRITIS.

URINE PROBLEMS

See BED-WETTING; CYSTITIS; INCONTINENCE; NON-SPECIFIC URETHRITIS; PYELONEPHRITIS.

See also KIDNEY DISEASE.

URTI (UPPER RESPIRATORY TRACT INFECTION)

An upper respiratory tract infection (URTI) is any bacterial or viral infection of the pharynx (throat). Tonsillitis, epiglottitis, glandular fever, sinusitis and the common cold can all be considered as different types of URTI. Each of these diseases is dealt with separately in this section.

Upper respiratory tract infections occur many times a year in everyone. Fortunately, most of us are able to destroy the infecting agent within a few days, or even hours, by using the body's natural defence mechanisms. The majority of these infections are so mild that we barely notice them, but when the defence system is overwhelmed by the disease, a doctor's assistance is necessary.

Infections in the mouth, throat, nose, sinuses and larynx (the upper parts of the respiratory tract) may be due to viruses, bacteria or fungi. Allergy reactions such as hay fever, can sometimes be confused with an URTI infection.

Viruses cause more than 90% of URTI cases. Viruses are unimaginably small particles of protein that are barely alive but have the capability of reproducing very rapidly, irritating tissue, and causing the owner of that tissue considerable distress. The body is invaded by viruses in every breath, every mouthful of food, and every time we touch our mouth or nose. Special cells in the blood stream and lymph glands rapidly produce antibodies to destroy the invading viruses, and only a minute proportion of those taken into the system cause disease. In their attempts to control an URTI attack, the glands in the neck may become swollen and tender.

Because viruses are barely alive and live within the tissue cells, it is exceedingly difficult to kill them. Medical science cannot cure any viral infection at present, be it measles, glandular fever, AIDS, or the common cold, but during the next decade we may see the greatest breakthrough since the development of antibiotics if some of the experimental drugs now under investigation prove to be effective against viruses. Because viral infections cannot be cured, colds, flu and viral URTI must run their course. Soluble aspirin and paracetamol will decrease the pain, fever and swelling in most sufferers, and combined with throat lozenges and decongestants may be the only treatment necessary. Doctors do not normally prescribe antibiotics, but can give medications that are effective in controlling the more distressing symptoms of URTI.

If the URTI is caused by **bacteria**, it is often described as pharyngitis, tonsillitis, sinusitis, etc. In these cases antibiotics are very effective in curing the disease in a few days, but the course of pills or mixture must be completed to prevent a recurrence. Bacterial infections generally cause more severe symptoms with high fevers, pain, swelling of tissues and foul phlegm.

Fungal infections are less common, and

are caused by microscopic plants that are distantly related to the algae that form scum on a stagnant pool. In one form, the mouth and throat become covered in a white plaque known as thrush. There are tablets, gels, mouth washes and paints available to cure most fungal infections as rapidly as antibiotics cure those caused by bacteria.

Unless there is severe pain or a high fever, it is reasonable to leave most attacks of URTI for a couple of days before seeing a doctor, but if the symptoms persist, appropriate help should be sought so that the victim can avoid discomfort and return to work or school as rapidly as possible.

See also COLD, COMMON; EPIGLOTTITIS; GLANDULAR FEVER; SINUSITIS; TONSILLITIS.

URTICARIA
See ALLERGY — Hives.

UTERINE FIBROIDS
The uterus (or womb) is made up of muscular tissue, fibrous tissue and glandular tissue. After childbirth, the uterus must shrink from a very large distended size back to its usual shape and size which resembles that of a small pear. It is thought that the stress on the uterus during pregnancy may result in some minor injury to the fibrous tissue in the uterine wall, and after the uterus contracts, this fibrous tissue may repair itself in an abnormal way. The result is the formation of one or more hard fibrous balls in the wall of the uterus, which may be the size of a golf ball or larger. When the uterus contracts to force out the blood and wastes during a period, these fibrous balls distort the uterus and cause the muscles to go into painful cramps.

If the uterine cramps and discomfort are very distressing, the uterus can be removed in a hysterectomy operation, or if the women wishes to have more children, the individual fibroid masses can be cut out of the uterus. Fibroids also often cause heavy menstrual bleeding, and surgery may be considered for this reason.

Fibroids are not cancerous, but they can certainly cause considerable distress to a woman, and because their symptoms can mimic a cancer, they should always be investigated.

UTERINE MOLE (HYDATIDIFORM MOLE)
One in every 750 pregnancies develops into a uterine (or hydatidiform) mole. Women with this unfortunate complication have a dramatic overdevelopment of the placenta (afterbirth) which fails to function correctly, and any embryo that is present dies at a very early stage. Multiple cysts develop in the placenta so that, when seen surgically, it appears like a large bunch of grapes. The woman may not be aware of the problem until it is well advanced, at 14 to 20 weeks of pregnancy, when an abnormal vaginal bleed or discharge may occur, and the womb feels much larger than expected. Occasionally, some of the grape-like cysts may be passed.

Once suspected, an ultrasound scan and blood tests will confirm the diagnosis, and surgical treatment is undertaken immediately. This will involve removing the abnormal placenta from the uterus (womb) through the vagina and cervix using a combination of suction and curettes (small sharp edged spoons). The tissue removed is sent to a pathologist for further microscopic examination. Careful follow-up of these women with blood tests and gynaecological examinations is essential, as a small percentage develop significant complications.

One complication is an **invasive mole**, in which the abnormal placenta penetrates through the wall of the uterus and damages it to the point where a hysterectomy is usually necessary.

A more serious complication that occurs in about 4% of women with uterine moles is the development of cancer in the abnormal tissue. This is called a **choriocarcinoma** and, if detected early enough, may be successfully treated with cytotoxic drugs (see Section 6). This type of cancer can also very rarely occur with an apparently normal pregnancy and a live baby.

UVEITIS
See IRITIS.

VAGINISMUS
See SEXUAL PROBLEMS.

VAGINITIS

Vaginitis is an infection or inflammation of a woman's vagina. Vaginal infections may be caused by fungi (see THRUSH), single-celled animals called *Trichomonas* (see separate entry), bacteria (see below) or warts (see separate entry). The most common form of inflammation is due to the menopause (atrophic vaginitis — see below).

Atrophic (post-menopausal) vaginitis

A woman's vagina is kept moist by the production of a mucus from glands in and around it. During sexual stimulation, these glands secrete more mucus to give added lubrication. After the menopause, the female hormone oestrogen is no longer produced by the ovaries. It is this hormone that stimulates the vaginal glands to produce the mucus. Without the oestrogen, the glands do not function, and many older women complain of a dry, sore, itchy vagina. Oestrogen also causes the formation of breast tissue and pubic hair. It is because oestrogen is lacking after the menopause that the breasts sag and the pubic hair becomes scanty.

The vaginal problem can be overcome in several ways. Simple moisturising creams can be purchased from chemists to apply when the vagina is irritated. A more effective treatment is to use creams containing oestrogen in the vagina. Although they are expensive, they often need to be used only once or twice a week. Excess use can cause absorption of the oestrogen, which may result in nipple soreness and other symptoms of oestrogen excess. The final method of treatment is to give oestrogen tablets in very small doses.

Bacterial vaginitis

A number of different bacteria can infect the vagina to cause a smelly grey vaginal discharge, soreness and redness. The diagnosis and type of bacteria present can be determined by the doctor taking a swab and sending it to a pathologist for further examination.

One of the most common bacteria causing vaginitis is called *Gardnerella vaginalis*, which causes a greyish, fish-smelling vaginal discharge. It is a slightly unusual bacterium in that it requires an environment that is oxygen-free and alkaline to grow. The upper end of the vagina can be oxygen-free, but normally the vagina is slightly acid, and this prevents the growth of any bacteria that may be present. However, if the vaginal environment becomes unbalanced and alkaline, problems may occur. The reasons for the vagina changing from acid to alkaline include the presence of semen after sex, changing sexual partners, hormonal changes at different times of the month, and the use of antibiotics.

Bacterial vaginitis infections can be readily treated by using the appropriate antibiotic tablets by mouth, and antiseptic douches (e.g. iodine solution, acidic jels) or creams in the vagina. Although the infections are not strictly speaking sexually transmitted diseases, in recurrent cases the male sexual partner may also need to be treated.

See also SEXUALLY TRANSMITTED DISEASE; THRUSH; TRICHOMONIASIS; WARTS.

VALVE DISEASE
See HEART VALVE DISEASE.

VARICELLA
See CHICKENPOX; SHINGLES.

VARICOSE ULCER
See ULCER, SKIN.

VARICOSE VEINS

Varicose veins never kill their owner, but they certainly cause a great deal of discomfort, and also a significant drop in ego and self-esteem when their owner finds others staring at the large, ugly, blue, knotted patterns they describe across the blotchy, red and sometimes ulcerated skin. Unfortunately, there are no magic cures for this very common problem, but doctors do have ways of reducing the symptoms and removing the veins that cause tired, aching, swollen legs.

The heart pumps blood out around the body through arteries. These become smaller and smaller until they are only one cell in diameter, when they are known as capillaries. In the capillaries, the oxygen and nutrition are removed from the blood, which then travels back to the heart through the veins. Two systems of veins are used in the legs to move the blood from the feet back to the heart. One system is deep inside the muscles of the calf and thigh, the other system is outside the muscles and just under the skin. It is in this superficial system that varicose veins occur.

The contraction of the muscles in the leg supplies the force to move the blood out of the legs. The muscle movement squashes the veins, and with the aid of one-way valves scattered through the superficial venous network, the blood is steadily pushed back towards the heart.

Pregnancy (because of the growing baby putting pressure on the veins in the pelvis) and prolonged standing (in jobs like hairdressing and shop assistant) make it difficult for the blood to move up from the legs into the body. The veins then become swollen with blood, and the one-way valves can become damaged. The damaged valves then allow more blood to remain in the veins, dilating them further and eventually causing the grossly dilated varicose veins.

Reducing the amount of standing, wearing elastic support stockings and regularly exercising the muscles in the legs while standing may prevent varicose veins. Once present, there are tablets that can reduce the aching that may be present in the dilated veins, but only surgical procedures can permanently remove the veins.

Injections may be used to destroy small, fine, spider-like networks of veins. This is rather like injecting a special type of glue into the veins, to stick the walls together. Larger isolated veins can be removed one at a time by a 'nick and pick' procedure, with a small cut being made over each vein to allow its removal. The most major procedure is stripping, where most of the superficial veins on one side of the leg from the groin to the ankle are removed. This procedure may be combined with a 'nick and pick'. After all these procedures, the leg must remain firmly bandaged for several weeks.

The operations are successful in most people, but they do not prevent the development of veins elsewhere in the legs, and the skin staining caused by the varicosities is usually permanent. It is sensible to discuss the matter with your general practitioner sooner rather than later if varicose veins worry you, so that referral to a surgeon can be arranged before too many of the tortuous veins develop.

VD (VENEREAL DISEASE)
See SEXUALLY TRANSMITTED DISEASE.

VENEREAL DISEASE
See SEXUALLY TRANSMITTED DISEASE.

VENOUS THROMBOSIS
See THROMBOSIS.

VERRUCAE
See WARTS.

VINCENT'S ANGINA (VINCENT'S DISEASE, VINCENT'S STOMATITIS, NECROTISING ULCERATIVE GINGIVOSTOMATITIS, TRENCH MOUTH)

Vincent's angina is a mixed infection of two or more different bacteria in the mouth. The infection is common in young adults at times of excessive stress and anxiety, and causes pain, soreness, ulceration and a grey membrane formation in the mouth, on the gums and the tonsils. The most obvious characteristic to others is the patient's very bad breath. The disease is named after the nineteenth century Parisian bacteriologist, Jean Vincent.

Vincent's angina is highly infectious and may spread rapidly through a group of people who are closely confined (e.g. school children, soldiers living in the trenches during the First World War — hence its alternative name of trench mouth).

The condition responds readily to antibiotic tablets (e.g. penicillin) and a hydrogen peroxide gargle.

VIRAL INFECTION

Every minute, millions of viruses enter your body through your nose and mouth. As they enter, the body's defence system uses its special cells and protein particles (known as antibodies) to repel the attack. Sometimes the defences are overwhelmed for a short time by the rapidly multiplying viruses. When this happens, you may have a day or two when you feel off-colour. If the virus numbers manage to totally defeat the defenders, you will develop a full-blown viral infection.

Viruses can cause diseases as diverse as measles, influenza, hepatitis, cold sores, chickenpox, glandular fever, the common cold, and AIDS. Virus particles are so small that they cannot be seen even by the most powerful light microscope, and special electron microscopes must be used. They are neither animal nor plant, but particles so basic they are classified into a group of their own. They are not alive in any sense we understand, but are overgrown molecules, intent on reproducing themselves at the expense of any host that happens along. Because they are not truly alive, they cannot be killed, and so the antibiotics that are so effective against the much larger living cells known as bacteria have no effect on viruses. For other than the few viruses that cause genital sores, some skin infections and cold blisters (against which idoxuridine and the very expensive new antiviral drug Zovirax are effective) we have no form of cure for viral infections. While you suffer from a viral infection, the body is busy producing the appropriate antibodies to fight the infection. Once the number of antibodies produced is adequate to destroy most of the viruses, the symptoms of your infection disappear, and you recover.

See also AIDS; CHICKENPOX; COLD, COMMON; CONJUNCTIVITIS; CYTOMEGALOVIRUS INFECTION; ENCEPHALITIS; GASTROENTERITIS; GLANDULAR FEVER; HEPATITIS; HERPES SIMPLEX INFECTIONS;

Section 5: Diseases

INFLUENZA; MEASLES; MENINGITIS; MUMPS; ROSEOLA INFANTUM; RUBELLA; SHINGLES.

See also VIRUSES, Section 7.

Vitamin-related Diseases

See BERI-BERI; CAROTENAEMIA; RICKETS; SCURVY.

Vitiligo

Vitiligo is a patchy loss of skin pigmentation that in pale-skinned northern Europeans may be barely noticed, but in southern Europeans, Arabs, Negroes and Chinese the resultant large white patches can be quite disfiguring. The disorder can occur in all races, in both sexes, and at all ages, but its onset is uncommon over 50 years of age. The white patches are sharply defined and may appear anywhere on the body, in any size and any number. Any overlying hair is usually white or grey. The affected areas of skin are very sensitive to sunlight, and burn easily. There are no other side effects or complications of the disease.

The cause of vitiligo is unknown, but it is probably an auto-immune disease, in which the body's defence mechanisms inappropriately attack cells and tissue that are normal tissue rather than invading organisms. In this case, the pigment-producing melanin cells (melanocytes) in the skin are destroyed.

The most effective treatment for vitiligo is to use cosmetic stains or dyes to disguise the affected areas of skin. A number of medical treatments are available, but these require long-term use of tablets and/or ultraviolet light exposure, and they have only moderate success.

The affected area of skin usually slowly extends to involve larger areas but eventually stabilises after several years. Spontaneous recovery is uncommon.

Von Recklinghausen's Disease of Multiple Neurofibromatosis

Besides having one of the longest names in any medical textbook, von Recklinghausen's disease of multiple neurofibromatosis has the characteristics of multiple light brown marks on the skin, soft fatty lumps under the skin, and, in some patients, nerves may be damaged. One in every 3000 people in Australia are affected by the condition. The lumps and spots are most commonly found on the trunk, pelvis and in the armpits. They also increase in size and number with age. The lumps grow from cells that form the soft sheath around every nerve in the body. The nerve damage is due to these soft lumps developing in the spinal canal, and in other areas (e.g. the auditory nerve that is responsible for hearing) where they can cause pressure on nerves to the point where the nerve is no longer able to function. Deafness, blindness and paralysis may be the long-term result in a small number of cases.

The disease passes from one generation to the next, but has a very variable result. About one third of patients merely have a couple of brown spots that never concern them, while about 10% are severely disfigured and disabled by large soft lumps under the skin, nerve weakness and multiple brown patches. Complications include scoliosis (curvature of the spine), bone cysts, uneven growth of the limbs (one arm or leg larger than the other), arthritis and mild mental retardation.

The diagnosis is confirmed by examining a sample (biopsy) of the patches or lumps under a microscope, where characteristic abnormal cells can be seen.

There is no treatment other than plastic surgery for any particularly bad lumps and patches. There is also no way in which you can determine whether a future child will have the condition, or how badly affected that child will be.

As the disease is transmitted genetically, anyone from an affected family should not marry someone who also has this condition in their background. Any family with members affected by this disease should seek further advice from a paediatrician, neurologist or geneticist.

Von Willebrand's disease

Von Willebrand's disease causes prolonged bleeding in affected people. It is an inherited disease, and may occur in both men and women. Most cases are mild, and patients complain of nose bleeds, heavy periods, bleeding gums and bleeding into the gut. Excessive bleeding also occurs with any cut or surgery and is dramatically worsened by aspirin. Patients lack one of the essential factors that are involved in the complex process of changing liquid blood into a clot. The diagnosis can be confirmed by the appropriate blood tests.

As the disease is normally mild, no treatment is required for the majority of patients, but aspirin must be avoided. If the patient is about to undergo dental or surgical procedures, it is necessary to give an injection of a blood extract that contains the missing factors, in order to avoid excessive bleeding during the operation. Other treatments are available for those who experience excessive bleeding from a severe case of the disease.

The long-term prognosis for patients with von Willebrand's disease is excellent, as even in the small number of victims who do need injections of the clotting factor the control achieved is very good.

Warts

A dense mat of spider webs, held onto the skin by a piece of paper fastened with string. Compresses of castor oil. The milk squeezed from the leaf of a wild lettuce. These are some of the treatments that were in use over a century ago for the age-old and most annoying of skin conditions, warts. There is no evidence that they may be caused by toads.

Warts are divided into three main types — genital warts, skin warts and plantar warts.

Genital warts (condylomata acuminata)

The human papilloma virus (HPV) is responsible for genital wart infections, and it is transmitted from one person to another only by sexual intercourse or other intimate contact. It is not possible to catch it from toilet seats or spa baths.

The obvious result of infection with the human papilloma virus is the growth of warts, sometimes of quite a large size, on the penis in men and in the genital area of women. They may appear as flat, pale areas on the skin, or as the dark-coloured, irregularly-shaped lumps more commonly associated with warts. After contact, the incubation period varies from one to six months, but may be even longer.

There are a number of hidden problems with this virus. In **men**, the virus may be present on the penis, but no warty growths may be obvious. They may only be seen if a doctor stains the area with a special liquid. The wart virus may also be present in the end of the urine tube (urethra) that runs through the penis, and in that position the warts are totally invisible. The warts can also be spread through sexual contact to other parts of the body.

Both men and women can be carriers of the virus from one sexual partner to another without being aware that they are infected. Only when the warts become large and obvious does the victim seek attention.

It is in **women** that the greatest, and deadliest, problems occur. If a woman is infected by HPV, she may develop genital warts not only around the outside of her genitals, but internally where they are difficult to detect. There may in fact be no warts present at all, but once the virus enters the vagina, it can attack the cervix, which is the opening into the womb (uterus). HPV infections of the cervix are associated with cancer of the cervix. It does not happen immediately and may take some years to develop, but a significant proportion of women with this infection will develop cancer. Cancer of the cervix has few early signs and is often not detected until it is well advanced and difficult to treat.

Every woman should have regular Pap smear tests every year or two while she is sexually active. These tests can detect this type of pre-cancer and cancer, genital wart infections and other gynaecological problems at an early stage. When detected early, the cancer can be treated effectively and completely cured. Any woman who knows that her partner has genital warts should be extremely careful to have Pap smear tests, and probably more frequently than normally recommended. Condoms can give reasonable, but not total, protection against catching an HPV infection.

The genital warts themselves, in both men and women, can only be treated by destroying the warts with acid paints or ointments, freezing the warts with liquid nitrogen, or by burning them away with an electric needle or lasers. Depending on the extent of the affected area, treatment with all except the acids and freezing will require either a local or general anaesthetic. Treatment is often prolonged, as the warts tend to recur, but with careful watching and rapid treatment of any recurrence the infection will eventually settle.

Anyone who is treated for genital warts should also have tests performed to check for the presence of other venereal disease, as a person carrying one type of VD could well carry another.

Skin warts

Warts on the skin are caused by a virus, a very slow-growing virus, which may take months or years to cause problems. Only a quarter of the population is susceptible to the wart virus, the rest of us have natural immunity. That is why some people never catch the disease, even though they may come into contact with warts frequently.

Warts are most common in children from 8 to 16 years of age. The virus is caught from someone else who has the disease, and months or years later, the wart develops. People with warts should not be isolated for fear of spreading the disease. The virus is widespread in the community, and isolation of victims is both impractical and ineffective.

Once a wart has developed, it will usually go away by itself without any treatment, but this may take many months or years. The average life span of a wart is about 18 months. The body gradually builds up antibodies against the wart virus, and when they reach a high enough level, the virus and wart are destroyed. Normally that person then has long-term resistance to further wart infections.

The most common sites for warts to develop are the knees, elbows, hands and feet. When warts develop on the soles of the feet they are called plantar warts or verrucae (see below).

Because warts can become both unsightly and painful, many patients wish them to be removed. The medical profession has progressed a bit further than using spider webs and wild lettuce, but the principle of wart removal remains the same. They cannot be cured by tablets or creams, they must be physically removed. The methods available are acid paints that are applied regularly to eat away the wart tissue, freezing the wart with liquid nitrogen to destroy its cells which causes it to fall off after a few days, burning the wart tissue away with a high voltage electric current in a process called diathermy, injecting a cell destroying substance under the wart, or cutting the wart out surgically. All these methods have their good and bad points, and if a wart is more than a few millimetres across, the various options should be carefully discussed with a doctor.

Because warts eventually disappear without any treatment, only those that are causing disfigurement or discomfort should be treated, as a scar may remain after any form of surgery, diathermy or freezing. Warts may also recur after all these forms of treatment.

In the future, it may be possible to have a vaccine against warts to prevent the development of this virus, in the same way that measles and influenza vaccines work today.

If you are not sure whether a lump on your skin is a wart, it should be checked by a doctor, as some forms of skin cancer may mimic a wart in appearance.

Plantar warts (verrucae)

Plantar warts (or verrucae) are warts on the soles of the feet, which tend to grow inwards rather than out. They tend to cause more problems than warts in other areas because they become painful with walking and so need treatment at an earlier stage than warts elsewhere on the body.

The treatment of plantar warts is the same as for skin warts, but a far larger hole than expected is usually left in the sole of the foot, as plantar warts tend to be a bit like icebergs, with only a small part showing on the surface. It may take some weeks after the surgery for the hole to heal.

WEGENER'S GRANULOMATOSIS

Wegener's granulomatosis is a rare disorder in which patients develop inflammation of blood vessels, kidney damage and ulcerating sores in the lungs, larynx, nose and sinuses. The symptoms include a fever, weakness, sinusitis, shortness of breath, cough, chest pain, coughing up blood and joint pain. Diagnosis is difficult, but it may be detected on a chest X-ray, or by taking a biopsy (sample) of one of the sores and examining the cells under a microscope.

The condition is invariably fatal without treatment, but good results have been obtained by using a drug called cyclophosphamide (see Section 6).

WERDNIG-HOFFMAN SYNDROME
See MOTOR NEURONE DISEASE.

WERNICKE-KORSAKOFF PSYCHOSIS (KORSAKOFF'S PSYCHOSIS, WERNICKE'S ENCEPHALOPATHY)

The Wernicke-Korsakoff syndrome is caused by a deficiency in vitamin B, particularly thiamine (vitamin B1), and occurs most commonly in alcoholics who neglect their diet. Elderly people who are malnourished may also fall victim to the condition. Karl Wernicke was a German neurologist and Sergei Korsakoff a Moscow physician in the latter half of the nineteenth century.

Patients develop a tremor, poor coordination, confusion, sudden eye movements, double vision, and pins and needles in the hands and feet. Blood tests can confirm the low levels of thiamine in the blood, but treatment is usually started immediately once the diagnosis is suspected. If alcoholics are not treated early, permanent brain damage may result. The treatment is to give thiamine by injection initially, and later by tablet, to replace that which is missing. A good well-balanced diet, no alcohol and good nursing brings most patients back to a reasonable lifestyle.

Section 5: Diseases

Whiplash injury

If a person is suddenly accelerated forwards (e.g. in a rear-end automobile accident), the head, because it is relatively dense and heavy compared to the rest of the body, has a tendency to remain behind. This results in the neck being bent backwards suddenly and excessively. The injury to the neck structures that results is described as whiplash. The sudden extension of the neck causes the ligaments and muscles on the front of the vertebral column and neck to be stretched and torn (sprained). In severe cases, the nerve fibres in the front half of the neck may also be overstretched and damaged. A whiplash injury may be worsened in a car accident if, after sudden acceleration, the car stops suddenly (e.g. is hit from behind and pushed into stationary car in front). The sudden bending of the neck may cause injury to the back of the neck as well.

The symptoms of whiplash injury vary dramatically from one person to the next. The pain, limited neck movement and stiffness that are common characteristics may commence shortly after the injury or be delayed by 24 hours or more. The pain may be felt not only in the neck, but also the shoulders, chest and back. Other possible symptoms include numbness in the fingers and forearm, difficulty in swallowing, blurred vision, dizziness, noises in the ears (tinnitus) and nausea. Unfortunately for patients, doctors and lawyers, X-rays are usually normal even in severe cases. The diagnosis is usually made on the doctors findings when the patient is examined.

Treatment of a whiplash injury (i.e. a sprained neck) is the same as for any other sprained joint — rest, immobilisation (neck brace), anti-inflammatory medications (NSAIDs — see Section 6), pain relievers, heat and physiotherapy. Most patients recover within a couple of weeks, but a very small number continue with long-term discomfort, pain and movement limitation.

Whitlow

See HERPES SIMPLEX INFECTIONS.

Whooping cough (pertussis)

For a week or two, a child with whooping cough seems to have a cold, but then the symptoms start to become more serious. The cough becomes steadily more severe and comes in increasingly distressing spasms, characterised by a sudden intake of breath before each cough, each spasm leaving the child exhausted. As it worsens, the child may become blue and lose consciousness. Thick stringy mucus is coughed up and may be vomited. The patient has no appetite and rapidly loses weight. The attacks of coughing occur for up to half an hour at a time, then there are a few minutes respite before the next attack begins. The cough may cause bleeding in the lungs, throat and nose, and the spasms may be severe enough to cause suffocation. If the child survives, the spasms start to ease off after a few weeks. For months later, mild recurrences may occur, and the victim may be left with permanent lung damage.

No treatment to cure this distressing disease is available, but it may be completely prevented. Even so, increasingly large numbers of children are being left unprotected because their parents forget to obtain the necessary course of injections or are poorly informed. Whooping cough is not a disease of the past. Hundreds of Australian children contract the disease every year, and many of them die or are left as invalids.

The bacterium that causes whooping cough is widespread in the community, and adults may have the disease and consider it merely a cold. Only in young children is the disease severe, and it is therefore important to start vaccinations as early as possible.

The vaccination against whooping cough is invariably combined with those for tetanus and diphtheria (see separate entries), and is given at two, four, six and 18 months of age. The triple antigen has minimal side effects, and the most common ones are a slight fever for 6 to 24 hours after the needle, and sometimes prolonged crying. Any other risks are minimal, and certainly far rarer than the serious complications of any of these three diseases. If the child has a fever or other illness, the vaccination may be delayed for a few days until it has recovered. The only children who should not be vaccinated are those with febrile convulsions, a history of epilepsy and allergies to certain elements of the vaccine. The course of four shots gives lifelong immunity against whooping cough, but boosters for tetanus and diphtheria are required throughout life every five to ten years.

If a child does contract pertussis (the technical name for whooping cough), the treatment will involve antibiotics to prevent the spread of the disease to others, oxygen, sedatives and careful nursing in isolation in hospital for several weeks.

The disease is spread from one person to another by the bacteria found in the microscopic droplets exhaled or coughed out in the breath of the patient and then inhaled by another person nearby. An adult with minimal symptoms may carry the disease from one infant to another, so careful nursing is essential. It takes from one to two weeks from the inhalation of the whooping cough organism for the disease to appear.

WILMS' TUMOUR (NEPHROBLASTOMA)

The Heidelberg surgeon, Max Wilms (born 1867), was the first doctor to adequately describe this form of kidney cancer that occurs in young children. More than 80% of patients with a nephroblastoma (the alternative name for Wilms' tumour) are under four years of age when diagnosed, and it accounts for nearly 10% of all childhood cancers. These children develop a swollen abdomen, but only one in five has pain, and even fewer develop the other possible symptoms of fever, bloody urine, weight loss and loss of appetite. The disease is usually detected by a doctor, or parent, feeling the large hard mass in the abdomen. The cancer arises not in the kidney itself, but in the tissues that immediately surround and support the kidney. It spreads to the liver and lungs, and in rare cases to the bone and brain. The diagnosis is confirmed by an X-ray of the kidney or a CT scan (see Section 4), followed by a biopsy (sample taken at operation).

Treatment requires the affected kidney to be removed surgically, followed by irradiation of the abdomen to destroy any remaining cancer cells. Chemotherapy with cytotoxic drugs (see Section 6) often follows the course of irradiation.

In years past, Wilms' tumour had an 80% mortality rate, but with modern techniques, this has been dramatically reduced so that 90% of patients now survive more than five years after diagnosis, and even if the cancer has spread to other organs, more than 50% survive for five years. The treatment methods are too new to be able to determine if these long-term survivals are actual cures.

WILSON'S DISEASE (HEPATOLENTICULAR DEGENERATION)

Wilson's disease is a rare, inherited disorder of the liver and brain that results in the excessive deposition of copper in these organs. It occurs in both males and females and is usually first diagnosed between 10 and 30 years of age. The disease is named after the London neurologist, Samuel Alexander Kinnier Wilson (born 1877). Patients may present with symptoms relating to the brain, the liver or both. The excess copper in the brain may cause symptoms of a psychiatric disorder, rigid muscles and tremor. The symptoms attributable to liver disease include jaundice (yellow skin), an enlarged liver and/or spleen, anaemia and hepatitis. One obvious characteristic is a brown/green ring (Kayser-Fleischer ring) around the iris (coloured part) in the eye, which is easily visible.

The diagnosis is confirmed by blood tests that detect the excessive levels of copper in the blood stream. Once diagnosed, the excess copper can be removed by one of a number of drugs (e.g. penicillamine — see Section 6), and a diet low in copper (i.e. avoiding shellfish, beans and offal). Lifelong treatment is necessary to keep copper levels low. The long-term outlook is good, but any damage to the brain or liver caused before the treatment is started cannot usually be reversed.

WISKOTT-ALDRICH SYNDROME
See IMMUNODEFICIENCY.

WOLFF-PARKINSON-WHITE SYNDROME
The Wolff-Parkinson-White syndrome is a form of abnormal heart beat that is diagnosed by doctors after examining an electrocardiogram (see Section 4). It is caused by a short circuit in the nerves connecting the upper chambers (atria) and lower chambers (ventricles) in the heart. The condition may be present from birth, or may develop as the result of a heart attack or infection.

Patients with the condition experience a very irregular heart rate, which in severe cases may limit their ability to exercise and adversely affect their quality of life.

Treatment involves taking regular medication (e.g. digoxin, procainamide, quinidine — see Section 6) to regulate the heart rhythm, or surgery to the heart to divide the abnormal nerve pathway.

XO SYNDROME
See TURNER'S SYNDROME.

YAWS
Yaws is a disease that is unknown in Australia, but it still occurs in some third-world countries with very poor hygiene. A similar bacterium to that which causes syphilis (see separate entry) is responsible for yaws, and some doctors theorise that syphilis evolved from yaws as hygiene standards improved during the European renaissance.

Patients with yaws develop sores on the skin and in the nose and mouth. These sores may become large, ulcerate, penetrate to the bone and cause permanent disfigurement. The glands in the armpits and groin are also inflamed.

The bacteria are transmitted from one person to another by close contact. Travellers need not take any additional precautions to protect themselves from the disease.

The disease can be readily treated with antibiotics (e.g. penicillin — see Section 6) and improved personal hygiene.

YELLOW FEVER
Yellow fever is a viral infection transmitted from one person to another by the *Aedes* mosquito. It occurs only in central Africa and tropical Central and South America. Although yellow fever is unknown in Australia, travellers to affected areas should

be vaccinated against the disease. Only one vaccination is necessary, and this gives protection for at least ten years.

After being bitten by a carrier mosquito, the incubation period for yellow fever is three to six days. Symptoms can vary from vomiting, headache, tiredness, and eye pain in mild cases, to severe generalised body pains, high fevers, bleeding from the gums and intestine, bruising, copious vomiting, delirium, kidney failure and liver failure. The liver failure causes yellow skin (jaundice) and gives the disease its name. Constipation is a common complication. The diagnosis may be difficult to make unless a doctor is aware that the patient has travelled in tropical Africa or America. Specific blood tests to confirm the diagnosis may not turn positive until a week or two after the symptoms develop.

There is no effective treatment or cure for yellow fever, and the patient must be carefully nursed, given fluids through a drip into a vein, and sedated until the disease passes. Death through massive internal bleeding and liver failure is common, even in good hospitals.

ZOLLINGER-ELLISON SYNDROME

The Zollinger-Ellison syndrome is a rare form of severe peptic ulceration (see ULCER, PEPTIC) in the stomach or small intestine, caused in most cases by a tumour in the pancreas that produces high levels of a hormone which promotes excessive acid production by the stomach. Robert Zollinger (born 1903) and Edwin Ellison (born 1918) were the American doctors who first described this condition. Patients have exaggerated symptoms typical of a peptic ulcer with severe pain in the upper part of the abdomen, bloating, nausea and diarrhoea. The onset is usually at a younger age than normal for a peptic ulcer.

A specific blood test can be performed to measure the amount of a substance called 'gastrin' in the blood. This hormone is responsible for stimulating the stomach to produce hydrochloric acid. Other tests will include examination of the stomach through a gastroscope (see Section 4) and measuring the amount of acid present in the stomach.

Treatment of the Zollinger-Ellison syndrome is the same as for normal peptic ulcers, but antiulcerants (see Section 6) must be used in far higher doses, and the need for surgery is more common. Treatment must normally be continued for life, but is very successful in controlling the disease.

SECTION 6

TREATMENTS

DRUG TREATMENT

565

SURGICAL TREATMENT

653

PSYCHIATRIC TREATMENT

676

OTHER FORMS OF TREATMENT

679

THERAPISTS

683

DRUG TREATMENT

Magic wands are unfortunately not yet available on prescription. Doctors are therefore limited in the ways they can treat patients. Treatment can be given by surgical procedures, by psychological counselling, by physical therapies, by irradiation, or by the modification of the body's processes with drugs.

The term 'drugs' can conjure up the image of a nasty, addictive capsule which has horrible side effects and which may cause serious damage to your body. In reality the drugs available on the Australian market today have undergone rigorous testing for many years before being released for public use. Most have also been extensively tested overseas. Doctors always try to weigh up any possible side effects of a drug against its potential benefits in order to avoid prescribing medications that may have adverse effects on the patient.

Many new drugs have become available in the last decade: cures for peptic ulcers, better drugs to combat high blood pressure, more effective antibiotics and antifungals, drugs to prevent heart attacks, anti-allergy tablets that do not sedate, and a new range of drugs that can actually cure some viral infections.

The greatest innovation now under way is changes to the way drugs are given. If a patient needs a medication in the body, it can enter as a tablet, liquid or capsule through the mouth; as an injection; or it may be introduced as a suppository and absorbed through the wall of the rectum. In the last few years, a new range of drugs has been introduced that can be absorbed through the skin into the bloodstream. An ointment or patch that contains the appropriate chemical is placed on the skin, and the drug is transported through the skin cells to the blood without causing any damage to the skin itself. Drugs that cause unpleasant side effects when taken by mouth or cannot be easily swallowed are obvious choices for this method of administration. Drugs to prevent angina (heart pain) and vomiting were the first to be introduced. Hormones and arthritis-relieving medications are due to follow. Some angina treatments cause unpleasant effects in the gut, and it is very awkward for people with vomiting to take a tablet when they cannot keep down a sip of water! The anti-vomiting skin patch is designed to be stuck on before a journey to prevent motion sickness, and lasts for up to three days.

Tablets have also been redesigned so that they do not break up until they reach a certain place in the gut. They can also dissolve at a set rate, releasing their active ingredients regularly into the body, so that only one or two tablets a day are necessary, rather than the three or four of earlier times. No-one (or almost no-one)

SECTION 6: TREATMENTS

likes taking tablets, but they are the most effective way medical science has of performing the modern miracles of curing infections, relieving symptoms and controlling diseases that crippled or killed our forebears.

Those who need regular medication should always carry suitable identification to show doctors in an emergency. Those with serious conditions should consider wearing a suitably engraved bracelet or pendant.

The drugs available in Australia are discussed in more detail on the following pages.

Drug groups

Every drug belongs to a particular class of drugs, all of which have similar properties, uses and actions. Nearly 100 drug classes are listed below, with a definition of the class, examples of drugs in that class, the uses of those drugs, the forms in which they can be found (tablet, cream, injection, etc.), their side effects, contraindications (when they should *NOT* be used), and any problems with their use.

To find the class to which a particular drug belongs:
1. Find the name of the drug in the alphabetical listing of DRUGS AVAILABLE IN AUSTRALIA in the next part of this section, and note the relevant drug class shown in the third column.
2. Then consult the drug classes listed below.

ACE INHIBITORS
See ANTIHYPERTENSIVES.

ACIDS
Acids are not commonly used internally in medicine today. Hydrochloric acid is naturally produced in the stomach to aid in digestion. It may be given by mouth in an extremely dilute form to patients with indigestion and a natural lack of stomach acid. Glutamic acid can also be used in this way. They are available in capsule or liquid form and, unless taken in excess or by those who do not require the medication, cause virtually no side effects.

Acid ointments (e.g. salicylic acid) and paints may be used on the skin to remove warts and small skin cancers. If the area being treated becomes painful, the acid should not be used for a few days until the pain subsides. Then it may be applied again.

ADRENERGIC STIMULANTS
Adrenergic stimulants are drugs that stimulate the nervous system. Adrenaline, dopamine and isoprenaline are the main drugs in this class. They are used to treat severe shock, low blood

pressure, severe allergy reactions, severe asthma and hypersensitivity reactions. They are available only as an injection. Side effects of a wide variety are common, and they interact with many other medications. They are used with great care in severe disease under the careful and constant supervision of a doctor.

See also STIMULANTS.

ALPHA RECEPTOR BLOCKERS
See ANTIHYPERTENSIVES.

ALKALISERS, URINE
Alkalisers are designed to raise the pH (acidity) of the urine from a low value to a high value, making it more alkaline and less attractive to bacteria. Common brands are Citravescent, Ural and Citralka. They act to control the burning experienced with bladder infections, and to control and prevent minor urinary infections. They are also used to control excess acid in the stomach. They are available as a liquid, or as a powder that mixes with water to make a palatable drink. They should not be used regularly in the long term, or in patients with kidney or heart failure. Side effects are rare.

AMINOGLYCOSIDES
See ANTIBIOTICS.

ANABOLIC STEROIDS
Anabolic steroids are drugs that build up body tissue. Oxymetholone and nandrolone (Deca-Durabolin) are common examples. They are used clinically to treat severe blood diseases (e.g. aplastic anaemia), some types of cancer, osteoporosis and kidney failure. They are used illegally by athletes and body builders to increase muscle mass. They are available as tablets and injections. There are many serious side effects and problems associated with their long-term use, including liver disease and damage, the development of male characteristics and cessation of periods in women, stunting of growth and early onset of puberty in children, swelling of tissue, water retention, infertility, personality disorders and voice changes.

ANAESTHETICS
Anaesthetics are drugs that cause the loss of sensation and pain. There are two main types, local and general.

Local anaesthetics are injections, creams, sprays or gels that remove sensation at one point in the body. Examples include

Xylocaine (injections, sprays and ointments), Citanest, Marcaine and lignocaine. They may be combined with adrenaline to restrict blood flow to an area and prolong the anaesthetic effect. General anaesthetics can be inhaled (e.g. halothane, nitrous oxide) or injected (e.g. thiopentone).

Side effects vary greatly from one agent to another but are rare with local anaesthetics. Adrenaline-containing local anaesthetics should not be used in fingers, toes, ear lobes or penis.

See also SURGICAL TREATMENT.

ANALGESICS

Drugs that reduce the sensation of pain are called analgesics. There are three main types — narcotics (see separate entry), salicylates (see NSAIDs) and paracetamol. Many analgesic preparations are combinations of two or more different medications. Paracetamol occurs in combination with many other types of drugs for the relief of cold symptoms and muscle spasm. Common presentations of paracetamol include Panadol, Panamax, Dymadon, Codral preparations, Capadex, Digesic, Codalgin, Fiorinal, Mersyndol, Migranol, Nembudeine and Panadeine. Paracetamol is available in tablet or syrup forms. Side effects are rare, and it can be used in the long term without problems, but overdosage has severe consequences, particularly in children.

ANORECTICS

Anorectic drugs are used to reduce appetite. Duromine, Ponderax, Sanorex and Tenuate are the commonly used drugs in this class in Australia. These drugs do *NOT* reduce weight but act as an aid to controlling appetite while the patient complies with a strictly controlled diet. They are available in tablet and capsule form only, and should not be used in patients who have high blood pressure, heart disease, thyroid disease or glaucoma.

Anorectics should not be used for long periods, as dependence can occur. They are stimulants, which may cause insomnia if used in the evening, and are used illegally by long-distance drivers and other who wish to remain awake for long periods of time. They should not be mixed with alcohol, and their use during pregnancy is controversial.

ANTACIDS

Drugs that neutralise acid in the stomach are antacids. A very large number of these medications are available without prescription, including Quick-Eze, Almacarb, Dexsal, Gastrogel, Meracote, Mucaine, Mylanta and Sodexol. They are used to treat bloating, flatulence, indigestion, hyperacidity and peptic ulcers, and are available as both mixtures and tablets. Sometimes they cause problems with the absorption of other medications if taken at the same time. Antacids should be used with care in patients with kidney disease. Constipation and diarrhoea may occur with overuse.

ANTHELMINTICS

Helminths are different types of worms that infect the human, usually found in the gut. The drugs that destroy these unwanted internal worms are called anthelmintics. There are many different types of helminths, including threadworms, hookworms, roundworms, and a number of rarer worms that are not normally found in Australia.

Combantrin and Vermox are the most common anthelmintics, and both can be purchased without prescription in mixture, tablet and granule formulations. They are relatively safe but should not be used during pregnancy or by patients with liver disease. It is important to treat all family members, and to carefully clean all clothing and bedding at the time of treatment. A number of prescription drugs are available for the treatment of resistant cases or rarer types of infection.

ANTIALLERGY EXTRACTS

Antiallergy extracts are extracts of many different pollens, venoms and other substances that can be used in very slowly increasing dosages to desensitise a patient who is allergic to a particular substance. Each individual patient must be tested before treatment to determine the specific extracts required. They are available as injections or drops that are placed on the tongue. A large range of allergies can be treated by these means, but they must be used under strict medical supervision as sudden severe allergic reactions may occur.

See also ANTIHISTAMINES.

ANTIANGINA MEDICATION

This large range of medications is used to treat angina (chest pain caused by a poor blood supply to the heart — see Section 5). Drugs in this group include the tablets Adalat, Anginine, Cardizem, Isordil, Peritrate and Pexid; the skin patches Nitradisc and Transiderm-Nitro; and the ointment Nitrolate.

The tablets come in two types — those that are swallowed whole on a regular basis to prevent angina (e.g. Adalat, Pexid) and those that are dissolved under the tongue to rapidly relieve acute attacks of angina (e.g. Anginine, Isordil).

Because some antiangina medications (e.g. Isordil) can cause stomach upsets, a new method of putting the medication into the body by passing it directly through the skin has been developed. Patches and ointments of various strengths are now available to prevent angina. Dosage can also be adjusted by wearing a patch for only a certain period of the day. These treatments have remarkably few side effects but may cause skin rashes in some people, particularly if they are applied to the same place too often.

Great care must be taken when using antiangina drugs in patients with glaucoma, anaemia, low blood pressure and heart failure. Another group of drugs, the beta-blockers (see separate entry), are also used to treat and prevent angina.

ANTIARRHYTHMICS

Antiarrhythmics are the drugs that keep the heart beating regularly. If the heart rhythm is uneven, beats are being missed, or extra beats are causing palpitations, doctors will prescribe an antiarrhythmic. There is a wide range of medications in this class, they work in different ways depending on the type of heart rhythm irregularity, and they are available in both tablet and injection form. The beta-blockers (see separate entry) can also be used for this purpose. Commonly used antiarrhythmics include Cordilox, Isoptin, Kinidin, Mexitil and Rythmodan.

Side effects do occur with antiarrhythmics, but they vary widely from drug to drug and patient to patient. It should be possible to vary the medication so that the effects of the drug are adequately helping the patient without causing significant side effects. These medications can also interact with other drugs, and some should not be used in certain diseases (e.g. thyroid disorders). A doctor treating a patient with one of these drugs must be fully aware of the patient's medical history and all the other drugs the patient is taking.

ANTIARTHRITICS

See ANTIRHEUMATICS; NSAIDs.

ANTIBIOTICS

Every sixth prescription written by doctors in Australia is for an antibiotic. They are thus the most widely prescribed group of drugs, but most patients understand very little about them.

Although there were chemical compounds used against infection before the second world war, the isolation of penicillin from a mould grown in a laboratory represented the first real exploitation of a purified natural substance that could kill bacteria. The very first supplies of penicillin came from the mould grown, due to wartime exigencies, in large numbers of bedpans. Most antibiotics today are produced as the result of chemical reactions (i.e. synthesised) as opposed to harvesting the drug from primitive life forms grown in bulk in areas that resembled mushroom farms.

Antibiotics are only effective against bacteria, and not against viral infections. Most of the infections seen by a general practitioner are caused by viruses, and there is no need for antibiotics in these cases.

Antibiotics are used by doctors in several situations:
- If the infection appears to be bacterial, the appropriate antibiotic will be selected to cure it. Samples or swabs may be taken so that the infecting bacteria and the correct antibiotic to kill it can be identified in a laboratory.
- If the problem is not clear-cut, or if there is some doubt as to the cause of a problem, an antibiotic may be prescribed to cover one of the possibilities. This may be the case with a severely sore throat.
- If a person has reduced immunity, is elderly, frail, liable to recurrent infections or due for an operation, an antibiotic may be used to prevent a bacterial infection. Women with recurrent bladder infections are one example.

Major problems can occur with the overuse of antibiotics. Cost is the first one, and as the government (i.e. you the taxpayer) pays part of the cost of everyone's antibiotics, this is a problem affecting you. Side effects are another problem. These can include rashes, diarrhoea (which can stop the oral contraceptive pill from working), nausea, fever and some rarer and more serious complications. The most important problem is the development of resistance which can enable bacteria to change in a way which makes them able to resist the actions of an antibiotic that was previously very effective. The need for new antibiotic agents is therefore always with us. Their development is a long and costly process involving huge investments by the drug companies. A good antibiotic deserves a long and effective life, and the needs of the public will be best served by the prescribing of antibiotics only when they are really needed, thus reducing the rate at which resistant strains develop.

Aminoglycosides
Aminoglycosides are a group of less commonly used antibiotics that can destroy certain types of bacteria causing infections in the urinary tract, skin and bloodstream. They are available as injections, tablets, powders and creams, and include gentamicin, Nebcin, neomycin and Soframycin. They are most commonly used as creams and powders on the skin, or as injections for very

severe infections. When used internally they can cause stomach upsets, skin rashes, pins and needles, and must be used with care in patients with kidney failure. They can interact with cephalosporin antibiotics. The creams and powders can sometimes cause adverse reactions and rashes too.

Beta lactams

The term beta lactams covers two closely related classes of antibiotics — the penicillins and the cephalosporins. If a patient is allergic to one of these, it is possible, but not certain, that they will be allergic to the other. They kill bacteria by breaking down the cell wall ('skin') around it.

Cephalosporins are a group of relatively strong antibiotics. They are divided by doctors into first, second and third generation cephalosporins. In general terms, they increase in strength and the number of types of bacteria they are active against decreases as you go from first to third generation drugs.

First generation cephalosporins are commonly used by general practitioners and include Ceporex and Keflex. They are active against a very wide range of bacteria, and are particularly useful in chest infections, urinary infections, skin infections and joint infections. They can interact with aminoglycoside antibiotics, and must be used with care in patients with kidney failure.

Side effects are uncommon with the first generation capsules and mixtures, but more likely with the third generation cephalosporins which are normally given by injection.

Penicillins are the most widely used antibiotics in the world. There are many different types of penicillin now available. They are broad-spectrum antibiotics that kill a wide range of bacteria, and have been used for almost every conceivable type of infection at some time. Unfortunately many bacteria are now becoming resistant to penicillin. Common brands include Amoxil, Moxacin, PVK, Augmentin, Flopen and Penbritin. They are available as tablets, capsules, drops, syrup, injection, and chewable tablets.

Side effects can include diarrhoea, skin rashes, fever, nausea and an allergy reaction. Allergies to penicillin are not more common than to other drugs, but appear to be so because it is so widely used. Patients who know they have a penicillin allergy should tell their doctors and wear a warning pendant or bracelet. Penicillin may cause a skin rash if given to a patient with glandular fever, and may start a vaginal thrush infection in some women.

Sulphas

Sulphas were the very first antibiotics developed, but the ones available in the late 1930s had severe side effects and were not very effective. Sulphas today are not as widely used as penicillins but still play a part in the treatment of some types of infections.

The most commonly prescribed sulpha preparations are Bactrim and Septrin, which have a sulpha antibiotic combined with a second type of antibiotic. They are used for chest, sinus and urinary infections most commonly. Pure sulpha antibiotics, such as Urolucosil, are still used for some urinary infections.

Side effects of sulphas are uncommon, but in rare cases serious problems can arise from their use. They should be avoided in patients with liver disease and used with caution in the elderly. They are available in tablet, mixture and injection forms.

Tetracyclines

Tetracyclines act by preventing the multiplication of bacteria. Other antibiotics act by directly killing the bacteria. As a result, tetracyclines are sometimes slower to act than penicillins or sulphas. They should *NOT* be used in pregnancy, during breastfeeding, or in children under 12 years of age, except in special circumstances. Prolonged use in children can cause yellow discolouration of teeth and nails. They can retard the development of the skeleton in a foetus if taken during pregnancy.

In other situations, tetracyclines are very effective in the treatment of many infections, particularly in the chest and sinuses. They are frequently used in the long term for the treatment of pimples in teenagers. Common brands include Achromycin, Doryx, Minomycin, Mysteclin, Rondomycin, Tetrex and Vibramycin. Some are combined with nystatin, an antifungal drug, to prevent the most common side effect — vaginal thrush in women. The more recently developed synthetic tetracyclines need be given only once or twice a day, and are far more effective than their antecedents.

Side effects of tetracyclines can include an increased sensitivity to sunlight and diarrhoea. They are most commonly used as capsules or tablets, but injections are available.

Others

The most common of the antibiotics that fall into the category of 'others' are the **erythromycins**. These act against bacteria by interfering with the way their internal chemical reactions occur. They are most commonly used in chest, sinus and ear infections. They can interact with theophylline, which is used by asthmatics and in some cough mixtures. Side effects can include nausea, diarrhoea, skin rashes and liver problems. Some people who are allergic to penicillin are also allergic to erythromycin. Common brands include EES, Eryc, Erythrocin and Ilosone. They are available as tablets, mixtures and injections.

Fasigyn and **Flagyl** are classed as both antibiotics and antitrichomonals. They destroy some microscopic animals as well as a select group of bacteria that survive without oxygen. They can be given in tablet form as a single dose. Side effects are uncommon, a bad taste and nausea being the most common.

A large range of other antibiotics that act against specific bacteria, or act only in certain organs, are also available to doctors. Flagyl and Fasigyn act against certain other microscopic animals that can infect the gut or vagina, and also kill bacteria that may be found deep inside the body where oxygen cannot reach. Dalacin and lincomycin are particularly effective against infections in bones and joints, as well as other organs.

A lot more of these antibiotics are rarely used, are mixed in skin creams, or have other very specific uses and cannot be adequately covered in this text.

ANTICHOLINERGICS

Anticholinergics are normally used in tablet form to treat conditions such as myasthenia gravis, chronic constipation, an underactive intestine and retention of urine. They may also be used to correct the side effects of atropine injections. Neostigmine, bethanechol and pyridostigmine are the most common anticholinergics.

ANTICOAGULANTS

Anticoagulants are drugs that stop blood from clotting at the normal speed. They are used in patients who have had strokes due to blood clots, clots in leg veins and clots in heart and lung arteries. Aspirin is a very mild anticoagulant and can be used in small doses to prevent strokes. All anticoagulants should be stopped before any surgical procedure.

Patients on the stronger anticoagulants, such as heparin (injection only) and warfarin (Marevan and Coumadin), must be monitored carefully by their doctors and have blood tests regularly to ensure that the clotting factors in their blood are kept at the desirable level.

Patients using anticoagulants will bruise and bleed more easily than normal, and care must be taken when using some antiarthritic medications, as they may cause bleeding into the gut while the patient is on anticoagulants. There are many precautions necessary with these drugs that make compliance with a doctor's instructions vital.

ANTICONVULSANTS

This large group of drugs is used to control and prevent fits and convulsions caused by epilepsy and other diseases. Barbiturates (see separate entry) and benzodiazepines (see ANXIOLYTICS) are also used for this purpose. Patients must sometimes take quite large quantities of anticonvulsants, or combinations of several drugs to control their problem, and blood levels are usually checked to arrive at the correct dosage. Anticonvulsants are nearly always used as tablets, but injections and mixtures of some drugs are available. Common examples include Dilantin (which is used mainly for grand mal epilepsy), Epilim, Mysoline, Ospolot, Rivotril, Tegretol and Zarontin.

Side effects from anticonvulsants vary widely from one person to another and between drugs. They are usually worst when treatment is first started, and wear off as time passes. Drowsiness, light-headedness, nausea and pins and needles are examples of possible side effects. Dilantin may cause gum problems if used in the long term.

All these drugs have a tendency to interact with other drugs, and the doctor must be made aware of all medications being taken and any other diseases (e.g. diabetes) that may be present.

ANTIDEPRESSANTS

Antidepressants are used to control depression (see Section 5). This is as much a disease as diabetes or high blood pressure but is often thought to be a mental disorder that patients can 'pull themselves out of'. Nothing could be further than the truth. Depression is caused by a biochemical imbalance in the brain, and requires appropriate medication to correct it before a tragedy occurs. There are two main types of antidepressants — tricyclics and MAOI.

Tricyclics

Tricyclics are the most widely used antidepressants and are very effective in treating most cases, but they are slow to act, taking to two to four weeks to reach full effectiveness. They also cause some sedation, and so are normally taken at night. The other most common side effects are a dry mouth, blurred vision, low blood pressure and excess sweating. Common examples are Allegron, Laroxyl, Nortab, Prothiaden, Sinequan, Tofranil and Tryptanol. Tolvon is a similar drug, but classed as a tetracyclic.

Some of the tricyclic drugs are very useful in treating bedwetting, but they must be used with care in patients with heart disease, epilepsy or glaucoma.

MAOI (monoamine oxidase inhibitors)

MAOI are potent antidepressants that are only used in severe and chronic cases of depression. They include Nardil, Marplan and Parnate. They are also slow in becoming effective, and their effects may persist for a couple of weeks after they are stopped.

They do not cause drowsiness, but they interact violently with many other drugs and some foods, including soy sauce, cheese, red wine and pickled foods. Any patient on MAOI should be given by their doctor a list of foods and drugs they must avoid. This list must be observed carefully, or serious side effects may occur.

MAOI should not be taken at the same time as tricyclic antidepressants, and only with extreme care by epileptic patients. Other side effects include insomnia, dizziness, palpitations, headaches, difficulty in passing urine, and a dry mouth. If taken correctly, they can dramatically improve a depressed patient's life.

ANTIDIARRHOEALS

Antidiarrhoeals are one of the most popular drug groups with patients. When you just have to go and go and go — and you want to stop — antidiarrhoeals such as Lomotil, Imodium and Lyspafen are just the thing to help. These are the most widely prescribed antidiarrhoeals, but they must not be overused. There are some types of diarrhoea that they are not suitable for, including those associated with jaundice (yellow skin), bacterial gut infections, and diarrhoea during pregnancy. They are dangerous in overdosage, but in the correct dose they usually only cause a dry mouth. They should not be used in children under the age of 12.

Diarrhoea has a vast number of causes (see Section 3), and the exact treatment chosen will depend on that cause. Many types of diarrhoea require no medication but a correct diet.

The milder over-the-counter antidiarrhoeals include the kaolin, codeine and pectin-containing mixtures and tablets. Codeine in high doses is a prescription item for the stopping of diarrhoea, as well as being a potent pain-killer (analgesic).

ANTIDIURETICS

The antidiuretics is a rarely used group of drugs that includes Minirin and Pitressin. They are used to reduce the amount of urine produced in a disease called diabetes insipidus and in some other even rarer conditions. They are unusual in that some forms are given routinely as a nasal spray. They must be used with extreme caution in pregnancy, and in patients with epilepsy, migraine or heart failure.

ANTIEMETICS

Antiemetics are medicines that stop you from vomiting. They are often difficult to give in tablet or mixture form, so many of them are also available as an injection or suppository (for insertion into the back passage) and even as a skin patch. There are many different drugs in this category, from the mild over-the-counter travel sickness pills such as Andrumin, Avomine and Dramamine, to the more effective and potent prescription drugs such as Stemetil, Motilium, Torecan and Maxolon. Care must be taken in using the prescription drugs in children and in epileptics. Overdosage can induce fainting, dizziness, blurred vision and collapse. Other side effects include spasms and twitches of neck and facial muscles. Otherwise, complications are few and seldom more than a dry mouth.

Scop is a new concept in the prevention of nausea in that it is a skin patch that is placed behind the ear before the nausea starts (e.g. before a sea journey). It is effective for three days.

Emetrol is a mild antiemetic that can be used safely in morning sickness.

ANTIFUNGALS

Fungi are members of the plant kingdom and are one of the types of microscopic life that can infect human beings in many diverse ways. The most common site of infection is the skin, where they cause an infection that is commonly known as tinea. Fungi are also responsible for many gut infections, particularly in the mouth and around the anus. It is a rare infant that escapes without an attack of oral thrush (see Section 5). Around the anus, the fungus can cause an extremely itchy rash, but in women it may spread forward from the anus to the vagina to cause the white discharge and intense itch of vaginal thrush or candidiasis (see Section 5). The most serious diseases develop when fungal infections occur deep inside the body in organs such as the lungs, brain and sinuses. These diseases are very difficult to treat and it may take many months with potent antifungal drugs to bring them under control. Fortunately, this type of condition is relatively rare.

Antifungals are divided into three broad groups — creams, powders, lotions and gels for use on the skin and in the mouth; creams and pessaries for insertion into the vagina to treat thrush; and tablets, mixtures and injections for internal fungal infections. All these are relatively slow to work, and in contrast to the dramatic improvement seen with antibiotics, it often takes many days or weeks with antifungals.

The skin preparations include Canesten, Pevaryl, Daktarin, Mycil, Enzactin, Nilstat, Tinacidin and many more. Most are available without prescription and are very safe, but must be used consistently until the rash has gone completely.

The vaginal preparations include Gyno-Daktarin, Gyne-Lotremin, Canesten, Ecostatin and Monistat. These are creams that are used around the vulva or are inserted into the vagina with the use of an applicator; or pessary tablets that are inserted into the vagina. There they kill off the fungus (called *Candida albicans*) that causes thrush. Most are very safe, but not all can be used during pregnancy.

There are only a small number of antifungals for internal use. Griseofulvin (Grisovin, Griseostatin) and Nizoral are the commonly used tablets. These tablets can be used to help treat fungal infections on the skin and in the vagina as well. Daktarin is available in an injection form for very serious internal fungal infections. There are no serious side effects associated with them, but they must be used with great care in patients with liver disease and pregnancy.

ANTIHISTAMINES

Antihistamines are some of the most commonly used drugs in Australia. They are often one of several drugs found in many cold and flu remedies that may be purchased from chemists.

Histamine is a substance, found in special cells in every part of the body, which is responsible for allergy reactions. If histamine is released from cells, it causes swelling, itching, spasm of muscles, dilation of blood vessels and secretion of phlegm. Histamine release in the nose causes a runny nose and sneezing; in the lungs it may cause asthma; in the skin it causes hives (urticaria); in the gut it causes diarrhoea. Histamines may be released in response to an insect bite, to inhaling pollen or dusts, eating certain foods or drugs, or touching some plants.

Antihistamines counteract the histamine released into the tissues, and so control allergy reactions. They work well in the nose, sinuses and throat; reasonably well in the skin; but not at all well in the lungs and gut. Antihistamines are therefore used for hay fever, sneezing attacks, skin allergies and drug rashes. Some can be useful in treating dizziness, itches, nausea and migraine.

Antihistamines should be avoided, if possible, during breastfeeding and in newborn babies. They should be used with care in children, and in patients with glaucoma, epilepsy and acute asthma. Most of them produce some degree of lethargy and drowsiness, so care must be taken when driving and operating machinery. Alcohol should be avoided while taking antihistamines. Children may be stimulated by antihistamines, in direct contrast to adults. The only other significant side effect is a dry mouth. Overdosage can cause confusion, convulsions and coma, but overdose symptoms may not become apparent for some hours after taking the drug. Common brands include Zadine, Avil, Polaramine, Periactin, Dilosyn, Fabahistin, Phenergan and

Dimetane. They are available as tablets and mixtures, and some come as injections for severe allergy reactions. Phenergan is also available on prescription as a cream for certain allergic skin conditions.

There are two antihistamines that do not cause sedation, Teldane and Hismanal, but they are only available on prescription. It is likely that more non-sedating antihistamines will be released in the future.

ANTIHYPERTENSIVES

Patients with high blood pressure (see HYPERTENSION, Section 5) have a higher incidence of strokes and heart attacks than those who have normal blood pressure. As a result, doctors are very keen to maintain blood pressure at a reasonable level by means of one or more different medications. There is a huge number of antihypertensive drugs available to keep blood pressure down. They work in different ways on the blood vessels, kidneys and brain. Diuretics and beta-blockers (see separate entries) are also used in treating hypertension, as well as the drugs listed below.

The major classes of antihypertensives will be discussed separately.

ACE inhibitors

Angiotensin converting enzyme (ACE) inhibitors are a class of drugs that prevent the contraction of the tiny muscles that circle around small arteries by blocking the action of the chemical that is essential for the contraction of these tiny artery muscles. Drugs in this class include Capoten and Renitec. They are used to treat both high blood pressure and heart failure, and are available as tablets and mixtures. Side effects include an excessive drop in blood pressure, cough, rashes, taste disturbances, headache, dizziness and kidney problems. They should be used with caution in patients with kidney disease and patients taking potassium supplements.

Alpha receptor blockers

Alpha receptor blockers are drugs that block the reception of certain nerve signals to the arteries, and if these signals are not received, the artery relaxes, allowing more blood to flow through at a lower pressure. These drugs have undergone considerable refinement over the years, and most of the earlier ones that had significant side effects are no longer used. Minipress is the most commonly used one today, and is very successful in controlling many hypertensives with minimal side effects. It must be started in a very low dose, which is slowly increased over several weeks. Side effects may include dizziness, headache, drowsiness, nasal congestion, palpitations and nausea. Alpha receptor blockers are available only as tablets.

Calcium channel blockers

Calcium is essential for the contraction of the tiny muscles around the arteries. When these muscles contract, the artery becomes smaller and narrower. Calcium channel blockers prevent the calcium from entering the muscle cells through tiny channels in the skin of the cell. These muscle cells cannot then contract easily, remain relaxed, and do not narrow the artery. The wider an artery, the less resistance is placed on the blood flowing through it, and the lower the blood pressure.

Cardizem, Agon, Plendil, Adalat, Isoptin and Cordilox are the main drugs in this group. Because they prevent the contraction of all arteries, they reduce the strain on the heart, and some of these drugs can therefore be used to treat angina, which is due to a lack of blood to the heart muscle.

Calcium channel blockers are quite safe and are normally used in tablet form, although some can be given as injections. They must be used with caution in patients with some heart diseases and diabetes. They can interact with a number of drugs, so doctors must be aware of all the patient's medications. Their side effects may include dizziness, headaches, hot flushes and constipation.

Methyldopa

Methyldopa is one of the older antihypertensives that works on the brain to prevent it from sending out nerve signals to the arteries. If these nerve signals are reduced, the arteries will relax and reduce the blood pressure.

Methyldopa is marketed by different companies as Aldomet and Hydopa. It should not be used in patients with liver disease, and should be used with caution in depressed patients. Side effects may include drowsiness, headache, depression, weight gain, sore tongue and impotence in men. It is normally used as a tablet, but an injection is available.

Other

There are a number of other antihypertensives that do not fit into the above classes. These include Apresoline, Declinax, and Loniten.

See also DIURETICS; BETA-BLOCKERS.

ANTILEPROTICS

Antileprotics are the drugs that are used to treat leprosy. This is now a rare disease in Australia but can be found in some Aboriginal and migrant communities. Clofazimine and rifampicin (which is also used for tuberculosis) are the only drugs routinely available in Australia for this purpose. They must be taken regularly for many months or years to cure the disease.

ANTIMALARIALS

Malaria is becoming an increasing problem in the world, as many forms of the disease are becoming resistant to the commonly used medications. Millions of people die of malaria in tropical countries every year, and the most resistant and virulent form in the world can be found in our nearest neighbour country, Papua New Guinea. It is essential for travellers to any tropical country to discuss with their doctor, at least a month before their departure, the appropriate medications necessary to prevent malaria. Because it is spread by mosquitos, insect repellents, protective clothing and mosquito nets also play an important part in preventing malaria. Generally speaking, the same drugs are used for both prevention and treatment of malaria, but they are given in much higher dosages for treatment.

Quinine, chloroquine and its derivatives (Plaquenil, primaquine, Lariam) have been the mainstay of malaria treatment since quinine was first isolated from the cinchona tree bark by Spanish missionaries in the sixteenth century. Chloroquine-resistant forms of malaria are now present throughout south-east Asia and the south-west Pacific regions. The newer synthetic quinine derivatives (e.g. Lariam) overcome this problem. A number of other antimalarials are available to travellers to these countries, and for those who do catch the disease. Pyrimethamine (Daraprim, Maloprim) and Fansidar are commonly used. These tend to have more side effects, and are better used for short periods of time if possible. They should not be used during pregnancy or breastfeeding.

Prevention requires taking one or two tablets a week for two weeks before entering a malaria infected area, and continuing until a month after leaving it.

ANTIMIGRAINE MEDICATIONS

Migraine can be treated when it occurs, or better still, in patients with frequent attacks, prevented by the regular use of medication.

Acute attacks can be treated by the use of pain-killers and sedatives, or the use of specific drugs that deal with the over-dilated arteries that cause migraine (see Section 5). The drugs that work in this way include ergotamine (Cafergot, Lingraine, Migral) and Dihydergot. Some are combined with other medications and pain-killers to improve their effect. All must be used as soon as a migraine attack starts, and they may cause significant side effects in some people. Side effects include nausea, pins and needles, light-headedness, and altered heart rate. The drugs should be avoided in pregnancy, breastfeeding, and patients with high blood pressure. They may also interact with other drugs, and are available as tablets (for both swallowing and dissolving under the tongue), suppositories (anal use), and injections.

Medihaler ergotamine is an inhaled form that is used like an asthma spray. It has fewer side effects than the tablets and works very quickly.

Drugs to prevent migraine include Deseril, Dixarit and Sandomigran. They are taken in the appropriate dosage on a regular basis for months on end to prevent the majority of (but not usually all) migraine attacks. Sometimes quite large doses are required. Side effects should be minimal, drowsiness, weight gain and difficulty in passing urine being the most common. Care must be taken with the use of these drugs during pregnancy and breastfeeding.

Catapres (used for high blood pressure) and Inderal (a beta-blocker) are also very effective in preventing migraine.

Antiparasitics

Antiparasitics are creams, shampoos or lotions that destroy microscopic animals (parasites) that can be found on the skin and in the hair. Scabies, crabs, head lice and body lice are the common parasites found in Australia. The medications are applied all over the body, or in just the affected area, depending on the parasite. The treatment is usually repeated after a few days, and other family members should be treated at the same time. Ascabiol, Eurax, Lorexane and Quellada are commonly used antiparasitics. When applied, the eyes, nostrils, mouth and vagina should be avoided. Side effects are almost non-existent, but some individuals can develop a skin sensitivity.

Antiparkinsonians

Parkinson's disease is a distressing condition that is relatively common in older people. Its characteristics include stiffness, a shuffling gait and mental deterioration (see Section 5). There are a number of types of antiparkinsonian drugs used to treat this condition. None of them cure Parkinson's disease — they aim to control it.

Levodopa acts to replace the missing chemical in the brain that causes the disease. It is sometimes combined in the same tablet with other medications that increase the effectiveness of the Levodopa and reduce side effects. It should not be given to patients with psychiatric problems, glaucoma, melanoma, liver or kidney disease. It can cause heart irregularities, changes in behaviour, nausea, weight gain, hallucinations, nightmares and hot flushes, and also slow, jerky, uncontrollable body movements. Madopar, Sinemet and Larodopa are the drugs in this group.

Bromocriptine (Parlodel) also acts to control Parkinson's disease. It is, strangely enough, also used to stop the production of breast milk and treat a bone overgrowth disease called acromegaly. Side effects of these tablets include nausea and vomiting, dizziness and a reduced tolerance to alcohol.

There are a number of other drugs used to treat Parkinson's disease, including Artane, Cogentin, Akineton, Norflex and Kemadrin. They must be used with caution in patients with glaucoma and heart problems. Side effects include inability to pass urine, blurred vision, dry mouth and constipation. All are available as tablets, a few as injections.

ANTIPSYCHOTICS

A psychosis is a serious mental disorder (see Section 5), in which the patients normally have no idea that there is anything wrong with them. There are a large number of specific mental diseases that fit into this category, and different antipsychotic drugs are known to be more useful in treating some types psychoses. Psychoses are often characterised by agitation, anxiety, tension, personality changes and emotional disturbances. Common psychotic diseases include mania, some types of depression, and schizophrenia. Drugs that can correct these problems include Anatensol, Largactil, lithium, Melleril, Mutabon D, Navane, Neulactil, Serenace and Stelazine. All are available as tablets, and some as mixtures and injections. Side effects include drowsiness, depression, tremor, skin rashes, dry mouth, stuffy nose, constipation and weight gain. Caution is required in patients who have liver disease or are pregnant.

Fluphenazine (Modecate) is a long-acting injectable antipsychotic that can be given on a monthly basis for long-term control of psychoses, particularly schizophrenia. This overcomes the problem of patients forgetting or refusing their medication.

ANTIRHEUMATICS

An amazingly diverse range of drugs can be placed in the category of relieving rheumatoid arthritis. Most of them have found their place here serendipitously, when patients being treated for other diseases found that their rheumatoid arthritis was improved. There is no cure for rheumatoid arthritis, but by the use of pain-killers, physiotherapy, NSAIDs (see separate entry) and the antirheumatic drugs, control is normally possible. Penicillamine (not related to the antibiotic), gold (e.g. Myocrisin or Ridaura) and chloroquine (normally used for malaria) fit into this category. All these medications are slow to act, have significant side effects, and patients using them must be monitored very regularly by their doctor. Because of these problems, they are only used in severe cases of rheumatoid arthritis where other treatment has failed. In the correct patients, remarkable relief from pain and swelling can be achieved.

Gold has normally been given by injection, but tablets are now available. It must be avoided in kidney and liver disease, and may cause skin rashes, eye problems, and other side effects. It can interfere with other medications, and because of its tendency to destroy white blood cells, blood tests are ordered regularly for patients on gold treatment. Penicillamine must not be used with gold, and blood and/or urine tests are required regularly. Skin rashes may occur and pregnancy must be avoided.

Chloroquine tablets can cause eye problems when used in the long term, so regular assessment by an eye specialist is normal.

ANTISEPTICS

Antiseptics are drugs that kill bacteria and other infecting organisms on the skin, in the mouth or other areas, without being absorbed into the body or blood. They may also be used to sterilise medical instruments and equipment. Something that is 'septic' is infected, so antiseptics act against infection.

They are available as lotions, creams, ointments, powders, pessaries (for vaginal use) and lozenges. A prescription is not normally required for their purchase. They have minimal side effects unless they are swallowed or otherwise used inappropriately. Allergy reactions (e.g. to iodine preparations) can occur. Commonly used antiseptics include Betadine, Isodine, Dequadin, Dettol, Savlon, Furacin, Phisohex and Vioform.

See also ALKALISERS, URINE.

ANTISPASMODICS

Antispasmodics prevent or treat painful muscular spasm of hollow tubes within the body, such as the gut and the urine-carrying tubes.

Gut antispasmodics

If the gut goes into spasm, severe intermittent pains can develop in the abdomen. Irritable bowel syndrome, infantile colic, gastroenteritis and gut infections are just a few of the diseases that can cause this problem. There are a large number of antispasmodic drugs for the gut that vary from mild over-the-counter tablet and mixture preparations such as Donnalix, Infacol and Mintec to potent prescription tablets such as Merbentyl,

Colofac, Buscopan, Librax and Pro-Banthine. Some of these are also available as injections.

The milder preparations have no significant side effects, but the stronger ones can sometimes cause a dry mouth, drowsiness and constipation. Care must be taken in patients with glaucoma, prostate problems and pregnancy.

Urinary antispasmodics

The only urinary antispasmodic available is Urispas. It relieves the painful muscle spasm of the bladder and urethra (urine tube) that occurs with kidney stones and infections, bladder infections and prostate disease. It may cause drowsiness, and must not be used in pregnancy and patients with glaucoma. It is available in tablet form only.

ANTITHYROID DRUGS

An overactive thyroid gland can cause a multiplicity of serious problems. The excess production of thyroxine hormone by the gland must be reduced before serious damage occurs to other organs in the body. The drugs that act against the thyroid gland are carbimazole and propylthiouracil. They should not be used in the long term, unless regular blood tests are performed to assess any potential damage to blood cells or other organs. Because of their significant side effects, these tablets are used only in the acute situation, until a cure by means of surgery or irradiation is undertaken.

ANTITUBERCULOTICS

Fifty years ago in Australia, tuberculosis (TB) killed thousands every year. Special hospitals were built in every capital and many regional centres, just to cope with the huge number of patients suffering from this lung disease. Today those hospitals have been converted to other uses, and thanks to X-ray screening, inoculations, pasteurisation of milk, better hygiene and effective antituberculotic drugs, tuberculosis has almost been eradicated. Tuberculosis does still occur in Australia though, usually in migrants from poorer countries and in Aborigines.

A number of drugs can be used for the treatment of TB. Normally two or three are given simultaneously, and in the early stages of treatment they may be given by injection. Treatment is very slow, and the medication must be taken for many months or years.

Isoniazid, ethambutol, rifampicin and pyrazinamide are the antituberculotics currently available. Regular blood tests and X-rays are necessary while on treatment, and sometimes side effects may necessitate alterations in dosage or choice of medication.

Because the side effects and precautions are so variable from drug to drug and patient to patient, it is not possible to list them in any meaningful way.

Antitussives

Antitussives are the mixtures, lozenges or tablets that stop coughing. They act by directly soothing the inflamed throat, decreasing the sensitivity of the part of the brain that triggers the spasm of coughing, decreasing the amount of phlegm in the throat, anaesthetising the throat, reducing inflammation, reducing pain, and by almost any combination of these methods. There are dozens of cough mixtures (antitussives). They differ from the expectorants (see separate entry), which are designed to increase coughing but make the coughing more effective so that phlegm can be cleared from the lungs and throat.

Codeine is one of the most common ingredients of cough mixtures and acts as a suppressor of the brain's cough centre and as a pain-killer. It is a mild narcotic, and its main side effect is constipation. There are a number of related drugs (e.g. pholcodine, dihydrocodeine, dextromethorphan) which act in a similar way. Most antitussives are available without prescription and have minimal side effects. Many have an alcohol base and also contain mild narcotics or antihistamines, so care must be taken with driving and operating machinery. Other cough suppressants may include guaiphenesin, senega, camphor and thymol. Antihistamines, decongestants, mucolytics and analgesics are often combined with these ingredients.

Hycomine and Ticarda are potent antitussives available on prescription only. They contain stronger narcotics, and are designed for short-term use in intractable, severe coughs. They can become addictive if used in the long term.

Antiulcerants

Antiulcerants control, soothe and heal the painful peptic ulcers that can eat into the wall of the gullet, stomach and small intestine. There are a number of different types that will be discussed below, but antacids (listed separately) also act in this way.

H2 receptor antagonists

One of the most significant advances in medication in the late 1970s was the introduction of cimetidine (Tagamet, Duractin), the first of the H2 receptor antagonists. Since then, ranitidine (Zantac) and famotidine (Pepcidine) have been released. These drugs are distantly related to antihistamines and act to cure ulcers by reducing the amount of acid secreted into the stomach.

This also enables them to control reflux oesophagitis, which may accompany a hiatus hernia.

H2 receptor antagonists are normally only prescribed after the presence of an ulcer has been proved by a gastroscopy (see Section 4) or X-ray of the gut. Cimetidine can sometimes interact with other drugs that control epilepsy and blood clotting. Side effects are not common, but may include dizziness, headache, rashes, tiredness, depression, increases in breast size (in both men and women) and liver problems. Treatment is usually rapidly effective, but must be continued for weeks or months to prevent relapses.

Other

There are a number of other anti-ulcer drugs, including Carafate, and De-Nol (available as liquid or tablet). These can also be used to prevent ulcers in patients taking the anti-arthritis drugs (e.g. NSAIDs — see separate entry) that have a tendency to cause them. Carafate and De-Nol should not be taken at the same time as antacids. De-Nol should be avoided in pregnancy.

Antivirals

Until very recently, drugs that killed viruses and cured viral infections were limited to the idoxuridine eye drops and ointments, and vidarabine. Acyclovir (Zovirax) is the first antiviral tablet/injection that can attack viral infections from within the body, but this only acts against herpes zoster and herpes simplex viruses that cause cold sores, genital herpes and shingles. Acyclovir appears to be a very safe drug, but its safety in pregnancy has not yet been established. Side effects are uncommon but can include nausea and headache.

Vidarabine is a potent injectable antiviral drug for use in severe infections only. It has significant side effects.

Idoxuridine is found in Stoxil, Virasolve and other eye drops and cold sore preparations. It is far more effective if used early in the disease when the virus is multiplying. It has minimal side effects.

Anxiolytics

Anxiolytics act to relieve anxiety and stress.

Benzodiazepine anxiolytics

This subgroup of anxiolytics includes a large number of drugs such as Valium, Serepax, Murelax, Ativan, Ducene, Frisium, Lexotan, Librium, Tranxene and Xanax. They all sedate and may cause dependency, and they also relieve anxiety, but the degree of sedation and dependency varies dramatically from one drug to another and one patient to another. Dependency should not be a problem unless the drugs are used inappropriately. Some of these drugs (e.g. Valium, Ducene, Librium) can also be used to relax muscle spasm and control convulsions.

Benzodiazepines such as Mogadon, Normison and Euhypnos are used primarily for their sedative property in inducing sleep in patients with insomnia. They are listed as hypnotics.

Benzodiazepines should not be used in patients with glaucoma, and with caution in patients with brain, liver, kidney and lung diseases. They should be stopped slowly, with a gradual reduction in dosage if they have been used for a long time. They will increase the effects of alcohol, and care should be taken with driving and using machinery while taking them. Side effects include drowsiness, forgetfulness, confusion, weakness, nausea, dry mouth, blurred vision and skin rashes. They are relatively safe in overdosages.

Other anxiolytics

The other anxiolytics include Buspar and Equanil tablets, designed for short-term use in anxiety states. They should be avoided during pregnancy and breastfeeding, and their side effects include sedation, interaction with alcohol, dizziness, nausea, blurred vision and weakness. Buspar does not cause dependence, but it is slow to act.

ASTRINGENTS

Astringents stop secretions and discharges, usually from the eyes. There are a number of eye drop preparations that control watery eyes and at the same time reduce the redness of the eye by causing contraction of the tiny arteries (vasoconstriction) that crisscross the whites of the eye. These include Albalon, Murine, Visine and Antistine Privine. These drops must be avoided in glaucoma and used with caution by patients with high blood pressure and diabetes. They should not be used continuously for more than two weeks, and if the condition does not ease within 48 hours, medical advice should be sought. A prescription is not required, and side effects are minimal, but stinging can occur when the drops are first introduced into the eye.

ATROVENT

See BRONCHODILATORS.

BARBITURATES

Barbiturates such as amylobarbitone and pentobarbitone are now used primarily to control convulsions and before operations, but they have been used in the past as sedatives and anti-anxiety drugs. They are addictive if given for long periods of time, and therefore have gone out of favour in recent years. The main side effects of these tablets and injections are overexcitement, a hangover on withdrawal, and pain at the site of injection. They increase the effects of alcohol, are dangerous in overdosage, and are available only on prescription.

BENZODIAZEPINES
See ANXIOLYTICS.

BETA-BLOCKERS
High blood pressure, migraine, irregular heartbeat, stage fright, prevention of heart attack, exam nerves, angina, overactive thyroid gland, tremors and glaucoma — all these diseases can be controlled, or treated, by the amazingly versatile group of drugs called beta- blockers. Some beta-blockers are very specific for particular diseases (e.g. timolol is used only in eye drop form for glaucoma; atenolol acts mainly on the heart), but others (e.g. Inderal/propranolol) can act in virtually all areas. The drugs in this class also include alprenolol, oxprenolol, pindolol, sotalol and metoprolol. They are available on prescription in tablet and injection forms.

Beta receptors are present on certain nerves in the body, and blocking the action of these nerves with beta-blockers produces the desired effects. Because they can control a fine tremor and anxiety over-performance, these drugs are banned in the Olympic and Commonwealth games, as they would give athletes such as archers and shooters an unfair advantage.

Beta-blockers are generally very safe medications but should not be used in asthmatics, patients with heart failure or with a slow heart beat. Care must be taken in their use by diabetics. Side effects include low blood pressure, slow heart rate, dizziness, insomnia, nightmares, nasal stuffiness, tiredness, nausea and impotence.

BETA LACTAMS
See ANTIBIOTICS.

BRONCHODILATORS
The bronchi are the tubes in the lung that contain air. Bronchodilators open these tubes to their maximum extent to allow more air to enter and leave the lungs. They are used to treat asthma and bronchitis. Bronchodilators are classified as either sympathomimetics or xanthinate derivatives.

Sympathomimetic bronchodilators

Ventolin, Bricanyl, Berotec, ephedrine and Respolin are the common sympathomimetic bronchodilators. They are available as pressure pack sprays, nebuliser additives, mixtures, tablets and injections. Ventolin is also available as a spincap — a capsule that can be ruptured and its contents are inhaled through a specially designed tube.

Sympathomimetics act very rapidly if inhaled or injected but more slowly, and with more side effects, if taken as a mixture or tablet. They should be used with caution in patients with high blood pressure and other heart disease. Side effects include palpitations, dizziness, headache, tremor, nausea and sweating.

Xanthinate derivatives

Theo-Dur, Nuelin, Choledyl, Brondecon, Elixophyllin and Somophyllin are the common drugs in this group. They are available as tablets, mixtures and injections. Nuelin is available as a sprinkle for adding to food. These drugs should be used with care in patients with high blood pressure and heart disease. Patients who smoke require higher dosages. Side effects include nausea (common), vomiting, headache, indigestion and palpitations.

Atrovent is a bronchodilator that does not fit into either of the above categories. It is an aerosol spray or nebuliser additive that increases the effectiveness of some sympathomimetics. Side effects are almost unknown.

CALCIUM CHANNEL BLOCKERS

See ANTIHYPERTENSIVES.

CARDIAC GLYCOSIDES

The foxglove flower has been known for centuries to control and assist patients with 'dropsy', which we now call congestive heart failure. Many medieval doctors made their reputation by curing the shortness of breath and swollen legs suffered by these patients by prescribing the regular use of foxglove tea. The active ingredient in the foxglove is digitalis, which has now been further refined to digoxin (also known as Lanoxin). This is the only commonly used cardiac glycoside, but Talusin is available for patients who cannot tolerate digoxin.

Digoxin is available in injection, tablet and mixture forms, and must only be used in the appropriate patients, as there are some heart diseases that it can aggravate. It can also interact with many other medications. Side effects are uncommon and usually associated with excess dosage, which may cause irregular heart beats, nausea, diarrhoea and abdominal pain.

CEPHALOSPORINS

See ANTIBIOTICS.

CHOLAGOGUES

Cholagogues promote the flow of bile from the gall bladder into the small intestine. Felicur is the only commonly used drug in this class. It is used in gall bladder infections and other liver diseases. It is available in capsule form, and there are no significant side effects, but it should be used with caution in early pregnancy.

CHOLINERGICS

Cholinergics are normally used in injection form to reduce the amount of saliva before an operation, to correct a very slow heart beat, and to relieve the spasm pain associated with kidney stones and gall stones. They are an old-fashioned treatment for asthma. Atropine is the only commonly used drug in this class.

CONTRACEPTIVES

See SEX HORMONES; SPERMICIDES.
See also Section 1.

CORTICOSTEROIDS

See STEROIDS.

CYTOTOXICS

The cytotoxics form a large, diverse group of drugs that are used to destroy cancer cells within the body in a process known as chemotherapy. 'Cyto' means cell, so 'cytotoxic' means toxic (harmful) to cells. They can be given by tablet or injection, and different drugs are used to attack different types of cancer. Unfortunately they are not all as specific in attacking cancer cells as we would wish, and normal cells may also be attacked and destroyed. The balance between giving enough of the drug to kill the cancer cells and not enough to kill too many normal cells is a very fine one.

The effectiveness of cytotoxic drugs varies dramatically from one patient to another and one disease to another. Some forms of cancer are very susceptible to cytotoxic drugs (e.g. acute leukaemias), while others are resistant. Side effects are very common, and again variable. Nausea, vomiting, diarrhoea, muscle pain, loss of hair, weight loss, fatigue and headaches are just a few of the many complications possible. Patients taking this type of medication will be closely monitored by their doctors through regular blood tests and clinic visits. Long-term treatment for many months is usually required, and other medications may be added to control the side effects.

DECONGESTANTS

Decongestants relieve stuffy noses, ease tight coughs and loosen mucus plugs. They are contained in a large number of proprietary cough and cold mixtures and work with varying degrees of efficacy.

Pseudoephedrine is a decongestant (and vasoconstrictor) found in nose drops, cough mixtures and cold tablets. Other decongestants include oxymetazoline and phenylephrine. They can cause stimulation and excitement as a side effect, and in nose drop form can actually increase congestion if used excessively.

See also MUCOLYTICS; BRONCHODILATORS; EXPECTORANTS.

DIGESTIVE ENZYMES

If the stomach, gall bladder and pancreas are unable to produce adequate enzymes to break down food into a form suitable for absorption, digestive enzymes (and acids) can be given in a tablet or capsule form during or after a meal. Because they are natural products (often obtained from pigs), side effects are rare unless they are taken in excess or away from meals.

DIURETICS

Diuretics are commonly called fluid tablets because they increase the rate at which the kidney produces urine, and therefore the frequency with which the patient has to visit the toilet to pass fluid. They are used to remove excess fluid from the lungs, legs and heart; to reduce blood pressure in hypertension; and to assist in the treatment of kidney failure. Common diuretics include Lasix, Chlotride, Moduretic, Navidrex, Burinex, Aprinox, Dyazide and Enduron. They all come as tablets, and some are available as injections. They must be used with caution in liver disease and diabetes.

The most common side effect of diuretics is washing out of the body (with the increased urine production) essential elements that should remain in the body. Potassium is the element most commonly lost, and as a result, many patients are given potassium (K) supplements to take while using diuretics. Some types of diuretics are not as likely as others to cause this problem, and others (e.g. Moduretic, Dyazide) are combined with a second drug to prevent the loss of potassium. This side effect may also be overcome by taking the tablets only five days a week, or in some other intermittent pattern. Blood tests are often ordered to assess the levels of potassium (and other elements) in patients on diuretics. Other side effects may include nausea, loss of appetite, headache, dizziness, cramps, muscle weakness, rashes and diarrhoea.

EXPECTORANTS

Expectorants aid the removal of phlegm and mucus from the respiratory passages of the lung and throat by coughing. They act by liquefying tenacious, sticky mucus so that it does not adhere firmly to the walls of the air passages, and can be shifted up and out by the microscopic hairs that line these passages and by the forced expiration of air in coughing. They are usually combined in a mixture with other medications such as mucolytics, decongestants, antihistamines, bronchodilators or antitussives (see separate entries).

The traditional expectorants include senega, ammonium chloride, and potassium iodide, all of which taste absolutely foul. Bromhexine and methoxyphenamine are more recently developed expectorants that have a slightly better taste.

The side effects of expectorants are minimal. Many different brands are available from chemists without a prescription.

FIBRINOLYTICS

Fibrinolytics are injections that are given into the veins in the immediate treatment of severe conditions involving blood clots in arteries (e.g. a heart attack). They prevent the further formation of blood clots, and begin the break-up of clots that have already formed by the destruction of a substance called fibrin in the blood clot. It is a process known as lysis (thus fibrinolytics).

HAEMOSTATICS

Haemo (blood) -static (stationary) drugs stop excessive bleeding. They include special injections of blood donation extracts to control patients with bleeding diseases such as haemophilia and Christmas disease (see Section 5), and tablets or injections to control bleeding in patients who have an excessive amount of anticoagulant drugs (see separate entry). They have been used in some types of snake bite where a venom that decreases blood clot formation (and therefore increases bleeding) has been injected.

Haemostatics may also be used as a lotion on exposed surfaces to reduce bleeding in surgery and in injection form for excessive bleeding after childbirth. They must be used with great caution and under careful medical supervision.

Hormones

Hormones are produced naturally in the body by many different glands, including the thyroid and parathyroid glands (in the neck), the pancreas (in the abdomen), the pituitary gland (in the brain), the adrenal glands (on top of the kidneys), the ovary and testes (sex hormones). Most of these are listed under their individual type of hormone (e.g. sex hormones). Hormones are chemicals that travel from the producing gland, directly into the bloodstream, and then around the body. They reach and act upon every cell in the body through the bloodstream.

Insulin is a hormone produced by the pancreas gland in the abdomen. Insulin allows sugar to pass from the blood into the cell. Every cell therefore requires this hormone, for without it the cell cannot obtain sugar, which is an essential source of energy and fuel for the cell. The thyroid gland produces thyroxine which acts to control the rate at which cells work. The pituitary gland produces a range of hormones, most of which control other glands. The pituitary gland is therefore the 'conductor' of the glandular and hormonal 'orchestra' of the body. Each of these hormone-producing glands is discussed further under the name of each gland in Section 2.

See also ANABOLIC STEROIDS; HYPOGLYCAEMICS; SEX HORMONES; STEROIDS; THYROID AGENTS; TROPHIC HORMONES.

H2 Receptor Antagonists

See ANTIULCERANTS.

Hypnotics

See SEDATIVES AND HYPNOTICS.

Hypoglycaemics

Hypoglycaemics are drugs that lower the level of sugar (glucose) in the bloodstream by allowing the sugar to cross the membrane surrounding a cell and to enter the interior of the cell. They are used in diabetes of both the maturity onset and juvenile forms (see Section 5).

Alteration to the dosage of all types of hypoglycaemics may be required with changes in exercise, or diet, surgery or the occurrence of other illnesses, particularly if a fever is present. A doctor should be consulted immediately in these situations.

As well as treatment with insulin or other hypoglycaemics, all diabetics must remain on an appropriate diet for the rest of their lives. Regular blood tests and urine tests are essential for the adequate control of all forms of diabetes. Some patients now use small machines, half the size of the average novel, to test their own blood sugar.

Hypoglycaemics fall into two main groups — insulin, which is normally produced by the pancreas; and other hypoglycaemic agents, which are tablets that can be used to perform the same task, but normally only in the mature form of diabetes that affects the middle aged and elderly.

Insulin

Insulin is a natural hormone produced in the pancreas. It is essential for insulin to be present in the blood, because without it, cells cannot absorb glucose. Unfortunately, insulin is destroyed by the acid and digestive juices in the stomach and gut, and therefore cannot be given in tablet form. It is only available as an injection.

Insulin has been derived from the pancreas of cattle or pigs for the last 60 years since it was originally identified and isolated by the American doctors, Banting and Best. Because it was derived from animals, there were occasional reactions to the foreign animal protein present in the insulin. In the last few years, genetically engineered human insulin has almost totally replaced the animal insulin. The new form causes virtually no adverse reaction after injection.

There are many different types of insulin available. They vary in their speed of action (how quickly they work after injection) and their duration of action (how long they last after injection). Some can be given by doctors as an injection directly into the bloodstream in acutely ill patients, others are combinations of long and short-acting insulins that enable diabetics to have only one or two injections a day, rather than four or more of the short-acting types. Each diabetic will have trials of a number of these combinations to find the one best suited to them.

There are a number of ways of administering insulin injections, including the traditional syringe and needle, injecting guns, and a new type of calibrated tube that looks like a ball point pen and is just as easy to carry in a pocket or purse but injects very precise doses of insulin.

Insulin is almost always required in the juvenile form of diabetes, but not usually in the maturity onset form.

Overuse of insulin, or a reduction in normal food intake or exercise, can lead to a sudden drop in blood glucose and collapse of the patient. Most diabetics are aware of the onset of a hypoglycaemic ('hypo') attack, and are prepared to deal with it by sucking a glucose sweet or swallowing a sweetened drink.

Other

There are a number of tablets that are used in maturity onset diabetes. They include Daonil, Diabinese, Diamicron, Euglucon and Rastinon. They must be used with caution in pregnancy, breastfeeding and kidney disease. Excessive use, or overdosage, can cause a 'hypo' attack as in insulin usage. Side effects are uncommon, but may include nausea and gut discomfort.

HYPOLIPIDAEMICS

The term 'hypo' means low (as opposed to 'hyper', meaning high), lipids are fats, and the term 'aemia' refers to the blood (compare 'anaemia' — lack of blood), so a hypolipidaemic is a drug that lowers fat in the blood. The fats include both cholesterol and triglycerides. An excess of either, or both, of these in the bloodstream can cause serious diseases such as strokes and heart attacks (see CHOLESTEROL EXCESS and TRIGLYCERIDE EXCESS, Section 5). A combination of diet and drugs are used to control excess levels of fat in the bloodstream. Diet alone may be sufficient in many patients.

Fat-lowering hypolipidaemics include Atromid S and Lurselle (tablets), Colestid and Questran (powders to mix with water). They are taken after meals to remove fats from the blood. They can be useful additive treatment in some diabetics and obese patients. They must not be used during pregnancy or breastfeeding, and should be used with caution in kidney, liver and gall bladder disease. They can interact with a number of other medications that may be essential for the patient's well-being. Side effects are uncommon but may include nausea and diarrhoea. The powders must always be mixed with water, and not swallowed dry.

HYPOURICAEMICS

Uric acid is the substance that, in excess, causes gout. Hypouricaemics are those drugs that reduce the level of uric acid in the blood, and treat or prevent gout. Colchicine can be used to both treat and prevent gout, but allopurinol (Zyloprim) and probenecid (Benemid) are used only for the long-term prevention of the disease. They are only available as tablets.

Once a patient has gout, regular medication should be taken for many years to prevent a recurrence of the joint pain and the kidney damage that may also occur.

Side effects of allopurinol include drowsiness and skin rashes. It should be avoided in pregnancy and breastfeeding. Colchicine may cause nausea and diarrhoea, and should be avoided in heart disease, kidney disease and the elderly.

Probenecid is also used to prolong the effectiveness of penicillin, as it prevents its excretion through the kidneys. Its side effects include headache, nausea, urinary frequency and hypersensitivity reactions, and it should not be used during an acute attack of gout or with aspirin.

IMMUNOSUPPRESSANTS

Immunosuppressants are used to suppress (control or reduce) the immune reaction that occurs after the transplantation of foreign tissue into a body. They may also be used in the treatment of some types of cancer and defects in immunity that allow a few rare diseases to arise within the body.

Immunosuppressants are the drugs that have made kidney, liver, heart and other transplants possible, as the body normally uses its immune system to reject these donated organs. They all have significant complications and precautions attached to their use, and are used only by doctors who specialise in this type of work. They are available both in tablet and injection form.

INSULINS

See HYPOGLYCAEMICS.

KERATOLYTICS

Keratolytics are skin preparations (creams, lotions, pastes, ointments) that are designed to remove the outermost layer of the skin (the keratin layer) and therefore act as the ultimate skin cleanser. Most are available without prescription and are used to treat diseases such as acne, psoriasis and some forms of dermatitis.

Excessive or inappropriate use may cause reddening, burning and discolouration of the skin, particularly on the face. It is wise to make a test application on an area of skin that is not cosmetically important before applying a keratolytic to the face.

LAXATIVES

When you've just got to go, but you can't go, a laxative may be the answer to a large bowel's prayer. Constipation is a relative matter, as some people consider it normal to pass faeces three times a day, while others consider once a week to be normal. If retained faeces and the attempts to pass them cause pain or discomfort, then constipation needs treatment. Laxatives should be the last resort in the treatment of constipation, after increased fluid intake and alterations to increase the bulk residue of the food in your diet have been tried.

Laxatives vary from simple lubricants, such as paraffin, to bulking agents that contain senna and other fibres, different sugars that draw fluid into the gut (e.g. lactulose, galactose), and gut stimulants (e.g. bisacodyl) that actually increase the contractions of the gut. They are available as tablets, mixtures, granules, suppositories and enemas (the last two for anal use). All are available without prescription.

The main complication with laxatives is their overuse. Patients may use laxatives to pass faeces excessively, and become dependent upon them for the natural functioning of the bowel. Patients trying to lose weight by increasing the rate of faeces output may create this type of dependence, and it is a practice to be deplored. Laxatives should never be used if there is any suspicion of more sinister disease in the gut. Many patients have treated a pain in the abdomen with laxatives, only to find that they have worsened a case of appendicitis. Laxatives should be used with great caution in children and during pregnancy.

LINIMENTS (RUBEFACIENTS)

Liniments are creams or lotions that are rubbed into the skin to create local warmth and skin redness. They include Finalgon, Ibu creme and Movelat which also have some pain-killing effect and are available on prescription only. There are scores of other liniments available from chemists to treat bruises, sprains, fibrositis and arthritic conditions. They should not be used on the face, near body openings (e.g. anus, vagina), or on grazes or cuts.

MAOI

See ANTIDEPRESSANTS.

METHYLDOPA

See ANTIHYPERTENSIVES.

MIOTICS

Miotics are eye drops that cause the pupil of the eye to contract (become smaller). They include pilocarpine and Prostigmin. Their main use is in the treatment of glaucoma, where they act to lower the pressure inside the eye. Sensitisation may occur with prolonged use. Side effects are uncommon.

See also MYDRIATICS.

MUCOLYTICS

Mucolytics liquefy mucus. Mucus produced during colds, flu, bronchitis and other infections of the airways, is often sticky and tenacious. Mucolytics make this phlegm watery and runny, so that coughing and sneezing can more easily clear it from the body. They are available as tablets, mixtures and as a liquid for use in a nebuliser.

Bisolvon and Mucomyst are probably the only pure mucolytics available, but this type of drug is often combined with decongestants and antihistamines (see separate entries) as a cold/cough mixture (e.g. Dimetapp, Triolix). They should be avoided in early pregnancy, and Bisolvon may aggravate peptic ulcers. Side effects are uncommon but may include nausea and diarrhoea.

Muscle relaxants

Muscle relaxants are used to relieve muscle cramps and the spasms associated with spasticity (cerebral palsy), paralysis (paraplegia and quadriplegia), multiple sclerosis and some rare brain diseases.

Quinine and orphenadrine are the most commonly used muscle relaxants to relieve night time cramps. They prevent the development of these cramps but do not relieve them once they have occurred. Quinine is also used in the treatment of some types of malaria. It should be avoided in pregnancy and breastfeeding, and used with caution in patients with heart disease.

Dantrium (injection and tablets) and Lioresal (tablets only) are potent muscle relaxants used in more severe and constant forms of muscle spasm. Dantrium may cause liver problems, and regular blood tests to check the liver must be undertaken while on treatment. There are many side effects and drug interactions with Dantrium, and these must be balanced against the benefits received by the patient. Lioresal has fewer problems, but should be used with caution in epileptics and patients with high blood pressure or kidney disease.

See also ANXIOLYTICS.

Mydriatics

Mydriatics are drops that cause dilation (an increase in size) of the pupil in the eye. They are the direct opposite to miotics (see separate entry). Atropine and cyclopentolate are the main mydriatics in use. They are used in examination of the eye to enable doctors to see into the eye, and during and after some types of eye surgery. They must not be used by patients with glaucoma. Side effects include blurred vision and a sensitivity to bright light.

Narcotics

Narcotics are strong, addictive and effective pain-killers. They are available as injections, tablets, suppositories (for anal use) and mixtures. They include morphine, pethidine, codeine, methadone, Omnopon, Endone and Temgesic. They are highly restricted in their use, and must be kept in safes by chemists and doctors. If they are used appropriately, they give relief from severe pain to patients with acute injuries, and pain from diseases such as cancer and kidney stones. They are often used before, during and after operations to ease the pain of the procedure. If used in this way, it is unlikely that addiction will occur. If used excessively, a psychological and physical addiction can rapidly develop. Heroin is an infamous illegal narcotic which is broken down to morphine in the body.

Narcotics not only relieve severe pain, they also reduce anxiety, stop coughs, sedate and cause euphoria (a 'high' — artificial happiness). Side effects include nausea, vomiting, constipation, dizziness, poor coordination, clouded mental ability, low blood pressure and muscle weakness. They should be used with caution in asthma and other lung diseases, liver disease and after head injuries.

See also ANALGESICS.

NSAIDs (NON-STEROIDAL ANTI-INFLAMMATORY DRUGS)

Despite their long name and unpronounceable acronym, the NSAIDs are some of the most widely used drugs in modern medicine. They are drugs that reduce inflammation in tissue, without being steroids (see separate entry), which are the most potent anti-inflammatory drugs available.

Inflammation is the redness, swelling, pain and heat that occurs in tissue that is subjected to some form of irritation or injury. NSAIDs not only reduce inflammation but also ease pain and lower fevers. Their main uses are in the treatment of rheumatoid and osteoarthritis, sporting injuries to joints, muscles and tendons, and to reduce the inflammation in the pelvis associated with menstrual period pain. They are all available as tablets or capsules, but some are also available as injections, and even as a rub-on lotion. Common brands include Indocid, Brufen, Voltaren, Naprosyn, Orudis, Feldene, Clinoril and Dolobid.

A subgroup of the NSAIDs are the salicylates, which are all derived from salicylic acid. The most commonly known member of this subgroup is aspirin, which acts as a pain-killer (analgesic), fever-reducing agent (antipyretic) and anti-inflammatory medication. It has the same side effects as the other NSAIDs.

The greatest problem with the use of NSAIDs is the possibility of causing peptic ulcers in the stomach or small intestine. Unfortunately, a significant proportion of the patients using these medications will develop some intestinal problem. This can be prevented to some extent by always taking the drugs after food, or in conjunction with an antacid or other ulcer-preventing medication. Any patient who develops stomach pains, vomits blood or passes black stools while on NSAIDs must cease them and see a doctor immediately. Other possible adverse reactions may include nausea, dyspepsia, diarrhoea, rashes, dizziness, sweating, itching and swelling of the legs. The NSAIDs must also be used with care in patients with heart failure, asthma and liver disease. They must not be used in conjunction with anticoagulants.

Despite the problems associated with the use of NSAIDs, many patients with arthritis find that these drugs have improved their lives dramatically by controlling their previously painful and swollen joints. They can also enable sportsmen and women to overcome painful sprains and strains to enable them to return to competition as quickly as possible.

See also ANALGESICS; ANTIRHEUMATICS.

ORAL CONTRACEPTIVES
See SEX HORMONES.

OTHER DRUGS
There are some important drugs that do not fit easily into other categories:

Acetazolamide
See *Diamox* below.

Antabuse (disulfiram)
Antabuse is used to deter the consumption of alcohol. Patients using Antabuse must be carefully selected and closely monitored by both doctors and family. The patient must have a strong desire to desist from alcohol, and usually has a history of spontaneous binge sessions that lead to severe intoxication and family or legal problems.

Antabuse is a tablet that is given daily on a regular basis for several months. It must be used with caution in patients with any other disease and on any other medication. If alcohol is taken while on Antabuse or for a week or more after the last dose is taken, the patient will immediately experience severe flushing, chest pains, headache, throat spasms, stomach cramps and vomiting. Overall, it is a most unpleasant experience and a great disincentive to alcohol intake.

Patients on Antabuse must be fully aware of what they are taking and why. Secret dosing of a patient can lead to severe reactions that may be life-threatening. When the medication is first taken, a small test dose of alcohol is often given to demonstrate to the patient the results of drinking.

Adverse reactions to the medication alone include drowsiness and numbness. Adjusting the dosage usually controls these problems.

Danazol (Danocrine)
Endometriosis is a painful and debilitating disease of women that may cause infertility (see Section 5). Its treatment was complex and often unsatisfactory until the development of Danocrine in the late 1970s. It is an extraordinarily expensive drug (approx $1.30 per tablet) but a very effective one. It can completely cure a woman with endometriosis after a course of six to nine months. It also has the ability to treat extremely heavy periods that fail to respond to other drugs, and it can be used in the treatment of a rare and sometimes fatal disease known as hereditary angioedema.

Danazol should not be given until the diagnosis of endometriosis has been proved by laparoscopy (see Section 4) or by surgery. It should be used with caution in patients with liver disease, cancer or pelvic infections. Liver damage may occur with very long term use. Side effects include acne, swelling of feet and hands, hair development on the face (temporary), rashes, nausea, weight gain, breast changes and vaginal irritation.

Danocrine
See *Danazol* above.

Diamox
Diamox tablets or capsules are used to control the swelling of the hands and feet that occurs in heart failure, to treat some types of epilepsy, and to control glaucoma of the eye — a rather diverse range of diseases. They should not be used during pregnancy. Side effects are minimal but may include frequency of passing urine, drowsiness, pins and needles sensation and loss of appetite.

Disulfiram
See *Antabuse* above.

Etretinate
See *Tigason* below.

Intal
See *Sodium cromoglycate* below.

Isotretinoin
See *Roaccutane* below.

Opticrom
See *Sodium cromoglycate* below.

Roaccutane (isotretinoin)
When acne is very severe and has failed to respond to every other remedy, Roaccutane may be the answer to a teenager's or young adult's prayers. This drug acts to prevent the function of the oil-producing glands in the skin and the rate at which the scaly substance known as keratin forms on the skin. It is given in tablet form for at least 16 weeks. This usually results in almost complete disappearance of the acne for many months. Further briefer causes may be required at a later date.

The greatest problem with Roaccutane is that it will definitely cause deformity in the child of any pregnant woman who receives it. Under no circumstances should this drug be used in a female unless it has been proved that the woman is not pregnant and is undertaking a very effective method of contraception (e.g. total sexual abstinence or regular use of oral contraceptives). The rhythm method is not an adequate contraceptive in this highly risky situation.

There are a number of other complications associated with the use of Roaccutane, so treatment is not undertaken lightly, and once commenced, the patient must be assessed carefully and regularly by a doctor. Side effects include dry mouth, nose, eye and other body cavities. Nose bleeds are often a consequence. Muscular pains, joint stiffness, peeling of skin and headache may also occur.

Rynacrom
See *Sodium cromoglycate* below.

Salazopyrin (sulphasalazine)
Ulcerative colitis (see Section 5) is a severe and potentially disabling disease that can be controlled by diet, steroids and Salazopyrin tablets. Crohn's disease of the large bowel may also be aided by this drug. It has not been proved safe in pregnancy, and must be used under close medical supervision with regular blood and urine tests to detect any early signs of kidney or liver damage. The most common side effects include nausea, vomiting and loss of appetite.

It is often necessary to continue treatment with Salazopyrin for long periods of time to keep the disease process under control.

Sodium cromoglycate (Intal, Opticrom, Rynacrom)
Sodium cromoglycate is available as an inhaled spray (Intal), as capsules suitable for inhaling through a device known as a spinhaler (Intal spincaps), as a solution for inhaling through a nebuliser (Intal solution), as eye drops (Opticrom) and as a nasal spray (Rynacrom).

The drug does not cure disease, but prevents asthma, hay fever and allergic eye conditions. As a result, if treatment is stopped, the disease may recur within a few hours or days. It must sometimes be used for several weeks before it reaches its peak preventative capacity, but in most patients it works to prevent these conditions in a few hours or days. Side effects are almost unknown, as it acts on the surface of the airways or eye, and does not enter the bloodstream. It is a remarkably safe and effective drug.

Sulphasalazine
See *Salazopyrin* above.

Tigason (etretinate)
Psoriasis can be a severe disfiguring disease that is difficult to treat. When other treatments for this chronic skin condition have failed, Tigason may be used to control (but not cure) the disease. It is also useful in a number of rarer skin conditions that are characterised by skin thickening and plaque formation. If used correctly, Tigason capsules can enormously improve patients' appearance, and therefore their attitude to life.

Tigason always causes damage to the foetus in pregnant women. Under no circumstances should it be used in a woman who is pregnant. Because it can remain in the body for up to a year after the last dose, Tigason is only used in fertile women in extenuating circumstances.

The drug can interact adversely with tetracycline antibiotics, which should be avoided during and after treatment. Its other problems include causing possible liver damage, an increase in blood fat levels and an increased risk of sunburn. For all these reasons, it is only used in patients who cannot be controlled in other ways. Other side effects include dryness of the mouth, temporary hair loss, sweating and thirst.

PENICILLINS
See ANTIBIOTICS.

RUBEFACIENTS
See LINIMENTS.

SALICYLATES
See NSAIDs.

SEDATIVES AND HYPNOTICS
Sedatives and hypnotics are overlapping groups of drugs that induce sleep (hypnotics), or reduce bodily awareness and activity

(sedative). They include sleeping pills such as Mogadon, Euhypnos, Normison, Rohypnol, chloral hydrate (also available as a mixture) and Dalmane.

Most sleeping pills are very safe provided they are taken in the recommended manner, but if used constantly for many weeks or months, patients may become dependent upon them. The greatest problem with the use of sleeping pills is that they are taken unnecessarily, particularly by elderly people who do not need large amounts of sleep. The pills are better taken intermittently when really needed, when they will work far more effectively.

Care must be exercised when taking hypnotics in the evening so that the patient is not still affected by the sedation the following morning.

See also ANXIOLYTICS; BARBITURATES.

SEX HORMONES

Sex hormones are produced by the ovaries in the woman and the testes in the man to give each sex its characteristic appearance. In men, they are responsible for the enlargement of the penis and scrotum at puberty, the development of facial hair and the ability to produce sperm and ejaculate. In women, the sex hormones that are produced for the first time at puberty cause breast enlargement, hair growth in the armpit and groin, ovulation, the start of menstrual periods, and later act to maintain a pregnancy.

If the sex hormones are reduced or lacking, these characteristics disappear. This happens naturally during the female menopause. During the transition from normal sex hormone production to no production in the menopause, there may be some irregular or inappropriate release of these hormones, causing the symptoms commonly associated with menopause such as irregular periods and hot flushes. After the menopause, the breasts sag, pubic and armpit hair becomes scanty, and the periods cease due to this lack of sex hormones. Men also go through a form of menopause, but more gradually, so the effects are far less obvious than in the female.

Uses of sex hormones

Sex hormones, and many synthesised drugs that act artificially as sex hormones, are used in medicine in two main areas — to correct natural deficiencies in sex hormone production; and to alter the balance between the two female hormones (oestrogen and progestogen) that cause ovulation, to prevent ovulation, and therefore act as a contraceptive.

It is now well recognised that hormone replacement therapy (HRT) in middle-aged women who are entering the menopause significantly improves their quality of life by not only controlling the symptoms of the menopause itself, but by preventing osteoporosis (bone weakening), reducing the apparent rate of ageing, and reducing the risk of cardiovascular disease (i.e. heart attacks and strokes).

Women who have both their ovaries removed surgically at a time before their natural menopause, will also require sex hormones to be given regularly by mouth or injection.

Female sex hormones can also be used to control some forms of recurrent miscarriage and prolong a pregnancy until a baby is mature enough to deliver, to control a disease called endometriosis, and to treat certain types of cancer.

Natural lack of the male sex hormone testosterone will cause the man to be impotent and sterile.

Types of female sex hormone

The female sex hormone oestrogen can be given as a tablet (Estigyn, Mixogen, Ogen, Orabolin, Premarin, etc.), as an implantable capsule that is placed under the skin (Oestradiol) or as an injection (Primogyn Depot).

If the woman has not had a hysterectomy, she will need to take a progestogen pill (Primolut, Proluton, Provera, etc.) in a cyclical manner every month or two. This may result in a bleed similar to that of a natural menstrual period (but usually much lighter) but gives the added benefit of protecting the woman against uterine cancer.

The side effects of oestrogen preparations include swelling of ankles and hands, weight gain, breast tenderness, dizziness, headaches and depression. Most of these can be overcome by adjusting the dosage. Progestogens have virtually no side effects.

Oral contraceptive pills

Sex hormones used as a contraceptive pill come in several different forms, but are mainly divided into the **combined pill** which contains both an oestrogen and progestogen, and the **mini-pill**. Some of the more widely used combined pills now have a two or three phase variation in their dosage during the month.

In 1961, a woman taking that first form of the oral contraceptive pill was taking more than 32 times the amount of hormone every month than the modern woman on the latest three-phase type of pill (Triphasil, Triquilar). Over the past three decades, the pill has been subjected to more clinical trials and more intensive investigation than any other medication used by womankind. There is no doubt that it is now much safer to take the contraceptive pill for many years than it is to have one pregnancy, and that is the realistic basis on which to judge the safety of any contraceptive.

Two different hormones control the menstrual cycle. At the time of ovulation, the levels of one hormone drops, and the other rises, triggering the egg's release from the ovary. When the hormones revert to their previous level two weeks later, the lining of the womb is no longer able to survive and breaks away, giving the woman a period. The pill maintains a more constant hormone level, and thus prevents the release of the egg. With the triphasic pills, the level of both hormones rises at the normal time of ovulation and then drops slightly thereafter to give a more natural hormonal cycle to the woman, while still preventing the release of an egg. When the pill is stopped (or the sugar pills started) at the end of the month, the sudden drop in hormone levels cause a vaginal bleeding to start.

The so-called mini-pill contains only one hormone (a progestogen) which is taken constantly without any sugar pills or break at the end of each month. This type of pill must be taken very carefully, as even missing it by four hours one day may drop the hormone levels sufficiently to allow ovulation and pregnancy. The failure rate of the mini-pill is significantly higher than that of the combined pill.

Although the sex hormones in the contraceptive pill are very safe, there are some women who should not use it. Those who have had blood clots, severe liver disease, strokes or bad migraines must not take the pill. Heavy smokers, obese women and those with diabetes must be observed closely, and probably should not use the pill after 35 years of age.

The pill has several positive benefits besides almost perfect prevention of pregnancy. It regulates irregular periods, reduces menstrual pain and premenstrual tension, may increase the size of the breasts, reduces the severity of acne in some women, and libido (the desire for sex) is often increased. It even reduces the incidence of some types of cancer.

A few women do have unwanted side effects from the pill. These can include headaches, break-through bleeding, nausea, increased appetite and mood changes. If these problems occur, they can be assessed by a doctor, and a pill containing a different balance of hormones can be prescribed.

If taken correctly, the pill is very effective as a contraceptive. But missing a pill, or suffering from diarrhoea or vomiting can have a very pregnant result. Some antibiotics can also interfere with the pill, as can vitamin C, so check this with your general practitioner. It is far better to be safe than sorry! There is no need these days to take a break from the pill every year or so, as may have been the case in earlier years.

The effects of the pill are readily reversible. If you decide to become pregnant, you could find yourself in that state in as little as two weeks after ceasing it, with no adverse effects on the mother or child.

See also CONTRACEPTION, Section 1.

Depo-Provera

Depo-Provera is an injectable progesterone that is approved for use in Australia to treat certain types of cancer and endometriosis. It is widely used overseas as an injectable contraceptive, given every three to six months. Some doctors are using it for this purpose in Australia, after discussing the pros and cons with their patients. Side effects include the cessation of menstrual periods, break-through vaginal bleeding, headaches, and possibly a prolonged contraceptive action (up to 15 months).

See also CONTRACEPTION, Section 1.

Male sex hormone

The male sex hormone (testosterone) is available in synthetic form as a tablet (Proviron), as an injection (Sustanon, Primoteston, Testoviron, etc.), and as implants. They are used to treat conditions such as failure of puberty to occur, pituitary gland dysfunction, impotence, decreased libido, and male osteoporosis. Side effects are unusual, but the prostate gland must be checked regularly for enlargement.

See also ANABOLIC STEROIDS.

SPERMICIDES

Spermicides are creams, gels and foams that are used in the vagina before sexual intercourse to kill sperm, and that therefore act as a contraceptive. They are not highly reliable, having a failure rate of up to 15%. Side effects are rare, except for local irritation in some men and women who are sensitive to the cream. They are often combined with the rhythm method, condoms or diaphragm to give added contraceptive protection. All are readily available from chemists without a prescription.

STEROIDS (CORTICOSTEROID HORMONES)

Cholesterol is the base substance from which the body produces natural steroids. There are many different types of steroids, including sex hormones (see above), anabolic steroids (that are often abused by athletes) and trophic hormones (see separate entries). The type being described here is more correctly called corticosteroid hormones. They act as powerful reducers of inflammation in damaged tissue. Artificial steroids have been synthesised to control a wide range of diseases, including asthma, arthritis, dermatitis, eczema, and severe allergy reactions.

Steroids are available as tablets (prednisone, prednisolone, etc.), injections (Celestone, Depo-Medrol, Kenacort, etc.), creams (Betnovate, Aristocort, Diprosone, hydrocortisone, etc.), nasal sprays (Aldecin, Beconase), inhaled sprays (Becotide), eye drops (FML), ear drops (Sofradex, Kenacomb) and suppositories (Ultraproct, Proctosedyl). They are therefore an extremely useful group of drugs in a wide variety of conditions.

The actions of steroids include shrinking down swollen, red tissue (e.g. in allergies, injuries, piles) to normal, reducing itching (e.g. in eczema and bites), and opening up airways by reducing mucus secretion and again shrinking swollen tissue (e.g. hay fever, asthma).

When used on the skin or on the surface of the airways (lungs, nose), side effects are uncommon. Overuse of sprays used for asthma is quite safe, but overuse in the nose can cause tissue damage. Creams and ointments that contain strong steroids should not be overused, particularly in children and on the face, as they can cause skin thinning and damage. Taken as injection into joints, steroids are very successful at controlling arthritis, but again, overuse may cause weakness and damage to the joint tissue instead of controlling the disease.

The greatest dangers occur when steroids are taken as tablets. Short courses, in which a high dose is given at the start and then reduced rapidly to zero over a couple of weeks, are quite safe. Low doses given for quite long periods of time are also relatively safe, but when high doses are given for months on end, damage can occur in the body.

Side effects of prolonged steroid tablet use include tissue swelling, an imbalance in blood chemicals, high blood pressure, weight gain, peptic ulcers, brittle bones (fracturing easily), heart failure, muscle weakness, delayed wound healing, headache, abnormal menstrual periods, fatty deposits under the skin, blood clots, cataracts, glaucoma and a host of rarer conditions. It is therefore obvious why doctors use these remarkably effective drugs with great caution. In some situations, the seriousness of the disease warrants taking the risk of using steroids to give a patient relief, or even saving a life.

There are several groups of patients in whom steroid tablets and injections must be used with great caution, if at all. They include those with diabetes, peptic ulcers, glaucoma, any serious infection (particularly fungal infections), high blood pressure, heart disease and liver disease. Patients using steroids should not undergo any form of vaccination or immunisation. If used judiciously, steroids can dramatically improve a patient's quality of life, but doctors must always be aware of the pros and cons of their use in every individual.

See also ANABOLIC STEROIDS; SEX HORMONES; TROPHIC HORMONES.

Stimulants

Stimulant tablets are used in medicine to treat mild depression, disorders of excessive sleep, some types of senility and (rather strangely) overactivity in children. They have been known to be abused by long-distance truck drivers and others who wish to stay awake for long periods of time. They are available as tablets such as Ritalin, No Doz and dexamphetamine.

Stimulants should not be used in patients with high blood pressure, thyroid disease, anxiety disorders or heart disease. Dependence upon these drugs can develop rapidly, and side effects include mouth dryness, difficulty in passing urine, irritability, muscle tremors and heart irregularities.

See also ADRENERGIC STIMULANTS.

Sulphas

See ANTIBIOTICS.

Sympathomimetics

See BRONCHODILATORS.

Tetracyclines

See ANTIBIOTICS.

Theophyllinates

See BRONCHODILATORS.

Thyroid agents

The thyroid gland in the neck produces the hormone thyroxine, which acts to control the rate at which every cell in the body works. It is the accelerator of the body. If thyroxine is lacking, the patient becomes tired and slow. This is a common condition in middle-aged and elderly women. The thyroid hormone not being produced by the thyroid gland can be given as a tablet (Oroxine, thyroxine) by mouth. If used at the correct dosage, as determined by regular blood tests, there should be minimal side effects. Overdosage can cause palpitations, sweating, anxiety and insomnia.

Tricyclics

See ANTIDEPRESSANTS.

Trophic hormones

Trophic hormones are given as injections to aid infertility, prevent miscarriages, stimulate sperm production in men, control breast pain due to hormone imbalances, to start puberty in cases where it has been delayed, and to control some patients with asthma and arthritis. There are a number of rarer diseases in which they are also useful.

Commonly used trophic hormones include Acthar, Humegon, Metrodin, Pergonal, Pregnyl and Synacthen. Adverse reactions are uncommon but severe when they do occur. They include nausea, headaches, peptic ulcers, fluid retention, high blood pressure, inappropriate sexual development and skin markings.

URINE MEDICATIONS
See ALKALISERS, URINE; ANTISPASMODICS

VACCINES
Vaccines are substances that are introduced into the body (by injection, tablet or mixture) to induce immunity to a particular disease. Vaccines have now been developed against a wide range of both bacterial and viral diseases.

Side effects vary between different vaccines but are usually confined to local inflammation at the site of the injection, fevers, irritability, and in rare cases, a very mild dose of the disease (e.g. measles).

See Table 6.1 over page.

VASOCONSTRICTORS (VASOPRESSORS)
Vasoconstrictors are drugs that constrict (reduce in size) blood vessels (arteries in particular) and raise blood pressure. When a patient collapses with a heart attack, severe allergy or shock, it is often due to the sudden overdilation of all the arteries in the body, which causes a very low blood pressure. This can be corrected by a doctor giving an injection of a vasoconstrictor such as adrenaline or Aramine.

Otherwise, vasoconstrictors are used mainly as drops in the eye and nose, and as additives (e.g. pseudoephedrine) to some cold and hay fever remedies. Vasoconstrictor eye drops (e.g. Murine, Albalon, Visine, Optazine, etc.) sting when first used, but this rapidly eases, and after the dilated arteries that have crisscrossed the white of the eye have been constricted, the eye is left looking and feeling much better. Nose drops and sprays containing phenylephrine shrink down the dilated arteries in the nose that develop with hay fever. They can therefore ease the congestion and stuffiness in the nose and allow victims to breathe more easily. Overuse can cause a rebound effect, and the nose becomes inflamed because the drops cause it to swell again. Always follow the directions on these drops and sprays carefully.

Section 6: Treatments

**TABLE 6.1:
VACCINATIONS**

Disease	Form	Frequency	Duration	Notes
Cholera	Injection	As required	6 months	Low-grade protection only.
Diphtheria	Injection	2,4,6 & 18 months, 5 & 15 years	10 years	Combined with tetanus & whooping cough as triple antigen.
Flu — see Influenza.				
German measles — see Rubella.				
Hepatitis B	Injection	3 doses at intervals of 1 & 6 months	Lifelong	Recommended for medical personnel and others exposed to blood.
Influenza	Injection	Every autumn	12 months	Different vaccine every year.
Measles	Injection	Once at 15 months	Lifelong	May be combined with mumps and/or rubella.
Meningitis	Injection	As required	12 months	For control of epidemics or travel to affected countries (see Section 7).
Mumps	Injection	Once at 15 months	Lifelong	Combined with rubella & measles.
Pertussis — see Whooping cough.				
Plague	Injection	2 to 3 doses	6 months	Residents of affected countries.
Pneumococcus	Injection	Once	5+ years	Patients susceptible to pneumonia.
Polio	Oral drops	2,4,6 months & 5 years	10 years	Called Sabin vaccine after inventor.
Rabies	Injection	2 inj. 1 month apart	1 year	Used for those likely to be exposed to affected animals overseas.
Rubella (German measles)	Injection	15 months & 12 years	Lifelong	Given alone or combined with measles and mumps in children.
Sabin — see Polio.				
Tetanus	Injection	2,4,6 & 18 months, 5 & 15 years	10 years	Given alone or with whooping cough & diphtheria as triple antigen.
Triple antigen — see Tetanus, Diphtheria and Whooping cough.				
Tuberculosis	Injection or skin scratch	Once	Lifelong	Not routine in Australia.
Typhoid	Injection or capsules	2 inj. 1 month apart; 3 cap. 2 days apart	3 years; 1 year	Travellers to affected areas.
Typhus	Injection	2 inj. 1 month apart	1 year	Residents in affected areas overseas.
Whooping cough (Pertussis)	Injection	2,4,6 & 18 months	Lifelong	Combined with tetanus & diphtheria as triple antigen.
Yellow fever	Injection	Once	10 years	Available from state government health departments for travellers.

Vasoconstrictors can be combined with surface-acting steroids in a spray (Tobispray) that is remarkably effective in clearing a blocked nose. Other vasoconstrictors (e.g. ephedrine) can also be used in creams to help shrink down piles (haemorrhoids). All vasoconstrictors should be used with caution in patients with high blood pressure, diabetes, thyroid disease or heart disease.

VASODILATORS

Arteries, and to a lesser extent veins, are surrounded by tiny muscles that control the diameter of the blood vessel tube by contracting and relaxing it. If arteries in the arms and legs are excessively contracted or blocked by plaques of cholesterol (atherosclerosis), the amount of blood reaching the distant parts of the body may be insufficient for them to work properly. The earliest sign of a poor blood supply is pallor of the skin. This is followed by muscle weakness and pain. Vasodilators will relax the tiny muscles around the artery, enabling it to dilate to its maximum extent and allowing the greatest possible amount of blood to reach the affected areas. Vasodilators can also be used in the emergency treatment of very high blood pressure.

Vasodilator tablets and injections include Dibenyline, Regitine and Serc, but many other drugs that have been classified elsewhere and may be used for high blood pressure (e.g. Adalat) and other purposes (e.g. Trental) can be used to dilate arteries and veins.

Dizziness and noises in the ears (tinnitus) can be caused by a poor blood supply to the ears, and using vasodilators can sometimes help this problem too.

VASOPRESSORS

See VASOCONSTRICTORS.

VITAMINS

Vitamins are a group of totally unrelated chemicals that have only one thing in common: they are essential (usually in tiny amounts) for the normal functioning of the body. All vitamins have been given letter codes, sometimes with an additional number to differentiate vitamins within a group. The missing letters and numbers in the series are due to substances initially having been identified as vitamins but later were found to lack the essentials for the classification.

Vitamin A, a fat-soluble vitamin, is found in milk, butter, eggs, liver and most fruit and vegetables. Very high levels are found in orange-coloured foods (e.g. pumpkin, carrots, pawpaw, etc.). It is essential for the normal function of the skin and eyes, but there is no evidence that extra amounts can improve vision in people with sight problems or can cure skin problems. High doses of vitamin A may cause a disease called carotenaemia which discolours the skin and may cause foetal abnormalities in pregnant women.

Vitamin B is divided into several subgroups numbered 1, 2, 6 and 12. All are water-soluble and occur in dairy products, meats and leafy vegetables. It is almost impossible to have a lack of only one in the group. If one is missing, all will be missing. A lack of these may cause anaemia and other blood diseases. Excess is rapidly excreted from the body through the kidneys and has no harmful effects. Vitamin B6 may be useful in mouth inflammation, morning sickness and nervous tension. Vitamin B12 is used as an injection to treat pernicious anaemia.

Vitamin C (ascorbic acid) is water-soluble and found in citrus fruits, tomatoes and greens, but its level in food is reduced by cooking, mincing and contact with copper utensils. It is essential for the formation and maintenance of cartilage, bone and teeth, and is used in moderate amounts to promote the healing of wounds and during convalescence from prolonged illnesses. Unfortunately there is no evidence to support its use in preventing or treating the common cold.

Vitamin D is a fat-soluble chemical found in egg yolks and butter, and it may be formed by a reaction of sunlight on skin. It is essential for the balance of calcium and phosphorus in the bones and bloodstream, but it is not used routinely in the treatment of disease.

Vitamin E is readily available in most foods. It is fat-soluble, and high doses may cause serious diseases and abnormalities including blood clots, high blood pressure, breast tumours and headaches. It is a quite dangerous drug, and is only rarely used in medicine.

Vitamin K is essential for the clotting of blood. It is fat-soluble and is found in most foods. It is also manufactured by bacteria living in the gut. A lack is very rare, and high doses may cause anaemia in infants and break down blood in adults. It is not commonly used clinically.

Nicotinic acid and **folic acid** are often classed as vitamins. Nicotinic acid is found in peanuts, meat, grain and liver. It is used in the treatment of certain types of headache, nervous disorders, poor circulation and blood diseases. Folic acid is essential for the basic functioning of cells, and extra amounts may be needed during pregnancy, breastfeeding, and in the treatment of anaemia and alcoholism.

There is no evidence that vitamin supplements benefit anyone on a normal diet and in good health. The cheapest and most effective way to obtain adequate vitamins is to eat a well-balanced diet. Most vitamin supplements are expensive, pass rapidly through the body, and merely enrich the sewers.

Xanthinate derivatives
See bronchodilators.

Drugs available in Australia

Most of the many thousands of drugs available in Australia that the average patient is likely to be prescribed or recommended are listed in Table 6.2 under both their trade or chemist name (in UPPER CASE) and generic or hospital name (in lower case). Every drug has at least two names, a generic name and a trade name. Some drugs are made by several companies, and so will have one generic name and several trade names (e.g. amoxycillin is the generic name for AMOXIL, IBIAMOX and MOXACIN). Every drug will therefore appear at least twice, under both its trade name(s) and generic name.

Each drug has the class to which it belongs listed, and whether it requires a prescription (Y) or not (N).

Some medications with many ingredients do not have all of them listed. The words 'et al.' after a drug name means 'and other' ingredients.

To find out more details about the uses, forms, side effects and complications of each drug: 1. Find the name of the drug in the left-hand column. 2. Note the relevant drug class shown in the third column, and then consult the listing of DRUG GROUPS in the preceding part of this section, where details about drugs are listed by drug class.

A small number of drugs that do not fit into any particular class have brief details about them in this list. Rarer drugs, common chemist lines, and drugs used in specialised situations (e.g. general anaesthetics) have been excluded.

TABLE 6.2:
DRUGS AVAILABLE IN AUSTRALIA

Name (TRADE/Generic)		Class	Prescription needed (yes/no)
ABBOCILLIN	Phenoxymethylpenicillin	Antibiotic/Penicillin	Y
Acetazolamide	DIAMOX	Other	Y
Acetic acid	ACI-JEL, AQUAEAR, PHYTEX, VOSOL	Antiseptic	N
ACETOPT	Sulphacetamide	Antibiotic/Sulpha	Y
Acetylcholine Cl	MIOCHOL	Miotic	N
Acetylcysteine	MUCOMYST, PARVOLEX	Mucolytic	N
ACHROMYCIN	Tetracycline HCl	Antibiotic/Tetracycline	Y
ACHROSTATIN	Tetracycline, nystatin	Antibiotic/Antifungal	Y
ACI-JEL	Acetic acid	Antiseptic	N
ACNACYL	Benzoyl peroxide	Keratolytic	N
ACNEDERM	Sulphur et al.	Keratolytic	N
ACT 3C	Ibuprofen, codeine	Analgesic/NSAID	N (Y Qld)
ACTACODE	Codeine phos. et al.	Antitussive	Y (WA only)
ACTAL	Aluminium compound	Antacid	N

Section 6: Treatments

TABLE 6.2:
DRUGS AVAILABLE IN AUSTRALIA (continued)

Name (TRADE/Generic)		Class	Prescription needed (yes/no)
ACTHAR GEL	Corticotrophin	Trophic hormone	N
ACTIFED	Triprolidine, pseudoephedrine	Antihistamine/Decongestant	N
ACTILYSE	Tissue plasminogen activator	Fibrinolytic	Y
ACTRAPHANE	Insulin	Hypoglycaemic	N
ACTRAPID	Insulin	Hypoglycaemic	N
ACTUSS	Pholcodeine	Antitussive	N
Acyclovir	ZOVIRAX	Antiviral	Y
ADALAT	Nifedipine	Antihypertensive/Calcium channel blocker	Y
ADIFAX	Dexfenfluramine	Anorectic	Y
ADM	Pectin, kaolin	Antidiarrhoeal	N
Adrenal extract	MOVELAT	Liniment	Y
Adrenaline	ADRENALINE, EPIFRIN, EPPY, RECTINOL	Mydriatic/Vasoconstrictor	Y
ADRIAMYCIN	Doxorubicin	Cytotoxic	Y
ADROYD	Oxymetholone	Anabolic steroid	Y
ADT	Diphtheria and tetanus toxoid	Vaccine	Y
AEROCORTIN	Polymyxin, neomycin, hydrocortisone	Antibiotic/Antifungal/Steroid	Y
AGAROL	Paraffin et al.	Laxative	N
AGIOLAX	Ispeghula/senna	Laxative	N
AGON	Felodipine	Antihypertensive/Calcium channel blocker	Y
AIROL	Tretinoin	Keratolytic	N
AKINETON	Biperiden	Antiparkinsonian	Y
ALBALON (A)	Naphazoline et al.	Vasoconstrictor	N
ALBAY	Venom extracts	Antiallergy	Y
Albumin tannate	TANNALBIN	Antidiarrhoeal	N
ALCAINE	Proxymetacaine, benzalkonium Cl	Anaesthetic	Y
ALCLOX	Cloxacillin	Antibiotic/Beta lactam	Y
Alcloxa	ACNEDERM	Keratolytic	N
ALDACTONE	Spironolactone	Diuretic. Also used for excess body hair and aldosteronism	Y
ALDAZINE	Thioridazine	Antipsychotic	Y
ALDECIN	Beclomethasone	Steroid (nasal or oral spray)	Y
ALDOMET	Methyldopa	Antihypertensive	Y
ALEPAM	Oxazepam	Anxiolytic/Benzodiazepine	Y
ALEXAN	Cytarabine	Cytotoxic	Y
ALGICON	Magnesium & aluminium compounds	Antacid	N
Alginic acid	GAVIGRANS, GAVISCON, MERACOTE	Antacid	N
ALKERAN	Melphalan	Cytotoxic	Y
ALLEGRON	Nortryptyline	Antidepressant/Tricyclic	Y
Allopurinol	ALLOREMED, CAPURATE, PROGOUT, ZYLOPRIM	Hypouricaemic agent	Y
ALLOREMED	Allopurinol	Hypouricaemic agent	Y
Allyloestrenol	GESTANIN	Sex hormone	Y
ALMACARB	Aluminium & magnesium compounds	Antacid	N
ALODORM	Nitrazepam	Hypnotic	Y
ALOPHEN	Multiple compounds	Laxative	N
ALPHACIN	Ampicillin	Antibiotic/Penicillin	Y
ALPHAMOX	Amoxycillin	Antibiotic/Penicillin	Y
ALPHAPRESS	Hydralazine	Antihypertensive	Y
ALPHOSYL	Allantoin, coal tar	Keratolytic	N
Alprazolam	XANAX	Anxiolytic	Y
Alprenolol	APTIN	Beta-blocker	Y
ALPRIM	Trimethoprim	Antibiotic	Y

DRUG TREATMENT

TABLE 6.2:
DRUGS AVAILABLE IN AUSTRALIA (continued)

Name (TRADE/Generic)		Class	Prescription needed (yes/no)
Alprostadil	PROSTIN	Used to maintain circulation in infants with heart defects	Y
ALUDROX	Aluminium & magnesium compounds	Antacid	N
Aluminium chlorhydroxide	MEDROL	Keratolytic	N
Aluminium hydroxide	Multiple tradenames	Antacid	N
Aluminium sulphate	STINGOSE	Soothing preparation for bites	N
ALUPENT	Orciprenaline	Bronchodilator/Sympathomimetic	Y
ALVERCOL	Sterculia	Antispasmodic	N
Amantadine	ANTADINE, SYMMETREL	Antiparkinsonian	Y
Amethocaine	MINIMS LA	Anaesthetic (local, eye)	Y
AMFAMOX	Famotidine	Antiulcerant	Y
AMICAR	Aminocaproic acid	Haemostatic	Y
Amikacin	AMIKIN	Antibiotic/Aminoglycoside	Y
AMIKIN	Amikacin	Antibiotic/Aminoglycoside	Y
Amiloride	AMIZIDE, KALURIL, MIDAMOR, MODURETIC	Diuretic	Y
Aminacrine	AMINOPT, CALISTAFLEX	Antibiotic (eye)	N
Aminophylline	CARDOPHYLLIN, SOMOPHYLLIN	Bronchodilator/Xanthinate derivative	Y
AMINOPT	Aminacrine	Antibiotic (eye)	N
Amiodarone	CORDARONE	Antiarrhythmic	Y
AMITRIP	Amitriptyline	Antidepressant/Tricyclic	Y
Amitriptyline	AMITRIP, ENDEP, LAROXYL, MUTABON, SAROTEN, TRYPTANOL	Antidepressant/Tricyclic	Y
AMIZIDE	Hydrochlorthiazide	Diuretic	Y
AMOXIL	Amoxycillin	Antibiotic/Penicillin	Y
Amoxycillin	AMOXIL, AUGMENTIN, CILAMOX, IBIAMOX, MOXACIN	Antibiotic/Penicillin	Y
AMPHOJEL/TABS	Aluminium hydroxide	Antacid	N
Amphoterecin	FUNGILIN	Antifungal	Y
Ampicillin	AMPICYN, AUSTRAPEN, PENBRITIN	Antibiotic/Penicillin	Y
AMPICYN	Ampicillin	Antibiotic/Penicillin	Y
AMPRACE	Enalapril	Antihypertensive	Y
Amsacrine	AMSIDYL	Cytotoxic	Y
AMSIDYL	Amsacrine	Cytotoxic	Y
Amyl nitrite	AMYL NITRITE	Antiangina. Cyanide antidote	N
Amylobarbitone	AMYTAL	Hypnotic	Y
AMYTAL	Amylobarbitone	Hypnotic	Y
ANAFRANIL	Clomipramine	Antidepressant/Tricyclic	Y
ANAPOLON	Oxymetholone	Sex hormone	Y
ANATENSOL	Fluphenazine	Antipsychotic	Y
ANCOLAN	Meclozine	Antihistamine	Y
ANCOTIL	Flucytosine	Antifungal	Y
ANDRIOL	Testosterone	Sex hormone	Y
ANDROCUR	Cyproterone	Reduction of male sex drive, prostate cancer etc.	Y
ANDRUMIN	Dimenhydrinate	Antiemetic	N
ANGININE	Glyceryl trinatrate	Antiangina	Y
ANPEC	Verapamil	Antihypertensive	Y
ANPINE	Nifedipine	Antiarrhythmic	Y
ANTABUSE	Disulfram	Other (alcoholism)	Y
ANTADINE	Amantadine	Antiparkinsonian	Y
Antazoline	ALBALON, ANTISTINE PRIVINE, OPTAZINE	Vasoconstrictor (eye)	N
ANTENEX	Diazepam	Anxiolytic/Benzodiazepine	Y
ANTHEL	Pyrantel	Anthelmintic	N

Section 6: Treatments

TABLE 6.2:
DRUGS AVAILABLE IN AUSTRALIA (continued)

Name (TRADE/Generic)		Class	Prescription needed (yes/no)
ANTI-SPAS	Benzhexol	Antiparkinsonian	Y
ANTISTINE PRIVINE	Antazoline	Vasoconstrictor/Astringent (eye)	N
ANTURAN	Sulphinpyrazone	Hypouricaemic agent	Y
ANUSOL	Zinc oxide, benzyl benzoate	Soothing preparation for piles	N
APRESOLINE	Hydralazine	Antihypertensive	Y
APRINOX	Bendrofluazide	Diuretic	Y
APTIN	Alprenolol	Beta-blocker	Y
AQUAMOX	Quinethazone	Diuretic	Y
ARAMINE	Metaraminol	Vasoconstrictor	Y
ARISTOCOMB	Triamcinolone, neomycin, gramicidin, nystatin	Steroid/Antibiotic/Antifungal (cream)	Y
ARISTOCORT	Triamcinolone	Steroid (cream)	Y
ARTANE	Benzhexol	Antiparkinsonian	Y
ARTERIOFLEXIN	Clofibrate	Hypolipidaemic	Y
ARTHREXIN	Indomethacin	NSAID	Y
ASA	Aspirin	NSAID/Analgesic	N
ASCABIOL	Benzyl benzoate	Antiparasitic	N
ASPALGIN	Aspirin, codeine	Analgesic	N
Aspirin	Multiple tradenames	Analgesic	N
ASPRO	Aspirin	Analgesic	N
ASPRODEINE	Aspirin, codeine	Analgesic	N
Astemizole	HISMANAL	Antihistamine	Y
ASTRIX	Aspirin	Prevents clots in bloodstream	N
ATARAX	Hydroxyzine	Antihistamine	Y
Atenolol	NOTEN, TENORMIN	Beta-blocker	Y
ATIVAN	Lorazepam	Anxiolytic/Benzodiazepine	Y
ATROBEL	Hyoscine, atropine, hyoscyamine	Antispasmodic	N
ATROMID S	Clofibrate	Hypolipidaemic	Y
ATROPINE	Multiple Trade names and forms	Cytotoxic Antispasmodic Antiemetic	y
ATROVENT	Ipratropium bromide	Bronchodilator	Y
AUGMENTIN	Amoxycillin, clavulanic acid	Antibiotic/Penicillin	Y
AURALGAN	Phenazone, benzocaine	Anaesthetic (ear)	N
Auranofin	RIDAURA	Antirheumatic	Y
AUREOMYCIN	Chlortetracycline	Antibiotic/Tetracycline	Y
Aurothioglucose	GOLD 50	Antirheumatic	Y
AUSTRAMYCIN V	Tetracycline	Antibiotic/Tetracycline	Y
AUSTRAPEN	Ampicillin	Antibiotic/Penicillin	Y
AUSTRASTAPH	Cloxacillin	Antibiotic/Penicillin	Y
AUSTYN	Theophylline	Bronchodilator	Y
AVIL	Pheniramine maleate	Antihistamine	Y Spray N Tabs
AVOMINE	Promethazine	Antiemetic	N
AZACTAM	Aztreonam	Antibiotic	Y
Azatadine	ZADINE	Antihistamine	Y (N NSW & Vic)
Azathioprine	IMURAN, THIOPRINE	Immunosuppressant	Y
AZIDE	Chlorthiazide	Diuretic	Y
Azlocillin	SECUROPEN	Antibiotic	Y
Aztreonam	AZACTAM	Antibiotic	Y
Bacitracin	MYCITRACIN, NEOSPORIN, SPERSIN, CICATRIN, NEMDYN, POLYBACTRIN	Antibiotic (on skin surface)	Y
Baclofen	LIORESAL	Muscle relaxant	Y
BACTIGRAS	Chlorhexidine	Antiseptic	N
BACTRIM	Cotrimoxazole	Antibiotic/Sulpha	Y
BACTROBAN	Mupirocin	Antibiotic (cream)	Y
BALNETAR	Coal tar	Keratolytic	N
BARBLOC	Pindolol	Beta-blocker	Y
BAYCARON	Mefruside	Diuretic	Y

TABLE 6.2:
DRUGS AVAILABLE IN AUSTRALIA (continued)

Name (TRADE/Generic)		Class	Prescription needed (yes/no)
BECLOFORTE	Beclomethasone	Steroid (spray)	Y
Beclomethasone	ALDECIN, BECLOFORTE, BECONASE, BECOTIDE	Steroid (spray)	Y
BECONASE/BECOTIDE	Beclomethasone	Steroid (spray)	Y
BENACINE	Diphenhydramine, hyoscine	Antiemetic	N
BENADRYL	Diphenhydramine	Antihistamine	N
BENATUSS	Multiple constituents	Antihistamine/Antitussive	N
Bendrofluazide	APRINOX	Diuretic	Y
BENEMID	Probenecid	Hypouricaemic agent; prolongs effectiveness of penicillin	Y
BENOXYL	Benzoyl peroxide	Keratolytic	N
Benserazide, Levodopa	MADOPAR	Antiparkinsonian	Y
BENYPHED	Multiple constituents	Antihistamine/Antitussive	N
BENZAC	Multiple constituents	Keratolytic	N
Benzalkonium chloride	Multiple trade names and forms	Antiseptic	N
Benzathine penicillin	BICILLIN	Antibiotic/Penicillin	Y
Benzhexol hydrochloride	ANTISPAS, ARTANE	Antiparkinsonian	Y
Benzocaine	Multiple trade names and forms	Anaesthetic	N
Benzoic acid	EGOMYCOL, MYCOZOL	Antifungal	N
Benzoyl peroxide	Multiple trade names and forms	Keratolytic	N
Benzotropine	COGENTIN	Antiparkinsonian	Y
Benzydamine HCl	DIFFLAM	Analgesic	N (Y Tas & Vic)
Benzyl benzoate	ASCABIOL	Antiparasitic	N
Benzyl nicotinate	PERGALEN	Cream for leg ulcers, thromboses & strains	N
Benzylpenicillin	BICILLIN	Antibiotic/Penicillin	Y
BEPANTHEN	Panthenol, Benzalkonium Cl	Soothing cream	N
BEROTEC	Fenoterol	Bronchodilator/Sympathomimetic	Y
BETADINE	Povidone iodine	Antiseptic	N
Betahistine	SERC	Vasodilator	Y
BETALOC	Metoprolol	Beta-blocker	Y
Betamethasone	CELESTONE, DIPROSONE, BETNOVATE	Steroid	Y
Betaxolol	BETOPTIC	Beta-blocker/Mydriatic	Y
Bethanechol	URECHOLINE, UROCARB	Anticholinergic	Y
BETNOVATE	Betamethasone	Steroid	Y
BETOPTIC	Betaxolol	Beta-blocker/Mydriatic	Y
BEX	Aspirin	Analgesic	N
BICILLIN	Several types of penicillin	Antibiotic/Penicillin	Y
BIOGLAN	Cyanocobalamin	Vitamin (treats pernicious anaemia)	N
BIORAL	Carbenoxolone	Antiulcerant (mouth)	N
Biperiden	AKINETON	Antiparkinsonian	Y
BIPHASIL	Levonorgestrel, ethinyloestradiol	Sex hormone (contraceptive)	Y
BIQUINATE	Quinine bisulphate	Muscle relaxant	N
Bisacodyl	BISALAX, COLOXYL, DUROLAX	Laxative	N
BISALAX	Bisacodyl	Laxative	N
Bismuth subcitrate	DE-NOL	Antiulcerant	Y(N SA & NSW)
BISOLVON	Bromhexine	Mucolytic	N (Y ACT)
BLENOXANE	Bleomycin	Cytotoxic	Y
Bleomycin	BLENOXANE	Cytotoxic	Y
BLOCADREN	Timolol	Beta-blocker	Y
BOLINAN	Polyvinylpolypyrrolidone	Antidiarrhoeal	N
BONJELA	Choline salicylate, cetalkonium Cl	Analgesic (gums)	N

Section 6: Treatments

TABLE 6.2:
DRUGS AVAILABLE IN AUSTRALIA (continued)

Name (TRADE/Generic)		Class	Prescription needed (yes/no)
Boric acid	HEMOREX	Soothes piles	N
BRASIVOL	Aluminium oxide	Keratolytic	N
BREDON	Oxolamine citrate	Antitussive	N
BREEZEAZY	Ephedrine, phenazone, aminophylline	Bronchodilator	N (Y NSW)
BRETYLATE	Bretylium tosylate	Antiarrhythmic	Y
Bretylium tosylate	BRETYLATE, CRITIFIB	Antiarrhythmic	Y
BREVINOR	Norethisterone, ethinyloestradiol	Sex hormone (contraceptive)	Y
BRICANYL	Terbutaline	Bronchodilator/Sympathomimetic	Y
BRINDALIX	Clopamide	Antihypertensive	Y
BROLENE	Dibromopropamide isethionate	Antiseptic (eye)	N
Bromazepam	LEXOTAN	Anxiolytic/Benzodiazepine	Y
Bromhexine HCl	BISOLVON, DURO-TUSS EXPECT.	Mucolytic	N
Bromocriptine RLODEL	Antiparkinsonian. Stops production of breast milk		Y
Brompheniramine	DIMETAPP, DIMETANE	Antihistamine	N
BRONCOSTAT	Killed Haemophilus influenzae	Prevents acute bronchitis	N
BRONDECON	Choline theophylinate	Bronchodilator/Xanthinate derivative	Y
BRUFEN	Ibuprofen	NSAID	Y
BRULIDINE	Multiple constituents	Antiseptic	N
Bumetanide	BURINEX	Diuretic	Y
Buprenorphine	TEMGESIC	Analgesic (v. strong)	Y
BURINEX	Bumetanide	Diuretic	Y
BUSCOPAN	Hyoscine-N-butylbromide	Antispasmodic	Y
BUSPAR	Buspirone	Anxiolytic	Y
Buspirone	BUSPAR	Anxiolytic	Y
Busulphan	MYLERAN	Cytotoxic	Y
BUTAZOLIDIN	Phenylbutazone	NSAID	Y
BUTESIN PICTRATE	Butyl aminobenzoate pictrate	Soothing cream	N
Butobarbitone	SONERYL	Sedative	Y
Butoxyethyl nicotinate	FINALGON, ACNE-SOL	Liniment	N
Butyl aminobenzoate	BUTESIN PICTRATE	Soothing cream	N
Butyl hydroxybenzoate	EGOMYCOL, HEXOPHENE, MYCODERM	Antifungal	N
CAFERGOT	Ergotamine, caffeine	Antimigraine	Y
Caffeine	CAFERGOT, DRIXINE, ERGODRYL, MIGRAL, NO DOZ, TRAVACALM	Antimigraine/Stimulant	Varies depending on form & strength
CALADRYL	Lignocaine, calamine, camphor	Anaesthetic (skin)	N
Calamine	CALADRYL, CALISTAFLEX	Soothing cream	N
CALCITARE	Calcitonin	Used for Paget's disease	Y
Calcitonin	CIBACALCIN, CALCITARE, CALSYNAR, MIACALCIC	Used for Paget's disease)	Y
Calcium carbimide	DIPSAN	Aid for alcoholism	Y
Calcium folinate	LEUCOVORIN	For anaemia and toxins	N
CALISTAFLEX	Aminacrine, lignocaine, calamine	Anaesthetic (skin)	N
CALMAZINE	Trifluoroperazine	Antipsychotic	Y
CALSYNAR	Calcitonin	For Paget's disease	Y
CANESTEN	Clotrimazole	Antifungal	Y
CANTIL	Mepenzolate bromide	Antispasmodic	Y
CAPADEX	Dextropopoxyphene, paracetamol	Analgesic	Y
CAPOTEN	Captopril	Antihypertensive	Y
Captopril	CAPOTEN	Antihypertensive	Y
CAPURATE	Allopurinol	Hypouricaemic agent	Y
CARAFATE	Sucralfate	Antiulcerant	N

TABLE 6.2:
DRUGS AVAILABLE IN AUSTRALIA (continued)

Name (TRADE/Generic)		Class	Prescription needed (yes/no)
Carbachol	ISOPTO CARBOCHOL	Miotic	Y
Carbamazepine	TEGRETOL, TERIL	Anticonvulsant	Y
Carbenoxolone	BIORAL	Antiulcerant	N
Carbidopa	SINEMET	Antiparkinsonian	Y
Carbimazole	NEO-MERCAZOLE	Antithyroid	Y
CARBOPLATIN	Carboplatin	Cytotoxic	Y
CARBRITAL	Pentobarbitone	Sedative	Y
CARDINOL	Propranolol	Beta-blocker	Y
CARDIPRIN	Aspirin, aminoacetic acid	Anticoagulant	N
CARDIZEM	Diltiazem	Antiangina	Y
CARDOPHYLLIN	Aminophylline	Bronchodilator/Xanthinate derivative	Y
Carica papaya enzyme	TROMASIN	Prevents inflammation	N
CAROBEL	Multiple constituents	Antiemetic	N
CARTIA	Aspirin	Anticoagulant	N
CATAPRES	Clonidine	Antihypertensive	Y
CDT	Diphtheria & tetanus vaccine	Vaccine	Y
CECLOR	Cefaclor	Antibiotic/Cephalosporin	Y
CEENU	Lomustine	Cytotoxic	Y
CEETAMOL	Paracetamol	Analgesic	N
Cefaclor	CECLOR	Antibiotic/Cephalosporin	Y
CEFAMEZIN	Cephazolin	Antibiotic/Cephalosporin	Y
Cefotaxime	CLAFORAN	Antibiotic/Cephalosporin	Y
Cefoxitin	MEFOXIN	Antibiotic/Cephalosporin	Y
Ceftazidime	FORTUM	Antibiotic/Cephalosporin	Y
Ceftriaxone	ROCEPHIN	Antibiotic/Cephalosporin	Y
CELESTONE	Betamethasone	Steroid	Y
CELLULONE	Methylcellulose	Fibre supplement	N
CELONTIN	Methsuximide	Anticonvulsant	Y
Cephalexin	CEPOREX, KEFLEX	Antibiotic/Cephalosporin	Y
Cephamandole	MANDOL	Antibiotic/Cephalosporin	Y
Cephazolin	CEFAMEZIN, KEFZOL	Antibiotic/Cephalosporin	Y
CEPORACIN	Cephalothin	Antibiotic/Cephalosporin	Y
CEPOREX	Cephalexin	Antibiotic/Cephalosporin	Y
CERUBIDIN	Daunorubicin	Cytotoxic	Y
Cetrimide	Multiple trade names	Antiseptic	N
CHENDOL	Chenodeoxycholic acid	Dissolves gallstones	Y
Chenodeoxycholic acid	CHENDOL	Dissolves gallstones	Y
CHININE	Quinine sulphate	Muscle relaxant	N
Chloral hydrate	DORMEL, NOCTEC	Hypnotic	Y
Chlorambucil	LEUKERAN	Cytotoxic	Y
Chloramphenicol	CHLOROCORT, CHLOROMYCETIN, CHLOROMYXIN, CHLORSIG, CHLOROPTIC	Antibiotic (normally eye)	Y
Chlordiazepoxide	LIBRAX, LIBRIUM	Anxiolytic	Y
Chlorhexidine	BACTIGRAS, HEXOL, SAVLON, HIBITANE, SILVAZINE, HEXOPHENE	Antiseptic	N
Chlormethiazole	HEMINEURIN	Sedative	Y
CHLOROCORT	Chloramphenicol, hydrocortisone	Antibiotic/Steroid (eye)	Y
CHLOROMYCETIN	Chloramphenicol	Antibiotic	Y
CHLOROMYXIN	Chloramphenicol, polymyxin	Antibiotic (eye)	Y
CHLOROPTIC	Chloramphenicol	Antibiotic (eye)	Y
Chloroquine	CHLORQUIN, NIVAQUINE	Antimalarial	Y
Chlorothiazide	AZIDE, CHLOTRIDE	Diuretic	Y
Chloroxylenol	DETTOL	Antiseptic	N
Chlorphenesin	MYCIL	Antifungal	N
Chlorpheniramine	DEMAZIN, PIRITON, ORTHOXICOL, SINUTAB	Antihistamine	N

Section 6: Treatments

TABLE 6.2:
DRUGS AVAILABLE IN AUSTRALIA (continued)

Name (TRADE/Generic)		Class	Prescription needed (yes/no)
Chlorpromazine	LARGACTIL, PROTRAN	Antipsychotic	Y
Chlorpropamide	DIABENESE	Hypoglycaemic	Y
CHLORQUIN	Chloroquine	Antimalarial	Y
Chlorquinaldol	STEROXIN	Antiseptic/Antifungal	N
CHLORSIG	Chloramphenicol, hypromellose	Antibiotic (eye)	Y
Chlortetracycline	AUREOMYCIN	Antibiotic/Tetracycline (skin)	Y
Chlorthalidone	HYGROTON	Diuretic	Y
Chlorthiazide	CHLOTRIDE	Diuretic	Y
CHLOTRIDE	Chlorthiazide	Diuretic	Y
CHOLEDYL	Choline theophyllinate	Bronchodilator/Xanthinate derivative	Y
Cholestyramine	QUESTRAN	Hypolipidaemic	Y (N NSW Vic)
Choline theophyllinate	BRONDECON, CHOLEDYL	Bronchodilator/Xanthinate derivative	Y
CHYMORAL	Trypsin, chymotrypsin	Prevents inflammation	N
Chymotrypsin	CHYMORAL, ZOLYSE	Prevents inflammation	N
CIBACALCIN	Calcitonin	Treats Paget's disease	Y
CICATRIN	Neomycin, bacitracin	Antibiotic (skin powder)	Y
CILAMOX	Amoxycillin	Antibiotic/Penicillin	Y
CILICAINE	Procaine penicillin	Antibiotic/Penicillin	Y
Cimetidine	DURACTIN, TAGAMET	Antiulcerant	Y
Cinchocaine	PROCTOSEDYL, SCHERIPROCT, ULTRAPROCT	Anaesthetic (anal)	Y
Ciprofloxacin	CIPROXIN	Antibiotic/Cephalosporin	Y
CIPROXIN	Ciprofloxacin	Antibiotic/Cephalosporin	Y
CIRFLO	Multiple ingredients	Improves blood circulation	N
Cisplatin	CISPLATIN, PLATAMINE	Cytotoxic	Y
CITRALKA	Sodium acid citrate, sodium benzoate	Alkaliser	N
CITRAVESCENT	Sodium citrotartrate, sodium bicarb.	Alkaliser	N
CLAFORAN	Cefotaxime	Antibiotic/Cephalosporin	Y
CLEARASIL	Multiple constituents	Keratolytic/Antiseptic	N
Clemastine	TAVEGYL	Antihistamine	N
Clemizole undecanoate	ULTRAPROCT, SCHERIPROCT	Soothes anal piles	Y
Clindinium bromide	LIBRAX	Antispasmodic	Y
Clindamycin	DALACIN C	Antibiotic	Y
CLINORIL	Sulindac	NSAID	Y
Clioquinol	HYDROFORM, SILIC C, VIOFORM	Antiseptic	Varies
Clobazam	FRISIUM	Anxiolytic/Benzodiazepine	Y
Clofazimine	LAMPRENE	Antileprotic	Y
Clofibrate	ARTERIOFLEXIN, ATROMID S	Hypolipidaemic	Y
CLOMID	Clomiphene	Causes ovulation	Y
Clomiphene	CLOMID	Causes ovulation	Y
Clomipramine	ANAFRANIL	Antidepressant/Tricyclic	Y
Clonazepam	RIVOTRIL	Anticonvulsant	Y
Clonidine	CATAPRES, DIXARIT	Antihypertensive/Antimigraine	Y
Clopamide	BRINDALIX	Diuretic	Y
Clorazepate	TRANXENE	Anxiolytic/Benzodiazepine	Y
Clotrimazole	CANESTEN, LOTREMIN	Antifungal	Y
Cloxacillin	ALCLOX, AUSTRASTAPH, ORBENIN	Antibiotic/Penicillin	Y
Coal tar	Multiple brand names	Keratolytic	N
CODALGIN	Paracetamol, codeine	Analgesic	N
CODATE	Codeine	Analgesic/Antidiarrhoeal	Y
Codeine	Multiple brand names	Analgesic/Antidiarrhoeal	Varies
CODIPHEN	Codeine, aspirin	Analgesic	N
CODIS	Aspirin, codeine	Analgesic	N

DRUG TREATMENT

TABLE 6.2:
DRUGS AVAILABLE IN AUSTRALIA (continued)

Name (TRADE/Generic)		Class	Prescription needed (yes/no)
CODOX	Dihydrocodeine tartrate, aspirin	Analgesic	N
CODRAL	Aspirin, codeine	Analgesic	Depends on strength
COGENTIN	Benztropine mesylate	Antiparkinsonian	Y
Colaspase	LEUNASE	Cytotoxic	Y
Colchicine	COLCHICINE, COLGOUT	Hypouricaemic agent	Y
COLESTID	Colestipol	Hypolipidaemic	Y
Colestipol	COLESTID	Hypolipidaemic	Y
COLGOUT	Colchicine	Hypouricaemic agent	Y
Colistin	COLY-MYCIN	Antibiotic	Y
COLOFAC	Mebeverine	Antispasmodic	Y
COLOXYL	Dioctyl sodium sulphosuccinate	Laxative	N
COLY-MYCIN	Colistin, neomycin	Antibiotic	Y
COMBANTRIN	Pyrantel embonate	Anthelmintic	Y
COMBIZYM	Pancreatin, aspergillus oryzae	Aids digestion	N
COMPAZINE	Prochlorperazine	Antiemetic	Y
CONTAC	Multiple constituents	Relieves cold symptoms	N
CORBETON	Oxprenolol	Beta-blocker	Y
CORDARONE X	Amiodarone	Antiarrhythmic	Y
CORDILOX	Verapamil	Antiarrhythmic/ Antihypertensive	Y
CORLAN	Hydrocortisone	Steroid (mouth ulcers)	Y
CORTATE	Cortisone	Steroid	Y
CORTEF	Hydrocortisone	Steroid	Y
CORTIC	Hydrocortisone	Steroid	N
Corticotrophin	ACTHAR GEL	Trophic hormone	N
Cortisone	CORTATE	Steroid	Y
COSANYL	Multiple constituents	Antitussive	N
COSMEGEN	Dactinomycin	Cytotoxic	Y
COTAZYM	Pancrelipase, protease, amylase	Aids digestion	N
Co-Trimoxazole	BACTRIM, SEPTRIN, TRIB	Antibiotic/Sulpha	Y
COUMADIN	Warfarin	Anticoagulant	Y
CRITIFIB	Bretylium tosylate	Antiarrhythmic	Y
Crotamiton	EURAX	Antipruritic/Antiparasitic	N
Cyanocobalamin	BIOGLAN, CYTAMEN	Vitamin (treats pernicious anaemia)	N
CYCLIDOX	Doxycycline	Antibiotic/Tetracycline	Y
Cyclizine	MIGRAL	Antimigraine	Y
CYCLOBLASTIN	Cyclophosphamide	Cytotoxic	Y
CYCLOGYL	Cyclopentolate	Mydriatic	Y
CYCLOPANE	Papaverine, atropine, paracetamol	Analgesic	N
Cyclopenthiazide	NAVIDREX	Diuretic	Y
Cyclopentolate	CYCLOGYL	Mydriatic	Y
Cyclophosphamide	CYCLOBLASTIN, ENDOXAN	Cytotoxic	Y
Cyclosporin	SANDIMMUN	Immune suppressant	Y
CYKLOKAPRON	Tranexamic acid	Treats hereditary angioedema	Y
Cyproheptadine	PERIACTIN	Antihistamine	N
Cyproterone	ANDROCUR	Reduction of male sex drive, prostate cancer etc.	Y
CYTADREN	Aminoglutethimide	Cytotoxic	Y
CYTAMEN	Cyanocobalamin (vitamin B12)	Vitamin (treats pernicious anaemia)	N
Cytarabine	CYTARABINE, ALEXAN, CYTOSAR	Cytotoxic	Y
CYTOSAR	Cytarabine	Cytotoxic	Y
Dacarbazine	DTIC	Cytotoxic	Y
Dactinomycin	COSMEGEN	Cytotoxic	Y
DAKTARIN	Miconazole	Antifungal	Y

Section 6: Treatments

TABLE 6.2:
DRUGS AVAILABLE IN AUSTRALIA (continued)

Name (TRADE/Generic)		Class	Prescription needed (yes/no)
DALACIN C	Clindamycin	Antibiotic	Y
DALMANE	Flurazepam	Sedative	Y
Danazol	DANOCRINE	Other	Y
DANOCRINE	Danazol	Other	Y
DANTRIUM	Dantrolene	Muscle relaxant	Y
Dantrolene	DANTRIUM	Muscle relaxant	Y
DAONIL	Glibenclamide	Hypoglycaemic	Y
Dapsone	MALOPRIM	Antileprotic/Antimalarial	Y
DARANIDE	Dichlorpheniramine	Used for glaucoma	Y
DARAPRIM	Pyrimethamine	Antimalarial	Y
DARTALAN	Thiopropazate	Anxiolytic	Y
Daunorubicin	CERUBIDIN	Cytotoxic	Y
Debrisoquine	DECLINAX	Antihypertensive	Y
DECADRON	Dexamethasone	Steroid	Y
DECA-DURABOLIN	Nandrolone	Anabolic steroid	Y
DECLINAX	Debrisoquine	Antihypertensive	Y
DECRIN	Aspirin, codeine	Analgesic	N
DELFEN	Nonoxynol 9	Spermicide	N
DELTASONE	Prednisone	Steroid	Y
DEMAZIN	Dexchlorpheniramine, pseudoephedrine	Antihistamine/Decongestant	N
Demeclocycline	LEDERMYCIN	Antibiotic/Tetracycline	Y
DE-NOL	Bismuth subcitrate	Antiulcerant	Y (N NSW,SA)
DEPO-MEDROL	Methylprednisolone	Steroid	Y
DEPO-PROVERA	Medroxyprogesterone	Sex hormone	Y
DEPTRAN	Doxepin	Antidepressant/Tricyclic	Y
DEQUADIN	Dequalinium	Antiseptic	N
Dequalinium	DEQUADIN	Antiseptic	N
DERALIN	Propranolol	Beta-blocker	Y
DERMACORT	Hydrocortisone	Steroid (cream)	Y
DERMAZOLE	Econazole	Antifungal	N
DESERIL	Methysergide	Antimigraine	Y
DESFERAL	Desferrioxamine	Iron poisoning and excess	Y
Desferrioxamine	DESFERAL	Iron poisoning and excess	Y
Desipramine	PERTOFRAN	Antidepressant/Tricyclic	Y
Desmopressin	MINIRIN	Diuretic	Y
DETTOL	Chloroxylenol	Antiseptic	N
Dexamethasone	DEXMETHSONE, MAXIDEX, SOFRADEX, TOBISPRAY, DECADRON	Steroid	Y
Dexamphetamine	DEXAMPHETAMINE	Stimulant	Y
Dexchlorpheniramine	DEMAZIN, POLARAMINE	Antihistamine	Y
Dexfenfluramine	ADIFAX	Anorectic	Y
DEXMETHSONE	Dexamethasone	Steroid	Y
DEXSAL	Multiple ingredients	Antacid	N
Dextromethorphan	Multiple trade names	Antitussive	N
Dextromoramide	PALFIUM	Analgesic (strong)	Y
Dextropropoxyphene hydrochloride	CAPADEX, DIGESIC, PARADEX	Analgesic	Y
Dextropropoxyphene napsylate	DOLOXENE	Analgesic	Y
DIABEX	Metformin	Hypoglycaemic	Y
DIABINESE	Chlorpropamide	Hypoglycaemic	Y
DIAFORMIN	Metformin	Hypoglycaemic	Y
DIAMICRON	Gliclazide	Hypoglycaemic	Y
DIAMOX	Acetazolamide	Other	Y
DIAZEMULS	Diazepam	Anxiolytic/Benzodiazepine	Y
Diazepam	ANTENEX, DIAZEMULS, DUCENE, PRO-PAM, VALIUM	Anxiolytic/Benzodiazepine	Y
Diazoxide	DIAZOXIDE, HYPERSTAT	Antihypertensive (inj.)	Y
DIBENYLINE	Phenoxylbenzamine	Vasodilator	Y

DRUG TREATMENT

TABLE 6.2:
DRUGS AVAILABLE IN AUSTRALIA (continued)

Name (TRADE/Generic)		Class	Prescription needed (yes/no)
Dibromopropramidine isethionate	BROLENE, BRULIDINE	Antiseptic	N
DICHLOTRIDE	Hydrochlorthiazide	Diuretic	Y
Diclofenac	VOLTAREN	NSAD	Y
Dicyclomine	INFACOL, MERBENTYL	Antispasmodic	Depends on form
Dienoestrol	DIENOESTROL	Sex hormone	Y
Diethylcarbamazine	HETRAZAN	Anthelmintic	Y
Diethylpropion	TENUATE	Anorectic	Y
Difenoxin	LYSPAFEN	Antidiarrhoeal	Y
DIFFLAM	Benzydramine	Analgesic	N (Y Tas & Vic)
Diflunisal	DOLOBID	NSAID	Y
DIGESIC	Dextropropoxyphene, paracetamol	Analgesic	Y
Digoxin	LANOXIN	Cardiac glycoside	Y
DIHYDERGOT	Dihydroergotamine	Antimigraine	Y
Dihydrocodeine	CODOX, PARACODIN, RIKODEINE	Analgesic/Antitussive	N
Dihydroergotamine	DIHYDERGOT	Antimigraine	Y
Dihydrostreptomycin	STREPTOMAGMA	Antidiarrhoeal	Y
Di-iodohydroxyquinolone	FLORAQUIN	Antiseptic (vaginal)	N
DIJENE	Aluminium & magnesium compounds	Antacid	N
DILANTIN	Phenytoin sodium	Anticonvulsant	Y
DILOSYN	Methdiazine	Antihistamine	N
Diloxanide	FURAMIDE	Antidiarrhoeal	Y
Diltiazem	CARDIZEM	Antiarrhythmic	Y
Dimenhydrinate	ANDRUMIN, DRAMAMINE, TRAVACALM	Antiemetic	N
DIMETANE	Brompheniramine	Antihistamine	N
DIMETAPP	Brompheniramine, phenylephrine, propanolamine	Antihistamine/Mucolytic	N (Y Qld)
Dimethicone	Multiple trade names	Skin soother	N
DINDEVAN	Phenindione	Anticoagulant	Y
Dioctyl sodium sulphosuccinate	COLOXYL	Laxative	N
DIPENTUM	Olsalazine	Laxative	Y
Diphemanil	PRANTAL	Antiperspirant	N
Diphenhydramine	BENACINE, BENADRYL, BENATUSS, BENYPHED, ERGODRYL	Antihistamine	Depends on form
Diphenoxylate	LOMOTIL	Antidiarrhoeal	Y
Diphenylpyraline	ESKORNADE, HISTALERT, SINUZETS	Antihistamine	N
Diphtheria toxoid	ADT, CDT, TRIPLE ANTIGEN	Vaccine	Y
Dipivefrin	PROPINE	Mydriatic	Y
DIPROSONE	Betamethasone	Steroid	Y
DIPSAN	Calcium carbimide	Aids alcoholism	Y
Dipyridamole	PERSANTIN	Anticoagulant	Y
DISIPAL	Orphenadrine	Antiparkinsonian	Y (N NSW)
Disopyramide	NORPACE, RYTHMODAN	Antiarrhythmic	Y
DISPRIN	Aspirin	Analgesic	N
Distigmine	UBRETID	Anticholinergic	Y
Disulfiram	ANTABUSE	Other (Alcoholism)	Y
Dithranol	DITHROCREAM, DITHRASAL	Keratolytic	N
DITHRASAL	Dithranol, salicylic acid	Keratolytic	N
DITHROCREAM	Dithranol	Keratolytic	N
DIULO	Metolazone	Diuretic	Y
DIXARIT	Clonidine	Antimigraine. Eases flushing	Y
Dobutamine	DOBUTREX	Adrenergic	Y
DOBUTREX	Dobutamine	Adrenergic	Y
DOLOBID	Diflunisal	NSAID	Y

Section 6: Treatments

TABLE 6.2:
DRUGS AVAILABLE IN AUSTRALIA (continued)

Name (TRADE/Generic)		Class	Prescription needed (yes/no)
DOLOXENE (CO)	Dextropropoxyphene, codeine	Analgesic	Y
Domperidone	MOTILIUM	Antiemetic	Y
DONNAGEL	Multiple ingredients	Antidiarrhoeal	N
DONNALIX	Hyoscyamine, atropine, hyoscine	Antispasmodic	N
Dopamine	DOPAMINE, INTROPIN	Adrenergic	Y
DORMEL	Chloral hydrate	Sedative	Y
DORYX	Doxycycline	Antibiotic/Tetracycline	Y
Dothiepin	PROTHIADEN	Antidepressant/Tricyclic	Y
Doxepin	SINEQUAN, DEPTRAN	Antidepressant/Tricyclic	Y
Doxorubicin	ADRIAMYCIN	Cytotoxic	Y
Doxycycline	CYCLIDOX, DORYX, VIBRAMYCIN, DOXYLIN	Antibiotic/Tetracycline	Y
Doxylamine	FIORINAL, MERSYNDOL, PANALGESIC	Analgesic/Antihistamine	N
DOXYLIN	Doxycycline	Antibiotic/Tetracycline	Y
D-PENAMINE	Penicillamine	Antirheumatic	Y
DRAMAMINE	Dimenhydrinate	Antiemetic	N
DRIXINE	Oxymetazoline	Decongestant	N
DRIXORA	Pseudoephedrine	Decongestant	N
DROLEPTAN	Droperidol	Antipsychotic	Y
Droperidol	DROLEPTAN	Antipsychotic	Y
DUCENE	Diazepam	Anxiolytic/Benzodiazepine	Y
DUOFILM	Lactic acid, salicylic acid	Keratolytic	N
DUPHALAC	Multiple ingredients	Laxative	N
DUPHASTON	Dydrogesterone	Sex hormone	Y
DURABOLIN	Nandrolone	Anabolic steroid	Y
DURACTIN	Cimetidine	Antiulcerant	Y
DUROLAX	Bisacodyl	Laxative	N
DUROMINE	Phentermine	Anorectic	Y
DURO-TUSS	Pholcodeine	Antitussive	N
DUVADILAN	Isoxsuprine	Vasodilator	Y
DYAZIDE	Triamterene, hydrochlorthiazide	Diuretic	Y
Dydrogesterone	DUPHASTON	Sex hormone	Y
DYMADON (CO)	Paracetamol, codeine	Analgesic	N
DYTAC	Triamterene	Diuretic	Y
Econazole	DERMAZOLE, ECOSTATIN, PEVARYL	Antifungal	Y
ECOSTATIN	Econazole	Antifungal	Y
ECOTRIN	Aspirin	NSAID/Analgesic	N
EDECRIL	Ethacrynic acid	Diuretic	Y
EES	Erythromycin	Antibiotic	Y
EFUDIX	5-fluorouracil	Cytotoxic	Y
EGOCORT	Hydrocortisone	Steroid	Y
ELDISINE	Vindesine	Cytotoxic	Y
ELIXOPHYLLIN (KI)	Theophylline, (potassium iodide)	Bronchodilator/Xanthinate derivative	Y
EMETROL	Fructose, orthophosphoric acid	Antiemetic	N
EMU-V	Erythromycin	Antibiotic	Y
Enalapril	AMPRACE, RENITEC	Antihypertensive	Y
ENDEP	Amitriptyline	Antidepressant/Tricyclic	Y
ENDONE	Oxycodone	Narcotic/Analgesic	Y
ENDOXAN-ASTA	Cyclophosphamide	Cytotoxic	Y
ENDURON	Methyclothiazide	Diuretic	Y
ENZACTIN	Triacetin	Antifungal	Y
Ephedrine	HEMOCANE, RECTINOL, FEDRINE	Vasoconstrictor	Depends on form
EPIFRIN	Adrenaline	Mydriatic	Y
EPILIM	Sodium valproate	Anticonvulsant	Y
Epirubicin	PHARMORUBICIN	Cytotoxic	Y

TABLE 6.2:
DRUGS AVAILABLE IN AUSTRALIA (continued)

Name (TRADE/Generic)		Class	Prescription needed (yes/no)
EPODYL	Ethoglucid	Cytotoxic	Y
EPPY/N	Adrenaline	Mydriatic	Y
EQUANIL	Meprobamate	Anxiolytic	Y
Ergometrine	ERGORTATE, SYNTOMETRINE	Causes uterine contraction	Y
Ergotamine	CAFERGOT, ERGODRYL, LINGRAINE, MEDIHALER, ERGOTAMINE, MIGRAL	Antimigraine	Y
ERGOTRATE	Ergometrine	Causes uterine contraction	Y
ERYC	Erythromycin	Antibiotic	Y
ERYTHROCIN	Erythromycin	Antibiotic	Y
Erythromycin	EMU-V, ERYC, EES, ILOSONE, ERYTHROCIN	Antibiotic	Y
Esculin	PROCTOSEDYL	Soothes piles	Y
ESKAMEL	Resorcinol, sulphur	Keratolytic	N
ESKORNADE	Multiple ingredients	Antihistamine/Decongestant	Y
ESTIGYN	Ethinyloestradiol	Sex hormone	Y
Ethacrynic acid	EDECRIL	Diuretic	Y
Ethambutol	MYAMBUTOL	Antituberculotic	Y
Ethinyoestradiol	Multiple brand names, including many oral contraceptives	Sex hormone	Y
Ethoglucid	EPODYL	Cytotoxic	Y
Ethosuximide	ZARONTIN	Anticonvulsant	Y
Ethyloestranol	ORABOLIN	Sex hormone	Y
Ethynodiol diacetate	OVULEN	Sex hormone	Y
Etidronate	DIDRONEL	Treats Paget's disease	Y
Etoposide	VEPESID	Cytotoxic	Y
Etretinate	TIGASON	Other (for psoriasis)	Y
EUGLUCON	Glibenclamide	Hypoglycaemic	Y
EUHYPNOS	Temazepam	Sedative	Y
EURAX	Crotamiton	Antiparasitic	N
EVENTIN	Propylhexidrine	Anorectic	Y
FABAHISTIN (PLUS)	Mebydroli (pseudoephedrine)	Antihistamine/Decongestant	Y (N NSW & Vic)
Famotidine	AMFAMOX, PEPCIDINE	Antiulcerant	Y
FANSIDAR	Sulphadoxine	Antimalarial	Y
FARLUTAL	Medroxyprogesterone	Cytotoxic	Y
FASIGYN	Tinidazole	Antibiotic	Y
FEDRINE	Ephedrine	Bronchodilator/ Sympathomimetic	N (Y NSW WA SA)
FEFOL	Ferrous sulphate (iron), folic acid	Treats & prevents anaemia	N
FELDENE	Piroxicam	NSAID	Y
FELICUR	Phenylpropanol	Stimulates bile flow	N
Felodipine	AGON, PLENDIL	Antihypertensive	Y
FENAMINE	Pheniramine	Antihistamine	N (Y ACT)
Fenfluramine HCl	PONDERAX	Anorectic	Y
Fenoterol	BEROTEC	Bronchodilator/ Sympathomimetic	N
FENOX	Phenyleprine	Decongestant	N
FERGON	Ferrous (iron) gluconate	Treats & prevents anaemia	N
FERITARD	Ferrous (iron) sulphate	Treats & prevents anaemia	N
FERRO-GRADUMET	Ferrous (iron) sulphate	Treats & prevents anaemia	N
Ferrous gluconate	FERGON	Treats & prevents anaemia	N
Ferrous sulphate	FEFOL, FERITARD, FERRO-GRADUMET, FESPAN, FGF	Treats & prevents anaemia	N
FESPAN	Ferrous (iron) sulphate	Treats & prevents anaemia	N
FGF	Ferrous (iron) sulphate, folic acid	Treats & prevents anaemia	N

Section 6: Treatments

TABLE 6.2:
DRUGS AVAILABLE IN AUSTRALIA (continued)

Name (TRADE/Generic)		Class	Prescription needed (yes/no)
FINALGON	Nonylvanillamide, butoxylethyl nicotinate	Liniment	N
FIORINAL	Paracetamol, codeine, doxylamine	Analgesic	N
FLAGYL	Metronidazole	Antibiotic	Y
FLAREX	Fluorometholone	Steroid (eye drop)	Y
Flavoxate	URISPAS	Urinary antispasmodic	(Y ACT)
Flecainide	TAMBOCOR	Antiarrhythmic	Y
FLOPEN	Flucloxacillin	Antibiotic/Penicillin	Y
FLORAQUIN	Di-iodohydroxyquinolone	Antiseptic (vagina)	N
FLORINEF	Fludrocortisone	Steroid	Y
FLOXAPEN	Flucloxacillin	Antibiotic/Penicillin	Y
Fluclorolone	TOPILAR	Steroid	Y
Flucloxacillin	FLOPEN, FLOXAPEN, STAPHYLEX	Antibiotic/Penicillin	Y
FLUCON	Fluorometholone	Steroid	Y
Flucytosine	ANCOTIL	Antifungal	Y
Fludrocortisone	FLORINEF	Steroid	Y
Flumethasone	LOCACORTEN-VIOFORM	Steroid/Antibiotic	Y
Flunisolide	RHINALAR	Steroid	Y
Flunitrazepam	HYPNODORM, ROHYPNOL	Hypnotic	Y
Fluocinolone	SYNALAR	Steroid	Y
Fluocortolone	ULTRALAN, ULTRAPROCT	Steroid	Y
FLUONILID	3,5-Dichloro-4-fluorothiocarbanilide	Antifungal	Y
Fluorometholone	FML, FLUCON, FLAREX	Steroid (eye)	Y
Fluorouracil	FLUOROURACIL, EFUDIX, FLUROBLASTIN	Cytotoxic	Y
Fluoxetine	PROZAC	Antidepressant	Y
Fluoxymestrone	HALOTESTIN	Sex hormone	Y
Fluphenazine decanoate	FLUPHENAZINE, MODECATE	Antipsychotic	Y
Fluphenazine HCl	ANATENSOL	Antipsychotic	Y
Flurazepam	DALMANE	Hypnotic	Y
FLUROBLASTIN	Fluorouracil	Cytotoxic	Y
FLUVAX	Influenza vaccine	Vaccine	Y
FML LIQUIFILM	Fluorometholone	Steroid	Y
FORTRAL	Pentazocine	Analgesic	Y
FORTUM	Ceftazidime	Antibiotic/Cephalosporin	Y
Fosfestrol	HONVAN	Cytotoxic	Y
Framycetin	SOFRADEX, SOFRAMYCIN	Antibiotic	Y
FRISIUM	Clobazam	Anxiolytic	Y
Frusemide	LASIX, UREMIDE, UREX	Diuretic	Y
FUCIDIN	Sodium fusidate/Fusidic acid	Antibiotic	Y
FULCIN	Griseofulvin	Antifungal	Y
FUNGILIN	Amphoterecin	Antifungal	Y
FURACIN	Nitrofurazone	Antiseptic	N
FURADANTIN	Nitrofurantoin	Antibiotic	Y
FURAMIDE	Diloxanide	Antiamoebic	Y
Furazolidone	FUROXONE	Antibiotic (gut)	Y
FUROXONE	Furazolidone	Antibiotic (gut)	Y
Fusidic acid	FUCIDIN	Antibiotic	Y
GARAMYCIN	Gentamicin	Antibiotic/Aminoglycoside	Y
GASTROBROM	Magnesium & calcium compounds	Antacid	N
GASTROGEL	Aluminium hydroxide, Magnesium compounds	Antacid	N
GASTROLYTE	Electrolyte solution	Corrects dehydration	N
GAVIGRANS	Multiple ingredients	Antacid	N
GAVISCON	Multiple ingredients	Antacid	N
GELUSIL	Aluminium & magnesium compounds	Antacid	N

TABLE 6.2:
DRUGS AVAILABLE IN AUSTRALIA (continued)

Name (TRADE/Generic)		Class	Prescription needed (yes/no)
Gemfibrizol	GEMFIBRIZOL	Hypolipidaemic	Y
GENOPTIC	Gentamicin	Antibiotic/Aminoglycoside (eye)	Y
GENOTROPIN	Somatropin	Hormone (induces growth)	Y
Gentamicin	GARAMYCIN, GENOPTIC	Antibiotic/Aminoglycoside	Y
GESTANIN	Allyloestrenol	Sex hormone (for miscarriages)	Y
GLAUCON	Adrenaline, benzalkonium Cl	Mydriatic	Y
Glibenclamide	DAONIL, EUGLUCON	Hypoglycaemic	Y
Gliclazide	DIAMICRON	Hypoglycaemic	Y
Glipizide	MINIDIAB	Hypoglycaemic	Y
Glucagon	GLUCAGON	Corrects low blood sugar	Y
GLUCOPHAGE	Metformin	Hypoglycaemic	Y
Glucose	DEXTROSE	Corrects low blood sugar	N
Glutamic acid	MURIPSIN	Acid	N
GLYCERIN	Glycerol	Laxative	N
Glycerol	GLYCERIN, numerous moisturisers	Laxative	N
Glyceryl trinitrate	ANGININE, NITRADISC, NITRO-BID, NITROLATE, TRANSIDERM-NITRO, TRIDIL	Antiangina	Y
Glycopyrrolate	ROBINUL	Antispasmodic	Y
GOLD	Aurothioglucose	Antirheumatic	Y
Gonadotrophin	HUMEGON, PROFASI	Hormone (infertility)	Y
Goserelin	ZOLADEX	Cytotoxic	Y
Gramicidin	ARISTOCOMB, GRANEODIN, KENACOMB, NEOSPORIN, SOFRADEX, SOFRAMYCIN	Antibiotic	Y
GRANEODIN	Neomycin, Gramicidin	Antibiotic	Y
GRANOCOL	Sterculia, frangula bark	Laxative	N
Griseofulvin	FULCIN, GRISEOSTATIN, GRISOVIN	Antifungal	Y
GRISEOSTATIN	Griseofulvin	Antifungal	Y
GRISOVIN	Griseofulvin	Antifungal	Y
Guaiphenesin	Numerous cold and cough mixtures	Antitussive	N
GYNE-LOTREMIN	Clotrimazole	Antifungal	Y
GYNO-DAKTARIN	Miconazole	Antifungal	Y
GYNO-TRAVOGEN	Isoconazole	Antifungal	Y
Haematoporphyrin	KH3	Tonic	Y
HALCIDERM	Halcinonide	Steroid	Y
Halcinonide	HALCIDERM	Steroid	Y
HALCION	Triazolam	Sedative	Y
Haloperidol	SERENACE	Antipsychotic	Y
HALOTESTIN	Fluoxymestrone	Sex hormone	Y
HEMINEURIN	Chlormethiazole	Sedative	Y
HEMOCANE	Allantoin, lignocaine, ephedrine etc.	Soothes piles	N
HEPARIN	Heparin	Anticoagulant	Y
Heparinoid	HIRUDOID, LASONIL	Superficial sprains, bruises & clots	N
HERPLEX	Idoxuridine	Antiviral (eye)	Y
HETRAZAN	Diethylcarbamazine	Anthelmintic	Y
Hexamine	HIPREX, MANDELAMINE	Antiseptic (urine)	N
HEXOL	Chlorhexidine	Antiseptic	N
HIBICLENS	Chlorhexidine	Antiseptic	N
HIBICOL	Chlorhexidine	Antiseptic	N
HIBITANE	Chlorhexidine	Antiseptic	N
HIDROSOL	Aluminium chloride	Excess sweating	N
HIPREX	Hexamine	Antiseptic (urine)	N

Section 6: Treatments

TABLE 6.2:
DRUGS AVAILABLE IN AUSTRALIA (continued)

Name (TRADE/Generic)		Class	Prescription needed (yes/no)
HIRUDOID	Heparinoid	Superficial sprains, bruises & clots	N
HISMANAL	Astemizole	Antihistamine	Y
HISTALERT	Diphenylpyraline	Antihistamine	N
HMS LIQUIFILM	Medrysone	Steroid	Y
HOMAT	Homatropine hypobromide	Mydriatic	N
Homatropine hydrobromide	HOMAT, ISOPTO HOMATROPINE	Mydriatic	N
Homatropine methylbromide	HYCOMINE	Antitussive	Y
HONVAN	Fosfestrol	Cytotoxic	Y
HOSTACYCLINE P	Tetracycline	Antibiotic/Tetracycline	Y
HUMEGON	Human gonadotrophin	Hormone (infertility)	Y
HUMULIN	Insulin	Hypoglycaemic	Y
Hyaluronidase	LASONIL	Superficial sprains, bruises & clots	N
HYCOMINE	Hydrocodone, homatropine, mepyramine, phenylephrine, ammonium Cl	Antitussive	Y
HYCOR	Hydrocortisone	Steroid (eye)	Y
HYDOPA	Methyldopa	Antihypertensive	Y
HYDRACYCLINE	Tetracycline	Antibiotic/Tetracycline	Y
Hydralazine	ALPHAPRESS, APRESOLINE, SUPRES	Antihypertensive	Y
Hydrochlorothiazide	AMIZIDE, DICHLOTRIDE, DYAZIDE, MODURETIC	Diuretic	Y
Hydrocodone	HYCOMINE	Antitussive	Y
Hydrocortisone	Multiple brands including: EGOCORT, HYCOR, PROCTOSEDYL, CORTEF, DERMACORT, SIGMACORT, CORLAN etc.	Steroid	Depends on strength
HYDROFORM	Hydrocortisone	Steroid	N
HYDROSONE	Hydrocortisone	Steroid	Y
Hydroxocobalamin	NEO-CYTAMEN	Treats pernicious anaemia	N
Hydroxychloroquine	PLAQUENIL	Antimalarial	Y
Hydroxyephedrine	TICARDA	Antitussive	Y
Hydroxyprogesterone	PROLUTON DEPOT	Sex hormone	Y
Hydroxyzine	ATARAX	Antihistamine	Y
HYGROTON	Chlorthalidone	Diuretic	Y
Hyoscine	SCOP	Antiemetic	N
Hyoscine-N-butylbromide	BUSCOPAN	Antispasmodic	Y
Hyoscine hydrobromide	ATROBEL, DONNAGEL, DONNATAB, KWELLS, TRAVACALM, TRAVS	Antiemetic/Antispasmodic	N
Hyoscine methobromide	PAMINE	Antispasmodic	N (Y Vic)
Hyoscyamine	ATROBEL, DONNAGEL, DONNATAL	Antispasmodic	N
HYPNODORM	Flunitrazepam	Hypnotic	Y
HYPNOVEL	Midazolam	Sedative	Y
HYPURIN	Insulin	Hypoglycaemic	Y
HYSONE	Hydrocortisone	Steroid	Y
IBIAMOX	Amoxycillin	Antibiotic/Penicillin	Y
IBU CREAM	Ibuprofen	Liniment	Y
Ibuprofen	BRUFEN, IBU CREAM, INFLAM, RAFEN	NSAID	Y
Idoxuridine	HERPLEX, STOXIL, VIRASOLVE	Antiviral	Y
ILOCAP	Erythromycin	Antibiotic	Y
ILOSONE	Erythromycin	Antibiotic	Y
IMFERON	Iron	Injection for anaemia	Y
Imipenem	PRIMAXIN	Antibiotic (injection)	Y

TABLE 6.2:
DRUGS AVAILABLE IN AUSTRALIA *(continued)*

Name (TRADE/Generic)		Class	Prescription needed (yes/no)
Imipramine	IMIPRIN, TOFRANIL	Antidepressant	Y
IMIPRIN	Imipramine	Antidepressant	Y
IMODIUM	Loperamide	Antidiarrhoeal	Y
IMURAN	Azathioprine	Immune suppressant	Y
Indapamide	NATRILIX	Antihypertensive	Y
INDERAL	Propranolol	Beta-blocker	Y
INDOCID	Indomethacin	NSAID	Y
Indomethacin	ARTHREXIN, INDOCID, RHEUMACIN	NSAID	Y
INFACOL	Simethicone	Antacid	N
INFLAM.	Ibuprofen	NSAID	Y
INITARD	Insulin	Hypoglycaemic	Y
INSULTARD	Insulin	Hypoglycaemic	Y
Insulin	Multiple trade names	Hypoglycaemic	Y
INTAL	Sodium cromoglycate	Other (prevents asthma)	Y
Interferon	INTRON, ROFERON	Treats some types of cancer	Y
INTRON A	Interferon	Treats some types of cancer	Y
INTROPIN	Dopamine	Adrenergic	Y
IONIL	Multiple ingredients	Keratolytic	N
Ipecuanha	ALOPHEN	Laxative	N
Ipratropium bromide	ATROVENT	Bronchodilator	Y
Iron	Multiple trade names including: IMFERON, FEFOL, FERRUM, FGF	(see under Ferrous)	N
Isocarboxazid	MARPLAN	Antidepressant/MAOI	Y
Isoconazole	GYNO-TRAVOGEN, TRAVOGEN	Antifungal	Y
ISODINE	Providone iodine	Antiseptic	N
Isoniazid	ISONIAZID	Antituberculotic	Y
ISOPHANE	Insulin	Hypoglycaemic	Y
Isoprenaline HCl	ISOPRENALINE	Adrenergic	Y
Isoprenaline sulphate	MEDIHALER ISO	Bronchodilator/Sympathomimetic	N
Isopropamide iodide	ESKORNADE, STELABID, TYRIMIDE	Antispasmodic	N
ISOPTIN	Verapamil	Antihypertensive/Antiarrhythmic	Y
ISOPTO CARBACHOL	Carbachol	Mydriatic	Y
ISOPTO CARPINE	Pilocarpine et al.	Mydriatic	Y
ISOPTO FRIN	Phenylephirine et al.	Astringent	N
ISOPTO HOMATROPINE	Homatropine et al.	Mydriatic	N
ISORDIL	Isosorbide	Antiangina	Y
Isosorbide	ISORDIL, ISOTRATE	Antiangina	Y
ISOTARD	Insulin	Hypoglycaemic	Y
ISOTRATE	Isosorbide	Antiangina	Y
Isotretinoin	ROACCUTANE	Other (severe acne)	Y
Isoxsuprine	DUVADILAN	Vasodilator	Y
Ispaghula	AGIOLAX, FYBOGEL	Laxative	N
ISUPREL	Isoprenaline	Adrenergic	Y
Itobarbitone	CAFERGOT PB	Barbiturate/Antimigraine	Y
KALURIL	Amiloride	Diuretic	Y
KAOFORT	Codeine phos., kaolin	Antidiarrhoeal	N
Kaolin	DONNAGEL, GLUCOMAGMA, KAOFORT, KAOMAGMA, KAOPECTATE, STEPTOMAGMA, ADM	Antidiarrhoeal	N
KAOMAGMA	Kaolin, aluminium hydroxide	Antidiarrhoeal	N
KAOPECTATE	Kaolin, pectin	Antidiarrhoeal	N
KAY CIEL	Potassium	Mineral supplement	N
KEFLEX	Cephalexin	Antibiotic/Cephalosporin	Y
KEFLIN	Cephalothin	Antibiotic/Cephalosporin	Y

Section 6: Treatments

TABLE 6.2:
DRUGS AVAILABLE IN AUSTRALIA (continued)

Name (TRADE/Generic)		Class	Prescription needed (yes/no)
KEFZOL	Cephazolin	Antibiotic/Cephalosporin	Y
KELOCYANOR	Dicobalt edetate	Antidote for cyanide poisoning	N
KEMADRIN	Procyclidine	Antiparkinsonian	Y
KENACOMB	Triamcinolone, neomycin, gramicidin, nystatin	Steroid/Antibiotic/Antifungal	Y
KENACORT	Triamcinolone	Steroid	Y
KENALOG IN ORABASE	Triamcinolone	Steroid (mouth ulcers)	Y
KENALONE	Triamcinolone	Steroid	Y
Ketoconazole	NIZORAL	Antifungal	Y
Ketoprofen	ORUDIS	NSAID	Y
KH3	Procaine, haematoporphyrin et al.	Tonic	Y
KINIDIN	Quinidine bisulphate	Antiarrhythmic	Y
K-MAG	Potassium	Mineral supplement	N
KOLPON	Oestrone	Sex hormone	Y
KONAKION	Phyomenadione	Haemostatic	N
KSR	Potassium	Mineral supplement	N
K-THROMBIN	Menaphthone sodium bisulphate	Haemostatic	N
KWELLS	Hyoscine et al.	Antiemetic	N
Labetalol	TRANDATE, PRESOLOL	Antihypertensive	Y
Lactulose	DUPHALAC	Laxative	N
LAMPRENE	Clofazimine	Antileprotic	Y
LANOXIN	Digoxin	Cardiac glycoside	Y
LARGACTIL	Chlorpromazine	Antipsychotic	Y
LARIAM	Mefloquine	Antimalarial	Y
LARODOPA	Levodopa	Antiparkinsonian	Y
LAROXYL	Amitriptyline	Antidepressant	Y
LASIX	Frusemide	Diuretic	Y
LASONIL	Hepainoid, hyaluronidase	Superficial bruises, sprains & clots	N
Latamoxef	MOXALACTAM	Antibiotic/Beta lactam	Y
LAXETTES	Phenolphthalein	Laxative	N
LEDERMYCIN	Demeclocycline	Antibiotic/Tetracycline	Y
LEDERTREXATE	Methotrexate	Cytotoxic	Y
LENTE MC	Insulin	Hypoglycaemic	Y
LETHIDRONE	Nalorphine	Counteracts narcotic poisoning	Y
LEUKERAN	Chlorambucil	Cytotoxic	Y
LEUNASE	Colaspase	Cytotoxic	Y
Leuprorelin	LUCRIN	Cytotoxic	Y
Levodopa	LARODOPA, MADOPAR, SINEMET	Antiparkinsonian	Y
LEVOPHED	L-Noradrenaline	Vasoconstrictor	Y
Levonorgestrel	BIPHASIL, MICROGYNON, MICROLUT, MICROVAL, NORDETTE, NORDIOL, SEQUILAR, TRIPHASIL, TRIQUILAR	Sex hormone (Contraceptive)	Y
LEXOTAN	Bromazepam	Anxiolytic/Benzodiazepine	Y
LIBRAX	Chlordiazepoxide, clidinium bromide	Antispasmodic	Y
LIBRIUM	Chlordiazepoxide	Anxiolytic	Y
Lignocaine	Multiple trade names and forms	Local anaesthetic	Varies
LINCOCIN	Lincomycin	Antibiotic	Y
Lincomycin	LINCOCIN	Antibiotic	Y
Lindane	LOREXANE, QUELLADA	Antiparasitic (scabies)	N
LINGRAINE	Ergotamine tartrate	Antimigraine	Y
LIORESAL	Baclofen	Muscle relaxant	Y
Liothyronine	TERTROXIN, TRIIODOTHYRONINE	For severely underactive thyroid	Y

Drug treatment

TABLE 6.2:
DRUGS AVAILABLE IN AUSTRALIA (continued)

Name (TRADE/Generic)		Class	Prescription needed (yes/no)
LIPEX	Simvastatin	Hypolipidaemic	Y
LITHICARB	Lithium carbonate	Antipsychotic	Y
Lithium carbonate	LITHICARB, PRIADEL	Antipsychotic	Y
LOASID	Aluminium & magnesium compounds, simethicone	Antacid	N
Lobeline	REFRANE	Aid to cease smoking	N
LOBETA	Penbutalol	Beta-blocker	Y
LOCACORTEN-VIOFORM	Flumethasone, clioquinol	Steroid/Antiseptic (ear)	Y
LOMOTIL	Diphenoxylate	Antidiarrhoeal	Y
LONAVAR	Oxandrolone	Sex hormone (promotes growth)	Y
LONITEN	Minoxidil	Antihypertensive	Y
Loperamide	IMODIUM	Antidiarrhoeal	Y
LOPRESOR	Metoprolol	Beta-blocker	Y
Lorazepam	ATIVAN	Anxiolytic/Benzodiazepine	Y
LOREXANE	Lindane	Antiparasitic (scabies)	N
LOSEC	Omeprazole	Antiulcerant	Y
LOTREMIN	Clotrimazole	Antifungal	N (Y Qld & Vic)
LPV	Phenoxymethylpenicillin	Antibiotic/Penicillin	Y
LUCRIN	Leuprorelin	Cytotoxic	Y
LURSELLE	Probucol	Hypolipidaemic	Y
Lypressin	VASOPRESSIN	Antidiuretic (nasal spray)	Y
LYSPAFEN	Difenoxin	Antidiarrhoeal	Y
LYTREN	Electrolyte solution	Corrects dehydration	N
MACRODANTIN	Nitrofurantoin	Antibiotic (urine)	Y
MADOPAR	Levodopa, benserazide	Antiparkinsonian	Y
Magnesium compounds	Multiple trade names	Antacid; Mineral supplement	N
MAGNOPLASM	Glycerol, magnesium sulphate	Poultice for abscesses	N
MALOPRIM	Pyrimethamine, dapsone	Antimalarial	Y
MANDELAMINE	Hexamine	Antiseptic (urine)	N
MANDOL	Cephamandole	Antibiotic/Cephalosporin	Y
MAREVAN	Warfarin	Anticoagulant	Y
MARPLAN	Isocarboxazid	Antidepressant/MAOI	Y
MAXIDEX	Dexamethasone	Steroid	Y
MAXOLON	Metoclopramide	Antiemetic	Y
Mazindol	SANOREX	Anorectic	Y
Mebendazole	VERMOX	Anthelmintic	N
Mebeverine	COLOFAC	Antispasmodic	Y
Mebhydrolin	FABAHISTIN	Antihistamine	N
Meclozine	ANCOLAN	Antihistamine	Y
MEDIFEM	Acidophilus culture, lactose, vinegar	Prevents vaginal thrush	N
MEDIHALER EPI	Adrenaline	Bronchodilator/Sympathomimetic	N
MEDIHALER ERGOTAMINE	Ergotamine	Antimigraine	Y
MEDIHALER ISO	Isoprenaline	Bronchodilator/Sympathomimetic	Y (N NSW)
MEDI PULV	Hexamidine, chlorhexidine, allantoin	Antiseptic	N
MEDROL ACNE LOTION	Methylprednisolone, sulphur	Steroid	Y
MEDROL TABS.	Methylprednisolone	Steroid	Y
Medroxyprogesterone	DEPO-PROVERA, FARLUTAL, PROVERA	Sex hormone	Y
Medrysone	HMS LIQUIFILM	Steroid (eye)	Y
Mefenamic acid	MEFIC, PONSTAN	Analgesic	Y
MEFIC	Mefenamic acid	Analgesic	Y
Mefloquine	LARIAM	Antimalarial	Y
MEFOXIN	Cefoxitin	Antibiotic/Cephalosporin	Y
Mefruside	BAYCARON	Diuretic	Y
Megesterol acetate	MEGOSTAT	Cytotoxic	Y
MEGOSTAT	Megesterol acetate	Cytotoxic	Y

Section 6: Treatments

TABLE 6.2:
DRUGS AVAILABLE IN AUSTRALIA (continued)

Name (TRADE/Generic)		Class	Prescription needed (yes/no)
MELLERIL	Thioridazine	Antipsychotic	Y
Melphalan	ALKERAN	Cytotoxic	Y
Menotrophin	METRODIN, PERGONAL	Induces ovulation and sperm production	Y
Mepenzolate	CANTIL	Antispasmodic	Y
Meprobamate	EQUANIL	Anxiolytic	Y
Mepyramine	ANTHISAN CREAM, HYCOMINE, NEO-DIOPHEN	Antihistamine	Depends on form
MERACOTE	Multiple ingredients	Antacid	N
MERBENTYL	Dicyclomine	Antispasmodic	Y Tabs, N Syrup
Mercaptopurine	PURI-NETHOL	Cytotoxic	Y
MERSYNDOL	Paracetamol, codeine, doxylamine	Analgesic	N
MESASAL	Mesalazine	Other (ulcerative colitis)	Y
Mesterolone	PROVIRON	Sex hormone	Y
MESTINON	Pyridostigmine	For myasthenia gravis	Y
MESTRANOL	NORINYL, ORTHO-NOVUM	Hormone (contraceptive)	Y
METAMIDE	Metoclopramide	Antiemetic	Y
Metaraminol	ARAMINE	Vasoconstrictor	Y
Metformin	DIABEX, DIAFORMIN, GLUCOPHAGE	Hypoglycaemic	Y
Methacycline HCl	RONDOMYCIN	Antibiotic/Tetracycline	Y
Methadone	PHYSEPTONE	Narcotic/Analgesic	Y
Methazolamide	NEPTAZANE	Additional glaucoma treatment	Y
Methdilazine	DILOSYN	Antihistamine	N
Methenolone	PRIMOBOLAN	Anabolic steroid	Y
Methicillin	METIN	Antibiotic/Penicillin	Y
Methionine	METHNINE	For paracetamol overdosage	N
METHNINE	Methionine	For paracetamol overdosage	N
METHOBLASTIN	Methotrexate	Cytotoxic	Y
Methocarbamol	ROBAXIN	Muscle relaxant	Y
METHOPT	Hypromellose	Artificial tears	N
Methotrexate	LEDERTREXATE, METHOBLASTIN	Cytotoxic	Y
Methoxamine	VASYLOX	Decongestant	N
Methoxsalen	OXSORALEN	Treats vitiligo	Y
Methoxyphenamine	ORTHOXICOL	Decongestant	N
Methsuximide	CELONTIN	Anticonvulsant	Y
Methyclothiazide	ENDURON	Diuretic	Y
Methyldopa	ALDOMET, HYDOPA	Antihypertensive	Y
Methylphenidate	RITALIN	Stimulant	Y
Methylphenobarbitone	PROMINAL	Barbiturate	Y
Methylprednisolone acetate	MEDROL, NEO-MEDROL	Steroid	Y
Methyltestosterone	ELDEC, MIXOGEN, TESTOMET	Sex hormone	Y
Metylundecenoate	MONPHYTOL	Antifungal	N
Methysergide	DESERIL	Antimigraine	Y
METIN	Methcillin	Antibiotic/Penicillin	Y
Metoclopramide	METAMIDE, MAXOLON, PRAMIN	Antiemetic	Y
Metolazone	DIULO	Diuretic	Y
Metoprolol	BETALOC, LOPRESOR	Beta-blocker	Y
METRODIN	Menotrophin	Trophic hormone	Y
METROGYL	Metronidazole	Antibiotic	Y
Metronidazole	FLAGYL, METROGYL, METROZINE, PROTOSTAT, TRICHIZOLE	Antibiotic	Y
METROZINE	Metyronidazole	Antibiotic	Y
Mexiletine	MEXITIL	Antiarrhythmic	Y
MEXITIL	Mexiletine	Antiarrhythmic	Y
MIACALCIC	Salcatonin	For Paget's disease	Y

TABLE 6.2:
DRUGS AVAILABLE IN AUSTRALIA *(continued)*

Name (TRADE/Generic)		Class	Prescription needed (yes/no)
Mianserin	TOLVON	Antidepressant	Y
Miconazole	DAKTARIN, MONISTAT	Antifungal	Depends on form
MICROGYNON	Levonorgestrol, ethinyloestradiol	Sex hormone (Contraceptive)	Y
MICROLAX	Multiple ingredients	Laxative	N
MICROLUT	Levonorgestrol	Sex hormone (Contraceptive)	Y
MICRONOR	Norethisterone	Sex hormone (Contraceptive)	Y
MICROVAL	Levonorgestrol	Sex hormone (Contraceptive)	Y
MIDAMOR	Amiloride	Diuretic	Y
Midazolam	HYPNOVEL	Sedative	Y
MIGRAL	Ergotamine	Antimigraine	Y
MIGRANOL	Paracetamol, atropine, papaverine, nicotinic acid	Analgesic	N
MILONTIN	Phensuximide	Anticonvulsant	Y
MINIDIAB	Glipizide	Hypoglycaemic	Y
MINIPRESS	Prazosin	Antihypertensive	Y
MINIRIN	Desmopressin	Antidiuretic	Y
Minocycline	MINOMYCIN	Antibiotic/Tetracycline	Y
MINOMYCIN	Minocycline	Antibiotic/Tetracycline	Y
Minoxidil	LONITEN	Antihypertensive	Y
MINTEC	Peppermint oil	Antispasmodic	N
MINTEZOL	Thiabendazole	Anthelmintic	N (Y Vic)
Misoprostol	CYTOTEC	Antiulcerant	Y
MITHRACIN	Mithramycin	Cytotoxic	Y
Mitomycin	MITOMYCIN	Cytotoxic	Y
Mitozantrone	NOVANTRONE	Cytotoxic	Y
MIXOGEN	Ethinyoestradiol, methyltestosterone	Sex hormone	Y
MIXTARD	Insulin	Hypoglycaemic	Y
MODECATE	Fluphenazine	Antipsychotic	Y
MODURETIC	Amiloride, hydrochlorthiazide	Diuretic	Y
MOGADON	Nitrazepam	Sedative	Y
MONISTAT	Miconazole	Antifungal	Y
MONODRAL	Penthianate	Antispasmodic	Y
MONOTARD	Insulin	Hypoglycaemic	Y
MORPHALGIN	Morphine, aspirin	Narcotic/Analgesic	Y
Morphine	ANAMORPH, MORPHALGIN	Analgesic	Y
MOTILIUM	Domperidone	Antiemetic	Y
MOVELAT	Salicylic acid et al.	Liniment	Y
MOXACIN	Amoxycillin	Antibiotic/Penicillin	Y
MOXALACTAM	Latamoxef disodium	Antibiotic	Y
MUCAINE	Oxethazine, aluminium & magnesium salts	Antacid	Y
MUCOMYST	Acetylcysteine	Mucolytic	Y (N NSW)
Mupirocin	BACTROBAN	Antibiotic (cream)	Y
MURELAX	Oxazepam	Anxiolytic/Benzodiazepine	Y
MURINE PLUS	Tetrahydrozoline et al.	Vasoconstrictor/Astringent (eye)	N
MURIPSIN	Glutamic acid, pepsin	Acid	N
Muromonab	ORTHOCLONE OKT3	Immune suppressant	Y
MUSTINE	Mustine hydrochloride	Cytotoxic	Y
MUTABON D	Perphenazine, amitriptyline	Antipsychotic	Y
MYAMBUTOL	Ethambutol	Antituberculotic	Y
MYCIFRADIN	Neomycin	Antibiotic/Aminoglycoside	Y
MYCIL	Chlorphenesin	Antifungal	N
MYCITRACIN	Bacitracin, neomycin, polymyxin B	Antibiotic/Antifungal	Y
MYCODERM	Salicylic acid, undecenoic alkanolamide, sodium propionate, bityl hydroxybenzoate	Antifungal	N

Section 6: Treatments

TABLE 6.2:
DRUGS AVAILABLE IN AUSTRALIA (continued)

Name (TRADE/Generic)		Class	Prescription needed (yes/no)
MYCOSTATIN	Nystatin	Antifungal	Y
MYCOZOL	Salicylic acid, benzoic acid et al.	Antifungal	N
MYDRIACYL	Tropicamide	Mydriatic	N (Y NSW)
MYLANTA	Simethicone, magnesium & aluminium salts	Antacid	N
MYLERAN	Busulphan	Cytotoxic	Y
MYLICON	Simethicone	Antacid	N
MYOCRISIN	Sodium aurothiomalate (gold)	Antirheumatic	Y
MYOQUIN	Quinine bisulphate	Muscle relaxant	N
MYSOLINE	Primidone	Anticonvulsant	Y
MYSTECLIN V	Tetracycline phosphate, nystatin	Antibiotic/Tetracycline/Antifungal	Y
Nalidixic acid	NEGRAM	Antibiotic	Y
Nalorphine	LETHIDRONE	Counteracts narcotic poisoning	Y
Naloxone	NARCAN	Counteracts narcotic poisoning	Y
Nandrolone	DURABOLIN, DECA-DURABOLIN	Anabolic steroid	Y
Naphazoline	ALBALON, CLEAR EYES, OPTAZINE, ANTISTINE PRIVINE	Vasoconstrictor (eye)	N
NAPROGESIC	Naproxen sodium	Analgesic/NSAID	N
NAPROSYN	Naproxen	NSAID	Y
Naproxen	NAPROSYN, NAXEN	NSAID	Y
Naproxen sodium	NAPROGESIC	Analgesic/NSAID	N
NARCAN	Naloxone	Counteracts narcotic poisoning	Y
NARDIL	Phenelzine	Antidepressant/ MAOI	Y
NATRILIX	Indapamide	Antihypertensive	Y
NATULAN	Procarbazine	Cytotoxic	Y
NAVANE	Thiothixene	Antipsychotic	Y
NAVIDREX	Cyclopenthiazide	Diuretic	Y
NAXEN	Naproxen	NSAID	Y
NEBCIN	Tobramycin	Antibiotic/Aminoglycoside	Y
NEGRAM	Nalidixic acid	Antibiotic	Y
NEMBUDEINE	Sodium pentobarbitone, paracetamol, codeine phos.	Analgesic/Barbiturate	Y
NEMBUTAL	Pentobarbitone sodium	Barbiturate/Sedative	Y
NEMDYN	Neomycin, bacitracin	Antibiotic (oint.)	Y
NEO-CORTEF	Neomycin, hydrocortisone	Steroid/Antibiotic	Y
NEO-CYTAMEN	Hydroxocobalamine	For pernicious anaemia	N
NEO-DIOPHEN	Mepyramine, phenylpropanolamine, dextromethorphan	Antihistamine/Antitussive	N (Y Qld)
NEO-HYCOR	Hydrocortisone, neomycin	Steroid/Antibiotic	Y
NEO-MEDROL	Methylprednisolone, neomycin, aluminium chlorhydroxide, sulphur	Steroid/Antibiotic	Y
NEO-MERCAZOLE	Carbimazole	Antithyroid	Y
Neomycin	Multiple trade names including: CICATRIN, KENACOMB, MYCITRACIN, NEOSPORIN, NEOTRACIN, SPERSIN etc.	Antibiotic/Aminoglycoside	Y
NEOPT	Neomycin	Antibiotic/Aminoglycoside	Y
NEOSPORIN	Neomycin	Antibiotic/Aminoglycoside	Y
Neostigmine	PROSTIGMIN	Anticholinergic	Y
NEOSULF	Neomycin	Antibiotic/Aminoglycoside	Y
NEOTRACIN	Bacitracin, neomycin, polymyxin	Antibiotic/Antifungal	Y
NEPTAZANE	Methazolamide	Additional treatment for glaucoma	Y

TABLE 6.2:
DRUGS AVAILABLE IN AUSTRALIA (continued)

Name (TRADE/Generic)		Class	Prescription needed (yes/no)
Netilmicin	NETROMYCIN	Antibiotic/Aminoglycoside	Y
NETROMYCIN	Netilmicin	Antibiotic/Aminoglycoside	Y
NEULACTIL	Pericyazine	Antipsychotic	Y
NEUR-AMYL	Amylobarbitone	Barbiturate/Sedative	Y
NEUROREMED	L-Tryptophan	Sedative (mild)	N
NEUTRALON	Aluminium sodium silicate	Antacid	N
NIAPREN	Ibuprofen	NSAID	Y
Niclosamide	YOMESAN	Anthelmintic	N
NICORETTE	Nicotine	Aid to smoking cessation	Y
Nicotine	NICORETTE	Aid to smoking cessation	Y
Nicotinic acid	CIRFLO, MIGRANOL, NO DOZ	Antimigraine/Stimulant	Varies
Nifedipine	ADALAT	Antihypertensive/Antiangina	Y
NILSTAT	Nystatin	Antifungal	Depends on form
NIPRIDE	Sodium nitroprusside	Antihypertensive	Y
NITOMAN	Tetrabenazine	Other (for brain diseases and tremors)	Y
NITRADISC	Glyceryl trinitrate	Antiangina (skin patch)	Y
Nitrazepam	ALODORM, MOGADON	Hypnotic	Y
NITRO-BID OINTMENT	Glyceryl trinitrate	Antiangina	Y
Nitrofurantoin	FURADANTIN, MACRODANTIN	Antibiotic	Y
Nitrofurazone	FURACIN	Antiseptic	N
NITROLATE	Glyceryl trinitrate	Antiangina	Y
Nitromersol	COLD SORE BALM, METAPHEN	Antiseptic	N
NIVAQUINE	Chloroquine	Antimalarial	Y
NIZORAL	Ketoconazole	Antifungal	Y
NOCTEC	Chloral hydrate	Sedative	Y
NO DOZ (PLUS)	Caffeine, nicotinic acid et al.	Stimulant	N
NOLVADEX	Tamoxifen	Cytotoxic	Y
Nonoxynol 9	DELFEN, ORTHO CREME	Spermicide	N
Nonylvanillamide	FINALGON	Liniment	N
Noradrenaline	LEVOPHED	Vasoconstrictor	Y
NORDETTE	Ethinyloestradiol, levonorgestrol	Sex hormones (contraceptive)	Y
NORDIOL	Ethinyloestradiol, levonorgestrol	Hormones (contraceptive)	Y
Norethisterone	BREVINOR, MICRONOR, SYNPHASIC, NORIDAY, NORINYL, ORTHO-NOVUM, PRIMOLUT-N	Sex hormone	Y
NORFLEX	Orphenadrine	Muscle relaxant	Y (N NSW)
Norfloxacin	NOROXIN	Antibiotic	Y
NORGESIC	Orphenadrine, paracetamol	Muscle relaxant	Y
NORIDAY	Norethisterone	Sex hormone (contraceptive)	Y
NORINYL	Norethisterone, mestranol	Sex hormone (contraceptive)	Y
NORMACOL	Sterculia, frangula bark	Laxative	N
Normethadone	TICARDA	Narcotic/Antitussive	Y
NORMISON	Temazepam	Sedative	Y
NOROXIN	Norfloxacin	Antibiotic	Y
NORPACE	Disopyramide	Antiarrhythmic	Y
NORTAB	Nortriptyline	Antidepressant/Tricyclic	Y
Nortriptyline	ALLEGRON, NORTAB	Antidepressant/Tricyclic	Y
NOTEN	Atenolol	Beta-blocker	Y
NOVANTRONE	Mitozantrone	Cytotoxic	Y
NUCOSEF	Codeine phos., pseudoephedrine	Antitussive/Decongestant	N
NUELIN	Theophylline	Bronchodilator/Xanthinate derivative	Y
NUROFEN	Ibuprofen	NSAID	Y

Section 6: Treatments

TABLE 6.2:
DRUGS AVAILABLE IN AUSTRALIA (continued)

Name (TRADE/Generic)		Class	Prescription needed (yes/no)
Nystatin	ACHROSTATIN, ARISTOCOMB, KENACOMB, MYCOSTATIN, MYSTECLIN V, NILSTAT, TETREX F	Antifungal	Depends on form
Octoxinol	ORTHO-GYNOL	Spermicide	N
OCUSERT	Pilocarpine	Mydriatic	Y (N NSW)
Oestradiol	MIXOGEN, PRIMODIAN, PRIMOGYN, PROGYNOVA	Sex hormone	Y
Oestriol	OVESTIN	Sex hormone	Y
Oestrogen	PREMARIN	Sex hormone	Y
Oestrone	KOLPON	Sex hormone	Y
OGEN	Piperazine oestrone	Sex hormone	Y
Olsalazine	DIPENTUM	Laxative	Y
Omeprazole	LOSEC	Antiulcerant	Y
OMNOPON	Papaveretum	Analgesic (strong)	Y
ONCOVIN	Vincristine	Cytotoxic	Y
OPERIDINE	Phenoperidone	Narcotic/Analgesic	Y
OPHTHAINE	Proxymetacaine	Anaesthetic (eye)	Y
OPHTHETIC	Proxymetacaine	Anaesthetic (eye)	Y
OPTAZINE	Naphazolin et al.	Vasoconstrictor (eye)	N
OPTICROM	Sodium cromoglycate	Other (allergic conjunctivitis)	Y
ORABOLIN	Ethinyloestrenol	Anabolic steroid	Y
ORADEXON	Dexamethasone	Steroid	Y
ORAP	Pimozide	Antipsychotic	Y
ORBENIN	Cloxacillin	Antibiotic/Penicillin	Y
Orciprenaline	ALUPENT	Bronchodilator/ Sympathomimetic	Y
OROXINE	Thyroxine	Thyroid agent	Y
Orphenadrine	NORFLEX, NORGESIC	Muscle relaxant	Y
ORTHOCLONE OKT3	Muromonab	Immune suppressant	Y
ORTHO-CREME	Nonoxynol 9	Spermicide	N
ORTHO-GYNOL	Octoxinol	Spermicide	N
ORTHO-NOVUM	Norethisterone, mestranol	Sex hormone (contraceptive)	Y
ORTHOXICOL	Methoxyphenamine et al.	Antihistamine/Other	N
ORUDIS	Ketoprofen	NSAID	Y
OSPOLOT	Sulthiame	Anticonvulsant	Y
OTICANE	Benzocaine, chlorhexidine et al.	Antiseptic	N
OTRIVIN	Xylometazoline	Decongestant	N
OVESTIN	Oestriol	Sex hormone	Y
Oxandrolone	LONAVAR	Anabolic steroid	Y
Oxazepam	ALEPAM, MURELAX, SEREPAX	Anxiolytic/Benzodiazepine	Y
Oxethazaine	MUCAINE	Antacid/Anaesthetic	N
Oxolamine	BREDON	Antitussive	N
Oxpentifylline	TRENTAL	Vasodilator	Y
Oxprenolol	CORBETON, TRASICOR	Beta-blocker	Y
OXSORALEN	Methoxsalen	Treats vitiligo	Y
Oxycodone	ENDONE, PERCODAN, PROLADONE	Narcotic/Analgesic	Y
Oxymetazoline	DRIXINE	Decongestant	N
Oxymetholone	ADROYD, ANAPOLON	Anabolic steroid	Y
OXY 5/10	Benzoyl peroxide	Keratolytic	N
Oxytetracycline	TERRAMYCIN	Antibiotic/Tetracycline	Y
Oxytocin	SYNTOCINON, SYNTOMETRINE	Causes uterine contraction	Y
PALFIUM	Dextromoramide	Analgesic (strong)	Y
PAMINE	Hyoscine	Antispasmodic	N (Y Vic)
PANADEINE	Paracetamol, codeine	Analgesic	Depends on strength
PANADOL	Paracetamol	Analgesic	N
PANAFCORT	Prednisone	Steroid	Y

TABLE 6.2:
DRUGS AVAILABLE IN AUSTRALIA *(continued)*

Name (TRADE/Generic)		Class	Prescription needed (yes/no)
PANAFCORTELONE	Prednisolone	Steroid	Y
PANALGESIC	Paracetamol, codeine, doxylamine	Analgesic	N
PANAMAX	Paracetamol	Analgesic	N
PANAMAX CO	Paracetamol, codeine	Analgesic	N
PANCREASE	Pancrelipase	Digestive enzyme	N
Pancreatin	PANAZYME, COMBIZYM, PHAZYME, POLYZYM, VIOKASE	Digestive enzyme	N
Pancrelipase	PANCREASE, COTAZYM-S FORTE	Digestive enzyme	N
PANCREX	Protease	Digestive enzyme	N
PANOXYL	Benzoyl peroxide	Keratolytic	N
PANQUIL	Paracetamol, promethazine	Analgesic/Antihistamine	N (Y Vic & Tas)
PANTHELINE	Propantheline	Antispasmodic	Y
Papaveretum	OMNOPON	Analgesic (strong)	Y
Papaverine	CYCLOPANE, MIGRANOL	Analgesic/Antimigraine	Y
Paracetamol	Multiple trade names including: CAPADEX, DIGESIC, DYMADON, FIORINAL, MERSYNDOL, PANADOL, PANAMAX, PARASPEN, TEMPRA	Analgesic	N
PARACHOC	Paraffin	Laxative	N
PARACODIN	Dihydrocodeine tartrate	Antitussive	N
PARADEX	Paracetamol, dextropropoxyphene	Analgesic	Y
Paraffin	Multiple trade names	Laxative/Moisturiser/Lubricant	N
Paraldehyde	PARALDEHYDE	Sedative	Y
PARALGIN	Paracetamol	Analgesic	N
PARASPEN	Paracetamol	Analgesic	N
PARLODEL	Bromocriptine	Antiparkinsonian. Stops breast milk	Y
PARMOL	Paracetamol	Analgesic	N
PARNATE	Tranylcypromine	Antidepressant/MAOI	Y
PAROVEN	Rutosides	Other	N
PARSTELIN	Tranylcypromine	Antidepressant/MAOI	Y
PARVOLEX	Acetylcysteine	Antidote for paracetamol poisoning	Y
Pectin	DIAREZE, DONNAGEL, GLUCOMAGMA, KAOMAGMA, STREPTOMAGMA, ADM	Antidiarrhoeal	N
PEDOZ	Zinc undecenoate, zinc oxide et al.	Antifungal	N
PENBRITIN	Ampicillin	Antibiotic/Penicillin	Y
Penbutolol	LOBETA	Beta-blocker	Y
Penicillamine	D-PENAMINE	Antirheumatic	Y
PENSIG	Phenethicillin	Antibiotic/Penicillin	Y
Pentaerythritol tetranitrate	PERITRATE	Antiangina	Y
PENTALGIN	Paracetamol, codeine, pentobarbitone	Analgesic/Barbiturate	Y
Pentazocine	FORTRAL	Analgesic (strong)	Y
Penthienate bromide	MONODRAL	Antispasmodic	Y
Pentobarbitone	CARBRITAL, NEMBUDEINE, NEMBUTAL, PENTALGIN	Barbiturate	Y
PEPCIDINE	Famotidine	Antiulcerant	Y
Peppermint oil	MINTEC	Antispasmodic	N
PEPSILLIDE	Liquorice, bismuth et al.	Antiulcerant	N
Pepsin	MURIPSIN	Digestive enzyme	N
PERCODAN	Oxycodone, aspirin, paracetamol	Analgesic (strong)	Y

Section 6: Treatments

TABLE 6.2:
DRUGS AVAILABLE IN AUSTRALIA (continued)

Name (TRADE/Generic)		Class	Prescription needed (yes/no)
PERGONAL	Menotrophin	Trophic hormone	Y
Perhexiline	PEXID	Antiangina	Y
PERIACTIN	Cyproheptadine	Antihistamine	N (Y ACT)
Pericyazine	NEULACTIL	Antipsychotic	Y
PERITRATE	Pentaerythritol tetranitrate	Antiangina	Y
Perphenazine	MUTABON D, TRILAFON	Antipsychotic	Y
PERSANTIN	Dipyridamole	Anticoagulant	Y
PERTOFRAN	Desipramine	Antidepressant	Y
Pethidine	PETHIDINE	Narcotic/Analgesic	Y
PEVARYL	Econazole	Antifungal	Depends on form
PEXID	Perhexiline	Antiangina	Y
PHARMORUBICIN	Epirubicin	Cytotoxic	Y
PHAZYME	Simethicone, pancreatin	Antacid	N
Phenazopyridine	PYRIDIUM	Antiseptic	Y (N NSW)
Phenelzine	NARDIL	Antidepressant	Y
PHENERGAN	Promethazine	Antihistamine	Depends on form
Phenethicillin	PENSIG	Antibiotic/Penicillin	Y
Phenindione	DINDEVAN	Anticoagulant	Y
Pheniramine	AVIL, FENAMINE, TRIOMINIC	Antihistamine	N
Phenobarbitone	PHENOBARB, DONNATAL	Barbiturate	Y
Phenolphthalein	AGAROL, ALOPHEN, LAXETTES, VERACOLATE	Laxative	N
Phenoperidine	OPERIDINE	Narcotic/Analgesic	Y
Phenoxybenzamine HCl	DIBENYLINE	Vasodilator	Y
Phenoxymethylpenicillin	ABBOCILLIN, CILICAINE, LPV, PVK	Antibiotic/Penicillin	Y
PHENSEDYL	Promethazine, pholcodeine, pseudoephedrine	Antihistamine/Antitussive	N
Phensuximide	MILONTIN	Antiparkinsonian	Y
Phentermine	DUROMINE	Anorectic	Y
Phentolamine	REGITINE	Vasodilator	Y
Phenylbutazone	BUTAZOLIDIN	NSAID	Y
Phenylephrine	Multiple trade names	Vasoconstrictor/Decongestant	N
Phenylpropanol	FELICUR	Cholagogue	N
Phenylpropanolamine	DIMETAPP, ESKORNADE, TRIOMINIC	Decongestant	Depends on form
Phenyltoloxamine	SINUTAB WITH CODEINE	Decongestant	N
Phenytoin	DILANTIN	Anticonvulsant	Y
PHISOHEX	Triclosan	Antiseptic	N
Pholcodine	ACTUSS, DURO-TUSS, TUSSINOL, PHENSEDYL, PHOLCODIN, TIXYLIX	Antitussive	N
Phthalylsulphathiazole	PHTHAZOL, THALAZOLE	Antibiotic/Sulpha	Y
PHTHAZOL	Phthalylsulphathiazole	Antibiotic/Sulpha	Y
PHYSEPTONE	Methadone	Narcotic/Analgesic	Y
PHYTEX	Zinc undecenoate, undecenoic acid	Antifungal	N
Phytomenadione	KONAKION	Haemostatic	N
Pilocarpine	OCUSERT, ISOPTOCARPINE, PILOPT	Miotic	Y
PILOPT	Pilocarpine	Miotic	Y
Pimozide	ORAP	Antipsychotic	Y
Pindolol	BARBLOC, VISKEN	Beta-blocker	Y
Pipenzolate	PIPTAL	Antispasmodic	Y
Piperacillin	PIPRIL	Antibiotic/Penicillin	Y
Piperazine oestrone	OGEN	Sex hormone	Y
Pipradrol	ALERTONIC	Tonic	Y
PIPRIL	Piperacillin	Antibiotic/Penicillin	Y
PIPTAL	Pipenzolate	Antispasmodic	Y
PIRITON	Chlorpheniramine	Antihistamine	N

Drug treatment

TABLE 6.2:
DRUGS AVAILABLE IN AUSTRALIA (continued)

Name (TRADE/Generic)		Class	Prescription needed (yes/no)
Piroxicam	FELDENE	NSAID	Y
PITRESSIN	Vasopressin	Antidiuretic	N
Pizotifen	SANDOMIGRAN	Antimigraine	Y
PLAQUENIL	Hydroxychloroquine	Antimalarial	Y
PLATAMINE	Cisplatin	Cytotoxic	Y
PLENDIL	Felodipine	Antihypertensive	Y
PLUSERIX	Mumps, measles, rubella vaccine	Vaccine	Y
POLARAMINE	Dexchlorpheniramine	Antihistamine	N (Y ACT)
Poloxalkol	COLOXYL	Laxative	N
Polymyxin B	AEROCORTIN, CHLOROMYXIN, MYCITRACIN, NEOSPORIN, NEOTRACIN, SPERSIN, TERRAMYCIN	Antibiotic	Y
PONDERAX	Fenfluramine	Anorectic	Y
PONSTAN	Mefenamic acid	Analgesic	Y
POSALFILIN	Salicylic acid, podophyllum resin	Keratolytic	N
Potassium clavulanate	AUGMENTIN, TIMENTIN	Antibiotic	Y
Potassium iodide	ELIXOPHYLLIN KI	Expectorant	Y
Povidone iodine	BETADINE, ISODINE, STOXINE	Antiseptic	N
PRAMIN	Metoclopramide	Antiemetic	Y
Prazosin	MINIPRESS	Antihypertensive	Y
PREDNEFERIN	Prednisolone	Steroid	Y
Prednisolone	Multiple trade names including: CORTEF, PREDNEFERIN, SCHERIPROCT, PREDSOL	Steroid	Y
Prednisone	DELTASONE, PANAFCORT, SONE	Steroid	Y
PREDSOL	Prednisolone	Steroid	Y
PREGNYL	Chorionic gonadotrophin	Trophic hormone	Y
PREMARIN	Oestrogen	Sex hormone	Y
PRESOLOL	Labetalol	Antihypertensive	Y
PRIADEL	Lithium carbonate	Antipsychotic	Y
Primaquine	PRIMAQUINE	Antimalarial	Y
PRIMAXIN	Imipenem, cilastatin	Antibiotic	Y
Primidone	MYSOLINE	Anticonvulsant	Y
PRIMOBOLAN	Methenolone	Anabolic steroid	Y
PRIMODIAN	Testosterone, oestradiol valerate	Sex hormone	Y
PRIMOGONYL	Chorionic gonadotrophin	Trophic hormone	Y
PRIMOGYN	Oestradiol valerate	Sex hormone	Y
PRIMOLUT N	Norethisterone	Sex hormone	Y
PRIMOTESTON	Testosterone	Sex hormone	Y
PRO-BANTHINE	Propantheline	Antispasmodic (excess sweating)	Y
Probenecid	BENEMID	Hypouricaemic agent. Prolongs effectiveness of penicillin	Y
Probucol	LURSELLE	Hypolipidaemic	Y
Procainamide	PROCAINAMIDE, PRONESTYL	Antiarrhythmic	Y
Procaine HCl	KH3, CELLAFORTE	Tonic	Y
Procaine penicillin	CILICAINE	Antibiotic/Penicillin	Y
Procarbazine	NATULAN	Cytotoxic	Y
Prochlorperazine	STEMETIL, COMPAZINE	Antiemetic	Y
PROCTOSEDYL	Cinchocaine, hydrocortisone, esculin	Steroid/Anaesthetic	Y
Procyclidine	KEMADRIN	Antiparkinsonian	Y
PROFASI	Chorionic gonadotrophin	Trophic hormone	Y

Section 6: Treatments

TABLE 6.2:
DRUGS AVAILABLE IN AUSTRALIA (continued)

Name (TRADE/Generic)		Class	Prescription needed (yes/no)
Progesterone	PROLUTON	Sex hormone	Y
PROGOUT	Allopurinol	Hypouricaemic	Y
PROGYNOVA	Oestradiol valerate	Sex hormone	Y
PROLADONE	Oxycodone	Analgesic	Y
Prolintane HCl	CATOVIT	Tonic	Y
PROLUTON	Progesterone	Sex hormone	Y
Promazine	SPARINE	Antipsychotic	Y
Promethazine	PHENERGAN, PHENSEDYL, PROTHAZINE, TIXYLIX	Antihistamine	N
Promethazine theoclate	AVOMINE	Antiemetic	N
PROMINAL	Methylphenobarbitone	Barbiturate	Y
PRONESTYL	Procainamide	Antiarrhythmic	Y
PRO-PAM	Diazepam	Anxiolytic/Benzodiazepine	Y
Propamidine	BROLENE	Antiseptic	N
Propantheline	PANTHELINE, PRO-BANTHINE	Antispasmodic (excess sweating)	Y
PROPINE	Dipivefrin, Benzalkonium chloride	Mydriatic	Y
Propranolol	INDERAL, DERALIN, CARDINOL	Beta-blocker	Y
Propylhexedrine	EVENTIN	Anorectic	Y
Propylthiouracil	PROPYLTHIOURACIL	Antithyroid agent	Y
Proscillaridin	TALUSIN	Cardiac glycoside	Y
PROSTIGMIN	Neostigmine	Anticholinergic	Y
PROSTIN VR	Alprostadil	Used to maintain circulation in infants with heart defects	Y
Protamine sulphate	PROTAMINE SULPHATE	Haemostatic	Y
Protamine zinc insulin	ZINC INSULIN	Hypoglycaemic	Y
PROTAPHANE	Isophane insulin	Hypoglycaemic	Y
Protease	BIOGLAN DIGESTIVE	Digestive enzyme	N
PROTHAZINE	Promethazine	Antihistamine	N
PROTHIADEN	Dothiepin	Antidepressant/Tricyclic	Y
PROTOSTAT	Metronidazole	Antibiotic	Y
PROTRAN	Chlorpromazine	Antipsychotic	Y
PROVERA	Medroxyprogesterone acetate	Sex hormone	Y
PROVIRON	Mesterolone	Sex hormone	Y
Proxymetacaine	ALCAINE, OPHTHAINE, OPHTHETIC	Eye surface anaesthetic	Y
PROZAC	Fluoxetine	Antidepressant	Y
Pseudoephedrine	Multiple trade names including: ACTIFED, BENADRYL, CODRAL, NUCOSEF, FABAHISTIN PLUS, SINUTAB, DRIXORA, SUDAFED, SINUZETS, SUDELIX, TUSSELIX	Decongestant/Vasoconstrictor	N
PSORIGEL	Coal tar, alcohol	Keratolytic	N
PURI-NETHOL	Mercaptopurine	Cytotoxic	Y
PV CARPINE	Pilocarpine	Mydriatic	Y (N NSW)
PVK	Phenoxymethylpenicillin	Antibiotic/Penicillin	Y
PYRALVEX	Anthraquinone glycosides, salicylic acid	Mouth ulcers	N
Pyrantel embonate	ANTHEL, COMBANTRIN	Anthelmintic	N
Pyrazinamide	ZINAMIDE	Antituberculotic	Y
PYRIDIUM	Phenazopyridine	Antiseptic (Urine)	Y (N NSW & Vic)
Pyridostigmine	MESTINON	Anticholinergic	Y
Pyridoxine HCl	Vitamin B6	Vitamin	N
Pyrimethamine	DARAPIM, FANSIDAR, MALOPRIM	Antimalarial	Y
QUELLADA	Lindane	Antiparasitic	N
QUESTRAN	Cholestyramine	Hypolipidaemic	Y (N NSW & Vic)

TABLE 6.2:
DRUGS AVAILABLE IN AUSTRALIA *(continued)*

Name (TRADE/Generic)		Class	Prescription needed (yes/no)
QUINATE	Quinine sulphate	Muscle relaxant	N
Quinethazone	AQUAMOX	Diuretic	Y
QUINIDEX	Quinidine	Antiarrhythmic	Y
Quinidine bisulphate	KINIDIN	Antiarrhythmic	Y
Quinidine sulphate	QUINIDEX, QUINIDOXIN	Antiarrhythmic	Y
Quinine bisulphate	BI-CHININE, BIQUINATE, MYOQUIN, QUINBISUL	Muscle relaxant	N
Quinine sulphate	CHININE, QUINATE, QUINOCTAL	Muscle relaxant	N
QUINOCTAL	Quinine sulphate	Muscle relaxant	N
QV	Paraffin, glycerol, alcoholet al.	Skin moisturiser	N
RAFEN	Ibuprofen	NSAID	Y
Ranitidine	ZANTAC	Antiulcerant	Y
RAPITARD	Biphasic insulin	Hypoglycaemic	Y
RASTINON	Tolbutamide	Hypoglycaemic	Y
RAUDIXIN	Rauwolfia serpentina root	Antihypertensive	Y
Rauwolfia	RAUDIXIN	Antihypertensive	Y
RECTINOL	Adrenaline, benzocaine, ephedrine	Vasoconstrictor/Anaesthetic	N
REFRANE	Lobeline	Aid to stop smoking	N
REGITINE	Phentolamine mesylate	Vasodilator	Y
RENITEC	Enalapril	Antihypertensive	Y
Resorcinol	CLEARASIL, EGOMYCOL, ESKAMEL	Keratolytic	N
RESPOLIN	Salbutamol	Bronchodilator/Sympathomimetic	N
RESPRIM	Co-trimoxazole	Antibiotic/Sulpha	Y
RETROVIR	Zidovudine	Antiviral (for AIDS)	Y
REVERIN	Rolitetracycline	Antibiotic/Tetracycline	Y
RHEUMACIN	Indomethacin	NSAID	Y
RHINALAR	Flunisolide	Prevents hay fever	Y
RIDAURA	Auranofin (gold)	Antirheumatic	Y
RIFADIN	Rifampicin	Antituberculotic	Y
Rifampicin	RIFADIN, RIMYCIN	Antituberculotic	Y
RIKODEINE	Dihydrocodeine tartrate	Antitussive	N
RIMEVAX	Measles vaccine	Vaccine	Y
RIMPARIX	Measles vaccine	Vaccine	Y
RIMYCIN	Rifampicin	Antituberculotic	Y
RITALIN	Methylphenidate	Stimulant	Y
Ritodrine	YUTOPAR	Stops uterus contracting in labour	Y
RIVOTRIL	Clonazepam	Anticonvulsant	Y
ROACCUTANE	Isotretinoin	Other (severe acne)	Y
ROBAXIN	Methocarbamol	Muscle relaxant	Y
ROBINUL	Glycopyrrolate	Antispasmodic	Y
ROBITUSSIN	Guaiphenesin, dextromethorphan	Antitussive	N
ROBUDEN	Stomach tissue extract	Antiulcerant	N
ROCEPHIN	Ceftriaxone	Antibiotic/Cephalosporin	Y
ROFERON A	Interferon	Cytotoxic	Y
ROHYPNOL	Flunitrazepam	Sedative	Y
Rolitetracycline	REVERIN	Antibiotic/Tetracycline	Y
RONDOMYCIN	Methacycline	Antibiotic/Tetracycline	Y
ROTER	Bismuth subnitrate, magnesium carbonate et al.	Antiulcerant	Y (N NSW & Vic)
Rubella vaccine	CENDEVAX, EREVAX, MERUVAX II	Vaccine	Y
RYNACROM	Sodium cromoglycate	Other (prevents hay fever)	N
RYTHMODAN	Disopyramide	Antiarrhythmic	Y
SALAZOPYRIN	Sulphasalazine	Other (ulcerative colitis)	Y

Section 6: Treatments

TABLE 6.2:
DRUGS AVAILABLE IN AUSTRALIA (continued)

Name (TRADE/Generic)		Class	Prescription needed (yes/no)
Salbutamol	VENTOLIN, RESPOLIN	Bronchodilator/Sympathomimetic	N
Salcatonin	CALSYNAR, MIACALCIC	For Paget's disease	Y
Salicylic acid	Multiple trade names	Keratolytic	N
SANDIMMUN	Cyclosporin	Immune suppressant	Y
SANDOCAL	Calcium lactate	Mineral supplement	N
SANDOMIGRAN	Pizotifen	Antimigraine	Y
SANOREX	Mazindol	Anorectic	Y
SCHERIPROCT	Prednisolone, clemizole undecenoate, cinchocaine	Steroid/Anaesthetic	Y
SCOP	Hyoscine	Antiemetic (skin patch)	N
SECUROPEN	Azlocillin	Antibiotic/Penicillin	Y
SEDATOL	L-Tryptophan	Sedative (mild)	N
SEDAURAL	Ephedrine, benzocaine, chlorbutol et al.	Anaesthetic/Vasoconstrictor	N
SEDU CAPS D	Salicylamide, diphenhydramine	Sedative (mild)	N
Selenium sulphide	SELSUN	Antifungal	N
SELSUN	Selenium sulphide	Antifungal	N
SEMILENTE	Insulin zinc suspension	Hypoglycaemic	Y
Semisodium valproate	VALCOTE	Anticonvulsant	Y
Senega	Multiple trade names	Expectorant	N
Senna	AGIOLAX, COLOXYL, SENOKOT	Laxative	N
SENOKOT	Senna	Laxative	N
SEPTOPAL	Gentamicin	Antibiotic/Aminoglycoside	Y
SEPTRIN	Co-trimoxazole	Antibiotic/Sulpha	Y
SEQUILAR	Ethinyloestradiol, levonorgestrol	Sex hormone (contraceptive)	Y
SERC	Betahistine	Vasodilator	Y
SERENACE	Haloperidol	Antipsychotic	Y
SEREPAX	Oxazepam	Anxiolytic/Benzodiazepine	Y
SETAMOL 500	Paracetamol	Analgesic	N
SH 420	Norethisterone acetate	Sex hormone	Y
SIGMACORT	Hydrocortisone acetate	Steroid (cream)	Y
SIGUENT NEOMYCIN	Neomycin	Antibiotic (eye)	Y
SILIC C	Clioquinol, dimethicone, glycerol et al.	Antifungal	N
SILVAZINE	Silver sulphadiazine	Antibiotic (cream)	Y
Silver sulphadiazine	SILVAZINE	Antibiotic (cream)	Y
SIMECO	Aluminium hydroxide, simethicone, magnesium hydroxide	Antacid	N
Simethicone	Multiple trade names including: GELUSIL, INFACOL, MYLANTA, SIMECO, SODEXOL	Antacid	N
Simvastatin	LIPEX, ZOCOR	Hypolipidaemic	Y
SINEMET	Levodopa, carbidopa	Antiparkinsonian	Y
SINEQUAN	Doxepin	Antidepressant	Y
SINEX	Xylometazoline	Decongestant	N
SINTISONE	Prednisolone	Steroid	Y
SINUTAB	Paracetamol, chlorpheniramine, (pseudoephedrine)	Antihistamine/Analgesic	N
SINUTAB WITH CODEINE	Paracetamol, phenylpropanolamine, codeine phos., phenyltoloxamine	ANTIHISTAMINE/ANALGESIC	Y
SINUZETS	Pseudoephedrine, phenylephrine, paracetamol	Antihistamine/Analgesic	N

DRUG TREATMENT

TABLE 6.2:
DRUGS AVAILABLE IN AUSTRALIA *(continued)*

Name (TRADE/Generic)		Class	Prescription needed (yes/no)
SLO-BID	Theophylline	Bronchodilator/Xanthinate derivative	Y
SLOW-Fe	Ferrous sulphate (iron)	Mineral supplement	N
SLOW-K	Potassium chloride	Mineral supplement	N
SODEXOL	Aluminium hydroxide, magnesium hydroxide, simethicone	Antacid	N
Sodium acid citrate	CITRALKA	Alkaliser	N
Sodium alginate	GAVISCON	Antacid	N
Sodium ascorbate (vitamin C)	Multiple trade names	Vitamin	N
Sodium aurothiomalate	MYCRISIN	Antirheumatic	Y
Sodium bicarbonate	Multiple trade names	Antacid/Alkaliser	N
Sodium citrotartrate	CITRAVESCENT	Alkaliser	N
Sodium cromoglycate	INTAL, OPTICROM, RYNACROM	Other	Y
Sodium fusidate	FUCIDIN	Antibiotic	Y
Sodium lauryl sulphoacetate	MICROLAX	Laxative	N
Sodium nitroprusside	NIPRIDE	Antihypertensive	Y
Sodium valproate	EPILIM	Anticonvulsant	Y
SOFRADEX	Dexamethasone, framycetin, gramicidin	Antifungal/Antibiotic/Steroid	Y
SOFRAMYCIN	Framycetin (gramicidin)	Antifungal/Antibiotic	Y
SOFRA-TULLE	Framycetin	Antibiotic	Y
SOLCODE	Aspirin, codeine	Analgesic	N
SOLONE	Prednisolone	Steroid	Y
SOLPRIN	Aspirin	Analgesic	N
SOLU-CORTEF	Hydrocortisone	Steroid	Y
SOLU-MEDROL	Methylprednisolone	Steroid	Y
SOLVIN	Aspirin, aminoacetic acid.	Analgesic	N
SOMATONORM	Growth hormone et al.	Increases growth rate in children	Y
Somatropin	GENOTROPIN	Hormone (induces growth)	Y
SOMOPHYLLIN	Theophylline	Bronchodilator/Xanthinate derivative	Y
SONERYL	Butobarbitone	Barbiturate	Y
SONE	Prednisone	Steroid	Y
SOTACOR	Sotalol	Antiarrhythmic	Y
Sotalol	SOTACOR	Antiarrhythmic	Y
SPAN K	Potassium chloride	Mineral supplement	N
SPARINE	Promazine	Antipsychotic	Y
Spectinomycin	TROBICIN	Antibiotic	Y
SPERSIN	Neomycin, bacitracin, polymyxin B	Antibiotic (skin)	Y
Spironolactone	ALDACTONE	Diuretic/Female excess hair	Y
SPRAY TISH	Tramazoline	Decongestant	N
SQUIBB-HC	Hydrocortisone acetate	Steroid (cream)	Y
SRA	Aspirin	Analgesic/NSAID	N
STAPHYLEX	Flucloxacillin	Antibiotic/Penicillin	Y
STELABID	Trifluoperazine	Antispasmodic	Y
STELAZINE	Trifluoperazine	Antipsychotic	Y
STEMETIL	Prochloroperrazine	Antiemetic	Y
Sterculia	ALVERCOL	Antispasmodic	N
Sterculia	GRANOCOL, NORMACOL	Laxative	N
STEROFRIN	Prednisolone	Steroid (eye drops)	Y
STEROXIN	Chlorquinaidol	Antiseptic	N
STOXIL	Idoxuridine	Antiviral	N
STOXINE	Providone iodine	Antiseptic	N
STREPTASE	Streptokinase	Fibrinolytic	N (Y Vic)
Streptokinase	KABIKINASE, STREPTASE	Fibrinolytic	N (Y Vic)

Section 6: Treatments

TABLE 6.2:
DRUGS AVAILABLE IN AUSTRALIA (continued)

Name (TRADE/Generic)		Class	Prescription needed (yes/no)
STREPTOMAGMA	Dihydrostreptomycin, attapulgite et al.	Antidiarrhoeal	Y
SUBLIMAZE	Fentanyl citrate	Analgesic	Y
Sucralfate	CARAFATE	Antiulcerant	N
SUDAFED	Pseudoephedrine	Decongestant	N
SUDAGESIC	Pseudoephedrine, paracetamol, triprolidine	Decongestant/Analgesic/Antihistamine	N
SUDELIX	Pseudoephedrine, guaiphenesin	Decongestant/Antitussive	N
Sulfadoxine	FANSIDAR	Antimalarial	Y
Sulindac	CLINORIL	NSAID	Y
Sulphabenzamide	SULTRIN	Antibiotic/Sulpha (cream)	Y
Sulphacetamide	SULTRIN, ACETOPT, BLEPHAMIDE	Antibiotic/Sulpha	Y
Sulphadiazine	SULPHADIAZINE	Antibiotic/Sulpha	Y
Sulphamethizole	UROLUCOSIL	Antibiotic/Sulpha	Y
Sulphamethoxazole	BACTRIM, Co-Trimoxazole, SEPTRIM, TRIB, RESPRIM	Antibiotic/Sulpha	Y
Sulphasalazine	SALAZOPYRIN, ULCOL	Other (ulcerative colitis)	Y
Sulphathiazole	SULTRIN	Antibiotic/Sulpha (cream)	Y
Sulphinpyrazone	ANTURAN	Hypouricaemic	Y
Sulthiame	OSPOLOT	Anticonvulsant	Y
SULTRIN	Sulphathiazole, sulphacetamide, sulphabenzamide	Antibiotic/Sulpha (cream)	Y
SUPRES	Hydralazine	Antihypertensive	Y
SURMONTIL	Trimipramine	Antidepressant	Y
SUSTANON	Testosterone	Sex hormone	Y
SYMMETREL	Amantadine	Antiparkinsonian	Y
SYNACTHEN DEPOT	Tetracosactrin	Trophic hormone	Y
SYNALAR	Fluocinolone acetonide	Steroid (cream)	Y
SYNFLEX	Naproxen	NSAID	Y
SYNPHASIC	Norethisterone, ethinyloestradiol	Hormone (contraceptive)	Y
SYNTOCINON	Oxytocin	Causes uterine contraction	Y
SYNTOMETRINE	Ergometrine	Causes uterine contraction	Y
TAGAMET	Cimetidine	Antiulcerant	Y
TALUSIN	Proscillaridin	Cardiac glycoside	Y
TAMBOCOR	Flecainide	Antiarrhythmic	Y
Tamoxifen	NOLVADEX	Cytotoxic	Y
TANNALBIN	Albumin tannate	Antidiarrhoeal	N
TARCIL	Ticarcillin	Antibiotic/Penicillin	Y
Tartaric acid	DEXSAL	Antacid	N
TAVEGYL	Clemastine	Antihistamine	N
TEGRETOL	Carbamazepine	Anticonvulsant	Y
TELDANE	Terfenadine	Antihistamine	Y
TEMAZE	Temazepam	Hypnotic	Y
Temazepam	EUHYPNOS, NORMISON, TEMAZE	Hypnotic	Y
TEMGESIC	Buprenorphine	Analgesic (strong)	Y
TEMPRA	Paracetamol	Analgesic	N
Teniposide	VUMON	Cytotoxic	Y
TENOPT	Timolol	Mydriatic	Y
TENORMIN	Atenolol	Beta-blocker	Y
Tenoxicam	TILCOTIL	NSAID	Y
TENUATE	Diethylpropion	Anorectic	Y
Terbutaline	BRICANYL	Bronchodilator/Sympathomimetic	Depends on form
Terfenadine	TELDANE	Antihistamine	Y
TERIL	Carbamazerpine	Anticonvulsant	Y
TERRAMYCIN	Oxytetracycline	Antibiotic/Tetracycline	Y

TABLE 6.2:
DRUGS AVAILABLE IN AUSTRALIA (continued)

Name (TRADE/Generic)		Class	Prescription needed (yes/no)
TERTROXIN	Liothyronine sodium	Thyroid agent	Y
TESTOMET	Methyltestosterone	Sex hormone	Y
Testosterone	SUSTANON, PRIMODIAN, PRIMOTESTON, TESTOVIRON, ANDRIOL	Sex hormone	Y
TESTOVIRON	Testosterone propionate	Sex hormone	Y
Tetrabenazine	NITOMAN	Other (for brain diseases and tremors)	Y
Tetracosactrin	SYNACTHEN	Steroid	Y
Tetracycline hydrochloride	ACHROMYCIN, ACHROSTATIN, AUSTRAMYCIN	Antibiotic/Tetracycline	Y
Tetracycline phosphate	HOSTACYCLINE P, HYDRACYCLINE, MYSTECLIN V, TETREX	Antibiotic/Tetracycline	Y
Tetrahydrozoline HCl	MURINE PLUS, VISINE	Vasoconstrictor/Astringent (eye)	N
TETREX	Tetracycline phosphate	Antibiotic/Tetracycline	Y
THALAZOLE	Phthalylsulphathiazole	Antibiotic/Sulpha	Y
THEO-DUR	Theophylline	Bronchodilator/Xanthinate derivative	Y
Theophylline	ELIXOPHYLLIN, NUELIN, SLO-BID, SOMOPHYLLIN, THEO-DUR	Bronchodilator/Xanthinate derivative	Y
Thiabendazole	MINTEZOL	Anthelmintic	N (Y Vic)
Thiamine (Vitamin B1)	Multiple trade names	Vitamin	N
Thiethylperazine maleate	TORECAN	Antiemetic	Y
Thioguanine	LANVIS	Cytotoxic	Y
THIOPRINE	Azathioprine	Immune suppressant	Y
Thiopropazate	DARTALAN	Antipsychotic	Y
Thioridazine	MELLERIL, ALDAZINE	Antipsychotic	Y
Thiotepa	THIOTEPA	Cytotoxic	Y
Thiothixene	NAVANE	Antipsychotic	Y
Thrombin	THROMBINAR, THROMBOSTAT	Haemostatic	Y
THROMBINAR	Thrombin	Haemostatic	Y
THROMBOSTAT	Thrombin	Haemostatic	Y
Thyroxine	OROXINE	Thyroid agent	Y
Ticarcillin	TARCIL, TICILLIN, TIMENTIN	Antibiotic/Penicillin	Y
TICARDA	Normethadone, hydroxyephedrine	Antitussive (strong)	Y
TICILLIN	Ticarcillin	Antibiotic/Penicillin	Y
Tiemonium iodide	VISCERALGIN	Antispasmodic	Y
TIGASON	Etretinate	Other (for psoriasis)	Y
TILCOTIL	Tenoxicam	NSAID	Y
TIMENTIN	Ticarcillin	Antibiotic/Penicillin	Y
Timolol	BLOCADREN, TIMOPTOL	Beta-blocker/Mydriatic	Y
TIMOPTOL	Timolol	Beta-blocker/Mydriatic	Y
TINACIDIN	Tolnaftate	Antifungal	N
TINADERM	Tolnaftate	Antifungal	N
TINEAFAX	Tolnaftate	Antifungal	N
Tinidazole	FASIGYN	Antibiotic	Y
Titanium dioxide	ACNE SOL, GRANUGEN	Keratolytic	N
TITRALAC	Calcium carbonate, aminoacetic acid	Antacid	N
TIXYLIX	Pholcodeine, promethazine	Antitussive/Antihistamine	N
TOBISPRAY	Tramazoline, dexamethasone	Vasoconstrictor/Steroid	Y
Tobramycin	NEBCIN, TOBREX	Antibiotic/Aminoglycoside	Y
TOBREX	Tobramycin	Antibiotic/Aminoglycoside	Y
TOFRANIL	Imipramine	Antidepressant	Y
Tolazamide	TOLINASE	Hypoglycaemic	Y

Section 6: Treatments

TABLE 6.2:
DRUGS AVAILABLE IN AUSTRALIA (continued)

Name (TRADE/Generic)		Class	Prescription needed (yes/no)
Tolbutamide	RASTINON	Hypoglycaemic	Y
TOLINASE	Tolazamide	Hypoglycaemic	Y
Tolnaftate	TINACIDIN, TINADERM, TINEAFAX	Antifungal	N
TOLVON	Mianserin	Antidepressant	Y
TOPEX	Benzoyl peroxide	Keratolytic	N
TOPILAR	Fluclorolone	Steroid	Y
TORECAN	Thiethylperazine	Antiemetic	Y
Tramazoline	SPRAY-TISH, TOBISPRAY	Vasoconstrictor	Depends on form
TRANDATE	Labetalol	Antihypertensive	Y
Tranexamic acid	CYKLOKAPRON	Haemostatic	Y
TRANSIDERM-NITRO	Glyceryl trinitrate	Antiangina	Y
TRANXENE	Clorazepate	Anxiolytic	Y
Tranylcypromine sulphate	PARNATE, PARSTELIN	Antidepressant/MAOI	Y
TRASICOR	Oxprenolol	Beta-blocker	Y
TRAVACALM	Dimenhydrinate, hyoscine, caffeine	Antiemetic	N
TRAVAD	Sodium dihydrogen phos. et al.	Laxative	N
TRAVOGEN	Isoconazole	Antifungal	N (Y Qld, Tas, Vic)
TRAVS	Dimenhydrinate, hyoscine	Antiemetic	N
TRENTAL	Oxpentifylline	Vasodilator	Y
Tretinoin	AIROL, RETIN-A	Keratolytic	N
Triacetin	ENZACTIN	Antifungal	N
Triamcinolone	ARISTOCOMB, KENACORT, ARISTOCORT, KENACOMB, KENALOG, KENALONE	Steroid	Y
Triamterene	DYAZIDE, DYTAC	Diuretic	Y
Triazolam	HALCION	Sedative	Y
TRIB	Co-trimoxazole	Antibiotic/Sulpha	Y
TRICHOZOLE	Metronidazole	Antibiotic	Y
TRIDIL	Glyceryl trinitrate	Antiangina	Y
Trifluoroperazine	CALMAZINE, PARSTELIN, STELABID, STELAZINE	Antipsychotic/Antispasmodic	Y
TRIIODOTHYRONINE	Liothyronine	Thyroid agent	Y
TRILAFON	Perphenazine	Antipsychotic	Y
Trimeprazine	VALLERGAN	Antihistamine/Sedative	N
Trimethoprim	ALPRIM, BACTRIM, RESPRIM, SEPTRIM, TRIB, TRIPRIM, Co-trimoxazole	Antibiotic	Y
Trimipramine	SURMONTIL	Antidepressant	Y
TRIOLIX	Dextromethorphan, pseudoephedrine, paracetamol	Antitussive/Mucolytic/Analgesic	N
TRIOMINIC	Phenylpropanolamine, pheniramine	Antitussive/Antihistamine	N (Y Qld)
Trioxysalen	TRISORALEN	Treats vitiligo	Y
TRIPHASIL	Levonorgestrel, ethinyloestradiol	Hormone (contraceptive)	Y
TRIPLE ANTIGEN	Tetanus, diphtheria & whooping cough vaccine	Vaccine	Y
TRIPRIM	Trimethoprim	Antibiotic	Y
Triprolidine	ACTIFED, SUDAGESIC, VASYLOX	Antihistamine	N
TRIQUILAR	Levonorgestrel, ethinyloestradiol	Hormone (contraceptive)	Y
TRISORALEN	Trioxysalen	Treats vitiligo	Y
TROBICIN	Spectinomycin	Antibiotic	Y
TROMASIN	Papaya enzyme	Prevents swelling after injury	N
Trypsin	CHYMORAL	Prevents swelling after injury	N
TRYPTANOL	Amitriptyline	Antidepressant	Y
Tryptophan	Multiple trade names	Sedative (mild)	N

DRUG TREATMENT

TABLE 6.2:
DRUGS AVAILABLE IN AUSTRALIA (continued)

Name (TRADE/Generic)		Class	Prescription needed (yes/no)
TUSSELIX	Dextromethorphan, guaiphenesin, pseudoephedrine	Antitussive/Decongestant	N
TUSSINOL	Pholcodine	Antitussive	N
Typhoid vaccine	TYPHOID VACCINE (inj), TYPH VAX (oral)	Vaccine	Y
TYPH-VAX	Typhoid vaccine	Vaccine	Y
TYRIMIDE	Isopropamide	Antispasmodic	Y
UBRETID	Distigmine	Anticholinergic	Y
ULCOL	Sulphasalazine	Other (ulcerative colitis)	Y
ULSADE	Calcium carbonate, aminoacetic acid	Antacid	N
ULTRALAN D	Fluocortolone	Steroid	Y
ULTRALENTE	Insulin zinc suspension	Hypoglycaemic	Y
ULTRAPROCT	Flucortolone, cinchocaine, clemizole	Steroid/Anaesthetic	Y
ULTRATARD	Insulin zinc suspension	Hypoglycaemic	Y
Undecenoic acid	PEDOZ	Antifungal	N
URAL	Sodium bicarbonate, sodium citrate, citric acid, tartaric acid, saccharin sodium	Alkaliser (urine)	N
Urea	Multiple trade names	Moisturiser	N
URECHOLINE	Bethanechol	Anticholinergic	Y
UREMIDE	Frusemide	Diuretic	Y
UREX	Frusemide	Diuretic	Y
URISPAS	Flavoxate	Antispasmodic (urine)	N (Y ACT)
UROCARB	Bethanechol	Anticholinergic	Y
UROLUCOSIL	Sulphamethiazole	Antibiotic/Sulpha	Y
VALCOTE	Semisodium valproate	Anticonvulsant	Y
VALIUM	Diazepam	Anxiolytic/Benzodiazepine	Y
VALLERGAN	Trimeprazine	Antihistamine/Sedative	N
VANCOCIN	Vancomycin	Antibiotic	Y
Vancomycin	VANCOCIN	Antibiotic	Y
VAREMOID	Rutosides	Treats piles	N
VASOPRESSIN	Lypressin	Antidiuretic	Y
Vasopressin tannate	PITRESSIN	Antidiuretic	Y
VASYLOX	Methoxamine, triprolidine, chlorbutol	Decongestant	N
VAXIGRIP	Influenza vaccine	Vaccine	Y
VEGANIN	Codeine, aspirin	Analgesic	N
VELBE	Vinblastine	Cytotoxic	Y
VELOSULIN	Neutral insulin	Hypoglycaemic	Y
VENTOLIN	Salbutamol	Bronchodilator/ Sympathomimetic	Depends on form
VEPESID	Etoposide	Cytotoxic	Y
VERACOLATE	Sodium tauroglycocholate	Laxative	N
VERADIL	Verapamil	Antihypertensive	Y
Verapamil	ANPEC, CORDILOX, ISOPTIN, VERADIL, VERPAMIL	Antihypertensive	Y
VERMOX	Mebendazole	Anthelmintic	N
VERPAMIL	Verapamil	Antihypertensive	Y
VIBRAMYCIN	Doxycycline	Antibiotic/Tetracycline	Y
VIBRA TABS	Doxycycline	Antibiotic/Tetracycline	Y
Vidarabine	VIRA-A	Antiviral	Y
Vinblastine	VELBE	Cytotoxic	Y
Vincristine	ONCOVIN, VINCRISTINE	Cytotoxic	Y
Videsine	ELDISINE	Cytotoxic	Y
VIOFORM	Clioquinol	Antiseptic	N
VIOKASE	Pancreatin	Digestive enzyme	N
VIR-A	Vidarabine	Antiviral	Y
VIRASOLVE	Idoxuridine, lignocaine	Antiviral/Anaesthetic	N

Section 6: Treatments

TABLE 6.2:
DRUGS AVAILABLE IN AUSTRALIA (continued)

Name (TRADE/Generic)		Class	Prescription needed (yes/no)
VISCERALGIN	Tiemonium iodide	Antispasmodic	Y
VISCOAT	Ephedrine, sodium citrate et al.	Decongestant/Antitussive	N
VISINE	Tetrahydrozoline et al.	Astringent	N
VISKEN	Pindolol	Beta-blocker	Y
VISOPT	Phenylephrine, hydromellose	Astringent	N
Vitamin A	Retinol — Many trade names	Vitamin	N
Vitamin B1	Thiamine — Many trade names	Vitamin	N
Vitamin B2	Riboflavin — Many trade names	Vitamin	N
Vitamin B6	Pyridoxine — Many trade names	Vitamin	N
Vitamin B12	Cyanocobalamin — CYTAMEN	Vitamin. Used in pernicious anaemia	N
Vitamin C	Ascorbic acid — Many trade names	Vitamin	N
Vitamin D	Sterols — Many trade names	Vitamin	N
Vitamin E	Tocopherol — Many trade names	Vitamin	N
Vitamin K	Phytomenadione, KONAKION	Haemostatic/Vitamin	N
VOLTAREN	Diclofenac	NSAID	Y
VOSOL	Acetic acid, propenandiol diacetate et al.	Drying agent for ears	N
VUMON	Teniposide	Cytotoxic	Y
Warfarin	COUMADIN, MAREVAN	Anticoagulant	Y
WAXSOL	Dioctyl sodium sulphosuccinate	Softens ear wax	N
WELLCOME ADM	Pectin, kaolin	Antidiarrhoeal	N
WINSPRIN	Aspirin	Analgesic/NSAID	N
XANAX	Alprazolam	Anxiolytic/Benzodiazepine	Y
XYLOCAINE	Lignocaine	Anaesthetic (local)	Y
XYLOCARD	Lignocaine	Antiarrhythmic	Y
Xylometazoline HCl	OTRIVIN, SINEX	Decongestant	N
XYLOPROCT	Lignocaine, hydrocortisone, aluminium acetate, zinc oxide	Anaesthetic/Steroid	Y
YOMESAN	Niclosamide	Anthelmintic	N
YUTOPAR	Ritrodrine	Stops premature labour	Y
ZADINE	Azatadine	Antihistamine	N
ZANTAC	Ranitidine	Antiulcerant	Y
ZARONTIN	Ethosuximide	Anticonvulsant	Y
Zidovudine	RETROVIR	Antiviral (for AIDS)	Y
ZINAMIDE	Pyrazinamide	Antituberculotic	Y
ZINCFRIN	Zinc sulphate, phenylephrine	Astringent	N
Zinc undecenoate	PEDOZ	Antifungal	N
ZOCOR	Simvastatin	Hypolipidaemic	Y
ZOLADEX	Goserelin	Cytotoxic	Y
ZOVIRAX	Acyclovir	Antiviral	Y
ZYLOPRIM	Allopurinol	Hypouricaemic	Y

Poisons Schedule

All medications, poisons and many chemicals in Australia are listed in a Poisons Schedule which gives a broad indication of how dangerous they are, where they can be marketed, who can sell or prescribe them, how they must be labelled, how they can be advertised, etc. All these products must have the schedule marked on them, and many medicines in your home medicine cabinet will be endorsed on the packet or bottle with lettering similar to that shown below:

The laws governing these schedules vary slightly from state to state. A brief summary of the eight schedules (based on the NSW law) follows:

SCHEDULE ONE (S1)
Poisons
Available only from pharmacies. Purchaser must be known to pharmacist and not under 18 years.

SCHEDULE TWO (S2)
Medicinal poisons — therapeutic
Available from pharmacies and stores with poisons licence on open shelving.

SCHEDULE THREE (S3)
Potent therapeutic substances
Available only from pharmacists. No prescription necessary. Stored out of public access. Purchaser must not be under 18 years. Purchasers of some of these products must be known to pharmacist.

SCHEDULE FOUR (S4)
Restricted substances
Available on prescription only from pharmacists. (Most drugs prescribed by doctors are in this category.)

SCHEDULE FIVE (S5)
Domestic poisons
No restriction on sale. Special packaging and warnings.

SCHEDULE SIX (S6)
Industrial, Agricultural and Veterinary poisons
No restrictions on sale, but must be stored 1.5 m above the floor. Special packaging and warnings.

SCHEDULE SEVEN (S7)
Special poisons
Special approval to prescribe required. Government approval for use may be required.

SCHEDULE EIGHT (S8)
Drugs of addiction
Available only on prescription from pharmacists. Careful records kept. Stored in approved safe.

Section 6: Treatments

Pharmaceutical Benefits Scheme

The Australian government introduced a pharmaceutical benefits scheme after the second world war to provide essential medications at a subsidised price. Since then, the scheme has been modified and reformed on innumerable occasions.

Every four months, every doctor and chemist in the country is circulated with a book which lists the drugs that may be prescribed under the scheme, how many tablets (or how much cream, etc.) may be prescribed, and how many repeats ordered. 36% of the drugs available are on a restricted list, which means they can only be prescribed for certain conditions, or the doctor must fill in a special prescription requesting authority from the government to prescribe the drug under the Pharmaceutical Benefits Scheme (PBS).

A doctor is allowed to write a prescription for almost any drug, in any reasonable quantity, and with any number of repeats, provided the patient is prepared to pay the full price of the drug. If the patient wishes to receive the drug under the Pharmaceutical Benefits Scheme, the doctor must prescribe the medication in line with the rules laid down by the government.

From November 1990, the average patient pays up to $15 for a prescription under the PBS (75% of drugs on the PBS list cost less than $15), and pensioners and those holding Health Care Cards pay $2.50. There is a small number of medications for which the government requires an additional patient payment. (These figures may have changed by the time this book goes to print).

The following table indicates how the PBS has changed over the past 20 years:

TABLE 6.3:
PHARMACEUTICAL BENEFITS SCHEME

Date	Max. price ($)	No. of drugs available	% of drugs restricted
1972	.50	684	26%
1975	1.00	689	22%
1978	2.00	648	25%
1981	2.75	596	28%
1984	4.00	586	30%
1987	10.00	542	31%
1990	15.00	518	36%

There are over 2000 drugs available in Australia, but only a quarter of them are available on the PBS. There are some classes of drugs (e.g. antitussives, antihistamines, vitamins, nasal steroids) that are totally unavailable, and some drugs that can be used for several purposes are only allowed to be used for a limited number of conditions under the PBS. The main reason for this apparent inequity is the high cost of pharmaceuticals. If more drugs were made available, and with fewer restrictions, the cost to the government (and then the taxpayer) would rise dramatically. The Government has the awkward task of deciding which medications are essential for the well-being of the average Australian, without unduly interfering in the doctor/patient relationship. The success of the scheme will be judged by doctors and patients in different ways, depending on their individual attitudes to state controls and subsidies.

Part of the cost of the prescription medications prescribed outside the PBS may be recoverable from private health insurance organisations (e.g. HCF, MBF, Medibank Private) if insurance in the appropriate table has been taken. Those who hold Veterans Affairs entitlement cards may receive a wider range (but still a restricted list) of drugs free of charge.

SURGICAL TREATMENT

Anaesthesia

Most patients who are told that they require surgery take the decision very calmly. There are some patients though, who are very apprehensive about the procedure. Often it is not the surgery that worries them, but the anaesthetic. They just can't cope with the thought of being put to sleep, even temporarily. Hopefully, explaining what happens during an anaesthetic and operation will reassure them.

It is normal to admit a patient who is having an operation under general anaesthetic to hospital 8 to 24 hours before the operation is scheduled. During this time, routine tests and checks are performed, and the anaesthetist makes a visit. The anaesthetist will check the heart, lungs and other vital systems to make sure there will be no problems during the anaesthetic. (Anaesthetists are doctors who have undertaken additional specialist training and study.) If the operation is an emergency one, these checks will be performed in the theatre to save time. If the surgeon is concerned about the patient, he or she may arrange for the patient to be seen in the anaesthetist's rooms several days before the operation so that any complications can be sorted out well in advance.

About an hour before an operation, you are changed into an easily removable gown and given an injection that will have been ordered by the anaesthetist. This will dry up the saliva so it does not cause trouble while you are asleep, and relax you in preparation for the anaesthetic. Shortly before the operation, you will be put onto a trolley and wheeled into the theatre suite. In some hospitals, your normal bed is wheeled all the way. Once at the theatre, you will be transferred into the care of the theatre staff,

Section 6: Treatments

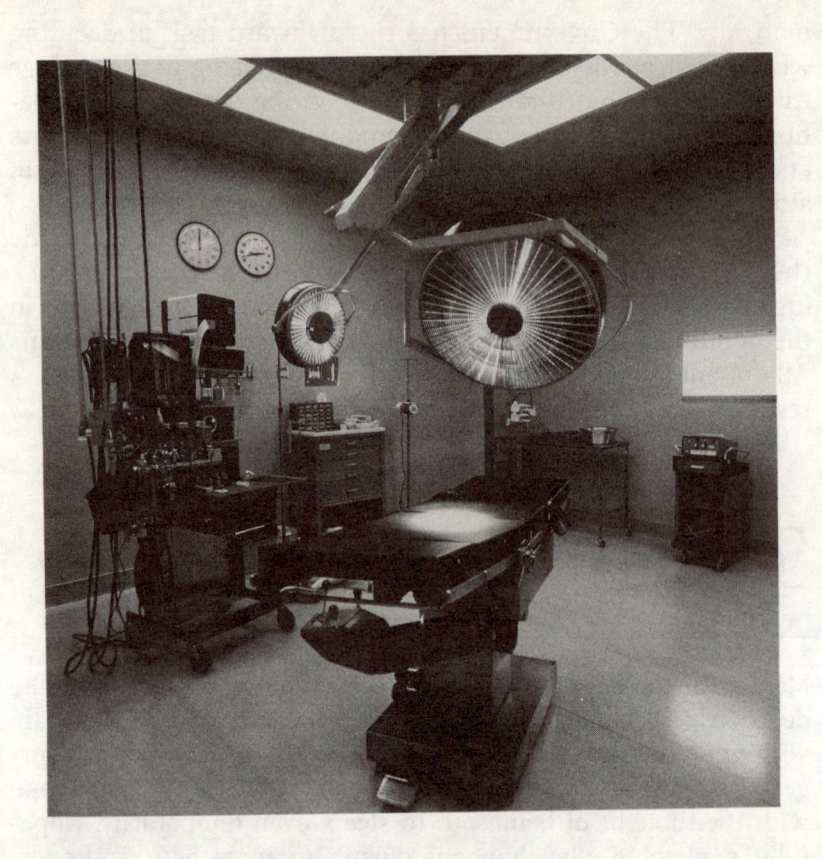

FIGURE 6.1: Operating theatre.

who all wear caps, masks, gowns and boots to keep the area as clean as possible.

In the theatre complex, you will be left in a small waiting room beside the theatre. Final paperwork and medication checks are performed there, and when everything is ready, you are wheeled into the theatre and transferred to the operating table, where you will lie under an enormous battery of powerful lights. Here you meet the anaesthetist again, but your memory of the meeting will be brief, as he or she will be busy putting you to sleep. A nurse assistant may get you to breathe oxygen through a mask while the anaesthetist places a needle in a vein in your arm or hand. Once all is ready, he or she will inject medication through the needle to make you drop off to sleep and relax your muscles. This is not at all frightening, and is just like going to sleep naturally. The drugs used to put you under last only a short time, and you are kept asleep by gases that are given through a mask or by a tube down your throat. You are very carefully watched all the time you are asleep, as the anaesthetist is regularly checking the pulse, blood pressure, breathing and heart. If there is any variation from the normal, the anaesthetist is trained to take the necessary steps to stabilise you again. When the operation is finished, the anaesthetist turns off the gases and gives you another injection to wake you up.

Your first memory after the operation will be of the recovery room. This is where you stay under the care of specially trained nurses and the anaesthetist until you are fully awake. You are then wheeled back to your ward to recover.

Side effects of a general anaesthetic can include a sore throat (from the tube that was placed down the throat to help you breath), headache, nausea, vomiting and excessive drowsiness (all side effects of the medication).

SPECIAL TYPES OF ANAESTHETIC

A **spinal anaesthetic** can be administered when operations below the waist are being performed. The patient remains awake, but is often sedated, while an anaesthetist or surgeon places a needle into the lower back. The needle is inserted between the vertebrae so that the tip enters the spinal canal, which contains cerebrospinal fluid and surrounds the spinal cord (see Section 2). The spinal cord carries all the nerve messages to and from the brain, and runs through the centre of the 24 vertebrae that form the backbone. A small amount of anaesthetic is injected into the spinal canal, so that the nerves below the level of injection no longer work and pain from the operation cannot be felt. The patient is often tilted slightly to prevent the anaesthetic from flowing further up the spine and affecting nerves above the level required for adequate anaesthesia.

The side effects of a spinal anaesthetic include low blood pressure, a headache for several days, and a slow heart rate. Nausea and vomiting are less common complications.

This type of anaesthetic is usually given when the patient is not well enough to stand a general anaesthetic, for caesarean sections, and in other circumstances when it is desirable for the patient to be awake.

An **epidural anaesthetic** is very similar to a spinal anaesthetic, but the injection into the back does not penetrate as deeply and does not enter the cerebrospinal fluid. The spinal cord is wrapped in three layers of fibrous material (the dura), and this anaesthetic is given into the very small space between the outer two layers. The procedure is technically more difficult, but the side effects are less severe. Epidural anaesthetics are used in the same circumstances as spinal anaesthetics.

Local anaesthetics are used in three ways:

1. A local area may be injected with anaesthetic solution to numb that area, e.g. while a mole is being cut out or a cut sutured. This method is commonly used by general practitioners,

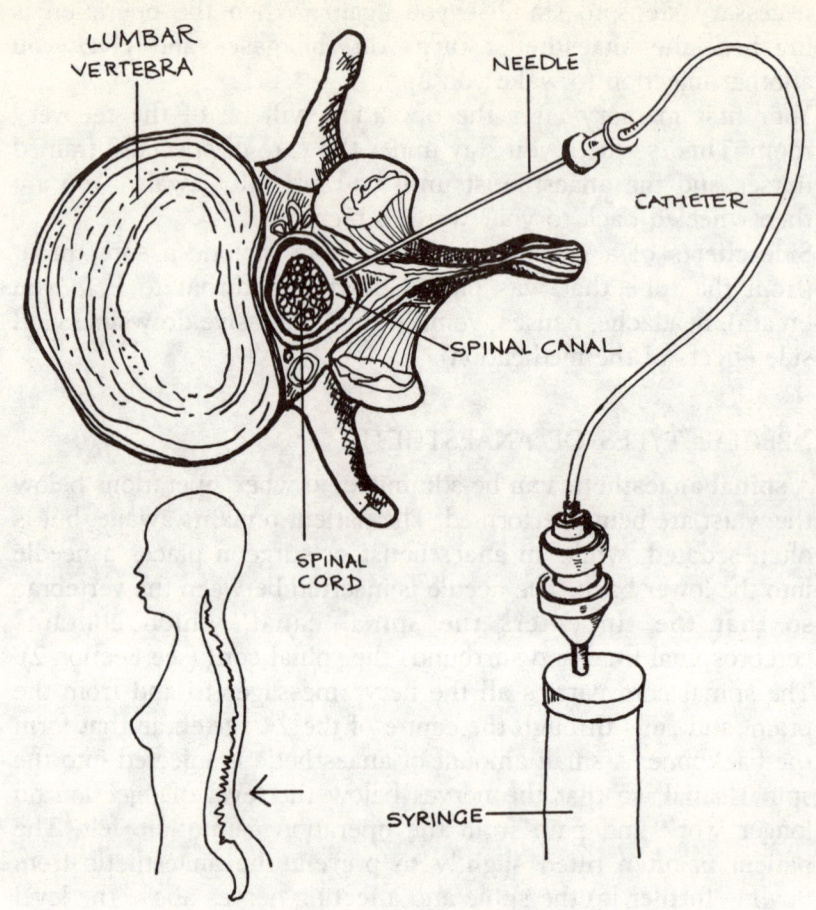

FIGURE 6.2: Spinal anaesthetic.

plastic surgeons, skin specialists and others for small procedures. The injection stings for a few seconds, but this sensation subsides rapidly as the anaesthetic takes effect.

The most commonly used local anaesthetic is lignocaine (see DRUGS AVAILABLE IN AUSTRALIA). This has an effect that lasts for one to two hours, depending upon the site of injection, the amount injected, and the concentration of anaesthetic used. Adrenaline may be added to the anaesthetic to reduce bleeding and prolong its effectiveness. Adrenaline cannot be used in toes, fingers and some other areas.

2. A local anaesthetic can be injected around a nerve to stop that nerve from receiving pain impulses from beyond the point of injection. These **nerve blocks** are commonly used in fingers and toes and in dental procedures, but almost any nerve in the body may be injected.

3. A tourniquet can be placed around the thigh or upper arm and a large amount of anaesthetic injected into the dilated veins below the tourniquet to give a **regional block**. This effectively

numbs the entire area below the tourniquet. This type of anaesthesia is commonly used to set minor fractures.

The anaesthetic used in a caesarean section (see below) can be a normal general anaesthetic, or a spinal or epidural anaesthetic, but if a general anaesthetic is used, special techniques are undertaken to make the anaesthetic as light as possible so that the baby is not anaesthetised when removed. After the mother is anaesthetised, the obstetrician will remove the baby as quickly as possible, and then the anaesthetic is deepened for the slow process of repairing the womb and other tissues that have been opened.

Day surgery is becoming more and more common for procedures as varied as in-vitro fertilisation and hernia repairs. The patient attends the day surgery centre early on the day of operation, a light general anaesthetic is administered, the operation is performed, and after three or so hours of recovery, the patient can go home again. The procedure is usually reserved for fit young and middle-aged people, and an assessment by the anaesthetist a few days before the operation is normal.

From the patient's point of view, the administration of an anaesthetic and undertaking an operation is simple and safe. Modern anaesthetics are improving all the time and complications are very rare.

Surgery

Surgery is performed to remove or repair tissues within or upon the body, to drain away pus or other unwanted substances, to remove foreign bodies or to insert artificial body parts. Any operation usually involves penetrating through tissue that contains nerves, so an anaesthetic of one type or another (see above) is necessary. The penetration may be very minor (e.g. a needle to drain an abscess or suck out a cyst), or a major part of the body may need to be widely exposed.

An operation may proceed by using a scalpel (a sharp, specially shaped knife), scissors, diathermy (electric needle) or laser (hot concentrated light beam) to cut through the tissues. Diathermy and lasers have the advantage of sealing most blood vessels as they cut, and therefore prevent bleeding. Any bleeding must be controlled or prevented as the operation proceeds by clipping and tying bleeding vessels, or by destroying them with diathermy or laser.

Once the operation has been performed, the wound is normally closed. This can be done by the traditional needle and thread, by staples, by special glues or by adhesive tape. The thread used can be absorbable or non-absorbable. Absorbable threads, such as catgut and more modern dissolving synthetics, are normally used internally; the non- absorbable threads such as silk, nylon and

Section 6: Treatments

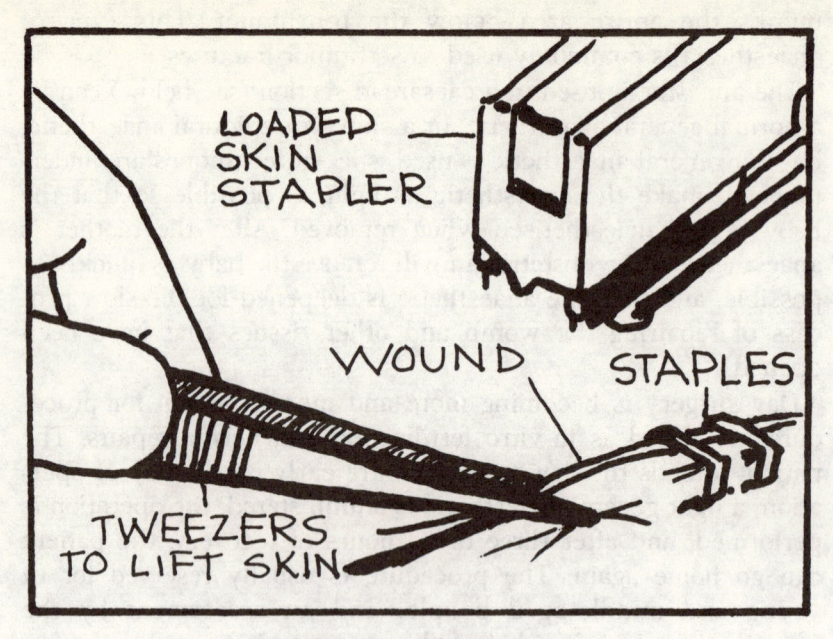

FIGURE 6.3: Stapling a wound.

other synthetics are commonly used on the surface, from where they must be later removed. Some non-absorbable sutures are used internally, and remain permanently, in areas where their continued support of a structure (e.g. hernia repair) is necessary.

Staples are applied by a special gun or forceps. Some sophisticated staple guns can now join together pieces of gut with one action. Internal staples are designed to remain forever, but external ones are normally removed. Glues are used mainly in eye surgery but are being used experimentally elsewhere. Tape is often used to close minor cuts or small wounds where only slight pressure is likely to be applied to the wound.

Drains are often inserted during or after an operation to remove any blood, secretions or pus that may slow the healing process. These drains empty into a sealed container or a clean dressing, and are usually removed after a few days.

Common operations

APPENDECTOMY (APPENDIX REMOVAL)

At the point where the small intestine enters the large intestine, there is a dead ending of large intestine (the caecum) going in one direction, and the main part of the large intestine leading to the outside is going in the other. Running off the caecum is a narrow tube about 12 cm long that is also a dead end. This tube is the appendix. The appendix is found only in humans and apes. In humans it serves no useful purpose, and a few people are even born without an appendix. If the narrow tube of the appendix becomes blocked by faeces, food, mucus or some foreign body, bacteria can start breeding in the closed-off area behind the blockage. This bacterial infection causes appendicitis (see Section 5).

The only effective treatment of appendicitis is surgery, and because of the serious consequences of a ruptured appendix, surgeons will remove the offending organ if there is a significant suspicion of appendicitis. Occasionally a normal appendix will be found is such cases, but it is far better to be safe than very sorry.

The operation is simple and takes about 20 minutes under a general anaesthetic. Unless there are complications, the patient should only have a small scar low down on the right side of the abdomen, often below the bikini line in women. Through this small incision, the appendix is found, the base is clamped, it is cut free of the surrounding structures and blood vessels, and then the base is cut through and the appendix removed. The stump of tissue from where the appendix was cut is carefully cleaned, and then oversewn to prevent any gut contents from leaking. The wound is then closed, with each layer of tissue being separately sutured.

The removed appendix will be sent to a pathologist for further checking under a microscope so that the diagnosis can be confirmed and any other disease excluded. You will be in hospital between two and four days, and you can return to work in seven to ten days.

Brain surgery

Brain surgery may be performed in various situations, including to remove a tumour, to treat infection, to deal with abnormal, blocked or bleeding blood vessels, to relieve chronic pain, modify behaviour, manage Parkinson's disease, or control epilepsy.

In operating on the brain for a tumour or cancer (see Section 5), the surgeon aims to reduce the amount (bulk) of tumour tissue present, and to reduce the excessive pressure in the patient's skull caused by the tumour. This initial operation is often followed by radiotherapy (see separate entry) and sometimes further surgery. Some growths in the brain are benign and not cancerous, and brain surgery may be able to totally remove them.

The actual surgery for a tumour may be performed in one of three ways:

1. In a recently developed procedure known as **stereo-tactic biopsy**, a small hole is made through the scalp and skull, and using a type of X-ray known as a CT scan (see Section 4) to precisely locate the tumour, a small amount of tissue is taken from the tumour for later analysis and diagnosis by a pathologist.
2. **Burr hole biopsy** is more traditional. In this procedure, a hole

is drilled in the scalp in the vicinity of the tumour, and through this a larger sample of tumour tissue may be taken for analysis.
3. A **craniotomy** is the third form of brain surgery. This involves the removal of a large flap of the scalp and a piece of the skull to reveal the brain. A large amount of tumour tissue can be removed, and pressure can usually be completely relieved by this technique. The removed piece of skull is replaced and held in position by sturdy stitches, and the flap of scalp is sewn down after the operation. Craniotomies are also used to gain access to the brain for some of the operations mentioned below.

An infection of the brain or surrounding tissues (e.g. middle ear infection) may cause an abscess (see Section 5) to form within or on the surface of the brain. Treatment involves drilling a small hole in the skull, and sucking out the pus from within the abscess. Antibiotics will also be prescribed.

Bleeding within or around the brain can be due to the rupture of a berry aneurysm (see Section 5), or damage to an artery caused by high blood pressure or hardening of the artery (see ATHEROSCLEROSIS, Section 5). Once the site of bleeding is located by special X-rays (angiograms — see Section 4), an operation can sometimes be performed to place a tiny silver clip on the bleeding artery or aneurysm and prevent further blood loss. The clip remains permanently on the artery and may be seen on later X-rays of the skull. This operation is considered to be major surgery, and there are some risks attached to it.

A partial or total blockage of an artery within the brain results in a stroke. In a small number of stroke victims, surgery may be possible to remove the blockage and restore function to the damaged area of brain.

Surgery on the brain may be performed to relieve some types of severe pain. Unfortunately only certain types of neuralgia (e.g. trigeminal neuralgia — see Section 5) that cause excruciating facial pain respond to this type of surgery. The procedure involves the very careful separation of the accompanying artery from the affected nerve, when the artery has been pressing on the nerve to cause pain. This is a very difficult procedure and may have complications.

Surgery to modify behaviour is rarely performed today, but a prefrontal lobotomy (cutting away the front of the brain) was a common form of treatment for severe personality disorders in past decades.

An operation known as stereo-tactic ablation can be performed on those who have an extremely severe form of Parkinson's disease (see Section 5) and who fail to respond to all medication. The malfunctioning control centres in the brain are destroyed in this operation, but locating the actual areas of the brain involved can be very complex and requires the assistance of a CT scan (see Section 4) and computer.

Some forms of epilepsy (e.g. temporal lobe epilepsy) can also be controlled by surgery. Through a craniotomy (see above), the short-circuiting part of the brain that is responsible for the fits can be partially or completely removed.

Neurosurgery (brain surgery) is now a routine surgical procedure at many moderate to large-sized Australian hospitals and has no greater risks than surgery to other major body organs.

CAESAREAN SECTION

See PREGNANCY COMPLICATIONS, Section 1.

CHOLECYSTECTOMY (GALL BLADDER REMOVAL)

The gall bladder is normally removed because there are stones in it that are causing pain or discomfort (see GALLSTONES, Section 5). Ideally, the operation is performed at a time when there is no infection present in the gall bladder, and after the patient has lost any excess weight. This is not always possible, and some of these operations must be performed while the patient is quite ill with cholecystitis. The operation can be considered to be of medium seriousness in the range of major to minor as far as surgery is concerned, but it is performed very commonly and routinely.

The incision is usually diagonal just below the edge of the ribs on the right side, but in some cases it may be vertical between the bottom of the breast bone and the umbilicus. Through this incision, the surgeon sees the liver, which must be pushed aside so that access to the gall bladder can be obtained. The gall bladder is carefully dissected away from the liver and removed, and then the duct that drains away the bile is cut. Through this opening into the common bile duct that connects the liver to the gut a fine tube is placed, and dye that can be seen on X-ray is injected into this duct to ensure that no other stones are present and that the bile will be able to flow freely after the operation. If no other stones are found, a drain will sometimes be left in the common bile duct to drain excess bile in the period after the operation when the damaged tissues may swell and cause blockages. The incision is closed with the other end of the drain left coming through the skin. The drain is removed after a few days when the common bile duct and surrounding structures have recovered from the operation.

Patients are in hospital for about five days, and off work for three to four weeks. Those involved in heavy manual labour may require six weeks to recover.

Section 6: Treatments

Coronary artery bypass graft (CABG, heart surgery)

Three main coronary arteries supply the necessary blood to the thick heart muscle. If one of these arteries becomes narrowed or partially blocked, angina (see Section 5) will occur. If it becomes totally blocked, the patient will suffer a heart attack. If a narrowed segment of coronary artery is discovered by special X-rays, this partial blockage can be bypassed by a graft using a vein from the leg. A coronary artery bypass graft (CABG) operation is a major but routine procedure in many Australian hospitals. It is successful in relieving angina and preventing heart attacks in thousands of Australians every year.

Under a general anaesthetic, the skin over the breast bone (sternum) is incised, and the breast bone itself is split open. Sometimes part of a rib is removed to give access to the heart. When the heart is seen, the blocked artery (or arteries in most cases) are identified, and a small piece of vein taken from the leg is sewn onto the side of the artery above and below the blockage. This allows the blood to bypass the blockage and to supply the heart muscle normally. The breast bone is stapled together and the skin is closed with sutures. The patients remain in hospital for about ten days, and will take up to six weeks to recover, but after that time they will find they have far more energy, no angina, and less shortness of breath than before. Most people claim it makes them feel ten years younger.

Close follow-up by the surgeons and/or general practitioner is necessary for some months after the procedure, and special tablets may be needed for the first few weeks or months.

Curette (dilation and curettage, D & C)

A curette is actually a sharp-edged spoon used by surgeons to clean out the inside of a small cavity within the body. The name of this surgical instrument is now often applied by gynaecologists to the actual operation of cleaning out the contents of the womb (uterus), which is probably the most common of all surgical procedures.

The uterus is a thick muscular sack, lined with special cells that rapidly multiply during the month to accept any pregnancy that may occur. If no pregnancy develops, the lining of cells breaks away, and causes bleeding that a woman recognises as her monthly period. If this delicate process is affected by one or more of several diseases and fails to operate correctly, many different complications can occur. A curette can be used to both diagnose and cure many of these problems.

The procedure only takes ten minutes, but will involve a visit to hospital, and a brief general anaesthetic. Once the patient is asleep, the doctor will use an instrument to look into the vagina. Through this, the opening into the uterus (the cervix — see Section 2) can be seen. This is normally closed, and a series of successively larger smooth rods are slid through the cervix to gradually dilate it. For this reason the operation is sometimes called a dilation and curettage. Once the cervix is wide enough, a small curette is passed into the uterus, and is scraped along the inside of the uterus in sweeping motions to remove all the cells and tissue inside the womb. These are collected for later examination under a microscope by a pathologist.

It is often difficult for doctors to exactly determine why a woman is having heavy, painful or irregular periods. The pathologist can report the type of cells that are present in the scrapings removed from the uterus, thus enabling an accurate diagnosis to be made. One common reason for problem periods is the failure of the uterus to clear all the cells and tissue during a period. The curette will give the uterus a very thorough cleaning, and as a result, the procedure often cures the period problems at the same time as the diagnosis is made.

It is normal to perform a curette after a miscarriage. When a miscarriage occurs, some unwanted tissue may be left behind, and it is necessary for this to be removed to prevent any infection in the uterus and allow another pregnancy to start. More than one in every ten pregnancies end prematurely as a miscarriage.

When termination of pregnancy (abortion) is indicated, it is performed by a dilation and curettage of the uterus. Suction is often used to empty the uterus before final curettage.

Infertility may be due to the incorrect development of the womb lining. A curette to remove and analyse this lining can help gynaecologists determine the cause of the infertility, and hopefully overcome the problem.

Cancer of the womb is not particularly common but very difficult to diagnose. It usually has the symptoms of abnormal vaginal bleeding and discharges. A curette would pick up the abnormal cancer cells, and these would enable a diagnosis to be made at an early stage when successful treatment is more likely.

Other than a slight ache low down in the abdomen, similar to a period cramp, there are no after-effects from a curette. Complications are rare, and your periods will start again three to six weeks after the operation.

EYE SURGERY

Most eye surgery is undertaken by ophthalmologists (eye doctors) who have undertaken many further years of training in this specialised area. Because of the small size of the eye, most eye surgery is carried out through an operating microscope and using

SECTION 6: TREATMENTS

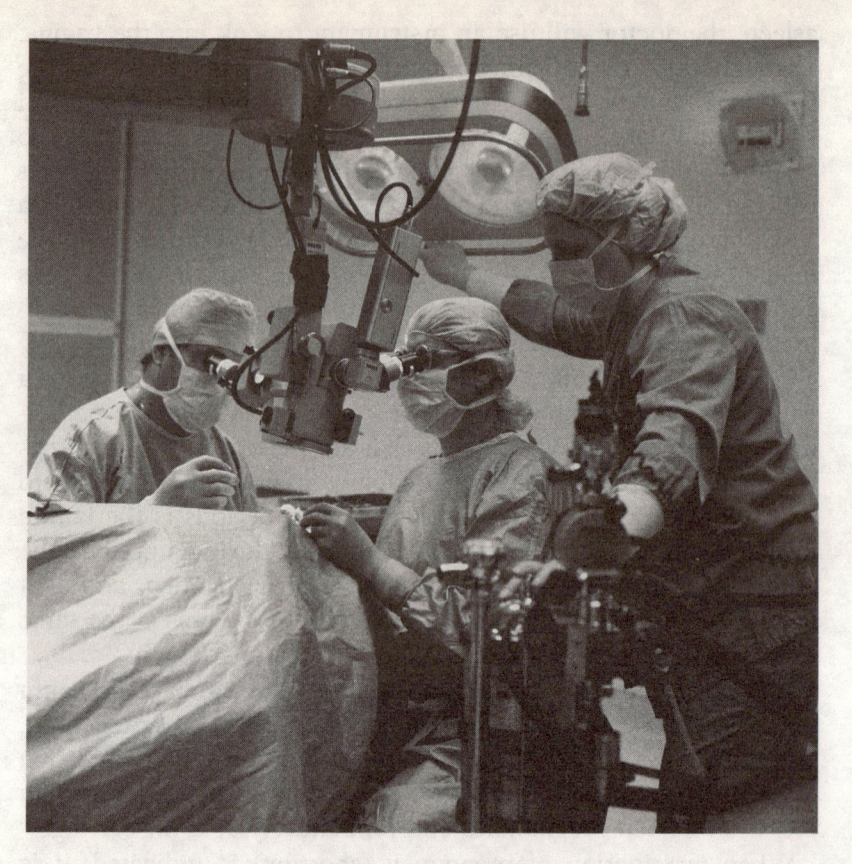

FIGURE 6.4: Eye operation.

extremely fine instruments, needles and threads.

Most procedures require a general anaesthetic, but in older people who are not good anaesthetic risks, quite major eye surgery (e.g. cataract removal) can be done using a local anaesthetic. Because the operation is limited to a very small area of the body, the patient recovers very rapidly from eye surgery, but special drops and eye protection may be necessary for some weeks. A lot of eye surgery is now performed as day surgery, with the patient arriving at the hospital in the morning and returning home the same day.

Eye surgeons operate on the front half of the eye as far back as the lens, and on the muscles and blood vessels around the outside of the eye. They can rarely operate directly on the inside of the eyeball itself, but they can use lasers in this area. The retina is the light-sensitive area at the back of the eyeball, and if this bleeds, separates from the back of the eye, or is otherwise damaged, lasers can be shone through the pupil and onto the bleeding or damaged area to repair it.

Incisions into the eye may be repaired by tiny sutures, or by special glues that bind together the edges of the wound.

The most common operation performed on the eye is cataract removal (see CATARACTS, Section 5).

GROMMETS (EAR VENTILATION TUBES)

A grommet is a short tube, ridged at both ends and often made of teflon, which is inserted through the eardrum to ventilate the middle ear.

The ear is one of the most complex organs, and is made from a diversity of materials found nowhere else in the body. Tiny finely balanced bones interact with super sensory nerve hairs and amazingly tough sheets of cartilage, but all on a microscopic scale (see Section 2). The ear is composed of three main parts. Interference with any of these three areas can cause deafness. The outer ear is the ear canal which leads into the eardrum. Beyond the solid sheet of tissue which forms the eardrum is the middle ear. This contains three tiny bones which magnify and transmit the vibrations of the eardrum, that are caused by a noise, across the cavity of the middle ear to a similar but much smaller membrane. This smaller membrane separates the middle ear from the inner ear. The inner ear is the third part of the ear structure, and contains a fine spiral shaped canal that gives us our ability to hear.

Except for the three tiny bones it contains, the middle ear is normally empty. To keep this space ventilated, a fine tube runs through the skull from the middle ear to the back of the nose. This is the Eustachian tube. When you drive up a steep hill, you swallow and your ears 'pop'. This is caused by air rushing through the Eustachian tubes to equalise the pressure inside and outside the ear. When a person has a cold, hay fever or other causes of excess phlegm and mucus production in the nose, the Eustachian tube may become blocked, and unable to function.

In some people, particularly children who have narrower Eustachian tubes, the middle ear may become full of a mixture of phlegm and mucus known as 'glue'. The glue material is too thick to pass easily back down the Eustachian tube to the nose, and if it remains in the middle ear, it may cause serious long-term problems. A general practitioner can try medications and nasal sprays to reduce the production of phlegm and liquefy the glue, but if the problem persists for more than a few weeks, he or she will send you to an ear, nose and throat (ENT) specialist.

Glue ears can be effectively treated by an ENT surgeon inserting grommets. Under a general anaesthetic, the surgeon puts a small hole in the eardrum (a myringotomy), sucks out most of the glue, and inserts a grommet into the hole in the eardrum. This grommet does not drain any further secretions from the middle ear but allows air to enter the ear so that there is no air pressure

Section 6: Treatments

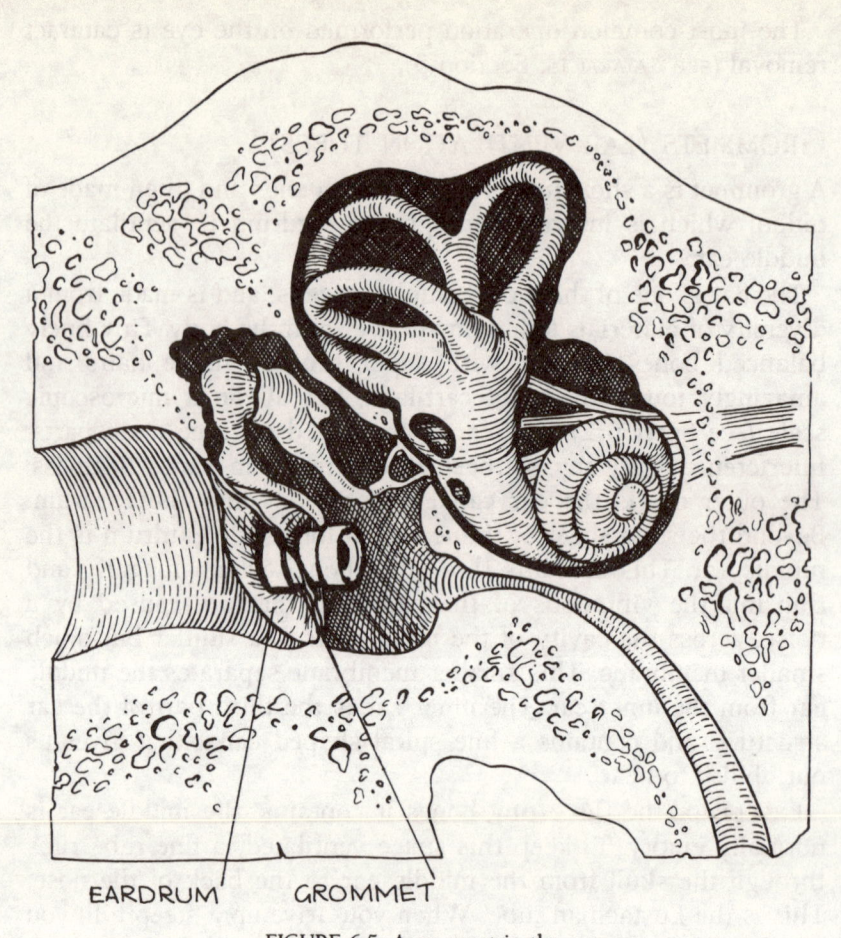

EARDRUM GROMMET

FIGURE 6.5: A grommet in the ear.

difference to push further rubbish up from the nose and into the ear.

After three to six months, the grommet falls out, and the eardrum usually heals up perfectly afterwards. It is then hoped that no further attacks of glue ear occur. These can be prevented by careful treatment of all colds and infections by the patient's general practitioner.

The use of the simple grommet, which is only 3 mm or so long, has prevented a great deal of deafness in children, and may prevent more serious complications, such as an abscess in the ear or brain.

Hysterectomy (removal of womb)

Hysterectomy is a term which many women misunderstand and fear, yet it is one of the most common surgical procedures performed.

The female sexual organs consist of four main parts — the

vagina which is used in intercourse, the womb (uterus) and its opening into the vagina called the cervix, the Fallopian tubes that carry the egg from the ovaries to the womb, and the two ovaries. It is only the uterus, tubes and one ovary that are removed from most women in a hysterectomy. Both ovaries and/or the vagina may be removed if the operation is for cancer.

Because the vagina and one ovary are normally left behind, the woman is able to have a normal sex life after the operation. The vagina remains the same size, and the female hormones that stimulate sexual responses and maintain the normal breast shape and body hair continue to be released in adequate amounts from the remaining ovary. Once she has recovered fully from the operation, the woman and her partner should notice no significant difference in their normal sexual relationships, and the woman will be able to obtain an orgasm just as easily as before the operation.

Women who have the operation before their menopause will still experience the problems commonly associated with the change later in their life, and the resultant hot flushes, depression, bloating, headaches and other symptoms may need further medical treatment.

Because the uterus is responsible for producing the blood loss that occurs with monthly periods, a hysterectomy stops any further bleeding, but a woman may still experience the symptoms of premenstrual tension, and sometimes detect the bodily changes associated with ovulation. This is because the remaining ovary continues to produce hormones in the normal cyclical manner, as though the uterus was still there to respond.

Hysterectomies are performed for many different reasons, the most serious being cancer (which may result in more major surgery to remove the surrounding glands as well). Most operations are for milder diseases and complaints that may still be very distressing to the individual woman. These problems include uterine growths (e.g. fibroids), endometriosis (a type of pelvic bleeding disorder), ovarian diseases, and most commonly for intractable heavy and painful periods.

A hysterectomy will take time to heal, as will any other major surgery, and it may be six to eight weeks before you can return to normal activities. You will probably have a scar on your abdomen, but if possible, the surgeon will make this a crosswise cut very low down so that all but the briefest of bikinis may still be worn. Sometimes the operation is performed through the vagina and leaves no visible scar.

Any woman who is contemplating a hysterectomy, or who has been advised to have one, should take along a list to ensure that her gynaecologist or GP adequately answers all her questions and concerns. In this way many problems can be avoided.

In vitro fertilisation — IVF (test-tube babies)

So called test-tube babies are now commonplace. After the initial development of the technique in the United Kingdom, Australian gynaecologists took the initiative and are now the world leaders in this area of medical technology. There are two main ways in which this technology can be used — IVF and GIFT.

In **IVF** (in vitro fertilisation — 'in vitro' means in glass, i.e. outside the body), an egg (ovum) is removed from the ovary of a woman at a precise time that is determined by hormones that are given to her in order to stimulate ovulation (production of an ovum or egg). The egg is removed under general anaesthetic in a process known as laparoscopy, in which two tubes, each about 1 cm in diameter and 20–30 cm long, are put into the abdominal cavity through small cuts on the surface of the abdomen. One cut may be placed in the umbilicus to minimise scarring. The gynaecologist looks through one telescope tube, and through the other operates to remove the egg.

The egg(s) obtained are placed in a special nutrient solution in a test tube or flat glass dish. To this is added sperm from the woman's husband, or if the husband is infertile, another donor's sperm may be used (AID — artificial insemination by donor). The eggs are examined under a microscope, and any eggs that are fertilised are then placed into the woman's uterus (womb) using a fine tube that is passed through the vagina and cervix into the uterus. From this position, it is hoped that the fertilised egg(s) (embryos) will implant into the wall of the uterus and grow into a baby (or babies). The success rate with any one IVF procedure is only about 20%, but in a series of procedures, success rates in excess of 70% have been achieved.

The newer technique is **GIFT** (gamete intra-Fallopian transfer). A gamete is a technical name for an ovum (egg) or a sperm. In this procedure, the egg is obtained in the same way as for IVF, but it is then placed into the woman's Fallopian tube along with a quantity of the husband's or donor's sperm, and fertilisation occurs in the biologically normal place — the Fallopian tube. The fertilised egg then migrates down to the uterus in the normal manner for implantation. The GIFT technique is only useful in women who have a normal Fallopian tube and a disease-free pelvis. Its success rate is 35% for each procedure.

Orthopaedic surgery (operations on bones and joints)

Orthopaedic surgery ranges from replacing worn out hip and knee joints with steel and plastic ones to screwing together the ends of broken bones and fusing together vertebrae in the back that are causing pain by pinching a nerve. The instruments used

DETAIL SHOWING SOCKET (OFTEN PLASTIC) AND BALL-SHAPED END OF METAL SHAFT →

ARTIFICIAL HIP JOINT GLUED INTO PLACE →

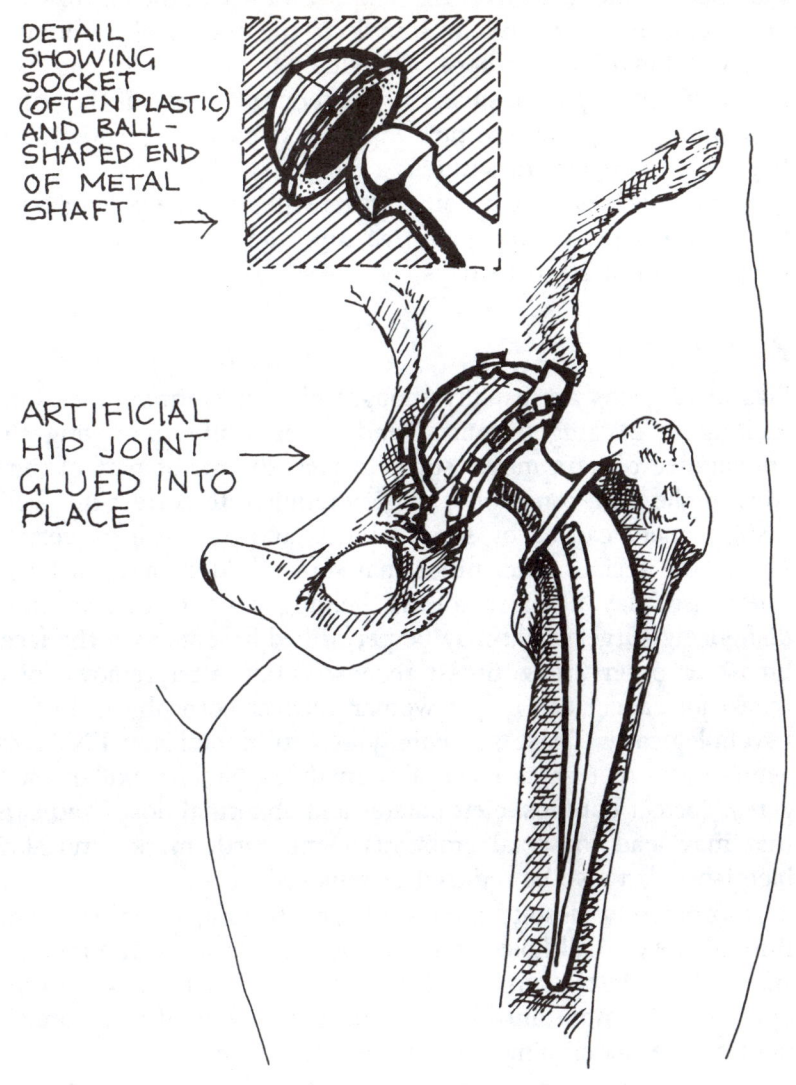

FIGURE 6.6: Artificial hip joint.

in this type of surgery are similar to, but far more sophisticated than, those of a carpenter. Saws, drills, screwdrivers and levers are necessary to cut through bones, drill holes for wires, insert screws and replace dislocated joints.

In a **hip replacement** operation for severe arthritis of the joint, a long cut is made along the outside of the thigh and over the hip joint. Through this, the top end of the thigh bone (femur) is exposed, and just below the start of the hip joint, the bone is sawn through to remove the top 1 cm of the femur and the part of the bone that forms the head of the femur and the hip joint itself. The inside of the femur (where the marrow is situated) is then reamed out for a distance of about 10 cm, and the hip joint socket on the side of the pelvis is partly drilled away. Special glue is then poured into the top of the femur from where the marrow has been removed, and the long spindle of the new steel hip joint is inserted down into the bone. The glue hardens rapidly and fixes it in position. A plastic socket is glued onto the side of the pelvis in a similar way, and the new hip joint is put into position. The tissues are closed with sutures.

Within a few days, physiotherapists will start the patient walking on the new, strong, pain-free hip, and most patients leave hospital within 10 to 14 days.

Plastic surgery

Plastic surgeons are usually thought of as performing face lifts, tucking in sagging tummies, and cosmetically improving the appearance of vain movie stars. In fact, the major part of their work is the time-consuming surgery required to correct the gross disfigurement caused by serious burns and the intricate correction of the serious deformities that some children have at birth. They also play a major role in helping patients recover from disfiguring surgery that may be performed for cancer of the face, breast or other areas. Breast reconstruction after removal of a breast for cancer can help a woman recover both physically and psychologically. These surgeons join with dental and ENT surgeons to correct gross facial abnormalities (facio-maxillary surgery), correct harelips, cleft palates and abnormal noses and ears that may lead to social embarrassment. Birth marks and skin blemishes can also be reduced or removed.

Unfortunately, despite their skills and techniques of operating through very small holes and in areas where scars will not easily show, even plastic surgeons leave some scar behind when they operate. It is important for a patient to be aware of these limitations before undergoing any form of plastic surgery.

One of the most common cosmetic operations is **breast enlargement**. If you're like Twiggy and want to be like Dolly Parton — forget it! But if you're a 32A and would like to be a 34B, then plastic surgery to increase your bust may interest you. Women desiring this operation fall into two broad groups — those who were born with small breasts, and those who have suffered a sagging or shrinkage of the breasts after breastfeeding or with age. There are also those who require breast reconstruction after surgery for breast cancer.

The operation involves a two or three day stay in hospital. Techniques vary from one surgeon to another, but normally a small cut is made under each breast, and through this a plastic bag of silicone gel is inserted as a prosthesis to increase the size and improve the shape of the breast. Often a small tube is left behind in the wound to drain off excess fluids that may accumulate. Bandages are tightly bound around the chest and breasts, so that when you wake after the general anaesthetic, you feel as if an elephant is sitting on your chest.

Recovery is normally at home, and the patient should rest for a week to ten days after the operation before returning to normal duties. The stitches are taken out in two stages about one and two weeks after the operation. After six weeks the breasts feel and look completely natural, and the tiny scar is hidden under the breast fold when you stand so that the briefest bikini can be worn.

Complications are unusual and are normally those of other types of surgery, such as bleeding and infection. The most common post-operative problem is breast capsule contraction. This occurs months after the procedure and is caused by the body laying down too much fibrous tissue around the implant, which results in the breast feeling firmer than normal. The treatment for this is called 'popping' and involves squeezing the breast so that the fibrous tissue tears, freeing up the prosthesis and softening the breast.

Breast augmentation is a relatively painless procedure. There has never been any link demonstrated between this operation and the development of breast cancer, you can still breastfeed after the operation, and you should still check yourself routinely for breast lumps. Except in special cases, Medicare and health insurance organisations do not cover any part of the cost.

TONSILLECTOMY (TONSIL REMOVAL)

The tonsils are glands, similar to those in your neck, armpit or groin, which lie in the throat on either side of the back of the tongue. They are made of lymphoid tissue which is responsible for producing antibodies to fight off infection. The tonsils are only 1% of the total body lymphoid tissue, so they are not essential from this point of view.

Tonsillectomy (often accompanied by the removal of other lymphoid tissue at the back of the nose — the adenoids) is a very old operation, the first ones being performed in Egypt around 3000 BC. It was a much more common operation in the pre-antibiotic era before the second world war, as tonsillitis without antibiotics was a severe disabling disease that could be life-threatening. Today the operation is still necessary under certain circumstances. These include:
- five attacks of tonsillitis in 12 months in a child, or three a year in an adult;
- an attack of quinsy (the formation of an abscess under the tonsil);
- obstruction of the airway or food passage by grossly enlarged tonsils;

- tonsillitis complicated by middle ear infections on two occasions;
- other rarer complications of tonsillitis.

Age is no barrier to tonsillectomy, provided the reasons for the operation are present, but it is unusual to perform it on babies under 12 months of age and on the elderly.

Tonsillectomy is normally done under a general anaesthetic. Adults stay in hospital for 2–4 days, children just overnight. Adults can return to work after two weeks, children can return to school after ten days. The degree of discomfort is about the same as an attack of tonsillitis, but without the accompanying fever and muscular aches. The operation would normally be postponed until any acute infection was controlled by antibiotics.

Complications are uncommon these days, the most common being bleeding from the operation site in the throat. This may be treated by local measures, or occasionally by a minor repeat operation. Bleeding may occur immediately after the procedure or a week to ten days later, and medical advice should be sought if it occurs.

Tonsillectomy is only performed to improve the quality of life in patients who suffer from repeated attacks of infection or constant discomfort from a blocked throat or ears. The canal that drains fluid from, and allows air to enter into the middle ear, opens into the back of the throat between the tonsils and adenoid glands. By removing the large amount of obstructing tissue, chronic ear diseases can also be helped by tonsillectomy and adenoidectomy.

Transplants and implants

It is not uncommon to hear jokes about patients who appear to have had every part of their body replaced by medical science, thus making them more robot than human. Many parts of the human can be replaced, but it will be centuries, if ever, before it will be possible to produce anything approaching an artificial person. Replacements can be of two types — **transplants**, where human tissue is transferred from one person to another (e.g. kidney and heart transplants); and **implants**, where totally synthetic material replaces a body part (e.g. artificial hip or heart valve). Many different medical specialties are involved in these fields, but the unsung heroes, particularly of the transplants, are the immunologists who have now developed means of combating the body's normal rejection processes.

Heart transplants were grabbing headlines a few years ago, but they have now moved out of the experimental area into accepted medical practice. Unfortunately the demand for this procedure will probably outstrip supply, as the supply of hearts from fatally injured people is limited.

The problem of supply has been overcome to some extent in **liver transplants**, where Australia led the way when a team of Queensland surgeons and anaesthetists performed an operation in which a part of a living adult's liver was successfully transplanted into a child. Liver transplants are now routine, and for more than 20 years, **kidney transplants** have been performed at Australian hospitals. Lungs can be transplanted along with the heart they belong to, as a **heart-lung transplant**, and sometimes the recipient's own heart can be transplanted to someone else, if it was only the patient's lungs that were damaged.

Orthopaedic surgeons perform more replacement operations than any other group of doctors. Almost every joint has been replaced experimentally, but the ones most commonly implanted are the hip and knee.

Artificial hips were first implanted 30 years ago by the Lancashire surgeon John Charnley. These days the operation is very common, and has made the lives of people with serious arthritis far more enjoyable. Patients who can barely crawl into their hospital bed find themselves walking normally only a couple of weeks after the operation (see above).

Knee joints are also replaced when necessary, as are the small joints of the fingers in victims of severe rheumatoid arthritis. There is even a small bone in the wrist (the scaphoid) that can be completely replaced if it is damaged by a fracture. Major whole bones of the arm and leg have been replaced experimentally.

Vascular surgeons bypass blocked **arteries** with pieces of vein taken from other parts of the body, or with specially prepared nylon tubing. This can enable those who have poor blood supply anywhere from the legs to the heart to recover normal use of those parts.

Ophthalmologists (eye doctors) have transplanted the **cornea** (the clear outer part of the eye that may become cloudy from age or disease) from the dead to the living for decades. The **lens** of the eye can also be replaced with an artificial one to cure cataracts. Ear nose and throat surgeons can replace the tiny bones in the middle ear with a plastic piston to restore hearing to some deaf patients.

Cardiac surgeons can replace faulty **heart valves** in newborn infants or elderly adults with those taken from animals, or with totally artificial valves.

Plastic surgeons can repair damaged noses and ears with artificial cartilage, or replace breasts lost by cancer. Operations to use part of your own body to replace those lost by disease or accident are legion (e.g. skin grafts, bone grafts).

Medical science is advancing at an exponential rate to meet the demands of a health conscious community. The experimental

Section 6: Treatments

PROFILE VIEW   **OUTFLOW VIEW**

FIGURE 6.7: Artificial heart valve.

procedures of today may well be the routine operations of the next decade.

Tubal ligation

See CONTRACEPTION, Section 1.

Vasectomy

See CONTRACEPTION, Section 1.

Stomas

Any opening in the human body is a stoma, but the ones doctors are concerned about are the artificial stomas (or stomata) that an increasing number of people must deal with, often for the rest of their lives. An artificial stoma occurs when surgeons bring part of the gut through the front wall of the abdomen so that the patient will pass faeces through this opening and not through the anus. It looks rather like a small pink doughnut sitting on the skin and is usually covered by a specially designed plastic bag that collects the waste products and gut secretions. No, it isn't a very pleasant topic to discuss, but it is even less pleasant for those in the community who must deal with the problem constantly.

Many varied diseases make a stoma necessary. Some babies are born without part of the gut and are unable to pass waste products. For their survival, the large intestine is opened to form a stoma on the abdomen. When they are older, it is sometimes possible to reconnect the gut or fashion a new anus for these

SURGICAL TREATMENT

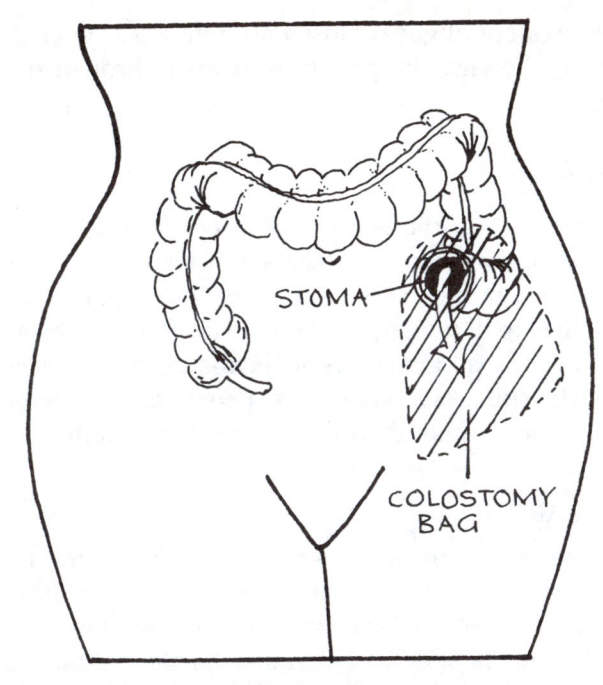

FIGURE 6.8: Colostomy.

children to enable them to lead a normal life. Cancer is a very common reason for a stoma.

COLOSTOMY

If the lower part of the bowel (the colon) is involved in a cancer, it may be impossible to reconnect the gut to the anus after the cancer has been removed, and thus a stoma, called a colostomy, is necessary. If the cancer is higher in the large intestine, the stoma may be temporary, as the gut can be reconnected after the cancer affected area has recovered from the initial operation.

GASTROSTOMY

If a person's gullet is damaged or missing and they are unable to swallow food, an opening can be made through the upper part of the abdomen into the stomach, and food is then placed directly into this and can continue on its normal way through the rest of the intestine.

ILEAL CONDUIT

Surgeons have devised some ingenious ways of helping patients with very difficult problems. One of these is for the patient who due to injury or disease has no bladder function. The ureter (the tube that carries urine from the kidney to the bladder) is implanted into the side of an isolated piece of gut. One end of this 30 cm segment of gut is closed off, while the other is formed into a stoma, allowing the patient to urinate through this into a plastic bag.

ILEOSTOMY

Some rare diseases of the bowel may necessitate the small intestine being made into a stoma. The small intestine is technically known as the ileum, and so this type of stoma is called an ileostomy. The small intestine is responsible for the absorption of food into the body and contains acids and digestive juices which may attack the skin. As a result these people have more problems dealing with their stoma than those with a colostomy.

OSTOMY CARE

There are two main problems affecting people with stomas — embarrassment if others find out about the problem (the person sitting next to you in the bus may have one without you knowing), and difficulties with the skin around the stoma caused by excoriation from the gut contents and the adhesives used to hold the collecting bag in place. A wide range of different bags, adhesives and deodorants are available to help with these problems. It is often a matter of trial and error to find the combination best suited to a particular patient.

PSYCHIATRIC TREATMENT

PSYCHIATRISTS AND PSYCHOLOGISTS

Psychiatrists are doctors who have undertaken several years of further study after graduation to become specialists in the area of mental disease and health. Psychologists are not doctors but have undertaken a course of training to obtain a Bachelor of Arts degree in psychology from a university. Many further their studies to earn postgraduate degrees.

Psychiatrists treat mental diseases (e.g. depression, phobias, schizophrenia) and teach patients how to maintain good mental health. Psychologists deal with behavioral, social and emotional problems (e.g. marriage counselling, dealing with badly behaved children, coping with stress).

To see a psychiatrist, it is necessary to see a general practitioner first, and to be referred to the psychiatrist. The fees charged by private psychiatrists are partly rebated by Medicare. Both general practitioners and psychiatrists refer patients to psychologists when appropriate, and patients may claim a rebate from some private health insurance funds in these circumstances but there is no Medicare rebate for psychologists. A person may see a psychologist without referral if he or she wishes, but most health funds do not give a rebate without a referral from a doctor.

Psychiatrists and psychologist both work in the public hospital system and in government clinics.

Abreaction

Abreaction (or catharsis) is a technique used during psychoanalysis (see below), in which the patient is desensitised to an unpleasant or disagreeable experience by thought, speech and action. An example of abreaction would be the following scenario:

If a person had an unpleasant encounter with a spider, and ever since has had an excessive fear of spiders, a psychiatrist would (over a period of weeks), gradually bring his patient closer and closer into contact with spiders in order to remove the fear.

Initially, the patient would be told merely to think about spiders, and associate the though of spiders with a pleasant thought (e.g. a holiday, nice meal, etc.). Once the patient was comfortable with thinking about spiders, he or she would be encouraged to talk about them.

The next step may be seeing pictures of spiders, drawing spiders, and seeing dead spiders in a bottle. The final stages could be holding a dead spider in the hand, and then allowing a harmless live spider to run across the hand.

The same technique can be used for a wide range of fears including fear of flying, heights, enclosed rooms or other situations.

Behaviour therapy

Behaviour therapy is used by both psychologists and psychiatrists to modify a patient's behaviour. In its basic principle, a patient is taught by rewards that acceptable behaviour is better than unacceptable behaviour, which may be punished by withholding a pleasure, or giving 'time out' to the patient. It is a modification of the 'carrot and stick' technique used with donkeys.

An example of behaviour therapy would be the following scenario:

A five-year-old child who is constantly urinating on the carpet or in other inappropriate places is taken to the toilet regularly. If the child urinates in the toilet, a small reward (e.g. food, use of a toy) is given.

If the child urinates in the wrong place, he or she is placed for a few minutes in a 'time out' situation, where the child is deprived of normal social contact with the parents and other children, and away from toys and other distractions. A laundry or bathroom may be used for this purpose.

The child soon learns that he or she is better off urinating correctly than incorrectly.

The same technique can be applied to intelligent adults (in a more sophisticated way that will be designed by the therapist), to subnormal people, or to the confused elderly. It is vital that any reward be far more significant than the punishment.

ECT

See ELECTROCONVULSIVE THERAPY.

ELECTROCONVULSIVE THERAPY (ECT, SHOCK TREATMENT)

Electroconvulsive therapy (ECT, shock treatment) has been used successfully by psychiatrists for 50 years to treat severe depression and other mental disease, but it has been subjected to much media criticism and vilification by consumer groups in the past decade or so. The adverse reactions to shock treatment come mainly from a misunderstanding of the procedure and what it can and cannot achieve.

A patient about to undergo ECT is thoroughly examined, and an electroencephalogram (see Section 4), and X-rays of the back and neck may be performed. The patient will be stopped from eating or drinking for eight hours before the treatment.

For the procedure, the patient is usually taken to a specially equipped room or theatre. They will be asked to empty their bladder. Electrodes are attached to the temples, and then a brief general anaesthetic is administered. During this anaesthetic, which lasts only a couple of minutes, an electric current is passed through the brain. This electric current causes the patient to have an epileptic-like seizure that lasts 5 to 15 seconds, but because the patient is anaesthetised, the actual body and muscle movement is only slight, and the patient has no pain or discomfort. The patient recovers rapidly from the anaesthetic, is confused for about an hour, may have lost any memory of events in the few hours before the shock treatment was given, and may suffer a dull headache for a day or two. There are no other side effects, and normal activity can be resumed an hour or so after the procedure.

The ECT is repeated up to three or four times a week for 8 to 12 or more treatments. Occasionally, more intensive programs of shock treatment are carried out under strictly monitored conditions. Up to 70% of patients with severe depression are significantly improved by ECT, and overall it is more effective than medication in these patients.

Psychoanalysis

In psychoanalysis, a patient sees a psychiatrist with further training in this area of psychiatry on a very regular basis (e.g. three to five times a week) for an hour or more at a time over several weeks, months or years. It is essential for a close rapport to develop between the doctor and patient. Only a small number of patients with specific character disorders or neuroses (see Section 5) are suitable for psychoanalysis.

The patient is placed in a comfortable position, sometimes lying down, sometimes in a comfortable chair, and the doctor usually sits out of the patient's sight. The patient is urged to express their thoughts, feelings, urges, desires, fantasies, memories and dreams. Using the free flow of thoughts between patient and doctor, the patient's personality and mind can be analysed (psychoanalysis).

The aim of the process is to give the patient insight into their lifestyle so that any problems and concerns can be worked through and controlled or rationalised. This process is called **psychotherapy**. The treatment is continued until the patient is content with their life and situation.

Shock treatment

See ELECTROCONVULSIVE THERAPY.

Other Forms of Treatment

Other forms of treatments include acupuncture, immunotherapy, lithotripsy and radiotherapy. For information on acupuncture, see NATURAL THERAPIES, Section 7. The others are discussed below.

Immunotherapy

Immunotherapy is the enhancement of the body's natural immunity as a method of preventing, or (more recently) of treating disease. Immunisation against a wide range of diseases such as polio, influenza, measles, typhoid, mumps, etc., is a well known role of this area of medicine. Immunisation against smallpox has resulted in the total elimination of this disease.

The new role of immunotherapy is in treating cancer, and specifically engineered antibodies are now being used to destroy some types of cancer cells. Antibodies are normally produced by the body as a reaction to an invading organism. Antibodies against the measles virus are produced by an attack of measles in order to destroy the invading virus, and these antibodies remain for the rest of the patients life to prevent a further attack of measles.

With genetic engineering techniques that have been developed within the last decade, specific antibodies have already been designed to detect certain types of cancer, and their use experimentally to treat these cancers is under way. Leukaemias and lymphomas (lymph gland cancers — see Section 5) are the main areas of success to date.

Immunotherapy is a new science, and medical practitioners are only just beginning to grasp its complexity and potential. Almost certainly immunotherapy will be as significant in the future as the first antibiotics were in 1940.

Lithotripsy

Stones are not normally part of the human anatomy, but those that may form in the kidney, gall bladder and salivary glands may be just as solid and hard as those found in the average quarry. Stones are formed by a compound being present in an excessively high concentration in a bodily fluid, such as urine, bile or saliva. The substance then comes out of solution as a crystal, or precipitates out of suspension and starts to grow with the deposition of successive layers of the substance to the original seed. Stones in the kidney and salivary glands tend to be angular in shape and crystalline, while those in the gall bladder are smooth and rounded, and grow by addition of successive layers of substance.

No matter where a stone forms, it makes its presence felt. Pain is the main symptom, but infections may accompany kidney stones and indigestion may occur with gall stones. Because of these symptoms, patients with a stone almost invariably require it to be removed.

Until recently, the only way to remove a stone was by an operation. These operations varied, depending on the site and size of the stone, but all required a general anaesthetic, several days in hospital, and several weeks recuperating. There is now a quick (but expensive) alternative for urinary stones and some gallstones — lithotripsy. Unfortunately this form of treatment cannot be used for salivary stones.

Lithotripters are now installed (at a cost of up to $2 million each) in several capital cities. They work by focusing high-intensity sound waves (shock waves) at the stone, and shattering it.

During lithotripsy, the patient is lightly sedated to make it easier to remain perfectly still, and placed in a warm bath of water (some newer machines do not require the water bath). The smooth cone of the machine is then placed against the skin, and with the aid of ultrasound or X-rays, is accurately focused on the stone. Care is taken in the positioning of the machine so that no

Other Forms of Treatment

bones or other vital structures are in the path of the shock wave. Once positioned, very powerful but very brief shock waves are passed through the body and stone. During this time the patient is awake and feels minimal discomfort. Every 15 to 30 minutes, further X-rays or ultrasound examinations will be performed to see if the stone has disintegrated.

The whole procedure takes anything from 15 minutes to two hours, depending on the size and hardness of the stone. Once the stone has been shattered, the remnants, which are the size of sand particles, can be passed normally through the urine or bile. The patient can go home the same day, can return to work the next day, and should have no further problems with the stone.

Radiotherapy

Radiotherapy had its beginnings when Madame Curie, the discoverer of nuclear radiation, noted the effect the radiation had upon her hands, and theorised on the possibility of these invisible rays being used to destroy unwanted tissue. Radiotherapy is the treatment of disease (usually cancer) with various forms of ionising radiation. Different types of radiation may be used for different degrees of penetration into the tissue. The time of exposure also varies, depending upon the depth and sensitivity of the cancer. Some cancers are known to be very susceptible to irradiation, while others are quite resistant.

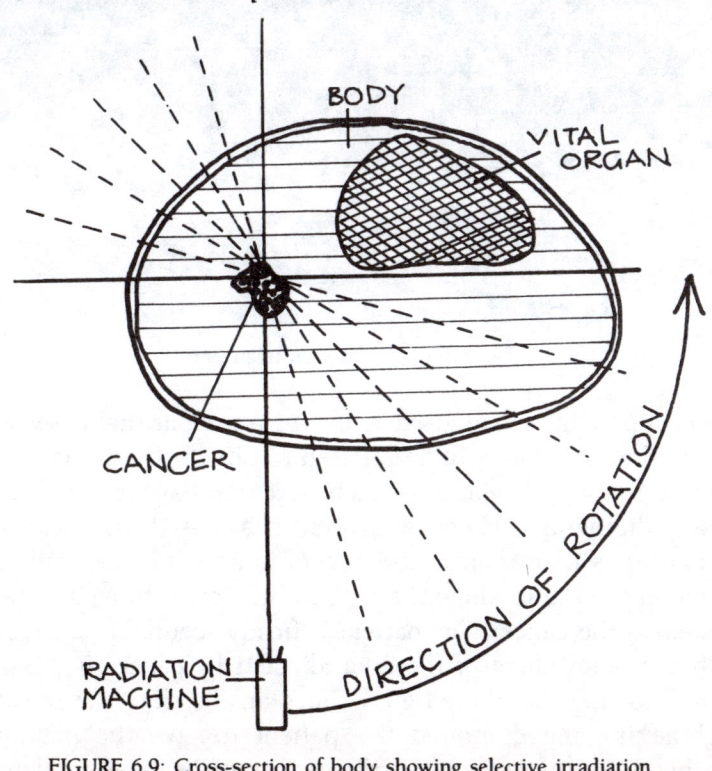

FIGURE 6.9: Cross-section of body showing selective irradiation.

Section 6: Treatments

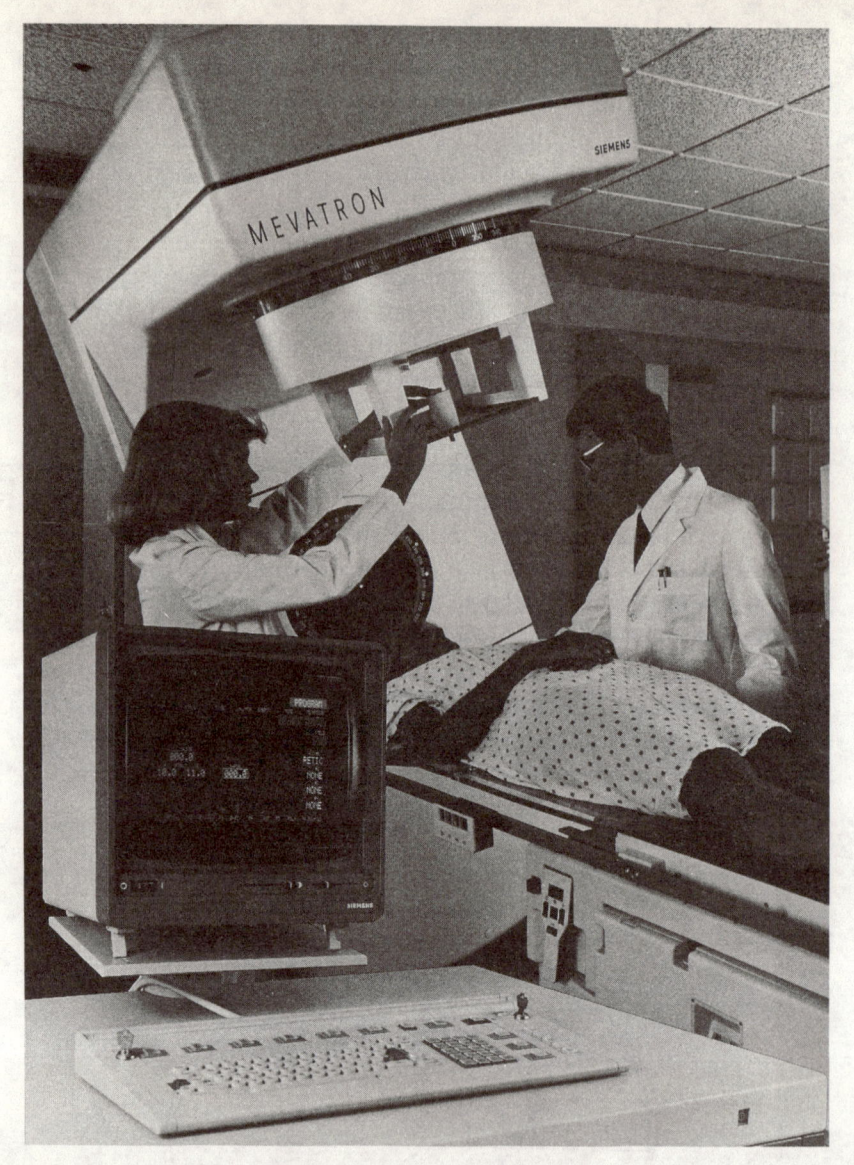

FIGURE 6.10: Radiation treatment.

Once a patient is diagnosed as having a tumour that is sensitive to radiotherapy, they will be referred to one of the special clinics attached to major hospitals in each state that have the facilities to apply radiotherapy. There the patient is assessed, the location of the cancer is determined, and special marks will be applied to the patient's skin to allow the beam of radiation to be accurately directed at the cancer. The patient is firmly secured to a stretcher so that no movement of the area affected by cancer is possible. Then following the plotted guide lines on the skin, the radiation machine is rotated around the patient to give the maximum possible dose of irradiation to the cancer, while avoiding damage to the skin and other vital internal organs. Depending on the site of the cancer, it may be attacked from only a few directions, or every imaginable direction that is safe. The aim is to destroy the cancer cells and allow the body's natural defence mechanisms and waste clearance cells do the rest of the work.

In other situations, a small amount of radioactive material may be briefly implanted into the cancer within the body, to destroy the surrounding malignant cells.

In Australia, the only source of these short-lived radioactive materials is the reactor at Lucas Heights, south of Sydney. These cannot be imported, as they have a radioactive life of only a few hours in some cases, and they must be airlifted to patients for immediate use.

See also RADIATION SICKNESS, Section 5.

THERAPISTS

Dieticians

Dietitians (or nutritionists) are professionals who have undertaken a course of training at a university or technical college, from where they have received a Bachelor of Science degree and/or a diploma in dietetics (or nutrition). Patients can attend a dietitian directly, or may be referred to one by a doctor. Some private health funds offer rebates for their services, but usually only on referral by a doctor.

Dietitians offer a range of skills that assist the normal medical treatment of many diseases, e.g. diabetes, high cholesterol levels, liver disease, gout, heart disease, constipation and diarrhoea. They can also offer advise on diets associated with food allergies, the correct diet for pregnant or breastfeeding mothers, the nutrition of babies, and correcting problems of obesity or underweight.

Dietitians work in private practice from city and/or suburban rooms, or are employed by hospitals or other large institutions.

See also DIET, Section 7.

Occupational therapy

Occupational therapy has no curative role in the way medicine is expected to have. Its underpinning rests with the assumption that the health level of individuals is affected by the activities and functions which are open to them or denied them. Occupational therapists therefore, through the use of therapeutic 'occupation' and specialised equipment and techniques, help individuals regain, maintain and develop functional competence which has been impaired or thwarted by disease, trauma, developmental abnormalities, psychological problems and social disadvantage.

The term 'occupational' embraces a wide spectrum of activities, including work, feeding, dressing and personal care, education, creative media, recreation, and social activities.

Occupational therapists may teach heart or AIDS patients ways of getting tasks done with less effort, help stroke victims with their movement problems, assist intellectually disabled to manage a variety of jobs by breaking them down into simple and easily handled units, educate the institutionalised patient on the use of community facilities, or use relaxation and other psychosocial techniques, individually or in groups, to improve the coping strategies or self-image of both children and adults.

Equipment commonly used includes devices for measuring performance, splints, a variety of aids to facilitate performance in daily living tasks (from cooking to driving), wheelchairs, and computers which may be used for clinical assessment, vocational training, communication, or as devices to facilitate the interface between the disabled and their environment.

Physiotherapy

Physiotherapists care for persons with physical disabilities and for those with pain and loss of function caused by physical disorders. Such disabilities and disorders can arise from a variety of causes, including injury, disease, congenital abnormalities, the ageing and degenerative processes.

People at any stage of their lifespan may present with movement disorders and functional loss. For example, physiotherapists may need to promote motor development in some children or treat their problems of incoordination. In teenagers and adults, the problems may be related to sports injuries, pain and disability from neck and back injuries, and arthritis, breathing problems associated with lung disorders, or movement disabilities arising from disorders of the nervous system, such as multiple sclerosis, stroke and spinal injury.

Physiotherapists use physical methods of treatment which include therapeutic exercise and motor retraining, manipulative therapy and electrophysical agents. Patient education and self-help procedures are an integral part of all management programs. Physiotherapists are also involved in the important areas of health promotion, injury prevention programs and clinical research.

METHODS OF ASSESSMENT, TREATMENT AND PREVENTION

The physiotherapist first undertakes a detailed assessment of the patient's movement disorder to provide the basis for the appropriate treatment and advice.

Therapeutic exercise and motor retraining

Human movement and locomotion require a highly sophisticated interplay between the brain and nerves, the joints of the body, and the muscle system. Injury or disease involving any of these systems can cause a range of physical disabilities.

The effect of injury or disease becomes very apparent in the muscle system. Muscles become weak and wasted, some may lose the capacity to stretch fully, or there may be a loss of coordination in the way the muscles work together to move the body. The nature and extent of the muscle and movement disability depends on the underlying cause. It may predominate in a limb (e.g. after a shoulder injury at sport or with an arthritic knee), in the trunk (e.g. after a back or neck injury), or it may be widespread when the nervous system is involved (e.g. cerebral palsy, stroke).

Therapeutic exercise aims either to restore the normal interplay between the nervous, joint and muscular systems, or to maximise their potential so that the person can function to the best of their ability whether they are returning to sport or learning to walk again.

Physiotherapists analyse the patient's locomotor system and ability to function in daily living, work, play or sport. Depending on the nature of the problem, the physiotherapy examination may include assessment of:
- muscle strength and endurance,
- muscle length,
- muscle tone,
- posture (including standing, sitting and working postures),
- automatic postural and balance reactions,
- joint movement (including the severity and influence of pain),
- movement and muscle coordination,
- gait.

Once the problems have been identified, the physiotherapist will begin a specific and graduated therapeutic exercise program with the patient.

Therapeutic exercise is different from general exercise. The latter, in the main, aims to improve the performance of normal muscles. In contrast, therapeutic exercise utilises various skills and techniques to bring abnormal muscles and movement to a normal level or to a maximum potential. Care is also taken with a patient's underlying pathology. For example, an exercise which may be easily performed by a healthy individual could be harmful for a person with back pain.

The patient often progresses through several stages to regain normal function. The physiotherapist helps the patient to learn again how to use muscles correctly to achieve good postures and movement. Special facilitation techniques may be used to help the patient activate muscles that are not working properly. Some muscles may need to be gently stretched.

Adequate muscle strength and endurance are needed both to produce movement and for protection from further injury. The physiotherapist may work the patient's muscles against the resistance of his/her hands or use the resistance of weights, pulleys, exercise machines, or water. The latter is called hydrotherapy. Safe and effective exercises are also designed for the patient to perform at home.

Physiotherapists stress preventative care and will provide ongoing exercise programs to help to prevent further problems and enhance quality of life. Additional special therapeutic exercise methods are used for persons suffering from neurological disorders which may have major effects on the muscle/motor control systems (e.g. people with motor coordination difficulties, cerebral palsy, spinal injuries causing paralysis and stroke). Techniques vary according to the condition and the presenting problems. In some instances, movement may be facilitated by the physiotherapist, or special techniques may be used to increase sensory input to help muscles work. In infants and young children, correct movement patterns may need to be established, and the physiotherapist can advise the parents about activities to assist the child's development. When exercise alone cannot achieve good and safe movement, the physiotherapist will advise on appropriate appliances (e.g. walking sticks, callipers, splints, wheelchairs).

Manipulative therapy

Manipulative therapy is the umbrella term for the techniques of passive mobilisation and manipulation. Mobilisation is a rhythmical movement gently applied to joints and soft tissues by the physiotherapist's hands. A manipulation is a single joint movement performed quickly.

The techniques of manipulative therapy are used to treat joints and muscles which have become painful and lack their normal range of movement. This dysfunction can occur in the spine or limbs, or indeed in the joint of the jaw. The pain and loss of movement can result from injury, overuse or poor use of the joints, or from osteoarthritis. Dysfunction in the small joints, discs and muscles of the neck can give symptoms of headache, neck pain and stiffness. The pain may spread into the arm. In the low back, the pain may spread down the leg.

When a patient seeks physiotherapy for a neck or back condition, the physiotherapist first conducts a thorough examination dealing with the nature and history of the symptoms. Descriptions of work, sporting and everyday activities are recorded, and the advice given regarding the best methods to relieve stress from the spine is based on this information.

Physical examination of the spine includes detailed analyses of posture, spinal movements and the muscle system. A neurological examination checks for any pressure on the nerves. The physiotherapist assesses the motion between each vertebra to find which joints of the spine are causing the pain and in which directions they have lost movement.

From the results of the examination, together with information from X-rays and other medical tests, the physiotherapist selects an appropriate manipulative therapy technique. Often this is a passive mobilisation technique, gently moving the joint to relieve its pain and help it regain movement. On occasion it is also necessary to manipulate the joint. Manipulation on the whole is a safe procedure, but as with any form of treatment, there are several conditions in which its use is unsafe (e.g. in dizziness caused by vertebral artery problems, spinal cancer, fractures, rheumatoid arthritis, and osteoporosis).

In conjunction with the manipulative therapy treatment, the physiotherapist teaches the patient specific, gentle exercises to help maintain and improve the spinal movement. As the pain and condition settles, therapeutic exercises are begun to ensure that the patient has a good muscle system and good general fitness to help support and protect the spine from further injury. The physiotherapist also teaches the patient good standing, sitting and working postures, and how to lift, carry and perform their work and daily activities safely without overstressing the spine.

Electrophysical agents

Physiotherapists use various electrophysical agents in the treatment of injured and painful joints, muscle and nerve tissue. These agents aim to relieve pain, reduce swelling and enhance healing and extensibility of the tissues. Basically, the electrophysical agents are used in one of three forms: heat, ultrasound, or electrical stimulation.

Heat may be delivered by the use of hot packs (a superficial moist heat), or, if deep warming of the tissues is required, by the administration of **short-wave diathermy**. The latter is particularly useful for chronically sprained and arthritic joints, and deep muscle problems. In this modality, high-frequency electrical energy is converted to heat within the tissues. There are, however, instances where the use of short-wave diathermy is contraindicated: i.e. where metal is present (e.g. in joint replacements and some intra-uterine devices), because it concentrates the electrical field and may cause local burning; where the electrical field may interfere with cardiac pacemakers; in pregnancy; and in patients who suffer severe circulatory disorders.

Ultrasound is the generation of high-frequency sound waves which impart a mechanical energy into the tissues. It is used to disperse swelling and enhance healing of injured tissue, and is commonly used in the treatment of sporting and other soft-tissue injuries.

There are various forms of electrical stimulation, e.g. **transcutaneous electrical nerve stimulation (TENS), interferential (IF) therapy, and high-voltage galvanic (HVG) therapy**. Many criteria govern which modality is selected and which intensities, waveforms or frequencies of current are used. These include whether the condition is acute or chronic, and whether the major aim is to suppress pain, reduce inflammation, enhance healing, or stimulate muscle contraction. Whilst the various forms of electrical stimulation are safe and without adverse side effects, there are some circumstances in which they should not be used. For example, IF should not be applied over the heart, in the region of cancers, or through the low back and pelvic regions during pregnancy.

Cardiopulmonary physiotherapy
Physiotherapists treat cardiopulmonary disorders and teach patients to correct abnormal breathing patterns or maximise their lung efficiency and exercise capability within the limits of a respiratory or cardiac disease. A person of any age (from premature babies to the elderly) may require physiotherapy for respiratory disorders such as cystic fibrosis, chest infection, chronic bronchitis, asthma or emphysema. Breathing difficulties can also occur after major surgery. Cardiopulmonary management is also an important part of rehabilitation following heart attacks or heart surgery.

The physiotherapist both observes and feels the patient's chest movement to analyse the breathing pattern, then listens to the patient's chest with a stethoscope to assess how much air is entering the lungs, and determines the presence and location of secretions (or phlegm).

In treatment, the physiotherapist teaches the patient how to breathe properly to increase the amount of air entering the lungs. The patient is taught relaxation and graduated exercises both for the mobility of the chest wall and for general exercise tolerance. Advice and direction is given on lifestyle changes such as attaining appropriate fitness and activity levels, and ceasing smoking.

When secretions are present in the lungs, the physiotherapist can use postural drainage to help remove them. To assist loosening and removal of secretions, the chest may be manually shaken, using techniques called vibration and percussion. The patient is also taught to cough or force air out effectively to help clear the lungs.

Health promotion and prevention of injury
The primary activities of physiotherapists in the workplace are health education and ergonomics. The physiotherapist evaluates the work site and how the worker physically performs the task. Potential problem areas are identified, and advice and instruction is given on the best method of performing the work. Strategies for prevention of injury are offered.

Physiotherapists are involved in many areas of women's health. They provide advice and instruction in the preparation for childbirth and instruct in fitness, back care and posture, both for the period of the pregnancy and for caring for the infant after birth. Education and exercise programs are also given for the prevention or management of such problems as stress incontinence and osteoporosis.

Physiotherapists instruct many groups in the community in the prevention of sporting injuries, including schools, clubs, and sporting associations. They frequently travel with teams to provide immediate assistance so that sportspersons may continue competing.

Physiotherapists advise on suitable forms of exercise and fitness programs, both for persons who may be recovering from a disability and for those who wish to maintain a healthy lifestyle but have concurrent problems, such as arthritis.

ACCESS TO PHYSIOTHERAPY

Many people have contact with physiotherapists in the hospital setting. Physiotherapists also practise in a variety of other settings within the community. These include:
- private practices,
- rehabilitation centres,
- community health centres,
- industrial and commercial premises,
- schools, including special schools,
- nursing homes,
- aged care centres,
- sporting venues,
- educational institutions.

Physiotherapists work in close association with doctors and other health professionals. They frequently work in multidisciplinary teams in both hospitals and the community.

Patients are commonly referred for physiotherapy by a medical practitioner, but medical referral is not essential to the practice of physiotherapy in Australia. Individual patients, medical practitioners, dentists and other health professionals may request physiotherapy.

Physiotherapy services delivered with the public hospital

system are covered under Medicare. Physiotherapy in the private sector is not covered by Medicare, but private health insurance funds offer a rebate for physiotherapy services. This rebate is available both to patients who are referred by a doctor and to those who present to the physiotherapist directly.

PHYSIOTHERAPY EDUCATION

Education programs in physiotherapy in Australia are offered either through universities or tertiary institutes. The undergraduate degree programs are of four years duration, and graduates receive either a Bachelor of Physiotherapy or a Bachelor of Applied Science (Physiotherapy) degree. Members of the Australian Physiotherapy Association are signified by the initials MAPA.

Higher degree studies in physiotherapy include a research Master's degree and a Doctor of Philosophy (PhD) degree. Postgraduate studies leading to the award of either a Postgraduate Diploma or a Master of Physiotherapy Studies are offered in many of the clinical specialty fields.

Specialisation

The Australian College of Physiotherapy, the scientific body of the Australian Physiotherapy Association, provides the formal process for a physiotherapist to reach the status of Specialist Clinical Consultant. Physiotherapists who have gained a higher degree in a specialty area may apply to enter the Fellowship process.

The Australian College of Physiotherapists is responsible for awarding fellowships in the areas of manipulative, sports, paediatric, neurological, orthopaedic and cardiopulmonary physiotherapy, as well as physiotherapy specialisation in the areas of gerontology and women's health. Physiotherapists who have successfully completed the process are signified by the initials FACP.

Podiatry

Podiatrists (previously called **chiropodists**) are responsible for the care of feet. They have been trained in their area of expertise by attending a course at a technical college, from where they receive the appropriate diploma. Patients can attend a podiatrist directly, or may be referred to one by a doctor. Some private health funds offer rebates for their services, but usually only on referral by a doctor.

Podiatrists can trim difficult nails, deal with some types of ingrown toenails, pare down corns and bunions, treat warts on the feet, and advise patients on footwear and general foot hygiene. A large part of their work involves the care of feet in the elderly.

Podiatrists work in private practice from city and/or suburban rooms, or are employed by hospitals.

Speech pathology

Speech pathology is also known as speech therapy. It involves the diagnosis and treatment of speech, language, stuttering and voice problems. The aim of speech pathology is to help a person to communicate as effectively as possible.

Speech pathology does not involve the art of fine speech — that is elocution. The latter is the term associated with such phrases as, 'how now brown cow'. Speech pathology does not involve diction or teaching English as a foreign language.

Children are often referred for speech pathology because they may jumble their sounds, which causes them frustration or embarrassment if they are unable to make themselves understood. There are generally recognised ages at which children acquire particular sounds. For example, many children do not master the sounds of 'r' and 'th' until the age of seven. A speech pathologist can recognise the difference between an immature sound pattern that will improve spontaneously and a confused pattern where therapy will be needed to teach the child to hear and correct wrong sounds.

Children may also need speech pathology to help in the development of language skills. They may be slow in acquiring words or in using sentences compared with their peers. Parents should also seek therapy if their child appears confused or is having difficulty understanding what other say.

Adults with speech difficulties can be limited in their choice of employment, as clear speech is essential in many careers. They may seek the assistance of a speech pathologist.

Sometimes accident, illness or injury interferes with speech and language which has been developing normally. A person who has had a stroke may have good hearing but because of brain damage may not understand what is heard. Also he or she may be confused in the use of words to express his/her thoughts and intentions and have a marked loss in speech. A speech pathologist will organise exercises to help the person re-learn to communicate to the best of his/her ability.

In some cases, therapy may not be able to help in the development of oral communication. For example, in severe cerebral palsy, the speech therapist may teach the use of alternative means of communication, such as word boards or electronic aids.

Speech pathology can help overcome the problem of stuttering. It can offer a person a new way of talking smoothly. It does not provide a cure.

Young children who are still refining their skills of speech and language, particularly during pre-school years, often repeat words and have hesitant speech. Parents should not worry unduly. Non-fluent behaviour is quite normal, and most children will grow out of it if ignored. However, if you or your child becomes anxious, it would be sensible to discuss the problem with a speech pathologist.

Adults and children can have problems with their voice. It may attract attention because it is nasal, hoarse or breathy. We are all subject to temporary changes in our voices, for example when we have a cold. However, if persistent change in voice occurs, a doctor should examine your nose and throat to try to identify the cause of this. The doctor will advise if help from a speech pathologist is needed.

If you have a problem in any of the above areas, ask your doctor, local hospital, school or child health centre to refer you to a speech pathologist. The pathologist will assess speech, language, voice and fluency skills. A diagnosis and decision on management will be made and a treatment plan organised. The frequency of therapy depends on the nature and severity of the problem. Whatever the difficulty, the involvement of the family members in therapy is important. They should try to understand the problem, therapy techniques and goals so they can assist the person with a communication problem make the best progress.

In Australia, becoming a speech pathologist involves four years of intensive study. Subjects undertaken include normal speech and language development, speech and language pathology, anatomy, physiology, and linguistics and psychology. During the course, practical experience is gained in various clinical settings. Once training is completed and exams are passed, a student graduates with a Bachelors degree in Applied Science in Speech Pathology.

There are five speech pathology training schools in Australia. They are based at:
University of Queensland
Cumberland College of Health Sciences, New South Wales
Lincoln Institute of Health Science, La Trobe University, Victoria
Curtin University of Technology, Western Australia
Sturt College of Advanced Education, South Australia

Once a person has qualified as a speech pathologist, he or she can become a member of the Australian Association of Speech and Hearing. This organisation encourages a high standard of clinical practice and assists therapists in keeping informed of the latest trends in therapy.

SECTION 7

MISCELLANEOUS

CHILD ABUSE
695

DENTISTRY
696

DIET
709

DOCTORS
720

GERMS
727

NATURAL THERAPIES
732

PATIENT ORGANISATIONS
736

PREVENTIVE MEDICINE
746

TRAVEL MEDICINE
757

Child Abuse

At some stage in the first few months of their baby's life, most parents feel like throwing their bundle of joy out of the window. Fortunately, the vast majority of parents resist this desire, but there is no doubt that children can become irritating, frustrating and maddening to the most loving of parents. Inexperienced parents and a new baby who cries day and night can lead to irrational thinking and spontaneous actions which are quite out of character and later will be profoundly regretted. Child abuse in this situation is understandable but still inexcusable. Parents must seek help from their doctor or child welfare officer before this stage is reached.

In other situations, child abuse may be more callous or sadistic. An unwanted child may be abused in order to extract unwarranted revenge. A father may hurt a child indirectly to hurt his wife or girlfriend. Some parents are simply nasty people who are violent in all their human relationships. Many child abusers were themselves abused as children.

Child abuse can be physical, psychological or sexual. Whichever form it takes, it can be difficult to detect and may continue for a long time before the child comes to the notice of a responsible person and is given protection. A person who abuses a child rarely does it when anyone else is around. If you become suspicious that a child is being abused, talk to a doctor or child welfare officer. You may suspect child abuse if a child has repeated bruising or burn marks and the parents delay or fail to obtain medical help, offer implausible or inconsistent explanations for the injuries, or if their reactions to the injuries seem strange. The most reliable indication of continued cruelty or neglect is often failure of the child to grow at the normal rate. Children made unhappy by repeated abuse do not thrive, and their weight drops well below the average for their age.

It sometimes happens that other members of the family are aware that a child is being abused and make excuses or close their eyes to what is going on. This is unforgivable. An adult who stands by and allows a child to be abused without getting help is as guilty and deserves as much condemnation as the abuser. Children are not only physically injured by abuse but may be emotionally scarred for the rest of their life.

Neglect is as much a form of child abuse as deliberate injury. Poor hygiene and under- or over-clothing an infant may be due to lack of knowledge, but lack of food and failure to obtain attention for illnesses, skin diseases, infected eyes and injuries is unacceptable abuse.

There is sometimes a fine line between discipline by the parents, temper tantrums by the child, and criminal abuse of the child. Casual observation by an outsider may give a false impression, but if the child shows signs of injury or the problem continues consistently, then the family requires help. This help is readily available from the family general practitioner, paediatricians, community nurses and welfare workers, and special teams attached to most children's hospitals.

Some parents realise that assistance in dealing with a difficult child is required, but are afraid to seek it because of the consequences. If help is sought voluntarily, it would be exceptional for any charges to be laid against the parents. Putting a parent in jail is rarely seen as a solution for either the child or the family as a whole. Rather, every effort is made to solve the problem by counselling, medications and care. Sometimes the child can be removed from the family for a short period, if it is thought this will help to relieve stress, modify abnormal behaviour patterns in the child, and lead to normal future family life. Only those who consistently refuse to accept their responsibilities as parents and reject offers of professional assistance are likely to find the law invoked against them.

Child abuse is not new, it has occurred throughout history, and is probably occurring less now than in Victorian times when child labour was the norm. However, society today is far more aware of the problem and less inclined either to accept it or sweep it under the carpet.

If there is child abuse in your family, or you suspect a child you know is being abused, or you yourself think you are at risk of abusing your child, talk to your doctor or the child welfare officer in your district. Many areas have a child abuse hot line that you can ring in an emergency. Whatever action you take, your approach will be confidential and assistance is available.

DENTISTRY

Dentistry is the art and science of caring for the teeth and jaws and their related structures.

Modern dentistry is one of the newer professions, not much more than a hundred years old. It is practised in Australia by a team headed by a university-trained dentist supported by various auxiliaries, such as dental hygienists, dental technicians, school dental therapists, dental chair-side assistants and receptionists. Most dentistry is carried out by private dentists. Government dentistry is provided in state dental hospitals and clinics and in the school dental service, which employs both dentists and school dental therapists. The latter receive two years full-time training to care for primary school children. The universities and some friendly societies also provide some dental services. Dentistry is controlled by dental boards appointed by the state governments. Nearly all dentists in the private and public sectors are members of the Australian Dental Association, a voluntary organisation.

Dentistry is practised by general practitioners in solo or group practices, and by a series of specialists in paedodontics (children's dentistry), endodontics (root fillings), periodontics (gum diseases), orthodontics (tooth straightening), prosthodontics (dentures and bridges), and oral and maxillofacial surgery (surgery of the mouth and jaws).

The standard of dental care in Australia compares favourably with any other country. Dental training is a full-time five-year university course which attracts the best students. Access to the latest overseas techniques, knowledge, materials and equipment is not only readily available but in many instances more widely available than in other countries. Australian contributions in these fields are also substantial, and modern communication systems ensure that the Australian population is kept abreast of new developments.

Many dental conditions are either incurable or irreversible. Preventive dentistry consequently has more application than in most health fields and forms a major component in the delivery of modern dental care.

Optimum dental health depends on a balanced input from government, profession and community. In particular, proven preventive measures such as the fluoridation of public water supplies and education programs aimed at every age group need to be applied at maximum possible level.

Dental care is needed right throughout life. It is not dental care that is expensive, but dental neglect. Appropriate dental care should therefore be available at each of the 'seven ages of man', from infancy to old age.

Paedodontics

Paedodontics is the provision of dentistry for children. Children have special dental needs as they produce two sets of teeth and hence have more teeth to care for than adults.

Teeth start forming at a very early stage before birth below the gums. As the teeth calcify and grow, they push their way into the mouth. The lower incisors or front teeth generally appear first, at about six months of age. By two and a half years, all the first or deciduous (because they are shed like autumn leaves) teeth are present. At six years, those front teeth are replaced by the permanent teeth, which coming up underneath resorb the root until there is none left, and the little crown that remains joins the tooth fairy market. At the same time, the permanent six-year molars appear at the back of the mouth behind the last of the deciduous molars. Those molars and the little eye teeth in front of them are not lost until about the age of twelve, when the second wave of permanent teeth appear. Again the twelve-year molars appear behind the six-year molars. The wisdom teeth appear many years later to complete the set.

As teeth are forming in the jaws, they should be exposed to an optimum amount of fluoride in the blood supply. Most water supplies in Australia have an optimum amount either naturally or artificially supplemented. In those areas which do not, mainly in rural areas and most of Queensland, the fluoride should be supplied by the children's guardians on a daily basis by tablets or drops. With optimum fluoride, the resulting enamel of the teeth is very much more resistant to attack from the acids causing tooth decay.

Teeth that come through crookedly will generally straighten themselves out as they grow, if they have enough room to move in. If not, they should be corrected by an orthodontist at about the age of twelve or when all the permanent teeth appear.

Faults can occur as teeth are forming. Some faults are hereditary. Some teeth do not form at all; others may be misshaped. Some teeth may fuse together. Other faults may be acquired. A disease suffered while teeth are forming may leave its mark on the teeth. Some antibiotics may affect teeth as they form, but this is less common as awareness grows.

Children's diet should be sensible. Foods rich in sugar are dangerous to teeth and poor nutritionally. Daily intake of sugar-laden foods can be easily reduced by not having them in the household at all. Parents can set a good example. Natural sugar such as in fresh fruits or vegetables is harmless, but sugar that comes from the refinery is not a natural part of life — it is by then a pure chemical and acts accordingly, breaking down in the mouth to acids which attack the enamel of teeth and start the decay process.

Children's teeth should be brushed from an early age and the habit firmly established. Self-brushing should be encouraged, but supervision is needed for many years.

Children should be introduced to the dentist at about the age of two and a half years, and then return every six months. Fear of dentistry is readily avoided and early detection of trouble makes correction easy. Children with complex problems should be treated by a paedodontist or children's dental specialist.

Endodontics

Endodontics is the treatment of the inside of a tooth. It is more commonly called root filling. Teeth with root fillings are dead.

In the middle of each tooth, underneath the enamel, dentine and cementum, lies the pulp of the tooth. It is very much alive and, because it is so sensitive, is popularly called the nerve of the tooth. However, as well as nerves it consists of arteries and veins and lymph glands and other normal tissues.

For a variety of reasons the pulp tissue in a tooth may die. Decay may proceed through the enamel until it reaches the pulp, allowing harmful bacteria access. The tooth may be cracked and also expose the pulp. A heavy blow on the tooth is capable of killing the pulp. When the pulp dies, it acts like all dead tissue and starts to putrefy. Very often pus is formed and starts to accumulate around the tip of the root. As it accumulates, it starts to build up pressure and hence cause severe pain. It is then called a dental abscess. If the pus builds up slowly it may not cause severe pain but turn into a chronic abscess, which starts to destroy the bone at the tip of the root. In either case, there are only two ways of treating the problem. One way is to extract the tooth, and the other is to do a root filling.

The specialist endodontist or the dentist opens up the pulp chamber of the tooth with a dental drill and proceeds to remove the dead tissue with long reamers and files which reach right to the tip of the root and clean and smooth the root canal removing the source of the infection. When it has been stabilised, the empty space is filled with a bland material, generally gutta percha, packed tightly into place with an antiseptic paste, and sealed. A well-treated root-filled tooth can last for many years. While not as good as a live tooth, it is vastly superior to any artificial substitute put in to fill the space.

Front teeth with a single straight canal are much easier to treat than posterior teeth with two, three or four curved root canals. Access to the back teeth is more restricted and such teeth are more expensive to treat. It is sometimes possible in special cases to amputate a faulty root of a multi-rooted tooth and keep the tooth to support a bridge or crown. Sometimes only the tip of the root is amputated to improve root fillings.

The main disadvantage of an endodontically treated tooth is its increased brittleness. It is often prudent to protect the dead tooth with a gold crown to minimise the risk of fracture. In some cases, especially where the crown of the tooth has been broken or weakened, a metal post is cemented into the root of the tooth above the root filling to provide extra support and strength.

In years past, dead teeth sometimes discoloured even to the extent of going black, but this is now uncommon. Nevertheless, dead teeth tend to lose their sparkle and appear dull and lifeless. Discoloured teeth can sometimes be bleached. Another way of improving their appearance is to cover them with a baked porcelain crown or a porcelain veneer over the visible surface.

Periodontics

Periodontics, as the name implies, deals with those parts of the mouth that lie around the teeth. It is important that the gums and bone are kept healthy to avoid periodontal disease. Dental decay is not the only cause of tooth loss. Periodontal disease causes enormous tooth loss, especially in later years. It is an insidious disease, for the most part painless, and often not recognised until it is too late. Like dental decay, it is preventable in most people.

Periodontal disease is really a series of different but related diseases, and is caused in the first instance by the accumulation of dental plaque around the teeth. Plaque is a soft deposit around the teeth caused by bacteria in the mouth. The mouth contains enormous numbers and varieties of bacteria, and each person has a different collection. Dental plaque can and should be constantly removed as it forms. Some of it is removed naturally. At one time when diets were more natural, a good deal was removed by the action of tough and fibrous foods. Wild animals and native tribes use this method, but modern man and domesticated animals need some further assistance. A professional mechanical removal with a scaler can be maintained by constant polishing with a very soft toothbrush, dental floss and soft wooden stimulators.

If plaque is left to accumulate, it causes irritation to the gums and bone. In many cases it is converted by other bacteria into a hard deposit called tartar or calculus, which no amount of brushing will remove. It must be scaled off with a sharp instrument by a dental hygienist, dentist, or periodontist (a dental specialist in this field). If left, tartar or calculus traps more plaque which is harder to remove and in turn becomes more calculus. Some people can build up enormous deposits in a very short time. Hard calculus deposits can trap not only plaque but food debris which can putrefy and cause bad breath or halitosis. Regular professional removal of calculus enables most people to keep their teeth clean, polished and healthy.

Gums that are irritated by plaque or calculus become inflamed and suffer from gingivitis. The gums look red and swollen, and bleed easily when touched. The bone underneath retreats towards the tip of the root. A pocket is formed between the gum and the tooth, which is impossible to keep clean and may become infected. The gingivitis turns into periodontal disease and causes pus and pain. If left untreated, the infection often becomes much worse and spreads over the whole of the mouth. The so-called trench mouth of the First World War, accelerated by the appalling hygiene conditions, was of this type. It is now known as Vincent's infection.

Apart from meticulous scaling and cleaning, the periodontist at times performs surgery to correct defects or prevent an ongoing problem. Pockets remaining after treatment can be surgically removed. The procedure is called gingivectomy.

While periodontal disease is seen less often in children, it is the lesson learnt in childhood that meticulous tooth cleaning is a part of civilised life that will help minimise the risk of trouble later in life.

Orthodontics

Orthodontics deals with the correction of teeth that are wrongly positioned. Ideally, teeth and jaws should match each other. As the face grows and the deciduous teeth are lost, the permanent teeth that replace them should slot neatly into place with no gaps and no crossing, forming a symmetrical elliptical arch like a string of pearls. The upper teeth should lock into the lower arch so that, when moved, the jaw joint moves smoothly in its socket. It is of course possible to be less than ideal and still be quite acceptable.

Treatment is needed when the appearance or the function of teeth is less than satisfactory. Things go wrong for a variety of reasons. Some faults are inherited. A small jaw may be characteristic of one side of the family, and large teeth a feature of the other side. A particular face shape and skeletal pattern may go back for generations. Other faults are acquired. A disease suffered while the teeth are growing in the jaws can affect their formation. Teeth may be lost prematurely from decay or an accident. At times some teeth do not appear at all. Some undesirable habits, such as mouth-breathing due to a permanently blocked nose, thumb-sucking, tongue-thrusting or lip-sucking, can easily displace some of the teeth temporarily or permanently.

The orthodontist is trained to predict the growth pattern of the jaws and how to re-direct it. Special X-rays of the head show how the teeth are lying in the skull and what influence they exert on the profile of the face. The jaw may be jutting aggressively forward, or lie too far back and give the appearance of a weak-looking chin. The orthodontist sets out to correct both the appearance and function of the misplaced teeth. If there is a shortage of room for all the teeth, either the arch is expanded to make more room, or some teeth are extracted. To expand the arch, small steel bands are cemented around the upper molar teeth. A detachable metal frame fits into the bands and, with the aid of an elastic strap passing behind the neck, the frame pulls those teeth backward and outwards to make a bigger arch and allow room for all the other teeth.

The optimum time for orthodontics is at puberty. There is a sudden spurt of body growth at this age, when the last of the permanent teeth appear and the face and jaws expand to their final adult shape. The growing bone can be re-directed to a desirable pattern. This is done by attaching wire springs to the teeth to guide them gently to their new positions. Under the small but constant pressure of the spring, the bone in front of the tooth is resorbed and the tooth moves into the space created. New bone is then formed behind the tooth to fill the space created by the movement. After several months when the teeth are in their new position, the bands are removed and often a temporary appliance is inserted to prevent the whole process from reversing to its original position. Orthodontics may be done at any age at all, but the best results are achieved at the optimum age.

Orthodontists sometimes move single teeth, particularly in adults, for reasons such as improving its position to take a crown or a bridge. At times an eye tooth may be held up in the palate, and in these cases a hook and spring are attached to its crown to pull it down into position.

Australian orthodontics is amongst the most advanced in the world, and some of the pioneers of the new techniques have been Australians whose work is copied overseas.

With the substantial current reduction in decay rates at puberty, orthodontics has become an attractive option for many people. Teeth that are correctly aligned are much easier to keep properly clean. They are more efficient for chewing, and their superior appearance contributes markedly to an enhanced self-image.

Orthodontics may sometimes seem expensive in the short term, but when amortised over a lifetime of perceived benefit, it is very cost effective.

Prosthodontics

Prosthodontics is the art of making artificial substitutes for teeth. There are two types — removable prostheses (false teeth), and fixed prostheses which are permanently cemented onto existing teeth or metal implants and cannot be removed.

Removable prostheses are either full dentures used when all teeth have been lost, or partial dentures which are attached by spring clasps to remaining teeth when only some teeth have been lost. Full dentures are made on a plaster model which is an exact copy of the patient's mouth, and consist of a pink acrylic resin base, to which are attached porcelain or acrylic resin teeth. Upper dentures are held in mainly by suction, and lower dentures mainly by muscle control. Partial dentures are similar, but are held in place by small wire springs which grip the remaining teeth. The best partial dentures are made from a cast chrome-cobalt metal or gold framework, to which the teeth are attached by acrylic resin.

It is now possible, where supporting teeth have been lost, to use a titanium implant to hold a denture. A hole is drilled into the jaw bone and a small cylinder of sterile titanium is dropped into place and sewn over. After some weeks, the surrounding bone attaches itself to the titanium. The gum is then cut back again and a small titanium extension is screwed into the implant. A denture can then be attached to the extension. It is very specialised work.

Australia is a world leader in a technique which uses tiny but very powerful magnets to help hold artificial teeth in place.

It is possible to provide very natural-looking teeth with the facilities now available. A common technique is to make a denture with an exact copy of teeth that need extracting, and place it in the mouth immediately the natural ones are removed. Some months later, when bone shrinkage has ceased, the dentures are re-lined with acrylic to make them fit very accurately once again. In this way the patient is never without teeth.

Fixed prostheses are crowns and bridges. To make a crown, the existing tooth is cut down to a cone shape, and the artificial crown (made from gold, acrylic resin, porcelain, or a combination of these) is cemented over the top. A bridge is a series of crowns linked together to bridge the gap made by missing teeth. It is cemented onto the remaining teeth and can only be removed with difficulty. It can also be attached to an implant of titanium or other metal.

A new type of bridge which is made of metal with teeth attached is simply cemented onto existing teeth without cutting them down to a cone shape. It uses a system of etching the enamel with an acid to allow a very strong cement bond to hold the bridge in place. It can only be used in favourable situations. A variation on this etching technique involves the use of thin baked porcelain veneers, which are cemented in the same way over the visible surfaces of ugly or stained teeth to give a perfect appearance.

Aesthetic dentistry

More and more it is becoming possible to improve people's dental appearance. A film-star smile can often be bought. Many film stars have done just that, and got their money back a hundredfold. People in many other fields are also well aware of the value of a good dental appearance, and countless personalities have benefited by a dramatic change in dental appearance, made possible by new technology.

Obviously individual cases vary enormously, from a simple re-shaping of some front teeth, to elaborate combinations of orthodontics, crowns, bridges and dentures. The use of thin veneers of porcelain or resin on the visible surfaces of ugly teeth can be quite dramatic, and unsightly fillings can readily be replaced.

Trauma

Teeth are so hard that they can easily last for a century in constant use, but they have a brittleness factor which is evident when they are abused. A heavy blow can either dislodge teeth altogether, or break sections off. Such fractures can be difficult to repair, and the repaired tooth is never as good as it was before. Prevention of damage is vastly preferable.

Teeth are always in danger in the vicinity of concrete. Falling on stairs or paths, or running into posts invariably causes severe damage. Swimming pools can also be hazardous zones, both when slipping and when diving into shallow areas, and care and awareness should be exercised.

During contact sports such as boxing, football, hockey, basketball, etc., a mouthguard made by a dentist which fits closely and allows normal speech and breathing should always be worn both while playing and training. It is cheap insurance.

A tooth that has been knocked out should immediately be replaced in its socket, before calling a dentist who can apply a splint and further treat as necessary. Time is most important and is measured in minutes. A quick wash of the tooth under a tap is all that is necessary before placing it back in place. The faster it is replaced, the better the chance of survival.

Temporomandibular joint

The lower jaw joint, which is located just in front of the ear, is called the temporomandibular joint, and is as complicated as its name. It does not have a simple opening and closing motion like some other joints, but slides both forwards and sideways on an S-shaped section of bone in the skull, from which it is separated by a piece of cartilage.

This joint can be damaged through wear or wrongly aligned teeth, and can then cause pains ranging from the face to the neck and shoulders, or severe headaches. Treatment of the condition is possible in most cases. Clicking of the joint is also common and sometimes precedes the painful period.

Oral and maxillofacial surgery

Oral and maxillofacial surgery is the treatment by surgery of diseased tissues of the mouth and jaws (e.g. the removal of benign tumours and cysts in the mouth), the correction of deformities and abnormalities, and the repair of fractures in the region. Most malignant tumours are removed by general surgeons, as they often extend beyond the region. The removal of teeth is a traditional surgical procedure by dentists. Teeth may be extracted with forceps or, in difficult cases, be surgically removed. In these cases the gum is peeled back, bone is removed from around the tooth or root to allow its easy removal, and then the gum is sewn back into place. The removal of impacted wisdom teeth is perhaps the commonest procedure carried out by oral and maxillofacial surgeons. A wisdom tooth is impacted when it does not have room enough to fit into place in the mouth and is jammed or impacted behind the tooth in front of it. This occurs mostly in the lower jaw. Removal is preferably carried out on people when they are young.

Some oral surgery is carried out to assist other dental specialists. For example, the surgeon may improve the shape of a jaw and re-shape tissue to allow a better denture to be made. Surgery to remove the tips of roots can help the endodontist do a better root filling. Exposing an eye tooth buried in the palate may assist the orthodontist to attach a spring to it and pull it into place. Transplanting a tooth from one part of the mouth to another can help the orthodontist, or the prosthodontist with a bridge. Preparing the jaws to take a titanium implant may help the prosthodontist fit a bridge where it could not be done otherwise.

Abnormalities may occur through developmental faults such as a cleft palate, which is due to bones not joining up when they should. A surgical team can correct this fault at an early age. A squat face can be lengthened by detaching the palate from the base of the skull, and inserting a bone graft made from a section of rib. The palate can be levelled if uneven, or moved to alter the shape of the face.

If the lower jaw juts out too far or recedes, giving a weak-looking chin, the surgeon can split the rear section of the jaw vertically and then move the front section backwards or forwards to the desired position. At the same time, the surgeon may cut a bit off a jutting chin or add a bone graft to a receding one. The jaw is then wired into place for a few weeks, while the patient is fed through a straw.

Problems with the temporomandibular joint (jaw joint) just in front of the ear are also often treatable by surgery.

Sometimes one side of the jaw keeps on growing after the other side has stopped, creating a lopsided appearance, and the teeth only meet on one side. Surgery can return all to normal. A bony growth called a taurus can also appear on the upper or lower jaws, and can be surgically removed.

The number of facial and jaw fractures has vastly increased with the road accident rate. Repairing and splinting these fractures calls for ingenuity and skill on the part of oral and maxillofacial surgeons. Some results are quite miraculous. Gunshot wounds to the face are also becoming more common and can be very severe. Industrial accidents and sporting injuries also keep the surgeons busy.

There are many other surgical procedures: clearing blocked

salivary ducts, treating the sinuses, removing foreign bodies which have become buried in the mouth and jaws, etc. The postgraduate training of the oral and maxillofacial surgeon is necessarily lengthy, wide-ranging, and continuous.

Fluoridation

Fluoridation of public water supplies is the adjustment of the natural fluoride level of the water upwards or downwards to the optimum level needed to minimise tooth decay in a population and maximise bone strength.

The discovery in the United States of America in the early part of the century that minute traces of the element fluorine in the form of fluoride ion drastically reduced dental decay in a population turned out to be probably one of the most significant discoveries in the field of public preventive medicine ever made. Until that time, dental decay was all but universal in its incidence, and devastating in its destruction of an important part of the body. With the realisation that a simple adjustment of fluoride level to match the level in naturally occurring waters which produced decay-resistant teeth, the way was open to bring under control one of the most widespread of the incurable diseases.

In Australia, the first community to apply the new-found method was Beaconsfield in Tasmania, which fluoridated its water supply in 1953. From that time, most of the nation (except Queensland) has followed suit. All capital cities (except Brisbane) have fluoridated water supplies, as have most provincial centres. The consequent reduction in tooth decay has been dramatic. It has not been eliminated, but so reduced that control of the disease appears possible.

In latter years, further assistance has been available by the almost universal incorporation of fluoride into toothpastes, conferring further benefits on those who use such pastes, and assuming particular importance in areas such as Queensland and the rural areas denied water fluoridation. Obviously the results in these cases are inferior to those achieved using the more natural method, but they are still significant. Further supplementation by the ingestion of fluoride tablets or drops in non-fluoridated areas is beneficial, and should be undertaken under professional guidance.

Preventive dentistry

Many dental disorders are incurable but preventable:
- Dental caries (tooth decay) can be reversed with the use of fluoride in its very early stages before it has become destructive, but later the only recourse is to cut away the diseased section of tooth and replace it with artificial substitutes of one kind or another.
- Periodontal disease in some of its manifestations can be

reversed in its early stages, but advanced bone loss around teeth cannot be recovered.

- Teeth injured by trauma either by accident or on the sporting field are seldom totally restorable, but can be repaired by the usual methods.

- Oral cancers and benign growths, if left unattended, may produce most serious results, but if treated early may be completely cured.

Preventive dental programs are carried out at community level, dental practice level, and at personal level. Community preventive practice consists of programs on fluoridation, education at school and adult level, dental health week presentations, displays at functions such as agricultural shows, community dental surveys, media announcements, and contributions on dental subjects and involvement in general preventive health measures through the National Health and Medical Research Council or other bodies.

Dentists in practice provide preventive services to their patients in the form of topical fluoride application on a regular basis, scaling and polishing teeth to prevent plaque and calculus deposition (the forerunner of dental diseases), regular oral examination to detect dental disorders and oral cancers, the application of sealants to fissures on tooth surfaces susceptible to decay, interceptive orthodontics to prevent malocclusion, the provision of custom-made mouthguards (the only really satisfactory method of decreasing the risk of tooth fracture among participants in contact sports such as hockey, football and boxing), and instruction in correct diet and oral hygiene methods.

Personal preventive methods involve meticulous cleaning techniques, a non-injurious diet (eliminating sugar and other harmful substances), sensible precautions to prevent trauma, and regular dental visits to spot deficiencies and remove accumulated soft and hard deposits and stains on the teeth.

Were a preventive program to be fully and properly applied, dental disorders would be all but eliminated.

Dental radiography

One only has to view a skull to realise how much of the teeth and jaws is hidden from view. What shows inside the mouth is only the tip of the iceberg. The magic of X-rays is able to unlock the hidden area and show clearly what lies out of normal sight. It is little wonder that dentistry was one of the earliest users of X-rays and still finds them indispensable for accurate diagnosis of dental conditions.

Specially designed dental X-ray machines are much smaller and less powerful than medical X-ray machines, as they deal with a smaller and more confined portion of the body. The modern machines with their heavy shielding and highly accurate exposure control mechanisms, coupled with the new fast photographic films used, ensure the lowest possible dose of radiation. Generally speaking, the dangers of radiation from dental X-rays are quite negligible. This view needs to be modified if, for example, other sources of radiation have been absorbed as well, or during pregnancy when exposure to radiation is inappropriate.

Most dental X-rays are taken with a small film inside the mouth, and show either views of individual teeth (periapical X-rays), or views of the crowns of all the back teeth both upper and lower (bite-wing X-rays). Larger X-ray films can be placed outside the mouth. One such picture is a side view of the whole of the head used at times by orthodontists to predict bone growth in the face. Another external type of X-ray uses a machine which rotates around the head and has the effect of stretching out the jaws and teeth in a straight line on a long oblong film.

X-rays are superb for searching out hidden decay leading to tooth loss, discovering buried teeth and old roots, finding bone fractures, looking for bone cancers and other conditions such as cysts of the jaws, and checking on bone loss around otherwise healthy teeth.

There is no facet of dentistry that does not use X-rays at some stage to assist in diagnosis and treatment. Modern preventive and constructive dentistry is dependent on the skilful interpretation of X-ray pictures. A further use is in the identification of dead bodies when other methods fail.

See also X-RAYS, Section 4.

Dentistry for the handicapped

Dentistry for the handicapped presents special problems because nearly all dental procedures involve dental equipment which is not readily mobile. This means that the handicapped person must be brought to the dental surgery and be able to adapt to equipment designed to cope with those who are not handicapped. Some dental practices are better equipped than others to handle the handicapped. For example, those on the ground floor with wide corridors are better able to cope with wheelchairs. Some patients may need to come in an ambulance. It is not always convenient to have supervisory staff from an institution available to accompany a patient.

There has been some improvement in mobile equipment which allows visits to the housebound and those in similar situations in institutions. There is some move to have dental surgeries included in the designs of some nursing homes, and this trend should be encouraged. With an ageing population the problems are likely to increase somewhat.

Forensic dentistry

Because of the indestructible nature of teeth, they form an important part of forensic science. Positive identification of bodies is often possible through dental records and X-rays of the teeth and jaws. There have been cases in Australia where fire after aircraft crashes has destroyed bodies beyond recognition, even as bodies, except for the teeth and jaws.

There have also been some cases in which bite marks have been matched with those of a suspect.

Oral medicine

Dentists are trained to recognise and treat all oral diseases, including many of the infectious diseases as well as tumours and inflammations. Any mouth disorder should be seen in the first instance by a dentist, who will readily refer the patient to an appropriate expert if the problem is outside the dental sphere.

DIET

A healthy diet

A healthy diet contains adequate quantities of six groups of substances: proteins, carbohydrates, fats, fibre, vitamins, and minerals. The first three contain kilojoules (i.e. produce energy) and the second three do not. It is also essential to have a supply of safe drinking water. You can live for weeks without food, but only a few days without water.

PROTEINS

Proteins are the chemical compounds that make up the body's structure. If you do not have a daily supply of proteins, the body cannot grow properly, nor can it repair damaged or worn-out tissues. Animal products (meat, fish, eggs, cheese) provide much protein in a form able to be used by your body. Vegetable proteins exist in peas, beans and other legumes, as well as in grains (and thus bread). If you eat more protein than your body needs it will provide extra energy, but if you do not use it up it will be converted to fat and stored.

CARBOHYDRATES

Carbohydrates are chemicals that contain carbon, hydrogen and oxygen. They are the body's preferred source of energy as the process of digestion converts them into forms of sugar that the body can use easily. Sugar, bread, pasta, potatoes and cereals are all foods rich in carbohydrates. Sugar, however, is not the best means of getting adequate carbohydrate as it has no minerals, vitamins or fibre, and is not always metabolised properly because it enters the bloodstream so quickly. It also gives rise to tooth decay.

Fats

The main function of fats is to provide energy, although minute amounts are used in growth and repair. Fats enable energy to be stored and play a role in insulation. Most fats come from animal products, although some are found in plant foods such as olives, peanuts and avocados. Excess fat is laid down in the body as fatty tissue and is the main cause of obesity.

Depending on chemical composition, fats are either saturated or unsaturated. Saturated fats are more likely to increase the amount of cholesterol in the body and therefore increase the risk of heart disease. Broadly speaking, animal fats, especially those in milk, butter, cheese and meat are highly saturated, and the fat in fish, chicken, turkey and vegetable products is unsaturated. Most of the fat in chicken and turkey is in the skin, which can be removed.

Fibre

Fibre is that part of the vegetable, cereal or fruit which is left over in the intestine, cannot be digested, and is passed out with the faeces.

Fibre food does not cause indigestion because it cannot be digested, and it does not always look stringy. For example, peas and beans are high in fibre, cucumber is very low, and celery is in between.

The average Australian eats 20 g of fibre a day, and should probably eat twice this much.

A high-fibre diet is one way of overcoming obesity, since it makes the stomach feel full so you feel less hungry, but there are fewer kilojoules to be absorbed from the food into your body. Furthermore, the fibre residue in the bowel increases the size and wetness of the stools, and so eases defecation and prevents constipation. The down side may be an increase in flatulence.

Diseases that benefit from a high-fibre diet include diverticulitis (small outpocketings of the large bowel), diabetes, gallstones, arteriosclerosis (hardening of the arteries), cancer of the bowel, varicose veins, piles and hernias. The incidence of these diseases is significantly less in populations who eat high-fibre diets, e.g. the natives of Africa. Moderation, however, is important. A diet made up entirely of fibre-based foods would lack essential nutrients, fats, carbohydrates and vitamins. It is important to tailor your intake of fibre to your specific needs.

If you are overweight, constipated or suffer from specific diseases, you will benefit from a high-fibre diet. The rest of us should balance our diets with an emphasis towards foods that are above average in fibre content.

TABLE 7.1:
FOODS HIGH IN FIBRE

Food	Grams of fibre per 100 g food
Pure bran	44.0
'All-bran'	26.7
Dried apricots	24.0
Prunes	16.1
Passionfruit	15.9
Puffed wheat	15.4
Soya low fat flour	14.3
'Weet-bix'	12.7
Shredded wheat	12.3
Potato crisps	11.9
Rye crispbread	11.3
Rock melon	11.0
High-fibre brown bread	9.5
Wholemeal flour	9.5
Parsley	9.1
Brazil nuts	9.0
Currants	8.7
Dried dates	8.7
Wholemeal bread	8.5
Peanuts	8.1
High-fibre white bread	7.6
Peanut butter	7.6
Baked beans	7.3
Sultanas	7.0
Spinach	6.3
Peas	6.3
'Special K'	5.5
Brown bread	5.1
Wheat biscuits	4.8
Fried onions	4.5
Olives	4.4
Broccoli tops	4.1
Mushrooms	4.0
White SR flour	3.7
Apple peel	3.7
Rich fruit cake	3.5
Plain white flour	3.4
Bananas	3.4
Broad beans	3.4
Chips (French fries)	3.2
French beans	3.2
Carrots	3.1
Spring onions	3.1
Beansprouts	3.0
Brussels sprouts	2.9
White bread	2.7
Baked potatoes	2.5
Rice	2.4
Sweet iced cakes	2.4
Apple pulp	1.4

SECTION 7: MISCELLANEOUS

VITAMINS AND MINERALS

Vitamins are chemicals of various kinds which are required (usually in tiny amounts) if the body is to function properly. All vitamins have been given letter codes, sometimes with an additional number to differentiate vitamins within a group, for example, vitamin A, vitamin B1, B12, vitamin C, D, E, K and so on. See also VITAMINS, Section 6.

Vitamins are contained in food, and in general most people who eat a balanced diet will get enough vitamins to service their body's basic needs. The virtue of added vitamins in the form of supplements has generated long, vigorous and as yet largely unresolved debate.

The **minerals** we need to remain healthy are mostly metals and salts, such as iron, phosphorus, calcium and sodium chloride (table salt). Like vitamins, minerals are needed in minute quantities and will be obtained from a reasonably well-balanced diet. In the case of salt, it has been found in recent times that too much can be bad for you and that adding salt to meals is not only unnecessary but may have a harmful effect, especially if you have high blood pressure.

Iron is a particularly essential mineral, since it is the core element in the manufacture of haemoglobin, the compound found in red blood cells which transports the oxygen from the lungs to the organs. If the iron levels are low, haemoglobin levels drop and the body becomes starved of oxygen, making you feel tired and weak. Iron is found naturally in many foods, including meat, poultry, fish, eggs, cereals and vegetables. Red meat, oysters, liver, beans, nuts and wheat contain particularly high levels of iron.

WHAT TO EAT

In broad terms, a healthy diet is a varied one. It is not possible to put forward a diet that is perfect for everyone, since people's needs vary according to the age and stage of life they are at, how active they are, and on many other factors. However, any diet should include, daily:
- protein from foods such as fish or other seafood, poultry, very lean meat, or eggs, dried peas, beans or lentils;
- some salad and three or four vegetables, including at least one serve of a green leafy variety and one yellow variety such as carrots;
- two or three pieces of fruit;
- cereal or grains, such as rice;
- bread (some dietitians recommend that this should be wholemeal or wholegrain but others are content with white bread);

- some dairy products, preferably low-fat for most adults (women in particular should ensure that they get an adequate supply of milk, yogurt or cheese to prevent the loss of calcium in their bones after menopause which causes osteoporosis).

CAFFEINE

As most users are aware, the caffeine in coffee, tea, cocoa and cola drinks acts as a stimulant. What most users do not know is that, depending on the strength, there is usually more caffeine in tea than in coffee.

Caffeine acts on the body to increase alertness, increase the rate at which the body metabolises (burns) food, and increase urine production. In large doses, it may produce headache, irritability, insomnia, psychiatric conditions and stomach upsets, and it can aggravate diabetes, heart disease, depression and anxiety disorders. If taken before going to bed, a short, less restful sleep can be expected. People who have any of the foregoing conditions should limit their caffeine intake.

There are some connections between moderate to large doses of caffeine and problems such as miscarriage, premature birth and stillbirth in pregnancy. Pregnant women should therefore limit themselves to two to four cups of tea, coffee or cola a day.

KILOJOULES

Kilojoules are simply the way the energy supplied by food is measured. One kilojoule is one unit of energy. Energy in food used to be measured in calories but the metric kilojoule is now internationally accepted. One calorie equals 4.2 kilojoules (kJ).

Different foods provide different amounts of energy and so have different kilojoule values. Fat generally supplies more than twice the number of kilojoules per gram that is provided by carbohydrates and proteins, while water and fibre have no kilojoules at all. There are innumerable charts showing the approximate kilojoule counts of various foods, and an estimate of how many kilojoules are expended in such activities as walking, jogging, doing housework and so forth. Kilojoule counting can help you to lose weight.

Every kilogram your body weighs equals 35 000 kilojoules. If you eat 2500 kJ less than you expend every day for a week, you will lose about 500 g.

Section 7: Miscellaneous

TABLE 7.2:
FOOD GUIDANCE CHART

Category A represents foods of low energy value. Category B contains foods of intermediate energy value. Foods in category C are of high energy value and/or low in nutrition and should be avoided if you need to lose weight.

Category	Food	Average helping	Kilojoules
Sweet Foods			
A	Artificial sweetener, liquid	Equivalent to 2 tsp	0
	Jelly, low-calorie	100 g	40
B	Artificial sweetener, granulated	Equivalent to 2 tsp	17
	Biscuit, plain	one	150
C	Biscuit, chocolate-coated/fancy	one	400
	Cake, fruit	80 g slice	1200
	Cake, plain	80 g slice	900
	Cake, rich/iced/cream-filled	80 g slice	1200
	Chocolate, any variety	30 g	680
	Custard/Junket	100 g	415
	Doughnut, plain	one	1140
	Health-food bar	one	745
	Honey/Golden syrup	tbsp	350
	Ice-cream, vanilla	scoop	475
	Jam/Marmalade	tbsp	310
	Jelly	100 g	400
	Sugar, any variety	2 tsp	165
Starch Foods			
B	Biscuits, cracker/crispbread/savoury	2–3	290
	Bread, any variety	1 slice	290
	Breakfast cereal, unsweetened (without milk)	cup	455
	Pasta, uncooked	2 tbsp	455
	Rice, uncooked	2 tbsp	455
	Rolled oats/Semolina, uncooked	30 g	455
C	Breakfast cereal, sweetened	cup	500
	Flour, any variety	1 tbsp	150
	Muesli, regular	2 tbsp	475
	Muesli, toasted	2 tbsp	580
Protein Foods			
B	Bacon, lean, grilled	40 g	500
	Beef, lean, raw	150 g	1000
	Cheese, cottage	60 g	330
	Cheese, hard (e.g. Cheddar)	30 g	500
	Cheese, soft (e.g. Edam)	30 g	400
	Chicken, raw	150 g	900
	Devon/Salami	30 g	400
	Egg, boiled/poached	one	300
	Fish, any variety, raw	150 g	650
	Fish fingers, grilled	2	455
	Fish, smoked	60 g	500
	Fish: Salmon/Tuna, tinned, drained	120 g	1000
	Frankfurters, boiled	2	1160
	Ham, lean, cooked	60 g	980
	Lamb/Mutton, lean, raw	150 g	900
	Liver/Kidney/Heart/Brains, raw	100 g	600
	Oysters, natural	dozen	340
	Oysters/Mussels, smoked	60 g	500
	Pork, lean, raw	150 g	1100
	Seafood: Crab/Lobster/Prawns, no shell	120 g	480
	Veal, lean, raw	150 g	990
C	Cheese, cream	30 g	435
	Duck, raw	150 g	2070

TABLE 7.2:
FOOD GUIDANCE CHART (continued)

Category A represents foods of low energy value. Category B contains foods of intermediate energy value. Foods in category C are of high energy value and/or low in nutrition and should be avoided if you need to lose weight.

Category	Food	Average helping	Kilojoules
	Fish: Herring/Sardine, tinned, drained	60 g	600
	Sausage, any variety, raw	100 g	1300
	Tongue/Sweetbreads, raw	100 g	850
	Turkey, raw	150 g	1600
FRUITS			
A	Lemon	15 g	20
	Lime	50 g	65
	Rockmelon	110 g	110
	Watermelon	110 g	110
B	Apple	100 g	220
	Apricot	100 g	190
	Banana	100 g	350
	Blackberries/Blackcurrants	100 g	240
	Cherries	100 g	260
	Custard apple	75 g	300
	Gooseberries	60 g	100
	Grapefruit	120 g	180
	Grapes	100 g	270
	Guava	90 g	240
	Honeydew melon	90 g	130
	Loganberries	100 g	250
	Mandarin	100 g	190
	Mango	100 g	280
	Nectarine	100 g	260
	Orange	130 g	220
	Passionfruit	30 g	60
	Pawpaw	100 g	120
	Peaches	110 g	190
	Pears	150 g	350
	Pineapple	80 g	130
	Plums	100 g	240
	Prunes	25 g	265
	Raspberries/Redcurrants	100 g	230
	Strawberries	100 g	160
	Tinned fruit, unsweetened	120 g	130
C	Dried fruit	20 g	290
	Tinned fruit	120	330
FATS AND OILS			
A	Coleslaw dressing, low-calorie	tbsp	45
	Salad dressing, low-calorie	tbsp	20
B	Butter/Margarine	tbsp	570
C	Cream, fresh	tbsp	310
	Mayonnaise	tbsp	570
	Oil, any variety	tbsp	700
	Salad dressing	tbsp	310
VEGETABLES			
A	Asparagus	6 spears	90
	Beans, green, raw	60 g	50
	Bean sprouts, raw	cup	120
	Beetroot, tinned	30 g	40
	Broccoli, boiled	60 g	65
	Brussels sprouts, boiled	60 g	95
	Cabbage, raw	60 g	60
	Carrot, raw	60 g	90

715

Section 7: Miscellaneous

TABLE 7.2:
FOOD GUIDANCE CHART (*continued*)

Category A represents foods of low energy value. Category B contains foods of intermediate energy value. Foods in category C are of high energy value and/or low in nutrition and should be avoided if you need to lose weight.

Category	Food	Average helping	Kilojoules
	Capsicum, raw	30 g	30
	Choko, boiled	60 g	60
	Cauliflower, boiled	60	60
	Celery, raw	30 g	30
	Cucumber, raw	60 g	40
	Eggplant, raw	60 g	62
	Leek, raw	60 g	95
	Lettuce, raw	30 g	10
	Mushrooms, raw	60 g	50
	Onion, raw	60 g	90
	Pumpkin, boiled	60 g	100
	Radish, raw	20 g	20
	Spinach/Silver beet, boiled	60 g	70
	Tomato, fresh/tinned	110 g	100
	Turnips, boiled	50 g	60
	Zucchini, boiled	70 g	50
B	Artichoke, tinned	200 g	365
	Beans, tinned/baked	60 g	280
	Corn, tinned	70 g	245
	Frozen mixed vegetables	90 g	175
	Olives	20 g	100
	Parsnip, boiled	60 g	165
	Potato, boiled	90 g	300
	Peas, boiled	60 g	150
	Peas, split, boiled	60 g	290
C	Avocado	100 g	660
	Potato, fried	90 g	990
	Sweet potato, boiled	90 g	430

DRINKS

Category	Food	Average helping	Kilojoules
A	Coffee/Tea, black	cup	0
	Cordial/Soft drink, low-calorie	200 mL	12
	Mineral water/Soda water	glass	0
	Tomato/Vegetable juice	120 mL	100
B	Coffee/Tea, white	cup	125
	Fruit juice, unsweetened	120 mL	250
	Milk, plain	200 mL	550
	Skim milk, plain	200 mL	290
C	Beer	middy	500
	Beer, low alcohol	middy	350
	Cider, alcoholic	200 mL	290
	Cider, sweet	200 mL	350
	Coffee/Tea, white with 2 sugars	cup	290
	Cordial/Soft drink	200 mL	380
	Hot chocolate	200 mL	670
	Milk, flavoured	300 mL	1000
	Spirits, brandy/gin/rum/whisky	30 mL	290
	Wine, dry	120 mL	360
	Wine, sweet	120 mL	400
	Wine, fortified	60 mL	330

MISCELLANEOUS

Category	Food	Average helping	Kilojoules
A	Fish paste	2 tsp	60
	Gelatine	7 g	100
	Soup, thin/clear	200 mL	110
	Soy sauce	tbsp	55
	Vegemite	tsp	40
	Vinegar	tbsp	0

TABLE 7.2:
FOOD GUIDANCE CHART (continued)

Category A represents foods of low energy value. Category B contains foods of intermediate energy value. Foods in category C are of high energy value and/or low in nutrition and should be avoided if you need to lose weight.

Category	Food	Average helping	Kilojoules
	Worcestershire sauce	tbsp	65
B	Peanut butter	tbsp	500
	Yoghurt, plain	200 g	650
	Yoghurt, skim milk, plain	200 g	440
	Yoghurt, skim milk, fruit-flavoured	200	680
C	Milk, condensed	tbsp	385
	Nuts, any variety	15 g	370
	Soup, thick/creamy	200 mL	500
	Tomato sauce	tbsp	90
	Yoghurt, fruit-flavoured	200 g	830
FAST FOODS			
C	Dim sim, fried	one	540
	Fish & chips	one serve	1660
	Hamburger	one	1370
	Meat pie	one	1560
	Pizza	215 g slice	1100
	Potato crisps	30	660
	Thick shake	cup	1140

Weight-reducing diets

Someone who is overweight is usually prescribed a low-energy diet. If the body has to draw on its reserves of stored fat for its energy needs, obviously the fat will be used up and weight will be lost. Many fad diets, however, eliminate carbohydrates which are essential for physical activity and the maintenance of a healthy body. This will certainly cause an initial weight loss, but mainly of the body's normal water content and muscle tissue rather than fat. Once the diet is discontinued (and it can't be maintained for more than a few weeks without giving rise to ill health), the lost weight rapidly returns.

A balanced diet containing all the requirements for a healthy body is a far more satisfactory way to lose weight and keep it off.

SUGGESTED DIET

- Lean meat, fish, egg or cheese (two servings per day);
- One small (boiled) potato;
- At least two servings of vegetables (steamed or boiled);
- Two to four pieces of fruit;
- Two to four slices of bread;
- 15 g of butter or margarine;
- 300 mL of milk (low-fat if preferred).

This will give you 5000–7500 kJ, depending on the size of the servings.

AVOID honey, chocolates, sugar or glucose, sweets, soft drinks, dried fruits, jellies, ice-cream, cakes, biscuits.

Section 7: Miscellaneous

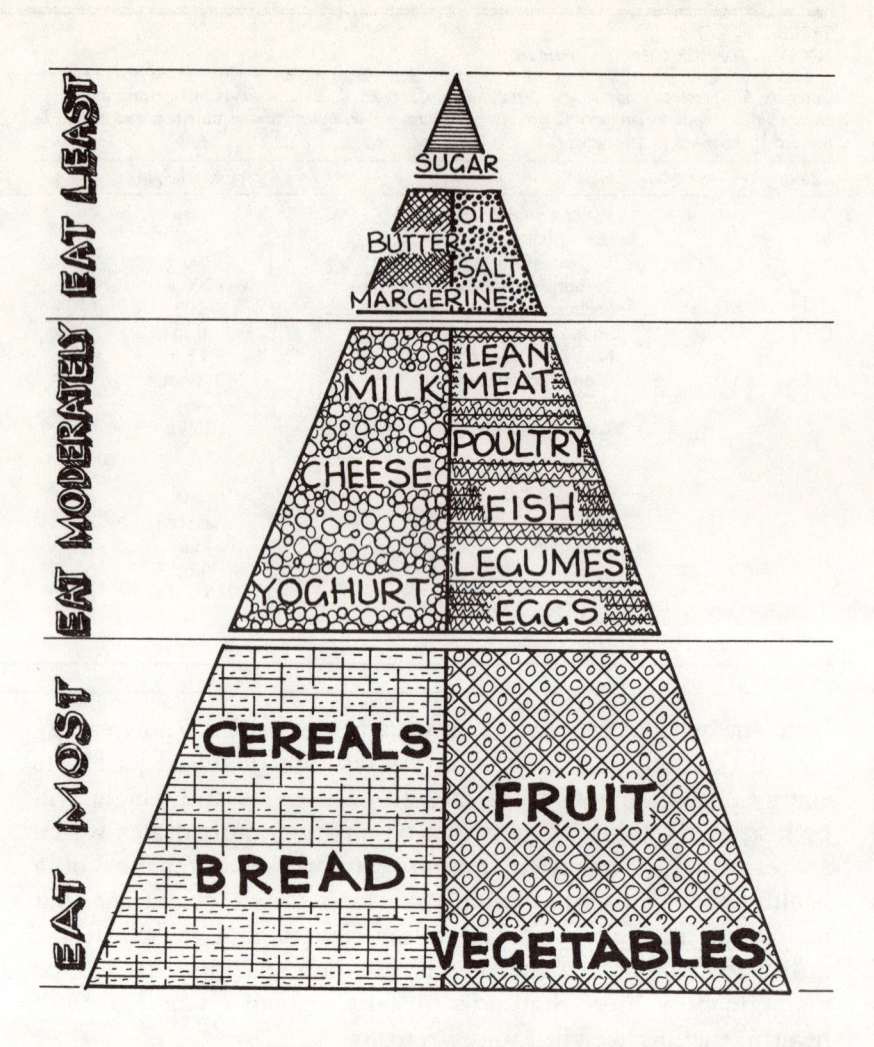

FIGURE 7.1: The healthy diet pyramid.

Vegetarian diets

There are far more vegetarians in the world than meat eaters, simply because vegetables, grains and the like are easier to keep without refrigeration and are usually more readily available. Australians, however, along with most of the developed Western world, for many generations have been enthusiastic consumers of meat. To a degree this is changing, for reasons including health, religion, environmental concerns and simple fashion.

There are three main types of vegetarian diet. The most common form is lacto-ovo-vegetarianism in which meat and fish are omitted from the diet, but eggs and dairy products are not. Pro-animal vegetarianism excludes meat while a vegan diet excludes all animal products, i.e. not only meat and fish but also dairy produce and eggs.

There is no reason why a vegetarian diet cannot be as healthy

TABLE 7.3:
ACCEPTABLE WEIGHT FOR HEIGHT FROM
THE AGE OF 18 ONWARDS

Height (cm)	Body Weight (Kg)
140	39–49
142	40–50
144	41–52
146	43–53
148	44–55
150	45–56
152	46–58
154	47–59
156	49–61
158	50–62
160	51–64
162	52–66
164	54–67
166	55–69
168	56–71
170	58–72
172	59–74
174	61–76
176	62–77
178	63–79
180	65–81
182	66–83
184	68–85
186	69–86
188	71–88
190	72–90
192	74–92
194	75–94
196	77–96
198	78–98
200	80–100

(from Ruth English, *Your Health and Your Figure. A Safe Guide to Weight Control*, AGPS 1988. Commonwealth of Australia Copyright reproduced by permission.)

as a diet containing meat, provided that, for example, the protein that non-vegetarians obtain from meat is obtained from some other source, such as nuts, cereals or pulses. Vegetarians also need to ensure they get adequate supplies of iron, zinc and calcium, which are found in good supply in meat and milk. Women in particular have double the iron needs of men and should take care to avoid iron deficiency. Women also seem to suffer more from loss of calcium. Generally an adequate supply of these minerals can be obtained from dairy products, but if these are not included in the diet, substitutes must be found. A vegan diet is likely to be deficient in vitamin B12, and supplements may need to be taken to avoid this.

Special diets for health disorders

There are various disorders which need special diets. The most common is probably diabetes (see Section 5), in which the level of glucose in the blood is too high due to lack of insulin. A diet for diabetics will control the intake of carbohydrate and also ensure that the time of consumption is such as to maximise the

Section 7: Miscellaneous

efficient use of the insulin when this is given by injection.

A high-protein diet containing large amounts of meat, fish and dairy products may be necessary in kidney diseases where protein is lost in the urine, after burns, and during recovery from illness that has caused the muscles to waste away.

Someone with a liver complaint such as hepatitis, or a gall bladder disease such as stones, may need to reduce their intake of fats. This will also apply to people who are suffering from narrowing of the arteries to the heart.

Mild attacks of diarrhoea can often be overcome by taking small amounts of food and fluids at frequent intervals rather than the usual three meals a day. The gastroenteritis diet plan can also be recommended.

TABLE 7.4:
GASTROENTERITIS DIET PLAN

Day 1   Clear fluids only
- (e.g. Gastrolyte, Lucozade, Repalyte, Staminade, clear soups, Bonox, very dilute flat lemonade, dilute cordial, frozen cordial, etc.).
- Do NOT drink plain water — it contains no nutrients.
- Isomil, ProSobee, Infasoy, etc., can be used as a milk substitute for infants. Breast milk is allowed for babies.

Day 2   Light diet
- Continue clear fluids and add bread, toast, cereals (with water or skim milk), dry biscuits.

Day 3   Add nutrition
- Boiled vegetables, high-fibre fruits, white meats (chicken breast, fish), cereals.

Day 4   Gradually increase food intake until it returns to normal.

AVOID all dairy products (milk, butter, cheese, ice-cream, yogurt), eggs, red meat, fatty and fried foods UNTIL COMPLETELY BETTER.

DOCTORS

The training of doctors

The medical course at the ten university medical schools in Australia lasts six years. The first three years are spent on biology and science subjects, and few patients are seen. The second three years are spent in hospitals, and patients are studied along with their diseases. Unlike students in many other courses, the medical students have no choice of subjects, but all must complete the same studies. This ensures an evenly high standard of graduates.

In the fourth, fifth and sixth years of the course, when the medical students spend most of their time at hospitals, they and the public meet each other. There is probably nothing more daunting to a patient than being faced by a wall of students around his bed, all anxious to examine the most private parts of his body! This experience can be equally unnerving for the students, because they are often unsure of what the patient, the accompanying doctor and the examiner expect. Medical students are very aware that their attentions may be unwanted by the patient, and this can make them even more nervous. It is hoped that everyone realises that cooperation can benefit both student and patient.

Once the students have completed six years of study and have passed all the exams, they graduate with the degrees of Bachelor of Medicine and Bachelor of Surgery, and are employed in our major public hospitals as interns. At the end of a year of long hours on duty, dramatic experiences and a great deal of practical learning, they are registered as fully fledged medical practitioners. The doctors must then embark on further hospital work and training before being able to enter private practice.

In past decades, many doctors left the hospitals after two or three years to enter general practice, but because of the vast increase in medical knowledge, and the great variety of cases they may see, most doctors who intend to enter general practice today complete a further three or four years training with the Family Medicine Programme of the Royal Australian College of General Practitioners, before they put up their shingle in your local shopping centre, 10 or 11 years after leaving school.

Those doctors who intend to enter specialist practice, have an even harder course to follow. They must first compete for one of the few training posts in the specialty they have chosen at one of the larger teaching hospitals. They then work as a registrar in that specialty for four or more years, passing very difficult exams at the beginning and end of this period, and attending lectures and courses during their very hectic working day. After obtaining their specialty fellowship, most specialists spend time gaining extra experience in hospitals overseas and interstate. This enables them to keep up with the latest techniques and ideas throughout the world so that they can apply them when they set up practice, 13 or more years after leaving school.

Once the doctors are established in private practice, the story does not end. Because the practice of medicine is changing at an ever increasing rate, they must keep up to date by reading journals, attending lectures, conferences and seminars, and listening to specially prepared tapes. This can take up a significant proportion of a doctor's spare time, particularly in general practice, when an extremely wide field of knowledge must be covered.

Qualifications

All medical practitioners are entitled to place letters after their names to indicate the qualifications they hold. This 'alphabet soup' after a doctor's name can give important information to

Section 7: Miscellaneous

patients about the doctor they are visiting, and his/her skills.

Sometimes an abbreviation for the city or university (e.g. Syd. for Sydney) follows the abbreviation for the qualification.

An explanation of the most commonly encountered qualification abbreviations follows.

TABLE 7.5:
MEDICAL DEGREES AND QUALIFICATIONS

Abbreviation	Qualification
BAppSc	Bachelor of Applied Science. An additional degree that may be taken during or after the medical course, on a specific area in medicine (e.g. biochemistry).
BCh	Bachelor of Surgery. Part of a basic medical degree, usually from a British University.
BChir	Bachelor of Surgery. Part of a basic medical degree.
BDS	Bachelor of Dental Surgery. The basic dental degree.
BDSc	Bachelor of Dental Science. An additional degree that may be taken during or after the dental course, on a specific area.
BHA	Bachelor of Health Administration.
BM	Bachelor of Medicine. Part of a basic medical degree.
BMedSc	Bachelor of Medical Science. An additional degree that may be taken during or after the medical course, on a specific area in medicine (e.g. biochemistry).
BOccThy	Bachelor of Occupational Therapy. The basic occupational therapy degree.
BPhty	Bachelor of Physiotherapy. The basic physiotherapy degree.
BS	Bachelor of Surgery. Part of a basic medical degree.
BSpThy	Bachelor of Speech Therapy. The basic speech therapy degree.
BVSc	Bachelor of Veterinary Science. The basic veterinary degree.
CFP	Certificate in Family Planning. Further study on contraceptive methods undertaken.
CHA	Certificate of Health Administration.
ChB	Bachelor of Surgery. Part of a basic medical degree, usually from a British University.
ChD	Doctor of Surgery. Higher degree in surgery from a British University.
ChM	Master of Surgery. Higher degree in surgery from a British University.
CPH	Certificate in Public Health.
DA	Diploma in Anaesthetics. Further study undertaken in Anaesthetics, but not a specialist anaesthetist.
DCH	Diploma in Child Health. Further study undertaken in child health, but not a specialist paediatrician.
DCP	Diploma in Clinical Pathology. Further study undertaken in pathology, but not a specialist pathologist.
DDSc	Doctor of Dental Science. Higher degree in dentistry.
DDU	Diploma of Diagnostic Ultrasound. Further study in the use of ultrasound equipment undertaken.
DFP	Diploma in Family Planning. Further study on contraceptive methods undertaken.
DipMedSurg	Diploma in Medical Surgery. From Papuan Medical College.
DM	Doctor of Medicine.
DO	Diploma in Ophthalmology. Further study into the diseases of the eye undertaken, but not a specialist ophthalmologist.
DObstRACOG	Diploma in Obstetrics from the Royal Australian College of Obstetricians and Gynaecologists. Further study into obstetrics undertaken, but not a specialist obstetrician.
DPH	Diploma in Public Health.
DS	Doctor of Surgery. Higher degree in Surgery.
DTH	Diploma in Tropical Health.
DTM	Diploma in Tropical Medicine.
FAAOO	Fellow of the American Academy of Ophthalmology and Otolaryngology. American specialist in eyes, ears and throat diseases.
FAAD	Fellow of the American Academy of Dermatology. American skin specialist.
FAAP	Fellow of the American Academy of Paediatrics. American children's diseases specialist.
FACA	Fellow of the American College of Anaesthetists. American specialist anaesthetist.
FACP	Fellow of the American College of Physicians. American specialist physician.
FACR	Fellow of the American College of Radiologists. American X-ray specialist.
FACS	Fellow of the American College of Surgeons. American specialist surgeon.
FAMAS	Fellow of the Australian Medical Acupuncture Society. Doctor who has undertaken further study in acupuncture.
FCAP	Fellow of the College of American Pathologists. American specialist pathologist.
FRACDS	Fellow of the Royal Australian College of Dental Surgeons.

TABLE 7.5:
MEDICAL DEGREES AND QUALIFICATIONS (continued)

FRACGP	Fellow of the Royal Australian College of General Practitioner. Doctor who has completed further course of study, and passed exams on general practice.
FRACOG	Fellow of the Royal Australian College of Obstetricians and Gynaecologists. Specialist in childbirth and women's diseases.
FRACP	Fellow of the Royal Australian College of Physicians. Specialist physician.
FRACR	Fellow of the Royal Australian College of Radiologists. Specialist in X-rays, etc.
FRACS	Fellow of the Royal Australian College of Surgeons. Specialist surgeon.
FRANZCP	Fellow of the Royal Australian and New Zealand College of Psychiatrists. Specialist psychiatrist.
FRCGP	Fellow of the Royal College of General Practitioner. English doctor who has completed further course of study, and passed exams on general practice.
FRCOG	Fellow of the Royal College of Obstetricians and Gynaecologists. English specialist in childbirth and women's diseases.
FRCP	Fellow of the Royal College of Physicians. English specialist physician.
FRCPath	Fellow of the Royal College of Pathologists. English specialist pathologist.
FRCPsych	Fellow of the Royal College of Psychiatrists. English specialist psychiatrist.
FRCS	Fellow of the Royal College of Surgeons. English specialist surgeon.
LM	Licentiate in Medicine. English basic medical qualification.
LMSSA	Licentiate in Medicine and Surgery, Society of Apothecaries. English basic medical qualification.
LRCP	Licentiate of the Royal College of Physicians. English basic medical qualification.
LRCPS	Licentiate of the Royal College of Physicians and Surgeons. English basic medical qualification.
MB	Bachelor of Medicine. Part of basic medical degree.
MCh	Master of Surgery. Higher qualification in surgery.
MD	Doctor of Medicine. Basic medical degree in North America and Europe. Higher qualification in Australia and Britain.
MS	Master of Surgery. Higher degree in surgery.
MSc	Master of Science. Higher degree in science.
PhD	Doctor of Philosophy. Doctorate degree in a special area of skill.

Choosing a doctor

There are times, often unexpected and unwanted, when your local general practitioner can become a very important and helpful person in your life. Choosing a good GP can therefore be a vital decision.

When moving into a new area, speak to neighbours and friends to see which doctor in the area they recommend. Do not rely entirely on their advice though, because doctors are human and personality clashes can occur. The GP that your neighbour can relate well to may not suit you at all. Once you have received these recommendations, visit the doctor for a routine matter so that you can assess her/him yourself. Can you communicate easily with him/her? Also check the surgery hours — do they suit you? What about after-hours cover — is it what you want? Are the surgery premises comfortable and relaxing?

Other factors you may wish to consider are the doctor's affiliations. Is he or she a member of the Australian Medical Association? Only about two out of three doctors belong to the AMA, but those who do agree to abide by a very strict ethical code, and the AMA may be able to help you if you have any problems with your doctor. The AMA cannot act in any way against doctors who are not members.

Is the GP a fellow or member of the Royal Australian College of

Section 7: Miscellaneous

General Practitioners? This academic college encourages excellence in general practice, and doctors who belong pledge to keep up to date with the latest advances in medicine. Those who are fellows of the college have undertaken further study in general practice, have passed a very strict set of exams, and have been in practice for a minimum of five years. Only 15% of Australia's GPs have this qualification, but the percentage will increase dramatically in the next few years with the introduction of incentives for further training in general practice. Look for the letters FRACGP after the doctor's name.

Once you have decided to use a particular doctor as your GP, let her/him know, so that appropriate files can be transferred from your old doctor and a good rapport can be established between you.

Getting the most from each visit to a doctor is also important. Any consultation will start with the doctor asking you in one way or another 'What is wrong, how can I help you?' Having a logical answer to this question, and being able to outline your problem concisely and simply helps both you and the doctor. Wisecracks such as 'You should be able to tell me that' or bland generalisations such as 'I'm not well' don't help anyone.

Most people have questions they wish to ask, but forget to ask all of them. Make up a list, and make sure that you have all your questions not only answered, but answered in a way that you understand. It is very easy for a doctor to use words or terms that you may not understand. If this happens, let him/her know.

If you don't get better with the initial treatment, it is far better to return to the first doctor than to start shopping around. Humans are not like machines, and they do not all react in the expected way. If problems arise, the original doctor will probably be in a better position to sort them out, rather than confusing yourself with a multitude of opinions and treatments from several doctors.

And finally, if you are not happy with a doctor, tell him/her so. Many a misunderstanding can be sorted out this way, and even if you do change doctors as a result, both you and the doctor may learn something to your mutual benefit if problems are brought out in the open.

Medicare

In February 1984, Australia was introduced to Medicare. Since then, Medicare has undergone some minor fine-tuning but has continued basically unchanged. It is the only form of medical insurance allowed in Australia. You can take out health insurance to cover hospital fees, dental fees, medical appliances, etc., but you cannot take out any other form of insurance to pay for doctors' fees.

A levy of $1.25 for every $100 of your taxable income is added to your tax bill every year to pay for Medicare. This fund pays for about a third of the costs incurred by Medicare. The balance is paid for out of the federal government's general revenue.

Under Medicare, each state is given a grant by the federal government to pay part of the cost of running its public hospital scheme. The state government and/or the public hospital patients pay the difference between the Medicare grant and the actual costs of running the hospital. Medicare pays nothing towards the cost of running private hospitals. If you want the convenience of care in a private hospital, it is necessary for you to take out additional hospital insurance or pay the costs yourself. A bed in a private hospital will cost between $200 and $350 per day, depending on the hospital and your illness. Other charges (such as theatre fees and dressings) are added to this account.

When you see a private general practitioner, specialist, radiologist or pathologist, a benefit can be claimed from Medicare. It is in this area that the greatest misconceptions arise. Doctors (like all other professionals and tradesmen) are entitled to set their own fees. These fees are usually within the limits set down by the Australian Medical Association. The federal government sets the refund a patient receives from Medicare for any particular service. These refunds are set without reference to the medical profession or any court of arbitration. There is thus a gap between the doctors fee and the Medicare refund that must be met by the patient. A refund may be claimed by mail or in person from Medicare offices after paying the doctor; or a 'pay doctor' cheque to pay Medicare's part of the fee may be obtained first, and forwarded with the patient's share of the fee to pay the doctor's account. Most doctors will direct-bill Medicare, or bill the patient at the lower refund level when they see pensioners or disadvantaged patients. Some doctors will direct-bill all patients.

Doctors' fees in Australia are very reasonable by world standards. A GP consultation in the United States will cost US$48 (A$68) and a private GP in England will charge £20 (A$44).

Australian Medical Association

The Australian Medical Association (AMA) evolved from the British Medical Association, and has been concerned with the health and rights of Australian patients for over a hundred years.

In each state, medical boards regulate the profession to ensure a uniform standard of patient care, and the AMA nominates delegates to many of these boards. AMA appointees sit on University Medical School boards to advise on the teaching of medical students, and has volunteer doctors participating in other citizen and government committees that protect the interests of a vast range of people and influence the general health of the community.

The AMA makes innumerable submissions to government, seeking to improve health care arrangements, the availability of medications, health insurance costs and the quality of hospital care. Policies on almost every aspect of medical practice and health care have been agreed upon by doctors in the AMA to serve as a guide for other doctors, corporations and government.

The AMA educates doctors through the *Medical Journal of Australia* and other postgraduate education programs, and undertakes public health education through the media on many topics. It encourages Australians to look after their own health and therefore save the cost of medications and consultations for diseases related to smoking, alcohol, obesity, traffic accidents, bicycle safety, drug abuse, etc.

Medical ethics

Inspire in me a love for my Art and for thy creatures. Let no thirst for profit or seeking for renown or admiration take away from my calling. Keep within me strength of body and soul, ever ready, with cheerfulness, to help and succour rich and poor, good and bad, enemy as well as friend. In the sufferer let me see only the human being.

The ethics of the medical profession have regulated doctor/patient relationships since the time of Hippocrates 2350 years ago. Today, the 1948 Declaration of Geneva is taken as the yardstick, but this is basically an updated version of the tried and true Hippocratic oath. The Australian Medical Association has expanded on these two oaths by compiling a code of ethics that covers, in detail, more areas of potential ethical conflict, and all the members of the AMA agree to abide by this strict code of conduct. The first item in the ethics of the AMA is the prayer of Maimonides that heads this article and was written in the twelfth century.

Unfortunately, most patients do not understand many of the intricacies of the medical code of ethics, and may become confused or annoyed at the way in which matters proceed as a result. The basis of the relationship between a doctor and his/her patients is that of absolute confidence and mutual respect. The patient expects the doctor not only to exercise professional skill, but also to observe secrecy with respect to the information acquired as a result of his/her examination and treatment of the patient. This means that a doctor has a strict obligation to refrain from disclosing to any person or organisation, without the consent of the patient (except where laws stipulate otherwise), any information which has been learnt in his/her consultation with the patient.

Ethics in the medical profession extend to the issuing of certificates, and under no circumstances may a doctor change the date, alter, or issue a certificate which is not true in every sense, as such certificates may be used to obtain unfair advantage for the patient, or disadvantage others.

Doctors must be in continual contact with their colleagues, and must exchange medical information freely in order to learn new techniques and better manage their patients. If a patient wishes to change doctors, he or she has a perfect right to do so. The correct procedure is for a patient to notify the present doctor (by mail if preferred) that he or she wishes to change to a new doctor. Relevant information can then be sent from the old doctor to the new one, so that there is no gap in care or confusion regarding the patient's case.

It is unethical for a doctor to hold himself/herself out to possess skills in a certain direction that he or she does not possess. For this reason, state medical boards regulate who can and cannot call themselves a specialist in certain areas of medicine that require higher levels of skill (e.g. surgery, obstetrics).

Doctors must not use the media or other methods to promote themselves as being better than other doctors in order to attract patients. As a result, most media doctors use a pseudonym to maintain their anonymity and therefore do not run foul of the ethical rules. If doctors were permitted to promote themselves in this way, the doctor most able to manipulate the media or to pay for the biggest advertisements would attract the most patients, and not the doctor best able to care for the individual.

Dichotomy is the splitting of medical fees between two doctors, and it is considered to be one of the worst possible breaches of medical ethics. An example of dichotomy would be the specialist who paid a GP to refer patients to him/her.

Any patient who is concerned about the ethics relevant to their particular circumstances should first discuss the matter with their own general practitioner, or they may be referred to a member of the ethics committee by the state AMA branch. Complaints about doctors can also be taken to your state Department of Health, and complaints relating to doctors in public hospitals can be taken to the Ombudsman.

GERMS

The human being can be infected with four totally different types of germs — bacteria, fungi, protozoa, and viruses. Viruses are by far the most common, followed by bacteria and fungi. The individual diseases caused by these germs are described in Section 5.

Bacteria

Tonsillitis, pneumonia, cystitis, school sores and conjunctivitis all have one thing in common. They may all be caused by bacteria. Bacteria are microscopic single-celled organisms that can penetrate into healthy tissues and start multiplying into vast numbers. When they do this they damage the tissue they infect, causing it to break down into pus. Because of the damage they cause, the involved area becomes red, swollen, hot and painful. The waste products of the damaged tissue and the bacteria spread into the bloodstream, and this stimulates the brain to raise the body temperature in order to fight off the infection. Thus a fever develops.

Millions of bacteria invade the body every day, but few cause problems because the body's defence mechanisms destroy most invading organisms. The white blood cells are the main line of defence against infection. They rapidly recognise unwanted bacteria and large numbers move to the area which has been invaded, to engulf the bacteria and destroy them. It is only when these defences are overwhelmed that a noticeable infection develops.

Hundreds of bacteria are known to microbiologists (the doctors and scientists who study them), but only a few dozen cause significant infection in the human race. All these bacteria have specific names and can be identified under a microscope by experts who can tell them apart as easily as most of us can identify different breeds of dogs.

When an infection occurs, the victim usually consults a doctor because of the symptoms. If the infection is bacterial, the appropriate antibiotics can be given to destroy the invading bacteria. Because different types of bacteria favour different parts of the body and lead to different symptoms, a doctor can make an educated guess about the antibiotic to use. When there is any doubt, a sample or swab is sent to a laboratory for expert analysis so that the precise organism can be identified, together with the appropriate antibiotic to kill it.

Many bacteria, particularly those in the gut, are beneficial to the normal functioning of the body. They can aid digestion and prevent infection with funguses (such as thrush) and sometimes viruses. Antibiotics can kill these good bacteria too, and common side effects of the use of antibiotics are diarrhoea and fungal infections of the mouth or vagina.

Viruses (see separate entry) are a totally different type of organism from bacteria. They are less than one thousandth the size of the average bacterium and antibiotics have no effect on them. Viral diseases, such as colds, flu, measles and hepatitis cannot be treated effectively.

The sooner any infection can be treated, the faster the recovery.

If you think you might have an infection, an early visit to the doctor is advisable.

Fungi

Mushrooms, the green slime that forms on stagnant pools, and tinea are all related. They are fungi. Fungi are members of the plant kingdom, and are one of the types of microscopic life that can infect human beings in many diverse ways.

The most common site of infection is the skin, where they cause an infection that is commonly known as tinea. The fungus that causes tinea (see Section 5) can be found everywhere in the environment in the form of hardy spores. These are microscopic in size and may survive for decades before being picked up and starting an infection. Between the toes the fungus causes a type of tinea commonly known as athlete's foot. This is because athletes sweat and wear close fitting shoes that lead to the ideal warm, damp environment favoured by fungi. Similar infections in the groin cause a red, itchy, rapidly spreading rash. In both situations, creams or lotions are used to kill off the fungus before it spreads too widely. The rash is often slow to clear, because the treatments destroy the fungus, and do not necessarily heal the rash. The body heals the rash itself once the infection is controlled.

Unfortunately, fungal skin infections tend to recur because the fungus in its cyst form is resistant to many types of treatment. The active forms of the fungus are killed, but the spores may remain in the skin pores to reactivate once the treatment is ceased. To prevent this condition, keep the affected areas cool by wearing the correct clothing and foot wear, and dry carefully when wet.

Fungi are also responsible for many gut infections, particularly in the mouth and around the anus. It is a rare infant that escapes without an attack of oral thrush (see Section 5). The white plaques that form on the tongue and insides of the cheeks are familiar to most mothers, and this is due to one of a number of fungi. Paints or gels used in the mouth usually bring it rapidly under control.

Around the anus, the fungus can cause an extremely itchy rash, but in women it may spread forward from the anus to the vagina to cause the white discharge and intense itch of vaginal thrush or candidiasis (see Section 5). The movement from the anus to vagina is aided by nylon underwear, tight clothing (particularly jeans), wet bathers and sex.

Fungi live normally in the gut, and are in balance with the bacteria that are meant to be there to help with the digestion of our food. Antibiotics may kill off the good bacteria, allowing the fungal numbers to increase dramatically; or they may migrate to unwanted areas. In these circumstances, they can cause trouble.

The most serious diseases develop when fungal infections occur deep inside the body in organs such as the lungs, brain and sinuses. These diseases are very difficult to treat and it may take many months with potent anti-fungal drugs to bring them under control. Fortunately, this type of condition is relatively rare.

The most obvious connection between the various forms of fungi occurs with the common ringworm. This is not really a worm, but a fungal infection growing outward from a central spore, in exactly the same way that mushroom rings form in the garden in damp weather.

Protozoa

Protozoa are microscopic single-celled organisms like bacteria, but they are significantly larger and closer to what we normally think of as animal-like. Most protozoa are harmless but a few are parasites (i.e. live on a host body) and cause disease, usually of a singularly unpleasant kind. They are found all over the world in the soil and in almost any body of water from moist grass to mud puddles to the sea.

There are various kinds of protozoa, depending on how they travel, either propelling themselves by one means or another, or in the case of the type that causes malaria, having no in-built means of propulsion but relying on a type of mosquito for transport. African sleeping sickness (affecting the nervous system) is caused by a species of protozoa and is transmitted by the tsetse fly, although the organism also has the ability to propel itself with a long whip-like tail.

Other diseases caused by protozoa are various gastrointestinal disorders and infections of the genitals such as vaginitis (inflammation and discharge from the vagina) or urethritis in men. A particularly unpleasant disease is called kala-azar which is transmitted by the bite of a sandfly, and leads to anaemia and an enlarged liver and spleen. Another form of the disease attacks the mucous membrane and skin of the nose and spreads to the lips and mouth, causing ulcers, and as it progresses the cartilage of the nose may be destroyed, resulting in severe facial damage.

Toxoplasmosis, which can be transmitted by cats and raw meat, and which can cause fatal or severe damage to an unborn child if a pregnant woman becomes infected, is also caused by a protozoan organism.

Another type of protozoa is the amoeba. This is a sort of irregularly shaped fluid blob enclosed in a membrane. There are several varieties of amoeba, one of which may live in the sockets of the teeth and give rise to gum disease, while others are a cause of brain disease. One variety is the cause of amoebic dysentery, a disorder characterised by severe diarrhoea, common in the tropics, and is frequently spread by drinking contaminated water, especially where human excrement is used as fertiliser. It can be an insidious disease in that it sometimes lives harmlessly in the intestines for many years and then, for no apparent reason, invades the intestinal wall and travels to the liver or other organs, where it forms an abscess.

Viruses

Let your imagination run wild! Imagine an entire world that is only the size of this full stop. A world that has millions of inhabitants, of a thousand or more different species. This is the world of the virus. It can be found anywhere in the environment. It could be in your body, or in a drop of sweat, a particle of dust, or the skin of your family dog.

If the viruses are in your body, they will be under constant attack by the body's defence system. Every minute, millions more viruses enter your body through your mouth or nose. As they enter, the defence system uses its special cells and protein particles (known as antibodies) to repel the attack. Sometimes the defences are overwhelmed for a short time by the rapidly multiplying viruses. When this happens, you may feel off-colour for a day or two. If the virus numbers manage to totally defeat the defenders, you will develop a full-blown viral infection. Viruses can cause diseases as diverse as measles, hepatitis, cold sores, chickenpox, glandular fever and the common cold.

Virus particles are so small that they cannot be seen by even the most powerful light microscope, and special electron microscopes have to be used. They are neither animal nor plant, but particles that are so basic that they are classified into a group of their own. They are not alive in any sense that we understand, but are overgrown molecules that are intent on reproducing themselves at the expense of any host that happens along. Because they are not truly alive, they cannot be killed, and so antibiotics that are effective against the much larger living cells known as bacteria have no effect on viruses. Other than for a limited number of viruses that cause genital herpes, shingles and cold sores, we have no form of cure for virus infections.

The common cold can be caused by any one of several hundred different viruses. They cause the lining of the nose, sinuses and throat to become red, sore and swollen; and phlegm and mucus are produced in great quantities to give you a stuffy head, sore throat and runny nose. The poisons created by the body destroying the viruses circulate around in the blood stream to cause the fever and muscular aches that we also associate with a cold. While you are suffering, the body is busy producing the appropriate antibodies to fight the infection. Once the number of antibodies produced is adequate to destroy most of the viruses, the symptoms of the disease disappear and you recover.

Doctors cannot cure the common cold or other viral infections, but they can help relieve the symptoms with medications to stop the runny nose, clear congestion, and ease the pains. It is also important for doctors to check that the infection has not worsened with a secondary bacterial infection developing in an already weakened body.

Doctors can vaccinate against some viral diseases, such as measles and influenza, to prevent you from catching them; but others such as the common cold cannot be prevented. The much touted vitamin C has not proved itself to be effective when subjected to carefully controlled clinical trials. Viral infections can best be avoided by a good, well-balanced diet, reasonable exercise, avoiding stress, protecting yourself from extremes of temperature, and avoiding those who already have the infection.

NATURAL THERAPIES

Natural therapy is a system of treating ill health and disease by using techniques and remedies which stimulate the body's innate ability to heal itself and without the use of pharmaceutical drugs or surgery. Many natural therapies have evolved from traditional medicine, i.e. indigenous systems of healing which are distinct from and often pre-date orthodox medicine. The natural therapies used in Australia today include some that have been borrowed from other cultures than our own, notably acupuncture, but also herbalism, which has an old European tradition as well as an ancient Chinese one.

Natural therapies are often called **alternative therapies**, especially by the medical profession, and are in general, with the common exception of acupuncture, not accepted by mainstream medical practitioners. Because this book is principally a medical guide, the natural therapies will not be covered in depth. Only those which either require registration or for which registration requirements are currently being sought will be briefly described.

The Australian Natural Therapists Association Ltd (ANTA) is an independent body which has defined the natural therapies as practised and taught in Australia, and also their interrelationships, in order to create a degree of order among the profusion of disciplines. According to ANTA, the natural therapies embrace the four principal disciplines of chiropractic, osteopathy, naturopathy and traditional Chinese medicine, and also include remedial therapies such as massage and exercise techniques. The disciplines include their own sets of sub-disciplines or modes of therapy.

Practitioners of chiropractic and ostopathy have to register with a board set up under existing legislation governing these disciplines in Australia in order to be able to practise. Corresponding legislation to regulate the practice of the other natural therapy disciplines has not yet been introduced but has been called for by ANTA, and the Australian Natural Therapists Accreditation Board (ANTAB) has been set up to set standards for natural therapies and to encourage practitioners who meet the standards to seek formal accreditation in anticipation of legislation.

Acupuncture

Acupuncture forms part of the natural therapy discipline of **traditional Chinese medicine** and is a system of healing in which the body's inherent defence, repair and maintenance systems are stimulated by means of the selective insertion of fine needles through the skin. The points for insertion are located along the meridians along which the energy (or chi), according to the ancient Chinese tradition, is perceived to flow through the body.

The art of acupuncture may be more than 4000 years old, but the oldest surviving description is the *Yellow Emperor's Classic of Internal Medicine* which was written in China about 100 BC. By the sixth century, the practice of acupuncture had been codified and standardised throughout China, and it remained one of the mainstays of Chinese medical practice until outlawed in 1929 by the nationalist government of Chiang Kai-shek. The practice of acupuncture continued in rural areas until the ban was lifted by Mao Tse-tung in 1949.

The first information in Europe about acupuncture was published by Dutch traders to Japan in the late eighteenth century. In 1821, the Englishman J.M. Churchill published *A Treatise on Acupuncturation* under the aegis of the Royal College of Surgeons and brought knowledge of the practice into the British area of influence.

In addition to the natural therapists who practise traditional Chinese medicine, many doctors in Australia now also use acupuncture. In China it is used to treat a very wide range of conditions. In the West it has come to be regarded as an effective adjunct in the treatment of chronic conditions such as asthma, sinus problems, arthritis, rheumatism, stress, migraine, and also of stomach complaints, non-specific muscle pains, insomnia, period pains, etc. Medical practitioners sometimes limit the use of acupuncture to the alleviation of pain (especially lower back pain, arthritis, headaches and facial pain). A series of treatment is usually required.

Traditional Chinese medicine has its own internal diagnostic system which arises out of the ancient philosophy and custom governing the discipline.

In addition to acupuncture, traditional Chinese medicine also uses **herbalism** (see NATUROPATHY below) and a combination of acupuncture and herbs in moxibustion or moxa treatment, in which acupuncture points on the body are stimulated by the heat from burning a stick of special herbs. The **remedial therapies** in this discipline include various massage techniques, acupressure, and shiatsu, and exercise and relaxation techniques such as tai chi.

There are currently colleges in Sydney, Adelaide, Brisbane and on the Gold Coast which offer courses in traditional Chinese medicine meeting the standards of education and training for accreditation by ANTAB.

Chiropractic and osteopathy

Chiropractic is a healing art designed to relieve human ailments by specific manipulation and adjustment of the spine. The technique and the fundamental theory that most human ailments result from a slight misalignment of the vertebrae, causing nerve interference, were developed by the American M.D. Palmer in 1895. He adjusted the spine of a man who had been deaf for many years, and the man regained his hearing.

Chiropractors believe that, because the nervous system (brain, spinal cord and nerves) controls all the other systems of the body, adjusting the spine can affect other more distant parts of the body. The adjustment of the spine is perceived as removing misalignments between the vertebrae called subluxations, or abnormal movements between vertebrae called fixations. When subluxations or fixations are removed, normal movement returns to the spinal joints, nerve and muscle irritations are eased and tension is relieved. It is claimed that subluxation in particular parts of the spine may induce disorders of other organs, such as the kidney, stomach, lungs and liver, and increase the body's likelihood of contracting disease.

Osteopathy is a system of manipulating the spine and other joints and their surrounding soft tissues to enhance nerve and blood supply activities and thereby improve back problems, other joint disorders and all body tissues.

Orthodox medicine looks upon manipulation as but one therapeutic action among a range of treatments available to patients with disorders of joints and muscles only. Manipulation is carried out by doctors and physiotherapists. Orthodox medicine does not accept that spinal adjustment can cure diseases within distant organs.

Chiropractors may be trained in one of two ways in Australia. Students may undertake a five-year course at the Phillip Institute of Technology in Melbourne, or obtain a Bachelor of Science degree, majoring in anatomy, at selected Australian universities, and follow it with a Graduate Diploma course at the Sydney College of Chiropractic. Many chiropractors in Australia have been trained in the United States. Osteopaths can be trained at the Philip Institute of Technology in Melbourne. Other osteopaths seeking registration by the various State Registration Boards of Chiropractic and Osteopathy qualify by sitting an examination set by the Boards or if they have recognised qualifications from overseas.

Naturopathy

Naturopathy is a natural therapy discipline which encompasses various modes or sub-disciplines, including nutrition, herbalism, homoeopathy, and remedial therapies such as massage and exercise. By the use of these, the naturopath aims to create the conditions within the body that are most conducive to healing.

The **nutrition** therapy consists of an assessment of the nutritional needs of the individual patient and any special requirements arising from the complaint for which help is sought. Advice is given (as by DIETITIANS, see Section 6) on how best to support the healing process by a sound diet, including adequate fluid intake, the avoidance of smoking and using other toxic or potentially toxic substances, etc. The advice may extend to the selective use of vitamins, minerals and other supplements, and in some cases to the use of fasting and hydrotherapy.

Herbalism is the use of plants and plant extracts (other than those used in pharmaceutical drugs, such as quinine, opium, digitalis, etc.) for the treatment of ailments. It is one of the forms of therapy used in naturopathy and also a sub-discipline within traditional Chinese medicine. In naturopathy it has developed mainly from a European tradition and is sometimes referred to as Western herbalism to distinguish it from Chinese herbalism. Herbalism as a form of traditional Aboriginal medicine in Australia has very limited application today.

Homoeopathy is a method of treating disease by the use of very small amounts of herbal, mineral or animal substances which in healthy individuals produce symptoms similar to those of the disease being treated. For example, someone who presented to a homoeopath with vomiting would be prescribed a very dilute mixture of a substance that was known to cause vomiting. This approach of treating like with like was introduced by a German doctor, Samuel Hahnemann (1755–1843), at the end of the eighteenth century. Some of the homoeopathic substances can be toxic when undiluted, but at the very high dilution of the therapeutically used dose the toxic properties are lost. The effectiveness of such preparations has not been supported by modern pharmacology. As a form of therapy used by medical practitioners, homoeopathy has not been as widespread in Australia as, for example, in Britain.

Western **remedial therapies** used by naturopaths include different forms of massage, exercise, postural and relaxation therapies (see REMEDIAL THERAPY).

Criticism of naturopaths is often aimed at their limited skills in diagnosing serious diseases and also at the **orthomolecular treatment** (i.e. the use of very large doses of vitamins and minerals) some of them recommend.

Colleges in Sydney, Melbourne, Adelaide, Perth, Brisbane and on the Gold Coast currently offer courses in naturopathy meeting the standards of education and training for accreditation by ANTAB.

IRIDOLOGY

Iridology is not a form of therapy but a diagnostic tool used by many naturopaths. It involves examining the condition of the iris (the coloured part) of both eyes of the patient. Photographs are often taken of the iris for later detailed examination.

Charts of the iris, divided into segments like a complicated clock face, are available, and were initially prepared by the American, Bernard Jensen. An abnormality, fleck or colour, or swirl of lines in an area of the iris can be interpreted from the chart to represent a problem in a particular part of the body.

Iridology is meant to be used in conjunction with other methods of diagnosis. There is no scientific evidence for the rationale behind iridology, but the diagnosis indicated can often be confirmed by other means once the problem area in the iris has been identified.

Remedial therapy

Remedial therapy is a generic term covering a number of massage, exercise and relaxation therapies. Remedial therapy does not involve the use of spinal manipulation or internal medicines.

Western remedial therapies include Swedish massage, deep tissue massage, sports massage, reflexology or zone therapy, the Alexander technique, relaxation therapy, and stress management therapy.

Oriental remedial therapies include Chinese massage, acupressure, shiatsu, and also yoga, tai chi, te kwan do, and transcendental meditation.

PATIENT ORGANISATIONS

There are many patient counselling, self help, health and welfare organisations for people with particular disabilities and their families. Your doctor or local medical centre can help you find the groups that may be relevant to you. The following list, which has been reproduced with the kind permission of IMS Publishing (Australia), represents a selection of the organisations contained in the *MIMS Services Directory 89/90*, published by IMS Publishing (Australia).

Because addresses and phone numbers are prone to change, it may be best to check the current phone book before contacting any of these. The phone book will also have the state and regional offices that there was not room for in this book.

Aboriginal Health Unit Department of Community Services and Health GPO Box 9848, CANBERRA ACT 2601 (062) 89 7875	Aboriginal health
Acoustic Neuroma Association of Australasia PO Box 259, BALWYN Vic 3103 (03) 846 1996	Acoustic neuroma
AIDS Policy and Information Section Department of Community Services and Health GPO Box 9848, CANBERRA ACT 2601 (062) 89 1555	Aids
The Albinism Fellowship and Support Group PO Box 717, MODBURY SA 5092 (08) 264 5743; (08) 265 3596	Albinism
Al-Anon Family Groups GPO Box 1002H, MELBOURNE Vic 3001 (03) 62 4933	Alcoholism
Alcoholics Anonymous General Service Office South Sydney Hospital Joynton Ave, ZETLAND NSW 2017 (02) 663 1206	
ADARDS 84 Eastern Road, SOUTH MELBOURNE Vic 3205 (03) 696 1696	Alzheimer's disease and related disorders
Anorexia Bulimia Nervosa Association — ABNA c/- Mental Health Resource Centre 35 Fullarton Rd, KENT TOWN SA 5067 (08) 42 6772	Anorexia nervosa and bulimia
Arthritis Foundation of Australia 4th Floor, Wingello House,	Arthritis/rheumatism

Section 7: Miscellaneous

	1–12 Angel Place, SYDNEY NSW 2000 (02) 221 2456
Asthma	The Asthma Foundation of NSW Wingello House 1–12 Angel Place, SYDNEY NSW 2000 (02) 235 1293; (02) 235 1202; (02) 235 1120 Asthma Foundation of Victoria 2 Highfield Grove, KEW Vic 3101 (03) 861 5666 The Asthma Foundation of Queensland 51 Ballow Street, FORTITUDE VALLEY Qld 4006 (07) 252 7677 Asthma Foundation of WA Suite 2, Heytesbury House 61 Heytesbury Rd, SUBIACO WA 6008 (09) 382 1666 The Asthma Foundation of SA 33 Pirie St, ADELAIDE SA 5000 (08) 51 4272 Asthma Foundation of Tasmania 82 Hampden Rd, Battery Point, HOBART Tas 7000 (002) 23 7725 Asthma Association ACT c/- Shout Office, Hughes Community Centre Wisdom St, HUGHES ACT 2605 (062) 81 2983 The Asthma Foundation of NT c/- Royal Darwin Hospital DARWIN NT 5790 (089) 20 7211
Autism	National Association for Autism (Australia) PO Box 339, EASTWOOD SA 5063
Blind/partially sighted	Australian National Council of and for the Blind PO Box 162, KEW Vic 3101 (03) 860 4444 National Federation of Blind Citizens of Australia 45 Wavereley Rd, EAST MALVERN Vic 3145 (03) 572 1044

Patient Organisations

Nursing Mothers Association of Australia 5 Glendale St, NUNAWADING Vic 3131 (03) 877 5011	Breastfeeding
Australian Cancer Society GPO Box 4708, SYDNEY NSW 2001 (02) 267 1944	Cancer
Camp Quality Camping Program for Children with Cancer (at no cost) 5 Taylor St, WEST PENNANT HILLS NSW 2120 (02) 872 5454	
Australian Cerebral Palsy Association PO Box 61, MOUNT LAWLEY WA 6050 (09) 443 0211	Cerebral palsy
Cleft Pals PO Box 475, LANE COVE NSW 2066 (02) 427 1097	Cleft palate and lip
Australian Council of Coeliac Societies PO Box 271, WAHROONGA NSW 2076 (02) 498 2593	Coeliac disease
Australian Crohn's and Colitis Association PO Box 201, MOOROOLBARK Vic 3138 (03) 726 9008	Crohn's disease and colitis
Australian Cystic Fibrosis Association's Federation PO Box 225, PADDINGTON Qld 4064 (07) 352 6322	Cystic fibrosis
Australian Deafness Council PO Box 60, CURTIN ACT 2605 (062) 82 4333	Deaf and hard of hearing
Diabetes Australia PO Box 944, Civic Square, CANBERRA ACT 2608 (062) 47 5655	Diabetes
Juvenile Diabetes Foundation Australia PO Box 1500, CHATSWOOD NSW 2067 (02) 412 4405	
ACROD (Australia's Council on Disability) PO Box 60, CURTIN ACT 2605 (062) 82 4333	Disabled/handicapped

Section 7: Miscellaneous

Australian Confederation of Sports for the Disabled
20a Ayr Avenue, TORRENS PARK SA 5062
(08) 272 4846

Australian Wheelchair Sports Federation
393 Burwood Rd, HAWTHORN Vic 3122
(03) 818 0297

Down's syndrome

Down's Syndrome Association of NSW
PO Box 2356, NORTH PARRAMATTA NSW 2151
(02) 683 4333; (02) 683 4533

Downs's Syndrome Association of Victoria
55 Victoria Parade, COLLINGWOOD Vic 3066
(03) 419 1653

Down's Syndrome Association of Queensland
GPO Box 1556, BRISBANE Qld 4001
(07) 275 1947

Down's Syndrome Association of WA
45 Adair Parade, COOLBINIA WA 6050

Down's Syndrome Association of SA
PO Box 65, BURNSIDE SA 5066
(08) 232 0293

Down's Syndrome Association of Tasmania
1 Power Rd, NEW TOWN Tas 7008

ACT Down's Syndrome Group
c/- ACT Council on Intellectual Disability
Shout Office, Community Centre
Wisdom St, HUGHES ACT 2605
(062) 81 2983

Down's Syndrome Association of Northern Territory
GPO Box 41545, CASUARINA NT 5792
(089) 27 9408

Drug abuse

Drug and Alcohol Foundation Australia
PO Box 269, WODEN ACT 2606
(062) 81 0686

National Campaign against Drug Abuse
Drugs of Dependence Branch
Department of Community Services and Health
PO Box 9848, CANBERRA CITY ACT 2601
(062) 89 1555

National Epilepsy Association of Australia PO Box 554, LILYDALE Vic 3140 (03) 735 0211	Epilepsy
Australian Red Cross Society 206 Clarendon St, EAST MELBOURNE Vic 3002 (03) 419 7533	First aid
St John Ambulance Association Cnr Canberra Avenue and Dominion Circuit FORREST ACT 2603 (062) 95 3777	
Haemophilia Foundation of Australia 1216 Toorak Rd, HARTWELL Vic 3125 (03) 29 2276	Haemophilia
Head Injury Council of Australia PO Box 304, PORT MELBOURNE Vic 3207 (03) 696 1388	Head injury/brain damage
National Heart Foundation PO Box 2, WODEN ACT 2606 (062) 82 2144	Heart disease
Australian Huntington's Disease Association c/- Lidcombe Hospital LIDCOMBE NSW 2141 (02) 646 8394	Huntington's disease
Infertility Federation of Australasia PO Box 426, WANNIASSA ACT 2903 (062) 91 6341	Infertility
AAMR (The National Association on Intellectual Disability) GPO Box 647, CANBERRA CITY ACT 2601 (062) 47 6022	Intellectual disability
Australian Kidney Foundation PO Box 62, GARRAN ACT 2605 (062) 82 2913	Kidney disease
Australian Federation of SPELD Associations (AUSPELD) PO Box 94, MOSMAN NSW 2088 (02) 969 7433	Learning difficulties
Lupus Association of NSW PO Box 271, CAMMERAY NSW 2062 (02) 92 7804	Lupus

Section 7: Miscellaneous

Victorian Lupus Association
PO Box 84F, MELBOURNE Vic 3001
(03) 560 8452

Lupus Group
c/- Queensland Arthritis Foundation
GPO Box 901, TOOWONG Qld 4066
(07) 371 9755

The Lupus Group of WA
17A Cambria St, KALLAROO WA 6025
(09) 401 5156; (09) 279 5387

South Australian Lupus/Scleroderma Group
c/- Arthritis Foundation of Australia
99 Anzac Highway, ASHFORD SA 5035
(08) 297 2488

Lupus Association of Tasmania
GPO Box 404, ROSNY PARK BELLERIVE Tas 7018

Mental health	Association of Relatives and Friends of the Mentally Ill PO Box 302, NORTH RYDE NSW 2113 (02) 887 5766 GROW — Australia's Community Mental Health Movement 209(a) Edgeware Rd, ENMORE NSW 2042 (02) 516 3733
Motor neurone disease	Amyotrophic Lateral Sclerosis (ALS) Society of Australia Suite 24, 2 Holden St, ASHFIELD NSW 2131 (02) 799 8519
Multiple birth	Australian Multiple Birth Association PO Box 105, COOGEE NSW 2034
Multiple sclerosis	National Multiple Sclerosis Society of Australia 34 Jackson St, TOORAK Vic 3142 (03) 249 7222
Muscular dystrophy	Muscular Dystrophy Association of NSW Box M10, SYDNEY MAIL EXCHANGE NSW 2012 (02) 698 9555 Muscular Dystrophy Association 208 Union Rd, ASCOT VALE Vic 3032 (03) 375 4560; (03) 370 0889

Muscular Dystrophy Association of Queensland
15 Sports Drive, UNDERWOOD Qld 4119
(07) 841 1098

Muscular Dystrophy Research Association of WA
Queen Elizabeth II Medical Centre
Verdun St, NEDLANDS WA 6009
(09) 382 2700

Muscular Dystrophy Association of SA
251 Morphett St, ADELAIDE SA 5000
(08) 212 6694

	Neurofibromatosis
Neurofibromatosis Association c/- 17 Kempe Parade, KINGS LANGLEY NSW 2147 (02) 624 7925	
Obsessive and/or Compulsive Neurosis Support Group (OCNSG) 33 Pirie St, ADELAIDE SA 5000 (08) 51 2796; (08) 231 1588; (08) 42 6772	Obsessive/compulsive disorder
Australian Quadriplegic Association 1 Jennifer St, LITTLE BAY NSW 2036 (02) 661 8855; (02) 661 8022	Paraplegia/quadriplegia
Parkinson's Syndrome Society PO Box 2408, NORTH PARRAMATTA NSW 2151 (02) 630 1192	Parkinson's disease

Parkinson's Disease Association of Victoria
583 Ferntree Gully Rd, GLEN WAVERLEY Vic 3150
(03) 562 0411

Parkinson's Syndrome Society of Queensland
PO Box 246, CARINA Qld 4152
(07) 349 6229

Parkinson's Association of Western Australia
5/154 Hampden Rd, NEDLANDS WA 6009
(09) 386 6485; (09) 330 1974; (09) 385 9835

Parkinson's Syndrome Society SA
37 Woodville Rd, WOODVILLE SA 5011
(08) 268 6222; (08) 274 1504

Parkinson's Association of Tasmania
2 Kallatie Rd, MONTAGU BAY Tas 7018
(002) 44 5192

Section 7: Miscellaneous

Prader-Willi syndrome	Prader-Willi Syndrome Association of Australia 14 Prospect Court, RINGWOOD Vic 3134 (03) 870 8428
Psoriasis	Psoriasis Association PO Box 387, SPRING HILL Qld 4004 (008) 77 7171
Scleroderma	Scleroderma Association of NSW PO Box 190, FRENCHS FOREST NSW 2086 (02) 929 7972 Scleroderma Foundation of Victoria World Trade Centre, Siddeley St, MELBOURNE Vic 3005 Scleroderma Association (Qld) c– 42 Chelmer St East, CHELMER Qld 4068 (07) 379 8570 Scleroderma Association (SA) 11 Tungara Ave, CROYDON PARK SA 5008 (08) 46 4081
Short stature	Little People's Association of Australia 7 Spurwood Rd, TURRAMURRA NSW 2074 (02) 44 4253
Spina bifida	Spina Bifida Association of NSW PO Box 15, CARLINGFORD NSW 2118 (02) 663 1311 Spina Bifida Association of Victoria 52 Thistlewaite St, SOUTH MELBOURNE Vic 3205 (03) 698 5222 Spina Bifida Association of Queensland 387 Old Cleveland Rd, COORPAROO Qld 4151 (07) 394 3822 Spina Bifida Association of WA PO Box 159, WEMBLEY WA 6014 (09) 387 3431 Spina Bifida Association of SA GPO Box 349, ADELAIDE SA 5001 (08) 267 2508

Spina Bifida Association of Tasmania
Box 31, Hampden House,
Hampden Rd, BATTERY POINT Tas 7000
(002) 23 4537

Stillbirth and Neonatal Death Support (SANDS) NSW PO Box 58, TERRY HILLS NSW 2084 (02) 450 1565	Stillbirth, neonatal death and miscarriage

Stillbirth and Neonatal Death Support (SANDS) Victoria
c/- Canterbury Family Centre
19 Canterbury Rd, CAMBERWELL Vic 3124
(03) 882 8338

Stillbirth and Neonatal Death Support (SANDS) Queensland
PO Box 708, SOUTH BRISBANE Qld 4101
(07) 207 1397; (07) 266 1788; (07) 848 6570

Stillbirth and Neonatal Death Support (SANDS) WA
c/- Agnes Walsh House, King Edward Memorial Hospital
Bagot Rd, SUBIACO WA 6008
(09) 447 9426; (09) 453 2310; (09) 342 8291

Stillbirth and Neonatal Death Support (SANDS) SA
Marion Community Centre
887 Marion Rd, MITCHELL PARK SA 5043
(08) 277 0304

Stillbirth and Neonatal Death Support (SANDS) Tasmania
PO Box 874, DEVONPORT Tas 7310
(004) 35 1263; (004) 27 2344; (004) 37 2620

Australian Speak Easy Association PO Box 113, MACLEAN NSW 2463 (066) 45 3022	Stuttering
Australian Tinnitus Association 288 Unwins Bridge Rd, SYDENHAM NSW 2044 (02) 516 3322	Tinnitus
Australasian Tuberous Sclerosis Society 17 Westmacott Parade, BULLI NSW 2516 (042) 67 3992	Tuberous sclerosis
Turner's Syndrome Association of NSW PO Box 112, FRENCHS FOREST NSW 2086 (02) 452 4196	Turner's syndrome

SECTION 7: MISCELLANEOUS

Ulcerative colitis

Australian Crohn's and Colitis Association
PO Box 201, MOOROOLBARK Vic 3138
(03) 726 9008

PREVENTIVE MEDICINE

Alcohol

Most societies, from the primitive to the highly developed, drink alcohol of one kind or another. It is a social lubricant which is almost invariably part of any gathering for purposes of relaxation, whether it be a native feast around a village fire, a business lunch, or a sophisticated cocktail party. Most people drink on such occasions to increase their feeling of conviviality and relaxation. If they feel they are losing their ability to control their actions, except on rare occasions, they will stop. People who do not stop and who are abnormally dependent on alcohol are alcoholics. Consistent overindulgence in alcohol has two deleterious effects — it damages and often destroys the social fabric of the alcoholic's life and usually that of their family, and it poisons the body's tissues and impairs their function.

There is no hard and fast definition of alcoholism. It can vary from a mild form, such as drinking socially whenever possible, to an advanced state where alcohol is necessary to start the day. Anyone who depends on alcohol even to a small extent should regard it as a problem. The regular need for a few more drinks than is wise can with astonishing ease develop into a full-blown problem of habitual drunkenness. In Australia, alcohol is second only to tobacco as a drug of addiction.

The reason why one person becomes an alcoholic and another does not has not yet been established, although there is some research indicating that a predisposition to alcoholism may be inherited. Apart from this, people seem to drink too much because they have problems which they find too great to cope with, so they seek solace and forgetfulness in drinking. Alcoholism is more common in men than in women, but women tolerate alcohol less well than men. Women's bodies contain less water and so their blood absorbs the same amount of alcohol more quickly.

A pregnant woman who is an alcoholic or heavy drinker subjects her baby to the risk of being physically or mentally retarded if she continues to drink during the pregnancy. The connection between an expectant mother's drinking and various abnormalities in newborn babies is well established and is called 'foetal alcohol syndrome'. The baby of an alcoholic mother may even suffer withdrawal symptoms when it is born and its supply of alcohol is cut off. Women who drink increase the risk of miscarriage, stillbirth, and having premature or low-birth-weight babies.

Alcoholism can be difficult to assess, both for the person concerned and for those around them. Generally speaking, the symptoms of an alcoholic are:
- heavy drinking, either at all times of the day, or in binges of several days at a time;
- blackouts or loss of memory (e.g. waking up in the morning and not being able to remember the night before);
- needing a drink to face the slightest difficulty;
- drinking alone;
- failure to fulfil family or work responsibilities because of drinking;
- unpleasant physical or mental reactions if drinking ceases for a period;
- irritability and/or aggression;
- secretiveness about drinking.

An alcoholic may display a red, blotchy face, the trembles, slurred speech and possibly a husky voice, although these are symptoms of other disorders as well. Alcoholics are also likely to make repeated assertions that they are giving up drinking, alternating with denials that they have a drinking problem.

The only way to stop being an alcoholic is to stop drinking, and the only person who can do this is the alcoholic themselves. No-one else can do it for them. However, help and support is available.

The first step in recovery from alcoholism is to recognise and admit that there is a problem. The next step is to see a doctor and possibly contact a voluntary association such as Alcoholics Anonymous (AA). Withdrawal from alcohol creates its own symptoms. There may, for example, be feelings of intense anxiety and panic, and the doctor will advise on the best course to follow. For alcoholics with a serious problem, a period in hospital to dry out is usually the first step. If necessary, sedatives and other drugs will be given under supervision to overcome the cravings and hallucinations that detoxification can bring on. The next step is usually counselling to help the alcoholic understand the problem and thus, hopefully, to control it. There is no cure as such for alcoholism, apart from the ability to refrain from drinking ever again.

Too much alcohol on a regular basis has terrible effects on the human body, especially on the liver, the brain and the nervous system. In its initial stages, over-heavy drinking leads to impaired judgment, blurred vision and speech, and a reduced ability to react quickly, making for example driving a car extremely hazardous. Later on there will be lapses of memory, and ultimately the brain may be unable to absorb anything new. The liver will be damaged irreparably, by cirrhosis (the build-up of scar tissue in place of injuredand dead cells). This in turn means that nutrients from food are not absorbed, so the alcoholic suffers from malnutrition. Hepatitis and cancer of the liver are also possible. The skin becomes warm and sweaty, the veins in the face become blotchy and purple and, in the later stages of liver failure the palms of the hands become permanently red. The lining of the stomach becomes chronically inflamed. Alcoholism tends to go hand in hand with an inattention to diet, and because alcohol itself contains only calories, ultimately an alcoholic becomes deficient in vitamins, especially vitamin B. This affects the muscles of the heart and the nerves of the lower legs and hands.

A person who wants to give up alcohol can — with the help of doctors, counsellors and ex-alcoholics. However, they really have to want to. Making the decision to give up may be impossible while the tensions causing the desire to drink remain. If this is the case, the only solution may be to reorganise family or working life.

Breast self-examination

Breast cancer is the most common form of cancer in women (one in every 15 women will be affected) and the best way of detecting it early, while it is still easily treatable, is for a woman to examine her own breasts regularly for lumps. All women of all ages should examine their breasts once a month, after their period if they are still menstruating (the breasts are less lumpy at this time).

If a lump is present, it is essential to see a doctor immediately. It is important to realise, however, that a lump does not necessarily signify cancer. There are many causes of lumps in the breast and indeed if a lump develops, especially in a young woman, the chances are that it is *NOT* cancer — about nine in ten lumps are benign. Nevertheless, because of that one in ten chance that the lump is malignant, it will be treated with suspicion until a precise diagnosis is made.

To examine your breasts, the first step is to look at them in a mirror. Stand in front of the mirror, first with your arms by your side and then with your arms raised above your head. Look at each breast to see if there is a lump, a depression, any swelling or dimpling, or a difference in texture. Get to know what your breasts look like, and be alert for any changes in appearance, particularly in the nipples.

Then lie down, and with one hand behind your head, examine the opposite breast with your free hand. This should be done by resting your hand flat on the chest below the breast and then

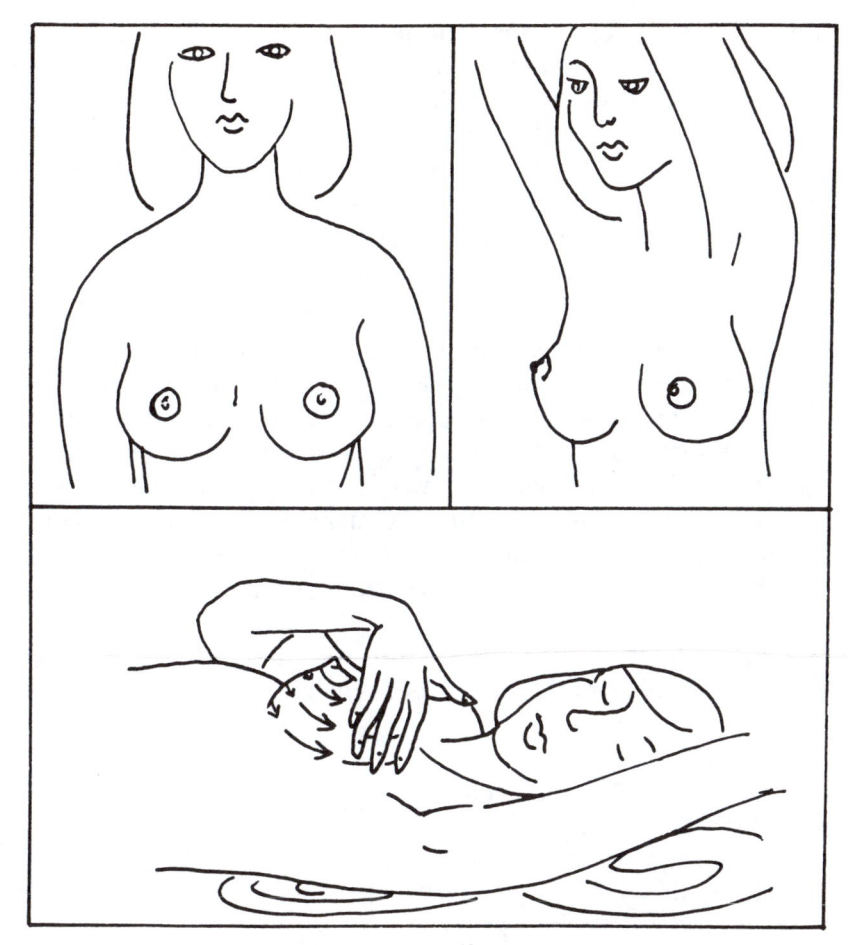

FIGURE 7.2: Breast self-examination.

creeping with the fingers up over the breast by one fingerbreadth at a time. You should do this twice, once over the inside half of the breast and once over the outside half. Check under the nipple with your fingertips and finally check your armpit. Repeat the procedure on the other breast.

Breast self-examination should take about five minutes a month and is one of the most effective forms of preventive medicine yet developed.

If you do find a lump, your doctor will conduct another examination of your breasts and may arrange for an X-ray mammogram, a needle biopsy or an ultrasound scan. These tests show the inside structure of the breast and can sometimes differentiate between cysts, cancers and fibrous lumps.

If all the features of the examination and investigations in a young woman indicate that the lump is benign, it is safe to watch the lump, with regular checks by the doctor, because many disappear after a few months. In an older woman, or if the lump persists, it should be removed by a small operation. If possible, this will be through a cosmetic incision that follows the line of the coloured area around the nipple or the fold under the breast so that the scar will be both tiny and concealed. In the majority of cases, this is the only treatment necessary.

If the lump is cancerous, more extensive surgery may be necessary, but unless the cancer is very extensive, surgeons no longer automatically remove the whole breast. Every effort is now being made to remove as little as possible.

Obesity

One of the modern preoccupations of people in the Western world is weight. Sometimes it seems as if everyone is trying to get thin. Magazines and newspapers expend inordinate amounts of paper and effort on the latest diet, and readers eagerly devour the hundreds of thousands of words that regularly make their appearance on the news stands. For many people, their concerns are more a matter of fashion and whim than a real need to lose weight. Weight, however, is a health problem for some people. Generally speaking, there is a range of weight according to age, sex and height, within which you should be to be healthy. Anyone who is more than 20% above their ideal weight is termed obese.

Obesity causes:
- increased risk of heart attack,
- liver deterioration,
- worsening of arthritis,
- poor circulation,
- strain on the lungs and joints,
- increased risk of diabetes,
- reduced ability to tolerate exercise or exertion,
- rashes in skin folds,
- gynaecological problems,
- increased risk of hernias,
- indigestion,
- increased risk from surgery and post-operative complications.

The more overweight you are, the greater the risk. A person who is more than 40% overweight is twice as likely to die from coronary artery disease as a person who is not overweight.

Mostly, obesity is caused by eating too much and exercising too little. The reason we eat is to get energy to maintain body temperature and to provide fuel so that our organs can function. Food also provides the raw material for building and repairing body tissues. If we eat more food than we need for the energy we expend, the surplus is stored as fat. How little 'too much' consists of is often not fully realised. If you eat one slice of bread more than you need every day, after ten years the stored food will weigh roughly 18 kg, and you will be that much over your ideal weight.

Obviously food requirements vary from individual to individual. A professional athlete or a manual labourer may need twice as much fuel as an office worker. Maintaining a healthy weight is simply a matter of balancing your particular fuel requirements with the amount you eat. There is no point in comparing the minuscule amount you eat with the huge amount consumed by your slender gluttonous neighbour, since your neighbour is different from you.

There are two ways of balancing your food and energy requirements. One is to reduce the amount you eat, and the other is to exercise more. A combination of both is probably ideal, but generally exercise on its own will not contribute too much to weight reduction since it is very much quicker to eat the food and take in kilojoules than it is to do sufficient exercise to burn the kilojoules up.

There are drugs that can combat obesity, but most doctors are reluctant to prescribe them since they can have major side effects. Furthermore, most such drugs are appetite suppressants and most obese people eat for reasons other than hunger alone.

In extreme cases of obesity, where the person's health is suffering and there seems no other solution, drastic treatments are sometimes tried. This includes wiring the person's jaw so they cannot open it and can fit only tiny amounts of food in, and so-called stomach stapling. This literally staples the walls of the stomach together, reducing it in size so that the amount of food that can be ingested is limited. Similarly, it is possible for an operation to be performed to by-pass part of the small intestine so that the area through which food can be absorbed is reduced. It also diminishes appetite. These operations are risky and meet with mixed success since the person's eating habits are not easily changed.

See also DIET.
See also Section 3 and Section 5.

Pap smear

Pap is short for Papanicolaou, the name of the Greek/American doctor who developed this cervical smear test. A Pap smear is used to detect any abnormality of the cervix, including infections and erosions (see also PATHOLOGY, Section 4). Chronic infections of the cervix of which the patient is not aware can cause infertility and other problems, and a Pap smear can enable the doctor to diagnose these and prescribe appropriate treatment. Unquestionably, however, the main value of the Pap smear has been its ability to detect pre-cancerous conditions of the cervix and cervical cancer at an early stage so that it can be treated. All women of any age who are sexually active should have regular smear tests — generally every year although once every two years may be enough for women who are past menopause.

The test is quite simple. The doctor introduces a collapsible metal tube, called a speculum, into the woman's vagina. This is painless although it may feel a touch intrusive. The speculum is usually metal or plastic and is shaped like a duck's bill. When the upper and lower blades are separated, the doctor can see the cervix, and a wooden stick or fine brush is gently inserted through the opening into the middle of the cervix. This lifts off a superficial layer of cells. The stick or brush is then wiped across a glass slide to form a smear on the glass. The slide is sent to a pathologist who examines the smeared cells under a microscope and sends a report to the doctor. The collecting of the cells takes only a minute or so, and the report is usually available within a week.

An abnormal result from a smear test does not mean that the woman necessarily has cancer, but it does mean that she should have a further test — this will usually be a colposcopy (see Section 4). If as a result of the colposcopy an early stage of cancer is detected, the abnormal cells may be burnt away by diathermy or laser, or a cone-shaped area of tissue may be excised. These forms of treatment will not interfere with a woman's normal sexual functioning or her ability to fall pregnant. Only if the cancer has already spread will she need to have the uterus removed in a hysterectomy, or undergo radiation therapy.

Cancer of the cervix is one of the more common forms of cancer in women, and yet if all women had a Pap smear regularly it could be totally prevented.

At the same time as a Pap smear is done, the doctor will usually insert two gloved fingers into the woman's vagina and feel for any abnormalities of the uterus or ovaries. The doctor may examine her rectum as well, and will probably check the blood pressure at the same visit.

Skin spots

Australians are among the most vulnerable people in the world in relation to skin cancer. Unlike the indigenous races of south-east Asia and the Pacific rim, Australians, with their fair skin, inherited from largely Anglo-Saxon or Celtic forbears and transported from the softer grey skies of Britain and Ireland, have little natural protection against the harsh and constant sunlight of the area.

Most of us have spots of one kind or another somewhere on our bodies, ranging from pimples and warts to more permanent freckles and moles. Most of these are harmless. Sometimes, however, a spot is cancerous, and occasionally a mole is a serious and deadly malignant melanoma. If diagnosed early, skin cancers have a very high cure rate and most deaths from the disease occur because the cancer was too far advanced before detection.

Melanomas can be flat or raised as lumps, and can be any colour from mid-pink to jet black. The signs to watch for in a spot or sore are:
- any change in colour;
- change in size;
- soreness or itchiness;
- bleeding or weeping;
- irregularity in colour or outline or of surface.

If any of these signs occur, see your doctor immediately. It is far better to check them out and find that they are harmless than to delay and be given a death sentence.

Smoking

If beetroot and strawberries, just for instance, were found not only to cause cancer in 10% of their heavy consumers, but eventually to bring 25% to an early death, no-one would consume them, and the government would long ago have legislated against growing them. Sadly, this is just what cigarette smoking does, but the sale of cigarettes is permitted, cigarettes have been heavily promoted by advertising, and large profits are made from their sale.

Over the centuries, since the introduction of tobacco to Europe in the 1590s, more and more people have become addicted to nicotine. Women started smoking in public only during the first world war, and the habit reached a peak during the second world war when 75% of the adult population of Australia were smokers. When today's grandparents were children, they were warned against smoking because 'it stunts the growth' (something it only does to the babies of smoking mothers), but generally it was not regarded as harmful, at least for adults. Cigarettes, cigars, lighters, pipes, ash trays, etc., were standard gifts at Christmas and birthday for a generation. Vast factories poured out billions of cigarettes that were made, packed, wrapped and boxed untouched by human hand. Multinational tobacco corporations gained enormous profits, and became powerful friends of government as tax payers and revenue earners. Governments even subsidised the growth of tobacco in some areas. Then came the crunch. It was found that smoking tobacco killed people. There was a long delay, and more than half the smokers escaped, but there was little doubt about it: for many people smoking was lethal.

Nicotine is a very powerful and toxic substance which acts initially as a stimulant on the central nervous system, but this effect is followed by a reduction of brain and nervous system activity. Nicotine causes narrowing of blood vessels, which then affects the circulation and causes blood pressure to rise. This is why regular absorption of nicotine through smoking can cause chronic heart problems and increases the possibility of heart attacks. In addition to nicotine, tobacco smoke contains many other chemicals which are harmful, including tar and carbon monoxide. Tar released in the form of particles in the smoke is the main cause of lung and throat cancer in smokers and also aggravates bronchial and respiratory disease.

We now know that 11% of smokers will get lung cancer, and 90% of them will die. Coronary heart disease will kill many prematurely. Chronic lung disease will cripple a large proportion of the remainder. The medical facts are conclusive — smoking is the biggest health problem in the Western world. It contributes to more deaths than alcohol and illicit drugs together, and costs the Australian economy $1000 million per year. If nobody smoked, there would be 30% less cancer.

Before anyone can stop smoking, they must really want to stop. No-one who is half-hearted about wanting to stop will ever succeed. Once you have decided to stop, set a time and date for the event. Tell everyone you know of your intentions, and take side-bets if you can to reinforce your incentive. Make lists of reasons why you must stop, and leave them everywhere at home and at work. Make sure that from the moment you stop, you have no cigarettes available to you, and resist the temptation to buy more. Start a savings account with the money you save by not smoking, and if you don't succeed, pay the balance to the Cancer Fund!

If these incentives are not sufficient, see your GP. He or she can prescribe nicotine-containing gum that will ease the craving for cigarettes. Group therapy sessions, hypnotherapy, psychological counselling, support groups, rewards at the end of each successful week and reinforcment visits to your GP can all help you wil the fight.

At present, 28% of the adult population smokes. One expert has predicted that by the year 2000, only 20% will smoke, and it will have become so antisocial that it will only be permitted by consenting adults in private! Let us hope that this prediction comes true.

See also BRONCHIECTASIS; BRONCHITIS; BUERGER'S DISEASE; EMPHYSEMA; HEART ATTACK; HYPERTENSION; LUNG CANCER; THROMBOSIS, Section 5.

SMOKING DURING PREGNANCY

There is no doubt that the babies of mothers who smoke are smaller (by 200 g on average) than those of non-smoking mothers. There is also an increased rate of premature labour (delivering the baby too early), miscarriage and stillbirth in these women. After birth, babies of smoking mothers continue to suffer both directly and indirectly from their mother's smoking. The smoking by the mother appears to reduce their resistance to disease, in particular to infection, so that babies born to smoking mothers die in infancy more often than average. By inhaling the smoke from either of their parents, these infants have more colds, bronchitis and other respiratory problems than babies in non-smoking homes.

Any woman who smokes should ideally cease before she falls pregnant, but certainly should do so when the pregnancy is diagnosed. This is far easier said than done, but if her partner stops at the same time, support and encouragement is given by family and friends, and assistance is obtained from the family doctor, women who are motivated to give their baby the best possible chance in life will succeed in kicking this very addictive habit.

Passive smoking

Almost everyone is forced to inhale fumes containing toxins such as formaldehyde, acetone, arsenic, carbon monoxide, hydrogen cyanide and nicotine at some time. You have no choice in the matter and have to suffer the consequences, because these chemicals are just a few of the scores of irritants found in cigarette smoke. Fortunately for most of us, the result of passive involuntary smoking is only a minor itch of the nose, a cough or a sneeze, but some people can develop life-threatening asthma attacks or have their heart condition aggravated by inhaling tobacco smoke. Being trapped in a vehicle or other enclosed space with a smoker can be a nightmare experience for such people. In some situations the non-smoker may be more affected than the smoker, because the smoke coming directly from a cigarette contains more toxins, nicotine and carbon monoxide than that inhaled by the smoker, which has been more completely burnt and passed through a filter.

The most unfortunate victims of passive smoking are the children of smokers. The incidence of pneumonia and bronchitis and the severity of asthma in children whose parents smoke are far higher than in the children of non-smokers. In babies of women who smoke, health problems caused by passive smoking begin before birth (see above).

In the workplace, more and more offices are becoming smoke-free zones. Unfortunately some people still smoke at work, and if their subordinates have adverse reactions to passive smoking, they may have to put up with it or change jobs. This situation may change in the future, as more and more workers are successfully claiming workers compensation payments for complications of passive smoking at work.

The non-smoking spouse or partner of a smoker is also at great risk. They have a significantly increased risk of lung cancer, reduced lung capacity, a higher incidence of asthma, and more respiratory infections than those whose spouses or partners do not smoke.

Smokers should now be aware of the health risks that they are taking every day, and they can no longer claim personal freedom to smoke where and when they like, as their habit is adversely affecting the health of those around them. All smokers should have the courtesy to only light up when there is no possibility of others inhaling the resultant toxic fumes. Legal suits by passive smokers against smokers for causing bodily harm have been successful in the United States.

Vaccination

Unless there are very good medical grounds not to vaccinate, all children should receive: the full course of triple antigen injections to protect them against tetanus, whooping cough and diphtheria; the measles, mumps and rubella vaccine; and the Sabin vaccine by mouth for polio. The risk of vaccination is infinitesimal, and when compared with the potential side effects of any one of these diseases, it is a far preferable course of action. Another person (adult or child) only has to breathe the infecting germs in the direction of your child and he or she may catch one of these dread diseases.

Tetanus is around us constantly in the soil. The bacteria causing this disease are carried by animals and are therefore not likely to be eradicated in the near future. The series of tetanus injections you receive as a child do not give you life-long immunity, and boosters are required every ten years, or more frequently if you injure yourself.

Most young doctors have never seen a case of diphtheria. The incidence of this disease is now low, but older citizens may recall losing childhood friends to it. Diphtheria is still around though, and many children still catch the disease each year, and suffer the difficulty in breathing, and possible heart complications that can accompany it.

Whooping cough is becoming a very worrying problem, as it is increasing in the community due to under-vaccination of many children. This is a potentially fatal disease, and even if the child survives the distress of weeks or months of severe coughing, they may be left with permanent brain or lung damage.

Measles is often considered to be a mild disease, but a small percentage of children even in Australia develop debilitating ear, chest and brain complications that may affect them for the rest of their lives. The measles vaccine is normally combined with the mumps and rubella vaccination at 12 to 15 months of age, but it can be given at a later age if vaccination has been neglected at the correct age.

Mumps is a relatively benign disease of childhood, but it too may have serious consequences, particularly if it is caught in adult life when it may spread to the testes and cause sterility, or infect the brain and cause permanent damage.

Polio was probably the most feared of childhood diseases. If it didn't kill your child, it probably left them crippled for life. The Sabin vaccine is now given by mouth to prevent this disease, but boosters are required into adult life every ten years.

German measles (rubella) vaccination is more important for girls as it can cause severe deformities to the foetus if contracted in pregnancy. To reduce the risk of spreading this disease, the vaccination is given in combination with measles and mumps at 15 months of age, and an additional booster is given to girls at twelve years of age.

Please take advantage of the protection against disease which is available. Are your children (or grandchildren) adequately protected?

TABLE 7.6:
CHILDHOOD VACCINATION SCHEDULE

Age	Vaccination
2 months	Triple antigen and Sabin
4 months	Triple antigen and Sabin
6 months	Triple antigen and Sabin
15 months	Measles, mumps and rubella
18 months	Triple antigen
5 years	Diphtheria, tetanus and Sabin
12 years	Rubella (girls only)
15 years	Diphtheria and tetanus

Travel Medicine

Getting sick on a holiday is always a major disappointment and in a strange environment can be very difficult to cope with. A few simple preparations can reduce the likelihood of disaster.

If you are going overseas, find out what the conditions are like in the country or countries you will be visiting. You should ask about the climate, the food, any local diseases against which you should be immunised, and the availability and cost of medical treatment.

Diarrhoea

Diseases

The most common ailment affecting overseas travellers is diarrhoea. Bali belly, Delhi belly, Cairo colic, Montezuma's revenge — the names are rueful testimony to the numbers of tourists whose main familiarity with their holiday destination is its lavatory facilities. Mostly diarrhoea is caused by contaminated water resulting from inadequate water and sewerage systems. Sometimes just the fact that you are drinking water that is different from the water you are used to, with different bugs in it, is enough to trigger a revolt in your intestines. If you are travelling in any third-world or tropical country, you should avoid drinking the water unless it has been boiled. Most reasonable hotels will provide a jug of boiled water in your room, but that still leaves the water you use to clean your teeth and ice blocks in all the long cool drinks you will undoubtedly consume. Don't have ice in your drinks, if necessary add mineral water from a bottle or can, and use boiled water to clean your teeth. If this is not possible, there are tiny purifying tablets you can pop into a glass, but these will give the water a 'taste' (which you may be able to overcome with a small sachet of fruit flavoured powder).

Food too can be a source of diarrhoea and food poisoning. Tempting as it is to try all those exotic dishes, steer clear of raw or underdone meat, uncooked seafood, unprocessed dairy products and uncooked fruits, vegetables and salad ingredients.

An attack of diarrhoea usually lasts only from one to three days but, especially if you are travelling around, it can be very uncomfortable and embarrassing. Ask your doctor to prescribe antidiarrhoea tablets before you go, and keep them with you in your personal baggage. If you are struck down with an attack, go on a fluid only diet for 24 hours and eat lightly for several days. You may have stomach pains, nausea and possibly vomiting as well.

Jet lag

Because of our geographic location and our relatively high standard of living, Australians spend proportionately more time on long-distance flights than the citizens of almost any other nation. To Americans, a long-haul flight is the seven hours it takes to cross the Atlantic, but we may spend 30 hours or more in a plane flying to Europe. These long flights lead to medical problems, many of which can be avoided.

Jet lag is the most common phenomenon encountered on intercontinental flights, and it is worse when flying east (against time) than flying west. Children are particularly upset by time changes and may take several days to adjust, becoming irritable and restless in the meantime.

The best way to deal with very long flights is to have a stopover. This enables you to recover from the confinement of the aircraft, and gives opportunities to experience additional cultures and scenery. If only one stopover is possible, it should be taken when flying east (from Europe to Australia or Australia to America).

The main symptoms of jet lag are tiredness, headaches, nausea, aching muscles, dizziness and disorientation. The best way to deal with the problem is to adjust to the local time zone as soon as possible. Start having the meals at the same time as the locals, even though you may feel like breakfast at 9 p.m., and go to bed near your normal time by the local clocks.

Meals rich in carbohydrates will aid your recovery, but alcohol will slow it. The normal analgesic preparations (paracetamol and aspirin), and a mild sleeping tablet (e.g. Normison, Euhypnos — see Section 6) may be useful. A new medication containing a substance called melantoin is being used experimentally to prevent jet lag. If it works, it should be on the market in the near future.

The air in aircraft is very dry and at a lower pressure than that on the ground. The dry air will dehydrate you rapidly, and you should ensure that you have plenty to drink on the flight, but once again, avoid alcohol. The low air pressure may cause severe pain and occasionally significant damage if you have blocked ears or a cold. If in doubt, check with a doctor.

Unless you are one of those lucky enough to be in the first class cabin, there will not be a great deal of leg room. As a result, you tend to remain in the one position for long periods of time. This will cause blood to pool in your feet and legs, and they will swell up to the point that it may be difficult to replace shoes removed for comfort. This problem can be minimised if you move around the aircraft as much as possible, without inconveniencing the other passengers and staff, and leave the aircraft for a long walk at every stop on route.

Accept the meals offered in flight, but do not overeat. Leave some food on the plate. When crossing many time zones, small amounts of food taken frequently are better than the normal three large meals a day.

Motion sickness (air sickness, car sickness, sea sickness)

Nausea and vomiting associated with any form of transport is caused by the same combination of factors. The main problem is that the two senses we use to balance — the eyes and the balance mechanism in the inner ears — do not synchronise. On a ship, the deck appears to be level, but we sense motion; in an aircraft, the interior of the plane appears to be horizontal, but the aircraft may be climbing steeply. Reconciling these conflicting

SECTION 7: MISCELLANEOUS

sensations from our eyes and balance mechanism helps to overcome motion sickness. In a ship, sitting on deck (ideally amidships) and watching the horizon will help. In an aircraft, a window seat from which we can see the earth below and a seat over the wings where there is least motion are helpful. In a car, sitting in the front seat or in the centre of the rear seat, from where the road can be easily seen, will assist.

Being overdressed, too warm, in a stuffy environment, eating too much, and drinking alcoholic drinks will aggravate motion sickness. You should be lightly dressed, slightly cold, have plenty of fresh air, eat small amounts of dry easily digestible food before and during the trip (no greasy chips or fatty sausages), and avoid alcohol. Fresh air is available by going on deck in a ship, opening a car window, and opening the air ducts wider on an aircraft (don't hesitate to ask a flight attendant for assistance).

If you still feel queasy, there are also a number of medications for the prevention or treatment of motion sickness. A wide range of antihistamines (see Section 6) are available in tablet, mixture and injection forms to both prevent and treat motion sickness. Milder ones are available without prescription, while stronger ones will require a visit to the doctor. Sedatives are used in some severely affected patients.

A small patch that is stuck on the skin behind an ear is the latest invention in the prevention of motion sickness. Called 'Scop', these patches are available from chemists without a prescription and last for three days. Prolonged, repeated use may cause problems though.

In chronic cases of motion sickness, the problem may be psychological as well as physical, and desensitisation by a psychiatrist or psychologist may be appropriate.

OTHER DISEASES

Many Australians have no conception of the hazards of travel to third-world countries. In most cases, medical facilities that we take for granted are simply non-existent. Anyone travelling outside Europe, North America or New Zealand should check carefully with their doctor about what vaccinations are necessary and what medications should be taken along just in case.

Typhoid and cholera are endemic in most of Asia, Africa and central America. A cholera vaccination is only necessary if you are living outside the major cities of third-world countries, or in third-rate accommodation. Only one shot is now required and is given two weeks before departure.

Cholera is a very severe disease that causes diarrhoea beyond your wildest imagination, and death can occur very rapidly from gross dehydration. The vaccine is only 60% effective and lasts for only six months. Therefore the fact that you have been vaccinated does not mean that you can forget about precautions with what you eat and drink.

Typhoid is a similarly unpleasant disease, but the vaccination is more effective and should be received by all travellers to third-world countries. The vaccine can be given as two injections 15 to 30 days apart, which lasts for three years, or by three capsules taken by mouth over five days, which gives twelve months protection. Both typhoid and cholera are caught by eating contaminated food.

Your doctor will give you a vaccination book and you should make sure that it is filled in correctly to keep track of your vaccinations and to prove to health authorities overseas that you have been vaccinated.

Yellow fever is found in Central America, central Africa and around the Red Sea. The vaccine for this lasts for ten years and is only available from State Health Departments. Yellow fever and cholera vaccinations are a condition of entry to some countries — if you land without proof of inoculation you will be sent away.

Malaria occurs in practically every tropical country. Particularly vicious forms that are resistant to many medications are occurring in south-east Asia and some Pacific islands. Our nearest neighbour, Papua New Guinea, has one of the world's nastiest forms of malaria. To prevent malaria, you need to take tablets regularly for a fortnight before you leave and for a month after you return. One or two tablets a week are normally prescribed. The malaria-carrying mosquito bites only between dusk and dawn, so take precautions against being bitten after dark — wear clothes that cover you as much as possible, avoid perfumes, and use repellents and insecticides.

If you have not had a tetanus vaccination within the past ten years, it is sensible to have a booster before you leave. Gashing your foot on a piece of barbed wire in a back alley in India is not the time to wonder when you last had one and where you can find a reputable doctor. An oral Sabin booster against polio at the same time is a wise precaution for third-world travellers.

If you are travelling to South America, central Asia or Africa, or intend to spend a long time in remote and primitive areas, you should consider an immunoglobulin shot to protect you from hepatitis. This is not a vaccine but boosts the body's defences against disease for a few months.

One of the great achievements of medical science has been the total eradication of smallpox. As a result, vaccination for this disease is no longer necessary, or indeed available, for travel anywhere in the world.

If you become ill within three months after you return from overseas, remember to tell your doctor where you have been so that all possible diseases can be taken into account.

Immunisation

A vaccination program for overseas travel should commence five weeks before departure but may be completed in two weeks if absolutely necessary. Vaccinations that may be required include:

Cholera — Two vaccinations, 7 to 28 days apart, give six months protection. Only one injection is required for a booster dose.

Immunoglobulin for hepatitis — One injection, a week before departure, gives protection for 6 to 12 weeks, depending on dose.

Japanese encephalitis — Two vaccinations, two weeks apart. It is required only for residence in rural areas of India, Nepal, China and south-east Asia.

Malaria — Start taking tablets two weeks before departure, and continue for four weeks after return from affected area.

Meningitis — One injection, five weeks before departure.

Typhoid — Three capsules, two days apart, gives 12 months protection. OR two injections, 7 to 28 days apart, gives three years protection. Only one injection is required for a booster dose.

Yellow fever — One injection, five weeks before departure, gives ten years protection.

All travellers should also ensure that their tetanus and polio (Sabin) vaccinations are up to date. Resistant malaria is resistant to chloroquine (see Section 5). Cholera vaccine may be compulsory for entry to a country but not a health requirement. Immunoglobulin may give short-term protection against hepatitis.

See Table 7.7 over page.

Insurance

Never travel overseas without health insurance. In developed countries you may be unlikely to be stricken with one of the more exotic third-world diseases, but medical treatment of any kind, e.g. in the United States, can be prohibitively expensive and you may find yourself unable to afford the care you need unless you are insured for the cost.

If you get ill in one of the less developed countries, you might need a hasty return home — even flying first class with special nursing care. Don't risk not being able to afford it.

TABLE 7.7:
IMMUNISATION REQUIREMENTS AROUND THE WORLD

Area/Country	Malaria	Resistant malaria	Typhoid	Cholera	Yellow fever	Meningo-coccus	Immuno-globulin
Australia, Bermuda, Canada, Europe, Fiji, Hong Kong, Israel, Japan, New Zealand, Samoa, Singapore, USA	No	No	No	No	No	No	No
Sao Tome, Togo	Yes	No	Yes	Optional	Yes	No	Optional
Bolivia, Cameroon, Colombia, Fr Guiana, Guyana, Panama, Peru, Surinam, Venezuela	Yes	Yes	Yes	Optional	Yes	No	Optional
Afghanistan, Argentina, Belize, Botswana, Costa Rica, Dominican Republic, El Salvados, Guatemala, Haiti, Honduras, Iraq, Libya, Maldives, Mauritius, Morocco, Nicaragua, Oman, Paraguay, Qatar, Saudi Arabia, Syria, Tunisia, Turkey, UAE, Yemen	Yes	No	Yes	No	No	No	Optional
Bangladesh, China, Iran, Indonesia, Kampuchea, Laos, Malaysia, Namibia, Pakistan, PNG, Philippines, Solomon Islands, South Africa, Sri Lanka, Thailand, Vanuatu	Yes	Yes	Yes	No	No	No	Optional
Angola, Benin, Brazil, Burundi, Congo, Gabon, Gambia, Ghana, Ivory Coast, Kenya, Nigeria, Rwanda, Senegal, Somalia, Sudan, Tanzania, Uganda, Zaire	Yes	Yes	Yes	Optional	Yes	Yes	Optional
Chad, Guinea, Liberia, Mali, Mauritania, Niger, Sierra Leone	Yes	No	Yes	Optional	Yes	Yes	Optional
Burma, Comoros, India, Madagascar, Malawi, Mozambique, Nepal, Vietnam, Zimbabwe	Yes	Yes	Yes	Optional	No	Yes	Optional
Djibouti, Egypt	Yes	No	Yes	Optional	No	Yes	Optional

SECTION 8

EMERGENCIES

FIRST AID

767

ACCIDENTS AND EMERGENCIES

781

BITES AND STINGS

803

WHEN TO CALL THE DOCTOR

811

HOME MEDICAL CHEST

813

First Aid

First aid is the initial care of someone who has been injured or become unexpectedly ill. Some injuries and illnesses are minor and require no more than first aid. Other emergencies are life-threatening, and prompt and appropriate first aid can mean the difference between life and death, or at the very least permanent disablement. Most of us find the prospect of being in a situation where someone is very ill or badly hurt and not knowing what to do alarming to say the least. And yet few of us take the trouble to learn basic principles of first aid.

First aid is not difficult and anyone can learn. A basic course takes only four hours to complete, and a full course only 15 hours of study over three or four days or nights. Courses are conducted by the Australian Red Cross, the St John Ambulance Brigade or your local ambulance service — their telephone numbers are in the phone book. The courses are not expensive — usually not more than $50, with the basic courses much less than this.

It is difficult to learn many of the necessary skills from reading about them. Nothing substitutes for hands-on experience. Nevertheless, even a theoretical familiarity with fundamental first aid principles and techniques may enable you to save a life — perhaps that of a child.

First aid does work. It is based on sound modern principles. Some of the people killed in road accidents would have survived if adequate first aid had been available. Similarly with near drowning it has been estimated that 60% of children resuscitated by a person trained in first aid survive, compared with only 30% if the rescuer is untrained.

The goals of first aid are: to sustain life, to prevent the illness or injury from becoming worse, and to promote recovery. It is important to recognise that reassurance and making the person as comfortable as possible is an important part of administering first aid.

Assessment

If you are at the scene of an emergency, keep calm and allocate priorities. Speed may be crucial, but panic and confusion will not help and may deny the injured person the attention they need.

The most important first step is to assess what the problem is and what immediate action is practicable. This is often no more than common sense. There is little point, for example, in diving in to save someone who is drowning if you cannot swim; or in rushing to the aid of a victim of an electric shock without cutting off the power so that you will not be electrocuted as well. When you have identified the problem, you can then carry out basic first aid procedures while someone else gets professional help.

The first step is to carry out the ABC of first aid (see below). Then control serious bleeding and take measures against shock. If the victim is unconscious, put them in the recovery position. Do not give anything to eat or drink (it may be vomited and cause the victim to choke if they lapse into unconsciousness or if they later have to be given an anaesthetic (e.g. to set a broken bone). Keep the victim warm and as comfortable as possible.

It is important to assess whether the victim is conscious or unconscious. You can do this by saying in a clear and reasonably loud voice things that require a response, such as 'Can you hear me? Open your eyes. What is your name?' If there is no response, gently shake the victim's shoulders, and if there is still no response they are unconscious. Never leave an unconscious person alone.

The ABC of first aid

Your main task in any emergency is to keep the victim alive. Whatever the injury, the victim will die or suffer irreparable damage to vital organs, in particular the brain, within three or four minutes unless oxygenated blood is kept circulating throughout the body. For this to happen, the victim needs three things:

1. a clear airway to let air into the lungs;
2. the capacity to breathe so that air is taken into the lungs to oxygenate the blood; and
3. a beating heart to pump the blood from the lungs to the body and brain.

This has given rise to the basic ABC of first aid — check the victim's Airway, Breathing and Circulation.

A — Airway

Make sure the airway is not being blocked by any foreign matter, e.g. false teeth, particles of food or vomit, seaweed, etc. Provided the neck has not been injured, turn the victim's head to one side and sweep your index finger around the inside of the mouth and under the tongue to remove anything that is there. Loosen any clothing around the neck, such as a tie or scarf. Make sure the tongue is not blocking the airway. To do this, tilt the head back by placing one hand on the forehead and the other hand under the angle of the lower jaw. Gently tilt the head back at the same time as you lift the jaw upward and forward.

It can be quite difficult to keep a child's airway clear. Generally the head of a small child should be kept horizontal without tilting the head. Support the lower jaw but be careful not to press on the tissues of the neck.

If it is safe to do so, place the victim in the recovery position

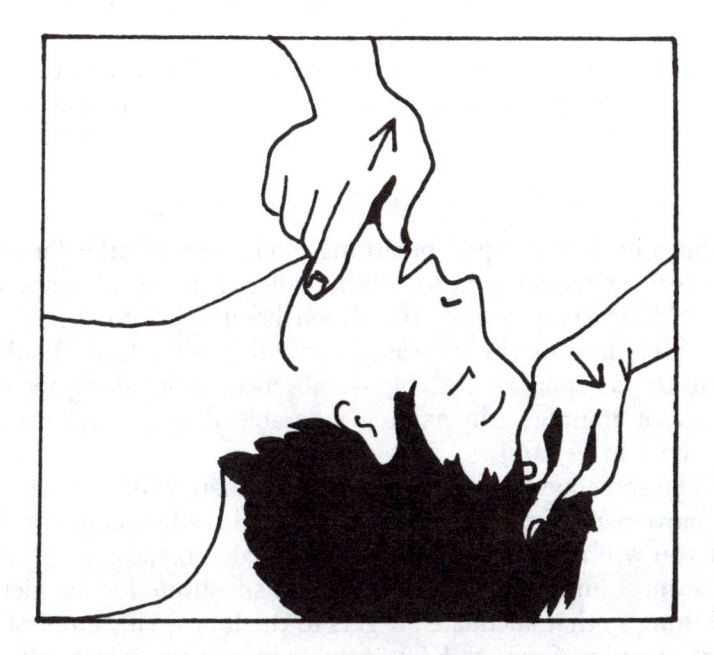

FIGURE 8.1: Head tilt.

(see UNCONSCIOUSNESS). This stops the tongue from falling backwards into the throat and ensures that any vomit or saliva cannot flow into the lungs. The recovery position should not be used if the victim might have a fractured neck or spine, unless their breathing becomes noisy, laboured or irregular.

B — Breathing

Make sure the victim is breathing — watch or feel the chest for movement. If none can be detected, place your ear close to the nose and mouth to hear whether there is any air passing in or out. If there is no sign of breathing start resuscitation (See EXPIRED AIR RESPIRATION).

C — Circulation

If the heart stops beating, the blood will stop circulating. The external indication of a beating heart is the pulse. The two most easily accessible pulses are in the wrist and the neck. The neck (carotid) pulse is usually the most appropriate, because if the person is seriously ill or shocked, the wrist pulse may be too weak to feel even though it is present. You can find the neck pulse by locating the thick cord of muscle running along the side of the neck; then find the larynx, which has the Adam's apple in

Section 8: Emergencies

front; place your first and second fingers lightly on the front of the muscle at the level of the Adam's apple. If there is no sign of a pulse, start external cardiac compression (see page 773). A victim who needs external cardiac compression will usually have stopped breathing as well, so you will normally have to carry out expired air respiration at the same time. The combined form of resuscitation is called cardiopulmonary resuscitation (see page 773).

Expired air respiration (EAR)

If someone has stopped breathing, you must breathe for them. The way in which you do this is called expired air respiration (EAR). Essentially it consists of you breathing into the victim's mouth or nose or (in the case of a child) both. EAR should be instituted as soon as possible — absence of breathing for more than four minutes can cause irreparable damage and over six minutes can be fatal.

When someone has stopped breathing, there will be no rise and fall movement of the chest, the face may be a bluish grey colour, and you will not be able to feel any exhaled breath.

The most important aim of EAR is to substitute for the victim's breathing so that adequate air gets to the lungs. The simplest and most effective form of EAR is to exhale your breath into the victim's lungs, in the the method known as mouth-to-mouth resuscitation, or the kiss of life.

Mouth-to-mouth resuscitation

(The numbers below refer to Figure 8.2 opposite.)

To perform mouth-to-mouth resuscitation, the victim should be lying on their back. Then:
- clear the mouth and throat of any obstruction(1);
- tilt the head backwards by placing one hand beneath the base of the head and lifting upwards(2);
- put your face at right angles to the victim's face so that you have easy access to the mouth and take a deep breath;
- pinch the victim's nose shut so that it does not provide an escape route for the air(3);
- seal your lips around the lips of the victim and blow firmly so that your exhaled breath is pushed into the victim's lungs(4);
- look to see if the chest rises — if it does not, check the airway again for any obstructions;
- if the chest rises, remove your lips and look to see if the chest falls. At the same time, place your ear close to the mouth and listen for air leaving the lungs(5);
- repeat the procedure again for four or five quick breaths;
- feel the victim's neck pulse(6). If it is present, continue at the rate of one breath approximately every four seconds. If you cannot feel the neck pulse, start external cardiac compression (see below).

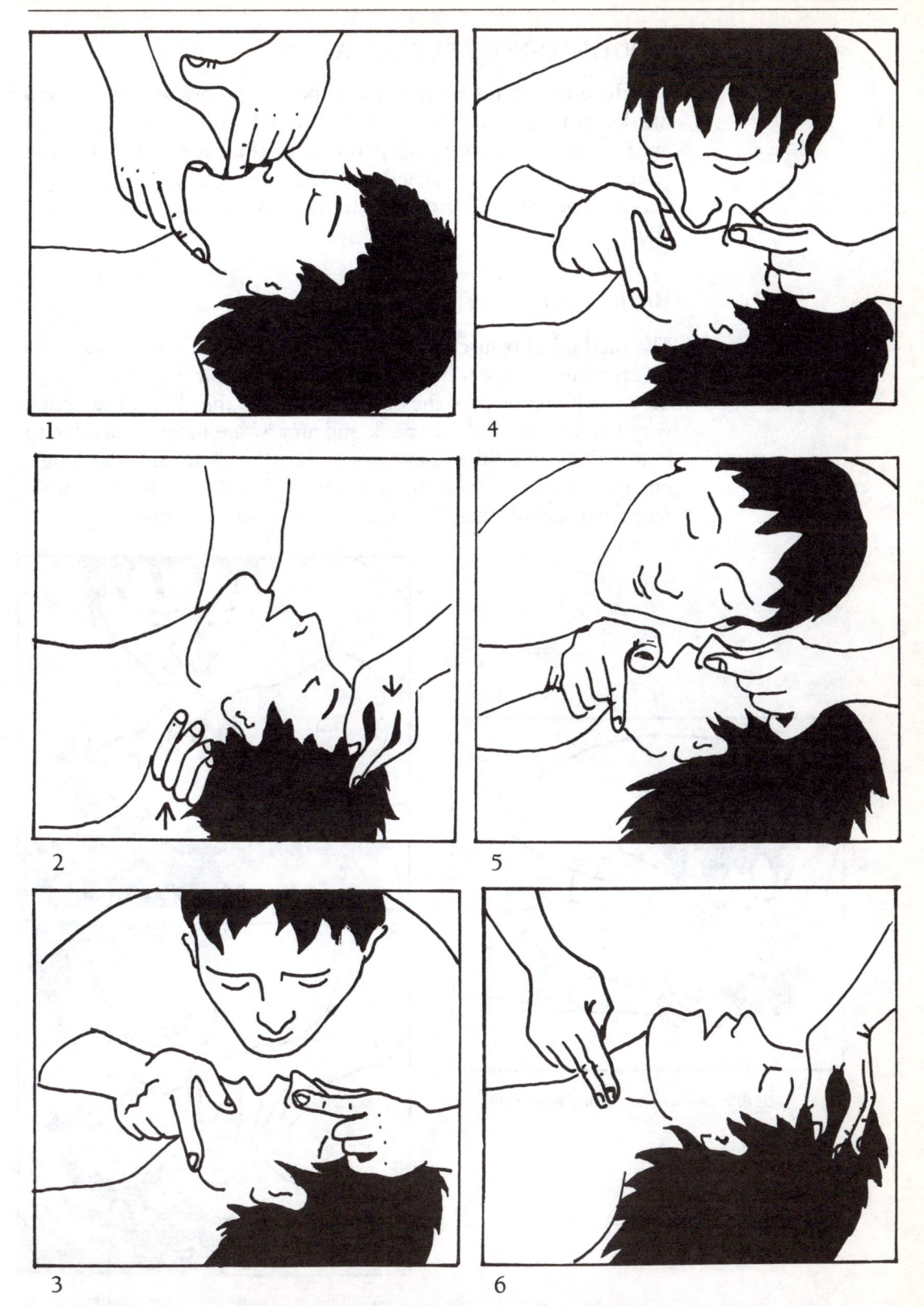

FIGURE 8.2: Stages of mouth-to-mouth resuscitation.

SECTION 8: EMERGENCIES

MOUTH-TO-NOSE RESUSCITATION

Mouth-to-mouth resuscitation may be inappropriate if the person has facial injuries or their face is covered with poison, or if you are trying to operate in deep water. In this case mouth-to-nose resuscitation can be carried out following the same technique except that air is blown into the nose while the mouth is held shut.

BABIES AND YOUNG CHILDREN

The method of resuscitating a baby or young child is the same as for an adult, except it may be easier to seal your mouth over both the mouth and nose of the child. Do not tip the child's head back very far, because a child's neck and airway are more vulnerable to injury than an adult's. Blow gentle breaths of air into the lungs, one breath every two or three seconds (20–30 breaths a minute). Stop each breath when the child's chest starts to rise.

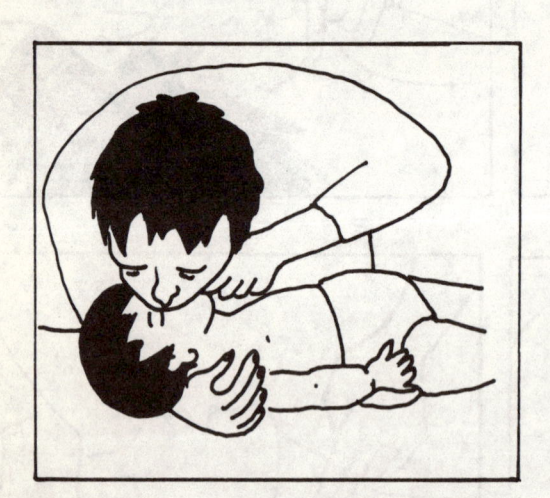

FIGURE 8.3: Resuscitation of a young child

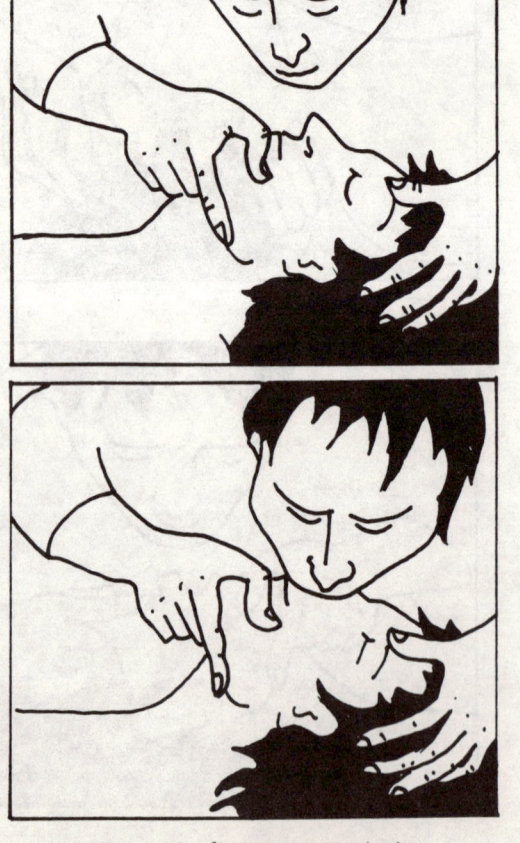

FIGURE 8.4: Mouth-to-nose resuscitation.

External cardiac compression (ECC)

When to use

External cardiac (heart) compression is a technique used to restart a heart that has stopped beating, and to maintain circulation so that damage caused by lack of oxygen to the brain and other vital organs is avoided. Basically it is intended to reproduce artificially the normal beating of the heart by rhythmically compressing the heart between the breastbone and the spine.

Before administering external cardiac compression it is important to ensure that the heart has stopped beating. If it is still beating, the procedure can be dangerous, even to the point of causing death. External cardiac compression can also damage vital organs as well as the ribcage if done incorrectly, so it should usually not be attempted unless you have learned how at an approved first aid course.

The need for external cardiac compression is indicated if the victim is unconscious, not breathing, and has no discernible pulse. Generally mouth-to-mouth resuscitation will be tried first. If the victim still shows no sign of life when the neck pulse is checked after the first five breaths, you should apply external cardiac compression together with the resuscitation. External cardiac compression must always be combined with mouth-to-mouth resuscitation.

Cardiopulmonary resuscitation (CPR)

Cardiopulmonary (heart-lung) resuscitation is a combination of expired air resuscitation and external cardiac compression. Essentially, it takes over both breathing and circulation in a person whose body has stopped carrying out these functions itself. It keeps vital organs supplied with oxygen and thus prevents death or brain damage. Although brain damage and death usually occur within 3–6 minutes there are cases where breathing and circulation have stopped for longer than this and the person has survived (usually young people and in very low temperatures), so CPR should always be administered.

It is possible for CPR to be undertaken by one person alone who alternates the two forms of resuscitation, carrying out expired air respiration for a period and then external cardiac compression before returning again to expired air respiration, and so on. However, it is difficult and tiring, and it is far better if two people can work together, one on the airway and one on the heart.

CPR should be learnt in an approved first aid course. It can be dangerous if inexpertly carried out.

Section 8: Emergencies

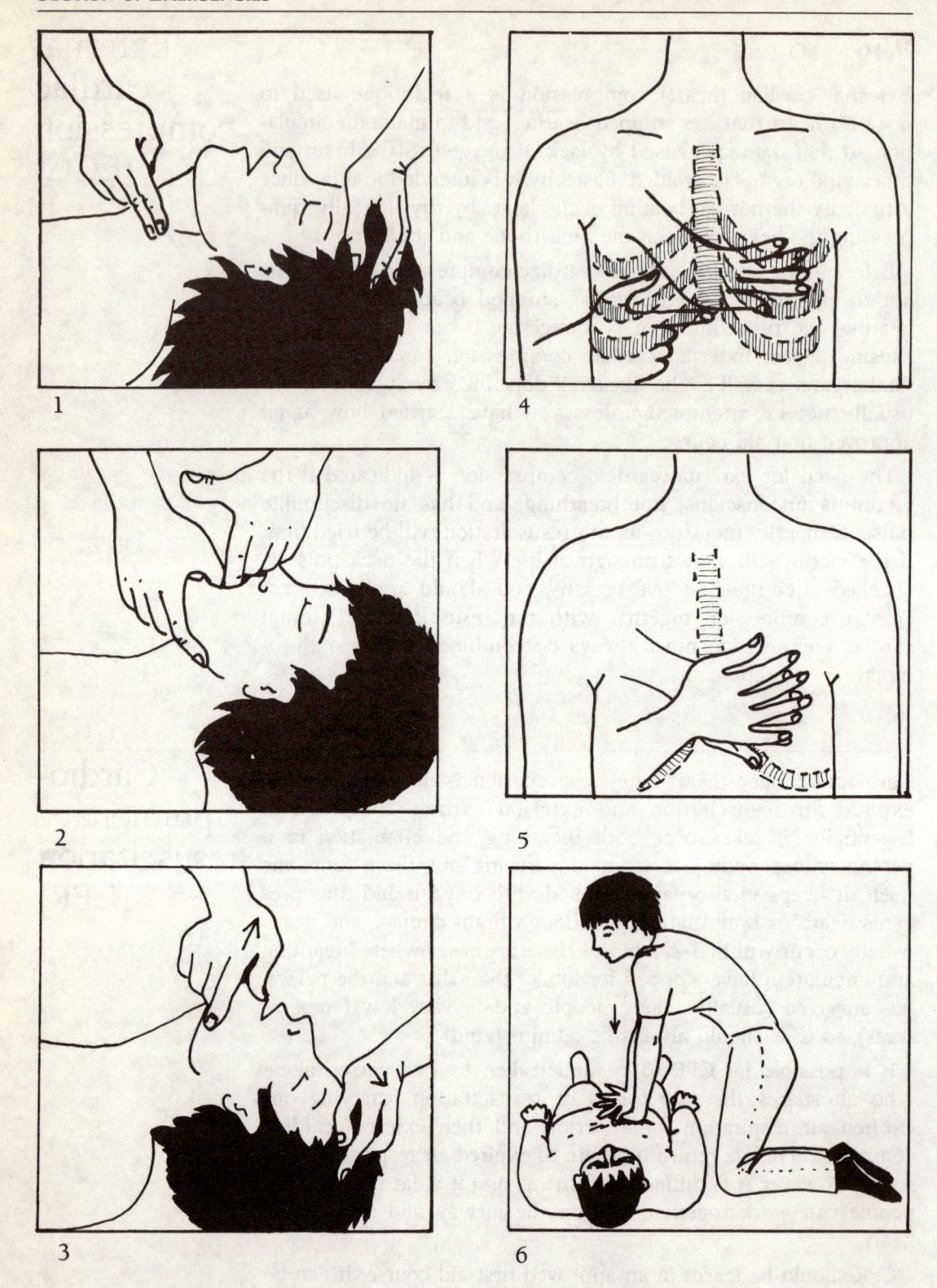

FIGURE 8.5: Stages of cardiopulmonary resuscitation.

FIRST AID

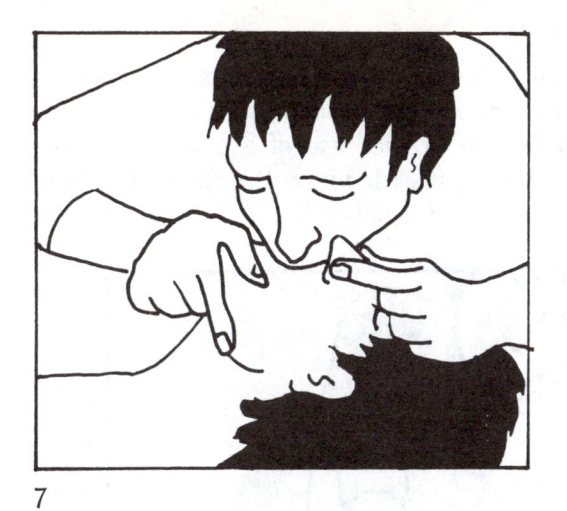

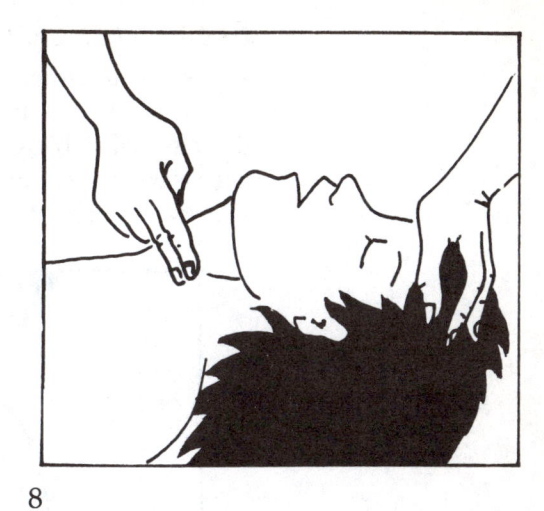

7   8

FIGURE 8.5: Stages of cardiopulmonary resuscitation (continued).

How to do CPR

(The numbers in the following refer to Figure 8.5 above).

Anyone proposing to give CPR should first check the victim's neck pulse(1). This is located between the Adam's apple and the large muscle running up the side of the neck. If there is no sign of a heartbeat and therefore CPR is indicated, you should:
- place the victim on their back on a firm surface;
- check that the airway is clear(2), and tilt the head back so that the passage to the lungs is unrestricted(3);
- place the heel of one hand on the middle of the lower half of the breastbone, keeping the palm and fingers raised clear of the chest(4). Place the heel of the second hand on top(5). With the arms straight, press down firmly so that the breastbone is depressed 4–5 cm(6). Keeping the hands in position, release the pressure;
- repeat 15 times, about one compression per second or slightly faster (about five compressions in four seconds);
- give two mouth-to-mouth breaths(7) (see EXPIRED AIR RESPIRATION, page 770);
- give another 15 chest compressions;
- continue with a pattern of 15 compressions to two mouth-to-mouth breaths;
- after one minute, check the neck pulse(8). If it has returned, stop the compression immediately;
- if the neck pulse cannot be felt, continue with the compression and check the pulse every two or three minutes. Stop as soon as the heart starts beating again;
- continue mouth-to-mouth resuscitation until the victim can breathe alone.

Section 8: Emergencies

BABIES AND CHILDREN

The same techniques of CPR can be used on babies and young children, but the breastbone should be depressed only 1 cm in the case of a baby and 2 cm in the case of a child. It is only necessary to use one hand to press down on the chest of a child, and two fingers are sufficient for a baby.

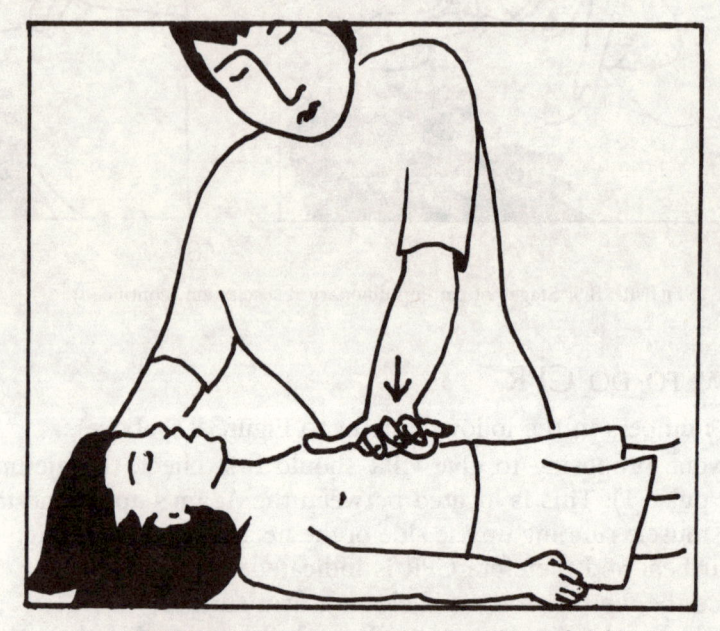

FIGURE 8.6: Putting pressure on breastbone of child.

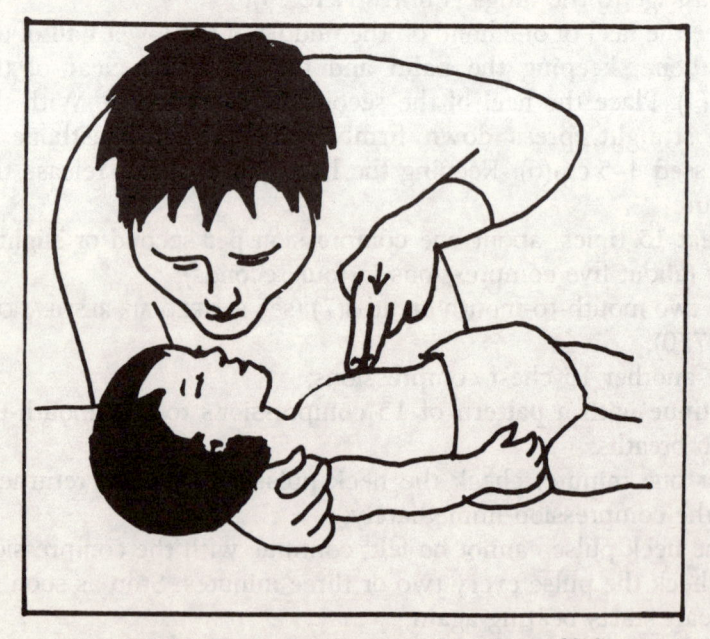

FIGURE 8.7: Putting pressure on breastbone of baby.

Control of bleeding

A person who is bleeding severely can die if it is not stopped, and this becomes a top priority once the ABC of airway, breathing and circulation have been attended to. Blood can be lost rapidly from a severed or torn artery, and it is vital to act quickly to avoid shock and unconsciousness. If an adult loses one litre of blood and a child as little as 300 mL, blood loss is severe.

There are three ways external bleeding can be controlled:
- you can press directly on the wound, which will stop the blood flow and encourage clotting;
- you can raise the wounded part so that the pressure is reduced;
- you can press on the artery supplying the wounded area so that the blood supply is cut off. However, this interferes with the natural healing process and should not be continued for longer than 15 minutes
- do not use a tourniquet.

Severe bleeding is often very alarming but it can be controlled relatively simply, and you should do your best to keep calm and carry out the necessary procedures. If you are attending someone who is bleeding uncontrollably, you should:
- lie them down flat and if possible raise the injured part (although not if you suspect a fracture since moving it may make it worse);
- apply direct pressure to the wound. Ideally you should use a dressing, but if none is available use a piece of clothing, or even your hand. Obviously you should use something that is as clean as possible, but do not waste time searching for sterile dressings or washing your hands — the victim may bleed to death during the delay. If the wound is gaping, hold its edges firmly together. If there is anything in the wound, try to press around it rather than directly on it. Unless the foreign body is lying loose on top of the wound, do not remove it — it may be plugging the wound and therefore reducing blood loss;
- bind the wound up so that pressure is maintained — use clothing torn into strips if there is no dressing;
- if blood oozes through the binding, add more, do not remove it. If you have a towel, use that. If you remove a dressing once it has been applied, it will dislodge the blood clot that will have formed and start the bleeding again;
- get medical help or take the victim to hospital as soon as you can;
- keep checking the victim for signs of shock or a cessation of bleeding or circulation. If necessary give EAR or CPR.

Arterial pressure points

If direct pressure on the wound is not effective, or the area of damage is too widespread for direct pressure, you can stop the

Section 8: Emergencies

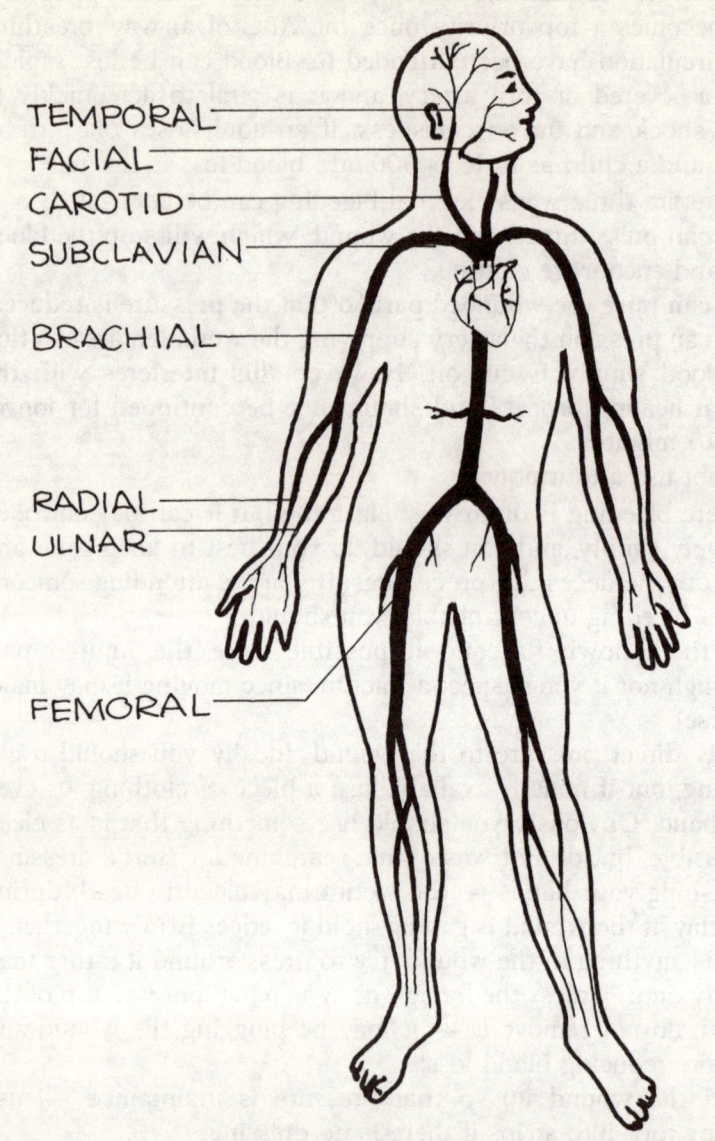

FIGURE 8.8: Arterial pressure points.

bleeding by applying pressure to the artery that supplies the area with blood. The best place to do this is to locate a pressure point between the wound and the heart where the artery can be pressed against a bone. The pressure point for the arm is halfway along the inside of the upper arm. For the leg, it is about halfway along the fold of skin in the groin that separates the thigh from the abdomen.

Shock

If a person loses so much blood that there is no longer enough to maintain adequate blood pressure, they are said to be in shock.

This is a medical condition (see Section 5) and has nothing to do with the emotional state of the person.

A person in shock is usually pale, feels faint, has a cold clammy skin and a weak rapid pulse. They may be thirsty, display signs of agitation and anxiety and become drowsy and confused, eventually losing consciousness. Shock is sometimes confused with a faint, but a person who has simply fainted will regain consciousness within a minute or so. Shock can follow any severe injury and is a medical emergency. Sometimes the bleeding is internal, in which case you will not see any blood. Anyone who has been badly injured should therefore be carefully watched for shock, and first aid should include measures to prevent or at least minimise shock.

WHAT TO DO
- Lie the victim down on their back.
- Keep the head flat on the ground and raise the lower part of the body so that blood will flow from the legs towards the head.
- Loosen any tight clothing and keep the victim warm by wrapping in a coat or blanket. Do not use a hot water bottle or an electric blanket.
- Do not give anything to eat or drink.
- Call a doctor or take the victim to hospital.

Electric shock caused by electrocution is discussed under ACCIDENTS AND EMERGENCIES below.

Unconsciousness

If a person is unconscious, they cannot respond to their surroundings in a normal way and their usual reflexes may not operate. This may mean, for example, that they cannot swallow or cough and so clear the throat of any mucus or foreign objects. An unconscious person's muscles relax and may be so floppy that if they are lying on their back their tongue will fall backwards, blocking the airway.

There are three levels of unconsciousness:
- the victim can be easily aroused but slips back into a sleepy state;
- the victim can only be aroused with difficulty;
- the victim cannot be aroused at all.

Any level of unconsciousness can lead to a difficulty in breathing, so it is essential to attend to the victim quickly and to get medical help. You can assess whether a person is unconscious by speaking loudly to them and shaking their shoulders. If they do not respond, they are unconscious (see ASSESSMENT above).

Leaving aside a temporary faint from which the person usually recovers quite quickly (see ACCIDENTS AND EMERGENCIES), reasons for becoming unconscious include a stroke or heart attack, a blow

Section 8: Emergencies

to the head, an overdose of alcohol or drugs, and diseases such as epilepsy or diabetes.

Do not move an unconscious person unless they are in immediate danger, and do not leave them alone (send someone else for help). Carry out the ABC of first aid as soon as you can. If necessary, administer mouth-to-mouth resuscitation or CPR. If the victim is breathing and has a pulse, put them in one of the **recovery positions** described below and keep them there to ensure that the airway is kept clear. Monitor the airway and pulse continually until help arrives. Do *NOT* give anything to eat or drink — do not for example try to revive them with sips of water; they will be unable to swallow and may choke.

Coma position

To put an unconscious person in the coma position,
- lie the victim on their back and kneel on one side;
- place the near arm straight down beside the body, tucking the hand, palm up, under the buttocks;
- cross the far arm over the chest;
- cross the far leg over the near one;
- protect and support the head with one hand, and with the other hand grasp the clothing at the hip furthest from you and pull the victim towards you so they roll onto the side;
- readjust the head to make sure the airway is still open;
- bend the upper arm into a convenient position to support the upper body. Bend the upper leg at the knee to bring the thigh well forward so that it supports the lower body;
- carefully pull the other arm out from under the body and leave it lying parallel so the victim cannot roll back.

Do *NOT* use the coma position if you suspect the victim has an injured back or neck, unless breathing becomes noisy, laboured or irregular.

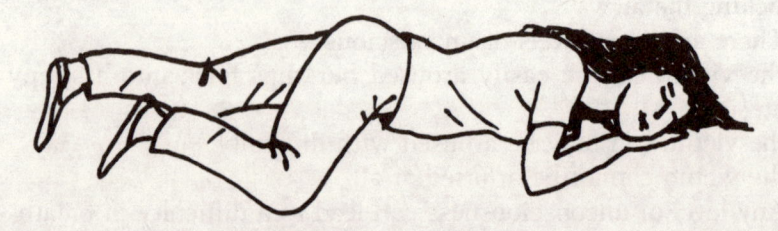

FIGURE 8.9: Coma position.

Lateral position

Provided there is adequate support for the head, an unconscious person may also be placed in the lateral position:
- place the victim on their back and kneel beside them;

- extend the far arm out at right angles to the body;
- place the near arm across the chest;
- bend the near knee so the leg is at right angles to the body, keeping the far leg straight;
- grasp the victim's near shoulder and hip and roll them on to their side so that they are facing away from you. Keep the back straight;
- place the top arm so that it rests comfortably across the lower arm;
- tilt the head backwards with the face slightly downwards to maintain a clear airway.

FIGURE 8.10: Coma position (lateral).

ACCIDENTS AND EMERGENCIES

See also the following section on BITES AND STINGS.

Allergic reactions (anaphylaxis)

Many of us have mild allergies of one kind or another. These are frequently irritating and inconvenient but no more than that. A few people suffer from anaphylaxis which is an immediate, severe and life-threatening allergic reaction. Death may occur within minutes without medical help.

Anaphylaxis usually occurs quite suddenly in response to something like an inoculation, drugs such as penicillin, or insect stings such as from bees or wasps. A victim suffering from anaphylaxis will become sweaty, develop widespread pins and needles, swell up (possibly in the tongue and throat), start wheezing, turn blue around the lips, lose control of their bladder, lose consciousness, convulse, stop breathing and die.

Swelling of the tongue and throat alone can cause death, and the most important first aid you can give is mouth-to-mouth resuscitation (see EXPIRED AIR RESPIRATION) and cardiopulmonary resuscitation (see separate entry). Get medical help as quickly as you can because the only action that can save the victim's life is an injection of something to reverse the effect of the allergy.

Section 8: Emergencies

A person who has had an anaphylaxic reaction previously may have an injectable form of adrenaline with them for use in an emergency.

See also Section 5.

Asthma

Asthma is a breathing problem caused by a spasm of the small air passages in the lungs, accumulation of mucus and swelling of the tissues. The victim becomes very distressed and gasps and wheezes, desperately trying to breathe. Most asthmatics carry medication with them and have been instructed how to manage an attack. However, asthma attacks can be, and not infrequently are, fatal and need careful attention.

Sit an asthma victim upright in a chair or leaning over a table or pillow. Reassure them and make sure they have plenty of fresh air. If they have medication, make sure it is given at once. Unless the attack is very short-lived, get medical help.

See also Section 5.

Burns and scalds

A burn is damage to body tissues by excess heat. A burn can be caused by fire, contact with something hot, electricity, the sun, excess friction. If the heat is moist such as from boiling water or steam, the burn is called a scald.

Burns are classified according to three degrees of severity. First degree refers to burns where the skin has reddened, such as in sunburn. Second degree burns are where the superficial layers of skin are damaged, such as in a blister from hot coffee. Third degree burns are when the full thickness of the skin has been burnt. See also Section 5.

Burns are painful and distressing, and all but minor burns are serious and need medical attention. Third degree burns are sometimes less painful as the nerve endings will have been destroyed. Extensive burns may lead to fluid loss and shock, and the victim will need urgent help.

FIRST AID

- If necessary put out the flames. Hold a rug or blanket in front of you as you approach so that you will not get burnt yourself, and envelop the victim in it. Wrap it tightly around the victim to smother the flames and lower them to the ground. You can also use water to douse the flames but make sure you do not create scalding steam.
- Remove hot clothing if it will come off easily, but do NOT remove any fragments sticking to the skin — you may remove the skin with it.
- Cool the burnt area with cold water. If the victim is comfortably

able to move and the burn is easily accessible, e.g. on an arm, hold the burn under cold water for at least ten minutes. If not, gently apply cold compresses.
- Do *NOT* prick or break any blisters and do not apply any lotions, ointments, or oily dressings — they will have to be removed later, which will be painful and damaging.
- Cover the burnt area with a clean (sterile if possible) non-stick dressing. If not available, use a wet cloth.
- Bandage the burnt area lightly — a torn up sheet is ideal. If the burns are on the face, cut holes for the eyes, mouth and nose.
- Allow the victim to rest in a comfortable position, if possible using pillows for support. Raise injured limbs to reduce swelling and fluid loss. If the face is burnt, try to keep the victim sitting up.
- Give frequent sips of water to replace lost fluids — but *NOT* alcohol.
- Watch for signs of shock and treat if necessary (see SHOCK).
- Give mouth-to-mouth resuscitation (see EXPIRED AIR RESPIRATION) or cardiopulmonary resuscitation (see separate entry) if required.

Choking

Choking occurs when a foreign body gets stuck in the airway so that breathing is obstructed. It is vital to remove the object immediately. In severe cases the victim cannot breathe at all, and if left untreated will die. Adults may choke on food or broken false teeth; children may choke on bits of toys they put in their mouth or foods such as peanuts or chewing gum.

When choking occurs, the victim may have a violent fit of coughing and the face and neck will become deep red, turning to purple. They will make a superhuman effort to breathe, and if unsuccessful will claw the air and clutch at the throat before turning blue in the face and collapsing.

Often the object will be dislodged by the coughing. If not, try to remove it with your finger — but be extremely careful not to push it down further. If that is unsuccessful, two or three sharp blows between the shoulder blades may clear it. Make sure the person is in a position in which the object can fall out easily — e.g. an adult should sit and lean forward. If the victim is lying down, turn them gently to one side.

If this fails, place your arms around the victim's chest from behind, with your clenched fists over the breast bone. As suddenly and as hard as you can, push on the breast bone and squeeze the chest. This will force the remaining air out of the lungs and up the windpipe so that (hopefully) the obstruction will be dislodged sufficiently for the victim to cough it up and out. If you are much bigger and stronger than the victim, try not to break too many ribs!

Section 8: Emergencies

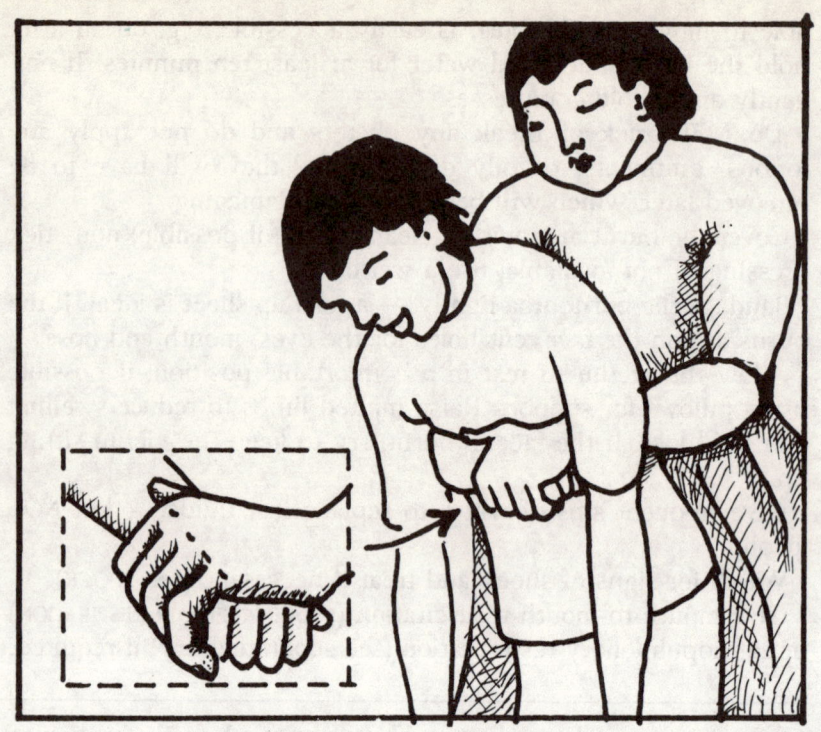

FIGURE 8.11: Chest compression.

If chest compression in this position does not work, place the victim on a table so that they are hanging over the edge from the waist up, with the top of their head on the floor. Try the chest compression again so that it is aided by gravity.

If all these measures fail and the victim is unconscious, lie them on their back and tilt the head backwards to maximise the airway. Sit astride the victim and place the heel of your hand on the upper abdomen just above the navel. Cover it with the heel of your other hand. Give a sharp downward and forward thrust towards the victim's head. Give up to four thrusts if necessary. If the victim does not splutter and start breathing, start mouth-to-mouth resuscitation.

As the victim starts breathing normally, place them in the recovery position (see UNCONSCIOUSNESS) and get medical help. It is especially important to tell the doctor if chest compression has been used, so that the internal organs can be checked.

If all efforts to dislodge the object fail, you will have to blow air past it by using mouth-to-mouth resuscitation until medical help is obtained.

BABIES AND CHILDREN

If you have a child who is choking, sit down and lie the child face down across your lap, with the head low. Give two or three blows between the shoulder blades with the heel of your hand. If this is unsuccessful administer chest compression. A baby can be held upside down in your arms while you slap it between the shoulder blades or administer chest compression.

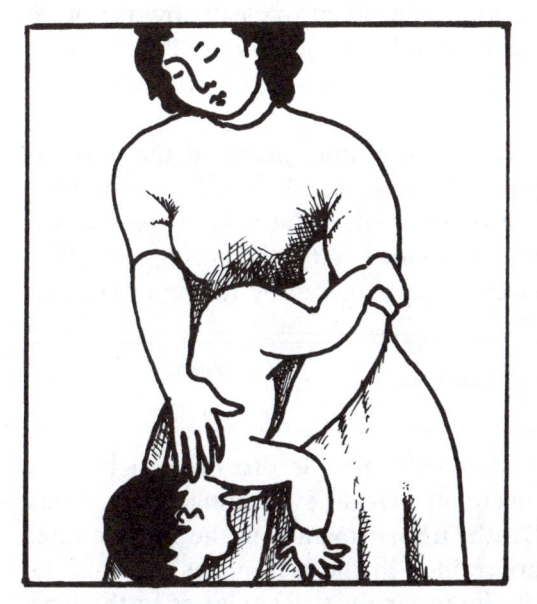

(a) infant

(b) child

FIGURE 8.12: Assisting choking child dislodge obstruction.

Concussion

See HEAD INJURIES.

Cuts

There are three essentials in dealing with any cut. The first is to stop bleeding, the second to prevent infection, and the third to repair the wound.

No matter how large the wound, the best way to stop bleeding is to apply pressure directly over the injury. Tourniquets should not be used. A piece of clean cloth several layers thick (e.g. a clean, folded handkerchief) is the best and usually most convenient dressing. Tissues tend to disintegrate and contaminate the wound.

The cloth should be applied over the bleeding area and held there firmly by the person giving first aid or the victim. If it is likely to be some time before further treatment can be given, the dressing can be held in place by a firm bandage, provided it is not so tight as to cause pain or restrict the supply of blood to the parts of the body beyond the bandage.

If an arm or a leg is involved, that part of the body should be elevated above the level of the heart. Unless the wound is minor,

Section 8: Emergencies

the patient should lie down to avoid fainting or shock.

Provided medical attention is readily available, no other first aid is necessary, as the doctor will ensure the cleanliness of the wound and its repair. If there is likely to be a significant delay before a doctor can be seen, it is prudent to clean any dirt out of the wound with a diluted antiseptic, or clean water if no antiseptic is available. Ensure that bleeding has stopped first, and do not disturb any clots that may have formed.

Minor cuts will heal without stitching, provided the edges of the wound are not gaping. If the edges do not lie comfortably together, if a joint surface is involved, if the wound continues to bleed, or if the scar may be cosmetically disfiguring, then it is essential to have the cut correctly repaired by taping or sutures.

Dislocation

See SPRAINS, STRAINS AND DISLOCATIONS.

Drowning

Every year in Australia about 400 people drown. Roughly two thirds of these deaths occur in private swimming pools, dams, rivers and waterholes. Deaths from drowning in the surf are rarer, mainly because lifesavers trained in the techniques of resuscitation are available. Despite increasingly strict rules as to the fencing of domestic swimming pools, a number of young children drown or nearly drown every year. It is astonishing how quickly a child can come to grief in a swimming pool.

A person will drown more quickly in cold water than warm and in salt water rather than fresh.

In almost all drowning accidents, the most important thing to do is to start artificial respiration quickly. Do not waste time trying to clear the victim's lungs of water. Drowning occurs because the larynx (windpipe) goes into spasm and blocks the air supply. In fact, very little water will have got into the lungs, and provided you breathe sufficiently strongly, the air will bubble through any water in the windpipe.

Obviously you should get the victim out of the water as soon as you can, but if this is likely to take several minutes, begin resuscitation in the water.

Resuscitation in the water

If you are in shallow water, begin mouth-to-mouth resuscitation (see EXPIRED AIR RESPIRATION) as quickly as you can. If there is any obstruction, clear the victim's airway with your fingers. Stand at the side of the victim's head, supporting the body with one hand, tilting the head back with the other, making sure that the jaw is supported. Depending on the depth of the water, you may be able to provide body support by kneeling on the bottom and raising one knee under the middle of the back. You may need to seal the nose with your cheek.

In deep water, resuscitation will have to be carried out while treading water and generally is within the scope only of trained lifesavers and strong swimmers. Do not try to do more than you are capable of doing — many unnecessary drownings occur because the rescuer gets into trouble. Mouth-to-nose resuscitation is more appropriate in deep water, because if the victim's mouth is open they may swallow more water.

A drowning victim is likely to vomit because of the large amount of water they have swallowed. They may also have solid matter such as seaweed caught in their airway, so as soon as you can get to dry land, turn the victim on their side and sweep your fingers around the mouth and tongue to remove any obstructions. Then turn them back and continue with the resuscitation, but clearing the mouth frequently. If they vomit during resuscitation, turn them on the side again at once. If the larynx is still in spasm, you will have to blow sufficiently hard to get past the spasm, but not so vigorously that the victim's stomach becomes distended.

If there is no pulse, begin cardiopulmonary resuscitation (see separate entry).

Once the victim is breathing, place them in the coma position (see UNCONSCIOUSNESS) and keep them warm with towels or blankets. Treat any injuries.

Keep a close watch on any drowning victim until medical help is available, since even someone who has responded to treatment can deteriorate rapidly. You should monitor their breathing and pulse every few minutes.

Drugs

See OVERDOSES.

Electric shock

The most important thing to remember about a person who has been electrocuted is that until they are removed from the source of the current they are likely to be 'live' and, if you touch them, you may be electrocuted too. Therefore the first thing you should try to do is switch off the power or break the connection between the victim and the appliance. If the accident involves low voltage current, such as that used in homes and for lights and heating in shops and offices, find the switch and turn it off, if possible by pulling out the plug. If you can't turn the power off, **do not touch the victim directly**, but stand on a rubber mat or wear rubber-soled shoes and try to separate the victim from the source of the current with something made from dry wood, e.g. a chair or a broom handle. Avoid anything damp or wet, since water is a very efficient conductor of electricity.

SECTION 8: EMERGENCIES

If the accident involves high voltage current, stay well away from the victim until an expert turns off the power — high voltage current can travel through the ground and give you a shock from up to six metres.

The seriousness of an electric shock depends on how strong the charge is, how long the victim was exposed to it, and how well they were insulated. Death by electrocution is most likely to occur if the victim was in contact with water.

Once you have separated the victim from the current, smother any burning clothes with a blanket or whatever is available, and then check through the ABC of first aid (see separate entry). Do whatever is necessary to resuscitate them. Then place the victim in the recovery position. The victim will almost certainly be suffering from burns, usually more severe than they appear on the surface. Get a doctor or go to a hospital as soon as possible.

Eye injuries

Any injury to the eye is potentially serious and should receive expert assessment and treatment. An injured eye should not be rubbed, nor should it be opened and examined since it is very easy to do further damage. If the victim is wearing contact lenses, they may be able to remove the lenses themselves, but otherwise it is best left to a doctor. It is especially important to act quickly if any chemical has entered the eye.

FOREIGN BODIES

Foreign bodies in the eye are relatively common and can usually be dealt with at home. Simply washing the face with cool water, ensuring some gets into the eyes, will often remove loose bits of grit. If a single bit is embedded in the under-surface of the upper lid and the lid is pulled back over a match, it may be possible to remove it with the moistened tip of a hanky. Do not touch the eye surface. If bits of grit adhere to the eye itself, unless they can be washed away easily, a doctor's attention is needed.

A BLACK EYE

A bruised or black eye can be relieved by an ice pack (not the traditional piece of steak). Be careful not to bring the eye into direct contact with the ice. Wrap the ice in a damp material and alternatively leave it on and remove it from the eye for about 20 minutes at a time.

If the eyeball seems to be injured or the victim is unable to see properly, get a doctor. The eye can be padded and bandaged shut while travelling to the doctor or hospital.

Chemical injuries

It is essential that chemicals in the eye are washed out immediately. Tilt the victim's head to the affected side, hold the eyelids gently apart and rinse the eye for at least 10 and preferably 20 minutes. Make sure that the water does not splash or flow into the other eye.

Fainting

By far the most common cause of a sudden lapse into unconsciousness is that the person has fainted. This is simply a temporary failure of blood supply to the brain and can be brought on by emotional situations, extreme heat, a stuffy room, and standing for long periods of time (e.g. soldiers on parade).

If a person has fainted, they should be made to lie flat with their legs raised to increase the flow of blood to the brain. Tilt the head backwards and make sure the airways are clear. Loosen any tight clothing. The person should regain consciousness within a few minutes. If the victim does not recover spontaneously within a short period, turn them on their side in the lateral position (see UNCONSCIOUSNESS) and get medical help.

Fever

The normal body temperature is approximately 37 degrees Celsius. This varies between individuals and even during the course of the day. It is usually at its lowest in the early hours of the morning. It may be higher in hot weather or after a physical work-out. A woman's temperature varies throughout her menstrual cycle. A temperature that is more than half a degree either way, however, is a warning signal. Low temperatures can occur after shock, severe bleeding or exposure. High temperatures are often a sign of disease, ranging from a common cold to flu to cancer. A high temperature is not dangerous in itself unless it exceeds 41 degrees.

If a person's skin is hot, they may have a temperature, but the only sure way to tell is to take their temperature with a thermometer. This is a small glass tube that has a mercury-filled bulb at one end and is marked with a temperature scale. Normal body temperature is marked with an arrow. As the mercury is heated in the patient's mouth, armpit or rectum, it expands and rises up the tube to a point on the scale that indicates the body temperature. A small kink in the tube prevents the mercury from sinking back into the bulb when the thermometer is removed. Before buying a thermometer, examine it carefully to make sure the mercury column and the markings on the scale are easy to see.

Before using a thermometer, wash and dry it and shake the mercury column down until it is below 37 degrees. Rotate the thermometer until you can see the top of the mercury column against the scale on the side.

In adults the most common place to take a temperature is in the mouth, but it can also be taken under the arm, in the groin, and in the rectum. In the rectum is sometimes easiest for babies. In small children under the arm may be preferable to the mouth, as they may bite the glass if the thermometer is placed in their mouth. Wherever you take the temperature, never leave a small child alone with a thermometer since both the glass and the mercury can be harmful if it is broken.

To take the temperature in the mouth, place the bulb of the thermometer under the tongue to one side of the mouth. The patient should hold it in place by closing the lips but not the teeth. Take a reading after three minutes.

To take the temperature in the rectum, smear the bulb of the thermometer with petroleum jelly. The patient should pull their knees up to their chest. Spread the buttocks with the thumb and forefinger of one hand so that you can see the opening of the anus and insert the thermometer, leaving it in place for 2–3 minutes.

To take the temperature under the arm, place the bulb under the patient's armpit and fold the arm across the chest so that the bulb is in contact with the skin all round. Record the temperature after five minutes. The reading from under the arm is slightly less accurate (about 0.5 degrees less than the true temperature).

Do not take the temperature immediately after the patient has had a bath, a meal, a hot or cold drink or a cigarette, because you will get a false reading.

See also Section 3.

Fits/ convulsions

A fit or a convulsion is a result of a disturbance in the functioning of the brain. Some people have fits regularly, or a fit may occur because of a particular event, such as a head injury or poisoning. Sometimes there seems to be no cause at all. A common reason for a seizure or fit is epilepsy (see Section 5). In this case, the sufferer will usually lose consciousness and fall to the ground, lying rigid for some seconds, often with the jaws clamped shut and the back arched. At this stage they may hold their breath until their face turns blue. As breathing begins again, there may be jerking muscular movements, they may froth at the mouth, bite their tongue and lose control of bowel and bladder. After the sufferer has regained consciousness, they may be confused and have no idea what happened.

PROTECTION OF THE SUFFERER

The main task of anyone present at an epileptic seizure is to protect the sufferer from harm. Do not restrict their movements, since the spasms and jerking are automatic and trying to stop them may cause injury. Simply move any objects that may be a

Cunjevoi plant (*Alocasia macrorrhizos*) flower

Cunjevoi plant (*Alocasia macrorrhizos*) seeds

African wintersweet (*Acokanthera oblongifolia*)

Castor oil plant (*Ricinus communis*)

Pineapple zamia palm (*Macrozamia miquelii*)

Angel's trumpet (*Brugmansia aurea*)

PLATE 8.1: Poisonous plants

Moreton Bay chestnut tree (*Castanospermum australe*)

Golden dewdrop (*Duranta erecta*)

Coral bush (*Jatropha podagrica*)

Arum lily (*Zantedeschia araceae*)

Oleander (*Nerium oleander*) white

Oleander (*Nerium oleander*) pink

PLATE 8.2: Poisonous plants

danger and, if necessary, remove false teeth (but do not prize the mouth open or force objects into it). Protect the head from banging against the floor by putting something flat and soft (such as folded jacket) under it. If possible loosen the person's collar so they can breathe more easily. Artificial respiration will probably be impossible, and the sufferer will breathe normally again at the end of the seizure, generally after a few minutes. The sufferer may fall asleep once the seizure has ended, in which case place them in the coma position (see UNCONSCIOUSNESS) and allow them to wake naturally. There may be a card or tag saying what to do if the person has a seizure — look for this and follow the instructions.

CONVULSIONS IN CHILDREN

Small children under the age of about four sometimes have convulsions because of a high temperature. These are called febrile convulsions (see Section 5) and generally consist of body rigidity, twitching, arched head and back, rolling eyes, a congested face and neck, and bluish face and lips. This can be extremely alarming for parents, but generally the seizure will end quite quickly.

You should:
- ensure that the airway is clear, and turn the child on to the side if necessary;
- remove the child's clothing;
- bathe or sponge the child with lukewarm water;
- when the child's temperature has been lowered, cover them lightly;
- call the doctor.

Fractures

A fracture is a broken bone. Generally the break is complete, but in young people whose bones are still flexible the bone may bend and only half break, in which case it is called a greenstick fracture. Most fractures are closed, i.e. the skin remains unbroken. If there is little damage to the surrounding tissues, it is a simple fracture. If the damage is extensive (e.g. if a lung is punctured by a rib), it is described as complicated. Open or compound fractures are where a bone protrudes through the skin or wound on the surface, and such fractures may lead to serious blood loss and are open to infection entering the wound (see also Section 5).

A limb or joint that is very painful, that looks out of shape, or that will not move following an injury or fall, is likely to be broken, and you should get the victim to a doctor or hospital casualty department as soon as possible.

While waiting for medical aid:
- keep the victim as warm and comfortable as possible;

SECTION 8: EMERGENCIES

- gently remove clothing from any open wound over the break and cover it with a clean (preferably sterile) dressing;
- do not try to manipulate the bone or joint yourself, as you are likely to cause further (potentially very serious) damage;
- move the affected area as little as possible and immobilise the fracture;
- if the injury is in the arm, use a sling (see SPRAINS, STRAINS AND DISLOCATIONS) or strap the arm to the body. If the leg is injured, strap the injured leg to the uninjured leg. Alternatively you can make a splint from a broom handle or a rolled-up newspaper (remembering to protect any open wound from the newsprint);
- do not give the victim anything to eat or drink, as the setting of the fracture may require an anaesthetic.

Head injuries

CONCUSSION

Concussion is a bruising of part of the brain as a result of a blow on the head (generally at the back) or a severe shake of the body. It can vary in severity from mere giddiness and a headache for an hour or two to a complete loss of consciousness, sometimes lasting for weeks. It can involve a loss of memory, possibly relating to events just before and after the accident, occasionally as to personal identity. A moderate to severe blow on the head will usually cause a degree of concussion. Symptoms include 'seeing stars', temporary, partial or complete loss of consciousness, shallow breathing, nausea and vomiting, paleness, coldness and clamminess of the skin, blurred or double vision, and a possible loss of memory.

You should lie the person down and keep them warm and comfortable. Cold compresses applied to the brow or the site of the injury may help. Do not give anything to eat or drink — if they lapse into unconsciousness and then vomit, they may choke. If the victim becomes unconscious, put them in the coma position (see UNCONSCIOUSNESS) and call the doctor.

Keep the victim under observation for at least 24 hours for signs of more serious injury to the brain or a fractured skull. The main symptoms include:
- a worsening headache;
- continued vomiting;
- drowsiness, stupor;
- deliriousness or other mental changes;
- collapse, fits, blackouts;
- giddiness;
- clear or bloodstained fluid draining from the nose or ears.

If any of these symptoms occur, get medical advice immediately.

Heart attack

A heart attack occurs if the supply of blood to the heart is reduced. This may be because the arteries carrying the blood to the heart have become narrowed or hardened or because a clot has formed. Generally the victim will have chest pains which may be described as an ache, pressure or a crushing feeling, and which often radiates to the arms, neck and jaw. They may be short of breath and have a weak or irregular pulse. They may experience nausea and vomiting and have a pale, cold, clammy skin. Feelings of anxiety and apprehension are common. Sometimes the victim collapses and becomes unconscious.

Carry out the ABC of first aid (see separate entry). If necessary, administer mouth-to-mouth resuscitation (see EXPIRED AIR RESPIRATION) or cardiopulmonary resuscitation (see separate entry). If the victim is conscious, help them into a position in which they are comfortable, and loosen clothing around the neck, chest and waist. If the victim is breathing but unconscious, place them in the coma position (see UNCONSCIOUSNESS). Get urgent medical help — preferably an ambulance to the nearest hospital with a coronary care facility.

See also Section 5.

Nosebleed

Bleeding from the nose may be the result of a blow to the nose, or because the nose has been blown too hard, causing the blood vessels to break, or the result of drying and cracking of the nose in hot, dry weather, or it may occur (especially in children) for no apparent reason at all. In elderly people, a nosebleed may be a side effect of high blood pressure.

Sit the victim down with the head leaning forward so that the blood does not flow into the throat. Loosen any clothing around the neck. The victim should then pinch the lower soft part of the nose between the finger and thumb for about 10 minutes, and then release the pressure slowly. This can be repeated if the bleeding continues. When the bleeding stops, the victim should be careful not to blow the nose, as this will dislodge the clot and start the bleeding again. If the bleeding does not stop or if you suspect a broken nose or other injury, the nose should be held while medical help is obtained.

Overdoses

A person who has taken an overdose of drugs may feel faint, slur their speech, have convulsions and gasp for breath. They will generally have a rapid, weak pulse. They may be unconscious.

Carry out the ABC of first aid and give mouth-to-mouth resuscitation (see EXPIRED AIR RESPIRATION) or cardiopulmonary resuscitation (see separate entry) as required. Get urgent medical help. Try to find out what drug has been taken and whether it has been swallowed, inhaled or injected. If you can find any containers, syringes or ampoules, send them to the hospital with the victim.

Section 8: Emergencies

TABLE 8.1:
OVERDOSES

Chemical/Drug	Consequence	Treatment
Alkalis (household bleaches)	Burning, vomiting, shock, difficult breathing.	Dilute with milk, allow vomiting, give vinegar.
Antidepressants (Tryptanol, Sinequan, Tofranil, etc.)	Coma, muscle spasm, convulsions, death.	Induce vomiting, assist respiration.
Aspirin (Aspro, Disprin, etc.)	Rapid breathing, brain disturbance, coma, kidney failure.	Induce vomiting.
Barbiturates	Drowsiness, confusion, coma, breathing difficulty.	Induce vomiting, give coffee, assist respiration.
Codeine (in pain-killers, cough mixtures, antidiarrhoeals)	Constipation, reduced breathing, stupor, coma, heart attack.	Induce vomiting, assist respiration.
Digoxin (Lanoxin)	Vomiting, irregular pulse, heart failure.	Dilute with milk or water, then induce vomiting.
Insecticides	Vomiting, diarrhoea, difficult breathing, convulsions.	Dilute with large amount of milk, induce vomiting, assist respiration.
Lysol and creosote	Burning of throat, vomiting, shock, breathing difficulty.	Dilute with large amount of milk. Do NOT induce vomiting.
Mushrooms	Varies depending on type.	Dilute with water, induce vomiting, assist respiration.
Narcotics (morphine, heroin)	Headache, nausea, excitement, weak pulse, shock, coma.	Induce vomiting if narcotic has been swallowed, assist respiration.
Paracetamol (Panadol, Dymadon, Panamax, etc.)	Vomiting, low blood pressure, liver damage, death (50 tabs).	Induce vomiting.
Petroleum products (petrol, kerosene, etc.)	Liver damage, lung damage.	Do NOT induce vomiting, dilute with milk.
Tranquillisers (phenothiazines)	Drowsiness, low blood pressure, rapid pulse, convulsions, coma.	Induce vomiting.

TREATMENT METHOD

Assisted respiration: Mouth-to-mouth or mouth-to-nose resuscitation. See EXPIRED AIR RESPIRATION

Dilution of poison: 500 mL + milk, flour in water or fruit juice.

Induce vomiting: Induce by giving syrup of ipecacuanha, using finger in throat, or upper abdominal pressure. Do not induce vomiting in an unconscious patient.

If the victim has vomited, try to collect a sample. However, do not induce vomiting unless you are sure it is appropriate. If the victim is unconscious, place them in the recovery position and continue to monitor breathing and pulse until help arrives.

The table below lists common medications and chemicals that may be taken in excess, the likely results of such overdoses, and the appropriate remedies to be used in an emergency.

Refer all cases to your doctor or the nearest Poisons Information Centre.

Poisoning

There are Poisons Information Centres in all states and territories. At the time of going to print, the phone numbers were:

NSW (02) 519 0466
(008) 25 1525 toll free for country callers
Vic (03) 345 5678
(008) 13 3890 toll free for country callers
Qld (07) 253 8233
(008) 17 7333 toll free for country callers

SA (08) 267 7000
(008) 18 2111 toll free for country callers
WA (09) 381 1177
(008) 11 9244 toll free for country callers
Tas (002) 38 8485
(008) 00 1400 toll free for country callers
ACT (062) 43 2154
NT (089) 27 4777

A person can be poisoned by taking an overdose of drugs, either accidentally or deliberately, or by swallowing or inhaling some substance that upsets the functioning of their body. You will need to act quickly to minimise the effect of the poison.

In children, a common cause of poisoning is raiding the family medicine chest, or the kitchen cabinet with its supply of cleaning fluids, solvents and so on.

If someone is poisoned, ring your nearest Poisons Information Centre or local doctor immediately, and ask them what to do in the case of the specific substance involved.

In general terms:
- if the victim is unconscious, place them in the coma position and check that the airway is clear;
- monitor their breathing and pulse constantly. If breathing stops, give expired air respiration, and if the pulse becomes weak or stops, give cardiopulmonary resuscitation (see separate entries).

DO NOT INDUCE VOMITING IF:
- you do not know what the poisonous substance is
- it is a corrosive substance such as battery acid, oven cleaner, toilet cleaner, a strong disinfectant or any acid or alkaline substance
- it is a petroleum based product, for example, kerosene, petrol, diesel oil, turpentine. If these substances are vomited up they will burn the throat a second time, or damage the lungs by inhalation.
- the patient is drowsy and may become unconscious. Such patients risk choking if they vomit.

Someone who has swallowed a corrosive substance can be given small sips of water or milk, but otherwise simply wipe the substance away from the mouth and face, make the victim as comfortable as possible and get urgent medical advice.

If the substance is a medicine or similar substance, it may help to induce vomiting, depending on the age of the victim and how long ago the substance was ingested — if possible ask the Poisons Information Centre or doctor first.

To induce vomiting, give syrup of ipecacuanha according to instructions on the bottle, or stimulate the back of the victim's throat with your finger. Do *NOT* give salt or soapy water to drink. Keep a sample of the vomit in a clean jar to send to the doctor or hospital.

SECTION 8: EMERGENCIES

If the poison has been inhaled, move the victim away from the fumes or turn the fumes (e.g. gas) off at the source. *DO NOT BECOME A VICTIM YOURSELF*. Once the victim is in the fresh air, loosen any tight clothing and check breathing and pulse constantly — if either ceases or becomes weak, administer artificial respiration.

Sometimes poisons are absorbed through the skin, e.g. pesticides, weed killer, etc. (See also ORGANOPHOSPHATE POISONING, Section 5). In this case, remove the victim's clothes and get them to wash or shower thoroughly. If they become dizzy or sick, or complain of blurred vision or show any other sign of distress, get medical help immediately. Wash the contaminated clothes separately from other clothes.

See also OVERDOSES.

See also LEAD POISONING; MERCURY POISONING, Section 5.

POISONOUS PLANTS

The plants found in many gardens are poisonous if they are eaten. One of the prettiest and deadliest trees is the oleander. These are widely grown throughout Australia as an ornamental tree, but are extremely poisonous. A leaf, a flower or a fruit is sufficient to kill a child, and the sap can be equally dangerous. The early symptoms of poisoning are vomiting, diarrhoea, palpitations and dilated pupils, which can lead to coma and death.

The castor oil plant grows wild in many scrub areas along Australia's eastern seaboard. It has seeds the size of a golf ball, which children often play with, but which if eaten can cause severe diarrhoea, cramps, vomiting and sometimes even death. Most councils consider it a noxious weed.

Dieffenbachia (sometimes called dumb cane) is a decorative shrub often found in indoor pots. Chewing or biting the large fleshy leaves of this attractive plant produces copious salivation and severe burning and irritation of the mouth which may last for many days.

Angel's trumpet is a small tree that may be 3 m or more high and has white trumpet-shaped flowers. Eating any part of the plant, especially the flowers, can caused severe gastrointestinal symptoms, delirium and death (see also FOOD POISONING, Section 5).

Other common plants that may cause severe illness, if not death, include the broad-leafed rainforest plant cunjevoi, the stunted pineapple zamia palm; the blue-black plumb-like fruit of the African wintersweet, the prickly *Duranta* or golden dewdrop, the attractive fruit of the pot or rock plant called coral bush or psychic nut, and the seeds of the Moreton Bay chestnut tree.

First aid in case of poisoning varies with the plant. Induction of vomiting is the normal immediate step if a child is found eating a potentially poisonous plant, but unless you are in a remote area, more details should be obtained from your doctor or the Poisons Information Centre.

See Plates 8.1 and 8.2 between pages 790–1.

Scalds

See BURNS AND SCALDS.

Splinters

Small pieces of wood, glass, thorn, prickles and the like often penetrate the skin and can cause infection if they are not removed. Most splinters can be removed at home, but if the splinter is very large or does not protrude from the skin, a doctor should be consulted.

To remove a splinter:
- sterilise a pair of tweezers by passing the ends through a flame or by boiling them in water for 10 minutes;
- wash the area around the splinter thoroughly with warm soapy water - wash away from the wound so that dirt is not carried into it - dry gently;
- pull the splinter out with the tweezers;
- wash the wound with a mild antiseptic and cover with an adhesive dressing.

If you are unable to dislodge a splinter, or if the wound swells or becomes painful after the spinter has been removed, see a doctor.

Sprains, strains and dislocations

A sprain occurs when a joint is severely wrenched so that the supporting ligaments are torn. Dislocation is when the ligaments are stretched so far that the bones of the joint are pushed out of normal contact with each other (see also DISLOCATION, Section 5). A strain is an overstretched muscle or tendon. These injuries often result from games or sport. The victim experiences severe pain, swelling and has difficulty in moving the joint. Discolouration from bleeding around the joint will probably be seen. If the joint is dislocated, it will usually look misshaped. It can sometimes be difficult to differentiate sprains and dislocations from a fracture, and if there is any doubt, a fracture should be assumed and medical attention sought. A doctor will usually order an X-ray. Never try to realign a dislocation.

While waiting for medical assistance, the RICE principles should be followed, i.e. Rest, Ice, Compression, Elevation:

Rest — place the victim in a comfortable position (if possible with the injured limb supported with pillows) and advise them to stay quietly;

Ice — apply cold packs (with the ice in damp material so that it does not come in direct contact with the skin);

SECTION 8: EMERGENCIES

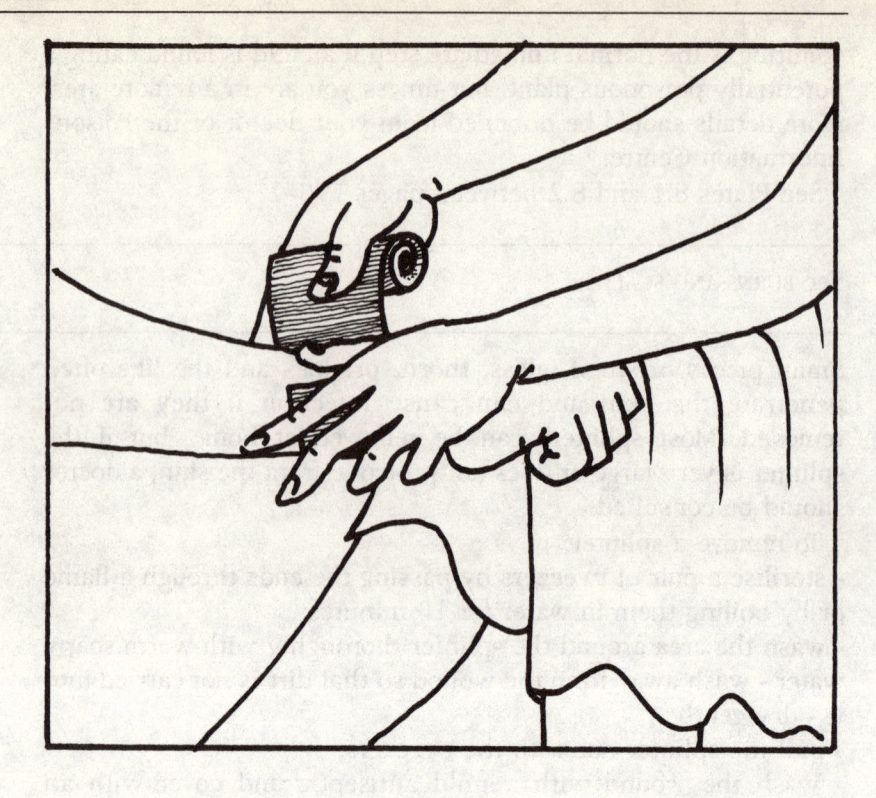

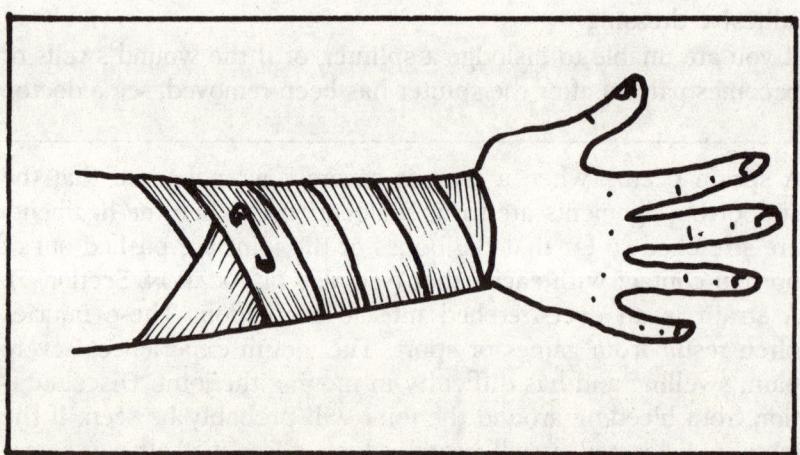

FIGURE 8.13: Strapping injured joint.

Compression — apply a firm bandage to the injured part;
Elevation — if possible, elevate the injured limb to reduce pressure and swelling. It is too tiring to hold a limb in the air without assistance, so pillows or a sling will need to be provided.

Most swelling in soft tissue is due to bleeding into tissue spaces. The purpose of RICE is to reduce this bleeding so that there is less swelling and less pain, and so that recovery is faster. Rest reduces the flow of blood around the body. Ice or any other form of cold causes the small blood vessels in the skin and other tissues to constrict so that the blood flow through those tissues is reduced. Compression bandages help to narrow bleeding vessels — good elastic bandages are best. Elevation helps to reduce the flow of blood in the elevated part.

STRAPPING AN INJURED JOINT

The best bandage to use for an injured joint is an elasticised roller bandage. Ideally, the size of the bandage should be related to the size of the injured limb, e.g. finger bandages should be small and body bandages should be wide. To strap an injured joint:
- place the joint in the position in which it is to remain;
- stand or sit opposite the victim, supporting the injury while bandaging;
- hold the roll in one hand and apply the outer surface on the bandage to the injured area, unrolling a few centimetres at a time;
- start about two or three bandage turns below the injury and bandage outwards from the victim's body, maintaining an even pressure. Finish two or three turns above the injury, overlapping each turn for maximum support. The bandage should be firm but not so tight that it will impede circulation.
- cut the end, tuck it in and pin;
- if there is no pin available, cut the end in two strips and make a reef knot.

See Figure 8.13 opposite.

SLINGS

Slings are used to rest, support or immobilise injuries to an upper limb or shoulder. They are triangular in shape and can be bought ready-made or adapted from any suitably shaped piece of material.

Arm sling. An arm sling is used to support an injured forearm in

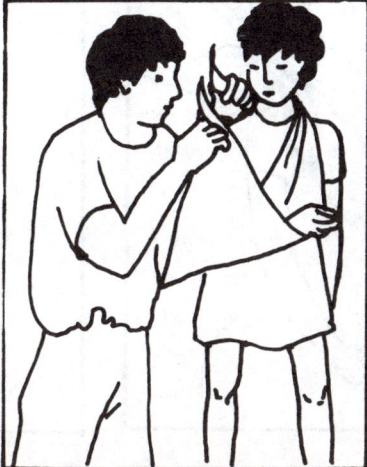

FIGURE 8.14: Tying an arm sling.

Section 8: Emergencies

a position roughly parallel to the ground.
- The victim should support the injured arm, with the wrist and hand raised higher than the elbow.
- Place the open sling between the chest and forearm, with the apex of the triangle stretching well beyond the elbow, the top point hanging over the shoulder on the uninjured side. The bottom point is towards the ground so that the long side of the triangle hangs down, parallel to the body.
- Bring the apex round the elbow so that it lies flat along the arm.
- Bring the base point up over the forearm and the top point

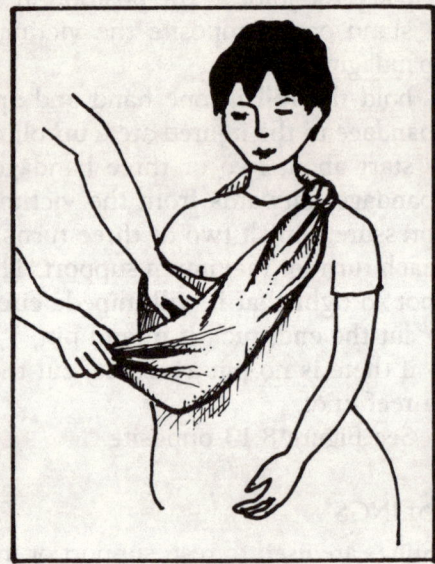

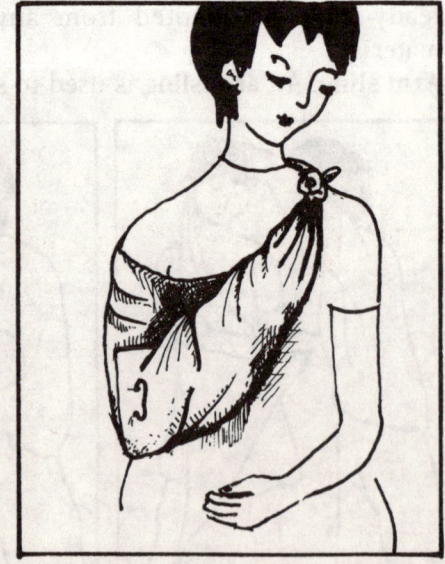

FIGURE 8.15: Tying an elevation sling.

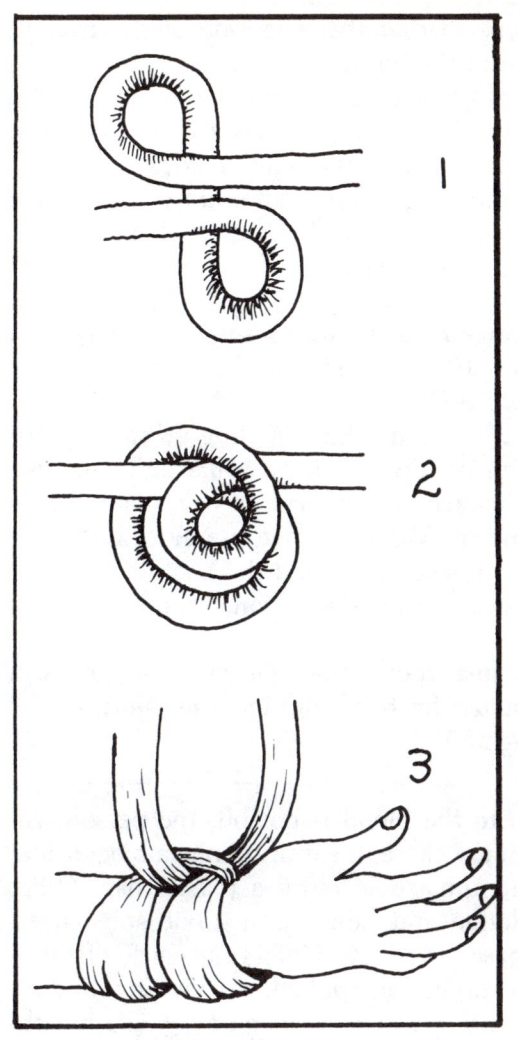

FIGURE 8.16: Tying a clove hitch for a collar-and-cuff sling.

around the neck so that the two points meet in the hollow just above the collar bone on the injured side.
- Tie the two ends in a reef knot.
- Make sure the victim's fingernails do not turn white or blue. If this happens, loosen the bandage or change the position of the hand.

Elevation sling. An elevation sling is used if the hand or forearm is injured, or to provide support for an injured shoulder without causing pressure on the shoulder or upper chest.
- The victim should rest the hand of the injured side on the opposite shoulder, with the elbow and upper arm held close against the chest.
- Cover the forearm and hand with a sling, with the apex of the triangle pointing towards the bent elbow, and the top point over the victim's shoulder on the uninjured side. The base point

SECTION 8: EMERGENCIES

should be hanging down, so that the long side of the triangle extends down the length of the body.
- Gently push the base of the sling under the hand, forearm and elbow of the injured limb. Then bring the lower end of the base up and around the victim's back on the injured side.
- Bring the two ends of the sling together around the back of the victim and secure with a reef knot on the uninjured side.
- Fold the top of the sling at the elbow, and fasten it with a pin or tape, or tuck it in.
- Check the victim's fingernails to make sure they have not turned blue. If they have, loosen the sling or bandage.
See Figure 8.15 on page 800.
Improvising a sling. If you do not have a sling or suitable triangular piece of material, improvise with a collar-and-cuff sling from a belt, tie, roller bandage or any piece of torn material:
- slip the bandage around the victim's wrist in a clove hitch;
- bring the ends of the bandage up around the back of the neck and tie in the hollow just above the collar bone on the uninjured side.
- The hand should be just above elbow level for upper arm injuries, and on the shoulder for hand and forearm injuries.
See Figure 8.16 on page 801.

Suffocation

If the supply of oxygen to the blood is cut off, the person will suffocate. The most common cause of suffocation is a blockage to the victim's nose and mouth, such as by a plastic bag. Other causes are smoke inhalation and fumes from toxic substances, such as gas and petrol-based products. Unless the cause of suffocation is removed and resuscitation applied, the victim will die.

A person who is suffocating will have laboured, noisy breathing, a swollen neck and head veins. Their face, fingernails and toenails will turn blue, and their pulse will be rapid, then weak before stopping altogether. Their breathing will change to shuddering spasms, and then cease. By this stage they will be unconscious.

The first thing to do if someone is suffocating is to deal with the cause. If it is a plastic bag, tear it. If they are breathing toxic fumes, get them outside or open the windows and doors. If the cause is smoke, make sure you do not become a casualty as well — protect yourself by tying a piece of cloth (preferably wet) over your nose and mouth before entering the room, and remove the victim as quickly as possible. In this case, do NOT open windows and doors as this will increase the risk of fire. Keep low to avoid the smoke. If the atmosphere is too contaminated, call the fire brigade.

Once you have the victim in a safe place, carry out the ABC of first aid (see separate entry). Remove any obstructions from the victim's mouth. If they have stopped breathing, carry out expired air resuscitation, and cardiopulmonary resuscitation if their pulse has stopped (see separate entries).

Once the victim is breathing, if they are still unconscious, place them in the coma position (see UNCONSCIOUSNESS) and send for medical help.

Sunburn

Australians with their fair skin and hot climate are very vulnerable to sunburn. The sun is extremely hot and will burn in the same way as fire, except that the sun is so far away we are not aware of the burning sensation that makes us draw back from fire. Obviously people with fair complexions are most susceptible to sunburn and should take extra precautions, especially in the middle of the day when the sun is at its height.

When the skin is burnt by the sun, it becomes red, painful and hot to the touch. If the burning is severe, the skin will blister. After a few days the skin dries and a layer peels off. Long-term effects of overexposure to the sun are permanent freckling, blotching and premature ageing of the skin.

Most cases of sunburn can be dealt with at home. The first step is to relieve the burning with a cool bath or shower, and apply cool compresses (although not iced since these may chill the victim) to the most affected parts. Calamine lotion or one of the commercial anti- sunburn creams will usually help. Paracetamol may reduce the pain. If the sunburn is severe, the victim may develop cold shivers and a temperature. Especially if a child is the sufferer, you may need to get medical advice.

Do *NOT* allow the victim of sunburn back in the sun without light-protective clothing until the burns have healed.

BITES AND STINGS

ANTIVENENE is available for bites and stings of:
- snakes
- funnel-web spider
- red-back spider
- box jellyfish.

DO use PRESSURE IMMOBILISATION (see over page) for bites and stings of:
- snakes
- funnel-web spider
- box jellyfish
- blue-ringed octopus
- cone shell
- insects (bees, wasps, ants, etc.) if the victim is allergic to them.

Section 8: Emergencies

Do *NOT* use pressure immobilisation for bites and stings of:
- red-back spider
- stonefish
- ticks.

PRESSURE IMMOBILISATION

1. Apply pressure to the bite until a bandage is available.

2. Bandage the limb firmly. The purpose of this is to restrict the venom as much as possible to the bitten area, so the bandage should be firm but not so tight that you cut off the blood supply completely. If you can use a crepe bandage, do so, but otherwise improvise with torn strips of clothing, pantyhose or the like. (a) Start at the bitten area and work to the fingers or toes. (b) Then return and cover the limb to the armpit or groin.

3. Immobilise the limb with a splint (e.g. a small branch of a tree) or by bandaging it to the other limb.

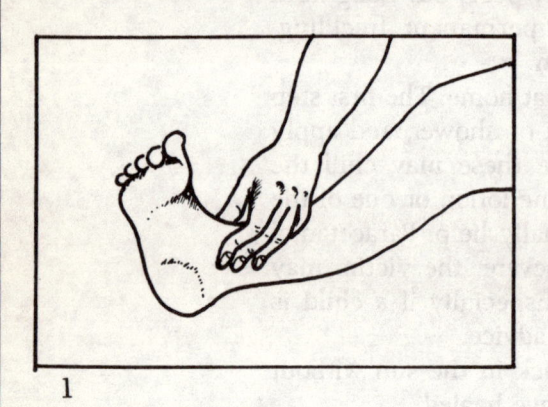

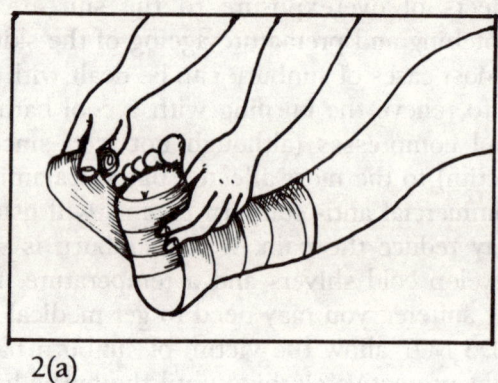

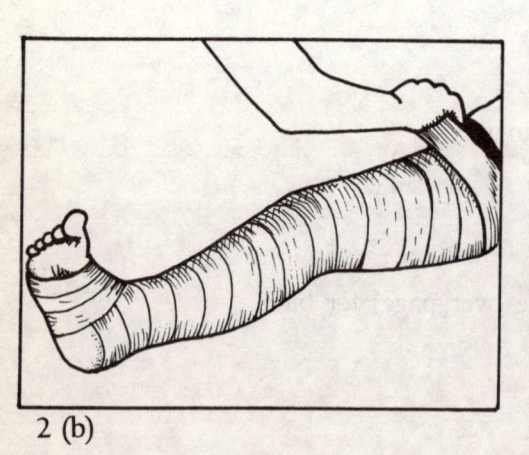

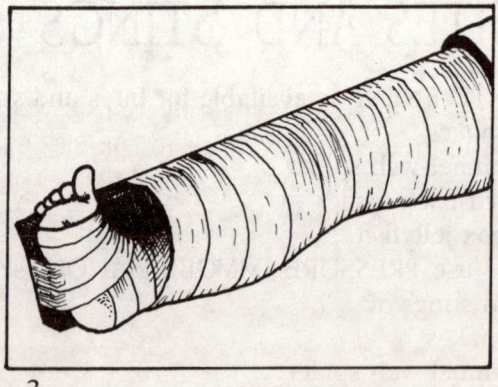

1

2(a)

2 (b)

3

Bees and wasps

A sting from a bee or wasp is often painful (in the case of a wasp, sometimes excruciatingly so) but recovery is swift and uneventful. However, a few people are allergic to such stings, and their reaction may be far more severe. They are likely to experience considerable local pain, swelling and irritation, puffy eyelids and wheezy breathing. If the reaction is severe, it can affect the breathing apparatus and the heart, and if breathing becomes difficult and/or the tongue starts to swell, get medical help immediately as the person's life may be in danger.

Bee stings are barbed and are usually left behind in the skin with the venom sac attached.

If someone is stung by a bee or wasp:
- remove the sting by scraping it sideways with your (clean) fingernail or the side of a knife. Make sure you do not pull or squeeze the sac of venom attached to the sting;
- wipe the affected area clean and apply a block of ice wrapped in damp material, e.g. a clean handkerchief;
- if the victim has an allergic reaction, apply pressure immobilisation (see above) and get them to a doctor;
- if their breathing or pulse stops, give mouth-to-mouth resuscitation (see EXPIRED AIR RESPIRATION) or cardiopulmonary resuscitation (see separate entry).

In recent years, European wasps have become a particular problem in Victoria and Tasmania. Unlike other wasps and bees, they do not release the sting into the skin of the victim but retain the ability to sting several times. This can be extremely painful and increase the possibility of an allergic reaction. The wasps are attracted to meat being cooked, and may be an unwelcome addition to barbecues. It is not unknown for them to crawl into an open can of drink, and then sting the victim in the mouth and throat. This can be extremely serious, since the airway may swell up and block. A wasp sting should be dealt with in the same way as a bee sting.

Dog and cat bites

Animal bites are extremely likely to be followed by infection, and it is important to take steps to combat this. Fortunately rabies is not a problem in Australia, but anyone bitten by an animal will need an injection against tetanus and so should see a doctor.

First-aid measures consist of thoroughly washing the wound with soap, followed by antiseptic, and then covering it with aclean dressing. Check for signs of infection for the first 24–48 hours. Most animal bites should be treated with antibiotics.

Marine stingers

Australian waters contain a number of marine stingers, mostly in the tropical waters but some in other areas. Marine creatures inflict their stings either by directly injecting the venom into the skin or by wrapping long tentacles containing stinging cells around the victim.

It is important to be aware that even if a fish is dead its venom may remain active, and poisoning can result from touching or treading on a dead fish.

Stonefish

Stonefish are found in the waters of the Australian tropics. They look astonishingly like a stone, and generally lie immobile in the sand under water, moving only if disturbed. Thongs or sandshoes should be worn if walking in Australian tropical waters. Prodding or kicking with bare feet a 'funny-looking stone' is a dangerous pastime.

A sting from a stonefish will cause intense pain spreading along the limb, blue or grey discolouration, swelling, sweating and signs of shock. The victim may become quite irrational as a result of the intense pain.

Anyone bitten by a stonefish needs urgent medical attention. While help is being obtained, you should relieve the pain by soaking the affected area in hot water, and remove any foreign body. Reassure the victim and keep them calm so that anxiety does not encourage the spread of the poison. Do *NOT* apply pressure immobilisation, as this increases the pain and may cause damage to the tissues. Be ready to apply mouth-to-mouth resuscitation if the victim's breathing falters.

Blue-ringed octopus and cone shell

Blue-ringed octopus and cone shells are often found in rock pools along the Australian coastline. They are extremely poisonous with venom that acts very quickly. A cone shell sting is usually painful, but that of the blue-ringed octopus is not necessarily painful at all. The blue-ringed octopus is an attractive creature that invites handling — *DON'T*. It is yellowish in colour, with blue bands that become iridescent when the octopus is disturbed.

Indications that a person has been stung include numbness of the lips and tongue (usually within minutes), muscular weakness, inability to breathe. You should:

- reassure and calm the victim as much as you can;
- send for medical help;
- make sure the victim is not left unattended;
- start mouth-to-mouth resuscitation as soon as breathing starts to weaken. Keep it up until medical help arrives — the victim will not be able to breathe for themselves;
- apply cardiopulmonary resuscitation (see separate entry) if the victim's pulse stops.

Tiger snake

Red-bellied black snake

Brown snake

Brown snake

Taipan

Death adder

PLATE 8.3: Venomous snakes

Red-back spider

Red-back spider: female and eggs

Funnel-web spider

PLATE 8.4: Spiders

Box jellyfish (sea wasp)

The box jellyfish is the most dangerous creature found in Australian tropical waters. A severe sting will lead to failure of the respiratory and circulatory systems in minutes. The box jellyfish has a small body with long tentacles. It is colourless and so can be difficult to see. It occurs in northern waters, especially between October and March, and bathers are generally warned to stay out of the sea during these months. However, increasingly beaches are being meshed to keep the jellyfish out, and then swimming is safe. Antivenene is available.

The most effective first aid treatment for all jellyfish stings, including the box jellyfish, is ordinary household vinegar — this renders the tentacles harmless within 30 seconds. Anyone who lives or is travelling in areas where dangerous jellyfish stings are a possibility should check that supplies of vinegar are available.

A box jellyfish sting will cause immediate and intense pain. The so-called 'frosted ladder' pattern from the tentacles can be seen along the line of the sting. (Tissue along this line will die in 24–48 hours.) The victim will quickly become irrational and find it difficult and then impossible to breathe.

You should *NOT*:
- try to remove the tentacles with your fingers, as undischarged venom cells may sting you;
- rub the sting, as this will spread the venom.

You should:
- liberally cover the affected area with vinegar;
- apply a firm compression bandage to the area;
- observe the victim closely and apply mouth-to-mouth resuscitation (see EXPIRED AIR RESPIRATION) if breathing stops and cardiopulmonary resuscitation (see separate entry) if the pulse stops;
- get medical help quickly.

If there is no vinegar available, apply a firm compression bandage above the sting. Remove any tentacles with tweezers (*NOT* your fingers) and then bandage the area itself.

Other jellyfish

Many jellyfish have stinging tentacles. Extensive stings can lead to respiratory failure and cardiac arrest, but most stings, although painful, are not life-threatening. One of the most common stingers in this category is the bluebottle or Portuguese man-of-war. Not surprisingly, the bluebottle is bright blue in colour, and consists of an air-filled sac with long thread-like tentacles. Often washed up on the beach by the tide, bluebottles are tempting targets for 'popping' by the unwary — a hazardous undertaking unless wearing shoes.

A person who has been stung by a jellyfish will usually have some surface indication of what has happened. The area subjected to the sting may display whip marks, goose pimples, or weals. The pain may vary from a mild burning to being severe or even intense. Minor stings may give rise to backache, pain in the chest, vomiting, aching limbs and sometimes loss of coordination, with some difficulty in breathing coming on 10–40 minutes after the sting.

Treatment is to pour household vinegar over the area of the sting. This destroys still active sting cells. Scrape off the remaining tentacles. Do not rub the area with sand, as this causes more venom to be absorbed. If no vinegar is available, pick off the tentacles with tweezers but not your fingers.

If the stings are severe:
- keep the victim at rest and calm them;
- treat for shock;
- if breathing or pulse stops, carry out mouth-to-mouth resuscitation (see EXPIRED AIR RESPIRATION) or cardiopulmonary resuscitation (see separate entry);
- get medical help.

Scorpions and centipedes

Stings from scorpions and centipedes can be very painful but, except in the case of allergy, the reaction is normally confined to the area of the sting. Apply ice to the affected area, and if symptoms persist see a doctor.

Snakes

Australia has some of the most dangerous snakes in the world. However, deaths from snake bite are comparatively rare, because the snake does not usually inject enough venom to be fatal. Of about 200 snake bites a year from potentially fatal snakes, five in fact cause death. A snake bite is more serious in a child than an adult, simply because the proportion of venom relative to size is greater in a child. However, whatever the age and stage of the person who is bitten, urgent medical assistance is imperative.

Anyone who suffers a snake bite should assume it is poisonous, since most non-venomous snakes do not bite (the carpet snake is an exception). Antivenene is now available for all poisonous bites.

Signs of snakebite include nausea, vomiting, headache, giddiness, double vision, drowsiness, tightening in the chest, diarrhoea, sweating, and difficulty in breathing. These may occur anything from 15 minutes to two hours after the bite. There will probably be puncture marks on the skin, but sometimes there is only a scratch, and sometimes no apparent mark at all. There may be some reddening, swelling, bruising or persistent bleeding at the site of the bite, but Australian snakes do not tend to produce any more than a minor local reaction.

The most important thing to remember in a case of snake bite is to keep the victim calm and move them as little as possible. This is because the body's natural reaction to stress and danger is to pump blood as fast as it can throughout the tissues to deal with the emergency, and this will spread the poison. So reassure the victim and make them as comfortable as you can.

At one time it was considered vital to find and identify the snake, but this is no longer so important as there are identification kits available. Looking after the victim is more important than looking for the snake. Do not wash the venom from the skin, however, as it may be needed for identification.

NEVER cauterise the bite or try to suck the venom out — this will cause the victim's blood to flow more swiftly as it hurries to plug the wound, and will only spread the poison.

If the bite is on a limb, apply pressure immobilisation (see above).

Check the victim's breathing and pulse regularly, and give mouth-to-mouth resuscitation (see EXPIRED AIR RESPIRATION) if breathing stops, and cardiopulmonary resuscitation (see separate entry) if the pulse stops.

Get medical help as soon as you can. It is better not to move the victim and to get an ambulance to come, but obviously this may be impossible if you are in an isolated spot.

See Plate 8.3 between pages 806–7.

Spiders

The only two Australian spiders that can cause death are the funnel-web, found around Sydney and on the Darling Downs of Queensland, and the red-back, found throughout Australia. Antivenene is available for both. The bites of other spiders may cause pain and irritation but will not usually be fatal.

See Plate 8.4 between pages 806–7.

FUNNEL-WEB SPIDER

The funnel-web spider is a large black, furry spider about 2–3 cm long. It lives in rock crevices, burrows, post holes, under houses or around dead tree roots. It sometimes wanders inside houses or toolsheds, and bites not infrequently result from a spider that has taken refuge in a boot or shoe.

The bite of a funnel-web spider is intensely painful, and a victim will usually be frightened and distressed. As with a snake bite, it is important to reassure and calm the victim, since the increased blood flow which is the body's reaction to fear and anxiety will tend to spread the venom more quickly.

Symptoms of a funnel-web bite include:
- tingling around the mouth;
- muscular spasm or weakness;

Section 8: Emergencies

- excessive sweating;
- profuse salivation;
- nausea;
- abdominal pain;
- numbness;
- coughing up of secretions from the lungs;
- weeping eyes;
- cold shivers;
- breathing difficulty.

Treat as for snake bite (see above) and get medical help quickly.

Red-back spider

The red-back spider is found in dark and protected areas, often hiding under cast-off tins and other rubbish. Only the female bites, and her body is the size of a pea, dark brown to black in colour, with the distinctive red or orange stripe running down the back.

The bite of the red-back spider may cause intense pain but not always. Symptoms of a red-back's bite include:
- tingling around the mouth;
- generalised pain;
- nausea;
- vomiting;
- profuse sweating;
- weakness and faintness;
- swelling around the bite;
- rapid pulse.

You should:
- reassure the victim;
- relieve the pain by applying an ice cube wrapped in damp material to the bite (but do not freeze or damage the skin);
- do NOT apply pressure immobilisation;
- get medical help urgently;
- watch for signs of shock and treat (see FIRST AID earlier in this section).

The venom of a red-back spider is relatively slow-acting, and provided there is no undue delay in obtaining the antivenene the victim should recover.

Ticks

Ticks are from the same family as spiders (arachnids) but are modified so much that they look nothing like their distant cousins. They have a large black body from which mouth parts protrude and grasp the skin. The tick does not have a head as such. A tube-like mouth part pierces the victim's skin to suck up blood. When the tick is full of blood, it drops off and waits for its next victim, which may be almost any warm-blooded animal, although some species preferentially attack certain animals. A full feed of blood may last the tick for a year or more.

Ticks are most active in the spring and summer. Bush ticks, which are the only dangerous form of tick, live on the eastern coastal strip of Australia. The most common victims of ticks are children playing in the bush, and golfers, since ticks shelter in foliage and drop on a victim and burrow in as they engorge themselves on blood. Ticks are usually found on the head, burrowing in amongst the hair, or in body crevices.

Ticks generally cause painful irritation and a raised lump on the skin. They may lead to paralysis if left untreated, especially in children.

Symptoms of tick bite are irritation and pins and needles at the site of the bite, nausea, double vision, unsteadiness, and eventually weakness and difficulty in moving first the lower limbs, then the upper limbs, and finally the face and breathing apparatus.

Do *NOT* attempt to pull the tick off or cut it out or squeeze it — this forces more venom into the system.

To remove a tick, wash it and the surrounding skin with an alcohol solution, such as methylated spirits. Place a pair of tweezers flat on the skin so that the jaws are on either side of the tick. Grasp the tick firmly, as close to the skin as possible, twist through 90 degrees, and then lift off. The tick will come away easily with minimal pain. Some tiny black marks, the mouth parts, may be left behind, but these rarely cause any trouble. Place some antiseptic cream or lotion on the bite and leave it alone to heal over the next couple of days. If the area becomes red and angry, it may have become infected, and a doctor should be consulted.

When To Call The Doctor

Illness can take on many different forms, so there can be no absolute rule about when the doctor should be called. If someone has an obvious injury or is very distressed, medical attention should be sought immediately. The problem arises with what appears to be relatively minor symptoms that may indicate a more serious underlying disease.

A raised temperature can occur with diseases as diverse as tonsillitis and the flu, to cancer and cirrhosis. The normal body temperature is 37 degrees Celsius. If the temperature is above 40 degrees, a doctor should be consulted immediately. If it is above 38 degrees, the patient can be safely watched for 12 to 24 hours. A fever below 38 degrees only requires a doctor's attention if it persist for several days or other symptoms are present.

Vomiting occurs in most people for one reason or another at frequent intervals throughout their lives. Food poisoning, gastroenteritis and overindulgence are the most common causes, and it will settle with starvation and time. However, once again more serious diseases may be responsible. In adults, it is safe to wait until the patient has vomited six to eight times before seeking attention. In infants, where dehydration can occur quite quickly, three or four vomits should be the limit.

Diarrhoea is also more serious in infants, and they should be checked if it does not cease in 12 hours. Adults can judge their need for attention by the degree of discomfort, but if the diarrhoea persists for more than 24 hours, they should visit their GP.

Headaches are another problem that plague the majority of mankind. Most will respond adequately to aspirin or paracetamol. Any headache that is not relieved by one of these simple medications should be checked within a day, and any headache that is relieved but returns repeatedly for three days or more needs investigation.

Shortness of breath when at rest needs immediate treatment, as it may be due to heart disease or lung problems.

Wheezing that recurs must also be investigated, and if it persists for more than a couple of hours without relief, urgent medical assistance should be obtained. Children can deteriorate rapidly with asthma and related conditions.

Pain of any kind without an obvious cause should also be checked if it persists for more than a couple of days. If the pain is severe enough to prevent you from sleeping or carrying on your normal daily activities, a doctor should be seen as soon as practical. Excruciating pain must be attended to immediately, day or night, as a few hours delay can often cause significant problems to deteriorate further.

It is particularly important for **chest pain** to be attended to as soon as possible. If there is a pressure or crushing sensation in the chest, particularly if combined with shortness of breath, you should seek medical attention instantly.

The most important reason to attend a doctor is if you are worried. Never feel that you are wasting a doctor's time. The doctor's job is to reassure you if nothing is wrong, and to take steps to deal with any problems that may be found. It is far better to be reassured today that there is nothing wrong than to wait for days or weeks and then have a serious disease diagnosed.

Home Medical Chest

A comprehensive medical chest for a family with children should contain:
Soluble aspirin tablets
Paracetamol tablets
Paracetamol liquid
Ipecacuanha (to induce vomiting)
Lotion for bites and stings
Anti-itch cream
Antiseptic cream
Antiseptic concentrated liquid
Pseudoephedrine tablets and/or liquid (for nasal congestion)
Oxymetazoline nose drops
Menthol inhalant
Cough syrup
Antiseptic ear drops
Antiseptic eye drops
Sun-screen lotion or cream
Splinter forceps
Triangular bandage (sling)
Adhesive dressing (various sizes)
Elastic bandages (wide)
Cotton gauze (*not* cotton wool)
Adhesive tape
Thermometer
Remember to replace antiseptic ear and eye drops regularly as their expiry date runs out, or sooner if they may have become contaminated by users.

INDEX

Abdomen
  abnormal mass in 121
  adhesions in 244
  ascites in 125
  borborygmi in 121
  colic in 303
  excessive noise in 121
  fluid in 125
  noise in 121
  pains in 121
  peritonitis and 468
  stomas in 675
  swelling in 122
Aboriginal health 737
Abreaction 677
Abscesses 277
  peritonsillar 488
Accidents
  first aid for 768
ACE inhibitor drugs 579
Acetazolamide 601
Achilles tendon 111
Acid drugs 566
Acne 241
  drugs for treatment of 603
Acoustic neurinoma 242
Acoustic neuroma 242
Acquired immune deficiency syndrome
  see AIDS
Acromegaly 243
Actinomycosis 243
Acupuncture 733
Adam's apple 87
Addiction
  alcoholic 246
  drug 327
  schedule of drugs of 651
Addison's disease 243
Adenitis 437
Adenoids 99
Adhesions 244
Adhesive capsulitis 357
Adolescence 50ff
Adrenal glands 65
  cancer of 469
Adrenergic drugs 566
Adrenitis 244
Afterbirth 20, 24
Agammaglobulinaemia 406
Ageing 56ff
  sense of smell in 105
Agraphia 189
AIDS
  categories of HIV 245
  condoms and 10
  nature of disease 245
  support groups 737
Air sickness 759
Albinos 737

Alcoholism 246
  drugs for treatment of 601
  preventative medicine and 745
  support groups 737
Aldosteronism 248
Alimentary tract 75
Alkaliser drugs 567
Allergic eczema 332
Allergic rhinitis 375
Allergies
  anaphylaxis 781
  desensitisers for 569
  severe and life-threatening 781
Allergy 248
Allergy tests 207
Alopecia 127
Alopecia areata 251
Alpha receptor blocker drugs 566, 579
Alternative therapies 732ff
Altitude sickness 253
Alzheimer's disease 252, 737
Amenorrhoea 157
Aminoglycosides 571
Amnesia 156
Amniocentesis 196
Amoebiasis 253
Amyloidosis 253
Anabolic steroids 567
Anaemia
  aplastic 254
  bone marrow biopsies and 198
  iron deficiency and 255
  nature of disease 254
  pernicious 255
  Schilling tests and 210
Anaesthesia 166
  nature of 653
  types of 654
Anaesthetic
  drugs 567
  epidural 26, 29
Analgesic drugs 568
Anaphylaxis 250, 781
Aneurysm 256
Angina 257
  drugs for 569
  Vincent's 553
Angioedema 250
Angiograms 223
Animal bites 805ff
Animals, human disease and
  brucellosis 283
  ornithosis 485
  rabies 488
  scabies 499
  sleeping sickness 518
  toxoplasmosis 539
  typhus 545
Ankles

815

Index

oedema in 165
Ankylosing spondylitis 258
Anorectic drugs 568
Anorexia nervosa
  nature of disease 258
  support groups for 737
  symptoms 125
Anosmia 175
Antabuse drugs 601
Antacid drugs 568
Antenatal checks 21
Antenatal classes 21
Anterior chest wall syndrome 537
Anthelmintic drugs 569
Anthrax 259
Anti-inflammatory drugs 600
Antiallergy extracts 569
Antiarrhythmics 570
Antibiotics
  acne and 242
  nature of 570
Antibodies
  immunotherapy and 679
Anticholinergic drugs 574
Anticoagulant drugs 574
Anticonvulsant drugs 574
Antidepressant drugs 575
Antidiarrhoeal drugs 576
Antidiuretic drugs 576
Antiemetic drugs 576
Antifungal drugs 577
Antigens
  in blood 68
Antihistamine drugs 578
Antihypertensive drugs 579
Antileprotic drugs 580
Antimalarial drugs 581
Antimigraine drugs 581
Antiparasitic drugs 582
Antiparkinsonian drugs 582
Antipsychotic drugs 583
Antirheumatic drugs 583
Antiseptic drugs 584
Antispasmotic drugs 584
Antithyroid drugs 584
Antituberculotic drugs 585
Antitussive drugs 586
Antiulcerant drugs 586
Antivenenes 803
Antiviral drugs 587
Anuria 184
Anus
  abscesses around 241
  bleeding from 122
  digestion and 75, 85
  fissures in 122
  itch in 123, 484
  pain in 123
Anxiety 123
  drugs for treatment of 587
  nature of disease 259
  neurosis and 451
Anxiolytic drugs 587

Aorta 66
  coarctation of 260
  disease of valve of 382
  narrowing of 260
Aortic stenosis 260
Aortic valve disease 382
Apgar score 24
Aphasia 177
Aphthous ulcers 546
Apnoea 176, 517
Appendix
  inflammation of 261
  removal of 658
Appetite
  excessive 124, 285
  loss of 124
Aqueous humour 77
Arms
  Erb's palsy in 344
  pain in 125
  slings for injured 799
  tennis elbow 530
Arrhythmia 381
Arteries 65, 74
  aneurysms and 256
  bypass grafts of 661
  gas embolism in 274
  inflammation of 262, 477
  pressure points in 777
  see also Aorta; Blood; Circulatory system
Arteriosclerosis 268
Arthralgia 154
Arthritis
  nature of disease 262
  support groups for 737
Arthroscopy 226
Asbestosis 266
Ascariasis 497
Aseptic meningitis 436
Aspirin damage 494
Asthenia 180
Asthma 267
  drugs for treatment of 589, 603
  emergencies involving 782
  support groups for 737
Astigmatism 79
Astringent drugs 588
Astrocytoma 279
Astrovent drugs 589
Ataxia 132
Atherosclerosis 268
Athetosis 189
Athlete's foot 358
Atrial filibration 166, 381
Atrophy 160
Auras 126
Australian Medical Association (AMA) 724
Australian Natural Therapists Association Ltd (ANTA) 732
Autism 270
  support groups for 738
Auto-immune diseases
  blood tests for 203

INDEX

Mikulicz's disease 514
pemphigoid 466
scleroderma 503
Sjögren's syndrome 514
SLE 428
Autonomic nervous system 95
Avulsion fractures 354
Babies
 see Infants; Labour and birth
Back
 abnormal curvature of 419, 426, 503
 ache in pregnancy 25
 bones of 106
 lumbago in 426
 nature of 106
 pain in 126, 270
 Scheuermann's disease in 500
Bacteria
 diseases caused by 727
 meningitis 436
Bad breath 126
Balance 136
Balanitis 271
Baldness 127, 251
Balls 111
Barbiturate drugs 589
Barium meals and enemas 223
Bartholin's cyst 272
Basal cell carcinoma (BCC) 514, 515
Becker's muscular dystrophy 445
Bed sores 272
Bed-wetting 272
Bee stings 805
Behavioural therapy 677
Bell's palsy 273
Bends 274
Benzodiazepine anxiolytics 587
Bereavement 61
Beri-beri 275
Beta lactams 572
Beta-blocker drugs 589
Bile 75, 88, 104
 drugs for problems with 591
 gallstones and 361
Bilharzia 276
Billings method of contraception 12
Biopsy
 bone marrow 198
 breast 199
 lymph node 199
 nature of 198
Birth breech 28
 by Caesarian section 28
 defects and caffeine 713
 multiple 4, 742
 premature 35
 see also Labour and birth
Bites animal 805ff
 first aid for 803, 808
 rabies and 488
Black death 473
Black eyes 788
Black spots

 seeing 186
Blackouts 143
Blackwater fever 429
Bladders
 cystitis in 66, 313
 function of 66
 ileal conduits and 675
Bleeding
 anal 122
 bruising 131
 drugs to stop 593
 during pregnancy 28
 emergency control of 777, 785
 excessive 127
 excessive vaginal 185
 from nose 164
 in urine 183
 in vomit 187
 into skin 171
 uterine 156, 185
 vaginal 185
 Von Willebrand's disease and 555
 see also Menstruation
Blepharitis 276
Blind spots 78
Blindness 128
 support groups for 738
Blisters 171, 340, 466
Bloating 122
Blood
 anticoagulant drugs and 574
 antigens in 68
 clotting test of 202
 emergency control of excessive 777, 785
 full count of 201
 functions of 67
 gas analysis of 202
 groups 68
 haemophilia 299, 374
 immune tests of 203
 in urine 183
 platelets 68
 poisoning 505
 polycythaemia vera and 478
 Rh negative mothers 69
 serum 67
 sugar test 202
 tests 200
 thalassaemia and 534
 transfusion reaction 540
 types of cells in 67
 urea test of 203
 vomiting of 187
Blood pressure
 diseases of 400, 403, 611
 nature of 83
Blue skin 172
Blue-ringed octopus stings 806
Body scans and X-rays 210ff
 arthroscopy 226
 bone scans 213
 bronchoscopy 226
 colonoscopy 226

INDEX

colposcopy 227
CT scans 210
culdoscopy 227
cystoscopy 227
densitometry 213
dual photon absorptiometry 213
echocardiography 213
endoscopy 224ff
gastroscopy 228
hysteroscopy 229
isotope scans 215
laparoscopy 229
magnetic resonance imaging (MRI) 214
nuclear scans 215
PET scans 217
radionuclide scans 215
ultrasound scans 218
X-rays 220ff
Boils general 277
in ear 360
Bones
ageing and 57
biopsy of marrow in 198
brittle 455
calcium and 71
cancer of marrow in 441
cancers of 277
first aid for fractures of 791
fractures of 353ff
in infants 70
in spine 106
infections of 456
lumps on 128
nature of 69
ossification in 69
osteoporosis in 456
Paget's disease of 461
scans of 213
surgery on 668
Borborygmi 121
Bornholm's disease 474
Bottle-feeding 37
Botulism 353
Bowel
abnormal colour of movements of 128
cancer of 675
colostomies and 675
diseases of 372
excessive desire to pass movements 129
irritable 121, 415
see also Large intestine
Box jellyfish stings 807
Bradycardia 169
Brain 71
cancer of 278
cerebellum 72
cerebrum 71
damage 741
electroencephalograms and 231
encephalitis and 337
meningitis and 481
stem 72
surgery 659

transient ischaemic attack (TIA) in 541
Wilson's disease of 559
Breakbone fever 316
Breastfeeding
compared with bottle feeding 37
how to 37
pregnancy and 14
problems with 39
support groups for 738
weaning 38
Breasts
biopsies of 199
cancer 280
changes in, during early pregnancy 17
enlargement of 129
infection 281
lumps in 130
mammograms and 223
nature of 72
pain in 130
self-examination of 748
surgery on 73, 670
tumours in 130, 224
Breathing
abnormal noises when 177
difficulties in 130
expelled air resuscitation (EAR) 770
hyperventilation 131
nature of lungs 88
stridor 177
suffocation 802
tests concerning 233
wheezing 189
Breech births 28
Bronchial carcinoma 427
Bronchiectasis 281
Bronchiolitis 281
Bronchitis 282
drugs for treatment of 589
Bronchodilator drugs 589
Bronchopneumonia 474
Bronchoscopy 226
Brucellosis 283
Bruises 131, 283
Bubonic plague 473
Buerger's disease 284
Bulimia 124, 285
support groups for 737
Bunions 181, 285
Burns 286
first aid for 782
to eye 350
Burping 132
Bursitis 125, 154, 287
Caecum 86
see also Large intestine
Caesarian sections 28
Caffeine 713
Caisson disease 274
Calcium
bones and 71
channel blocker drugs 579, 580
deficiency diseases 456

818

INDEX

Calculi
  gall stones   361
  kidney stones   417
  salivary stones   498
Cancer
  adrenal gland   469
  bone   277
  bone marrow   441
  brain   278
  breast   199, 280, 748
  cervical   74, 227, 293
  colo-rectal   304
  drugs for treatment of   591
  general nature of disease   288
  kidney   559
  liver   386
  lung   427
  lymph gland   394
  mesothelioma   437
  nipple   461
  ovarian   459
  Pap smears and   751
  parathyroid gland   399
  radiotherapy and   681
  skin   416, 514, 752
  stomach   522
  support groups for   738
  testicles   532
  thyroid   537
Candidiasis   536
Cannabis
  abuse of   329
Capillaries   74
Car sickness   759
Carbohydrates
  diet and   709
Carbuncles   277
Carcinoid syndrome   289
Carcinoma
  see Cancer
Cardiac failure   380
  see also Heart
Cardiac glycoside drugs   590
Cardiac stress test   232
Cardiomyopathy   289
Cardiopulmonary physiotherapy   688
Cardiopulmonary resuscitation (CPR)   773
Cardiovascular system   74, 81
Carotenaemia   289
Carpal tunnel syndrome   290
Cartilage   69, 83
Cat bites   805
Cat scratch disease   291
Cataracts   128, 290
Catarrh   291
Catharsis   677
Cells, blood   67
Cellulitis   292
Centipede stings   808
Central nervous system   94
Cephalosporins   572
Cerebellum   72
Cerebral palsy   292

  support groups for   739
Cerebrospinal fluid tests   204
Cerebrovascular accident (CVA)   524
Cerebrum   71
Cervical cancer   293
Cervical caps   10
Cervical osteoarthritis   143
Cervical smear tests   751
Cervical vertebrae   106, 107
Cervix
  colposcopies and   227
  disorders of   74
  during labour   23, 35
  nature of   73
Cestodes   530
Chalmydial infections   295, 540
Chancroid   293
Change of life   54
Charcot-Marie-Tooth disease   294
Cheeks
  infection in   345
Chemotherapy   591
Chest
  anterior wall syndrome   537
  compression of, to stop choking   783
  pain in   132
  pleurisy and   473
  pleurodynia   474
  pneumothorax in   475
  x-rays of   221
Chickenpox   294, 510
Chilblains   295
Children
  abuse of   695
  aspirin damage to   494
  autism and   270
  bronchiolitis and   281
  choking in   784
  convulsions in   134, 348, 791
  croup in   310
  dates for vaccination of   757
  dentistry and   697
  diabetes in   321
  febrile convulsions in   348
  fits in   791
  hyperactivity in   398
  immunisation of   49, 757
  impetigo and   502
  knock knees in   419
  resuscitation of   772, 776
  rheumatoid arthritis in   266
  rickets in   456, 495
  scarlet fever in   500
  scoliosis and   503
  teeth in   110
Chiropodists   690
Chiropractic   734
Chloasma   18, 173
Choking
  first aid for   783
Cholagogue drugs   591
Cholecystectomy   661
Cholecystitis   361

INDEX

Cholelithiasis   361
Cholera   296
  travel and   760
Cholesterol excess   297
  nature of   65
Cholinergic drugs   591
Chondromalacia   298
Chorea   153, 396
Choriocarcinoma   550
Chorionic villus sampling   205
Christmas disease   299
Chromosomes   5
  defects in   544
Chronic fatigue syndrome (ME)   445
Chronic hypoadrenocorticism   243
Chronic pulmonary heart disease   307
Ciguatera poisoning   300
Cilia   95
Circulatory system
  first aid and   769
  heart and   81
  nature of   74
Circumcision   98
Cirrhosis   300
Clap   369
Cleft palate   739
Climacteric   54
Clostridial myositis   363
Clots
  blocking veins and arteries   535
  drugs for treatment of   593
  lung   335
Clotting test   202
Club foot   301
Clubbing of fingers   144
Clumsiness   132
Cluster headaches   301
Coagulation test   202
Coarctation of aorta   260
Cocaine
  abuse of   328
Cochlea   76
Coeliac disease   302
  support groups for   739
Coitus interruptus   11
Cold sores   389
Cold, common   302
Colic   121
  intestinal   303
Colitis
  drugs for treatment of   603
  support groups for   739
  ulcerative   547
Colles' fractures   355
Colo-rectal cancer   304
Colon   86
  cancer of   304
  X-rays of   226
Colonoscopy   226
Colostomy   675
Colostrum   37
Colour blindness tests   237
Colposcopy   227

Coma   133
Coma position   780
Comforters   44
Compound fractures   354
Conception   4
  artificial   4, 410, 667
  Down's syndrome and   326
Concussion
  first aid for   792
Condoms   9
Condylomata acuminata   555
Cone shell stings   806
Confusion   133
Congenital syphilis   528
Conjunctivitis   140, 141
  allergic   251
  infected   305
  trachoma   540
Conn's syndrome   306
Constipation
  abnormal, in infants   393
  drugs for treatment of   597
  in general   133
  pregnancy and   25
Contraception   6ff
  Billings method   12
  cervical caps   10
  coitus interruptus   11
  condoms   9
  Depo-Provera   8, 608
  diaphragms   10
  fallacies concerning   14
  future developments in   15
  IUDs   11
  male pill   15
  menopause and   55
  oral   6, 605
  reliability of different methods   14
  rhythm method   11
  spermicides   9
  sponges   11
  the pill   6, 605
  tubal ligation   13
  vasectomy   13
Contraceptive drugs   8, 605, 608
Contractions   22
Convulsions   133
  drugs to prevent   574, 588
  epilepsy and   342
  febrile   348
  first aid for   790
Cor pulmonale   307
Cords
  see Umbilical cords
Corneas   77
  transplants of   673
  ulcers on   347
Coronary artery bypass graft   661
Cortex
  hormones produced by   65
  nature of   71
Corticosteroid drugs   608
Cortisone

INDEX

nature of 65
Coryza 302
Cosmetic surgery
　breasts 73
　teeth and 703
Costochondral syndrome 537
Cot death 308, 744
Cough 134
　croup 310
　drugs for treatment of 586
　whooping 558
Crabs 309
Cramps
　muscular 134
　nocturnal 134
Cretinism 309
Crohn's disease 309
　support groups for 739
Crotch rot 358
Croup 310
CT scans 210
Culdoscopy 227
Curettage 32, 662
Cushing's syndrome 149
　nature of disease 311
Cuts
　first aid for 785
Cyanosis 172
Cystic fibrosis 312
　support groups for 739
Cystinosis 312
Cystitis 66, 313
Cystocele
　prolapse and 482
Cystoscopy 227
Cysts
　Bartholin's 272
　eye 434
　hydatid 396
　in breasts 130
　in general 312
　kidney 477
　ovarian 460, 521
　sebaceous 104, 505
Cytomegalovirus infections (CMV) 314
Cytotoxic drugs 591
Danazol 602
Dandruff 314
Danocrine 602
Deafness 134
　support groups for 739
Death 59ff
Decongestant drugs 592
Defecation 86
Deficiencies
　calcium 456
　iodine 147
　see also Vitamin deficiencies
Dehydration 315
　when flying 758
Deja vu 135
Dementia 135
　Alzheimer's disease 252

nature of disease 315
Dengue fever 316
Densitometry 213
Dentistry 696ff
　forensic 709
　preventative 706
Depigmentation of skin 172
Depo-Provera 8, 608
Depressed fractures 354
Depression 135
　drugs for treatment of 574
　mania and 431
　nature of disease 316
　shock treatment and 678
Dermatitis 317, 426
Dermatomyositis 319
Dermis 103
Dermographia 175
Diabetes
　drugs for treatment of 594
　support groups for 739
Diabetes insipidus
　nature of disease 319
Diabetes mellitus
　appetite and 124
　blindness and 128
　in pregnancy 29
　nature of disease 320
　thirst and 179
　tremors and 182
Diabetic ketoacidosis 323
Diagnosis
　process of 194
　see also Body scans and X-rays; Electrical tests;
　　Endoscopy; Pathology; Physical tests
Diamox 602
Diaphragms 10
Diarrhoea
　anxiety and 124
　drugs for treatment of 576
　nature of 136
　when travelling 757
Diet 709ff
　diabetes and 321
　for health disorders 719
　pyramid 718
　vegetarian 717
　when travelling 757, 758
Dieticians 683
Digestion
　nature of 75
　stomach and 108
　X-ray of upper tract 228
Digestive enzymes 592
Dilation and curettage (D&C) 32, 662
Diphtheria 323, 756
　Schick test for 207
Diplopia 186
Discharge
　ear 138
　eye 140
　nipple 163
　nose 164

821

INDEX

urethral 182
vaginal 185
Dislocation 324, 354
  first aid for 797
  hip 393
  shoulder 512
Disulfiram drugs 601
Diuretic drugs 592
Diverticulitis 325
Dizziness 136
Doctors
  how to choose 723
  qualifications of 721
  training of 720
  when to call 811
Dog bites 805
Double jointedness 84
Double vision 186
Down's syndrome 326
  support groups for 739
Dropsy 165
Drowning
  first aid where 786
Drugs
  addiction to 327
  available in Australia 615
  categories of 566
  first aid for overdoses of 793
  list of 615
  overdoses 793
  pregnancy and 16
  support groups where abuse of 740
  tests 17
  treatment by
Drugs, medicinal
  list of 615
  types of 566
Dry eye 140
Dry mouth 159
Dry skin 174
Dual photon absorptiometry 213
Duchenne's muscular dystrophy 445
Dummies 44
Duodenum
  nature of 75
Dupuytren's contracture of hand 330
Dwarfism 148
Dysarthria 176
Dysentery 331
Dysidrosis 479
Dysmenorrhoea 157
Dyspepsia 137
Dysphagia 177
Dyspnoea 130
Dystrophy 344, 444
Dysuria 184
Ears
  aches in 137
  deafness 134
  discharge from 138
  dizziness and 136
  furunculosis in 360
  glue 665

grommets in 665
infections 457ff
mastoiditis 432
Ménière's disease and 434
nature of 76
noises in 138
surgery on 665
tinnitus in 138
vertigo and 136
wax in 138
Echinococcosis 396
Echocardiography 213
Eclampsia 34
Ectopic pregnancy 30, 79
Eczema 331
  allergic 332
  atopic 332
  hypostatic 334
  irritant 333
  photosensitive 334
  seborrhoeic 334
  varicose 334
Ejaculation 3
  lack of 139
  problems with 506
Electrical tests 320ff
Electrocardiogram (ECG) 230
Electroconvulsive therapy (ECT) 678
Electrocution first aid for 787
Electroencephalogram (EEG) 231
Electromyogram (EMG) 232
Elephantiasis 335
Embolism
  arterial gas 274
  lung 335
  pulmonary 335
Embryo
  see Foetus
Emergencies 768
Emphysema 336
Encephalitis 337
Endocarditis 338
Endocrine glands 80
Endodontics 698
Endometriosis 339
  drugs for treatment of 601
Endoscopy 224ff
Energy
  lack of 180
Engorgement of breasts 39, 40
Enophthalmos
  watery 141
Enterobiasis 472
Enuresis 272
Enzymes
  digestive 75
  production of 98
Epidemic polyarthritis 496
Epidermis 103
Epidermolysis bullosa 340
Epididymo-orchitis 341
Epidurals 26, 29
Epiglottis 86

INDEX

Epiglottitis 341
Epilepsy 342
   auras and 126
   grand mal 343
   narcolepsy 448
   partial seizures where 344
   support groups for 740
Epistaxis 164
Erb's muscular dystrophy 344, 445
Erb's palsy 344, 445
Erection, lack of 507
Erysipelas 345
Erythema 174
Erythema multiforme 345, 522
Erythema nodosum 346
Erythromycins 573
Ethics, medical 726
Etretinate drug 602, 604
Eustachian tubes 99
Ewing's tumours 278
Exophthalmos 141
Expectorant drugs 593
Expelled air resuscitation (EAR) 770
Exposure 303, 404
External cardiac compression (ECC) 773
Eyelid, diseases of 141ff, 446
Eyes
   allergic conjunctivitis in 251
   black 788
   blepharitis and 276
   blindness in 78, 128, 738
   cataracts and 290
   conjunctivitis 140, 141, 251, 305
   damage due to premature birth 36
   detachment of retinas 493
   disorders of 78
   drugs for problems with 588, 598, 599
   dry 140
   first aid for injuries to 788
   flash burns to 350
   floaters in 351
   foreign bodies in 346, 788
   glaucoma 367
   Horner's syndrome in 395
   inflammation of iris 413
   iridology and 735
   iritis 413
   meibomian cysts and 434
   nature of 77
   pain in 140
   photosensitive 494
   protruding 141
   red 141
   squints and 520
   sties in 141, 526
   sunken 141
   surgery on 663
   trachoma and 540
   ulcers in 347
   watery 141
   see also Corneas; Vision
Face
   Bell's palsy and 273

   inflammation of 243
   pain in 143
   rosacea in 496
Factor IX deficit 299
Factor VIII deficit 373
Faeces
   incontinence of 406
   pathology testing of 206
   see also Bowel
Failure to thrive in babies 143
Fainting 143, 789
Fallopian tubes
   nature of 79
   pregnancy in 30
   tying of 13
Fallot's tetralogy 383
Familiarity 135
Farting 145
Fasciculation 182
Fat
   abnormal gain of 165
   in diet 710
Fatigue 180
   chronic 445
Fears 144
Febrile convulsions 348
Feeding
   bottle 37
   breast 37
   solid 47
Feet
   bunions and 285
   club 301
   flat 351
   ganglions on 362
   gout in 371
   metatarsalgia in 438
   pains in 145
   podiatry and 690
   smoker's foot 284
Felty's syndrome 349
Femoral hernia 387
Fertilisation 4
Fevers 144
   blackwater 429
   breakbone 315
   dengue 316
   first aid for 789
   glandular 366
   Lassa 420
   need for doctor 812
   Q 486
   rheumatic 494
   Ross River 496
   scarlet 500
   typhoid 544
   undulant 283
   yellow
Fibre
   diet and 710
Fibrinolytic drugs 593
Fibrocystic disease 312
Fibroids

Index

uterine 550
Fibrositis 350
Fingernails 161
Fingers
  clubbing in 144
  pains in 154
  swollen 144
First aid 740, 767ff
  accidents 781ff
  asthma attacks 782
  bites and stings 803ff
  bleeding 777
  choking 783
  concussion 792
  cuts 785
  drowning 786
  electric shock 787
  eye injuries 788
  fainting 789
  fevers 789
  fits and convulsions 790
  fractures 791
  heart attack 792
  nosebleeds 793
  overdose 793
  recovery positions and 780
  severe allergic reactions 781
  shock 778
  slings 799
  splinters 797
  sprains 797
  strapping injured joints 799
  suffocation 802
  sunburn 803
  unconsciousness 779
Fissures, anal 122
Fits 133
  epilepsy and 342
  febrile 348
  first aid for 790
Flatulence 145
Floaters, eye 351
Flu 410
Fluid
  drugs for treatment of 592
  excess 125, 165
  in abdomen 125
  on ankles 122
Fluoridation 706
Flushes 145
Foetus
  amniocentesis and 196
  chorionic villus sampling and 205
  development of 19
  hydramnios and 31
  skeleton in 69
  spina bifida and 519
  untrasound scans of 219
  see also Pregnancy
Folic acid 614
Follicles
  hair 80
Folliculitis 352

Food guidance chart 714
Food poisoning 352
Forceps deliveries 27
Forensic dentistry 709
Fractures
  first aid for 791
  treatment of 356
  types of 353ff
Frigidity 507
Frostbite 357
Frozen shoulder 357
Full blood count 201
Fungal infections 358, 394, 408, 523
  drugs for treatment of 577
  nature of 728
Funnel-web spider bites 809
Furuncles 277
Furunculosis, ear 360
Gait, abnormal 187
Galactorrhoea 163
Gall bladder 87
  removal of 661
Gallstones 361
Gamete intra-Fallopian transfer (GIFT) 410
Ganglions 362
Gangrene 363
Gastric juices 108
Gastritis 364
Gastroenteritis 121, 364
  diet for 720
Gastrointestinal tract
  see Digestion; Large intestine; Small intestine
Gastroscopy 228
Gastrostomy 675
Genital herpes 390
Genital warts 555
Genu valgum 419
German measles 498
Germs 727ff
Giantism 147
Giardia infection 365
Giardiasis 365
Gingivitis 148
Glands
  adrenal 65
  Bartholin 272
  lymph 394
  parathyroid 112, 399
  pituitary 99
  prostate 100
  salivary 91, 170
  sebaceous 103
  spleen 107
  sweat 103
  swollen 146, 244
  thyroid 112
  types of 80
Glandular fever 366
Glaucoma
  nature of disease 367
  tests for 236
Glomerulonephritis 368
Goitre 147

Gonorrhoea 369
Goose pimples 103
Gout 181, 371
   drugs for treatment of 596
   pseudogout and 484
Grand mal epilepsy 343
Grave's disease 401
Greenstick fractures 354
Grief 61
Groin
   femoral hernia in 387
   pain in 147
Grommets
   insertion of, into ears 665
Growth
   excessive 147, 243
   pains 372
   reduced 148
Guillain-Barr syndrome 372
Gullet 96
   by-passing of 675
Gums
   diseases of 467
   pains in 148
Gut
   see Digestion; Large intestine; Small intestine
Gynaecomastia 129
H2 receptor antagonist drugs 586
Haematemesis 187
Haematuria 183
Haemochromatosis 372
Haemolytic anaemia 254
Haemophilia
   Christmas disease and 299
   nature of disease 373
   support groups for 741
Haemorrhage 127
Haemorrhoids 123
Haemostatic drugs 593
Hair
   excessive 148
   infection of follicules 352
   loss 127, 251
   nature of 80
   touch and 114
Halitosis 126
Hallucinations 149
Handicapped
   dentistry for 708
   support groups for 739
Hands
   carpal tunnel syndrome and 290
   Dupuytren's contracture of 330
   ganglions on 362
   left-handedness 420
   pain in 149
   tremor in 182
Hansen's disease 422
Hash
   abuse of 329
Hay fever 375, 603
Head
   first aid for injuries to 792

   injuries to 377, 741
   lice 425
   water on 397
Headache 150, 301, 376
Hearing 76
   loss 134
Hearing tests 238ff
Heart
   abnormal beat of 560
   angina and 257
   attack 378, 790
   cardiac stress test 232
   chest pain and 137
   chronic disease of 307
   drugs for problems with 570, 590
   electrocardiograms and 230
   endocarditis in 338
   failure 380
   fast beating of 150
   irregular rhythm in 381
   ischaemic disease of 415
   muscle infection 446
   nature of 81
   pericarditis and 467
   resuscitation by external compression of 773
   sudden rapid beating of 464
   surgery on 661, 673
   transplants 672
   triglyceride excess and 542
   valve diseases 382, 673
Heart attacks
   first aid for 792
Heart disease support group 741
Heart-lung resuscitation 773
Heartburn 150
   pregnancy and 25
Height
   of children 49
   of infants 42
Hemiplegia 166
Hepatitis 384
   travel and 761
Hepatolenticular degeneration 559
Hepatoma 386
Herbalism 733, 735
Hernias
   hiatus 96
   nature and types of 386
Heroin
   abuse of 328
Herpangina 523
Herpes simplex infections 389
Herpes zoster 510
Hiatus hernia 96, 391
Hiccups 151
High blood pressure 400
High-fibre diets 710
Hips
   artificial 673
   dislocation of 393
   fractures of 355
   pain in 151
   Perthes' disease of 469

Index

Hirschsprung's disease 393
Hirsutism 148
Histoplasmosis 394
HIV, categories of 245
Hives 175, 250
Hoarseness 152
Hodgkin's disease 394
Home medical chest 813
Homeopathy 735
Hookworm 395*
Hordeolum 526
Hormones
  adrenal gland, in 65
  aldosterone 306
  as drugs 594, 605
  cortisone 65
  disease due to insufficiency of 243
  female 97
  menopause and 55
  produced by cortex 65
  sex 605
  steroids 65, 608
  treatment of infertility by 610
Horner's syndrome 395
Hospices 60
Hunger, excessive 124
Huntington's chorea 396
  support group for 741
Hyaline membrane disease 492
Hydatid cysts 396
Hydatid of Morgagni 397
Hydatidiform moles 550
Hydramnios 31
Hydrocele 532
Hydrocephalus 397
Hydrocortisone
  Addison's disease and 244
Hyperactivity 398
Hyperaldosteronism 306
Hypercholesterolaemia 297
Hyperglycaemia
  blood tests for 202
Hypermetropia 78
Hyperparathyroidism 399
Hypertension
  drugs for treatment of 579
  high blood pressure 400
  pulmonary 307
Hyperthyroidism 401
Hypertrichosis 148
Hyperventilation 131
Hyperviterminosis 289
Hypnotic drugs 604
Hypoadrenocorticism 243
Hypoglycaemic drugs 594
Hypoglycaemia
  blood tests for 202
Hypolipidaemic drugs 596
Hypoparathyroidism 403
Hypotension 403
Hypothermia 303, 404
Hypothyroidism 405
Hysterectomy 666

  placenta accreta where 33
Hysteroscopy 229
Ichthyosis 174
Icterus 175
Ileal conduits 675
Ileostomy 676
Ileum 104
Immune blood tests 203
Immunisation 49, 611, 761, 755
Immunodeficiency 406
Immunoglobulin 761
Immunosuppressant drugs 597
Immunotherapy 679
Impacted fractures 354
Impetigo 502
Implants 672
Impotence 507
In vitro fertilisation (IVF) 4, 410, 667
Incontinence
  of faeces 406
  urinary 184, 272, 407
Incoordination 132
Indigestion 121, 137, 132, 137, 150, 710
Induction of birth 31
Infants
  24-hour 'wogs' in 496
  blue at birth 465
  bones in 70
  bottle-feeding of 41
  breastfeeding of 37
  brittle bones in 455
  choking in 784
  colic in 303
  congenital syphilis 528
  constipation in 393
  cot death and 308
  diarrhoea in 136
  dummies and comforters for 44
  failure to thrive in 143
  Fallot's tetralogy in 383
  gangrene in 449
  growth and development of 42ff
  height of 42
  Hirschsprung's disease in 393
  lungs in 89
  PKU tests of 470
  premature 35
  respiratory distress syndrome and 492
  resuscitation of 772, 776
  sleep problems 48
  solid foods for 47
  teething in 45
  temper tantrums in 45
  thumb sucking by 44
  toilet training of 46
  walking by 43
Infarct 378
Infections
  bacterial 408
  chalmydial 295, 540
  cytomegalovirus 314
  ear 457ff
  fungal 358, 394, 408, 523

giardia 365
herpes simplex 389
in general 408
pseudomonas 485
staphylococcal 521
streptoccocal 523
throat 470
viral, see Viral infections
Infectious mononucleosis (IM) 366
Infective hepatitis 384
Infertility 409
Depo-Provera and 9
diabetes and 30
drugs for treatment of 610
support group for 741
Inflammation
artery, of 262, 477
drugs for treatment of 600
eye iris 413
face 243
muscle 478
nerve 372
Reiter's syndrome and 492
sarcoidosis and 499
vaginal 551
Influenza 410
Inguinal hernia 387
Inguinal pain 147
Innoculation 755
Insecticide poisoning 454
Insemination artificial 4
Insomnia 153, 412
Insulin 595
production of 97
Insurance
travel and 762
Intal drug 375, 602, 603
Intellectual disability support group 741
Inter-uterine devices (IUDs) 11
PID and 465
Intercourse 3
painful 508
Intestine
see Digestion; Large intestine; Small intestine
Intetrigo 413
Intravenous pyelograms (IVP) 222
Involuntary muscles 91
Iodine deficiency 147
Iridology 735
Iritis 413
Iron
deficiency 255, 413
excessive storage of, in body 372
poisoning 413
Irritable bowel syndrome (IBS) 121, 415
Ischaemic heart disease 415
Isotope scans 215
Isotretinoin 603
Itches 153
anal 123, 484
vulval 187
IUDs 11
IVF 4

Jaundice 175, 415
Jejunum 75
Jellyfish stings 807
Jerking movements 153
Jet lag 758
Joints
arthritis and 262
arthroscopy and 226
bursitis in 287
double 84
fractures involving 354
gout in 371
nature of 83
painful and swollen 154
pigmented villonodular synovitis and 471
strapping of injured 799
surgery on 668
synovitis and 528
temporomandibular 704
Juvenile diabetes 321 321
Juvenile rheumatoid arthritis 266
Keratoacanthoma (KA) 416
Keratolytic drugs 597
Kidney stones 115, 417
Kidneys
cancer of 559
failure of 416
glomerulonephritis 368
infection in 184
nature of 84
nephrotic syndrome and 449
pain in 155, 183
polycystic 477
pyelonephritis in 486
support group where diseases of 741
transplants of 85
X-rays of 222
Kilojoules 713
Klinefelter's syndrome 418
Knees
arthroscopy of 226
chondromalacia and 298
pain in 154
replacement of joints in 673
Knock-knees 419
Korsakoff psychosis 557
Kwashiorkor 431
Kyphosis 419
Labour and birth 22
breech births 28
Caesarian sections 28
face presentation 31
forceps deliveries 27
induction of 31
pain relief during 26
premature birth 35
premature labour 34
problems with placenta during 32ff
prolapsed cord 35
prolonged 35
vacuum extraction 28
Lactation 37, 163
Laparoscopy 229

INDEX

Large intestine
  appendicitis and   261
  bowel blockage and   121
  digestion and   75
  nature of   85
  X-rays of   223
Laryngitis   419
Larynx   86, 177
Lassa fever   420
Lateral epicondylitis   530
Laxative drugs   596
Lead poisoning   420
Learning difficulties
  support group for   741
Left handedness   420
Leg pain   155
  in children   372, 455
Legionnaire's disease   421
Legs, restless   493
Leprosy   422
  drugs for treatment of   580
Leptospirosis   422
Lethargy   180
Leucocytes   67
Leucorrhoea   180
Leukaemia
  bone marrow biopsies and   198
  nature of disease   423
Libido, reduced   508
Lice   425
Lichen simplex   426
Ligaments   nature of   87
Light-headedness   136, 143
Limb girdle dystrophy   344
Limb pain   125, 155
  syndrome   372
Liniment drugs   598
Lithotripsy   115, 680
Liver
  cancer of   386
  cirrhosis   300
  leptospirosis in   422
  nature of   87
  porphyria and   479
  Wilson's disease of   559
Lockjaw   533
Loin pain   155
Lordosis   426
Louse, head   425
Low blood pressure   403
LSD
  abuse of   330
Lumbago   426
Lumbar puncture test   204
Lumps
  on bones   128
  in breasts   130
  in lower legs   346
  in neck   163
  in testicles or scrotum   178
Lungs
  asthma and   267
  bronchiectasis and   281

bronchiolitis and   281
bronchitis and   282
bronchoscopy and   226
cancer of   395, 427, 793
embolisms in   335
emphysema   336
nature of   88
pleurisy and   473
pneumoconiosis   474
pneumothorax in   475
pseudomonas infections in   485
respiratory distress syndrome and   492
sarcoidosis and   499
silicosis and   513
Lupus erythematosis, systemic (SLE)   428, 741
Lymph glands
  cancer of   394
Lymph nodes
  biopsies of   199
Lymphatic leukaemia   423
Lymphatic system
  nature of   90
Lymphogranuloma venereum   296
Lymphoma   394
Magnetic resonance imaging (MRI)   214
Making love   3
Malabsorption   155
Malaria   429
  drugs for treatment of   581
  travel and   761
Male pill   15
Malnutrition
  abnormal weight loss and   188
  in babies   143
  loss of appetitie and   124
  nature of   431
Mammograms   223
Mania   431
Manipulative therapy   686, 734
Mantoux tests   207
MAOI (monoamine oxidase inhibitor) drugs   575
Marasmus   431
Marfan's syndrome   432
Marijuana   abuse of   329
Marine stingers   806
Mastitis   281
Mastoiditis   432
Masturbation   3
Measles   433, 498
  vaccination and   756
Medical ethics   726
Medical practitioners   720
Medicare   724
Medulloblastoma   279
Meibomian cyst infections   434
Melaena   122, 129
Melanin   103
Melanoma   516
  detection of   752
Memory
  ageing and   58
  loss of   156
Ménière's disease   434

Meningioma 279
Meningitis 435
Menopause 54
Menorrhagia 158
Menstruation
   in adolescent girls 51
   premenstrual tension syndrome (PMT) 480
   problems with 156
   swelling before 122
Mental illness
   anxiety 259
   attempted suicide 526
   depression 2316
   multiple personality disorder 441
   neurosis 451
   obsessive compulsive neurosis 453
   paranoid disorders 463
   phobias 471
   psychosis 496
   schizophrenia 501
   support groups for 742
   treatment of 676ff
Mercury poisoning 436
Mesenteric adenitis 437
Mesothelioma 437
   asbestosis and 267
Metabolism
   thyroid gland and 112
Metatarsalgia 438
Methyldopa 579, 580
Micturation, frequent 183
Middle ear
   infections in 138
   nature of 76
Migraines 438
   auras or premonitions and 126
   drugs for treatment of 581
   see also Headache
Mikulicz's disease 514
Minerals 712
Minimata disease 437
Miotic drugs 598
Miscarriage 32
   curette after 663
   support groups for 744
Mitral valve stenosis 383
Moles
   uterine 550
Molluscum contagiosum 440
Mongolism 326
Moniliasis 536
Mononucleosis
   infectious 366
Morbilli 433
Morning sickness 25
Mosquitoes
   dengue fever and 316
   malaria and 429
Motion sickness 759
Motor neurone disease 440, 742
Mountain sickness 253
Mouth
   dry 159

infections 523
nature of 90
pigmentation of 159
sore 159
stomatitis 523
swollen 159
teeth 110
thrush in 536
trench 553
ulcers 160, 546
see also Dentistry; Teeth
Mouth-to-mouth resuscitation 770
Movement, abnormal
   gait 187
   jerking 153
   restless legs 493
   tic 180
   tremor 182
   writhing 189
Moxibustion 733
Mucolytic drugs 598
Mucus
   drugs to liquefy 598
   in cervix 73
Multiple myeloma 441
Multiple personality disorder 441
Multiple sclerosis
   support group for 742
Multiple sclerosis (MS) 442
Mumps 443
   vaccination and 756
Munchausen's syndrome 444
Murine typhus 545
Murray Valley encephalitis 338
Muscles
   convulsions in 133
   cramps in 134
   drugs to relax 599
   electromyograms and 232
   inflammation of 478
   nature of 91
   pains in 160
   skeletal 92
   spasm 160, 376
   sphincter 108
   tics in 180
   wasting of 160, 344
   weakness in 166, 180
Muscular dystrophy 444
   support groups for 742
Musculoskeletal system
   see Bones; Joints; Ligaments; Muscles; Spine;
      Vertabrae
Myalgia 160
Myalgic encephalomyelitis (ME) 445
Myasthenia gravis 446
Mycoplasma pneumonia 446
Mydriatic drugs 599
Myelograms 222
Myeloid leukaemia 424
Myelotmatosis 441
Myocardial infarct 378
Myocarditis 446

Index

Myopia 78
Myxoedema 405
Nails
  abnormalities in 161
  infections in 447
  ingrown toe 447
  nature of 93
Nappy rash 448
Narcolepsy 448
Narcotic addiction 327
  see also Drugs
Narcotic drugs 599
Natural therapies 732ff
Naturopathy 735
Nausea
  in general 162
  pregnancy and 25
Neck
  lump in 163
  pain in 163
  whiplash injury of 558
Necrotising enterocolitis 449
Necrotising ulcerative gingivostomatitis 553
Nematode infestations 497
Neoplasm 288
Nephritis 369
Nephroblastoma 559
Nephrolithiasis 417
Nephrotic syndrome 449
Nerves
  inflammation of 372
  motor neurone disease of 440
  nature of 94
  neuralgia and 450
  optic 78
  sciatica and 502
  spinal cord 106
Nervous complaints
  see Mental illness
Nervous system
  brain and 71
  nature of 94
  spinal cord and 106
Neuralgia 450
Neurofibromatosis 554, 743
Neurones 94
Neurosis 451
  obsessive compulsive 453
Nicotinic acid 614
Nipples
  cracked 39
  discharge from 163
  inverted 40
  Paget's disease of 461
Nitrous oxide
  during labour 26
Nocturnal cramps 134
Nodules in skin 172
Noises
  abdominal 121
  in ears 138
Noses
  bleeding from 164, 793

  discharge from 164
  disfiguring enlargement of 495
  drip from 291
  hay fever and 375
  nature of 95
  obstruction of 164
  smell and 105
NSAID drugs 600
Nuclear scans 215
Numbness 166
Nutritionists 682
  alternative 735
Obesity 165, 453, 710
  diet for 710
  health risks of 750
Obsessive compulsive neurosis 453, 743
Occupational therapy 683
Octopus stings 806
Oedema 165
Oesophagus
  nature of 96
  reflux oesophagitis and 490
Oligohydramnios 31
Oliguria 184
Opthalmoscopy 235
Optic nerves 78
Opticrom drug 603
Oral contraceptive drugs 6, 605
Orf 454
Organophosphate poisoning 454
Orgasm 3, 508
Ornithosis 485
Orthodontics 701
Orthomolecular treatment 735
Orthopaedic surgery 668
Osgood Schlatter's disease 455
Ossification 69
Osteitis deformans 461
Osteoarthritis 262
Osteogenesis imperfecta 455
Osteogenic sarcoma 278
Osteomalacia 456, 495
Osteomyelitis 456
Osteopathy 734
Osteoporosis 126, 456
Osteosarcoma 278
Ostomies 674ff
Otitis externa 457
Otitis media 459
Ovarian cancer 459
Ovarian cysts 460, 521
Ovaries
  nature of 97
  pain in 167
Overdoses
  first aid for 793
Overeating 124, 165, 480
Overweight 165
Paedodontics 697
Paget's diseases 154
  of bone 461
  of nipple 461
Pain

INDEX

abdominal   121
anal   123
arm   125
back   126, 270
breast   130
chest   132
   drugs for treatment of   599
ear   137
eye   140, 187
facial   143
feet   145
fingers   154
groin   147
gums   148
hands   149
hips   151
inguinal   147
joint   154
kidneys   155, 183
knee   154
leg   155
loin   155
muscle   160
neck   163
nerve   450
ovaries   167
pelvic   167
penis   167
RSI and   492
shoulder   171
toes   180
touch and   113
see also Anaesthesia
Pallor of skin   166
Palpitations   166
Pancreas
   nature of   97
Pancreatitis   461
Pap smears   74, 751
Papules on skin   172
Paralysis   166
   Erb's palsy and   344
   motor neurone disease and   440
   polio and   476
Paranoid disorders   463
Paraplegia   167, 462, 743
Parasites
   drugs for treatment of   582
Parasthesia   168
Parasympathetic nervous system   95
Parathyroid
   excess activity of   403
   glands   112, 399
Parkinson's disease   463
   drugs for treatment of   582
   support groups for   743
Paroxysmal atrial tachycardia (PAT)   464
Passive smoking   755
Patent ductus arteriosus (PDA)   465
Pathological fractures   354
Pathology
   amniocentesis   196
   biopsy   198

   blood   200
   cerebrospinal fluid   204
   chorionic villus sampling   205
   faeces   206
   pregnancy   210
   process of   195
   skin   207
   sperm   206
   sputum   208
   urine   208
Patient organisations   736
Pediculosis   309, 425
Pelvic floor exercises   483
Pelvic inflammatory disease (PID)   465
Pelvic pain   167
Pemphigoid   466
Pemphigus   466
Penicillins   572
Penis
   discharge from   182
   ejaculation and   3, 139
   infection of head of   271
   nature of   98
   pain in   167
   painful urination and   184
   sexual problems involving   506ff
Peptic ulcers   546, 561
   drugs for treatment of   586
Pericarditis   467
Periodontics   700
Periodontitis   467
Periods
   see Menstruation
Peripheral nervous system   94
Peritonitis   121, 468
Peritonsillar abscess   488
Perthes' disease   469
Pertussis   558, 756
PET scans   217
Petechiae   171
Phaeochromocytoma   469
Pharmaceutical benefits scheme   652
Pharyngitis   470
Pharynx   90, 99
Phenylketonuria (PKU)   470
Phobias   144, 471
   spiders and   677
Photophobia   186
Photosensitive eyes   174
Physical tests   232ff
Physiotherapy   684
   access to   689
   cardiopulmonary   688
   education   690
Pigmentation
   of mouth   159
   skin   172, 173
Pigmented villonodular synovitis   471
Piles   123
Pill, the   6, 605
Pimples   241
Pins and needles   168
Pinworm   472

INDEX

Pituitary glands   99
   tumours of   243
Pityriasis rosea   472
Pityriasis versicolor   359
Placentas   20, 24
   abruption of   33
   accreta   32
   praevia   33
   retention of   33
Plague, bubonic   473
Plantar warts   557
Plasma   67
Plastic surgery   670
Platelets   68
Pleurisy   473
Pleuritis   473
Pleurodynia   474
Pneumoconiosis   266, 474
Pneumonia
   fungus and   394
   Legionnaire's disease and   421
   mycoplasma   446
   nature of disease   474
Pneumothorax   475
Podiatry   690
Poisoning
   blood   505
   ciguatera   300
   copper   559
   emergency information services   794
   food   353
   insecticide   454
   iron   413
   lead   420
   mercury   436
   organophosphate   454
   schedules of poisons   651
Poisonous plants   796
Polio   vaccination and   756
Poliomyelitis   476
Poliomyositis   319
Polyarteritis nodosa (PAN)   477
Polycythaemia vera   478
Polydipsia   179
Polyhydramnios   31
Polymenhorrhoea   158
Polymyalgia rheumatica (PMR)   478
Polyuria   183
Pompholyx   479
Porphyria   479
Postnasal drip   291
Postural hypotension   404
Pot   abuse of   329
Potent therapeutic substances   651
Pott's fractures   355
Poultry   human disease and   485
Prader-Willi syndrome   480, 744
Pre-eclampsia   34
Pregnancy
   antenatal checks   21
   antenatal classes   21
   appetite during   124
   bleeding during   28
   breastfeeding and   14
   development of foetus in   19
   diabetes in   29
   drugs and   16
   ectopic   30
   first signs of   17
   health during   21
   placentas and   20
   pre-pregnancy check-ups   16
   problems during   25
   quickening   19
   Rh negative mothers   69
   sex during   22
   sleeplessness and   18
   smoking and   16, 754
   stretch marks and   18
   tests for   210
   ultrasound scans and   219
   urination and   17
   see also Conception; Foetus
Premature birth   35
Premature ejaculation   506
Premature labour   34
Premenstrual tension syndrome (PMT)   480
Premonitions
   epilepsy and   126
Presbyopia   78
Pressure immobilisation   804
Pressure points
   control of bleeding by   777
Pressure sores   272
Preventative dentistry   706
Preventative medicine   745
Priapism   167
Progressive systemic sclerosis   503
Prolapse   482
Prostate
   cancer of   228, 483
   diseases of   483
   enlargement of   483
   glands   100
   infection of   484
Prosthodontics   702
Proteins
   diet and   709
Protozoa
   nature of   730
Pruritus   153
Pruritus ani   484
Pseudogout   484
Pseudomonas infections   485
Psittacosis   485
Psoriasis   485, 743
Psychiatric disease
   see Mental illness
Psychiatric treatment   676ff
Psychiatrists   676
Psychoanalysis   678
Psychologists   676
Psychosis   486
   drugs for treatment of   583
Ptosis   142
Puberty   50ff

INDEX

delayed 169
early 169
in boys 52
in girls 51
Pulmonary function tests 233
Pulmonary hypertension 307
Pulmonary valve stenosis 383
Pulse 82
   fast 150, 166
   first aid and 769
   slow 169
Purpura 171
Pustules in skin 173
Pyelonephritis 486
Pylorus 75
Pyrexia 144
Q fever 486
Quadriplegia 167, 462, 743
Quickening 19
Quinsy 488
Rabies 488
Radiation sickness 489
Radiography dental 707
Radionuclide scans 215
Radiotherapy 681
Rashes 173, 440, 448, 466, 472, 544
Raynaud's phenomenon 150, 489
Recovery position 780
Rectocele 482
Rectum 75, 85
   cancer of 304
   prolapse of 482
Red-back spider bites 808
Reflux oesophagitis 490
Regional enteritis 309
Reiter's syndrome 492
Remedial therapy 736
Renal failure 416
Renal pain 155
Repetitive strain injury (RSI) 492
Reproduction 3ff, 5ff
   female 100
   male 101
Reproductive system, female
   ultrasound examination of 217
   X-ray examination of 227, 229
Respiratory distress syndrome 492
Respiratory function tests 233
Respiratory systems
   blood gas analysis of 202
   drugs for contol of asthma and hay fever 603
   drugs for removal of phlegm and mucus from 593
   nature of 101
   noses and 95
   physiotherapy and 688
   sputum tests and 208
Respiratory tract infections 549
Restless leg syndrome 493
Restricted substances 651
Resuscitation 768
   drowning and 786
   heart 773
   heart-lung 773

mouth-to-mouth 770
mouth-to-nose 772
Retinal detachment 493
Retinas 77
   detachment of 493
Retinitis pigmentosa 494
Retrolental fibroplasia 36
Reye's syndrome 494
Rh incompatibility 69
   amniocentesis and 196
Rheumatic fever 494
Rheumatoid arthritis 263
   drugs for treatment of 583
   support groups for 737
Rhinitis 375
Rhinophyma 495
Rhythm method of contraception 11
Rickets 456, 495
Rickettsal infection 487
Rickettsiosis 545
Rigor mortis 60, 92
Ringworm 358
Roaccutane drug 603
Rodent ulcers 515
Root fillings 699
Rosacea 466, 496
Roseola infantum 496
Ross River fever 496
Rotator cuff syndrome 497
Roundworm infestations 497
Rubefacient drugs 598
Rubella 498, 756
Rubeola 433
Rynacrom drug 603
Salazopyrin drug 603
Salicylate drugs 604
Saliva 91
Salivary glands
   swollen 170
Salivary stones 498
Salmonellosis 544
Salpingitis 465
Sarcoidosis 499
Sarcoma 277
Satus epilepticus 343
Scabies 499
Scalds
   first aid for 782
Scalp dandruff and 314
Scans
   see Body scans and X-rays
Scarlet fever 500
Scheuermann's disease 500
Schick test 207
Schilling test 210
Schistosomiasis 276
Schizophrenia
   multiple personality disorder and 442
   nature of disease 501
School sores 502
Sciatica 502
Scleroderma 503, 743
Scoliosis 503

Index

Scorpion stings 808
Scrofula 504
Scrotal pain 178
Scrub typhus 545
Scurvy 504
Sea sickness 759
Sea wasp stings 807
Sebaceous cysts 505
Sebaceous glands 103
Sedative drugs 604
Seizures 133
  epilepsy and 342
Self-examination of breasts 748
Sensation 113
  loss of 166
Senses 102
Septic arthritis 265
Septicaemia 505
Serum hepatitis 385
Serum sickness 505
Sex
  elderly and 509
  hormones 605
  in general 3ff
  lack of ejaculation during 139
  problems with 505ff
  while pregnant 22
Sexually transmitted diseases (STDs) 510
Shakes 182
Shigellosis 331
Shingles 510
Shivering 170
Shock
  first aid for 778
  syndrome 511
Shock treatment 678
Short-wave diathermy 687
Shortness of breath 130
  tests of 235
Shortness of stature 148, 744
Shoulder
  dislocation of 512
  frozen 357
  pain in 171
  rotator cuff syndrome 497
  slings for injured 799
Sight
  see Eyes; Vision
Sight tests 235ff
Silicosis 266, 513
Sinusitis 513
Sjögren's syndrome 514
Skeletal muscles 92
Skeleton 69
Skin
  abscesses on 241
  acute redness of 345
  bed sores on 272
  bleeding into 171
  blistered 171
  blue 172
  cancers of 416, 514, 752
  depigmentation of 172
  dermatitis and 317, 426
  disease in elderly women 466
  drugs for problems with 596
  dry 174
  eczema 331
  epidermolysis bullosa 340
  first aid for sunburn 803
  hives on 250
  impetigo and 502
  itchy 153, 479
  loss of colour in 172
  nature of 102
  pain 172
  pallor of 166
  papules 172
  pigmentation of 173
  pityriasis rosea and 472
  psoriasis and 485
  pustular 173
  rashes 40, 173, 440, 466, 472, 544
  red 174
  redness of face 496
  scaly 174
  spots 752
  sun-sensitive 174
  tests of 207
  thickened 174
  thinned 174
  ulcers 547
  vitiligo 554
  Von Recklinghausen's disease of 554
  warts on 556
  weals on 175
  yellow 175
SLE (Lupus erythematosis, systemic) 428, 741
Sleep
  apnoea 176, 517
  problems in children 48
  tests concerning 235
Sleeping sickness 518
Sleeplessness 153, 412
  drugs for treatment of 605
  pregnancy and 18, 27
Slings
  first aid for 799
Small intestine 75
  Crohn's disease of 309
  ileostomy and 676
  nature of 104
  sprue in 302
  X-rays of 223
Smallpox 518
Smell, sense of
  in general 105
  loss of 175
  taste and 105
Smith's fractures 355
Smoker's foot 284
Smoking
  ageing and 56
  dangers of 752ff
  passive 754, 755
  pregnancy and 16

INDEX

Snake bites 808
Snoring 176
Sodium cromaglycate drug 603
Sores
  bed 272
  boils 277
  cold 389
  school 502
Spasticity 292
Speech
  difficulty with 176
  loss of 177
  pathology 691
Sperm 111
Sperm tests 206
Spermicides 9, 608
Sphincter muscles 108
Sphygmomanometer 400
Spider bites 809, 810
Spina bifida 519, 743
Spinal anaethetic 655
Spinal cord 106
  cerebrospinal fluid tests and 204
  myelograms and 222
  paraplegia and 167
Spinal tap test 204
Spine 106
  see also Back
Spleen
  abnormal enlargement of 349
  nature of 107
  rupture of 519
Splinters
  first aid for 797
Spondylitis 258
Sponges
  contraception using 11
Spontaneous abortion 32
Spots
  black, in eyes 186
  blind, in eyes 78
  seeing 351
Sprains
  first aid for 797
Sprue
  non-tropical 302
  tropical 520
Sputum tests 208
Squamous cell carcinoma 515
Squint 520
Stammering 525
Staphylococcal infections 521
Stein-Leventhal syndrome 521
Sterility
  male 418
Steroid drugs 567, 608
Steroids
  nature of 65
Stevens-Johnson syndrome 522
Sties 142
Still's disease 266
Stillbirth support groups for 744
Stimulant drugs 610

Stings
  first aid for 803ff
Stomach
  cancer 522
  gastritis and 364
  gastroenteritis and 364
  nature of 108
Stomas 674ff
Stomatitis 523
Stonefish stings 806
Stones
  kidney 115, 417
  lithotripsy and 680
  salivary 498
  see also Gallstones
Stools
  see Bowel
Strabismus 520
Streptoccocal infections 523
Stress 523
  ageing and 56
  drugs for treatment of 587
Stretch marks 18
Stridor 177
Stroke 524
Stuttering 525, 745
Sty 526
Sub-dural haematoma 378
Sudden infant death syndrome (SIDS) 308
Suffocation 802
Sugar diabetes 320
Suicide attempt 526
Sulpha drugs 570, 572
Sulphasalazine drug 603
Sulphazaloprin drug 603
Sun spots 752
Sunburn
  first aid for 803
Support groups 737
Surgery
  description of process of 657
  oral 704
  theatre for 654
  types of 658ff
  see aslo Anaesthetic; Cosmetic surgery
Swallowing difficulty in 177
Sweat
  excessive 178, 527
  glands 103
Swelling
  abdomen 122
  drugs for treatment of 601
  eyelids 141
  fingertips 144
  glands 146, 244
  joints 154
  lower legs 346
  mouth 159
  Raynaud's phenomenon 489
  RSI and 492
  salivary glands 170
  testicles 178
Swimmer's ear 457

Index

Sympathomimetic bronchodilator drugs 590
Syncope 143
Synovitis 528
Syphilis 528
Tachycardia 150
Talcosis 266
Tapeworm 530
Taste, sense of
  abnormal 178
  nature of 109
  waterbrash 188
Teenagers
  see Adolescence
Teeth
  broken 704
  dentistry and 696ff
  false 702
  fluoridation and 706
  nature of 110
  pain in 182
  periodontitis and 467
  root filling of 696
  surgery on 704
  temporomandibular joint and 704
  see also Dentistry; Mouth
Teething 45
Temper tantrums 45
Temperature, high 144, 812
Temporomandibular joint 704
Tendonitis 531
Tendons 111
Tenesmus 129
Tennis elbow 530
Tenosynovitis 125, 531
Tension headache 376
Test tube babies 4, 410, 667
Testicles
  diseases of 532
  epididymo-orchitis in 341
  nature of 111
  painful or swollen 178
  torsion of 179, 397, 533
  undescended 533
Tests
  see Body scans and X-rays; Electrical tests; Endoscopy; Hearing tests; Pathology; Physical tests; Sight tests
Tetanus 533
  animal bites and 805
  vaccination and 756, 761
Tetany
  muscle spasm and 160
Tetracycline drugs 573
Thalassaemia 534
Theophyllinate drugs 589
Therapeutic hypotension 404
Thirst
  excessive 179
Thoracic pain 132
Thoracic vertebrae 106, 107
Threadworms 123
Throat 90, 99
  epiglottitis and 341

first aid for choking 783
  hoarseness 152
  infection 470
  sore 179
  tonsilitis and 538
Thromboangiitis obliterans 284
Thrombosis 535
Thrush 536
Thumb sucking 44
Thymus 90
Thyroid
  cancer of 536
  cretinism and 309
  drugs for treatment of problems with 585, 610
  excess activity of 401
  nature of 112
  underactivity of 405
Thyrotoxicosis 401
Tic 180, 182, 541
Tietze's syndrome 537
Tigason 604
Tinea 358
Tingling sensation 168
Tinnitus 138, 435, 745
Tiredness, abnormal 180
Toes, pain in 180
Toilet training 46
Tongue 90, 109
  discoloured 181
  sore 181
Tonometer 236
Tonsilitis 538
Tonsillectomy 671
Tonsils 99
  abscesses on 488
Toothache 182
Touch
  nature of 113
Toxic shock syndrome 539
Toxoplasmosis 539
Trachea 114
  diphtheria and 324
Trachoma 540
Transfusions
  reactions to 540
  serum sickness and 505
Transient ischaemic attack (TIA) 541
Transplants 672
Travel medicine 757ff
  medications to pack 760
  vaccinations 761
Tremor
  in face 180
  in hands 182
  Parkinson's disease and 463
  writing and 189
Trench mouth 553
Trichomoniasis 541
Tricuspid valve
  incompetence 383
  stenosis 383
Tricyclic drugs 575
Trigeminal neuralgia 541

Triglyceride, excess 542
Trisomy 21 326
Trophic hormone drugs 610
Trypanosomiasis 518
Tubal ligation 13, 79
Tuberculosis (TB) 542
  drugs for treatment of 585
  Mantoux test for 207
  scrofula and 504
Tuberous sclerosis 544, 745
Tubes, Fallopian
  ligation of 13
  pregnancy in 30
Tumours
  black cell 469
  bone 128, 277
  brain 182, 242
  breast 130, 224
  chest 437
  Conn's 306
  cystoscopy and 228
  Ewing's 278
  neck 163
  pituitary gland 243
  testicle 178
Turner's syndrome 544, 745
Twins 4
Twitches 180, 182
Typhoid fever 544
  travel and 760
Typhus 545
Ulcerative colitis 547, 745
  drugs for treatment of 603
Ulcers
  eye 347
  mouth 160, 261, 546
  peptic 546, 561
  rodent 515
  skin 547
  stomach 122
Ultrasound scans 217
  physiotherapy and 688
Umbilical cords
  cutting 24
  hernias and 388
  meaning 20
  prolapsed 35
Umbilical hernia 388
Unconsciousness 133, 143
  first aid and 779
Undulant fever 283
Uraemia 417
Ureters
  nature of 115
Urethra
  bladder and 66
  discharge from 182
  nature of 115
  pain in 167, 184
Urethritis 115, 182, 295, 548
  non-specific 452
Urinary tract
  cystoscopy and 227

Urination
  early pregnancy and 17
  excessive or frequent 183
  in children 47
  painful 184
  prostate and 100
Urine
  abnormal colour of 183
  antispasmodic drugs and 584
  bed-wetting and 272
  bloody 183
  drugs to alkalise 567
  gassy 184
  inability to pass 184
  incontinence 184, 407
  lack of 184
  purple 479
  tests of 208
URTI (upper respiratory tract infections) 549, 550
Urticaria 250
Uterus
  culdoscopy and 227
  endometriosis in 339
  fibroids in 550
  moles in 550
  nature of 115
  prolapse and 482
  surgery on 662
  ultrasound scan of 219
Uveitis 413
Uvula 99
  snoring and 176
Vaccination 49, 611, 755
  travel and 761
Vaccines 611
Vagina 100, 116
  colposcopies and 227
  discharge from 185
  excessive bleeding from 185
  prolapse and 482
  thrush in 536
Vaginismus 510
Vaginitis 551
Varicella 294, 510
Varicose veins
  in general 552
  pregnancy and 27
Vasectomy 13
Vasoconstrictor drugs 611
Vasodilator drugs 613
Vasopressor drugs 611
Vegetarian diets 717
Veins 65, 74, 116, 552
Venereal diseases
  gonorrhoea 369
Verrucae 557
Vertebrae 106
  pain in 126
Vertigo 136
Vincent's angina 553
Violence
  abnormal 186
Viral infections

INDEX

adenitis 437
  drugs for treatment of 587
  encephalitis 338
  in general 314, 408, 553
  mononucleosis 366
  mumps 443
  oral 523
  orf 454
  shingles 510
Viruses
  general nature of 731
Vision
  black spots in 186
  blind spots in 78
  blurred 186
  colour blindness tests 237
  double 186
  opthalmoscopy and 235
  pain with bright light 186
  tests of acuity of 237
  tonometer and 236
Visual acuity tests 237
Vitamin deficiencies
  anaemia and 255
  beri-beri 275
  carotenaemia 289
  rickets and 456, 495
  Schilling test for 210
  scurvy and 504
Vitamins
  diet and 712
  nature of 613
Vitiligo 172, 554
Vocal cords 87
Voice box 86
Voluntary muscles 91
Vomiting
  blood 187
  bowel blockage and 121
  drugs for treatment of 576
  in general 162
  poisoning 793
Von Recklinghausen's disease of multiple
  neurofibromatosis 554, 743
Von Willebrand's disease 555
Vulva 100
  itch in 187
Walking
  abnormal 187
  by infants 43
Warts 555
Wasp stings 805
Waterbrash 188
Wax in ears 138
Weakness, muscular 166, 180, 189

Weals on skin 175
Weaning 38
Wegner's granulomatosis 557
Weight
  abnormal gain in 188
  abnormal loss of 124, 188
  kilojoules and 713
  of children 49
  of infants 42
  pregnancy and 22, 124
  table of acceptable 719
Wernicke's encephalopathy 557
Wernicke-Korsakoff psychosis 557
Wheezing 189
Whiplash injury 557
Whitlow 389
Whooping cough 558
  vaccination and 756
Wilm's tumour 559
Wilson's disease 559
Wind in bowel 122
Windpipe 114
Wiskott-Aldrich syndrome 406
Wolff-Parkinson-White syndrome 560
Womb
  nature of 115
  removal of 666
  X-ray of 229
  see also Uterus
Worms
  anal itch and 123
  drugs to kill 569
  hook 395
  pin 472
  round 497
  tape 530
Writhing movements 189
Writing difficulties 189
X-rays 220ff
  angiograms 223
  barium meals and enemas 223
  dental 707
  endoscopy 224ff
  intravenous pyelograms 222
  mammograms 223
  myelograms 222
  womb 229
  see also Body scans and X-rays
Xanthinate bronchodilator drugs 590
XO syndrome 544
Yaws 560
Yellow fever 560
  vaccination for 760
Zollinger-Ellison syndrome 561
Zygotes 4